U0929824

甘肅年鑒

GANSU YEARBOOK

1994

甘 肃 年 鉴 编 委 会 编

中国统计出版社

(京)新登字 041 号

图书在版编目(CIP)数据

甘肃年鉴 1994 年/甘肃年鉴编委会编
北京:中国统计出版社，1994.8
ISBN 7-5037-1563-4

Ⅰ.甘…
Ⅱ.①甘…②甘…
Ⅲ.甘肃-1994-年鉴
Ⅳ.Z524.2

中国统计出版社出版
(北京复外三里河月坛南街 38 号)
甘肃省统计局印刷所印刷
兰州广告装璜美术设计所美术编辑
*
787×1092 毫米 16 开本 46.5 印张 168 彩页 160 万字
1994 年 8 月第一版 1994 年 8 月兰州第一次印刷
印数 1-2000 册
*
ISBN 7-5037-1563-4/C.904
定价:86 元

地址：甘肅省蘭州市農民巷 105 號
電話：8415001 8415144
傳眞：8825849
郵編：730000
Add : No. 105 the Peasant Lane,
Lanzhou, Gansu
Tel : 8415001 8415144
Fax : 8825849
Post Code: 730000

總經理、黨委書記：李連維
Director, Party Secretary: Li Lian Wei

GANSU MECHANICAL GROUP COMPANY

簡介

甘肅機械集團公司是 1992 年經甘肅省政府批準成立的集工、貿、科、金融、服務于一體的大型企業。公司核心層由 50 家企事業單位構成，員工 7 萬人。集團公司對附屬核心層單位實行資產統一經營管理。

公司產業基礎雄厚，機電產品種類達 3600 多個，其中許多為國家和地方優質名牌產品。近年來，公司順應市場經濟規律，幾大業務領域均有建樹，發展形勢良好。

優勢互補，合作共榮。集團公司矢志于同海內外各界朋友在互惠互利原則下，開展寬領域多層次的經濟技術合作，共創美好事業藍圖。

GANSU MECHANICAL GROUP COMPANY

The company, approved to set up by Gansu provincial government in 1992, is a large scaleenterprise with industry, trade, science and technology, finance and service. Its core unit isformed of 50 enterprises and institutions, with 270000 staff and workers. The company exercisesunified management and administration of the assets over the subsidiary core units.

The company is with rich industry base, over 3600 varieties of mechanical and electricalproducts, among whom there are many good quality and famous brand products of the state andlocal. In recent years, the company conforms to the market economy regular, several businessfields all make a contribution, the development situation is good, "Superiority is mutuallycomplementary. Cooperation and common prosperity" The company likes to develop economictechnology cooperation of wide fields and many administrative levels and draw a beautifulblueprint together with the friends both at home and abroad under the mutually beneficialprinciple.

中國人民銀行甘肅省分行

趙春生，高級經濟師，中共黨員。1935年生，滿族。現任中國人民銀行甘肅省分行行長，中共甘肅省委第八屆委員，省八屆人大代表。
Zhao Chun Sheng ·· Senior economist, President.
The committee member of the eighth provincial Party committee in Gansu. The deputy to the Eighth People's Congress.

簡 介

中國人民銀行甘肅省分行是總行在甘肅的派出機構，是貫徹實施國家貨幣政策；按照授權代表省政府領導和管理全省金融事業的行政機關。

中國人民銀行甘肅省分行發揮中央銀行職能，當好政府的經濟參謀，為政府提供科學的决策依據，通過不斷加強和改善金融宏觀調控措施，運用經濟、法律和行政手段，維護全省的金融秩序，領導、管理、監督、轉換、協調全省的金融機構，為我省各類金融機構穩健經營和金融市場有序運作提供完善服務，以推動地方經濟持續、快速、健康地發展。

GANSU BRANCH OF CHINA PEOPLE'S BANK

The branch is an agency of China People's Bank in Gansu, also is an administrativeorganizations of following the national money policy, leading and managing the provincialfinance cause on behalf of the provincial government according to the authorization.

The branch plays the central bank function, is a good economy chief of the government, provides scientific policy basis for the government. Through continnousely strengthening andimproving financial macrocontrol measure, applies economic, law, administrative means to defendthe provincial finance order, lead, manage, control, check, concert the provincial financesetup. It also provides perfect service for firmly managing of various finance organs andmoving in turn in the finance market so as to promote the local economy's developingcontinuously, quickly and healthfully.

定期分析我省貨幣流通形勢，促進市場繁榮發展。圖為劉世安副行長在貨幣流通形勢與政策理論座談會上作專題發言。

Regularly analysing the money circulation situation of our province. Bringing about a richmarket advance.

The vice prisident of Liu Shi An is making a report on a special topic at the forum on themoney circulation situation and policy theory.

中國人民銀行甘肅省分行

貫徹國家貨幣政策，安排、部署我省金融工作。圖為在蘭州召開的全省銀行行長、保險公司經理會議，傳達貫徹總行會議精神。

Following the state money policy, planning, disposing our provincial finance work. The meeting of the provicial bank presidents and insurance company managers convening in Lanzhou is relaying and following the gereral meeting' s spirt.

努力增加同國際金融組織的聯系，充分利用外資，促進我省經濟健康發展。圖為亞洲開發銀行中國處官員來我省考察時同行領導合影留念。

Hardly ncreeasing the connetion with the international finance organizations, fullyutilizing foreign funds, bringing about a health advance in Gansu economy. China officers of Asian Developing Bank have a group photo taken to make the occasion with the bank leaders Whenthey visited in Gansu.

中國人民銀行甘肅省分行積極促進甘肅證券業的健康發展，1993 年批準我省六家證券商成為上海、深圳證券交易所會員單位，并在蘭州設立證券交易大廳，公開掛牌交易。圖為崔正華、許飛青、盧克儉等省上領導視察甘肅證券公司證券交易廳。

Gansu People's Bank actively brings about a health advance in Gansu stock trade. In 1993, it approved six stock trading companies in Gansu becoming the member units of Shanghai 、 Shenzhen stock exchange and built stock exchange hall in Lanzhou, publicly hung out its shingleto exchange.

The provincial leaders of Cui Zheng Hua, Xu Fei Qing, Lu Ke Jian visit the stock exchangehall of Gansu Stock Company.

甘肅機械集團公司 蘭州電機廠

廠長：陽貽華 Director: Yang Yi Hua

國家銀獎產品－TEH 系列交流同步發電機
Product of the State Silver Prize·· TEH series of synchronous alternator

新產品－交流伺服電機
New product· alternating current esrvo electric machinery

簡介

蘭州電機廠是國家機械工業部布點在西北地區制造電機和發電設備的大型骨干企業，始建于 1958 年。工廠現有職工 6000 多人，其中有各類工程技術人員和專業管理人員 1200 多人，125 人具有專業高級職稱。工廠占地面積 55 萬平方米，固定資產一億多元。

蘭州電機廠產品共有十大類，即大中型交流電機、大中型直流電機、一般交流發電機、柴油發電機組、移動電站、中頻發電機、低壓控制屏、特殊專用電機、交流伺服及主軸電機、中小型水輪發電機組共計 88 個系列，330 個品種，2000 多個規格，年綜合生產能力達二百萬千瓦。

地址：甘肅省蘭州市七里河區民樂路 66 號
電話：2336951
傳真：0931---2335068
郵編：730050

LANZHOU ELECTRIC MANUFACTORY

The manufactory, set up 1958, is a key, large-scale enterprise making electric machine andgenerated electricity equipment in the northwest China fixed by the National Machinery IndustryDepartment. Now it has over 6000 staff and workers, among whom there are over 1200 variousengineers and technicians and specialized management personnel, 125 personnel with senior specilized post. The manufactory has 550000 m2 area and 1 hundred million yuan fixedassets.

Its products has ten kinds, such as large-medium alternating current machines, large- mediumdirect current machine, general alternator, diesel generating set, moving power station, intermediate frequency generator, low-pressure control screen, special purpose electric machine, alternating current esrvo and spindle motor, medium-small turbine generating set, altogether88 series of 330 varieties of over 2000 standards. The annual production capacity reaches 2million kw.

Add: No. 66 Minle Road, Qilihe District, Lanzhou Gansu
Tel : 2336951
Fax : 0931---2335068
Post Code: 730050

LANZHOU ELECTRIC MANUFACTORY

甘肅機械集團公司

THE GREAT WALL CONTROL APPLIANCE PLANT IN TIANSHUI

簡介

主要產品：KYNI 高壓櫃、GCK4 低壓抽屜開關櫃、起重機電氣控制設備；CJ12、24、20、35 交流接觸器； CZ18、CZO、CZ2、CZ10、TCC1 直流接觸器；YWZ2、ZWZ10 制動器； JL15、JT3A、JT18 繼電器。

地址：天水市秦城區南廓路11號
電話：214511 212763
傳眞：212766
電掛：2235
郵編：741018

廠長：劉玉民 Director : Liu Yu Min

天水長城控制電器廠

THE GREAT WALL CONTROL APPLIANCE PLANT IN TIANSHUI

Main products: KYNI high- pressure case, GCK4 low- pressure drawer switch case craneelectricity control equipment, CJ12, 24, 20, 35 alternating current contactor CZ18, CZO, CZ2, CZ10, TCCIdirect current contactor, YWZ 2, ZWZ 10 brake, JL15, JT3A, JT18 relay.

Add: No, 11 Nankuo Road, Qincheng District, Tianshui
Tel : 214511 212763
Fax : 212766
Cadle: 2235
Post Code: 741018

GCK4 低壓抽屜開關櫃 GCK4 low-pressure drawer switch case

裝配生產綫 The assembly line

甘肅機械集團公司　天水長城開關廠

簡介

本廠為機械部中壓等級(0.4～36KV)開關設備及電器元件定點專業制造廠，重點骨干企業。產品遍布全國幷出口亞非八國。四種產品分獲部、省優質產品稱號。企業榮獲“部工藝管理先進企業”、“省質量管理獎”等榮譽。為國家二級企業。

地址：甘肅省天水市秦城區長開路 6 號
電話：212942
傳眞：212870
郵編：741018

天水長城開關廠廠長 高級工程師梁國恆
Director: Liang Guo Heng (Senior engineer)

THE GREAT WALL SWITCHGEAR PLANT IN TIANSUI

The plant is a key enterprise, a fixed specialized plant making medium-pressure grade (0.4～36KV) switch equipments and appliance cells of the Mechanical Department. Its products areselling well throughout the country and has been exported to eight countries of Asia and Africa. Four kinds of products have been awarded the ministry and provincial prizes of good qualityproducts. The enterprise has been awarded the honours of the ministry technological managementadvanced enterprise and the provincial quality management, etc. It's the second- class, stateenterprise.

Add : No. 6 Changkai Road, Qincheng District,
Tiansui, Gansu
Tel: 212942
Fax: 212870
Post Code: 741018

JYN3-10 手車式高壓開關櫃配 ZN5/13/28---10/630A---3000A 眞空開關手車

JYN3-10 handcart, high-pressure switch ZN5/13/28---10/630A---3000A Vacuum switchhandcart

具有國際八十年代末期先進水平的 FMS 板材柔性加工自動生產綫

The automatic production line of softly processing FMS boards with the internationaladvanced level by the end of the eighties.

THE GREAT WALL SWITCHGEAR PLANT IN TIANSUI

蘭州手扶拖拉機廠

LANZHOU WALKING TRACTOR PLANT

簡介

蘭州手扶拖拉機廠是機械工業部重點農機企業，甘肅機械集團公司緊密層成員廠家，地處七里河工業區，分東、西兩個廠區，占地面積 23 萬平方米，現有職工 2400 多人。主要生產經營的品種有：農機類、摩托類、工程機械類、配件類等四大類，三十余種規格，其中農用運輸車被中國質量管理協會用戶委員會評為“全國百家用戶滿意產品”。

地址：蘭州市七里河區民樂路 8 號
電話：2334721
傳真：2338634
郵編：730050

LANZHOU WALKING TRACTOR PLANT

The plant is a key farming machine enterprise of the Mechanical Industry Department, themember factory of Gansu Mechanical Group Company. It lies in Qilihe industrial district, divided into east and west factory areas with 230000m2 area, over 2400 staffand workers. Its main varieties are farming machines, motocycles, engineering machinery, fittings, four types of more than 30 standards among whom farming transport car is elected thesatisfied product of the national hundred customers by the customer committee of China qualitycontrol committee.

Add : No. 8 Minle Road, Qilihe District, Lanzhou
Tel : 2334721
Fax : 2338634
Post Code : 730050

廠長：吳永高 Director: Wu Yong Gao

質檢人員一絲不苟檢查質量
The workers were inspecting quality seriously

LT2810D 蘭駝牌自卸農用車
LT2810D Lantuo self-unload farming vehicle

甘肅機械集團公司

甘肅機械集團公司　蘭州汽車齒輪廠

LF06S 六檔全同步變速箱齒輪及軸
LF06S six-grade synchronous gearbox gears and axles

廠長：汪海洋 Director : Wang Hai Yang

LANZHOU CAR GEAR PLANT

引進日本東方工程公司具有八十年代國際先進水平的 unic 可控氣氛連續滲碳箱式熱處理自動生產綫。
Unic automatic heat-treatment production line of controlled atmosphere continuing carburingbox with the international advanced level in the eighties form Japan East Engineering Company.

簡介

蘭州汽車齒輪廠是國家生產汽車變速箱總成及其齒輪的重點企業之一，已有 50 余年的歷史。產品有 CA—141、EQ—140、BJ—130 汽車變速箱總成及其齒輪和後橋螺傘齒。新產品有 CA—141 後橋單級減速螺傘齒；LCS—520、MSA—5P、LF06S 汽車全同步變速器總成及其齒輪。

LANZHOU CAR GEAR PLANT

The plant is one of the key enterprises producing car gearbox assembly and its gears inChina. It has lasted for over 50 years since the plant set up. The products include CA—141, EQ—140, BJ—130 car gearbox assembly and its gears and rear axle spiral bevel gears. The newproducts include CA—141 rear axle single retarded spiral bevel gears, LCS—520, MSA—5P, LF06Scar synchronous gearbox assembly and its gears.

MSA—5P 變速箱總成(日本五十鈴) MSA—5P gearbox assembly

地址：蘭州市安寧區桃村 89 號
電報：3635
電話：7666456
郵編：730079
Add: No. 89 Taohua Village, anning District, Lanzhou
Cable: 3635
Tel: 7666456
Post Code: 730079

甘肅機械集團公司

天水鍛壓機床廠

TIANSHUI FORGING PRESS PLANT

廠長: 陳三國 Director: Chen San Guo

簡介

本廠是國家"三五"期間投資建設的三綫企業。1993年6月21日被國家經貿委賦予進出口自營權，并成為國家機電產品出口基地，專業生產各種剪、折整形機床。主要生產QC12Y系列液壓剪板機、W67Y系列液壓板料折彎機以及國內獨家生產的龍門移動式液壓機、液壓切口機、無芯模封頭旋壓機、楔形模橫軋機等，還可承接以上產品的非標及變形機種的設計制造。

地址: 甘肅省天水市北道區
電話: (0938) 736873
傳眞: (0938) 735086
郵編: 741020

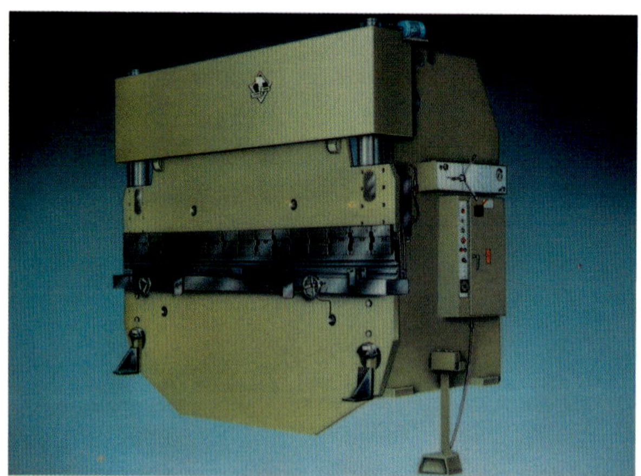

W6TY—160/ 3200 液壓板料折彎機
W6TY—160 / 3200 hydraulic board breaking machine

QC12Y—25× 4000 液壓剪板機
QC12Y—25× 4000 hydraulic board cutting machine

TIANSHUI FORGING PRESS PLANT

The plant is a three–line enterprise invested and built by the state during the period ofthe third–five–year plan. On June, 21, 1993. The state Economic and Trade Committeeentrusted to the plant its own business power of import and export. The plant becomes an exportbase of the state machinery and electrical products, specially produces various cutting andbreaking plastic machine–tools. It mainly produces QC12Y series of hydraulic board cuttingmachine, W67Y series of hydraulic board breaking machine, as well as gantry moving hydraulicmachine, hydraulic cutting machine, non–wick sealing head spinning machine, etc. only producedby the plant in the state. It also contracts to design and make the non– standard and deformedmachinery kinds of the above products.

Add : Beidao District, Tianshui, Gansu
Tel : 736873
Fax : (0938) 735086
Post Code : 741020

地址：甘肅省蘭州市七里河區任家莊 23 號
郵編：730050
電話：2336941
傳眞：2337668

Add : No. 3 Renjiazhuang, Qilihe District, Lanzhou, Gansu
Post Code : 730050
Tel : 2336941
Fax : 2337668

LANZHOU BEARING PLANT

廠長：王鶴德 Director: Wang He De

簡介

蘭州軸承廠是國家大型骨干企業之一，占地 20 萬平方米，現有職工 3300 余人，固定資產原值 5200 萬元，重要生產設備 800 余臺，具有先進、齊全的檢測手段，采用國際(ISO)標準和最新國家標準，生產"0、1、2、6、7、8"六大類，G、E、D 三個精度等級，外徑尺寸在 28mm——300mm 以內的近千個品種的工業軸承，產品暢銷全國，遠銷四十多個國家和地區。

LANZHOU BEARING PLANT

The plant is one of the key, large-scale enterprises of the state with 200000 m2, over 3300staff and workers, 52 million yuan fixed assets, over 800 key production equipments, also withadvanced and complete examination and test means. It adopts international (ISO) standard andthe newest state standard, produces "0, 1, 2, 6, 7, 8," six big types, G, E, D three precisiongrades, near one thousand varieties of the outside diameter size within 28mm——300mm industrialbearings. Its products are selling well throughout the country and have been exported to over40 countries and regions.

各類軸承 Vairous kinds of bearings

辦公大樓 Office building

甘肅機械集團公司

GANSU ENGINEERING INDUSTRY SUPPLY AND MARKETING COMPANY

簡介

甘肅省機械工業供銷總公司為全民物資流通企業。該公司主要經營：金屬、非金屬原材料、化工、機床設備、工程機械、電綫電纜、電工儀器、軸承、儀器儀表、汽車、摩托車以及成套設備等。公司與全國各大生產廠家、鋼廠有着密切的業務聯系。是 1990 年至 1993 年蘭州市工商行特級信用企業。

總公司地址：甘肅省蘭州市中山路 360 號
電話: 8467375
郵編: 730030

總經理：朱寶德 Manager: Zhu Bao De

GANSU ENGINEERING INDUSTRY SUPPLY AND MARKETING COMPANY

The company is a material circulation enterprise of the whole people. It mainly managesmetal, nonmetallic materials, chemical industry, machine tool equipment, engineering machinery, wire and cadle, electric industry equipment, bearing, instrument and meter, car, motorcycle, and complete set of equipments, etc. The company have close business connections with each largeproduction and steel plant all over China. It also was a special- class credit enterprise ofLanzhou Industrial and Commercial Bank from 1990 to 1993.

Add: No.360 Zhongshan Road, Lanzhou, Gansu
Tel: 8467375
Post Code : 730030

公司大樓 Office building

甘肅省汽車工業總公司

簡介

甘肅省汽車工業總公司(甘肅省汽車貿易總公司)是以經營汽車、汽車配件為主，兼營摩托車和配件以及汽車横斷產品的實體性專業流通公司。注冊資金3570萬元，流動資金9758萬元，總公司營業展銷樓位于蘭州市中山路360號。營業辦公場所寬敞，倉儲設施齊全。下設二十四個經銷公司、五十多個經營網點遍布全省各地。年銷售收入達兩億多元，與名優汽車配件生產廠家建立了長期穩固的聯營關系。

地址：蘭州市中山路360號
電話：8462763
傳真：8463414
郵編：730030
電掛：3086

GANSU CAR INDUSTRY COMPANY

The company is a entity, specialized circulation company mainly managing cars and car fittings, also managing motorcycle, motorcycle fittings and car cross products, with 35.7 million yuanregistered funds, 97.58 million yuan circulating funds. The company's business exhibition andsales building lies in the No. 360 Zhongshan Road, Lanzhou. Its office place is commodious andthe goods installation is complete. The company is composed of 24 selling companies, over 50business places which spread all over the province. The annual sales income reaches over 2hundred million yuan. The company has established long-term, firm, combined business relationswith famous-good car and fittings factories.

Add: No. 360 Zhongshan Road, Lanzhou
Tel: 8462763
Fax: 8463414
Post Code: 730030
Cable: 3086

總經理趙方閣(高級經濟師)
President: Zhao Fang Ge (Senior economist)

GANSU CAR INDUSTRY COMPANY

甘肅省汽車工業總公司營業展銷大樓
The exhibition and sales business building

公司部分領導成員在汽車展銷場檢查工作
The leaders of the company are checking up on work in the car exhibition and sales place.

甘肅機械集團公司

甘肅機械集團公司

甘肅省農機總公司

GANSU AGRICULTURAL MACHINERY COMPANY

簡介

甘肅省農業機械總公司是集省、地、縣三級 98 個農機公司統營的經濟實體。流動資金 1 億多元，年銷售額 8 億多元。以經營農、林、牧、副、漁各業所需農機商品為主，并發展成營銷汽車、工程機械、建材和金屬材料、機電、機床和非標設備、農機和汽車配件等 15 個大類、3000 多個品種的綜合性、多元化、集團化的農機流通企業。

地址：甘肅省蘭州市濱河東路 209 號
電話：8413467
傳眞：8886634
郵編：730030
Add: No. 209 Binhe East Road, Lanzhou, Gansu
Tel : 8413467
Fax : 8886634
Post Code: 730030

總經理：武成忠 General president: Wu Cheng Zhong

GANSU AGRICULTURAL MACHINERY COMPANY

The company is a economic entity unified run by 98 agricultural machinery companies of province, district, county, grade–3 with over 1 hundred million yuan circulating funds, 8 hundred million yuan annual sales volume. It mainly manages agricultural machinery products for the needs of farming, forestry, animal husbandry, sideline and fishery and develops to an agricultural machinery circulation enterprise of synthesis, pluralism, group managing and selling cars, engineering machinery, building material, metal material, machine electricity,machine tools, non–standard equipments, agricultural machines and car fittings, 15 kinds of over 300 varieties.

展銷現場 The exhibition and selling site

公司經銷的部分產品 Some products sold by the company

中国工商银行甘肃省分行

中國工商銀行甘肅省分行行長：張文軒
President: Zhang Wen Xuan

ICBC

GANSU BRANCH OF THE INDUSTRAL AND COMMERCIAL BANK OF CHINA

簡介

中國工商銀行甘肅省分行自 1985 年與人民銀行分設以來，已發展成為甘肅省最大的專業銀行。分行機關現設有 25 個處室及附屬機構，轄 14 個地、州中心支行、市支行。1 個省轄辦事處 101 個縣(市)支行和支行級辦事處，149 個分理處和縣轄辦事處，605 個儲蓄所，全部機構達 866 個；現有職工 11381 人，現任行長張文軒，副行長李延齡、馮茂霖，總經濟師徐壬良。

到 1993 年 7 月末該行各項存款余額達 134.2 億元，占甘肅省國家銀行的比重達 48.9%。其中儲蓄存款余額達 83.67 億元,企業存款余額達 50.53 億元。各項貸款余額達 134.45 億元，占甘肅省國家銀行的比重達 42.6%。其中工業流動資金貸款 110.65 億元，固定資產貸款達 23.8 億元。共建成電子化網點 350 個電子化網點覆蓋率已達 40%；基本上在地、市行及重點行處實現了儲蓄監櫃聯網和通存通兌。目前已同全省 87953 戶企、事業單位和 588 萬戶職工居民建立了長期穩定的信用關系。除為生產、流通、消費提供系統的金融服務外，還開辦了信托投資、房地產、委托、代理、租賃、代發工資、牡丹信用卡、信息咨詢和國際金融等業務，目前已同世界上 200 多家金融機構建立了代理關系，為社會提供了更廣泛的金融服務。

GANSU BRANCH OF THE INDUSTRIAL AND COMMERCIAL BANK OF CHINA

Gansu Branch has been the largest spcialized bank since it was parted from the People's Bank inMarch, 1985. The branch organization now has 25 departments and its subsidiaries with thecentral branches, city branches of 14 regions and prefectures, one office under Gansu province,101 county branches and branches offices, 149 small local branches and the offices under thecounties, 605 savings banks. The branch has total 866 structures and 11381 staff and workers.Now the president is Zhang Wen Xuan, the vice presidents are Li Yan Ling, Feng Mao Lin, thegeneral economist is Xu Ren Liang.

By the end of July, 1993, the remaining sum of various savings reached 134.2 hundredmillion yuan making up 48.9 per cent of the total remaining sum of the state banks in Gansuamong whom the remaining sum of savings deposit reached 83.67 hundred million yuan and theremaining sum of enterprise deposit reached 50.53 hundred million yuan. The remaining sum ofvarious loans reached 134.45 hundred million yuan making up 42. 6 per cent of the totalremaining sum of the state banks in Gansu among whom industrial circulating funds loans reached110.65 hundred million yuan and fixed assets loans reached 23.8 hundred million yuan. 350electron networks have been built and the cover rate has reached 40 per cent. Savings controlcounters have been basically realized joint-net in the region or city banks and the key banks ordepartments and you can deposit and exchange money at any banks of the whole system. Now it hasbuild long-time, stable credit relation with 87953 enterprises and institutes and 588 workersand residents. Besides supplying systematic finance service for production, circulation andconsumption, the branch has opened trust investment, " Mudan" credit cards, news consultation,international finance, etc. Now the branch has built acting relation with over 200 financialstructures in the world and supplied wider finance service for society.

ICBC

中國工商銀行甘肅省分行

1993 年新落成的工商銀行甘肅省分行營業大樓夜景

Night view of the business building newlyset up in 1993

在全省率先實行櫃員制，提高了工作效率，縮短了辦理業務時間，增強了服務功能。

The branch first carried out counter staff system and raised work efficiency, shortenedhandling business time, strengthened service function in Gansu.

自動取款機為廣大客戶提供了方便.
Automatic drawing-money engine supplies convenience to vast consumers.

發放貸款支持重點建設、重點項目。 圖為貸款支持的甘肅煤礦機械廠建成年產 2000 噸摩擦焊鑽杆生產綫，產品獲全國首屆科技貸款優秀成果金箭獎。

Grant credits to support key construction and items.

The picture is providing a loan to support Gansu Coal Mechanical Plant building the annualproduction capacity of 2000 tons of the friction welding pipe production line.

The products have won "Gold Arrow " prize of excellent achievements in China firstscientific and technological credite.

規範化的工作，優質高效的服務，贏得了廣大客戶的信賴。
Standard work, good quality and high efficiency servicehave won vast consumers' trust.

GANSU BRANCH OF THE INDUSTRAL AND COMMERCIAL BANK OF CHINA

GANSU BRANCH OF THE INDUSTRAL AND COMMERCIAL BANK OF CHINA

“儲蓄之花”燦爛絢麗
“Savings flowers” are bright.

大力開展業務知識競賽，不斷提高職工的業務技能和素質。圖為獲得業務知識競賽團體第一名的省分行機關代表隊在領獎臺上。
Vigorously develop business knowledge competition and continuously raise the workers’business skill and quality.
The picture is that the office representative team of Gansu Branch won the first team titlein the business knowledge competition and were receiving the prize on the stage.

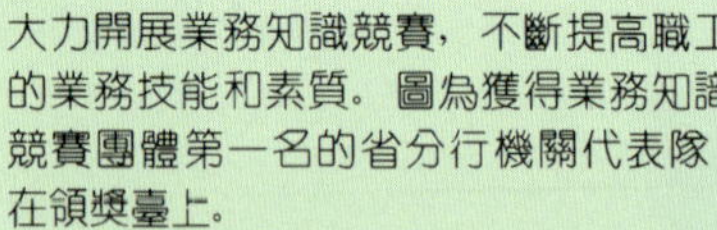

貸款支持“蘭化”晴綸生產綫改造裝置
Provide a loan to support Lanzhou Chemical Industry Company rebuilding the installationof acrylic production line.

大力發展國際業務，積極支持具有地方民族特色的外貿創匯產品
Vigorously develop international business and actively support the achieving exchangeproducts of Foreign Trade with the local national features.

ICBC

中國工商銀行甘肅省分行

全神貫注，一絲不苟。圖為：獲得全省、全國業務技術比賽會計揭打傳票第一、第五名的選手 唐旭紅在比賽中。

Be absorbed, be conscientious and meticulous.

The picture is that Tang Xu Hong is in the competition who is the first and fifth contestantfor opening and tapping vouchres in Gansu provincial and China Business Skill Competition.

地址：蘭州市靜寧路 218 號
電話：8410011—6806
郵編：730030
Add: No.218 Jingning Road, Lanzhou
Tel: 8410011 · 6806
Post Code: 730030

牡丹卡業務長足發展，已與全國近百個城市聯網。

"Mudan" Care business develops rapidly and has joined the nets with near hundred of citiesin China.

GANSU BRANCH OF CHINA AGRICULTURAL BANK

簡 介

我行辦理農村金融，服務城鄉經濟，并受中國人民銀行委托，領導和管理全省農村信用社。

我行堅持信譽至上、竭誠服務、高效廉潔，文明辦行的方針，發揮國家銀行和農村集體金融組織整體功能，應用微機并率先在全省金融系統采用自動取款等現代化手段，利用遍及城鄉的分支機構網絡，為農工商企事業單位、個人及國內外廣大客戶提供優質、高效、完善的服務，存貸業務發展迅速，業務領域不斷拓寬，并加快步伐，嚮國有商業銀行的改革目標邁進。1993年底，全省農業銀行和信用社存款達93.6億元，占全省各金融機構存款總額的30.85%，信貸資產達107.4億元，占全省金融系統信貸資產總額的29.2%。

我行適應改革開放的要求，立足國內業務，積極發展國際業務。目前，我行已與30多個國家和地區的24家銀行及其分支機構建立了代理行關系，外匯存款574萬美元，年辦理各類國際結算業務數千萬美元。

地址：蘭州市中心廣場統辦二號樓
電話：8418386
電掛：1053
郵編：730030

中國農業銀行
甘肅省分行

中國農業銀行甘肅省分行辦公大樓
The office building of Gansu Agriculturial Bank.

中國農業銀行甘肅省分行行長：羅正亞
President : Luo Zheng Ya

GANSU BRANCH OF CHINA AGRICULTURAL BANK

The branch handles rural finance, serves urban and rural economy and leads, managesGansu rural credit houses with the commission of China People's Bank.

The branch insists on the policy of "credit supreme, serving wholeheartedly, highefficiency and honest, running bank civilized, plays the whole function of the National bankand rural collective finance organization, applies microcomputer, is in the first to use modernmeans of drawing money automatically in Gansu finance system, supplies good quality, highefficiency and perfect service to agricultural, industrial and commercial enterprise units, individual and all customers at home and aboard with the branch setup network all over city andvillage. Its existing stock business is developing quickly, business fields are continuouslyopening widely. The branch is quickening its steps to stride forward towards the reform goal ofthe national commerce bank. By the end of 1993, Gansu savings of the agricultural banks and thecredit houses reached 93.6 hundred million yuan and made up 30.85 per cent of the total savingsvolume of Gansu financial setup. The credit assets reached 107.4 hundred million yuan and madeup 29.2 per cent of the total volume of Gansu financial system.

We are suiting the needs of reform and opening, are based on the national business andactively developing international business. Now, we have established agent bank relations with24 banks and its branches of over 30 countries and regions. The foreign exchange savings is5740 thousand $, various international settling accouts business of the anual handling is thousands of thousand $.

Add : No.2 the United Office Building, the Centre Square, Lanzhou.
Tel : 8418386
Cable : 1053
Post Code : 730030

GANSU BRANCH OF CHINA AGRICULTURAL BANK

分行領導檢查基層工作。
President are in specting

分行領導(右一)與意大利客人洽談有關業務。
President are holding talks with Italian

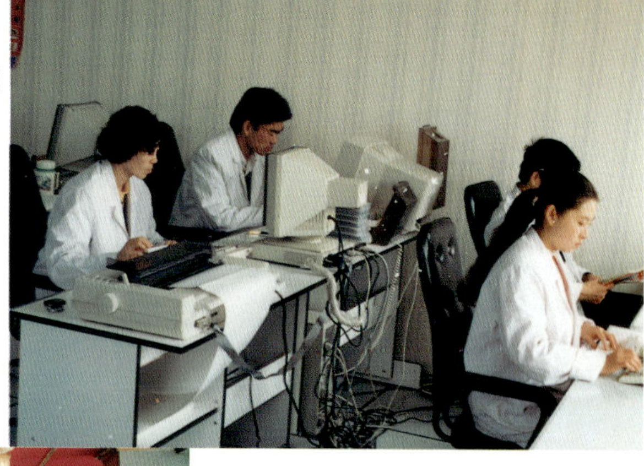

電子化建設有突破性進展，開通了環球間金融電訊通訊網絡。

The electronics construction is developing penetratively and opening the financialtelecommunication networks in the earth.

分行營業部營業廳
The business hall of the branch'es business department.

中國農業銀行甘肅省分行

位于市中心中央廣場的分行培訓中心暨國際業務部、營業部。
The training centre and the international business department lying in the centre square, Lanzhou.

在科技開發一條街的農行服務機構
The service setup of Lanzhou Agriultural Bank is in the street of scientific and technicaldeveloping.

GANSU BRANCH OF THE CHINESE PEOPLE'S CONSTRUCTION BANK

地址：蘭州市中心廣場統辦二號樓
郵編：730030
電話：8418095 8418293
傳真：8418086
Add : No. 2 the United Office, Building the Centre Square, Lanzhou
Post Code : 730030
Tel: 8418095 8418293
Fax : 8418086

中國人民建設銀行甘肅省分行 行長、黨組書記　張宗祥
President and Party Secretary : Zhang Zong Xiang

中國人民建設銀行甘肅省分行

簡介

中國人民建設銀行甘肅省分行是以經營中長期投資業務為主，既管理政府投資又經營信貸業務，既經辦國內業務又經營國際業務，具有多功能、綜合性的國家專業銀行。全行現有職工8000人，機構、網點665個，其中地州市中心支行14個，專業支行4個，縣支行、辦事處、分理處170個，儲蓄網點477個。另有國際業務部及代辦點15個，房地產信貸部130個，城市信用社31個。還有信用卡、信托投資、租賃、房地產開發、信息、咨詢等多種服務項目和服務機構。目前全行總資產達200多億元。隨着金融改革的不斷深化，甘肅省建行將進一步開拓業務，逐步嚮商業銀行發展，以更新、更優、更全的水準竭誠為社會各界服務。

GANSU BRANCH OF THE CHINESE PEOPLE'S CONSTRUCTION BANK

The branch mainly manages long-time investment business, and manages government investment aswell as credit business, also manages home business as well as international business, It's aNational professional bank with various functions and synthesis. It now has 8000 staff andworkers, 665 net places among whom there are 14 central branches of region, prefecture and city, 4 professional branches, 170 county branchess, offices, and small local branches, 477 savingsnet places. It also has 15 charge affairs offices of international business department, 130real estate credit departments, 31 city credit houses and various service items and structuresof credit card, credit investment, rent, real estate developing, news advice and etc. The totalassets of the branch now reaches over 200 hundred million yuan. With the deeping of finance reform, the branch will further open up business, progressively develop to commercial bank, whole heartedly scvice for various society sections with newer, more excellent, more total standard.

甘肅省建設銀行辦公大樓
The office building to Gansu Construction Bank

行長：平　岳 President: Ping Yue

中國銀行甘肅省分行

簡介

國家外匯外貿專業銀行中國銀行甘肅省分行的分支機構已遍及全省除甘南州以外的13個地(州)市，網點總數達85個，并與世界上50多個國家和地區的100家銀行的60多個分、支機構建立了業務往來關系。主要業務有：各項外匯和人民幣進出口貿易、非貿易國際結算；國際匯兑；國內結算；單位、個人外幣和人民幣存款；華僑存、匯款；外匯和人民幣貸款；國際信托投資、租賃咨詢、擔保見證；發行金融債券；代客叙做外匯買責；發行人民幣長城信用卡等。近年來，還辦理外國政府貸款、混合貸款、出口買方信貸業務，并嚮省內各單位積極提供國際經濟、金融行情及信息。建行17年來，累計發放各項人民幣流動資金貸款130多億元；支持甘肅省出口創匯14億美元；累計上繳國家税利1.9億元人民幣。

地址：蘭州市平凉路577號
郵編：730030
傳真：8418096
電傳：72128 LZBOC CN
電話：8418675

GANSU BRANCH OF CHINA BANK

GANSU BRANCH OF CHINA BANK

The branch organizations of Gansu Branch of China Bank·· The National Foreign Exchange AndForeign Trade Specialized Bank, have spread all over 13 prefectures, cities except Gannan. Thesum total reaches 85 networks. The branch has built business contact relations with 60 branchorganizations of 100 banks of over 50 countries and regions in the world. Its main businessincludes various foreign exchange, RMB import and export trade, nontrade international settlingaccounts, international collection, domestic settling accounts, unit and individual foreignmoney and RMB savings, overseas Chinese savings and remittance, foreign exchange and RMB loans, international trust invests, rent consultation, assurance and witness, issuing financial bond,issuing RMB Great Wall credit cards, etc. In recent years, the branch also handles foreigngovernment loans, mixture loans, export buyer credit business and actively providesinternational economy, financial quotations and information to each unit in Gansu.Since settingup for 17 years, the branch has total issued over 130 hundred million yuan of various RMBfloating funds, supported 14 hundred million $ export foreign exchange to Gansu, total turned 1.9 hundred million yuan tax profit over to the state.

Add: No. 577 Pingliang Road, Lanzhou
Post Code: 730030
Fax: 8418096
Telex: 72128 LZBOC CN
Tel: 8418675

我行利用日本買方信貸 22.65 億日元，支持蘭州化學工業公司化肥廠改擴建項目于 1993 年 12 月 30 日在蘭州舉行了簽字儀式。

The branch utilized 22.65 yen of Japan buyer credit to support the Chemical Fertilizer Factoryof Lanzhou Chemical Industry Company to rebuild and extend the items. The signing ceremony tookplace in Lanzhou on Dec. 30, 1993.

我行利用西班牙政府混合貸款 2891 萬美元支持甘肅省引進 10 萬門程控電話交換機設備項目簽字儀式于 1993 年 6 月 4 日在蘭州舉行。

The branch utilized 28.91 million $ mixture loans of Spain Government to support Gansu toimport the equipment item of 100000 programme control telephone switchboard. The signingceremony took place in Lanzhou on June 4, 1993.

我行長城信用卡業務自 1989 年陸續開辦以來，發展迅速。截止 1994 年 4 月末信用卡存款余額達 12589 萬元人民幣，有效卡發行數達 11427 張，各類特約商戶 315 家，僅 4 月份交易額就達 15135 萬元人民幣。

Since Great Wall credit card business opened in 1989, it has developed quickly. By the endof April, 1994, the remaing sum of credit card saving reached 125.89 million yuan. The issuenumber of effective cards reached 11427 copies, various kinds of 315 special commercialconsumers. Only in April, trad volume reached 151.35 million yuan.

GANSU BRANCH OF CHINA BANK

中國農業銀行蘭州市支行

LANZHOU AGRICULTURAL BRANCH OF CHINA AGRICULTURAL BANK

行長、黨委書記、高級經濟師張勇
Economist: Zhang Yong President, Party Secretary, Senior

簡介

蘭州市農業銀行自 1979 年恢復建行後，已發展成為資金實力雄厚、服務功能齊全、企業信譽和經濟效益良好的國家專業銀行，營業網點遍布蘭州城鄉各地。

業務範圍包括：

辦理城鄉機關、團體、部隊、企業、事業單位存款、城鄉集體、個體工商戶存款及個人儲蓄存款；辦理工業企業、商業企業、農業企業、鄉鎮企業和集體經濟組織、供銷合作社以及農戶和個體工商戶各項貸款；

辦理轉帳結算、現金結算及票據貼現業務。

辦理委托、代理、租賃、咨詢、信托、房地產、(金穗)信用卡等業務；

辦理資金拆借和金銀收售；經批準後，可發行金融債券，代理發行債券和股票及其轉讓業務。

正積極開辦國際業務和農村保險業務。

蘭州市農行在嚮商業銀行轉軌期間，始終堅持經濟效益和社會效益并舉的方針，本着一流素質、一流服務、一流質量、一流效率的目的，竭誠為社會各界服務，與企業和廣大客戶一起共創輝煌未來。

具有現代化服務水平的電腦服務中心
The electric-head sevice centre with modern service level.

市農行辦公樓外景
Outdoor view of the branch office building.

中國農業銀行蘭州市支行

市縣領導出席榆中農行辦公樓落成典禮并剪彩。
The city and county leaders are attending inauguration ceremony of Yuzhong AgriculturalBank's office building and cutting the ribbon.

規模較大的職工運動會
Larger scale labour sports meeting

聞名中外的安寧桃鄉，其發展中有農行、農村信用社的一份貢獻。
Famous Anni Peach Country. Its development has the contribution of the Agricultural Bankand the rural credit house.

LANZHOU AGRICULTURAL BRANCH OF CHINA AGRICULTURAL BANK

The branch has developed to a National specialized bank with strong funds, complete servicefunction, good enterprise credit and economic benefit since it returned to set up in 1979, Itsbusiness stations spread all over Lanzhou.

Business scope:

Handling deposit of government, organization, army, enterprise, institution, urban and rural collective, individual industry and commerce unit and individual savings.

Handling various loans of industrial enterprises, commercial enterprises, agriculturalenterprises, village and town enterprises, collective economy oganizations, supply and marketingcooperatives, peasant household, and individual industry and commerce units.

Handling settling accounts of transfer accounts and cash, discount business of bills.Handling commission, action, rent, consultation, trust, real estate, credit cards and so on.

Handling fund loan and collecting and selling gold and silver.

Issuing financial bonds, stocks and its transferation after ratification.

Now starting international business and countryside insurance business.

During the branch is turning into commercial bank, it throughout insists on both economic and social benefit polices, servers for the social wholeheartedly in line with the purpose offirst-class quality, first-class service, first-class quality, first- class efficiency. andcreates glorious future with enterprises and consumers.

Add : No. 31 Gulou lane, Lanzhou.
Tel : 8461721
Post Code : 730030

中國人民建設銀行蘭州市支行

簡介

中國人民建設銀行蘭州市支行成立于1955年1月，是蘭州地區以經營中、長期投資信用為主同時開展多種金融業務的國家銀行。1993年底各項存款余額達163.257萬元，撥貸款業務總量達到了20多億，從1986年到現在，累計經辦大中型項目和省列重點項目37個。1993年，我行經辦的大中型項目有永登引大入秦工程、蘭州生物制品所疫苗生產綫工程、蘭州電信樞紐工程等5個項目，共完成投資額2億多。

到1993年底，蘭州市建設銀行已擁有1587名干部職工，21個科(室)，下屬建行房地產開發公司、城市建設信用部、住房信貸部，下轄3個縣支行，11個辦事處，27個分理處，82個儲蓄所(櫃)。

我行隨着全國金融事業發展也不斷采取改革措施，拓寬城市金融業務領域，壯大資金實力，經營管理水平和職工隊伍素質不斷提高，為支持蘭州地區經濟建設作出了應有貢獻。

地址：蘭州市城關區金昌路47號
電話：8825882（辦公室主任程光夏）
傳真：8820412
郵編：730030

行長：焦正明 President :Jiao Zheng Ming

建行蘭州市支行辦公大樓 The Office Building of Lanzhou Construction Branch

LANZHOU BRANCH OF CHINA PEOPLES CONSTRUCTION BANK

LANZHOU BRANCH OF CHINA PEOPLES CONSTRUCTION BANK

Lanzhou Branch of the Chinese People's Construction Bank, set up in Jan, 1955, is a Nationalbank of mainly managing medium and long-time investment credit as well as developing financcbusiness.

By the end of 1993, the bank has 1587 staff and workers, 21 offices, subordinate real estatedeveloping company, city construction credit department, housing credit department, 3 countybranches, 11 offices, 27 small local branches, 82 savings banks, Its various deposit volumereaches 1632570000 yuan. Allocations and loans business volume reaches 20 thousand million yuan.

Since 1986, the bank has managed 37 large-medium scale items and provincial key items. In 1993, it managed items of Yongdeng Yindaruqin Project, The vaccine production line of Lanzhou Biological Product Institute, Lanzhou telecommunication control project, etc. It has completed 2 hundred million investment volume.

With the deeping of finance reform, we'll actively open up city finance business field, strenthen fund strength. The management level and personnel quality has continuously raised andmade contribution to Lanzhou economy.

Add: No.47 Jinchang Road, Chengguan, Lanzhou
Tel: 8825882
Post Code: 730030
Fax: 8820412

蘭州支行支持建設的蘭州電信樞紐工程,完成投資4300萬元

Lanzhou telecommunication control project

蘭化公司毫秒樓,完成投資19256萬元。

The millisecond building of LanzhouChemistry Company

建行蘭州市支行領導班子焦正明(左二),副行長徐香英(左一),白興周(右三),張蘭生(右二)紀檢組長馬建國(右一)研究興行大計。

The leading group : Jiao Zheng Ming (left 2), vice–president ·· Xu Xiang Ying (left 1), BaiXing Zhou (right 3), Zhang Lan Sheng (right 2), and discipline inspecting leader ·· Ma Jian Guoare studying to strengthen bank plan.

建行蘭州市支行積極配合蘭州地區房改的全面起步,積極提供優質服務,1993 年共吸收住房存款 17600 萬元,以抵押形式為建房單位和個人發放貸款 8915 萬元,較好地支持了蘭州地區住房建設。

The branch actively cooperates housing reform with Lanzhou and offers excellent quality service.

1993年8月建行蘭州市支行嚮蘭州各界隆重推出了萬事達 VZSA 信用卡，到目前，已發卡 3000 余張,特約商戶 120 家。

In Aug. 1993, the branch distributed Wanshida, VZSA credit cards and has distributed over3000 copies by now.

1994年3月底，建行蘭州市支行儲蓄存款突破十億元大關，支行領導親自參加儲蓄宣傳活動。

In the end of March, 1994, Lanzhou Branch'es savings topped 10 hundred million yuan. Theleaders took part in disseminating savings activity.

中國人民建設銀行蘭州市支行

交通銀行蘭州分行

LANZHOU BRANCH OF TRAFFIC BANK

簡介

交通銀行蘭州分行于 1989 年經中國人民銀行批準對外營業。新成立的蘭州交行以社會主義商業銀行為目標，開拓進取，努力發展，積極走綜合性銀行之路，有力地支持了蘭州地區經濟建設。

交通銀行蘭州分行經過不懈的努力，業務已由蘭州輻射到周圍經濟區域，業務品種也發展到從人民幣存款、放款 、匯兌、結算到證券交易、信托投資、信息咨詢、租賃、擔保、代保管、外匯業務和保險、房地產等綜合性業務，嚮跨地區、跨行業、多功能、外嚮型的方嚮發展。到目前，蘭州交行已擁有總資產 13.38 億元，為蘭州及周圍經濟輻射地區累計發放各項貸款達 67.8 億元，創利稅共 9680.6 萬元，1993 年人均創利 15 萬元，成為甘肅省金融界的一支新興力量。

交行蘭州分行營業辦公大樓

The business office building of Lanzhou Traffic Bank.

地址：甘肅省蘭州市慶陽路 124 號
電話：8820345 8820084 8827102
傳眞：(0931) 8820172
電掛：3340
郵編：730030

Add : No. 124 Qingyang Road, Lanzhou
Tel : 8820345 8820084 8827102
Fax : (0931) 8820172
Cable : 3340
Post Code : 730030

交行蘭州分行營業廳

The business hall of Lanzhou Traffic Bank

LANZHOU BRANCH OF TRAFFIC BANK

Lanzhou Traffic Bank wsa granted to external business by China People's Bank in 1989. Ittakes the socialist commerce bank as the aim, opens up and keeps forging ahead, develops hard, actively takes synthetic bank road, supports Lanzhou economic construction strongly.

After unremitting efforts, its business has spread from Lanzhou to around economic fields, business varieties has developed from RMB savings, loans, remittance, settling accounts, to stock exchange, trust investment, news consultation, rent, assurance, substitute storage,foreign exchange business, insurance, real estate. It's developing to across regions, across trades, various functions, extroversion type. By now it has total asset of 13.38 hundred million yuan, has granted various credits of 67.8 hundred million yuan to Lanzhou and around economic regions,made profits tax of 96,806,000 yuan. In 1993, the branch made 150000 yuan profits tax per capita.It has become a new force in Gansu financial field.

甘肅省農業廳

地址：蘭州市秦安路 1 號
電話：8823911
郵編：730030

廳長：劉興邦 Director: Liu Xing Bang

簡介

甘肅農業歷史悠久，農作物品種資源豐富，糧食作物主要有小麥、玉米、洋芋、谷子等三十多種。經濟作物主要有棉花、油料、甜菜、黑瓜子、藥材、水果等。蘭州百合、河西發菜、隴南黑木耳、隴東黃花菜等為本省特產。蘭州白蘭瓜、黑瓜子、天水花牛蘋果、甘谷辣椒干、民樂蘋果梨和紫皮大蒜等產品遠銷國內外。藥材種類較多，主要有當歸、黨參、黃(紅)芪、甘草等。

1993 年，全省農業總產值為 130.43 億元，農民人均純收入達到 556 元。農村面貌發生了歷史性的變化，人民安居樂業。

GANSU AGRICULTURAL OFFICE

Gansu agriculture has a long history. The resources of the crops is rich. The grain cropshave over 30 kinds, such as wheat, cron, potato, millet, etc. Economic crops mainly includecotton, oil, beet, black melon seeds, medicinal materials, fruits, etc. The specialities ofGansu have Lanzhou lily, Hexi hair vegetable, Longnan black edible fungus, Longdong day lily, etc. Lanzhou Bailan melon, black melon seeds, Tianshui Huaniu apples, Gangu dried chilli Minleapple–pears and violet garlics, etc. are selling well both at home and abroad. Main medicinalmaterials include Chinese angelica, dangshen, As tragalus membranaceus, licorice root, etc.

In 1993, the total output value of Gansu agriculture was 130.43 hundred million yuan, Percapita net income of the peasants reached 556 yuan, The rural face has historically taken place. The people live and work in peace and contentment.

Add: No. 1 Qinan Road, Lanzhou.
Tel: 8823911
Post Code: 730030

GANSU AGRICULTURAL OFFICE

白蘭瓜主產于甘肅省蘭州、靖遠、民勤、安西等地。其果面呈乳白色，瓤色翠綠，單瓜重 1.5—2 公斤，含糖量 12—16%。并富含鈣、磷、鉄及多種維生素。

Bailan melons, are from Lanzhou, Jingyuan, Minqin, Anxi etc. Its surface is milky white, and its pulp is jade green, Per melon weighs 1.5· 2kg with 12· 16 Per cent sugar, also withrich calcium, phosphorus, iron and many vitamins.

花牛蘋果產于甘肅省天水市。其果色滿紅，果形高樁，五棱突出，果肉質密，脆而爽口，味甜多汁。平均單果重 241.6 克。

Huaniu apples are from Tianshui, Gansu. Its colour is red, its shape is high pile, its fiveedges stick out and its pulp is fine–grained, The apples are crisp, tasty and refreshing, sweetand juicy. Per apple weighs 241.6g.

GANSU LOCAL TAX BUREAU

甘肅省地方稅務局

GANSU LOCAL TAX BUREAU

地址: 蘭州市皋蘭路 76 號(統辦 3 號樓)8 樓 801
電話: 8415628
郵編: 730000
Add: Room 801, 8th Floor, No.3 United Office Buil ding No.76 Gaolan Road, Lanzhou
Tel: 8415628
Post Code: 730000

地方稅務局局長吴碧蓮 Director: Wu Bi Lian

簡介

甘肅省地方稅務局(正廳級)成立于1994年4月，為省政府的直屬機構，受省政府和國家稅務總局雙重領導，以省政府領導為主。省以下各級地方稅務局實行省級地方稅務局垂直管理的領導體制。

1994年4月21日省政府任命吳碧蓮同志為省地方稅務局局長，王維國、郝發忠、徐挺鵬同志為副局長。

甘肅省地方稅務局的主要職責是：貫徹執行國家的各項稅收法律、行政法規和規章；組織各項稅收收入，運用稅收杠杆對經濟進行宏觀調控和監督；負責全省地方稅務局征收的稅種和地方國有企業所得稅的征收管理工作；負責全省地方稅務局系統的機構、編制、人員和經費的管理，按干部管理權限負責系統內干部的考核、任免工作；負責全省地方稅務局系統的稅收計劃，統計報表工作等。

甘肅省地方稅務局將不斷強化征收管理，調動各方面的積極性，使稅收工作更好地適應社會主義市場經濟發展的需要，確保甘肅的財政收入穩步增長，促進甘肅經濟持續、健康發展。

GANSU LOCAL TAX BUREAU

The bureau, set up in April, 1994, is an organization directly under Gansu Provincial Government, under the double leadership of Gansu Provincial Government and the State Tax Bureau, mainlyunder the leadership of Gansu Provincial Government. The various-class local tax bureaus underthe province practise the leadership system of the vertical management of the Local tax bureaus.

On April 21, 1994, the provincial government appointed Wu Bi Lian director. Wang Wei Guo, Hao Fa Zhong, Xu Ting Peng vice directors of the Local Tax Bureau.Its main duty is to implement the state tax laws, administrative laws and regulations, toorganize various tax income, to wield tax lever to conduct macroscopic control and regulationon economy, to be in charge of collecting tax kinds of the provincial Local tax bureau, andcollecting management of local state enterprises' income tax, to be in charge of the managementof local tax system's organizations, establishment, personnel and funds, to be in charge ofappointing, removing and checking on the cadres according to cadre management jurisdiction, tobe in charge of tax plan, statistical report forms of the local tax system.

The bureau will continuously strengthen collect management, arouse various enthusiasm inorder to make tax to suit the needs of the social market economy better, ensure steadilyincreasing of Gansu financial income, bring about a continuous, healthful advance in Gansu economy.

甘肅省文化廳

GANSU CULTURAL OFFICE

甘肅省文化廳廳長：張炳玉 Director: Zhang Bing Yu

簡介

甘肅省文化廳是甘肅省人民政府下設的管理文化藝術事業的職能部門。主管全省的戲劇藝術、群眾文化、文物、圖書、電影、文化市場、文化外事等工作。下設藝術處、群眾文化處、文化市場管理處、電影處、外事處、演出管理處、省文物局(為廳屬二級局)、研究室、多種經營辦公室、辦公室、人事處、計劃財務處、廳直黨委、紀律檢查組、監察室。全省現有專業藝術表演團體 80 個，群眾藝術館 15 個，文化館 83 個，文化站 1269 個，博物館 50 個，圖書館 86 個，電影發行公司 93 個，電影放映隊 2300 個。

GANSU CULTURAL OFFICE

The office is a function department managing cultural and artistic undertakens under theleadership of Gansu People's Government. It mainly manages theatrical art, mass art, cultural relic, books, film, cultural market, cultural foreign affairs, etc. The office includes ArtDepartment, Mass Cultural Department, Cultural Market Management Department, Film Department, Foreign Affairs Department, Programme Management Department, Gansu Cultural Relic Office, Research Office, Various Management Office, Office, Personnel Division, Plant and FinanceDepartment, Office Party Committee, Inspecting Discipline Group, Control Office in Gansu. Nowthere are 80 specialized art performance groups, 15 mass artistic galleries, 83 culturalcentres, 1269 cultural stations, 50 museums, 86 libraries, 93 film releasing companies, 2300film projection teams.

地址：蘭州市東崗西路 284 號
郵編：730000
電話中繼綫：8886773
Add: No. 284 Donggang West Road, Lanzhou.
Post Code: 730000
Tel: 8886773

甘肅省文化廳廳長張炳玉(右)，省文物局局長馬文治，1993 年 5 月為省文物局成立揭牌。

現代隴劇《天下第一鼓》劇照。

The stage Photo of Modern Long Opera ·· "The First Drum Under Heaven"

甘肅省隴劇團在香港演出《鼓舞太平》(1993年)

Gansu Long Opera Troupe performed "Fire Drum Dance" in Hongkong in 1993

甘肅省隴劇團創作演出的隴劇現代戲《天下第一鼓》,1992年參加第三屆中國藝術節演出獲得好評,1993年在全國第三屆文華獎評選中,榮獲"文華新劇目獎"和"文華導演獎"。

Modern opera ·· "The First Drum Under Heaven" written and played by Gansu Long OperaTroupe was well received in the First China Artistic Festival in 1992. In 1993 it won theprizes of "Wenhua New Operas" and "Wenhua Directors" in the Third Choice of Wenhua Prizes.

甘肅省文化廳舉行紀念《文物保護法》頒布十周年宣傳日活動。(1992年)

The office held propaganda day activity marking"Law of protecting cultural relic" issuedfor ten years in 1992.

甘肅省文化廳

甘肅省敦煌藝術劇院創作演出的《敦煌古樂》，此劇根據該院院長席臻貫破譯的敦煌藏經洞中 25 首唐代樂曲創編而成，集歌、樂、舞為一體，1993 年赴香港演出。
"Dunhuang Ancient Music" written and played by Gansu Dunhuang Artistic Opera Troupe. It wasperformed in Hongkong in 1993

敦煌莫高窟全景
Full view of Dunhuang Mogao Grottoes

嘉峪關全景
Full view of Jiayuguan

《敦煌古樂》劇照。
The stage photo of "Dunhuang Ancient Music"

麥積山石窟第 44 窟、佛
The 44th grotto of Maiji Mountains.

麥積山石窟全景
Full view of Maiji Mountains

甘肅省雜技團在香港演出雜技《雙鑽桶》(1993 年)
Gansu Acrobatic Troupe performed the acrobatics · · "Double Jumping Through Bucket" in Hongkong in 1993

甘肅省雜技團在香港演出雜技《飛天造型》(1993 年)
Gansu Acrobatic Troupe performed the acrobaticsお "Feitian Modelling" in Hongkong in 1993.

GANSU AUDIT BUREAU

甘肅省審計局黨組書記、局長高存弟
Party secretary and Director: Gao Cun Di

地址：蘭州市民主東路 89 號
電話：8418672 8418681
傳真：8414644
郵編：730000
Add: No. 89, MinZhu East Road, Lanzhou.
Tel: 8418672 8418681
Fax: 8414644
Post Code: 730000

甘肅省審計局

簡介

甘肅省審計局組建于 1983 年 9 月，依照《憲法》和法律的規定獨立行使審計監督權，對全省財政金融、行政事業單位、基本建設、工交商貿企業、利用外資、農林水利等領域的財政財務收支及國有資産管理使用情況進行審計監督，并對地縣審計機關、社會審計組織、内審機構進行管理和業務指導。現任局黨組書記、局長高存弟，副局長龐一娟、孫永廉、韓汝坤。

GANSU AUDIT BUREAU

The bureau, set up in Sep. 1983, lonely exercises audit and supervision authority accordingto the Constitution of the People's Republic of China and the legal provisions. It audits andsupervises the management and use condition of the national assets and financial income of thewhole provincial finance, administrations and institutions, capital construction, industry, traffic, commerce, trade, utilizing foreign money, farm, forestry, water conservancy and otherfields. It also manages and guides business of the region and county audit bodies, social auditorganizations, internal audit bodies. The Bureau Party Secretary and Director Gao Cun Di, ViceDirectors Pang Yi Juan, Sun Yong Lian, Han Ru Kun.

省審計局黨組一班人在研究審計工作
The group of the bureau Party organization is studying audit work.

審計人員對引大入秦工程光明峽倒虹吸進行現場審計。
The auditors are going on spot audit to Yindaruqin works

我局所屬甘肅省審計事務所是全國百強審計事務所之一。圖為該所所長艾曉明同志。
The bureau is under Gansu Audit Affairs Institute which is one of the hundred best auditaffairs institutes.The picture is director Ai Xiao Ming.

局領導和省審計事務所的領導在一起研究社會審計工作。
The bureau leaders are studying social audit work with the leaders of Gansu Audit AffairsInstitute.

蘭州供電局

LANZHOU POWER SUPPLY BUREAU

局長王步全(左)、黨委書記賈義號在部署全局工作
Director Wang Bu Quan (left) and Party Secretary Jia Yi Hao are assigning the bureau's work

簡介

蘭州電網地處西北電網和甘肅電網的中心，是西北四省一陝、甘、寧、青的電力交換樞紐。作為全國特大型供電企業的蘭州供電局，現有職工 3707 人，下屬 12 個基層單位，擔負着甘、青兩省 5 個地(市)和 20 個縣(市、區)的供電任務。平均供電半徑約 150 公里，電網覆蓋面積 10 萬平方公里；現有 35 千伏及以上變電站 51 座，主變壓器 95 臺,總容量為 4163900 千伏安，輸配電綫路 4000 多公里；擁有固定抄表用戶 9.5 萬戶；固定資產原值 10.49 億元，年售電量達一百多億千瓦時。全年最高負荷 169 萬千瓦，供電可靠率 99.68%；年銷售收入 14 億元。

地址：蘭州市七里河區西津東路 355 號
電話：(0931) 2334311 (0931) 2335321
傳眞：(0931) 2337010
郵編：730050
電掛：9722

LANZHOU POWER SUPPLY BUREAU

The bureau lies the centre of the Northwest electrified wire netting and Gansu electrifiedwire netting. It is the power change hub of four provinces of Shan, Gan, Ning, Qing in theNorthwest. The bureau as the largest state-scale power supply enterprise with 3707 staff andworkers and 12 basic units, holds power supply task of Gan, Qing provinces, 5 districts (cities) and 20 counties (cities and regions), also with 150 km average power supply radius, 100000square km electric net covered area. It now has 51 substations of 35 kv, 95 main transformers, 4163900 kv total capacity, over 4000 km trans mission line, 95000 fixed users, 1049 million Yuan original value of fixed assets, over 100 hundred million kw / h annual selling electricity volume, The annual highest load is 1690000 km. Power supply reliable rate is 99. 68 percent. The annual sales income is 1400 million yuan.

Add : No.355 Xijin East Road, Qilihe, Lanzhou
Tel : (0931) 2334311 (0931) 2335321
Fax : (0931) 2337010
Post Code: 730050
Cable: 9722

蘭州供電局辦公大樓
Office building of Lanzhou Power Supply Bureau

LANZHOU POWER SUPPLY BUREAU

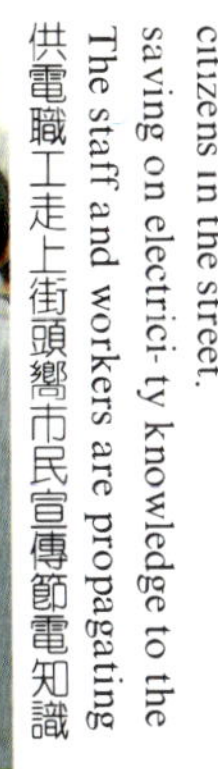

供電職工走上街頭嚮市民宣傳節電知識

The staff and workers are propagating saving on electrici- ty knowledge to the citizens in the street.

為保證安全用電，專業技術人員深入用戶單位檢查用電設備。

The professional technicians are checking electrial equipment in the consumers' unit in orderto pledge using electricity safely.

定期培訓社會電工，提高他們的技術水平。

In order to raise their technical level, social electricity workers are trained regularly.

變電檢修職工在冲洗高壓設備

The repairing workers in the substation are washing high–pressure equipment.

蘭州供電局多種經營工作飛速發展。圖為永登電力局漁場。

The various management works of the bureau are developing rapidly. It is the fish yard ofYongdeng Power Bureau.

甘肅省財政科學研究所

GANSU FINANCE SCIENTIFIC RESEARCH INSTITUTE

簡介

甘肅省財政科學研究所是隸屬于甘肅省財政廳領導的全民所有制事業單位，業務上受國家財政部財政科學研究所指導。目前主要承擔廳內下達的科研課題任務，以及省政府、省委調研部門有關財經方面的分課題任務，省科委及有關部門下達的課題任務，并編輯出版《財會研究》刊物。

甘肅省財政科學研究所內設辦公室、研究部、編輯部、發行科四個職能部門，共有正式職工 18 人。其中高、中級技術人員 9 人，助理 7 人；大專以上學歷人員 16 人，其中碩士學歷 4 人。

由本所主辦的《財會研究》(月刊) 目前在國內公開發行 20000 册，并在 1993 年度全國財政系統 50 多種刊物評比中榮獲二等獎。

地址：蘭州市東崗西路 340 號
電話：8829690
郵編：730000
Add: No.340 Donghang West Road, Lanzhou
Tel: 8829690
Post Code: 730000

法人代表：郭玉安 Legal person: Guo Yu An

省財政科研所領導及各科室領導在研究工作。
The leaders both of Gansu Financial Scientific Research Institute and each office arestudying work.

GANSU FINANCE SCIENTIFIC RESEARCH INSTITUTE

The institute is an ownership institution under the leadership of Gansu Financial Office andunder the leadership of the Finance Scientific Research Institute of the State Financial Ministry on business. Now it mainly undertakes scientific research subject task assigned by the office, the part subject task on financial economy assigned by the Findings and Research department of the provincial government and committee, the subject task assigned by the provincial scientific committee and the department concerned and edits, publishes the publication of Finance and Accounting Research.

The institute has four function departments of Office, Research Department, EditorialDepartment, Publishing Department with 18 staff and workers among whom there are 9 senior andmedium technical personnel, 7 assistants.

Finance and Accounting Research directed by the institute is published for 20000 copies inChina and won the second-class prize in over 50 publications appraisal of the state financesystem in 1993.

《財會研究》雜志獲全國財政系統刊物評比二等獎。圖為獎品及獎狀。
Finance and Accounting Research won the second-class prize of publications appraisal in theState financial system. The picture is the prize and certificate of merit.

《甘肃年鉴》编纂委员会

《甘肃年鉴》编辑部

序

甘肃地处我国的腹部地带，地域辽阔，自然、旅游资源等都具有一定的优势，特别是矿产、水能，位居全国前列，有较大的开发潜力；是中华民族发祥地之一，人文历史源远流长，人民勤劳友好，民族风情特色鲜明。

经过各族人民的辛勤劳作，特别是改革开放以来，甘肃的经济发展较快，具有一定的发展基础，1993年全省国民生产总值（GNP）已接近360亿元，从而强化了甘肃在我国西北地区开发的纽带和依托地位。

为适应甘肃改革开放的需要，省政府决定，自1994年起编辑出版《甘肃年鉴》，期望通过她来全面记载甘肃政治、军事、法律、经济建设、社会发展的进程，反映甘肃先进的企业，优良的产品，介绍甘肃的风土人情，使她不但成为内容比较丰富、可靠，实用性较强，能够提供大量信息的参考书，而且能够成为甘肃对外交流、宣传的一个“窗口”，树立甘肃的形象，让更多的人们了解甘肃，加深印象，我认为，出版这样一本书一定会起到积极的作用。

甘肃省省长：（签名）

一九九四年七月

PREFACE

Gansu lies in the abdomen of our country with vast district, natural, and tourist resources have some superiority, specially minerals and water energy stand in the forefront of China and have considerable development potentialities. It's one of the birthplaces of the Chinese nation . Its humane history goes back to ancient times. The people areindustrious and friendship. Its national features are bright.

After working hard of each nationality people, specially since reformation and opening to the outside world, Gansu economy has developped faster and has certain development base. In 1993, the total value of Gansu national production was near 360 hundred million yuan and strengthened Gansu to be the link and the prop place in the northwest area of our country.

In order to suit the needs of Gansu reformation and opening to the outside world, the Provincial Government decides to publish GANSU YEARBOOK from 1994 and wishes that Gansu Yearbook can record Gansu politics, militray affairs, law, economic construction and social development process, can mirror Gansu advanced enterprises, good products, introduce Gansu local conditions and customs. We shall make it to be not only the reference book with rich, reliable and stronger practical contents providing enormous message, but also to be a Window of Gansu external exchange and propagande, set Gansu image, make more people to know Gansu and get a deeper impression . I think the book will paly a positive role..

Zhang Wu Le

July, 1994.

编者说明

《甘肃年鉴》是一部集《统计年鉴》和《经济年鉴》等诸功能于一体，全面、系统、客观反映甘肃国民经济和社会发展情况的资料性年刊。内容丰富、涉猎广泛、资料翔实可靠，是融知识、资料、信息多功能于一体的综合工具书。它的出版发行，将为各级党政部门、企事业单位和科研部门提供科学决策、咨询和研究的可靠依据。它荟萃了全省各条战线、各个部门和各地区一年来取得的新成就、新进展和新经验，其内容不仅包括甘肃省基本的省情省力状况，而且囊括了全省社会主义现代化建设成就，以及全省在建立社会主义市场经济体系过程中所取得的丰硕成果。同时也是介绍甘肃地理、气候、资源优势、基础设施等软硬环境的投资指南。它为国内外客商来甘肃投资、合作开发提供了详实的论证咨询资料，将有力地推动甘肃经济建设和社会发展，为积极参与国内、国际经济大循环创造条件。本《年鉴》为甘肃省人民政府的地方性年刊，自今年起，将一年一刊，由中国统计出版社统一公开出版发行。

《甘肃年鉴》共分三大部分：其中全省各厅局、各地、州、市、县和省内各专业银行、省内大中型企业的发展概况和经济运行综述为第一部分。并特载了阎海旺书记在第八次党代会上的报告和张吾乐省长在人代会上的工作报告。精炼、生动、客观地记述了甘肃省的政治、经济、法律、人文、科技和生态等诸方面的基本发展情况，颇值一读。第二部分以大量准确、可靠、翔实、权威的统计资料，大容量密集型的信息，分别由综合、人口和劳动力、固定资产投资、能源原材料消费与库存、财政税收、物价、人民生活、城市概况、农业、工业、建筑业、交通运输邮电通讯业、批发零售贸易和餐饮业、对外经济贸易和旅游业、金融、保险、教育、科技以及文化、体育、卫生及其他事业、少数民族、分地县主要指标及附录等十九个篇章组成。统揽无遗、全面系统地描述了1993年甘肃国民经济和社会发展的整个运行状况和发展态势，是一年来甘肃省各族人民在各条战线上奋力拼博所取得成果的真实写照。插图为《甘肃年鉴》的第三部分。为了更有效地宣传、介绍甘肃，为国内外各界人士了解和研究甘肃提供全方位信息服务，追求达到最佳信息咨询效果，本刊增设了大量高清析度明快、形象的彩色插图，并对插图的文字部分全部作了中英文译释对照处理，以生动、活泼、色彩纷呈的形式将甘肃省名、特、优、新、异产品和科研部门及其最新研究成果展示给国内外各界读者，以期提高甘肃及其工农业产品的知名度。

为了尽量满足各方面和各界人士的需要，本《年鉴》在资料内容和编排顺序上，加大了地、州、市、县篇的内容，并增加了表式指标，增加了科学的细分类和分组，增大了宏观经济运行信息和微观经济效益、财务信息容量。为求《年鉴》在内容和外观上更加实用和完善，使编辑质量更上一层楼，我们在总结以往经验的基础上竭尽全力作了较大的改进。时值举国上下认真学习《邓小平文选》第三卷关于社会主义市场经济理论之际，本《年鉴》就是一本理论联系实际有用的参考书。《甘肃年鉴》的问世，对全省人民抓住机遇、迎接挑战、奋博进取，勇敢地面对21世纪和加速全省经济腾飞，将起到积极的促进作用。在这由计划经济向社会主义市场经济转变的历史关头，我们恳切希望有志于改革、开放、振兴甘肃经济的各界有识之士，利用本《年鉴》提供的资料，为重振甘肃丝路之雄风，作出自己的贡献。

《甘肃年鉴》在编纂过程中，受到了有关领导和各部门及热心统计人士的大力支持和热情帮助，在此深表谢意。因时间仓促，内容涉及面广，编撰工作难免遗珠，衷心希望读者批评指正。

编者说明

目录

特载

甘肃概况

·基本情况·

·国民经济社会发展·

政治

·中共甘肃省委·

·中共甘肃省纪律检查委员会·

·甘肃省人民代表大会·

·甘肃省人民政府·

·中国人民政治协商会议甘肃省委员会·

·民主党派和工商联·

·甘肃省总工会·

·甘肃省妇女联合会·

法律

民　族

·民族工作·

地县概况

统计资料

一、综 合

二、人口与劳动力

三、固定资产投资

四、能源原材料消费与库存

五、财政税收

六、物价

七、人民生活

八、城市概况

九、农 业

十五、金融、保险

十六、教育、科技及文化事业

十七、体育、卫生及其他事业

十八、少数民族

十九、分地县主要指标

附录　私人企业概况

大事记

CONTENTS

Special Publishings

Gansu Survey

Basic Condition

National Economy and Social Development

Politics

Gansu Provincial Committee

Gansu Commission for Inspecting Discipline

Social Facilities

Finance and Tax

Finance and Insurance

STATISTICAL MATERIALS

Chapter 1 GENERAL SURVEY

Chapter 2 POPULATION AND LABOR FORCE

Chapter 3 INVESTMENT IN FIXED ASSETS

Chapter 4 CONSUMPTION AND INVENTORY OF ENERGY ORIGINAL MATERIALS

Chapter 5 PUBLIC FINANCE AND TAX REVENUE

Chapter 6 PRICE

Chapter 7 PEOPLE'S LIVELIHOOD

Chapter 9 AGRICULTURE

Chapter 13 WHOLESALE, RETAIL SALES AND CATERING TRADES

Chapter 18 MINORITY NATIONALITIES

Chapter 19 MAIN INDICATORS BY PREFECTURE AND COUNTY

Appendix STATISTICS OF PRIVATE ENTERPRISES

特　　载

大力发展社会主义市场经济
为实现第二步战略目标努力奋斗

——在中国共产党甘肃省第八次代表大会上的报告

（1993年12月19日）

阎海旺

同志们：

现在，我代表中共甘肃省第七届委员会向大会作报告。

中国共产党甘肃省第八次代表大会，是在全省深入贯彻党的十四大和十四届三中全会精神，改革开放和现代化建设事业进入新的发展阶段的大好形势下召开的。这次大会的主要任务是：以邓小平同志建设有中国特色社会主义的理论为指导，认真总结省第七次党代表大会以来的工作，确定今后一个时期的主要任务、基本思想和工作部署，选举产生中共甘肃省第八届委员会的纪律检查委员会。动员全省共产党员和各族人民继续全面正确地贯彻党的基本路线，全面落实党的十四大和十四届三中全会提出的各项任务，加快建立社会主义市场经济体制的步伐，推进党的建设和精神文明建设，推动经济建设持续快速健康地向前发展，为实现第二步战略目标努力奋斗。

一、过去五年工作的回顾和总结

1988年省第七次党代表大会以来，在党中央领导下，在党的十一届三中全会以来全省各项工作取得重大成就的基础上，各级党组织带领广大共产党员和人民群众，以邓小平同志建设有中国特色的社会主义理论为指导，继续坚持"一个中心，两个基本点"的党的基本路线，围绕治穷致富的近期目标，大力推进改革开放和现代化建设，全省呈现出经济发展、政治稳定、民族团结、社会进步的可喜局面，省第七次党代表大会确定的主要任务基本完成。

——经济持续健康发展，实力明显增强。过去的五年，省委和各级党委把大力发展社会生产力、治穷致富作为头等大事，用主要的时间和精力抓经济建设。在国内出现政治风波和国际风云变幻的复杂情况下，保持清醒的头脑，正确处理各种社会政治矛盾，始终坚持以经济建设为中心。特别是在邓小平同志南巡重要谈话和党的十四大以后，进一步确立发展才是硬道理的思想，把握新的机遇，确定了提前一年实现"八五"计划，提前三年实现国民生产总值翻两番的奋斗目标，经济发展步伐明显加快。预计1993年，全省国民生产总值达到340.88亿元，五年年均递增8.13%；国民收入达到305.53亿元，年均递增7.92%；农业总产值达到128.52亿元，年均递增5.5%；工业总产值达到440亿元，年均递增9.17%；财政收入达到45.8亿元，年均递增8.54%。

——农村面貌发生重大变化，农民生活水平明显提高。过去的五年，我们始终把农村工作和发展农村经济作为战略任务，把改变农业生产基本条件作为重点。坚持因地制宜，分类指导，积极调整农村产业结构，大力发展乡镇企业，全面推进"两西"建设，有计划地实施扶贫开发的温饱工程。提高农业生产水平，增加农民收入。预计1993年，全省农民人均纯收入达到550.26元，比1988年增长59.43%。特别可喜的是，长期困扰我们的吃饭问题得到很大缓解，实现了全省粮食基本自给、大部分地区解决温饱的目标。这些年粮食总产先后登上60、65、70亿公斤三个台阶。今年预计可以达到73亿公斤以上。

——改革不断深化，对外开放打开了新局面。过去的五年，我们始终注意正确处理改革与发展的关系，尤其是在遇到新情况、新问题时，坚持用深化改革的办法去解决。整个改革以经济体制改革为重点，相应推进科技、教育、文化和社会保障制度等各项改革。现在，我省经济体制发生了很大变化，打破了所有制结构单一的状况，出现了以公有制为主体，个体、私营、三资企业等多种经济成份共同发展的局面。农村经济体制改革不断深入，稳定家庭联产承包为主的责任制，完善双层经营体制，建立健全社会化服务体系，放开种植计划和农副产品价格，进一步扩大农民生产经营自主权。紧紧围绕贯彻《条例》，转换国有企业经营机制，积极进行股份制试点。在中小国合商业企业普遍推行各种经营方式的改革。城乡各类市场发展迅速，市场在资源配置中的作用逐步扩大。坚持把扩大对外开放作为促改革、促发展的重要举措，投资环境有所改善，渠道不断增加，领域不断拓宽，多层次对外开放的格局初步形成，招商引资和“三资”企业有了较快发展，对外经济技术交流与合作广泛开展。

精神文明建设取得新的成果，社会各项事业有了较快发展。过去的五年，我们在抓好物质文明建设的同时不放松精神文明建设，在改革开放的过程中坚持四项基本原则。省委制定并实施了同“八五”经济社会发展计划相配套的政治工作规划。在农村用三年时间集中进行了广泛深入的社会主义思想教育，在企业普遍开展基本路线和基本国情教育，在高等学校比较系统地进行马克思主义、爱国主义和社会主义教育，在广大党员和干部中普遍进行建设有中国特色社会主义理论的学习和教育。普遍加强思想政治工作，开展多种形式的精神文明建设活动。科技、教育、新闻出版、广播电视、文化艺术、体育和医疗卫生等各项事业进一步繁荣和发展。

——加强了民主法制建设，安定团结的政治局面得到巩固和发展。过去的五年，省委一直努力加强党内的团结、领导班子的团结、干部队伍的团结、军政军民团结和各民族的团结，维护社会政治稳定。省委领导班子团结统一，省上几大班子协调一致，各级领导班子的团结不断得到加强。认真贯彻落实民族宗教政策，大力发展民族地区经济文化事业，促进各民族人民的团结。重视做好统一战线的工作，充分发挥各民主党派、各人民团体和社会各界、各方面在改革开放和现代化建设中的重要作用。重视党管武装的工作，深入开展国防教育，促进民兵工作“三落实”。注意妥善处理各种人民内部矛盾，重视解决群众关心的热点问题和难点问题，把群众的积极性引导到改革和建设上来。加强民主法制建设，严厉打击各类刑事犯罪和经济犯罪活动。持续开展以禁毒、反盗窃为重点的除“六害”斗争和“扫黄”专项斗争，为改革开放和经济建设创造了比较好的社会环境。

——党的建设得到加强，各级领导班子整体素质进一步提高。过去的五年，省委坚持不懈地抓了党的思想建设、领导班子建设、基层组织建设、党员队伍建设和党风廉政建设。坚决维护党中央的集中统一领导，服从党和国家的统一部署，在思想上、政治上自觉地同党中央保持高度一致。在1989年春夏之交的政治风波中，省委采取坚决措施制止动乱，各级党组织和广大党员立场坚定，经受住了考验。认真坚持民主集中制原则，不断增强党的团结统一。坚持把思想建设放在首位，各级领导干部的理论学习做到经常化、制度化。选拔了一批德才兼备的干部，充实和加强各级领导班子。采取多种形式加强党的基层组织建设。通过学习教育、整顿作风、查处案件、健全制度、加强监督等措施，开展反腐败斗争，推动了党风和廉政建设。各级党委加强对工会、共青团、妇联等群众团体的领导，充分发挥他们各自的作用。

——干部群众在改革开放和经济建设和实践中增强了信心，精神面貌发生深刻变化。过去的五年，我们在全省范围内先后开展了关于生产力标准，关于正确理解和把握党的基本路线，关于全面理解和贯彻邓小平同志南巡重要谈话、抓住机遇加快发展等几次大讨论，不断加深对建设有中国特色社会主义理论的理解，破除“左”的影响和旧的传统观念，思想不断得到解放。改革开放更加深入人心，艰苦奋斗，加快治穷致富已成为全省上下的自觉行动。各级党组织和广大干部，在条件艰苦、困难较多的情况下，发扬党的优良传统和开拓进取精神，为改变甘肃面貌，兢兢业业，勤奋工作，做出了贡献。

过去的五年，虽然取得了很大成绩，但也应当清醒地看到，工作中还存在着不少差距和不足，前进中的困难和矛盾还很多。我们的思想解放程度和开拓创新精神，还不适应加快改革开放和发展社会主义市场经济的需要，改革在一些方面还没有大的突破。对解决影响经济快速健康发展的一些重要制约因素，虽然做了很大努力，取得了一定成效，但对有些重大问题调查研究不深，措施不够得力，矛盾仍然相当突出。经济实力不强，财政十分困难，各项经济社会事业的发展受到很大制约。农业生产基本条件、基础设施。产业结构不能适应发展的要求。社会治安形势比较严峻，特别是吸毒、贩毒、盗窃等问题多年屡禁不止，群众很不满意。党风和廉政建设仍然存在一些严重问题，某些腐败现象没有得到有效遏制。工作中抓组织落实下功夫不够，一些好的工作思想和正确决策还没有完全落实，等等。我们必须保持谦虚谨慎的作风，高度重视存在的问题，努力加以解决。

回顾过去的工作，总结五年来的实践，从成功的经验和存在的问题中我们深深体会到：

必须始终坚持解放思想，实事求是的思想路线。解放思想、实事求是是建设有中国特色社会主义理论的精髓。没有思想的不断解放，观念的不断更新，就不可能有工作上的新突破和事业上的新发展。在我们这样一个商品经济不发达、旧传统观念影响比较深的省份，解放思想更为重要。我们同发达省份相比，确实有很大差距。这既有思想解放程度上的差距，也有客观条件的制约。因此，必须坚持思想解放和实事求是的辩证统一。既要有加快发展的紧迫感，力求发展得更好更快一些，又要从自己的实际出发，不盲目攀比；既要敢想敢干，大胆探索，不因困难失掉信心，又要有科学的态度，脚踏实际，稳步前进，不因近利而盲动；既要打破封闭守旧观念，虚心学习外地经验，又不能照抄照搬、简单模仿。只有这样，才能避免片面性的盲目性，把中央精神同当地实际紧密结合起来，创造性地开展工作，把甘肃的事情办好。

必须牢牢把握经济建设这个中心。生产力水平低，经济落后，财力薄弱，群众生活水平不高，是我们省的主要问题。改变贫困落后的面貌是甘肃各族人民最大的愿望和根本利益所在，把经济搞上去是解决我省诸多矛盾和困难的根本之道。因此，任何时候任何情况下，以经济建设为中心的思想不能动摇，抓紧治穷致富的主要任务不能放松。只有不断强化"发展才是硬道理"的思想，形成集中精力抓经济建设的强大舆论和合力，才能团结和凝聚全省上下各方面的力量，加快经济发展步伐，带动和促进各方面的工作。

必须把深化改革、扩大开放作为推动经济发展的强大动力。改革就是解放和发展生产力。我们省这些年的发展和进步，从根本上说得益于改革开放。现在存在的一些矛盾和问题，主要是旧体制的弊病没有完全克服，新体制还没有完全形成。要解决体制上和经济运行中深层次的矛盾，加快经济社会发展步伐，根本出路仍然在于深化改革、扩大开放。我们要把更大的精力集中到加快改革上来，勇气要更大一些，步子要更快一些。

必须始终坚持两手抓、两手都要硬的方针。加强社会主义精神文明建设，是建设有中国特色社会主义的内在要求。越是深化改革、扩大开放，越要加强精神文明建设。只有端正党风，加强廉政建设，搞好社会治安综合治理，保持健康的社会风气，保持社会政治稳定，才能为改革开放创造良好的社会环境。我们任何时候都要防止和克服一手硬一手软的问题。

必须充分发挥党的核心领导作用。搞好党的自身建设，加强党的领导，是改革开放和现代化建设的根本保证，我省这些年之所以社会政治稳定，改革和建设不断发展，主要是各级党组织发挥了核心领导作用，广大共产党员发挥了先锋模范作用，全省人民在各级党组织的领导下发扬艰苦奋斗的精神。建设好各级领导班子，坚持党的群众路线，不断密切党同人民群众的血肉联系，增强党的吸引力、凝聚力和战斗力，提高总揽全局、驾驭矛盾、协调各方的能力，更好地发挥党的核心领导作用，是保证党的基本路线全面贯彻的关键。

同志们，我省五年来工作的成绩和进步，是在邓小平同志建设有中国特色社会主义理论的指导下取得的，是全省各级党组织和各族人民群众在党中央领导下团结奋斗的新成果，是在党的十一届三中全会以来大量工作的基础上的新进展，这里，我代表中共甘肃省委，向全省工人、农民、知识分子、解放军指战员、武警官兵、公安干警、以及各条战线的广大共产党员、各级干部和各民主党派、各人民团体、各界人士、各族人民群众表示衷心的感谢和崇高的敬意！

根据党的十四大精神，今后不再设立党的顾问委员会。省顾委成立以来，协助省委为推进我省两个文明建设和加强党的建设，维护和发展安定团结的政治局面，做了大量卓有成效的工作，做出了重要贡献。我代表省委对省顾委的同志表示衷心的感谢和崇高的敬意！

二、经济发展的基本思路和指导方针

今后五年，我省现代化建设处在一个非常重要的历史阶段。这五年，是由计划经济向社会主义市场经济转轨，初步建立起社会主义市场经济体制框架的关键时期；是全省解决温饱，摆脱贫困，向小康迈进，全面实现第二步战略目标的决战决胜时期；是在现有基础上构筑适应社会主义市场经济发展的新结构，为下世纪全省经济的振兴和腾飞奠定基础的重要时期，我们一定要珍惜和把握国内和国际的有利时机，大力发展社会主义市场经济，使甘肃经济持续健康发展，在今后五年内再登上一个新台阶。

我省今后经济社会的发展，既有很多有利条件和潜在优势，又有不少制约因素。突出的问题是：第一，农村实现小康的任务十分艰巨，扶贫攻坚的难度很大。第二，国有大中型企业活力不强、后劲不足，地方工业主要是地县工业、乡镇企业十分薄弱，整个工业结构不够合理，效益不高。第三，基础设施建设滞后，瓶颈制约突出，对外开放受到很大限制。第四，建设资金严重不足，财政困难，积累能力差。这是我省今后经济发展的难点，也是我们需要着力解决的重点。

为了扬长避短，发挥优势，转变劣势，突出重点，解决难点，适应发展社会主义市场经济的总趋势，今后五年我省经济发展的基本思路是：以邓小平同志建设有中国特色社会主义理论为指导，按照党的十四大提出的发展社会主义市场经济的要求，进一步深化改革、扩大开放，强化农业基础，继续改变生产基本条件，改善基础设施，改造传统产业，努力搞好国有大中型企业，加快发展地方工业、轻工业、乡镇企业和城市集体经济，大力发展第三产业和新兴产业，形成比较合理的经济结构，全面提高全省经济的整体素质和整体实力，推动经济的持续快速健康发展，推进本世纪末小康目标的基本实现。

今后五年我省经济发展的奋斗目标是，在提高效益、优化结构的基础上，提前一年实现"八五"计划，提前三年实现国民生产总值翻两番。实现这一目标的主要指标是：以1993年为基数，到1998年，国民生产总值平均每年增长9.3%，达到490亿元；国民收入年均增长7.5%，达到407亿元；工业总产值年均增长10%，达到645亿元，其中地方工业年均增长11%，总产值达到429亿元；农业总产值年均增长5.5%，达到170亿元；粮食总产量达到80——85亿公斤；乡镇企业总产值年均增长26.9%，达到470亿元，农民人均纯收入年均增长9.6%，达到870元；财政收入在1993年计划数的基础上年均增长9.5%，达到68亿元。到那时，我省经济将出现一个新局面，全省的面貌发生更加深刻的变化：交通、能源、通信等基础设施和农业生产基本条件有较大改善，经济发展主要制约因素基本得到解决，为进一步加快发展创造较好的物质基础条件；农村经济全面发展，全省基本稳定地解决温饱，部分地区步入小康；新的具有我省特点的主导产业和发展优势基本形成，地方工业、乡镇企业和城市集体经济有更大的发展；地县经济实力明显增强，财政困难的局面趋于缓解，城乡人民生活水平有较大提高，经济将迈上一个新台阶。

为了实现上述任务和奋斗目标，在经济建设中必须坚持以下指导方针和重大措施。

(一)强化农业基础，促进农村经济全面发展

在发展社会主义市场经济中，农业仍然是整个国民经济和社会稳定发展的基础，我省实现小康的重点在农村，难点也在农村。必须坚定不移地贯彻以农业为基础的方针，坚定不移地把农业放在经济工作的首位，多渠道增加农业投入，做到粮食总产量必须稳定增长，农民收入必须不断增加，根据不同类区的差异性和分类指导的原则，今后我省农村经济发展的总体部署和要求是：河西等一些条件较好的地区要逐步实现小康；中部、陇东和陇南一部分地区要在稳定解决温饱的基础上向小康迈进；高寒阴湿和少数民族地区要力争基本解决温饱。

要把大力提高农村社会生产力，加快农村经济发展，不断增加农民收入，作为农村工作的出发点和落脚点。围绕发展高产优质高效农业，在努力提高粮食单产、稳定增加总产的同时，按照市场经济的规律和特点，大力调整农业产品结构和农村产业结构，进行农业综合开发，大力发展畜牧业、林果业、渔业和多种经营，发展创汇农业，大幅度提高农业的综合经济效益。实行农科教、内外贸、种养加、贸工农四结合，加快名优特产品的商品基地建设，建立支柱产业。在有条件的地方发展集约化规模经营。继续把乡镇企业摆在地县经济的主体地位，作为振兴农村经济、发展和壮大集体经济、实现小康目标的战略重点。全党动员，全社会大办，全面推行股份合作制，因地制宜，中小起步，“多轮驱动”注重效益，走超常规、快速发展的路子，加快提高乡镇企业在全省经济中的比重，提高乡镇工业在乡镇中的比重。坚持发展与提高并重的原则，加快乡镇企业的技术改造和产品开发，提高管理水平，提高产品档次和质量，提高规模效益，增强企业的竞争能力。要加强规划，引导乡镇企业适当集中，充分利用和改造现有小城镇，建设新的小城镇，带动农村第三产业的发展，促进农村剩余劳动力的转移。要一手抓增加收入，一手抓减轻农民负担各项政策措施的落实，切实保护和更加充分地调动广大农民的积极性。

继续重视改变农业生产基本条件。坚持实施“22274”工程，特别是抓好建成两千万亩水地的各项措施的落实。实行大中小并举，省地县协同，国家、集体、农民结合的方针，拓宽投资渠道，坚持不懈地进行农田水利基本建设，积极做好各项前期工作，加快骨干水利工程和配套设施建设。在灌区必须积极推广节水农业，逐步形成以水养水、良性循环的水利运行新机制，努力扩大灌溉面积和其它基本农田。坚持种草种树，搞好小流域治理，继续抓好两西建设，保质保量完成分年度任务。

(二)认真实施“四七计划”，打好扶贫攻坚战

现在全省仍有400多万农村人口收入在300元以下，处于贫困状态，主要集中在高寒阴湿、少数民族地区和部分老区。我们要以引导全省人民逐步实现共同富裕的高度责任感，怀着关心群众疾苦的深厚感情，下决心解决这些地区的脱贫问题。要通过实施扶贫攻坚的“四七计划”，即用七年时间，力争解决400多万贫困人口的温饱问题，要认真调查研究，找出症结，选准发展项目，走开发扶贫的路子。大力进行农业综合开发，积极发展二三产业，组织好劳务输出，促进劳动力的转移。对确实解决不了问题的地方，要有计划地实行移民。多渠道增加扶贫投入。各项扶贫资金要相对集中，重点倾斜，主要用于修建公路和基本农田，解决人畜饮水，兴办各类扶贫实体，培养当地人才。严格扶贫开发项目管理和审计制度，禁止挤占和挪用，保证扶贫效益。加强对扶贫工作的组织领导，省上和有关地县要制定规划，建立和完善领导责任制和对口帮扶责任制，稳定和加强扶贫开发工作机构，抽调大批干部到乡村蹲点扶贫。采取特殊优惠政策，推动人才、技术等生产要素向扶贫攻坚的主战场流动。

(三)加大工业结构调整力度，提高经济效益

以国有大中型企业为主体的有色金属、石油化工、机械加工、煤炭电力和钢铁冶金等基础工业，是我省长期形成的主导产业和发展优势，在全省经济发展和财政收入中

有着举足轻重的作用。但相当多的企业设备老化、技术落后、产品陈旧、负担沉重、后劲不足，处于生产增长缓慢、效益下降、亏损增多的被动局面。必须下决心有计划有重点地进行技术改造和产品结构调整，广泛应用新技术、新材料、新工艺，按市场需求确定和开发主导产品，全面提高生产技术水平和产品档次，提高经济增长中的科技含量，提高管理水平。要通过技术改造和加强管理双重手段，加快发展速度，提高经济效益，重振雄风，更好地发挥这批国有大中型企业在全省经济发展中的带动辐射作用。

要把加快发展地方工业，提高县级经济实力，放在全省经济工作的重要地位，要增加投入，增加贷款额度，力争今后几年内各地县能够建成一个或几个带动当地经济、缓解财政困难的骨干企业。新建企业一定要按市场需求，选准项目，提高成功率和投资效益。对现有地县工业企业要进行改造提高，跟踪研究市场需求变化，加强产品的更新换代，提高市场份额占有率，增强竞争能力。

要大力发展新兴产业，使之尽快成为新的发展优势。集中一定的力量，高起点、高标准地建设一批与我省原材料工业配套的加工骨干企业，尤其要注重发展市场容量大的终极产品和产业，形成一批具有我省特点的名优新特产品。从经济技术发展趋势出发，综合分析我省资源和技术条件，要把有色金属加工业、电子工业、医药工业的农副产品加工业作为主导产业重点发展。

（四）适应国民经济发展和对外开放的需要，加快基础设施建设

加快基础设施建设，不仅是当前经济发展中亟待解决的问题，也是保证经济长远发展的战略性措施。要通过加强宏观调控，集中资金，重点保证铁路、公路、航空、通信建设和城市改造。抓住国家一批骨干交通、通信通道建设经过我省境内的有利条件，积极配合和支持铁路、公路、航空、邮电等重点工程的建设，确保建设项目的按期竣工。多渠道筹集资金，增加投入，改造和兴修公路以及县乡公路，加快山区道路建设步伐，努力形成以主干线为骨架，地方道路为网络，铁路、公路、航空相互配合的综合运输体系。加快邮电通信网的技术改造和建设，实现省际省内干线传输数字化，县以上城市基本实现电话交换程控化，建成以兰州为中心的快速高效的通信网。努力解决城市基础设施不配套的问题，搞好城市的规划和管理，提高城市的综合服务功能。

（五）加强科技、教育工作、加速人才培养和科技成果向现实生产力的转化

要坚定不移地贯彻科学技术是第一生产力的方针，把经济建设真正转移到依靠技术进步和提高劳动者素质的轨道上来。重点加强应用研究和各种实用技术的推广应用。地方和企业都要加大科技投入，逐步形成结构优化、布局合理、精干高效、适应市场经济需要的新的研究开发体系和科技推广体系，力争在发展“两高一优”农业、大中型企业技术改造、地方工业和乡镇企业产品开发、原材料深加工技术等方面有所突破。对我省经济发展中的重大和关键技术课题，要统一协调组织科研力量进行攻关，抓好技术引进项目的消化、吸收和创新，鼓励科研机构、高等院校和企业合作进行技术开发。要在企业内部建立起市场、科研、生产一体化的技术进步机制，使企业成为技术开发的主体。推动技术市场的发展和技术成果商品化的进程，大力突破转化过程中的中间试验环节，加速科技成果向现实生产力的转化。积极发展各种所有制形式和经营方式的科技企业，发展科技服务组织，进一步放开搞活技术市场，加强技术中介机构建设，更多地组织科研单位、高等院校和企业参加技术交易、技术洽谈活动。要办好兰州高新技术产业开发区，促进和带动全省高新技术产业的发展。

要把教育放在优先发展的战略地位，把加速各类适用人才的培养作为加快经济发展的重大措施。全面贯彻《中国教育改革和发展纲要》，逐步加大对教育的投入，宁肯牺牲一些其他方面的利益，也要把教育方面存在的突出问题解决得好一些。积极提倡和鼓励多种类型的社会力量办学。统筹规划，合理布点。加强基础教育，重视农村教育，本世纪末全省基本普及初等义务教育，70%的人口地区普及初级中等教育，绝大多数地区基本扫除青壮年文盲。调整教育结构和专业设置，积极发展职业技术教育、各类成人教育和高等教育，努力培养适应我省改革和建设需要的各类合格人才，要努力创造更加有利于知识分子施展聪明才智的良好环境，在全社会进一步形成尊重知识、尊重人才的良好风尚。

（六）继续实施双带整推，促进生产力合理布局和经济协调发展

双带整推有利于发挥大中型企业和城市的优势，有利于改变二元经济结构，有利于促进生产要素的合理流动和优化配置，要继续坚持。今后要在深化上做文章，进一步拓宽领域，使之在更广的范围和更深的层次上开展起来，要按照市场经济的内在要求和互惠互利的原则，重点在产品、技术、人才、管理和闲置设备等方面，推动不同所有制、不同类型的企业进行跨行业、跨地区的联合与合作，形成一批以大中型企业为核心，地县企业、乡镇企业与之配套服务的格局，促进各类企业共同发展。要进一步增强中心城市的经济实力和综合功能，充分发挥城市对乡村的辐射带动作用，充分发挥乡村对城市的服务作用，使城

乡经济融为一体。要根据经济发展的内在联系，打破旧体制的分割与束缚，突破行政区划的界限，按照资源优化配置和生产要素合理组合的原则，实行联合开发，逐步形成各具特色的区域经济和生产力布局。加快主要铁路和公路干线沿线地带的经济开发，继续办好已定的开发试验小区，使之成为资源综合开发和带动全省经济发展的新的生长点。

（七）千方百计增加财源，努力缓解财政紧张状况

财政困难一直是我省经济社会发展中的一个主要问题，近些年来矛盾更为突出。今后五年，要把增加财政收入，缓解财政困难，作为一个重大问题认真对待。增加财政收入的根本出路在于发展经济，提高效益。要按照省上制定的扭补规划，用好扭补资金，办好扭补项目。通过发展地方工业、乡镇企业和第三产业，培植和扩大财源，不断提高县级财政的积累能力。努力提高投资效益、生产效益和经营效益，增加收入。依法加强税收征管，减少流失。加强资金的统一管理和调度，在管好预算内资金的同时，切实管好预算外资金。要根据国家财税体制改革的新情况，按照“一要吃饭，二要建设”的原则，妥善处理好积累与消费的关系，统筹安排财政支出。建设资金的安排，要尽力而为，量力而行，保证重点，突出效益，把有限的资金管好用好。要结合机构改革，精简机构，分流人员，压缩行政事业经费，减轻财政负担。大力提倡艰苦奋斗、勤俭节约，反对大手大脚、铺张浪费。

（八）不断改善各族人民生活，做好计划生育和环境保护工作

加快经济发展，治穷致富，实现小康，都是为了满足我省各族人民日益增长的物质文化需要。今后五年，随着生产的发展，城乡居民收入水平、消费水平和生活质量要有比较大的提高。特别要抓好居住条件的改善和物价水平的宏观调控，保证人民的实际生活水平逐年有所提高。

人口问题是关系经济社会发展全局的重要问题，是造福后代、功在千秋的事业。我省计划生育工作取得了不小的成绩，但人口形势依然十分严峻，工作难度很大。计划生育工作的重点在农村。要把计划生育同发展农村商品经济，农民勤劳致富奔小康，建设幸福文明家庭结合起来，大力推行男到有女无儿家结婚落户，妥善解决纯女户的实际困难。要稳定计划生育政策，实行目标管理责任制，落实党政负总责的要求。要突出抓好中部、东部、“老少边穷”地区和人口大县的计划生育工作，确保实现既定的人口控制目标。坚持优生优育，提高人口质量。

要增强全民的环境保护意识，进一步健全环保法规，加强环保执法监督和管理，保护环境，保护生态。积极防治工业污染，依法保护和合理利用水、矿产、森林、草原等各种自然资源，做到经济建设、城乡建设、环境保护同步发展。切实保护耕地，依照法定权限和程序，严格用地审批制度，坚决制止乱占、滥用耕地。

三、改革开放的重点任务和主要措施

党的十四届三中全会作出的《中共中央关于建立社会主义市场经济体制若干问题的决定》，为我们指明了经济体制改革的方向。今后五年，我们要按照《决定》提出的总体目标、主要环节和基本要求，随着形势的发展和改革的深化，不断提出措施办法，及时总结经验，加快社会主义市场经济体制的建立。在工作中，必须坚持整体推进和重点突破相结合的原则，既注意改革的循序渐进，又不失时机地在重要环节取得实质性突破，带动改革全局。根据我省实际，今后一个时期我省改革开放要抓好以下重点任务和主要措施。

（一）建立与生产力水平相适应的所有制结构形式

在社会主义制度下，坚持以公有制为主体，多种经济成份共同发展，是我们党的一个长期方针。我们必须坚定不移地贯彻执行。同时也要看到，集体经济和非公有制经济发展缓慢，是制约我省经济发展的重要因素，也是我省同发达地区差距拉大的一个重要原因。历史的经验证明，所有制结构必须同生产力水平相适应，越是经济不发达地区，越要注重发展集体经济和非公有制经济。我们要以是否有利于发展社会主义社会的生产力，是否有利于增强社会主义国家的综合国力，是否有利于提高人民的生活水平为标准，来判断各方面工作的是非得失，思想更解放一些，手脚更放开一些。采取多种形式，放手发展集体经济、混合经济，大力发展并依法保护个体、私营、“三资”等非公有制经济，逐步提高在国民经济中的比重，使之成为推动我省生产力发展，繁荣城乡经济的重要经济成份。

农村改革要稳定、完善以家庭联产承包为主的责任制和统分结合的双层经营体制，进一步明晰产权关系，加强以土地为主的各项制度建设，保障和规范农村的基本经济关系。在坚持土地集体所有的前提下，延长耕地承包期，允许继承开发性生产项目的承包经营权，允许土地使用权依法有偿转让。本着“积极支持，正确引导，不断完善，逐步发展”的原则，大力推行多种形式、多种类型的农村股份合作制，用股份合作制改造乡镇集体企业，并由乡镇企业向农业、林果业、饲养业、水产养殖业以及农副产品加工业和第三产业扩展。同时，对一切有利于农村经济发展的经营形式，都要大胆实验，在实践中不断完善。

要区别不同情况，对国有企业进行所有制结构调整。军工产品、特殊产品的生产以及一些重要基础产

业和公用设施，由国家独资经营。对国有大中型企业，在理顺产权关系的基础上，分别采取国家控股参股、公有法人持股、公开向社会发行股票等多种形式，逐步改造为股份制企业，对国有小型企业，有的可以改造为股份合作企业。有的可以实行租赁，有的可以通过出售、拍卖等形式转为集体或个人所有。

发展非国有经济继续实行不限比例、不限规模、不限速度的政策。新办企业适合哪种所有制形式就办成哪种形式。对商业、饮食、服务业和生产社会化程度较低的制造业，要大力发展集体经济以及个体、私营企业，积极拓宽引进外资的渠道，采取优惠政策，鼓励发展“三资”企业。对一些投资规模较大的企业，采取股份制方式筹资兴办，大力发展混合所有制经济形式。

(二)建立适应市场经济要求的现代企业制度

以公有制为主体的现代企业制度是社会主义市场经济的基础，是发展社会化大生产和市场经济的必然要求，是国有企业改革的方向。当前一个时期，要把主要精力放在继续贯彻《全民所有制工业企业法》和《全民所有制工业企业转换经营机制条例》上，切实转换企业经营机制。要把属于企业的权力和责任不折不扣的落实下去，确保企业的法人地位和生产经营活动的自主决策权，使企业真正成为自主经营、自负盈亏、自我发展、自我约束的法人实体和市场竞争主体。加快国有资产产权管理体制改革，理顺产权关系和国家与企业的关系，探索国有资产管理经营的有效形式，实现国有资产的保值、增值，有效地防止国有资产流失。现代企业按照财产的结构，可以有多种组织形式，国有企业实行公司制是建立现代企业制度的有益探索，具备条件的国有大中型企业，单一投资主体的可依法改组为独资公司；多个投资主体的，可依法改组为有限责任公司或股份有限公司。企业要不断完善内部经营管理，提高经营决策水平，提高经营素质。全心全意依靠工人阶级，加强职工队伍建设，造就企业家队伍，形成企业内部权责分明、相互制约的机制。

(三)培育和发展市场体系

市场经济是通过市场发挥价值规律、供求规律、竞争规律的作用，优化资源配置，因此，必须把建立健全市场体系，作为今后改革和发展的主要任务来抓。

要加快价格改革，放开绝大部分中间产品和最终产品价格，按照市场需求变化由企业自主定价。放开农副产品价格，对主要农产品实行最低保护价，建立国家储备制度，逐步取消现行的合同定购制。生产资料除国家控制的个别产品外，其余全部放开。对少数关系国计民生的主要产品以及能源、交通、公用基础设施的价格和服务性收费，按价值规律和市场供求关系的变化，由政府进行管理和调整。

要建立各种有形市场，特别是大力培育各类要素市场，形成新型的市场组织形式。加快建立适合农村市场经济发展的多行业、多层次、多功能的社会化服务体系，促进农业专业化、商品化、社会化。提高农民进入市场的组织化程度，鼓励农民个人或合伙联办各类经济技术服务和中介机构，为农村经济发展提供产前、产中、产后服务。进一步发展和完善商品市场，在大宗商品的产地有重点地发展一批面向全国的批发市场，根据我省优势，积极试办瓜果蔬菜和有色金属产品期货市场。发展以国合商业为骨干、大中小批发相结合的批发市场。发展多种所有制形式和多种经营方式并存的商品零售市场。有计划地发展经纪行、拍卖行等流通中介组织。突出抓好各类生产要素市场建设，重点发展和完善资金、生产资料、劳动就业、技术、产权交易、房地产、信息市场等，形成完整的综合性的生产要素市场体系。要加强市场管理，规范市场行为，反对不正当竞争，创造平等竞争的环境，形成统一、开放、竞争、有序的大市场。

(四)改善和加强宏观调控

加强宏观调控是建立和完善社会主义市场经济体制的重要组成部分。宏观经济调控体系的建立，要按照国家统一的部署，近期在财税、金融、投资和计划体制改革方面迈出重大步伐。计划管理体制改革重点是进一步转变管理职能，从直接的行政调控向间接的经济调控转变，从直接管理微观经济活动向间接调控宏观经济运行转变，从主要定指标、批项目、分投资、分物资，转向重点研究制定经济发展总体规划、重大方针和政策、供求关系平衡、经济结构和布局调整的规划方案。投资体制改革重点是建立投资主体责、权、利相统一的自我约束机制和风险责任。按照产业政策调整投资结构，防止低水平的重复建设，管好投资规模，提高投资效益。金融体制改革重点是尽快建立和完善我省多种形式的金融机构，拓宽筹资和融资渠道。积极为国家专业银行的改革创造条件，鼓励专业银行积极有效地投入地方经济建设。财税体制改革重点是认真落实中央分税制和税收制度、企业利润分配制度等改革措施。适应分税制的需要，改革财政预算体制，建立省、市、县独立的分级预算管理体系，划清经常性预算和建设性预算的收入来源和支出范围，防止互相挤占。

加强宏观调控，必须切实转变政府职能。要认真解决经济管理中长期存在的政企不分、“两权”不分的问题，把政府的职能从直接管理具体经济活动转到主要是制定和执行宏观调控政策，搞好基础设施建设，创造良好的经济发展环境上来。政府要运用经济手段、法律手段和必要的行政手段管理国民经济，不直接干预企业的生产经营活动。要按照精简、统一、效能的原则，力争1995年完成机构改革任务，并逐步实行公务员制度。要按照新职能的要求定编、定岗、定责，真正做到转变职能，理顺关系，精兵简政，提高效率。要做好思想政治工作，广开门路，妥善解决富余人员的安置问题，保证机构改革的顺利进行。

（五）进一步扩大对外开放

扩大对外开放是建立社会主义市场经济体制，加速经济发展，深化改革的强大推动力。我们要抓住有利机遇，坚持国内国外开放并举，国内国际市场并重，省内省外资源并用，东进西出，内联外引，形成向国外开放、省外开放、省内地区之间相互开放的格局。利用一切可以利用的条件，加强同国外的联系，拓宽对外开放的渠道和领域。继续贯彻执行省委、省政府制定的发展"三资"企业的各项优惠政策，努力改善投资环境，招商引资，吸引国外厂商来我省投资建设。用足用活兰州市内陆开放城市政策，充分发挥兰州市在我省对外开放中的"龙头"作用。大力开展省际之间的经济技术协作与交流，利用我省的优势，积极引进技术、人才、资金等。加强西北五省区的联合协作，利用第二条亚欧大陆桥开通的有利条件，共建"国际大通道"联合"走西口"。要努力改变出口产品结构单一的状况，在巩固、发展现有出口产品的同时，根据我省资源和技术优势，着力开发技术含量高、在一定时期内具有较强竞争能力的新产品，提高出口产品的质量，提高产品信誉，增强占领导市场的能力，提高创汇能力。加强出口产品基地建设，在资金和政策上给予适当倾斜。进一步改革外贸体制，加强和改进海关、商检、口岸等各项工作，加速转换各类企业的对外经营机制，赋予具备条件的生产和高科技企业的对外经营权。积极开发旅游资源，扩大对外交往，增加旅游创汇。

（六）建立合理的个人收入分配和社会保障制度

个人收入分配要坚持以按劳分配为主体、多种分配方式并存的制度，体现效率优先、兼顾公平的原则。劳动者的个人劳动报酬要引入竞争机制，打破平均主义，实行多劳多得，合理拉开差距。坚持鼓励一部分地区一部人通过诚实劳动和合法经营先富起来的政策，提倡先富带动和帮助后富，逐步实现共同富裕。建立适应企业、事业单位和行政机关各自特点的工资制度与正常的工资增长机制。

建立多层次的社会保障体系，对深化企业改革，保持社会稳定，顺利建立社会主义市场经济体制具有重大意义。要在完善企业养老和失业保险制度方面有大的进展。逐步将目前主要对国有企业职工实行的养老和失业保险，扩大到城镇非国有企业的全体职工，对各类职工实行统一的养老保险制度。逐步建立国家机关和事业单位工作人员的保险制度。在农村逐步建立以个人交纳费用为主、集体补助为辅的养老保险制度。建立社会医疗保险制度，扩大医疗保险的覆盖面，提高社会化程度，保证职工的基本医疗。建立适用于城乡各类企业和用工形式的工伤保险制度。建立统一的社会保险管理和经办机构，制定统一政策，加强管理监督，逐步形成保险基金筹集、运营的良性循环机制。实行以出售公有住房为重点，"售、租、建"并举的方针，加快城镇住房制度改革。要从我省城镇居民收入水平的实际出发，合理确定住房价格，加快住房商品化进程。

同志们，以建立社会主义市场经济体制为目标的经济体制改革，是一场涉及经济基础和上层建筑许多领域的深刻革命。党的十一届三中全会的《决定》，将为根本解决制约我省经济发展的深层次矛盾创造有利的环境和条件，提供历史性的机遇。抓住机遇，不仅要抓住发展的机遇，更要抓住改革的机遇。同时，也要清醒地看到，社会主义市场经济体制的建立，必然要改变旧体制固有的和体制转变过程中形成的多种不合理的利益格局，不可避免地会遇到困难和阻力。尤其是在我们这样一个生产力水平较低、商品经济不发达、市场发育不充分、深受传统经济体制束缚的省份，建立社会主义市场经济体制难度很大，任务非常艰巨。我们要在建设有中国特色社会主义理论的指引下，抛弃那些超越社会主义初级阶段的不正确思想，继续转变传统的计划经济观念，主要摆脱"左"的束缚，冲破因循守旧的习惯，同时警惕右的干扰。要尊重群众的首创精神，及时总结群众创造出来的实践经验，尊重群众意愿，重视群众的切身利益，使改革具有广泛而深厚的群众基础。要紧紧抓住重点领域的改革，制定具体方案，大胆探索，勇于实践，不断开拓前进。

四、积极推进社会主义精神文明和民主法制建设

发展社会主义市场经济，我们始终面临着两个最严峻的考验：一个是经济能不能搞上去，一个是社会风气能不能搞好。经受住这两个考验的根本所在，就是要以建设有中国特色社会主义理论为指导，坚持一手抓改革开放，一手抓打击犯罪；一手抓经济建设，一手抓民主法制；一手抓物质文明，一手抓精神文明等一系列两手抓、两手都要硬的基本方针。

（一）充分发挥思想政治工作的优势

思想政治工作是我们党的优良传统和政治优势。大力加强思想政治工作，是加强思想道德建设，防止社会不良风气滋生蔓延的有效措施。要有针对性地进行党的基本路线教育，突出爱国主义、集体主义和社会主义思想教育的主旋律，搞好近代史、现代史教育和国情省情教育。在发展社会主义市场经济的过程中，要坚决抵制资本主义和封建主义腐朽思想的影响和侵蚀，坚决反对拜金主义、享乐主义和极端个人主义，树立为人民服务，为国家富强努力奋斗的信念和正确的人生观、价值观。要在全社会提倡有理想、有抱负、有高度的事业心和责任感，大力发扬艰苦奋斗的精神。各行各业都要切实重视职业道德建设，逐步形成自身特点的职业行为和道德规范。切实加强社会公德教育，发扬民族传统美德，大力表彰具有时代精神的先进模范人物。要在全体人民中进行有理想、有道德、有文化、有纪律的教育，特别要重视对青少年的教育和培养，使他们从小养成良好的习惯，做社会主义"四有"新人。要坚持不懈地普及法律常识，增强全社会的法制意识，养成遵纪守法的良好习惯。继续广泛进行国防教育，增强全省人民的国防意识。

正确处理好各种人民内部矛盾，是新时期思想政治工作的重要任务。要通过深入细致的思想政治工作，解惑释难，化解矛盾，协调关系，理顺情绪。采取民主的方法、说服教育的方法，引导人民群众正确对待、处理个人利益和集体、国家利益的关系。眼前利益和长远利益的关系，局部利益和全局利益的关系。要经常研究分析和解决苗头性、倾向性的问题，把属于人民内部矛盾引起的各种纠纷解决在萌芽状态，解决在基层，解决在当地，防止事态扩大。要善于调动一切积极因素，克服和化解消极因素，切实把群众的积极性引导好、发挥好、保护好，促进团结、稳定、民主、和谐局面的巩固和发展。

精神文明重在建设，重在效果。要坚持高标准、经常化，切实防止和克服形式主义。要根据各行各业的特点，有针对性地开展各种共建活动。继续广泛开展拥政爱民、拥军拥属活动。大力提倡尊老敬贤、扶困济贫等社会互助活动，恢复和发展团结友爱互助的社会风尚。通过开展创建文明城市、文明单位、文明村户活动，搞好社区文化、村镇文化、企业文化、校园文化建设，改变不文明、不健康、不道德等不良社会风气，有效抵制封建迷信和各种陈规陋习。

(二)切实做好宣传舆论和文化工作

宣传舆论和文化建设是社会主义精神文明建设的重要组成部分。文学艺术、新闻出版、广播影视、卫生、体育、文物、图书馆、博物馆等各项文化事业，都要坚持为人民服务、为社会主义服务的方向和"百花齐放、百家争鸣"的方针，与社会主义市场经济体制相适应，符合社会主义精神文明建设和自身发展的规律，正确处理好经济效益与社会效益的关系，把社会效益放在首位。要旗帜鲜明地反对、抵制和批评消极的、不健康的东西，以正确的舆论和具有时代精神的作品，引导和激励广大人民群众奋发向上，开拓进取。报纸、广播。电视等新闻媒介要坚持团结、稳定、鼓劲和正面宣传为主的方针，更多地采用总结推广典型的方法，生动活泼地宣传党的路线、方针、政策，宣传我省改革开放和经济建设的成就，宣传人民群众在两个文明建设实践中的丰富经验和创造精神，把握正确的舆论导向。广大文化艺术工作者要积极投身到经济建设和改革开放火热的生活中去，创作健康有益、生动活泼、丰富多采的精神产品，以陶冶人们的情操，提高人们的精神境界，满足人民群众文化生活各方面的需求。进一步继承和发扬中华民族优良的思想文化传统，充分挖掘我省丝路文化、现代革命斗争史和多民族地域文化等丰富资源，创作出一批高质量的具有地方特色的艺术精品。要提倡社会科学工作者围绕发展社会主义市场经济，围绕我省改革、建设中的理论和实践问题，进行研究，大胆探索，繁荣社会科学。

(三)加强社会主义民主和法制建设

发展社会主义民主，健全社会主义法制，是建设有中国特色社会主义的重要方面，是推进社会主义现代化建设，保持社会稳定、人民安居乐业的重要保证。人民代表大会制度是我国的根本政治制度。各级党委要加强对各级人大及其常委会的领导，积极支持人大依法行使职权，充分发挥人大在管理国家事务中的作用，善于把党的主张通过法定程序变为国家意志。要根据我省改革开放和发展社会主义市场经济的需要。进一步加强法制建设，加快立法步伐，特别是加快经济立法。要加强人大及其常委会对"一府两院"的监督，用法律法规和监督手段，引导、推进和保证改革开放和经济建设的顺利进行。巩固和发展新时期的爱国统一战线，坚持和完善共产党领导的多党合作与政治协商这一基本政治制度，充分发挥人民政协在政治协商和民主监督中的作用。继续实行重要决策协商在前和向民主党派、无党派人士通报情况和征求意见的制度，支持和鼓励他们积极参政议政。重视培养非中共干部，有计划地安排民主党派和无党派人士在国家机关、司法部门担任领导职务，并保证他们有职有权。注重研究和解决社会主义市场经济条件下统一战线面临的新情况、新问题，充分调动党外各方面人士的积极性，为推动全省经济发展和改革开放贡献力量。进一步加强党对工会、共青团、妇联等群众团体的领导，支持他们按照各自的章程独立负责地开展工作。

(四)坚决维护社会政治的长期稳定

没有稳定的社会环境，改革难以推进，经济建设无法进行，什么事情也干不成。各级党委一定要高度重视当前广大人民群众反映最强烈的社会治安问题，把保一方平安作为一项关系全局的大事来抓，加强领导，高度重视，紧抓不放，力争在近期内见到明显成效，让全省人民都高兴。要建立和完善社会治安综合治理的领导责任制，落实《甘肃省社会治安综合治理条例》，紧紧依靠广大人民群众和社会各方面的力量齐抓共管，群防群治。强化人民民主专政职能，充分发挥专政机关的作用，严厉打击各种犯罪活动。当前要重点打击严重经济犯罪，遏制贪污受贿势头的蔓延。打击严重刑事犯罪，特别是团伙犯罪和暴力犯罪，遏制重大恶性案件上升势头。坚持不懈地开展打击毒品犯罪、抢劫盗窃、车匪路霸等专项斗争，伸张正义，保护人民。以扫黄禁毒为重点，查禁和扫除卖淫嫖娼、吸贩毒品、制黄贩黄、赌博、拐卖妇女儿童等社会丑恶现象。要加强文化市场的管理。要大力宣传表彰见义勇为的英雄人物和模范事迹，扶正祛邪，弘扬社会正气。切实加强政法队伍建设，从严治警，努力提高政治素质和业务素质。要教育公、检、法、司干警廉洁奉公，忠于职守，严格执法，秉公执法，文明执法，在人民群众中树立良好形象，当好人民民主专政的坚强卫士。人民解放军是人民民主专政的坚强柱石。驻甘部队是我省两个文明建设的重要力量。各级党委和政府要积极支持部队建设，加强军政军民团结。进一步做好民兵预备役工作，不断加强国防后备力量建设。继续加强安全工作，加强人民武装警察部队建设，更加有力地维护国家安全和社会稳定。

(五)认真做好民族宗教工作

在社会主义条件下，正确处理民族问题是一个带根本性的问题，加强民族团结是一个需要长期努力的重要任务。加快少数民族地区经济文化发展，推动民族地区社会进步，提高群众生活水平，是民族工作的核心，也是实现各民族真正平等、共同繁荣的基础。要把民族地区干部群众的注意力和精力吸引到这方面来，共同为之奋斗。继续对民族地区实行优惠政策，帮助民族地区发展经济、文化和各项社会事业。要认真贯彻落实党的民族政策，全面贯彻落实《民族区域自治法》和我省的实施办法。在全省范围广泛深入地进行马克思主义民族观和党的民族政策的教育，进行民族平等、互助、团结和"两个离不开"的教育，不断增强民族团结。对不利于民族团结的言行要进行批评教育。对破坏民族团结、危害民族关系的犯罪活动，对国内外民族分裂势力相互勾结进行的渗透破坏活动，要进行针锋相对的斗争，坚决依法打击。

继续重视和加强宗教工作。深入宣传和全面贯彻党的宗教信仰自由政策，保证公民有信教自由，也有不信教自由，尊重宗教信仰的民族习俗。宗教信仰自由政策不适用于共产党员，党员信仰宗教是党的纪律所不容许的。要积极引导宗教与社会主义社会相适应，充分发挥爱国宗教团体的作用，团结引导广大信教群众和宗教界人士积极参加两个文明建设活动，为保持社会稳定，促进经济发展多作贡献。依法加强对宗教事务的管理，对正常的宗教活动加以保护，对利用宗教进行违法犯罪活动的要加以限制和打击。宗教必须在宪法和法律规定的范围内活动，不允许宗教干预国家行政、司法、学校教育和社会公共教育。鼓励宗教走自养的道路，防止宗教活动加重对信教群众的经济负担。

五、全面加强新时期党的建设

进一步深化改革，扩大开放，建立社会主义市场经济体制，推动经济和社会全面发展，必须加强党的建设，改善和加强党的领导。我们要根据党的建设面临的新情况，针对全省党组织和党员队伍存在的突出问题，以加强领导班子建设和思想作风建设为重点，坚持从严治党，提高执政水平和领导水平，把党建设成为社会主义现代化事业的坚强领导核心。

(一)坚持用建设有中国特色社会主义的理论武装党员干部的思想

邓小平同志创立的建设有中国特色的社会主义理论，是我国社会主义改革和建设实践经验的结晶，是进行社会主义现代化建设的强大思想武器和科学指南。是当代中国的马克思主义。坚持用建设有中国特色社会主义理论武装全党，是新时期党的建设首要的和根本的任务，也是当前和今后深化改革、加快现代化建设步伐的根本保证。当前，各级党委和广大党员、干部，都要按照中央关于学习《邓小平文选》第三卷的决定提出重点和要求，认真学习《邓小平文选》第三卷。要在认真研读原著上多下功夫，力求融会贯通，掌握精神实质；要在理论联系实际上下功夫，紧密结合我省改革开放、经济建设、精神文明建设和党的建设的实际，增强工作的预见性和创造性；要在统一思想上下功夫，联系思想实际和工作实际，总结经验教训，澄清模糊认识，增强执行"一个中心、两个基本点"的基本路线的自觉性和坚定性，保持思想上、政治上的高度一致。学习必须坚持要精、要管用的原则，不搞形式主义和繁琐哲学。各级领导干部特别是县上领导干部，要带头学好理论，掌握基本观点和基本方法，带动和促进广大党员干部的学习。

(二)坚定不移地开展反腐败斗争

在发展社会主义市场经济的条件下，反腐败斗争始终是党面临的一项长期的艰巨任务。我省各级党的组织和绝大多数党员、干部是好的。但是，也确有少数经不住物质利益和金钱的诱惑，经不住资产阶级腐朽思想的侵蚀，滋长了以权谋私，权钱交易，贪污受贿，徇私枉法，吃拿卡要，挥霍浪费，公款吃喝旅游等消极腐败现象，损害了党和政府的形象，败坏了社会风气，对党的执政地位和社会政治稳定构成了严重威胁。不清除消极腐败现象，任其发展蔓延，党就会走向自我毁灭。我们一定要按照中央的要求和部署，下更大的决心，采取坚决有效的措施，集中解决好存在的突出问题。当前，要进一步抓好领导干部廉洁自律、查处大案要案、纠正不正之风三项任务，努力取得反腐败斗争的阶段性成果。开展反腐败斗争，一定要坚持一要坚决、二要持久的方针，坚持不懈地抓下去。各级党委要加强对纪检、监察、检察工作的领导，支持他们查处大案要案。各级领导机关和各级领导干部要带好头，严格要求自己，模范执行中央的要求和规定，做廉政勤政的表率。要对自己管理单位的廉政建设全面负责，逐步形成一级带一级，一级抓一级，敢抓敢管的局面，对各种腐败现象，要坚决斗争，决不能熟视无睹、麻木不仁。对腐败分子，不管是什么人，都要依法依纪惩治，决不能心慈手软，姑息迁就。对严重干扰、阻碍案件查处的，对搞诬告陷害的，也要绳之以法纪。要坚持标本兼治，对广大党员和党员领导干部，经常地进行党的宗旨教育，不断提高防腐拒变的自觉性，加强廉政建设的法规和制度建设，反腐倡廉纳入法制轨道。逐步建立有效的约束机制，发挥法律监督、组织监督、群众监督和舆论监督的作用，动员各方面的力量综合治理。要全党动手，党政主要领导干部全面负责，纪检、监察、司法、审计、执法监督部门各司其职，协调配合，发挥整体效能，切实抓出成效，取信于民。

(三)努力把各级领导班子建设成为坚强的领导核心

当前和今后一个时期，领导班子建设总的目标要求是：以思想作风建设为重点，针对薄弱环节，从解决突出问题入手，使班子在思想上政治上达到高度一致，组织上行动上达到高度统一，成为全面贯彻党的基本路线的坚强领导核心。

要继续贯彻执行干部队伍“四化”方针和德才兼备的原则。对坚决执行党的基本路线，有高度的事业心和全心全意为人民服务强烈责任感，在改革开放和现代化建设中政绩突出、群众信任的干部，要大胆提拔重用。对经过群众评议、组织考核不胜任的干部要及时调整。对那些以权谋私、群众反映强烈、工作不负责任的干部，要果断地调整下来，对构成违法违纪的要坚决查处。对个人主义严重、思想作风不纯的人，坚决不能提拔重用。选拔任用干部要坚持实践观点、群众观点，严格按照规定程序办事，坚决抵制和克服用人问题上的不正之风。要注意把那些政治上强、懂经济管理的人才选拔充实到各级领导岗位，提高班子领导经济工作的水平。要打破论资排辈、求全责备的陈腐观念，放开视野，多渠道、大范围地选拔优秀年轻干部。通过专业培训、岗位交流、挂职锻炼等多种形式，提高年轻干部的工作能力，帮助他们尽快成熟起来。重视培养选拔妇女干部、少数民族干部。坚持实行干部交流和培训制度。认真执行干部离退休制度，对老同志政治上、生活上要关心，使他们老有所为，安度晚年。

坚持和健全民主集中制，完善党内民主生活制度，是加强领导班子思想作风建设的重要内容。要大力发扬党内民主，增强决策的民主化、科学化。同时又要强调集中统一。必须重申党员个人服从党的组织，少数服从多数，下级服从上级组织，全党各级组织和全体党员服从全国党的代表大会和中央委员会的组织原则，任何时候，任何情况下党员组织都必须严格遵照执行。各级党委都要坚持健全集体领导制度，个人有不同意见允许保留，但必须服从和执行集体的决定。全省各级党组织特别是党员领导干部，都要自觉地增强党性原则，维护党和国家的利益，维护党中央的权威，坚定不移地贯彻执行中央和上级党组织的各项方针政策，保证全党上下高度一致，集中统一，政令畅通，要进一步加强党内团结，领导班子成员之间要互相信任、互相支持，有意见应开诚不公地摆在桌面上，心平气和地讨论，求得统一的认识和看法，对闹无原则纠纷，搞内耗，经过教育不改，严重影响工作的，要果断处理。各级领导干部都要自觉地接受党组织和党员的监督，坚持过好双重组织生活，开展认真的批评与自我批评，增强党内生活的政治性和原则性。

(四)加强党的基层组织建设

党的基层组织是党的全部工作和战斗力的基础。党的路线、方针、政策的贯彻执行，各项工作部署的落实，都要靠基层党组织团结带领广大党员群众去实践。在做好经常性工作的同时，每年都要集中一段时间，坚持不懈地抓好基层组织建设，使其成为坚强的战斗堡垒。

加强党的基层组织建设，要紧紧围绕党的基本路线，根据建立社会主义市场经济体制的要求，针对农村、厂矿企业、街道、科研院所、学校、机关承担的任务和各自的特点来进行。农村要在这几个整顿提高和社会主义教育的基础上，结合农村示范村建设规划，搞好以党支部为核心的村级组织配套建设，努力带领广大农民群众脱贫致富奔小康。国有企业党组织充分发挥政治核心作用，围绕企业改革和生产经营开展工作，保证监督党和国家方针、政策的贯彻执行，充分调动广大职工群众的积极性。企业集团、“三资”企业和其他各种经济组织都要抓紧建立健全党的组织，制定适合各自特点的工作制度和活动方式。机关、学校、科研院所、街道等基层党组织，要加强自身建设，组织、教育、团结党员在各项工作中发挥先锋模范作用。要继续重视做好在生产一线和青年中发展党员的工作。各级党委要加强对基层党组织建设的领导，经常分析研究和解决基层党组织建设中存在的突出问题，切实解决好少数基层党组织软弱无力的状况。

改革和建设的新形势对共产党员提出了更高更严的要求。每个共产党员都应当站在改革开放和现代化建设的前列，在改造客观世界的同时，努力加强自身的党性修养和锻炼。在任何时候、任何情况下，共产党员都要做解放思想、实事求是的模范，做艰苦奋斗、无私奉献的模范。做顾全大局、团结合作的模范，做勤奋工作、忠于职守的模范，做遵纪守法、清正廉洁模范，成为两个文明建设的带头人。

（五）努力改进领导作风

发展社会主义市场经济，我们经验不足，知识不多。各级党的领导干部要认真学习社会主义市场经济基本知识和现代科技知识，努力提高领导现代化建设的水平。要相信群众，依靠群众，充分走群众路线，密切党同群众的联系。要切实加强调查研究，经常深入实际，深入基层，了解真实情况，及时总结群众创造出来的实践经验，提高作群众工作的本领。要进一步改进领导作风和工作作风，反对形式主义，反对官僚主义，反对形而上学，提倡干实事，抓落实，求实效。各级领导干部要时刻想到我们是一个贫穷落后的省份，时刻想到我省还有几百万人民群众没有解决温饱，时刻想到我们是人民的公仆，以为甘肃各族人民谋利益作为自己光荣而神圣的职责，以全心全意为人民服务的饱满政治热情，经常关心群众疾苦。要始终保持认真负责、积极向上的精神状态，无私奉献，兢兢业业，勤奋工作。

同志们，大力发展社会主义市场经济，提前实现第二步战略目标，为下个世纪甘肃经济的腾飞奠定坚实的基础，这是摆在全省二千三百万各族人民和近百万共产党员面前的光荣而艰巨任务。我们要紧密地团结在以江泽民同志为核心的党中央周围，坚定不移地贯彻党的基本路线，坚定不移地走建设有中国特色的社会主义道路，为实现这次大会确定的宏伟目标而努力奋斗！我们深信，只要全省上下同心同德，聚精会神，励精图治，艰苦奋斗，蕴含着巨大发展潜力的陇原大地、丝绸古道就一定会兴旺发达，繁荣昌盛！

政府工作报告

——1994年4月2日在甘肃省第八届人民代表大会第二次会议上

张吾乐

各位代表：

我代表省人民政府向大会作工作报告，请予审议，同时请各位政协委员和列席人员提出意见和建议。

一九九三年的工作

过去的一年，政府工作以党的十四大精神为指针，围绕建立社会主义市场经济体制的总目标，深化改革，扩大开放，抓住机遇，加快发展，努力克服前进中的各种困难，完成了省八届人大一次会议批准通过的主要任务和奋斗目标。

一、国民经济持续较快健康发展

全省国内生产总值完成349亿元，比上年增长10.7%。财政收入52.16亿元，增长30.5%。农业生产又是一个丰收年，总产值完成140.4亿元，增长8.6%。粮食总产量达到75亿公斤。多种经营有了新的发展，畜牧业继续稳定增长。引大入秦、景电二期等大型水利工程和小型水利建设取得了新进展，全年净增有效灌溉面积22.3万亩，“三田”94万亩。乡镇企业发展较快，总产值达到178亿元，增长58.4%。农业综合开发进展顺利，商品基地和农产品深加工业有了一定规模，促进了农业经济效益的提高和农民收入的增加。农民人均纯收入达到563元，净增60元。“两西”建设全面完成了年度任务，一部分条件较好的地区开始实施“小康工程”，老区贫困地区和民族地区的经济有了新的发展。工业生产在资金、运输比较紧张的情况下实现了较快增长，全部工业总产值完成501.8亿元，增长14.7%。产业和产品结构继续得到调整。产销率达到96.7%。销售收入、实现利税的增长超过了产值的增长幅度。全省预算内工业企业销售和利税分别比上年增长42.6%和50.7%。市场紧俏的名优工业产品增幅较大，钢产量首次突破100万吨。重点产品质量稳定提高率达到92.1%，开发省级新产品624项，新产品产值率10.3%。工业企业全员劳动生产率比上年提高11.2%。全省

26个重点建设项目有一半建成或部分建成投产。社会商品零售总额达到161.9亿元，比上年增长20.4%。城乡集市贸易、专业市场和要素市场得到进一步发展，各类市场总数达到1775个，新增150多个。城乡居民储蓄增加，全年银行各项存款余额达到303.4亿元，比上年同期增长17.9%；各项贷款余额达到367.8亿元，增长21.8%。一些企业和建设项目按照国家规定所发行的股票、债券，对缓解资金供求矛盾发挥了一定作用。贯彻落实中央宏观调控措施收到了初步成效，金融秩序和经济秩序明显好转，农产品收购资金基本得到保证。交通运输、邮电通信、城市公用设施等基础设施建设有了新的进展，省境内国道部分路段的改扩建工程提前完成。宝中铁路和兰新铁路复线建设加快了进度。兰州电信枢纽建成投入使用，全省新增市话改制扩容10.47万门，大部分县市实现了长话、市话和农话的自动化，市内和农村电话用户增幅较大。

二、改革开放迈出了新步子

按照建立社会主义市场经济体制的要求，继续推进了各方面的改革。以贯彻《条例》、落实《企业法》为重点的企业改革，促进了经营机制的转换。在进一步深化企业内部三项制度改革的同时，实行了资产经营承包以及国有民营和社有自营等多种资产经营形式。股份制试点迈出了实质性步伐，规范化的股份制企业已有125户，长风股票上市交易获得了成功。住房制度改革进入了实施阶段，商品化进程加快。社会保障制度改革进展顺利，职工养老保险实现了地级统筹。计划、财税、金融、物资、物价等体制也相应地进行了一些改革，促进了政府职能的转变。对外开放继续扩大。国外经济组织在兰州设立的办事机构达到87个；我省在国外兴办的各类企业已达60多家。全省新注册三资企业500家，累计达723家，资金总额9.6亿美元。其中外资额4亿美元。对外贸易在比较困难的情况下，完成了出口总值4.8亿美元，其中出口创汇2.8亿美元。旅游、技术交流、引进国外智力、利用外国政府贷款、对外援助、对外承包工程和劳务输出都取得了一定成绩。多种形式的横向联合向纵深发展，企业之间、工贸之间、农贸之间、生产与科研之间的合作与协作更加密切，新组建了一批经贸、科研联合体。开发小区建设进展良好，筹资规模已达20亿元，建成各类开发项目近600个，兴办企业987个，去年实现产值14亿元，利税2亿元。

三、科技教育等各项社会事业协调发展

科技工作适应经济发展的需要，深化改革，加快调整，推动技术开发和技术服务走向市场，促进了生产和科研的紧密结合。科技成果的推广应用率有所提高，技术贸易合同额突破2亿元。省列科研课题和重点技术攻关项目进展良好，一大批科研成果通过了鉴定，其中有138项获得省级奖励。社会科学研究活跃，取得了一批优秀成果。基础教育得到进一步加强，全省新增普及初等义务教育的县2个，普及初级中等义务教育的县3个，适龄儿童入学率达95.8%，在校学生巩固率和合格率也有一定提高。普通高校和中等专业教育面扩大，成人教育、职业教育、职工岗位技术培训教育有了较大发展。扫盲达标县达到45个。办学条件继续得到改善。计划生育工作同发展农村经济、脱贫致富和创建文明家庭结合得更加紧密，全省人口自然增长率为13.32‰，完成了国家下达的人口计划。依法对工业污染和城市环境进行综合治理，自然生态环境有了新的改善，土地工作重点抓了土地资源的保护、开发和合理利用，不断纠正乱占耕地的现象，近年来全省耕地面积每年都有增加。文化体育事业有了新的发展。围绕筹办第四届中国艺术节，扩建和改造了一批文艺演出场馆和设施，创作了一批优秀作品。全省已基本开通了电视微波线路，出版了一批优秀书刊和艺术作品。群众性的体育运动日益普及，竞技体育有了较大突破，在第七届全运会上，我省获得西北五省区总分第一。卫生工作贯彻预防为主、依靠科技进步、动员全社会参与、中西医并重、为人民健康服务的方针，重点抓了农村医疗、乡镇卫生院建设以及计划免疫、传染病管理、地方病、职业病防治和卫生执法监督。不断加强和完善新形势下的社会保障工作，对灾区群众的生产生活做了妥善安排。双拥工作、国防教育、预备役和民兵工作取得了显著成绩，军民共建活动深入开展，军政、军民团结不断得到加强，涌现出了34个双拥模范县。民族团结、宗教、参事、文史、地方志、侨务、文物保护与开发等工作都有所加强，取得了一定成绩。

四、民主法制建设有了新的进展

各级政府自觉地把政府工作置于人大监督之下，加强了与各民主党派、工商联、无党派爱国人士和群众团体的密切联系，促进了决策的科学化和民主化。政府法制建设不断加强，行政立法、执法监督、行政复议、法制教育、法律服务等工作迈出了较大步伐，对与建立市场经济体制有关的法规执行情况进行了重点检查。查处了一批重点违法案件。“二五”普法教育面继续扩大，群众法制意识有所增强。坚持“两手抓、两手都要硬”的方针，妥善处理了一些影响较大的突发事件，有组织、有重点地进行了以禁毒、反盗窃、打击车匪路霸、扫除社会丑恶现象为重点的专项斗争，严厉打击了各种刑事犯罪活动。

五、反腐败斗争初步取得成效

按照中央提出的近期反腐败斗争的三项任务，在省委统一部署下，重点抓了领导干部廉洁自律和自查自纠。对县处级以上干部在各类经济实体中兼职问题进行了清理，查办了一批以权谋私、贪污受贿的大案要案。各级监察机关共立案受理各类违法违纪案件1569件，已结案1271件，结案率为81%。狠刹行业不正之风取得明显效果，先后公布取消不合理收费项目282项，乱摊派、乱收费现象得到一定遏制。严格出国出境审批制度，基本刹住了用公款出国出境旅游的不正之风。加强和改善了信访举报工作，共受理群众来信21475件，接待来访群众4318人次。

各位代表，过去的一年，甘肃的改革开放、经济建设和其它各项事业能够取得一定的成绩，这是全省人民认真贯彻党的十四大精神和国家的各项方针、政策，锐意改革、努力奋斗的结果；是各级人民代表监督帮助和政协委员通力合作的结果；各民主党派、工商联、无党派爱国人士积极参政议政，工会、共青团、妇联、科协以及其它群众团体、驻甘人民解放军和武警官兵围绕经济建设这个中心做了大量工作。在此，我代表省人民政府，表示衷心的感谢。

在回顾和总结一年来工作的时候，我们清楚地看到，在工作中还存在着不少问题。一是思想观念转变的还不快，未能较好地适应建立社会主义市场经济体制的需要；二是改革和发展的措施还不够得力，企业经营机制转换比较慢，经济效益不高和财政紧张的状况还没有根本好转；三是政府职能转变和机关作风不能适应发展市场经济的要求，工作效率还不高，抓落实不够；四是社会治安问题较多，综合治理有待进一步加强；五是物价上涨过快，给城乡居民生活增加了一些困难。我们要在今后的工作中，采取切实有力的措施，用改革的办法逐步解决好这些问题，促进我省经济和各项社会事业持续快速健康发展。

一九九四年的主要任务

1994年是全面推进改革、加快建立社会主义市场经济体制的关键一年，国家在财税、金融、计划、投资、外贸、物价和企业制度等方面实行了一系列重大改革，我省各方面工作面临着重大转折。做好今年的政府工作有不少有利条件和新的机遇，但也面临着严峻的考验：一是对中央出台的一系列重大改革措施，我们还缺乏足够的思想和工作准备，适应能力较差；二是农业基础薄弱，生产力水平低，扶贫攻坚难度很大；三是资金、运输供求矛盾突出，组织生产困难较多；四是地方财源十分薄弱，收支差额较大，财政工作压力很大；五是农业比较利益下降，居民对价格改革承受能力较弱，平抑价格的任务很重。面对新的形势，全省经济和社会发展的指导思想是：全面贯彻党中央确定的“抓住机遇，深化改革，扩大开放，促进发展，保持稳定”的方针，正确处理改革、发展和稳定的关系，进一步加快改革步伐，扩大对外开放，继续强化农业基础，大力调整经济结构，加速科技进步，努力提高经济效益，推动全省经济和各项社会事业的持续、快速、健康发展。主要奋斗目标是：国内生产总值增长9.5%；工农业总产值增长8.7%，其中工业总产值增长10%，农业总产值增长5%；乡镇企业总产值增长40%以上，农民人均纯收入达到613元；财政收入按同口径计算略高于上年实际完成数；社会商品零售总额增长14.3%；零售物价总指数上涨幅度控制在10%左右；年末人口严格控制在国家下达的计划以内。在推动经济较快发展的同时，进一步改善人民生活，协调发展各项社会事业。为了保证实现上述奋斗目标，省人民政府准备主要抓好以下几方面的工作：

一、确保农村经济稳定增长

在发展社会主义市场经济的过程中，农业的基础地位任何时候都不能动摇。各级政府一定要把农业摆在国民经济的首要位置上，采取得力措施，夺取今年农业的全面丰收。一是在确保粮食生产稳定增长的前提下，积极调整农村产业结构。继续贯彻努力提高单产、稳定增加总产的方针，立足抗旱防灾保丰收，积极推广丰产、高产的农业耕作技术，抓好各种形式的科技承包，努力减轻农民负担，搞好农用生产资料价格的宏观调控，促进粮食生产稳定增长。河西地区、沿黄灌区、陇东和徽成盆地等小片商品粮生产基地要继续高度重视粮食生产，为保证全省粮食大局的稳定做出贡献；缺粮地区要努力改善农业生产条件，提高粮食自给水平，减少粮食调入量。继续抓好“菜篮子”工程和农副产品商品基地建设，加快发展商品畜牧业和林草业。把市场机制引入农业，引导和支持农民因地制宜地调整种植结构和作物布局，积极发展有市场需求的经济作物和高附加值产品，开展农副土特产品的系列开发和深加工，千方百计增加农民收入，提高农业生产的综合经济效益，大力发展高产优质高效农业。二是保持农业有一个合理有序的投入，努力做到投入总量每年都有新的增长。继续实施“22274”工程，集中力量确保重点水利工程的建设，大中型骨干工程做到在建一个、准备一个、收尾一个，不断改善农业生产基本条件，发动和依靠群众大搞小型水利和“三田”建设，开展小流域综合治理，植树种草，治沙治水，建设稳产高产基本农田。景电二期工程年内要全部收尾，引大入秦工程确保在冬灌前发挥效益。继续搞好农村交通、能源、通信、市场、人畜饮水工程等基础设施建设。积极推广节水灌溉和干旱地区农田集流灌溉技术，推动灌溉农业和雨养农业有新的发展。进一步抓好“两西”建设，确保完成今年的各项任务。三是继续深化农村改革，进一步稳定家庭联产承包责任制，完善统分结合的双层经营体制。对“三荒”地的开发经营实行更为优惠的政策，加快培育农村经济的市场主体，进一步搞活农产品流通，积极发展贸工农一体化的经营实体，推动农业和农村经济向市场化阶段迈进。四是实行分类指导，确定不同类型地区的战略重点和主攻方向。河西地区，沿黄灌区、城市郊区和其它条件较好的地区，要努力提高农业生产的综合水平，加快向市场经济过渡，在全省率先奔小康。中部、陇东和陇南、天水的部分地区，要在稳定解决温饱的基础上，搞好区域综合开发，向小康目标迈进。高寒阴湿和少数民族贫困地区，要努力实施“四七”扶贫攻坚计划，发扬自力更生、艰苦奋斗的精神，开创全社会扶贫济困的新局面。坚持以城带乡，以川带山、以富带贫，发挥资源优势，兴办各类扶贫开发经济实体，搞好农村剩余劳动力的转移，通过生产自救、劳务输出、发展多种经营等多种方式，增加经济收入。

二、大力发展乡镇企业

继续坚定不移地把乡镇企业作为振兴全省经济的战略重点，把全面推行股份合作制作为乡镇企业快速发展的突破口，把加快城市郊区、交通沿线、中小城镇、商品集散地、资源富集地区乡镇企业的发展作为全省乡镇企业上台阶的重要依托，把解决人才和资金缺乏问题作为发展乡镇企业的关键措施，把推进技术进步、加强内部管理、提高工业比重作为乡镇企业上规模、上水平的重点，把乡镇企业建设和小城镇建设紧密结合起来。继续鼓励机关干部和科技人员承包、领办、创办乡镇企业。继续坚持效益第一、中小起步、多轮驱动、多轨运行、集中布局、连片发展的方针，一手抓扩大发展，一手抓改造提高。扩大对外开放，多渠道引进境外资金、先进技术和管理经验，适应市场变化，积极开发新产品，努力提高产品质量，不断增强企业的变能力和竞争能力。紧密结合“双高一优”农业的发展，加快农牧业资源的综合开发利用，搞好农副土特产品的深度加工，建设一批高起点的现代化企业，提高农副产品的商品转化率。

三、提高经济效益，加快工业发展

今年工业生产要以优化结构、继续搞好大中型企业和加快发展地方工业为重点，以增加有效供给和财政收入为目标，努力提高经济效益，保持持续、健康、较快发展的势头。一是坚持实行“双带整推”，进一步搞好大中型企业。积极探索在新形势下和中央在甘企业继续合作的方式，理顺利益关系，一如既往地支持中央在甘企业的发展，更好地发挥其对地方经济的带动辐射作用。依托大中型企业，实行加工增值，进行系列开发，用企地联合的办法发展地县工业，把大中型企业的优势转化为地方经济的优势，促进各类企业共同发展。二是大力发展地方工业。从各地实际出发，以市场需求为导向，以产业政策为指导，选择一批市场前景广阔的项目，有重点、分步骤地安排建设。坚持效益第一的原则，项目要选准，论证要充分，算帐要有动态观念。三是加快调整产品结构。依靠科技进步，大力开发高产值、高利润、高出口创汇、高市场占有率和质量优的产品，促进产业结构的优化。四是加快技术改造的步伐。继续提高技术改造投资在整个投资中的比重，宁可少上几个新项目，也要集中一部分资金搞技术改造，从技术进步中求效益。对现有工业企业特别是地方企业摸底排队，有重点地进行脱胎换骨的技术改造，加速产品的更新换代，提高市场占有率，提高地方工业的整体素质。五是加强工业生产调度工作。积极摸索在市场经济条件下调控经济运行的办法，搞好经济运行的综合协调工作。加强对经济走势的监测和预报，对出现的矛盾及时加以解决。优化生产要素的分配和组合，把有限的能源、原材料用于支农产品、出口创汇产品、人民生活必需品和市场紧俏的名优产品的生产。继续抓好限产、压库、促销工作，落实促销政策，讲究营销策略，搞好产品销售，以销促产。搞好交通运输的协调、衔接和调度工作，确保重点物资的运输。六是进一步加强企业管理，引导企业眼睛向内，苦练内功，狠抓扭亏增盈，努力提高劳动生产率，提高企业素质和经济效益。

四、加快第三产业发展步伐

把第三产业作为增加财政收入、增强地方综合实力、改善人民生活的重要支柱，多渠道、多形式地增加对第三产业投入，加快其发展步伐。抓好各类市场建设重点培育和完善专业批发市场、金融市场和产权交易市场。大力发展交通通信、商品流通、保险、信息咨询、证券、房地产、旅游和其它新兴产业，开办新的服务项目，分流社会购买力，满足人民群众多方面的需求。巩固和发展流通体制改革的成果，继续完善国有民营和社有自营，对大中型商业企业进行股份制改造。进一步疏理和扩展流通渠道，积极发展大型流通产业集团，鼓励个体经营者扩大经营，鼓励农民进入流通领域，组织好工业品下乡和农副产品进城。简化登记审批手续，鼓励事业单位、社会团体、科研机构、大专院校和各类群众组织，以及从党政机关分流出来的人员，兴办第三产业，拓宽城镇就业渠道。企业内部服务系统和设施要由福利型、公益型、事业型向经营型转变，减轻企业负担，提高劳动效率，促进后勤服务工作走向产业化、社会化和商品化。

五、放手发展个体、私营经济

积极落实国家和省上有关加快发展个体、私营经济的政策措施，充分发挥个体私营经济在搞活经济、扩大就业中的重要作用，努力提高个体、私营经济在整个经济中的比重。在国家允许的范围内继续实行不限身份，不限规模，不限速度，不限比例，不限领域的政策，大力发展集体、个体、私营等多种经济成份。鼓励社会各界利用闲散资金、闲置厂房设备，兴办非国有企业，引导个体、私营经济跨领域、跨行业、跨所有制开展横向联合；允许具备经营能力的私营企业和个体工商户直接同外商打交道，合资、合作办企业，承接“三来一补”业务。

六、推进各项社会事业健康发展

在持续快速发展经济的同时，推进科技、教育、文化、卫生、体育等各项社会事业健康协调发展，进一步加强社会主义精神文明建设，提倡助人为乐、见义勇为、勤俭朴素、艰苦奋斗的精神，树立良好的社会风尚，随着经济的发展，不断增加对社会各项事业的投入。

坚定不移地确立科教兴省的战略，尽快把经济建设转移到依靠科技进步和提高劳动者素质的轨道上来。科技工作继续贯彻“稳住一头，放开一片”的方针，适应发展社会主义市场经济需要，促进科技经济一体化。以科技转化为重点，调动广大科技人员的积极性，推动科研单位和科技人员，到经济建设主战场建功立业。加强技术市场、技术咨询、科技信息交流机构和成果推广服务体系建设，继续抓好中试基地建设，重视先进科技成果的推广和专利技术的开发。鼓励科技人员创办民营科研企业，支持发展各类群众性科研组织。积极组织科研单位、大专院校和大中型企业，向乡镇企业、城市集体企业、地方小型企业，转让有效益、有市场的科技成果和扶贫开发项目。进一步完善科技承包，促进科教单位同生产经营单位之间多种形式的联合协作。搞好重大科研课题攻关，重视和支持基础研究、应用研究、社会科学研究等工作。

把教育放在优先发展的战略地位，牢固树立百年大计，教育为本的思想，深化教育体制改革，培养合格人才，增强教育适应社会主义市场经济的能力。加快招生分配制度改革步伐，逐步提高自费生、定向生、委培生比例，调整教育结构，完善专业设置。积极倡导和鼓励多种类型的社会力量办学，支持学校同企事业单位挂钩，探索教育同社会结合的新途径。继续加强基础教育，稳步推进九年制义务教育，不断提高学龄儿童的入学率、在校生的巩固率和合格率，搞好初中后、高中后职业培训。全面落实《教师法》和《中国教育改革和发展纲要》，努力增加教育投入，及时兑现教师工资，积极改善办学条件。统筹安排好农村各类教育，发展民族地区教育，继续搞好希望工程和扫盲工作，着力培养一批农村实用技术人才和经济建设人才。认真落实好知识分子政策，稳定现有人才队伍，特别是关键岗位的技术人员和学术带头人。大胆放手地起用各类能人，保护和调动他们的积极性。

深入开展爱国卫生运动，积极发展民办医疗和中医药事业，加强乡镇卫生院的建设。高度重视对传染病、地方病、职业病及其它各种严重危害群众身体健康疾病的防治。认真搞好妇幼保健、食品卫生、劳动卫生、公共场所卫生和以消灭脊髓灰质炎为重点的计划免疫等工作，提高群众健康水平。完善医疗卫生监督机制，加强思想政治工作，教育广大医务工作者，努力改善医德医风，促进医疗水平和服务质量的提高。加强医药市场的监管工作，严厉打击伪医假药，保障人民身体健康。

本着节俭、精彩、突出特色的原则，办好第四届中国艺术节，发展城乡文化事业，采取多种形式，为群众提供丰富的精神食粮，广泛开展群众喜闻乐见、健康有益的文娱体育活动，增强人民体质，强化文化市场管理，深入持久地开展“扫黄”斗争，打击各类非法出版活动，清除精神垃圾，净化社会环境。搞好文物的保护、研究和开发，加强基层图书馆、文化馆(站)和广播电视转播台(站)建设，巩固和发展农村有线广播。

认真贯彻落实三大基本国策。继续坚持“三为主”的方针，抓紧抓好计划生育，稳定各项政策，加强基础工作和“六好”村建设，完善人口计划目标管理责任制，坚决制止早婚、私婚，杜绝多胎生育和计划外生育，提倡优生优育，提高人口素质。增强全民环境保护意识，依法强化环境监督管理，对重点污染源实行限期治理，开展城市环境综合整治，搞好环境保护。依法加强土地管理，严禁乱占滥用耕地，大力开发土地资源，稳定全省耕地面积；积极培育和规范地产市场，充分利用土地生财聚财。

其它各项社会事业在新的一年里也要有新的发展。

七、发展民族经济，加强民族团结

各级政府要把民族工作作为关系政治经济全局的重大问题来对待，从民族平等、民族团结、民族进步、共同繁荣出发，以经济建设为中心，全面发展少数民族地区的经济和各项社会事业，不断巩固社会主义的新型民族关系。充分发挥民族地区的各种优势，落实支持民族地区发展经济的优惠政策，拓展经济技术协作的领域和渠道，多方筹集资金，增加对民族地区的投入。加强基础设施建设，改善农牧业生产条件，培植民族地区自身发展的造血机能。认真贯彻民族区域自治的各项法律法规，广泛深入地开展民族平等、互助、团结和“两个离不开’的教育，进一步加强民族团结。正确区分两类不同性质的矛盾，妥善处理各类纠纷，坚决依法打击破坏社会安定、破坏民族团结、危害民族关系的犯罪活动和国内外民族分裂势力相互勾结进行的渗透破坏活动。认真贯彻党的宗教政策，实施《甘肃省宗教事务管理暂行规定》，依法加强对宗教活动的管理，团结宗教界爱国力量，引导信教群众和宗教界人士积极参加两个文明建设活动。坚决取缔一切非法宗教活动和地下宗教势力，不允许宗教干涉行政、司法、教育等政治和社会事务。

八、进一步加强民主法制建设

各级政府要自觉接受人大监督，重视和发挥人民政协、各民主党派、群众团体在政治协商、民主监督中的作用，虚心听取人民代表和各界人士对政府工作的意见和建议，使广大人民群众的意志在政治和社会生产中得到充分体现。不断增强政府工作的透明度，坚持政府部门与各民族党派的对口联系制度，互通情况，提高政府决策的科学化、民主化水平。进一步重视和加强政府法制工作，健全执法监督检查体系，坚决纠正有法不依、执法不严和违法不纠等现象。积极维护社会政治稳定，进一步落实社会治安综合治理责任制，为改革开放和经济发展创造良好的社会环境。毫不动摇地坚持"严打"方针，以"抓禁毒、破大案、打团伙、追逃犯"为重点，组织好专项斗争和区域性打击行动，坚决查禁和扫除卖淫嫖娼、赌博、拐卖妇女儿童等社会丑恶现象，严厉打击各种违法犯罪活动，扭转部分地区治安差的状况。正确处理人民内部矛盾引发的各种事件，密切注意社会动向，把矛盾解决在基层。解决在萌芽状态。继续开展"二五"普法教育，增强公民的法制观念。切实加强政法队伍建设，从严治警，努力提高政策素质和业务素质。

进一步加强军政、军民团结，深入开展双拥活动和国防教育，增强全民的国防观念。认真做好民兵预备役工作，不断加强国防后备力量建设。

甘肃省1993年国民经济和社会发展执行情况和1994年计划报告（摘要）

甘肃省计委主任

朱作勇

一、1993年全省国民经济和社会发展计划执行情况

1993年，全省国民经济在调控总量、调整结构、保证重点、提高效益的基础上，保持了持续稳定的发展态势，同时，各项社会事业也得到了协调发展。全年全省国内生产总值达349亿元，比上年增长10.7%。其中，第一产业增长6.8%；第二产业增长10.9%；第三产业增长13.8%。

——农业生产获得丰收，粮食总产量创历史最好水平，达75亿公斤，比上年增产6亿公斤。乡镇企业快速发展，产值达177.2亿元，超额完成省委、省政府确定增长50%的奋斗目标，农民人均纯收入达563元。工业总产值完成501.8亿元增长14.7%；工业主要产品产量均有较大幅度的增长，钢、有色金属、原煤、发电量等增长都在两位数以上。

——全年全省全社会固定资产投资完成112.4亿元，比上年增长32.1%；其中，第一产业投资增长4.5%，第二产业投资增长10.9%，第三产业投资增长92.2%。地方国有单位基本建设投资完成26.1亿元，增长43.6%；更新改造投资完成12.1亿元，增长9.8%。

——对外贸易完成出口创汇2.8亿美元。全省累计借用外资正式签约5.23亿美元，累计入境外资2.9亿美元．注册"三资"企业累计达到723户，其中93年新增500户。投资总额达9.6亿美元，其中外资额4亿美元。

——市场建设有了新的进展，全省已累计建成各类生产资料市场和集贸市场1770多个，成交额达100亿元左右，全省实现社会商品零售总额161.9亿元，比上年增长20.4%；财政收入完成52.1亿元，增长30.5%。年末全省银行各项存款增加46.2亿元，各项贷款增加65.7亿元。股份制试点有所突破，全省批准的股份制企业达125户。

在经济发展的同时，科技、教育、文化、卫生、体育等各项社会事业也取得了新的成绩。但是，1993年我省经济运行中还存在一些突出的矛盾和问题。一是农业基础依然脆弱，基本生产条件还未得到根本改善。二是各项资金短缺。三是铁路运输紧张，运力与运量之间的矛盾仍然非常尖锐。四是部分企业亏损扩大，效益下滑。五是石化、机械、纺织等一批老企业由于改造资金投入不足，产品结构不合理。六是物价总水平持续上升，部分居民和贫困地区的农民生活水平相对下降。

二、1994年计划安排的指导思想和主要目标

1994年计划安排的指导思想是:贯彻党的十四届三中全会《决定》精神,全力推进各个领域的重大改革,进一步扩大对外开放,立足于国际国内两个市场、两种资源、两类资金,转换机制、优化结构、提高效益;适当集中建设资金,切实保证重点建设,继续强化农业生产基础,加快发展地方工业、乡镇企业和第三产业,促进国民经济持续、快速、健康发展,促进经济与社会协调发展。

1994年国民经济和社会发展的主要目标是:

——国内生产总值增长9.5%,其中第一产业增长5%(农业总产值增长5%);第二产业增长9.6%(工业总产值增长10%);第三产业增长13%。

——全省全社会固定资产投资年初规模为96.90亿元,同口径相比,较去年增长32.1%。地方固定资产投资73.38亿元,其中,国有单位投资52.4亿元,增长51.7%;集体单位投资9.91亿元,增长41.6%;个体投资11亿元,增长22.2%;在国有单位固定资产投资中,基本建设29.47亿元,增长66.2%;技术改造13.5亿元,增长17.4%;商品房建设投资6.85亿元,增长95.7%;其它投资2.65亿元,增长47.2%。

——财政收入预算53.5亿元,同口径比去年略有增长。

——社会商品零售总额185亿元,增长14.3%;全社会零售物价总指数上涨幅度控制在10%左右。

——外贸进出口总额4.72亿美元,增长18%,出口3.3亿美元,进口1.42亿美元,其中技术引进4300万美元。

——全省年末人口控制在2385万人以内,人口自然增长率为14.9‰。

——农民人均纯收入613元,增加50元。

实现上述目标,全省国民经济主要指标均可提前一年实现"八五"计划和经济上新台阶的目标。

三、1994年国民经济和社会发展的主要任务和措施

(一)、强化农业基础,大力发展农村商品经济

1.绝不放松粮食生产,保夏争秋、提高单产、增加总产。做好国家商品粮基地县的建设工作,扶持省内商品粮基地的生产。

2.增加政策、资金、物资等综合投入。确保国家提高的粮棉收购价格和粮棉合同订购"三挂钩"以及国家扶持农业发展的其他各项优惠政策真正落实到农民手中,并继续做好农业生产资料供应。

3.继续推广各项科技增产措施,把提高农业产品的产量和质量建立在依靠科技基础上。要进一步扩大种植业、养殖业和林果业先进适用技术的推广应用,加快优良高产新品种更新换代步伐。

4.坚持一手抓粮、一手抓钱。以市场需求为导向,积极调整农业生产结构,发展啤酒花、杂豆等高附加值、高商品率、高创汇率的产品。

5.加强农村市场建设。健全和完善粮食、蔬菜、皮毛、药材等专业批发市场;同时,进一步开拓和发展农村消费品市场。

6.进一步加快引大入秦、景电二期等重点续建和收尾项目的建设进度。继续搞好小流域综合治理等水土保持工作。抓紧疏勒河流域综合开发等项目的前期工作。

(二)、大力发展乡镇企业和地方工业,增强地方经济发展实力

1.坚持把加快乡镇企业发展作为振兴全省经济的战略重点。通过股份合作制、以劳带资、横向联合、引进资金以及增加银行信贷等多种途径,扩大对乡镇企业的投入。加快产品结构调整,提高规模效益和经济效益,提高乡镇工业在乡镇企业中的比重,增加地方财政收入。加强规划,引导乡镇企业适当集中,把发展乡镇企业和乡村小城镇建设结合起来,提高城镇化水平。

2.拓宽思路,加快发展地方工业。要以效益为中心,立足省内原材料和农副产品资源,重点发展加工增值型、利用当地资源型、配套服务型、结构转移型、高科技型等多种类型原材料深度加工和高附加值产品的地方工业企业。要加强对现有地县工业的存量调整,跟踪市场变化。采取多种形式,广开筹资渠道,增加对地方工业的投入。

(三)、进一步加强基础设施建设,为经济发展和对外开放创造更加良好的外部环境

今年煤炭、电力、交通、通信、民航、城市建设等方面重点安排靖远、窑街、华亭等重点矿井、大峡水电站、中川高速公路、程控电话等一批基础设施项目。同时争取利用外资建设兰州煤制气管网,二热管网和兰州环境整治工程。

(四)、搞好大中型企业,加快现代化企业制度改革的步伐

深化企业产权制度的改革和企业内部的配套改革,开展建立现代化企业制度的试点工作,继续推进股份制改革,发展多种形式的股份制和股份合作制企业。大力调整企业组织结构,在企业联合、兼并、破产、拍卖上争取有实实在在的突破,促进企业生产要素以及产权的合理流动和有效配置。同时深入开展"抓管理、练内功"活动,提高企业的管理水平和经济效益,努力减少企业亏损。

(五)、推进对外开放向高层次、宽领域、纵深化方向发展

努力扩大出口,合理进口。对出口产品的生产,在资金、能源、原材料、运输、结汇等方面继续给予支持。同时充分发挥各级外贸公司、自营出口企业和三资企业的出口积极性,搞好重点出口产品基地建设。要积极利用国外资金、资源、技术和市场,扩大利用外资规模,引导外资更多的投向创汇行业,基础设施、基础

产业、高新技术产业和现有企业的技术改造；引导外资投向国有企业，特别是大中型企业；提高外商资金到位率。同时，加强对外债的管理，按照“谁借谁还”的原则举借外债，并逐步争取建立偿债基金，增强偿还外债的能力。

（六）、拓展城乡市场，加快发展第三产业，改善人民生活

要重点发展具有我省产地优势的生产资料和生活资料批发交易市场、金融市场、要素市场、再生资源市场。坚持国家、集体、个人一起上，谁投资，谁得益的原则，打破地区封闭和部门垄断，提高第三产业的开放度。继续加快社会保障制度的改革，逐步建立起多层次、多形式的社会保障体系。通过发展农村经济、发展小城镇、推行公务员制度等，稳步增加城市职工和农民的收入，提高生活水平。要加快住房商品化改革和住房建设，逐步改善城镇居民住房条件。

（七）、大力促进高科技产业化，协调发展各级各类教育，推动各项社会事业健康发展

1. 积极促进科技经济一体化，抓好一批先进适用技术的推广应用，并在投资、信贷等方面给以支持，使其尽快转换为生产力。

2. 继续把教育摆在优先发展的战略地位，进一步加强基础教育，重点抓好九年制义务教育、大力发展中等职业教育，成人教育，重视特殊教育，继续鼓励多渠道、多形式社会集资办学和民间办学。

3. 确保第四届中国艺术节的场馆建设。安排好文化、卫生、体育、新闻、出版、广播、电视等各项社会事业，继续抓好计划生育工作，切实严格控制人口增长，搞好社会治安。保护和合理利用自然资源，加强环境保护、改善生态环境。

（八）、抓好“四七”扶贫攻坚规划，并认真组织好实施，为奔小康奠定基础

把两西地区农业建设和老区贫困的扶贫开发结合起来，提高扶贫资金投入强度，及时向特困地区倾斜。充分利用贫困地区已经形成的生产基础和资源优势，将扶贫开发纳入市场经济的轨道，提高稳定脱贫的比例。把农村奔小康摆在农村工作的重要位置，坚持因地制宜、分类指导、分步实施、分层推进的原则，根据区域经济发展现状，确定不同的奋斗目标。抓好一批小康工程的示范乡、村建设，为全省奔小康树立样板，提供经验。

（九）、深化各项改革，进一步加强和改善宏观调控

——深化省情认识，面对市场调整和完善发展思路，用新观点、新思路、新方法，抓紧制定全省以及地区、行业“九五”计划和到2010年长远发展规划。

——积极稳妥地推进价格改革，努力把物价总水平上涨幅度控制在10%左右。千方百计增加农副产品的生产供应，特别是要继续抓好大中城市的“菜篮子”工程；对关系广大居民基本生活的必需品和服务价格，实行价格监审制度。

——深化投资体制改革，扩大资金运筹总量。按照保重点、保效益的原则，集中力量搞好地方的基础设施和基础产业项目。要大胆进行企业法人责任制试点工作，落实企业法人的决策权限和投资风险。

——对部分重要生产资料实行国家订货制度，同时，努力创造条件，逐步建立和完善重要生产资料的专项储备和风险调节基金，增强宏观调控实力。

积极发挥各经济综合部门在协调宏观经济政策方面的功能，保证各项改革的协调配套和顺利实施。同时，加快地方经济立法工作。要进一步转变职能，继续深化计划体制改革，努力使计划适应市场变化趋势，弥补市场功能不足，引导市场正常有序运行，加强对经济走势的监测和预警、预报，及时提出宏观调控的对策建议。

甘肃省党政群团机构及领导人

省委及各部门主要负责人名单

省委书记：阎海旺

省委副书记：张吾乐　孙　英　杨振杰

省委常委：阎海旺　张吾乐　孙　英　杨振杰　李虎林　饶凤翥　仲兆隆　石宗源　陆　浩　梁培禛　杨怀孝　牟本理

省委秘书长：仲兆隆

中共甘肃省纪律检查委员会书记：饶凤翥

中共甘肃省委办公厅主任：郭方忠

中共甘肃省委组织部部长：陆　浩

中共甘肃省委宣传部部长：石宗源

中共甘肃省委统战部部长：杨振杰　（兼）

中共甘肃省委研究室主任：姚恭荣

中共甘肃省委政法委员会书记：杨怀孝　（兼）

中共甘肃省委直属机关工作委员会书记：仲兆隆　（兼）

中共甘肃省委副秘书长、中共甘肃省委保密委员会主任：孙田民

中共甘肃省委党史资料征集研究委员会主任：石星光

中共甘肃省委老干部工作局局长：

韩玉玺 （兼）

甘肃省第八届人民代表大会常务委员会组成人员

甘肃省人大常委会主任：卢克俭

甘肃省人大常委会副主任：马玉海

嘉木样·洛桑久美·图丹却吉尼玛

王金堂　穆永吉　李　萍　姚文仓

胡慧娥

甘肃省人大常委会秘书长：汤九夫

甘肃省人大常委会副秘书长：

张国定　王凤鸣　尚志仁　韩肇文

甘肃省第八届人大常委会委员：

丁生才　丁言章　马进龙　马怀西

马冠洛　王凤鸣　王正之　王作山

王松山　王国祥　王应国　王新中

王翠兰　马依尔　艾努瓦尔

石怀川　刘　燕　安国增　关铭涵

孙兆霞　李嘉宾　张天理　张定国

陈以南　尚志仁　周林科　赵逵夫

赵燕翼　皇甫斌　俞夕云　顾　竺

郭宪章　高金荣　崔　岩　韩肇文

蒋维模　戴云鹏

甘肃省人大常委会各工作部门及其领导成员：

办公厅主任：王凤鸣

民族侨务工作委员会主任：王应国

法制工作委员会主任：石怀川

司法民政工作委员会主任：皇甫斌

教科文卫工作委员会主任：王松山

财经工作委员会主任：王国祥

农业工作委员会主任：崔　岩

代表工作委员会主任：马怀西

研究室主任：韩肇文

庆阳地区工作委员会主任：宋廷杰

平凉地区工作委员会主任：张新民

陇南地区工作委员会主任：王在鹏

武威地区工作委员会主任：裴永俊

酒泉地区工作委员会主任：武惠民

甘肃省人民政府组成人员名单

代省长：张吾乐

副省长：路　明　杨怀孝　陈绮玲

郭　琨　崔正华

秘书长：孔令鉴

省计划委员会主任：朱作勇

省经济贸易委员会主任：李文治

省农业委员会主任：丁　齐

省建设委员会主任：张国杰

省教育委员会主任：阎思圣

省科学技术委员会主任：魏庆同

省经济体制改革委员会主任：

冯亦兵

省体育运动委员会主任：张维国

省物价委员会主任：尹霖初

省计划生育委员会主任：赖学忠

省民族事务委员会主任：李　膺

省人民政府外事办公室主任：

叶绍裘

省国防科技工业办公室主任：

王一兵

省财政厅厅长：张文启

省对外贸易经济合作厅厅长：

程有清

省石油化学工业厅厅长：黄树德

省冶金工业厅厅长：柳宏克

省商业厅厅长：邵克文

省交通厅厅长：胡国斌

省农业厅厅长：刘兴帮

省林业厅厅长：朱耀光

省水利厅厅长：薛映承

省畜牧厅厅长：周明辉

省公安厅厅长：贺明保

省安全厅厅长：马兴中

省司法厅厅长：张　忠

省民政厅厅长：胡培玉

省监察厅厅长：朱毓贤

省文化厅厅长：张炳玉

省广播电视厅厅长：杨德儒

省卫生厅厅长：王陇德

省审计局局长：高存弟

省统计局局长：吴士起

省劳动局局长：祝晏君

省人事局局长：张国维

省工商行政管理局局长：惠树人

省土地管理局局长：金学有

省物资局局长：毛春荣

省粮食局局长：杜　颖

省建材局局长：乔龙德

省环境保护局局长：张　坤

省乡镇企业管理局局长：李万林

省旅游局局长：卫孺牛

省新闻出版局局长：韩效文

省宗教局局长：马德祥

政协甘肃省第七届委员会

主　席：中效曾

副主席：

黄正清（藏族）　黎　中　韩正卿

朱宣人　贡唐仓·丹贝旺旭（藏族）

王　平　陈剑虹　应中逸　杜大仕

拜玉凤

秘书长：徐尚和

办公厅主任：刘　福

提案法制委员会主任：杨　立

文史资料委员会主任：刘郁采

经济科技委员会主任：马超铭

农业委员会主任：李佐栋

教文卫体委员会主任：于忠正

民族宗教委员会主任：蒲　泽

祖国统一联谊委员会主任：杨拯美

中共甘肃省纪律检查委员会

书　记：饶凤翥

副书记：朱毓贤　吴泉祖　张瑞堂

常务委员：饶凤翥　朱毓贤

吴泉祖　王金堂　蒙庆银　王廷钰

阎正芳　田振玺　樊佩君（女）

秘书长：阎正芳

甘 肃 概 况

基本情况

甘肃自然概况

一、优越的自然

甘肃，以古甘州(今张掖)、肃州(今酒泉)而得名。秦设陇西郡，唐代置陇右道，简称陇。元代始建甘肃行省，省制由此肇基。

甘肃位于祖国地理中心，地处黄河上游，地域辽阔，历史悠久。介于北纬 32°31′～42°57′、东经 92°13′～108°46′之间。东接陕西，东北与宁夏毗邻，南邻四川，西连青海、新疆，北靠内蒙，并与蒙古人民共和国接壤，总面积 45.4 万平方公里。全省设 7 个行政公署、2 个自治州、5 个省辖市，68 个县(7 个民族自治县)、11 个市辖区、7 个地辖市。首府兰州。

甘肃地貌复杂多样，山地、高原、平川、河谷、沙漠、戈壁，类型齐全，交错分布，地势自西南向东北倾斜。复杂的地貌形态，大致可分为各具特色的六大地形区域：

陇南山地。这里重峦叠峰，山高谷深，植被丰厚，到处清流不息。这一区域大致包括渭水以南、临潭、迭部一线以东的山区，为秦岭的西延部分，面积近 4.8 万平方公里，山地和丘陵是这一地区最明显的地形特征。整个地势西高东低，绿山对峙，溪流急荡，峰锐坡陡，说似江南风光，却也胜似五岭逶迤。南疆的“纤秀”，北国的“粗犷”，在这里得到了完美的融合。

陇中黄土高原。位于本省中部和东部，东起甘陕省界，西至乌鞘岭畔。这里曾经孕育了华夏民族的先民，建立过炎黄子孙的家园，亿万年的地壳运动变迁和历代战乱，灾害侵蚀，使它支离破碎，尤以定西中部地区成了祖国最贫瘠的地方之一。但在这 11.3 万平方公里的土地上，蕴含着无尽的宝藏，有着全省 70% 的耕地。这里有苍松翠柏，有潺潺溪流，有丰富的石油、煤炭，也有闻名遐迩的名山大川。黄河从这里穿流而过，造就了多少天险夜渡，雄关要塞，峪口大峡。刘家峡、盐锅峡、八盘峡的水轮，把无穷无尽的动力和光明，奉送给这块土地，唤发它新的青春，改变着它昔日的贫困。

甘南高原。它是“世界屋脊”——青藏高原东部边缘一隅，地势高耸，平均海拔超过 3000 米，是个典型的高原区。这里草滩宽广，水草丰美，牛肥马壮，是本省主要畜牧业基地之一。

河西走廊。斜卧于祁连山以北，北山以南，东起乌鞘岭，西迄甘新交界，是块自东向西、由南而北倾斜的狭长地带。海拔在 1000～1500 米之间。长约 1000 余公里，宽由几公里到百余公里不等，面积 11.1 万平方公里。这里地势平坦，机耕条件好，光热充足，水资源丰富，是著名的戈壁绿洲。有着发展农业的广阔前景，是甘肃主要的商品粮基地。

祁连山地。在河西走廊以南，长达 1000 多公里，面积 7 万多平方公里，大部分海拔在 3500 米以上，终年积雪。冰川逶迤，是河西走廊的天然固体水库，植被垂直分布明显，荒漠、草场、森林、冰雪组成了一幅色彩斑斓的立体画面。

河西走廊以北地带。这块东西长 1000 多公里，海拔在 1000～3600 米的地带，人们习惯称之为北山山地。这里地近腾格里沙漠和巴丹吉林沙漠，风高沙大，山岩裸露，荒漠连片，一块块山间平原，尽是些难事耕作之地。人烟虽然稀少，却能领略“大漠孤烟直，长河落日圆”的塞外风光。

甘肃是个多山的省，地形以山地、高原为主。最主要的山脉首推祁连山、乌鞘岭、六盘山，其次诸如阿尔金山、马鬃山、合黎山、龙首山、西倾山、子午岭等，多数山脉属西北——东南走向。省内的森林资源多集中在这些山区，大多数河流都从这些山脉形成各自分流的源头。

甘肃的主要河流有 20 多条，分归两大流区，三大流域。即外流区和内流区；长江流域、黄河流域和内陆流域。内陆流域特指发源于祁连山，流经河西走廊，最终消失在沙漠中的诸河流流域，如石羊河、黑河、疏勒河等。这些河流主要由祁连山冰雪融水补给，季节性强。甘南高原东南部和陇南山区属长江流域，主要是白龙江长 500 多公里，水量大，水流急，落差大，季节变化小，它与秦岭、淮河同为我国的南北地理分界线。陇中黄土区属黄河流域，包括黄河干流、渭河、泾河三个水系，水量季节变化明显，含沙量大，有冰期，灾害多，域内水土流失严重。

甘肃深居西北内陆，海洋温湿气流不易到达，成雨机会少，大部分地区气候干燥，属大陆性很强的温带季风气候。冬季寒冷漫长，春夏界线不分明，夏季短促，气温高，秋季降温快。省内年平均气温在 4～14℃之间。各地海拔不同，气温差别较大，日照充足，日温差大。

全省各地年降水量在 300～860 毫米之间，大致从东南向西北递减，乌鞘岭以西降水明显减少，陇南山区和祁连山东段降水偏多。受季风影响，降水多集中在6～8月份，占全年降水量的50～70%。全省无霜期各地差异较大，陇南河谷地带一般在280天左右，甘南高原最短，只有140天。

甘肃历史上就是一个多民族聚居之地。包括汉族在内，现有41个民族，其中千人以上的少数民族有回、藏、东乡、土、裕固、保安、撒拉、满、蒙、哈萨克、维吾尔族等十一个，东乡、保安、裕固族，则是我省特有的三个民族。全省总人口2135.70万人，其中少数民族190万人。

二、丰富的资源

甘肃幅员辽阔，土地资源丰富。从陇东高原到河西走廊，从北山山地到陇南山区，分布着各种各样的山地、丘陵、高原、平川、荒漠、戈壁、森林、草原、绿洲、沼泽、冰川等，无所不有。适于种植的农业土壤多达15种。人均耕地2.57亩，比全国人均1.45亩多1.1亩。草原面积2.4亿亩，占本省土地总面积的30%，为全国第五大牧区，草地面积广，水草质量好。林地面积5949.75万亩，木材蓄积量近2亿立方，主要分布在长江、黄河、内陆河三大流域的白龙江、小陇山、洮河、西秦岭、子午岭、关山、祁连山等110个林区，近年来人造林面积逐年扩大，重砍轻造的局面有所改变，育用结合已初见成效。

甘肃地貌形态多异，地质构造复杂，在地质构造带形成过程中，发育生成了极为丰富的矿产资源，主要是有色金属、黑色金属，能源矿藏、化工原料，以及冶金辅助原料、建筑原料和其它非金属矿藏。据统计，全省共发现各种矿产地1975处，其中有色金属矿产490处，黑色金属542处，能源矿产391处，非金属矿产552处。在已探明储量的66个矿种中，有23个矿种探明储量居全国前五位，其中镍、铂、钽、铱、锇、钌、硒、铸型粘土重晶石等十种矿的储量居全国首位。铅、锌、铜、钴、铬、锑、金、钒、伴生流等10多种的矿产储量都在全国占居重要地位，故有我国有色金属之乡的称号。

在陇原大地上，还蕴藏着丰富的能源资源。煤、油页岩、泥炭、石油的储量相当可观，煤矿产地65处，主要分布在靖远、窑街、阿干镇、华亭等地，总储量67.3亿吨，并伴生着一定数量的油页岩。石油产地两处，可开采的储量2.7亿吨，玉门油田为0.6亿吨，长庆油田为2.1亿吨。

甘肃境内黄河、白龙江等水系。水量充沛，落差集中，发展水电建设有得天独厚的优越条件。全省已建成水电站29座。黄河上游的刘家峡、盐锅峡、八盘峡水电站和白龙江的碧口水电站，总装机容量达212.5万千瓦，加上其它火力发电厂、小水电、小火电，省内总装机容量已超过300万千瓦，年发电量达140多亿度，同时，座落在黄河上游的黑山峡、积石峡等也都是建设水电的理想地段。除丰富的水能资源外，由于省境内大部分地区晴天多，日照长，有20%的地区风速每秒在4米以上，就为利用太阳能和风能提供了有利条件。

甘肃是全国中药材重要产区之一，有野生药材951种，居全国第二。已经营450多种，主要的有当归、大黄、党参、甘草、红芪、黄芪、贝母、天麻、杜仲、灵芝、冬虫夏草等，其中“岷当”、“文党”产量大、质量好，是闻名中外的出口药材，仅当归一项，在国内外市场年平均供应量达500多万公斤。此外，还有可作为药用的动、植物及矿物中药材约1080余种。在充分利用野生药材的同时，积极推广家种药材，到1988年，全省家种药材面积达30多万亩，并建立了许多特种药物的自然保护区，在一定程度上缓和了毁灭性的滥采行为。丰富的药材资源，为甘肃发展医药工业提供了良好的条件。

甘肃有野生动物650种，鸟类441种，属于国家保护的稀有珍禽异兽20多种，其中属一类保护的有32种(动物24种，鸟8种)，二类保护的有36种(动物24种，鸟12种)，三类保护的有近50种(其中鸟类6种)。主要分布在陇南山区、河西走廊、祁连山区以及甘南高原的森林地带。陇南地区的野生动物，以大熊猫、金丝猴最为珍贵。大熊猫是我国独有、世界驰名的珍贵动物，号称“国宝”，仅存于川、陕、甘接交的局部山区，总数量不足1000只，是国家最重要的保护动物之一。在甘肃仅产于文县境内的白水江以北的一片山区及迭部县的极少数地方，主要以箭竹的茎、叶、笋为食。大熊猫性情温顺，活泼可爱，寿命一般在20年左右。金丝猴也是我国特有的一种珍稀动物，其美誉仅次于大熊猫，素有“国宝”、“猴中之王”的称号。在甘肃仅产于文县、康县、武都县。外形瘦长而壮实，因其背上有金黄色丝状长毛而得名。为拯救和保护这两种举世珍贵动物，国家已把文县白水江一带18万公顷的地方，定为大熊猫和金丝猴的自然保护区，以使其更好地生息繁衍，与人类共生共存。此外，陇南山区还生活着牛羚、苏门羚、青羊、大鲵(娃娃鱼)等大量稀有动物，集中了全省大部分野生珍稀鸟类。生活在河西戈壁滩上的野马、野驴、野骆驼、滩黄羊、鹅喉羚、藏原羚等珍贵动物和祁连山区的白唇鹿、马麝、野耗牛、雪豹等。以及陇南山区大量的珍稀鸟类给寂寞、幽静的大自然增添了生机，给甘肃人民增添了生活的乐趣，激发了人们对甘肃的热爱，吸引着国内外各阶层人士对甘肃的向往和神秘的兴趣。

甘肃丰富多彩的土特产诸如白兰瓜、醉瓜、冬果梨、花牛苹果、百合、黑瓜子、大接杏、猕猴桃、蕨菜、发菜、黄花菜等，都深得国内外人士称赞。还有独具特色的手工艺品，兰州的洮砚、酒泉的夜光杯、兰州的雕刻葫芦、保安腰刀和临夏回族的砖雕等，工艺精美绝伦，风格特异，在我国手工艺品中独树一帜。别具风味的地方食品，如兰州清汤牛肉面、陇西腊肉、静宁锅盔、泾川罐罐馍、静宁烧鸡、高三酱肉等，久已名传天下，脍炙人口。

甘肃是中华民族文化的发祥地之一。据考古发掘的材料证明，早在10万年前，我们民族的先民就在这里生活。新时器时代文化遗址在甘肃的大量发现进一步佐证，甘肃灿烂的远古文化与中原的仰韶文化是一脉相承的。甘肃的仰韶文化以马家窑、半山、马厂类型为代表。这类文化最具特色的是制陶业，这里出土的彩陶，造型精美，色彩逼真，是甘肃制陶艺术的瑰宝。秦安大地湾遗址的发掘向世人表明：早在公元前7000～4000年之间，甘肃境内的居民就已经创造了令后人惊叹的古代文明。当华夏民族文化进入青铜器时代，陇东一带的周民族逐渐强大，控制关陇。等到武王伐纣，建立周王朝，分封诸侯之时，秦国便受封于九州之一的雍州，即今天水一带。秦汉时代，关陇地区是国家的政治、经济、军事、文化中心。汉武帝击破匈奴，在河西走廊署武威、酒泉、张掖、敦煌四郡，史称“河西四郡”，河西遂并入汉朝版图，西汉王朝开始对河西进行了大规模的经营开发，实施了移民河西，加强边防设施，实行大规模军屯等措施。经过数十年经营，河西走廊出现了仓廪丰足、牛马遍野的富饶景象。汉代的开边政策及张骞通西域的成功，丝绸之路由此开通，出现了丝绸西去，天马东来的盛况。河西诸郡随着中西交通的开辟，中外商人的往来，变成了一个个商品贸易中心和商品集散地。汉末至隋初，中原战乱，而河西地区相继建立的一系列地方割据政权则相对稳定，河西的经济文化仍然得到了某些发展。隋唐时期，丝绸之路畅通无阻，进入了繁荣鼎盛时代，中西交往呈现出一派空前盛况。大唐帝国盛极一时，河西的武威、敦煌成为经济文化十分繁荣的国际性贸易城市。整个河陇地区，农桑繁盛，士民殷富，史书为此大书特书，“天下称富庶者无如陇右”。中国有句哲言，叫做物极必反，唐代末年，国势倾颓，吐蕃内侵，河陇沦陷，陆上丝绸之路日趋衰落，国家政治、经济重心东移，河陇地区远离帝都，逐渐沦为荒僻之地，贫困从此扎下了根，直到今天依然困扰着甘肃前进的步伐。

历朝历代的兴亡变迁，在甘肃大地上留下了引人深思的古代遗迹。有世界闻名的石窟艺术，有巧夺天工的出土文物；有雄关要塞，和名城古堡；也有佛教遗迹和道教名山；还有文人绝唱、英雄悲歌，以及地方艺术奇葩和许多美妙的历史传说。甘肃是石窟艺术之乡，敦煌则是世界文化艺术的宝库。甘肃六大石窟各具特色，惟以敦煌莫高窟和麦积山石窟最为引人注目。莫高窟栩栩如生的彩塑和优美动人的壁画，千姿百态的麦积山雕塑，显示了我国古代艺术家高超的艺术创造才能，召唤着多少海外游子，吸引着多少中外游人学者。武威出土的东汉铜奔马更是我国古代的艺术珍品。居延汉简、武威西夏碑的出土，解开了许多历史疑迷。唐代大诗人杜甫在甘肃写下了110多首“山川历落、居然在眼”的现实主义诗篇，留下了一串闪光的足迹，陇南的成县至今还有一个香火不断的杜甫草堂。王维、岑参、高适、李益、李梦阳等历代诗人雄浑豪迈的边塞诗句，更为甘肃文化史增添了绚丽多彩的篇章。人们常说燕赵之地多出悲歌慷慨之士，其实陇原大地上也出现过无数闪光的历史巨人和忠臣良将，有的功垂青史，有的沉冤千年，关于他们的种种奇妙的历史传说，早已成为整个中华民族有口皆碑的民间故事。

甘肃不仅保留了丰富的历史遗存，而且为中国革命的胜利建立了不朽的功勋。刘志丹在这里点燃了革命的火种，六盘山迎来了“红旗漫卷西风”，西路军悲壮的历史留下了祁连山不灭的回声，红军三大主力会师的纪念塔，则是革命走向胜利的永久象征。

甘肃有着辉煌的历史，现在却是这样落后，甘肃有过富庶的历史，今天却是如此贫困。孙中山先生说过：“世界潮流浩浩荡荡，顺之则昌，逆之则亡”，只要我们在所取得成就的基础上，立足实地，乘改革开放之春风，发展经济；只要我们顺乎历史潮流，做到天尽其时，地尽其利，物尽其用，人尽期才，振兴甘肃的伟大事业，就可指日而待。

三、建置沿革

春秋战国及以前

商代，居于泾河、渭河流域尚处于氏族部落阶段的周朝的祖先周部落，改善耕作，开拓了我国最早的农业。这一时期，甘肃境内有羌方、共（今泾川县北）、密（今灵台县西）等方国部落。

西周时，秦人的祖先在省境东部今天水地区定下来，开始了由游牧经济向农业经济的缓慢过渡，而游牧生活仍占居主要的地位。

春秋时期，省境属秦国和西戎。前688年（秦武公十年）秦国在已被征服的邽戎、冀戎地区，设邽县（今天水市北道区南）、冀县（今甘谷县）。这是甘肃历史上建立最早的两个县。

战国时期，秦国的疆域已达今甘肃的东南部。秦昭王二十七年（公元前280年）设置陇西郡，时过9年，于秦昭王三十五年（公元前272年）再建立北地郡。

秦汉时期

秦统一六国，建立起统一的、多民族的封建中央集权国家，全面推广春秋战国时期已出现的郡县制，分全国为36郡(后增为40郡)。当时,省境行政区划为郡、县两级制,共设陇西、北地两郡。

西汉时期的行政区划同秦代一样,仍为郡县两级制。公元前205年,汉高祖始占有陇西、北地两郡。公元前121年置武威、酒泉两郡。过了10年,于元鼎六年(公元前111年),分武威郡置张掖郡,析酒泉郡置敦煌郡。同时迁徙内地贫民到河西4郡,在沿黄河自朔方以西至令居(今永登县),广泛实行军事屯田,军农结合,巩固边防。河西4郡的设置,对切断匈奴与西羌的交通,开辟我国通往西域的走廊,对于开发河西,促进这一地区经济和文化的发展,具有十分重要的意义。其后于汉武帝元鼎三年(公元前114年)又增置天水、安定郡;元鼎六年(公元前111年)设武都郡;汉昭帝始元六年(公元前81年),从天水、陇西、张掖3郡各分出两个县建立金城郡。这样,就使省境郡的数目由秦代的两个郡增为10个郡,共辖115县、10道(县一级、在少数民族地区设置)。

东汉时,行政区划大体上是州、郡、县三级制。汉灵帝中平五年(公元188年),为了加强地方官的实力,镇压农民起义,改革地方行政制度,扩大刺史权力,并将刺史更名为州牧,确定州为郡上面的一级地方政权。这就使实行了400年之久的郡县两级制扩大为州、郡、县三级制。

三国和魏晋南北朝时期

三国和魏晋南北朝时期,基本上实行的是州、郡、县三级制。

魏、蜀、吴三国鼎立时期,省境共置凉州1州(另有一部分地方分属雍州和益州),12个郡、77个县。大部分地方属魏国,南部的部分地区属蜀国。

西晋,省境设凉州、秦州、兼属雍州,统12个郡、72个县。凉州,治姑臧(今武威市),辖6个郡、41个县,即金城郡、武威郡、张掖郡、敦煌郡、酒泉郡、西郡(分山丹一带);秦州,治冀县(故治在今甘谷县东南,后迁至上邽,即今天水),统六个郡、24个县,即陇西郡、南安郡、天水郡、略阳郡(原广魏郡,晋武帝时更名)、武都郡。阳平郡(今文县和四川省平武县)。属雍州(治长安,今陕西省西安市)的为安定郡,治临泾(今镇原县),统7个县。进入东晋,社会动乱,北方形成分裂割据局面。从西晋末到十六国时期,跨境或在甘肃境内先后建立的割据政权有:后赵、前秦、后秦,各占有约当今甘肃一部之地;前凉(公元314年—公元376年),历时62年,治姑臧(今武威市),辖区东至秦陇,北及居延,南逾河湟,西至葱岭;西秦,都苑川(今榆中县东北),辖区约当今甘肃西南部;后凉(公元386年—公元403年),都姑臧,建国18年,初有前凉旧地,后除姑臧外,仅有仓松(今古浪西),番禾(今永昌西)2郡;南凉(公元397年—公元414年)立国18年,都廉川堡(今青海省乐都县),辖地东至金城,西到青海,北据广武(今永登东南),南有河湟;北凉(公元397年—公元439年),历时43年,初都张掖,后迁姑臧,据有武威、张掖、敦煌、酒泉、金城、西海、西平、乐都等郡地;西凉(公元400年—公元420年),立国21年,都敦煌,后迁酒泉,辖区约有今酒泉、玉门、安西、敦煌几县地。

南北朝时期,甘肃先后为北魏、西魏、北周的统治地区。这一时期,行政建置十分混乱。

北魏,甘肃境设置8个州、35个郡、91个县。北周,甘肃境设22州、56郡、104县。

隋唐五代时期

到隋唐五代,又回到秦汉的郡县两级制。

隋初,隋文帝为改变南北朝时期州、郡、县三级体制过于分散的状况,根据"存要去闲,并小为大"的原则,开皇三年(公元583年)裁并州郡,取消郡一级建制,实行以州统县,使东汉末年以来实行的三级地方政制,重新恢复为州、县两级制。隋炀帝大业三年(公元607年),又改州为郡,以郡统县,并分郡为上、中、下三等。另设司隶和刺史分部巡察主掌监察。经裁并,省境共设16郡、76县。

唐朝,初改郡为州,唐玄宗时又改州为郡,唐肃宗时再改郡为州,终唐之世,仍为州、县两级制,郡只是地理区域的名称。类似这样的划分,一直延续到清代。当时省境共设22州,辖67县。全省设置的州是:秦州(今天水市)、河州(今临夏市)、渭州陇西郡(今陇西、渭源、武山、漳县)、兰州(今兰州市、皋兰县)、阶州(今武都县)、洮州(今临潭县)、岷州(今岷县和临潭县南部)、叠州(今临潭县西南和白龙江上游)、宕州(今舟曲以西、宕昌东南)、凉州(今武威市、金昌市、古浪县)、沙州(今敦煌县)、瓜州(今安西县)、甘州(今张掖市、山丹县)、肃州(今酒泉市、玉门市)、泾州(今泾川、灵台、平凉市、镇原县)、原州(今平凉市西北和宁夏回族自治区固原县)、渭州(分原州平凉县置,今平凉市)、宁州(天宝元年即公元742年改北地郡置,今宁县,正宁和镇原县东部)、庆州(今庆阳地区大部)、凤州(今两当、徽县和陕西省凤县),文州(今文县)和狄道府(今临洮县西)。除了行政区,唐代还设有监察区。

宋元明清时期

宋金辽时期,行政区划大体上是路、州(府)、县三级制。

北宋初分全国为10道,至道三年(公元997年)改10道为15路(后增为26路),甘肃属陕西路。但宋代的路与唐代的道有所不同。宋初的路是财政区兼有监察的职能,后来才逐渐变成地方最高一级建制。

11世纪初叶,党项族西夏(公元

1038年——公元1227年)崛起，于宋仁宗明道元年建国，都兴庆府(今宁夏回族自治区银川市)，辖区有22州，其中在甘肃境内的有甘(西夏改为宣化府)、凉(西夏改为西凉府)、肃、瓜、沙、会等6州。西夏的统治约有190年之久，后为蒙古所灭。

南宋时，甘肃大部隶属金朝。属南宋利州西路(北宋时称秦凤路)的有文州、阶州、西和州(今西和，礼县)、凤州、同庆府(今成县)，天水军(绍兴初因秦州为金占领，遂置南天水县，北天水县，嘉定元年即公元1208年改县为军，今天水市)。

金朝，在甘肃境置4路，16州(府)，50个县。

元代，甘肃行政区划大体上是省、路、府(州)、县四级制。省辖7路，5个直隶州，4个府，22属州，24县。

明初，沿用元朝的行省制。明太祖洪武二年(公元1369年)置陕西等处行中书省(辖甘肃)。

甘肃属陕西承宣布政使司管辖。原甘肃境内共设置5府、9属州(隶属于府)、50县。5府是庆阳府、平凉府、巩昌府、临洮府、灵州(直隶州)。9个属州是：宁州(隶属庆阳府)、泾州、静宁州、固原州(以上3州属平凉府)、秦州、阶州、徽州(以上3州属巩昌府)、兰州、河州(以上2州属临洮府)。除府(直隶州)、属州、县外，还设有卫、所。

清朝的地方行政制度是省、府(直隶州、直隶厅)、县(散州、散厅)三级制。清德宗光绪十年(公元1884年)，从甘肃分出新疆单独建省。分置以后的甘肃省辖8府6直隶州，1直隶厅、61县。8府是：兰州府、平凉府、巩昌府、庆阳府、宁夏府、西宁府、凉州府、甘州府。6直隶州(与府同级)是：泾州、固原州、阶州、秦州、肃州、安西州。1个直隶厅(与府同级，在少数民族聚居地区设置，不领县)，即化平川直隶厅(平凉、华亭、固原、隆德4州县地)。除了直隶厅，全省还设8个属厅(散厅、隶属于府，不领县)：洮州厅(属巩昌府，今临潭县)、庄浪厅(属凉州府，今永登县南)、抚彝厅(属甘州府，今临泽县)、宁灵厅(宁夏府，今宁夏回族自治区吴忠市)、贵德厅(属西宁府，今青海省贵德县)、循化厅(属西宁府，今青海省循化撒拉族自治县)，丹噶尔厅(属西宁府，今青海省湟源县)，巴燕戎格厅(属西宁府，今青海省化隆县)。

民国时期

辛亥革命以后，废除了清代的府、州、厅制。民国元年(公元1912年)，甘肃共设7道，下辖77县。

北伐战争以后，民国16年(1927年)，废除道的建制，改县的行政长官县知事为县长。1928年，划甘肃西宁道属之西宁，大通、乐都、循化、贵德、巴燕、湟源等7县，另建青海省；同时划甘肃宁夏道属之宁夏、宁朔、灵武、盐池、平罗、中卫、金积、豫旺(原镇戎县，今固原县)等8县和宁夏护军使所辖的阿拉善额鲁特，额济纳土尔扈特2部地，成立宁夏省。区划调整分置以后，甘肃省辖64县，1929年增置到68县。

大革命时期，甘肃就有中国共产党领导的革命活动。1935年11月，根据中华工农民主共和国中央执行委员会的决定，陕甘边区根据地划为陕甘省。1936年7月，改陕甘省为陕甘宁省，驻地迁往甘肃曲子，辖区在甘肃境内的有华池、环县、曲子、固北、赤庆、定环等县。1937年1月，中共关中特委派代表与国民党代表谈判，将正宁、宁县"一分为二"，国民党在其白区设两个县，共产党在红区设新宁、新正县，隶属关中分区。同年，陕甘宁省划分为三边分区和庆环分区。庆环专署辖华池、曲子、固北(后并入环县)，赤庆(后并入华池)、环县、定环(后分别并入环县和定边)6县，另在原统战区设陕甘宁边区陇东办事处，领导庆阳、合水、镇原、宁县的抗日救亡运动。1940年3月，庆阳、合水、镇原3县正式建立抗日民主政权。同年4月，陕甘宁边区政府决定建立陇东分区，在庆阳设立陇东分区行政督察专员公署，辖华池、环县、曲子、庆阳、合水、镇原6县。1949年6月，宁县、正宁两县划归陇东分区管辖。

中华人民共和国成立以后

中华人民共和国成立，开始了我国行政制度的新阶段。在摧毁旧政权以后，党和人民政府总结了革命根据地行政建设的经验，结合社会主义革命与社会主义建设的实际情况，逐步形成省、专区(州、市)、县(市、区)三级地方行政体制。

1949年8月甘肃省解放以后，即成立甘肃行政公署，下辖庆阳、平凉、天水、武都、岷县、定西、临夏、酒泉、武威、张掖、兰州11个分区(专区、市)，73县(局)。甘肃行署隶属于西北军政委员会(后改为西北行政委员会，1954年撤销)。1950年成立甘肃省人民政府，1954年根据内务部的通知精神，将撤销的宁夏省合并于甘肃省，1955年，甘肃省人民政府更名为"甘肃省人民委员会"。以后，根据第一届全国人民代表大会第四次会议关于成立宁夏回族自治区的决定，1958年划3个专区(自治州)、19个县市归宁夏回族自治区管辖。"文化大革命"中，省人民委员会更名为"甘肃省革命委员会"，1979年更改为甘肃省人民政府。

气候影响评价

【气候概况】甘肃1993年的气候特征是：年平均气温除陇东和陇南正常略偏低外，其他地区接近常年。年降水量河西(以黄河为界)偏多，河东正常略偏少。年日照时数接近常年。冬季偏暖，降雪多，日照正常。春季河西正常偏暖，河东正常偏冷，降水西多东少，日照全省正常偏少。夏季全省偏凉，多雨，日照略偏少。秋季偏凉，少雨，多日照。主要气象灾害是冰雹、暴洪、黑风暴、冻害、干旱。气候条件属正常年景。

1.气温

全省各地年平均气温在0.0℃(乌鞘岭)—14.5℃(文县)之间。除陇东和陇南偏低0.2—0.5℃外,其他各地接近常年。

气温各月分布不匀,1月全省寒冷,月平均气温偏低1.0℃—3.7℃。2月全省气温偏高1.6—5.6℃,有隆冬不冷之感。3月大多数地方气温偏高0.5—3.2℃,春意荡洋。4月风和日暖,气温偏高0.3—1.6℃。5月气候偏凉,全省绝大多数地方气温偏低1.0—2.6℃。6月气温接近常年。7和8月气温分别偏低0.5—1.8℃和1.0—2.3℃,三伏不热。9月河西和甘南高原气温偏低0.3—1.0℃,其他地方偏高0.5—1.7℃。10月全省偏凉,气温偏低0.5—2.0℃。11月河西和陇东气温偏低0.3—2.7℃,其余地方偏高0.2—2.3℃。12月全省绝大多数地方气温接近常年。

2.降水

全省各地年降水量在63.6(安西)—851.4毫米(康县)之间。河西偏多3—7成,陇南偏多2成左右,其余地区比常年偏少2成左右。

降水各月分布不匀,1月除酒泉、武威两地区北部和陇南南部偏少2至9成外,其余地方降水均偏多5成至3倍,其中中部和甘南高原北部偏多1至3倍,个别地方偏多4至8倍。2月酒泉、武威、庆阳三地区的北部偏少2成至1倍,其余地方偏多1成至2倍,个别地方偏多3至6倍。3月河西偏多8成至3倍,个别地方比常年偏多达20多倍;河东大多数地方偏多2成至1.5倍。4月全省各地降水普遍偏少2至9成。5月河西中部和西部、陇东北部、陇南北部和东部降水偏少1至8成,其余地方偏多2成至1倍。6月河西中部、中部的南部、陇东东南部偏多2成至1.6倍,其余地方偏少1至8成。7月河西降水偏多5成至3倍,河东大部分地方偏多2成至1倍。8月河西偏多5成至2.5倍,河东大多偏少1至6成。9月全省各地降水偏少2成至1倍。10月陇东和陇南偏多1至8成,其余地方偏少1成至1倍。11月河西、陇东和中部三地区的西北部偏多1成至1倍,个别地方偏多达4倍,其余地方偏少1成至1倍。12月除个别地方比常年偏多1至2倍外,其余地方偏少3成至1倍。

3.日照

全省各地年日照时数在1437.9小时(成县)——3300.3小时(马鬃山)之间,基本接近常年。冬季除兰州市日照偏少35%外,其他地方正常。春、夏两季全省日照正常略偏少。秋季全省日照正常略偏多。

【气象灾害及其影响】

1.冰雹、暴洪

冰雹、暴洪是本年危害最重的气象灾害,开始早(4月29日),结束迟(10月5日),危害地区广,灾情重,主要集中在6、7月,占全年总次数的2/3。据统计,全省近70县市(次)不同程度遭受冰雹、暴洪危害。全省受害人数达240多万人,死亡30人,受害牲畜3900多头(只),损坏房屋6400多间,倒塌房屋3900多间,农作物受灾面积430万亩,成灾面积280万亩,减产粮食1.5亿公斤,损失粮食1500多万公斤,农、林、牧等产业直接经济损失约3亿元,给铁路和公路的交通运输也造成一定影响。

2.黑风暴

5月5日在河西走廊的金昌至中部的白银一带发生了一次有气象记录以来少见的黑风暴。这次黑风暴是西西伯利亚强冷空气南下,在冷锋加速中形成的强风和强沙尘暴相结合产生的一种灾害性天气。黑风暴所到之处,瞬间最大风速达34米/秒,强劲的西北风席卷沙尘,黑浪翻腾,狂奔呼啸,挟石带沙,'沙暴壁'高达300米左右,能见度为0米,天昏地暗、伸手不见五指。

我省的金昌、永昌、民勤、武威、古浪、天祝、景泰、靖远、白银等县市受其危害极大。据统计,在这次黑风暴中有50人死亡,14人失踪,153人受重伤。农作物和经济林果受灾面积达30多万公倾。丢失、伤亡各类牲畜6万多头(只)。吹倒(断)电杆786根,毁断电线78公里,导致金川公司35千伏供电线路中断,致使100个厂矿企业停电停产20多小时。武威市上城乡发生火灾,烧毁民房145间,烧死牲畜240头(只)。兰新铁路部分路段被大风吹起的流沙埋压,造成客、货车迟发、晚点和停运达42列。这次黑风暴给上述地区造成直接经济损失达2.36亿元。

3.干旱

4月—5月上旬在陇东、陇南北部、中部一些地方因降水偏少,出现了不同程度的春旱。旱灾与往年相比虽然较轻,但对一些地区的农业生产仍然造成了一些影响。庆阳、平凉和天水三地市由于春旱冬小麦长势差,影响了其正常拔节、孕穗发育及大秋作物的按时播种、出苗和正常生长。

4.初秋的雪灾和霜冻

8月29日—9月6日先后在民乐、天祝、榆中、临洮县大雪纷飞并出现了霜冻天气。民乐县沿山的夏粮晚熟区20多万亩粮油作物受害,减产粮油1000万公斤,经济损失1000多万元。天祝县32万亩小麦、青稞、油籽、洋芋全部受冻,粮食减产3010万公斤,直接经济损失3685万元。榆中县南山一带和临洮县东北部遭受历史上罕见的大雪袭击,使长势良好,可望丰收的小麦、豌豆、胡麻、洋芋等共27990亩全部冻死,损失粮食130.83万公斤,油料作物经济损失18万元。

【气候影响综合评价】

1.气候与农业

对农业生产有利的气候条件

是：上年伏秋雨水多，底墒好，冬小麦播种适时，出苗齐壮。入冬后降雪多，对冬小麦安全越冬十分有利。春季回暖早，降水普遍较多，土壤墒情好，大部分地方春小麦播种适时，出苗整齐，长势良好，对冬小冬麦返青拔节也十分有利。4月虽然降水偏少，由于土壤底墒好，加之有几场适时透雨，大部分地方天旱地不旱，大秋作物播种顺利。5月——8月大部分地方降水偏多，没有出现高温和干热风天气，对小麦成熟和大秋作物的生长十分有利。入秋以后大部分地方降水偏少，但土壤底墒较好，对大秋作物的成熟和冬小麦播种影响不大。对农业生产不利方面是：在一些地方遭受冰雹、暴洪、黑风暴、冻害及干旱等灾害的危害比较严重。综合全年和生长季的光照、温度、降水等主要气象要素分析，气候条件属于正常年景。

2. 气候与林业

冬季降了几场好雪，春、夏两季降水较多，土壤墒情好，对植树造林和林木生长有利。各地植树造林成活率比较高，如中部干旱地区的定西县植树造林的成活率在8成以上。林业部门充分利用了春末夏初各地降水偏多的有利气候条件，在清水、秦城、武山、礼县、西和、灵台等县（区）和榆中县兴隆山等地进行了飞播造林试验，效果较好。气候对林业不利的方面是：低温、寒潮、黑风暴等。低温冷冻使幼苗发育不良，一些地方的树木被积雪压断。5月5日的黑风暴使一些地方的林木被风刮断，有的连根拔起，防风固沙林被风沙埋压，有些经济林木的花蕾被风沙吹落，造成一些地方的果品减产。

3. 气候与畜牧业

冬季气候偏暖，有利于牲畜越冬，春季升温快，降水多，使得牧草返青早、生长好。夏季降水多，牧草生长旺盛，抓膘好、仔畜成活率高。秋季降水较少，多晴朗少云天气，为牧草的收割、晾洒、储运提供了有利的气候条件。由于气候条件有利，因而大多数牧业县牧草生长良好，牲畜膘肥体壮，各类牲畜的保活率、繁成率、总增长率都比较高。气候条件对牧业的不利影响主要是3月中旬的连阴雨雪天气，由于积雪较厚，牲畜无法出圈采食，使肃北、肃南、天祝等县牲畜被冻饿死2万多头。玛曲、碌曲两县由于五月低温阴雨天气多，牧草生长缓慢，6月——9月降水偏少，牧草生长受阻，植株矮小，提前枯黄，产量低，是近10年来第二个低产年。

4. 气候与水利

本年大多数地方降水正常偏多，水库蓄水量也比较多，全省各水库总蓄水量比1992年增加26.5%。刘家峡水库因为上游降水多，库区来水较丰，到10月底水位为1725米，蓄水量达33.89亿立方米，为今冬明春的发电、灌溉提供了有利条件。气候对水利的不利影响是冰雹、暴洪灾害比较严重，对各地水利设施和水电站造成的损害比较重。

5. 气候与交通

综观全年，大多数时间气候对铁路和公路交通运输的影响是利大于弊。

气候对铁路的不利影响，主要是暴洪对铁路造成的水害比较严重，其次是黑风暴。4月下旬—9月上旬我省局地性的暴洪较多，因水害在铁路正线上共发生断道28次，其中陇海线3次，中断行车152小时；兰新线25次，中断行车379小时，在支线上发生断道9次，中断行车390小时。5月5日在河西出现的黑风暴，由于风大和能见度极差，武威分局全线停车3.5小时，客、货车迟发、晚点和停运42列之多，经济损失达百万元以上。

气候对公路运输的不利影响，主要是大雪、暴洪和黑风暴等造成的危害。3月中旬的大雪天气，使柳（园）—（西）藏公路敦煌至当金山段的部分路段积雪厚达1米，阻断交通3天。7月20——21日在河西境内连降2天大雨，在古浪县造成山体滑坡，公路行车中断2天，被堵车辆达几百辆。兰州至武威公路段因水害冲毁桥梁1座，堵车几百辆。陇南地区因暴洪毁坏公路路基20多公里，桥涵10余座，中断行车30次。4月28日——5月5日的雷雨天气，引起的泥石流冲毁国道212甘川公路新城子—白阳坝5处，长2.5公里，桥梁6座、涵洞18个，县乡公路46处，长40余公里。

（刘德祥）

土地资源概况

甘肃位于中国西北内陆腹地，总土地面积45.44万平方公里。属典型的山地黄土高原。山地多，沙漠、丘陵、戈壁分布广。全省地处青藏高原、内蒙古高原、黄土高原交汇地带。域狭长，地跨北亚热带、暖温带、温带和寒带气候区。一般海拔在1000—3000米之间，年均气温0—14℃，年降雨量36.8—800.7毫米，无霜期48—238天。依干燥度指标划分有三分之二的地区属于干旱、半干旱和极端干旱的荒漠地带。又因受流域河流的分割和气候地貌形态变化影响，自东南向西北大致区分为长江流域、黄河流域、内陆河流域，不同流域的特征造成明显的多种土地类型。东南和西南部的省界边缘地带为山地；中部和陇东属于深厚土层的黄土高原；西部的河西走廊为绿洲与沙漠戈壁相间，还有零星分布和盐碱滩。此外还有丘陵、盆地、河谷、平原等土地类型。

一、土地资源主要特点

1. 土地资源总量大，难利用土地多

甘肃土地总面积居全国第七位，人均占有土地31.9亩，比全国人均占有土地13.4亩，高出1倍多。但耕地面积小，仅占全省土地总面积的10%，垦殖系数低居全国第26位。而沙漠、戈壁、高寒石山、裸岩冰川、低洼盐碱、沼泽等难利用的土地占总面积的36%以上。土地利用率不到60%。境内虽有一定面积的宜农、宜林、宜牧荒地资源，其中受缺水、风沙、盐碱等有障阻因素影响的三等地多，约占一半以上。可垦的耕地后备资源不足，开发利用难度大。

2. 山地多平地少，土地质量差

全省山地和丘陵占总土地面积78.2%。其中：地面坡度大于25度的占33.7%，平川地只占21.8%。现有耕地中山地占65%、川塬地仅占35%、低洼湿地占2.7%、盐碱地占1.26%、风沙地占1.64%、高寒阴湿地占14.9%、中低产田占耕地面积68.9%。另外林地比重小，草地退化生态破坏问题严重。

3. 土地的光热条件虽好，水土资源分布不平衡，土地生产力低

全省大部分地区光照充足，年日照时数平均为1700——3300小时，太阳年平均总幅射量每平方米4800——6400兆焦，高于我国同纬度的东北、华北地区，热量方面除高寒地区外，完全可以满足耐寒作物生长对积温的要求。并能种植多种喜温作物对积温的要求。但灌溉水源缺乏，且分布不平衡，成为限制土地生产力的主要因素。全省总水量309.5亿立方米，人均1500立方米，比全国平均水平低44%。耕地亩均水资源占有量422立方米，相当全国人均、亩均水资源量的56%和32%。陇南水多地少，土地分散坡陡，利用困难。水的利用率为3.22%，水土流失严重；河西地区水少地多水的利用率已高达123%（含重复用水量和地下超采量）。因而土地开发利用受到水利条件制约。陇中、陇东黄土高原区也是地多缺水，沟谷水位低，提水困难。水利投资效益差。

二、土地利用现状

1993年全省土地总面积67727.39万亩。各类土地面积变化情况分述如下：

1. 年耕地总面积为5221.73万亩。其中山地3370.31万亩，川地1459.02万亩，塬地392.4万亩。

2. 土地面积339.62万亩，与1983年49.8万亩相比，10年间果园面积年平均递增率为21%。发展速度较快；今后应适当控制防止与粮争地。

3. 林地总面积7619.98万亩。其中森林面积6069.68万亩，人工营林面积2434.30万亩。

4. 草地总面积为23222.54万亩。其中：天然草场21668.04万亩，人工草场911.86万亩。半人工草场307.60万亩。

5. 水域面积765.07万亩。

6. 居民点、工矿用地1078.93万亩。

7. 公路、铁路和机场用地301.64万亩。

8. 未利用的土地2577.51万亩。

三、土地资源保护利用情况

1. 1993年共开发新增耕地107200亩

其中：开荒80275亩，围垦6193亩，废弃地利用12552亩，其他6715亩。年内减少耕地65980亩，其中：国家建设占用耕地11811亩，集体建设占用耕地2476亩，灾害毁耕地5933亩，农业结构调整34510亩。年内耕地增减相抵，全省净增耕地39740亩。

2. 各类建设用地面积

1993年全省各类建设占用土地为56778亩，比1992年46606亩增加10172亩。其中国家建设用地29142亩，比上年增加825.4亩；集体建设用地7914亩，比上年增加4904亩；农村个人建房占地19154亩，比上年减少893亩。农民建房用地乱占问题，得到了有效控制。以上各项用地均未超过国家下达的用地计划指标。

3. 开发区和用地

由国务院和省政府批准建立的七个经济开发区规划占地总面积为168000亩。其中连海、白银西区、金昌东区、西成铅锌矿区为工业开发区。兰州宁卧庄为高新技术开发区、临夏为民族经济开发区、敦煌市为旅游开发区。在现有基础上，加快步伐，按已确定的重点，增强自我发展和辐射吸引能力，积累经验，探索路子，以推动黄河上游的经济发展，在开发区推行土地使用制度改革，有偿使用土地筹集建设资金，合理利用土地等方面起着典范作用。1993年累计土地开发建设面积达到41300亩，由于开发建设资金不到位，开工建设面积只占开发区总面积的24.5%。

4. 土地使用制度改革步子加快

由过去无偿使用变为有偿使用土地，为经济建设筹集了资金。据1993年10月不完全统计全省出让土地2695亩，收取出让金8519万元。兰州市利用土地出让吸引外资和社会闲散资金走出了一条以地生财聚财，加快城市建设的路子，已通过土地出让为政府筹集建设资金4489万元。引资达10亿元。1993年，敦煌市利用土地出让，为政府筹集资金804.4万元，已占到财政收入的29.4%。

5. 全省重点农田保护区划定界累计完成56个县占农业县（市、区）79个的70.9%

省级土地利用总体规划编制工作于1993年10月完成。并经省政府审定已报国务院待批。有18个县（市、区）也完成了县级土地利用总体规划，有的已经上级政府批准组织实施。另外在土地利用规划、农田保护、开发复垦等方面有7个县（市、区）分别获得省和国家土地管理局的奖励。其中：榆中县和正宁县、清水县的土地利用总体规划分别获得优秀成果一、二等奖。为各级

政府宏观控制和管理土地资源提供了科学依据。

四、土地利用存在的主要问题

长期以来,缺少土地统筹规划和综合协调,土地利用结构与布局不尽合理,在新的形势下,土地管理方面也出现了新的不适应问题,如开发区占地面积大,实际开工建设用地少,果园面积扩大过快。1993年已扩大为339万多亩,超过了我省国民经济"八五"计划和"九五"规划,2000年的发展水平。出现了果粮争地,城郊菜地面积逐年缩小趋势。由于人口增加人均耕地逐年减少至今人均耕地地下降为2.3亩。耕地利用"重用轻养",农业投入不足,地力下降普遍存在;在旱作农业区,经营粗放,陡坡种植,输荒种植,有的种撞田,广种薄收。破坏植被尚未完全制止。林区"重伐轻育",采育失调,林地生产力低下;牧区超载,草场退化;还有工业"三废"污染土地现象加剧。土地资源和土地资产管理缺乏有效的措施;各类房地产开发公司和国家建设及集体建设用地,乱占滥用土地的现象时有发生。今后,必须加强统一规范化的管理。

(甘肃省土地管理局规划处)

甘肃省矿产资源特征远景及其开发利用

省地矿局副局长

殷先明

甘肃是我国矿产资源大省之一,尤以有色和稀贵金属为最。

地质勘查证实,全省已找到145种有用矿产,发现矿产地2500多处。探明D级以上储量的矿产达82种(不含铀、钍及水气矿产),产地470多处,其中大型矿床51处,中型128处。

据矿产储量表的保有储量统计,列全国前十位的有46种,其中镍、钴、铂族、硒、铸型粘土和饰面蛇纹岩等11种的储量居全国首位,锌、铬、铜、锑、重晶石、菱镁矿等15种分列全国2—5位,具明显优势。

对经济建设起重要作用的45种常用矿产,除铝土矿、硼、金刚石和硅藻土等外,我省均探明有一定储量,并能基本或部分满足建设之需。就人均占有量而论,石油、铬、钒、镍、铜、铅锌、钴、钨、锑、金、萤石、硫、水泥灰岩等近20种矿产均高于全国人均占有量的1倍以上。如此丰富的矿产资源为我省经济高速发展,奠定了雄厚的物质基础。

一、矿产资源的基本特征

1.探明资源丰富,经济潜在价值高。依据探明的能源、金属和非金属三大类共46种矿产的保有储量进行经济潜在价值的计算约3600多亿美元,人均约1.7万美元。从三大类矿产的价值构成看,能源矿产2310亿美元,占64%;金属矿产955亿美元,占26%;非金属矿产370亿美元,占10%。金属矿产中,以有色金属最高达640亿美元,约占金属矿产总值的67%,其余为黑色(23%)和贵金属(10%)。这一构成反映出甘肃矿产资源结构的特色。

2.许多重要矿产,特别是金属矿产的探明储量高度集中于一个地区或产地,而小型矿床(点)则遍布全省,既有利于建设规模矿业基地,又便于发挥地方优势。如金川矿床集中了我省全部的镍、铂族和80%的铜储量,成为我国镍和铂族金属的提炼中心。再如西成地区赋存着全省66%的锌和36%铅储量,该区即将建成为我国大型铅锌基地之一。

3.共(伴)生矿产或组份复杂的综合矿床多,极大地提高了矿床的经济价值,但也相应加大了开采和选冶的难度。据统计,几乎全部大中型金属矿床和部分非金属矿床均共伴生有多种有益组份。如金川铜镍矿床含有13种有益元素,其中铂族和钴的储量分别为全国总量的50%和20%以上。有些矿床的共伴生组份的经济价值已接近或超过主金属的价值。如小铁山矿床,除铜外,共伴生的铅、锌、金、银、镉、硒等储量均达大中型以上规模,其经济价值高于主金属。近年来,由于加强了金、银的回收,矿山出现扭亏增盈,创造出良好的经济效益。

4.某些大宗矿产贫矿、难选矿多,富矿少,有的存在矿种不配套。以铁矿为例,占92%属非磁性贫铁矿,选矿工艺较复杂。又如,农用化肥矿产明显不足,探明的磷储量少且矿石贫(一般含P_2O_5仅8—12%)多为难选的胶磷矿,致使目前难以利用。

5.有色金属探明矿种齐全并具品位富、易选冶的特点,是甘肃的一大优势。全国探明的有色金属共13种,除铝以外,我省均探明有储量,其中镍、钴、铜、铅锌、锑、汞的保有储量居全国前列。就矿石品位论,省内铜矿床含Cu>1%的富矿占总储量的70%以上;铅锌矿石P_6+Zn品位大多在7—8%,某些重要矿床(如厂坝等)品位>8%的原生硫化矿石占全矿的90%以上,选冶回收率高,开发利用条件优越。

6.矿床地质工作程度偏低,一定程度制约了矿业的发展。据统计,目前已编入矿产储量表的产地仅580余处,为发现产地的20%强,探明储量的矿种只占发现矿种的60%。有些矿床由于地勘程度低,无法满足矿山建设需要。以金矿为例,大多为普查储量,致使黄金开采处于"等米下锅"。尤为突出的是,大部分乡镇集体或个体矿山所开采的产地,工作程度更低,有的甚至没有做过地勘工作,对矿山发展带来不利影响。

二、矿产资源的远景

甘肃国土辽阔,地质构造复杂,成矿条件优越,显示良好的勘查和开发前景。现就主要矿产作一简要介绍:

1. 能源矿产：我省能源矿产品种齐全，既有常规能源如石油、天然气、煤、油页岩、泥炭及地热，又有新能源如铀、钍等。能源结构以煤为主，油(气)与煤比例为1∶16，明显偏低。就探明储量，石油和煤在国内不具优势。但煤炭资源远景十分可观，预测资源总量达1870亿吨，居全国第6位。空间分布上，主要集中于陇东地区，这对即将建成的陇东能源重化工基地提供了可靠的后备资源基础。

甘肃铀探明储量居全国第6位，资源保证程度较高，且内外部条件较好，但至今尚未利用。从能源工业发展趋势看，应尽早开发这一新能源，尤其河西地区条件更为有利，应予以重视。

2. 有色金属矿产：从资源条件和有色金属工业发展对资源需求分析，甘肃有色金属资源前景是优劣并存。其具体表现在如下几个方面：

一是在甘肃有色金属工业中占主导地位的铝冶炼业，没有资源保证，应当继续坚持利用省外乃至国外资源的政策；

二是镍资源十分丰富，只要保持合理开发规模(年产电镍4万吨)，坚持贫富兼采，作为全国最重要镍基地的优势可持续到下世纪中叶。目前，在北山及其邻区(新疆哈密)相继发现有远景的铜镍矿产地，对我省镍工业的发展创造了有利条件。

三是铜矿资源不足，后备基地短缺，急待找到一批大型矿床。据预测，找矿潜力很大，目前已探明的储量大致是远景资源量的20—30%。在祁连山西段和北山地区，铜资源量在数百万吨以上，有找到新矿床可能。事实上，已在镜铁山和柳沟峡发现若干具中型规模的矿床，只要加强地勘工作，振兴甘肃铜工业指日可待。

四是一个新的铅锌矿业基地在西成地区初具雏型，该区铅锌储量可望达到2000万吨，发展远景极其乐观。

3. 贵金属矿产：贵金属是我省优势资源，其中铂族具明显现实优势，由于以共伴生矿为主，资源开发受到制约。经近年勘查，省内独立岩金矿远景可观，初步证实具一定规模的产地达49处，大中型规模的有13处，预测资源量在千吨以上，现已探明的储量尚不及10%，找矿潜力巨大。西倾山、礼(县)—岷(县)、北山南带及文(县)—康(县)等地区已构成重要金矿带，随黄金的大规模开发，有望成为全国主要产金基地之一。

4. 黑色金属：作为钢铁工业原料矿产，省内探明矿种齐全，资源保证程度较高。但以贫矿和难选复杂矿为主，利用难度大。不过目前已开发出较完善的工艺流程，大规模工业开发已不存在问题。区域成矿条件有利，而地勘工作总体水平偏低，尚有一定发展前景。钢铁工业的发展所需资源一般有保证。

5. 化工和建材非金属矿产：按探明资源，我省非金属不具优势，尤其是大宗农用矿产和玻陶原料矿产，难以满足工业需要。而且就勘查和开发前景而论，上述两类矿产的找矿潜力还很不明朗，必须采取合理的资源政策。水泥原料及部分化工矿产(如芒硝、重晶石、硫铁矿等)则资源充足且开发潜力大，有很好的发展远景。

三、矿产资源的开发利用

甘肃作为以能矿资源为依托的资源产业省，其经济的发展，一定程度上依赖于对矿产资源的开发。

我省矿业开发已具相当规模，在国内占居重要地位。据统计，已开发利用的矿产达64种，约占探明矿种数的80%。已正规开发的矿产地218个，占探明储量产地的39%。另外，在数以千计的小矿床(点)中，约70—80%已被乡镇和个体采矿所利用，总之矿产资源开发程度较高。

全省国有矿山247个(含31个在建矿山)，乡镇集体矿山2500多个，个体采点1100多个。近年矿石开采量约8000多万吨，其中甲类矿产5300多万吨，约占全国同类矿产开采总量的2.47%；乙类矿2700多万吨，占全国0.8%。1992年矿业及相关原材料工业总产值(现价，下同)达185.67亿元，占全省工业总产值的50.28%，其矿业产值28.16亿元，占7.63%，矿业已成为支柱产业。

尽管矿业开发已取得了明显进展，但从总体开发水平上与全国相比，尚有一定差距。突出表现在资源综合利用程度不高，在我省矿山企业中，除金川和白银两个直属企业较成功地开展了资源的综合利用外，大多数矿山，特别是地方和集体矿山，因缺乏资金和技术，未能有效地回收有益组份。此外，从反映资源利用水平的"三率"指标看，我省矿山企业普遍要比全国平均水平低5—10个百分点，加剧了资源的短缺。

根据经济社会发展总体规划，从资源配置特点出发，甘肃矿业开发的重点是：加快煤炭和油气的勘查和开发，建设强大的能源工业，推进有色、贵金属和非金属矿产的开发利用，建立从资源采选到加工，直到综合利用的产业群，形成以有色和稀贵金属、石油化工、钢铁及建材为主体的，在国内外有重要影响的产业优势。建设好四大综合矿业基地和十四个重点矿业开发区，它们分别是：河西有色、贵金属、黑色和化工基地，中部有色、石油加工和建材基地，陇东能源重化工基地和陇南有色、贵金属和化工基地；金昌镍、铂族、盐磷化工及建材开发区，嘉酒玉钢铁、石油化工、盐类矿产和其他非金属开发区，北山煤、金、有色及非金属开发区，张掖煤、盐类矿产及建材非金属开发区，天祝煤、黑色和建材非金属开发区，兰州石油加工、有色冶金和建材开发区,白银煤及有色金属开发区,连海煤、冶金及非金属开发区,平凉煤和建材非金属开发区,庆阳石油(天然气)开发区,西成铅锌、金及非金属开发区,文康金及化工非金属开发区,西倾山黄金开发区。

为了合理利用矿产资源,搞好综合矿业基地及矿业开发区建设,应采用两类资源开发循环模式,即:地质勘查(货币投入)→矿山开发→矿产品加工和商品生产→销售(货币增值)→地质勘查再投入;省外(或国外)输入矿产资源(货币投入)→矿产品加工和商品生产→销售(货币增值)→矿产品再输入。

上述前一类循环是以省内资源为基础的地质勘查一矿业开发模式,亦是现行最重要的开发模式,目前我省大多数矿业基地的建设,适宜采用这一模式。后一类的矿业原料供应立足于省外或国外,如我省已高度发展的铝和稀土冶炼业以及石油加工业等属此类模式。随矿业的发展和资源不断耗竭,后一模式将日益重要。

国民经济·社会发展

1993年甘肃省国民经济运行情况综述

1993年,全省围绕建立社会主义市场经济的总体目标,面对新的形势,努力加强和改善宏观调控,从而使国民经济得到了持续、健康、较快地发展,对外开放继续扩大,经济体制改革稳步深入,全年实现国民生产总值358.53亿元,比上年增长11.6%,达到近几年来的较高水平。但是,我们也应清醒地看到,由于经济发展的条件、环境等的制约,我省国民经济运行中的一些问题和矛盾仍突出存在,我们在全国经济中的地位仍很微弱,这对我们今后的发展无疑会产生多方面的影响,必须以积极的姿态全面深化改革。

一、国民经济的总体运行状态

总体而言,虽然年内全省经济运行的环境发生了一定的变化,宏观调控的力度有所调整,外加我省经济仍处于新旧体制相互交织、作用的情况下,但由于认真贯彻中央关于经济工作的一系列政策措施,及时整顿经济秩序,从而使社会总供给和总需求基本平衡,全年供需差率为-3.82%,国民经济运行的态势良好。根据季度测算,全省国民生产总值相对处于较为合理的增长状态,与上年同季相比,1—4季度分别增长10.1%、11.1%、10.0%和11.6%,基本平稳。从国民经济综合景气评分变动图所显示的结果,经济运行在一季度平稳的基础之上,二季度开始加快,由绿灯区进入黄灯区,6月份达到了顶峰,之后9月份出现回落,第四季度仍处于黄灯区,我们同样可以看出,全省经济处于较快的增长状态,但一直未进入红灯区。

二、生产稳步发展,社会供给能力增强

全省工业生产持续快速增长,乡及乡以上工业累计3月末、6月末、9月末、12月末的增长速度分别达到9.1%、10.8%、11.5%、9.8%。全年工业生产增加值实现136.74亿元,增长14.1%;实现总产值505.25亿元,增长14.2%;工业生产增长的主要动因来自于重工业,重工业增长速度达到16.0%,而轻工业为9.4%。生产的加速发展使社会供给能力进一步增强,工业基础行业和重点行业在市场竞争中取得了良好的成绩,全省钢产量首次突破百万吨大关,达到106.45万吨,比上年增长14.0%;发电量达到227.91亿千瓦小时,增长13.8%;原煤产量增长17.1%,达到1805.58万吨;水泥产量达到543.11万吨,增长10.9%。

建筑业生产不断发展,经营状况稳定,全年实现增加值23.22亿元,比上年增长10.2%,一些县的建筑业已成为群众脱贫致富和增加财政收入的重要行业,从业人员多,作业范围广。国有建筑施工企业在改革中不断探索,克服困难,创造了良好的成绩,全年房屋施工面积在530万平方米以上,同时,房屋竣工面积大幅度增加,总面积在460万平方米以上。

全省第二产业全年完成增加值159.96亿元,比上年增长13.6%,生产水平的提高,使整体的经济效益水平也有所改善,企业劳动生产率提高,资金使用效率提高。但是,存在的问题仍然相当明显,我省企业的微观生产经营状况令人不安,一是企业管理水平处于较低的层次,费用大,浪费多,而且一些企业的内部管理还有所放松,经营机制转换的步伐较慢;二是企业的活动资金全面紧张,同时企业产成品的积压也较为严重,相当的企业开工不足甚至停产,年末,全省乡及乡以上独立核算工业企业产品成库存价值占同期工业总产值的16.4%;三是企业间的差距扩大,中央企业普遍好于地县企业,亏损企业增多,亏损面扩大,年末全省乡及乡以上独立核算工业企业亏损面达11.9%,亏损额达12.86亿元,其中大中型企业占78.1%。同时,轻重工业相差较大,如果促进轻工业的稳健发展是宏观调控中应当注重的问题。

全省农业生产随着种植计划的放开进入新的时期,由于重视了保护农民积极性,减轻农民负担,增加农业投入,引导农业生产,因而再获丰收,全年农业增加值比上年增长8.8%,达到87.43亿元。主要农产品除棉花因灾减产外,均有所增长,其中粮食总产量达到750.26万吨,比上年增产 8.9%，油料 37.53 万吨，增产 2.9%，受收入的驱动，主要经济作物，特别是药材、水果和产量增加较多。全省畜牧业生产继续稳步发展，提供的肉、禽、蛋、奶增加，牧产品商品率已接近 60%，年末大牲畜存栏 596.38 万头，生猪存栏 645.10 万头，羊只存栏 1025.58 万只，均比上年增加。

三、市场流通进一步活跃

经过多年的实践，全省上下对流通的重要性不断增强，1993 年形成了市场建设热潮，一些地区将发展流通，带动第三产业发展，作为振兴本地区经济的突破口。全省消费品市场繁荣活跃，但不稳定，全年社会消费品零售额达到 156.11 亿元，比上年增长 21.7%，城市增长幅度大大高于农村，生产资料市场交易活跃，年末全省县及县以上物资企业生产资料购进与销售速度分别为 16.1%和 17.7%。

1993 年全省对外贸易出现了一定的困难，全年外贸进出口总额为 4.8 亿美元，比上年增长 14.3%，其中进口额比上年大幅度增长，达 2.0 亿美元，而出口额虽经努力达到 2.8 亿美元，但比上年呈负增长。

同生产企业相似，流通企业在市场竞争中也出现了许多问题，主要表现在各项资金紧张，从而使企业拖欠增加，农副产品收购、外贸出口等受到直接影响；消费市场层次鲜明，地区间、企业间相差较大，受居民收入水平限制，地县、特别是农村市场消费水平不足，1993 年全省居民人均消费水平为 631 元，其中农业居民仅为 412 元；国有流通企业的作用发挥不充分，管理水平不高；对外贸易发展不稳定，一个明显的原因是自宣传不够，固定贸易对象少，流动性大。

四、投资需求适度增长

据测算，1993 年全省投资需求为 152.27 亿元，比上年增长 12.1%，其中，固定资产投资需求为 97.37 亿元，而当年全社会固定资产投资额实现 122.08 亿元，比上年增长 43.41%，其中国有单位投资额为 81.55 亿元，比上年增长 13.7%。全省大中型和重点建设项目进展顺利，基础建设受到重视，固定资产投资结构较为合理，基本符合甘肃的实际，一批新的生产能力通过固定资产投资得到实现。但是，投资项目的审查应进一步强化，并加强监督，提高投资效率和效益。

五、财政收入增幅大，金融形势趋稳

1993 年全省财政收入达到 52.11 亿元，比上年增长 30.4%，这一形势是在年初收入进度迟缓的情况下，经多方努力而取得的。但是，全省财政困难的局面并未得到扭转，全年 63.'7 亿元的财政支出主要用在"吃饭"上，2/3 左右县的行政事业单位职工工资不能按时发放，这自然使财政支出中用于建设的资金份额相当小。

全省金融在整顿秩序、深化改革中得到发展，金融市场建设加快，融资渠道、手段向多元转化，金融形势出现了存款增加，现金投放减少的良好局面，年末，银行各项存款余额达 303.4 亿元，比上年增长 17.9%；各项贷款余额达 367.8 亿元，比上年增长 21.8%，其中，流动资金 236.7 亿元，增长 18.5%，固定资产 100.9 亿元，增长 31.5%；银行累计现金收入增长快于支出，现金净投放 19.1 亿元，比上年少投放 3.2 亿元，金融事业的发展，有力地支持了全省的经济建设。

六、居民收入继续增加，物价水平持续上涨

随着经济的发展，全省城乡居民的收入水平继续增加。从总量上看，1993 年全省人均国民生产总值为 1541 元，比上年增加 226 元。抽样调查表明，农民人均纯收入达到 562.85 元，比上年增长 12.0%，城镇居民人均生活费收入 1839.4 元，比上年增长 17.4%。然而，1993 年的物价形势却令人不安，全省物价水平呈逐月持续上涨的局面，而且表现出起点高、全面上涨、涨幅较大的特点，成为 1988 年以来的第三个高峰年，全年零售物价指数为 113.0%，比上年高 7.2 个百分点；生活费用价格指数为 115.4%，比上年高 8.2 个百分点。由于物价水平的上涨较高，使居民的实际收入增加不多，部分居民甚至生活水平下降，这已引起人们的关注。

回顾 1993 年的经济发展形势，全省宏观形势良好，在国内经济中的地位稳定，按国内生产总值排序，在全国 30 个省、市、区中列第 26 位。我们应在这一基础之上，从甘肃的实际出发，全面深化改革，加强宏观调控，强化手段，把宏观经济与微观经济紧密结合起来，加快向新体制过渡的进程，努力缓解各种矛盾和问题，实现国民经济的健康快速发展，使人民的生活水平有较大的提高。

1993 年甘肃省乡镇企业发展情况

省乡镇企业局局长

李万林

一、乡镇企业概况

1993 年，在邓小平同志南巡谈话精神鼓舞下，各地县认真贯彻国务院中西部乡镇企业经验交流会和乡镇企业工作会议精神，发展乡镇企业积极性空前高涨，各级领导真抓实干乡镇企业大好局面前所未有，创造了我省乡镇企业发展史上的最好水平。

全省乡镇企业数达 274658 个，比上年增加 35186 个，增长 14.69%。其中占乡镇企业个数 91%的个体企业增长 15.22%，乡办、村办企业分别增长 12.44%、16.24%，合作企业个数比去年略有增加。

乡镇企业从业人数达到 166.46 万人，比上年增加 22.82 万人，增长 15.89%，占农村总劳动力的 19.35%，约占剩余劳动力的 50%左右；乡办、村办、合作、个体办从业人数分别占从业人员的 24.9%、12.6%、9.6%、52.9%，分别比上年增长 12.96%、13.85%、13.2%、18.34%。

乡镇企业总产值达 177.22 亿元，比上年增加 65.32 亿元，增长 58.37%。其中合作企业在维持原有规模的条件下，增长速度最快，高达 63.66%。分行业来看，农业、工业、建筑业、交通运输业、商饮业产值分别为 1.88 亿元、88.99 亿元、34.72 亿元、25.80 亿元、25.89 亿元，分别比上年增长 76.7%、53.38%、61.79%、51.59%、80.17%；其中第二产业——工业、建筑业是乡镇企业的支柱产业，占乡镇企业总产值的 70%。

乡镇企业营业收入达到 155.4 亿元，比上年增长 58.28%，产值收入率为 87.69%。

乡镇企业主要产品产量比上年有所增加。原煤 741.72 万吨，比上年增加 167.87 万吨，增长 29.3%，水泥 155.95 万吨，比上年增加 30.03 万吨，增长 23.85%，砖 605434.9 万块，比上年增加 134008.2 万块，增长 28.4%。瓦 150147.05 万片，比上年增加 37769.25 万片，增长 33.6%。机制纸及纸板 78285.8 吨，比上年增加 8347.4 吨，增长 11.94%。

出口产品交货值 1.6 亿元，比上年增加 0.54 亿元，增长 50.9%

实际上交国家税金 4.84 亿元，比上年增加 1.5 亿元，增长 44.74%。

实现纯利润 10.72 亿元，比上年增加 2.91 亿元，增长 37.27%。

职工工资总额 23.16 亿元，比上年增加 5.89 亿元，增长 34%。

固定资产原值 50.63 亿元，比上年增加 12.85 亿元，增长 34%。

乡村股份合作制企业 1098 个，职工人数 35563 人，资本金 34159.2 万元，总产值 62008.2 万元。

总产值上亿元的县 58 个，比上年净增 17 个，产值总计 152.11 亿元，占乡镇企业总产值的 75%。

总产值上亿元的乡 14 个，比上年净增 7 个。产值总计 21.85 亿元，占乡镇企业总产值的 13%。

总产值 500 万元以上的村 293 个，比上年净增 156 个，产值总计 32.48 亿元，占乡镇企业总产值的 18.3%。

总产值 1000 万元以上的企业 70 个，比上年净增 40 个，产值总计 12.1 亿元，占乡镇企业总产值的 6.8%。其中产值超过 5000 万元的企业 3 个（上亿元的企业 1 个）。

乡村亏损企业个数 204 个，占乡村企业 1.3%，比上年减少 37 个，亏损金额 1404 万元，比上年增加 206 万元。

乡镇企业全员劳动生产率 10646 元/人，比上年净增 2855 元/人，增长 36.64%。其中工业全员劳动生产率 12887 元/人，比上年净增 3221 元 /人，增长 33.32%。

乡镇企业的发展，使它在全省经济特别是在整个农村经济中的地位和作用，日益显示出来。

一是已经成为全省国民经济的重要组成部分。乡镇工业异军突起，自成体系，在生产能力，企业布局，产品结构等方面，对全省工业起到了填空白、补缺门、增实力的作用。1993 年乡镇工业产值达到 89 亿元，占全省工业总产值 505.25 亿元的 17.62%，占地方工业总产值的 52.43%，乡镇企业的某些产品，如原煤、水泥、石膏、罐头、地毯、机制砖、机制纸及纸板，已分别占全省 30%——95%，玫瑰油占全国产量 80%。乡镇建筑业形成了一支广为瞩目的建筑大军，开创了与国有、城市集体建筑公司争雄的局面，大大活跃了建筑市场，1993 年乡镇建筑业从业人数达到 44.39 万人，占全省建筑业的 70%，完成总产值 34.72 亿元，占全省建筑施工产值的 45%，超过国有建筑企业总产值。由农民兴办的交通运输、商业、饮食、服务、旅游等第三产业，冲破了国有企业一统天下，成为多形式、多渠道、多层次兴办第三产业的一支主力军，1993 年营业收入达到 59 亿元，对促进生产，方便生活，解决城乡人民买难卖难问题起到了很好的作用。在流通搞得好的几个县，集市贸易的成交额实际已超过了国有与供销合作商业的营业额。

二是已经成为农村经济的重要支柱。1993 年全省乡镇企业总产值是农业总产值的 1.3 倍，基本上形成了“二分天下有其一”的局面。乡镇企业的发展引起了传统农业的巨大变革，使我省农业开始由单一经营向农工商综合经营转变，由生产初级产品逐步向深度加工、综合利用转变，由自然经济向社会主义的市场经济转变。据 1993 年统计，乡镇企业应付利润中上交乡村 5788 万元。其中用于补农、建农、村镇建设、文教和集体福利事业资金共 5361 万元，有利地促进了农村公益事业的发展。

三是已经成为农村劳动力转移的主要场所。1993 年，全省乡镇企业从业人员占农村剩余劳动力 350 万人的 47.4%，对安置农业剩余劳动力、增加农民收入、解决农民温饱起到了重要作用。据 1993 年统计，乡村企业从业人员中，初中以上文化程度的占 42.5%，已有 2.14 万名工程技术人员。乡镇企业为农村剩余劳动力找到了出路，为劳动剩余时间的有效利用创造了条件，为农民企业靠勤劳致富提供了用武之地。

四是已经成为农民致富的重要途径。1993 年，全省乡镇企业营业收入达到 155.4 亿元，占到农村经济总收入的 51.90%，其中从业人员得到的工资收入 23.16 亿元，每个农业人员平均 121 元占全省农民人均纯收入的21.5%。部分县、乡占到三分之一,高的达到一半以上。乡镇企业为合理组合各种生产要素,进一步解放农村生产力,有效地开发和利用农村各种资源,较快的增加农民收入开辟了道路。凡是乡镇企业搞得好的地方,群众基本上是一年解决温饱,三年脱贫致富。

五是已经成为地方财政收入的重要来源。乡镇企业的发展不仅使农民得到了实惠,而且为地方财政开辟了一个新的财源。1993年全省乡镇企业的税金达到4.84亿元,为农业税的1.3倍,占财政收入的9.2%,皋兰、榆中等乡镇企业发展快的县乡已占到财政收入的50%以上,已初步改变了地方财政拮据的困境。

二、乡镇企业发展中存在的突出问题

1993年,我省乡镇企业发展出现了良好的势头,但和全国迅猛发展的势头相比,还是有很大差距,总产值位居全国第24位,其增长速度比全国平均增长速度低7.9个百分点,一些基数较大的省其增长速度高于我省。目前存在的主要问题是:

1.资金投入不足。根据乡镇企业"八五"后三年计划和"九五"发展规划,总产值每年要净增60亿,按投入产出1:2资金投入至少要保持30亿元以上,1993年各种资金只落实了15亿元,占总投资的50%。因此,一批新建项目和技改项目因资金缺口较大或没有资金而不能开工建设,制约了乡镇企业的发展。

2.科技人才缺乏。1993年底,乡村企业职工中,工程技术人员21425人,占职工总数的3.4%。其中中级职称以上的3574人,占职工总数的0.5%,这些专业技术人员有相当一部分还是土生土长的能人,经过系统、正规专业培训的很少。有些县乡镇企业职工中,只有几名大中专毕业生。企业厂长、经理文化程度普遍较低,专业知识贫乏,不适应乡镇企业大发展的需要。科技人员领办、创办和承包乡镇企业进度缓慢。

3.政策有待进一步落实。近十年来,省委、省政府和省有关部门先后出台扶持乡镇企业发展的政策有130多条。对乡镇企业的发展起了重要作用。但一些"含金量"高的政策到位率差。乱收费、乱摊派、乱罚款现象仍在发生,企业负担沉重。据有的县对采矿、选矿企业调查,矿山企业要向12个部门和单位交纳36种税费.这些税费占企业当年销售收入的38——41%。上收乡镇企业、改变企业隶属关系问题,省人大、省政府和农业部多次发文件要求认真执行国务院颁布的《条例》,坚决予以纠正,但问题仍然不断发生。

4.企业整体素质差。我省乡镇企业起步晚,规模小,经济管理水平低,从总体上看,大都处于起步、发展阶段,许多经济指标落后于全国平均水平,自我积累、自我发展能力微弱。

三、乡镇企业发展思路和原则

党的十四大以来,随着我国社会主义市场经济体制的建立,把国有企业逐步推向市场,乡镇企业的发展面临着强大的竞争对手,同时,改革、开放搞活也给乡镇企业带来良好的发展机遇。我省乡镇企业发展的基本思路是:

1.充分利用我省丰富的矿产和农、林、牧等农业资源和各种原材料,产量大、品种多、质量好的优势,走开矿生财,加工增值的路子。

2.充分利用欧亚大陆桥开通的机遇,打破地区、行业界限,走横向联合的路子,开展跨地区、跨部门。跨所有制界限的横向经济联系,大力引进人才、引进技术、引进资金、引进设备,发展外向型经济和三资企业。

3.充分利用平等竞争的条件,实行多轮驱动、多轨运行,大力发展股份合作企业、个体、私营企业和第三产业,走以商促工、综合经营的路子。

4.充分利用人力资源,走劳务输出的路子。为了促进我省乡镇企业的发展,我们的发展原则一是速度不限。在保证企业经济效益和社会效益的前提下,发展速度能搞多快就搞多快。二是所有制性质不限。不管是哪一种所有制形式、哪一种经营方式,只要能促进当地生产的更快发展,能够较快地增加农民收入、能较快地增加当地经济实力,都要一视同仁,积极支持。三是产业不限。除国家法律规定不许生产的产品和经营行业外,能发展什么就发展什么,适合发展什么就发展什么。四是规模不限。能大则大,能小则小,尤其是要鼓励企业上规模、上水平、上档次、上大项目。

1993年甘肃省经济体制改革概要

省体改委主任

冯亦兵

1993年,甘肃省经济体制改革按照中央和省委、省政府的部署。围绕建立社会主义市场经济体制目标,在各个方面都取得了新进展。

一、深入贯彻《条例》,促进企业转换经营机制

1.结合甘肃实际,依据《条例》制定了我省《实施办法》,3月10日以省政府第1号令发布实施。《实施办法》集中了我省企业改革的有益经验,有重点、有针对性地对《条例》进行了细化和延伸,增强了操作性。

2.各级政府部门对照《条例》共清理规范性文件3524件,其中认定继续有效的2588件,需要修改的189件,予以废止的777件。

3.采取具体措施,推动《条例》的贯彻落实。一是抓点带面,推动企业自主权的落实。全省共选择了198户企业作为贯彻《条例》的重点企业,制定了带有共性的落实企业自主权的8条政策规定。二是省级综合部门改革现行的管理办法提出了向企业放权的配套措施。三是开展执法检查工作,督促对《企业法》、《条例》和《实施办法》的落实。

4. 企业贯彻《条例》和自主经营的意识增强。一是一些企业能够依据《条例》规定行使和维护自己的合法权益,在企业自主权不落实或权益受到侵犯时,能根据《条例》规定向主管部门要权或抵制侵犯企业合法权益的行为。二是结合贯彻《条例》进一步深化内部三项制度改革,到年底全省有80%左右的企业程度不同地深入进行了劳动人事和分配制度等内部改革。三是相当一批企业主动适应市场变化,根据市场需求自主调整生产经营决策。

5. 企业组织结构调整有了新的起色。根据不完全统计,全省关闭4户企业,停产整顿7户,转产2户,兼并45户(对),破产4户。同时还尝试和探讨了新的企业组织结构调整形式,如把小企业交给有较严格的科学管理制度的大企业承包、经营和管理,或者卖给私人经营等。企业组织结构调整的进行,不仅促使企业转换经营机制,而且有助于资产结构的合理化和运营效果的提高。

二、国有企业推行多种资产经营形式

1. 进一步完善承包经营责任制。省煤炭工业总公司和国防工办等企业主管部门主动改进企业承包指标,强化和突出了对资产保值增殖的要求。财政厅根据国家要求在酒泉地区和天水市选择40户企业,推行"税利分流"试点。

2. 积极试行股份制。1993年,全省共批准较规范化股份制试点企业125户,超过年初100户的计划。股份有限公司11户,有限责任公司114户。股本总额15.6亿元,其中国家股2亿元,法人股10.6亿元,个人股3亿元。甘肃长风宝安实业股份有限公司和兰州黄河企业股份有限公司分别成为我省公众股和法人股首家上市企业,标志着我省股份制试点进入一个新阶段。

3. 国有小型商业企业推行国有民营。这项改革1992年首先在兰州、定西、平凉等地市推开。到1993年,全省14个地州市已有2640多户国有小型商业企业实行了国有民营,占全部国有商业企业的86%,实行国有民营的粮食企业占8%,实行社有自营的供销社企业占到55%。国有民营的实行为提高我省商业企业的经营效果探索到一条有效途径。

三、个体、私营、"三资"企业等多种经济成份发展较快

1993年,省上多次提出要把大力发展多种经济成份作为我省改革和发展的战略任务来抓,各地根据各自特点,采取得力措施,推动了非国有经济的蓬勃发展。

1. 个体、私营经济的新发展。到1993年底,全省已有持照个体工商户28.27万户,48万多人,比1992年底增长23.8%和30.1%;私营企业2453户,投资者6477人,雇工4.6万多人,比1992年底分别增长41.8%、41.5%和32.8%。个体私营经济从业人员达53.5万人,占全省社会劳动力的4%,个体私营商业修理等服务网点占社会网点总数的80%以上。

1993年,个体私营经济注册资金14.4亿元,创产值13.4亿元,约占全省工业总产值的3%;年营业额62.3亿元,其中商品零售额占社会零售总额的28%,比1992年提高10个百分点;上缴税金2亿多元,增加25%,占全省工商税收的5.2%。

2. 股份合作企业取得突破性进展。为使我省股份合作制企业健康规范的发展,省体改委会同有关部门研究起草了《甘肃省城镇股份合作制企业暂行办法》。全省各地采取政策引导、能人先行、他人效仿、整体推动等方式和措施,使股份合作制企业得到了迅速发展。全省农村股份合作制企业已达7300多家,入股资本11.5亿多元,从业人员8.8万人。与此同时,股份合作制形式在城镇集体经济中也在积极推行。

3. 其它非国有经济,特别是"三资"企业发展迅速。1993年底,全省"一厂两制"集体企业5549户,当年新办603户;职工23.67万人,当年新就业人数4.4万多人。完成社会总产值34.36亿元,比1992年增长30.67%,完成工业总产值24.08亿元,销售收入20.91亿元,分别增长21.44%和49%。到年底批准的"三资"企业数累计达823家,其中当年新批准的556家,是1992年底前"三资"企业数的两倍多;投资总额累计10.8亿美元,其中1993年的投资总额为6.3亿美元,增长1倍多。

四、市场体系建设有了新的发展

1993年全省市场建设出现了五个特点:一是各级领导重视;二是市场建设的投资增加,多方投资、多方建设;三是市场建设由单纯追求数量转向上规模、上档次;四是市场建设结构得到改善,生产要素市场有了较快发展;五是市场管理、监督机制进一步加强。

1. 以商品市场为主要内容的市场建设步伐明显加快。当年全省动工新建、扩建、改建商品市场212个,一批跨地区跨行业的大型专业批发市场陆续投入使用。西北石化产品物资交易市场开业当天就成交2.89亿元,标志着我省商品市场向大规模、高档次发展。全省集贸市场发展到1600多个,其中,专业批发市场370多个。在全省十大市场中,交易额上亿元的有7个。

资金市场扩大,资金融通量、有价证券发行券种和数量增加。资金市场会员单位由1992年的14家增加到29家，会员基金达14250万元，新增4350万元，融资总额62亿元，比1992年增长两倍，其中，拆入33亿元，拆出29亿元。甘肃证券公司、兰州市信托投资公司等6家证券机构分别成为上海、深圳证券交易所会员单位，公开进行股票交易业务。

科技成果市场交易日趋活跃，兰州、白银、天水、金昌等地举办多种类型技术交易会13次，成交额达5000多万元。在4月份“93”甘肃香港经贸洽谈会上科技成果签约项目20个，成交额3259.9万美元。

人才交流中心、职业介绍所、不定期的人才市场等各种形式的劳动力市场全面发展，各种职业介绍机构150多个，登记人员50多万。

2.价格形成机制发生了质的变化。到年底，预计由市场形成价格的比重在社会商品零售总额中将占到96%，农副产品收购占到85%，生产资料销售占81%；价格体系进一步合理，基础产品价格继续提高，生产资料价格指数高于生活资料和轻工产品，农副产品价格又有所提高，粮油销价基本放开。对不合理收费进行清理，取消了11项对农民的不合理收费，减轻农民负担1900多万元，取消了80项不合理的行政事业收费。

3.市场管理、监督和服务工作有所加强。起草出台了有关拍卖、国有小型企业产权转让、商品房价格管理、技术市场管理等规范市场行为的法规性、政府规章性规定，用法律和法规逐渐规范我省市场秩序。

与市场经济发展相配套的社会中介服务组织建设也相应发展。全省已有会计师事务所23个，注册会计师126人，从业人员350人；审计师事务所90个，从业人员500多人；律师事务所108个，从业人员510多人；职业介绍所152个，登记人员50多万；资产评估机构23个，劳动争议仲裁机构89个。其中有3家会计师事务所和律师事务所由中国证监会等有关部门认可，具有从事证券业务的资格。

市场的监督管理有所加强。全省到1993年，共考核命名“重合同、守信用”企业7526户，当年新申请注册商标468件，核准217件，注册商标累计达2664件。

五、宏观体制改革走向深入

1993年，我省宏观体制改革朝着市场经济目标，按照中央改进和加强宏观经济调控的决策进行了大量的工作。

计划投资体制的改革是进一步缩小指令性计划和指导性计划的范围，省管计划指标由343项减为154项，计划产品由262种减少为92种，分别比原来减少55.1%和65%。同时，在我省经济发展计划中增设了反映全省经济结构和总量的一、二、三次产业增加值和工农业增加值及其增长率指标，以及全社会(包括全民、集体、个体)固定资产投资规模和全省新增贷款规模等一系列宏观调控目标。

财政体制改革主要是扩大财政建设资金实行有偿使用范围，发挥投资公司对建设资金实行信用管理的作用；实施《企业财务通则》和《企业会计准则》，省贯彻《条例》20户重点企业率先实行新财务制度，28户企业进行了清产核资试点。

按照中央宏观经济调控的布置，我省大力整顿金融秩序贷款逐步向重点项目倾斜。国家专业银行开始建立风险管理机制，省农行选择一批基层机构进行政策性贷款和商业性贷款分帐管理试点。

政府部门一方面制定省级机构改革方案，进行县级综合改革试点，另一方面转变政府职能，改进管理制度，明确各自的责任，从直接管理企业的方式转向间接管理的方式。

六、社会保障体系建设和房改步伐加快

全省养老保险14个地州市都实现了地级统筹，近三分之二的县实行养老保险金直接发放。除行业统筹外，有9.7万个单位、85万职工参加了养老保险，占应参加单位的93.8%。集体企业有2891户、5.6万人参加了养老保险，5户企业的352名职工参加了个人储蓄性养老保险。省劳动局、体改委制定下发了《加强外商投资企业中方职工社会保障工作的若干意见》和《企业职工社会工伤保险试行办法》，进一步扩大了社会保险范围。参加失业保险的已有1万个单位，126万人，到三季度领取保险金的有1200多人。同时进行了公费医疗制度和医院卫生体制改革的研究准备工作。

住房制度改革在国家批准《甘肃省房改总体方案》后又陆续出台了《提租补贴暂行办法》等5个配套政策。以提租补贴、建立公积金、缴交保证金、出售公有住房为主要内容的房改在全省城镇开始实施。房改起步的县(市、区)有63个，中央在甘单位27家，省直单位63家，分别占73.3%、67.5%和59.4%。

当前甘肃省投融资体制改革概述

省计委副主任　张忠敬

省计委综合处处长　武毅

根据党的十四届三中全会精神，针对投资领域存在的投资总量控制不住、投资结构不合理，投资效益不高等方面的突出问题，按照建立社会主义市场经济体制的目标，投融资体制改革的主要内容是：规范投资行为，强化投资风险约束机制，完善投资总量和结构的宏观调控，建立投资服务体系。

一、规范投资行为，改革投资方式

按照投资的使用方向和不同投资主体的投资范围，新的投融资体制将投资大体划分为竞争性项目投资、基础性项目投资和公益性项目投资三大领域。

1竞争性项目投资。主要有黑色、有色、建材、机电、轻纺、石化、医药等行业的项目，这类项目的投融资要逐步推向市场，以企业作为基本的投资主体。商业性银行是这类项目投融资的重要渠道，并实行企业与银行双向自主选择的方式。同时，允许企业根据国家有关规定，通过发行企业投资债券和股票等有价证券，在长期资金市场上直接融资。政府原则上不参与竞争性项目的投资，对这部分投资主要是加强政策指导。

2.基础性项目投资，大部分属于政策性投融资范围，主要由政府集中必要的财力物力，通过经济实体进行投资，并广泛吸收地方、企业参与投资；鼓励以大型骨干企业为主进行投资；有的还可吸引外商直接投资，对交通运输、能源等新建基础性项目，鼓励合资建设，并组建有限责任公司或股份有限公司。基础性项目中关系国计民生、跨地区性的项目和地方性项目，按谁受益、谁投资的原则，分别由中央政府投资主体和地方政府投资主体承担。

3.公益性项目投资，主要由政府用财政资金安排。除了特别重要的项目和必须由中央政府安排投资的项目由中央政府承担投资外，绝大部分项目应按受益范围由所在地方政府承担投资。科技、教育等公益事业，在政府不搞摊派的前提下，鼓励捐赠和由企业、个人投资兴办。公益性项目的投资应根据各级政府财政状况量力而行，并建立标准化、规模化的投资管理制度。

二、强化投资风险约束机制

1.积极推行企业法人责任制。建设项目要首先明确投资责任主体，即先有法人后定项目。由企业法人对建设项目的筹划、筹资、建设实施直至生产经营、归还贷款和债券本息以及资产的保值增值，实行全过程负责，承担投资风险。改、扩建和新建项目，都要尽可能依托现有企业进行，项目建议书由企业或由新组成的法人提出。合资建设的项目要积极推行法人持股的股份制形式。凡不同投资方合资建设的新建、扩建项目，都要创造条件，组建符合规范的有限责任公司或股份有限公司，各投资者按投资比例或入股比例分享权益。

2.规范项目融通资金的行为。为强化投资风险约束，对建设项目实行资本金制度。资本金必须使用企业自有资金，严禁使用借入资金注册。企业资金来源统一规范为企业自有资金和企业对外筹措资金两部分。新开项目除资本金外，还需一定比例的铺底流动资金，要积极推行贷款资产抵押和担保制度，增强风险意识。要培育和建立资产拍卖市场。

3.建立严格的投资决策责任制。实行谁决策、谁负责的原则，对项目建设过程和投资以后出现投资不足，产品滞销等问题，由决策者自己负责处理。

三、加强和完善对投资总量和结构的宏观调控

要建立中央和省两级负责的宏观调控体系。在方法上，综合运用经济政策、经济法规、计划指导和必要的行政管理手段进行间接调控。在投资总量调控上，采用资金调控、规模调控和总量监测的方式，以资金源头调控为主。采用投资率、综合建设周期和投资规模扩大率三项指标监测投资活动和总量变化。在对投资结构调控上，运用价格政策、税收政策、产业政策、规划和计划的指导等调控手段。同时加强投资活动的信息反馈，建立科学的项目审批制度，全面推行招标投标制。

四、加快建立和培育投资市场服务体系

要建立咨询服务体系、设计服务体系、审计组织体系、工程监理服务体系等，从信息上、技术上、质量上、法律上保证投资活动的顺利进行。

根据新的投融资体制改革的要求，我省采取的配套改革措施是：

——进一步调整和完善我省经济发展思路，努力开辟地方财源。

一是要正确处理中央企业与地方企业的关系，在全面清理地方与中央合资项目的基础上，理顺中央企业与地方的权责利关系。同时，为中央企业的发展创造更加良好的外部环境。二是要把工作的重点和地方投入的重点转向发展地方工业上来，坚持量力而行、效益第一的原则，以产业政策为指导，以当地的实际为基础，选择一批市场周期性长的项目，开发高新技术产品和人无我有的产品。三是要大力发展第三产业。重点培育和完善各类市场体系以及证券、房地产业、旅游业和社会化服务体系。四是大力调整产业和产品结构。充分挖掘现有企业的内在潜力，走内涵扩大再生产的路子，五是大力发展各种所有制的企业。因地制宜地发展股份制企业、股份合作制企业、联营企业和私营企业，优化投资环境，想方设法招商引资。

——对在建的地方项目认真进行审核排队，确定扶持重点。

按照以经济效益为中心的原则，把效益好、对地方经济发展作用显著、辐射功能强的项目筛选出来，集中财力、物力加快建设进度，使其尽快发挥效益。效益比较差、消耗高、市场前景不明朗的项目要停缓建。效益差、技术陈旧的盲目建设、重复建设项目，已经立项而未开工的要下决心停下来；已经开工的，要做过细的工作，寻求新的生产门路或暂缓建设。

——认真加强建设项目的前期工作

依托社会智力资源，提高科学决策水平，紧紧追踪国内外市场的

新技术、新产品，筛选一批市场前景广阔、附加值高、经济效益显著、能为地方财政增加收入的建设项目，并加快前期工作进度。同时完善项目库和建立固定资产项目登记备案制度，定期发布投资信息。

——适当加大现有资金的综合平衡力度，保证重点建设的资金需要。

要在淡化行业基数的基础上，坚持按项目争取和安排资金，确保重点项目建设。各类建设资金和建设基金要加大综合平衡力度，优先保证重点建设资金的需要。加强各类专项基金的管理，尽快研究出台一些新的建设基金。

——积极筹办地方融资机构

在省内农村选几个办得比较好的信用合作社，组建农村合作银行进行试点，拓宽地方筹融资领域。在城市选择二至三个省辖市组建城市合作银行，按国家规定的有关条例开展城市筹融资业务，取得经验后再逐步扩大。同时积极向国家争取扩大我省发行债券和提高融资权限。

——搞好大中型企业，千方百计增加自身积累

要抓好现代企业制度改革，强化经营管理，不断提高经济效益，增加自身积累，吸引商业性银行贷款搞建设。必须大力培植地方财政收入的来源，多搞一些增加地方财政收入的项目，逐步缓解地方财政的紧张状况，为扩大再生产创造条件。

——下决心扶持新的经济成长点

继续办好开发小区，要在研究政策和资金投入方面有新的措施和办法，真正把开发小区办成所在区域的经济成长点，带动区域经济的快速发展；加快房地产开发，随着住房制度的改革，要重点开发适应当前居民收入水平的中低档商品房建设，拓宽消费领域，发展一批相关产业；努力开拓农村市场，增加适应广大农牧民需要的轻纺产品，创造市场机遇，促进我省轻纺工业的发展。

——继续争取国家对我省的投入

积极向国家产业政策靠扰，重点选择一批骨干公路、通讯设施、能源、原材料工业、新兴材料、高科技产业等方面的建设项目，积极争取国家开发银行和各商业银行对我省的投入。

——选择一批新建项目，积极推行企业法人责任制，强化投资风险约束机制

要着手选择一批投资少、周期短、效益比较好、符合国家产业政策的项目进行企业法人责任制的试点，落实企业法人的决策权限和投资风险，强化企业法人在保证工程质量、控制投资、降低造价、加强经营、达产达标、盈利还贷，以及资产保值、增值方面的责任，并逐步推广。

——继续扩大利用外资规模

要加快改善我省利用外资的投资环境，不断提高偿债信誉，继续扩大吸引外资能力。同时，要组织力量，本着立足当地资源、面向两个市场的原则，选择一批经济、科技和社会事业方面的好项目，进行招商引资，扩大与外商合作的领域和范围。

甘肃的著名边关古城遗址

玉门关和阳关。是汉代建筑在丝绸之路南北道上的重要关隘。唐代著名诗人王之涣的《凉州词》中的“羌笛何须怨杨柳，春风不渡玉门关”，王维的《渭城曲》中的“劝君更尽一杯酒，西出阳关无故人”的诗名中指的就是这两座关隘。这两首唐代边塞诗中悲壮苍凉的怨情和凄楚幽深的别绪，总是深深勾起人们对河西走廊西端这两座古关的向往。玉门关也叫小方盘城，在河西走廊西端的敦煌市境内。相传和阗玉经此输入中原，故得名。自汉魏以来，它是通往西域诸国最西边防上的重要关隘，也是丝绸之路北路必经之关口。现在的玉门关是一座四方形小城堡，全用黄土垒筑而成，面积600平方米。阳关位于敦煌市城西南70公里处，因在玉门关之南，以南为阳，故称“阳关”。阳关遗址现在已不复可寻，只在一座红色砂石峰上，矗立着一个古代烽火台。遗址地面不是见断壁残垣，只可见沙丘之间露出的板结地面有墙基痕迹。

嘉峪关是万里长城西止点的重关，位于嘉峪关市。因其南北各有终年积雪的祁连山、连绵起伏的马鬃山，地势险要，巍峨宏伟，故称“天下雄关”。嘉峪关是中国古代的伟大建筑之一。现存的嘉峪关城楼建于公元1372年，至今有600多年的历史。整个城墙由大理石条和砖块砌成，分内外两城，城东西各有城关、城楼、城头四角各有一座“角楼”，南北城墙中段各有一座“敌楼”。整个建筑飞檐凌空、遥相对峙，非常精巧。嘉峪关是历代王朝设防之地，也是古丝绸之路必经关隘和东西文化交流要道。

政　治

中共甘肃省委

1993年甘肃省组织工作情况综述

省委组织部

1993年，是组织工作任务十分繁重的一年，也是组织工作取得重要进展的一年。全省各级组织部门以建设有中国特色社会主义理论为指导，积极探索社会主义市场经济条件下搞好党的组织工作的新路子、新方法，解放思想、实事求是，更新观念，锐意进取，紧紧围绕经济建设这个中心开展工作，突出抓好领导班子建设和党的组织建设，从组织上保证了全省改革开放和经济建设的顺利进行。

一、党的基层组织建设和党员教育管理

1.党的基层组织状况

1993年，全省基层党组织比上年增加772个。党的基层组织按行业分类，农林牧、水利业占33.78%，工业、地质、建筑、交通、邮电占25.27%，教育、科研、卫生占10.81%，商业、金融、服务占10.05%，党政机关、社会团体占18.35%，其他占1.73%。

2.党员队伍状况及党员发展

在全省党员中，女党员占13.43%；少数民族党员占5.03%。

全省党员的构成情况：年龄构成：35岁以下的党员占全省党员总数的20.18%；36岁至45岁的党员占26.38%；46岁至55岁的党员占25.24%；56岁以上的党员占28.2%。

文化程度：具有大中专文化程度的党员占17.26%；高中文化程度的党员占15.02%；初中以下文化程度的党员占56.68%。

职业分布：工人、农牧民中的党员占全省党员总数的57.93%；国家行政、管理干部中的党员占28.07%；各类专业技术人员中的党员占10.58%；其他职业的党员占1.42%。

1993年，各级党组织重视做好发展党员工作，全年发展党员占党员总数的3.05%，其中女党员占发展党员总数的19.16%；少数民族党员占5.65%；工作在企业农村生产一线的党员占51.85%；35岁以下党员占66.9%；大专以上文化程度的占20.27%；各类专业技术人员占21.33%。普通高校本专科学生党员占学生总数的比例由上年的1.8%上升到2.1%。

3.密切围绕经济建设，进一步加强企业、农村、机关、高校、街道党组织的建设

农村基层党组织建设得到加强。组织3个调查组，到全省12个地、州、市的25个县、46个乡和56个村调查，对《1991—1993年甘肃省农村村级组织建设规划》实施情况进行了调查，并提出选题，约请22位地、县委书记进行专题调查。在此基础上，召开了"全省农村基层党组织建设座谈会"，回顾总结了几年来农村基层党组织建设工作，对社会主义市场经济条件下加强农村基层党组织建设进行了全面安排和部署。围绕实施《条例》、贯彻落实1992年全省企业党的建设工作座谈会精神，积极探索在社会主义市场经济条件下，围绕生产经营加强企业党建的途径和路子。先后到一些大型企业、城市集体企业、乡镇企业和外商投资企业进行调查，提出了加强这些企业党的建设的意见。以转变作风为重点，加强了机关党的建设。代省委、省政府起草了《关于进一步加强省直机关作风建设的意见》。同时，注意了科研院所、高等院校党的建设工作。按照党的十四大提出的用邓小平同志建设有中国特色社会主义理论武装全体党员这个总的要求，积极开展党员教育管理工作。加强了对全省发展党员工作的指导，扩大了入党积极分子队伍。据统计，目前全省有18万入党积极分子，年轻党员少，生产一线党员少的问题开始受到各级党组织的重视并逐步改善。重视了党的制度建设，抓了党代表大会制度、县以上党和国家机关党员领导干部双重民主生活会制度的落实。积极开展党员电化教育工作，在推进全省党员电教工作基础建设的同时，组织交流了《邓小平在广东》、《伟大的实践》、《中国必由之路》等100多部电教片；推广了天水、张掖、敦煌、泾川、宁县等地市县开展电教工作的经验，统筹解决了部分地县的电教设备。

二、领导班子和干部队伍建设

1.全省干部的构成情况：

政治状况：干部中党员占38.1%；团员占15.3%；民主党派和无党派占46.6%。

年龄构成：35岁以下的干部占干部总数的47.9%；36岁至45岁的占26.4%；46岁至54岁的占18.5%；55岁以上的占7.2%。

文化程度：大专以上的干部占干部总数的29.7%；中专占36.2%；高中占16.4%；初中以下占17.7%。

专业分布：全省各类专业技术干部占干部总数的61.8%，其中，

中级职称的占专业技术干部总数的23.7%，初级职称的占60.5%。

干部分布：行政机关占24.5%；事业单位占22.9%；企业单位占27.6%；中小学校占25%。

2.领导班子建设

按照省委的总体部署，从1992年冬开始，用一年多时间完成了省人大、省政府、省政协和市(州)县乡四级领导班子换届选举工作。这次换届坚持贯彻党的干部“四化”方针和德才兼备的原则，自觉服从和服务于经济建设这个中心，在改善领导班子年龄、文化、专业结构，坚持干部离退休制度上狠下功夫。突出了一、二把手的选配，突出了年轻干部的选配，突出了经济管理干部的选配，积极推进干部交流，增强了领导班子的整体功能和领导经济工作的能力。换届后的地县党政领导班子，文化程度有较大幅度提高，年龄档次明显拉开，群体结构进一步改善。目前，14个地州市党政领导班子形成以50岁上下的干部为主体的年龄结构，大专以上文化程度的占83.5%；85个县市区党政领导班子形成以40岁左右的干部为主体的格局，具有大专以上文化程度的占61.9%。班子中熟悉经济工作的同志明显增加。地州市、县市区党委班子都配备了主管经济工作的副书记，政府班子都配备了熟悉和分管工业、农业、商贸流通等行业的干部，地县党政一把手中至少有一名同志熟悉经济工作。

认真抓了省第八次党代表大会各项组织工作。精心组织指导代表的推荐选举，精心做好会前各项组织准备工作，精心组织会议期间的选举事项，从而保证了省第八次党代表大会顺利选举产生了新一届省委、省纪委领导集体。

针对部分省直班子年龄老化和结构不够合理的问题，结合换届，集中力量抓了省直部门领导班子调整配备。着重对接近离退休年龄的一把手和缺额较多的班子进行了考察和调整。不失时机地抓了领导班子的思想作风建设，采取相应措施，下决心解决了部分班子成员中存在的思想涣散，纪律松驰，不负责任，推诿扯皮，内耗严重，形式主义和民主集中制坚持不好等问题。以反腐败和加强党风廉政建设及健全民主集中制为主要内容，省委专门发出通知，督促县以上领导班子开了两次民主生活会。省委组织部会同省纪委派出工作组，分赴各地各单位参加和检查了民主生活会。通过调查研究，提出了加强和考核领导班子思想作风建设的意见。

围绕班子建设，采取多种形式开展了干部交流。第二批同天津互派挂职交流了61名干部，为两地经济协作，培养干部做了大量的工作。在对干部交流工作进行总结的基础上，根据我省的实际，起草下发了《关于加强与外省市干部交流工作的通知》，对干部交流工作的原则、形式、管理等方面提出了具体要求，使我省干部交流工作逐步健全、完善和发展。目前我省同近十个省市挂职交流干部共260多人。

改进和强化了干部培训工作。针对换届后地县党政领导干部的状况，下发了《关于调整全省干部培训五年规划的通知》，调整了培训规划。举办了2期地厅级领导干部培训班和2期县委书记、县长岗位职务培训班和4期省直部门处级干部进修班，600多名县处级以上干部参加了培训。去年，全省共培训各级各类干部9.9万人次，占干部总数的20%。全省已形成了能够适应不同岗位、不同层次干部需要的各种类型、各种形式、各种渠道的干部教育格局。到1993年底，全省已有各级各类党校、干部院校166所，教职员4679人，专职教师1009人。组织各方力量，编撰出版了地县党校和企业党校教材，解决了全省学校系统缺乏统一教材的问题。

去年在做好补充调整工作的基础上，大胆启用了一大批年轻优秀的后备干部。针对后备干部名单中缺额较大的情况，组织力量先后到10个地市州进行调查，基本摸清了省管后备干部队伍的变化情况，并就此提出了抓好这项工作的意见，促进了后备干部名单的补充。去年，继续从省内外大专院校选调了44名应届大学生赴基层锻炼。从我省中青年干部的实际出发，举办了中青年干部、中青年女干部培训班和中青年党政干部研究班，有计划、有目的的加强了对青年干部的培养教育。

牵头抓总，知识分子工作上了一个新台阶。与省人事局一起开展了“甘肃省人才外流现状及对策”调查，对近几年外流到沿海地区的部分知识分子进行跟踪调查，提出了稳定知识分子队伍的对策和建设性的意见。制定下发了《关于进一步做好部分高级专家延长退(离)休年龄工作的通知》，完善了享受政府特殊津贴的有关规定。去年又有345名优秀知识分子享受了政府特殊津贴。由省委组织部发起成立的省高级专家协会，已发展会员746名，并积极为科技成果转化为生产力牵线搭桥，到目前，已收集整理科技成果项目170项。有的已经转让或联营，取得了较好的经济效益。

结合省级机构改革，指导和作好国家公务员制度的试点和党委机关参照试行的前期准备工作。下发了《关于在机构改革中加强干部机构、编制管理的通知》，贯彻《条例》精神，积极推进企业干部人事制度改革。根据“管少、管好、管活”的精神，加强了对改革试点企业的调查研究，探索在市场经济条件下企业领导班子的管理办法，下放了部分大、中型企业的干部管理权限。干审工作总结推广了一些地市和县的经验，建立了联席会议制度，加强了同执纪执法部门的工作联系，为全省各级组织部门选拔干部和解决领导班子存在的问题，提供了重要信息。慎重稳妥地解决了一批疑难案件，解决了一些重信重访问题。

振奋精神真抓实干 开创宣传思想工作的新局面

——93年甘肃省宣传思想工作回顾

省委常委宣传部部长

石宗源

1993年，全省宣传思想战线以建设有中国特色社会主义的理论和党的基本路线为指导，认真贯彻党的十四大精神，切实加强理论学习、宣传和研究，把用建设有中国特色的社会主义理论武装广大干部、党员和群众的思想放在首位，服从并服务于经济建设和改革开放，坚持正确的舆论导向，加强思想道德教育，繁荣文化艺术事业，取得了很大成绩，形势是好的。主要表现在以下几个方面：

第一，用建设有中国特色的社会主义理论武装思想、指导工作，已成为广大干部和群众的自觉要求。在学习邓小平同志南巡重要谈话和党的十四大精神的基础上，全省各级党组织和宣传思想工作部门，以《邓小平文选》第三卷的出版发行为契机，把用邓小平同志建设有中国特色社会主义理论武装全党的任务逐步落实到实处。省委举办了省、地主要领导干部研讨班。省、地、县三级党委中心学习组坚持学习制度，各地、各单位主要领导带头学习，带头作辅导报告，带头谈心得体会。广大干部认真研读原著，把握精神实质，努力学习和掌握邓小平同志关于解放思想、实事求是的思想路线，紧密联系实际，查自己思想观念更新的程度，看改革开放、抓住机遇、加快发展的意识浓不浓；查自己"三条标准"树立的牢固程度，看在经济建设中的作为是大是小；查自己处理"两手抓、两手都要硬"关系的自觉程度，看在精神文明建设方面干劲足不足。通过认真刻苦地学习，广大干部群众特别是各级领导干部逐步认识到，只有学好建设有中国特色的社会主义理论，才能纠正对马克思主义的教条式理解，才能纠正对社会主义的不科学的甚至扭曲的认识，才能纠正那些超越社会主义发展阶段、不切实际的思想和政策，从而解放思想，轻装上阵，把全部精力投入到两个文明建设中去。

第二，"两手抓、两手都要硬"的方针得到进一步贯彻。全省各级党政组织认真贯彻省委关于"在建设和完善社会主义市场经济新体制的过程中，宣传思想工作关系全局，具有特殊重要性"的指示，切实加强了对宣传思想工作的领导。党委主要负责同志亲自过问，经常分析研究社会动态和干部群众的思想脉博，确定宣传思想工作的重点和宣传口径，支持和引导宣传思想战线的同志深入改革开放和经济建设第一线，加强思想政治工作。广大宣传思想工作者抓重点、抓典型、抓载体、抓质量，在全省上下掀起了学习建设有中国特色社会主义理论的热潮，使干部群众改革开放和经济建设的热情日益高涨，团结稳定的政治局面更加稳固。社会主义精神文明建设非抓不可、不抓不行，已成为绝大多数干部和群众的共同愿望和自觉行动。

第三，服从并服务于经济建设这个中心，已成为宣传思想工作者的共识。近几年来，宣传思想战线上的同志自觉地投身到改革开放的洪流之中，满腔热情地为经济建设这个中心服务。围绕深化农村改革，搞活国有大中型企业，大力发展乡镇企业和第三产业，建立和完善社会主义市场经济体制等重大经济决策，开展了丰富多彩、生动活泼的宣传教育活动。省委宣传部组织力量，抓了全省十大农贸市场的调查，并通过新闻媒介作了广泛宣传；酒泉地区开展了"走向市场"的大邀传、大学习、大讨论活动；张掖地区开展了"争当富民支部、创建文明新村"和"双文明评议"活动；白银公司、兰炼、兰化、酒钢等大中企业在职工中普遍开展了社会主义市场经济理论教育，等等，都取得了明显成效。在经济建设和改革开放的宣传中，各地、各单位坚持搞好深入的调查研究，准确掌握经济活动中社会各阶层人们的思想动态，抓住阻碍市场经济发展的思想认识问题，有针对性地引导人们解放思想、转变观念，进一步焕发了广大干部群众投身经济建设和改革开放的积极性、创造性。

第四，"团结、稳定、鼓劲"和坚持正面宣传为主的舆论氛围初步形成。

各级宣传文化部门和新闻出版单位，紧密围绕省委、省政府和各级党政部门的中心工作，充分发挥大众传播媒介覆盖面广、传播速度快和影响大的特点，各司其职，各展其长，形成合力，生动活泼地宣传党的理论、路线、方针和政策，深入浅出地阐释一系列改革开放举措，实事求是地总结推广群众在实践中创造的新鲜经验，热情讴歌各条战线的先进典型，既反"左"又防右，在引导社会舆论、开展思想教育方面发挥了应有的作用。广大新闻工作者，对群众关心的热点、疑点问题，进行实事求是、入情入理的分析，把握分寸、不搞人为"加温"，坚持正面引导，循循善诱，典型引路，匡扶正义，旗帜鲜明地为改革开放鼓与呼。在理顺群众情绪，沟通党和政府与人民群众的血肉联系方面，起到了不可替代的作用，产生了比较满意的效果。

第五，爱国主义、集体主义、社会主义的时代精神日益弘扬光大。

按照“精神文明重在建设”的方针，各级党委把爱国主义、集体主义、社会主义教育作为加强社会主义精神文明建设的核心内容，开展了多种形式的宣传教育活动。在企业，教育职工从爱岗爱厂做起，发扬主人翁精神，树立全局观念，增强奉献意识。在农村，通过“算国家投入帐，集体扶持帐，家庭收入帐”，引导农民正确处理国家、集体、个人三者利益之间的关系。尤其在青少年中，各级各类学校和团队组织，认真组织学生学习中国近代、现代史，进行爱国主义和革命传统教育，大力开展“爱我中华、振兴中华、热爱家乡、建设家乡”的专题思想教育活动、“两史一情”知识竞赛活动、100部革命历史题材影视片观看活动等等。省内涌现出一大批以李洪生、刘水为代表的先进典型。最近“2·16”兰州南湖抢救落水儿童的英雄群体又为我们谱写了一曲社会主义精神文明的正气歌。这些，都是我们近些年来在青少年中广泛开展爱国主义、集体主义、社会主义教育的成果，是用正确的人生观、价值观和崇高理想塑造一代新人而结出的硕果。

第六，高唱时代主旋律的一批优秀精神产品，受到人民群众的欢迎。各级宣传文化工作部门，把反映时代主旋律的精神产品繁荣创作、繁荣文艺作为文化工作的指导思想，组织作家、艺术家、记者深入改革开放和经济建设第一线参观、采访、考察，推出了反映“引大入秦”宏伟工程的好新闻、好通讯和大型报告文学《西部：一条彩河的诞生》；组织挖掘民族优秀文化遗产，推出了《敦煌古乐》、《敦煌艺术之最》等具有鲜明地方特色和民族特色的优秀出版物；电视剧《艰难的抉择》、《白马》、《走进香巴拉》和讴歌团结奋进的时代精神、展现西北人博大胸襟和黄土高原民族风采的现代陇剧《天下第一鼓》等得到省内外观众的一致好评。自1992年以来，在全国各种文艺比赛、演出活动中，我省获奖剧目达30多个，为甘肃各族人民争了光。为鼓励作家、艺术家创作出更多、更好的的作品，我们举办了“甘肃省首届敦煌文艺奖”，对200多部新作品和100多名作者进行了奖励。与此同时，群众性文化活动也日益活跃，以纪念毛泽东同志诞辰100周年为契机，各地、各单位举办了丰富多彩的文艺演出活动，把群众文化活动推向了新高潮。地繁荣文艺的同时，各地十分重视和加强了对文化市场的管理，一度出现的黄色书刊、非法出版物泛滥的现象开始得到初步遏制。

这些成绩的取得，是在各级党委的领导和政府的支持下，全省宣传思想战线的同志们共同努力的结果。同志们的辛勤劳动，为我省改革开放、经济发展、社会稳定提供了强有力的思想保证和舆论支持。但是，我们也应当清醒地认识到，与党中央和省委的要求相比较，同广大人民群众对我们的期望相对照，我们的工作还存在不少差距和问题，亟待研究、解决和改进。主要表现在：

一是从全局看，“两手抓、两手都要硬”的思想还没有成为全体同志的自觉意识，忽视精神文明建设的现象相当普遍。有些同志片面认为，市场经济必然要冲击精神文明建设，市场经济发展要优先于精神文明建设，经济搞上去了精神文明自然而然会上去的。这种认识在不少地方和一些领导同志的思想上，包括宣传思想部门一些同志的思想上，还不同程度地存在着。由此而产生的轻视宣传思想工作，忽视政治理论学习，放松对广大群众特别是青少年进行思想教育的倾向还没有根本扭转。

二是我们面临着建立社会主义市场经济体制的巨大变革，宣传思想工作的解惑释疑的任务远没有完成。一方面，广大干部群众迫切需要进一步解放思想，更新观念，掌握市场经济知识，以适应市场经济发展的需要；但另一方面，我们从事宣传思想工作的同志却对市场的理论、知识、政策、法规等了解不多，知之不深，难以对群众关心的热点、疑点问题作出有说服力的、通俗易懂的宣传解释工作。同时要看到，市场经济的负效应使金钱万能的思想渗透到了社会生活的众多领域，导致拜金主义、享乐主义、极端个人主义等腐朽思想滋生蔓延，腐败现象、不正之风屡禁不止，道德水准有所下降，人民群众很有意见。在这种新形势、新情况面前，我们的宣传思想工作缺乏系统的、有效的教育方法和防范措施。一系列改革的重大举措相继出台，涉及到社会各方面利益关系的调整，引发了群众心理上的失衡和思想上对改革的困惑，而我们从事宣传工作的同志，对如何化解群众的思想疑虑，统一人们的思想，保持社会的稳定，还缺乏应有的研究，缺乏必要的预见，缺少得当的措施和办法。

三是从我们队伍自身看，还存在思想观念、精神状态不适应的问题。加之工作难度大，工作条件差，手段落后，物质待遇低，一些同志的精神状态不够振作，宣传思想工作队伍不稳的情况也比较突出。

四是一些同志忙于琐碎事务，对学习政治理论和现代经济、科技知识热情不高，对经济和社会发展全局了解不够，对群众思想脉络理得不清，唯书唯上、坐而论道的现象时有发生。

五是主旋律唱得还不那么宏亮。具体表现在文化精品还很少，精神产品质量有待进一步提高；作家、艺术家、记者的笔锋、镜头，与人民群众的火热实践也还不同程度地存在着距离，特别是对文化市场还缺乏得力、有效的管理，扫除黄色、非法出版物和音像制品的任务仍相当艰巨。

这些问题都需要我们认真对

待，尽快扭转被动局面。现在，全国宣传思想工作会议精神给我们指明了方向，省委、省政府对我们提出了具体要求，我们一定要认真总结经验，发扬成绩克服缺点，振奋精神，真抓实干，把全省宣传工作提高到一个新水平。

1993年甘肃省统战工作综述

中共甘肃省委统战部副部长

吴廷富

按照中央和省委关于新形势下统一战线工作的要求，1993年全省各级统战部门积极开展了大量统战工作，巩固和扩大了党领导的爱国统一战线，为维护全省政治社会的稳定、促进经济发展做出了新贡献。

一、召开了全省统战工作会议。各级统战部门积极组织力量，用主要精力调查研究了在建立社会主义市场经济体条件制下民主党派工作、党外人士的培养选拔工作、民族地区的稳定与发展工作、宗教事务的管理工作、工商联转变职能和非公有制经济代表人士的思想政治工作、非党知识分子工作、对台和海外联谊工作等方面出现的新情况和新问题，提出了加强各项工作的政策性意见。在充分调查研究的基础上，于12月7日至9日召开了全省统战工作会议，出席会议的有200多人，是近年来规模最大的一次。会上，传达学习了全国统战工作会议精神和江泽民、李瑞环、王兆国同志的讲话，省委书记阎海旺、省委副书记兼统战部长杨振杰就做好新形势下我省的统战工作讲了话。这次会议，分析了我省统战工作的形势，探讨了新形势下统战工作的新特点，明确了统战工作各个领域的政策原则和工作任务，是从理论思想、政策原则上指导当前和今后一个时期全省统战工作的重要会议。

二、继续进行了完善共产党领导的多党合作和政治协商制度的工作。到1993年底，我省有民革、民盟、民建、九三学社、民进、农工6个民主党派，共有成员8900余人，民主党派各级委员会47个。各级党委和统战部门在坚持已经建立的民主协商会、谈心会、情况通报会和“季度学习恳谈日”制度的同时，进一步完善了政府有关部门与各民主党派的对口联系制度，省政府办公厅下发了《关于进一步加强民主党派对口联系的通知》，有15个省直厅局与民主党派建立了对口联系。各民主党派加强了思想、组织、作风和机关建设。组织各民主党派主要负责人赴南方考察学习。民主党派成员和无党派人士在政府及其部门和司法机关担任领导职务的工作有新进展，到年底，有副省长1名；有6人在省政府有关部门担任专、兼职领导职务；兰州、嘉峪关市各有1名党外副市长；有15人担任了副县(市、区)长；200余人在省、地(市、州)直机关担任处级职务。还有100余人被聘为特约监察员、检查员、审计员、教育督导员和人民陪审员。完成了省政协七届委员会换届的党外人事安排工作。七届委员会共有委员503名，其中非中共人士303名，占60.2%；共安排常委109名，其中非中共人士70名，占64.2%；有主席、副主席10名，其中非中共人士5名，占50%；推荐全国政协委员28名，常委4名。

三、积极稳妥地处理民族、宗教方面的突发性事件，维护了全省的稳定，全省共有45个民族成份，其中少数民族人口185万人，占全省总人口的8.3%。聚居的少数民族有回、藏、东乡、土、满、裕固、保安、蒙古、撒拉、哈萨克10个民族，其中东乡、裕固。保安族是我省的特有民族。全省有伊斯兰教、佛教(包括藏传佛教)、道教、天主教、基督教五种宗教，信教群众约为223万人，约占全省总人口的10%。有寺欢教堂3700余处，各级爱国宗教组织129个，其中省级7个。民族、宗教工作是我省统战工作的重点。1993年，在省委、省政府领导下，各有关部门和有关地区密切配合，按照疏导教育、化解矛盾的原则，妥善处理了几起民族、宗教方面的突发性事件，维护了全省的稳定。加强了对宗教事务和宗教活动场所的管理，取得了明显的成效。继续稳妥地进行了藏传佛教转世工作。加强了对归国藏胞的审批登记、立案建档工作。调查研究民族地区经济社会发展问题，提出了意见建议。研究提出了加强民族干部选拔培养的意见，并组织民族干部到经济发达地区挂职锻炼和到香港学习考察。通过各方面的工作，维护了民族地区的稳定和各民族的团结，巩固和扩大了党同宗教界的爱国统一战线。

四、积极推进工商联转换职能，做好非公有制经济代表人士的思想政治工作和经济领域的统战工作。根据中央精神，研究提出了工商联转换职能、发挥民间商会作用的意见和措施。对全省非公有制经济状况做了调查摸底，发现和掌握了一批有影响的代表人士。省工商联顺利地进行了换届，扩大了非公有制经济代表人士的安排。到1993年底，全省各级工商联组织69个，共有会员9300余人，其中新会员6247人，新会员中非公有制经济代表人士3898人。有100余名非公有制经济代表人士在各级人大、政协和有关组织中作了安排。民主党派和工商联组织继续开展智力支边、培训办学、咨询服务活动，取得了明显的成效。

五、认真开展党外知识分子工作。对全省非党知识分子代表人物进行了摸底调查，建立了“非党知识分子人才库”，有38442名中级以上职称的民主党派和无党派知识分子入库，其中高级职称4446人。并确定了214名党外知识分子代表人物名单，加强了联系，扩大了联谊面。同时，帮助解决了一些非党知识分子代表人物在工作、生活方面的实际困难。

六、对台和海外统战工作取得了新进展。我省有台胞140多人，去台人员5548人，台属5万多人。有国外华人2万余人，省内归侨、侨眷2万多人，侨胞、归侨、侨眷中回族、藏族、哈萨克族、东乡族等少数民族占有较大比重。从事对台和海外统战工作的群众团体和民间组织有甘肃省台湾同胞联谊会、甘肃省华侨联谊会、甘肃省黄埔同学会、甘肃省海外联谊会。1993年，对台工作重视各种形式的对台宣传和教育工作，向新闻媒体提供各种文稿、图片550篇(幅)；举办各种形式的对台宣传座谈会、报告会、讲座150多场(次)。新增台资企业50余家。吸收台胞捐赠600多万元人民币，用于资助文化教育事业。广泛开展了“写一封信，提供一条信息，引进一个项目”的活动，收到了良好的效果。共接待台胞23000余人(次)。农村台属脱贫率达70%以上。通过这些工作，扩大了我省与台湾的交流，增加了彼此的了解。遵循“不忘老朋友，结交新朋友，扩大联谊面，着眼二三代”的工作方针，积极开展海外联谊工作，加强了与海外及港澳各界人士的联系。群众团体和民间组织在海外统战工作中发挥了积极作用，兰州、定西、天水还成立了海外联谊会。

七、重视了省参事室、文史馆和社会主义学院的工作。省政府参事室有参事42人，主要是原国民党中上层军政人员和社会上有一定影响的知名人士。省文史馆有馆员37人，主要是社会上有一技之长的老年知识分子。甘肃社会主义学院主要培训民主党派干部和各界党外人士、统战干部，有教职员工46人。省参事室和文史馆发挥参事、馆员作用，积极参政议政，开展文史研究工作，取得了很大成绩。省社院共举办6期培训班，培训党外和党内干部268人。

八、加强了统战部门的自身建设。省。地、县党委和部分高等院校、厂矿企业、科研单位党委设有统一战线工作部，是在党委领导下主管统战工作的综合部门。省和有关地、县设有民族、宗教事务管理部门和对台工作机构。各级统战干部认真学习邓小平同志建设有中国特色的社会主义理论和党的统一战线理论、方针和政策，政治素质和业务水平有新的提高。各级统战部门适应建立社会主义市场经济体制的新形势，努力加强自身建设，认真履行职责，解放思想，实事求是，开拓进取，为党的统一战线事业做出了应有的贡献。

1993年省委常委会议

△3月7日，七届二一二次常委会议，学习讨论中央、国务院关于当前经济情况和加强宏观调控的意见。讨论通过了顾金池同志在全省经济情况通报会结束时的讲话、阎海旺同志在全省经济情况通报会上的讲话稿。

△10月30日，七届二二六次常委会议，讨论通过了贯彻《中央关于建立社会主义市场经济体制若干问题的决定》的意见。

△12月29日，八届一次常委会议，评论通过了省政府关于一九九四年计划安排中几个问题，以及推进各项改革加快我省经济发展的对策和措施。

以决策研究为重点 服务党委中心工作

省委研究室主任

姚恭荣

经过近十年的建设，全省党委系统调研网络基本形成。甘肃省委研究室成立于1985年11月，系省委直属的职能部门。室内设九个处室，干部49人。研究人员的结构特征是：文化结构以大专为主，年龄结构以中青年为主，干部职务结构以处级为主。根据工作性质和人员结构特点，除行政领导职务外，还设有地、县、科三级调研员。全省14个地、州、市和77个县(市)区的党委也设立了研究室，现有工作人员395人。

党委系统调研部门的主要职责是：围绕党委的中心工作搞好决策服务，发挥参谋助手作用；根据党中央制定的路线、方针、政策和各个时期的工作部署，结合当地实际，为党委提供两个文明建设的科学决策依据和贯彻落实的措施；跟踪调查各部门和各地党委贯彻落实中央和省委确定的方针、政策情况；协同有关部门调查研究党的建设、思想政治工作、民主法制建设和群众工作的重大方针、政策，提出工作建议；负责起草或协同起草重要文稿，参与有关重要会议的筹备工作；协调和指导辖区党委系统的调研工作。按照上述职能，党委调研系统在经济建设、政治工作和党的建设等方面，较好地发挥了参谋助手作用。

一、努力适应新任务、新目标的要求，紧紧围绕党委中心任务开展工作

党委研究部门属于党委决策的参谋咨询机构。紧紧围绕党委中心任务和领导决策活动开展工作，是其首要的工作。这些年的工作重点是：按照中央的方针政策，结合甘肃不断发展变化的形势，主动为党委提出指导工作的重大思路、解决突出矛盾和问题的决策、建议；针对全省或区域性的倾向性问题，抓住需要解决的关键性问题，提出解决的意见和办法，形成决策预案，提交领导审议和决策；始终以领导和广大人民群众最关心的现实问题为重点，集中力量抓好全局性的经济社会发展思路研究，同时，抓住经济生活中的重点、难点问题进行对策研究，变为党委决策；重视全面发挥“调研、服务、协调”职能，通过经常随同领导下乡、下厂，参与领导同志联系点的工作，充分了解领导意图和群众愿望，总结点上的经验，推动面上的工作。省委研究室在全省党委系统的调研活动中，努力做好协调组织工作，对重大调研任务联合作战，发挥网络作用。省委研究室每年都召开一次地县党委研究室负责人会议，选择几个全省性的重大问题，进行深入探讨，交流研究成果。同时广泛吸收、储备社会各方面、各专业研究部门的调研成果，并及时把这些成果综合、反映到各级党委的决策服务中去。

二、坚持以经济建设为中心，着重结合省情、县情研究基本思路和重大决策

坚持以经济建设为中心，是我们党在整个社会主义初级阶段的基本任务。各级党委对经济建设的领导，主要是坚决贯彻中央的路线、方针、政策，紧密结合甘肃实际，制定正确的发展思路，解决事关全局的重大问题，把全省现代化建设推向前进。这就决定了党委研究室的任务就是要着力在中央精神与甘肃各地实际上下功夫，深入调查研究，为制定全省经济社会发展规划、基本思路和解决重大问题，提供决策服务。这些年的主要研究成果有：

在农村经济研究上，从甘肃农业条件差，干旱多灾，“三料”俱缺的实际出发，始终突出脱贫致富这个主题，唱了“四部曲”。第一部曲，省委提出“三年停止植被破坏，五年基本解决温饱”目标后，联合对中部地区 18 个县进行全面调查，提出了综合治理的配套政策和实施方案；第二部曲，围绕“兴河西之利、济中部之贫”的“两西”建设目标，集中进行河西商品粮基地建设和河东地区生态农业开发研究；第三部曲，在“两西”建设取得突破性进展后，及时地把全省农村工作的调研重点放在高寒阴湿地区和少数民族地区的开发扶贫上；第四部，在全省温饱问题基本得到解决后，集中研究河西地区、沿黄灌区和陇东地区的商品粮基地建设，提出建设甘肃三大粮仓的战略构想。这些基本思路和战略方面的研究成果，都转变为省委重大决策，对推动全省农村经济发展产生了深远影响。

在工业经济研究上，侧重于研究搞活国有大中型企业、发展地县工业和乡镇企业的问题。从全省经济发展的现状出发，认真借鉴东南沿海省区的先进经验，于 1988 年向省委提出了“放开胆量搞改革，加快步伐求发展”的八条思路。被省委采纳并在全省贯彻后，对促进全省思想的解放、观念的转变，加快建设和改革步伐，产生了积极的促进作用。根据甘肃经济结构的特点，在多年研究的基础上，于 1991 年提出了“强化农业基础，搞好大中型企业，以城带乡，以大带小，整体推动甘肃经济发展”的建议。省委、省政府作出了实施“双带整推”战略方针的重大决策。

在发展战略研究上，主要围绕制定“八五”发展计划和第二步战略目标，进行分阶段研究。确定“八五”计划和第二步战略目标的战略思想、战略重点、主要目标和改革措施；研究阶段性任务和措施，提出了全省在经济建设中近期要办好的十二件大事，经全省党员代表大会讨论通过，并形成决议；邓小平同志南巡重要谈话之后，按照经济上台阶的要求，对省委提出的“全省提前一年实现‘八五’计划，提前三年实现翻两番”的目标，作了跟踪调查，及时研究实施中的重大问题。

三、按照“两手抓、两手都要硬”的方针，强化综合研究服务功能

全面贯彻执行党的基本路线，是全党的根本任务，也是党委研究部门决策服务的根本任务。党委研究部门始终从党委总揽经济、政治、文化等建设全局的需要出发，在调研工作指导思想上，力求正确处理经济与政治关系，既突出经济研究的主题，又不忽视政治工作如何保证、促进经济建设的工作研究。省委确定全省经济社会发展第二步战略目标后，研究室从如何保证第二步战略目标实现的角度思考问题，调查研究了同经济建设目标配套的全省“八五”期间及今后十年的政治建设规划，从政治思想建设、党的自身建设、廉政建设，文化建设等方面提出了建设性意见。针对一度时期甘肃社会治安问题突出的状况及时协同有关部门调查形成了全面加强社会治安综合治理，严厉打击“三害”的意见，为改善和加强全省社会治安综合治理发挥了重要作用。针对经济建设和改革开放中出现的一些倾向性思想问题，先后为省委提供了关于加强企业政治思想工作、加强高校政治教育、加强中青年知识分子思想教育的工作建议，为省委加强政治思想建设的工作指导起到了重要作用。如何加强新时期党的建设，一直是党委研究部门着力研究的一个重大问题，先后对加强农村基层党组织建设、企业党的工作、高校及机关党的工作，提出了许多有价值的建议。

四、坚持决策研究和实施调查相结合，着眼于推动各项决策的落实

党委调研部门，不仅全力以赴做好党委决策前的各项调查研究、参谋咨询等服务工作，而且十分重视决策贯彻实施过程的跟踪调查、经验总结、完善改革措施和信息反馈等服务工作。在张(掖)、临(泽)、高(台)进行了农村综合改革的试点；牵头组织了农村社会主义思想教育；对“双带整推”战略方针的实施，从宣传发动，制定规划和政策、

总结推广典型经验等方面组织推动；对经济运行中的重大问题，及时了解，帮助协调解决。

中共甘肃省纪律检查委员会

围绕经济建设中心搞好纪检监察

纪检委办公厅副主任

康建成

1993年，在中纪委和省委、省政府的领导下，我省各级纪检监察机关紧紧围绕经济建设这个中心，全面履行纪检监察机关的职能，做了大量的工作，取得了一定成效。

集中力量开展反腐败斗争 本年度特别是8月中纪委第二次全体会议之后，省纪委、省监察厅，集中力量抓了反腐败斗争。

一.抓自查自纠，领导干部的廉洁自律有了明显进步。按照中央关于党政机关县以上领导干部廉洁自律的五条规定，从9月下旬到10底，省上几大班子和14个地、州、市及省直各单位，都在认真学习、提高认识、充分准备的基础上，召开了领导班子的民主生活会，开展自查自纠。省委先后两次召开常委民主生活会进行自查自纠，会前向各地、州、市和省直各部门党委、党组发出通知，征求意见，会后又向全省专题通报了民主生活会情况，听取反映和批评，接受群众的监督。全省党政机关、事业单位15265名县(处)级以上领导干部进行了自查，占同级干部总数的98%。

二.抓专项治理，群众反映强烈的一些不正之风得到了有效遏制。

1.协同有关部门抓了减轻农民负担的工作。全省农民负担比上年减少6000多万元。负担降到5%，实现地、县、乡无超标。

2.全省共清理出行政事业性乱收费项目2541个，收费标准3300个。经省政府批准，分4批宣布取消了155个乱收费项目。

3.重点整治了带有行业特点的不正之风，认真清理和纠正了公费出国(境)旅游的不正之风，9月份以来用公款出国(境)的团组明显减少，比上年同期减少20批92人。多年来没有解决的一些不正之风得到了明显纠正。

三.抓案件查处，严肃处理了一批违法违纪的党员、干部。

1.加强领导，集中精力查办案件。省纪委4名常委直接抓查案工作。常委会坚持每月至少听取一次案件检查汇报，审定立查案件，及时研究解决查案中遇到的困难和问题。省纪委先后两次发出通知，要求各级纪检监察机关抓住时机，抓紧案件检查特别是大案要案查处工作，并就加强领导、突出重点、强化措施等，提出了要求。省纪委3次抽调人员，组成督查组，由常委带队，分赴地、县和省直单位督促检查，促进了查案工作。

2.加强案件审理工作，提高办案质量。

3.加强和改进信访举报工作。各级纪检监察机关共受理群众来信来访25793件次，其中检举控告19073件次，比上年分别增长48.02%和53.55%。对反映比较具体的重要信件，及时组织调查核实，获得了一批党员、干部违纪违法案件线索，发挥了党内外群众的监督作用。

全省各级纪检监察机关和广大纪检监察干部振奋精神，排除干扰，下大气力查处违反党纪政纪的案件1569件，处分党员961人。其特点是：

经济案件居高不下。贪污、受贿、违反财经纪律案件尤为突出。查处经济案件568件，处分党员425人，分别占全年案件总数和党员人数的36%和44%。因经济问题受处分的党员中，排在前3位的贪污、违反财经纪律和受贿，分别占因经济问题受处分党员的42%、22%和16%。

县处级以上党员干部受处分的人数比例上升。涉及地厅级干部5人，县处级干部52人，占受处分党员总数的6%，比1992年上升了一个百分点。

受三大处分的党员人数比例增长。占全年处分党员总数的51.6%，比上年度所占比例增长了4个百分点。开除党籍的人数比上年度增长7%。

官僚主义失职渎职案件呈增长趋势。此类案件120件，处分党员76名，比上年度分别增长50%和55%。

党员受行政处分和受刑事处分的人数上升。255名党员受到行政处分，比上年度增长55%。94名党员受到刑事处分，比上年度增长24%。

开展对党的路线方针政策和国家法律法规执行情况的监督检查

1.围绕减轻农民负担开展监督检查。省监察厅会同省农业厅督促省直22个相关部门，对涉及农民负担的文件、项目进行清理，宣布废除、修改了一些涉及农民负担的文件。取消不合理的农民负担项目66项，部分取消20项，同地县有关部门查处伤农坑农案件384起。

2.围绕全民所有制工业企业转换经营机制条例的贯彻落实开展监督检查。重点对一些单位及其工作人员中设置障碍、勒卡干扰企业转换经营机制的行为进行了认真地查纠，解决了一些比较突出的问题。

3.围绕中央和省上的方针政策的贯彻落实开展监督检查。较好地解决一些地方和单位存在的有令不行、有禁不止、弄虚作假，以及形式主义、严重官僚主义等问题。

深入党纪和廉政勤政的宣传教育

1. 开展了以学习《党章》为主要内容的党风党纪教育活动。对全省党员进行党的纲领、宗旨、理想和优良传统作风教育。

2. 开展了反腐倡廉宣传教育活动。选择了一些有普遍教育意义的典型案例，充分利用新闻媒介，集中宣传报道。各级纪检监察机关摄制、购买、录制电视教育片1046部，撰写教育文章769篇。省纪委拍摄的《高墙下的悔恨》电视专题片，真人真事现身说法，有较强的针对性和感染力。

3. 开展了以《党性在改革中闪光》为主题的教育活动。省纪委《党风通讯》充分利用刊物优势，积极配合中心工作，开展多方面的宣传教育活动，全年共发行刊物和《反腐败学习材料专辑》100多万册，发挥了积极作用。

加强调查研究和理论研究

省纪委常委和监察厅正副厅长，围绕反腐败斗争、党风廉政建设、减轻农民负担、案件检查、合署办公等，带领机关干部，分赴各地开展调查研究，对涉及全局性的一些问题，研究提出了解决的措施和意见。省纪委和各级纪检监察机关对50家非正常亏损企业进行调查，向省委、省政府提交了《关于对我省部分亏损企业的调查报告》，省委下发引起各地党政领导的重视。在调查研究的基础上，对反腐败斗争中的一些深层次问题进行研究，及时向省委、省政府提出了解决的意见和建议，推动了反腐败斗争的开展。

搞好纪检监察机关的自身改革

根据中央决定精神，省纪委、省监察厅和14个地(州、市)86个县(市、区)纪检监察机关全部合署办公，实现了党政监督体制上的重大改革。党政监督体制的整体效能正在逐步显示出来。各级纪检监察机关认真抓了干部队伍的思想、作风建设。

1. 加强思想政治工作，搞好机关作风建设，提倡奉献精神，干部职工的工作责任性和纪律性有明显增强。省纪委主要领导同志还明确提出，各级纪检监察机关要成为当地机关中思想作风建设最好的单位之一。

2. 从改革入手建立健全各项规章制度和办事程序，用制度管人、管事、管机关，工作质量进一步提高。

3. 鼓励和支持纪检监察干部面向社会，调查研究，学习业务，练好基本功。工作效率和工作水平有了提高。

1993年12月，中共甘肃省第八届代表大会选举产生了由33名委员组成的中共甘肃省纪律检查委员会。

甘肃省人民代表大会

省人大常委会1993年工作概况

一、甘肃省第八届人民代表大会常务委员会组成人员

甘肃省人大常委会主任：卢克俭

甘肃省人大常委会副主任：马玉海　嘉木样·洛桑久美·图丹却吉尼玛　王金堂　穆永吉　李萍　姚文仓　胡慧娥

甘肃省人大常委会秘书长：汤九夫

甘肃省人大常委会副秘书长：张国定　王凤鸣　尚志仁　韩肇文

甘肃省第八届人大常委会委员：

丁生才　丁言章　马进龙　马怀西　马冠洛　王凤鸣　王正之　王作山　王松山　王国祥　王应国　王新中　王翠兰　马依尔　艾努瓦尔　石怀川　刘燕　安国增　关铭涵　孙兆霞　李嘉宾　张天理　张定国　陈以南　尚志仁　周林科　赵逵夫　赵燕翼　皇甫斌　俞夕云　顾竺　郭宪章　高金荣　崔岩　韩肇文　蒋维模　戴云鹏

二、甘肃省人大常委会各工作部门及其领导成员：

办公厅主任：王凤鸣

民族侨务工作委员会主任：王应国

法制工作委员会主任：石怀川

司法民政工作委员会主任：皇甫斌

教科文卫工作委员会主任：王松山

财经工作委员会主任：王国祥

农业工作委员会主任：崔岩

代表工作委员会主任：马怀西

研究室主任：韩肇文

庆阳地区工作委员会主任：宋廷杰

平凉地区工作委员会主任：张新民

陇南地区工作委员会主任：王在鹏

武威地区工作委员会主任：裴永俊

酒泉地区工作委员会主任：武惠民

三、甘肃省人大常委会1993年召开的主要会议

(一)1993年1月8日至17日，甘肃省第八届人民代表大会在兰州举行第一次会议。出席这次会议的省八届人大代表447人，因病因事请假99人。

甘肃省第八届人民代表大会代表名单(共546名)

兰州市(86名)

丁存德(回族)　丁言章　万声德　马玉英(女、回族)　马玉贵(女、回族)　马志博(东乡族)　马金城(女、回族)　马锦玲(女、回族)　王世俭　王国良　王金堂　王道义　王翠兰(女)　王德华　史振业　白玉珍(藏族)　冯鹤林　吕全福　吕胜西　任侠(女)　刘燕(女、回族)　刘玉林　刘济刚　刘铁军　齐有兰(女)　孙骥　牟原勋　李琳(女)　李廷禄　李秀山(女)　李虎林　李得元　李登瀛　杨玉平　杨树龙　肖尽善　何虎　何纪文　何荣素(女)　宋伯言　张忠　张俊　张弼　张友智　张志乐　张国威

张国娣(女)　张宦廷
张春玲(女)　周敏霞(女)
岳淑芳(女)　赵　福　赵文华
皇甫斌　贺明保　姚文仓
姚秀珍(女)　秦　炳　徐永坚
霍永禄　穆永吉(回族)　魏庚禄
魏致中

白银市(32名)
王民强　王松山　王重国　卢友人
白　银　仲兆隆　米胜德(回族)
杜永春　李伯荣(回族)　李　桂
吴尚惠　何俊芳(女)
张兰英(女)　张有礼　张廷魁
张振英　张锡勋　苗其荣　赵玉柱
胥继明　胡安魁　饶凤翥
索正秀(女、土族)　高维俊(回族)
黄罗斌　彭凌云　董桂芝(女)
韩修国　路　明　摆文华(回族)
瘳安安(女)　蔡子明

金昌市(15名)
王义理　冯兴儒　许飞青　刘生多
杨金义　张　坤　吴金生　李其清
李　琪(女、回族)　赵俊谋
姜爱琴(女)　高言琪(女)
敦建浩　贾笑天　赵敬中

嘉峪关市(9名)
马忠朴　王　平　王晓琴(女)
孙一峰　李善平　李福盛　高　复
敦能祺　吕常胜(锡伯族)

临夏回族自治州(28名)
丁生才(保安族)　丁明昌(回族)
马白克(东乡族)
马玉海(回族)　马正峰(回族)
马世德(回族)　马进龙(东乡族)
马进瑶(回族)
马法土麦(女、保安族)
马尚英(东乡族)　王世文
王发杰(土族)　王建梅(女)
方永铭　石宗源(回族)　孙矿生
李连维　杨怀孝(回族)
汪益宝(东乡族)　张道贞(女)
赵　群(女)

拜玉凤(女、回族)　敏　政(回族)
韩哲民(撒拉族)　傅绍琪　颜宗伯
李文治　马瑞莲(女、回族)

甘南藏族自治州(23名)
丹正嘉(藏族)
丹智草(女、藏族)　仁青才让(藏族)
卢克俭(藏族)　代　茂(藏族)
杨丹珠(藏族)　杨复兴(藏族)
杨镇刚(藏族)　杨九次日(藏族)
李边玛(藏族)　张国定
贡卜扎西(藏族)　宗　者(藏族)
罗　赛(藏族)　单秉忠(回族)
卓玛草(女、藏族)　堪布仓(藏族)
雷如平
嘉木样·洛桑久美·图丹却吉尼玛(藏族)
张文启　王素琴(女)
徐梅芳(女)　班地牙(藏族)

庆阳地区(43名)
西峰市(7名)
马兆林(回族)　王国祥　王宣宗
李　玉(女)　李克勇　张甫虎
惠树人

正宁县(4名)
王常桂(女、回族)　赵世选
赵春生(满族)　樊旺鹏

华池县(3名)
李爱玲(女)　赵秉璋　流　萤

合水县(3名)
王九锡　白麟炳　郭　琨

宁　县(7名)
许明学　李翰林　杨德儒
荀玉巧(女)　赵明峰　韩根兴
黄续祖

庆阳县(6名)
王世泰　王吉泰　尤　恺　佘文成
宋　华(女)　贾兰玥(女)

镇原县(7名)

张文汉　张吾乐　陈桂梅(女)
段红英(女)　郭继芳　阎帅家
李　峰

环　县(6名)
史昌林　许敏华(女)　李兆军
李海德(回族)　俞夕云(女)
敬廷年

平凉地区(43名)
平凉市(10名)
王一兵　白荣琴(女、回族)　李平安
杨万青　杨振杰　刘思荣　郑华民
段全福　黄登贵(回族)
翟　明(女)

泾川县(5名)
马全福(回族)　王新中　李思正
张秉科　康小玲(女)

灵台县(7名)
马进文(回族)　冯忠和　胡昌林
胡淑香(女)　葛士英　徐栓龙
张新民

崇信县(3名)
代志敏　刘玉民　张荫农

华亭县(5名)
丁泽生(回族)
马秀春(女、回族)　苗宗杰　徐丕豪
景　泰

庄浪县(6名)
万乔娃　李雪英(女)　杨新林
张力学　崔正华　魏治林

静宁县(7名)
丁　齐　马　斌　吕忠厚
李佩红(女)　段积昌　景宗健
翟沪兰(女)

陇南地区(46名)
成　县(6名)
刘醒初　何光第　杨巧素(女)
张　娟(女)　胡慧娥(女)

赵麟祥

两当县(4名)
王志胜　石怀川　刘　雄
陈绮玲(女)

徽　县(5名)
王正之　王彩琴(女、回族)　杨万春
温恩仲　杨继雄

西和县(5名)
李平珍　赵双桂(女)　高孔岗
阎海旺　魏永平

礼　县(7名)
马谦卿(女)　刘守业
虎炳班(回族)　赵　权
黄冬梅(女)　康世荣　靳百龄

康　县(4名)
吴土改　张菊梅(女)　高玉峰
魏庆同

武都县(7名)
王凤鸣　权维洲　关康基
李千菊(女)　辛心田
者全福(回族)　唐友辉

文　县(4名)
马　曦　关铭涵(满族)　袁怀进
班慧婷(女、藏族)

宕昌县(4名)
王守义　朱宗贤
杨兰琴(女、藏族)　顾　竺

定西地区(42名)

定西县(9名)
左俊文　申效曾　朱作勇　刘生荣
安巧兰(女)
苏凤英(女、回族)　李兰图　吴神沙
董世德

通渭县(6名)
马新元　田应龙　张　鹤　敬根年
韩肇文　张思义

陇西县(8名)
王志诚　乔华北　李光尧　汪　鉴
沙秀梅(女、回族)　宋淑珍(女)
高金荣(女)　曹宗周

漳　县(3名)
王永泰　吕芝芳(女)　岳自新

渭源县(5名)
王兴泰　李子奇　沈仲梅(女)
周志祥　赵学科

临洮县(5名)
田得如　冯秀兰(女、东乡族)
杨得生　袁乃斌　雷　炯

岷　县(6名)
王　纪　邓淑芳(女)　邢安民
严登明　何兆科(回族)　郝朝喜

武威地区(32名)

武威市(15名)
马俊海(回族)　白玉珍　孙玉宝
刘毓汉　李万林　李文辉　李光辉
李清心(女)　张宏科　张景发
何水平(女)　赵相才　俞存乃
郭玉琴(女)　唐光禄(满族)

古浪县(6名)
王三福　他玉璞　齐康然　李进堂
张　秀(女)　赵燕翼

民勤县(6名)
祁子湘　李连菊(女)　李嘉宾
杨兴昌　赵明贤　屈登程

天祝藏族自治县(5名)
李向忠　李桑吉(藏族)
张廷祥(土族)　张金义(女)
戴云鹏

张掖地区(32名)

张掖市(10名)
王克孝　王应凤　孔令鉴
李怀玲(女)　李建萍(女)
杨惠兰(女)　张伯壬(满族)
张新民　崔　岩　彭尔笃

山丹县(4名)
丁丹凤(女)　王兴明　毛郁生
孙兆霞(女)

民乐县(5名)
马怀西　汤九夫　张玉德　梁国安
窦锦绣(女)

临泽县(4名)
王作山　李天东　李宝峰　杨　荣

高台县(4名)
马冠洛　尚仁志　周国康
盛翠萍(女)

肃南裕固族自治县(5名)
安国增(裕固族)　李德奎(藏族)
秦治国(藏族)
顾秀花(女、裕固族)
安维堂(裕固族)

酒泉地区(33名)

酒泉市(10名)
方秀兰(女)
冯芝兰(女、回族)　李宗绩　肖　麟
张德仁　陆　浩　苟守忠　武文梁
武惠民　赖学忠

玉门市(8名)
马　刚　王占昌　李永江
许冬兰(女)　沈　洁(女)
秦志成　郭富才　褚　江(女)

金塔县(3名)
许万福　曹天福　梁守信

安西县(3名)
李建忠　张天理　陈　伟(女)

敦煌市(5名)
王成业　刘治国　孙　英
娄　婕(女)　程有清

肃北蒙古族自治县(2名)

巴依尔(蒙古族)　韩宝忠(蒙古族)

阿克塞哈萨克族自治县(2名)

艾努瓦尔(哈萨克族)　　明道信

解放军(33名)

才仁普措(藏族)　王清宇　王振先

白胜才　石银华　马建凤(女)

刘万贵　刘顺尧　纪海亮　成福顺

李太忠　李　刚　周林科

周嘉秀(女)　　陈孟超　郑　中

范宏洲(土家族)　张应斗　张高明

张树理　张德功(东乡族)　禹喜华

海连龙(彝族)　　柴发旺　袁景楠

阎多本　黄培圣　晏成忠　傅金保

韩筱玉(女)　　魏汉璋　史滨海

梁培祺

列席这次大会的人员225**名**:

省人民政府组成人员(14名)

尹霖初　物价委员会主任

张维国　省乡镇企业局局长

张克鲁　省局法厅厅长

黄树德　省石化厅厅长

叶绍袁　省轻纺厅厅长

刘兴邦　省农业厅厅长

蒲　泽　省林业厅厅长

王　军　省治金厅厅长

张炳玉　省文化厅厅长

杨　立　省审计局局长

袁吉璋　省统计局局长

金学友　省土地管理局局长

赵力德　省环保局局长

马超超　省乡镇企业局局长

省七届人大常委会委员(不包括省八届人大代表)(21名)

马少青(保安)　　马进福(东乡)

白占彪　权增述　朱　瑜　刘涤行

却太尔(蒙)　　李　彦　李寿文

张金榜　张昌言　张清岱　张应举

陈中清　钟永棠　都大昌　郭秀哲

麻　韬　肖叔泽　童若兰(女)

窦恒通

省高级人民法院副院长、省人民检察院副检察长(2名)

张树兰　省高级人民法院副院长

李来凤　省人民法院副检察长

省人大常委会各工作部门负责人,省人大常委会部分地区工作委员会负责人(24名)

杨效忠(藏)　省人大常委会民族侨务工作委员会副主任

孙启明　省人大常委会法制工作委员会副主任

王同礼　省大常委会司法民政工作委员会副主任

牛养惠　省人大常委会财经工作委员会副主任

夏玉滨　省人大常委会财经工作委员会副主任

石国柱　省人大常委会财经工作委员会副主任

包文林　省人大常委会农业工作委员会副主任

何瑞生　省人大常委会农业工作委员会副主任

巩广禄　省人大常委会办公厅副主任

白永发　省人大常委会办公厅副主任

安晨光　省人大常委会办公厅副主任

张文麟　省人大常委会办公厅副主任、研究室副主任

傅柏清　省人大常委会办公厅副地级研究员

王耀轩　省人大常委会办公厅副地级研究员

马耕夫　省人大常委会代表工作委员会副主任

梁尊中　省人大常委会代表工作委员会副主任

罗继成　省人大常委会研究室副主任

王富金　省人大常委会庆阳地区工作委员会副主任

闫　革　省人大常委会平凉地区工作委员会副主任

杨映春　省人大常委会陇南地区工作委员会副主任

邢汝贤　省人大常委会定西地区工作委员会副主任

徐积德　省人大常委会武威地区工作委员会副主任

闫德铭　省人大常委会张掖地区工作委员会副主任

任会琮　省人大常委会酒泉地区工作委员会副主任

省委、省政府各部门和各群众团体及有关单位负责人(51名)

李如汇　省委研究室副主任

刘学福　省委统战部副部长

罗祖孝　省委宣传部副部长

于忠正　省人民政府副秘书长

赵胜勤　省人民政府副秘书长

韩福俊　省人民政府副秘书长

吴　浩　省人民政府副秘书长

魏武峰　省政府研究中心主任

陈宝生　省政府研究中心副主任

赵国祯　省直机关工委副书记

彭世秀(女)　省委老干部工作局副局长

丁燕琴(女)　省保密工作委员会副主任

魏职高　省委党史资料征集研究委员会副主任

马世峰(保安)　省民族事务委员会副主任

高才大　省老龄工作委员会副主任

石允蒲　省公安厅副厅长

吴溪达　省财政厅副厅长

蔡志清　省商业厅副厅长

郑宝宿　省水利厅副厅长

张晋卿　省卫生厅副厅长

彭效忠　省畜牧厅副厅长

王通智　省旅游局副局长

李培芳　省人事局副局长

汪同建　省物资局副局长

祁连峰　省建材局副局长

于淮仁　省新闻出版局副局长

海　飞　甘肃电视台台长

邢同义　甘肃人民广播电台副台长

姜文明　中国工商银行甘肃省分行行长

李文光　中国农业银行甘肃省分行行长

崔永熙　中国银行甘肃分行副行长
吴立中　中国人民建设银行甘肃省分行纪检组长
张喜坤(女)　中国人民保险公司甘肃分公司副总经理
崔志英　省建筑总公司总经理
苏志希　省电子集团公司总经理
赵春林　省医药总公司副经理
马荣兴(回)　省农垦总公司党委副书记
司天义　省供销联社副主任
胡继文　省气象局党组书记
唐丰年　省地震局副局长
魏万进　省储备局局长
党长生　省电力局副局长
李清波　省邮电局纪检组长
殷国平　省地矿局副局长
康和生　省民航局副局长
张立燕　兰州铁路局局长助理
郝玉屏　省地方志编委员会副主编
马梅荃(回、女)　省科学技术协会副主席
延　涛　省社会科学联合会副主席
王松龄　省科学院院长
任安国　省社会科学院副院长

出席政协甘肃省七届一次全委会议的全体委员(名单略)

部分县、市(区)人大常委会负责人(43名)

赖全章　永登县人大常委会主任
孙有林　清水县人大常委会副主任
秦虎生　北道区人大常委会副主任
杨　恺　会宁县人大常委会主任
谈嘉言　景泰县人大常委会主任
张　俊　平川区人大常委会主任
杨茂林　永昌县人大常委会主任
曹文光　金川区人大常委会主任
马永澜　临夏市人大常委会副主任
张廷辉　永靖县人大常委会主任
马维清(回)　东乡县人大常委会主任
马克祥(回)　康乐县人大常委会主任
马进瑶(回)　广河县人大常委会主任
吕国仁　临夏县人大常委会主任
吴丕忠　积石山县人大常委会副主任
其　饶(藏)　碌曲县人大常委会副主任
阿　老(藏)　玛曲县人大常委会副主任
赵宝玺　镇原县人大常委会主任
宋维斌　宁县人大常委会副主任
高文科　庆阳县人大常委会副主任
杨天荣　西峰市人大常委会副主任
杨发录　华亭县人大常委会主任
唐克昌　庄浪县人大常委会副主任
范秀玲(女)　灵台县人大常委会副主任
李志东　泾川县人大常委会副主任
张一炯　武都县人大常委会主任
张成福　文县人大常委会主任
马　骏　宕昌县人大常委会主任
马俊玉　康县人大常委会副主任
唐世忠　成县人大常委会副主任
赵维新　徽县人大常委会副主任
康耀宗　礼县人大常委会副主任
何继忠　西和县人大常委会副主任
田　龙　渭源县人大常委会主任
窦克明　漳县人大常委会主任
何立臻　民勤县人大常委会副主任
葛正泰　天祝县人大常委会主任
马长海　民乐县人大常委会主任
赵延华　临泽县人大常委会主任
范国斌　安西县人大常委会主任
李万寿　金塔县人大常委会主任
刘　贵　敦煌市人大常委会副主任
哈　泰(哈萨克)　阿克塞县人大常委会副主任

省政府参事室参事、文史研究馆馆员(70名)

省政府参事室参事(37名)

省政府参事室参事

高登霄(藏族)　省政府参事室副主任
许建勋　省政府参事室副主任
齐天然　省政府参事室参事
史镜清　省政府参事室参事
郑毅民　省政府参事室参事
刘中仁　省政府参事室参事
邱复兴　省政府参事室参事
张子丰　省政府参事室参事
周定志　省政府参事室参事
吴振英　省政府参事室参事
秦怀玺　省政府参事室参事
石德安　省政府参事室参事
彭培根　省政府参事室参事
郭汾祥　省政府参事室参事
王连耒　省政府参事室参事
赵文源　省政府参事室参事
王香亭　省政府参事室参事
刘大奎　省政府参事室参事
李惠平　省政府参事室参事
朱介宾　省政府参事室参事
马希范　省政府参事室参事
于俊杰　省政府参事室参事
王静波　省政府参事室参事
冯文山　省政府参事室参事
刘移山　省政府参事室参事
王绍义　省政府参事室参事
何炎武　省政府参事室参事
刘广毅　省政府参事室参事
王天任　省政府参事室参事
王　昶　省政府参事室参事
魏永理　省政府参事室参事
刘锦淘　省政府参事室参事
常建勋　省政府参事室参事
马悼忻　省政府参事室参事
欧阳骥华(女)　省政府参事室参事
蒋景琪　省政府参事室参事
于文瑞(女)　省政府参事室参事

省文史馆馆员(33名)

张思温　省文史馆名誉馆长
邵文龙　省史馆副馆长
王惠科　省文史馆副馆长
赵志凡(女)　省文史馆副馆长
水天长　省文史馆副馆长
魏永康　省文史馆馆员
王九菊(女)　省文史馆馆员
纪新青(女)　省文史馆馆员
马玠璧　省文史馆馆员
柴木兰(女)　省文史馆馆员
张令瑄　省文史馆馆员
马礼常(女)　省文史馆馆员
党维新　省文史馆馆员
刘敬先　省文史馆馆员
曹　恭　省文史馆馆员

张尚瀛　省文史馆馆员
王君实　省文史馆馆员
曹　麓　省文史馆馆员
李东岳　省文史馆馆员
赵世英　省文史馆馆员
王焕文　省文史馆馆员
石佩久　省文史馆馆员
周恩棠　省文史馆馆员
胡希蕴　省文史馆馆员
斐广铎　省文史馆馆员
王先江　省文史馆馆员
骆石华　省文史馆馆员
刘九畴　省文史馆馆员
汉国华　省文史馆馆员
牛华生　省文史馆馆员
师　纶　省文史馆馆员
匡　扶　省文史馆馆员
王沂暖　省文史馆馆员

这次会议审议通过了省七届人大常委会主任许飞青所作的关于省七届人大常委会工作报告，甘肃省省长贾志杰所作的关于甘肃省人民政府工作报告省计划委员会主任郭琨所作的关于甘肃省1992年国民经济和社会发展计划执行情况及1993年国民经济和社会发展计划草案的报告，省财政厅厅长崔正华所作的关于甘肃省1992年财政预算执行情况和1993年财政预算草案的报告，省高级人民法院院长秦炳所作的关于甘肃省高级人民法院工作报告，省人民检察院检察长王平所作的关于甘肃省人民检察院工作报告；审查批准了甘肃省1993年国民经济和社会发展计划，原则批准了甘肃省1993年财政预算。这次会上还进行了一系列的换届选举事项，按照组织法和选举法的有关规定，选出了甘肃省第八届人大常委会主任、副主任、秘书长、委员（名单见前）；选举阎海旺为甘肃省省长，张吾乐、路明、杨怀孝、陈绮玲、郭琨、崔正华为甘肃省副省长；选举王世文为甘肃省高级人民法院院长，李德奎为甘肃省人民检察院检察长。会议还选举了甘肃省出席第八届全国人民代表大会的代表（共43名）：

丁泽生　马玉贵　马邦才　马全翠
马靖宇　王永银　王国良　王家达
王福成　卢克俭　齐茂忠　安　锋
许飞青　孙　英　孙一峰　李万林
李文成　李吉均　杨小琴　杨丽青
杨全义　杨德儒　吴全衡　张吾乐
陈可言　陈耀仁　郑锦霞　赵俊谋
郝洪涛　柯茂盛　哈布塞来木
聂大江　贾志杰　顾　军　顾金池
倪安民　郭锡廉　陶进美　阎海旺
韩修国　温家宝　德畦仓　魏宝文

（二）1993年1月18日，省八届人大常委会在兰州举行了第一次会议，新当选的八届人大常委会主任卢克俭主持了会议。会议审议批准了省人民政府《关于省政府换届后各委办主任、厅局长任命前有关问题的报告》，并对此作出了决议。

（三）甘肃省第八届人民代表大会常务委员会第二次会议于3月8日至10日在兰州召开。

省人大常委会主任卢克俭主持了会议。本次会议上，委员们首先认真学习了《中华人民共和国地方各级人民代表大会和地方各级人民政府组织法》、《中华人民共和国全国人民代表大会和地方各级人民代表大会代表法》和《甘肃省人民代表大会常务委员会议事项规则》、《甘肃省人民代表大会常务委员会人事任免暂行办法》等法律、法规；审议和原则通过了《甘肃省人大常委会1993年工作要点》；听取了副省长杨怀孝、省人大常委会秘书长汤九夫、省人民检察院副检察长郑长生关于提请本次会议决定任命的有关人选的情况说明。

会议以举手表决的方式通过了甘肃省第八届人民代表大会常务委员会代表资格审查委员会主任委员、副主任委员、委员名单，通过了甘肃省第八届人民代表大会常务委员会副秘书长及工作部门负责人任命名单，决定任命了甘肃省各地区中级人民法院院长和检察分院检察长；会议以无记名投票方式决定任命了省人民政府秘书长等组成人员。会议还通过了其他人事任免事项。通过任命：

张国定任甘肃省人大常委会副秘书长；

王凤鸣任甘肃省人大常委会副秘书长兼办公厅主任

尚志仁任甘肃省人大常委会副秘书长；

韩肇文任甘肃省人大常委会副秘书长兼研究室主任；

王应国任甘肃省人大常委会民族侨务工作委员会主任；

关铭涵任甘肃省人大常委会民族侨务工作委员会副主任。

石怀川任甘肃省人大常委会法制工作委员会主任；

马　斌任甘肃省人大常委会法制工作委员会副主任；

孙启明任甘肃省人大常委会法制工作委员会副主任。

皇甫斌任甘肃省人大常委会司法民政工作委员会主任；

李嘉宾任甘肃省人大常委会司法民政工作委员会副主任；

王同礼任甘肃省人大常委会司法民政工作委员会副主任。

王国祥任甘肃省人大常委会财政经济工作委员会主任；

王作山任甘肃省人大常委会财政经济工作委员会副主任；

戴云鹏任甘肃省人大常委会财政经济工作委员会副主任；

石国柱任甘肃省人大常委会财政经济工作委员会副主任。

崔　岩任甘肃省人大常委会农业工作委员会主任；

包文林任甘肃省人大常委会农业工作委员会副主任；

何瑞生任甘肃省人大常委会农业工作委员会副主任。

王松山任甘肃省人大常委会教科文卫工作委员会主任；

罗继成任甘肃省人大常委会教科文卫工作委员会副主任。

马怀西任甘肃省人大常委会代表工作委员会主任；

马耕夫任甘肃省人大常委会代表工作委员会副主任；

梁尊中任甘肃省人大常委会代表工作委员会副主任。

张文麒任甘肃省人大常委会研究室副主任。

巩广禄任甘肃省人大常委会办公厅副主任；

白永发任甘肃省人大常委会办公厅副主任；

安晨光任甘肃省人大常委会办公厅副主任。

决定任命：

孔令鉴为甘肃省人民政府秘书长；

郭　琨为甘肃省计划委员会主任(兼)；

尹霖初为甘肃省物价委员会主任；

丁　齐为甘肃省农业委员会主任；

阎思圣为甘肃省教育委员会主任；

魏庆同为甘肃省科学技术委员会主任；

张维国为甘肃省体育运动委员会主任；

赖学忠为甘肃省计划生育委员会主任；

朱作勇为甘肃省经济体制改革委员会主任；

程有清为甘肃省人民政府外事办公室主任；

王一兵为甘肃省国防科技工业办公室主任；

张文启为甘肃省财政厅厅长；

黄树德为甘肃省石油化学工业厅厅长；

王　军为甘肃省冶金工业厅厅长；

邵克文为甘肃省商业厅厅长；

刘兴邦为甘肃省农业厅厅长；

朱耀光为甘肃省林业厅厅长；

薛映承为甘肃省水利厅厅长；

周明辉为甘肃省畜牧厅厅长；

贺明宝为甘肃省公安厅厅长；

张　忠为甘肃省司法厅厅长；

胡培玉为甘肃省民政厅厅长；

朱毓贤为甘肃省监察厅厅长；

张炳玉为甘肃省文化厅厅长；

杨德儒为甘肃省广播电视厅厅长；

王陇德为甘肃省卫生厅厅长；

高存弟为甘肃省审计局局长；

吴士超为甘肃省统计局局长；

张国维为甘肃省人事局局长；

惠树人为甘肃省工商行政管理局局长；

金学有为甘肃省土地管理局局长；

毛春荣为甘肃省物资局局长；

杜　颖为甘肃省粮食局局长；

乔龙德为甘肃省建材局局长；

张　坤为甘肃省环境保护局局长；

李万林为甘肃省乡镇企业管理局局长；

卫孺牛为甘肃省旅游局局长；

韩效文为甘肃省新闻出版局局长；

决定任命：

傅景华为酒泉地区中级人民法院院长；

杨志明为张掖地区中级人民法院院长；

周述曾为武威地区中级人民法院院长；

郭思礼为定西地区中级人民法院院长；

成　峰为陇南地区中级人民法院院长；

安　统为庆阳地区中级人民法院院长。

冯建新为甘肃省人民检察院酒泉分院检察长；

高新民为甘肃省人民检察院张掖分院检察长；

尚敏学为甘肃省人民检察院武威分院检察长；

黄　琨为甘肃省人民检察院定西分院检察长；

王　旭为甘肃省人民检察院平凉分院检察长；

张应堂为甘肃省人民检察院庆阳分院检察长；

师春善为甘肃矿区人民检察院检察长。

通过任免：

吴碧祥任定西地区中级人民法院经济审判庭庭长、审判委员会委员。免去其定西地区中级人民法院经济审判庭副庭长职务。

杨渊吉任定西地区中级人民法院执行庭副庭长。

张学军、查明巧任定西地区中级人民法院审判员。

葛家勇任庆阳地区中级人民法院审判委员会委员。

张　有任武威地区中级人民法院告诉申诉庭副庭长。

张承安任甘肃矿区人民检察院检察委员会委员、检察员；

丁克祥、张敏、王平、王浩春任甘肃矿区人民检察院检察员。

赵志坚任甘肃省子午岭林区人民检察院副检察长、检察委员会委员。

批准任命：

李存科任定西县人民检察院检察长；

李俊德任通渭县人民检察院检察长；

王友瑞任渭源县人民检察院检察长；

边明德任临洮县人民检察院检察长；

刘志俊任岷县人民检察院检察长；

张树堂任漳县人民检察院检察长；

杨伯英任陇西县人民检察院检察长；

黄胜平任平凉市人民检察院检察长；

张清录任泾川县人民检察院检察长；

张学明任灵台县人民检察院检察长；

苟宗信任华亭县人民检察院检察长；

陈贵录任静宁县人民检察院检察长；

郑德里任庄浪县人民检察院检察长；

殷占隆任张掖市人民检察院检察长；

杨　鹏任民乐县人民检察院检察长；

何多敏任山丹县人民检察院检察长；

黄进荣任肃南裕固族自治县人民检察院检察长；

张文有任临泽县人民检察院检察长；

谢福生任高台县人民检察院检察长；

免去张鸿儒、胡慧娥的甘肃省高级人民法院副院长、审判委员会委员职务；

免去希文的甘肃省人民检察院定西分院检察委员会委员、检察员职务；

免去张益功的甘肃矿区人民检察院检察委员会委员、检察员职务。

（四）甘肃省第八届人民代表大会常务委员会第三次会议于5月18日至22日在兰州举行。

省人大常委会主任卢克俭主持了会议。会议审议通过了关于批准《兰州市人民代表大会常务委员会监督市中级人民法院和市人民检察院工作的暂行办法》、《兰州市南北两山绿化开发管理实施办法》、《阿克塞哈萨克族自治县施行婚姻法部分条款的变通规定》的决定；审议通过了关于批准甘肃省1993年财政预算的决议。听取和审议了省人民政府关于甘肃省一九九三年财政预算和元至四月份财政收支执行情况的报告、关于全省贯彻《全民所有制工业企业转换经营机制条例》的情况汇报、关于全省乡镇企业工作情况的汇报、关于全省体育情况的汇报。

会议已无记名投票和举手表决的方式，任免了政府、两院组成人员。会议结束时，省委书记顾金池到会并作了重要讲话。决定任命：

朱作勇为甘肃省计划委员会主任；

张国杰为甘肃省建设委员会主任；

李文治为甘肃省经济贸易委员会主任；

李　膺为甘肃省民族事务委员会主任；

程有清为甘肃省对外贸易经济合作厅厅长；

胡国斌为甘肃省交通厅厅长；

通过任命：

张新民任省人大常委会平凉地区工作委员会主任；

裴永俊任省人大常委会武威地区工作委员会主任；

陈兴洲任省人大常委会定西地区工作委员会主任；

张俊基任省人大常委会酒泉地区工作委员会主任；

通过任免：

陈锦秀任平凉地区中级人民法院院长；

韩世贵任陇南地区中级人民法院分院院长；

杨建中任甘肃矿区人民法院院长。

孙春升任甘肃矿区人民法院审判员。

李功德任甘肃省高级人民法院审判员。

张荣正任陇南地区中级人民法院审判委员会委员；

刘汉祖任陇南地区中级人民法院分院审判委员会委员；

邓汉武任陇南地区中级人民法院审判员。

赵小平、冯海平、金孟虎、王萍英、郭建民任平凉地区中级人民法院审判员。

刘叔权任定西地区中级人民法院经济审判庭副庭长。

杨新安、唐开福任张掖地区中级人民法院审判员。

孙继跃任甘肃矿区人民法院审判委员会委员，免支其甘肃矿区人民法院刑事审判庭副庭长职务；

刘宪奎任甘肃矿区人民法院刑事审判庭庭长，免去其甘肃矿区人民法院经济审判庭庭长职务；

王金华任甘肃矿区人民法院经济审判庭庭长；

季如华任甘肃矿区人民法院刑事审判庭副庭长；

王　英任甘肃矿区人民法院行政（告诉申诉）审判庭副庭长；

张国华任甘肃矿区人民法院执行庭副庭长；

批准任命：

曾　琳为甘肃省人民检察院陇南分院检察长；

邓玉杰为甘肃省人民检察院兰州铁路运输分院检察长；

钱子和为甘肃省人民检察院白龙江林区分院检察长。

马学正任兰州市人民检察院检察长。

邢葆材任甘肃省人民检察院武威分院副检察长；

张　亭任甘肃省人民检察院武威分院副检察长；

张洪伟任甘肃省人民检察院酒泉分院检察员；

杜立栋任甘肃省人民检察院平凉分院检察员；

杨旭红、赵马雄、张英龙任甘肃省人民检察院庆阳分院检察员；

王长庆任舟曲林区人民检察院检察长；

魏周礼任洮河林区人民检察院检察长；

李耀东任迭部林区人民检察院副检察长、代理检察长；

陈育民任白龙江林区人民检察院副检察长、代理检察长，检察委员会委员。

康连庄任迭部林区人民检察院副检察长、检察委员会委员。

纪国武任敦煌市人民检察院检察长；

伍守齐任玉门市人民检察院检察长；

王金玉任金塔县人民检察院检察长；

杨德昌任安西县人民检察院检察长；

胡　布任肃北蒙古族自治县人民检察院检察长；

罗　锋任阿克塞哈萨克族自治县人民检察院检察长；

魏生广任民勤县人民检察院检察长；
刘志庆任天祝藏族自治县人民检察院检察长；
史有全任古浪县人民检察院检察长；
李百堂任武都县人民检察院检察长；
石清泉任文县人民检察院检察长；
刘　述任宕昌县人民检察院检察长；
王生敬任康县人民检察院检察长；
赵维玺任成县人民检察院检察长；
刘　红任西和县人民检察院检察长；
王居书任礼县人民检察院检察长；
刘礼义任徽县人民检察院检察长；
马俊祥任两当县人民检察院检察长；
张　弛任西峰市人民检察院检察长；
朱书考任宁县人民检察院检察长；
郭广玉任庆阳县人民检察院检察长；
李振荣任华池县人民检察院检察长；
许明义任环县人民检察院检察长；
张文科任合水县人民检察院检察长；
苏世龙任正宁县人民检察院检察长；
曹步效任镇原县人民检察院检察长；

会议决定：批准接受刘秉衡辞去兰州市人民检察院检察长职务的请求。

会议决定免去：

朱作勇的甘肃省经济体制改革委员会主任职务；
郭　琨的甘肃省计划委员会主任职务；
程有清的甘肃省人民政府外事办公室主任职务。
刘生荣的省人大常委会武威地区工作委员会主任职务；
宋德寿的省人大常委会定西地区工作委员会主任职务；
王宽心的酒泉地区中级人民法院审判员职务；
韩治荣的甘肃矿区人民法院行政审判庭庭长职务；
李兴文的甘肃矿区人民法院民事审判庭庭长职务；
石文义的甘肃矿区人民法院刑事审判庭庭长职务。
李永茂的甘肃省人民检察院武威分院副检察长、检察委员会委员职务；
韩　运的甘肃省人民检察院定西分院检察员、检察委员会委员职务；
刘鹤平的迭部林区人民检察院检察长职务。

(五)1993年7月20日至24日，省人大常委会在兰州召开了第四次会议。会议由卢克俭主持。会议审议通过了关于批准《甘南藏族自治州食盐加碘防治碘缺乏病管理办法》的决定，审议通过了关于批准甘肃省1992年财政决算的决议。会议批准任免：

张秀兰任甘肃省人民检察院张掖分院副检察长、检察委员会委员；
刘福发任甘肃省人民检察院平凉分院检察员。

免去

宋池林的甘肃省人民检察院定西分院副检察长职务；
陈　彦的甘肃省人民检察院张掖分院副检察长、检察委员会委员、检察员职务；
刘永革的甘肃省人民检察院检察员职务。

(六)甘肃省第八届人民代表大会常务委员会第五次会议于9月25日至29日在兰州举行。

省人大常委会主任卢克俭主持了会议。会议审议通过了《甘肃省劳动保护监察暂行条例》、《甘肃省实施水土保持办法》；听取和审议了省人民政府关于贯彻中央加强宏观调控政策措施的情况报告，省高级人民法院关于审理经济犯罪和经济纠纷案件的情况报告、省人民检察院关于元至八月全省查处贪污贿赂等经济犯罪情况的汇报。会议以举手表决的投票表决的方式通过了关于接受阎海旺辞去甘肃省省长职务的请求的决定和关于由副省长张吾乐代理甘肃省省长职务的决定。会议通过任免：

李永昌、金秀馥、邢恩杰任甘肃省高级人民法院副院长、审判委员会委员。
牛兴全任定西地区中级人民法院副院长；
马呈祥任定西地区中级人民法院民事审判庭庭长、审判委员会委员，免去其定西地区中级人民法院民事审判庭副庭长职务；
冉旺玺任定西地区中级人民法院民事审判庭副庭长；
杨凤杰任陇南地区中级人民法院刑事第一审判庭副庭长；
王奇福任陇南地区中级人民法院审判员。
姜　荣任张掖地区中级人民法院刑事审判庭庭长；
张志忠任张掖地区中级人民法院刑事审判庭副庭长；
田　伟任张掖地区中级人民法院民事审判庭副庭长；
丁耀明任张掖地区中级人民法院经济审判庭副庭长；
赵治荣任张掖地区中级人民法院告诉申诉庭副庭长；
杨志坚任张掖地区中级人民法院执行庭副庭长；
杨学明任张掖地区中级人民法院审判员；
申志忠任甘肃省人民检察院定西分院检察委员会委员。
免去陈文笔的定西地区中级人民法院民事审判庭庭长、审判委员会委员职务。
免去宋之堂的张掖地区中级人民法院刑事第一审判庭庭长职务。
免去邢恩杰的甘肃省高级人民法院执行庭庭长职务。

会议批准：

免去杜仲德的甘肃省人民检察院副检察长、检察委员会委员职务；

免去赵国诚的甘肃省人民检察院副检察长、检察委员会委员职务。

免去黄启毅的甘肃省人民检察院平凉分院副检察长、检察委员会委员职务。

免去史　联的甘肃省人民检察院检察员职务。

(七)甘肃省第八届人民代表大会常务委员会第六次会议于11月22日至27日在兰州召开。

省人大常委会主任卢克俭主持了会议。

会议审议通过了《甘肃省社会治安综合治理条例》、《甘肃省实施残疾人保障法办法》、《甘肃省农民承担费用和劳务监督管理办法》；通过了《甘肃省人大常委会关于1993年—1997年地方立法规划的决定》和《甘肃省人大常委会关于进一步贯彻执行<药品管理办法>严禁生产、销售、使用假劣药品的决议》；听取和审议了省人民政府和省高级人民法院、省人民检察院、省人大常委会作的关于1993年全省政府系统开展执法监督检察工作的情况汇报，关于全省法院系统1993年执法检察工作情况汇报，关于全省检察机关执法检察工作情况的报告，关于我省开展反腐败斗争的情况汇报，关于环境保护工作情况的汇报和关于1993年在全省范范围内组织代表视察的情况报告。会议还通过了几项人事任免。

决定任命

柳宏克任甘肃省冶金工业厅厅长。

免去王　军的甘肃省冶金工业厅厅长职务。

会议通过任免：

王志清任甘肃省高级人民法院刑事第二审判庭庭长，免去其甘肃省高级人民法院刑事第二审判庭副庭长庭长职务；

蔡秋香任甘肃省高级人民法院行政审判庭庭长；

冯耀习任甘肃省高级人民法院执行庭庭长。

免去姚　桢的甘肃省高级人民法院刑事第二审判庭庭长职务；

免去魏中扬的甘肃省高级人民法院行政审判庭庭长职务。

党传新任酒泉地区中级人民法院刑事第二审判庭庭长，免去其酒泉地区中级人民法院刑事第一审判庭副庭长职务；

马吉祖任酒泉地区中级人民法院经济审判庭副庭长；

田春明任酒泉地区中级人民法院民事审判庭副庭长；

李发泰、杨正明、成永贵、王有林任酒泉地区中级人民法院审判员；

朱进文任武威地区中级人民法院刑事第一审判庭副庭长；

吴一凡、王国锋、何世杰任武威地区中级人民法院审判员；

姜会堂、梁　勇、尚书录任庆阳地区中级人民法院审判员。

刘韶青任甘肃省人民检察院定西分院副检察长、检察委员会委员。

免去肖印堂的酒泉地区中级人民法院民事审判庭庭长、审判委员会委员职务。

四、甘肃省人大常委会1993年开展的主要工作

第一，制定地方立法五年规划。八届全国人大一次会议用根本大法的形式把“国家实行社会主义市场经济”肯定下来，这就标志着我国经济体制改革进入了加速建立社会主义市场经济的新阶段。这个新阶段的特点就是重视体制和政策的规范化，用法律引导、推进和保障改革的顺利进行，迫切要求加快立法，特别是经济立法。地方立法作为国家法律体系的重要组成部分，在适应这一新形势发展，为此，常委会按照宪法的要求，把制定立法规划放在了十分重要的位置，组织有关专家、学者及实际工作者，从总体上、法理上对社会主义市场经济法律体系构想进行了研究，并在广泛调查研究的基础上经过充分讨论，制定出1993年——1997年五年立法规划。

新制定的立法五年规划有以下几个特点；一是突出经济立法。兼顾其它立法；二是突出本省特点，在针对性上下功夫；三是突出制定与国家法律相配套的实施细则，使之更具有操作性；四是突出民族自治地方单行条例的制定，保障和促进民族地区的经济和社会发展。立法规划的主要内容包括建立社会主义市场经济体制、规范市场主体、维护市场秩序、加强宏观调控、完善社会保障以及加强社会主义民主政治建设、健全国家机构组织制度、惩治各种犯罪活动、维护社会治安、促进教育科学文化发展、保护环境等十个方面共67件地方法规。

为了确保立法规划的实施，常委会要求各有关部门借鉴外地经验。抓好年度立法计划编制和落实，集中力量，加快立法进度。同时，实行实际工作和理论工作相结合，注意发挥专家学者在立法工作中的作用，不断改进立法手段，使我省的立法工作有重点、有计划地进行。

第二，完成全年立法任务。一年来，常委会结合本省实际，坚持积极慎重、急需先立的原则，围绕我省改革开放和社会发展的具体任务，先后制定和批准制定的地方性法规和民族自治地方单行条例11件，初审地方性法规2件。其中有关经济方面的地方性法规5件。

为了加快立法步伐，常委会与“一府两院”有关部门共同商讨年度立法计划，采取统一规划，分工负责，各司其职，协同工作的措施，积极进行工作。在法规的起草过程中，常委会提出解放思想，开拓创新，着眼针对性，立足可行性，增加超前性，强调计划性的要求，调动各法规起草单位的积极性，保证立法任务顺利完成。

我省农业基础比较薄弱，干旱和水土流失严重。为了尽快改变这种状况，常委会制定了《甘肃省实施水土保持法办法》。这个法规对于加快改变我省农业生产条件，控制和治理水土流失，增强农业后劲，促进粮食生产持续、稳定发展起到积极的作用。农民负担过重是我省农村存在的突出问题之一，国务院和省政府多次发出紧急通知，并明文取消了乱摊派、乱收费、乱罚款的项目。为了把农民的合理负担及劳务管理纳入制度化、法律化的轨道，促进农村经济改革的深入发展，常委会有关工作委员会与政府有关工作部门密切合作，起草了《甘肃省农民负担费用和劳务监督管理办法》，并经常委会第六次会议通过颁布实施。这个法规对于减轻农民负担，调动农民生产积极性，发挥了较好的作用。随着社会主义市场经济的发展，商品流通越来越活跃，为了加强引导、规范、保障商品流通的健康发展，常委会于第七次会议制定了《甘肃省经纪人管理暂行条例》。通过上述法规的制定，我们认识到制定规范市场经济行为、加强宏观调控的经济法规，虽然难度很大，但只要从实际出发，加强调查研究，重视借鉴国内外的经验，就能够加快经济立法的步伐。

此外，常委会承办了全国人大常委会交办的19件法律草案征求意见的工作。经过认真的办理，共收集各种修改意见近百条，及时转送全国人大法工委，为制定有关法规反映了广泛的意见。

第三，听取和审议"一府两院"工作汇报和专题报告。一年来，常委会紧紧围绕建立社会主义市场经济体制和全省不同阶段的主要工作以及群众普遍关心的重大问题，及时听取和审议了"一府两院"的工作汇报和专题报告。常委会在去年5月举行的第三次会议上，听取和审议了省政府《关于甘肃省1992年财政预算和1993年元至4月份财政预算执行情况的报告》，并根据省人大八届一次会议的授权，审查批准了关于1992年我省财政决算的报告，常委会还先后听取和审议了关于贯彻全民所有制工业企业转换经营机制条例的情况、贯彻中央加强宏观调控政策措施的情况、环保工作情况、开展反腐败斗争情况，以及审理经济犯罪和查处贪污贿赂经济犯罪情况等29项工作汇报。

为提高审议水平，增强监督实效，每次例会之前，常委会组成人员都围绕议题实地进行调查。如在审议反腐败斗争情况汇报之前，常委会一名副主任和几名委员去白银等地进行调查，对反腐败斗争所取得的成绩及存在的问题作了全面了解，写出了调查报告。因此，在审议汇报时，提出了有事实、有依据、有分析、有措施的意见和建议。为了掌握我省工业企业转换经营机制的情况，做到审议报告时心中有数，常委会主任、副主任和部分委员分赴金昌、天水和兰州等地区，进行了广泛深入的调查研究，提出了一些切实可行的意见，增强了常委会审议的力度。回顾一年来的工作，常委会在听取审议'一府两院'工作汇报和专题报告的过程中，基本上做到了审议前有调查，审议中有建议，审议后有检查，对"一府两院"既起到监督制约作用，又达到了促进和支持的目的，为推动全省社会经济的发展作出了积极努力。

第四，组织代表进行视察。代表视察是代表联系人民群众，了解实际情况，反映人民群众意见和要求，认真履行职责的重要形式。去年常委会组织的代表视察活动，又有新的改进。

（一）广泛动员，统一认识。为了把视察工作落实到实处，常委会召开动员会和电话会，由省委书记、人大主任和省长在会上作动员，反复阐明代表视察的重要意义，动员省人民关心和支持代表视察，要求各级政府密切配合并自觉接受代表视察。省委、省人大、省政府的主要领导同志都以普通代表身份同其大家一起深入机关、单位、厂矿、企业视察，使代表视察活动更加富有成效；

（二）分段安排任务，有计划的进行工作。为了使视察工作有计划、有目的进行。从6月初开始到10上旬，分三阶段进行，并分级提出了要求。即第一阶段为视察了解情况，提出意见阶段，第二阶段为转交"一府两院"办理视察提出问题阶段，第三阶段为检查落实意见办理情况阶段，使代表视察活动善始善终，取得更好的成效。

（三）突出重点，全省上下统一进行视察。常委会主任会议在广泛听取各方面意见的基础上，确定了以企业转换经营机制、农民承担费用和劳务管理、社会治安综合治理和打击假冒伪劣商品等四个方面的内容为重点，在省人大常委会组织四个视察组进行视察的同时，要求各级人大常委会组织本级人民代表与省人大代表共同开展视察工作。

（四）广泛宣传视察活动，动员全省人民共同努力发展社会主义民主。为了使代表视察活动在全省范围内迅速开展起来，广播、电视、报纸等新闻单位，广泛开展宣传，及时报道代表视察活动情况，增强了人民群众当家作主的意识。

由于采取了上述措施，使代表视察活动收到较好的效果。全省共有1976名县级以上四级人大代表，视察了80个县(市、区)的340个乡镇、1164个行政村和664个企事业单位，召开汇报会、座谈会1121次，走访群众1447人次，提出建议、批评和意见785件。这些建议、批评和意见转交各级"一府两院"后，已全部办理完毕，得到答复的有706件，占总量的89.9%。其中有84件是由各级政府部门在陪同代表视察的现场办理的。如代表在酒泉地区视察时，了解到夹山子水库工程资金不落实，工期拖长，农民负担加重，群众意见很大，将此问题向省政府转告后，得到了妥善的解决。毒品犯罪是群众深恶痛绝而且反映最为强烈的问题，常委会根据视察中群众反映量刑偏宽等意见，会同有关部门向全国人大常委会和最高人民法院作了汇报，向司法部门提出从严执法的建议，有关部门采取了相应的措施，这对严厉打击毒品犯罪活动、维护社会稳定是个有力的推动。常委会还针对视察中了解到全省医药市场管理混乱、医疗事故屡屡发生、广大群众意见很大的状况，及时作出《关于进一步贯彻执行＜药品管理法＞严禁生产、销售、使用假冒伪劣药品的决议》。这个决议对于加强市场管理，制止不正当竞争行为，遏制、销售伪劣药品，保障公民合法权益起到了积极的促进作用。总之，通过这次视察，拓宽了视察思路，强化了监督力度，增强了代表意识，提高了地方国家权力机关的威信。

第五，在全省范围内进行执法检查监督。开展执法检查中法律监督的一种形式。当前，改革开放在深化，新旧体制转换过程在加快，更需要发挥这种监督作用、。一年来，常委会围绕"一府两院"工作和人民群众关心的热点、难点问题，有组织地开展了以贯彻《企业法》和《企业转换经营机制条例》、《农民承担费用和劳务监督管理条例》、全国人大常委会和省人大常委会关于社会治安综合治理的决定、决议及贯彻《产品质量法》等法律法规执行情况为重点的执法检查监督。同时，按照全国人大和国务院的部署，组织了对环保方面执法的检查。这次执法检查是在常委会统一领导，统一部署，采取自查、抽查、重点检查以及和代表视察相结合的方法进行的。常委会各有关工作委员会，受常委会主任会议的委托，还多次赴各地对执法检查情况进行了检查和督促。通过执法检查监督，增强了执法机关和工作人员的责任感和自觉性，对广大干部和群众进行了一次法制教育，纠正了一些错案。查处了一批违法犯罪分子，发现了一些执法不严、违法不究的问题。仅政府系统就查处违法违纪案件7000多件，追回违纪资金400多万元，依法追究了53人的刑事责任，给予党纪、政纪处分的109人，维护了法律的尊严。

在法律监督过程中，常委会注意通过信访渠道掌握监督信息。信访案件中。检举、控告和申诉案占绝大多数，对于这类案件，常委会都及时转交"一府两院"办理，特别重大的案件由常委会主任、副主任亲自批阅，要求答复办理结果，直至问题完全解决。去年常委会共受理人民来信来访3360件次。经领导批示的案件84件，要求报告办理结果的211件，收到办理结果报告183份。通过办理信访案件，保障了公民、法人和其他组织的合法权益，增强了司法机关的公仆意识，对于改变一些部门"有法不知道，知道不执行，执行不坚决"的状况，起到了明显的作用。

第六，依法任免国家机关工作人员。换届后人事任免面宽、量大，常委会认真贯彻党管干部的原则，并严格按照法律规定办事，在充分酝酿的基础上进行民主表决，认真履行人事任免职权。一年来，常委会共决定任命代省长1人、政府其他组成人员48名，地区中级法院院长、地区检查分院检察长21名；任命省人大常委会各工作部门和地区人大工委负责人41名；批准任命州、市和县级检察院检察长48名；任命两院其他工作人员101名；免去省人大常委会、省政府及两院国家机关工作人员59名。从这些任命的干部的情况看，中青年干部比例有所上升，年龄明显下降，知识结构更趋合理，其中有不少同志是近几年在改革开放、发展经济中脱颖而出的优秀人才。这些同志进入工作岗位后，大都能够解放思想，更新观念，锐意改革，开拓进取，担负起人民交付的重大担，为我省社会经济的全面发展注入了新的活力。

第七，加强和改进代表工作。代表工作是人大工作的基础。做好人民代表工作，使代表能够充分发挥作用，这就从根本上保障了人民当家作主的主人翁地位。

一年来，常委会从以下几个方面加强了代表工作：一是重视对代表活动的组织工作。换届之后，常委会从方便代表履行职责的角度出发，根据实际需要和可能，将省八届人大代表编为106个活动小组，重申和修定了联系代表办法和代表联系选民制度等，使代表活动有组织地进行。二是牢固树立常委会为代表服务的观念。为代表服务最根本的问题是为代表行使职权创造良好的环境和条件。首先，让代表学法、知政，熟悉全省和本地区的情况。为此常委会除通过机关报刊《人民之声报》、《人大研究》杂志和各种文件、材料及时向代表通报人大和"一府两院"工作情况外，去年10月，常委会还专门召开情况通报会，由省政府负责人向代表通报全省政治、经济发展形势和政府工作情况，常委会领导向代表通报省人大常委会工作情况，并将这些通报材料印发每个代表。其次，为代表行使职权提供条件，如去年组织的大规模视察活动，就是本着这种思路所进行的具体工作。再次，常委会组成人员深入各地区调查研究时，登门走访代表，召开座谈会，听取代表的意见和建议，使上情下达，下情上达。这项工作已形成制度。一年来，组成人员联系代表百余人次，听取反映了代表建议、意见一百多条。三是认真办理代表议案和建议、意见。省八届人大一次会议期间，代表共提供议案和建议、意见735件，其中议案85件，经过大会议案委员会审查，均按建议和意见处理。截止去年12月底，所有建议和意见全部办理完毕。

其中解决的建议和意见164件，有245件正在解决之中，向全国有关部门反映的84件，还有242件因条件所限一时还解决不了。这些都一一向代表本人作了答复。

第八，全面完成指导县乡换届工作。我省这次县乡换届是从1992年9月开始的，全省85个县(市、区)和1550个乡(镇)中，任期届满的82个县(市、区)，除崇信县1993年底换届外，其余81个县(市、区)和1462个乡(镇)都在1993年3月底结束了换届工作。共选出县级人大代表14868名，乡(镇)级人大代表62889名，选出县级领导班子成员1030名，乡级领导班子成员4262名。

从全省情况看，绝大多数县乡严格依法办事，换届选举工作进行顺利，广大群众满意。也有个别县乡的换届选举出现了一些不符合法律规定的做法，选民和代表有意见，并多次上诉省人大常委会。对这些不符合法律规定的做法，基本上都得到了纠正。各级人大常委会在换届结束后，本着实事求是的精神，总结了本地区的县乡换届选举工作。普遍认为，这次换届选举，由于党委重视，人大常委会精心组织，充分发扬民主，严格法依法办事，使换届选举工作得以顺利进行。从选举的结果看，县乡各级领导班子组成结构、年龄结构、知识结构进一步优化。他们思想解放，精力充沛，敢管敢抓，富有朝气，成为带领全省各族人民进行社会主义现代化建设的中坚力量。

第九，密切同上下级人大常委会的联系和对外交往。在过去的一年里，常委会重视同全国和下级人大常委会的联系。主动向全国人大常委会汇报工作，积极承办全国人大常委会交办的事宜；每次都邀请部分下级人大常委会主任列席；召集下级人大常委会主任座谈会，研究每个时期人大工作出现的新情况、新问题；及时帮助下级人大常委会纠正本行政区域发生的重大违法事件；重视解决下级人大常委会一些实际困难。从而达到了相互学习，相互促进，取长补短，共同前进的目的。

加强同兄弟省区人大常委会的学习交流，是改进常委会工作的一项重要措施。去年8月，常委会牵头召开了西北五省区人大财经工作座谈会。为了学习沿海和经济发达地区人大常委会财经工作的经验，还特邀了10个兄弟省区的常委会有关负责同志列席会议。同时，有部分组成人员和工作部门的负责人，先后赴云南、山东、江苏、广东、海南、山西、四川等省市学习，并参加了人大系统召开的座谈会、经验交流会以及理论研讨会，使我们开阔了视野，学到了经验，拓宽了工作思路。去年我们接待了来我省视察的全国人大常委会孙起孟、李锡铭副委员长。两位副委员长对我省人大建设工作的一些做法给予了充分的肯定。一年来，常委会共接待全国人大有关委员和兄弟省市区人大常委会的访客人73批676人。

积极开展对外联络，加强与国外议会的交往，是学习、借鉴国外议会经验，为我省改革开放和经济建设创造良好环境的一项重要工作。去年，常委会接待了新西兰莱斯特彻奇市议会友好访华团和其他国家地区议会代表。通过相互交流，加深了外国朋友对我省的了解，增进了友谊，为常委会与国外议会的友好往来开了个好头。

第十，加强常委会自身建设。本届常委会组成人员有四分之三的同志是新当选的，全心全意大多数是长期从事党委政府工作的，对人大工作比较生疏。为了使大家尽快熟悉人大工作，更好地依法履行职责，常委会坚持了中心学习小组学习制度，组织成员集中学习了建设有中国特色社会主义的理论，学习了宪法和法律、法规以及有关人大工作方面的知识。为了加深对党的十四大精神和十四届三中全会有关建立社会主义市场经济决议实质内容的学习，正确理解社会主义市场经济的内涵，主任会议请来学者，讲解有关市场经济的知识，通过学习，使大家增长了法律意识和人大工作意识，增长了有关市场经济的知识，使之很快熟悉适应人大工作。常委会重视改进工作作风，坚持群众路线，加强调查研究，组成人员先后有90多人次，深入70多个地州市、县市区进行调查研究，共写出100余份调查报告，为常委会审议"一府两院"工作提供了有力的依据。人大常委会和政府的工作，既有监督和被监督的关系，又有密切不可分割的工作联系。为此，常委会坚持和改进了主任和省长联系制度，邀请"两院"主要负责人列席会议。去年共召集了两次主任、省长联席会议，解决了一些重要问题。

为了使各工作部门适应新形势下人大工作的需要，常委会特别重视加强和改进机关工作。主任和分管副主任先后召开机关干部会议对机关建设提出要求，一年来，常委会组织职工认真学习《邓小平文选》三卷、学习宪法和法律，提高对人大工作的认识，树立为社会主义民主和法制建设献身的精神；调整个别工作机构，充实了领导班子；制定和修改了22个工作制度，汇集成《机关工作手册》。发至每个职工遵照执行；各工作部门分工明确，恪尽职守，为开好"三会"付出了辛勤的劳动。人大理论研究和宣传工作有所加强，召开了人大制度理论研讨会，专题研讨了市场经济下的地方人大工作；成立了"甘肃省市场经济法制研究会"；充分利用《人民之声报》和《人大研究》这两块舆论阵地，有计划、有组织地宣传了我省各级人大工作和由常委会制定的地方性法规。后勤服务工作也有较大改进，这些都有力地促进了常委会工作健康、有序的发展。

甘肃省人民政府

省政府全体会议

甘肃省第八届人民政府第一次全体会议

1993年10月7日下午在省政府办公厅召开。会议由副省长杨怀孝主持,代省长张吾乐、副省长陈绮玲、郭琨、崔正华及政府组成人员35人出席了会议,原甘肃省委书记顾金池、省委书记阎海旺应邀参加了会议。列席会议的有,兰州市政府、省政府部门归口管理的事业单位、公司、联社、总会,国务院业务主管部门与省政府双重领导的部门的主要负责同志;应邀参加会议的还有省法院、省检察院、省纪委、省委宣传部、省委研究室、省人大财政经济工作委员会、省政协经济科技委员会、省总工会、团省委、省妇联、各民主党派和工商联的负责人及部分新闻单位的记者,共计141人。

会上,张吾乐代省长代表省政府安排部署了全省第四季度的工作,主要是:1.要全面完成全年国民经济和社会发展的各项任务;2.根据国家即将出台的改革措施对关系经济发展全局的重要工作,要超前做好预测分析,确定四季度应该采取的措施,为明年乃至今后经济的发展做好准备;3.要千方百计扩大全省资金运筹规模,加强资金调度,确保工业生产、流通和建设的需要;4.编制好明年的计划;5.筹备开好老区工作、教育工作、农村工作、经济工作等四个会议;6.要特别注意处理好社会敏感问题,保持社会安定;7.按照中央要求和省委的部署,认真开展反腐败斗争;8.根据国家深化改革的总体设想,调查研究,按照建立社会主义市场经济的框架,进一步完善全省经济和社会发展的思路。

顾金池、阎海旺同志在会上也作了重要讲话。

省政府1993年常务会议

第1次 2月8日上午,阎海旺省长主持召开,主要分析了我省农业形势,研究提出了当前农村及农业生产工作重点和措施。一是全力以赴抓好春耕生产;二是抓紧解决"打白条"问题;三是继续把乡镇企业作为发展农村经济的突破口;四是继续搞好农田水利基本建设;五是继续推行农村改革,切实安排好群众生活。会议决定对当前农业生产资料生产供应中存在的问题给予解决。

第2次 3月2日下午,阎海旺省长主持召开,主要研究了4项议题。一是传达国务院粮食购销政策发布和定货会精神,确定了贯彻意见;二是听取了关于赴北京争取艺术节给予支持的情况汇报;三是听取了第八届人代会甘肃代表建议、议案收集筛选情况的汇报;四是听取了省政府办公厅几项工作的汇报。

第3次 3月8日上午,受阎海旺省长委托,常务副省长张吾乐主持召开,讨论通过了《甘肃省全民所有制工业企业转换经营机制实施办法》(试行)。

第4次 4月26日下午,阎海旺省长主持召开,主要研究了3项议题。一是讨论通过了《甘肃省人民政府会议规则》、《甘肃省人民政府关于减少领导同志事务性活动的实施办法》和《甘肃省人民政府关于改进公文处理工作的若干规定》等三个工作规则;二是听取审议了对几位同志所犯错误处理的复议意见;三是讨论了《关于改革省级会议费管理办法的意见》。

第5次 5月10日上午,阎海旺省长主持召开,主要研究了5项议题。一是利用国外资金改造中川机场问题;二是靖远电厂引进外资问题;三是讨论通过了《甘肃省实施城市房屋拆迁管理条例细则》;四是讨论通过了《甘肃省劳动保护监察条例》;五是讨论通过了《甘肃省农村计划生育优待办法》。

第6次 5月24日下午,阎海旺省长主持召开,主要研究了3项议题。一是讨论通过了《甘肃省实施防汛条例细则》;二是讨论通过了《甘肃省实施河道管理条例办法》;三是讨论通过了《甘肃省小型水利工程管理办法》。

第7次 7月2日上午,阎海旺省长主持召开,主要议题两个。一是讨论修改了《在全省经济情况通报会上的讲话》;二是传达学习中共中央〔1993年〕第6号文件。

第8次 7月12日上午,阎海旺省长主持召开,讨论通过了《甘肃省实施水土保持法办法》。

第9次 8月23日下午,阎海旺省长主持召开,主要研究了3项议题。一是讨论通过了《关于我省涉及农民负担项目审核的处理意见》;二是讨论通过了《甘肃省社会治安综合治理条例》(草案);三是讨论通过了《甘肃省实施残疾人保障法办法》(草案)。

第10次 9月1日下午,阎海旺省长主持召开,听取了人事部西安片工资改革座谈会精神,研究了工资改革问题。

第11次 9月27日上午,阎海旺省长主持召开,通报了省级领导变动情况,推荐了代省长候选人。

第12次 10月8日下午,张吾乐代省长主持召开,主要研究了4项议题。一是听取了省教委《关于贯彻<中国教育改革和发展纲要>的几个问题的汇报》，讨论决定了支持全省教育事业发展的几项政策措施；二是听取了省计委《关于对庆阳老区会议需要解决的问题协调情况的汇报》，原则同意了第8次庆阳老区会议解决的有关问题；三是听取并原则同意了省人事局《关于全国推行公务员制度和工资制度改革工作会议精神及贯彻意见的汇报》；四是听取了省政府法制局《关于第二次全国法制工作会议精神的汇报提纲》，原则同意贯彻落实会议精神的具体意见。

第13次10月30日下午，张吾乐代省长主持召开，主要研究了6项议题。一是讨论通过了《甘肃省人民政府关于进一步贯彻落实党中央国务院部署深入开展反腐败斗争的通知》；二是听取并原则通过了《甘肃省设市预测与规划》，同意上报国务院；三是讨论了省建委《关于省建筑勘察设计院和省水利水电勘测设计院级别升格的报告》，同意"两院"由现县级级别升格为副地级级别，报省委审批；四是讨论通过了《长风宝安实业股份有限公司社会公众股票发行总体方案》；五是同意甘肃工业大学成立技术工程学院；六是同意省财政厅为筹措中国第四届艺术节经费，开展社会捐资活动的意见。会上张吾乐代省长还通报和安排了当前的工作。

第14次11月12日上午，杨怀孝副省长受张吾乐代省长委托主持召开，主要研究了5项议题。一是讨论通过了《甘肃省农民负担监督管理办法》(草案)，同意提请省人大审议；二是讨论通过了《甘肃省实施归侨侨眷权益保护法办法》(草案)，同意提请省人大审议；三是讨论通过了《甘肃省经纪人管理暂行条例(草案)》，同意提请省人大审议；四是讨论通过了省政府《关于进一步清理整顿窑街、靖远、阿干矿区国有煤矿井田范围内乡镇小煤矿的方案》；五是讨论通过了全省第一批取消的收费项目。

第15次11月25日上午，张吾乐代省长主持召开，主要研究了3项议题。一是原则同意了省计委关于1994年计划安排的初步意见；二是原则同意了省农委关于全省农村工作会议的筹备意见；三是讨论通过了全省第二批取消的55项乱收费项目。

第16次12月14日上午，张吾乐代省长主持召开，主要研究了4项议题。一是原则同意了农村救灾粮及补贴款方案；二是原则通过了《甘肃省城镇股份合作制企业暂行办法》；三是通过了有关人事任免事项；四是同意给在我省工作的中科院学部委员颁发省政府津贴。

第17次12月27日上午，张吾乐代省长主持召开，主要研究了4项议题。一是原则通过了1994年全省宏观经济管理和调控中采取的11条措施；二是原则同意省计委关于1994年计划安排意见；三是原则同意了全省经济工作会议的安排意见；四是布置了有关部门近期要抓好的重点工作。

（甘肃省人民政府办公厅秘书处）

为适应建立社会主义市场经济体制积极稳妥地推进甘肃省机构改革工作

一、全省行政和事业单位机构编制的基本概况

1993年全省各级党政群机关和事业单位机构编制总规模为：党政和事业机构共31277个，行政、事业总编制598099名，实有人数590362人。

(一)、行政机构与编制

全省各级党政机构共4706个，其中省直74个，地(州、市)级722个，县(市、区)级3910个。全省行政机关总编制为122103名，实有124969人，其中省直编制6791名，实有8060人；地(州、市)级编制21872名，实有22919人；县(市、区)级编制60494名，实有62585人；乡镇编制32946名，实有31405人。

(二)、事业机构与编制

全省共有事业机构26571个，其中省直属457个，地(州、市)属1913个，县(市、区)属6933个，乡镇属17208个。全省共有各类事业编制475996名，实有465393人。其中省直编制66303名，实有64939人；地(州、市)编制73474名，实有69102人；县(市、区)编制143713名，实有149023人；乡镇编制192506名，实有182329人。

按经费开支划分，全省事业单位中，由财政全额拨款的有318917人，占实有人数的68.5%；差额拨款(补贴)的81725人，占16%；自筹资金的64697人，占15.5%。

按岗位性质划分，教育系统229965人，占总人数的49.4%；卫生系统56783人，占12.2%；文化系统11383人，占2.5%；科技系统17142人，占3.7%；农林牧水系统74953人，占16.1%；其它系统75167人，占16.1%。

二、机构改革工作

为了全面落实党的十四大提出的三年内完成机构改革工作的要求，积极稳妥地推进我省机构改革工作，一年来，我省机构编制部门，在省委的领导下，认真抓了机构改革的调研、试点和准备工作。

(一)、调整、充实、加强了领导和办事机构

去年以来，由于班子换届，原省编委部分成员工作有了变动，为了加强对机构编制工作的领导，省委对编委成员做了调整，调整后的编委由阎海旺同志任主任，孙英同志、杨怀孝同志任副主任，确定了共有10名同志组成的省机构编制委员会，加强了对机构编制工作的领导。

为了充实编委办事机构，在原编委办公室的基础上，又从省属有关部门抽调了10多名同志，成立了省直、事业、地县、综合四个组，加强了力量，改善了办事机构。

（二）、对全省机构改革工作做了安排部署

根据省委七届八次全委扩大会议关于加快改革步伐，尽快完成全省机构改革的总体要求，提出了《关于全省机构改革的安排意见》，6月份，省委、省政府已正式印发全省执行，要求全省机构改革大体分三个阶段进行。第一阶段调查研究，制定方案；第二阶段组织实施，实行“三定”；第三阶段检查验收，巩固完善。并对机构改革的指导思想，内容重点，组织领导，审批程序和方法步骤等提出了明确要求。6月8日，编委办公室召集省直各厅局人事处长、办公室主任参加的打招呼会，会上传达了党的十四届二中全会关于党政机构改革的精神，介绍了我省编制现状，提出了需要各部门尽快做好的三项工作，一是抓住一个重点，即转变职能，下放权力；二是突出两个难点，即兴办实体、分流人员；三是搞好一个方案，即各部门的“三定”方案。会后，各部门即着手进行调查研究，转变职能，分流人员和制定“三定”方案的工作，截止年底，已有30多个部门提出了机构改革的初步设想，10多个部门上报了初拟的本部门的“三定”方案。

（三）、开展了调研、试点和测算工作

调研工作。2、3月份，由编委办公室牵头，从有关部门抽调人员，组织力量，分成四个组，先后对14个地、州、市和14个机构改革试点县做了调查。通过调查，对14个地、州、市的机构改革工作和机构改革试点县的改革进度、收到的效果，存在的问题和建议有了较全面的了解。并向省委、省政府写了专题报告。

为了把我省机构改革方案设计的更科学、合理、更能切合我省实际和掌握大量第一手资料，编委办公室上半年，先后对省直22个部门机构改革的整体设想、转变职能、精简撤并、人员分流、存在问题和困难等做了调查。下半年，就地、县、乡机构改革方案，事业单位机构改革的基本思路，分流人员的若干意见，机关后勤部门如何改革等方面的问题，又先后到9个地、州、市，30个县、乡，50多个事业单位和部分省直机关，广泛听取了各方面的意见，为方案的进一步修改完善提供了第一手资料。

确定了省直事业单位机构改革有试点。7月份，经与有关部门协商，初步确定了西北师范大学、工业专科学校、兰州医学院第一附属医院、兰州市第一人民医院、省科技情报所等五个具有代表性和不同类型的事业单位作为机构试点单位，让这些单位先行引路，为事业单位面上的机构改革提供经验。

分类定编测算工作。根据中央对市、县、乡各级分类定编的标准，对我省13个城市、67个县、1554个乡镇进行了分类测算，结合我省实际，对测算结果进行了论证分析，提出了符合我省实际的分类定编意见。在此基础上，对全省编制总规模和精减幅度情况做了测算。通过分类定编测算工作，对下一步各级改革工作的实施和审批创造了必备条件。

（四）、草拟了10个我省机构改革方案和实施意见（征求意见稿）

根据中央有关机构改革的精神和要加快机构改革步伐的要求，联系我省实际，分别草拟了《甘肃省省级党政机关改革方案》、《省级党政机关机构改革实施意见》、《地、州、市机构改革方案》、《县级机构改革实施意见》、《乡镇机构改革方案》、《事业单位机构改革的基本思路》、《专业经济部门转为实体的若干意见》、《分流人员的若干意见》、《机关后勤部门机构改革的意见》、《清理省直非常设机构的意见》。这些方案几经论证修改，其中《甘肃省省级党政机构改革方案》；已在省委常委和部分副省长范围内征求了意见；《县级机构改革实施方案》，因着手较早，并在10多个省、地、县的有关部门和单位开了论证会，几经论证修改，这个方案已基本成熟，有待审议批准；《清理省直非常设机构的意见》，经多次酝酿论证，也已成熟，待审议批准后即可实施；《事业单位机构改革的基本思路》，分别在省教委、省卫生厅、省科委及其所属事业单位请示了意见，并做进一步修改。截止年底我省机构改革所需的各类方案已草拟齐备。

总的看，1993年我省机构编制工作，是在党的十四大精神指引下，积极推进我省机构改革工作的一年。各级各部门本着精简、统一、效能的原则，紧紧围绕转变职能、理顺关系、精兵简政、提高效率的改革内容，努力探索，积极进取，大力开展调查研究，抓紧制定本地区、本部门的“三定”工作。机构改革正在有序在进行，各项机构改革的准备工作大体就绪，改革的大气候已在全省形成。

（省编委：李志民、梁祖贵、何怡）

适应市场经济要求 推进人事制度改革

省人事局局长

张国维

1993年，我省人事工作以党的十四大精神为指针，紧紧围绕建立社会主义市场经济体制和人事工作为经济建设服务这个中心，以抓好推行国家公务员制度、机构改革、工资制度改革的准备工作为重点，进一步加强干部管理、知识分子工作、军转干部安置、退休干部管理、人才市场建设、人事调研宣传、反腐倡廉和机关自身建设，各项人事工作取得了较好的成绩，为我省改革开放和建立社会主义市场经济体制提供了服务。

一、对三项改革做了充分的准备工作

推行国家公务员制度和机构改革、工资制度改革是我国政治体制改革的重要内容，也是建立社会主义市场经济体制、加快经济发展的重要条件。为了保证三项改革的顺利进行，我省做了实施前的各项准备工作。在推行国家公务员制度方面，经省委、省政府研究决定，成立了甘肃省推行国家公务员制度工作办公室，加强了领导。根据国家推行公务员制度的实施方案精神，结合我省实际，确定了我省推行国家公务员制度的指导思想、主要内容、实施范围和方法步骤，提出了争取用三年或更多一点时间在我省推行国家公务员制度的实施意见；积极培训骨干，系统学习公务员制度的基本内容，派出有关人员到北京、香港、加拿大参加公务员制度的培训，组织有试点条件的厅局人事干部参加人事部举办的培训班；利用报刊、电台等宣传媒介，公开宣传国家公务员制度，创造推行的舆论环境。在机构改革方面，主要抓了安排部署和方案的起草工作。根据省委七届八次全委扩大会议要求，研究起草了《关于全省机构改革的安排意见》，对我省机构改革的指导思想、内容重点、组织领导、审批程序、方法步骤等提出了明确的意见和要求，由省委、省政府正式印发全省各地。根据中央关于机构改革的精神，通过认真调查研究和广泛征求意见，起草了《甘肃省省级机构改革方案》、《县级机构改革实施方案》、《清理非常设机构意见》、《事业单位机构改革基本思路》等方案和实施办法。其中，《县级机构改革实施方案》在省、地、县10多个部门和单位召开了论证会；《清理非常设机构意见》几经酝酿，业已成熟；《事业单位机构改革基本思路》在省直有关部门及其所属事业单位征求了意见。开展了试点和测算工作，继续加强了对十四个机构改革试点县的指导工作。根据中央对市、县、乡各级机构分类定编的标准，对13个城市、67个县、1554个乡镇进行了分类，并对全省定编精简幅度作了测算。在工资制度改革方面，我们主要作了六项准备工作：第一，根据改革的主要内容，深入到我省十四个地、州、市和部分省直单位及中央在甘单位，调查工资、津贴、补贴等方面的情况，并协同人事部调查了我省部分县、市、区的地区津贴情况；第二，筹办并参加了人事部在兰州、西安召开的工资制度改革工作座谈会，参与了全国机关、事业单位工资制度改革方案及实施办法和地区津贴实施办法等五个征求意见稿的讨论，充分反映了我省在工资改革中存在的问题；第三，对全省机关事业单位增资情况，先后三次进行了选点、抽样测算，确定了各职务人员平均增资水平；第四，按照改革的主要精神，草拟了《甘肃省机关工作人员工资制度改革若干问题的处理意见》、《甘肃省事业单位工资制度改革中有关具体问题的处理意见》、《甘肃省关于机关事业单位工改中有关离退休人员增加离退休费若干问题的处理意见》、《甘肃省机关事业单位工资制度改革中有关地区津贴问题的处理意见》；第五，举办了工资业务骨干培训班，为工资制度改革培训了158名业务骨干。经过大量的准备工作，我省三项改革的推行实施工作，任务已经明确，条件已经具备，时机已经成熟，为省委、省政府全面安排部署创造了良好的条件。

二、知识分子工作得到了进一步加强

广大知识分子是我省经济建设和各项事业发展的重要力量。1993年，我们围绕尊重知识、尊重人才、为广大知识分子办实事、办好事、充分调动知识分子积极性的主题；进一步加强了知识分子工作。

(一)选拔评选了享受政府特殊津贴人员和省级优秀专家。根据国家和省上有关精神，在全省范围内继续开展了选拔享受政府特殊津贴人员的工作。组织初选和专家评议，经省委研究同意，向国家人事部报送了368名享受1993年政府特殊津贴人员。在全省范围内开展了评审省级优秀专家工作。

(二)继续做好延长部分高级专家退休年龄的工作。为缓解我省高级人才资源缺乏的矛盾，根据国家有关规定和省委领导同志的指示，我们与省委组织部一起，在广泛征求各方面意见的基础上，结合我省实际，联合下发了《关于进一步做好部分高级专家延长退休年龄工作的通知》，对高级专家延长退休年龄问题做了具体规定，重新明确了按条件、经报批延长年龄的高级专家不占用本单位专业技术职务限额的规定，为50名高级专家办理了延长退休年龄的审批手续，报经国家人事部批准4名杰出高级专家暂缓退离休，为这些同志继续在工作岗位上发挥学术带头人作用和培养中青年专业技术人员提供了条件。

(三)继续完善专业技术职务聘任制，加强了任职资格的审查及专业技术人员考核工作。在1992年下放部分单位专业技术职务评审权的基础上，进一步出台了一些配套政策。对评审任职资格做了补充规定，制定了评聘分开的具体办法，调整了破格晋升条件。全年新组建或调整高级评委会17个，组织召开高评会65次，评审通过正高级职务资格178人，副高级职务资格2639人。其中破格晋升正高职务16人，副高级职务326人。全省各级人事部门共评审通过中级职务任职资格6000人，初级职务任职资格8000人左右，为新就业的大中专毕业生考核定职12000人左右。审定高级专业技术名誉资格180多人。加强了资格考试的组织指导工作，经省编委批准成立了省职称考试中心，全年共组织全国统一的资格考试5次，参考51779人；举行外语统考2次，32992人；不具备规定学历的基础理论和专业知识考试5次，12865人。考试组织严密，纪律良好。同时，对全省的专业技术人员进行了任期考核和年度考核，为职称工作的制度化、规范化做了大量的具体工作。

（四）建立了专家人才库。组织力量对全省所有专家和具有高级任职资格人员进行了建档入库工作，并逐步录入计算机进行管理，为准确掌握高级专业技术人才状况，促进科学技术转化为生产力等方面打下了良好的基础。

（五）重视了专业技术干部队伍的建设。草拟了《关于促进我省中青年专业技术人才迅速成长的意见》，提出了9条措施；参与了甘肃科技人员外流情况及对策研究课题的调研；在《甘肃日报》、甘肃电台开辟专栏，宣传优秀专家的事迹。

三、人才市场开始起步运行

建立和培育人才市场是建立社会主义市场经济体制的客观要求。1993年进一步加快了改革步伐。第一，加强了人才市场的内部建设。省、地两级人事部门共建立人才市场13个，出台了《人才市场管理暂行规定》，确定了人才市场的服务方式和供需双方协议成交的办理方式，界定了人才市场的调节服务范围和对象，确定了人才市场的人才信息储存传递功能、人才流动调节功能、服务功能和管理功能等四大功能；建立了人才市场信息员队伍和人才供求信息网络，聘请了218名人才信息员，及时为省人才市场提供人才供求信息，服务于人才流动；指导全省各级人事部门的人才市场建设，为各地筹措17万元经费，帮助建立人才奖励基金；加强宣传，提供服务，全年共印发《甘肃人才市场信息》25000多份，编发了《甘肃国营大中型企业概况与人才需求》、《甘肃高校概况与人才培养》等书刊。第二，积极为人才交流提供服务。制定了《甘肃省招聘引进人才暂行规定》，为700多人办理了流动手续，受理人才流动仲裁60余起，推荐安排非在职“五大”生760多人，管理流动人员档案490余份，引进省外专业技术人才21人，办理辞职、辞退手续40余份，办理出国政审手续50多人次。组团参加“全国人才市场首届人才技术交流大会”，签定引进人才协议350份。组织省机械、电子、冶金、石化、建筑、建材、轻纺等行业及兰州、白银、天水、定西等地市人事部门的同志，先后四次到全国各地高等院校，引进我省急需专业的大学毕业生，通过艰苦细致的工作，外省高校回甘肃地方工作的毕业生占甘肃生源总数的28.89%。第三，积极稳妥地将非师范类大中专毕业生就业推进各级人才市场。通过双向选择落实就业去向，打破了传统的计划分配体制，对在市场调节下实现合理的人才资源配置进行了有益的尝试，使毕业生就业制度改革迈出了较大步伐。省内10所高校2400多名非师范类毕业生在省上举办的两次人才交流会上签定了1670多份就业合同，占统招毕业生的70%。全省共为毕业生就业举办人才市场会议23次，进入市场的毕业生30000多人次，签定合同与协议9000多份。在全省部分地区和部分高校成立了大中专毕业生择业指导机构，加强了毕业生就业的指导服务工作。加强了对政策导向和宏观调控，对自愿来我省工作，主动要求到边远、基层单位去的毕业生，筹集5万元给予了奖励，为生活基础不在甘肃的毕业生提供800——1000元的安家补助。为国有大中型企业、重点建设单位分配了1000多名毕业生，基本保证了这些单位的用人需求。人才市场的建立和运行，为促进人才合理流动，更好地发挥各类人才的作用创造了良好的条件。

四、继续做好干部队伍的宏观管理

加强干部队伍宏观控制和各项管理是人事工作的重要内容。1993年，我们继续加强了这方面的工作，较好地适应了我省改革开放和经济建设的需要。

（一）继续加强了干部队伍的宏观调控。在机关、事业单位职工人数和工资总额上，采取了分类管理、区别对待的管理办法。对县以上党政机关增加人员严格控制，对事业单位实行分类管理，从严格控制全额拨款事业单位增加职工，适当放宽差额拨款事业单位增人，对自收自支单位实行用人自主，放开内部分配。加强基层人员力量，制定了《关于乡镇农业技术推广机构定编后补充人员的实施意见》，草拟了《关于动员各类人员到乡镇企业工作的若干规定》，为充实基层干部力量提供了政策依据。同时，还为乡镇基层各站下达招聘干部计划5500余名，占国家下达我省干部指标总数的43%。进一步认真贯彻《全民所有制工业企业转换经营机制条例》精神，调查研究了给企业下放人事管理权后出现的新情况和新问题，加强了对企业人事制度改革的指导。

（二）搞活干部调配工作。1993年，干部调配工作认真贯彻执行1992年出台的各项政策措施，在实践中注意配套完善，研究解决实际执行中出现的问题，有效地避免了一放就乱，一管就死的被动局面。全年共为企业、事业和中央在甘单位审批调兰州干部1145人，这些人员流动比较合理，大多数充实到了科研和生产第一线。

（三）加强干部考录工作。根据国家人事部、公安部通知精神。研究提出了全省公检法、劳改劳教、林业公安系统以工代警人员考试录用干部的具体实施意见；组织了 4500 人的考试，按指标和条件录用了 2892 名干部；组织了银行系统的招干考试，审查录用了 1364 名干部。

(四)认真开展干部培训、任免、奖励工作。根据各系统新录用干部的实际，分期对 300 多名新录用干部进行了岗前培训。协同省教委对有关部门和行业举办的专业证书培训班进行了审查和验收。依照法律程序，在省政府换届中，按时完成了省直委办厅局主要领导的任免手续。参与了省审计局、省财政厅等 6 个系统的先进个人和先进集体的评比奖励活动。根据有关规定，会同省委组织部、省农委为获得农业丰收奖的 140 多名领导干部办理了奖励升级手续。

(五)进一步加强了退休干部管理工作。会同省委组织部制定了《关于进一步严格执行干部退(离)休制度的通知》，要求各地、各部门在实际工作中严格把关，坚持到龄即退。全年共为 23 名厅局级干部、322 名县处级干部办理了退(离)休手续。调整了我省国家机关、事业单位工作人员和离退休人员的护理费标准。成立了省退休人员服务公司，为退离休人员发挥余热、开展老有所为活动提供了条件。

(六)妥善安置军转干部。全年共安置军转干部 543 名，其中师职 5 名，团职 138 名，专业技术干部 138 名。对 5 名师职干部全部安排了实际职务。支持 22 名军转干部走自我安置的路子，还妥善安置了 86 名随调家属。

甘肃省监察工作为地方经济建设服务

省监察厅厅长

朱毓贤

1993 年 5 月底以前，根据中央机构改革的决定精神，全省各级监察机关与同级党的纪律检查机关合署办公，实行一套机构、两块牌子、两种职能。合署后，各级纪检监察机关在不断加强自身建设，以适应新体制要求的同时，以邓小平同志建设有中国特色社会主义理论为指导，认真贯彻党的十四大和中央纪委二次全会精神，紧紧围绕经济建设这个中心，全面履行纪检监察机关的职能，为维护全省政治稳定，促进改革和经济建设作了大量工作，取得了一定成效。

一、以查处违法违纪案件为重点，集中力量开展了反腐败斗争

1. 抓自查自纠，领导干部的廉洁自律有了明显进步。抓好党政机关县(处)级以上领导干部的廉洁自律是反腐败斗争的主要任务之一，省纪委、省监察厅要求各单位在自查自纠中把领导干部自查自纠同党内外群众监督相结合；把本单位的自查自纠和上级的督促检查相结合；把自查自纠与制定整改措施相结合。到年底，全省有 224 名在企业兼职的县(处)级以上领导干部已经辞去了一头的职务；党政机关创办的经济实体已有 1000 多个与原单位彻底脱钩。通过自查自纠，绝大多数领导干部在思想上受到了一次深刻的廉洁自律教育，抵制腐败的免疫力普遍有所增强。

2. 抓专项治理，群众反映强烈的一些不正之风得到有效遏制。一是积极配合农业部门，以纠正侵害农民利益的不正之风为突破口，重点查纠乱摊派、乱集资、乱收费问题，制止了一些行业“吃拿卡要罚”的违法违纪行为。二是集中整治了行政事业性乱收费问题。全省共清理出行政事业性乱收费项目 2541 个，收费标准 3300 个。到 12 月底，省上先后向社会公布取消了三批共 141 项收费项目。三是重点整治了带有行业特点的不正之风。各行各业结合各自实际，认真开展专项治理。如党政机关着重纠正了用公款大吃大喝和在公务活动中以权谋私问题；公检法和行政执法部门集中查纠了徇情枉法，吃拿卡要问题；医疗单位注重查纠了坐吃回扣、搭车开药和乱收费问题；金融系统集中纠正了以贷谋私、拆借资金问题；粮食系统狠刹了压级压价、短斤少两的问题；水电系统着重查纠了以水以电谋私的问题。四是认真清理和纠正了公费出国(境)旅游的不正之风。针对一些地方、机关和团体违反规定，巧立名目组团公费出国(境)旅游的问题，5 月份，省上及时发出了严格制止公费出国(境)旅游的通知，从 8 月份开始，又组织力量进行了清理纠正，取消了一些不符合规定的出国(境)团组，使这一不正之风得到了遏制。

3. 抓案件查处，严肃处理了一批违法违纪干部和党员。一年来，全省纪检监察机关共立案查处违法违纪案件 1569 件，其中 52 名县(处)级干部和 5 名地(厅)级干部受到了处分。一批违法案件及时移送司法机关处理。特别是下半年以来，各级纪检监察机关紧紧围绕中央和省委关于开展反腐败斗争的部署，认真抓了对违法违纪案件的查处。仅 9 至 12 月，共查处违法违纪案件 610 件，有 550 名党员干部受到了党纪政纪处分，其中县(处)级干部 41 人，地(厅)级干部 4 人。

二、开展了对党的路线、方针、政策和国家法律、法规执行情况的监督检查

一是围绕减轻农民负担开展监督检查。省监察厅会同省农业厅督促省直 22 个相关部门，对涉及农民负担的文件、项目进行清理，在此基础上，宣布废除、修改了一些涉及农民负担的文件。省上取消不合理的农民负担项目 66 项，部分取消 20 项，同地县有关部门查处伤农坑农案件 384 起。各地还对夏季粮油农副产品收购工作开展了执法监察，督促金融、财政、粮食、供销等部门，从资金筹措兑现、粮油调运销售等环节入手，加强协调管理，保证了夏季粮油等农副产品收购工作的顺利进行，全省基本没有出现“打白条”问题。

二是围绕全民所有制工业企业转换经营机制条例的贯彻落实开展监督检查。重点对一些单位及其工作人员中设置障碍，勒卡干扰企业转换经营机制的行为进行了认真地查纠，解决了一些比较突出的问题。省监察厅还制定下发了《甘肃省监察机关处理国有工业企业对侵犯其合法权益的行政行为申诉的办法》，在实践中收到了比较好的效果。

三是围绕中央方针政策的贯彻落实开展监督检查。省纪委、省监察厅根据中央纪委、监察部《关于严格遵守党纪政纪，保证党中央、国务院有关经济工作的各项政策和措施贯彻落实的通知》精神，结合实际提出并印发了具体贯彻意见。各级党委、政府和纪检监察机关把执行党纪政纪情况作为反腐败斗争的一项重要内容，认真地开展监督检查，较好地解决了一些地方和单位存在的有令不行、有禁不止、弄虚作假，以及形式主义、严重官僚主义等问题。

三、大张旗鼓地开展廉政勤政的宣传教育，并加强了调查研究和理论建设工作

全省纪检监察机关结合学习贯彻党的十四大和中央纪委二次全会精神，利用各种形式，有计划、有目的地在全省范围内开展党风党纪和反腐倡廉的宣传教育活动。先后多次举办了报告会、演讲会和知识问答，摄制、购置、录制电视教育片1046部，撰写教育文章769篇，发行省纪委、省监察厅主办的《党风通讯》(与《甘肃监察》合刊)杂志和《反腐败学习材料专辑》100多万册。同时，省上和各地还有选择地在广播、电视、报纸上公开集中宣传报道了一批有普遍教育意义的典型案例，弘扬了正气，震慑了邪恶。

为适应社会主义市场经济体制的要求，各级纪检监察机关面对新情况、新问题，深入基层，深入实际，认真开展调查研究，积极探索新的工作方法和途径。在围绕反腐败斗争、党风廉政建设、减轻农民负担、案件检查、合署办公等问题开展调查中，对涉及全局性的问题，均研究提出解决的措施和意见，增强了工作的指导性。各级纪检监察机关还从本地实际出发，注重加强对新形势下反腐倡廉的理论研究，制定了一些政策规定，对促进经济发展起到了积极作用。

发挥侨务优势 振兴甘肃经济

省人民政府副秘书长、省政府侨务办公室主任
石作峰

全省各级侨务办公室是同级人民政府领导和管理侨务工作的部门，其基本任务是：保护华侨和归侨、侨眷的正当合法权益，广泛团结海外华侨和归侨、侨眷，增进同外籍华人的友好情谊，为振兴中华、统一祖国，发展同各国人民的团结友好与合作交流而奋斗。侨务部门的主要工作对象包括：国(境)外的华侨、华人和港澳同胞；国内归侨、侨眷和定居内地的港澳同胞及港澳同胞眷属。

1979年，省政府外事办公室下设侨务处，1982年改为侨办。1984年7月省委中发1984(15)号文决定省侨办为正地级单位，划归政府序列。1986年省编委下文侨办设秘书处和侨政处，并将原来的5人编制扩充到12人。1991年5月，经有关部门批准，成立了“甘肃海外交流协会”，实现一套人马两块牌子。

1993年的全省侨务工作，以邓小平同志建设有中国特色的社会主义理论为指导，认真贯彻十四大精神，围绕省委、省政府的中心工作以及1993年国务院侨务工作会议精神，以经济建设为中心，从甘肃省情、侨情实际出发，解放思想，开拓创新，进一步发挥侨的优势，强化服务，取得了较好的成绩。

一、制定符合本省侨情的侨务法规

《中华人民共和国归侨侨眷权益保护法》于1990年9月7日第七届全国人民代表大会常务委员会第十五次会议通过，正式颁布实施。这是我国第一部关于保护归侨、侨眷合法权益的政策性法规。1993年7月19日，中华人民共和国国务院第118号令，公布了《中华人民共和国归侨侨眷权益保护法实施办法》。这充分体现了党和政府对广大归侨、侨眷和海外侨胞的关心和侨务工作的重视，在社会上产生了广泛的影响。甘肃省地处内陆。经济比较落后，归侨、侨眷较沿海省份少。为充分发挥全省归侨、侨眷们在对外开放中的积极作用，有利于本省经济振兴和社会发展，省侨办在各级侨务部门大力宣传《中华人民共和国归侨侨眷权益保护法》、《中华人民共和国归侨侨眷权益保护法实施办法》的同时，历时三年多的时间，八易其稿，完成了《甘肃省实施归侨侨眷权益保护法办法》(以下简称《省实施办法》)的定稿工作，1994年1月29日经甘肃省八届人大常委会第七次会议审议通过。这对我们贯彻国务院的侨务工作会议精神，立足国内、面向海外三千万华侨、华人，树立大侨务思想，做好甘肃的侨务工作，尤其做好归侨、侨眷知识分子工作，充分发挥其海外关系优势，对加快甘肃经济发展具有十分重要的意义。此法公布后，在归侨、侨眷中引起了热烈的反响。一致认为，这是全省侨界政治生活中的一件大喜事。既反映了全省广大归侨、侨眷、海外侨胞和侨务工作者的共同愿望

和要求，而且也符合全省人民的利益。充分体现了党和政府对归侨、侨眷的关心和爱护，有利于激发广大海内外侨胞的爱国热情。在《省实施办法》中，根据我省情况，对部分条款适当地放宽了照顾幅度，如第十九条规定：回国工作30年以上的归侨职工在我省退休时，其退休金与原工资的差额，由所在单位补足；第十七条中规定的“三侨”考生以及全国、全省劳动模范侨眷的子女报考省内各类大学、大专、中等专业学校和技工学校按本省招生有关规定给予照顾。

二、开展以经济建设为中心的全方位服务

在邓小平同志建设有中国特色社会主义理论指引下，侨务部门抓住大发展的机遇，开展以经济建设为中心的全方位服务。

据不完全统计，省侨办1993年年内共接待奥地利、美国、加拿大、马来西亚、印尼、泰国、缅甸、印度、尼泊尔等国家和香港、澳门地区的侨胞、港澳同胞43批，计140多人次。促成了合资合作项目3个，外商总投资额2000万美元，促进了甘肃经济发展。1993年10月，经省侨办牵头组织，郭琨副省长率团赴深圳华侨城参加国务院侨办等单位举办的“中国大中型企业对外经济技术合作洽谈会”，兰州炼油厂、酒泉钢铁公司、兰州平板玻璃厂等10家大中型企业参加了会议。会上与外商签订意向性协议两项，总投资额6123万美元，协议外资额1808万美元。

由省侨办牵线，兰州饭店与外商合资的“丽都大酒店”开业；省侨办为敦煌市中旅社引进510万美元筹建的“敦煌国际大酒店”年初破土动工；甘肃省侨汇公司与香港东兴行投资有限公司合资创办、港方投资35万美元的甘肃侨港旅游娱乐有限公司成立。同时，为进一步积累侨务资金，按照政企分开的原则，省侨办所属“甘肃中旅商场”、甘肃华侨经济发展公司的“华侨商场”开业，该公司与外商合资的“金厦房地产有限公司”及“甘肃奥侨汽车修配有限公司”也相继营业。《甘肃省人民政府侨务办公室贯彻全民所有制工业企业转换经营机制实施办法》出台实施。各地、州、市侨务部门也相继根据不同情况，创办了经济实体，全年新创经济实体14个，注册资金400万元。既解决了部分归侨、侨眷子女的就业问题，又为侨务工作顺利发展创造了条件。

甘肃海外交流协会是中国海外交流协会的团体会员。海协会的宗旨是：广泛联系海外华侨、华人、港澳台同胞及其团体，增进了友好情谊，发展合作交流，为统一祖国，振兴中华服务。发挥海协民间社团的优势，可以弥补侨务工作方面的某些不足。海协会通过广交朋友，开展海外联谊。增进了我们与海外侨胞的友谊。聘请的海协海外理事，也正积极为海协做大量有益的工作。

三、不断深化、加强侨务宣传工作

由于历史的原因，世界以致有的沿海省市对我省缺乏了解，一些旅居海外的原甘肃籍华侨、华人对我省疑虑重重。只知敦煌莫高窟而不知甘肃，家中挂着“陇西堂”而不知陇西就在甘肃。这无疑给我们的侨务工作的开展带来了一定的困难。要吸引外资，必须首先使世界了解甘肃，这方面做了以下几点工作：

开展一封信活动。我省旅居海外的华侨、华人分布在美国、印尼、马来西亚、日本以及港澳等54个国家和地区，他们在省内的眷属与我们侨务工作有密切的联系。通过归侨、侨眷向他们在海外的亲友介绍甘肃改革开放以来的大好形势和巨大变化，欢迎他们来省内探亲访友，宣传来去自由的方针。对个别仍存疑虑的重点人，侨务部门主动出面向他们介绍国内情况，打消他们的顾虑，使得有的人毅然回乡，康慨解囊，资助办学。有的表示将在有生之年为家乡经济建设多做贡献。

寓宣传于接待之中。近年来，来甘肃省探亲、旅游、洽谈经济合作项目的华侨、华人、港澳同胞逐年增多，各级侨务部门通过热情接待，强化对他们的思想感染力，唤起他们对甘肃的理解和支持。积极来甘肃省投资办厂。

以宣促联。省侨办和甘肃海外交流协会通过“走出去、请进来”及函电、信件等多种形式的联络，密切了与海外华侨、华人社团和知名人士的联系，先后与香港南源永芳集团公司、奥地利华人总会、香港扶轮社、泰华妇女联合会、新加坡李氏宗亲社团、世界（陇西）青商会等十多个社团建立了友好关系。

通过对李氏文化的宣传，激发了世界李氏华侨、华人的寻根访祖热情，增进了他们对甘肃省的感情，一批海外李氏知名人士期待着来甘肃省寻根，这将有利于甘肃省的对外改革开放，也将会给甘肃省的旅游业带来契机。

1993年甘肃省外事工作概述

省人民政府外事办公室主任

叶绍袁

1993年，我省外事部门在省委、省政府和外交部、全国友协的领导下，认真贯彻执行党的外交路线和方针、政策，坚持对外开放，努力为经济建设服务，使全省外事工作有了新的发展。

1993年，全省共接待来自30多个国家、地区和国际组织的公费邀请外宾206批，1185人，其中从事经济技术、科技交流、洽谈进口贸易、来甘投资以及各类专家学者的人数，占来访总人数的70%以上。全省因公出访人数达1176批，4284人。出访人员中执行经贸任务、劳务输出、科技文化和体育交流及其它业务活动的人数，占全部出国人数的90%以上。

1993年，我省对外友好城市工作有了新的发展。天水市与澳大利亚本迪戈市正式结好。白银市、嘉峪关市与哈萨克斯坦齐姆肯特市、江布尔市的结好，已获全国友协批准。金昌市与澳大利亚库尔加迪市已经开始友好交往。敦煌市与日本臼杵市、镰仓市发展友好关系的意见已上报全国友协。另外，与非洲国家的城市结好工作已初步开展起来。

1993年，我省地市外事工作迈出了新的步伐。兰州、天水、白银、金昌、嘉峪关等市充分利用已有的渠道，积极扩大对外交往，进行经济、贸易、技术方面的合作。先后在国外办起一批工厂、宾馆、商店和餐馆，初步获得经济效益。

一、加强对外事工作的领导，充分发挥外办的归口管理作用

对外开放的不断扩大，对外交往的日益增多，越来越要求外事工作必须加强宏观管理。为此，我们在工作中注重发挥本部门上下勾通、政策指导、工作协调和服务这三个方面的作用。在及时传达贯彻党和国家外交政策的同时，我们先后连续出台了三个政策性文件，并着重解决了实施中的具体问题。通过涉外部部门负责人会议、干部培训班、国际形势及政策通报会等形式，宣传政策、传递信息。全年出版《甘肃外事》杂志6期，指导了工作，密切了与基层的联系。遇到涉外单位重要外事活动，我们积极参加，进行现场协调和指导。

二、加强对因公出国(境)工作的监督和管理，为经济建设服务

近两年来我省因公出访团组和人数大幅度增加。我办根据中央、国务院和省委、省政府的有关政策和规定，加强了对此方面工作的监督和管理。一是把审核报批工作同促进经济建设、反腐倡廉有机地结合起来。对于符合政策规定、有实质内容的出访，或涉及我省经济建设的重要项目及关系到交往全局的出访，我办“开绿灯”，给予及时审批，并认真做好服务。使其顺利成行。否则，我们不予审批，并做好解释工作。我省于1993年4月在香港举办了经贸洽谈会，我办与省外经贸厅一起，在短时间内，完成了250人的赴港审批、办照及其它手续，保证了洽谈会的顺利进行。二是把宏观管理和分类指导结合起来。出国任务的审批工作，我们全面实行了由省外办、外经贸厅、省科委和兰州市分别审批，省外办统一审核办照的办法，简化了程序，提高了效率。另外，还对各单位在护照保管等具体工作上，给予指导和帮助。三是把出国审批与后续服务结合起来。我办采取出国审批和办理护照签证及代订国际机票、车票一条龙的办法。在北京设立签证办事机构，使出国团组一次委托全程收益。全年我们自办签证415批，1487人次，受到有关方面的好评。

三、发挥友城工作优势，拓宽对外交往渠道

首先把为省辖市发展友城作为近期的工作重点。在调查摸底、友好交往的基础上，选择适合对象，并做好了前期准备工作。其次讲求实效，努力为经济建设服务。我办组织了省政府代表团赴独联体四国访问，为我省在这些国家开展经贸合作和科技文化交流摸清了情况，找到了对策。另外，还通过友城渠道向日本、新西兰派出了医学、建筑、语言、果树等方面的留学人员。同时还协助省国际公司向日本选派了建筑行业的研修生33名。另外，还积极开展民间结好活动，接待了几十个国外民间友好团体的来访。

四、搞好接待服务工作，为引进人才和资金打下基础

我办在接待外宾过程中，注意把重点落实在扩大甘肃在国际上的影响和提高甘肃的知名度上，寓宣传于接待之中。除较高规格的团组外，我们还邀请10多名外国常驻记者来甘肃参观、采访。我们根据其合理要求，客观、主动、热情地为他们展示甘肃各方面的发展、变化，使他们写出一批较客观、友好的文章，在国内外产生良好影响。与此同时我办还利用接待，积极为有关单位提供信息、牵线搭桥，取得了经济效果。另外，还从促进经济发展的角度，在14个大专院校进行了聘请外籍教师资格认可的调查研究和审批工作，并协同有关部门积极审核报批，使我省年内新增开放县区14个，这样使我省对外国人开放地区已达整个县区的60%以上。

1993年秋天，我办利用与美国工商界及驻美使、领馆的关系，促成省政府赴美招商小组的成功访问。为1994年我省在美举办的经贸洽谈会的成功，打下良好的基础。

中国人民政治协商会议甘肃省委员会

政协甘肃省第七届委员会

【七届一次会议】1993年1月7——14日在兰州举行。本届委员503人。实际到会484人。1月6日下午，分别举行预备会议和首次主席团会议。预备会议由六届省政协主席葛士英主持，中共甘肃省委副书记孙英介绍了七届委员会全体委员构成状况和会议主席团建议组成人员的基本情况。会议通过了主席团和秘书长名单。首次主席团会议推选申效曾等11人为主席团常务主席，通过了会议议程(草案)、日程和分组办法等事项。1月7日，大会正式开幕。大会的执行主席是申效曾、黄正清、黎中、韩正卿、朱宣人、贡唐仓·丹贝旺旭、王平、陈剑虹、应中逸、杜大仕、徐尚和。申效曾主持会议，朱宣人致开幕词。省上党政军领导和老同志应邀出席开幕大会。中共甘肃省委书记顾金池同志作重要讲话。他说，5年来，我省六届各级政协组织，各民主党派、无党派爱国人士，始终不渝地坚持党的领导，坚决认真地履行"政治协商、民主监督"的职责，紧紧把握和围绕经济建设这个中心，在促进甘肃的改革开放和维护社会安定团结等方面，做出了积极贡献。希望七届政协组织很好地总结和坚持上一届包括历史上其它各届成功的经验和做法，并且在原有的基础上再发展、再创造，进一步推进政协各项工作开展。1月8日，全体委员列席省八届人大一次会议。会议期间，委员们认真学习了中共十四大会议精神，讨论了顾金池的讲话和贾志杰省长在省八届人大一次会议上所作的《政府工作报告》，以及计划、财政报告等。委员们就我省经济上新台阶提出了许多意见和建议。主要有：转变观念，发展社会主义市场经济；要高度重视农业和农村工作；要重视培养人才，大力发展教育事业；进一步加快个体私营经济发展；努力做好民族宗教工作。此外，委员们还就我省矿产资源的开发、转换国有企业经营机制、发展科技、文化、医疗卫生、体育事业以及人民政协自身建设等发表了许多意见、建议。1月12日举行了第二次主席团会议。会议通过了主席、副主席、秘书长和常务委员候选人名单(草案)，通过了选举办法(草案)等。14日上午，大会进行选举。会议选举申效曾为主席，黄正清、黎中、韩正卿、朱宣人、贡唐仓·丹贝旺旭、王平、陈剑虹、应中逸、杜大仕为副主席，徐尚和为秘书长，丁毓国等98人为常委。14日下午，大会闭幕。会议通过了七届委员会提案委员会关于七届一次会议提案情况和审查意见的报告，通过了七届一次会议决议。决议指出，人民政协要按照省委、省政府的战略部署，充分发挥综合人才库的作用，坚持为经济建设服务，为发展社会生产力服务，为加快我省改革开放步伐，加快建立社会主义市场经济体制做出贡献。申效曾主席在闭幕会上讲话中对会议取得的成果进行了总结。要求全体政协委员和各级政协组织，深入学习十四大精神，认真履行"政治协商、民主监督"职能，积极参政议政，为推进经济体制改革，为我省九十年代经济上新台阶做贡献；会议期间收到提案329个，是历届会议较多的一次。

【常务委员会议】七届第1次会议1993年1月15日在兰州举行。会议研究讨论并原则通过了1993年常委会的工作要点，主要内容为：1993年工作总的思路是：深入学习、贯彻中共十四大精神，用邓小平同志建设有中国特色社会主义理论武装思想，指导人民政协工作；高举爱国主义、社会主义旗帜，坚持党的基本路线，认真履行"政治协商，民主监督"职能，为推进社会主义民主和法制建设服务；进一步解放思想，振奋精神，发挥政协综合人才库的优势，为加快全省改革开放步伐，提前一年完成"八五"计划，提前三年实现国民生产总值翻两番，促进经济上新台阶做贡献。围绕省委、省政府的工作部署。重点抓好以下几个方面的工作：一、深入学习、贯彻中共十四大精神，用建设中国特色社会主义理论统一思想，增强贯彻党的基本路线的自觉性和坚定性。二、紧紧围绕我省经济建设的中心任务，充分发挥政协的人才智力优势，为甘肃经济上新台阶献计出力。三、继续贯彻执行《中共中央关于坚持和完善中国共产党领导的多党合作和政治协商制度的意见》和全国政协制定的《关于政治协商、民主监督的暂行规定》，积极参政议政，在推进社会主义民主政治建设中发挥应有的作用。四、发挥人民政协团结协调功能，为维护我省团结稳定的政治局面服务。五、利用各种生动有效的形式，开展祖国统一联谊工作。六、坚持两手抓、两手都要硬的方针，积极为社会主义精神文明建设服务。七、加强政协自身建设，进一步改革工作方法，不断提高政协工作水平。

第2次会议 1993年4月26—29日在兰州举行。省政协常委85人出席了会议。这次会议的主要议题是讨论兰州市改革开放、加快经济建设问题。会议传达学习了全国政协八届一次会议精神和中共甘肃省委七届八次全委扩大会议精神；听取讨论了省政协委员关于兰州对外开放工作情况的视察报告；任命了省政协副秘书长、办公厅及各专门委员会正副主任，通过了各专门委员会委员名单。会上，常委们就兰州市改革开放工作的情况进行了两天的大会讨论，他们一致认为，1992年以来，兰州市认真贯彻中共十四大精神，充分利用国家给予的政策，以开放促改革、促开发，内陆开放城市建设的路子对头，起头良好，改革开放的大环境正在逐步形成。兰州市的基础条件和地理位置同沿海、周边地区相比，在改革开放方面有它不利的一面，要想经济建设更快地发展，改革开放就必须要有突破性的进展，走超常规、跳跃式的发展路子，加大改革开放力度，采取更加有力的措施和办法，促进经济更好更快地发展。为此，常委们提出如下建议：一、以建设有中国特色的社会主义理论为指导，进一步解放思想，更新观念。二、兰州市作为内陆开放城市，要进一步增强开放意识，"软、硬件"并重，努力改善投资环境。三、加快经济建设步伐。四、发挥科教优势，加快兰州发展。会议结束时申效曾主席和全国政协常委李子奇讲了话。

第3次会议 1993年9月22——25日在兰州举行。省政协常委74人出席了会议。会议期间，副省长崔正华向常委们通报了全省经济形势和发展农村社会主义市场经济的情况，省委常委、省纪委书记饶凤翥介绍了省委关于反腐败斗争的安排部署和全省的反 腐败情况。会议的主要议题是讨论发展农村社会主义市场经济问题。会前，省政协就此问题组织委员们进行了视察并写出了视察报告。在两天的大会讨论中，常委们就加强农村科技开发、建立农村服务体系，搞活流通以及反腐败等问题提出了建议，会议还通过了人事任免事项。会议结束时，省委副书记杨振杰和省政协副主席黎中讲了话。杨振杰在讲话中指出，各级党委要进一步重视统战工作，为他们开展工作创造良好的环境和条件。各级政协组织要找准位置，抓住重点，发挥优势，提高参政议政水平。黎中在讲话中强调，人民政协在为农村发展市场经济服务方面是大有可为的。要继续加强对农村基础地位的认识，继续调整农村经济结构，培育市场主体，按产业化组织农村市场经济，对农业实行政策保护与扶持，加强精神文明建设，各级政府要转变职能，加强对农村市场经济的领导。

第4次会议 1993年12月28——30日在兰州举行。77名常委出席了会议。会议的中心议题是学习贯彻中共十四届三中全会精神。会议认真学习了《中共中央关于建立社会主义市场经济体制若干问题的决定》和中共甘肃省第八次代表大会精神；通过了《关于认真学习贯彻中共十四届三中全会精神的决议》和《关于召开中国人民政治协商会议甘肃省第七届委员会第二次会议决定》。会议表示完全拥护并坚决执行中共十四届三中全会精神。会议要求全省各级政协组织和政协委员，更好地履行协商监督职能，围绕建立社会主义市场经济体制的宏伟目标，选好角度，发挥优势，做出贡献。会议结束时申效曾主席和王平副主席讲了话。申效曾在讲话中要求在参与建设社会主义市场经济的伟大实践；打好扶贫攻坚战；做好民族宗教工作，巩固安定团结的政治局面；发展甘肃教育事业；积极参与反腐败斗争等方面积极探索，做出努力。会议决定于1994年3月下旬或4月上旬在兰召开政协甘肃省第七届委员会第二次会议。

【专门委员会工作】

提案法制委员会

一年来，通过多种形式宣传引导，提倡围绕党和政府的中心任务搞调研、选题目，使委员提案普遍质量较高，层次较深。在办案中实行联合办案、现场办案、开门办案、跟踪办案，加强了党派、团体提案工作；对贴紧党和政府的中心任务、人民群众普遍关心的重要提案，实行重点交办和催办，收到了较好的效果。七届一次会议以来，共收到提案353件，立案351件，提案中属于经济建设方面的194件，占总数的55.3%。截止11月底，已办理答复329件，占提案总数的93.7%，其中已落实102件，占办复提案数的31%。对筛选出的22件重要提案，已落实采纳和列入计划的20件，如省民盟《建议我省采取实际措施，扩大高校办学自主权的提案》，省教委已列为高等教育改革重点。选择了委员意见集中、人民群众反映强烈、对我省社会经济关系重大的兰州市大气污染问题，经调查论证，起草了《关于防治兰州市大气污染的建议案》，经主席会议讨论后，作为省政协建议案送省政府，有关部门正在制定具体落实方案。在法制工作方面，组织人员对甘肃省三资企业基本情况及当前存在的问题进行了两次调查；配合了全国政协常委俞雷同志率队的调查组在甘肃对危害社会治安的严重犯罪和执法问题进行的调查；组织委员讨论了省政府送交的《甘肃社会治安综合治理条例》，提出了具体的修改意见；法律服务所为委员和社会群众积极提供法律服务和咨询。

学习宣传妇女青年委员会

今年根据省政协常委会工作要点的安排，负责筹办了全省县级政协领导工作研讨班，在研究安排、撰写讲稿、编印材料、筹集经费、组织管理、各项服务等方面做了大量工作。有74个县(市、区)的政协主任或副主席参加了研讨学习。研讨班取得了良好的成效，委员们把组织委员和基层政协组织学习领会邓小平同志建设有中国特色社会主义理论作为主要任务。一年来共编发学习资料7期、1.37万份、26.74万字。为了加深理解党的十四大报告精神，还印发了中共中央学校十位同志编写的十讲辅导材料。《邓小平文选》第三卷出版发行后，筹办了省政协中心学习组召集的在兰部分常委、委员200多人参加学习《邓选》第三卷和中共十四届三中全会《决定》讨论会。为了帮助委员和基层政协领会社会主义市场经济理论，将江泽民总书记的文章《当前的经济工作》、陈锦华同志在全国经济体制改革座谈会上的讲话等学习材料印发给委员和基层政协；同时邀请兰州大学经济系教授李育良向在兰委员作了辅导报告。年初各级政协换届后，为了使新一届政协委员和基层政协及时了解党在新时期的统一战线理论、方针、政策，认真贯彻好全国政协八届一次会议精神，印发了李瑞环、叶选平、吴学谦同志在全国政协八届一次会议和八届一、二次常委会上的讲话，汇集印发了省委、省政协领导同志在全省县级政协领导工作研讨班上的讲话、讲课材料。

文史资料委员会

出版了《甘肃文史资料选辑》两

辑(第36、37辑);派员参加了八届全国政协第一次文史资料工作会议,为《中华文史资料文库》选送稿件;完成了全国大型协作书《侵华日军暴行总录》有关甘肃的稿件征编任务;调查和组织了《中华老字号》的有关资料。

经济科技委员会

一年来围绕甘肃的改革开放和经济建设完成专题调查4项。配合省、市政协联合视察团,对兰州市建设内陆开放城市的工作进行了视察,提出了进一步解放思想,转变观念;加强基础设施建设,"嫁接"改造老企业、开发现代农业积极大胆地引进吸收国际国内先进技术和管理经验;抓好开发区建设;深化外贸体制改革,大力培育和完善市场体系等8条建议。与此同时,对兰州市的环境污染治理,进行了专题调研,提出了加快"二热"管网建设和煤制气尽快发挥效益的建议。组织部分委员,对平凉、庆阳地区农村经济发展情况进行了专题视察,在视察中委员们提出,要使平、庆地区农村经济更快地发展,应解决进一步解放思想、转变观念;严格控制农业生产资料价格,调动农民种粮积极性;减轻农民负担;加强和完善农村社会化服务体系等问题。调查报告列为七届三次常委会的主要议题之一。在对兰州、白银等科技成果转化情况的调查中,针对两地存在的一些问题,提出如下建议:1.建立常设技术信息市场,沟通技术的供需渠道;2.疏通银行科技开发贷款的渠道,建立科技成果扩大基金;3.制订切实可行的扶持科技成果转化的优惠政策;4.鼓励科技人员向经济建设主战场——基层转移。还向兰州地区的委员发函,围绕加快兰州改革开放问题开展献计献策活动,先后有20余名委员提出了意见和建议。

农业委员会

年初,举行全体委员会议,讨论通过了委员会《工作简则》和1993年《工作要点》。委员会把工作重点放在调查研究上,抓住对全省农业生产发展有重要意义的问题,组织委员进行视察、调查。提出了意见和建议,受到了有关方面的重视和采纳。先后对张掖、武威地区农村社会主义市场经济发展情况;河西农民负担情况;对联系点会宁县工农业发展情况;对兰州、白银沿黄灌区加快开发农业水土资源情况等进行了4次视察和调查活动。《关于张掖、武威地区农村社会主义市场经济发展情况的报告》列为省政协七届三次常委会议的主要议题之一,作为大会重点发言,其主要意见和建议,省政协会后向省委、省政府的报告中作为重要内容。先后3次召开座谈会,对全省农业问题、扶贫工作进行专题讨论和研究,提出了意见和建议。为了引导农民走向市场,收集整理《景泰县八道泉乡王庄村积极发展集体经济快速致富奔小康》、《张掖市上秦乡安里闸村转换农业劳动力兴办集体合作及股份制企业》、《和政县城关镇西关村农民马亦天大规模租赁土地种养加综合开发创效益》3个典型材料,印发全省,收效良好。

教育文化卫生体育委员会

根据委员会工作要点,今年在教文医卫等方面,组织委员进行了以下调查研究工作。教育方面,在全省教育工作会议之前,先后组织教育界委员进行四次座谈讨论,提出了扩大高校办学自主权;解决高校教师队伍建设中亟待解决的问题;进一步加强基础教育,控制高中,发展职业技术教育;进一步加强少数民族教育工作等6条意见、建议。甘肃省贯彻落实《纲要》的意见公布以后,又先后举行了7次调查座谈会,征询了8所高校、9所中学、幼儿园中的90多位省、市、区政协委员以及院校中各民主党派负责人、无党派人士和学校领导同志意见,经认真研究论证,对贯彻实施《纲要》和《教师法》又提出了4项建议:1.广泛进行"百年大计,教育第一"的宣传教育;2.增加教育投入,减轻学校负担;3.采取积极有力措施,稳定教师队伍;4.切实改进和加强各类学校的管理,抓好学生的德育工作。文化方面,为办好第4届中国艺术节举行了"环境艺术研讨会",对美化兰州环境,从绿化、雕塑、市容与卫生,兰州市人文景观的发挥利用方面提出了意见。省上和兰州市采纳了不少建议。医卫方面,为了发展甘肃医药学业,举行了小型座谈会,对中药专家作了访问。11月中、下旬省卫生厅依据卫生部的通知,为贯彻落实党中央、国务院关于开展反腐败斗争,认真纠正部门和行业不正之风精神,在全省进行了医疗机构行业作风抽样调查,委员会派员参加了此项工作。

民族宗教委员会

民族宗教工作在多民族的甘肃省有着特殊重要的地位,委员会围绕增进民族团结,稳定全局和振兴少数民族地区经济积极开展工作。组织部分委员,对临夏民族经济开发试验区的建设情况,进行了专题视察和调查研究,产生了《关于临夏民族经济开发试验区的视察报告》。《报告》提出了以下建议:对市场经济发展中出现的繁荣和不景气交替的现象,应有正确的认识和相应的对策措施;对少数民族地区地方的财政能力呈下降趋势的问题,应引起足够的重视等。下半年对兰州地区的委员进行了访问,广泛听取意见和建议,将了解到的有关重视发挥科研部门委员作用的建议,以及要求进一步落实好宗教房地产遗留问题的呼吁,及时向省委、省政府有关部门作了反映,全国统战工作会议以后,召开了在兰委员"学习《邓选》第三卷和贯彻全国统战工作会议精神座谈会"。结合学习《邓选》第三卷重点讨论了搞好民族、宗教工作问题。

祖国统一联谊委员会

发挥委员优势，为“三引进”牵线搭桥，先后引进台资、港资在甘肃地区兴办宾馆、农贸中心、农副产品加工、食品等产业，为甘肃的经济建设做贡献。进一步对“陇西堂”的筹建情况进行调查。陇西县是我国李氏族生息繁衍的祖地，省政协通过几年来的各种会议、委员提案等形式，呼吁并促进省委、省政府批准在陇西筹建“陇西堂”，以利海内外李姓同胞寻根敬祖，发展与台港和海外的联谊。今年委员会两次去陇西县，对“陇西堂”的筹建情况做进一步的调查了解，帮助解决具体问题，促进建设进程。组织部分委员赴敦煌，对敦煌旅游开发区进行了专题调查，就影响开发区发展的交通不便、电力供应不足、水源开发危及自然景观、合资合作项目资金不能到位等问题，提出了解决意见和对策，报请省政府参考。一年中共接待台、港及海外客人9批15人。编辑出版了《陇原乡音》一书，向台、港、澳及海外同胞宣传甘肃改革开放以来的巨大变化。

民主党派和工商联

民革甘肃省委员会概况

中国国民党革命委员会(简称民革)是由原中国国民党民主派和其他爱国民主人士所创建，是具有政治联盟特点的、致力于建设有中国特色社会主义和祖国统一事业的政党。

民革在现阶段的政治纲领是，高举爱国主义和社会主义旗帜，遵循建设有中国特色社会主义理论，坚定不移地贯彻执行以经济建设为中心，坚持四项基本原则；坚持改革开放的基本路线，动员全体党员，团结所联系的人士，发扬孙中山爱国、革命和不断进步的精神，发挥自己的特点和优势，履参政议政，民主监督的职责，为巩固和扩大爱国统一战线，维护安定团结的政治局面，推进改革开放和社会主义现代化建设，健全社会主义民主和法制。促“一国两制”和平统一祖国，把我国建设成为富强、民主、文明的社会主义现代化国家而奋斗。

一、甘肃民革沿革

1951年4月10日，民革兰州市分部筹备委员会正式成立，推选筹备委员12人，李翰园为召集人。

1954年12月31日，民革甘肃省分部筹备委员会正式成立，委员17人，邓宝珊为召集人，李翰园、袁金章为副召集人。甘肃省分部筹委会下辖银川市、天水市、武威县3个支部筹备委员会和兰州市11个基层小组。

1956年6月，在兰州召开了民革甘肃省第一次代表大会。选举出委员31人，候补委员7人，组成民革甘肃省第一届委员会，推选邓宝珊为主任委员，李翰园、袁金章、水梓、王治岐为副主任委员，俞方皋为秘书长。

1958年9月，在兰州召开了民革甘肃省第二次代表大会。选举出委员17人，候补委员5人，组成民革甘肃省第二届委员会。邓宝珊任主任委员，李翰园、卢忠良任副主任委员，马光宗为秘书长。

1961年9月，在兰州召开了民革甘肃省第三次代表大会。选举出委员27人，候补委员5人，组成了民革甘肃省第三届委员会。邓宝珊任主任委员，李翰园、卢忠良任副主任委员，马光宗为秘书长。

1966年—1976年的十年动乱期间，甘肃民革被迫停止活动。中共十一届三中全会后，在中共甘肃省委的关怀下，1978年9月，甘肃民革成立临时领导小组，卢忠良、沈求我为召集人，重新开展工作。当时，成员只有171人，在落实政策中，陆续恢复了一部分成员的党籍，到1979年底，成员人数增加到205人。

1979年12月，在兰州召开了民革甘肃省第四次代表大会。选举出委员28人，候补委员8人，组成民革甘肃省第四届委员会。卢忠良任主任委员，沈求我、马光宗、杨汉烈、苏杰儒任副主任委员，周化南为秘书长。1982年举行的四届三次全委会上，又增选周化南、蒋云台为副主任委员。到1983年底，成员总人数增加到804人。

1984年3月，在兰州召开了民革甘肃省第五次代表大会。选举出委员47人，候补委员10人，组成民革甘肃省第五届委员会。卢忠良任主任委员，蒋云台、马光宗、杨汉烈、马丕烈、马冠洛、马耀南任副主任委员，马耀南兼秘书长，还推选了省委会顾问22人。在1985年举行的五届二次全委会上，又增选王治岐为副主任委员。1985年年底，全省成员总数达992人。

1986年6月，在兰州召开了民革甘肃省代表会议，增选委员14人，候补委员4人。在会议期间举行的五届三次全委会上，增选常务委员11人，增选高葆英(女)为副主任委员；选举省委会执行组成员5人，马冠洛任组长，马耀南任副组长。还推选了省委会顾问8人。

1988年6月，在兰州召开了民革甘肃省第六次代表大会。选举出委员50人，候补委员11人，组成民革甘肃省第六届委员会。马丕烈任主任委员，马冠洛、马耀南、高葆英(女)、赵晓柯、邓炎喜任副主任委员。在1989年12月举行的五届二次全委会上，又增选白照为副主任委员兼秘书长。

1992年7月，在兰州召开了民革甘肃省七次代表大会。选举出委员51人，候补委员6人。马冠洛任主任委员、邓成城、马耀南、高葆英(女)、俞正、倪安民(女)任副主任委员。

二、1993年甘肃民革概况

一年来，各级民革组织和广大党员，以中共十四大精神为指导，遵循民革八大提出的要求和任务，继续贯彻中共中央《关于坚持和完善中国共产党领导的多党合作和政治协商制度的意见》。在民革中央和中共甘肃省委的领导下，坚持“一个中心、两个基本点”的基本路线，为推进改革开放和现代化建设，为统一祖国大业，为健全参政党机制和发挥参政党作用而加强自身建设，为甘肃经济做出了一定的贡献。

1.积极参政议政，开展民主监督。

(1)民革党员中的各级人大代表和政协委员共182人。他们通过调查研究，参与视察和各类检查活动，就如何加快改革步伐，把我省经济工作搞上去提出了许多内容翔实，水平较高的意见、建议和提案。特别是在省、市(县)政协会议上，以民革的名义提出的一些提案，由于集思广益，质量较高，受到各级政府和主管部门的重视，有的已被采纳和实施。

(2)由省委会从民革党员中聘任的专家和学者组成的政策研究委员会，发挥群体功能，编发《参政简报》，结合我省的经济建设和社会热点问题，诸如“三资企业的发展”，“煤炭资源的破坏”，“假冒伪劣商品的泛滥”，“铺张浪费现象的蔓延”等方面提出的意见和建议，受到政府主管部门的好评。

(3)省委会领导应邀参加中共甘肃省委、省政府、统战部主要领导同志主持的协商会、通报会、恳谈会、座谈会共18次。他们解放思想，坦城直言。在融洽信任的气氛中与中共党政部门领导人共同探讨社会主义市场经济理论和民主党派工作如何为经济建设服务的问题；座谈香港问题和台湾问题。同时，就国家和我省的重大方针政策、经济形势、反腐倡廉、维护本省安定团结局面和省政府、省政协的重要人事等问题提出意见和建议。民革市(县)委员会的主要领导同志也经常参加当地中共党委召开的座谈会、茶话会，就发展本地区经济和地方事务提出意见。

(4)民革党员中的36位省参事室参事、省文史馆馆员和其他同志，列席和旁听省人大会议，参加一些视察活动，深入实际，调查研究，直接参与本省两个文明建设中有关事务的协商和国家政策法规的贯彻落实。

(5)为贯彻中共中央意见精神，在各级政府部门担任领导职务和被聘为各级特约检察员、监察员、审计员、教育督导员的30位党员，在各自的岗位上，尽心尽职，努力工作。同时，参加税收、财务、物价大检查的党员，也以认真负责的态度履行职责，受到好评。此外，一些地方组织坚持开展“议政会”和“参政议政卡”活动，也拓宽了民革的参政议政面。

2.努力为经济建设和祖国统一事业服务。

(1)根据民革中央的有关指示精神，省委会加强了对经济工作的领导，完善了领导和管理经济实体所必需的规章制度，采取积极慎重的态度组建和扩大经济实体。省委会的中山咨询公司下属5个实体。另外，兰州市民革创办了装饰、琴行、房地产开发、饮食服务等实体；定西县民革创办了购销公司；白银市民革创办了咨询服务部；临夏市民革创办的中山文艺社和中山医院，以及各级组织兴办的其它医疗机构，开辟了民革为经济建设服务的新途径和新领域，取得了良好的经济效益和社会效益。

(2)社会办学方面，除继续办好现有学校外，又开办了国家承认学历的中山职业学校。截止1993年底，甘肃民革创办的学校有中山辅导学院(大专层次，中山职业学校、中山职业技术学校、中华业余学校、武威中山业余学校以及临夏民族联合学校。

(3)积极宣传“一国两制”方针，促进祖国和平统一大业。《台湾问题与中国的统一》白皮书发表后，省民革召集在兰部分委员和台胞台属进行座谈，表示坚决反对台湾独立，强烈遣责台湾当局不顾客观事实，企图分裂祖国，给两岸和平统一制造障碍的错误行径。港督彭定康和政改方案发表后，省民革及时召开座谈会，遣责港英当局的“三违背”行径，坚决拥护我国政府在香港问题上的原则和立场。

(4)省委会领导同志还给民革党员和市(县)民革组织及统战、政协和兄弟党派等部门宣讲台湾政情和祖统形势，收到了良好的效果。省委会除了不定期地编印台情资料《宝岛了望》分发基层组织外，还适当扩大了台情录像资料片的播映范围，使更多的人能及时了解台湾政情，便于有针对性地开展祖统工作。省委会还搜集整理出《西北马家海内外亲友简况》，为做好西北马家海内外亲友的统战工作提供了重要资料。

3.努力加强自身建设，健全参政党机制。

(1)一年来，省委会紧紧围绕中共十四大精神，结合民革八大会议决议和民革党章，以及李鹏总理的工作报告开展思想政治工作，增强了民革党员坚持基本路线的自觉性，提高了为改革开放和现代化建设服务的积极性。

(2)省委会创办的刊物《甘肃民革》以及兰州市民革创办的《兰州民革》、临夏市民革创办的《临夏民革》和武威市民革创办的《民革之窗》也为党员的思想建设起了促进作用。《团结报》甘肃记者站及时报道了甘肃民主党派和统战系统的消息。

(3)组织状况:

截止1993年底,甘肃民革共有党员1468人,各级组织88个。

其中:教育界359人,科技界53人,工程技术界158人,财经界95人,医药卫生界181人,文化艺术界98人,出版界3人,工商企业240人,政府机关92人,党派机关112人,社会团体13人,其他64人。

其中:高级职称的166人,占11.3%,中级职称的459人,占31.3%。

其中:全国人大代表1人,全国政协委员2人;省人大代表7人,省政协委员21人;省参事室参事17人,省文史馆馆员23人;市级以下人大代表和政协委员119人。

(4)人事变动:

1993年11月,在民革甘肃省七届二次全委会上,选举邓成城同志为甘肃省民革主任委员,推举马冠洛同志为甘肃省民革名誉主委,使省委会领导班子向年轻化迈出了可喜的一步。

(民革甘肃省委员会:鲁 晋)

甘肃省工商业联合会概况

省工商业联合会、
省民间商会会长
周怀仁

甘肃省工商业联合会也称甘肃省民间商会,是中华全国工商业联合会的地方组织,是人民政协的组成单位之一,是中国共产党领导的具有统一战线性质的人民团体和民间商会。

解放前甘肃省各市县就有商会组织。那时的商会在联合民族工商界反帝爱国、兴利除弊、繁荣民族工商业方面,发挥过有益的作用。中华人民共和国诞生以后,人民政府接管并改组了旧商会、旧工业会、旧同业公会。根据建国方针和经济建设的需要,1951年10月,周恩来总理在全国政协一届三次会议的《政治报告》中提出,工商业联合会将逐渐成为全体工商界的组织。1952年8月,中央人民政府政务院公布《工商联合会组织通则》,这是新中国颁布关于建立工商联的第一部具有法律效力的规定。我省工商界人士经过协商酝酿,于1952年12月底召开了甘肃省工商业联合会筹备代表会议,成立了筹备委员会。1954年1月,甘肃省工商业联合会第一届会员代表大会在兰州召开,宣告甘肃省工商业联合会正式成立。此时,全省77个县、市中,已有63个县、市正式成立了工商联。

省工商联成立后,认真贯彻执行了党的过渡时期总路线,辅导私营企业纳入国家资本主义的轨道,积极团结、推动推动会员接受社会主义改造。到1956年,全省有20519(户)人原工商业者顺利地实现了全行业公私合营,为完成国家对资本主义工商业的社会主义改造,起到了积极的配合作用。1956年9月,中国共产党第八次全国代表大会召开,我国对资本主义工商业的社会主义改造基本完成,社会主义制度已基本建立。这一时期以及以后的工商联基本任务有所调整。省工商联适应形势的发展,在思想教育和为社会主义建设服务两大方面继续发挥作用,团结、教育广大工商业者,"听毛主席的话,跟共产党走,走社会主义道路"和"顾一头,一边倒",一心一意为社会主义服务,开展了爱国主义、国际主义、社会主义的思想教育,为实现对国民经济调整的"八字方针",为企业增产节约,克服三年经济困难,争取工农业生产的发展,做出了一定的贡献。

"文化大革命"的十年动乱中,省工商联被迫停止了活动。1978年9月,甘肃省和兰州市工商联相继恢复活动。1979年12月,省工商联召开了第四届会员代表大会。为了贯彻执行党的十一届三中全会精神,遵照全国工商联提出的"坚定不移跟党走,尽心竭力为四化"的行动纲领,省工商联适时地把工作重点转移到调整全体成员的积极因素,为巩固安定团结的政治局面,加快社会主义现代化建设上来。积极参与了对全省大政方针的协商讨论;协助党和政府落实了对原工商业者的政策;开展对老、少、边、穷地区的经济发展和工商企业的咨询服务;举办工商学校,培训工商专业人才;兴办集体企业;开展对港、澳、台工商社团和工商界人士的联络,扩大对外开放以及加强工商联组织建设等方面,都取得了显著的成绩。

随着改革开放的深入和经济的发展,我国出现了新的非公有制经济成份,这不但是公有制经济的有益补充,也为具有中国特色的社会主义增加了新的内容。1991年7月6日,中共中央发出了关于工商联若干问题的指示<即中发(1991)15号文件>。这一指示指出,在我国,非公有制经济成份作为公有制经济的有益补充,将在相当长的历史时期内存在和发展。现在亟需有一个党领导的、主要是做非公有制经济代表人士思想政治工作的人民团体。工商联作为党领导下的以统战性为主、兼有经济性、民间性的人民团体,可以配合党和政府承担这方面的任务,成为党和政府管理非公有制经济的助手,联系非公有制经济代表人士的一个桥梁。中央指示明确了新时期工商联的性质、任务、组织结构和主要职能。确定新时期工商联的会员对象,除了原工商业者外,主要应是私营企业、个体工商户、"三胞"投资企业和部分乡镇企业。因对外交往的需要,大中型国营企业负责人可以个人名义入会,中小型国营企业可以自愿参加工商联,个体劳协、私营企业协会、乡镇企业协会、外商投资企业协会可作为团体会员自愿参加工商联。中央指示规定工商联的主要职能有七项,即参政议政;反映会员的意见和要求,维护会员的会法权益;协助政府进行专题调研,开展经济服务活动;加强自身建设,帮助会员自觉遵守国家的政策法令,引导教育会员爱国、敬业、守法,履行社会职责;开展与港、澳、台工商社团和工商界人士的联系,协助政府引进资金、技术和人才;办好工商联自办企业;经政府委托和批准,参与具体的经济活动。党中央的指示,指明了工商联自身改革和发展的道路、工作重点和努力方向。我省各级工商联组织进行了认真学习和广泛宣传,并按中央指示精神进行会员结构的调整和工作职能的转变。1993年7月,甘肃省工商联召开了第七届会员代表大会,选举产生了新一届领导班子,为开创工作新局面打下了基础。

1993年10月,全国工商联第七届会员代表大会在北京召开,党和国家领导人李瑞环、荣毅仁、田纪云、李岚清等在开幕前会见了全体代表。全联"七大"根据新时期的新任务,修改了《中国工商业联合会章程》,选举了执行委员会领导成员。

全国工商联"七大"是工商联历史上一次具有继往开来重要意义的会议,它总结了工商联和中国共产党风雨同舟四十年的历史过程;丰富了新时期工商联工作的内容;确立了以经济建设为中心,以重点做好非公有制经济代表人士工作为已任,以促进社会主义市场经济体制的建立和完善为目标的总方针;掀开了九十年代工商联历史新的一页。

继中共中央关于工商联若干问题的指示下达以后,邓小平同志南巡发表重要谈话,进一步丰富了建设有中国特色的社会主义理论,明确提出了加快改革开放和经济建设的战略思想和政策原则,调动了各方面深化改革,扩大开放,争取国民经济迈上新台阶的积极性和创造性。中共十四大和十四届三中全会,提出了建立社会主义市场经济体制的总目标,明确了九十年代改革和建设的总任务。中央一系列重大决策,对加快改革步伐,加速经济发展至关重要,对工商联组织如何为改革开放和经济建设服务,如何在社会主义市场经济中发挥民间商会作用,提出了新的更高的要求。

一学习《邓小平文选》三卷,贯彻落实中共十四届三中全会决定和全联"七大"精神。省工商联指导各级工商联组织专职干部和广大会员学习,把专职干部和会员的思想统一到十四届三中全会精神和建立社会主义市场经济体制上来。

一对非公有制经济人士的联系工作有了很大进展。各级工商联在对本地区非公有制经济情况普遍调查的基础上,与大多数非公有制经济人士建立了经常性的联系,每个市县联系的代表人士达到或超过了50名。

一加强调查研究,积极参政议政。省工商联多次参加省委、省政府召集的有关会议,就反腐倡廉,加快经济发展等问题提出建议。

一积极开展以经济建设为中心的各种服务。六月间组织6家会员企业参加了"中国青岛通讯电子新产品新技术交易会",成交金额120万元;七月组织16家会员企业参加'93广东省工商联经贸洽谈会,成交金额380万元;10月组团参加全国工商联经贸洽谈会,28个不同经济成份企业参加,成交金额850多万元,被评为优秀成交奖。并利用这次机会,与港、澳、台客商进行了广泛的接触,拓宽了联络渠道。

一工商联组织建设,会员发展工作有了新进展。截止12月底,全省已经恢复和建立工商联组织75个(其中筹备组织6个),专职干部226人。有会员10178个(其中企业会员2155个,团体会员278个、个人会员4882人)。企业会员中,既有国营、集体、也有私营、"三胞"和外商投资企业,涉及工业、商业、林牧、科技、建筑、交通运输和服务等行业。团体会员中,有个体劳动者协会、乡镇企业协会、私营企业协会,私营企业公会、私营企业联谊会和外商投资企业协会。

一工商联自办企业增多,并在巩固中得到发展。截止12月底,全省各级工商联共有自办企业64个,职工人数1639人。其中省工商联自办企业35个,职工人数761人;地、市、县(区)工商联自办企业29个,职工人数878人。

甘肃省总工会

做好工会工作
振兴甘肃经济

1993年,我们在党的十四大精神鼓舞下发挥工会优势,体现工会特色,充分履行工会的四项职能,继续把全心全意依靠工人阶级的根本指导方针落实到基层。全面落实了省总确定的1993年工会工作的指导思想和各项工作任务,为振兴甘肃,发展社会主义市场经济,建设社会主义精神文明,保持社会稳定等方面,发挥了重要作用。

1993年,我们重点抓了以下几方面的工作:

一、深入学习贯彻党的十四大精神,用有中国特色的社会主义理论武装思想

各级工会以解放思想、更新观念、实事求是、加快发展为主线,充分发挥工人报刊、广播、电视、文化宫、俱乐部的优势,采用多种形势宣传党的方针政策。全体工会干部深入基层,组织学习、培训、辅导和讲座,紧密联系企业实际,联系十多年来改革开放和经济建设取得的成绩，教育广大职工明确社会主义市场经济的基本概念和理论，明确在建立社会主义市场经济体制中担负的重要历史责任，增强贯彻党的基本理论和基本路线的自觉性。

二、坚持把工会工作做到转换企业经营机制的全过程中去

各级工会组织在企业改革的全局中，组织开展了形式多样的社会主义劳动竞赛、群众性的合理化建议、技术革新和技术协作等活动。1993年，全省共有30余万人参加了工会组织的技术比武、竞赛活动，涌现出各类技术能手2.6万余人。全省三千多个基层单位开展了劳动竞赛，参加人数达75万余人，双增双节活动创效益近4亿元。各行各业职工提出合理化建议26万余件，其中有12万件被采纳实施，创造价值1.2万余元，各项职工发明创造活动创价值近亿元。

各级工会主动参与协调劳动关系工作，处理解决好改革中涉及职工利益的各种问题，在深入调查研究的基础上，及时准确地向党和政府反映职工的意见和愿望，为改革的稳步、扎实进展出了力，尽了责，为稳定职工队伍，维护安定团结、推进改革和建设，调动广大职工的生产积极性做出了贡献。

三、关心职工生活，维护职工合法权益

在深化改革当中，各级工会本着在维护全国人民总体利益的同时维护职工合法权益的原则，认真研究解决进一步落实和保障工人阶级主人翁地位问题，协助党和政府、企业行政采取积极措施，在力所能及的范围内，积极为职工说话、办事。各级工会一方面及时向党和政府反映部分停产、半停产、亏损企业的职工生活困难问题，另一方面积极组织职工扶贫救济活动。采取提供技术培训、技术咨询、帮助技术改造、解决技术难关等方式方法，为困难企业增强“造血”功能。全省成立职工扶贫组织500余个，筹集扶贫资金400万元，扶持困难职工2万多人。省总还开展了职工互助补充保险试点工作，开展“送温暖”活动，切实帮助企业解决职工的生活困难。省总、全总还推广了定西地区工会帮厂扶贫，帮助企业扭亏、扶持职工脱贫的经验，在维护职工合法权益，维护改革开放大局上，各级工会发挥了积极作用。

四、依法办事，提高工会参政议政能力

社会主义市场经济是以法律为规范和保障的经济体制，工会要从整体上代表和维护职工的权益，就必须依法办事，以增强参政议政力度。

1993年，省总积极组织各级工会和职工群众参与了《劳动法》、《最低工资保障法》等10多项法律法规的修订工作，形成了许多建设性意见，表达了工会和职工的意愿。

《工会法》颁布后的一年当中，各级工会组织利用多种形式，广泛宣传，各级工会举办《工会法》学习培训班23期，参加培训人数为1350多人。各级基层工会还结合企业转换经营机制，从贯彻《条例》入手，举办了一批“三项制度改革”、“劳务市场趋势”、“待业保险”等为内容的普法学习班、研讨会，教育职工支持改革、投身改革。

各级工会认真落实《企业法》、《全民所有制企业职工代表大会条例》、《城镇集体企业条例》等一系列法律法规，进一步健全和完善职代会制度，落实职代会五项职权，凡是涉及企业改革和职工利益的重大举措，事先都是交职代会审议、讨论或通过，求得职工群众的理解和支持。1993年，全省400多个基层工会建立了职代会制度，职代会普及率达74%。部分乡镇企业、外资企业的民主管理制度逐步建立健全。职工的民主参与、管理企业的权力正在进一步提高。

五、贯彻分类指导方针，使工会工作迈上新水平

为了贯彻实施省总提出的“以企带县、以大带小、技协扶持、帮厂扶贫、扭亏增盈”的“双带整推”战略目标，各级工会采取得力措施，通过产地结合、企地结合，发挥各自优势，为提高工会工作整体水平做了大量扎实有效的工作，取得了显著成绩。

1993年3月15日，省总召开全省国有大中型企业工会主席联席会议，会议总结了自1989年以来省总以国有大中型企业工会为重点，辐射、带动全省工会工作的工作，交流了在转换企业经营机制中积极发挥作用的经验。实现了我省工会工作由一个模式到分类指导的重大转变，一个以大企业工会为重点和依托，全面推进全省工会工作的新格局已经形成。

1993年3月22日，省总又组织召开了全省地县工会暨民族地区工会工作会议，会上兰州市等七个地、市、县工会做了专题经验介绍，省总推广他们的经验，要求地、县工会在经济改革的大潮中，找准位置，紧紧围绕本地、县改革和建设，积极主动地开展各项工会工作，为发展地方经济，增进民族团结，提高工会整体水平做贡献。这次会议对加强我省地、县工会工作，开创新时期地、县工会工作新局面起到了积极作用。

1993年8月17日，省政府与省总工会第三次联席会议召开，这次会议的主要议题是：研究部署帮助企业扭亏增盈工作。这次联席会议是在省总多方考察、研究了我省经济形势的基础上向省政府提议召开的。通过各级工会组织和广大职工同各级政府的有效合作，为切实解决我省经济发展中的问题，维护职工的切身利益，维护职工队伍的稳定，化解矛盾，增进理解起到了重要作用。

六、大力兴办工会企事业，增强工会自我发展能力

1993年，省总和各级工会组织坚持"为改革开放、发展社会生产力服务，为职工群众服务，为推进工运事业服务"的宗旨和社会效益与经济效益相统一的原则，按照"全面起步，稳妥发展"的兴办企事业方针，走"服务——发展——更好地服务"的路子，抓住时机，合理规划，兴办各类经济实体309个，固定资产10193万元，从业人员4000余人，营业收入达6013万元，实现利润760万元，上缴税金140万元，积累基金480万元，上缴各级工会105万元。工会企事业的大力发展，拓宽了新时期工会工作的路子，显示了工会组织的优势，锻炼培养了工会经济人才，增强了工会经济实力。

七、加强职工教育，提高职工队伍素质

1993年，全省工会宣传工作立足为深化改革和经济建设服务，着力提高职工队伍的整体素质，努力满足职工精神文明需求，开展了一系列形式多样的活动。一是召开了全省职工思想道德教育座谈会和研讨会，在深入基层调查研究的基础上，对职工思想状况和政治思想工作的形势进行分析研究；二是进行了职工读书自学表彰奖励，评出自学成材者19名，自学成果6项，读书自学先进集体(小组)13个，读书自学积极分子60名；三是组织开展纪念毛泽东同志诞辰100周年的活动。根据全总和省总的安排部署，各级工会从实际出发，举办了多种形式的纪念活动近千次。充分表达了广大职工群众对毛主席的深切怀念和崇高敬意，歌颂了老一辈无产阶级革命家的丰功伟绩。

各级工会教育职工立足本岗位，搞好本职工作，并广泛发挥各类职工兴趣小组的作用，组织开展各类各项有益的文体活动，丰富职工业余文化生活，富教于乐，陶冶职工高尚情操，为培养四有职工队伍做了大量工作。

八、搞好工会自身改革和建设，努力提高整体水平

截止1993年年底统计，我省共有基层工会组织12300个，工会会员168万余人，我们还拥有一支1万余人的工会专职工作人员和20多万名工会积极分子队伍。在经济体制改革的新形势下，我省各级工会组织，以增强基层工会活力为中心环节，推进和加强了自身的建设和发展，扩大了工会组织在社会上的影响，为甘肃工运事业发展做出了积极贡献。

甘肃省工会第八次代表大会在省委、省政府和全总的亲切关怀和指导下，于1993年8月21日至23日在兰州隆重召开。大会认真总结了省总七大以来的各项工作，讨论确定了今后一个时期我省工人运动和工会工作的方针任务，动员广大职工发扬工人阶级的主力军作用，积极投身改革开放和现代化建设，为发展甘肃经济而奋斗。出席这次大大会的500名代表来自全省工业、交通、基建、农林、财贸、文教、科技、卫生、体育及党政机关等各条战线，具有广泛的群众性、代表性。会上，代表们畅所欲言、集思广益、民主讨论、统一了思想，明确了目标，振奋了精神，大会选举产生了新的一届省总领导班子，圆满完成了各项预定议程。大会的胜利召开标志着甘肃工会工作进入了一个新的发展阶段。

改革开放任重道远，工会组织和广大职工肩负着十分光荣而重大的使命。我们要充分发挥工会组织的优势，动员团结全省职工群众积极投身改革建设事业，为振兴甘肃经济，为把我们的国家建设的更加繁荣富强而不懈努力！

(甘肃省总工会调研室)

甘肃省妇女联合会

1993年甘肃省妇女工作跃上新台阶

甘肃省妇联主任

孙兆霞

1993年，全省各级妇女组织以邓小平同志建设有中国特色的社会主义理论为指导，坚持党的基本路线，围绕经济建设中心，认真贯彻党的十四大和中国妇女七大会议精神，全面履行"代表、维护、服务、参与、联谊"职能，带领广大妇女积极投身改革开放和现代化建设。在妇女参政、培养选拔妇女干部、维护妇女儿童权益、发动妇女参与经济建设等方面取得了明显成效，为促进我省社会政治稳定，加快经济发展，繁荣各项事业，做出了积极的贡献。

一、认真学习、贯彻十四大精神，加强思想政治工作，促进精神文明建设

1993年，全省各级妇女组织把认真学习、宣传和贯彻十四大精神作为首要任务来抓，围绕加快改革开放和经济建设步伐的主题，组织城乡妇女学习《邓小平文选》第三卷和党的十四大、十四届三中全会精神，使广大妇女树立起社会主义市场经济观念、效益观念和竞争观念。同时，广泛深入生动地开展了爱国主义、集体主义、社会主义教育和"四有"、"四自"教育，提高了妇女的思想政治素质，推动了社会主义精神文明建设。

二、培养选拔女干部工作有新的进展，推动了妇女参政议政

1993年全省县、乡换届后，85个县(市、区)中，有84个县(市、区)领导班子配备了女领导干部125名，占同级干部的7.43%，比上届提高了3.6%，其中50个县(市、区)党政班子中配备女领导干部51名，占85个县的58.8%。全省28.9%的乡党政班子中有了女领导干部，占同级干部的8.19%。我省妇女参政开始走出低谷，各级领导班子中女干部比例过低的状况得到初步改变，培养选拔女干部工作逐渐步入健康发展的轨道。

全省有妇联干部2306人，其中少数民族干部271人，具有大专以上文化程度的462人，占妇联干部总数的20%，具有高中、中专文化程度的1513人，占妇联干部总数的65.61%；招聘妇联干部589人，占妇联干部总数的25.54%。1993年加强了妇联干部的岗位培训，在努力提高妇女干部素质上下功夫。省妇联与省委组织部联合开办了全省中青年干部培训班。组织全省各地、省直单位100多名妇委会主任参加了全国妇联干部培训基地的培训。组织14个地(州、市)的90多名地、县、乡妇女干部赴浙江、上海、广东培训和考察；派出了20名地、县妇联主任赴大连市挂职锻炼。省妇联举办了以学习市场经济知识为主的培训班，59名地、县妇联主任参加了培训。

为适应改革形势的要求，加强了妇联组织的自身建设和整体功能建设。1993年召开了甘肃省第九次妇女代表大会，选出了新一届省妇联领导班子。各地、县妇联也普遍进行了换届。进一步加强了基层妇女组织建设，在党政机关、科教文卫事业单位建立了妇委会，与各民主党派、港澳、台胞、宗教界高层妇女建立了联系，在女领导干部和女知识分子中开展了联谊活动。

三、做好新形势下的维权工作，推动《妇女法》全面实施

(一)继续以"双学双比"、"巾帼建功"两项活动为载体，提高广大妇女的经济地位和政治地位。

在农村妇女中开展的"双学双比"活动，围绕发展"两高一优"农业，以提高妇女素质，增强妇女生产技能，加强农村妇女科技队伍为重点，向纵深发展。全省共办妇女扫盲班3621期，参加扫盲妇女13.5万人，其中9.5万多人脱盲。共举办实用技术培训班21501期，培训妇女57万多人次，掌握一至两门技术的妇女36.13万人，60%的村妇代会主任已成为"双学双比"女能手，评定女农民技术员2516人，累计达到9000多人。继续把"双学双比"与扶贫开发工作相结合，全省妇联系统建立1613个扶贫点，帮助17700多农户脱贫，办起了以妇女为主体的扶贫实体155个，有12.5万多人次的女劳力转向城镇服务和外出做季节工。省妇联与省扶贫抽纱工贸有限公司配合，将钩锈项目作为12个贫困县的龙头项目进行扶持，共培训妇女10000多名。"三八"绿色工程活动又有新发展，全省有221.19万妇女参加此项活动，建"三八"绿色基地458个。在城镇妇女中开展的"巾帼建功"活动，围绕城市经济建设的中心，以岗位建功、岗位成才为基本形式开展各种竞赛活动。她们立足本职，刻苦钻研业务，大胆改革新创造，参加技术比武；提合理化建议10.2万多条，创价值2508万元；技术攻关741项，创价值56678万元；"双增双节"活动创效益11924万元；举办各类培训班1715期，7.7万多名妇女参加了培训。

(二)认真宣传、贯彻《妇女法》，全面维护妇女儿童合法权益

1993年，进一步推动《妇女法》的学习、宣传活动，促使全社会了解维护妇女权益的重要意义和法律规定。各级妇联组织协同有关单位，对全省贯彻实施《妇女法》的情况进行了检查，敦促各级党委、政府，各部门、单位采取切实措施，解决妇女权益保障方面存在的问题，取得了成效。劳动、人事、教育等部门在招工、招干就业安置、受教育等方面采取有效措施，使男女平等的政策初步得到落实。省妇联与有关部门共同起草了《甘肃省妇女权益保障法实施办法(草案)》。积极参与社会治安综合治理与解救被拐卖妇女儿童工作，开展了打拐禁娼专项斗争。省妇联和省公安厅联合召开了全省"打拐"工作会议，制定了《全省打击拐卖妇女儿童犯罪工作三年规划》。各级妇联配合公安机关积极解救被拐卖的妇女儿童，全省破获拐卖妇女儿童案件63起，解救被拐卖妇女249人，儿童76人，初步遏制了拐卖人口的犯罪活动。充分发挥了各级妇联信访、法律顾问组织的维权职能。开展了心理咨询、法律咨询、婚姻家庭咨询、代书、参与诉讼外调解等业务的服务。

四、继续做好儿童工作，进一步推进儿童事业的发展

1993年，我省儿童工作努力协调有关方面认真实施《九十年代甘肃儿童发展规划纲要》(简称NPA)，围绕家庭教育，继续开展优生、优育、优教工作。全省14个地(州、市)和47个县(市、区)及省级有关部门相继制定了"NPA"实施方案，开展了大规模的培训及宣传学习活动。全省举办各种培训班524期，培训宣传员2.3万多人培训地域覆盖面以乡为单位达到95%。省妇联、省教委、省广播电台联合举办了甘肃省广播家长学校，有10万名家长参加学习。省妇联、省家教协会组织教育、卫生系统专家学者编写省广播家长学校系列教材，其中，《小学生家庭教育》已印发10万册。全省办家长学校1578所，广播父母学校74所；建立妇女儿童活动阵地86个，兴办为妇女儿童服务的企业、事业共25个。妇联办托幼园所37个，2674名儿童入托。

五、层层表彰树立典型，妇女中大批先进模范人物脱颖而出

1993年，全省层层表彰树立了一批先进妇女典型，并且注重通过新闻媒介宣传她们的事迹。3月5

日，省妇联召开纪念“三八”国际劳动妇女节83周年大会，会上表彰了61名“双学双比”先进女能手，40个“双学双比”先进协调组织和单位，20名优秀妇联干部，13个“巾帼建功”先进单位，50名“巾帼建功”标兵和13个新时期妇女拥军先进集体，26名新时期妇女拥军模范。全省儿童工作现场会表彰了18个《九十年代儿童发展规划纲要》培训宣传工作先进单位。省妇联和省公安厅联合召开的全省“打拐”工作会议表彰了7个“打拐”工作先进集体。全省涌现出县以上“双学双比”活动先进女能手4398人、先进协调组织171个、先进协调单位178个，县以上“巾帼建功”活动先进个人2613名、先进单位348个；县级以上“三八”红旗手1783名、“三八”红旗集体106个，“五好家庭”35.51万户。有30人获得绿色奖章。她们中佼佼者不仅在省内各项建设中成绩突出，而且赢得了全国以及世界性的荣誉。甘肃妇女已成为甘肃经济和社会发展的一支举足轻重的力量。

甘肃的石窟艺术

甘肃素有“石窟艺术之乡”的美称。在河西走廊、陇东高原、陇南大地都可以看到古代能工巧匠留下的石窟艺术造型和壁画瑰宝。中国四大石窟中，甘肃就占了两个。

敦煌莫高窟，又称千佛洞，位于甘肃省敦煌县东南25公里的鸣沙山崖壁上。洞窟分上、下两层，高低错落，南北长1600多米，岩壁高达50多米，共存洞窟492个，壁画45000多平方米，彩塑2400多尊。据记载，莫高窟始建于前秦建元二年(366年)，历经隋、唐、宋、元各代不断扩建重修。历代艺术家们呕心沥血，建造出的我国规模最大，内容最丰富的石窟群——莫高窟，以壁画、泥塑著称。壁画内容除有佛象及佛教故事外，还有民间故事和反映古代各民族生活、习俗、风尚的画面。彩塑有佛、菩萨、弟子、天王、力士等，造型精致，生动传神。莫高窟的艺术是人类文明的曙光。目前，已形成了一门独立的学科——敦煌学。

麦积山石窟，麦积山位于天水市东南45公里，是秦岭山脉西端小陇山的一座独立山峦，山头略呈圆锥形，很像农家的麦垛，故名麦积山。石窟开凿于后秦(公元384～417年)，为我国著名的大型窟群之一。共有洞窟194个，内有7000多座石雕，1000多平方米壁画。最大石窟横宽30多米，最小洞窟则仅能容身。石窟分布在悬崖峭壁上，上下左右之间靠栈道或千佛廊连结通达，在现存石窟中最为惊险陡峭。塑像有高浮塑、圆塑、粘贴塑、壁塑等。数以千计的与真人大小相仿的圆塑，极富于生活情趣，被视为珍品。从高16米的阿弥陀佛，到10多厘米的小影塑，个个精巧绝伦，栩栩如生，充分体现了我国古代雕塑的艺术风格。

炳灵寺石窟位于兰州市西南100公里的永靖县积石山中，和黄河上游著名的刘家峡水库相连。石窟开凿于西秦建弘元年(420年)，历代均有扩建，现存龛窟183个，大小石雕像694尊，泥塑82尊，壁画900多平方米。以唐代作品最多。其造像构思精巧，雕刻精细；壁画内容丰富，线条流畅，色泽鲜丽，生动喜人，为我国现存最早的壁画，其中169窟高15米，满布佛龛、佛像，是我国最早的洞窟。石窟临黄河北岸，分布于南北2公里的峭壁之上，有凌空栈道连接各个洞窟。1964年在窟前修筑200米长的石坝，以防水患。炳灵寺石窟为甘肃著名的旅游胜地，已被列为全国重点文物保护单位，为我国六大石窟之一。

甘肃著名石窟除上述三者外，还有陇东的庆阳北石窟、平凉南石窟、泾川王母宫、安西榆林窟、武山水帘洞、庄浪云崖寺石窟、张掖马蹄寺石窟、武威天梯山石窟、敦煌西千佛洞石窟等十几处，甘肃石窟之多，类型齐全，这在全国首屈一指。

法　律

公安机关

适应经济建设的新形势改进加强治安管理工作

省公安厅副厅长

石允蒲

社会主义市场经济体制的建立，必将引起上层建筑、意识形态和社会生活各个方面的重大变革，尤其给社会治安秩序、治安管理机制等方面带来许多新情况、新问题和新任务，面对这种新形势，1993年，全省治安管理工作以党的十四大和十四届三中全会精神为指针，紧紧围绕建立社会主义市场经济体制这个中心，坚持强化职能，改进方法，强化改革意识和创新精神，有效地维护了全省社会政治稳定，为改革开放和经济建设创造了良好的治安环境。

治安管理必须紧紧围绕经济建设这个中心，始终把维护社会政治稳定放在首位。治安管理工作涉及社会方方面面，与经济建设息息相关，治安管理工作的好或差，服务质量的优与劣，直接影响到经济的发展和社会政治的稳定。1993年，全省的治安管理工作以服从服务于经济建设为中心，始终把维护社会政治稳定放在首位，努力提高对社会治安的管理效能。各级公安机关充分发挥专政职能作用，大力加强治安管理工作，侦破了一批反革命案件，严厉打击了严重刑事犯罪活动，加强了各项治安防范控制，及时粉碎了境内外敌对分子在甘肃的破坏阴谋。同时紧紧抓住民族分裂、宗教渗透和群体性事件等影响政治稳定的主要问题，坚持制定周密对策，积极疏导，化解矛盾，在努力减少各种不安定因素的同时，协助党委、政府妥善处置了90起因人民内部矛盾引发的上访、请愿、游行、罢工和械斗等群众性治安问题，有效地维护了全省的社会政治稳定。

治安管理必须以"严打"为首要措施，保持治安大局的稳定。严厉打击刑事犯罪，是治安管理的首要措施，也是为改革开放和经济建设服务的重要方面。1993年，全省公安机关始终把严厉打击严重刑事犯罪作为保证社会治安持续稳定的重要环节，针对不同时期刑事犯罪活动的特点，以严重危害经济建设和社会治安的案件为重点，以大要案件为主攻目标，大力加强侦查破案，突破了一批影响大、危害严重的恶性案件，并结合进行重点整治，及时解决了一些突出的治安问题，保持了治安大局稳定。1993年全省公安机关共立刑事案件18145起，破获了15648起，破案率为86.2%；共立重大刑事案件6004起，破获了4221起，破案率为81.9%；与1992年相比，刑事案件总破案率提高了5.1个百分点，重大案件破案率提高了2.7个百分点。通过侦查破案挖出各类犯罪团伙1789个，抓获成员6834人，依法打击处理了一大批刑事犯罪分子，为国家、集体和个人挽回了三千多万元的经济损失。同时，全省各级公安机关针对刑事犯罪活动中的突出问题，组织开展了以打击毒品犯罪为重点的禁毒专项斗争，侦破贩毒案件1886起，抓获毒品犯罪分子2046名，缴获了近30公斤的海洛因和鸦片。并抓住时机，适时开展了禁种和铲除毒品原植物工作，基本控制了私种罂粟问题。对一些地区一度突出的"车匪路霸"，团伙犯罪，盗割破坏通信线路，拐卖人口，盗掘古墓葬和古遗址、走私文物等问题，都在一定范围内开展了专项斗争和集中打击，集中整治了重点地区的治安秩序，解决了突出问题，收到了明显的社会治安效益。经对全省86个县、市(区)1993年社会治安状况的的分类评估，治安状况良好或基本良好的有64个，占74.4%；一般的有21个，占24.1%；治安状况较差的只有1个，占1.2%。

治安管理必须突出重点，加强防范控制，进行综合治理。在治安管理中，突出重点，打防并举，进行综合治理，是维护城乡治安秩序的基本途径。1993年，在重大政治、经济、文化活动较多，安全保卫工作任务繁重，治安管理面临许多新问题的情况下，各级公安机关以重大活动的安全保卫工作为重点，依法加强治安管理，强化防范控制，形成了人口、危险物品、特种行业管理和公共治安控制相配套的工作机制，减少了犯罪的空隙和漏洞，提高了对违法犯罪活动和治安灾害事故的预防能力。1993年全省公安机关结合严厉打击刑事犯罪斗争，对废旧金属收购、旅店等特种行业全面进行整顿，严密了管理；根据节令特点在公共复杂场所建立了治安控制网络，有效地监控、防范、打击了社会面上的违法犯罪活动；在枪支弹药、易燃易爆危险物品的管理上，集中进行整顿，定期开展安全检查，消除隐患，确保了安全；同时，根据重大节庆活动安全保卫工作和治安形势的需要，适时开展治安清查行动，查禁各种社会丑恶现象，清理各种不安定因素。1993年，共查处治安案件24349起，治安处罚35180人。各项治安管理措施的加强，确保了"兰交会"、"嘉峪关国际滑翔节"。"甘南州庆"等重大活动的安全和来甘重要警卫对象的安全。交通管理部门以"压事故、反违章、保畅通"为中心，反复整顿了全省道路交通秩序，对拖拉机和农用三轮车、无牌无证车辆、军用车辆进行了专项治理，并抓住事故多发季节，开展了"百日无特大事故"竞赛活动，使交通事故比1992年减少10.4%。消防监督工作进一步加强，消防基础设施进一步完善，火灾事故比1992年减少10.7%。

治安管理必须适应经济建设新形势的需要，不断改进旧的管理办法，建立新的管理机制。改革和加强各项治安管理工作，既是巩固公安工作治安效益的重要措施，又是实现公安工作治安效益的具体途径。1993年，全省公安机关提出了"四个为主"的方针，即坚持动静结合，以动态管理为主；坚持灵活多样，以规范化管理为主；坚持条块结合，以块块管理为主；坚持突出实践，以探索改革为主。同时，提出了新形势下治安管理工作的基本思路，即在人口管理工作上，正确预测户口观念在人们心目中逐渐淡化、户口管理进一步开放、户口成份更加多样化的趋势，努力跳出旧的管理框框，着力探索以对人的管理为主、居住地管理为主、证件化管理为主的新路子；在特种行业管理上，要面对高度开放的客观形势，着力推行行业许可证制度，健全管理规范；在治安基层基础工作上，大力加强派出所三项基本建设，推行警务区制度；在面上治安工作中，着力于以巡警体制为主的巡逻网络化建设。按照这些新的思路，各级公安机关进行了大胆的探索和实践。1993年，在省辖五市组建了巡警工作，初步开展了多种形式并存，徒步巡逻为主，分片包干，责任到人的工作机制，面上治安控制能力明显提高，深受人民群众和各界的欢迎。在兰州、金昌等地进行了改革派出所勤务制度的试点，设立了警务区，并向全省城市推广，有力地推动了派出所规范化建设，基础工作进一步得到加强。省公安厅还制定下发了《出租房屋治安管理暂行办法》、《暂住人口管理办法》、《区市级系统计算机正规化建设方案》、《保安服务业管理暂行规定》及公共场所、集贸市场、刻字业等方面的管理规定和办法，在特种行业和公共娱乐场所实行了许可证制度，强化了管理。消防、边防、交通、出入境等治安行政管理方面又出台了一些改革和管理措施，在服务经济建设中较好的发挥了职能作用。

治安管理必须建设一支强有力的管理队伍，不断提高管理水平和质量。治安管理工作能否落实到实处，治安管理队伍的建设是重要的保证，面对商品经济的冲击，治安管理之所以能够适应客观形势的发展变化，在繁重的任务面前取得胜利，很重要的一条就是狠抓了治安管理队伍的自身建设。1993年全省公安机关在首次评授警衔之后，狠抓了干警的思想教育工作，引导干警把思想和精力集中到本职工作上，立足岗位，为经济建设和改革开放建树功勋。根据新形势下公安工作的需要，加强了各级公安机关领导班子建设，配齐配强了基层领导干部，保证了政令和警令的畅通；加强了队伍的正规化和制度化建设，积极探索制定了适应市场经济需要的队伍管理制度和办法；建立了内外监督制约机制，增强了治安管理工作的透明度。反腐败斗争的深入开展，有效地纠正了治安管理中不正之风，密切了警民关系，推动了公安机关的廉政建设。治安管理队伍的不断加强，使管理水平和质量进一步提高，保证了各项治安管理工作任务的顺利完成。

1994年，是我国改革开放和现代化建设关键的一年，维护政治稳定和社会安定的任务将更加繁重、艰巨。全省公安机关将以邓小平同志建设有中国特色的社会主义理论为指针，坚持解放思想，实事求是的思想路线，坚持党委领导下的专门工作与群众路线相结合的方针，从严治警，充分发挥职能作用，坚决打击敌对势力和各种犯罪活动，强化改革，强化服务，强化管理，全力维护政治稳定和社会安定，为保卫社会主义经济建设作出不懈的努力。

检察工作

甘肃省检察工作概述

省人民检察院检察长

李德奎

1993年，全省各级人民检察院在省委、高检院、省人大的正确领导和监督下，认真贯彻党的十四大和八届全国人大会议精神，按照最高人民检察院的部署，严格执法，狠抓办案，强化监督，真抓实干，以严格执法统揽检察工作的全局，集中力量查办贪污贿赂等经济犯罪大案要案，严厉打击刑事犯罪活动，依法查处"侵权"、渎职犯罪案件，强化执法监督，为维护我省政治稳定和社会安定，促进改革开放和经济发展做出了积极贡献。

一、贪污贿赂检察

深入开展惩治贪污贿赂等经济犯罪的斗争，集中力量查办了一批大案要案。全省检察机关坚持把惩治贪污贿赂犯罪作为第一位的工作，重点查办了发生在党政领导机关、司法部门、行政执法部门和经济管理部门的贪污贿赂等经济犯罪案件，集中侦破了一批大要案件，有力地推动了反腐败斗争的深入开展。全年共受理贪污贿赂等经济犯罪案件1491件，经审查立案684件826人。其中，贪污贿赂案390件，挪用公款案149件，偷、坑、骗税案95件，假冒商标案38件。在决定立案侦查的案件中，大要案337件446人，占立案总数的49%和案犯总数的54%，比上年分别上升33.2%和27.4%。其中，犯罪金额5至10万元的58件，10至50万元的56件，50至100万元的8件，100万元以上的3件；侦破要案34件，涉及县处级干部32人，副地级干部2人。通过办案为国家挽回经济损失2100多万元。特别是8月，党中央作出进一步开展反腐败斗争的决定后，省院根据省委和高检院的安排，就全省检察机关查办大要案工作作了全面部署。省委及时批转了省院的贯彻意见。各地检察机关态度坚决，行动迅速。广泛开展举报宣传，适时召开新闻发布会，公布立案查办的大要案，很快形成反腐败斗争的声势。广大干部、群众热情支持，积极举报贪污贿赂等经济犯罪分子。9至12月，全省检察机关收到举报2031件，占全年举报总数的74.75%，比上年同期上升4.6倍，出现了署名举报多、到检察机关上门举报多和举报线索成案率高的好势头。各级检察机关抓住有利时机，及时调整工作步骤，加强对查办大要案工作的领导，实行检察长办案责任制，集中精力突破了一批大案要案。9至12月，共立案侦查贪污贿赂万元以上、挪用公款5万元以上大案133件，占此类案件立案总数的53%，比上年同期增加1.9倍，为全省反腐败斗争取得阶段性成果发挥了重要的职能作用。

二、刑事检察

充分发挥法律监督职能作用，加强与公安、法院的配合，坚持依法从重从快的方针，严厉打击严重刑事犯罪活动，积极参加各种专项斗争和社会治安综合治理。坚持对重特大案件提前介入，及时批捕、起诉了公安机关提请逮捕和移送起诉的严重刑事案犯，全年受理公安机关提请逮捕的人犯12599名，审结12060名，其中批准逮捕11261名；受理公安机关移送起诉案犯罪12003名，审结10865名，提起公诉10111名，为维护我省社会治安的稳定发挥了积极作用。在严厉打击刑事犯罪斗争中，一是把握重点，严厉打击杀人、抢劫、强奸、重伤害等严重危害社会治安的暴力犯罪。共批捕这类案犯2101人，重特大案犯1283人。分别占批捕人数的18.7%和11.4%。其中，杀人犯304人，占2.7%，抢劫犯1162人，占10.3%，强奸犯350人，占3.1%，重伤害犯285人，占2.5%。在办理这些案件中，检察机关坚持"基本事实清楚、基本证据确凿"的原则，在保证办案质量的前提下，力求快捕、快诉，加大打击力度，不在检察环节上贻误战机。二是坚持贯彻全国人大常委会《关于禁毒的决定》，严厉打击制、贩、运毒品犯罪活动。全年共批捕毒品案犯1062人，占捕人总数的9.4%，比上年的437人增加了1.4倍，是近年来批捕毒品罪犯最多的一年。针对我省毒品犯罪猖獗，犯罪分子为逃避打击，采取化整为零等形式贩卖毒品的特点，检察机关认真执行省人大关于毒品犯罪起刑点的意见，对制、贩、运1克海洛因、20克雅片的，坚决批捕、起诉。为了充分体现从重从快的方针，省院提出对毒品犯罪被告人一般不作免诉处理的原则，有力地打击了毒品犯罪的嚣张气焰。三是开展专项斗争，打击盗窃犯罪和拐卖妇女儿童犯罪，保护人民财产安全和公民人身安全。全年共批捕盗窃案犯5513人，占捕人总数的49%，比上年同期上升19.6%，其中重大盗窃犯1336人，特大盗窃犯245人，分别比上年上升39.9%和27.6%；批捕拐卖妇女儿童案犯79人。四是切实履行侦查监督和审判监督职能，保证严格执法。充分运用法律规定，行使侦查监督权和审判监督权，对有罪不究和提请批捕、移送起诉经审查无罪的，依法予以纠正，全年不批准逮捕799人，不起诉82人；追加逮捕人犯84人，追加起诉犯罪分子21人。对有关执法部门有罪不究、以罚代刑经提出意见仍不纠正的，检察机关依法直接立案侦查，决定逮捕，提起公诉，推动严格执法。对法院有罪判无罪，重罪轻判和轻罪重判等错判案件提起抗诉。全年对58件认为确有错误的刑事判决提出了抗诉，对审判活动中的违法行为及时提出纠正意见。

三、法纪检察

认真查处"侵权"、渎职案件。查处"侵权"、渎职等法纪犯罪案件，是检察机关保护人权、履行法纪监督职能的重要工作之一，也是严格执法，加强廉政建设，深入开展反腐败斗争的重要任务。全年共受理各类法纪案件679件，立案侦查174件，其中大要案23件，比上年上升35%；特大案件8件。重点查办了影响恶劣、群众反映强烈的徇私舞弊、刑讯逼供、非法拘禁、玩忽职守和重大责任事故等五类重点案件，共立案132件，占立案总数的75.9%。其中，追究司法人员26人。在查处"侵权"、渎职案件的同时，注意在法纪罪案中发现和查处贪污贿赂犯罪，扩大办案效果。

四、监所检察

坚持"一手抓执法监督、一手抓办案"的指导思想，及时检察纠正了部分监管场所利用职权对减刑、假释罪犯和保外就医、缓刑人员乱收费，部分看守所违反规定截留已决犯搞生产等违法问题；积极查处了监管改造场所发生的各类犯罪案件；立案查处了个别监管人员贪污、贿赂、"侵权"、渎职犯罪案件，配合监管改造机关坚决打击"牢头狱霸”，依法从重从快地打击被监管改造人员的又犯罪活动；监督和促进对罪犯、劳教人员依法文明管理，保护被监管人员的合法权益。全年共办理在监管改造场所发生的各类犯罪案件137件243人；向监管改造单位发出书面检察建议103人(次)，提出口头检察建议829人(次)；纠正了204名人犯的超期羁押问题。维护了监管改造秩序。

五、民事行政检察

民事行政检察工作较上年有较大的发展。在抓紧健全机构、培训干部、克服困难、积极办案的同时，加强了对民事审判和行政诉讼活动的监督。全年共受理不服法院判决的民事行政案件168件，经审查立案54件，已提起抗诉7件。在对民事、行政诉讼活动的监督中，提出检察建议13件，有3件被法院采纳，改变了原审判决。

六、控告申诉检察

控告申诉检察工作在及时处理群众来信来访的同时，把办好各类控申案件作为严格执法、强化监督职能的重点工作来进行。全年共办理控申案件352件，其中，复查刑事申诉案件102件，依法纠正24件。根据高检院要求，在全省开展了文明接待活动，取得了较好的效果。张掖分院控申接待室被最高人民检察院授予“全国文明接待室”称号。

七、检察科学技术

检察科学技术工作配合惩治腐败，严厉打击贪污贿赂等经济犯罪和其它各类刑事犯罪斗争中，全年受理各类现场勘查、文证审查和检验鉴定案件614件。出具各类鉴定书、检验报告、分析意见书291份。为检察机关履行法律监督职能查处各类犯罪案件提供了科学依据，促进了办案效率，提高了办案质量。

八、加强队伍建设，提高执法水平

加强检察队伍建设是履行法律监督职责的重要组织保障。全省各级检察院在抓好业务建设的同时，坚持依法建院、从严治检的方针。按照建设一支政治强、业务精、纪律严、作风硬的检察队伍的要求，加强了队伍的思想、组织、制度和作风建设。在突出加强干警思想政治工作中，切实加强了各级领导班子的建设，与此同时，围绕严格执法，搞好自身反腐败工作。各级检察院进一步加强勤政廉政制度建设，健全内部监督制约机制，从制度上保证了检察人员廉洁自律。

司法行政

深化改革 强化职能 努力搞好法律保障和法律服务工作

省司法厅厅长

张 忠

司法行政工作是社会主义法制建设的重要组成部分，在发展社会主义市场经济中，担负着法律保障和法律服务的繁重任务。1993年，全省各级司法行政机关和广大干警，认真学习贯彻邓小平同志南巡重要谈话，认真学习贯彻党的十四大精神，进一步解放思想，开拓创新，深化各项工作改革，在过去工作的基础上，各项业务都有了新的发展，为维护社会稳定，服务改革开放和社会主义市场经济作出了积极贡献。

一、劳动改造

劳动改造工作始终坚持“改造第一、生产第二”的方针，坚持依法、文明、严格、科学管理，坚持实施《罪犯改造行为规范》和《监管场所环境规范》，推行了对罪犯的分押、分管、分教工作，对罪犯进行了百分考核，依法奖惩，确保了监所的安全稳定，提高了改造质量。罪犯脱逃率在0.1%以下，重新犯罪为4——7%。在全省劳改单位的罪犯中，实行分押纯度平均达56.3%；实行分级管理的犯人达押犯总数56.3%；实行分类教育的犯人达63.2%。“三分”工作调动了罪犯改造的积极性，促进了改造质量的提高。在坚持“三课”(政治课、文化课、技术课)教育的同时，积极开展创建“优秀特殊学校”活动。全省押犯单位都办成了特殊学校；省二监和省劳改四支队、六支队，经过验收，达到了省级优秀特殊学校标准；全省劳改单位对罪犯进行政治教育、文化教育和技术教育课的入学率分别达到97.8%、92.5%和73.8%。“三课”教育和开展创建“优秀特殊学校”活动，既使教育改造工作更加规范化、系统化，又促进了劳改经济发展，也为社会输运了人才。

二、劳动教养

劳动教养工作认真贯彻执行“教育、感化、挽救”的方针和“三象”原则，始终把提高教育改造质量放在一切工作的首位，把劳教经济改革作为重点工作来抓，使教育改造和劳教经济都有新的起色，取得了较好成绩。劳教人员逃跑率为0.64%。根据我省吸毒劳教人员较多的实际，各劳教单位进一步完善戒毒管理制度，采取单独编队，集中管理，严格制度，堵源截流，强制戒毒和药物戒毒相结合等方法，保证了戒毒工作的顺利进行，年内无一例戒毒事故，使所内吸毒劳教人员安全戒除了毒隐，戒毒率达98%。全年劳教人员参加政治课学习的入学率达100%；参加文化课学习的入学率达100%；参加职业技术课学习的入学率达89%。

三、法律服务

社会主义市场经济的建立，为司法行政机关提出了一项艰巨而紧迫的任务，这就是要尽快建立与市场经济相适应的法律服务体系。1993年，律师、公证、基层法律服务工作，紧紧围绕为社会主义市场经济服务，在深化改革，强化服务职能，增强法律服务工作的生机与活力上作文章、下功夫。司法部"六月会议"之后，深入开展调查研究，结合实际，按照"解放思想，实事求是，吃透省情，分类指导，合理布局"的基本思路，于10月制定下发了《甘肃省司法厅关于深化和推进律师、公证、基层法律服务工作改革的意见》，从而加快、推动了法律服务工作的改革步伐，使律师、公证和基层法律服务工作在深化改革中取得了突破性的进展。

律师工作大胆突破了使用生产资料所有制、行政级别概念界定的束缚，放开手脚发展律师和律师工作机构，开展各项业务。全省专兼职律师已发展到850人，比上年增加100人。律师事务所发展到123个，其中不占国家编制、不要国家经费的"四自"律师事务所15个，比上年增加11个。律师为各级政府、国家机关、社会团体、企事业单位担任常年法律顾问3534家，比上年增加27.9%；办理刑事辩护3437件，下降14.3%；民事诉讼代理2420件，增长18.6%；经济案件诉讼代理2382件，增长24.5%；行政诉讼代理182件，增长17.4%；非诉讼法律事务2546件，增长77.5%；代写法律事务文书8400件，下降8.4%。

公证工作实行了主任负责制、目标管理责任制、效益浮动奖金制等多种形式的改革。经过试点，公证工作发展势头良好，办证数量平均提高了30%，办证质量也有很大提高。年内，公证工作机构已发展到98个，比上年增加8个。公证人员已发展到432名。全省共办理各类公证事项86153件，其中经济公证46275件，比上年增长3.11%；民事公证37163件，比上年下降31.91%；涉外和涉港、澳、台公证2715件，比上年增长12.11%。

乡镇基层法律服务，通过加快和深化改革，机构增加，队伍发展，业务进一步拓宽。全省已建立乡镇、街道法律服务所528个，比上年增加91个。乡镇、街道法律服务所共有法律服务工作者1339名，比上年增加56名。全年共担任乡镇政府、乡镇、村办企业常年法律顾问1252家，比上年增长14.1%；协办公证15035件，比上年下降21.5%；民事诉讼代理786件，比上年增长26.8%；非诉讼代理1501件，比上年增长60.7%；调解纠纷13603件，比上年减少280件；代写法律文书6224件，比上年增长1.7%；宣讲法律9898场次，受教育人数达570多万人次。

四、"二五"普法

1993年，是全省实施"二五"普法规划的关键性一年，省委、省政府领导亲自过问，省人大八届四次常委会专门听取了"二五"普法的情况汇报。由于领导重视，主管部门精心组织，各业务部门大力协作，新闻单位积极配合，使"二五"普法自觉地服从和服务于改革开放和社会主义市场经济建设，取得了明显的成效。一是各级干部的法制教育进一步深化。全省各级党校把法制教育列入教学计划，使轮训干部能受到较系统的法制教育；县以上领导干部中心组确定了学法"学习日"制度，保证每月一次；组织副厅级以上干部法制讲座6次，有3000多人次听讲；各地、各部门在普遍学习的基础上，组织不同层次的考试和考核，全省参加的干部达21万人次。二是专业法学习全面开展。各地、各部门坚持条块结合、分别实施的原则，采取组织讲座、法律知识竞赛等多种措施，认真落实。省直部门中有70多个单位结合自己的业务学习了专业法律法规，培训骨干24300余名，购买发行教材77500多册，参加学习的干部职工占总人数的90%以上。三是依法治理工作有了新的进展。截止年底，全省依法治理工作已在9个地州市、28个县市区全面展开。白银市、天水市代表我省出席了第三次全国部分城市学法、用法、依法治市座谈会。白银市政府把依法治市纳入政府四项基本政策之一，得到全国依法治市会议的肯定。四是宪法学习教育取得了新的成果。九条宪法修正案通过后，及时下发了学习通知，通过学习，广大干部群众充分认识了把社会主义市场经济等内容纳入宪法，以根本大法的形式确定下来的重要意义，提高了全体公民的学宪、护宪、按照宪法精神规范行为的自觉性。

五、人民调解

人民调解工作认真贯彻执行"调防结合，以防为主"的方针，以预防纠纷激化为重点，充分发挥了在社会治安综合治理中"第一道防线"的作用。1993年，全省农村、街道和厂矿企业共有调解委员会组织23106个(其中农村17777个、街道居委会1856个、厂矿企业3048个)，共有调解人员156086名，培训调解人员84648名。经过对调解组织整顿，一类调解组织13384个，占调解组织总数的57.9%；二、三类调解组织9722个，占42.1%，比上年减少5.2%。全年共调解婚姻、继承、赡养、抚养、邻里、房屋、宅基地、债务等各类民间纠纷109268件，调解成功101435件，成功率达92.8%，比上年增长1.6%。全年共防止民间纠纷转化为刑事案件1460件，2584人；防止民间纠纷引起非正常死亡665件，826人。

军　事

武装警察

努力提高部队写政素质，为甘肃经济建设和社会稳定服务

中国人民武装警察部队甘肃总队

总队长：何虎　　政委：王永银

1993年，是我省武警部队全面建设取得显著进步的一年。一年来，在武警总部党委和省委、省政府及省公安厅党委的正确领导下，坚持用党的十四大精神和邓小平同志建设有中国特色社会主义理论武装部队，坚决按照江总书记"五句话"的总要求和"陇原卫士、丝路哨兵"题词精神，牢牢地把握总部党委提出的在部队建设中必须坚持"与江泽民为核心的党中央保持高度一致；努力把武警部队建设成为'政治合格、军事过硬、作风优良、纪律严明、保障有力'的钢铁之师；履行武警部队职能，为维护国家安全和社会稳定做出贡献"的三条原则。始终坚持以执勤和处置突发事件为中心，全面落实总部的工作部署，圆满完成了维护国家安全和社会稳定的各项任务。尤其是担负跨区执行任务的部队，经受了锻炼和考验，圆满完成了各项任务。

一.认真学习十四大精神，广大官兵执行和捍卫党的基本路线的自觉性进一步增强

总队党委把学习贯彻党的十四大精神，用邓小平同志建设有中国特色社会主义理论和新时期军队建设的思想武装官兵的头脑，作为部队建设的根本大事来抓。坚持以总队、支队两级党委、机关和团以上领导干部为重点，采取中心组学习、集中教育和办集训班等形式，系统学习了十四大报告、邓小平同志建设有中国特色社会主义理论和新时期军队建设思想。《邓小平文选》第三卷出版后，两级党委集中时间学习了中共中央《决定》、江泽民总书记的讲话和《邓选》第三卷，并及时安排部署了部队的学习。各级领导带头通读了《邓选》三卷，基层学习也不断深入。在定西支队进行试点后，深入开展了坚持党的基本路线教育。先后有268名领导和机关干部深入基层宣讲辅导，较好地统一了广大官兵对一些理论和实践问题的认识，进一步提高了对确立建设有中国特色社会主义理论指导地位重大历史意义的认识，明确了党的基本路线是国家的生命线和人民的幸福线，建立社会主义市场经济是发展生产力的必由之路，更加牢固地树立了坚持和捍卫党的基本路线一百年不动摇的观念。在完成以执勤和处置突发事件为中心的各项任务中，表现出很高的政治觉悟和良好的精神风貌。

二.狠抓惩治腐败、加强廉政建设工作，党委班子和干部队伍建设进一步加强

贯彻民主集中制和党委统一的集体领导下的首长分工负责制，采取定期考察讲评和个别帮助相结合的方法，继续抓了《支队级党委(常委)会工作规则》、《党委成员管理规定》和各项生活制度的落实，支队级党委核心领导作用普遍发挥较好。按照总队部署，狠抓了党风和廉政建设。年初，两级党委和机关集中学习了军委13号文件，进行对照检查，逐级制定了落实措施。总队党委《发扬优良传统加强廉政建设的措施》被总部《政工简讯》刊登。中央作出开展反腐败斗争决策后，总队及时召开纪律检查工作会议，认真传达贯彻江总书记重要讲话、中纪委二次全会、全军、公安部和总部纪检工作会议精神，部署总队惩治腐败、加强廉政建设工作。依据总部、总队党委的《实施意见》和年内达到的阶段性目标，以总队、支队党委、领导干部和机关为重点，采取召开民主生活会、集中学习教育和征求基层意见等方法，上下结合，突出抓了自查自纠、对照检查、正面教育和违纪问题的查处。针对工作作风、干部使用、战士关注的"热点"问题(如考学、学技术、转志愿兵)、执行政策规定和生活待遇等五个方面检查出的问题，从杜绝吃、拿、卡、要、占、报、借等方面入手，进行了专项清理。查处党员违纪问题6起，处理遗留案件2起，6名党员干部受党纪和政纪处分。通过扎实有效的工作，一些突出的不正之风得到了遏制和纠正，党风廉政建设的阶段性目标基本达到。分两期对新提团职干部进行了上岗前的教育培训。认真做了院校招生、转业干部和老干部的安置工作。及时调整、充实、培训基层干部，干部队伍素质进一步提高。

三.忠实履行维护社会稳定的神圣使命，圆满完成了以执勤和处置突发事件为中心的各项任务

坚决贯彻江总书记"居安思危"的思想，积极抓了处置突发事件的各项准备工作。总对在四支队和兰州市支队抓了贯彻总部山东战备执勤工作会议精神、落实"三个规定"的试点，7月中旬召开现场会作了推广，促进了各项战备执勤法规的落实。组织驻兰机动部队进行了首

长机关和部分实兵处置突发事件演习，锻炼提高了部队快速反应能力。积极参与并有效处置了临夏、西吉、西固区新城、白银平川区等突发事件。四支队、兰州、临夏、平凉、天水、定西、白银等支队广大官兵坚决执行中央和上级的有关指示，一声令下，迅速出动，在情况复杂、地域生疏、各种保障十分困难的情况下，严格遵守政策纪律，忍辱负重，风餐露宿，团结奋斗，圆满完成了执勤任务，受到了公安部、武警总部及地方党政领导的充分肯定和表扬。赴西吉部队创造和总结的“四位一体”及“稳定后方、支援前方”等收缴武器的成功战例和经验，得到了中央政治局和军委的肯定。先后5次围歼持枪杀人案犯，都圆满完成了任务。统一部署，进行了为期一个月的勤务教育整顿。清理撤收非执勤和有偿执勤用兵，充实了一线兵力。坚持开展“执勤先进中队”、“执勤标兵中队”评比竞赛活动，提高了固定目标执勤安全系数。执勤先进中队、标兵中队分别达到70%和10%。机动部队投入部分兵力担负兰州等大中城市和重点地区巡警巡逻勤务，与公安干警一起抓获各类违法犯罪分子1235人，制止流氓滋扰和打架斗殴514起，收缴各种凶器826件，赃款43148元，为群众提供服务3000余次，受到社会各界好评。全省武警部队积极参加抢险救灾88次，抢救遇险群众162人、受灾物资近百万吨，为保护国家和人民生命财产安全做出了贡献。涌现出了酒泉支队藏族班长李洪生舍亲舍己救出6名遇险群众的英雄壮举。

四.切实加强教育训练，部队军事业务素质明显提高

部队各级党委坚持把教育训练摆到战略地位来抓。总队集中20天时间对100名教导队长、中队长进行了教学法集训，举办了参谋业务和通信专业骨干培训班，受训116人。各支队以教导队为基地，重视抓好干部骨干训练，广泛开展了“四会”教练员评比竞赛活动，85%以上的干部骨干基本达到“四会”要求。依据《军事训练大纲》，突出抓了部队训练、专勤专训、机动部队应急训练和战法研究，使训练更加适应执勤和处置突发事件需要。经考核，部队训练成绩良好率100%，优秀率55%，总评优秀。10个全训中队和31个执勤中队达到训练全优。指挥学校按照“一个服务，两个适应”的办学思想，着力解决学员第一任职需要，加强实践性环节，教学内容、手段、效果不断得到改进和提高。经总队对教员教学能力和应届毕业学员进行考核，优秀率比上年提高9.2%。

五.坚持不懈抓好经常性思想工作和管理工作，部队集中统一思想稳定

针对社会主义市场经济条件下部队官兵的思想反映，深入进行了发扬优良传统、“五种革命精神”、“64字创业精神”、革命人生观和价值观教育。结合学雷锋活动，采取多种形式，大力宣扬李洪生舍亲舍己抢救群众的英雄事迹。总部、总队在北京和兰州召开了李洪生事迹新闻发布会，组成李洪生事迹报告团，在首都北京和省内巡回报告40余场次，直接听众达5万余人，引起社会各界强烈反响，有效地抵制了拜金主义、享乐主义、极端个人主义的侵蚀。适时抓了执行紧急任务部队和落榜考生的思想政治工作。抓了《宪法》、《刑法》、《兵役法》等七个法律条规的学习教育。以纪念“双拥”活动50周年为主题，“拥政爱民月”和警民共建活动广泛深入，警政警民团结进一步增强。7个支队、44个中队被县以上人民政府评为拥政爱民先进单位，5个部队所在地县市被国家命名为“双拥模范城(县)”。

经常性管理以作风纪律建设为核心，以预防事故、保证安全为重点，狠抓条令条例的学习教育和贯彻落实，部队战备、训练、工作、生活秩序趋于正规。针对部队管理中出现的问题，狠抓专项治理，相继进行了车辆驾驶员、武器、兵员管理教育整顿。广泛开展尊干爱兵、警容风纪整顿月活动，严肃认真地纠正打骂体罚战士、索要战士钱物和侵占士兵利益的不良倾向，进一步密切了官兵关系。始终坚持积极预防的思想，把安全防事故工作当作保持部队稳定和促进部队建设上新台阶的大事来抓，多次召开安全工作电话会议部署、讲评，先后两次集中时间进行安全教育整顿，持续开展“百日安全无事故”活动，进行安全检查。总队制定了《事故案件惩戒规定》，对发生事故、案件的责任者予以严肃惩处，有效地遏制了各类事故、案件的发生，11个支队达到“三无”。庆阳、平凉、甘南支队连续五年以上，定西、武威、张掖支队连续二年以上保持“三无”，确保了部队内部安全。

六.同心协力落实《纲要》，基层建设稳步发展

坚持把加强党支部建设作为基层建设的关键。重视配齐配强基层干部，及时健全了组织。采取建立组织生活登记、《党员手册》和举办“党员之家”等形式，较好地落实了各项组织生活制度。认真抓了党支部骨干和党员发展对象培训，坚持开展创先争优活动，有33个先进党支部和43名优秀党员受到总部、总队通报表彰。各级团组织和广大团员青年认真贯彻落实共青团十三大精神，争做新时代“四有”军人，在基层建设中发挥了突击队作用。总队机关年内派出4批36个工作组119名机关干部深入基层，认真开展调查研究，解决基层实际困难。支队机关充分发挥一线指挥部作用，实施对基层面对面的领导。通过抓点带面，调查研究，合力解难，促进了未达目标中队、非建制单位和弱点项目的建设，解决了在人员管理、伙食管理、营区管理和物质文化生活方面存在的突出问题，促进了《纲要》的落实。经考评，有81.7%的中队达标，达标先进中队27个，庆阳、甘南、平凉、第四支队被评为达标先进支队。

人民防空

解放思想 深化改革 人防工作再上新台阶

人民防空是国防建设的重要组成部分，它兼有战时保护人民生命安全，避免或减少国民经济损失和平时为国民经济建设服务的双重职能。我省自开展人防工作以来，特别是党的十一届三中全会以来，在国家人防委、兰州军区人防委和省政府、省军区的正确领导下，经过全省人防战线的干部职工和广大军民的共同努力，建设了百万平方米以上的人防工程；建立了以省会为中心的全省八个人防重点城市的无线电数据传输网，以重点目标为中心的警报报知网络和兰州天马无线寻呼台；制订、修改、完善了城市防空袭预案，组建了七种人防专业队伍；在全省人防重点城市初级中学普及了“三防”常识教育，开展了以《人民防空条例》为主要内容的人防宣传教育活动。人防工程、设备、设施的开发利用，扩大了平战结合的成果，为城市建设、国民经济建设做出了一定的贡献。随着人防建设的不断发展，人防工作在未来战争和城市建设、经济建设中的地位越来越重要。

过去的一年里，我省人防工作认真贯彻邓小平同志南巡谈话和十四大精神，坚持“长期坚持，平战结合，全面规划，重点建设”的方针，抓住机遇，加大改革力度，人防事业有了长足的发展。

一、面向市场经济，深化投资和内部体制改革。在人防建设上，采用“借鸡下蛋”、利用外资、合资的办法，修建了10000多平方米的地下工程。省人防通信站面向市场，在竞争中求发展，与一家企业合资建成了容量为3万门的BP机无线寻呼网。这些项目的建设，不仅发展了人防事业，而且为城市居民提供了规模较大的商娱中心和通信服务，发挥了人防建设的战备效益，经济效益和社会效益。省人防设计科研院不断深化内部体制改革，从1986年实行自收自支以来，经济效益逐年上升。1993年改革组织管理和分配办法，极大地调动了技术人员的积极性，全办设计收入达到40万元，年人均产值1.5万元，比上年增长25%，创造了设计收入新纪录。

二、落实人防建设政策，拓宽资金来源渠道。人防工作是一项全民性的工作，人防建设是造福子孙后代的千秋伟业。因此，人防建设需要全社会的关心和支持。1992年，我省与兰州军区人防委联合制定下发了《进一步贯彻落实国家人防建设有关政策规定》。1993年，各级人防部门把落实文件精神作为头等大事来抓。多数城市制订下发了实施意见。酒泉市人防办与有关部门协商，落实了地方自筹资金，从1994年起，酒泉地区财政和酒泉市财政分别按所辖人口每年每人一元的标准拨出人防建设费。酒泉、玉门落实了动员城镇职工总人数的1～2%的人员，参加人防公共工程的建设维护义务劳动。对派人有困难的单位，允许按应参加义务劳动人员比例，向人防部门缴纳工资、福利、劳保用品、零星工具等四项费用，由人防部门统筹安排进行人防建设。兰州、天水、金昌等城市从“抓结合民用建筑修建防空地下室”入手，制定了应建范围和标准，基本杜绝了不建、漏建和不按标准建设的现象。一年来，修建防空地下室10000多平方米。因其他原因不能修建的，人防部门按物价部门规定的标准，收取易地建设费200多万元。

三、全面完成了人防工程建设任务。兰州火车站、天水市广场人防工程，主体工程已经完成。全年续建人防工程2281平方米，加固改造工事775平方米，维护管理工程22.3万多平方米，处理遭水灾工事1950平方米。省人防和兰州市人防办对兰州市结合民用建筑修建的防空地下室建设质量进行了检查。

四、指挥通信工作有新进展。各重点城市着手对原防空袭预案进行修订，通过调查研究，初步掌握了第一手资料，兰州市完成了防空袭预案基本方案的修订任务。大多数城市对人防专业队伍进行整组，结合岗位练兵，进行专业训练。微机控制无线数据传输网络过几年的试通后，于1993年正式开通。人防警报的社会化管理水平有了进一步提高，全省警报完好率和覆盖率分别达到90%和75%以上。

五、宣传教育工作常抓不懈。各人防重点城市继续认真贯彻落实省委宣传部、省军区政治部、省人防办联合制定的《关于深入开展全民人防教育的实施细则》，并逐步将人防教育纳入国防教育体系。酒泉地区在行署机关举办国防、人防教育专题形势报告全，2000多名机关干部受到了教育。金昌、玉门、白银、酒泉继续开展人防宣传周活动，受教育面达到80%以上。全省普及了初级中学人防知识教育，开展教育学校共158所，受教育学生28140余人。

六、经济效益，社会效益明显上升。一年来，各级人防部门进一步扩大人防工程、设备、设施的对外开放面，利用技术、设备等优势，发展第三产业，创办经济实体。全年实现产值营业额3400万元，实现利税400万元，平战结合收入130万元，新增平战结合工程10000多平方米。先后建设的11个大中型骨干工程，被用作商场、娱乐场所，方便了群众生活，促进了经济建设。

经 济

农林牧渔水利业

农业(种植业)概况

省农业厅厅长

刘兴邦

1993年,我省农业生产在建立社会主义市场经济体制中,参与了市场竞争,给自身的发展注入了新的活力,有了新的发展。特别是粮食、油品等主要农产品价格的逐步放开,调动了农民的生产积极性,使农业生产向着"高产、优质、高效"的路子稳定发展,获得第十一个丰收年。其主要特点是:

一、农村经济持续、稳定、协调发展。

1993年,我省农业和农村工作贯彻中央农村工作会议和全国农业工作会议精神,以社会主义市场经济为导向,以继续深化农村改革为动力,以发展农村经济为目标,使农村经济持续、稳定、协调地发展。据统计,全省农业总产值(按1990年不变价计算)达到134.51亿元,比上年增加10.7亿元,增长8.64%。其中,农业产值达到91.65亿元,比上年增加15.21亿元,增长19.89%。农业产值占农业总产值68.14%,比1992年提高了6.4个百分点。全省农民人均纯收入562.9元,比上年增加60.2元,增长11.98%。

二、农作物播种面积基本稳定,产量增加

1993年全省农作物播种面积5458.09万亩,比上年减少34.3万亩,减0.62%。其中,粮食作物播种面积4269.04万亩,粮食总产量达到746.15万吨,比上年增加49.19万吨,增长7.06%,再创历史最高水平。分品种来看,与上年比较有增有减:小麦面积2105.34万亩,增加27.52万亩,产量394.7万吨,增加57.26万吨,增长16.97%,平均亩产增加25公斤;玉米、高粱分别减产5.13%和9.38%;大豆面积129万亩,增加23.58万亩,产量10.81万吨,与上年基本持平;蚕豆面积140.45万亩,增加26.43万亩,产量23.7万吨,增长41%。经济作物播种面积688.49万亩,比上年增加52.81万亩,增长8.31%。经济作物中除棉花减产以外,其他均保持了增长的势头。其中,油料、烤烟、甜菜、药材产量分别达到37.53万吨、4.53万吨、104.62万吨和5.29万吨,分别比上年增长2.88%、4.59%、11.04%和63.74%。蔬菜面积116.77万亩,产量249.4万吨,分别比上年增长3.48%和7.27%;蚕、茶、果生产均有不同程度的增长,水果丰收,创历史最好水平,果园面积325.83万亩,比上年增加47.31万亩,增长16.99%,水果总产量59.66万吨,增加12.54万吨,增长26.61%;蚕茧产量312.76吨,茶叶产量170.83吨,分别比上年增长6.49%和7.02%。

三、农业生产条件有所改善,投入不断增加

1978年之前,由于我省农业底子薄、基础差、条件落后,制约着农业生产的发展。改革开放以来,农村实行家庭联产承包责任制,给农村和农业生产发展输入了新的活力,调动了农民的生产积极性。特别是近年来,党中央、国务院强调农业在国民经济中的基础地位,国家和广大农民对农业投入逐年增加,农业生产条件得到进一步改善。1993年全省耕地面积5221.78万亩,虽比上年减少1.77万亩,减0.03%,但比1978年以来最低年份的1990年5213.36万亩增加8.42万亩,增长0.16%。有效灌溉面积达到1349.7万亩,比上年增加22.33万亩,增长1.68%,比1986年的1238.74万亩(1978年以来的最低年份)增加110.96万亩,增长8.96%。1993年有效灌溉面积占耕地面积的25.85%,比上年提高了0.44个百分点,比1986年提高2.12个百分点。保灌面积达到1124.69万亩,比上年增加17.31万亩,增长1.56%,占有效灌溉面积的83.33%。化肥施用量(实物量)153.94万吨,比上年增加14.93万吨,增长10.7%,其中,氮、磷、钾、复合肥分别为67.46万吨、64.61万吨、2.67万吨、19.2万吨,分别增加4.98万吨、5.34万吨、1.29万吨、3.32万吨,增长7.97%、9.02%、93.36%和20.91%。每亩耕地施用化肥29.48公斤,比上年增加2.87公斤。农用塑料薄膜使用量28293吨,比上年增加7338吨,增长35.02%,其中,地膜23336吨,比上年增加5905吨,增长33.88%,塑料薄膜覆盖面积达到340.81万亩,增加33.19万亩,增长10.79%。农村用电量21.84亿度,比上年增加1.45亿度,增长7.13%,其中,农业生产用电17.24亿度,增加0.98亿度,增长6%。

四、服务功能进一步增强

90年代以来,我们紧紧围绕"农业工作为农业生产服务,为农民服务,为农村经济服务"的方针,加强农业社会化服务体系建设,增强农业部门的综合服务功能,乡镇农技农经服务站建设有了新的进展。1993年初安排194个“四有”乡站建设任务，到目前为止，全省累计投建“四有”乡站1200个，建成836个，分别占农业乡镇总数的81.6%和56.9%，有49个县已完成“四有”乡站投建任务。现有县级农业技术推广站17个，农业技术推广中心64个，有农民技术员5.4万人，科技示范户36.44万户。乡站在搞好技术服务的同时，绝大多数都通过兴办经济实体，帮助农民引进新技术、新品种，积极开展经营服务，在组织引导农民进入市场，增加收入中发挥了重要作用。

五、种植结构趋于合理

近年来，我省农业生产认真贯彻“决不放松粮食生产，积极发展多种经营”的方针。1993年初，从全省实际出发，确定了粮食播种面积坚持“大稳定、小调整”的原则，提出了全省粮食播种面积警戒线不能低于4200万亩，经济作物按照市场需求适度发展。粮食生产在稳定面积、提高单产、增加总产的前提下，调整品种结构，发展适销对路和经济效益高的优质小麦、玉米、啤酒大麦、小杂粮、大豆等品种，调减劣质油料面积，稳定甜菜，扩大棉花，大力发展瓜果、蔬菜及名优新特产品。通过调整，农作物种植结构发生了较大变化，由传统的“粮食——经济作物”二元结构逐步转向“粮食——经作——饲料绿肥”的三元结构。全省粮食作物与经济作物的比例，粮食、经作与其他农作物的比例由1990年分别为88：12和80：11：9到1993年分别为86：14和78：13：9。农作物种植结构逐步趋于合理，产量也同步增长。

六、以发展“两高一优”农业为目标，大力推广实用增产技术

据不完全统计，1993年全省安排大面积推广项目12项，累计完成6366万亩次，其中“丰收计划”、“温饱工程”、地膜覆盖、水稻旱育稀植、种子包衣、综合高产栽培技术、立体栽培技术、配方施肥、病虫草鼠害综合防治等增产技术措施，上规模、上水平，技术进步在农业生产中所占比重有较大幅度增加，在全年粮食丰收中产生了重要作用。由于实用增产技术的大力推广和广泛应用，我省农业逐步向着“高产、优质、高效”的方向发展。1993年全省小麦产值(按90年不变价计算)达到23.29亿元，比上年增长16.98%，小麦产值占粮食作物产值的54.7%，比上年提高3.9个百分点。经济作物中的甜菜、烤烟、药材产值分别达到1.6亿元、1.38亿元、2.59亿元，比上年分别增长10.97%、4.59%、62.54%。蔬菜、水果产值分别达到7.73亿元和7.17亿元，比上年分别增长7.29%和25.91%。农业商品化程度明显提高，据统计，1993年农业(种植业)商品产值达到44.28亿元，比上年增加14.02亿元，增长46.33%。粮食商品量达到170.27万吨，商品率为22.82%，比上年提高2.22个百分点；商品油16.07万吨，商品率42.82%，比上年提高1.71个百分点；蔬菜商品量175.5万吨，商品率为70.36%，比上年提高4.58个百分点；瓜类商品量为42.3万吨，商品率为80.92%，比上年提高6.72个百分点。由于种植业商品化程度的提高，推动了农村经济的繁荣和农民收入的增加。

七、农业商品基地建设进展顺利

1993年全省投放发展粮食生产专项资金(农业部分)1389万元(不含周转金)，继续用于省列商品粮基地建设。重点扶持开展新技术推广、良种繁育推广、中低产田改造、仪器设备购置和农民技术员的培训。1993年基地范围内向国家交售商品粮110.39万吨；调入商品粮比上年同期减少2.9万吨，减42%；向国家交售油料8万吨。1993年我省三个国家级商品粮基地县总投资1250万元，主要用于农业科技推广建设，发展“两高一优”农业综合开发等，保证了基地建设和效益的充分发挥。

甘肃林业在改革中迅速发展

省林业厅厅长

朱耀光

重点改革措施

【大力推行工程造林】我省从1989年开始推行工程造林，到1993年已占造林总任务44.8%。据林业部核查，推行工程造林以来的近四、五年时间，全省造林面积核实率平均在95%以上，成活率85%以上的合格面积占核实面积的80%左右，造林核实率、合格率和当年成活率比八十年代以前提高10%以上。

【不断调整生产结构】全省各地在安排林业生产时，注意市场要求，突出发展“两高一优”林业，促使经济林迅猛发展，经济林在造林总任务中的比重由八十年代初期约5%发展到现在的40%，主要品种保存面积达40多万公顷，户均0.1顷，已成为全省农村经济主要的支柱产业和最受群众欢迎的小康工程。

【加快“四荒地”造林绿化进程】各地在巩固林业“三定”工作成果的同时，将尚未造林绿化的“四荒地”面向社会租赁、拍卖，加快了荒山绿化步伐。全省已租赁、拍卖集体宜林“四荒地”1.83万公顷。其中庆阳、天水两地市起步较早，取得明显成效。

【注重科技兴林】各地把林业科技推广，林业生产和产品加工销售有机地结合在一起，大搞产加销一条龙服务，全省部分地区从地到乡成立科技生产一体化的林果产品经销实体，把分散的产品组织起来，形成规模，发挥优势，扩大了市场，增强了竞争力。仅平凉地区，1993年就组织外销果品3000多万公斤，实现产值4000多万元。

主要工作成就

【森林培育】1993年,全省计划造林13.5万公顷,实际完成15.7万公顷,占计划的118%。其中,工程造林6.9万公顷,占造林总任务的44.8%。在人工造林面积中,防护林5.8万公顷,用材林3.6万公顷,经济林5.3万公顷。完成义务植树5894万株,四旁植树4523万株。

【重点工程】(1)三北防护林体系二期工程。全年完成造林11.4万公顷,占计划的101.6%。其中工程造林4.6万公顷,完成工程项目36个。完成育苗0.5万公顷,容器育苗557.8万袋。封山育林2.44万公顷,中幼林抚育4.76万公顷,补植造林2.38万公顷,新建乡村林场110个。二期工程还剩两年时间,9月份按照林业部要求,开始编制三期工程规划,止年底,各地、县完成外业调查和内业整理,全省三期规划方案雏形基本完成。(2)长江中上游防护林体系工程。全省属"长防林"工程范围的共13个县(区),现已启动8个县。全年完成"长防林"建设6.8万公顷。其中:重点营造林任务4.1万公顷(包括防护林2.7万公顷,用材林0.5万公顷,经济林0.4万公顷,薪炭林0.4万公顷);面上营造林2.7万公顷。分别占计划任务的100.88%和118.03%。是我省"长防林"建设启动以来,完成造林质量好、数量多的一年。(3)沙漠综合治理工程。是1992年新启动的国家重点工程项目之一。全年完成人工造林0.7万公顷,是计划任务的1倍多。封沙(滩)育林(草)13.55万公顷。(4)国营林场脱贫工程。我省是林业部确定的国营林场脱贫试点省之一。1993年,全省国营林场完成造林2.91万公顷,占年计划的112.7%,其中速生丰产林0.4万公顷。育苗0.23万公顷,占年计划的109.0%。完成中幼林抚育3.33万公顷,低产林改造0.31万公顷,经营采伐0.12万公顷,生产木材26万立方米。销售总收入达到1.05亿元,比1992年增长23.5%,实现利润1800多万元,首批启动的55个贫困林场,已有23个基本实现脱贫。全省已有17个林场年产值突破100万元,有100多个林场年产值突破50万元;国营林场的贫困面已由工程启动前的56.4%下降到1993年的35.95%。

【森林保护】全年共发生森林火警3次,创造了全年无森林火灾的好成绩。全省林业公安机关共立案1368起,查处1310起,综合查处率95.7%,为国家挽回经济损失184.7万元。防治森林病虫鼠害17万公顷,防治率为55.1%,比林业部下达的39%指标高出16.51%;实施森林病虫害监测代表面积103.7万公顷,监测覆盖率为53.61%;实施产地检疫种苗面积0.7万公顷,种苗产地检疫率为77.17%;杨树蛀干天牛防治面积完成3万公顷,防治率达到67.71%。

【林产工业】1993年,全省完成锯材0.4立方米;纤维板0.59万立方米;纸板561吨。

【木材生产】全年生产商品材53.94万立方米,其中森工出材23.84万立方米。

【林业产值】全年实现林业产值13亿元,较去年增长近20%。

甘肃畜牧业发展综述

省畜牧厅厅长

周明辉

1993年,甘肃省畜牧业以提高效益为中心,走产业开发及贸工牧一体化的路子,畜产品产量全面增长,城乡肉食市场进一步繁荣,全省畜牧业获得第十二个丰收年。

肉蛋奶毛全面增产。全省肉类总产达到52.7万吨,首次登上50万吨台阶,禽蛋产量突破10万吨(10.2万吨),鲜奶产量9.9万吨;与上年相比,肉蛋奶分别增长11.7%、4.1%和15.1%,呈现出较高的增长势头。其中牛羊禽肉在肉类中的比重上升到25.4%,比上年提高1个百分点,肉类结构进一步优化。绵羊毛产量结束了1990年以来连续三年减产的颓势,恢复到15411吨,比上年增长3.7%。

畜禽出栏持续增长。年内出栏肉猪539.6万头、肉牛52.8万头、肉羊316.2万只,分别比上年增长6.0%、3.9%和4.3%。家禽出栏数达到3407万只,比上年大幅度上升,增幅达34.6%。

牲畜存栏稳中有增。年末存栏大牲畜596.4万头,其中:牛345.3万头;生猪645.1万头,其中能繁母猪47.2万头,占7.3%;绵山羊1025.6万只。与上年相比,牛增长0.8%,羊增长1.3%,猪增长2.9%,能繁母猪增长1.5%。

一.奶肉牛业发展速度加快。由于牛肉市场持续看好,乳品企业重现生机,牛产业发展迅速。全年牛肉产量达到5.6万吨,牛奶产量达到9.5万吨,分别比上年增长7.7%和13.1%。牛饲养量净增5.3万头。张掖、临泽等地利用氨化秸秆等饲草资源大力发展肉牛生产,集体养牛势头很旺,张掖市新办肉牛育肥场9个,养牛669头,出栏516头,临泽养牛10头以上的集体养殖场达到10多个。临夏州帮助乳品企业渡过难关,有力带动了奶牛业的发展,牛奶产量比上年增长31%。黄土高原宁县、镇原苜蓿带家庭牛场已初具规模。平凉、泾川、灵台等市县肉牛以成为外贸出口的拳头产品,全区养牛业收入占牧业收入的比重由上年的16.3%上升到32.2%,提高15.9个百分点。

二.抓流通建市场形成热潮。全省各地抓流通建市场热情很高。白银市开展"畜牧年"活动,将市场建设当作重点来抓,新建了景泰县畜产品批发市场,白银区个体定点屠宰场等专业市场,全市五县区有畜禽及其产品交易的农贸市场达到39个。平凉市组建肉牛专业交易市场，并通过肉牛公司的购、宰、卖牛，连接养牛户与市场，形成牛产业一条龙经营。张川镇、龙山镇、三甲集、平凉市四大皮毛交易集镇，皮毛成交量大幅度上升，年交易额逾2亿元。全省参与畜产品季节贩运的农民有3万多人，畜产品活畜专业市场及有畜产品与活畜禽交易的综合农贸市场达到806个，其中专业市场132个。皮毛肉蛋奶生意红火，价格上扬。

三.兴办实体增强服务实力。全省畜牧系统新办各类兴牧实体52个，实体总数达到210个，四分之三的县中心(站)兴办了实体，二分之一的乡站开展了综合办站，盈利乡站的比重上升到60%。各级畜牧服务实体在开展综合服务的同时，自身实力不断增强，全年创收额达1.4亿元。酒泉地区畜牧部门把兴办实体作为服务体系建设的突破口来抓，服务实体发展到424个，经营额达1771万元，纯收入136万元，并且呈现出向产加销一体化全程服务、横向联合、外向型方向发展的新趋势。

四.牧业支柱产业地位上升。不少地区把发展牧业，作为增加农民收入的主要途径和农村奔小康的突破口，从投入、服务等多方面支持畜牧业经济发展，使畜牧业支柱产业地位明显增强。甘南、陇南、临夏、定西、张掖、白银等地、州、市牧业产值占农业总产值的比重已上升到30%以上。白银市牧业产值比重一年增长3个百分点；张掖地区人均畜牧业纯收入达到254元，占农民人均纯收入的29.8%；平凉地区在552元农民人均纯收入中，牧业有114元，占20.7%的份额，仅次于粮经种植业收入，居第二位。全省牧业产值和牧业总收入分别达到37.5亿元和33.7亿元，占农业总产值和农业总收入的28%和26%，在农业经济中处第二位，在农村居民现金收入中占有“三分天下有其一”的地位。畜牧业商品率达到59.7%，比种植业高15个百分点。

五.牧业科技转化有新进展。农牧民对科学技术的接受程度与良种普及程度和专业化、规模化、商品程度是相适应的。依靠科技进步，是发展内涵畜牧业的根本途径。为此，我省将科技兴牧贯穿于畜牧业全过程与全方位，提高牧业科技含量。一是大力推广良种畜禽。兰州、临夏、山丹、民乐等地当年从山东引进繁殖率较高的小尾寒羊5000多只；平凉、庆阳等地从陕西大量引进产蛋性能较好的罗曼鸡种；定西地区年内引进良种猪593头，种牛250头，种羊422只，引进调剂种鸡22.6万只，孵化育雏推广良种鸡15万只。全省良种猪鸡牛羊的规模分别达到262万头、2409万只、84万头和412万只，良种化程度相应提高，猪为41%、鸡达66%，牛羊分别达到34%和40%。二是建立科技示范点，推广畜牧实用技术。白银市建立科技示范点30个，发展畜牧科技示范户1万户，有重点地推广了13项养殖业综合配套技术；张掖地区把青贮氨化秸秆养牛和双推五改养猪作为重点，实行区域推进，全年青贮氨化饲料32.6万吨，比上年增长63.9%，新增改圈养猪农户7.8万户，累计达到16万户，占应改农户数的80%。全省畜牧科技成果应用率、科学技术覆盖率普遍提高，科技在畜牧业增产中的作用不断增强，有力促进了畜禽饲养周期的缩短，加快了出栏周转，提高了产品率和商品率。三是通过层层举办培训班，壮大畜牧科技队伍，提高农牧民科技素质。全省年内举办各类畜牧科技培训班4300期，培训技术人员和农牧民35万人次。

六.适度规模养殖上新档次。养殖业是长效薄利产业，只有适度规模，才能取得较好效益。改革开放以来，我省始终没有放松对规模养殖的扶持、忽视适度规模养殖的发展。武威地区将适度规模养殖与庭院经济结合起来，使规模养殖连年上新台阶，1993年全区适度规模养殖户达1.3万户，比上年增加3276户，增长35%，年内出栏猪牛羊28.6万头(只)。其中规模养猪户7455户，养猪14.6万头，出栏率达126%。全区规模养殖户均牧业纯收入达1600元。省会兰州各类畜禽养殖场达70个，饲养量逾273万头只。张掖地区机关事业单位办养殖企业的势头较好，全区乡以上机关事业单位与农场兴办养殖场84个，饲养家畜2.5万头只，家禽13.9万只，实现利税40多万元；临泽县制订了“畜牧业率先奔小康”规划，办起养鸡500只以上、养猪100头以上、养牛10头以上的集体养殖场50多个，并以新华种猪场为依托，建成一批育肥专业村及百头规模育肥户。1993年全省各类畜禽养殖场达到1048个，出栏家畜7.6万头只，家禽246.5万只；养殖大户达到8.9万户，比上年增加1.8万户，增长25%，收入万元以上的专业大户达到1607户，出栏家畜110.3万头只，家禽133.8万只，分别占全省家畜家禽出栏总量的13%和11%，肉蛋奶毛商品量占社会商品总量的22%。规模养殖已成为我省现代商品畜牧业的主导力量。

七.牧业商品基地效益突出。为了向市场提供集中批量产品，我省先后分层次有重点地建设了7大类型10个商品畜牧业基地，1993年这些基地在市场经济大潮推动下，进一步发挥了较好的效益.基地内畜产品商品量又有新的增加，占社会商品量的份额上升到35%。平凉地区关山肉牛基地和静宁、庄浪瘦肉型猪基地建设，面向市场，突出效益，抓商品出栏，通过牛、猪品种改良，短期育肥，科学饲养和全程服务等配套措施的落实，获得了新发展。

关山肉牛基地牛饲养量达38万头，出栏商品牛7.2万头，比上年增长3%，分别占到全区的88%和98%，出栏商品牛收入过亿元，创历史最高水平。静宁、庄浪两县猪存栏29万头，出栏商品猪25万头，分别占全区的56%和60%。其中瘦肉型猪饲养量达到22万头，占两县猪饲养量的40%，比上年增长1.7倍，出栏瘦肉猪收入3000万元。全区两基地商品收入共计1.3亿元，占畜牧业总收入2.5亿元的52%，比上年增长40%。商品基地在畜牧业市场经济中的地位与作用日益突出。

八.畜禽疫病防治趋向规范。兽医防检部门认真贯彻执行《家畜家禽防疫条例》，按照因病设防，预防为主的原则，扎扎实实地开展了免疫驱治，疫病监测和兽医卫生监督管理工作，推广了免疫新程序，有效地控制了危害我省畜禽健康的疫病和寄生虫病的发生与流行。全年共免疫接种各类畜禽7977万头只，驱治畜禽寄生虫2762万头只，共检活畜禽1350万头只、肉类8万吨，查处违法案件1000余起。严格的防检驱治，使猪、鸡、羊及大牲畜的病死率降至1.0%、2.3%、1.2%和0.8%。

甘肃水利在改革中前进

省水利厅厅长

薛映承

改革开放15年来，我省水利建设无论速度、质量和效益，都是建国以来最好的时期。国家在“八五”计划和十年规划中把水利同交通、能源、原材料等放在优先发展的基础产业地位。水利投入机制、价格体系、水政建设、综合经营都有了新的突破。主要表现在：一是内部结构不断调整，服务领域扩大。现有水利工程在坚持为农业基础服务不动摇、供给城乡生产生活用水和动力的同时，农村改水项目开始起动，水电建设向规模化发展，综合经营发展势头良好，水土保持和防汛抗旱工作有了新的发展，水利产业开始展示为国民经济和社会发展全面服务的格局。二是多元化的水利投入机制开始起步，国家、集体、个人对水利的投入有所增加，出现了股份制和农民投入兴修小型水利、开发水电、租赁荒山荒坡的典型，利用外资范围扩大。三是基本建设新建工程项目普遍推行投资包干和招标承包，特别是引大入秦和一批新建项目推行项目法施工和合同管理，质量效益提高，标志着基本建设改革的逐步深化。四是灌区管理水平提高，自我维持、自我发展能力增强，水费改革、节水措施和晋等升级制度的推行，增强了灌区活力。五是水利综合经营方兴未艾，势头良好，综合经营已成为水利经济的一大支柱。六是水政建设有了突破，水法规、水资源管理、水利执法三大体系逐步健全，水利工作开始走上法制轨道。

1993年，我省水利事业围绕抗旱保粮、夺取农业丰收这个中心，省委、省政府多次召开会议，专题研究水利工作，党政军领导和机关干部带头参加农田水利基本建设劳动，推动了群众性农田水利基本建设。各级水利部门注重调查研究、规划协调、督促检查和发动群众，在计划下达迟，资金到位晚、到位率低的情况下，仍然较好地完成了各项建设任务。截至年底，全年共新增有效灌溉面积40万亩，提高保灌面积21.24万亩，恢复改善面积8.01万亩，新修“三田”93万亩，治理水土流失面积2133平方公里，解决了23.25万人和22.86万头牲畜的饮水困难。

水利设施在抗旱防汛中发挥了重要作用。1993年，全省近2/3的县受旱，受旱农田面积一度达1600万亩，成灾300万亩，有120万人、110万头畜的饮水发生严重困难。在抗旱斗争中，全省派出5万多名干部奔赴抗旱生产第一线，帮助指导生产，全省共投入4.2万项各类抗旱设施。维修提灌3000多处，机电设备3800多套，整修各级渠道9800公里。现有水利设施在抗旱生产中发挥了突出作用，全省已推广雨水集流技术3348户，解决了干旱山区1.7万人、2.5万畜的饮水困难。灌区节水又迈出了新的步伐，全省完成常规节水面积310万亩，完成低压管道输水灌溉技术7.9万亩，累计达到32.4万亩。在河流来水减少，水库蓄水不足的情况下，由于实行了水资源统一调配，合理协调上下游、工农业之间的用水矛盾等一些得力措施，灌溉任务仍然按计划完成。完成春灌380万亩，夏灌1230万亩，秋灌450万亩，实灌面积达到1300多万亩。同时，以水补旱，以秋补夏等多种抗旱措施得到落实。再创历史最好水平。

1993年，全省经历两次长时历主汛期，中小河流及山洪沟边因局地暴雨形成的洪灾频繁，共有69个县受灾，受灾人口243万，农作物430万亩。在防汛斗争中，各级政府认真贯彻“安全第一，常备不懈，以防为主，全力抢险”的方针，领导高度重视，汛前准备充分，渡汛措施落实，坚持依法治汛，着力推行防汛工作正规化、规范化、制度化和量化考核，保证了防汛工作顺利进行。据不完全统计，全省各渠道投入防汛资金442万元，投入工日115万个，加固、修复水毁工程50多项，抢修水毁渠段1.6万米，清理河、沟道469条、394.7公里。减免洪涝灾害损失4000多万元，为国民经济和社会安定提供了保障。

今后一个时期，我省水利建设的基本方针是：坚持以经济效益为中心，巩固与发展、除害与兴利结合，治理与开发、建设与管理、服务与经营并重，确立水利的基础产业地位，搞活致富水利行业，初步建立起充满生机和活力的水利市场经济体制。重点在五个方面深化改革：一是以产权明晰、事企分开、权责明确、管理科学为目标，改革水利固定资产经营管理体制。二是以社会投入为主体，建立多元化、多渠道、多层次的水利投入格局。三是以市场为导向，尊重价值规律，深化价格改革。四是以贯彻《水法》为重点，加强水政，依法治水。五是以专业化、商品化为目标，建立优质高效的水利服务体系。

工　业

1993 年供电行业发展简述

兰州供电局局长

王步全

电力工业是国家的能源基础工业。我们甘肃省有着丰富的资源，具有发展电力工业的广阔前景和巨大潜力。

兰州电网地处西北电网和甘肃电网的中心，是西北四省——陕、甘、宁、青的电力交换枢纽。作为全国特大型供电企业的兰州供电局，现有职工 3707 人，下属 12 个基层单位，担负着甘青两省 5 个地(市)和 20 个县(市、区)的供电任务。平均供电半径约 150 公里，电网覆盖面积 10 万平方公里；现有 35 千伏及以上变电站 51 座，主变压器 95 台，总容量为 416. 39 万千伏安，输配电线路 4000 多公里；拥有固定抄表用户 9. 5 万户；固定资产原值 10. 49 亿元，年售电量达 100 多亿千瓦时。全年最高负荷 169 万千瓦，供电可靠率 99. 68%；年销售收入 14 亿元。

兰州供电局坚持以安全生产为基础、以优质服务为宗旨，以提高经济效益和社会效益为目的，全体职工走团结协作、艰苦创业的道路，挖潜改造、发展电网，为国民经济的发展和人民生活用电做出了积极努力。随着加快改革、扩大开放，社会用电需求也在不断加大，特别是解决市区电网的建设与改造问题尤为突出。为此，经与市政府领导共同研究，1993 年成立了兰州市城市电网建设协调领导小组，负责资金筹集、电网规划和工程建设的协调领导，为兰州市区电网建设创造了新的有利条件。

供电行业是公用事业，发生电力事故是国民经济的灾难。“安全第一，预防为主”是供电行业多年实践的经验和奉行的基本工作方针。通过全局职工的艰苦努力，特别是通过近年来全国电力系统开展的“安全、文明生产达标”活动，企业的管理水平有了显著提高，安全生产责任制得到了进一步落实，逐步形成了自上而下逐级监督，自下而上逐级负责的安全生产局面。1993 年，系统安全基本稳定，面对较为严重的缺电局面，坚持以提高社会经济效益和全社会的稳定为前提，千方百计抓好事故防范，以改革促安全，以安全促发展，杜绝了大面积停电、重大设备损坏、系统稳定破坏等影响社会稳定和威胁人民生命财产的事故发生，保证了电网安全可靠运行。

“人民电业为人民”是供电企业的服务宗旨，“严细、文明、团结、争优、求实、创新”是兰州供电局的局风。多年来，兰州供电局各级党政工团领导发动和带领全局职工，深入开展职业道德教育，坚决纠正行业不正之风，广泛开展了优质服务活动。向社会公布了“四公开”（即电价、电费标准公开，办理用电业务程序公开，处理窃电与违章用电公开，处理违犯供电纪律公开）和“四监督”（即领导监督、舆论监督、用户监督和内部监督，并监督“四公开”内容的执行情况，监督执行各种规定制度和政策情况，监督服务作风、服务态度和服务质量情况，监督供电企业为工农业生产和人民生活用电服务情况）以及监督举报电话号码，受到了社会各界的欢迎。由于优质服务工作取得了较好成绩，曾被电力部评为优质服务先进单位，在兰州市窗口行业服务竞赛中连续多年被评为先进单位，在 1993 年兰州市窗口行业优质服务竞赛中荣获第一名。

当前，随着改革的深化，兰州供电局正在从劳动、人事、工资三项制度改革入手，积极推进企业经营机制的转换。在深化企业内部改革的过程中，引入了竞争机制和激励机制，进一步改善了企业内部劳动关系，调动了广大职工的积极性，为适应建立社会主义市场经济的新形势和供电企业的长远发展注入了新的活力。同时，通过“三项制度”改革，走减人增效的道路，使兰州供电局的多种经营工作得到了长足发展。多种经营已经形成了一定的规模，经工商注册的多种经营企业已发展到 80 多个，范围扩展到电气、电子、冶炼、饮食、印刷、养殖、商业等多种行业，并在香港、珠海、海口、无锡、威海建立了多种经营企业，为多种经营的高速发展和供电企业的自身发展增强了后劲。

回顾 1993 年，我们供电企业既有喜悦也有困忧。特别是电网建设与改造的资金较为紧张，远远难以满足实际需要；企业陈旧设备的老化问题相当突出，设备的更新完善和电网技术改造的任务繁重；拖欠电费问题突出，严重影响了企业的经济效益和电网建设的发展。这些问题，在一定程度上制约了供电企业的发展。今后，我们将按照中央、部、省的有关政策，着力解决好这些问题，为甘肃电力事业的发展和国民经济的腾飞做出应有的贡献。

煤炭工业发展综述

省煤炭工业局局长、
省煤炭工业总公司经理
苗宗杰

1993年,全省煤炭战线的广大职工群众,以邓小平同志南巡重要谈话和党的十四大精神为指针,发扬煤矿工人艰苦奋斗、无私奉献和吃大苦、耐大劳、特别能战斗的优良传统和作风,围绕经济效益这个中心,深化内部改革,转换经营机制,优化产业和产品结构,努力减少亏损,上下团结一致,克服重重困难,顽强拼博,全面完成了煤炭生产、建设、安全、经营等多项任务,取得了十分喜人的成绩。

一、原煤产量增加,生产效益提高

1993年,全省原煤产量达1806.61万吨,比1992年增长17.13%,比历史上产量最高的1990年多产240多万吨。其中:国有重点煤矿产煤641.86万吨,比上年增加20.67万吨;省营煤矿产煤105.35万吨,比上年减少2.95万吨;地、县煤矿产煤248.91万吨,比上年增加10.99万吨;乡镇集体及其他煤矿产煤796.64万吨,比上年增加384.97万吨。省属煤炭企业实现工业总产值57548万元,比上年同期增长3.21%;商品煤质量进一步提高,灰分为13.29%,含矸为0.19%,分别比上年同期下降0.46%和0.03%;全员效率首次突破1吨大关,达到1.1吨/工;煤炭多种经营、集体经济和第三产业跃上新台阶,完成产值1.5亿元,比上年增长66.6%,上缴税金504.9万元,比上年增长81.5%,当年新安置企业富余人员及待业青年2575人。全省煤矿原煤生产百万吨死亡率为2.685,比上级下达的控制指标降低33.16%,其中国有重点煤矿为1.875,省营煤矿为0.948,地县煤矿为5.385;省属总承包煤炭企业实现销售收入62188万元,比上年增长33.44%;省营煤炭企业实现销售收入7430万元,比上年同期增长32%;全省出口原煤3.36万吨,创外汇105万美元。

二、煤炭基本建设取得新进展

全省共完成煤炭基本建设计划投资22572万元,完成基建井巷进尺15234米,特别是年设计能力45万吨的陈家沟矿井和150万吨的海石湾矿井经国家批准并按时开工建设,对国家"八五"重点建设项目我省华亭煤炭基地的大规模开发、窑街衰老矿井的接续和缓解甘、青两省用煤紧张局面都具有重要意义。

三、深化内部改革,转换经营机制

从1993年开始,省属煤炭企业全面实行了新一轮的"投入产出总承包",与13户企业和4个直属公司、2个事业单位签订了承包经营责任书,一包三年,一次包定,并本着"生产型向生产经营型"、"粗放型向效益型"转变的原则,围绕经济效益定指标、定任务,把原有的十几项承包指标减化为四项承包硬指标,省煤炭总公司只考核企业的产值、产量、亏损和安全,其他的经济技术指标和任务均作为考查指标,把权力下放给基层,由企业根据实际自行决定,从而大大地加强了企业经营的自主权,取得了良好成效。窑街、靖远、阿干、山丹等4个国有重点煤矿的产量、产值上升,亏损减少,比计划减少亏损2610万元;人员减少,效率提高,共减少原煤生产人员和非生产人员6892人,全员效率达到1.1吨/工,创历史最好水平;安全生产状况进一步好转,原煤生产百万吨死亡率为1.875,比控制指标降低38.56%。

同时,全省煤炭系统还在干部人事、劳动用工、工资分配、精简机构、分流人员、财务管理、成本核算以及住房、医疗制度等方面,进一步加大了改革力度,出台了许多相应的改革政策和方案,采取了许多切实可行的措施和办法,使全省煤炭工业深化内部改革工作开始整体推进,迈出了新的步伐。为了调整产业和产品结构,坚决走减人提效、扭亏增盈和集中生产、高产高效的发展我省煤炭工业的路子,提出了全省煤炭工业"八五"期间的奋斗目标,力争在"八五"末建成2——3个年产超过100万吨的生产矿井或生产工作面,全省省属煤矿原煤产量达到1700万吨,人员减少2——2.5万人,效率达到1.2吨/工;到2000年全省原煤产量达到2300万吨,人员减少3.5——4万人,效率达到1.5吨/工。为适应市场经济需要,强化产品销售,增强煤炭企业的整体利益、整体效益和竞争实力,省煤炭总公司与有关地区和企业,组建了我省第一个区域性的运销联合体——甘肃省陇东煤炭销售联合会,为培育、建立我省煤炭交易市场体系奠定了基础,提供了经验。为了充分发挥科技是第一生产力的作用,切实重视人才和知识分子工作,表彰奖励了全省煤炭系统100名优秀中青年知识分子,这在我省煤炭发展史上尚属首次;评选出科技进步成果38项,也给予了表彰和奖励。总之,经过广大干部、知识分子和工人群众的共同努力,全省煤炭工业的改革和建设都取得了新的成绩,呈现出"两手抓、两手硬,两个文明一起抓,两个成果一起要"的新局面。

我省是全国预测煤炭储量在1000亿吨以上的省区之一。到1993年底,全省已累计探明煤炭储量100亿吨左右,主要分布在陇东、河西、靖远和兰州地区,适合大规模开采,而且煤质优良,是属低灰、低硫、高活性、高发热量的优质动力煤。全省已建成生产原煤能力3万吨以上的矿井58对,核定生产能力为1272万吨,累计生产原煤2亿多吨,为甘肃国民经济的发展做出了突出贡献。

1993年甘肃省石化工作综述

省石油化学工业厅厅长
黄树德

1993年,全省石化行业17.8万名干部职工,以经济建设为中心,解放思想,转变观念,深化改革,扩大开放,抓住机遇,加快发展,完成了年初确定的主要奋斗目标,各项经济指标都有较大幅度增长。

——生产经营持续发展。全行业完成工业总产值73.25亿元,比上年增长8.82%,约占全省工业总产值的18.31%;"八五"前三年平均年递增率为10.36%。集体经济完成社会总产值8.07亿元,比上年增长6.24%。

主要产品产量完成较好。其中:原油、纯碱、电石、油漆产品提前完成年计划;原油加工、纯碱、黄磷、电石、盐酸等产品产量,分别比上年增长14%以上。

——经济效益稳步提高。1993年,全行业实现利税总额11.08亿元,比上年增长60.57%,"八五"前三年平均年递增率为19.23%;销售收入达111.43亿元,比上年增长59.79%;产销率为106.6%,平均年递增33.93%。

——重点项目进展良好。1993年,计划完成固定资产投资16.09亿元,实际完成16.02亿元,占年计划总投资的99.59%。其中完成基本建设投资7.99亿元,用于技术改造8.03亿元。兰炼第一套常减压炼油改造、兰化1万吨ABS改造、刘化10万吨合成氨、16万吨尿素、甘肃电石厂9万吨电石、张掖农药厂1000吨有机磷农药等39个项目建成投产。兰化30万吨合成氨、52万吨尿素、16万吨乙烯、兰炼4万吨聚丙烯、玉门局150万吨炼油配套,庆化50万吨炼油、金昌12万吨磷二铵等一批重点工程正在加紧前期准备和施工。

——油气勘探继续扩大战果。长庆局油气勘探取得新成果,新获天然气探明储量415亿立方米,控制储量874亿立方米。保证了原油产量稳中有升,全年生产原油180.3万吨,比上年增长12.6%,陇东油田原油产量首次突破百万吨大关。玉门局在酒东盆地见到工业性油流;在酒西盆地有新发现;在吐鲁番盆地的勘探获重大战绩,葡北一井喜喷高产油气流,日产原油137立方米,天然气4万多立方米。

——科研开发富有成效。1993年,全行业完成30项。其中4项达到国内先进水平,有17项新产品通过省级鉴定。7项新产品分别荣获"优秀新产品奖"和"1993年省科技进步奖"。实现新产品产值2.96亿元,利税1800万元,新产品率达10.6%。固体碘伏系列、甘草精、聚乙烯醇包装膜、PVC型材,乙苯脱氢345催化剂等一批具有代表性的精细化工新产品已开发成功,投入市场,取得经济效益。精细化工"一条龙"年产值达1.4亿元,利税3300万元,比上年增长25.85%。进入兰州高新技术开发区的企业和科研单位逐年增多,在区内组建了石化行业首家集科工贸与一体的高新技术企业——甘肃三星石化集团股份有限公司。

——改革开放不断推进。省厅结合企业实际,研究制定了贯彻落实《甘肃省全民所有制工业企业转换经营经营机制实施办法(试行)》的具体意见,对14项自主权中属于省厅管理的部分,全部下放给企业。企业内部的各项配套改革进一步深化,兰炼、兰化、刘化、油漆、盐化、轮胎、庆化等企业的岗位技能工资改革已进入实施阶段。住房和医疗制度改革初见成效。外向型经济的发展有了新突破。1993年新批"三资"企业12户,投资总额达3800多万美元。省厅组织力量,参加了省政府4月初在香港举办的招商引资洽谈会;配合有关企业和科研单位参加了"93兰交会"。全行业石化产品出口创汇达3867万美元。

——学吉化学刘化活动迈出了新步伐。1993年初,全行业有22个单位被省厅树为"双高"(速度、效益)旗帜。一年中,他们不断总结经验,继续开拓前进,有力地促进了企业经济效益和管理水平的提高。刘化总厂、省轮胎厂、金昌化工总厂以经济效益为中心,内抓管理,外拓市场,不失时机,加快发展,工业总产值均突破亿元大关,提前两年实现了"八五"计划确定的奋斗目标。西北油漆厂、金昌化工总厂、刘化总厂已跨入国家大二型企业行列。省厅继续引导企业坚持开展"三创"活动;在全行业开展了首次环境执法检查:定期进行安全生产大检查;超额完成了年度大中小修计划,全部设备和主要设备完好率分别为95.12%和96.65%。

1993年,甘肃石化工业发展中存在的主要矛盾和问题:

(一)产业结构性矛盾仍很突出。一是原材料产品多,深度加工增值步伐跟不上。表现为:初级产品多,低档产品多,高附加值产品少,系列产品少,精细化工产品少,出口创汇产品少。二是中央企业比重大,地方化工实力薄弱。1993年中央企业产值占全省石油化工产值的70.81%;利税占全省石油化工企业利税的86.17%;销售收入占全省石油化工企业销售收入的88.07%。三是技术改造任务相当繁重。我省大部分石油化工企业都是五、六十年代建成的,工艺比较落后,设备老化,产品陈旧,负担沉重,后劲不足。地县化工企业更是采用传统工艺生产,规模小,技术素质和管理水平较差,能耗、成本高,质量、效益低。企业技术结构的调整迫在眉捷。

(二)石化工业产值在全省工业产值中所占比重由1980年的28.

2%下降到1993年的18.31%。

深化改革 勇于开拓 努力开创甘肃省成品油销售工作新局面

省石油总公司总经理
王新权

甘肃省石油总公司是我省销售成品石油的大型企业，承担着全省成品石油供应任务。主要经营汽油、煤油、柴油、润滑油、石油及其制品，特种油品；兼营化工产品、化纤、金属材料、中介服务。

甘肃省石油总公司具有四十余年的历史。四十多年来，随着我国社会主义经济建设事业的发展，不断发展，不断前进。1987年率先实行承包经营，企业进入了新的振兴发展时期。七年来，全省油品购销总量创历史最高纪录，年平均增长15%，确保了甘肃工农业生产和建设发展的需要；超额完成了承包经济指标，保证了上交利税逐年增长；推进技术进步，加强经营设施建设，有力地增强了企业发展后劲。在提高企业经济效益的同时，职工的生活福利也得到一定改善，进一步增强了企业的凝聚力。

1993年，我省油品市场经历了先是紧俏后又疲软的变化。在复杂严峻的市场形势下，石油公司系统职工以党的十四大精神为指针，在省委、省政府和中石化销售公司的领导下，努力适应社会主义市场经济的新要求，积极转变观念，坚持深化企业改革，转换经营机制，狠抓市场经营与内部管理，克服了资金紧缺，铁路运力紧张等困难，在困难重重的条件下，较好地发挥了主渠道作用，取得了税收与上交利润持续增长的良好成绩，为甘肃国民经济持续、快速、健康地发展，为稳定市场、保障供应做出了应有的贡献。

一、进一步发挥主渠道作用，以市场为导向，强化购销工作，积极参予市场竞争

去年，国家进一步削减成品油计划，计划外油品销量不断增大，加之省内油品市场多头经营，资源分散，竞争更为激烈。面对复杂多变的市场形势，石油公司系统职工更新观念，勇于探索，千方百计促销增效。

（一）全力以赴抓调运，搞好货源落实。根据去年年初测算，我省成品油缺口约55万吨。省总公司加强宏观调控指导，充实了调运队伍，实行责任包干，派专人常驻油田、炼厂抓催调。为了弥补铁路运力不足，省总公司系统充分利用铁路自备槽车和公路罐车，采取公路、铁路运输并举，抢运油品，保证了全省货源的及时到位。

（二）强化市场意识，在立足省内销售的同时，开拓省外市场，拓宽了销售渠道。在省内销售上，各级公司本着薄利多销的原则，主动上门了解用户需求，实行让利销售，重视售后服务，稳定了省内销售渠道；进一步加强了加油站的经营管理工作，对油品数质量严格把关，赢得了顾客的信任；根据市场需求，组织适销对路的灯用煤油和润滑油品投放市场，取得了较好的经济效益。在省外销售上，各级公司采取联营、代销等灵活方式。积极拓宽省外销售渠道，扩大了市场占有率。

（三）充分发挥主渠道作用，重视社会效益。我省自然条件差，经济不发达，财政紧张，市场发育尚不完善。省石油总公司在解放思想，开拓经营，增创效益的同时，从成品油这一重要的战略物资和特殊商品的特点出发，坚持严格管理市场，统筹安排市场供应的原则，继续发挥国有企业的主渠道作用。首先是始终把支援农业作为一项长期任务来抓，去年在国家平价农柴油不能及时到位的情况下，各级石油公司采取议价转平价供应，保证了农柴油的供应兑现进度。其次是对平凉、庆阳、陇南、甘南、临夏等老少边穷地区和无电区实行倾斜政策，在资源调运和价格上给以优惠，减轻当地群众的负担，保证了当地工农业生产和群众生活用油的需要。再次是积极配合当地政府、行署执行省政府整顿石油市场的通知精神，清理了一批不合格的加油站和供油网点，使社会广泛了解了政府对石油市场的管理政策，遏制了全省滥建加油站的势头。

（四）大力兴办第三产业，开拓经营新领域。随着改革的进一步深入和向市场经济的逐步过渡，石油公司系统越来越重视从单一经营向多元化、多品种方向发展。坚持以油为主，积极兴办第三产业和集体企业，在多种经营上积极探索，逐步形成主营业务和多元化经营两条腿走路的新格局。我们积极向其他行业渗透，在兰州新办了宾馆、酒店业，新建了西北首家小高尔夫球场，在敦煌集资新建了沙洲大酒店。这些投资项目将为省石油公司系统的开拓发展增添生机与活力。

二、深化三项制度改革，转换经营机制，适应市场经济新形势

在人事、用工制度上，全系统进行了企业内部机构改革。各级公司按照“精简、统一、效能”的原则，定编定员，精减机关管理机构和人员，组建经济实体，分流富余人员，加强营销力量，增加经济效益。省总公司机关率先将原有15个处室精减为7个，将原有179名管理人员分流100名，形成了“小管理大经营”的格局。

在分配制度上，全系统开展了岗位技能工资制为主要内容的分配制度改革。去年在5家单位先行试点，在总结经验的基础上，全系统已全面铺开。与此同时，各级公司积极探索加油站内部分配制度改革，实行了加油站职工收入同经济效益挂钩的分配形式，适当加大了工资、奖金浮动范围，部分单位试行了吨油工资含量,全员风险抵押。通过实行岗技工资制和其他有效的分配形式,初步打破了平均主义思想观念,体现了奖勤罚懒,向一线和苦、脏、累、险工作岗位倾斜,调动了职工的积极性。

三、以管理为基础,完善内部约束机制,加强储运设施建设,确保库、站安全

(一)加强财务基础工作,理顺系统财务管理体系,确保了全系统上交省财政任务的完成。去年,为了适应国家财会制度改革的要求,省总公司多次举办各类学习班,组织全系统财会人员学习、掌握新会计制度,进行了新旧帐务接轨处理,保证了新会计制度的顺利实施。在资金紧张时,建立了系统内部的财务指标考核体系,对各地公司的上缴利润及其它各项资金使用的考核指标,都作了月度分解,加强对系统财务管理的监督,压缩了费用开支,清理了拖欠款,有效遏制了系统利润滑坡趋势。发挥财务审计职能,加强国有固定资产的管理,开展了清产核资工作,划清了国有企业与集体企业、第三产业固定资产的界线,对国有资产实行有偿使用,杜绝了国有资产的流失。

(二)狠抓制度落实、加强了油库、加油站的安全管理。石油商品具有易燃易爆的特性,安全管理尤为重要。为了抓好油库、加油站的安全管理工作,省总公司一是明确提出各级企业法人代表是企业安全的第一责任人,把安全工作与企业领导的工作政绩和经济利益挂起钩来。二是对油库设备实行承包责任制,把设备承包到人,加强了设备的档案管理。三是重视安全常规教育,及时向职工通报省内外典型事故案例,播放安全教育录像,对照各项规章制度查苗头堵漏洞,强化了职工的安全意识。四是开展了第三次油库、加油站千日安全无事故竞赛活动。通过落实安全管理工作,去年全系统主要设备完好率达到100%,其他设备达到95%以上,全系统事故发生率比上年下降50%。

(三)强化成品油数质量意识,维护了石油公司主渠道的信誉。全系统统一实行了以"升"为单位的计量标准,并坚持定期对计量器具进行鉴定。严禁从非石油经营渠道进货,严把出入库关。全面检查了系统内加油站和经销点的数质量,对数质量不合格单位进行了严肃处理。对优秀油库的评比实行数质量一票否决制。这些措施维护了广大消费者的利益,发挥了国有石油销售企业应有的作用。

(四)缩减投资规模,保证重点储运设施建设。全系统去年克服资金紧张、三材涨价等困难,压缩基建项目,集中资金,保证重点项目和已开工项目的按期完工。省总公司加强宏观调控,发挥行业技术优势,对平凉、武威、张掖、嘉峪关等地、市公司的油库进行更新改造及建设,从工程设计到材料配套供应提供一条龙服务。全年完成生产性项目48项,新建加油站19座,基层供油网点9个,投资574万元,增强了企业的竞争实力和发展后劲。

1994年,是我国加快建立社会主义市场经济体制的关键性一年。在新的一年里,我们要进一步发挥石油公司的主渠道作用,加强宏观调控,整顿石油流通领域,实行行业管理,建立统一、有序的成品油市场。在建立新的成品油流通体制的过程中,我们将进一步强化行业管理,抓紧做好建立现代企业制度的各项基础工作,加强企业集团建设,最大限度地发挥主渠道优势,全方位开拓经营,全面加强企业内部管理,完善内部激励和约束机制,确保油库、加油站安全,端正行业作风,开展优质服务,加快建设一个有改革开拓的精神,有雄厚的竞争实力,有灵活的经营策略,有科学的管理手段,有合理的人才结构,有良好的职工素质的新型石油集团公司,力争全面完成今年的各项工作任务,为甘肃国民经济的发展再作新贡献。

1993年兰州炼油化工总厂发展综述

兰州炼油化工总厂厂长

李文成

兰州炼油化工总厂(简称兰炼)是我国"一五"期间156项重点工程之一,1958年建成投产,是新中国成立后建成的第一座现代化大型炼油厂。

建厂35年来,党和国家十分关怀兰炼的建设和发展。老一辈无产阶级革命家周恩来、朱德、彭德怀、邓小平以及党和国家领导人江泽民、朱镕基等曾先后到该厂视察,对兰炼做出的成绩给予了充分肯定。1992年8月,江泽民总书记在视察该厂时,挥笔题写了"发扬高严细实厂风,创办一流石化企业"的题词,对兰炼的进一步发展寄予了厚望。30多年来,兰炼依靠科技进步,不断进行技术改造,把一个单一的炼油企业,逐步发展成为一个以炼油为主,既有裂化催化剂、石油添加剂生产,又有机械、仪表、压力容器制造、炼厂建筑安装以及科研、设计的特大型综合企业。

30多年来,兰炼坚持不懈地依靠技术进步,对老企业进行挖潜改造,生产规模不断扩大,技术装备水平不断提高,经济技术实力不断增强。先后建成投用了第二套常减压、硫化烷基酚钙等10多套炼油化工生产装置,还对一套催化裂化等16套主要炼化装置和储运、动力等辅助系统进行了技术改造。目前,炼油化工装置由原设计的16套发展到65套;原油一次加工能力由原设计的100万吨/年发展到500万吨/年;能生产360余种石化产品和350多种机械仪表产品;职工人数发展到20000余人。自建厂至1993年底累计加工原油6348.4万吨，完成工业总产值274.7亿元，实现利税90.49亿元。为支援全国石化企业和政府有关部门培养输送管理人才和技术骨干10000余人，全国凡有炼厂处就有兰炼人，被誉为“中国石油工业的摇篮”。

1993年，兰炼认真贯彻落实党的十四大和十四届三中全会精神，继续坚持科技兴厂的方针，把技术进步作为增强企业活力与发展后劲的支柱和先导，不断开发中高档新产品、改进老产品，以满足社会和用户需求，提高企业在市场竞争中的应变能力，从而保持了旺盛的发展势头。在外部环境依然不大宽松，内部机制没有理顺的情况下，创出了原油加工量、实现利税、销售收入和工程建设四个新水平。在摆脱计划经济体制羁绊，适应市场经济需求的紧要关头赢得了新的主动权。

——千方百计争取资源，生产任务全面超额完成。在计划内原油欠供51万吨，兰新铁路运力十分紧张，原油进厂和成品油出厂多次受阻的情况下，采取多种方式，通过多种渠道争取到计划外原油78万吨，原料油15万吨，并积极与有关部门接触，疏通运输，创造条件坚持生产。全年共加工原油312万吨，比上年增长0.6%，生产汽、煤、柴、润四大类产品195万吨，比上年增长11.05%；生产催化剂1.12万吨，比上年增长27.21%；生产添加剂2.07万吨，比上年增长17%；机械产品完成682吨，完成计划的150.5%；生产仪表11782台(件)，完成年计划的148.80%。全厂的原油加工量和主要产品均创造了兰炼建厂以来的最高纪录。

——积极开拓市场，经济效益明显提高。1993年，兰炼加快走向市场的步伐，加速“四位一体”的销售网络建设，进一步加强了与汽车制造、冶金、水电、煤炭等行业直供大用户的产销合作，在主要市场区域内兴建了一批仓储设施，在主要城市开办了一批特油经销点，从而提高了市场应变能力，市场占有率得到巩固和提高，大大促进了经济效益的提高。全年实现销售收入43.67亿元，比上年增长50.84%；实现利税5.04亿元，比上年增长43.8%，均达到兰炼建厂以来的最高水平；出口创汇1000万美元，比上年多创汇145万美元，国内创汇达到500万美元，创历史新水平。

——积极主动创造条件，工程建设创历史最好水平。全年完成工程建设投资4.2亿元。一套常减压装置改造，1万吨/年半合成催化剂，3000吨/年分子筛、背压发电、生活水处理等5套新装置相继建成投产；丁烷脱沥青、制氢、两酸处理工程等3套装置完成主体施工。尤其是一套常减压装置改造工程在短短5个月的时间里，浇铸了2600立方米混凝土，安装设备260台，完成投资5300多万元，并实现了一次试车成功，创造了兰炼工程建设的最高水平。同时还完成了五年一次系统大检修和12套装置的检修任务。

——突出技术成果向生产的转化。认真贯彻石化总公司科技工作会议和“十条龙”的攻关会议精神，坚持面向生产狠抓技术攻关，面向市场，加快产品开发，编制了兰炼500万吨/年原油加工改扩建工程总体方案和8年科技进步规划；完成科研开发成果109项，其中75W/90GL—5车用齿轮油、10W30QF/CD通用发动机油和油膜轴承油通过国际台架试验和现场使用试验；开发了15W/40CD柴油机油等14个新产品，其中80W/90GL—5车用齿轮油等已开始批量工业生产。1993年石化新产品创利税4064万元。

——加强领导，精心组织，“151”改革目标全面实现。按照党的十四大精神和国务院《条例》的要求，加强对改革工作的领导，采取一系列有效措施，加速企业内部深化改革的步子。对催化剂厂、添加剂厂、机械厂、仪表厂等非炼油生产分厂实行投入产出包干，内部工效挂钩，放开经营；促使石化研究院、自动化研究院、设备研究所等科研单位走上合同结算，企业化经营的路子；将三联公司、运输公司、兰苑宾馆、设备维修公司转制、剥离，推向市场，从总厂分离到集体企业3500余人，占职工总数的20%；初步建立了炼油化工生产系统的厂内模拟市场运行机制；组建了建安、机械两个企业集团；实行了总厂机构改革方案；全面推行了岗位技能工资制度，开办了厂内劳动力市场；组建了三星石化(集团)股份有限公司；推行了住房制度改革。

——努力发展外向型经济。与香港中旅集团有限公司签订了合资兴建40万吨/年聚丙烯装置的协议；与全国50多个单位合作建加油站代销点60多个，组建了10个联营销售公司；与34个县级石油公司建立了长期销售协作关系；在香港建立了兰炼经贸公司。还与其他科研单位及大专院校签订技术合作合同26项，其中与兰州化物所合作开发的Y—911热管氧化试验仪达到国际先进水平。

——从严治内，狠抓“三基”，强化管理。根据企业全方位进入市场和内部改革不断深化出现的新问题，重申管理是企业发展基础的观点，提出了简现管理形式，强化管理实效，理直气壮抓管理的要求；采取了“抓好管理，搞好生产，带好队伍”稳定生产分厂的强有力措施；通过多种途径强化企业本质安全管理；结合贯标进一步健全和完善了全厂的质量保证体系、质量审核工作，有效地提高产品的实物质量，确保石化产品出厂合格率连续15年保持100%；坚持“抓三基、创四奖、争五优”活动和每季一次的岗位责任制大检查;在炼化系统深入持久的开展了“四查五整顿”工作,巩固了企业管理的基础地位。

在发展生产,提高效益的同时,职工的物质条件和生活健康水平也有进一步提高。

1994年3月30日,《人民日报》在头版头条显著位置以“‘共和国长子’再展风采”为题刊登了兰炼以靠科学技术力量,走出一条旧厂改造、老厂新生的希望之路的长篇通讯,并为此加了编者按,认为兰炼在过去有过辉煌的年代,为国家实现工业化出了产品,出了资金,出了人才,出了技术,建立了不朽的功绩,不愧为“共和国长子”。在历经艰辛,饱经沧桑之后,又通过大规模技术改造和改革内部运行机制,以精良的装备,先进的技术、优质的产品,雄厚的实力,向世人展示了诱人的魅力和青春风采,对兰炼给予了极大的鼓舞和鞭策。

不断开拓 锐意进取 再创新绩

1993年兰州钢铁集团公司进一步解放思想,紧紧围绕“生产和发展”这一主题,始终抓住“双增双节”这一关键,经受住了外部经济环境和市场条件巨变的考验,胜利实现了年初确立的“4034”奋斗目标,提前两年实现兰钢“八五”规划目标,并为甘肃省钢产量1993年首次突破100万吨大关,做出了自己应有的贡献。一年来,兰钢无论是生产经营工作,工程建设进度,还是逐步深入的企业内部深层次改革,都取得了引人瞩目的成绩,公司全体员工用自己的辛勤汗水和勤劳的双手,再次在兰钢的发展史册上,书写下了具有深远意义的一页。

一、工业总产值和经济效益指标持续增长,钢和钢材产量再创新高

1993年,我们既迎来了新的发展机遇,也经受了外部经济环境剧变的洗礼,全年钢材市场大起大落,对於承受能力较强的企业来说也是举步维艰,我们更是受到了生产规模,原材料供应、资金短缺等诸多不利因素的影响,在巨大的压力面前,公司及时召开动员大会,正确剖析形势,说明对策,消除了职工的疑虑,激发了职工的生产热情,全公司的生产经营成绩硕果累累,工程建设蒸蒸日上,开创了兰钢全面大发展的新局面。

1993年全年累计完成工业总产值49100万元,完成省下达年计划的109.11%,比上年增长18.03%。全年实现销售收入12.79亿元,比上年增长92.72%。全年利税总额突破2亿元大关,达2.2亿元,比上年增长97.32%,全年实现利润1.03亿元,比上年增长2.1倍,均创兰钢最好历史水平。

1993年生产钢40.15万吨,完成省下达计划的125.47%,比上年增长20.17%,净增产钢6.2万吨。其中连铸坯全年生产14.3万吨,完成年计划的113.41%,比上年增长37.52%。全年生产钢材34.15万吨,完成省下达计划的136.60%,比上年增长40.53%,净增产钢材5.6万吨。钢和钢材均创历史最好水平,全年共7次刷新月产纪录,并分别提前66天和64天完成省下达的计划任务,提前两年实现了兰钢“八五”规划目标和第二轮承包任务,从而使兰钢的生产能力跨上了一个新台阶。

二、主要技术经济指标进步明显,促进了经济效益的不断提高

“科技是第一生产力”的思想日益深入人心,科技攻关,技术改造,推广应用“四新”成果和群众性的小改小革成绩显著,技术进步意识普遍增强。这一切都极大地促进了技术经济指标的提高。全公司1993年综合成材率达88.09%,在1992年86.84%的基础上,连跨87%和88%两个台阶,比年计划提高了3.07个百分点,比上年提高了1.25个百分点,公司重点考核的17项技术经济指标全部比上年有所进步或改善,其中转炉钢铁料消耗等18项指标超过了历史最好水平,连铸坯收得率和电炉冶炼电耗等13项指标进入了全国地方骨干钢铁企业的前列。通过技术经济指标的进步,有效地降低了成本,促进了企业经济效益指标的提高,国家衡量企业经济效益的综合指标名列全省第三,其余6项经济效益指标,均处全省前矛。

三、全员质量意识普遍增强,产品质量有了新的进步

在1993年生产中,尽管我们的产品产量增长幅度较大,但我们紧紧抓住质量这个中心问题不放松,全员质量管理意识普遍增强,各项管理制度和措施进一步得到了加强和完善,产品质量有了进一步提高,上级考核的产品质量稳定提高率的6项指标,全部达标,稳定提高率为100%,优质产品率达87.78%。1993年国家技术监督局和中国质量管理协会授於兰州钢铁集团公司“质量效益型先进企业”称号,这是全省唯一被授於这种荣誉的单位。1993年,在全公司范围开展的“废品减半”活动,搞得扎实有效,全年计划减少废品1136吨,实际减少废品2929吨,国家技术监督局和中国质量管理协会授於我公司为“全国降损工作先进单位”,全省享有这一荣誉称号的单位仅有4家。

四、双增双节持之以恒,深挖内潜积极创收

1993年,我们坚持把双增双节工作作为企业增加效益的主攻重点。通过内部增产,节能降耗,狠抓成本管理,积极开拓外部创收业务等一系列卓有成效的工作,全面超额完成了年初确定的各项双增双节任务,全年累计增收节支4206万元，完成全年计划目标的145.13%。为了把双增双节工作做实做细，公司每月定期召开由各单位领导参加的双增双节分析会，针对生产经营中出现的问题及时进行总结分析并予以解决。各二级单位都将开展双增双节放在各项工作的首位，把增产增收，节能降损作为自己的工作重点。公司也加大了经济责任制考核的分量，实行重奖重罚。通过狠抓组织落实，大部分单位都超额完成了公司下达的任务。能源消耗、物料消耗平均比上年有较大幅度降低，全年吨钢可比能耗和吨钢综合能耗分别比上年下降了10.82%和6.62%，相当于节约成本1582万元。公司考核的16项双增双节技术经济指标有15项完成了计划，完成率为93.75%。1993年扣除物价上涨等因素，公司可比产品总成本比上年降低了946万元，降低1.97%，公司辅助生产单位在搞好内部服务的同时。进一步拓宽了创收渠道，有效地增加了企业外部利润，全公司还严格控制费用支出，坚持财务"一支笔"审批，狠抓紧"跑、冒、滴、漏"。另外，各基层单位进一步强化物资管理，开展清仓查库，减少二级库存，大力修旧利度，仅此全年累计就实现利润640万元。

五、科技攻关取得新的突破，重点工程建设进度加快

由我公司承担的一项国家级重点科技攻关项目和一项省级重点科技攻关项目在1993年都取得了突破性进展，有的项目已由科研攻关阶段进入了半工业化生产阶段，科研成果正在向现实生产力转化。薄板坯连铸实现了多炉连浇，金川弃渣综合利用研究通过中期评估，重点工程建设进度快，技术改造成效显著。

六、加强管理苦练内功，巩固完善改革成果

管理和改革是相辅相成的一个问题的两个方面。旧的不适应的管理制度要通过改革来打破，改革的成果要通过建立新的管理制度来巩固。1993年，兰钢的改革和管理都取得了新的进展，各级领导干部和广大职工认真学习邓小平同志建设有中国特色的社会主义理论和十四届三中全会精神，通过学习，使大家增强对加快建设社会主义市场经济体制的认识，看到改革的必要性和紧迫性。在管理方面，公司开展了以整顿财经纪律为主要内容的'五整顿"工作，并结合反腐败斗争，广泛深入地开展了廉政建设教育，对严重违反财经纪律的干部作了严肃处理；对立项在建项目，进一步严格了概算审批，结合清产核资工作，全面摸清公司家底，建立用户记录，减少了物资流失，与此同时，还开展了质量，设备管理大检查，加强了班组建设，涌现出71个优秀班组，11个特级班组，促进了公司各项管理工作的提高.在改革方面，1993年进一步巩固完善了以"三项制度"为突破口的改革成果，对下岗位后富余人员进行了妥善安排，实现了"在岗、试岗、下岗"三类人员劳动管理的动态化。完善了岗位技能工资，制定了新的动态管理办法，实行了工龄工资。1993年还成立了公司股份制改造领导小组，初步构筑了兰钢股份公司的基本框架为实现股份制做了积极的准备工作。另外，为了积极发挥集团公司多元化功能，增设对外窗口，壮大集团整体实力，成立了兰钢集团公司深圳昌明工贸公司。与哈萨克斯坦普罗斯托公司签订了生铁及球团矿长期供货协议，有效地利用了"两个市场"、"两种资源"，为今后进一步开展国际贸易做好了铺垫。同时，我们还积极探索住房制度发展办法，初步草拟了住房制度改革方案，预计1994年上半年可望出台实施。

1993年在兰钢的发展史上是不平凡的一年，是值得回顾的一年，每一个公司员工都在各自的工作岗位上，尽职尽责，埋头苦干，促进了公司整体工作的发展，赢得了生产经营的巨大成就。但是，成绩只代表昨天，我们的工作还有很多不足，新的问题还需要我们认真研究对策，不少困难还有待我们去克服。我们坚信，十四届三中全会已经给企业发展指明了方向，不断深入的改革是我们强大的动力源泉，我们只要继续发扬兰钢人的光荣传统，坚持不懈地为兰钢的繁荣和发展扎实工作，兰钢必将以新的姿态屹立於中国钢铁工业之林，为我国的经济建设和钢铁工业的发展做出更大的贡献。

（冯清伟）

在改革中不断发展的甘肃烟草业

中国烟草总公司

甘肃省公司经理

张效善

甘肃烟草业主要包括全省烟草及其制品的生产、收购、调拨、运输、销售和烟草市场的管理。1984年9月，根据国家关于烟草实行专卖制度和集中统一管理的规定，成立了甘肃省烟草专卖局和甘肃省烟草公司。下属企业有4户烟厂、10个烟草专卖分局(分公司)，56个县(市、区)烟草专卖局(公司)，省局(公司)直属单位有卷烟销售公司、商贸总公司和西北烟草质量监督检测站。

九年多来，党中央关于改革开放的英明决策和国家对烟草实行专营的制度，使我省烟草事业同甘肃省的其他事业一样得到了蓬勃发展。1993年，完成卷烟产量30.4万箱，比省烟草专卖局(公司) 成立之初的1985年的15.46万箱增长了96.6%；卷烟销量46.83万箱，比1985年的22.85万箱增长104.9%；烟叶收购58.8万担，比1985年的5.9万担增长8.97倍；实现利税3.56亿元,比1985年的6560万元增长4.83倍,九年累计实现利税18.74亿元。

卷烟产品结构得到调整。各工业企业立足于提高经济效益,紧紧围绕市场需求,增产畅销而且盈利的产品,限制平销产品,停止和压缩滞销产品。坚决停止单箱亏损100元以上的产品的生产,积极推行配方改革,有计划地研制和开发新产品。目前,全省卷烟产品共有44个牌号,雪茄烟有6个牌号,混合型和新混合型卷烟有3个牌号,规格有100mm、84mm、81mm、70mm4种。烤烟型甲级烟"海洋"、"奔马",乙级烟"兰州"、"凤壶"等四个牌号先后被评为省优产品。形成了等级品种比较齐全,产品结构趋于合理,产品质量不断提高的新局面。

卷烟销售稳步增长。根据甘肃烟草业发展的实际情况,省烟草公司明确提出了销售工作要立足地产烟,立足本区划,以地产烟销售为主体,省外烟为补充的经营思想,各地烟草工商企业,根据这个经营思想,积极培育地产烟市场,注意供需平衡,加强市场调查和预测,进行余缺调剂,下伸批发网点,健全销售网络,开拓农村市场,发挥了国有商业主渠道的作用,使全省卷烟销量不断上升,烟草商业的经济效益逐年稳定增长,基本满足了不同层次的消费需求。

卷烟工业技术改造初见成效。省烟草公司成立以后,总投资19593万元,重点改造了四户烟厂的制丝、卷接包设备及配套设施。兰州卷烟厂在"七五"期间引进西德梗丝膨胀设备、意大利6000型横包机组、英国莫林8卷接机组,卷烟生产能力由年12万箱增长到20万箱。"八五"期间主要是进一步完善制丝生产线,将滤嘴烟生产能力由现在的9.4万箱提高到12万箱;天水卷烟厂在"七五"期间增强了国内先进的真空回潮、打叶、切丝、烘丝、卷接包设备,卷烟生产能力由2.5万箱增加到10万箱;"八五"期间主要引进科马斯制丝线,改造旧的制丝线和部分卷接包设备,卷烟生产能力将达到15万箱。经过改造,全省卷烟工业技术装备整体水平有较大的提高,企业实力进一步增强。

烤烟种植有了较大的发展。甘肃省烤烟种植已有40多年的历史,主要分布地庆阳、平凉地区。这里种植烤烟曾几起几落,发展缓慢,收购量一直徘徊在2——5万担之间。省烟草公司成立以后,把发展烟叶生产放在了重要地位,坚持"计划种植、主攻质量、提高单产、增加效益"的烟叶生产的指导方针,推广"良种化、规范化、区域化"生产和先进的种烟技术,增加种烟投入,制定优惠政策。使烟叶的收购量和等级合格率有了较大的提高,对缓解烟叶供需矛盾,增加地方财政收入,帮助老区人民脱贫致富起到了积极作用。

企业改革有了新的进展。1986年我省烟草行业部分企业实行了厂长经理负责制。从1987年开始全省烟草工商企业全部实行了承包制,并实行了厂长经理负责制。为了进一步提高经济效益,增强企业活力,充分调动广大职工的积极性,1989年实行了工资总额同经济效益挂钩。同时,积极改革干部制度和人事制度,各级领导班子实行了目标责任制。对领导干部实行了任期制和试用制,对技术干部实行了聘任制,对处级以下干部(不含处级)实行了岗位责任制。根据《全民所有制工业企业法》和《全民所有制工业企业转换经营机制条例》的要求,从1992年开始进行了以干部聘任制为主要内容的干部人事制度改革,以全员劳动合同制为主要内容的劳动用工制度改革和岗位技能工资制为主要内容的工资分配制度改革。在经过工商企业分别试点,取得经验的基础上,1993年在全系统推开,1994年,全省烟草行业将重点进行落实《企业法》和《条例》规定的各项经营权,进行清产核资,为建立现代企业制度打基础、做准备工作。

专卖管理不断得到加强。我省烟草行业实行专卖管理制度和集中统一管理以来,认真贯彻党和国家的各项方针政策,广泛宣传和坚决执行《烟草专卖法》,强化专卖管理体制,逐步建立健全了专卖管理网络。随着国家深化改革。扩大开放和社会主义市场经济形势的发展,社会上有些人对是否坚持专卖制度提出了怀疑,各级专卖管理机关统一思想,稳定队伍,坚持专卖制度不动摇,与公安、工商等部门密切配合,集中清理整顿卷烟自由批发市场,严厉打击了卷烟走私、无证经营、无证运输、非法批发等违法活动。1993年共查处种类卷烟违法案件2751起,其中大要案66起,罚没款374万元,收缴走私、进口卷烟123件,没收假冒卷烟183件,捣毁制造假烟窝点4处,取缔无证批发、无证经营户612户。省局(公司)十分注意专卖队伍内部的建设,把内部管理放在专卖管理的重要位置,内外结合,标本兼治,健全了内部管理制度,做到依法生产和经营,使我省烟草专卖管理工作初步走上了制度化、规范化、法制化的轨道。

甘肃轻纺工业在改革中奋进

省轻纺总会会长

韩福俊

甘肃省轻纺工业经过40多年的建设,已形成门类比较齐全的工业生产体系,为国家积累资金、安排就业、繁荣市场、改善和提高人民生活水平都做出了重大贡献,已成为我省国民经济的重要支柱之一。

改革开放以来,甘肃轻纺工业有了长足发展。截止1993年,全省轻纺工业拥有40多个行业,系统内有1200多个企业、近20万名职工,固定资产原值17.66亿元。通过10年多来的改革与发展，主要轻纺产品的年生产能力大幅度提高:机制纸及板纸13万吨,啤酒10万吨,日用搪瓷制品0.2万吨,日用陶瓷制品2000万件,保温瓶370万个,灯泡3200万只,合成洗涤剂4万吨,酒精3.5万吨,火柴82万件,日用玻璃6万吨,肥皂0.5万吨,食糖12万吨,原盐7万吨,乳制品0.24万吨,白酒3万吨。全省纺织工业年产棉纱32000吨,精纺呢绒1000万米,粗纺毛呢350万米,毛毯(含纯毛、混纺、化纤毯)300万条,各种毛衫139万件,毛线(含纯毛、混纺、化纤线)0.8万吨,针棉织品562万件,棉布6000万米,化纤2.5万吨。

近年来,经过不断改革和探索,出现了一些具有地方特色的轻纺工业发展模式:利用地产资源、羊毛资源,建立粉丝、味精、淀粉、盘纸、地毯、草编等多家轻纺企业的通渭模式;利用资源优势,发展杏经济的镇原模式;利用旅游热线,开发旅游产品的敦煌模式;以名酒陇南春为龙头,配套发展地方工业的徽县模式;利用名胜古迹,多渠道、全方位引进资金、技术、管理,“嫁接”、状大地方经济的泾川模式;把工业与流通紧密结合,前店后厂的武威模式;利用军工企业的技术优势与开发地方优势资源深加工增值相结合的临泽模式。

1993年,在总量相对过剩、结构矛盾突出、市场竞争激烈、原辅材料涨价、流动资金匮乏的情况下,全省一轻、纺织工业完成工业总产值25.85亿元(按1990年不变价计算),其中一轻工业完成销售产值14.78亿元。

——抓改革,一厂一策,增强发展后劲。一是继续贯彻落实《企业法》和《条例》,深化了“三项制度”改革,落实了企业14项经营自主权,根据企业不同情况,引进外资“嫁接”了一批,开发三产转向了一批,为建立现代企业制度奠定了良好的基础;二是分类指导,抓影响企业的关键问题。对经济效益较好的企业帮助创造有利于放开经营、放手发展的条件:三毛厂进一步发挥行业排头兵作用,在生产一流产品的同时推动管理上台阶,创出了一流效益;兰维厂把建设甘肃轻纺行业原料基地作为办厂目标,一手抓管理、降消耗、增效益,一手抓改革、改造、产品开发,开拓国际市场;甘谷油墨厂瞄准国内外先进水平,加快技术改造步伐,不断扩大优势产品产量,初步形成了酞青兰为主导产品的我国有机颜料基地。对效益一般的企业加大了改造的力度。一毛厂精纺分厂狠抓技术改造,使产品质量不断上档次,粗纺分厂出口、来料加工、部分工序向精纺转移三管齐下。对亏损企业按“主业精、副业兴、多种经营”的发展思路,重点抓了重组和改造工作。兰棉厂实行分厂制,划小核算单位,“分灶吃饭”,现已分设成兰州纺织厂和兰州印染厂,龙头蛇尾平等竞争。兰州毛条厂扩大了来料加工,并采取租赁、合资等办法,逐步发挥了现有厂房的效益;白银棉纺厂、白银针织厂在调整结构、开发新产品和多种经营上寻求新的出路。三是借鉴北京一轻总公司“退二进三”、“退四进二”的经验,纺机厂、毛条厂充分利用“级差地租”调整产品结构和产业结构的优势,增强了企业活力和发展后劲。

——抓稳定,立足发展,理顺工作秩序。甘肃省轻纺总会是根据中央改革精神,参照轻工业部、纺织工业部机构改革方案,在原省轻纺工业厅的基础上,撤厅建会而来的。作为省政府直属事业单位,其主要任务是搞好行业规划,实施行业政策,进行宏观指导,为企业提供服务,并且继续承担政府授予原轻纺厅行使的行政职能。厅改总会后,一是观念更新、稳定队伍、明确职责,统一认识,振奋精神,加强总会机关的思想作风建设,使机关精神面貌有了明显改观。二是根据“精简、统一、效能”的原则,结合我省轻纺实际,研究制定了总会机构改革方案,对职责不清,职能重迭、交叉的处室进行了精减、合并,将处室精简28%,将一些年龄较轻,政治、业务素质好,懂经济、会管理,具有改革意识的干部充实到处室负责工作,使处室领导平均年龄下降了7.9岁,文化专业结构也更趋合理。三是从抓发展规划入手,逐步理清我省轻纺工业的发展思路。四是研究探讨在社会主义市场经济条件下,加强行业管理的方法和路子,即从以前注重抓直属单位单纯行政性直接管理,逐步转向了面向全省大轻纺工业的宏观行业性管理,强化规划指导、组织协调、科技开发、人才培养、咨询服务、监督检查,逐步建立起适应社会主义市场经济发展的管理体制和运行机制。

——抓调整,优化结构,壮大经济实力。1993年,企业的市场意识、竞争意识普遍增强,围绕市场调整产品结构的自觉性显著提高,新产品开发周期大大缩短,对滞销和亏损产品采取了限产或停产的果断决策。各企业除抓紧改造项目的收尾、达产达标外,普遍重视开发新产品,把它作为调整产品结构的主要措施来抓。兰州三毛厂把系列化、高档化作为调整产品结构的主攻方向,精纺呢绒又开发出驼丝锦、毛绒贡缎、羊绒、毛丝等24个系列,新产品更新率达85%,新产品产值率为19.33%。兰州一毛厂开发新产品200多项,新产品更新率达58.94%,新产品产值率为36.87%。省纺机厂及时研制开发市场前景看好的双螺杆挤出机。省纺研所狠抓产品上档次、上水平,严把质量关,开发的新产品走俏市场,在北京、东北等地很受欢迎。甘肃毛纺厂依据市场行情,集中力量开发玻璃钢制品,收到了好的效果。

——抓营销,扩大出口,增强创汇能力。1993年在由计划经济向市场经济转换的过程中,新旧体制磨擦、碰撞与多年沉积的矛盾相互交织,使得轻纺工业十分困难。困境面前,全省轻纺系统的各级领导和广大职工在深化改革的征程中不断进取,在市场经济的大潮中经受磨炼,全省纺织工业销售产值(现值)完成11.06亿元,同比增长7.4%;一轻工业完成14.78亿元,同比增长38.52%,销售产值比产值的增长速度高出32.31个百分点。省属企业实现产品销售同比增长14.6%,其中毛纺增长9.1%,棉纺增长31.8%。面对国内市场供过于求的现实,企业逐渐认识到扩大出口是走出困境的一条重要途径,千方百计拓宽出口渠道,出口创汇有显著增长。1993年,全省轻纺产品出口交货值达到1.25亿元,同比增长40.44%,其中,总会直属企业完成8452.67万元,占出口交货总值的67.6%,同比增长46.81%。兰棉、白棉、白针、兰维、甘谷油墨厂等企业都有较大增幅。省纺机厂的产品历史上第一次走出国门。甘谷油墨厂对出口产品酞青兰精益求精,成为全国有机颜料出口最多的厂家,他们还充分利用自己的技术优势,走出国门到印尼办厂,仅技术入股的股份即达25%。

——抓清欠,盘活资金,提高资金利用率。近年来,资金短缺和"三角债"困扰成为企业生产经营的最大障碍。针对这种情况,各企业一方面普遍实行销售大包干,强化销售力量,扩大销售网点;一方面组织得力人员催收清欠,收到了显著的效果。省轻纺供销总公司成立了专门负责清欠的分公司,复活资金;甘谷油墨厂由领导、技术干部和销售人员组成三结合小组,开展"访百家用户活动"。去年底,全省34户县以上纺织企业产成品资金比上年降低25%,108户县以上轻工企业比上年降低15%,省属企业降低25%,其中毛纺下降5.8%。棉纺下降65.4%。同时,企业上缴三税明显增加,省属企业上缴所得税、调节税比上年增长了5.9%,其中毛纺增长5.6%,产品销售税金增长29.96%,其中毛纺增长27.16%,棉纺增长69.16%。在毛纺企业中,兰州三毛厂一枝独秀,上缴利税2930万元,同比增长15.4%,名居全国毛纺同行业前列。

轻纺行业是竞争性较强的行业。1994年是改革关键的一年,改革、发展、稳定仍然是1994年的主旋律。困境与希望同在,机遇与挑战并存。我省轻纺工业由于相对发育程度低,新兴行业成长慢,适应能力差,困难就更大一些,由于总量相对过剩,结构矛盾突出,原辅材料涨价等,轻纺工业所面临的形势依然严峻,作为加工工业的轻纺工业,责无旁贷地应当起好弥合"断层"的桥梁和"二传手"作用。我们要按照国家产业政策,规划和建设好下游工业,在解决甘肃经济强烈的二元反差和致力于贫困地区脱贫致富,富民强省中承担起应负的责任,增强信心,把握机遇,拓宽思路,再造辉煌。

持续、快速、稳定发展的甘肃冶金工业

省冶金工业厅厅长

柳宏克

甘肃冶金工业从"一五"起步,历经国民经济的调整,几起几落,已经走过了36年的历程,在这36年中,相继建成了西北地区最大的钢铁联合企业——酒泉钢铁公司和生产规模在全国同行业中名列前茅的兰州炭素厂、西北铁合金厂,以及地方骨干企业——兰州钢铁集团公司和甘肃省铝业公司、山丹焦化厂、甘肃锑厂、白龙江金矿等省部属大中型企业,各地还建成了200余家中小冶金企业。自1983年有色金属工业分离上划后,在党的改革开放政策的推动下,全行业基本建设和技术改造步伐明显加快,生产规模不断扩大,企业内部改革逐步深化,对外开放日趋拓宽,品种结构得到优化调整,经济效益显著增长。已经形成了钢铁采矿、冶炼、轧材和辅助产品基本配套的生产体系。36年里,仅省部属大中型企业的总投资就达到43亿多元,形成固定资产31亿元。每年可为国家提供20多种总量达760多万吨的冶金产品,年创工业总产值23亿多元。从1986年到1993年的八年间共给国家上缴利税13.4亿元。冶金工业已在全省国民经济中占有重要的地位。

抓住机遇,努力工作,创造历史最好水平

1993年,是我国经济体制改革具有转折性的一年,也是我们大踏步前进的一年。在这一年里,我们冶金系统在党的十四大精神指引下,坚持用建设有中国特色社会主义理论和党的基本路线统一思想认识,认真学习《邓小平文选》第三卷,增强发展冶金工业的责任感和使命感。全面贯彻落实《全民所有制工业企业转换经营机制条例》,进一步深化企业改革,努力转换经营机制,坚持面向市场,增强竞争能力,切实把注意力集中到深化改革、转换机制、优化结构、提高效益上来。紧紧围绕"八五"计划的实施和100万吨钢奋斗目标的实现,及时根据市场供求变化调整营销策略和品种结构,克服资金短缺,能源原材料涨价等困难,抓住机遇,努力工作,使生产建设和经济效益都取得了较大的成绩,创造了历史最好水平。

——发展速度大大加快,钢产量首次突破100万吨,我省冶金工业开始登上了新台阶。1993年,冶金系统共完成工业总产值23.2亿元,比上年增长了13.4%。主要产品产量都稳定增长,其中钢101万吨,生铁111.6万吨,钢材72.3万吨,铁

合金7.3万吨，焦炭84.5万吨，铁矿石379.1万吨，炭素制品5.96万吨，铝3.76万吨。全省黄金完成3.8万两，超额完成了国家计划。按工业增加值计算的全员劳动生产率平均达到15601元/人年。

——经济效益显著增长，实现利税创造历史最好水平。全年共实现销售收入43.14亿元，实现利税7.1亿元，实现利润3.2亿元，分别比1992年增长了91.8%、121.94%和234.01%。共上缴利税5.6亿元，出口创汇达1875万美元。

——加强领导，保证重点，基本建设和技术改造取得了较好的成绩。1993年，在建设资金迟迟不能到位的情况下，为了确保“八五”登上新台阶目标的实现，我们千方百计筹措建设资金，加快工程进度。全年共完成基建技措投资3.98亿元，省部列入计划的12项工程中有10项完成了建设进度任务。其中有五项单项工程建成投产，年新增生产能力钢4万吨，连铸坯30万吨，铝型材800吨。在下半年，我们按照国家加强宏观调控的政策，正确处理“吃饭”与建设的关系，坚持量力而行的原则，把有限的资金用在“刀刃上”，一保生产。二保建设。到年底，“八五”计划中确定的酒钢高炉达产配套和中板工程，兰钢电炉扩建改造，兰炭一万吨高功率大电极，陇西铝厂二期等五项省级重点建设项目都有了较大进展。

一年来，我们把深化改革和加强管理有机地结合起来，努力克服“以改带管”、“以转代管”的消极倾向坚持从严治企业，夯实基础管理工作，进一步深化了企业改革。在贯彻落实转机《条例》中，我们做到三不一多，即凡是《条例》中规定应放给企业的权力，厅里不留，全部放给企业；凡是省上各级综合部门下放给企业的权力，厅里不截，积极协助企业落实；凡是需要厅里协调解决的问题，厅里不推，主动帮助解决，做到多服务，服好务。各企业也努力克服计划经济体制下形成的思想羁绊和工作束缚，充分发挥自己的主观能动性，放开手脚，大胆主动地用足用好自主权。酒钢和兰钢作为省上率先进行贯彻《条例》的试点企业，进行了大力度、深层次的改革，在巩固、完善、提高“三项”制度改革成果的基础上，分别开展了股份制改造的准备工作，进行了清产核资。酒钢还按照“发展主体、搞活辅助、放开后勤”的经营战略方针，对医疗、住房、养老保险等制度进行了一系列的改革。各企业都普遍推行了新的财会制度，开展了劳动用工、干部人事和工资奖金分配等“三项”制度的改革。

不断挖掘内部潜力，开拓市场，增加效益是我们全年工作的主旋律。各企业都从大处着眼，小处着手，严格各项经济承包责任制，加强了资金、物资的集中统一管理，严肃财经纪律，减少浪费，努力消化各类涨价因素。全系统138项技术经济指标与1992年相比，改善和提高的有83项，持平的有8项，其中新创和达到历史最好水平的有53项。32项可比产品质量稳定提高率达到100%。同时，还坚持科学技术是第一生产力的方针，大力开发新产品，推广应用新技术，加强技术攻关和科研项目向生产力的转化，不断推进技术进步。全系统共有三项技术攻关项目获得省部级科技进步奖，开发新产品8项，创造新产品产值32624万元，两种新产品获省优秀新产品奖。

深化改革，促进发展，提前一年完成“八五”计划

今年，是全国上下深入贯彻党的十四届三中全会和全省人民贯彻落实省第八次党代会精神的一年，是深化改革、加快发展、建立社会主义市场经济体制的攻坚年、突破年。同时，也是要继续保持我省冶金工业快速、健康发展的非常重要的一年。我们的指导思想是：以邓小平同志建设有中国特色社会主义理论为指导，加大改革力度，加快发展步伐，切实转变机关职能，转换企业经营机制，积极探索建立现代化企业制度的路子；以技术改造、优化结构为重点，苦练内功，强化管理，努力提高各项经济技术指标，力争速度、销售收入和实现利税三同步增长，全面提高经济效益，确保提前一年完成“八五”计划，为全省实现第二步战略目标做出贡献。我们的目标是：完成工业总产值25亿元，速度达到8%；力争产钢110万吨，产铁120万吨，产材80万吨，实现销售收入37亿元，实现利税5.45亿元。出口创汇2170万美元。完成投资10亿元，确保酒钢高炉达产配套、中板工程、高炉喷吹煤粉和改质沥青，兰钢70吨电炉及配套项目，兰炭高功率电极，西铁12500KVA电炉烟气治理，甘铝陇西铝厂二期等八项重点建设和改造工程完成进度任务。

“抓住机遇、深化改革、扩大开放、促进发展、保持稳定”是今年全党工作的大局，我们要牢牢把握这个方针，继续推进企业改革。总体思路是认真贯彻执行转机《条例》和固定资产监督管理《条例》，深入开展“三项”制度和企业各项管理制度的配套改革，争取尽快建立起适应社会主义市场经济要求的企业管理制度；要按照精干主体、搞活辅助、剥离后勤的原则，大力推进企业内部组织结构的改革，提高劳动生产率，形成人、财、物三要素合理流动的新机制；在建立现代企业制度方面要在认真搞好清产核资的基础上，采取国家独资公司、有限责任公司和股份有限公司三种形式，抓好两个试点，即一是按照省上部署抓好酒钢建立现代企业制度的试点工作，二是其它企业有条件的要选择一、两个二级厂矿或公司开展内部试点，逐步把我们的冶金企业建设成公司化、集团化、多元化的开放式企

业，达到产权明晰，责权利明确；政企分开，自主经营、自负盈亏的市场竞争主体的目的。要认真研究财税、金融、投资、外贸等体制改革政策，正确分析新的改革举措给我们冶金企业带来的利弊得失，抓住机遇，加快发展步伐。冶金厅机关要适应社会主义市场经济的要求，解放思想，转变观念，探索新的工作思路和工作方法，积极搞好宏观调控方面的工作。要将工作重点转到行业管理上来。一方面要帮助企业和促进冶金企业，特别是地县中小企业增强活力，加快发展；另一方面，还要严格按照国家产业政策，管好行业建设和发展上的重大问题。要建立行业监督、管理体系，加强行业法制工作；建立信息体系，加强信息指导，为企业的发展提供决策依据。要加强行业的规划，找准优势，扬长避短，增畅限滞，优化产品结构，引导全省冶金工业健康协调地发展。

在改革中发展，在改革中前进，是不可抗拒的潮流。充分利用我省金属矿产资源丰实等优势，进一步发展甘肃冶金工业是全省冶金战线广大职工的共识。我们深信，在党的改革开放政策的指引下，在省委、省政府的正确领导下，有全省人民的大力支持，我省冶金工业会取得更加辉煌的成就。

1993年甘肃省有色金属工业发展综述

1993年，甘肃省有色金属工业以改革和发展总揽全局，克服了电力、原材料、运输涨价、资金紧张、有色金属市场平淡等各种困难，使改革、生产经营和建设都保持了良好的发展态势。

一、生产完成情况及发展状况

（一）产量、产值稳步增长，经济效益取得好成绩

1993年，全省有色金属工业完成工业总产值（1990年不变价）65.03亿元，比上年同期增长12.74%。其中有色兰州公司直管的6户生产企业完成工业总产值（1990年不变价）50.01亿元，比上年同期增长9.9%。

全省十种常用有色金属产量完成39.67万吨（其中铜6.96万吨、铝21.0万吨、铅1.1万吨、锌7.94万吨、镍2.65万吨），比上年同期增长27.60%。其中有色兰州公司直管的6户生产企业完成十种有色金属33.8万吨，比上年同期增长22.46%。有色金属加工材完成3.44万吨；稀土化合物完成1.52万吨，创历史最好水平。

在产量、产值快速增长的同时，有色兰州公司6户直管生产企业产品销售收入达到43.2亿元，比上年同期增长17.38%。全年实现利税总额6.74亿元，其中产品销售税金4.22亿元，比上年增长16.10%。由于受能源、原材料涨价、风灾等因素，特别是独联体低价抛售镍等市场因素的影响，实现利润2.52亿元，比上年下降。但扣除能源、原材料上涨和实行新财会制度的影响，若按可比口径计算，实现利润仍比上年有一定的增长。值得提出的是西北铝加工厂在多年大幅度亏损，1993年全国铝加工行业普遍不景气的情况下，摘掉了亏损“帽子”；甘肃稀土公司继1992年扭亏之后，1993年利润大幅度增长，实现利润305.4万元。实现了有色兰州公司6户生产企业无一亏损。

（二）基本建设、技术改造取得新进展

1993年，基本建设全年完成总投资58654万元，是重点建设项目完成投资计划比较好的一年。金川有色金属公司完成基本建设投资3.75亿元，比上年增长了15.74%，创历史最好水平；矿山掘进量完成2180米/70000立方米，闪速熔炼、铜熔炼热电站等一批重点建设工程均完工或交付使用。去年建成的我国第一座镍闪速炉，得到中外专家的一致好评。

白银有色金属公司西北铅锌冶炼厂完成投资12000万元，锌系统、硫酸系统生产流程的完善和填平补齐项目完成了任务，有效地保证了试车的顺利进行，全年生产阴极锌5.5万吨。厂坝铅锌二期完成投资7500万元，东山头大爆破清理完毕，采矿系统完成630米通风排水平硐。白银铝厂去年8月份通过了有色总公司和甘肃省的验收，全年生产铝锭4.1万吨。

重点技术改造项目全年完成投资25239万元，比上年增长37.76%。金川有色金属公司龙首矿西采区露天转井下工程开始试车生产；白银有色金属公司冶炼厂电解扩建工程建成投产，使铜电解能力由4.25万吨增加到5万吨；甘肃稀土公司6000吨工程生产线已达产达标；兰州铝厂连海铝业股份有限公司、连城铝厂宝川铝业股份有限公司相继建成投产。增加了企业发展后劲。

（三）地方有色金属工业和集体经济稳步发展

近年来，我省地方有色金属工业蓬勃发展，成为振兴当地经济的一支重要力量。1993年地方矿山企业面对激烈的市场竞争，认真贯彻落实省公司召开的第三次管理经验交流会议精神，坚持“整顿、巩固、提高、发展”的方针，向管理和科技进步要效益，在降低矿产品成本、提高矿产品质量上狠下功夫，在调整产品结构、发展多种经营上开拓思路，使主要经济技术指标又有较大的提高，列入行业管理的地方矿山企业完成工业总产值12760万元，生产铜、铅、锌矿产品金属含量4万吨，实现利税2713.3万元，采选配套的企业户户盈利。

集体经济和多种经营快速增长，在产品深加工、综合利用和第三产业方面已形成全方位、多功能、多

层次的企业系列，开始由速度型、安置型向效益型发展，较好地完成了生产经营任务。1993年全系统集体经济社会总产值突破10亿元，比上年同期增长25.6%，全年实现利税5575万元，其中上交税金4271万元。

二、深化改革和发展的主要措施

(一)人员分流，调整结构

有色兰州公司根据全系统的实际，把企业人员分流、调整结构作为深化改革、降低成本、提高劳动生产率、增强在国内外两个市场上竞争的重要举措。兰州公司根据全系统的实际，从十个方面划清政策界限，引导企业加快分流步伐。各企业普遍把辅助生产、后勤、生活服务等单位划出去自主经营、自负盈亏，面向企业内外搞有偿服务。各企业发挥自身优势，以市场为导向，开拓新的生产和经营领域，或扩大主业生产规模，或对产品进行深度加工，综合利用，或强化销售力量，在外开办窗口，或开发与有色金属相关的，市场有需求效益的项目，有的企业还打入其他行业。1993年在人员分流、结构调整方面一个新的特点是：不仅对企业二、三线人员中的富余人员进行分流，而且还对一线富余人员进行分流。有的企业为了调动二级单位分流的积极性，采取了诸如减员不减工资总额、工资总额分流等有力措施，促进了二级单位把富余人员从岗位上分流出来，去开发其他新项目，增加经济收入。据统计，有色兰州公司6户直管生产企业当年劳动生产率提高了11.87%，分流人员11623人，组建独立核算的经济实体191个，实现利税6133万元。

(二)劳动保险制度改革开始起步

有色兰州公司职工养老保险统筹工作，已于1993年7月份开始。到年末，已将直、协管14个企事业单位，88024名职工和14094名离退休人员纳入养老保险统筹范围，并征集到部分统筹调剂基金。兰州铝厂、兰州连城铝厂等企业已足额上交了统筹基金。

(三)开展股份制企业的试点

1993年，甘肃省有色金属工业企业体制改革迈出了重要一步，开展了股份制企业的试点工作。试点的几户股份制企业在股份制的建立、资金筹措、基本建设、试车生产以及管理上发挥了股份制企业的优越性，为建立现代企业制度积累了宝贵经验。连海铝业股份有限公司从1992年9月28日破土，到1993年6月28日竣工，仅用了九个月时间就建成投产，当年生产出10088吨电解铝；宝川铝业股份有限公司建设也速度快，质量好。金川冶金股份有限公司、白银有色工贸股份有限公司和白银氟化盐有限公司组建后已显示出产权改革的巨大威力。三佳稀土有限公司机制转换明显，效益很好。

(四)强化企业内部管理基础工作

企业在外抓市场的同时，眼睛向内，继续加强财务、成本、质量、科技、生产调度、机动能源、安全环保等生产经营各个环节的管理工作，使企业内部工作得到加强。各企业根据自身情况，改进经营管理模式，巩固和发展了诸如划小核算单位，内部模拟市场、对二级单位委托法人自主经营等行之有效的改革措施，对调动多层次的积极性发挥了作用。据统计，在21项物耗指标中18项物耗单位耗量稳定或下降，7种产品的电耗指标，稳定或下降的有6种。

三、科技进步得到进一步重视，取得一批科技成果。

企业走向市场，增强了推进科技进步的压力和动力。各企业把科学技术看作第一生产力，围绕生产建设中的技术难题，围绕提高经济效益这个中心，大搞科技攻关，加大科技投入。据统计，有色兰州公司直管的6户生产企业投入科技开发资金2000多万元。1993年全省有色系统获总公司科技进步奖的科技成果有10项，获省科技进步奖的科技成果有3项。这些成果大部分达到了国内先进水平，个别项目达到了国际先进水平，由于这些科技成果具有很强的针对性和实用性，应用到生产中，很快就转化为生产力。白银有色金属公司小铁山矿，上向巷道式采矿法实验研究成功，提高了资源利用率，降低了贫化损失率；金川有色金属公司，通过一、二矿区富矿选矿新工艺工业试验，降低了精矿中氧化镁的含量，满足了闪速熔炼的生产要求；兰州连城铝厂侧插自焙铝电解槽干糊技术大面积推广，使阳极上部沥青挥发物减少30%；兰州铝厂侧插自熔铝电解槽新型阳极糊工业实验，在不改变现有生产工艺和设备的条件下，改善了工艺性能，提高了产品质量。

振兴和发展甘肃有色金属工业，是全省有色行业方方面面的事情。设计、施工、机修和设备供应等单位在比较困难的情况下，顾全大局，为发展甘肃有色金属工业尽心竭力，并面向市场千方百计开发任务，取得了较好的经营业绩。地勘局在找矿取得新进展的同时，调整人员结构和产业结构迈出较大步伐；科研单位围绕生产建设开展多种形式的科研和科技活动，加速科技成果向生产力转化，既出了成果，又出了效益。

(中国有色金属工业兰州公司)

甘肃机械工业

省机械集团公司总经理：

李连维

甘肃机械工业是全省工业的支柱产业之一。按照国家统一划分的制造业分类，包括金属制品业、普通机械工业、交通运输设备制造业、电气机械及器材制造业、仪器仪表及其他计量器具制造业五个大类。全省共有乡及乡以上独立核算机械企业999个，职工17.98万人，固定资产原值29.26亿元，年产值(90年不变价)41.21亿元，占全省工业总产值的11.5%。分属于机械、冶金、电力、石化、电子、司法、交通等多个部门管理。由甘肃省机械工业总公司归口管理的企业(以下称“甘肃省机械工业系统企业”)总产值比重占到全省全部机械工业的80%左右。

1993年全省机械工业系统归口管理企业225户，其中大中型企业35户；全部职工12.71万人，其中工程技术人员9千人；固定资产原值23亿元，固定资产净值13.9亿元；拥有各类主要加工设备26347台，其中，金属切削机床11810台，锻压设备2524台。按生产的产品用途分类分为农业机械、工程机械、仪器仪表、石化通用、重型矿山、机床工具、电工电器、食品及包装机械、汽车工业、其他机械等十二大行业，生产门类比较齐全，下分为64个具体制造业，能生产二百多类种上万种不同型号规格的产品。

甘肃省机械集团公司是带动全省机械工业发展的主要力量。甘肃机械集团公司是在甘肃省机械工业总公司多年发展基础上组建，并经省委、省政府批准成立的，是由集团公司本部、紧密层、半紧密层、松散层组成的集科工贸一体的全民所有制企业。甘肃机械集团公司成立一年多来，坚持走调整、高效发展经济的道路，充分显示了整体优势。经过一年多的发展，截止1993年底，集团公司已拥有紧密层工业企业29户，半紧密层工业企业72户，松散层工业企业22户，成员工业企业资本金100193万元，拥有固定资产原价15.46亿元，实现工业总产值(90年不变价)230613万元，主要经济指标(销售收入、实现利税等)均占全系统的70%以上。1993年甘肃机械集团公司不断深化改革，强化企业管理，调整产品结构，积极引进外资，引进技术，增强企业发展后劲，为今后进一步的发展奠定了坚实的基础。

一、1993年全省机械系统经济运行概况

1. 工业生产与销售

1993年上半年，在全国经济高速发展的推动下，我省机械工业平均月增长速度达12%。三季度，由于国家金融政策的调整，宏观经济运行形势偏紧，全系统增长速度也在逐月回落。截止1993年底，实现工业总产值(90年不变价)31.75亿元，比上年增长9.39%，以现行价计算的工业总产值为36.66亿元，增长速度达到24.65%。在不变价产值中，电工电器与机床工具行业的增长速度分别达到24.69%和31.61%。农业机械行业基本与上年持平。而石化通用、仪器仪表、汽车工业、机械基础件行业出现了负增长。其中占我省机械行业产值比重较大的石化通用行业、机械基础件行业分别下滑1.54%和14.6%，对全局影响很大。全系统工业增加值仅比上年增长4.95%。

1993年底，全系统销售产值(现行价)为35.71亿元，比上年增长24.72%，产品销售率为97.4%，产销基本衔接。库存总额8.25亿元，比上年增长31.34%。库存当量(库存总额/月平均销售额)为2.83个月。

占全系统不变价工业总产值比重86%的115类种主要产品中，生产量(实物量)与去年相比增长和持平的有71类种，下降的有44类种，总价值量(不变价)比上年增长了7.54%。农产品资金不到位，农民负担过重，影响了农机产品的需求量。主要的24类种农机产品中，除农用机动三轮车、农用运输车、拖内配件等四类产品比上年有所增长外，其余产品均有不同程度的下降。电工电器行业是产品结构调整比较成功的行业，其产品中，交流电动机增长19.7%，交流发电机增长33.53%。金属切削机床、机床电器的产量分别增长了12.84%和64.1%。照相机产量下降了34.70%。轴承产量下降26.31%。石油钻采设备下降了40.23%。汽车行业产品中，改装汽车下降幅度达51.71%，而汽车配件则增长35.81%。

2. 产品出口

1993年底，全系统出口交货值为11838万元人民币，基本与上年持平，出口创汇折合美元1981.56万美元，却比上年下降8.16%。全系统出口企业21户，产品出口到美国、香港、东南亚、西欧等30多个国家和地区。从出口产品结构来看，出口交货值(现价人民币)中机床类产品出口占23.14%，轴承占10.09%，电机占15.88%，石油钻采设备占15.68%。这四大类产品占全部出口额的70%以上。

3. 新产品开发及产品结构调整

1993年全系统根据市场需求，结合新产品开发，加快了产品结构调整的步伐。全年共组织开发新产品178项。其中，甘肃机械集团公司紧密层企业开发新产品109项，新产品产值率达到36%。全年完成了一批技术水平高、经济效益好的项目，如天水风动工具厂的TROC712HC－01履带式液压露天钻车、天水锻压机床厂生产的W67YK－100/3200、800/10000数控板料折弯机、Q12YK－6×3200数控液压剪板机，甘肃长城电器工业公司生产的JYN□－10/630～1000、10/1250～3000间隔型金属封闭开关、CJ20－200、600、630交流接触器，兰州石油化工机器总厂生产的JY4800金刚石压机，平凉印刷机械厂生产的QZK130微机控制切纸机等。有一些新产品已大量投入生产，如：兰州手扶拖拉机厂生产的

2815四轮运输车，天水长城开关厂生产的F－C回路开关柜、天水213机床电器公司生产的交直流操作接触器等。

几年来，全省机械系统特别是甘肃机械集团公司紧密层企业普遍重视产品结构调整工作。甘肃机械集团公司把调整产品结构做为企业兴亡的关键问题常抓不懈。通过产品结构调整，涌现出了一批具有优势产品的企业，如兰州手扶拖拉机厂、天水213机床电器公司、兰州真空设备厂、甘肃长城电器工业公司、兰州电机厂、天水锻压机床厂、天水风动工具厂等。1993年，全系统开发性调整完成70项，实现工业总产值(不变价)12144万元，比上年增长11.8%；适应性调整完成92项，实现产值64402万元，增长36.29%，外向型调整创汇1148万美元，折合人民币6653万元。

4.技术改造与技术引进

1993年甘肃机械工业围绕着产品结构调整和技术进步，在资金非常困难的情况下，坚持技术改造，全年完成更新改造投资11345万元，比上年增长15.54%。全年列入国家和地方更新改造措施计划项目有20项，计划投资额10345万元，实际完成投资6296万元，占年计划的60.86%，项目计划资金自筹率为26.6%。

全省全年技术改进项目主要集中在甘肃机械集团公司。共完成技术引进项目7个，总计312.36万美元。主要有兰州通用机器厂的涡旋压缩机技术改造项目，兰州电机厂交流伺服及主轴电机的技术改造工程，甘肃长城电器工业公司、天水213机床电器公司引进的气体保护自动焊机、热固注射机等“八五”技改项目关键设备，天水锻压机床厂的救灾恢复能力项目大型落地铣床等，这些关键技术设备引进成为增强企业发展的后劲，提高企业技术水平和产品竞争力的有效措施。

5.引进外资

甘肃地处西北内陆，由于自身条件的限制，引进外资比较困难。甘肃机械集团公司本着互惠互利原则，多渠道招商引资。1993年全系统共建成四个合资企业，均由甘肃机械集团公司成员单位组建，总投资246.1万美元，其中引进外资118万美元。建成的四个合资企业分别是甘肃光学仪器工业公司与香港合资的深圳金达电器金属制品有限公司；甘肃光学仪器工业公司与美国合资成立的金威电器有限公司；天水轴承仪器厂与香港合资的天水兴田橡塑机械有限公司；甘肃机械集团公司本部甘肃润达实业开发公司与俄罗斯合资成立的兰州西格拉特娱乐有限公司。

6.产品质量

1993年，全系统企业产品质量基本稳定。全年实查考核品65种，全部合格，其中一等品45种。全年省级监督抽查119种产品，不合格品14种，占11.76%，主要集中在地县企业，其主管部门正在积极组织整改、整顿。

甘肃机械集团公司引导企业贯彻GB/T1900－ISO9000系列质量管理标准，并通过示范作用和产品质量监督取得了很好的效果。国家产品抽查合格率为100%。1993年中国质量管理协会组织的全国用户满意产品一百家企业评选中，兰州手扶拖拉机厂的“兰驼牌”农用运输车榜上有名。兰州电机厂生产的LD牌1FT5系列交流伺服电机、LD牌TZH系列三相交流发电机、LD牌TFX－H系列船用三相交流发电机，天水213机床电器公司生产的石林牌CJX4－09/12N机械联锁交流接触器，天水长城低压电器厂生产的环宇牌CJ20－16交流接触器，天水风动工具厂生产的燎原牌S60型气砂轮等6项产品获甘肃省实物质量赶超国际先进水平奖。天水海林轴承厂生产的海林牌7308E、7508E、7510E圆锥滚子轴承等10类产品获甘肃省实物质量赶超国内先进水平奖。兰州电机厂、天水长城开关厂被评为甘肃省质量效益型企业。

7.深化改革与企业管理

1993年甘肃机械集团公司朝着翻两番的奋斗目标，脚踏实地，大胆探索，做了许多扎实而富有成效的工作，带动了全省机械工业系统整体素质和水平的提高。一些成功的经验和作法在全系统推广。甘肃机械集团公司所做的主要工作：

一是按照《全民所有制工业企业转换经营机制条例》要求和省政府《实施办法》，不断完善符合本集团实际的贯彻意见，积极放权于企业，并指导企业用好自主权，转机制，抓管理，练内功，增效益。集团公司坚持对企业抓好领导班子建设、经济合同书的落实、企业产品结构及组织机构的调整、基础管理与科学管理四件大事。主要领导分工负责，深入企业调查研究，进行分类指导帮助，取得了一定效果。股份制改造的选点和前期准备工作也在积极进行。

二是抓两头、抓调整，求得集团公司的整体发展。鼓励经营形势好的企业抓住机遇加快发展，开拓市场，多超多留，为集团公司整体发展做出贡献。奋力减亏扭亏是全年的工作重点。集团公司通过多种方式进行企业组织机构调整，大胆探索帮助部分亏损企业摆脱困境的有效途径。在1993年将甘肃省筑路机械厂成功地并入兰州手扶拖拉机厂之后，又将甘肃省电影机械厂整体划归兰州油泵油咀总厂；将天水长城电工仪器厂与天水213机床电器厂合并成立天水213机床电器公司；帮助兰州柴油机厂缩小生产规模，向兰州电机厂、兰州手扶拖拉机厂、兰州真空设备厂分流人员；支持天水长城精密电表厂、甘肃光学仪器工业公司迅速进行转换内部经营机制的试验。这些改革措施有的获得成功，有的已初见成果，对促进生产要素的合理流动、壮大优势企业实力起了积极的作用，体现了集团公司对国有资产实行统一经营管理的优越性。

三是以保值增殖为目的，完善运行机制，加强国有资产管理。集团公司为确保财政上交，制定了国有资产在价值形态上的考核办法，全面推行工效挂钩，提高整体效益，并制定了《防止国有资产流失，加强干部廉洁自律的有关规定》和《关于企业经营活动中几个值得注意的问题的通知》，帮助企业在发展第三产业、开展多种经营的过程中划清资产界限和经营责任，确保国有资产和企业利益不受损害。

四是狠抓基础管理和科学管理工作。从全国范围来看，在给企业放权后，不少企业以包代管，以改代管，出现了管理滑坡的现象。在这种情况下，甘肃机械集团公司部分企业仍自觉地抓住管理工作不放松，形成了各自的管理特色和管理优势。甘肃长城电器工业公司所属的天水长城开关厂、天水长城控制电器厂以其过硬的基础管理工作受到机械部领导的高度赞扬，并在全行业推广。

五是集团公司本部新办经济实体正常起步，顺应了改革的潮流。继1992年兴办十个实体公司后，又成立了经营部，利用集团公司的营业执照合法创收。通过一年多的经营实践，集团公司大部分实体公司运转正常。

8．经济效益

1993年甘肃省机械工业系统虽然在扭亏增盈上做了很多工作，也取得了一定效果。但由于国家宏观金融政策调整，并受新旧财会制度衔接过渡的影响，全系统仍未彻底扭转经济效益下滑的局面。1993年底全系统销售收入达38.2亿元，比上年增长41.29%，但其中应收帐款6.7亿元，占全部销售收入的17.52%。百元销售收入成本费用含量达到91.4元。经济效益发展很不平衡。全系统盈利企业171户，盈利额14405万元，比上年增长20%。兰州电机厂、甘肃长城电器工业公司、天水风动工具厂三厂实现利润逾千万元，占全省盈利企业盈利额的42.61%。利税总额21970万元，比上年增长7%，其中实现利润为5852万元，比上年下降20.83%。全省全年亏损企业54户，比上年增长23户，亏损额达8553万元，比上年增长92.07%。从投资者投资收益角度来看，全系统投资收益率（税后利润/资本金×100%）仅为0.45%，大大低于当年存款利息水平。盈利企业的投资收益率也只有8.56%。

从资产负债状况来看，全系统流动资产占用额达到39.1亿元；存货为23.8亿元；产成品存货为7.2亿元。全部资产总额58.97亿元，负债总额43.53亿元，资产负债率高达73.82%。全系统有近三分之一的企业处于资本金亏空状态（即所有者权益小于资本金），资本金亏空15209万元，其中有4户企业出现了资不抵债（即所有者权益小于0）。

二、经济发展的主要制约因素及存在的困难与问题

1.资金紧张。1993年下半年，由于全局性的资金紧缩，加之上半年生产资料价格总水平很高，资金紧张成为企业最突出矛盾。部分市场需求形势好、产品利润率较高的企业由于缺乏资金购买原材料，处于停产、半停产状态。企业组织生产困难重重，货款回收不力，相互拖欠的债务链加剧。资金紧张造成了一部分企业出现了非正常亏损。例如，轴承生产企业，1993年轴承市场虽然旺销，但上半年特钢厂减少轴承钢的生产，企业买不来原材料，下半年轴承钢供给虽有缓解，但企业贷不到款，无力购买。由于资金短缺，导致基础件行业出现了全行业亏损。企业生产周转资金尚不能满足，技术改造投入更无从谈起，难以走向健康的自我发展的道路。

2.成本费用高。1993年全系统百元销售收入成本费用（指财务费用、管理费用）含量比1986年高出13元。成本费用上升的主要原因是企业变动成本上升很快，原材料价格一涨再涨。1993年以来，轴承钢涨价80%以上，电费上涨60%，银行贷款利率两次上调，企业难以承受。成本费用上升对农机行业冲击尤为明显，由于农村市场承受能力低，长期以来农机产品一直处于保本微利状态，天水拖拉机厂生产的15马力四轮拖拉机售价仅6千多元，和一吨钢材价格差不多。我省大部分机械产品处于买方市场，市场竞争激烈，价格效益低。成本费用大幅度上升，而产品价格却不能相应上涨，超过了企业消化吸收能力，侵蚀了利润。

3.亏损局面相当严重。1993年底全系统企业亏损面为24%，亏损额为8553万元，比上年增长92.07%。全年农业机械、仪器仪表、石化通用、机械基础件、汽车等五大行业都出现全行业性亏损。造成亏损的客观原因主要有四方面。一是原材料货紧价扬，企业资金紧张。二是技术改造投入不足，造成企业设备老化、工艺落后、成本上升。三是个别长期亏损的特困企业，进行产品结构调整缺乏资金支持，短期内很难扭转亏损局面。四是一些“三线”企业负担沉重。大部分亏损企业经营机制转换慢、产品结构调整跟不上市场需求，也是主观上导致亏损的重要原因。此外，由于新旧会计制度衔接过渡，对1993年实现利润影响也很大。

4.资产增量投入严重不足，市场应变能力低。长期以来，我省机械工业系统企业固定资产更新改造投入严重不足，相当一部分企业设备老化、技术水平低。全省机械工业

系统企业中约有半数人均固定资产净值不足6千元。"八五"期间,很多技改、基建项目急需进行,而资金到位率却很低。在这种固定资产存量结构和增量投入水平下,企业市场应变能力普遍偏低。

城建环保测绘

深化体制改革 加快城乡建设

省建设委员会主任
张国杰

1993年,是全省城乡建设事业持续发展的一年,也是加强宏观调控取得明显成效的一年。一年来,各级建设部门和广大职工,认真贯彻党的十四届三中全会精神和党中央关于加强宏观调控的重大决策,促进了城市建设和村镇建设事业的全面发展。

一.城市市政公用基础设施的建设取得一定成绩

1993年,各级建设部门积极推进城市建设投资体制改革,通过建立国家财政投入、市政公用设施有偿使用和公用事业合理计价为主要内容的多渠道投资体制,使城市市政公用基础设施建设得到持续发展。全省城市建设完成固定资产投资18020万元,建成了嘉峪关市供水一期工程,新增日供水能力1.4万吨,白银市、西峰市、平凉市等三个城市供水工程的形象进度完成了年度计划。到1993年底,全省城市供水综合生产能力为253万吨/日,非农业用水人口为253.6万人,每人每天平均生活用水量为147公斤,用水普及率为97.2%。建成了西和、合水、武都、康县县城以及陇西县城文峰水厂等5个县镇供水工程,新增日供水能力9845吨。到1993年底,全省68个县镇中,按正式设计建成自来水设施的县城43个,日供水能力为12.9吨,用水人口为53.6万人。

城市燃气、集中供热工程建设有所发展。兰州煤气工程敷设市区低压管线15公里,新增用户4万户。到1993年底,兰州、嘉峪关两个城市煤气供气总量为2666万标立方/年,用气人口为23.7万人;兰州、金昌、白银、玉门、武威等5市液化石油气供气总量为46733吨/年,用气人口为63.9万人,民用燃料气化率为33.6%。兰州市"二热"集中供热管网工程完成了东岗小区三个街坊热力站及管网敷设工程。到1993年底,全省兰州、嘉峪关、白银、玉门、金昌、酒泉、张掖等7个城市集中供热能力为1132兆瓦/小时,供热面积为1466万平方米。

城市公共交通设施建设取得新的成绩。1993年,全省城市新增公共交通车辆34辆,新增出租汽车989辆,新增运营线路170公里。到1993年底,全省城市公共交通标准运营车辆为1017辆,出租汽车2620辆,每万人拥有公共交通车辆4.5标台。

城市道路、排水、防洪设施建设速度有所加快。兰州、天水、白银、金昌、嘉峪关、平凉、西峰、张掖、临夏等城市以及武都、永昌等县城,通过多渠道筹集资金,建成了一批城市道路、排水、防洪等市政工程,全省新增城市道路长度8.3公里,新增排水管道9公里,新增和加固城镇防洪河堤42公里。到1993年底,全省城市长度1669公里、面积1497万平方米,每人平均拥有道路面积5.7平方米;城市排水管道1108公里,排水管道密度为3公里/平方公里,城市污水日处理能力为23.3万吨,污水处理率为21.6%;城市防洪堤328公里,桥梁286座,路灯29581盏。

二.城市环境综合整治全面展开,城市市容市貌有所改观

1993年,全省设市城市按照建设部、爱国卫生运动委员会、卫生部、国家环保局等有关部门的统一部署,广泛动员群众,全面开展城市环境综合整治目标管理考核活动,促进了环境卫生管理和生态环境建设,扭转了部分城市脏、乱、差的状况。据不完全统计,全省城市和县城全年植树416万株,新增园林绿地面积162公顷。到1993年底,全省城市建成区绿化覆盖面积为2920公顷,绿化覆盖率为7.4%,公共绿地面积811公顷,每人平均公共绿地面积3.1平方米。全省城市有垃圾无害化处理厂9座,日处理能力1379吨,环境卫生清运机械364辆,公共厕所992座,民办保洁队伍2625人,垃圾粪便无害化处理率为21.1%。嘉峪关市、临夏市分别被评为全省1993年度城市环境综合整治地级市、县级市第一名,受到建设部通报表扬。

三.城市房地产业和住宅建设持续发展

1993年,全省各城市认真贯彻党中央关于加强宏观调控的决策和国务院关于发展房地产业若干问题的通知精神,开展了对城市房地产开发企业的全面检查和房地产市场的宏观调控,按照国家确定的控制规模、调整结构、依法办事、规范行为、调节收益的界路,促进房地产业继续健康发展。通过检查和宏观调控措施的落实,引导房地产市场行为向规范化方向发展,促进了土地使用制度由无偿划拨转为有偿出让的改革,加快了城镇住宅建设和房地产投资结构的改善。全省城镇住宅建设年度总投资约8.3亿元,竣工面积266万平方米,每人平均居住面积7.1平方米。全省现有房地产开发经营机构337个,1993年度开发土地面积123公顷,施工房屋面积345万平方米,竣工房屋面积97万平方米,其中住宅竣工面积81万平方米。年内销售商品房屋面积

53万平方米，其中住宅49万平方米，销售收入4.75亿元，土地转让收入75万元，房屋出租收入221万元，其他收入3780万元，合计经营总收入5.16亿元，缴纳税费2831万元，实现利润1994万元。各城镇继续加强了城镇房屋产权产籍管理和房地产市场管理。尚未完成房屋产权登记发证工作的少数城镇，继续抓紧了登记发证工作；已完成此项工作的城镇，开始对房屋产权产籍实行动态管理。各城市推行了《房屋租赁许可证》、《房地产买卖契约》、《房地产租赁契约》等三个规范文本，规范了房地产交易行为。兰州、金昌、白银、酒泉等城市房地产交易机构开展了房地产市场估介管理工作。

四.城市市政公用企业转换经营机制步伐加快，企业内部改革逐步深化

1993年，各城市建设主管部门进一步贯彻实施国家有关部门共同颁发的城市供水供气供热企业、城市公共交通企业、市政工程施工企业转换经营机制实施办法，取得了积极成效。市政公用企业面向市场，逐步从单纯社会效益型向社会效益与经济效益结合型转变，成为自主经营、自负盈亏、自我发展、自我约束的商品生产和经营单位。兰州市公交总公司在企业内部全面推行承包责任制，对39条线路、606台公共汽车实行单车承包，社会效益和企业经济效益有了显著提高，“乘车难”状况有所改善。兰州市自来水总公司完善各项内部改革后，进一步增强了企业活力和对外竞争能力，服务质量有了明显提高，城市供水状况有了较大改善。

五.村镇建设进入新阶段，村镇基础设施进一步得到改善

随着农村经济的发展和乡镇企业的相对集中建设，带动了全省村镇建设的全面发展。到1993年底，全省有69个建制镇完成了总体规划调整工作，305个集镇完成了集镇建设规划调整工作，6363个村庄完成了村庄规划调整工作，规划设计水平都有不同程度的提高。全省新修乡镇道路7.88万公里，建成了59个建制镇、205个乡镇、3050个村庄的简易供水设施，年供水能力达3亿多吨，其中建制镇供水普及率达54%。村镇住宅建设持续发展，截至1993年底，全省村镇新建住宅35473万平方米。经过各地抓点带面，出现了一批新型集镇和农民新村。

1994年，是全面推进改革，加快建立社会主义市场经济体制的关键一年，我们要进一步深化改革，加快发展，把全省城乡建设事业推上新的台阶。一要强化城市和村镇规划意识，切实抓好规划，使其充分发挥指导城市建设和发展的“龙头”作用，逐步建立和完善与社会主义市场经济体制相适应的城市规划调控机制，促进城市经济、社会协调发展。二要大力加强城市市政公用基础设施建设，进一步提高城市功能和环境质量，努力缓解部分城市群众吃水难、用气难、乘车难等问题。三要继续推动城镇房地产业健康发展，建立与社会主义市场经济相适应的住宅建设运行机制和住房供应体制，努力提高城镇人民群众居住水平。四要加快农村集镇建设，促进农村经济和社会的全面发展。

环境保护

【综述】1993年，甘肃省各项建设事业取得新的成就，全部工业总产值完成501.8亿元，增长14.7%。重工业、轻工业分别完成增加值117.9亿元和27.9亿元，占80.9%和19.1%，消耗高、污染重的行业在本省经济发展中仍具优势和主导地位。面对改革开放步伐加快和经济建设迅速发展的局势。甘肃省以党的十四大精神和环境与发展十大对策为指针，积极探讨并着力调整环境保护工作的指导思想和发展战略，紧紧围绕经济建设这个中心，把工作着眼点放在正确处理环境与发展辩证关系上，全面推进环境保护事业，推动可持续发展战略的实施，取得了成效。

经过全省上下共同努力，环境污染和生态破坏没有随着生产发展而同步增加。工业“三废”排放量均控制在计划目标以内，除工业废气年排放量比上年增长11%外，工业废水年排放量比上年降低4%，工业废渣年排放量与上年持平。工业“三废”处理和综合利用率均比上年提高，全省“三废”综合利用产值达到2.47亿元，比上年增长55%。省内主要城市中，除兰州市冬季大气污染仍较严重，金昌、白银两市的二氧化硫污染居高不下以外，其他城市的环境质量基本保持稳定，黄河甘肃段、渭河、北大河、石油河、黑河、泾河、大夏河等主要河流的水污染物浓度未发生大的变化，交通与生活噪声扰民以及固体废弃物污染问题开始得到控制与治理，从而为全省经济建设和改革开放创造了较好的环境条件。

【环境规划与计划、目标责任制】甘肃省坚持并不断完善把环保计划。城市环境综合整治计划纳入国民经济和社会发展年度计划，各级政府层层分解，逐一落实。省计委与省环保局编制完成并正式下发了《甘肃省环境保护“八五”计划和十年规划》，省经贸委与省环保局联合下发了《甘肃省22个重点企业污染防治规划》，省环保局还参与编制和审查了全省国土规划，省统计局把环境保护计划完成情况正式纳入全省国民经济和社会发展统计公报，向全社会通告，省环境保护局发布了《1992年度全省环境统计公报》和《1992年全省环境状况公报》，从而增进了全社会对于环境保护的关注程度。

从本年度开始，甘肃省对业已实行八年之久的年度环境保护目标责任制实行重大改变，由每年签订一次责任书改为每三年签订一次。省政府同14个地、州、市(矿区)和12个省直工业厅、局(总公司)签订了1993年——1995年度环境保护目标责任书。各地及厅局把环境保护责任制与环境规划、计划有机地结合起来，又分别同所辖市区和企业、事业单位签订了年度责任书(个别地区改为三年一签订)，从而使省上确定的环境保护目标与任务落实到基层。

【建设项目环境管理】继续实行分级管理，抓全过程监督，坚持"先评价，后建设"、"增产不增污"和"以新带老"原则，环境影响评价和"三同时"管理工作逐步加强，特别是大中型企业的环境影响评价审批率和"三同时"执行率继续巩固并有所提高。据统计，全省新上320个建设项目中，已有235个执行了环境影响评价制度，233个应执行"三同时"的建设项目中，从环保部门对221个项目检查情况看，已执行"三同时"的有203个，省管8个项目全部执行了"三同时"。管理范围已由工业项目扩大到农业、能源、交通、社会事业以及自然资源开发和中外合资项目等。

【工业污染防治】经过多年探索，甘肃省基本形成了"以环境质量为中心，环境计划为依据，污染物总量控制为重要途径，不断强化环境管理"的新机制，1993年工业污染防治取得较大进展。

一是坚持结合技术改造，开展资源、能源的综合利用，对重大污染源实行限期治理，减少"三废"排放量。在对占全省工业污染总负荷75%左右的211家重点工业污染企业"对号入座"的基础上，实行"政府下达，责任承包，齐抓共管，奖罚分明"的办法，省政府年内下达了第11批省级污染限期治理项目共6项，总投资达1472万元，完成后年回收价值可达589万元。

【城市环境保护】1993年，全省各城市以通过加强组织领导、制订和完善规划、抓好骨干工程建设和完善基础设施、增加综合整治投入和加强城市环境法制建设等措施，推动环境综合整治不断深入。道路交通、绿化美化以及基础设施建设普遍有了发展，涌现出2个国家级、7个省级城市环境综合整治优秀项目。截至年底，各城市累计建成烟尘控制区79个，总面积245平方公里，民用型煤年生产能力达到40万吨，建成环境噪声达标小区32个，累计面积80平方公里。各城市普遍制订了烟尘控制区整改三年规划，完成了地面水环境保护功能区划报告，推行集中供热和联片供暖有了新的进展。临夏市建成太阳能住宅实验小区，建筑面积1572平方米。武威市政府发布了《武威市城市地下水饮用水源保护区污染防治管理规定》，基本建成城市垃圾无害化处理一期工程，城市烟尘控制区覆盖率达到85.6%。敦煌市将市区38个石棉掺拌经营点搬出城外，将街头卡拉OK全部搬入室内，大大改善了旅游城市环境质量。酒泉地区制定发出了《关于工业生活锅炉采用先进设备的有关规定》、《关于对城区卡拉OK和舞厅噪声管理的规定》和《酒泉地区建筑施工设备及其噪声污染管理办法》，并在全区推行了建筑机械设备使用许可证制。

五个省辖市就各自重点环境问题攻关取得新成绩。金昌市四大环境问题中，金川公司尾矿坝覆盖、电厂粉煤灰综合利用和化工总厂含碱废水治理基本完成。白银市投资150万元，完成银光路污水沟改造工程，使东市区60万吨废水由明渠排放改为暗渠排放。兰州市政府对大气污染防治极为重视，做到"早抓、狠抓、冬病夏治，争取主动"，仅四城区开展大气污染治理项目124项，查封了已具备联片供热条件而未停运的30台锅炉房，各街道办事处和城郊乡镇共向8万多居民发出了《关于小火炉禁烧有烟煤的通知》，加强监督检查，开展群防群治。此外，还恢复了已中断多年的汽车尾气路检工作，煤气工程累计安装已达6万户，使用5万户，新增供热面积20万平方米，总面积将达到50万平方米。天水、嘉峪关等市的烟尘控制区建设质量有了新的提高。

【排污收费与排污申报登记】1993年，甘肃省排污收费持续增长，通过执法大检查，有效地促进了拖欠、漏征、少征和排污量不实等问题的解决，全省排污染收费开征户达到3624户，收费额达到3951万元，分别比上年增长19%、11.5%，当年安排污染治理资金2846万元。据统计，1984～1993十年间，全省累计征收排污费2.31亿元，带出其他资金用于环保4.32亿元，共安排污染治理项目1697个。基层环境监理工作发展迅速。

排污申报登记工作采取抓好试点、逐步推开的办法，已对365个排放水污染物的企业完成了申报登记。在兰州市对饮用水源上游的10家企业首批发放临时排污许可证取得成功的基础上，白银、武威又相继开展了试点工作。

【自然环境保护】1992年，甘肃省自然生态环境的保护有了新发展。生态农业模式得到进一步推广，泾川县成为全国生态农业试点县。永昌县编制的《乡镇环境保护规划》年内正式通过国家环保局组织的验收，迈开了乡镇环境综合整治的步子。

乡镇企业环境管理工作有所加强。不少地、市的环保、计划、乡镇企业和工商等部门配合协作，建设项目的环境影响评价审批率和"三同时"执行率有了提高，天水市当年30个集体、乡镇新上建设项目全部执行了环境影响评价制度。平凉地区行署明文规定，乡镇企业不准上小造纸、小电镀、土冶炼等严重污染环境的项目，华亭县据此否决了原计划兴建的河西乡造纸厂、安口镇黄板纸厂项目、许多地方积极推行乡镇企业的技术改造、工艺改造、节能降耗和综合利用，先后进行了一些治理老污染源的示范工程。

野生动植物和自然保护区保护与管理工作取得新成绩。结合环境执法大检查，重点抓了临夏、夏河皮毛市场销售野生动物皮张、康县乱捕倒卖大鲵、武都县倒卖大熊猫皮张、肃南乱捕驯养马鹿等问题的调查与处理。据统计，1988～1992年，全省共查出乱捕滥猎、倒卖偷运国家一、二级保护动物案件20余起，涉及近400人次。安西戈壁荒漠自然保护区等24个自然保护区的建设与管理保持稳定。新成立的省级自然保护区评审委员会年内开展了活动，完成了2个申报省级、国家级自然保护区的评审工作。

【环境科学技术与环境监测】全省各级环境保护部门致力于把环境科研的重点转向为污染治理和管理服务，坚持开展黄河、渭河、泾河、大夏河及石油河等主要河流的环境容量和污染防治对策的研究，取得显著成效。省环境保护研究所发挥"主力军"作用，承担了16项环境科研课题，其中3项成果已完成鉴定。

环境监测进一步发挥了"耳目"、"哨兵"作用。各级环境监测站完成了所担负的环境质量监测、重点污染源例行监测以及企业排污收费监测和核查、环保设施竣工验收监测、城市定量考核监测等任务。省环境监测中心站编制完成了1992年度《环境质量报告书》以及全省重点工业污染源排污状况报告书等，顺利通过了国家环保局与省质量管理局组织的计量认证。

【环境宣传教育】1993年，甘肃省环境宣传教育好戏连台。先后掀起了爱鸟周与4.22地球日、六五世界环境日、八月五日环境保护事业开创20周年以及12月31日环保定为基本国策10周年纪念四次活动高潮。省内新闻界对环境问题给予前所未有的关注，中央电视台《中华环保世纪行》采访组深入陇南山区，对当地矿产资源开发中正反两方面典型在《新闻联播》中播出，引起了很大反响；《中国环境报》对连海铝业公司违犯"三同时"问题予以曝光，促进了这一问题的处理；《中国青年报》、《南方周末》及国外新闻媒介对兰州市兰泉化工厂污染纠纷事故予以报道；兰州市新闻单位紧密配合冬季大气污染防治工作，《兰州晚报》推出"金城环保行"专栏，《兰州日报》设立"大气环境观察哨"栏目，兰州电视台播出《金城环保扫描》专题节目，从而形成了环境保护舆论监督的强烈氛围。省环保局及有关单位先后拍摄完成了《呼唤》、《黄河从我身边走过》、《兰天、大地、人》等环境保护题材的电视专题片。各地、市、州还组织了规模颇大的环境保护法规及科学知识考试，参考率普遍达到90%以上。

（甘肃省环保局）

甘肃测绘事业发展概况

省测绘局局长

张昶生

测绘是测量与地图制图的总称，它是人类了解自然、改造自然、利用自然的重要手段。其主要任务是运用科学的理论、方法和技术获取地球整体或局部的陆地、海洋及空间的各种数据资料和图形资料，是国家行政管理的基础工作之一。其成果广泛运用于反映国土疆界、资源调查、环境监测、农业建设、能源、交通、水利等大型工程建设、城乡规划建设、土地开发利用、重大灾害监测预报和科学研究、国防建设等各个方面。同时，它与人们日常生活也有着密切的关系，特别是地图的用途日益广泛，如教学用图、旅游图、城市交通图、邮编图、商业网点分布图等等，这些都直接为群众工作生活提供了方便。随着改革的深入和经济的发展，它在经济建设、国防建设和科学研究等方面越来越发挥着重要作用。

我省测绘队伍分布在14个地州市和铁路、煤炭、石油等19个系统、140多个单位，全行业拥有常规测绘仪器几十种2000多台（件），已形成了开展大地、重力、地形、地籍、形变、工程等20个专业的测绘能力。近几年，又添置了九十年代国际最先进的GPS全球卫星定位系统和大型内业成图设备，在我省已推广应用。1993年度，经全省测绘职工的艰苦努力，主要完成各种水准测量2280.28km，普通导线测量1786.47km，地形测量（各种比例R地形图）2316幅/5364.61km2，工程测量（资源勘测、地区规划、工程建设、施工运营、管理等所需的各种测量）6325.24km2，地籍测绘18209km2。省测绘局在技术力量、设备仪器、服务项目等方面，发挥了主力军的作用，在全面完成国家指令性任务的同时，还编制出版了各种类型地图、地图集、分区图、旅游图、商务图和各种专业用图。省测绘档案资料馆全年为省内外各用图单位提供了各种比例尺地形图17908幅1784张，各种挂图6738张，底图929幅（袋），洗印航空像片5706张，航片149筒，大地成果414点，从而为我省经济建设提供了可靠的测绘保障。同时，为适应社会主义市场经济发展的需要和改善发展测绘事业的条件，进一步转变观念、开阔眼界、拓宽测绘领域，发展第三产业，弥补经费不足。许多单位以抓住机遇，参与竞争，突破本省，面向全国，加快发展为目标，在我省测绘市场疲软，任务严重不足，取费又很低的情况下，从全国各地，特别是经济发达的东南沿海省区抢任务、争项目，取得了较好的经济效益和社会效益。

作为全省测绘管理部门的省测绘局，在搞好各项测绘保障的同时，进一步转变政府职能，深化改革，提高服务水平，在加强行业宏观调控，统筹规划，信息引导，培育市场，监督指导的过程中，认真学习、宣传、贯彻了《中华人民共和国测绘法》，重点抓了地方测绘法规的完善和地州市测绘管理机构的建立，还开展了执法检查、行业调研、质量监督检验等工作，使我省测绘行业管理迈上了新台阶。在6月20日全国《测绘法》宣传日活动中，邀请了郭琨副省长发表了广播电视讲话，还分别在兰州市、天水市、嘉峪关市设立了五个宣传点，出动数百人上街，散发材料13万份。通过大力宣传《测绘法》，使社会对测绘工作有了一定的了解和认识，也扩大了测绘的社会影响；为尽快制定我省贯彻、实施《测绘法》实施细则，专门组织人员调研论证，收集参考省内外的立法资料、广泛征求了各方面意见，拟定了《甘肃省测绘管理工作条例》上报省人大待批；9月初召开了地州市测绘管理工作座谈会，交流了建站经验，至年底，在14个地州市中已建立测绘管理站的达75%，绝大部分开展了工作；先后对13个单位拟出版的专业地图进行了审查，对个别单位在地图绘制上出现的错误及时进行了处理。还完成了全省三项测绘产品质量检验工作。省测绘学会在年初召开了全省第五次会员代表大会，选出了新一届理事会，同时各专业委员会有效地开展了技术咨询等服务工作，组织了地籍培训班、GPS技术演示会和两次技术交流活动，有力地推动了我省测绘事业的发展。

各行各业都离不开测绘成果。准确及时的测绘资料能够使决策者得到最佳的选择、使生产者获得最优的设计，可以降低成本，减少工程造价和节省生产费用，避免不应有的损失和浪费，但它的效益更多是从建设部门的工作中体现出来的，因此它的实际效益是无法估量的。

运输邮电业

交通事业的新发展

甘肃省交通厅厅长

胡国斌

1993年，全省交通战线广大干部职工在党的十四大精神指引下，以邓小平同志建设有中国特色的社会主义理论为指导，团结一致，深化改革，加速发展，使全省公路、水路交通运输事业有了新的发展。

一、交通基础设施建设继续保持了良好的发展势头，各地修路建桥，发展交通的热情进一步高涨

公路建设超计划完成了任务。全年共完成重点建设投资27226万元，比1992年增加7776万元。列为部、省重点建设项目的国道312线柳园至星星峡段、兰州至灿口段，国道109线唐家台至刘寨柯段，马鬃山边防公路都提前竣工，通过了部、省组织的验收，质量均被评为优良。在时间紧、任务重的情况下，胜利完成了兰郎公路一期改建工程，为甘南州四十周年大庆献了一份厚礼，为临夏、甘南两个少数民族地区的经济发展筑起了一条通畅的交通大道。天北高速公路一幅混凝土路面已铺通。中川一幅高速公路完成了路基及大部分桥涵和构造物工程，隧道超额完成了年进度计划。标志着我省高速公路建设实现了零的突破。其他公路建设项目也都如期完成了年投资计划。由于在施工中加强管理，层层落实责任制，保证了施工安全，取得了全年未发生重大伤亡事故的好成绩。

地方道路建设，全年共完成投资4234.73万元，新改建公路201.38公里，新改建桥梁21座713.14米，使地方交通条件得到不断改善。

交通支持保障系统及站点建设进展顺利，交通科技通信中心大楼已建成交付使用，省货运中心主体工程已完工，并部分投产使用。1993年又建起了张掖、秦安、成县等地、县两级汽车站。

截止1993年底，全省公路通车里程已达到34857公里，其中二级公路达到2115公里，比1992年的1809公里增加了306公里，占到总里程的6.06%，三级公路达到8931公里，占总里程的25.61%，各种桥梁达到3263座96410延米。三级以上公路比重达到31.6%，公路整体质量水平有了进一步提高。

1993年6月全国公路建设工作会议后，省政府于9月召开了全省公路建设工作会议，制定了到本世纪末我省公路建设的方针和目标。即：建成"两纵、两横"干线公路为骨架，连通全省主要城乡的公路网。

"两纵"：一是从甘宁交界的刘寨柯开始，经靖远、白银、兰州、临夏、合作至郎木寺；二是从甘宁交界的甜水堡开始，经庆阳、长庆桥、庄浪、秦安、天水、成县至武都。

"两横"一是从陕甘交接的牛背开始，经天水、馋口、兰州、武威、张掖、酒泉、安西至甘新交界处的星星峡；二是从陕甘交界的凤翔路口开始，经泾川、平凉、会宁至灿口。

这四条主干线贯穿全省14个地、州、市，连接48个县、市、区，全长3531公里，对全省经济和社会发展具有十分重要的意义。其中"一横"牛背至星星峡也是国家"两纵、两横"公路主骨架规划路线，全线长1600多公里，基本横穿了我省东西，这对我省来说是一个很好的机遇。全省公路建设工作会议起到了统一思想，提高认识，动员群众的作用。会议之后，各地修路建桥，发展交通的热情进一步高涨，不少地县政府提出了各自的奋斗目标，制定了优惠政策，民工建勤蓬勃开展，为公路建设创造了良好的条件。

二、公路养护质量稳步提高，路政管理逐步走上以法治路的轨道

继续坚持了“全面养护、常年养护、突出重点、预防为主”的方针。通过抓好春运安全，水毁修复，开展百日养护竞赛活动，巩固扩大标准化养路成果，保证了路况质量稳步上升。省养公路好路率达到73.2%，县乡公路好路率达到54.5%，分别比1992年提高了1.5和1.9个百分点。

加强路政管理，坚持“管养一体、群专结合、综合治理、预防为主、依法治路”的原则，做到专业管理与群众监督相结合。针对存在的突出问题，省政府向全省批转了省交通厅、省公安厅、省建委、省工商局、省土地局提出的《关于进一步加强公路路政管理工作的几点意见》，使路政管理有了更加可靠的依据。兰州市中级人民法院还在兰州公路总段设立了我省第一家公路巡回法庭，使路政管理逐步走上了依法治路的轨道。

三、客货运输进一步繁荣，公平有序的运输市场在竞争中进一步得到发展

截止1993年底，全省民用汽车拥有量已达12.50万辆。全社会公路、水路货运量和货物周转量分别达到1.7亿吨和88亿吨公里，比上年分别增长8.3%和11.7%；客运量和旅客周转量分别达到8677万人和45.7亿人公里，比上年分别增长3.9%和9.1%。公路货运已实现了进出市场自愿，车货双方择优成交。公路客运短途线路已全面放开，长途客运基本上实现了公平竞争。机动车维修、搬运装卸、运输服务已全面进入市场。在培育和完善运输市场过程中，加强了健全市场规则，规范经营行为方面的工作。同时，注意建立有形市场，提高市场组织化程度，取得了良好的社会效益和经济效益。

在水运安全管理方面，严格执行国家有关法规，加强检查监督。按照谁主管、谁负责的原则，认真落实责任制，重点加强乡镇船舶管理，保证了水上运输安全，使水运安全管理水平进一步提高。

四、深化企业内部改革，促进企业经营机制的转换

各级地方政府和交通管理部门，认真贯彻《条例》，落实企业的14项自主权，积极为企业进入市场创造条件。各交通企业从深化内部改革入手，实行经理(厂长)负责制，打破干部工人身份界限，合理配置劳动力，优化用工结构，改革分配制度，打破工资等级，强化内部管理。划小核算单位，调整企业内部产权结构。全面推行经营承包责任制，完善租赁经营和单车承包经营。全省14家地以上国营运输企业大部分通过租赁或单车承包提高了经济效益。同时大力发展延伸服务，扩大经营范围，坚持一业为主，多种经营，努力改善经营结构。随着各项改革的不断深化，进一步增强了企业的市场竞争能力和市场的适应能力。

五、各项交通规费征收情况良

认真贯彻落实省政府甘政发(1992)162号文件精神，改革了征费方式，全面推行养路费包缴制度。积极运用法律手段保证征费工作顺利开展，全省已在征稽所站建立44个法院执行室，为依法行政，按章征费提供了法律保证。经过努力，进一步稳定了费源，促进了增收，全年完成养路费收入比年计划增长8.12%。其它，除客运附加费外，车辆购置附加费、拖位机养路费、运管费都按计划完成了征收任务。

六、科技进步在生产实践中的作用进一步加

结合我省公路建设和养护的实际情况，积极引进和采用了符合省情的新工艺、新技术和新材料。转体桥的设计施工、水泥混凝土路面、控制爆破技术、南河川旧桥检测、旧油皮再生剂、抗剥落剂和高速公路的施工等利用新技术后，进一步降低了工程造价，保证了工程质量，加快了公路发展。微机更广泛地应用于养路费征稽、工程设计、计划统计、汽车站售票、客货运输服务系统等各个方面，对促进各项事业发展发挥了积极的作用。

工程监理系统进一步健全，监理制度进一步完善，交通工程监理工作已开始走上轨道。

七、坚持“两手抓、两手都要硬”，加强了精神文明建设

以学习邓小平同志建设有中国特色的社会主义理论为重点，加强理论学习，提高全体职工坚持党的基本路线的自觉性。特别注意加强基层单位和生产第一线的思想政治工作，开展多种形式的岗位竞赛活动。为群众办实事、解决职工住房和子女待业等突出问题，稳定了职工队伍，增强了凝聚力，为重点工程建设提供了政治保证。

针对存在的行业不正之风和“三乱”现象，对全省交通系统行政性收费项目进行了认真全面的清理，取消了特种车辆报停费和养路费缴讫塑封费等收费项目。组成省、地、县厅局长联合检查组，对全省11条国道、16条省道及19条县乡道路8721公里路线的“三乱”情况进行了检查。促进了行业风气的不断好转。

加强管理、提高效益，推动整体工作健康发展

兰州铁路局局长

王国良

1993年，兰州铁路局认真贯彻党的十四大和十四届三中全会精神，以经济建设为中心，以改革为动力，以安全、运输、路风和基本建设为重点，务本求实，团结拼博，开拓创新，取得了较好的成绩。

一、深化改革逐步推进，转换经

营机制开始起步

根据铁道部的部署和铁路运输企业的特点，制定了《兰州铁路局转换经营机制实施细则》，确定了全局贯彻《条例》、转换机制的基本框架。在充分试点和精心准备的基础上，在全局平稳实施了岗位技能工资方案，在贯彻按劳分配、克服平均主义方面取得了重要突破。局、分局、站段三级的"三定"工作全面完成，明确了职能，精干了机构，提高了效率，减少机构26个、减少行管服务人员1769人。在用工制度改革方面，推行了上岗合同制，为实行全员劳动合同制创造了条件；同时，采取招聘集体劳务工的办法，解决了新线用工来源。住房制度的改革逐步展开，先后实行了集资建房、有偿分房和建立公积金"三个办法"，提租补贴和出售公有住房的实施方案也基本确定。在运输组织工作的改革取得一定进展，工程、工业、生活部门走向市场，进行了积极探索。多元经济稳步发展，多种经营取得了较好效益，集体经济进一步巩固，对外经贸有了良好的开端。

二、迎难而上，组织会战，全面完成运输生产任务

1993年，在运用车不足，施工干扰大，自然灾害频繁的困难条件下，全局干部职工立足于抓早赶前，精心组织，挖潜扩能，尤其是在前三个季度欠帐较多的严峻形势下，全局上下紧急动员，组织会战，在铁道部及兄弟局的大力支持下，经过广大干部职工的努力拼博，超额完成了全年运输生产任务，主要运输指标创造了历史最高水平。全年旅客发送量完成1302万人、超年计划5%，比上年增长2.3%；完成货运发送量4605.6万吨，为年计划100.1%，比上年增长1.5%；完成客货换算周转量531.76亿吨公里，超年计划3.5%，比上年增长3.5%；完成运输收入15.7亿元、超年计划8.4%，比上年增长14.4%；完成清算收入21.2亿元、超年计划20.5%，比上年增长17.8%，提供建设资金7146万元。其它经济技术指标也好于往年。

三、运输安全工作在错综复杂的条件下保持了基本稳定

1993年，全局安全工作既有艰巨繁重的施工改造的不利影响，又有比较严重的自然灾害干扰，但在各级组织和广大干部职工的共同努力下，取得了建局以来除1985年外的最好成绩。主要表现在：行车事故特别是重大、大事故件数大幅度减少，安全周期有所延长，"六大安全"均有好转。全年共发生行车事故268件，其中重大事故2件，险性事故12件，一般事故254件，与1992年相比，事故总件数减少27件，即减少9.2%；其中：重大事故减少4件，大事故减少1件，险性事故减少3件，一般事故减少19件，分别减少66.7%、100%、20%和7%。全年消灭了责任重大路外伤亡事故、责任旅客伤亡事故、货运重大、大事故和特大火灾事故。职工因工死亡率为0.008‰，因工重伤事故率为0.055‰，分别比部定指标降低86.7%和54.2%。

四、重点工程建设进展顺利，基建任务全面完成

1993年，局管内重点工程全面进入建设高潮。年初，路局召开了国家重点工程计划会议，作出了"东取天兰、西战复线、南打青藏、北攻包兰"的战略部署。设计、施工、运营部门密切配合、协同作战；施工大军战酷署、斗严寒、风餐露宿、英勇奋战，创造了西北铁路建设史上的又一奇迹。全年完成基建投资10.6亿元。

——全国十大重点工程之一的兰新复线武疏段完成投资9亿元。土石方完成967.5万方，全线路基已成型，7座大桥全部完成，1993年中桥完成83座，其余正在收尾，小桥涵全部完成，铺轨已达370公里。预计1994年基本建成。全线铺通后，近期能力为1700万吨，远期能力为5000万吨以上。

——包兰线中干复线，是宝中线的相关工程全线长63公里，投资1.2亿元，于1992年9月28日开工，1993年10月31日建成，11月8日全部投入运营，比部定工期提前两个月。

——包兰线电气化工程投资3000万元，已按计划完成了前期工程。同时，技改工程完成投资3010万元。

——天兰二期扩能工程于1992年11月开工，1993年3月26日竣工，保证了新运行图的实施。

——宝中线全长498公里，投资42亿元，现在已完成土石方3388万立方米，设计总量基本完成。大中桥219座已全部完成，隧道68座，完成了67座。六盘山隧道正在收尾。铺轨完成了349公里，还剩149公里，预计1994年5月底全线铺通，比部定时间可提前一个月，年输送能力为1500万吨。

五、基础工作不断加强，职工生活水平逐步提高

全年投资3.4亿元，用于强化安全设施和运输设备，举办各类培训班4044期，培训职工147581人(次)，全年培训率达9.3%、脱产培训率达4.4%。班组建设工作进一步加强，146个不合格班组已有105个跨入合格及先进班组行列。职工住宅建设进展较快，全年竣工18.7万平方米，文教设施建设完成投资620万元；医疗卫生建设投资完成946万元；边远水电建设完成投资1216万元，解决了37个车站的职工吃水问题。职工人均收入扣除物价上升因素，保持了适度增长。安置待业青年1443人，临时从业人员达7524人。

六、依靠科技发展生产力，加快科技进步

路局全年下达科研和推广项目109项，已鉴定成果15项，验收3

项，有5项科研成果已通过部、省、局级鉴定。兰西编组场尾部自动调速系统经过技术审查，确定了扩大试验的规模、方案和进度，已开始施工。货车车号识别系统已确定了方案和技术指标，正在试制样机。

1993年新编运行图，与1992年运行图相比，客货列车分别增加3.5对和17.5对，旅速提高1公里/小时，技术速度提高1.5公里/小时，货运机车日车公里提高14.7公里。10月份，中干复线开通后，结合春运临客开行方案，相应地调整了运行图，提高了运输能力。

在新设备的应用管理上，红外线轴温探测装置使用率达98.6%，预报热轴9045辆，准确率100%，兑现率72.8%。无线列调防止各类行车事故636起，其中：防止险未构成的重大、大事故19件，防止折角塞门关闭92件，防止燃轴14件；防止险性事故143件，防止路外伤亡事故53件，行车惯性事故大幅度减少。先进技术设备的推广使用，为安全运输提供了可靠的设备保障。

在推进现代化管理上，全局共举办质量管理培训班226期，3851人参加全国统考取得合格证。全局现有QC小组3094个，参加职工25044人，取得成果1015项，其中：获得局优81项，部优20项，国优5项，创造可计算的经济效益506万元。

七、路风建设和治安综合治理取得新成绩

按铁道部的部署，大力开展了整顿路风和治安秩序工作。全局清理各类收费项目160项，停止了46项违规违价项目。局。分局、站段制订各类规范办法56项，客货窗口单位实行了挂牌服务，公布了收费项目和标准，设举报电话107部，强化了内部监察和外部监督。通过加强综合治理，职工违章率、犯罪率、内部治安事件率分别较1992年下降33%、39.6%和28.2%；“三无单位”达到80%。

总之，1993年，全局各项主要工作都取得了比较好的成绩，形成了加快发展的好势头，为西北地区经济振兴做出了积极的贡献。

1993年甘肃民航事业发展综述

1993年，民航甘肃省管理局走深化改革之路，加强航空业务工作建设，狠抓安全管理，促进了各项工作的正常开展，确保了空地安全，提高了服务质量，加强了基础建设，较好完成了各项任务。

一、生产任务完成情况

截止1993年12月31日，民航甘肃省管理局共保证各种飞行9922架次，其中：班机464架7次，专机20架次，加班493架次，包机214架次，训练飞行3938架次，调机、公务、急救198架次，军航56架次，其它356架次。区域管制室保证飞行13176架次。

计划飞行2564航班，取消240班，正常2093班，不正常231班，其中：天气原因影响55次，机械故障103次，机务原因13次，空勤原因5次，油料原因5次，下站原因2次，其它48次，全局放行正常性为90.1%，除去非机场原因正常性为99.9%。

全年完成旅客发运量216594人，比上年增长3.5%；货邮发运量2904.7吨，比上年增长－2.9%；换算旅客吞吐量51.22万人次，比上年增长5.7%。

二、开展“安全年”活动确保空地安全。

按照民航总局的要求，我们统一布置，开展了多层次、全方位的“93安全年”活动。通过活动，促进了全局安全形势的良性发展，并取得了良好成效。

我省成立了“93安全年”活动领导小组，下发了《“安全年”活动安排》，规定了1993年的安全总目标及各业务保证单位具体任务。整个安全年活动过程中，各单位利用闭路电视、黑板报、问卷考试调查、技术比武、岗位练兵、安全劳动竞赛等形式扎实细致地保证安全，各个单位制（修）订了管理标准和工作标准，完善并落实了《综合奖惩办法》，实行重奖重罚。

“安全年”活动中，对机场铁丝网围界进行了多次大修补和补充，对停机位和行车路线进行了重新划定，重新测量修建了观测目标物，对各项通信导航设施进行了大检查和维护修理，加强了航行管制人员的业务培训和执照考核，组建了局机务科并适合适航要求投入工作，加强水电管理确保机场供电正常，汽车运输严抓地面安全一年无差错、无事故，安全检查站加强对旅客、行李的检查与监控，年内查获旅客违法携带枪支弹药及其它违禁危险品共计3522件。

一年来，全局没有因机场原因发生飞行等级事故、空防事故及地面严重事故，确保了空地安全。

三、运输服务工作

1993年，我局继续推行“全方位开放”的政策，积极做好引进其它航空公司前来开辟新航线的工作。至今已为新疆航空公司、四川航空公司提供代理客货销售业务，并在兰州市新增一处售票点，实现了计算机售票的联网工作。在现有条件下，全局重点做好了不正常航班情况下的保障服务工作，严格运输服务人员的管理，清理、整顿了收费项目，停止了不合理收费八项，服务质量有较大提高。

四、基础建设工作

1993年，新建投资项目完成了中川浴池工程，中川淡化水工程，日贷中川航管楼土建工程。

敦煌机场跑道因鼓包问题严重，自5月11日零时起停航抢修，8

月26日复航。另外，敦煌机场改（扩）建工程环境评价报告，已于9月15日经民航总局、国家环保局联合审议，初审终审一次通过。现已完成改（扩）建前期工作，等待国家计委批准立项。兰州中川机场跑道病害严重问题由西安公路研究所进行了全面的综合检测。10月30日至11月3日，由民航总局、西北管理局领导及专家联合认定，必须对现跑道进行整修加固，且立即加快中川机场改（扩）建前期准备工作。会后，立即成立了工程领导小组，跑道整修加固工程的准备工作也同时展开，争取1994年4月份正式开工。

五、加强企业管理

1993年，按照民航总局和西北管理局指示，完成了油料系统分立的交接任务；将生活服务中心、安全检查站、经营管理处、卫生处调整为省局二级机构，接收原民航西北管理局兰州留守处，合并成立了省局兰州办事处。调整中，省局妥善安排人员，合理清理财产，工作进行顺利。

1993年，我省相继制定了《综合奖惩办法》、《中川机场暂住人口管理规定》、《省局干部管理暂行规定》、《省局QC活动实施办法》、《加强水电管理规定》。研究确定了干部定编及基层单位分队、班组设置、定编，实行岗位（职务）津贴，进一步完善了管理体制。

积极推行方针目标管理、标准化管理及全面质量管理工作。把QC攻关活动做为加强企业管理的突破口，1993年注册登记QC小组78个，占全局班组总数的76%，共获国家级优秀QC小组奖一个，省级奖六个，民航总局奖三个，省局优秀QC小组奖十三个。

六、构筑新的经营格局

1993年6月，确立了《民航甘肃省局党委关于发展多种经营构筑新的经营格局的建议》，《建议》明确了"一业为主"，多种经营是全局经营格局的基本方针。省局强调以保证安全、保证航空运输正常为主的关系不能颠倒，同时大力提倡和扶持兴办各种经济实体。全年省局共批准设立经济实体14个，涉及旅游、宾馆、餐饮、工程设计、电器维修、广告等行业。与台商合资兴建的"中川山庄"也破土动工。

认清形势 加快发展 为提前实现甘肃省邮电"八五"计划而奋斗

省邮电管理局党组书记、局长

姚学礼

1993年，全省邮电部门深入学习贯彻党的十四大和十四届三中全会精神，认真落实部、省有关会议提出的工作任务，坚持以通信发展为中心，"两个文明"一起抓，加快建设，发展业务，深化改革，改善服务，全面超额完成了各项经济计划指标，各方面工作都取得了较大的进步。

一、注重经营，开拓市场，主要经济指标有了较快的增长

1993年，全省完成邮电业务总量3.68亿元，比上年增长37.31%。其中，中央国营部分完成3.47亿元，比上年增长38.14%；农村电话部分完成2100.3万元，比上年增长24.95%。全省完成邮电通信总量3.06亿元，比上年增长31.13%。中央国营邮电业务收入完成3.53亿元，比上年增长42.6%；农村电话业务收入完成1773.5万元，比上年增长17.24%。中央国营自有收入完成4.56亿元，超额8.6%完成全年计划，比上年增长33.7%。通信企业全员劳动生产率达到1.9万元，比上年提高34.16%。

1993年，全省邮电通信发展有以下几个比较明显的特点：一是长、市话业务的主导地位更加突出，占全部邮电业务总量的比重继续上升。全省净增市话用户4.5万多户，长途有权用户4万多户，无线移动电话2000多户，市话通话次数增长58%，国内长话张数增长55%。长、市话业务价值量占到全省邮电业务总量的54%。二是省辖市局的业务发展速度加快，带动和促进了全省业务的发展。兰州等五个省辖市的邮电业务总量、业务收入占全省的比重分别达到66%和70%，业务总量，业务收入的增长幅度除天水外，均超过全省平均增长幅度。省辖市局在全省业务发展中具有越来越重要的作用，为全省的业务发展做出了贡献。三是企业营销工作进一步加强，服务方式比以前灵活多样。各单位结合当地通信市场实际情况，确定了营销工作目标和重点，制订了业务发展激励办法，开展了"满意在邮电"等竞赛活动。一些局改变等客上门的官商作风，组建营销队伍，到党政机关、大中型企业上门服务。一些年内开通程控电话的局，基本做到边投产、边放号；尚未开通程控电话的局，积极采取过渡措施扩容放号；各局都根据市场需求，积极开发新业务。全省县以上城市全部开办了礼仪电报和传真业务，十五个地市县局开办了国际国内特快专递业务，六个地县局开办了450兆集群式移动电话，35个地县局开办了无线寻呼业务；一些地市局开办了货运通知单和银行结算单特快专递业务和储蓄代缴电话费业务。邮电服务的覆盖面更加扩大，形式更加多样。

二、加快建设，增强能力，通信网的规模及技术装备、服务水平进一步提高

1993年，全省邮电部门坚持依靠政策扶持，依靠科技进步，依靠企业自身的努力，进一步加快通信建设，增强通信能力，取得了显著成效。

固定资产投资规模有了较大的提高。1993年，我省邮电完成固定资产投资5.92亿元，比上年增加一倍多。其中，基本建设投资完成2.72亿元，技改投资完成3.2亿元。兰州电信枢纽土建工程通过初步验收，开始工艺和设备安装；张掖、酒泉通信生产楼主体完工；省内数字微波工程基本完成年内进度，进入调测阶段；引进10万门程控电话工程进度加快，已有五个局相继开通；还完成了兰州市话3万门扩容和移动电话扩容等重点工程。全年新增邮政生产场地1.2万平方米，新设支局所42处，整修邮电局所120处；新增更新邮运汽车31辆；净增农话业务电路1077条；新增长途自动交换机2730路端；完成市话改制及扩容10.87万门，净增市话交换机容量7.82万门；全省市话交换机容量已达到24.24万门，比上年增长47.65%。全省程控交换机占市话自动交换机总容量的比重达到56%。

通信技术及服务水平得到进一步改善。全省共有邮电局所1164个，每一局所平均服务面积达到309平方公里，平均服务人口2.1万人，报刊零售点达到201处，邮政储蓄点283处，其中有20个储蓄点实现了营业微机处理，全省设投币式公用电话亭128个，磁卡电话103部，公用电话总数达1068部。

全省县(市、区)局市话自动化已达到85.7%，比上年提高了15.7个百分点，农村电话交换点自动化达到11.66%，省到地区、地区至县的平均电话电路数分别比上年增长50%和40%，全省每百人拥有话机1.38部(含用户交换机上的话机)，比上年提高21.05%。移动通信交换机达到7500门，无线寻呼发射机44部。

三、转换机制，加强管理，企业内部改革工作有了新的进展

1993年，全省邮电部门本着积极稳妥、分步实施的原则，重点进行了人事、劳动工资、内部分配、计划管理、财务制度等方面的企业内部改革。各级领导班子的结构更加合理，年轻化步伐加快，领导班子的整体素质有了提高；改革用人制度，企业重点吸收大中专毕业生和专业技术人才，一定程度上缓解了专业技术人才短缺的矛盾；修改完善了省内工效挂钩办法，实行了岗位技能工资制，进一步克服了分配中平均主义；改革计划管理办法，实行了固定资产计划分级分类管理、计划指标分级负责办法，下放了部分技术改造项目投资计划管理权限，进一步增强了企业活力；对第三轮承包经营责任制办法进行了修改，调整了部分专项基金的留用比例；进一步扩大了企业的资金留用使用权；按照部、省统一部署实行了新的财务管理办法和会计制度，完成了新旧财务制度的过渡转换；劳动保险制度进一步深化，建立了邮电职工个人缴纳基本养老保险金制度。此外，各单位还结合实际，在企业内部机构设置、搞活用工形式、优化劳动组合、搞活内部分配等方面进行了积极的改革与探索。邮政重点抓了新的邮件、报刊投递频次时限规定的落实，对省内的火车干线邮路和汽车干线邮路进行了调整，将部分委办汽车邮路改为自办邮路，使邮政网路更趋合理。重新编制了转口局综合作业时间表，围绕时限和规格加强视察、检查工作，全程时限逾限率和处理规格不合格率都比上年有明显降低。电信重点抓了设备维护和网路运行管理，完成了省网管中心二期工程，进一步提高了通信质量和全网运行效率。此外，还加强了对开放经营的电信业务的管理，做好公用网与专用网的协调发展工作，通信行业管理工作逐步走上正轨。

1993年是我省邮电通信发展较快的一年，无论是完成固定资产投资和新增通信能力，还是业务发展速度都比上年有较大幅度的提高。这些成绩的取得，主要是改革开放给邮电通信发展提供了广阔的市场，各级地方政府为邮电通信发展创造了较好的外部环境，以及全省邮电职工的努力进取。但也存在一些困难问题，主要是通信能力和技术装备水平仍然不适应社会发展需要，大多数地市州长途电路严重不足，部分城市市话待装户有增无减，供需矛盾突出，一些局邮件处理场地紧张、邮运能力不足；通信建设资金短缺，特别是各项分摊的资金不能按期到位，大多数企业还不具备自我发展能力；经营服务与市场要求不相适应，经营意识不强，缺乏对市场的分析预测，对用户缺少分层次服务措施；和东部省市通信水平和业务发展相比，形成了新的差距，并在逐步拉大。这些问题要在新的一年里继续认真解决和改进。

1994年是我省邮电发展极为关键的一年，也将是我省邮电在“八五”期间投资规模最大、建设任务最重、新增通信能力最多、业务发展最快的一年。经过全年的努力，我省邮电争取实现“一超、两转、三化、四翻番”，即主要经济计划指标和通信能力提前一年超额完成“八五”计划；电信通信网基本实现由人工交换向自动交换转变，省内二级干线邮运网由委办运输向自办运输转变；地市州长市电话交换实现程控化，省到地的干线传输实现数字化，县(市)电话实现自动化；邮电固定资产投资、新增市内电话机交换容量、新增长途电路数、市内电话放号都比上年实际增长翻一番。可以说，1994年将是我省邮电通信迈大步、登台阶、上水平、大发展的一年。无论是企业现有的物质技术条件，还是市场的客观需求，都使我们有可能比过去发展得更快、更好。

国内商业物资流通

甘肃商业

一、基本情况

1993年,我省国有商业的基本特点是:商品丰富充裕,购销稳中见旺,市场起伏波动较大,企业经营困难增加,全省商业呈现三升一降局面,即费用上升、上交利税上升、亏损额上升,实现利润下降。

1. 主要经济指标完成情况。全年商业商品购进完成51.68亿元,比上年增长4.93%;商品销售完成62.32亿元,比上年增长8.6%,其中省级商业完成13.24亿元,比上年增长23.88%,地市商业完成49.09亿元,比上年增长5.1%;费用水平10.1%,比上年上升1.3个百分点;利润总额5522万元,比上年下降29.3%,其中省级商业1790万元,比上年下降12.21%,地市商业3484万元,比上年下降38.17%;缴纳利税总额17573万元,比上年增长11.25%,其中省级商业2539万元,比上年增长8.73%,地市商业15034万元,比上年增长11.9%;期末亏损单位241个,比上年增加33个,增长15.87%,亏损总额为5014万元,比上年增长29.69%;企业流动负债率为89.1%,比上年增加4.53个百分点。需要说明的是造成去年全省商业利润大幅度下降的主要原因是国家政策调整带来的企业税费增支。据测算,全年因零售营业税率、贷款利率和运杂费等提高共多支出2728万元,如果剔除这些增支因素,去年利润为8250万元,同比增长5.62%。

2. 市场形势。受全国、全省经济快速发展及国家宏观调控政策措施的影响,1993年全省商业的经营情况是:购销基本稳定,零售活于批发,城市旺于农村,商品销售呈马鞍之势,部分主要副食品货源偏紧,年末货紧价扬。全年日用工业品丰富充裕,部分副食品如猪肉、牛肉、羊肉、食糖、鲜菜,由于受国家货币紧缩,农副产品收购资金短缺,以及货源偏紧影响,库存急剧下降。全省商业猪肉库存月平均4035吨左右,比上年减少54.49%,食糖库存月平均4022吨,比上年减少43.52%,羊肉、牛肉、鲜菜、纯碱库存也降至历史最低水平,上述商品价格大幅度上升,蔬菜尤甚。与上年相比,兰州市蔬菜市场价格八月份上涨35.1%,九月份上涨22.3%,十月份上涨8.6%,十一月份上涨33%。从商品销售情况看,零售好于批发,全年国有商业零售额比上年增长9.51%,而批发销售只增长3.72%。兰州市民百、工贸、兰百三大商场全年销售额分别达到2.6亿、2.1亿和1.6亿元,增幅均超过两位数。从城乡消费来看,城市旺于农村,全省商业市以上零售额达19.07亿元,比上年增长13.42%,高于县及县以下14.83个百分点。从季节看,商品销售与上年相比,三至七月增长,九至十一月下降,十二月增长幅度达1.21倍,前旺后平,年末猛增。十二月份销售大幅度上升的原因,一方面是消费者怕税制改革后引起物价上涨集中购物所致,另一方面是企业将为下年结转的一块销售列到当年所致。

3. 商品经营。1993年增支减利因素猛增的情况下,全省各级商业企业千方百计扩销增效。一是继续调整经营结构,拓宽经营领域,坚持"一业为主,综合经营",在抓名优产品上下功夫,在扩大多种经营中找出路,巩固、扩大各类形式的总经销、总代理,以商为主向加工业、旅游业、房地产等领域渗透、发展,全方位、多渠道进行开拓经营。食品行业转轨变型步伐加快,初见成效,与上年相比亏损单位和亏损额分别下降10.99%和9.39%。二是不断改进和创新营销方式。不少企业在购销业务中采取了适度有奖销售、保险销售、敞架销售、预约销售、邮寄销售等灵活多样的促销手段和措施,许多企业整修店容店貌,增设新的经营服务项目,提高服务质量,以整洁新颖的面貌和良好的服务吸引顾客,扩大销售。三是积极发展外向型经济,1993年全省商业开办合资企业22户,总投资4.67亿元人民币,其中外资合3358万美元,全年商业进出口额达1500万元,创汇150万美元。四是加速商办工业技术改造和设备更新,积极开发新产品。全年商办工业总产值3.11亿元,销售收入3.02亿元,实现利税1035万元;开发省级新产品21项,产值1456万元,销售2400万元,新产品产值率达8.3%,利税率达14.13%。

4. 基础建设。1993年,各级商业部门和企业千方百计筹集资金,加快商业基础设施建设,使我省国有商业基础设施建设迈上了一个新台阶。全年全省商业系统固定资产投资总额达3.7亿元,建设规模40万平方米,实际完成投资1.7亿元,新增固定资产1亿元。其中,省列建设项目28个,投资3317万元,实际完成2675万元,占计划的80.6%;在建项目施工面积10.43万平方米,竣工5.14万平方米,占49.20%;新增商业网点4.52万平方米,新增固定资产5300万元。建成或基本建成的省列重点项目有景泰糖酒副食商场、武山洛门蔬菜批发交易市场、泾川温泉服务楼、省蔬菜公司陇西恒温库、省商业储运公司药贸大厦等。各地也通过多种途径,兴建和改造了一批商业网点和设施。永昌县商业系统基本建成各类营业楼11座,1.67万平方米,总投资1000多万元,超过前四十年的投资总额。根据当地实际需要和有利条件,各地商业还兴办建设了一批综合、专业批发市场。年内建成的有陇西县小百货批发市场、定西县汽车东站综合批发市场、天水肉禽蛋水产批发交易市场、靖远县蔬菜瓜果批发交易市场等，总投资1215万元，建筑面积36660平方米。

二、商业改革

1. 在小型商业企业中大力推行"国有民营"改革。年初，省商业厅会同省体改委等部门提出《关于国有小型商业企业实行国有民营的意见》，经省政府批转下发后，小型商业企业"国有民营"改革在全省迅速展开，成为小型商业企业改革的一种主要形式，到年末全省已有2600多户小型商业企业实行了"国有民营"，推行面达80%以上。兰州市二商局系统适宜搞"国有民营"的210户小型商业企业全部实行了此项改革，定西地区的264个门店已有249个实行了"国有民营"。平凉、庆阳、张掖、天水等地市的推行面都达到70%～90%。实行"国有民营"改革，资产出租，资金自筹，定额上交，超收归已，充分调动了小型商业企业职工的经营积极性，给企业注入了活力，加速了企业经营机制的转换，促进了企业经济效益的增长，是小型企业比较理想的一种选择。全年"国有民营"企业商品销售额33065万元，比上年增长216.5%；实现利润248万元，比上年增长181.8%。

2. 贯彻《条例》，加快企业转换经营机制步伐。在充分落实企业各项经营自主权的同时，进一步深化企业三项制度改革，加大力度推进企业转轨建制。据不完全统计，全省542户大中型商业企业约有50%实行了一般干部和中层干部聘任制，绝大多数企业精简压缩了管理机构和人员，分配上普遍实行了联销联利计酬、百元销售或利税工资含量、提成工资、计件工资等办法，职工收入中浮动部分逐步增大。部分企业实行了企业经理由主管部门聘任，副职由经理提名，主管部门审核同意后，经理直接聘任的新机制，全省商业企业经营机制程度不同地得到转换。

3. 积极探索批发企业改革新路子。全省商业在总结以往批发二、三级联营、发展企业集团、实行批零合一等有效措施的基础上，按照"优化经营、两头延伸、甩开包袱、分离裂变、调整结构、重构体系"的思路，着重推行了母体裂变、新老划断，组建单体公司，兴办加工实体，建设批发市场等，并取得一定成效。

4. 积极开展股份制、组建企业集团及企业兼并、拍卖等项改革试点。兰州民百、兰百、工贸三大商场已经兰州市政府批准改组为股份有限公司。各地选择了一些企业实行股份合作制试点。酒泉市糖酒公司、食品公司和食品厂自愿合并成立了酒泉市糖酒食品总公司，下设7个分公司（厂），全年销售达6000万元，利润250万元。一些地县还进行了跨系统、跨行业的企业兼并，对个别偏远、无利的小门店进行了拍卖。

三、饮食服务业

1993年，全省商业系统共有饮食服务网点1157个，人员15309人，完成营业收入30957万元，比上年增长13.27%，其中饮食业11942万元，比上年增长7.14%；服务业10477万元，同比增长17.5%；其他收入8557万元，同比增长17.48%。实现利润净额1645.8万元，比上年同期增加184.2万元，增长12.6%，其中饮食业472.6万元，比上年下降2.72%；服务业1223.1万元，比上年增长16.99%；其他业亏损49.8万元，比上年减亏19.8万元。

1. 饮食业。各地国有饮食企业面对粮价放开、部分副食品供应紧张及公款消费锐减等因素，及时采取对策，改变经营方式，翻新门店、门面，坚持薄利多销，增加名优小吃和大众化品种，不断拓宽市场领域，千方百计参与市场竞争，增加营业收入，在市场形势和外部环境比较严峻的情况下，仍取得良好效果，全年营业收入11942.2万元，比上年增长7.14%。

2. 旅店业。在全社会兴办宾馆，市场竞争日趋激烈的形势下，国有旅店业企业充分发挥传统优势，在增加设施、设备，改造原有客房、卫生间，加速硬件建设的同时，积极采取措施，走出店门联系会议，争取旅游团组，实行全程、系列化服务，不断改善服务质量和服务档次，加强软件建设，受到了顾客的青睐。全年营业收入5823万元，比上年增长23.78%；利润净额859.9万元，比上年增长17.06%。

（甘肃省商业厅）

甘肃粮食工作迈向市场经济的历史性一年

省粮食局局长

杜　颖

1993年是我省粮食工作朝着社会主义市场经济目标大步前进的一年。各级粮食部门以价格改革为突破口，以宏观调控为保证，以转换企业经营机制为关键，积极落实各项工作指标，主动发挥主渠道作用，保证了全省的军需民食，为发展我省经济做出了贡献。

粮油价格改革迈出了关键的一步。根据省政府的决定，从1月1日起，我省全面放开食油购销价格，取消国家油品定购任务、定购价格、统销价格和定量供应；从4月1日起，放开城乡粮食销售，取消城镇居民、经牧民、菜农和农村返销粮平价供应，价格随行就市。为了保证改革政策的顺利出台，各级粮食主管部门在当地政府的领导下，与有关部门紧密配合，组成精干、高效、运转灵活的指挥班子，狠抓了调运、加工、销售及宣传解释等环节的工作，从而使我省在粮价改革两年迈出两大步的基础上，又顺利迈出了关键的一步。全省粮食工作结束了四十年来高度集中的计划经济模式，步入了全新的社会主义市场经济领域。

粮食收购计划完成较好。今年我省夏粮和粮食总产均创历史最高水平，从而为收购工作奠定了物质基础。粮食部门认真贯彻省政府“稳购放销”的粮改方针，在全省7.45亿公斤定购任务保持不变的前提下，向76个县的359万农户分解下达了定购任务，发放预购定金4420多万元，较前6年年均实发额多1085万元。夏粮上场后，省政府领导多次召集会议研究资金问题，有关银行对定购资金逐段作了安排，全省基本做到了不打白条。由于玉米走俏、多渠道经营等原因，全省收购工作一度出现产区慢于销区、市购慢于定购、秋粮慢于夏粮的情况，河西普遍采取了以夏补秋的措施，个别完成任务确有困难的县收取差价款买市价粮补交定购任务。国家定购和市场收购总量达到12.26亿公斤，基本满足省内总量平衡的需求。其中定购小麦入库6.49亿公斤，超额21.8%完成任务，东部9个地、市为自求平衡，超交定购粮3300万公斤。全省河西5个地区欠交定购粮7600万公斤。加上市价购入的5.41亿公斤粮食，全省收购总量达到2.26亿公斤，基本满足省内总量平衡的需要。

粮食销售经受了考验，确保了市场供应。销价放开前的三月份，全省实销粮食4.17亿公斤，比正常销量增加3倍多，由于加工、调运及时，保供措施有力，各地基本没有出现脱销断供现象。12月，沿海销区和南方产区粮价暴涨波及我省，全省当月粮食销量猛增到1.65亿公斤。根据国务院和省政府的决定，我局下发了平抑粮油价格、稳定市场的紧急通知，规定了粮油销售最高限价，推广了兰州市印发“信誉卡”、实行“五保”的做法。各地明码标价，挂牌经营，敞开供应，并对大专院校学生食堂予以优惠，全省粮食市场货源充足，供应平稳。年末兰州市每公斤粮价特一粉1.32元，特二粉1.28元，为全国省会以上城市最低价；每公斤菜油7.20元，与各省基本持平。在平时的供应工作中，基层粮食企业努力克服多渠道竞争、销量锐减等困难，对城市供应网点布局进行了调整，增加供应品种，推广粮油小包装，开展上门服务，积极推行供产销一体化和连锁经营，使城镇粮食销量由4月的1233万公斤逐步上升到十一月的4447万公斤。全年共安排农村粮食销售0.43亿公斤，其中1150万公斤粮食按定购价供应灾区，群众生活没有发生大的问题。全省全年粮食销售总量9.31亿公斤，比收购总量少2.95亿公斤。

粮食调拨产销直接定货办法开始推行。我局先后4次召开协调会议，完善合同调拨办法，对定购粮实行了调拨数量由产销双方直接商定、调拨管理和价格按省局统一规定执行的双重管理办法。根据全省产销定货会签约数量，制订了分季度、分月粮食发运计划，由各地区组织实施。为了加强对合同双方的监督制约，试行了省内区间调拨保证金制度。经省政府协调，工商银行、农业银行注入资金2381.89万元，对省内粮食调拨拖欠款中的两行互欠部分进行了清理，进口粮拖欠款也清付了2300多万元。全年共从河西运出定购粮食1.85亿公斤；同时，完成了接收省外和进口粮1.85亿公斤的计划。保证了省内地区间的粮食余缺平衡。

国库粮油保管有了加强。年度末全省粮食库存14.1亿公斤（不含储备粮），比上年增加2.1亿公斤。食油库存1741万公斤，比上年减少3818万公斤。全省粮油综合库存最多时超过30亿公斤，其中露天存放5亿公斤以上。各地在放开粮食销价后，继续认真抓了仓储管理工作，春秋两季在全省范围开展了粮油安全大普查，对发现的虫粮、高水分粮及时进行了处理。根据内贸部通知，在先行试点的基础上，全省组织200多个调查组，投入4000多人次，对库存粮食进行了全面清查。全省“双低”储粮1.96亿公斤，低温储粮3.25亿公斤，机械通风储粮7400万公斤，科学保粮率26.5%，77个县达到“四无”粮仓县标准，24个大库达到“四无”粮库标准，分别占到总数的90%和96%。

转换经营机制工作有了新的进展。14户有代表性的企业进行了贯彻“条例”试点，企业的各项权利基本得到落实。经过清理，废除了36个与“条例”精神不符的文件。各级粮食财务部门在“五包干”办法停止执行后，及时建立、完善了费用定额补贴办法，为实行新会计制度做好准备。通过挖潜、节支、增收，完善各项管理制度，开展了扭亏增盈工作。粮油加工企业积极转换经营机制，提高产品质量，适应市场需要，完成产品产量56万吨，实现利润1433万元；饲料工业完成产品产量10.98万吨，实现利润274万元。运输企业实现利润93万元，比上年增加58万元。

多种经营工作成绩显著。粮食销价和经营放开后，企业把多种经营作为“半壁江山”对待。按照“主营养家、多营发家”的思路，陆续投入近半数工作力量。据不完全统计，各地粮食部门多渠道筹集资金2800多万元，新增门占815个、营业面积79180平方米。全省粮食系统现有种植场74个，种植各种果木17.8万株；养殖场178个，存栏猪1.6万头、鸡6.4万只、牛900余头、羊1700只；副食加工点152个，饮食服务点258个，综合性商店172个。经营范围已扩展到采矿、汽车配件、建材加工、种植养殖等近300个项目，共实现利润1419万元。有三分之一的单位靠多种经营使企业增添了活力，职工增加了收入。

宏观调控机制正在形成。根据我省粮情，在放开销价的同时，稳住了定购，从而掌握了粮源，保证了供应，也保护了农民的利益；配合有关部门初步建立了省级粮食风险基金，并将其中的大部分用于灾区返销粮供应补贴，对稳定农村起了积极作用；继去年7个库挂牌后，今年又有7个库被命名为“国家粮食储备库”，按照适当集中的要求，将分散存放在河西的部分专储粮集并到储备库保管；省级7.5亿公斤储备粮、600万公斤储备食油的划转工作基本完成，先后动用3650万公斤储备粮、248万公斤储备食油投放兰州等地市场，保证了元旦、春节期间的供应；全年下达粮食基建、技措计划7批，安排项目38个，计划投资3413.5万元，完成投资3124万元，竣工项目9个，新增粮食仓容1.38亿公斤、油罐容量5000吨；继张掖、酒泉、兰州之后，武威粮食批发交易市场建成开业，县及县以下建成初级市场163个，省内粮食市场体系初具规模。

我省是在经济基础薄弱的情况下，与东部较发达省市同步进行粮价改革的，由于遗留的问题和新出现的矛盾比较多，配套政策滞后，企业经营机制的转换一时还跟不上，销价和经营放开后，粮食工作面临很大的困难，存在不少问题：多年积累的巨额财政挂帐尚未解决，上亿元的进口粮欠款和省内调拨粮欠款久拖未付，企业资金短缺，负债经营；粮食销量较上年下降31.7%，实现利润下降55.7%，粮食企业、特别是城镇粮站经营困难；经营网点不足，设施陈旧的问题也十分突出。在1994年的工作中，我们要认真学习邓小平同志建设有中国特色的社会主义理论，紧紧围绕发展社会主义市场经济这一目标，以强化宏观调控为保证，以建立现代企业制度为突破口，进一步深化粮食流通体制改革，积极研究解决历史遗留问题和改革中的深层次问题，使我省的粮食工作朝着经营市场化、调控系统化的格局发展，努力完成省委、省政府交给我们的各项任务。

供销合作社引导农民进入市场是新形势下的重要使命

省供销联社主任

黄德友

在社会主义市场经济体制的新形势下，如何引导广大农民尽快进入市场，主动适应市场，逐步成为农村市场经济的主体？这是当前培育农村市场的核心问题，也是供销社深化改革的一项艰巨任务。

一、供销社引导农民进入市场责无旁贷

首先，供销合作社引导农民进入市场是发展农村经济的需要。这几年，农民的商品经济意识虽然较之过去大大增强，但还仅仅处于起步阶段。他们往往还是根据上一年得到的信息安排当年生产，带有很大的盲目性。即使获得了准确的信息，如果没有社会化协作和中介组织，不善于全面分析和正确运用信息，千家万户的生产经营活动一旦在较大程度上趋同，就难免造成农副产品生产和市场的剧烈波动，使农民蒙受损失。自八十年代以来，我省农产品出现了多次剧烈波动。某个产品走俏，多家抬价抢购，形成“大战”；某个产品滞销，各家压级压价，出现“卖难”。这不仅使农民受到伤害，也不利于农村经济和整个国民经济的健康发展。可见，农民要进入市场，迫切需要一个强有力的中间组织，为他们提供产前产中产后服务，在小生产与大市场之间架起一座桥梁，积极帮助他们学会游泳，适应市场。

其次，引导农民进入市场是农民对供销社的新要求。随着市场经济的发展，农民不仅要适应市场，还应该过渡到主动影响市场。卖难则说明农民既不能影响市场，也不能适应市场。现在，农民强烈要求供销社在产、供、销、储、运、加各个环节、各个方面为他们提供服务，解决他们在生产流通中遇到的困难。因此，我们必须顺应农民的愿望和要求，在更大程度上、更大范围内去满足农民生产、生活需要，并依靠合作社组织的力量，共同去承担农民的市场风险。

再次，供销合作社引导农民进入市场也是自身发展的需要。供销合作社存在的价值就在于为农民生产生活服务，在服务中壮大发展自己。离开了农民，离开了农业，供销社就成了无源之水。改革开放以来，供销社只所以取得今天这样大的成绩，根本的一条就是恢复了农民集体所有制性质，较好地坚持了服务宗旨，急农民之所急，想农民之所想，为农民办了许多实事、好事，取得了广大农民的支持和信赖。经济发达国家的经验也表明，合作社是农民自我服务、自我保护的最佳形式。所以，供销社只有扎根于农民之中，引导组织农民发展市场经济才能根深叶茂。

二、供销社在引导农民进入市场方面做出了积极贡献

这几年，全省供销社积极引导和组织农民发展商品生产，并为之提供多方面的服务，使农民在生产经营活动逐步走向市场，按照市场需求，调节农业生产和农产品流通，在小生产与大市场之间发挥了桥梁纽带的作用。

1.兴办骨干商品生产基地，通过示范、引导，把农民的生产经营活动纳入市场轨道。在骨干商品生产基地建设上，发放扶持基金、提供种植技术、供应生产资料，合同定购产品，把生产与市场连接起来。有的扶持农民办，有的与农民联办，供销社还自办示范性商品基地。在土地较多的地方新办了一批农商联营，连片种植，统一管理，集约经营的“园林式”实体型基地。到目前，全省

供销社共筹集投放商品基地建设资金4000余万元，已扶持建成棉花、苹果、黑瓜籽、生漆、黄花菜等各类骨干商品生产基地100余个，总面积600万亩，占全省农作物播种面积的11.2%。初步形成河西走廊以黑瓜籽、红枣、葡萄、葵花籽为主，陇东以黄花菜、杏产品、白瓜籽为主，陇南以生漆、木耳、柑桔、苹果、核桃、花椒为主；甘南、临夏地区以畜产品为主；中部干旱地区以瓜果、百合、草编制品为主的商品生产基地服务格局。累计十年农牧民从基地获得收入达40亿元。这些基地，引导农民逐步发展适度规模经营，由小而全向专业化转变，提高了集约化生产水平。

2.提供科技、信息服务，为农民步入市场牵线搭桥。省、地、县供销合作社分别成立了科研所和科研小组，拥有科技人员200多人，基层社还与1500多名乡、村级技术人员长期开展技术交流和技术合作。近年来，在有关部门的配合下，完成科研项目51项，其中16项分别获得国家、部级和省级科研成果奖。与此同时，各级供销社不断健全信息服务网络。目前全省100多个单位编辑发行了《信息导报》、《市场情况》、《商品信息》等信息刊物60多种。省供销合作联社设立了信息服务中心，拥有省内外信息通讯员1100名，向农民传递生产、技术和市场信息，开展咨询服务，形成了上下连贯、纵横交错的信息服务网络。省社还与《甘肃农民报》共同开辟了《农家富》专版，成为指导农民发展商品生产的重要媒介。

3.大力发展农产品加工业，积极发展出口业务，把甘肃农产品推向国际市场。全系统已兴办650多个加工厂点，加工项目扩展到棉花、畜产、土产、果品、粮油等九大类。1993年，加工产值达3亿元。已有4个产品被评为部优产品，5个产品在全省获奖。社办工业的发展，不仅促进了农副产品转化增值，而且也扩大农副产品销路开拓了新的途径。引导农民进入市场，不仅限于地方市场、区域市场、国内市场、还必须包括国外市场。近几年，我省供销社先后在深圳、上海、北京、福州、海南开设了窗口企业，在省内办了10余户合资企业、8户挂靠出口业务企业，通过多种形式把甘肃农产品打入国际市场，引导农民参与国际竞争，收到了积极的效果。

4.建立批发交易市场，让农民进入市场学游泳。近年来，全省供销社采取自筹、统筹、贷款、扩股集资等办法，建立了一批批发交易市场。大的集镇基层供销社利用现有大院推广了“前店后市，商场市场一体”的做法，组织农民进入市场，产销直接见面。目前，全省供销社建起种类批发交易市场140多个，年成交额5亿多元。尽管这些市场还处于初期阶段，但这些市场已逐渐成为商品交易集散中心，带动了周围地区经济的发展，为广大农民进入市场提供了便利条件。通过这种形式，农民学到了市场的基本知识，了解和掌握了来自各方面的信息，懂得了产品只有通过市场交换才能变成商品的道理，锻炼和提高了参与市场竞争和应变能力。

5.以庄稼医院为主体，开展技物结合、多形式的农资系列化服务。各级供销社按照“管供、管用、管效果”的要求，建立完善了省、县、基、村四级服务组织。省上设立了农资系列化服务总站，在77个农业县中已全部建立了服务中心站，911个基层社中建立了918个服务站。还建成村级农资服务站2024个。各级服务站共建庄稼医院1078所，技术咨询处820处，租赁维修站446个，配药配肥点1964个。目前，有近一半的“庄稼医院”达到了“十有”标准，即有庄稼医生、店堂柜台、宣传手段、规章制度、服务档案、诊断处方、试验示范点、土壤和农药速测箱、植保机械和商品供应。农资商品销售总额比1986年增长1.5倍，化肥、农膜供应量逐年增加，满足了农业生产的基本需要。

此外，供销合作社在全省广大村镇建立了饮食、旅店、理发、照相、租赁、储运等各类服务网点4700多个图书代销点600个，以及阅览室、电影院等文娱场所，既为农民的生产服务，也为农民的生活服务，以提高他们适应市场，走向市场的自觉性和主动性。

三、在新形势下，供销社在引导农民进入市场方面的新思路

1.按照市场经济需要，进一步完善农业系列化服务体系。农民要走向市场，必须要以完善的社会化服务为条件。我们已建立了骨干商品基地、棉花全程服务、农产品加工、农产品出口、科技、信息、农资系列化和村级服务八大服务体系，初步形成了供销社为农服务体系的基本框架，比较好地适应发展农村市场经济的需要。今后要在继续完善和巩固已有成果的基础上，重点抓好以下一些服务项目。

(1)以市场为导向，大力发展优质名牌农产品。一是在稳定粮食生产的基础上，扩大适销对路的经济作物生产，调整种植结构。特别要注意发展区域特色的名、特、优、新产品，创农产品名牌。二是要狠抓科技兴农政策的落实，努力增加农产品的科技含量，重点推广农作物和畜禽良种，以此来不断提高农产品的质量，以适应市场的需求。

(2)搞好农产品的深加工和转化，把农产品名牌最大限度地转化为工业品的名牌。这是把农业推向市场的关键一环。要改变过去单纯向社会提供初级产品的状况，将种植业、养殖业、加工业有机结合起来，形成种养加结合的产业格局，实现农产品的多层次、大幅度增值。我们将根据供销社实际，重点帮助省内农产品主产区发展各类加工业，包括供销社社办工业和乡镇企业，唱好自己的"拿手戏"，打好自己的"优势仗"，更高起点、更高档次地进行优质名牌农产品的精加工、深加工，生产出能够走向国际市场的名牌产品。

(3) 搞好产销信息的发布和产销合同的签订。要为农民提供及时准确的市场信息，引导他们按照市场要求进行生产和经营，变追求数量为数量、质量并重，生产流通一齐抓。要按照市场经济的规律，努力用经济、法律手段来理顺供销社同农民的关系，通过与农民订立产销合同，明确各方的权利和义务，建立较稳定的产销关系，用市场供求拉动生产发展，以从根本上解决"卖难"问题。

(4) 进一步发展专业合作社和专业协会。改革以来，我们按照自愿互利的原则，以供销社为依托，以专业户为重点，以服务为宗旨，在全省建立了100多个专业合作社和专业协会，这些组织一方面为专业生产提供多方面的服务，另一方面组织他们进行生产技术信息等方面的相互交流。从这几年的情况看，它有利于发展社会分工与协作，促进生产专业化和适度规模经营，实现农产品销供产、贸工农一体化。也便于供销社为其提供系列化服务。

2. 培育和完善以农产品批发市场为中心的市场体系。当前农民走向市场的一个重要制约因素是市场体系发育不够。今后必须加快培育和完善农产品市场体系。一是要在办好初级市场的基础上，在农产品集中产区和主要销区，特别是县一级建设一批专业批发市场。有条件的地方逐步建立起一批在全国有影响的大型专业批发市场。并把这些大型市场逐步过渡到期货贸易市场，以做到按需生产，克服产销脱节。供销社要增设农产品贮藏仓库和加工设施，为农民进场交易提供多方面的服务，切实让农民真正得到经济实惠，让利于农。

3. 行农产品代理制。这是世界合作社成功之路。供销社要为农民代购、代销、代运，开展代理业务。形式可以多样。可以实行供销社将农民的产品销售后，扣除应得手续费后的全部销货款交给农民；可以实行将农民产品先购进来，待销售出去后，将利润还给农民。后一种近几年个别地方做过一些。效果比较好，农民也满意。推行代理制，就把供销社同农民的经济关系结成了一体，进一步密切了同农民群众的关系。这就为供销社代理农民进入高层次规范化的批发交易市场和期货市场，当好农民的代理商，打下了基础。

4. 一步深化供销社改革。就是要按照市场经济要求和合作社原则，继续坚持民办方针，坚持服务宗旨，积极探索在市场经济条件下搞好为农服务的路子。这是个首要问题。其次，要按照《条例》精神。转换经营机制，增强活力，使企业真正成为市场经济的主体，走向市场，肩负起引导农民进入市场的重任。第三，要强化民主管理，让农民更广泛地参与供销社重大决策。第四，各地要按照中央、国务院精神办事，重农民利益，维护供销合作社合法权益，任何改变基层社隶属关系、平调供销社财产的做法都要立即改变。

甘肃物资工作在开拓市场中取得新进展

1993年，全省物资系统销售额完成53.8亿元，比上年增长49.4%；上交利税完成6667万元，比上年增长37.7%；主要物资实物供应量也有所增长。其中钢材供应量完成53万吨，汽车6857辆，水泥完成44万吨，木材完成19万立方米，铜铝铅锌4种有色金属完成4万吨。较好地保证了我省工农业生产和人民生活所需的物资供应。特别是地县物资工作发展迅速，成为全省物资工作上台阶的主要力量。

一、解放思想，转变观念，综合发展能力明显增强

1993年全省物资工作以解放思想、观念转变为前提。以发展社会主义市场经济新体制下的大市场、大流通、大贸易为基本思路，紧紧围绕市场转变观念，使全省物资企业已基本摆脱了计划经济体制下形成的经营思想，企业的发展思路已集中到如何以适应市场为中心，围绕市场抓资源，围绕市场促销售，围绕市场求发展上来。一是彻底摒弃了过分依赖计划内物资经营的观念，全力以赴拓展市场物资经营，主要物资的市场经营比重进一步提高，达到90%以上。二是跳出了当地市场的局限，积极发展外购外销。特别是一些工业基础薄弱，地域偏僻的县级物资企业，全力以赴拓展外地市场，取得了长足发展，搞得好的企业外销份额达40%以上。外地设点工作也取得了较大进展，据不完全统计，全省物资企业在省外设点已达100多个，许多企业已涉足于沿海城市。一些县级物资企业纷纷进入大城市及"三沿"开放城市，设立网点，拓展业务。三是摆脱了过分依赖经营主业的限制，面对多元化的竞争格局，强化主产品经营，积极开展多种经营，企业抗御市场风险的能力进一步增强。四是开展多种形式的联合成效显著，系统内的联合、工物联合进一步向紧密型发展。进入七月份，国家宏观调控措施出台，面对销售难上、效益难争的严峻形势，及时采取措施，以变应变，积极调整经营结构，大力压缩库存，果断放弃无销路品种。开发适销对路的新品种。并积极发展联营，以代理商、销售公司等多种形式，与大中型生产企业攀亲，建立联营联销关系。以上情况表明，物资企业开拓市场，参与大流通、大市场的经营思想和观念发生了转折性变化，为物资工作的长远发展打下了比较扎实的思想基础。

二、因地制宜，完善功能，生产资料市场建设有了进展

一年来，全省物资部门认真贯彻中共中央、国务院《关于加快发展第三产业的决定》，不等不靠，因地制宜，狠抓生产资料市场建设，建成了一批具有地方特色的生产资料市场。目前全省物资系统已建成各类生产资料市场38个，其中综合市场8个，专业市场30个，成交额突破15亿元。直接进驻市场的省内外大中型企业已超过300户，并且大部分市场运营情况良好。同时发展城乡网点1000多个，初步形成了不同层次，不同规模，不同形式的生产资料市场网络。在抓好生产资料市场建设的同时，在提高市场档次，扩大辐射面，完善服务功能上也取得了进展。省政府批准以省物资局为主筹办的兰州有色金属交易市场，筹备工作进展顺利，1994年可望正式开业。酒泉地区物资局投资2000多万元兴建的商贸大楼已投入使用成为我省西部地区最大的生产资料市场。省有色金属总公司在积极参与上海和深圳交易所交易活动和建立期货经纪公司的基础上，建立了上海金属交易所兰州交易厅，已开始代理期货业务。省物资局克服原材料涨价，资金紧张的严重困难，加紧省物资交易大厦工程的建设，建成后的甘肃物资大厦，将成为西北乃至辐射全国的多功能综合性商流、物流、信息流中心。在市场建设上，加强了基础设施的建设，现代化通讯手段有了提高，不少市场购置了传真机、计算机和其他先进设备，规范了市场交易，提高了运作水平。市场网络的形成为把生产和流通企业推向市场提供了重要条件，为促进物资流通产业的发展提供了极为有利的条件。

三、深化改革，转换机制，企业进入市场的步伐明显加快

深化改革，转换企业内部机制是1993年物资工作的一个重点。一年来，各地物资部门和企业在这方面做了大量工作，特别是在贯彻落实《企业法》和《条例》上，在人事、用工、分配三项制度和试行“国有民营”改革上，勇于实践，敢闯敢试，摸索出了许多行之有效的办法，推动了全省物资流通产业的发展。在人事制度上许多地区和企业打破“铁交椅”，重德重才，确立了主要以经济效益定干部升降的标准，中层干部全部实行了聘任制。使一批年富力强、敢开拓、善经营、会管理的同志走上了领导岗位，提高了企业的经营管理水平。在用工制度上，不少企业面向社会，公开招聘，择优录用新职工，先试用，后上岗；对现有职工实行双向选择、择优上岗和待岗制；还有一些企业实行全员劳动合同制，有力地促进了企业职工的合理流动和优化组合。在分配制度上，不少企业采取费用包干、风险抵押、分档计奖、岗位工资等多种办法，使职工报酬与工作实绩、经济效益挂钩，对有突出贡献的人员实行重奖，调动了职工的积极性。实践证明，转换经营机制已成为全省物资企业拓宽市场，扩大销售，提高效益，增强发展后劲的主要途径。

四、夯实基础，健全制度，企业管理工作得到加强

多年来物资流通企业的实践证明，凡是企业管理基础扎实、管理严格有方的，企业就有生机和活力，效益就提高，企业就发展。各级领导普遍重视加强企业管理。一是完善了各种形式的经济责任制，普遍建立了企业的激励机制和约束机制。二是从物资流通的各个环节把关，加强制度建设，不断健全和完善各项规章制度和管理办法，对经营活动实行制度化、规范化管理。许多物资企业着力加强企业的安全经营，对购销合同的签订、购销渠道、付款提货等经营环节都做出了明确的规定，减少了经营风险。三是加强了财务管理，突出抓了资金的统一管理和有效使用。大部分企业建立了内部银行，资金统一调度，有偿使用；组织专人清理债权债务；并结合新会计制度的执行，重新制定完善了企业的财务管理制度。四是抓了现代化手段的运用和人才培训。微机数量增加，应用范围扩大，各级领导重视现代管理方法的学习，促进了管理水平的提高；采取多种形式，培训人才，提高了职工素质。企业管理工作的加强，有力地促进了各项任务的完成。

五、不等不靠，积极主动，物资体制改革进展顺利

八届人大一次会议之后，随着国家物资管理机构的改革，我省各级物资局中，绝大部分成建制的转为经济实体，作为独立的企业法人直接进入市场。14个地州市物资局，原来有4个为两块牌子，一套人员，有10个为事业编制，企业开支的物资局建制。现在有9个地州市物资局已挂了两块牌子，并正在做成立以直属企业为核心、延伸到县级物资企业的物资集团公司的准备工作。全省80个县市物资局已有78个转为物资总公司或实行两块牌子、一套人员，向走向市场迈出了扎实的一步。

过去的一年，尽管市场形势多变，机构变动，困难较大，但经过卓有成效的工作，仍取得了较大的成绩。实践证明，我省物资系统的大多数企业在激烈的市场竞争中，是有一定的应变能力和竞争能力的。

（张世俊）

对外经济贸易

1993年甘肃省对外经济贸易工作综述

国际贸易促进委员会

甘肃省分会会长

许飞青

1993年,甘肃省对外经济贸易全面发展,外经、引进外资都有了长足进步;外贸出口克服重重困难,经济效益开始好转;国际贸易促进工作也取得了新成绩,在我省对外经济贸易和国际交往中发挥出日益重要的作用。

一、外经,1993年共执行项目243项,比1992年增加11项

对外工程承包、援外和劳务合作,逐步从单一的执行对外援助项目,发展到多种行业的承包工程与劳务合作。1993年,经贸部批准的我省外经公司已由1家增加到6家,业务范围涉及24个国家和地区,派出人员有土木建筑、公路、化工、地质、林业、农业、铁路、石油机械、电力安装及饮食服务行业。全年共执行项目57项,比1992年增加10项,合同金额25173万美元,比1992年增加16.93%,带动设备出口55.23万美元,援外机电产品457件(台),外派人员1710人次,营业额5200万美元,比1992年增长25.97%,特别是省建总公司承建的津巴布韦契诺伊师范学院,被经贸部评为援外工程的样板。

接受多、双边无偿援助项目,1993年执行59项,受援总金额1372.3万美元,比计划超5项。这些项目主要是由联合国人口基金会儿童基金会,开发计划署,粮农组织粮食计划署,欧共体及加拿大、日本、英国等国家提供无偿援助,与我合作在扶贫、农、林、牧、水利、机械以及文化、教育、卫生、妇女参与发展等领域进行,涉及到全省14个地、州、市。这些项目的执行,收到良好的社会效益和经济效益。

国际技术交流计划执行17项,实际执行47项;创办海外非贸易企业,1993年新批24户,累计达40户,其中:独联体27户,东欧5户,蒙古1户,非洲5户;新加坡1户,澳大利亚1户,合同总金额1509.246万美元。外经工作在各类项目的执行中,得到了省直各有关部门,有关地、州、市及项目单位的高度重视和大力支持与合作,建立了良好的工作关系,并为今后奠定了基础。

二、引进外资

1993年底我省累计利用国外贷款,已签约29项,借用外资合同总额为4.57亿美元。其中1993年签约3项,借用外资合同总额为1.96亿美元;外商投资企业发展较快,"三资"企业总数累计达823家;投资合同总额10.79亿美元,其中外资额为4.76亿美元。仅1993年新增外商投资企业556家,新增投资额6.3亿美元,外资额2.92亿美元,分别相当于过去十三年企业总和的两倍,投资总额的1.4倍,外资额的1.58倍。投资合作领域拓宽。由过去兴办农副产品加工、轻工、电子产品为主逐步扩展到石油化工、能源交通、原材料加工、高新技术产品等领域,第三产业作为外商投资重点,已占外商投资的41.6%;投资的国别和地区由以前的4至5个国家和地区扩大到23个国家和地区;投资的布局由以前的以兰州地区为主逐步向全省14个地、州、市延伸,一批规模较大的生产型企业,如年产18万吨混合饲料的兰州正大有限公司,年产2万吨铝锭的华兴铝业公司和投资1850万美元的陇明型材有限公司等已建成投产。全省三资企业年出口创汇总额达1837万美元,接近于1992年的3倍。另外,去年我省技术进出口也有了良好的起步,全年技术出口共计9项,总金额1270万美元。

三、外贸出口

1993年外贸出口工作,在狠抓出口创汇进度的同时,注重抓外贸企业内部经营管理,通过处理库存,催收国内外帐款,加速资金周转,减少资金不合理占用,提高省内收汇率,努力降低换汇成本以减少亏损,力求逐步摆脱效益不好的处境。从当年经营状况看,除少数公司仍有较大亏损外,应该说,其他大多数省级外贸公司都有不同程度的减亏或盈利。

全省对外贸易共完成进出口总值48410万美元,其中出口完成28347万美元。一般贸易出口25135万美元,占全省出口总值的88.7%;易货贸易出口1375万美元,比1992年增长69.13%,占全省出口总额的4.8%;三资企业出口1837万美元,占全省出口总值的6.4%,18家省市外贸公司完成19821万美元,占出口总值的70%;18家经营权企业完成1574万美元,占出口总值的5.5%;中央工贸公司完成4198万美元,占出口总值的14.8%。出口的主要大宗商品有:硅铁,4.1万吨,2100万美元;手工羊毛地毯26万平方米,1300万美元,无毛绒321吨,1029万美元;锌锭3700吨,346万美元;锌精矿10486吨,202万美元;铝锭9000吨,980万美元;煤炭4万吨,123万美元。

全省进口到货20063万美元,其中外贸企业进口6688万美元,易货贸易进口1375万美元,三资企业进口12000万美元。进口增长幅度相当可观。

出口收汇率有所提高,截至去年11月,全省各类外贸企业平均收汇率为实际创汇额的65%。其中:省市外贸公司高于平均收汇率的依次有:兰州市,广告、土畜、地毯、设备、粮油、化工7个公司;有经营权企业有兰州电机厂、西北铁合金厂、一毛、炭素、长风5家企业;中央工贸公司有兰炼、冶金、包装、有色等4个公司。

出口退税工作进展顺利,全年共退税16690万元人民币。

与1992年相比,有10个公司出口创汇率出现增长趋势,省市外贸公司有:机械增长83%;包装增长33%;有经营权企业:兰石,增长10%;炭素,增长109%;西北铁合金,增长53%;兰州电机厂,增长205%;海林轴承厂,增长81%。中央工贸公司:冶金,增长26%;兰炼,增长17%;煤炭公司,增长9%。这些公司出口增长的原因:一是有的1992年出口基数比小,1993年主动出击,在开拓市场,联系客户,收购货源,狠抓成交等方面采取了切实措施。二是一些机电产品生产企业,兰石、兰州电机厂、海林轴承厂等产品质量逐步提高,占领国际市场的竞争能力逐步增强,这为优化我省出口产品结构开了个好头。三是以五金、矿产为主的原材料生产企业,如西北铁合金、炭素厂等出口增长比较稳定,显示了较强的出口实力和潜力。

四、贸促工作

随着我省对外经济贸易的发展和市场经济的确立,中国贸促会甘肃省分会,中国国际商会甘肃商会,作为联系政府与企业的桥梁,联络国内国外经贸界、金融界的纽带作用越来越重要。截至1993年底,甘肃贸促会已与世界40多个国家和地区的有关机构、工商会、贸易协会等对口组织建立了长期的业务合作关系。

1993年,省贸促会先后组织了兰化、西北铁合金、煤炭、酒钢等10多家企业和有关部门的46人次及一些私营企业、个体户,到日本、韩国、新加坡、美国、加拿大、沙特阿拉伯、南非、独联体等国家和地区进行市场考察,签订合作项目协议29份,协议金额3210万美元,签订贸易合同300多万美元。邀请国外企业、工商、金融和对口组织来我省考察,洽谈贸易和经济合作,先后邀请接待10多个国家的19个代表团180多人次,与我省20多家企业和单位进行了洽谈和交流。

出国展览工作,省贸促会与外经贸厅共同举办"甘肃省香港对外经贸洽谈会",并邀请了在企业界有影响的霍英东等人出席。组织我省10家企业参加了美国洛杉矶、阿根廷布宜诺斯艾利斯、阿联酋迪拜等3次国际展览会、博览会,共租用摊位8个,签订成交合同28份,373.18万美元,签订项目协议5份,180万美元,结识新客户400多家。与有关单位联系,成功地举办了"兰州国际汽车展览会",共展出6个国家的50种不同型号的客车、小轿车、客货两用车、货车52辆,大大方便了三资企业购买免税车的需要。成功地举办了"兰州国际医疗器械展览会",受到省上医务界的欢迎。

法律事务工作也有了新发展,1993年共签发原产地证800多份,认证140份。申报单位已从1992年的16家发展到36家。举办涉外经贸法律培训班一期,参加人员有企业厂长、经理和业务人员30多名,并承担了部分会员企业的国际经贸法律咨询工作和代理国际贸易纠纷仲裁和调解工作。

前进中的
甘肃商检事业

省商检局局长

陈　鹏

甘肃进出口商品检验局成立于1957年。三十多年来,在艰难曲折的前进道路上,它为甘肃经济建设和对外贸易的发展做出了积极的贡献。

根据《中华人民共和国进出口商品检验法》的授权,甘肃商检局一直把检验把关视为自己的首要任务,坚持依法施检、热情服务,赢得了国内外各有关方面的信赖,创造了良好的社会经济效益。从1989年《商检法》颁布实施以来,检验的出口商品24000多批,价值30多亿元;进口商品2000多批,价值1.2亿多美元。在它的严格检验监督下,有700多批不合格的出口商品被堵在国门之内,避免造成经济损失和不良影响;有250多批有问题的进口商品对外出证索赔,共赔回440多万美元;与此同时,还签发普惠制原产地证书4500多份,对方给惠后大大增强了我出口商品的竞争能力。通过上述工作,每年约为社会创造经济效益6000万元左右。

甘肃商检不仅重视进出口商品的检验把关,而且重视进出口企业监督管理。从甘肃的实际出发,严格按照管、帮、促、相结合的原则,对不同企业采取了不同的管理办法。领导质量意识较强、生产条件较好,管理体系完善、产品质量稳定的企业,实行宽松管理,不定期地进行抽查;反之,则实行加严管理,结合检验工作随时进行检查,帮助攻克难关,促其迅速转变;特别对那些弄虚作假、欺骗顾客的企业,则毫不手软,一经发现就一追到底,在查清事实的基础上严肃处理,以儆效尤。在一些涉及安全卫生的重点企业中,还实行了质量许可和卫生注册制度,对其技术管理、设备管理、质量管理、人员素质等进行严格考核,符合条件的发给证书,从而有效地促进了产品质量的提高。截止目前,全省获得质量许可证的企业已有67家,获得卫生注册证的企业已有26家(有2家还获得德国和英国卫生注册),这些企业的产品质量普遍符合出口要求。为使我国复关后能与国际市场接轨,还在出口商品生产企业中开始推行ISO9000系列标准,先后举办培训班7期,有300多家企业500多人次参加了学习,这对促使企业完善质量管理体系已经或正在发挥着积极的作用。

甘肃商检始终把加强自身建设当作关系事业兴旺发达的大事来抓。多年来,已经培养和造就了一支百人以上具有多学科多门类的检验技术队伍,建立了2个二级实验室、6个三级实验室,搜集了4000多册各种检验标准和图书资料，配备了较先进的检测设备100多台(件)，不仅能够快速准确地完成法定检验鉴定任务，而且还能承担社会委托业务。为了进一步改善服务态度，提高服务质量，还本着新事新办、特事特办、难事帮办的精神，采取了很多方便措施，如受理电话、传真报验，缩短检验签证周期，开展送证上门业务，实行跟踪检验和售前预验，应用户要求出国监造监装，帮助企业进行客户资信调查，协助签订质量检验和索赔条款，开展外商投资财产价值评估等等。所有这些，都得到了贸易关系人的一致好评。

旅游服务

甘肃旅游

【旅游业概述】1993年，甘肃旅游系统全体干部、职工，以党的十四大精神和邓小平同志南巡谈话精神为指针，在省委、省政府和各级地方政府的直接领导和支持下，在国家旅游局的指导下，解放思想，真抓实干，克服困难，不断努力，促进全省旅游业跨上新台阶，逐步完善和发展旅游市场经济体制，提高经济效益和服务质量，完成了各项经济指标和工作任务。

1993年，全省旅游系统接待海外旅游者10.39万人次，接待人天数为16.78万人天。其中接待外国人为8.04万人次，接待外国人人天数为13.2万人天。全省各市、县接待旅游人数中，兰州市37618人次，嘉峪关市10717人次，酒泉市5948人次，敦煌市37000人次，天水市2174人次，武威市1795人次，张掖市1522人次，平凉市462人次，夏河县6713人次。

在接待海外游客中，日本游客?949人次，韩国游客92人次，北美游客5544人次，西欧游客22687人次，澳大利亚及新西兰游客1246人次。

1993年，全省旅游营业收入1.2亿元，外汇收入5000万元外汇人民币，利润1680万元，结汇4000万元人民币。其中旅行社营业收入2263万元，创汇2263万元外汇人民币，利润490万元；宾馆、饭店营业收入7279万元，创汇2737万元外汇人民币，利润1123万元；其他旅游企业营业收入2393万元，商业性营业收入1500万元外汇人民币；餐饮营业收入5229万元外汇人民币。

全省各市县旅游收入和创汇分别是：兰州市营业收入5963万元，创汇3101万元外汇人民币；敦煌市营业收入2020万元，创汇1221万元外汇人民币；嘉峪关营业收入1436万元，创汇295万元外汇人民币；酒泉市营业收入985万元，创汇194万元外汇人民币；武威市营业收入339万元，创汇0.5万元外汇人民币；天水市营业收入327万元，创汇78万元外汇人民币；平凉市营业收入814万元，夏河县营业收入132万元，创汇72万元外汇人民币。

1993年，甘肃国内旅游继续呈现蓬勃发展势头，全年营业收入达1.77亿元，接待国内外游客254万人次。产业规模也逐渐壮大，三类旅行社已由1992年的24家发展到72家。文化、教育、统战、侨联、司法、公安、交通、电力、林业等行业和部门，以及全省14个地、州、市都相继成立了三类旅行社。国内旅游业已成为促进各地区扩大对外开放的重要窗口，并逐步列为各地区经济和社会发展的重点和支柱产业。各地、州、市及县的主要领导同志亲自抓旅游工作，制定旅游资源开发和发展规划，协调解决当地旅游业发展中遇到的困难和问题，勘察和调研旅游景点的维修和建设。充分利用各地的旅游资源优势，完善旅游景点设施和提高接待能力，特别是南线旅游景区中的甘南、临夏、陇南地区积极兴办国内旅游业务，促进当地的对外开放和经济建设，带动相关产业的发展。

【旅游客源市场开发与促销】1993年，甘肃旅游市场的发展与促销，本着从实际出发，继承传统旅游产品，增加新产品，开发新项目，抓住客源市场，重点开拓的原则，采取各种灵活方式，增强宣传促销力度，扩大宣传媒介范围，形成全方位开发格局。5月下旬，在兰州召开了出国参展工作研讨会，总结了近几年外联促销的经验，分析了国际、国内旅游市场形势，提出了今后外联促销工作的意见，认为：要认真研究对策，转变观念，调整经营策略和经营方式。在竞争激烈的形势下，要有紧迫感，掌握信息，在主要客源国建立基地，加强宣传。要提高外联促销人员的政治、业务素质，使其成为甘肃旅游事业的“先锋”。

在国内的旅游产品推销活动中，以国家旅游局推出的“'93中国山水风光游”为重点。6月初，由西藏自治区主办，甘肃、青海、新疆三省区旅游局参加，召开了'93中国山水风光游拉萨汇合点活动筹备会议，提出了具体活动方案，拟定了联合开发的10条线路，以适应不断变化的市场需求，增强市场开发的持续性，国外抓促销，国内抓产品，形成文化性观光产品系列，使山水旅游产品质量逐步提高，客源市场不断扩大，加快西北地区和甘肃旅游业的发展。在推出的旅游线中有：加德满都——拉萨——格尔木——西宁——兰州——香港；成都·拉萨——格尔木——敦煌——嘉峪关——兰州——香港；西安——兰州——敦煌——嘉峪关——吐鲁番——乌鲁木齐——喀什——红其拉甫口岸；兰州——西宁——格尔木——拉萨——樟木口岸；北京——西安——敦煌——嘉峪关——吐鲁番——乌鲁木齐——喀什；兰州

——西宁——格尔木——若羌——和田——乌鲁木齐;兰州——西宁——拉萨——林芝——山南——拉萨。经过积极的准备,各省区分工协作,于9月顺利完成了活动,取得了联合推销,共同受益的效果。

在宣传促销中以丝绸之路为主线,广为宣传被国家旅游局列为1993年精选的旅游节会活动中的甘肃嘉峪关国际滑翔节、天水伏羲文化节、夏河拉卜楞寺大法会和浪山节、敦煌之夏等具有吸引力的传统拳头旅游产品,以扩大影响,吸引和招徕海外游客到甘肃观光旅游。

在积极开展省内外各项旅游宣传活动的同时,大力开展国外旅游宣传活动。全省旅游系统先后派出14个展销团组64人次,参加了柏林、香港、日本、新加坡、马来西亚、泰国、法国等7个国际旅游展销会和韩国组织的第一届"中国旅游展"交易会。各个展销团组积极宣传推销,洽谈业务,重点宣传和推出了甘肃汽车、摩托车、滑翔、狩猎、寻根访祖、民族风情等特殊旅游项目。

在走出宣传促销的同时,不失时机的邀请外国客商、接待海外记者到甘肃来考察采访。先后接待了美国、日本、法国、新加坡、香港、台湾等国家和地区的记者10多人。并且邀请国内主要旅游报刊的编辑记者和中央电视台记者到甘肃进行考察采访,拍摄专题片,在海内外报刊杂志及电视台刊登发表文章和播放专题片,宣传甘肃旅游资源和景点,更进一步扩大和提高甘肃旅游业在海内外的知名度,促进全省旅游业的发展。

【旅游基本建设与商业开发】1993年,甘肃旅游业基本建设出现了新的变化。在旅游景点和接待设施的开发上采取各种措施和办法,积极多方筹资和引进外资,不断加快建设步伐。兰州金城宾馆与香港维加投资有限公司合资后,对设备陈旧的中楼和接待大厅进行了改造装修,总投资达1811万元。其中港方投资100万美元。中楼改造后,拥有各种档次的客房154间,硬件设施达到四星级客房标准。为了更进一步提高接待能力,金城宾馆采取集资入股的方式,成立了股份制性质的金鼎旅游服务有限公司。共投资50万元人民币,对原宾馆招待所进行了改造装修。嘉峪关旅游局为适应迅猛发展的旅游业,满足国内外旅游者逐年增长的需求,提高接待能力,嘉峪关宾馆于1992年年底开始改造工程,总投资达2700万元,建筑面积15573平方米。截止1993年年底,已完成投资770万元,建筑面积7580平方米。省民航局与台湾丰霖股份有限公司在中川机场合资兴建中川山庄,按三星级旅游涉外宾馆标准修建。

按照国家旅游局的计划安排,甘肃"中华故土园工程"开始启动。并确定在酒泉市的西汉胜迹——泉湖公园动工修建。

在加快旅游业的发展建设中积极引进外资,先后成立了合资企业甘肃丝绸之路旅游服务有限公司、甘肃旅游航空服务有限公司、华澳娱乐有限公司、甘肃侨澳娱乐有限公司、甘肃金纬旅游服务有限公司、甘肃金顺工艺饰品发展责任有限公司、兰州天马图片影印有限公司等9个合资项目,共吸引外资4693万元人民币。已登记注册并正式开业的5家公司及金城宾馆有限公司的外商资金已到位1350万元人民币。

旅游业的迅猛发展,带动了其他行业兴办旅游的积极性。先后批准了刘电宾馆、地质宾馆、陇林宾馆、民族饭店、骊靬宾馆为新的旅游涉外宾馆。批准兰州云峰清真餐厅、兰州天元大酒楼、兰州亚西亚大酒店、云海酒楼、甘肃旅游服务公司旅游餐厅、兰州海外城酒楼、富士大酒店、民族餐厅、麦积山植物园餐厅为涉外餐厅。批准旅游涉外定点商店有:甘肃省中旅商贸公司、甘肃省地毯进出口公司飞天地毯展销厅、敦煌市飞天工艺美术开发公司、敦煌聚雅堂、兰州书林斋、兰州华侨商场、敦煌画院展销厅、敦煌藏经阁。批准的涉外定点医院有:兰州军区总医院、甘肃省兰州急救中心、敦煌市医院。批准的涉外定点车船公司有:甘肃黄河旅游汽车公司。

为了充分发挥全省旅游资源的优势,适应现代旅游的需求,1993年年初,省旅游局组织了一次较大规模的资源调研工作,针对各地、市旅游资源的优势和存在的问题,提出了发展规划和建议,并与有关部门共同落实了120万元的旅游资源建设专项资金,对各地18个资源项目进行了开发和建设。特别是旅游业起步比较晚的庆阳、定西地区,为了加快旅游业的发展速度,适应改革开放的需要,各级领导进一步解放思想,转变观念,认真贯彻中央和省委关于"大力发展旅游业"和"把旅游业作为大产业来办"的精神,加快了旅游业发展步伐。

【旅游行业管理】甘肃旅游系统在注重基础建设,不断提高服务质量,树立良好的甘肃旅游业形象的同时,加强了旅游全行业的管理工作。1993年年初,省旅游局、省工商行政管理局联合对全省19家一、二类旅行社认真进行了业务年检和审计验证。对旅行社的业务经营、经济指标、服务质量和其他方面进行了全面检查和审计,重新核定了5家更改名称的一、二类旅行社。为了适应国内旅游业蓬勃发展的需要,1993年全省新批准成立三类旅行社46家。根据全国旅游行业管理工作会议精神,按照国家旅游局的安排,向全省转发了国家旅游局《国内旅游行业服务质量基本标准》(讨论稿),广泛征求了三类旅行社的建议和意见。并对全省的254名导游人员进行了严格的换证考核,对201名导游人员进行了资格考试,促使导游人员不断学习,提高业务知识和工作能力，保证了导游人员的接待服务质量。

1993年，为了加强星级和旅游涉外饭店、宾馆的管理，不断提高服务水平和经营管理水平，对全省15家星级宾馆进行了复审及评定。还对主要经济指标完成情况进行统计审核。在旅游旺季组织专门人员跟踪检查服务质量，下发宾客意见调查表，征求宾客的意见，监督服务质量。同时，组织开展了全省第二届旅游行业烹饪服务技能竞赛和旅游团队正餐质量评比活动，促使涉外星级宾馆、饭店服务质量的不断提高。并对全省89家旅游涉外定点宾馆、饭店、餐馆、商店、车船公司进行不定期的抽查和业务年检、审计验证工作，加强了涉外定点单位的管理，促进了服务质量的提高。根据国家旅游局旅游价格“一控制、六放开”的改革方案，为了便于全省旅游企业在经济运行中利用价格杠杆，适应市场的竞争，经过认真研究，提出了全省星级宾馆、饭店、主要游览点及旅游相关单位的收费项目的指导协调价格；与此同时，积极会同省物价、文物、园林、民航等部门通报价格信息，为旅游企业走向市场提供服务。

（阎赤 刘理）

经济管理与监督

适应需要 抓住机遇 甘肃省统计改革与现代化建设又上新台阶

省统计局局长

吴士起

1993年，全省各地、各部门统计机构和广大统计人员，以邓小平同志建设有中国特色的社会主义理论为指针，认真学习和贯彻党的十四大和十四届三中全会精神，认真落实省委、省政府和国家统计局的工作部署，解放思想，转变观念，加快统计改革与建设的步伐，提高统计服务水平，在综合协调、经济预测、建立健全省一级新国民经济核算体系，以及加强宏观经济监测、预警和统计制度方法改革方面作了大量工作，取得了可喜成绩。

一、统计制度方法改革取得重大突破

（一）新国民经济核算体系由试点试算进入实施阶段，建立起了省一级核算体系基本框架。

建立健全新国民经济核算体系，是党政部门加强宏观调控的迫切需要，也是推动统计工作向适应社会主义市场经济方向转变的关键环节。为建立适合我省省情的新国民经济核算体系，我们克服起步晚、时间紧、难度大的困难，积极组织各地、各部门联合攻关，打破常规，采取“跳跃式”前进的方法，着手研制完成了新国民经济核算体系基层调查一套表，并在酒泉市进行了试点。酒泉地、市统计部门及有关部门为试点做了大量工作，试点工作圆满成功，为全面推行取得了经验。在试填、试算、试点的基础上，对核算体系一套表进行修订后，已在去年年报中正式实施。新国民经济核算基层调查一套表既符合我省社会主义市场经济发展的需要，又满足了上报国家统计局报表的需要，与原有的核算制度相比，在核算范围、内容、方法等方面都有重大突破。同时，这种根据新国民经济核算体系的要求设置基层单位一套表的方法，使得整个国民经济核算形成一个基层资料——帐户——基本表的工作流程，使其所形成的指标体系呈扇形结构，既减轻了基层负担，又使得整个工作达到了规范化、科学化的要求，为准确、快捷地完成国民经济核算体系的转轨打下了基础。我省这项工作受到了国家统计局有关部门的肯定，被认为在全国居于前列。在今年的全国统计工作会议上作了发言，与会者很感兴趣。此外，我们完成了国内生产总值及其使用表、资金流量表、对外经济往来表等的编制工作，建立了省一级国民经济核算体系框架。

（二）积极实施新的国家统计报表制度。

按照国家统计局的统一部署，从去年年报起开始实施新的国家统计报表制度。新的统计报表制度在改革统计指标体系、统一统计标准、理顺专业之间的关系等方面进行了较大的改革，初步克服了长期以来在计划经济体制下形成的各专业统计彼此分割、自成体系、互不衔接配套的弊端，从整体上提高了统计制度的标准化和规范化程度。实施新的统计制度，是我国统计制度的一项重要改革，组织实施难度很大，我省各级政府极为重视和支持，省政府专门下发了新报表制度实施工作的明传电报，大部分地、县政府也下发了有关文件，提出了实施要求，各地、各部门统计机构对这项工作极为重视。采取有力措施，克服重重困难，作了大量的、艰苦的组织协调工作，进行了广泛的动员、培训和周密的布置，使新报表制度在我省的贯彻实施基本顺利。

全省各部门统计机构适应加强科学决策和宏观调控的需要，根据上级部门的部署，积极配合当地统计改革，在改革和完善部门及行业统计制度方面，也做了大量工作，取得了好的效果。

（三）专项统计制度实施效果良好，适应了加强宏观管理的需要。

为适应党政部门加强宏观管理的需要，根据国家统计局的部署，我们在全省建立并实施了工业增加值、工业销售产值、工业企业经济效益评价统计制度，和国内生产总值季度核算制度，以及根据我省实际情况制定的粮食、供销、商业、外贸、旅游企业经济效益评价统计制度，经过两年的实施和完善，效果良好，基本达到了预期目的，对改善我省宏观经济管理，纠正片面追求产值增长、盲目攀比速度的倾向，起到了积极的作用。

二、统计咨询服务水平进一步提高

一年来，各地、各部门统计机构紧紧围绕经济建设这个中心，积极开展统计调查，大力加强统计分析研究，不断拓展统计服务领域，进一步提高了统计咨询服务水平。

（一）统计分析研究重点保证了党政领导在宏观经济决策中的需要。

一是为党政领导加强宏观调控提供了大量的具有量化特点的咨询意见和建议。随着市场经济的发展和政府职能的转变，各级党政领导为适时适度地进行宏观调控，迫切需要准确、及时地把握经济发展态势。各级统计机构积极适应这一要求，加强了对国民经济运行的监测预警，及时反馈新情况、新问题。去年上半年，我们根据各地、各部门提供的统计数据和信息，在对上半年全省经济形势准确分析的基础上，适时提出了《经济在上升区运行、宏观调控面临新考验》的意见；针对一些重点能耗企业超耗严重的情况，及时向省政府呈送了《关于目前我省重点能耗企业能源超耗情况的汇报》；针对我省取消农作物种植计划后，粮食生产没有出现大的波动的情况，我们写了调查报告，进一步坚定了有关部门彻底取消种植计划的决心；针对东西部经济发展的差距、甘肃经济落后的原因等问题，向中央在兰州召开的有关会议，来甘肃视察的中央领导同志等提出了统计部门的看法和建议；我们在调查的基础上，提出的甘肃经济市场化、建立资本市场的建议，得到省委、省政府主要领导的肯定，等等。从经济运行的实际情况看，我们的这些分析观点是基本符合实际的，基本正确的，对省委、省政府判断经济形势、进行宏观决策，把握宏观调控的方向和力度发挥了参谋作用。

二是紧密围绕社会、政治、经济生活中出现的新情况、新问题进行分析研究。各地、各部门统计机构在搞好宏观经济分析的同时，紧密围绕社会、政治、经济生活中出现的新情况、新问题进行研究，就制定经济发展战略、发展第三产业、优化产业结构、提高经济效益等重大课题，以及房地产热、开发区热等热点问题，深入调查研究，搞好专题分析，为当地党政领导提供了一批选题准确、观点鲜明、分析深刻、对策建议比较全面的统计分析报告。这些分析报告受到了领导同志的肯定，并在有关的工作报告中采用。

三是统计系列分析报告质量不断提高。各地、各部门统计机构充分发挥统计资源丰富和调查网络分布广的优势，广泛开展统计系列分析和追踪调查，形成了一批内容丰富、质量上乘的系列调查报告。一是居民生活小康系列报告。我们分别对全省城市和农村居民生活小康标准进行了分析论证，提出了城市、农村居民生活小康标准、已实现程度、达到小康标准应做的工作等，形成了一系列报告，被有关部门所采用。二是固定资产投资与建筑系列报告。先后就固定资产投资增长高于工业总产值增长，如何延长经济增长周期等问题进行了调研活动，形成系列分析报告数十篇，先后被有关刊物、省委、省政府的信息刊物所采用。三是儿童基本情况调查系列报告。有调查的初级报告和最终报告，有反映儿童生长、生活、教育、计划免疫等情况的分析报告，这些报告以观点客观、资料翔实等特点而成为我省在儿童基本情况方面具有权威性的材料，受到省教委、卫生厅、妇联等部门的肯定与好评。

（二）大型统计调查取得丰硕成果。

一是圆满完成了投入产出调查。根据国家统计局的部署，在各级统计部门的精心组织下，在全省各级党政领导和各部门的大力支持下，经过全省数万名调查人员的辛勤努力，圆满完成了全省投入产出调查任务，及时处理上报了有关数据，我省投入产出办公室被国家评为质量管理一等奖和组织协调优秀奖。目前正在进行投入产出数据资料的开发应用工作。

二是完成了儿童基本情况抽样调查。根据国家统计局的部署，为配合《九十年代中国儿童发展规划纲要》的贯彻实施，省城乡调查队完成了 1992 年我省儿童基本情况抽样调查，调查结果反映了我省在儿童保护和发展方面取得的成就，同时也反映了存在的一些问题，对推动我省儿童事业发展具有重要意义。

三是首次开展了全省第三产业普查。虽然这次普查时间紧、任务重、难度大，但在全省各级政府的重视和有关部门的大力支持下，经过全省各级统计机构和广大普查人员的努力，在较短的时间内做了大量艰苦细致的工作，目前已完成了清查摸底、调查登记及主要数据汇总工作。

（三）统计信息咨询服务工作进一步发展。

在过去的一年里，统计信息资源的开发应用，在广度和深度上都有所拓展，咨询服务的质量明显提高，赢得了社会普遍赞誉。全省各级统计部门，特别是地、县统计部门，纷纷成立了统计信息咨询服务机构，目前已有 20 多家，全省第一个统计事务所在兰州市统计局成立，第一个经济统计书店在省调查队开业。这些咨询服务机构，承担了大量的社会经济调查，开展了多层次、多类型的地区、企业经济和企业排序活动，为统计工作和社会各界提供了多种多样的事务服务，取得了较好的经济和社会效益。部分地市统计部门主动联合有关部门，积极组织社会力量，建立跨行业、地区、省的统计咨询服务机构，开发以统计信息为主体的信息资源，拓宽了统计信息咨询服务的领域，推动了统计信息产业的发展。

甘肃省审计工作简述

省审计局局长

高存弟

1993年，全省审计工作认真贯彻邓小平同志重要谈话和党的十四大精神，坚持改革，转变观念，解放思想，开拓奋进，紧紧围绕经济建设这个中心，积极开展审计监督，推进了审计事业的发展。

一、国家审计机关紧紧围绕经济工作中心，认真履行监督职能，依法查处各种违纪问题。

1993年，全省各级审计机关认真贯彻执行审计署关于强化审计监督的十八条意见，开展了对财政金融，基本建设，工交商贸、行政事业、利用外资，农、林、水利等领域的审计监督。全省共审计了4944个单位(项目)，审计总金额487亿元，查出各类违纪资金39799万元，其中应上缴财政2879万元，已上缴财政1526万元；应减少财政拨款和补贴833万元；应追还挪用专项资金6729万元；查出损失浪费金额6277万元；对违纪单位和违纪责任人处以罚款62万元；被审计单位采纳意见建议893条。

(一)、把审计监督的重点放在财政、金融和重点建设项目上。

1993年7月，省政府批转了省审计局《关于强化审计监督更好地为经济建设服务的意见》，要求全省各级审计机关都要围绕适应社会主义市场经济的要求，充分发挥审计监督的宏观调控作用，保证中央和省上经济政策的贯彻落实，着重审计和调查当前经济生活中的主要矛盾和问题，更好地为改革开放和经济建设服务。

全省各级审计机关根据审计署的统一部署和省政府的要求，加强了对财政、金融和新开工建设项目资金来源的审计，对整顿金融秩序、控制固定资产投资规模起了积极作用。全省共审计财税部门128个，其中地级10个，县级46个，乡(镇)72个，达到审计署提出的地、县财税每年审计三分之一的要求。查出违纪资金3787万元，经审计，可增加财政收入981万元。各级审计机关针对审计中发现的越权减免税收，承包流转税，隐瞒财政收入、财政赤字不实，财政资金体外循环和财政信用资金管理混乱等问题，积极提出意见、建议，受到政府和有关部门的重视。各级审计机关认真贯彻中央6号文件精神，组织力量，统一行动，对金融系统“四行一司”的违章拆借资金，占用联行汇差资金、压单压票，擅自设立金融机构和占用银行资金兴办经济实体等五个方面的情况进行了专项审计。全省共审计金融单位418个，查出信贷超规模、违章拆借、信贷投向不合理等有问题资金102542万元，应追回侵占挪用资金355万元。同时，省局还承担了金融系统118个单位的财税大检查任务。

按照国家宏观调控的要求，全省共审计开工前项目343个，审计在建项目、竣工项目106个，查出偷税漏税、转移侵占挪用基建资金等违纪金额3808万元，经审计减少项目投资70万元，核减工程预决算189万元。

(二)、改进对国有企业的审计方法，促进企业转换经营机制。

全省各级审计机关认真贯彻《全民所有制工业企业转换经营机制条例》和审计署、国家经贸委、体改委《全民所有制工业企业审计监督规定》，重点审计占有国家资产数额较大的和亏损较多的企业，其他国有企业逐步委托社会审计组织审计。在财务收支审计的基础上向检查企业内控制度和经济效益延伸。审计的内容主要是企业的资产负债和损益的真实、合法性，监督国有资产的保值增值。

全省共审计各类企业757个，并对3个股份制企业开展了试审。被审计的企业中，国有资产增值的179个，损失的46个，盈亏不实单位192个。查出各类违纪资金21260万元，其中应上缴财政的935万元。查出企业因经营决策失误、物资管理差、经济往来损失等原因造成损失浪费金额达3723万元。

通过审计监督，维护企业的法定经营自主权，反映企业的困难，帮助改善外部环境。各地审计机关不仅依法处理企业的自身违纪问题，还对有关部门严重失职和弄虚作假侵犯企业权益的行为提请政府有关部门依法处理。同时，及时总结企业改革中成功的经验，反映企业的现状、困难和问题，有针对性地提出扭亏措施和对策，对企业转换经营机制起到了促进作用。

(三)、围绕改革和经济发展中的重要问题开展审计和审计调查，为领导决策当好参谋

各级审计机关注意围绕改革试点、经济活动热点。工作中的难点进行审计和调查，全年共提交各类综合报告、审计调查报告和审计信息1323篇，其中被各级政府、上级审计机关、新闻单位、有关部门采用批转的752篇，内部通报和对外公布的80篇。

我省经济活动的重点是农业，各级审计机关，特别是地、县审计机关坚持把农业资金的审计放在重要位置上。1993年全省统一组织对敦煌、泾川等18县(市)1991——1992年农业资金的投入情况进行了审计。通过对127个财政、银行。农业主管部门的审计，查出各类违纪资金3445万元,其中应归还原资金渠道3001万元。这项审计揭示了当前我省农业资金投放、管理、使用中存在的问题,分析了原因,提出了改进的意见和措施。

为了掌握我省利用外资的情况,全省共对世界银行贷款项目和世界粮农组织援款项目的129个执行单位进行了审计。

(四)、积极参加反腐败斗争,促进廉政建设。

全省各级审计机关根据省委,省政府的统一安排,在认真开展自查自纠和同时,配合有关部门,检查纠正不正之风,查处大案要案。1993年,全省审计机关共移送贪污贿赂案件12起,移送司法、监察等部门处理的违纪责任人16人。各级审计机关还通过对全省1750个行政单位、796个事业单位的经常性审计监督,查出挪用专项资金建住宅楼、预算外收入不入帐,扩大补贴范围,提高补贴标准,公费旅游吃喝、滥发钱物请客送礼等违纪资金2892万元。

二、社会审计进一步发展

1993年,全省审计事务所和注册审计师有了较快发展。全省已建立审计事务所92个,比上年同期增长96%;从业人员705人,比上年增长2倍。完成各类委托项目6934项,其中,财务收支审计、承包离任审计1089项,清理债权债务55项,协助司法、监察机关完成经济案件鉴定67项,验资年检、资产评估5325项,基建预决算验证105项,为企业提供咨询服务、建帐建制、担任常年顾问等293项。经审计核减虚假注册资金3190万元,核减基建预决算金额368万元。

各级审计机关加强对社会审计的管理和指导,促进上规模、上水平。审计机关向审计事务所分流一部分骨干和从事审计工作多年的老同志,还补充了一批大中专毕业生,增加了职龄人员,改善了从业人员的专业结构。1993年底,全省已有注册审计师523名。

三、因势利导,推动内部审计工作继续发展

党的十三届七中全会提出改进企业内部审计制度的要求后,内审工作越来越受到企业的重视,内审工作得到了继续发展。1993年底,全省内审机构已发展到1242个,配备专(兼)职内审人员2967名。1993年,全省内审机构共完成审计单位(项目)2471个,已纠正违纪余额15896万元,查出损失浪费675万元,促进提高经济效益831万元,查出贪污贿赂案件7起,移送监察、纪检、司法部门处理11人。

今后全省审计机关要以党的十四届三中全会、全国经济工作会议和全国审计工作会议精神为指针,强化审计监督,严格审计执法,保证中央和省上经济政策的贯彻落实。

1993年甘肃省工商行政管理工作综述

【各类市场的培育和建设继续保持良好的发展势头】1993年,全省各级工商行政管理部门继续积极参与组织、培育、建设各类市场,重点发展各类专业批发市场,有力地促进了市场的发展。到年底,全省集贸市场总数达1682个,其中专业、批发市场401个,年成交额70亿元,比上年增长59.09%,占全省社会商品零售总额43.41%。全省成交额亿元以上的有市场13个。1993年市场建设有以下几个特点:一是投资规模大,建设档次高。全省共完成市场建设投资2.98亿元,在兰州、白银、金昌、定西等地,建成了一批投资数百万元乃至上千万元的设施全、多功能的大型市场。二是建设速度快。当年动工新建、扩建、改建的市场达267个,到年底新建、扩建、改建投入使用的有168个,建设周期比往年缩短。三是生产资料市场有了较大发展。全省从甘肃资源、能源大省的优势出发,加快发展生产资料市场,到年底,全省共有生产资料市场93个,年成交额达30多亿元;还建成了西北石化物资交易市场,正在筹建兰州有色金属交易市场等跨地区、辐射面广的区域性市场。

【监督管理社会主义大市场取得初步成效】在市场管理中,全省工商行政管理部门开始从侧重于管理集贸市场向监督管理社会主义统一大市场转变。广大市场管理人员认真学习社会主义市场经济理论,转变观念,改革市场管理方式,从以往的侧重管理上市商品范围向侧重管理市场行为转变。各地还积极探索生产资料、生产要素市场管理办法,向参与这些市场的监督管理迈出了一步。各级工商行政管理部门还注意研究解决大市场流通中的一些问题,比如针对一些地方建关设卡,阻碍商品流通的问题,坚决撤关撤卡,打破地区封锁,促进了货畅其流。为了加强商品市场的宏观管理,省工商局根据国家工商局发布的《商品交易市场登记管理暂行办法》,制定了《甘肃省开办市场登记管理暂行办法》,对市场登记工作提出了明确的要求,登记工作取得了初步成效。

【改革企业管理登记制度,促进各类企业发展】各级工商行政管理部门根据企业登记管理改革的目标,积极探索,大胆试验,弱化前置审批,减少许可证,支持企业转换经营机制,促进企业走向市场。积极支持企业组建企业集团,进行股份制试点。1993年全省新组建企业集团26户,新增股份制企业131户,促进了企业的组织结构、产业结构和产品结构调整。各地还积极试行无主管部门企业的登记工作,为一批无主管部门企业办理了登记注册手续。天水市还制定了无主管部门企业登记管理试行办法,促进了企业的发展。到年底,全省内资企业发展到10.2万户,注册资金645.5亿元,从业人员 351.83 万人，分别比上年增长 24.9%、28.6%和 19.0%。

全省各地根据国家工商局"简化登记手续、强化年检年审"的要求，加强了以年检年审为重点的监督管理工作，进行年检的企业数占应年检企业总数的 93.16%。各地严格按照《企业法人登记管理条例》及其《施行细则》的规定，对一些经多次督促仍然不按要求办理年检的企业进行了严肃处理，从而维护了工商法规的严肃性，增强了监督管理的力度。

【外商投资企业继续快速增长】1993 年，在外商投资企业登记管理工作中，从"三个有利于"出发，认真落实各项优惠政策，同其他有关部门共同努力，不断改善投资环境，吸引外商来甘肃投资。同时，改革登记管理办法，尽量向国际惯例靠拢，为依法独立登记创造条件。从甘肃的省情出发，适当放宽登记条件，尽可能放宽经营范围，为企业生产经营创造条件。省工商局认真总结了近年来"三资"企业发展的经验，对存在的问题进行了深入的调查研究，就落实优惠政策、改善管理、加强服务，促进"三资"企业发展，向省政府提出了建议，受到省上领导的重视。在促进发展的同时，加强了以年度检验和出资检查为主要内容的监督管理工作，重点抓了企业出资率和投产开业率。按时完成年检任务，使年检率达到 78.5%，年检企业实际出资额占注册资金总额的比例及企业开业率均居全国前 5 名。由于投资环境的改善，去年全省"三资"企业仍然保持了快速增长的势头，到年底，新登记"三资"企业 500 户，投资总额 5.7 亿美元，注册资本 4.6 亿美元，其中外方认缴 2.5 亿美元。全省"三资"企业总数达到 723 户，投资总额 9.59 亿美元，注册资本 7.52 亿美元，其中外方认缴 3.97 亿美元，分别比上年增长 3.2 倍、2.2 倍、2.6 倍和 2.7 倍。外国(地区)企业常驻代表机构也由上年的 10 家增加到 91 家。

【进一步放宽政策，放手发展，促进个体私营经济再上新台阶】1993 年，全省各级工商行政管理部门认真贯彻省委、省政府《关于加快个体私营经济发展的决定》，进一步解放思想，大力宣传党和国家对个体私营经济的政策。各地在工作中坚持放宽政策，放手发展，对发展个体、私营经济中的限制进行了大胆突破，进一步放宽了从业人员条件，放宽了经营范围，简化了登记手续，缩短办照时间。在边远落后地区按照"先放开，后规范"的原则，采取了更为宽松的政策。同时还采取措施，创造条件，欢迎外来，支持外出。各地工商行政管理部门还积极为个体私营企业解决各种实际困难，提供咨询、信息等服务，为他们创造公平竞争的条件。1993 年，全省个体、私营经济的发展出现了前所未有的好形势。到年底，全省个体工商户已发展到 28.27 万户，从业人员 48.07 万人，注册资金 9.83 亿元，年产值 9.26 亿元，营业额 60.01 亿元，分别比上年增长 23.8%、30.1%、37.7%、63.2%和 77.1%，发展速度是我省近 10 年来最快的。私营企业的发展也打破了前几年徘徊不前的局面，发展到 2453 户，从业人员 5.25 万人（投资者 6477 人，雇工 46022 人），注册资金 4.52 亿元，年产值 4.13 亿元，营业额 2.29 亿元，分别比上年增长 41.8%、33.8%、80.2%、164.3%和 78.2%。个体、私营经济从业人数已占全省总人口的 2.3%，年产值约占全省工业总产值的 3%；商品零售总额达 42.3 亿元，占全省社会商品零售总额的 26.6%。1993 个体、私营经济纳税 2.3 亿元，占全省工商税收的 4.9%。

【改革商标、广告、经济合同管理，帮助企业增强市场竞争能力】1993 年，全省各级工商行政管理部门积极帮助企业增强商标、广告意识，运用商标、广告开拓市场，扩大企业和商品的知名度，增强企业的竞争能力。各地继续加强了对商标工作的领导，积极引导企业进行商标注册和商标续展，帮助企业争创驰名商标。全年共向国家工商局申请注册商标 419 件，经国家局核准注册商标 249 件，续展商标 171 件，使全省注册商标总数达 2696 件。为了搞好服务商标注册工作，省工商局和省商标事务所共同举办了服务商标培训班，并动员企业及时申请注册服务商标。到年底，全省共受理申请 17 件。

在广告管理工作中，进一步放宽了广告的经营条件，鼓励以多种形式从事广告经营。支持新闻单位开辟了新的广告宣传媒体，扩大广告容量。在全省推广了广告发布示范合同文本制度，促进了广告经营活动的规范化。到年底全省新发展广告经营单位 135 户，累计达到 393 户，广告从业人员达到 4235 人，广告经营额 4680 万元。

根据国家工商局《关于在部分城市进行广告代理制和发布前审查试点工作的意见》，省工商局在兰州市开展了这两项改革的试点工作。经省编委 9 月 1 日批准，省工商局同兰州市工商局共同组建了甘肃省广告审查委员会和广告审查中心，12 月 15 日正式开展业务工作。结合换发《广告经营许可证》，对兰州地区 75 户广告公司按照经营资质标准进行审查。赋予其中一部分具备条件的以广告代理权。同时，指导兰州地区新闻单位积极理顺内部经营机制，为全面实行广告代理制奠定基础。

经济合同管理主要围绕增强全社会的合同意识，提高合同履约率，维护合同当事人的合法权益积极开展工作。新修改的《经济合同法》颁布后，全省通过各种形式，开展了学习、宣传活动，收到了良好效果。继续开展了"重合同、守信用"活动，参加这项活动的企业已占全省法人企业总数的 40%，被命名的企业有 2392 户。各级工商行政管理部门积极推行合同示范文本，三年来，累计发放合同示范文本 1200 万份，社会合同示范文本使用率达 90%以上。继续开展了合同鉴证工作，全省共鉴证合同 12345 份，金额 55.76 亿元。积极推行法人委托代理证书制度，规范了企业的签约行为，提高了履约率。合同仲裁逐步向规范化发展，办案质量有明显提高，全年共受理合同纠纷案件 228 起，前期结转 31 起，结案 229 起，解决争议金额 2151 万元。

【深入开展打假、打私斗争，维护经济秩序】1993 年，全省各地继续深入开展了打击制售假冒伪劣商品、走私贩私和骗买骗卖活动的斗争。各级工商行政管理部门继续发挥在“打假”中的牵头、组织、协调作用，堵源截流，端窝挖点，重点查处制售假劣药品、食品和假劣农业生产资料、建筑材料等违法行为。全年共端掉制假窝点 160 个，查处的假冒伪劣商品价值 1850 万元。全年共立案查处各类经济案件 378 起，其中万元以上的大案 68 起。全国打击走私工作会议以后，省局及时制定了《甘肃省开展打击走私贩私活动行动方案》，各级工商行政管理部门积极行动，同有关部门密切配合，查处走私贩私活动。全省共查处走私案件 31 起，查获各类进口小轿车 106 辆，进口录放像机近百台，以及部分彩电、黄金、卷烟等走私物品，罚没款 235.3 万元，有力地打击了走私贩私活动。

【法制建设取得新成绩】1993 年，各级工商行政管理部门大力抓好法制建设，认真搞好法制教育，广大干部依法行政的自觉性进一步提高。按照市场经济法制建设的要求，省工商局积极参与经济立法工作，大力推进地方经济立法的进程，参与了《反不正当竞争法》、《公司法》等 20 多项法律、法规的修改工作。根据省人大和省政府的要求，在认真调查研究的基础上，起草了《甘肃省经纪人管理暂行条例》和《甘肃省拍卖条例》。《甘肃省经纪人管理暂行条例》已在省八届人大常委会六次会议上经过了一审。《反不正当竞争法》、《消费者权益保护法》出台后，各级工商行政管理部门认真搞好学习培训，利用各种形式广泛开展宣传活动。省局还举办了全省工商行政管理系统《反不正当竞争法》培训研讨会，为全省学习该法培训师资，取得了明显效果，认真开展了执法检查，促进了系统执法监督检查工作的制度化和规范化。

【开展反腐败斗争，加强廉政建设】1993 年，全省各级工商行政管理部门按照中央、省委和国家工商局关于开展反腐败斗争的部署，结合本部门的特点，狠抓了反腐倡廉、纠风治乱工作。省工商局及时提出并下发了《关于近期落实反腐败斗争三项工作任务的安排意见》和《关于把反腐败斗争工作进一步引向深入的通知》，对全省工商系统提出了明确、具体的要求。同时派出反腐败工作督察组到兰州、天水、定西等地进行了检查。各级工商行政管理部门联系，实际针对群众反映强烈的问题，扎扎实实开展反腐败斗争，取得了较好的成效。对工商行政管理系统行政性收费进行了认真清理，明令取消 21 个收费项目。对工商行政管理部门办经济实体的情况进行了模底，到年底，大部分实体已与原机关脱钩。为了接受社会监督，各地认真做好群众举报工作，设立了举报电话、举报箱，鼓励群众反映问题。各地还认真抓好违法违纪行为的查处工作，查处了一批案件。

【基层建设进一步加强】1993 年，各级工商行政管理部门把基层工商所建设作为加强自身建设的一项基础工作，继续抓紧抓好。各地结合实际认真贯彻落实《工商所初级规范达标验收标准》。6 月底至 7 月初，国家工商局对我省首批达标工商所进行了抽查，对我省落实《工商所条例》和初级规范达标工作给予了充分肯定，并同意我省 119 个工商所为达标工商所。各地继续开展了“双先”活动，调动了广大干部职工的积极性，并涌现出 49 个先进集体和 58 名先进个工作者。省工商局对这些先进集体单位和先进工作者进行了表彰。

（省工商局：赵长寿　白春鸣）

天下黄河第一桥

位于兰州市白塔山下的黄河铁桥，历史悠久，素有“天下黄河第一桥”之称。始建于明洪武年间。明洪武 5 年(1372 年)，在兰州城西 3.5 公里处建浮桥。明洪武 9 年(1376 年)，将此浮桥移至城西 5 公里处。明洪武 18 年(1385 年)，将浮桥移至白塔山下。至今还存有当时建桥时所遗的重数吨、长 6 米的铸铁浮桥柱 3 根，人称“将军柱”。清光绪 33 年(1907 年)，由德商承建，将浮桥改建为铁桥，桥长 233.3 米、宽 7.5 米，桥下设四墩，共花去白银 30 多万两。1954 年对铁桥进行了整修加固，增加了弧形钢架拱梁，使铁桥更加显得气势雄伟，绚丽多彩。

社 会 事 业

体 育

锐意进取、大力发展甘肃体育

省体育运动委员会主任

张维国

1993年全省广大体育工作者，以党的十四大精神为指针，以建设有中国特色的社会主义理论为指导，一手抓改革，一手抓“七运”，勇于开拓，锐意创新，使全省体育事业有了突破性进展。这一年是圆满实现“打好四个战役，实现一个突破”（一青会、二青会、六运会、七运会为四个战役，突破甘肃没有运动员参加奥运会的历史）的全省体育近期奋斗目标的一年，也是胜利完成“七运会”任务和体育事业全面发展的一年。竞技运动技术水平得到进一步提高，业余训练及体育宣传、体育科研、体育教育、体育交流等各项工作也有了新的进展。

一、竞技体育成绩显著

在第七届全国运会上全省有219名运动员参加了18个项目的决赛，获奖牌16枚，其中金牌4枚、银牌7枚、铜牌5枚，4——8名28个，团体总分189分，1人1次刷新一项亚洲纪录、4人2次刷新两项全国纪录、获得体育道德风尚奖的运动员25人。从本届运动会看，全省获决赛权的人数比六运会的92人翻了一番还多，参加决赛的项目、获得奖牌的总数、团体总分都超过了“六运会”。金牌数列全国45个代表团的第23位，总分比“六运会”增加了83分，上升了四个位次，列全国第21位，首次居西北之首。

此外，年度比赛也取得了好成绩，获得第一名6个，第二名10个，第三名8个，4——8名14个。有8个项目31人次参加国家队集训，其中5个项目32人次代表中国队到7个国家和地区进行交流和比赛，在各类国际比赛中共获金牌2枚、银牌1枚，铜牌2枚，4——8名3个。

“七运会”结束后，省体委既着手对参赛1997年“八运会”的有关问题进行了研究，并于10月在白银召开了“全省体育改革发展与研讨会”，对参赛第八届全国运动会的项目进行了论证分析，并做出了相应的战略部署，提出了“奋力拼博八运会，决心挤身二十位；重点项目夺金牌，一般项目争奖牌；成绩再上新台阶”的奋斗目标和“缩短战线，突出重点，扬长避短，发挥优势，效益设项，稳步发展”的指导思想以及完成大赛任务的对策和措施，从而为完成“八运会”任务保持全省竞技体育的持续发展奠定了理论和策略基础。

二、群众体育蓬勃发展

全省体育人口达710万人，占总人口的30.7%，施标学校达17594所，施标率为92.4%，比1992年增长9.8%，达标学生214.2万人，达标率为95.7%，比1992年上升1%，通渭、皋兰等14个县（市、区）达到达标先进标准。建成4个省级体育先进县、市、区（玉门市、山丹县、陇西县、北道区），44个先进乡（镇）。白银公司、兰州一中、省农民体协等36个单位获国家级群体先进；傅延民、郝兰芳等20名获国家级群体先进个人，并受到国家体委的表彰；三所中学（天水三中、兰州三十三中、武威二中）被评为全国贯彻《学校体育工作条例》先进学校；天水一中、武威六中、兰州六中、靖远二中被评为全国体育传统项目学校先进集体；四个乡镇在全国亿万农民健身活动评选中上了光荣榜。

在全国第七届中学生运动会上，获银牌2枚、铜牌3枚、4—8名26个，团体总分居全国第11位。

残疾人体育迅速发展。在1993年全国残疾人田径、射击赛中，田径获金牌16枚、银牌7枚、铜牌1枚，团体总分居分区赛第一。在射击赛中获1金、4银、1铜的好成绩，在羽毛球赛中夺得LBA2组男子双打亚军、男子单打第4、第5名。

成功地组织了“争奥运迎七运全民健身”活动。据统计，全省城乡共组织丰富多彩的体育竞赛60419次，约984万人次参加。4月3日，兰州市体委同有关部门组织了“兰州市青少年支持北京申办2000年奥运会万人签名”活动，全市30000多名青少年参加。

职工体育有了新发展，逐步实现了活动时间业余化、活动形式大众化、活动经费系统化、管理工作规范化的目标。此外社区体育也有新的启动。

三、体育竞赛进步明显

组织正常比赛8项9次1412人次，承办全国七运会男子柔道竞赛1次176人次，组织辅助性竞赛21项23次2554人次，业余队参加全国比赛21项24次303人次，及单项协会举办各类竞赛81次10873人次，其中承办全国比赛2项2次400人次，省级竞赛42次4094人次。

充分发挥社会办竞赛的优势，使竞赛工作逐步向社会化迈进。省围棋协会以兰州市网点经营开发公司为赞助单位，全面承担了全省竞赛、业余训练和组队参加全国各类比赛任务。省自行车协会以"兰州民百股份有限公司"为依托，举办了"民百杯"自行车系列赛。省羽协、舞协、台协、门协、乒协、武协等也通过各种渠道举办各种形式的比赛。

行业体育竞赛范围不断扩大，已有9个行业系统举办竞赛，有的还形成了制度。

竞赛效益有所提高。在竞赛安排上突出重点，研究制定了田径竞赛制度，传统项目比赛制度，做到了小学、中学、业余体校层层有比赛、层层有重点，同时，改革了竞赛方法，计分和奖励办法，调动了训练单位的积极性。1993年共有18人打破4项省最高纪录，有14人被批准为运动健将，15人被批准为一级运动员，有4项创全省最好成绩。

裁判队伍发展迅速，全年共有46人被批准为一级裁判员，11人被批准为国家级裁判员，16人分别担任了"七运会"各项比赛的裁判工作。

四、业余训练人才辈出

全省业余训练基本形成了一个以体育运动学校为最高层次、重点体校和重点项目训练点及普通业余体校互相衔接的业余训练体系，培养输送了一批优秀体育人才。在"七运会"中，获决赛权的209名运动员中，业余体校输送的就达172人，占决赛总人数的82%。获金牌运动员李文凯、刘学海、朱正军、李向东、郑生荣、李茹红、杨春香、李彦新等均是各级业余体校培养输送的。

1993年共有10个代表队参加6项全国青少年比赛，取得了12个第一名、9个第二名、19个第三名的好成绩，从而培养和锻炼了后备人才。

加强了体育运动校建设。对全省10所运动校进行了合格评估，全部达到了国家规定的标准。同时对1025名在校学生进行了六门课程统考，及格率均达90%以上。

五、体育改革不断深化

一是在体育社会化方面进一步开拓了路子。鼓励和引导体育社团向实体化或自收自支方向发展。目前已逐步减少了对省级单位运动协会的投入，部分体协已基本做到自收自支。动员社会各部门、各方面办体育，多方面、多渠道筹措体育经费，为体育事业的发展开拓了新路；二是将竞争激励和风险机制引入运动训练中去。参赛七运会上至省体委领导，下至基层干部和教练领队均层层承包任务，并落实到具体人，按不同职别交纳不同数量风险金，奖罚分明。这一措施改变了"吃大锅饭"的现象，增强了广大干部的风险意识和竞争意识，调动了抓运动训练的积极性，收到了良好的效果；三是注重机关职能转变，加强了宏观指导、省体委领导机关开始由"办体育"向"管体育"转变，省体委领导同志主持的"西北竞技体育效益"研究获国家体委科技进步奖。在"甘肃体育发展与改革研讨会"上，对全省竞技体育的发展战略以及项目的设置也进行了改革。

1993年是"七运年"、"奥运年"，体育宣传围绕这两大任务展开，取得了良好的效果。

此外，还较好地组织了省体工二大队搬迁和七里河体育场改造工程。体育科研、体育教育、体育对外交流、体育经营创收等工作也取得了较好的成绩。

卫　生

医疗卫生事业发展概况

基本情况

1993年全省共有医疗卫生机构4141个，比1992年减少51个。其中县及县以上医院352个，乡镇卫生院1547个，卫生防疫站104个，妇幼保健站93个，医学科研所9个，专科防治所28个，药品检验所56个，高等医学院校2所，医学大专班3个，中等医药学校14所，县卫生学校18所，卫生职业技术学校19所。全省医院病床总数51293张，比1992年增加2174张，平均每千人拥有床位2.18张，卫生工作人员94723人，比1992年增加2250人，卫生人员中有专业技术人员77807人，平均每千人拥有卫生技术人员3.31人，其中每千人口有医师1.08人，有护士0.74人。1993年全省共报告乙类传染病31206例，发病率199.02/10万，比1992年下降27.57%。没有发生甲类传染病。以县为单位全省"四苗"全程接种覆盖率97%以上。1993年省级行政事业单位享受公费医疗的有115221人，公费医疗支出1863万元，年人均支出166.11元，比1992年多支13.60元。省级综合医院平均每一门急诊人次费用为24.1元，每一出院病人医疗费用为1799元。

卫生改革

1993年主要抓了五件事：

1.在保证基本医疗服务的前提下，普遍开展了适应不同层次需求的服务，如专家门诊、专科专病门诊、家庭温馨病房、特殊服务、院外服务、业余服务、保健咨询服务等。按照"一院两制"的管理办法，开办分院，扩大服务领域。1993年仅省属医疗单位开办"一院两制"医疗机构6个，筹资260余万元，购置大型设备5台(件)，诊治患者1万余人次，纯收入80多万元。

2.制定了《甘肃省一、二、三级综合医院评审标准》等配套文件，完成了医院分级管理试点工作，对4所医院进行了评审，确定酒泉地区人民医院为三级乙等医院，金塔县人民医院、敦煌市人民医院为二级甲等医院。酒泉地区卫生处确定总寨乡中心卫生院为一级甲等医院。

3. 兴办各种经济实体，全省各级卫生事业单位共创办各种类型经济实体43个，从业人员495人，年利润264万多元。

4. 14个地、市、州均制定了公费医疗制度改革意见或办法，多数开始实施。卫生厅与有关部门共同制定了《甘肃省学生和幼儿园儿童住院医疗保险办法》，在全省范围内开办了中、小学学生和幼儿园儿童住院医疗保险业务。

5. 省直有16个单位被批准出台住房制度改革实施方案，并开始全面实施。

农村卫生建设 **甘肃省政府把农村卫生"三项建设"列为全省重点工作之一。主要措施和成效：**

1. 重点改造建设了210所乡镇卫生院。年初省政府召开全省乡镇卫生院建设天水现场会议，现场参观了天水市5所乡镇卫生院，总结交流了1991年以来全省乡镇卫生院建设的基本经验，对在卫生院建设中做出突出成绩的75个先进集体和102名先进个人给予表彰奖励。会后，各地继续发动社会筹资修建、改造卫生院，全省共落实建设资金1884.3万元，新建、扩建和维修改造乡镇卫生院210所，完成房屋建筑面积84841平方米。

2. 通过"几个一点"的办法，筹集防保机构建设资金490万元，用于10个县卫生防疫站和7个县妇幼保健站的改造建设，完成建筑面积17577平方米。

3. 重点扶持民族地区发展卫生事业。1993年7月，副省长陈绮玲率省政府5部门主要领导，亲临甘南藏族自治州参加农牧区卫生工作会议，决定从1993年起设立专项经费，每年100万元，连续3年，为甘南州培训卫生技术人才，购置医疗设备；为两个牧业县购置两辆综合服务车，开展巡回医疗；省城7所大医院为甘南7县实行对口技术支援。

4. 为加强对村级卫生人员的规范化管理，组织完成了全省第三次乡村医生业务知识统一考试，17000多名乡医参加统考。对考试合格的4666人发给《乡村医生证》，8233人发给《乡村医士证》。

1993年，村卫生所和医疗点恢复发展到22075个，占行政村总数的92.8%。

传染病、地方病防治

1993年，计划免疫在"四苗"接种率以县为单位达到85%的基础上，重点抓了消灭脊髓灰质炎工作。1——4月，各地先后开展了两轮脊灰强化免疫活动，投服率分别达到97.94%和97.93%。10月，省政府在张掖召开全省消灭脊髓灰质炎工作会议，在兰州召开全省儿童计划免疫工作协调小组会，动员部署消灭脊髓灰质炎工作，要求糖丸投服工作做到"村不漏户，户不漏人，送药到手，看服到口，咽下再走"。11月20日，省政府转发了省卫生厅《关于全省开展消灭脊髓灰质炎强化免疫日活动的安排意见》，并拨款50万元用于开展这项活动。12月5日全国强化免疫日，省、地、县、乡主要领导亲临接种点，与防疫人员一起为250万4岁以下儿童投服疫苗。1993年全省脊髓灰质炎发病确诊6例，发病率比去年降低40%。

传染病防治管理工作进一步得到重视和加强。据统计，1——11月全省共发生乙类传染病31206例，较去年同期下降27.57%。其中肝炎、痢疾、伤寒、麻诊、流脑、猩红热、黑热病等11个病种的发病率较去年同期下降，淋病、梅毒、乙脑、流行性出血热及斑疹伤寒等5个病种发病率较去年同期上升。流行性出血热疫情发生早，来势猛，有10个县(市)、60个乡(镇)发病1051例。其中岷县的发病及死亡人数分别占全省发病及死亡人数的76.6%和23.81%。岷县疫情发生后，卫生厅和地县有关业务部门先后组派15批人员赴岷县等地指导防治工作，由于抢救及时，治疗得当，病死率比去年同期下降34.06%。同时，由于采取了以灭鼠为中心的综合防治措施，使该县疫情呈下降趋势。

碘缺乏病防治是1993年地方病防治工作的中心任务，为此，省政府于10月召开了全省消除碘缺乏病工作会议，在全省范围内建立健全了碘盐监测网，加强碘盐市场监管，碘盐普及率由去年的60%提高到80%以上。制定了《甘肃省2000年消除碘缺乏危害规划纲要》，我省已被确定为国际组织联合支援我国消除碘缺乏病的三个受援省之一。

妇幼卫生

1993年妇幼保健工作围绕《九十年代中国儿童发展规划纲要》，以执行妇幼卫生合作项目为突破口，推广适宜技术，提倡母乳喂养，创建爱婴医院，搞好计划生育技术服务，促进各项妇幼卫生工作的开展。省妇幼保健院通过国家的评估，取得了"爱婴医院"称号。妇幼卫生合作项目进展顺利，效果显著，基层妇幼卫生机构工作条件改善，人员素质及服务质量提高，群众的自我保健意识增强。项目实施四年来，孕产妇死亡率由1989年的31万下降到19万，婴儿死亡率由55‰下降到29‰。

中医工作

1993年3月，省政府在天水召开了全省中医工作会议，讨论提出了加快中医事业改革和发展的意见。省卫生厅划拨51万元专款，重点扶持了12所中医(藏医)医院的专科专病建设。举办了中医医院分级管理学习班，确定了省、地两级试点医院。省中医学校开办了农村不包分配中医中专班，招收学员49名；继续开展中医师带徒工作，给32位老中医药人员配备45名中青年医生；设立"甘肃省中医药学皇甫谧基金奖"，经过评选，12名德高望重的专家荣获皇甫谧中医药学基金奖和荣誉证书。制定颁布了《甘肃省气功医疗管理若干规定实施细则(试行)》,规范了全省气功医疗活动的开展。

纠正行业不正之风

重点对"红包"、"处方回扣"、"药品回扣"和乱收费等四个问题开展了专项治理。年初,省卫生厅抽调20余人,分3组,历时2个月,对全系统医德医风情况作了专题调查。从3月起,先后制定公布了《关于开展医德规范教育的通知》、《关于医务人员违反职业道德的处罚规定》、《关于立即停止医疗单位根据检查申请单给医务人员提取回扣的通知》、《关于进一步加强医疗单位药品采购管理工作的通知》和《关于卫生行业清理纠正乱收费的意见》等五个文件。由各级卫生行政部门精心组织落实,逐项进行治理。经年底检查验收取得了一定成效。据对省、地、县医院不完全统计,3——12月医务人员拒收"红包"401人次,涉及金额8.26万元;收受非法回扣现象得到明显遏制,如兰州医学院第一附院药剂科一年上交医院药品让利回扣款81.3万元;取消18个不合理收费项目,查处了一些乱收费问题,金额40余万元;对一些违反职业道德的人和事公开曝光。

其他工作

1.开展了打击制售假劣药品的专项斗争,全年共出动人员5116人次,检查医疗单位及药品经营企业6992家,查处各种违法案件290起,假劣药品总值56.5万元,罚没款总额20多万元。

2.开展食品质量监督大检查,1——9月共监测食品8500件,合格7152件,合格率84.1%。1——9全省共发生食物中毒11起373人,死亡1人,与去年相比中毒人数减少50.8%。公共场所卫生采样合格率为81.1%,化妆品抽验合格率为76.92%。

3.完成了1992——1993年度省卫生厅医疗卫生科技进步奖的评奖工作,93项科研成果获奖,其中一等奖2项,二等奖31项,三等奖60项。有15项获省科委科技进步奖。

4.邀请美国6名眼科医生在兰州、天水市和夏河县工作,接诊病人1553人,手术129例。卫生厅与农业部农牧渔业国际合作公司合办"柬埔寨金边中国友谊医院",已正式开业。

(乔公先)

教　育

甘肃教育事业

【教育发展概况】1993年,全省教育战线认真学习、贯彻《中国教育改革和发展纲要》和省委、省政府《关于贯彻落实中国教育改革和发展纲要的意见》精神,确立在社会主义市场经济体制下教育改革和发展的思路、政策措施与目标任务,按照大力加强基础教育,积极发展职业技术教育、高等教育和成人教育的原则,进一步解放思想,加快改革步伐,各级各类教育又有了新发展。

1993年,全省共有幼儿园717所,学前班6652个,接受学前教育的儿童34.6万人,其中六周岁接受学前教育的儿童27.4万人,占六周岁儿童总数的65%;有盲聋哑学校11所,小学附设特教班57个,在校(班)学生1721人;小学23948所,在校学生250万人,学龄儿童入学率为95.75%,其中少数民族学龄儿童入学率为85%,小学毕业生升初中的比例为82.65%;有独立初中1140所,在校学生71.6万人,初中毕业生升普通高中的比例为26.31%;有完全中学460所,在校学生15.65万人。与上年相比,幼儿园增加122所,学前班增加308个,接受学龄前教育的儿童增加了3.20万人,六周岁儿童接受学前教育的比例提高了5.90个百分点;特殊教育学校增加了2所,特教班增加了20个,残疾少年、儿童在校学生增加了694人;小学学龄儿童入学率提高了0.47个百分点,其中民族地区学龄儿童入学率提高了1个百分点。有普通中等专业学校115所,在校学生5.51万人,职业中学191所,在校学生4.34万人,技工学校74所,在校学生2.63万人,与上年相比,职业中学增加2 所,技工学校增加7所,在校学生均略有减少;高中阶段职业技术教育和普通高中招生之比为0.91∶1。有高等学校17所,在校本专科生4.05万人,研究生1027人,本专科和研究生在校人数分别比上年增加5923人和75人。有成人中等专业学校96所,在校学生3.34万人;成人高等学校21所,在校学生1.20万人,成人中专比上年减少2所,在校学生增加2081人;成人高校在校生增加3318人。

【普及九年义务教育的新进展】1993年,肃南、会宁两县普及初等义务教育,高台、金塔、安西3县普及初级中等义务教育。至此,全省54个县(市、区)普及了初等义务教育,14个县(市、区)普及了初级中等义务教育。根据《中国教育和改革发展纲要》精神,结合甘肃实际,在实施"八五"规划的基础上,按照国家教委实施义务教育规划到县、落实到乡的原则,修定了《甘肃省普及九年义务教育年度规划》,并提出了具体贯彻实施意见,力争全省在本世纪末基本普及初等义务教育,占人口70%地区普及初级中等义务教育。按照《义务教育法》实施细则的要求,省上先后制定了《义务教育目标责任制》、《义务教育入学通知书制度》、《九年义务教育评估验收及表彰奖励制度》、《教育经费筹措、改善办学条件情况通报制度》、《教育检查汇报和督导评估制度》等一系列配套政策措施，从制度上保证了《义务教育法》的实施。在小学和初中全面实施《九年义务教育课程方案》。制定了甘肃省实施《课程方案》的意见，确定自1993——1994新学年开始，全省全日制小学、初级中学的起始年级一律开始执行国家教委印发的《课程计划》，制定了各种学制初中、小学的课程安排表，并给各级教研部门和学校配发了教学大纲，对各地教师进行了义务教育教材的培训。

【贫困地区小学教育项目终期评估】 1993年，省教委对项目县进行了终期抽查评估。评估结果表明，项目工作实施4年来取得了显著成效。一是全省64所项目学校的办学条件从根本上得到了改善，成为全省边远贫困地区的示范性学校。项目学校建设共投资487.8万元(其中中方投入407.75万元，联合国儿童基金会投入80.05万元)。二是通过多种形式的教师培训活动，使教师队伍的素质有明显改善，教师的教学教研能力有了较大提高。三是项目学校在贫困地区发挥了带头作用和辐射作用；促进了当地初等义务教育的普及。

【初高中毕业会考制度逐步完善】 1993年，全省贯彻调整后的教学计划，完善会考制度，初、高中毕业会考工作全面展开。省教委根据《中国教育改革和发展纲要》及国家教委《关于稳步推进普通高中毕业会考工作的意见》，制订了一系列政策措施。经省政府同意，报国家教委批准，实行高中毕业会考制度后的首届毕业生，1994年将按新的高考科目设置参加高考。在高校录取新生时，参考高中会考成绩。同时，省教委与省人事局、省劳动局、省军区司令部联合发文规定，从1994年起，在招工、招干、征兵时承认省教委统一颁发的高中毕业证书和会考成绩。

【中小学师资队伍建设取得成效】 1993年，为了加快初中教师学历培训步伐，开展了函授、卫星电视教育、自学考试三沟通的专科学历培训。"三沟通"是教师培训工作改革的重要举措，是一种新的培训模式。省教委印发了《关于加快我省初中教师学历培训步伐的实施意见》，成立了甘肃省初中教师学历培训领导小组。全省报名参加学习的学员共17200多人。8月，严格按照国家级考试要求，进行了首次期终考试，平均及格率为63%。

全省开展了中、小学教师继续教育、骨干教师培训等各种形式的培训工作，加强了县、乡、校三级培训网络的建设，有组织地进行了中小学在职教师的业务进修、教研活动、基本功训练等。1993年，全省教师进修院校和师范院校计划内学历教育招收中小学教师3390人。由于新教师补充和多种渠道的学历培训，中小学教师的学历合格率有了新的提高。小学教师学历合格率达到81.8%，初中54.1%，高中42.8%，分别比上年提高了1.5、3.7和1.3个百分点。

【职业技术学校的规范化建设】 1993年，省教委在上年对普通中专办学水平评估的基础上，根据甘肃实际，对职业中学的评估标准、评估程序等进行了完善和调整，全省新上等级学校12所，达到B级标准的骨干职业学校已达75所，占全省职业中学总数的39.3%，其中21所B级以上学校的校均规模达到600人以上，办学水平和办学效益有了较大幅度的提高。

【职业技术学校的专业布局和专业设置的调整改造】 1993年，按照社会主义市场经济的发展和城乡产业结构调整、乡镇企业迅速崛起的要求，省教委组织对全省普通中专及各地职业中学的专业设置情况进行了全面调查和研讨，布置和安排了职业高中和普通中专专业布局和专业设置的调整、改造工作。要求县镇和相当一部分农村职业高中的专业，按照当地乡镇企业的需要进行调整和充实，初步形成对口培养适用人才的专业布局。农业类专业经过不断改造和完善，在培养目标、教学内容和方法等方面更加适应发展"高产、优质、高效"农业和进行家庭综合生产经营的要求。城市职业高中的专业(工种)设置适应发展和调整二、三产业、行业和地区经济结构的需要。要求普通中专结合国家教委新颁布的《中华人民共和国普通中等专业学校专业目录》进行专业调整和归并。1993年秋季，由省上直接指导的8个试点学校的乡企类专业已开始招生。

【职业技术教育改革步伐加快】 中共甘肃省委、省人民政府下发了《关于改革发展职业技术教育若干问题的意见》及《甘肃省职业技术教育五年规划纲要》(1993——1998)，要求到"八五"末，高中阶段的职业技术学校招生数与普通高中招生数之比达到1：1，到本世纪末达到5.5：4.5。特别是从甘肃实际出发，制定、提出了三个项目计划，包括：百所重点职业中学建设计划；职教产业开发的"6156"计划，即在全省范围内建立职教系统的6大产业基地(高效、优质、高产农业，林果业，农副产品加工业，农业社会化服务体系，城乡第三产业，高新技术产业)，100所职业技术学校年创收超过50万元，全省职校年创收总额达到6000万元以上；职教为乡镇企业服务计划，从而使未来五年甘肃职教发展有了一个实事求是的奋斗目标。此外，还在办学、招生、就业、分配、校办产业开发等方面制定了有力的措施，为职业技术教育的改革与发展奠定了基础。

【高等学校新生缴费上学试点】 1993年，经省人民政府批准，兰州医学院、兰州工业高等专科学校进行了新生缴费上学的改革试点。即从上述两校的1993年国家招生计划中确定了200名本科生、150名专科生国家任务计划作为试点，所招学生在其国家任务的计划形式不变、迁转粮户关系、毕业后由国家统一分配和培养经费仍由省财政按现行办法拨付的前提下，实行缴费上学，缴费标准与自费生相同。学校所收费用全部纳入学校财政，主要用于改善办学条件。同时促进学校积极进行奖学金、贷学金的改革，开展勤工助学活动。

【高校招生计划和专业设置调整】1993年全省招收本专科学生15391人，其中省属高等学校招生8661人。为满足本省经济建设的需求，特别是对工科类专门人才的需求，1993年全省高等学校又安排了省列调节性招生计划2095人，比去年增加105.9%，其中给部委属高等学校安排825人。同时进行了依托有条件的成人高等学校发展我省普通高等工程教育的尝试，1993年通过招生计划挂靠兰州工业高等专科学校的办法，依托兰炼职工大学，开办了机械制造和机电一体化专业，招生90人。

进一步调整了专业结构和层次结构，拓宽了现有专业的服务面向，以适应本省地方经济的发展和产业结构调整。在师范院校内开办了非师范专业，1993年在西北师范大学等5所师范院校设置了化工工艺、应用电子技术、计算机应用与维护、电算会计与统计、外贸英语等32个本省经济建设和社会发展所需要的非师范类专业；将西北师范大学计算机教育(本科)专业调整为计算机及应用(本科)专业，其培养方向调整为为本省以经济建设为中心的社会主义现代化建设培养计算机及应用方面的应用人才；在甘肃政法学院等校新设了经济法(本科)、侦察学(本科)和中医食疗专科等4个专业。

【“产学研联合开发工程”取得新进展】1993年，省教委会同省经贸委、科委等部门在调整“产学研”领导班子，开展调查研究，编印《甘肃省科技优势指南》、《高校科技成果汇编》、《企业难题汇编》等配套资料的同时，组织高校走出去，请进来，深入企业，了解学校，互通“有无”，联合攻关。当年，仅西北师范大学、甘肃工业大学、兰州铁道学院、兰州医学院4所院校，即从社会各界的工矿企业获得横向开发及研究课题90多项，合同金额700余万元，使企业提高了效益，学校得到了资助，也促进了成果转化，企业、学校双向受益。

【高校参与、支持农村教育综合改革见成效】1993年，全省17所高校，投入较多人力、物力和财力，分别对11个贫困、对口实验县进行了人才培养、培训和学校建设、科研开发等物质和技术的支援。西北师范大学、甘肃农业大学、甘肃联合大学接受培养大专以上各类人才2000余名，编印多门类近百项成套技术培训资料15万份，举办现场培训、专题讲座600多场次，培训农村技术骨干万余人。兰州大学、西北师范大学、甘肃农业大学、兰州医学院等，除派人下乡巡回开展学术交流、技术服务外，还提供50多万元的仪器设备，捐赠图书资料3万余册，课桌凳百余套，解决了农村中、小学的急需。甘肃农业大学大力开展科技咨询和示范，使当地农民人均收入由220元提高到400元，初步改变了贫困面貌。甘肃农业大学承担完成的“河东地区‘吨粮田’、‘双千田’”成效显著，年底已通过技术鉴定，达到国内领先水平。兰州大学、西北师范大学为当地企业技术革新改造提供技术服务，提高了产品质量，新产品代替了旧产品。

【学位授权点有所增加】根据国务院学位委员会部署，甘肃省高校新增硕士点1个，博士生指导教师14名，其中兰州大学12名，西北师范大学、甘肃农业大学各1名。至此，全省高校共有硕士点123个，博士点19个，博士生指导教师48名。

经国务院学位委员会审查批准，授予甘肃政法学院学士学位授予权。全省10所本科院校均成为学士学位授予单位。

【农村扫盲和实用技术培训广泛开展】1993年，全省农村成人教育抓发展求实效，为地方经济建设服务。全年扫盲23.53万人，比上年增加3.41万人，完成责任指标的131.13%；又有7个县非文盲率达到85%以上，全省青壮年非文盲率达到85%的县总数达到45个；高标准扫盲县、市7个(待验收)；青壮年文盲率由上年的21.6%下降到18.6%。农民技术培训学校发展到3233所，比上年增加977所，增长43.31%。其中乡农民文化技术学校发展到882所，增加37所，增长4.37；招生57.79万人，增长31.9%；毕业(结业)51.11万人；在校学员40.26万人，比上年增长27.2%。村农民文化技术学校发展到2313所，增加928所，增长67%；招生40.72万人，增长311%；毕(结)业41.20万人，增长110.2%；在校学员22.74万人，增长183.2%。

【燎原计划实施情况】“燎原计划”实施工作有了进一步发展，“燎原苹啊笔痊断缬啥5个增加到195个，增长200%；随项目进行技术培训10万多人；论证确立新开发项目17个。据4个地区统计，“燎原计划”项目年产值2701.26万元，利税294.45万元，群众收益310.15万元。

【促进全省成人高中等教育为经济建设服务】1993年，全省高、中等成人教育在提高质量、更好地为经济建设服务方面采取了一系列措施。省教委、省计委、省人事局根据市场经济的需要，发出了《关于处理好当前成人高等教育改革中12个政策性问题的通知》，进一步明确从甘肃实际出发，把为乡镇企业、中小型企业和农村服务作为改革和发展甘肃成人高等教育的重点，出台了有关支持和照顾政策。在普通高校、成人高校开办了第二专业专科学历教育，在广播电视大学试办以专科为主的基础段教育。根据甘肃农村、乡镇企业以及部分关键岗位对人才的特殊需要，试行了由用人单位(地区)委托，培养急需、短缺人才的办法。全省14所普通高校、成人高考共招生4000余人。为理顺成人高、中等学历教育质量调控、服务机制，成立了“甘肃省成人教育质量服务中心”，全面加强质量管理。全年对成人高、中等学校进行了4次统(抽)考。

【严格成人学历教育颁证制度】制订了“全国成人高等教育统一证书”的验印审批制度，验发高、中等学历教育毕业证。审批核报了4所高等专科学校夜大函授教育和甘肃农业大学的函授部。根据目前市场经济需要核批了一批新专业。论证了省党校即将成立的“甘肃市场经济管理干部学院”。3所普通高校成立了成人教育学院。新建了兰州阿语成人中专，调整了原省机械职工中专，组建了甘肃成人中等专业学校，强化了部分学校为地方经济服务的机能。

【职工教育与社会力量办学的制度建设】1993年，全省岗位培训以完善制度，加快岗位规范标准建设为重点，取得了可喜成绩，全年培训60多万人次。

进一步完善社会力量办学制度，加强管理，保证质量，提高社会效益。省教委起草了《社会力量办学管理条例》，制订了规范的科学管理制度。对已批准的社会办学进行重新登记，对不符合条件的进行相应的处理，社会力量办学开始走向规范管理轨道。

【办学条件又有新的改善】1993年，全省地方教育总投入13.82亿元，其中教育事业费支出为8.30亿元，教育基建投资为4140万元，分别比上年增长12.01%和5.84%。贯彻国家教委和国家计委《关于全面消除和杜绝中小学危房的规定》，全省多渠道筹措改善办学条件经费2.1亿元，新建、改建、维修中小学校舍66.1平方米，添置课桌6.6万双人套，全省中小学危房比例由上年的3.86%下降到3.79%。继续加强教育费附加的征收管理工作。全年征收教育费附加1.20亿元，其中城市4573万元，农村7456万元。各学校积极开展勤工俭学育人富校活动，加快校办产业发展，中小学勤工俭学开展面达到90%，比上年增长5个百分点，总收入4000万元，生均收入11.4元，分别增长20%。高等学校校办产业发展到177个，其中高新科技产业107个，纯收入达到1000多万元，比上年翻了一番。在教学仪器设备配套工作中，继续实行“筹二奖一”的原则，各地自筹150万元，完成全年配备400万元仪器设备任务。全省92%以上的小学配备了“两箱三仪”，比上年提高了2个百分点；80%以上的独立初中达到理科仪器三类配套标准，比上年提高近20个百分点。全省新建教育电视台、站7座，总数已达26座。师范院校标准化建设稳步推进，世界银行给甘肃的2000万美元贷款，经过6年实施，已完成95%，取得明显成效。5所师专和23所中师基本完成基建规模，师范院校办学条件有了较大改善。

全省教育经费的投入虽然实现了“两个增长”，但公用经费继续呈下降趋势，改善办学条件所需经费的缺口依然很大，教育投入与事业发展之间的矛盾仍很尖锐。对甘肃这样一个经济、文化不发达的省份来讲，如何采取切实有效的措施，多渠道筹措教育经费，加快改善办学条件的步伐，促进教育的改革与发展，是当前和今后一个时期所面临的艰巨任务。

(马光荣)

文化工作

文化工作概述

省文化厅厅长

张炳玉

1993年，全省文化工作坚持以党的十四大精神和建设有中国特色的社会主义理论为指针，解放思想，转变观念，开拓创新，以文化体制改革为突破口，全力以赴地开展第四届中国艺术节的筹备工作，各项业务工作取得显著的成绩。全省文化工作在服务于建立社会主义市场经济体制的新形势下，逐步探索繁荣、发展文化事业的路子。

文化体制改革工作

《甘肃省文化事业单位改革的若干意见》由省委办公厅、省政府办公厅转发，省文化厅又制定了《甘肃省文化事业单位改革的若干意见实施细则》。全省文化系统认真贯彻文件精神，推进了文化体制改革的进程。文化事业单位，特别是艺术表演团体的改革得到深化。北道区剧团、正宁县剧团、高台县剧团、榆中县文工团、靖远县剧团、金昌市艺术团、张掖七一剧团等一大批剧团，在经营方式、内部机制、创作演出、以文补文方面，都结合自己的实际，迈出了步子，取得了明显的成效。其中北道区剧团推行内部经营承包的改革措施，实行承包人风险抵押，自主经营，自负盈亏，逐年减少财政补贴，推向市场。从7月份推行改革以来，起步平稳，运转正常。剧团内部实行优化组合，层层承包，职工有了风险意识，压力变动力，使整个剧团有了活力和凝聚力，半年演出125场，演出收入4万元，超额完成了全年任务。

第四届中国艺术节筹备工作

筹备工作将剧目生产放在首

位，本着“荟萃艺术精品，弘扬民族文化”的主旨，从创作，评审、排练三个环节上下功夫，成立了创作一、二、三部，组织了特邀剧作者队伍和专家评审组，对创作和征集到的剧本进行筛选、评审，从中精选出10个作为重点剧目，经过加工提高，已陆续开始排练。各地区也出现了一些好的剧目。艺术节的开幕式设计经过征集方案、考察借鉴、集体构思、分头创作，题为《黄河潮》的开幕式总体方案已经完成。文物精品展、民间民俗美术展、书画摄影展的设计已经完成，开始征集展品。大型群众文化活动场景和群众文艺组台演出正在筹备之中。供艺术节使用的文化系统6个场馆经过考察，提出了扩建、维修和改造方案，招标建设工作已全面铺开。

戏剧艺术工作

甘肃省陇剧团1991年创作演出的大型现代陇剧《天下第一鼓》，在文化部第三届“文华奖”评选中荣获“文华新剧目奖”和“文华导演奖”，这是甘肃首次获得专业舞台艺术的政府最高奖。省政府给予省陇剧团10万元重奖。甘肃省杂技团、甘肃省陇剧团、敦煌艺术剧院同时在香港演出，引起轰动。其中，省杂剧团3个月商业性演出356场，演出纯收入20多万港元。全省80个专业艺术表演团体全年演出1.38万场（农村演出1.12万场），观众2402万人次。演出及其他收入506.3万元，平均经费自给率22.67%。

群众文化工作

全省15个群众艺术馆、83个文化馆全年举办展览402个，组织文艺演出722次，举办训练班256次，结业0.93万人，放录像2.38万场。1992年，省文化厅提出了建设丝绸之路文化长廊工程的规划，东起泾川县窑店乡，西到安西县柳园镇，中间经过9地、市，24个县、市、区，172个乡、镇（街道），全长1900多公里。计划经过8年奋斗，逐步建成，辐射全省。1993年修订下发了丝路文化长廊建设计划和实施意见，召开了全省丝绸之路文化长廊建设座谈会，带动了长廊沿线各地的区段建设，各地都制订了工程规划，进行试点和工程的起步工作。1993年，在文化部组织实施的争创全国标准文化馆活动中，酒泉市、武威市、山丹县、庆阳县文化馆被评为全国标准文化馆。通渭县被文化部命名为“中国书画艺术之乡”，镇原县、庆阳县被命名为“中国民间艺术之乡”。1993年，在全国、全省群众文化比赛活动中获得14项奖。

公共图书馆工作

全省86个公共图书馆总藏书量664.8万册，全年接待读者243万人，图书流通234.8万册，为读者举办各种活动465次，参加人数24万人。召开了全省图书馆工作会议，研究部署了全省图书馆事业深化改革的问题，安排了全省地县图书馆定级评估试点工作。会后对16个地县图书馆进行了定级评估。由省文化厅等单位共同发起的“捐献百万册书”活动，收到捐书64.40万册、捐款19.14万元。全部书、款都已分配到县图书馆。

文物保护和考古发掘工作

狠抓文物安全管护工作，重点整治了礼县、西和县盗掘古墓葬事件。积极做好古建筑抢救维修工作，榆林窟加固维修、炳灵寺加固维修、大地湾遗址抢险加固、天梯山石窟原址修复分别完成了当年计划、前期工作、设计方案、省级论证。完成省级和全国重点文物的公布及呈报工作。公布了第五批（217处）省级重点文物保护单位，呈报了第四批全国重点文物保护单位。配合基本建设，完成田野考古发掘任务。清理发掘了武威塔儿湾西夏遗址7000多平方米，出土200件西夏瓷器，在酒泉西沟发掘了3座晋代墓，出土铜器、陶器100多件，在玉门白土梁发掘了3座晋墓，出土文物70多件。全省50个博物馆，馆藏文物29万件。办文物陈列45个、展览64个，参观人数60.8万人（其中外宾6.9万人），总收入93.2万元（其中门票收入39.9万元）。全省文物保护管理单位25个，参观人数63.6万人（其中外宾4.2万人），总收入430.8万元（门票收入410.66万元）。

电影工作

贯彻广电部关于深化电影行业机制改革精神，召开了全省电影工作会议，制订了《甘肃省关于深化电影行业机制改革的若干意见》，由省政府批转。加强了电影市场的管理，制定了管理办法，放开了电影票价。全省完成观众8611.9万人次，放映22.4万场次，放映收入1911.2万元，发行收入1038.2万元。电影生产完成了8部27本集影视片的拍摄。

文化科技工作

组织完成了《甘肃省科技志》中“舞台、电影科技”和“文物保护科技”的编写任务。

文化市场管理工作

全省现有各类文化管理经营网点14000余个，其中歌舞厅509家；卡拉OK厅309家；书报刊网点2835个；印刷厂667家；音像制品批发、零售、出租放映点3200个；台球室2291家，4061台；电子游戏机室829家，3824台；营业性艺术培训36家；文化个体户647家。初步形成了包括传统演出市场、书报刊市场、电影市场、文物市场和新兴的娱乐市场、中外文化交流市场、文化艺术培训市场在内的综合性文化市场体系；初步形成了以国家为主，集体、个人为辅开发文化市场的经营格局。随着文化市场的发展，管理不断加强，全省现有县以上文化市场管理机构144个，专（兼）职管理人员369人，有文化稽查队25个，文化稽查人员883人。初步形成了省、地、县、乡四级文化市场管理网络。1992年甘肃省政府颁布了《甘肃省文化、娱乐市场管理暂行规定》,文化主管部门相继制定了配套的管理办法,使全省文化市场管理开始步入法制化、规范化的管理轨道。1993年授予西北宾馆卡拉OK歌舞厅等29个舞厅"甘肃省文明舞厅"称号。同时,西北宾馆卡拉OK歌舞厅、玉门市文化馆歌舞厅被评为全国文明娱乐厅,兰州市文化稽查队被评为全国文化市场管理先进集体,白银市文广局葛根才等3人被评为全国先进个人。

对外文化交流工作

进一步加强了对外文化交流的归口管理,制定了加强归口管理和改革的意见和办法。组织办理了15起209人次的文化出访团组的报批手续,主要有敦煌艺术剧院、省杂技团、省陇剧团赴港演出,省艺校高金荣赴加拿大和台湾进行学术交流,省群艺馆常垦赴美国举办个人摄影作品展,敦煌研究院赴日研修和参加合作保护研究等。组织协助接待来华团组8起77人次。主要有哈萨克斯坦钢铁飞车团,俄罗斯大棚马戏团等。

档案工作

1993年档案事业发展概述

省档案局局长

王爱彦

我省档案事业是1978年恢复、发展起来的,现已初具规模。截至1993年底,全省共有各级档案行政管理部门93个,各级各类档案馆117个,机关档案室9248个;拥有档案工作人员10954人,其中专职人员2501人;馆(室)档案资料总藏量达到933.68万卷。

省档案局是全省档案事业行政管理机构。现为省委、省政府直属机构,列入政府序列,归省政府办公厅管理。各地、州、市均设有档案局(处),各县、市、区设有档案局(有少数在机构改革中与有关部门合并)。各级档案行政管理部门的职责是:主管本行政区域内的档案事业,并对本行政区域内机关、团体、企业事业单位和其他组织的档案工作实行监督和指导。

依法治档初见成效。《中华人民共和国档案法》及其《实施办法》的颁布实施,为我国依法治档提供了法律依据。近几年来,我省从各方面加强了依法治档工作。首先,建立了法制机构,配备了专职人员,负责全省档案法制工作;在全省各地、县档案部门设了法制监督员,形成了全省性的法制监督网络,为有效地开展档案执法提供了组织保证。其次,大力开展档案法制宣传。采取上街宣传咨询、印发宣传材料、举办培训班、利用报刊、广播、电视等新闻媒介多种形式,宣传《档案法》和《档案法实施办法》以及其他档案法规、政策,增强了社会的档案意识和法制观念。第三,研究制订了我省档案法规体系方案,为进一步加强我省档案法制建设、增强档案立法工作的计划性、科学性与统一性打下了基础。第四,对一些违犯《档案法》的事件进行了及时有效的查处,强化了档案法律、法规的威慑作用。

职工教育上新台阶。培养一支高素质的档案专业队伍,这是我省档案事业发展的关键所在。多年来,采取统一安排、分级负责、多渠道培训、"两条腿"(专业教育、在职培训)走路、多层次(提高班和普通班)结合的方法,坚持不懈地开展职工教育,取得了显著的成效。1993年,委托兰州大学举办了在职干部档案大专班,招收学员37名;举办各种培训班10期,培训各类档案人员745名。大部分地区也都举办了各种类型的培训班。持续不断的职工教育,使我省档案干部队伍的文化结构和档案专业程度发生了很大变化。目前,全省各级档案行政管理部门和档案馆以及省级以上机关档案部门中,大专文化程度的人员已占23.7%,大专以上档案专业的人员占11.5%。

档案馆建设取得新进展。档案馆是档案工作的主体。1993年,我们采取档案馆上等升级等有力措施,加强了各级档案馆的建设,取得了四个方面的新进展:一是扩大了档案开放范围。截至1993年,全省开放档案的单位达到73个,应占开放档案单位总数的76%;开放档案的数量达170913卷,占应开放档案总数的39%。二是档案馆馆库建设成绩显著。自1985年采取省、地、县三级投资建设地、县档案馆库以来,至1993年底,已投资近1600万元,新建馆75个,占应建馆总数的76%,新建馆建筑总面积74349平方米,大大改善了档案保管条件。三是档案抢救进展迅速。据统计,我省各级档案馆保存的档案中,全国重点档案有22万卷,其中需要抢救的有14万卷。数年来,各级档案部门在有限的经费条件下,积极努力,进行抢救,至1993年,已抢救档案8.43万卷,占应抢救档案总数的60%。四是现代化管理迈开步伐。实现档案的现代化管理是档案工作适应不断发展的新形势的主要手段。全省各级档案部门在改进传统的管理方法,尽可能地向档案利用者提供高质量服务的同时,积极创造条件,购置配备电子计算机等现代化管理设施。至1993年,全省各级各类档案管理机构拥有微机116台,小型和中型机终端10个,复印机215台。省档案馆还拥有缩微摄影机8台及其辅助设备14台,形成了本省范围内设备先进、技术力量较强的缩微中心。1993年,又投资20余万元,购置了7台微机,建成了省档案馆档案管理电子计算机网络系统。为了全面提高我省档案管理的综合水平,在全省档案馆开展了档案管理上等升级工作。截至1993年，全省达标档案馆有73个，其中省一级30个，省二级36个，省三级7个，占应上等升级档案馆总数的76%。

机关和企事业单位档案工作得到加强。机关和企事业单位档案工作是国家档案工作的基础，是整个档案事业的一个有机组成部分。截至1993年，全省县级以上机关和事业单位档案室档案资料总藏量达到600万卷以上；共有档案人员9805人，其中专职档案人员1352人。在上等升级中，全省县级以上机关档案管理达标单位已有3434个；国有工业企业档案管理达标单位共有746个，其中国家一级5个，国家二级103个，省一级367个，省二级271个。为了适应新的发展形势，进一步加强了企业和经济部门的档案工作，召开了全省企业档案工作座谈会，提出了关于进一步加强企业档案工作的意见，并由省政府办公厅批转各地执行。与此同时，还对乡镇企业和三资企业档案工作的建立采取了相应的措施。

档案开发利用取得效益。保管档案的最终目的在于向社会提供利用。各级档案部门按照《档案法》的规定，采取灵活多样的方式，开展全方位服务，较好地发挥了档案的社会效益和经济效益。据1993年统计，各级各类档案馆提供档案资料265640卷(册)，利用者达23031人次。省档案局1993年编印的《档案利用效益典型事例选编》，收集了我省档案利用方面的典型事例50件，其所创造的经济效益约达3亿元。档案编研是向利用者提供高层次服务的一个重要方面。各级档案部门十分重视档案编研工作。1993年，全省共完成编研成果209种，在各项工作中发挥了重要作用，得到各方面的好评。如省档案馆配合我省“引洮”工程的重新上马，编纂了《甘肃省引洮上山水利工程概况简介》，受到省政府领导的较高评价。

学会工作气氛活跃。省档案学会是挂靠在省档案局下面的由我省档案工作者组成的群众性学术团体，是中国档案学会和省社科联合会的团体会员。截至1993年底，共有会员2085名，其中74名同时为中国档案学会会员。全省各地、州、市除少数地区正在筹备外，其他地区均已成立了档案学会。多年来，省、地两级档案学会围绕档案工作的中心任务，积极组织广大会员，开展形式多样、丰富多采的活动，在学术研究、档案宣传、业务培训等方面发挥了重要作用，成为省、地档案行政管理部门业务工作上的得力助手。

广播电视

甘肃省广播电视事业发展概况

省广播电视厅厅长
杨德儒

1993年，全省各级广播电视部门和广播电视工作者全面贯彻落实党的十四大精神，充分发挥广播电视的宣传舆论作用，在促进我省深化改革，脱贫致富，振兴甘肃经济，建设社会主义精神文明中做出了应有的贡献，各方面的工作取得了新的进展。

一、广播电视宣传

1993年，全省29座广播电台共开办31套节目，平均每日播音223小时42分，其中转播中央台节目47小时14分，日均自办节目132小时03分。甘肃人民广播电台3套节目平均每日播音35小时12分，比上年增加2小时，日均自办节目31小时33分，比上年增加2小时33分。全年共播发新闻稿38464条，其中自采新闻3192条；播发《对农村节目》稿件307组；播出各类文艺节目1621个(组)；播发各类专题节目365组。28座地、县级广播电台平均每日播音188小时30分，其中自办节目每日播音100小时30分，日播音量均大大超过上年。

全省12座电视台共开办14套节目，平均每周播出435小时30分，比上年增加81小时50分；其中转播中央台节目110小时27分，周均自办节目291小时23分。甘肃电视台2套节目平均每周播出57小时28分，其中转播中央台节目4小时16分；自办节目53小时12分。全年共播新闻5046条，其中录像新闻4550条，占90%，口播新闻496条；被中央电视台采用441条，其中63条在《新闻联播》节目中播出。播出各类专题节目1013部(集)，其中自制专题节目640部(集)。播出文艺、娱乐性节目608个(期)。播出电视剧1814部(集)。

1993年的广播电视宣传，突出并主要抓了以下几年方面：

1. 精心组织较好的完成了各项重大宣传任务

各级广播电视台站，坚持正确舆论导向，充分发挥广播电视的宣传优势，按照省委、省政府的工作部署，对《邓小平文选》第三卷的发行、组织学习活动，党的十四届三中全会的召开及省人大、政协“两会”、省第八次党代会等重大活动，进行了及时报道和深入宣传。甘肃人民广播电台为宣传《邓选》第三卷的学习，开设了《邓选》第三卷读书班，并恢复了《理论学习》节目。在省人大、政协“两会”、省第八次党代会宣传活动中，电台负责人带队进行了7次现场直播。甘肃电视台及时播发了《邓选》第三卷在甘肃的发行仪式，并及时报道了全省各地、各级党组织和广大党员干部学习《邓选》第三卷的活动情况。在省第八次党代会召开期间，《甘肃新闻》开辟了《党代表风采》专栏，并在《社会博览》、

《党旗飘飘》栏目中开展深度报道。共播出新闻46条。专题22个,现场直播一场。对反腐倡廉的宣传,两台均进行了及时准确的报道;对揭露出来的与腐败有关的人和事,从宣传舆论上进行了有力打击,同时歌颂了一批严于律己、廉洁奉公的典型。在坚持正面宣传为主的前提下,对社会上存在的丑恶现象进行了有力的揭露和抨击。甘肃人民广播电台新闻部开办的《质量监督台》在群众中引起强烈反响,成为联系各阶层群众的纽带和桥梁。甘肃电视台的《社会博览》、《新闻大观园》等栏目,抓住群众关心的热点、难点问题,大胆揭露、触动社会生活,促进了一些问题的尽快解决,如对兰州市磨沟沿小区群众吃水难问题、省人民医院医德医风差等问题,经报道后促进了问题的解决和重视。

2. 自始至终突出了改革开放和经济建设的宣传

各级广播电视台站在宣传内容上,突出了改革开放和经济建设这个中心,大张旗鼓的为改革开放和经济建设鸣罗开道,制定了"三个结合"和"五个加强"的宣传措施。"三个结合"即把大量的成就事实报道和党的十四大精神的宣传有机地结合起来,把省内重大活动、事件的宣传和日常宣传有机地结合起来,把典型报道和整体宣传结合起来;"五个加强"即在广播电视宣传中加强了建设有中国特色社会主义理论的宣传,加强了经济建设和改革开放的宣传,加强了农业和农村工作的宣传,加强了"双带整推"战略措施的宣传,加强了社会主义精神文明建设的宣传。围绕突出经济建设宣传,甘肃人民广播电台抓了贯彻《全民所有制工业企业转换经营机制条例》和《中共中央关于建立社会主义市场经济体制若干问题的决定》的宣传。《路在何方》系列报道反映了企业在转换经营机制中所面临的现实问题。《经济大世界》板块节目容量大,现实感强,收到了较好的宣传效果。为发展第三产业和乡镇企业,新闻、农村等节目采播了大量报道、评论。《空中彩虹》开辟了《"甘草杯"乡镇企业有奖征文》栏目,新闻部报道了依靠政策、依靠科技、依靠人才脱贫致富的成就和经验。甘肃电视台的新闻节目,以改革开放和经济建设为内容的宣传占全部新闻播出的80%。为配合"双带整推"战略方针的贯彻实施,拍摄制作的三条消息播出后,被中央台在《新闻联播》节目中连续三天播出。在贯彻《企业法》和《条例》的宣传中,《社会博览》、《经济纵横》、《经济了望》、《经济动态》和《甘肃大地》等栏目,都从不同角度摄制播出了一系列专题报道,其中对甘肃省十大市场的专题报道等,有机地配合了省委、省政府的中心工作。

3. 大力加强精神文明建设的宣传

各级广播电视台站大力加强精神文明建设宣传,突出了爱国主义、集体主义和社会主义的宣传教育,结合建党72周年、建国44周年、老一辈无产阶级革命家为雷锋同志题词30周年、纪念毛泽东诞辰100周年进行了深入广泛的宣传。甘肃人民广播电台为《纪念毛泽东同志诞辰100周年"供销合作杯"全省广播台站文艺节目大联展》,甘肃电视台筹措播出的《毛泽东传》等10多部纪录片,40多部(集)专题,30多条纪念活动的报道及主办的《世纪太阳》大型文艺晚会等,都从不同角度、不同侧面缅怀了老一辈无产阶级革命家的壮阔活动,同时也讴歌了现实生活中的先进典型,弘扬了爱国主义、集体主义和社会主义精神。

4. 进一步繁荣文艺、文化娱乐性节目

遵循文艺"双百"方针,为不断丰富人民群众精神文化生活,尽可能满足不同层次听(观)众的需求,甘肃人民广播电台先后推出《银河知音》、《梨园内外》等挂牌文艺节目及其他一些优秀节目。文艺节目专题直播《歌儿唱给毛主席听》、音乐《羊倌》,也都受到社会各界的好评。甘肃电视台《擂台争春》等文艺晚会、反应西北风情的音乐艺术片《大戈壁》、综艺栏目《花好月圆》、新辟《艺苑风采》、《体育世界》及《今宵点歌台》等播出后,深受观众的喜爱。制作的电视剧《跨越》、《黄河从身边走来》,译制的电视连续剧《古堡情怨》、拍摄的中篇电视连续剧《白马》、少儿电视连续剧《我们长大了》等,都对观众有较大吸引力。

5. 节目质量不断提高

全省各级广播电台、电视台不仅节目制作能力加强而且在提高节目质量上下功夫,取得了较好的成绩。全省各级电台年制作广播节目31362小时40分。甘肃人民广播电台年制作节目5354小时54分,日制作节目能力比上年增加12分。全省各级电视台年制作电视节目2442小时41分。甘肃电视台所制作节目475小时54分,日均节目制作能力1小时18分,较上年增加18分。《酒泉人民新观念》等25个广播节目(稿件)在全国评奖中获奖,其中甘肃人民广播电台的节目占76%;《解决我省中部地区人畜饮水一项战略措施开始付诸实施》等35个电视节目在全国评奖中获奖,其中甘肃电视台的节目占66%。甘肃电视台摄制的《白马》、《我们长大了》等电视剧也在全国评奖中获奖。

6. 深化宣传改革,增强宣传效果

全省广播电视台站为了拓宽宣传途径,扩大宣传效果,在改革节目形式,扩大节目容量方面做了积极的探索和努力。1月23日甘肃电视台的第2套节目即甘肃飞天经济台试播;5月1日,天水电视台开办的第2套节目正式播出。在节目改革方面,甘肃电视台几乎所有的节目进入了相应的栏目，并规范了栏目长度，使全台节目实现栏目化播出。同时，增辟新栏目，改进和推出了一批专栏节目，如《社会博览》、《经济纵横》、《艺苑采风》、《今宵点歌台》等，内容和形式适应了广大观众多层次、多方面的需求和喜爱。据统计，全年各栏目共收到观众来信6万多封，甘肃人民广播电台新开办了《经济大世界》、《陇上人家》、《星期天，你好》三个主持人直播板块节目及《午夜温馨》节目，并在《经济大世界》开设了《经济短波》、《空中商业街》、《观察与透视》、《改革与思考》等栏目。这些节目上的改革，使节目更具容量大、现场感强、真实的特点。

7.加强横向联系和对外交流

甘肃人民广播电台为纪念毛泽东诞辰100周年，与甘肃广播电视学会、甘肃省供销合作社联办了《供销合作杯》节目；为加强全省交通管理，与省公安厅交警总队在《陇上人家节目》中联办了《交通短波》；还与甘肃省乡镇企业管理局、甘肃日报社联办了《甘草杯有奖征文》等活动，都收到了较好的宣传效果。甘肃电视台继续加强与省级兄弟台的联系和合作，成功地举办了中国西部电视集团年会，完成了《长城内外》、《中华之最》、《中国历史文化名城》、《舞韵》、《中国笑星大奖赛》、《中国歌星大汇串》、《西部娃》、《西部之乐》等电视片。为宣传甘肃，扩大甘肃在全国和全世界的影响，同时使我省人民更多地了解世界，起到了积极作用。加强了与一些国家和地区电视界的友好往来和业务交流，年内曾组团赴日本秋田参加了第四届甘肃——秋田电视友好交流周活动；和法国电视三台建立了友好往来和业务关系；与韩国江陵电视台和日本秋田电视台协助摄制了大型电视系列片《藏传佛教》30集（前期拍摄已近尾声）；在《美州东方卫星电视》中播出了甘肃电视台自制节目30个小时，打开了一扇面向世界宣传甘肃的窗口。

二、广播电视事业建设

1993年甘肃的广播电视建设。由于省委、省政府的重视和各级党委、政府及广播电视部门的努力，在财力紧张的情况下，仍取得了一定发展。

1.无线广播。全省共有广播电台29座，比上年增加2座，其中省级1座，地（州、市）级6座，县（市）级22座，新增建嘉峪关人民广播电台和金昌人民广播电台；全省有中波发射台、转播台24座，总功率674.1千瓦，较上年增加2千瓦；有调频广播发射台、转播台37座，总功率107.55千瓦，和上年基本持平。中波、调频广播混合覆盖率达到65%，较上年的63.2%上升了1.7个百分点。

2.电视广播。全省有电视台12座，其中省级1座，地（市）级10座，县（市）级1座；有电视发射台、转播台1042座，比上年增加49座；发射总功率152.09千瓦，较上年增加22.25千瓦。全省有卫星电视地面站1295座，比上年增加298座。全省电视人口覆盖率达到70%，比上年的68.4%上升了1.6个百分点。

3.微波线路。年内开通了张掖至嘉峪关、兰州至临夏至甘南合作、兰州至白银等地（州、市）的微波线路，全省广播电视专用微波站达到48个，线路总长度达到1869.5公里，微波站比上年增加12个，线路增加了423.9公里。

4.有线电视。全省已建起有线电视系统636家，其中行政区域性有线电视台2个、企业有线电视台20个、有线电视站418个、共用无线系统196个，已连结终端用户32.6万户。甘肃有线电视台的用户目前可收看15套电视节目。

5.有线广播。全省有县级广播站63个，乡镇广播放大站1422个，村广播室3200多个，乡镇以下广播专线57371公里。通有线广播的行政村占全省行政村总数的57.1%，有55.1%的农户可通过有线广播收听中央、省、县级的广播。

科学技术

改革发展中的甘肃科技事业

省科学技术委员会主任

魏庆同

1993年，全省科技工作以党的十四大精神为指针，以小平同志"科学技术是第一生产力"的理论为依据，认真贯彻落实党和国家的科技发展方针和政策，在深化科技体制改革、加速科技成果转化步伐、组织实施重大科技攻关项目、发展高新技术及其产业化、推进经济建设和社会发展等方面的科技进步，取得新的进展。全民的科技意识有了很大的提高，各行各业、各地区依靠科技发展经济的良好势头正在兴起。

一、科研院所面向市场、面向经济、面向社会的主动性进一步增强

社会主义市场经济体制的确立，给科研院所的改革和发展带来了新的机遇和挑战。

一年来，遵照国家"稳住一头，放开一片"的科技体改方针，围绕优化科技资源配置、转换管理职能和科技运行机制，深化内部改革等，落实各项改革措施，进一步调动了科研院所和广大科技人员面向市场、面向经济、面向社会的积极性、主动性和创造性。全省94个县以上政府部门所属的独立自然科学研究机构中，实行所长负责制的有63个；实行任期目标制的有39个；实行承包经营责任制的有25个；建立中试场所的有5个；进入企业或企业集团的有5个；兴办各种类型的技术经济实体达242个；实现事业费基本自立的有22个；发展状况较好的有15个，基本解决自身生存问题的有49个，生存比较困难的有30个。省建材研究院面向中小企业和乡镇企业大力开展技术开发工作，全年创收198万元，获纯利63万元。省机械研究院坚持走以科技为先导、科工贸一体化的道路，共组织科研与开发项目99个，其中已经完成55项，创收80万元。

民营科技在改革与发展中日趋壮大，已成为我省科技战线上的一支重要的生力军。1993年，新组建的民营科技企业近300家，总数达到800余家，从业人员1.4万人，年技工贸总收入达到4亿元，利润8000万元，上交税金1000万元。民营科技已覆盖到农、林、牧、建材、食品、医药、化工、生物制品、机械、交通。电子、建筑、能源、环保等46个行业，企业的素质有了明显提高，有不少企业正在向集团化、产业化、国际化的方向迈进。

二、技术成果商品化的发展势头良好

大力培育、发展技术市场，不断活跃技术贸易活动，促进科技成果商品化并转化为直接的生产力，是社会主义市场经济体制赋予科技战线的一项重要任务之一。

各级科技行政管理部门认真贯彻"放开、搞活、扶持、引导"的技术市场发展方针和"甘肃省技术市场管理条例"，不断地加强了技术市场的宏观管理和指导工作，技术市场管理体系，技术市场的培育、技术贸易活动都取得了新的进展。甘肃省技术市场管理办公室、甘肃省技术合同仲裁委员会已相继组建；许多地、县正在抓紧筹建技术市场管理机构，兰州、白银、天水、平凉、金昌、甘南等地市的技术市场管理机构已开展工作。全年省地两级的技术交易额达到2.1亿元，其中各地区共举办14次技术交易活动，交易额突破6000万元。四月份，由科技管理部门、科研单位、大专院校、民办科技企业等组成的"甘肃省'93香港经济贸易洽谈会"科技分团，首次在香港开展了对外技术贸易活动，取得了显著成效。在这次香港经贸洽谈会上，共展出项目306个，与美国、日本、新加坡、泰国、英国、法国、加拿大及港澳等20余个国家和地区的2600名客商进行了洽谈和交易，成交项目20项，总成交额3259.9万美元(其中合同成交额1325.93万美元)，在甘肃科技走向世界方面迈出了重要的一步。

为了发展技术市场，促进科技转化，从9月份开始，省科委、省经贸委、省农委、省社科联组织了"抓联促转，科技万里行"活动。这项活动按照"先进、实用、实效"的原则，通过组织科技分队深入地县中小企业和乡镇企业现场诊断和考察，举办技术贸易、推广科技成果等形式，推进科技转化。先期进行的武威、白银两地市已取得了明显的成效。

三、高新技术产业开发区的建设取得了新的进展

"发展高科技、实现产业化"是实现我国第二步战略目标的一项重大战略措施，是"科技兴陇"的一项重要任务。

兰州高新技术产业开发区是国务院批准的52个国家级高新技术产业开发区之一。区内的企业已发展到350家，其中高新技术企业为268家("三资"企业45家，股份制企业2家)，从业人员达11000多人，其中科技人员有5000多名，初步形成了国有、集体、私营、股份制、"三资"等多种经济成份并存的高新技术企业群体。几年来，开发区内累计开发高新技术项目达300个，有200个产品投产。以生物技术、精细化工、新型材料、同位素、中医药的研究与开发为主体的产业体系正在形成。全年技工贸总收入达到3.45亿元，利税3592万元。区内的一批骨干企业已脱颖而出，兰炼三星公司等5家企业的年技工贸总收入已超千万元，兰化兰达公司等32家企业的年产值已超百万元以上，兰炼三星公司的年产值已超过5000万元，国家科委授予实施"火炬计划"先进高新技术企业称号。基础设施建设正在抓紧进行，已有110家企业进入科技一条街进行科技开发。生产和经营活动；南河滩产业基地建设已完成720亩土地的规划设计和场平工程；医药高科技一条街的建设已完成16万平方米建筑的总体规划工作。

四、科技兴农、科技兴企取得良好成效

科技兴农、科技兴企、科技兴地、科技兴县正日益成为各级领导、各行各业乃至全社会的共识，特别是农村和企业的科技进步有了新的发展，取得了良好的成效。

科教兴农战略的实施，推进了农村的科技进步。以乡镇科技管理体系、科技服务体系、科技示范体系、科技培训体系建设为主体的科教兴农活动呈现出方兴未艾的局面。全省已组织乡镇科委1144个，占乡镇总数77%；配备科技副乡镇长860名，占乡镇总数的58%；配备科技专干1573名。全省各类乡镇科技服务组织达4713个，从业人员2万人；组织专业技术服务队1096个，从业人员7805人；各类农民技术经济合作组织达到5385个，参加的农户达到8.4万户；农民专业技术研究会(协会)5383个，会员近9万人。全省已建立农业综合示范基地126个、示范乡241个、示范村1931个、科技示范户15万户、示范面积480万亩、辐射带动面积达865万亩。全省地、县、乡三级农村科技培训体系已初步形成。近几年来共举办培训班1.3万期，有122万人次受到了技术培训。1993年全省共有420个单位的27942名科技人员、管理人员和农民技术员参加科技承包，承包面积达1500万亩，取得经济效益8.3亿元。全省有770个乡镇开展了科技达标活动，其中已验收合格的乡镇达235个。

为了推进企业的科技进步，不断提高企业的技术素质，和产品更新换代的能力，企业内部的科技体系建设有了新的发展。全省170个大中型企业中，已有96个建立了技术开发机构；有75个建立了技术开发基金；有145个企业实行了总工程师技术责任制。创建科技型企业的活动正在全省范围内由点到面逐步开展，经有关部门或地市命名的科技型企业达59家。随着市场经济的发展，依靠科技振兴企业已越来越受到企业家的重视，企业科技进步考核指标已成为规范企业行为，纳入企业承包和厂长任期目标考核的重要内容。

五、三个层次的科技发展计划执行情况良好，取得一批重要科技成果

全年共组织面向经济主战场、高新技术及其产业化、基础研究和应用基础研究三个层次的省级科技攻关、星火计划、火炬计划、中试基金、成果推广、软科学、自然科学基金及中青年科学基金等六大科技计划项目506项，投入科技三项费1150万元，中试基金100万元，贷款3300万元，承担单位自筹7592万元，其它拨款288万元。据对项目实施情况的跟踪调查和动态管理，80%以上的项目均按期完成了年度任务。

据对“八五”重大科技攻关项目中期检查和评估结果分析，绝大多数项目取得了突破性的进展。三年来，科技攻关计划共取得成果102项，其中农业科技攻关成果47项，工业科技攻关成果为55项。“蚕桑工程”、“绿洲工程”、“小康工程”、“扭补工程”及星火计划的实施进展情况喜人，为区域性支柱产业的发展和科技扶贫工作，发挥了科技先导和示范作用。全年共组织实施了国家级和省级火炬计划75项，项目完成可新增产值3.2亿元，有50个火炬计划项目及高新技术产品在北京参加了“中国火炬计划成果及高新技术产品展览会”，向国内外展示了我省高新技术产业化的成就。为解决中间试验“断层”问题，建立了中试基金，组织实施15个中试基金项目，其中有9项中试基地建设起步良好。全年组织实施重大科技成果推广项目28个，“浙农一号畜、禽全价饲料”、“不锈钢微丝生产线”等项目已在生产中产生了显著的经济效益和社会效益。为增强我省科技发展后劲，培养脱颖而出的科技人才，自然科学基金和中青年科学基金计划资助基础和应用基础研究项目143项，“两金”计划已有16项通过科技成果鉴定，其中4项达到国际先进水平，12项处国内领先水平。

全年共取得各类科技成果632项（含中央在甘单位），其中达到国际领先水平2项、国际先进3项、国内领先45项、国内先进97项、省内先进96项。经省科技进步奖和星火奖评审委员会评审共有138项成果获奖，其中科技进步奖为112项，星火奖为26项。全省专利申请量累计达到2769件，国家授权的为1242件，有165项专利技术已在生产中实施应用，有83个优秀专利项目分别参加了国内外的专利成果博览会。

六、科技事业的自身建设稳步发展

归口省科委管理的省级科研院所科学事业费共60个财务核算单位，在省财政比较困难的情况下，1993年科学事业费实拨额度达3512.9万元，比1992年度增长7.43%。这些科研院所全年创收的纯收入达243.9万元，比1992年度增长5.6%，解决了部分困难及事业发展中的实际问题。

社会科学

前进中的甘肃省社会科学院

省社会科学院院长　支克坚

省社会科学院情报研究所所长

郭宝宏

1993年，全院在邓小平建设有中国特色社会主义理论和党的基本路线指引下，在省委宣传部和院党委的领导下，认真贯彻党的十四大和十四届三中全会精神，坚持改革开放，坚持理论工作与我省改革实践相结合，努力为本省两个文明建设服务，调动各方面的积极性，使社会科学研究工作又取得新的成就。1993年，全院共承担院级以上研究课题25项，其中国家“八.五”哲学社会科学规划重点项目和中华社科基金项目10项，省社会科学规划办和省科委研究课题4项，省有关部门、地区和大企业委托的研究课题6项，院级研究课题5项。这些课题都比较鲜明地体现了在邓小平建设有中国特色社会主义理论指导下，为我国及本省改革开放和两个文明建设服务的特点。其中有的直接为本省改革开放和经济建设中的迫切问题进行对策研究；有的在广泛调查的基础上，对本省乃至西部地区和全国经济和社会发展中的重大问题做了系统的、具有超前性质的研究；有的研究了本省以及西北政治、经济、文化史上的重要问题，对于当前的两个文明建设也有借鉴和启迪作用；有的为我国高等院校的理论教学提供了新鲜的教材或参考资料；有的结合当代实践、对我国社会科学有关学科的基础理论提出了新颖的观点，推动社科基础研究的前进步伐；还有的为省委、省政府深入了解国情、省情，制定政策，提供了科学依据。据统计，1993年全院科研人员共完成各类著作15部，约350万字；撰写学术论文140多篇，约15.5万字。一些跨学科、跨部门的重大课题，如由支克坚教授、穆纪光研究员、刘敏研究员担任主编，由国情室、社会学法学所、农经所承担的国家“八.五”社科规划重点项目《中国百县(市)经济·社会调查·永昌卷》、由支克坚教授、周述实副研究员牵头，经济所、农经所承担的国家课题《中国百家企业调查·兰炼卷》，课题组全体成员多次深入基层，调查研究，充分占有第一手资料，并对资料进行认真的分析综合，因而已完成的著作经专家评审，认为达到较高的水平。由吕胜利副研究员牵头，农经所部分同志承担的《武威地区石羊河流域水资源与工农业协调发展的动力学模拟研究》，直接服务于武威地区水利和工农业建设，得到地方有关部门的大力配合，成果已通过专家鉴定。由岳青副研究员牵头，社会学法学所承担的《西北民族地区的社会稳定与社会发展》，紧紧抓住西北民族地区各少数民族在改革开放中的一系列问题，结合民族历史、民族心理、民族特征进行深入的调查研究，其成果也起到了为改革开放和经济建设服务的作用。

在哲学研究方面，在以往进行的“邓小平哲学思想研究”、“社会主义纵横谈”、“改革开放中的伦理道德”等项研究的基础上，由邓兆明副研究员牵头，哲学所承担的《社会主义市场经济与人》一书，也已完成。这部著作既是学习和宣传邓小平有中国特色社会主义理论和党的十四届三中全会精神的教材，又是一部研究、拓展和贯彻邓小平有中国特色社会主义理论的专著。它围绕社会主义市场经济与人的关系，阐述了经济基础的变革导致人以及人的思想观念发生变化的一系列理论和实践问题。此外，由尚乐林研究员牵头，哲学所部分同志承担的“思维与现代科技”的研究，力求运用马克思主义哲学观点，提炼、概括和抽象现代科技最新成果的范畴，阐述人类思维活动的机理，所发表的一系列论文，有的已引起国内学术界的关注。

在文学研究方面，1993年，文学所在以往对甘肃古代作家、甘肃古代诗歌、甘肃古代散文、历代咏陇诗作进行系统研究和整理的基础上，集体撰著并出版了《甘肃古代文学概览》一书。在多年来编辑《敦煌语言文学通讯》(内刊)，开展敦煌学研究、编写出版《敦煌文学》的基础上，由颜廷亮研究员牵头，组织院内及全国敦煌学专家，撰著出版了《敦煌文学概论》一书。这些研究成果，对理清“文革”十年遭到严重破坏的本省历史上的文学遗产，加强本省精神文明建设，促进今后的地方文学研究工作，都起到很好的作用。

在历史学研究方面，本院建院以来一直把研究力量集中于三个方面，即陕甘宁边区历史研究、西北社会经济史研究和西路军研究。1993年，上述三个方面继续取得可喜成果。如在陕甘宁边区历史研究方面，编辑出版了论文集《陕甘宁革命根据地史研究》(第二辑)在西北社会经济史研究方面，王致中、魏丽英两位副研究员继专著《明清西北社会经济史研究》之后，又出版了专著《中国西北社会经济史研究》；在西路军研究方面，董汉河副研究员在以往取得成绩的基础上，又进一步向纵深拓展，相继发表了《西路军战俘问题研究》、《西路军与西安事变》等论文多篇。其中《西路军与西安事变》一文，从西路军与西安事变的关系这一新的视角研究探讨西路的有关问题，已在学术界引起较大反响，先后有10余家报刊转摘。

在法学研究方面，为配合我省民主与法制建设和改革开放，以往曾组织撰写和发表了《高度民主概念和目标》、《普及法律知识手册》、《法律社会学概述》、《农村专业户法律顾问》、《犯罪学》等论著，为我省民主政治建设和法律知识的普及做出了贡献。1993年以来，社会学法学研究所为贯彻党的十四届三中全会精神，配合全省市场经济体制的建设，组织力量撰写《市场经济与地方法制建设》(研究报告)，目前已完成；由该所法学研究室主任张谦元等组织撰写的著作《甘肃经济发展与地方立法研究》也已全部完稿，待出版。

从1986年起，本院承担省方志办委托的《甘肃省社会科学志》研究编撰任务，这项工作涉及历史年代长、学科领域广，且史料整理分析工程量大、志述准确性要求高。经艰苦努力，到1993年底，由支克坚教授担任主编的《甘肃省社会科学志》(80万字)已完成初稿。

在围绕经济建设和改革开放的主战场，积极开展学术研究的同时，为活跃本省和院内学术空气，促进社科研究事业的发展，1993年，全院有计划地开展了学术交流活动。截止1993年12月底，全院共举办院际、省际、院内、所级学术会议计35次，参加人数达470余人(次)。其中较为突出的如“全国第二届社科志编纂理论研讨会”，本院与省委宣传部联合召开的，有部分大、中型企业经理、厂长及政府有关部门负责人和高校、科研单位专家学者参加的“‘复关’对策研讨会”，本院与金昌市等联合发起召开的“全国资源型工矿城市发展战略研讨会”，哲学研究所主办的全国性的“社会主义市场经济与人研讨会”，《甘肃社会科学》杂志编辑部主办的“王符及汉末社会批判思潮国际学术讨论会”，本院举办的“青年科研人员学术成果报告会”等等，都收到很好的效果。此外，院内科研人员的一些优秀论文，还被国际性、全国性和全省性的学术会议选中，并参加了交流。如周述实副研究员关于甘肃产业结构研究的论文，参加了在香港举行的“中国地区经济发展学术讨论会”的交流；吕胜利副研究员的被国内专家鉴定为“达到国内领先水平”的论文《草地生产力与中国草地生产力的模拟》，参加了“国际草地资源学术会议”的交流；他的《中国草地生产力的动力学模拟》一文，参加了“系统科学与系统工程第二届国际学术讨论会”的交流；周述实关于社会主义市场经济与“双带整推”的论文、姜安印关于社会主义市场经济与新资源观的论文，参加了省委宣传部召开的“发展甘肃社会主义市场经济研讨会”的交流；邓兆明副研究员的《论毛泽东的调查研究理论》、尚乐林研究员的《毛泽东关于质的“安定性”的辩证探索》等论文，参加了中宣部等单位在京举行的“纪念毛泽东诞辰100周年学术讨论会”的交流。通过这些学术会议和学术交流，使得全院科研队伍能够及时了解全国社科研究领域的最新动态，使得全院科研工作经常保持勃勃的生机，也使得科研人员扩大了视野，互通了信息，交流了经验，因而是十分有益于整体科研事业的发展的。

在1993年举行的全省第三次社会科学优秀成果评奖中，甘肃省社会科学院共有15项研究成果获奖，其中由颜廷亮研究员担任主编的《敦煌文学》获一等奖；由甘棠寿、时正新、穆纪光三位研究员担任主编的《中国国情丛书——百县(市)经济社会调查·静宁卷》、刘敏研究员担任主编的《中国不发达地区农村的社会发展》、时正新等合作完成的《甘肃农业技术政策研究》等三项获二等奖；另有11项成果获三等奖。

总之，在1993年，甘肃省社会科学院的各项科研事业取得了较大成绩。省委副书记孙英在8月视察本院时充分肯定了省社科院历年来的成绩，同时指出，邓小平有中国特色社会主义理论的指导、改革开放和发展社会主义市场经济的丰富实践，为社会科学研究提供了难得的大发展的良好机遇。要求省社科院抓住这一机遇，努力培养和造就一支坚持以马克思主义为指导、用中国特色社会主义理论武装起来的、有较高学术水平的社会主义的社会科学工作者、理论家，推动社会科学研究大繁荣、大发展。现在，全院上下正在认真贯彻孙英同志的指示精神，力求在1994年为全省改革开放和现代化建设做出更多的贡献。

甘肃的名寺古庙古塔

拉卜楞寺位于甘肃省夏河县城西大夏河畔，依山傍水，风景秀丽，为我国西藏佛教格鲁派(黄教)六大寺之一。建于清康熙四十八年(1709年)。整个寺院占地面积为1300多亩。由六座学院、七大佛殿、嘉木样活佛的佛宫以及许多僧舍组成。其中闻思学院的大经堂，可容四千余喇嘛同时诵经。寺内有佛像二万四千多尊。珍藏文物数万件，藏文经典，书籍6万多册。居西藏佛教寺之首位。其建筑均为金瓦朱甍。红黄墙垣，金彩飞檐，寺顶四角立铜质镏金宝瓶，极为富丽堂皇。寺院座落在河北岸，凤、龙二山南北拱峙，相映成趣，为一座优美的庭园。拉卜楞寺高大宏伟、巍峨壮观，是我国佛教圣地之一。

天水伏羲庙。位于天水市西关，始建于明代，清代也曾几次复修，但基本保持了明代建筑风格。伏羲是传说中的中华民族的始祖，据考证他降生在成纪(今天水市秦安县以北)，从他才开始了观天地之象，有了历法。又画八卦，创造了文字，教人民知礼节，从事渔猎畜牧生产，而且还创造出琴、瑟乐器。数千年来，伏羲被列为三皇(伏羲、神农、黄帝)之首，视为创造华夏民族文明的始祖。伏羲庙为一座两进三门的建筑群，自南向北牌坊、庙宇、月台、碑亭、玉殿、古柏等，占地3700多亩。院中太极殿是一座高大建筑，殿内有伏羲像一尊。每年农历七月十九日，是伏羲祀典日，这一天群众纷纷前来朝拜，表达对这位人文始祖的崇敬。

王母宫山。位于泾川县西郊的“回山”。关于西王母的传说，在中国民间有着十分广泛的影响。这里便是传说中西王母“下凡”之处。据史料记载，自唐汉以来，这里就已香火旺盛，被信奉西王母的善男信女们视为顶礼膜拜的真正圣地。回山王母宫始建于汉代，到宋代已形成一个规模宏大的建筑群。因回山系西王母圣地，故历代十分重视修葺，一直延传至清代同治年间，不幸毁于当地一次战乱。但现存历代有关王母传说及王母宫建筑的石碑、遗文、遗址及诗作，其数量之多，年代之久，内容之丰富，可谓独一无二，是“回中降西王母处”的重要资证。每年农历三月二十，来自四面八方朝圣谒拜的香客络绎不绝。

甘肃古塔较多。其中著名的有武威罗什塔、张掖木塔、华池双石塔、宁县政平塔、兰州白塔等。其中武威罗什寺塔、张掖木塔等都是唐代修建的名塔。

财 政 税 务

财政

深化财政改革 加强收支管理

省财政厅厅长

张文启

1993年，我省各级财政部门在省委、省政府的正确领导下，认真贯彻党中央和国务院的各项方针、政策，强化收支管理，加快财政改革步伐，整顿财税秩序，严肃财经纪律，保证了财政预算任务的完成。1993年，全省财政收入实际完成52.17亿元，为调整预算的119.98%，超收8.63亿元，比1992年增长30.50%。全省财政实际支出63.17亿元，为调整预算的90.26%，比1992年增长18.12%。

一、千方百计筹措资金，促进生产经济发展

生产经济的发展是财政增收的根本，因此1993年，各级财政在资金、财力都十分紧张的情况下，努力增加发展生产经济方面的投入。在农业方面，重点支持了基础设施建设、综合开发、多种经营、农村社会化服务体系和科技兴农，对于促进"两高一优"农业和乡镇企业的发展起到了积极作用。从投入总量上看，当年预算安排的支农资金全部到位。对一些重点建设和技改项目，从资金上给予了重点保证，省级基建支出圆满完成了全年预算。在扶持地县经济发展方面，积极抓好财政"扭补"和地县财政收入上台阶工作，尽力拨付扭补资金。到1993年底，全省有12个县市的财政收入分别登上了3000万元，5000万元和1亿元的台阶，另有二个县提前一年实现了财政扭补。在利用世界银行贷款方面，全年共提回美元折合人民币近1.3亿元，促进了工农业生产和教育卫生事业的发展。

二、积极深化财税改革，支持和配合其他改革

《企业财务通则》和《企业会计准则》的颁布，是企业财会改革的必然要求，也是深化财政改革的一项重要内容。围绕"两则"的颁布实施，财政部门狠抓了"两则"的培训和实施工作，并深入企业了解情况，解决问题，保证了这次企业财会改革的顺利进行。进入1993年下半年以后，按照中央的统一部署，投入了大量精力，进行认真的调查摸底和测算，为税制改革、分税制改革以及国有企业利润分配制度改革打下了基础。

另外，配合机构改革，支持事业单位和经济管理部门转换职能，兴办经济实体，减轻财政负担；配合住房制度改革，参与了房改中政策办法的制定工作，先后会同有关部门制定了《甘肃省住房公积金管理试行办法》、《甘肃省城镇公有住房提租补贴试行办法》、《甘肃省住房租赁保证金管理试行办法》等。同时，进行了认真细致的公积金、提租补贴等数据的测算工作。

三、大力组织财政收入，积极清理拖欠税利

从年初开始，各级财政部门就把组织工作抓得很紧。六月，省财政厅与省税务局联合召开了加强税收征管、大力组织财政收入的电话会议，十月，省政府下发了加强宏观调控、狠抓增收节支的通知；进入四季度后，召开了全省财政处(局)长会议，对后几个月的工作做了重点布置，并下发了明传电报。按照省上统一部署，各有关部门与财税部门密切配合，集中主要力量，深入重点欠税大户，抓收促缴。部分地县对收入进度实行目标管理，层层分解，落实到人，坚持按旬按月进行分析考核，保证了各项收入任务的完成。

为有效组织收入，控制收入流失，还从以下几方面进行了努力。一是税收财务物价大检查工作主要检查了收入流失问题，对欠税欠利大户，订出规划，限期清交，对有意拖欠拒缴的，由税务部门通知银行依法强行扣缴。二是认真清理各项税收减免和优惠政策，杜绝乱开口子，停止了对企业临时性、困难性税收减免的审批。三是狠抓了"两金"的征管。四是专项检查了固定资产投资方向调节税和营业税税率提高后的征管工作。五是采取了对专控商品征收附加费的办法，增加收入，控制集团消费的过快增长。

四、合理调度资金，严格控制支出

1993年，财政资金十分紧张，各级财政部门想方设法调度资金，并合理、灵活地利用部分预算外间歇资金，基本保证了人员工资的发放和重点建设的支出。

为了从严控制各项非生产性支出，对各项事业行政开支精打细算，对省级行政单位的经费支出实行了定额考核管理，在兰州、天水和金昌三市进行了行政经费"下管一级"的试点工作；制定了综合财政预算管理办法，引导和鼓励事业行政单位用预算外资金和自有资金补充正常经费；调整了差旅费包干办法；对会议费继续执行财政审批制度，严格了会议费的计划管理；对专控商品从严控制，从1993年5月1日起，开征了专控商品附加费，有效地遏制了社会集团购买力的过快增长；对小汽车实行定点维修，部分地区对行政事业单位的超编人员和超编车辆不供给经费；根据中央关于开展反腐败斗争的各项规定，各级财政部门在制止用公款请客送礼、公费旅游、随意提高费用开支和各种津贴、补贴标准以及扩大补贴范围等方面也做了大量工作。这些措施都有效地控制了非生产性支出的增长势头。

五、充分发挥财政职能，做好各项财政工作

一是认真贯彻落实中央6号文件精神，积极行动，对照"约法三章"对财政部门自身进行了认真的检查，全面清理了财政信用资金的使用及管理情况；整顿了财政机关兴办的经济实体。二是千方百计完成国库券销售任务。1993年上半年，在国库券一度滞销的情况下，各级财政部门组织大量人力，采取宣传动员和上门服务等促销形式，超额完成了国家分配我省4.05亿元的认购任务。三是开展税收、财务、物价大检查工作。截止1993年12月底，税收、财务、物价大检查共查出各类违纪金额1.22亿元，应入库6675万元，实际入库6419万元。通过对粮食企业财务物价大检查，初步核实了粮食企业亏损挂帐的底数，查出违纪资金5000多万元。四是积极开展反腐败斗争和治理"三乱"工作。按照省委、省政府的统一部署，在认真学习的基础上，开展了廉政教育。根据中央的要求，会同有关部门清理取消了一批乱收费项目，并制定了《甘肃省罚款没收财务管理规定》、《关于行政性收费纳入预算管理的有关规定》、《关于加强行政事业性收费管理有关规定》等办法。五是国有资产管理工作进一步加强；注册会计师事业得到进一步发展。

1993年财政工作的主要问题及1994年财政工作的指导思想

一是企业经济效益低下的状况没有大的转变，企业亏损仍很严重，应上缴的税利不能及时、足额地收缴入库。二是机构人员继续膨胀，全省财力的四分之三以上被机构、人员经费所占用，维持"吃饭"和机构正常运转已成为各级财政的头等大事。三是财权财力过于分散，使本来就十分有限的财政资金，被分散在十多个部门多头管理，难以发挥资金的规模效益。四是部分地县赤字增加，财政困难加剧。五是一些单位花钱大手大脚，铺张浪费，违犯财经纪律的现象仍很严重。

1994年，我省财政工作的指导思想是：认真贯彻党的十四届三中全会和省第八次党代会精神，坚持"抓住机遇，深化改革，扩大开放，促进发展，保持稳定"的工作方针，积极推进以分税制体制为主要内容的各项财政改革，大力培植和开辟新的财源，狠抓增收节支，调整支出结构，努力保吃饭、保稳定，适当增加农业、教育、科技投入，促进国民经济持续、快速、健康发展。

国有资产管理

国有资产管理局局长

张文武

国有资产管理的主要职责是：贯彻执行国家国有资产管理的方针、政策、法律、法规和各项管理制度，并组织实施，检查、监督执行情况，对违法事件依法进行行政处罚；组织对本省国有资产的现状和变动情况的调查研究及登记管理工作，对国有资产的运营情况实施检查，促进国有资产经营、使用单位提高资产的经营、使用效益，监督、保障国有资产的保值、增值；参与国家投资的分配和回收投资的再分配；会同有关部门对企业进行承包、租赁、合资、参股经营等项工作，并参与决定国营企业税后利润分配和合资企业国有资产股权收益的分配；审批国营企业承包、租赁、合资、参股经营和兼并、拍卖、破产清理等经济活动中涉及国有资产的评估、产权变动和财务处理；审批行政事业单位国有资产产权转移、评估和财务处理；组织推动企业闲置国有资产的处理，提高国有资产的利用率；管理本省设在中华人民共和国境外的国有资产，维护国家财产的合法权益；承办地方政府和财政部门交办的其它事项。

一、国有资产的存量、分布及结构。

到1993年底，我省国有资产存量已达244.54亿元，其中：经营性资产148亿元，占资产总量的60.52%；非经营性资产96.54亿元，占资产总量的39.48%。

经营性资产的分布及结构是：

1.按行业部门来分，工业部门68.21亿元，占经营性资产的46.09%；建设、建筑工程部门30.44亿元，占经营性资产的20.57%；铁、交、邮部门4.72亿元，占经营性资产的3.19%；商粮贸金融部门22.28亿元，占经营性资产的15.05%；农林水部门5.16亿元，占经营性资产的3.49%；文教卫生部门1.93亿元，占经营性资产的1.30%；城市公用部门2.50亿元，占经营性资产的1.69%；房地产及经营开发单位12.23亿元，占经营性资产的8.26%；其它部门0.53亿元，占经营性资产的0.36%。

2.按资产的管理权限来分，兰州市14.99亿元，占经营性资产的10.13%；白银市3.06亿元，占经营性资产的2.07%；天水市4.90亿元，占经营性资产的3.31%；金昌市1.07亿元，占经营性资产的0.72%；嘉峪关市0.5亿元，占经营性资产的0.34%；酒泉地区4.11亿元，占经营性资产的2.78%；张掖地区3.14亿元，占经营性资产的2.12%；武威地区2.66亿元，占经营性资产的1.80%；陇南地区2.72亿元，占经营性资产的1.84%；定西地区2.19亿元，占经营性资产的1.48%；平凉地区2.62亿元，占经营性资产的1.77%；庆阳地区1.67亿元，占经营性资产的1.13%；临夏州1.62亿元，占经营性资产的1.09%；甘南州1.41亿元，占经营性资产的0.95%；省级101.34亿元，占经营性资产的68.47%。

非经营性资产的分布及结构是：

1.按资产的构成来分，固定资产90.69亿元，占非经营性资产的93.94%；流动资金5.35亿元，占非经营性资产的5.54%；专项资产0.50亿元，占非经营性资产的0.52%。

2.按资产的管理权限来分，

兰州市15.36亿元，占非经营性资产的15.91%；白银市4.36亿元，占非经营性资产的4.51%；天水市5.23亿元，占非经营性资产的5.41%；金昌市9.39亿元，占非经营性资产的9.73%；嘉峪关市0.47亿元，占非经营性资产的0.49%；酒泉地区6.33亿元，占非经营性资产的6.56%；张掖地区6.07亿元，占非经营性资产的6.29%；武威地区6.72亿元，占非经营性资产的6.96%；陇南地区5.05亿元，占非经营性资产的5.23%；定西地区4.28亿元，占非经营性资产的4.43%；平凉地区4.05亿元，占非经营性资产的4.20%；庆阳地区5.91亿元，占非经营性资产的6.12%；临夏州2.94亿元，占非经营性资产的3.05%；甘南州2.97亿元，占非经营性资产的2.89%；省级17.59亿元，占非经营性资产的18.22%。

二、国有资产管理进展

1993年，我省国有资产管理在促进转换企业经营机制，维护国有资产权益，优化资产配置，推进国有资产管理体制改革等诸多方面有了新的进展，主要表现在：

1.全面开展行政事业单位财产清查登记。遵照国务院清产核资领导小组《关于印发<国家行政事业单位财产清查登记工作方案>的通知》要求及国家国有资产管理局等部门的有关文件精神，上半年，在全省范围内开展了行政事业单位财产清查登记工作。这次进行财产清查登记的有86个省级有关部门，14个地(州、市)和85个县(市、区)所属共计38999个国家行政事业单位。其中：行政单位18243个，占总户数的46.78%；事业单位20326个，占总户数的52.12%；社团单位430个，占总户数的1.1%。清查核实后全部资产为112.17亿元，其中：

国有资产为104.04亿元，占全部资产的92.75%。清查核实后的资产比清查前帐面资产90.16亿元，增加了22.01亿元，增长24.41%。通过财产清查登记，规范了我省行政事业单位财产管理工作，严格了财产的购置、领用和报废的审批手续，建立健全了财产管理制度，从而保障了国有资产的权益。

2.国有资产产权年检。国有资产产权登记是国有资产管理部门代表国家对国有资产进行登记，依法确认国家对国有资产的所有权以及企业单位占用、使用国有资产的法律行为。1993年在上年度开展国有资产初始产权登记的基础上，对全省国有企业和实行企业化管理的事业单位进行了产权登记年检。据统计，1993年度共办理各类产权登记4143户，登记国有资产94.71亿元。其中：年检登记3816户，占登记总户数的92.11%，登记国有资产90.63亿元，占登记总资产的95.69%；开办登记300户，占登记总户数的7.24%，登记国有资产3.07亿元，占登记总资产的3.24%；变动登记12户，占登记总户数的0.29%，登记国有资产0.81亿元，占登记总资产的0.86%；注销登记15户，占登记总户数的0.36%，登记国有资产0.20亿元，占登记总资产的0.21%。产权登记的持续开展，既理顺了国家与企业法人之间的产权关系，又强化了对国有资产的监督管理，同时增强了人们产权管理及维护国有资产权益的意识。

3.企业清产核资。企业清产核资是党中央、国务院决定在"八五"期间进行的一项重要工作。为了摸索经验，1993年选定省级8个厅(局)、总公司所属24户大中型企业，地县市所属4户小型企业，进行了企业清产核资扩大试点。经清查，参加扩大试点的28户企业清查前的帐面资产总值70.31亿元，查出固定资产净值盘盈8182万元，盘亏991万元；流动资产盘盈1875万元，盘亏1.08亿元；专项及其它资产盘盈3万元，盘亏50万元。清查后的资产总值为71.08亿元，比原帐面数增加7872万元，增长1.12%。清查后各类待报废、待核销的资产损失为2.59亿元，占资产清查值的3.64%。经重估，固定资产原值增值13.13亿元，增幅为53.31%，固定资产净值增值7.85亿元，增幅为49.36%。经清查核实，1993年3月31日清查时点，28户试点企业实际占用的资产价值总量为73.68亿元，其中：各项负债40.51亿元，占54.98%；所有者权益为33.17亿元，占45.02%。通过企业清查扩大试点，发现了企业经营管理中存在的问题，初步掌握了企业保值增值及损失挂帐情况，为加强企业管理，转换经营机制，建立现代企业制度试点提供了切实依据。

4.资产评估。随着社会主义市场经济体制的建立，国有企业之间和不同所有制企业之间出现的企业兼并、联营，资产出售、拍卖，股份制经营，中外合资、合作经营，资产租赁、抵押、担保等国有资产产权变动和经营主体对资产的优化配置活动，迫切要求对有关资产进行评估定价，以维护双方的产权权益。在这种形势推动下，1993年我省资产评估工作发展很快。据统计，1993年我省评估立项共215项，确认121项，分别较上年的立项36项，增加了179项，增长497.22%，确认15项，增加了106项，增长706.67%。其中：确认中外合资、合作经营9项，占确认总数的7.44%；确认股份制改组6项，占确认总数的4.96%；确认联营5项，占确认总数的4.13%；确认资产转让12项，占确认总数的9.92%；确认公房出售89项，占确认总数的73.55%。评估确认值为8.54亿元，增值率达58.6%。在做好评估立项、确认工作的同时，我们加强了对评估机构的管理。

5.产权交易市场。产权交易是优化资源配置，提高企业资产运营效益，盘活存量资产，消灭企业亏损的重大举措；是转换企业经营机制，把企业推向市场，实现产权市场化的实际步骤；是深化产权制度改革，理顺产权关系，推动产权流动的有效途径。1993年，组建了2家产权交易中心，并在天水市举办了甘肃省首届产权交易会，会议期间已达成意向或签订合同的有86台(件)，价值达320万元，预计会后通过看货、面议还会有更多的项目成交。会上还举行了整体企业联合、兼并的签字仪式以及三家企业成功兼并的经验交流。通过这次产权交易会，增强了产权交易意识，积累了组织大型交易活动的经验，同时，为进一步打开产权交易局面，举办下届全省的产权交易会奠定了基础。

6.股份制试点。为了切实加强股份制试点企业的国有资产的管理，在国有企业股份制改组中，我们积极与省体改委联系，共同对实行改组的33户企业进行摸底调查，参与其股份制改组的审批。对批准改组的股份制企业，督促其严格按照国家国有资产管理局《关于在股份制试点中加强维护国有资产权益的通知》、《股份制试点企业国有资产管理暂行规定》等有关文件的要求，规范其股份制改组行为，与此同时，积极实施国务院91号令，对实行改组的企业进行资产评估，在资产评估确认的基础上界定产权，确认国家股股本。

税　务

加强税收工作
促进甘肃经济发展

国家税务总局甘肃

省分局局长　刘思义

1993年，对于甘肃的税收工作来说是极不平凡的一年。在这一年里全省广大税务干部认真贯彻执行中央领导关于加强税收工作的指示，紧紧围绕组织收入这个中心，按照国家税务总局和省委、省政府对税收工作的部署和要求，结合本部门实际做了大量艰苦细致的工作，取得了令人瞩目的成绩，创下了我省税收史上税收收入、增长幅度、起收幅度三项最高纪录，为平衡我省财政收支，促进甘肃经济发展，支援国家建设做出了积极贡献。为了保证税收任务的完成，促使税款及时、足额地入库，全省税务干部坚持依法治税，廉洁自律，勤奋工作，在抓好组织收入的同时，努力做好其他各项二作，加强对个体税收、投资方向调节税及个人收入调节税的征管，取得了显著成效。在全省范围内推行地方税规范化管理，加强了对地方税及其他各税种的监控管理。按照中央和国家税务总局的要求，及时清理了我省自定的税收优惠政策，并停止了一切不符合税法规定的减免税的审批，增加了收入。为了及时掌握了解工作中出现的新情况，各级税务部门经常组织工作组深入基层、企业，做细致的调查研究，发现问题及时解决，为领导决策提供依据。在加强队伍建设方面，我们注重对税务干部的培训，提高其政治思想素质和业务素质，为保证收入的完成打下了良好的队伍基础。

一、积极组织收入，平衡财政收支

1993年，我省各级税务部门共组织各项收入53.07亿元，比1992年增长22.82%，增收9.98亿元。其中，工商税收完成47.90亿元，完成国家税务总局下达年计划38.07亿元的125.82%，超收9.83亿元，比上年增长36.19%，增收12.73亿元。中央级收入完成9204万元，完成国家税务总局下达年计划1.21亿元的76.07%，短收2896万元，比上年增长41.86%；地方级工商税收完成46.98亿元，完成国家税务总局下达年计划36.86亿元的127.45%，超收10.12亿元，比上年增长36.08%；完成省政府下达年计划38.26亿元的122.87%，超收8.72亿元。国营企业所得税完成3.07亿元；能源交通基金完成9734万元；预算调节基金完成1.05亿元；粮食补贴基金完成646万元；教育费附加完成6662万元；烟酒专项收入完成21万元。

1993年全年收入进度很不均衡，一季度完成年计划的18.69%。二季度完成31.22%。三季度完成23.92%。四季度完成51.98%。从主要税种看，来自生产环节的产品税、增值税收入为30.75亿元，比上年增长35.94%；来自流通环节的营业税收入为11.17亿元，比上年增长44.76%。特别是上半年，收入进度一直吃紧，税收收入大幅度滑坡，针对这种情况，省局及时召开了税收收入分析会和全省税务局长会议，认真分析了收入下滑的原因，教育广大税务干部要认真处理好三个关系，即税收与经济改革的关系，税收与市场经济的关系，税收与社会的关系，使广大税务干部提高了思想认识。在具体工作中做到了既抓好大中型企业的重点税源，同时又抓紧零星分散的个体税收。并争取各级党政部门对税收工作的支持，协调好各方面关系。通过各地税务部门的严抓细管，实现了时间过半，完成税收任务过半的目标，受到了省委、省政府的高度评价。下半年以后，各级税务部门十分重视收入分析制度，针对组织收入工作中出现的问题，及时分析，并采取措施贯彻落实，保证了税收收入有较高的增长势头。

1. 全省工业生产速度持续增长，生产环节的税收增长幅度较快。1993年全省工业总产值完成360.2亿元，比上年增长9.8%，一些工业支柱产品产量保持了一定的增长幅度，全年征收产品税、增值税30.75亿元，比上年增长35.94%。

2. 全省城乡市场活跃，购销两旺，使营业税收入大增。1993年社会商品零售总额达到161.88亿元，比上年增长20.42%；来自流通环节的营业税完成11.17亿元，比上年增长35.94%，其中商业零售和其他饮食业营业税税率提高两个百分点后，增收8413万元。

3. 外商投资项目和投资额不断增加，投资领域不断拓宽，全年共征收工商统一税2900万元，比上年增长4.66倍。

4. 1993年基本建设投资规模扩大，建材产品受市场影响，产品价格上扬，增加税收收入6780万元。

5. 积极清理企业欠税。各级税务部门都把清理欠税工作当头等大事来抓，全年共清缴企业欠税3.63亿元。

6. 1993年我省认真贯彻中央6号文件精神，清理越权自定税收优惠政策，停止临时性和困难性减免税的审批，共增收2.9亿元。

7. 开展各项税收大检查，贯彻落实《税收征管法》及其实施细则，强化征收管理，增收税款5456万元。

二、加强征收管理，保证收入，减少税款流失

1. 加强《税收征管法》的学习宣传

1993年年初，我们在《甘肃经济报》上刊登了《税收征管法》知识连载，在全省范围内广泛开展了《征管法》知识竞赛，参赛人数达1500多人，有力地促进了征管法及其实施细则的学习和贯彻执行。结合税法宣传月活动，我们组织人员编写印发了《税收征管法学习手册》及大量的宣传辅导材料，使更多的人掌握和了解了《税收征管法》。

2. 清理税收优惠政策

为了保证税法的统一性，强化宏观调控，促使企业公平竞争，实现财政收支走两条线的政策。根据中央6号文件、国务院51号文件精神，对我省自1988年以来，省委、省政府为发展经济而制定的一系列税收优惠政策进行了清理，共清理出23个文件、38条规定属于越权制定的优惠政策。并将清理结果如实地向省委、省政府和国家税务总局作了汇报。并立即停止了对不符合税法规定的减免税的审批，包括困难性、临时性的减免税，进一步加强了宏观调控，增加了税收收入。

3. 加强重点税源和个体税收的征管

甘肃重点税源占总收入的70%左右，对这部分税源，我们始终紧抓不放，及时进行全面系统的分析，安排收入进度。在七八月份召开了重点税源分析会，对全省的重点税源都逐一摸底排队，做到了心中有数。对于有潜力可挖的企业，通过详细的分析研究，安排了合理的收入计划。个人收入调节税、投资方向调节税、个体税收的征管问题，在我省是薄弱环节，并且问题比较突出，针对这种情况，首先，我们组织有关人员，深入10个典型企业，对个人收入调节税的征管工作进行了详细的调查，分析了情况，制定了具体措施，强化了征收管理。其次，对投资方向调节税，严把税目税率审核关，并多次进行了调查了解，催缴税款，超额完成了任务。全省有个体户11.4万户，对这部分税款，我们一直抓得较紧，做到合理核定，有序征收，结合大检查，对个体税收进行了全面系统的清理检查，使全年个体税收收入达2.32亿元，完成计划任务1.94亿元的119.59%。

三、积极稳妥地做好新税制出台前的各项准备工作

全国税制改革方案于1993年下半年下发，全面性、结构性的税制改革将在1994年元月1日起正式实施，时间紧而任务重，为了能够使新税制顺利到位并正常运转，我们主要做了以下几方面的工作。

1. 加强宣传，搞好测算工作

为了宣传税制改革的的重要意义和新税制的优越性，让广大税务干部对税制改革有一个比较全面的、系统的了解，我们抽调有关人员组成工作组，分头做思想发动和组织动员工作，并在《甘肃日报》上刊登了13讲税制改革专题讲座，同时还在《甘肃经济报》上多次刊登新税制辅导材料，多次在广播电台、电视台发表讲话，召开新闻发布会进行宣传。组织我局有关人员，进行调查研究，先后三次进行摸底测算，掌握实施新税制后对我省税收收入的影响，为领导及时了解税改前后税源变化情况和实行分税制提供了准确的数据资料。

2. 开展培训学习工作，为新税制出台作准备

全国税制改革实施方案和部分税收条例及实施细则出台后我省税务系统紧急行动起来，自上而下，全面开展了大规模的培训工作，对新税制的有关内容进行了系统的学习，并组织考试，收到了良好的效果。据不完全统计，到1993年底，全省税务干部的培训面达到98%，同

时还培训企业厂长、经理和财会人员53500多人次,培训个体户65000人次,基本上达到了预期的要求。另外,我们还进行了发票印制和一般纳税人的认定工作,初步统计,全省共印制增值税专用发票800多万份,并及时发放到一般纳税人手中,共认定一般纳税人10821户。

提高认识 统一行动 积极推进税制改革

省地方税务局局长

吴碧莲

迎着改革的大潮,我们跨入了1994年。

在我国经济体制改革的关键阶段,国务院作出了《关于实行分税制财政管理体制的决定》,这是建立社会主义市场经济体制的一项重大举措,是经济体制总体改革的一项重要内容。它对进一步理顺中央和地方的财政分配关系,更好地发挥国家财政的职能作用,增强中央的宏观调控能力,促进社会主义市场经济的发展关系极大。可以说,税制改革是一项伟大的创造性事业,是一项艰巨复杂的社会工程。我们要充分认识实行分税制财政体制的重大意义和改革的急迫性,积极投入到税制改革的大潮中。

一、税制改革是发展社会主义市场经济的客观要求

党的十四大明确提出,我国经济体制改革的目标是建立社会主义市场经济体制,随着市场经济的发展和各项改革的顺利进行,我国原有税制在加快改革开放的新形势下,已难以适应市场经济发展的要求,因而必须进行改革。市场经济的快速发展给税收提出了新的要求:

1.建立、发展、完善社会主义市场经济,必须建立一套符合市场经济客观要求的新税制。社会主义市场经济是统一和完整的,它要求我们必须统一税法、公平税负、简化税制、合理分权、理顺分配关系、规范分配格局。

2.建立社会主义市场经济必须要有宏观调控。在当前加强宏观调控是一个非常紧迫的问题,只有做到这一点才能使经济走上健康发展的轨道。当前,经济生活中已经产生的矛盾主要是新旧体制转换过程中国家宏观调控弱化造成的。因此,要从根本上解决这些矛盾,只有靠深化改革。其中建立一套新的、完善健全的税制对于解决当前的矛盾是十分必要的。

3.税制改革是健全社会分配体制的需要。目前,我国的分配制度尚不健全,制约了经济的发展。为维护国家权益,增强中央宏观调控能力,在保证国家财政收入合理增长的同时调动地方积极性,必须在划分事权的基础上划分财权,确保地方靠自身的努力去组织财源,发展地方经济。

4.市场经济是开放的经济,税制改革应与国际惯例衔接。目前外商投资企业所适用的一些税收条例是改革初期历史条件的产物。现在看来有一些已经很不适应经济发展的需要,直接影响到引进外资和进一步开放,因此必须与国际上大多数国家一样,按照公平税负的原则和操作上的方便,对内对外两套税制并存的情况尽快完成并轨。

二、新税制是建立社会主义市场经济体制的必要条件

当前,我们进行税制改革的一个重要目的就是要充分发挥财政调节经济的杠杆作用,将为进一步改善和加强中央的宏观调控,保证整个国民经济持续、快速、健康地发展和社会主义市场经济体制的最后建立提供可能,创造必要条件。

基于历史上进行的多次财税体制改革经验教训,使我们清醒地认识到,在整个发展社会主义市场经济的过程中,对旧税制不进行改革,不建立起适应社会主义市场经济发展的新税制是不行的。虽然旧的财税体制曾为保证财政收入的增长,促进国民经济的发展起过积极的作用,但随着社会主义市场经济的发展,逐步暴露出一些弊端:一是虽经多次改革,许多地方仍是多种财税体制并存,未能实现统一税法,公平税负的目标,致使地区之间财政分配苦乐不均,国家财政收入占国民生产总值、中央财政收入占全国财政收入的比重逐年下降,国家宏观调控能力弱化,地方本位主义、保护主义泛滥;二是财政行为发生扭曲,经济发达地区与落后地区两极分化现象严重,上有政策,下有对策,收入多的地方自行减免税,而困难的地方为了吃饭甚至搞"竭泽而渔",严重干扰了社会主义市场经济的健康发展;三是财政体制与税收体制不配套,财权与事权不衔接,造成了一些地方越权减免税,变相承包税收,自定各项优惠政策,使国家财政流失严重;四是由于各行其事的减免税助长了地方争项目、争投资,自筹资金上项目等无政府状况,政府控制基本建设规模成了"空话",消费需求的过快增长又导致"通胀"的急剧上升;五是强化了地方利益机制,促使地方为了追求更多的财政收入,投资向加工企业倾斜,社会资金也向价高利大的房地产业集中,而关系到国家整体发展的交通能源建设却资金不足,造成资源配置的不合理和财力的大量浪费,直接影响国家产业政策的贯彻和产业结构的调整。而分税制的建立,可以改变以往财税改革出现的弊端。一是中央财政通过分税制可以适当集中一些财力,可以改变中央财政依赖于向地方"要饭吃"和被迫向银行借款来解决困难的窘境。同时,既可以为国家有效地实施产业政策和区域开发政策提供财力保证,又可以避免国民收入的超分配,减轻通货膨胀的压力;二是分税制把主体税种流转税列为中央收入或中央与地方的共享收入，这样可以杜绝地方发展经济只着力于追求产值的增长，单纯依靠流转税的增加来增加财政收入的偏向，从而把地方发展经济的积极性引导到大力提高企业素质、加强企业管理、提高经济效益，靠实现利润来增加地方收入；三是中央同地方的分税，破除了目前存在的以流转税为主体的地方既得利益的束缚，中央可以超越各地局部利益，更放手地按照全国资源合理配置的要求，按照市场竞争优胜劣汰的规律，全面实施经济发展的产业政策。这便为整个国民经济快速健康的发展提供了必要保证，同时为地方经济稳定发展创造了良好的客观环境。

三、税制改革的指导思想、目的和主要内容

这次税制改革的指导思想是统一税法、公平税负、简化税制、合理分权、理顺分配关系，保障财政收入。税制改革的目的是加强中央宏观调控能力，理顺中央与地方、国家与企业的分配关系，加强税收法制和征收管理，防止税收流失，实现税制简化和高效。税制改革的主要内容：一是建立以增值税为主体、包括消费税和营业税的流转税体系。增值税的改革，是整个税制改革的关键，新的增殖税为价外税将成为我国的主体税种。新的流转税规定对商品的生产、批发、零售和进口普遍征收增值税；在此基础上，有选择地对部分消费品交叉征收消费税；对不实行增值税的劳务交易和第三产业征收营业税；扩大资源税征税范围，提高部分税目的税额，使之与增殖税相配套、相衔接。新的流转税制统一适用于内外资企业，取消对外资企业征收的工商统一税，逐步做到内外一致，与国际惯例相衔接，同时，废止了部分与经济发展不相适应的税种。二是统一所得税制度。首先，统一各类内资企业所得税，用税法规范企业税前列支的项目和标准，稳定和拓宽税基，实行合理的比例税率，企业所得税按33%的比例税率实行计税，在条件成熟时，统一内外资企业所得税。其次，合并现行的有关税种，建立统一的个人所得税制度。三是改革其它税种。主要包括开征房地产增殖税、证券交易税、遗产和增予税，改革城市维护建设税。取消盐税等10多个税种，原32种工商税变为17种。

四、统一行动，抓好机构的分设工作

职能决定机构，机构体现职能，按照税制改革的要求和工作需要，在国家机构改革的统筹安排下，坚持精简、效能的原则，当务之急是加速建立中央税务局和地方税务局两套税务机构，更好地肩负起中央和各级地方税收任务。根据国家的要求，现有税务局做为国家税务局的基础，那么，地方税务局的组建工作将是更加艰巨的任务。

五、精心操作，确保新税制正常进行

实行分税制财政管理体制，旨在建立起适应社会主义市场经济要求的财税运行机制，这是一项十分艰巨、复杂的创造性工程，它既需要整个财税体系各环节的紧密衔接，又要国民经济各综合部门的大力合作。为了保证新税制的健康运行，各级财政部门无论遇到多大困难，都必须顾全大局，确保改革措施及时到位。要严格遵循中央确定的体制框架和基本政策，实事求是地核定收入基数，坚决执行税收返还的原则和比例，自觉纠正弄虚作假现象，杜绝违背原则的各种变通，要尽快学习领会掌握各项改革政策、措施，熟悉新税种、新税率，要精心操作，把握好改革中财税联动的特点，妥善解决操作中遇到的新问题，做到全力以赴、确保新税制正常运行。

社会主义市场经济四要素

1. 发育的市场环境，包括形成商品市场和要素市场，这就需要一系列相关体制的配套改革。

为了形成商品市场，需要改革计划体制、流通体制和价格管理体制。

为了形成要素市场，首先是资金市场和劳务市场，需要改革投资体制、金融体制和人事体制、社会保障体制。

2. 市场活动的主体是企业，但企业必须自主经营、自负盈亏，才能成为合格的市场主体。

3. 完善市场规则，有两个层次：

一是微观层次上的市场规则，有些需要国家制定法规，有些仅需要同业认同的公约，还有些是约定俗成的做法。

二是宏观层次上的市场规则，其作用是保证竞争的适度。这些方面的市场规则，一般都需要以国家法规形式出现。如垄断法、制止不正当竞争法等等。

4. 对市场进行有效的调控，主要是为了减少盲目性，提高市场运行效率。

在市场经济条件下，要由直接调控改为间接调控。即国家调控市场，市场引导企业。

从直接调控到间接调控，需要各级政府转变职能；也需要随着职能的转变，调整组织机构。直接管理企业微观经济活动的机构要精简，进行宏观管理和间接调控的机构要加强。

金融保险

人民银行

稳步推进金融改革 支持甘肃省经济持续快速、健康的发展

中国人民银行

甘肃省分行行长

赵春生

1993年，全省各级金融部门认真贯彻中央(1993)6号文件和党的十四届三中全会精神，紧紧围绕"从严控制总量，优化结构，面向市场，转换机制，提高效益"的货币信贷方针，加强了宏观调控，整顿了金融秩序，严肃结算纪律，积极筹措资金，调整信贷结构，使一、二季度出现的严峻的金融形势很快好转。

一、大力筹措资金，优化贷款投向，基本保证了全省经济发展的合理资金需要

各行采取有效措施，抓住两次利率调整的有利时机，加强宣传，改进服务，积极组织存款，信贷资金来源不断扩大。到年底，全省金融机构各项存款余额达360.64亿元，比年初增加57.40亿元，增长18.93%，其中银行各项存款比年初增加46.15亿元，增长17.94%，余额达303.38亿元。在银行存款增加额中，城镇储蓄存款增加36.03亿元，增长26.73%，余额达170.82亿元，当年增加额创历史最高纪录，储蓄存款增加额占各项存款增加额的比重达78.08%，成为银行信贷资金的主要来源。

同时，进一步开拓和发展了金融市场，扩大了有价证券的发行，增加了上市转让的券种和数量。全年累计发行国库券4.05亿元，比上年增长8.87%，发行财政债券995.6万元，首次发行了中央银行融资券1.04亿元。配合有关部门进行了企业股份制改造，有6家金融机构经批准成为上海、深圳两市证券交易所异地会员单位，并在兰州市建立了股票交易大厅，公开挂牌交易，为企业到市场直接筹资融资创造了条件，也为居民选择新的投资方式提供了方便。甘肃金融市场全年累计拆借资金62亿元，推动了资金的相互融通。

在大力筹资融资，不断增加信贷资金来源的同时，进一步调整贷款结构，严格执行"五优先"、"五从严"、"八不贷"的政策，适时合理发放贷款，支持了全省经济的发展。到年底，全省金融机构各项贷款余额达419.43亿元，比年初增加79.42亿元，增长23.36%，其中银行各项贷款比年初增加65.71亿元，增长21.74%，余额达367.83亿元，其中流动资金贷款增加36.94亿元，比上年多增加8.03亿元，重点解决了效益好的国有大中型企业和地方企业的正常生产经营的资金需要，保证了农副产品和外贸出口产品收购的资金需要，支持了乡镇企业的发展；农业贷款增加2.04亿元，支持了农业生产和农村经济的全面发展；固定资产贷款增加24.15亿元，比上年多增加10.27亿元，其中基本建设贷款增加19.47亿元，技术改造贷款增加3.92亿元，保证了国家、省重点建设和技术改造的资金需要。

全省净投放货币19.12亿元，比上年少投放了3.16亿元，控制在下达的计划以内，保证了正常合理的现金供应。

二、积极推进了金融体制改革

适应市场经济发展和经济体制改革的需要，有计划、有步骤地发展了多样化、多层次的金融机构，积极引进省外金融机构在我省设立了派出机构，加快了组建城市信用联社的试点工作，向农村信用联社颁发了《经营金融业务许可证》，促使其在合法、合规的基础上开展业务活动，稳健经营。实行大额款项汇划通过人民银行转汇，加强了汇差资金管理，在大中城市开办银行本票，为个体工商户和个人在银行立帐户提供方便，扩大了转帐结算，减少了现金使用。在省内部分地区陆续开办了职工养老统筹保险，拓展了新的服务领域。逐步扩大了抵押贷款业务，加强了贷款风险管理。完善了资金管理体制，部分试行了贷款限额管理下的资产负债比例管理和资产风险管理办法。同时进行了机构、人事和劳动用工、分配等三项制度改革，促进了各项业务的发展。

三、整顿金融秩序，严肃金融纪律，促进了金融形势的逐步好转

去年下半年以来，全省各级金融部门，严格按照党中央、国务院指示精神和朱镕基副总理提出的"约法三章"，以及人民银行总行党组提出的"三要"、"十不准"的规定，认真开展了整顿金融秩序，严肃金融纪律的工作。

认真清理、坚决纠正了违章拆借资金的问题。根据人民银行总行《关于进一步整顿和规范同业拆借秩序的通知》的有关规定，各金融机构对拆借资金的期限、利率、用途、对象等方面进行了认真的检查和清理，停止了省以下资金市场的直接拆借和对非银行金融机构的资金拆

借及其它违章拆借。到年底，已收回违章拆借资金3.01亿元，占1992年以来违章拆借资金的58.67%，7月份以后，全省再未发生过违章拆借。

撤并了未经人民银行批准擅自设立和越权审批的金融机构，对非法设立的金融机构及其它违规行为进行了处罚。对部分金融机构进行了年检。在合格的基础上重新换发了《经营金融业务许可证》，进一步加强和规范了对各类金融机构的管理。

各行、司与所办经济实体脱钩的工作进展比较顺利。到年底，全省金融系统办的360个经济实体，已撤销、转让137个，保留的223个大部分已经脱钩，有714名干部辞去了兼任的职务，占兼职干部数的90.1%。

按照整顿结算秩序的要求，重点对压票压汇、无理拒付、少扣或不扣滞纳金问题进行了查处，并对邮政汇兑资金设立了专户，保证了及时兑付，较好地解决了"绿条子"问题。加强了利率管理，对违反利率政策的问题进行了认真的查处，并在《甘肃日报》等报纸上公布了人民银行制定的存贷款现行利率，把执行利率政策的情况置于群众和舆论的监督之下，维护了利率政策的严肃性。

四、强化了稽查监督工作，保证了各项宏观调控政策、措施的有效落实

在全省范围内重点进行了金融宏观调控政策、措施执行情况的专项稽核，在各行普遍进行自查的同时，人民银行省分行组成工作组，对三个单位进行了重点稽核。对超规模发放贷款、违反利率政策、违规拆借资金、发放假委托贷款、违规开展住房信贷业务等问题进行了认真的查处。加强了常规稽核，试验推广了非现场稽核和信贷资产质量稽核。同时各行、司结合本系统业务，自选了部分稽核项目，围绕"两防一保"工作，加强了内部稽核。通过以上工作，较好地发挥了稽核监督职能，保证了各项宏观调控政策、措施的有效贯彻落实。

五、保险事业有了新的发展

1993年，全省保险系统进一步深化内部改革，强化经营管理，加快经营机制转换步伐，不断拓宽服务领域，各项业务在连续五年保持较快发展的基础上，提前实现了全省保险业"八五"规划奋斗的目标。到年底，全省保险业务收入达5.04亿元，比上年增长33.29%，其中保费收入2.8亿元，超额16%完成全年计划。全年共处理各种赔付案件31.95万起，赔款和给付2.05亿元，分别比上年增长35.64%和45.82%，较好地发挥了保险的经济补偿职能和抗灾防灾的重要作用。

六、认真开展了"两防一保"活动，内部管理工作得到加强

全省各级金融部门始终把"防诈骗、防盗窃，确保银行资金安全"作为一项重要任务来抓，加强了领导，狠抓了各项措施的落实。通过组织学习和宣传教育，完善内部制约机制，签订"两防一保"责任书，对要害岗位、要害人员进行行为考核等措施，增强了全体职工的"防""保"意识，堵塞了漏洞，初步形成了内外结合、齐抓共管、综合治理的良好局面。有效地制止了一些金融诈骗活动，保证了国家资产的安全。

七、加强了各项基础建设，工作质量和工作水平进一步提高

1993年全省各级金融部门认真学习党的十四大和十四届三中全会精神以及《邓小平文选》第三卷，用邓小平同志建设有中国特色社会主义理论武装全体职工的思想；加强了领导班子建设。按照干部"四化"方针和德才兼备原则，一批懂金融会管理、有开拓创新精神的干部被提拔到领导岗位，保证了领导班子的新老交替。同时狠抓了领导班子的思想作风建设，重视了职工教育和业务培训工作；加强了调查研究和统计分析工作，对经济、金融运行中出现的新情况、新问题，进行了深入、认真的调查研究和综合反映，为各级党政领导和上级行决策提供了第一手资料和依据。

在正确分析形势和估价去年工作成绩的同时，我们还要清醒地看到存在的问题，看到工作中的不足。主要是一些单位执行制度不严，内部管理松驰，有章不循，以致发生了重大案件；在推进金融体制改革中，金融部门自身在思想观念等方面还有许多不适应的地方，转换职能在具体操作上也还有一定的难度。同时我省企业经济效益普遍比较差，而资金需求又很大，在专业银行向商业银行转换的过程中，如何进一步提高资金使用效益是摆在我们面前的一项亟待解决的问题。对此，我们要加倍努力工作，克服困难，坚定信心，认真做好各项工作，决不辜负省委、省政府和各总行、司对我们的期望。

外汇管理

1993年甘肃外汇管理

1993年，在国家外汇管理局和省政府的领导下，我们认真贯彻执行中央、国务院关于加强和改善外汇管理的方针政策，全面落实全国外汇管理分局长会议提出的各项工作任务，围绕支持甘肃经济发展和扩大对外开放的需要，在稳定人民币汇率、平抑外汇调剂价格，加强出口收汇监督、强化金融机构外汇业务管理以及开展外汇检查等方面做了大量的工作，并取得了较好的成绩。

【外汇收支】1993年，全省外贸出口

28347万美元，出口收汇19750万美元，其中地方外贸、工贸公司出口21395万美元，净收现汇12875万美元。全年无偿上缴中央外汇2162万美元，有偿上缴4671万美元，地方留成外汇6042万美元；非贸易外汇收入1619万美元，留成719万美元；全年各类外汇额度总收入15186万美元，总支出16700万美元，其中因公出国团组476个，批汇465万美元。

1993年全省外汇收支主要有以下几个特点：一是非贸易外汇收入大幅度增长。全省非贸易外汇收入在1992年突破了千万美元关口的基础上，1993年又有新的发展，外汇收入达1619万美元，比上年增长30.60%。二是出口下降，贸易留成外汇减少。1993年全省外贸出口和出口收汇分别比上年减少6821万美元和6018万美元，下降19.40%和23.35%。三是外汇额度总收支均比上年减少。1993年，在贸易留成外汇减少的情况下，中央和国拨专项外汇也大幅度减少，减少比例达57.50%。全省外汇额度总收入比上年减少11.80%；外汇总支出比上年减少15.80%。

【积极做好有偿上缴中央外汇的人民币兑付工作】国务院决定从1993年6月起，有偿上缴中央外汇由人民银行负责收购，实行“高来高去”政策，人民银行授权外汇管理局具体实施。为了使这项工作顺利展开，一方面及时与有关单位取得联系，进一步做好外汇核拨工作，以保证出口企业能及时得到有偿上缴中央外汇的人民币资金，另一方面召开了省级各专业银行会议，研究解决人民币资金汇划的具体问题。同时，在内部建立健全了有关的核算帐户，严密人民币兑付工作的核算手续。从6月到12月，全省共计兑付有偿上缴中央外汇的人民币资金6761万元，有效地缓解了外贸出口企业人民币资金紧张的矛盾。

【外汇留成制度】1991年1月1日起，我国外贸体制进入了新的一轮改革，实行自负盈亏的经营机制。在外汇留成方面，取消了出口供货企业10%的留成外汇，也取消了经济特区的优惠留成比例，全国实行统一的留成比例，为外贸企业创造了平等竞争的条件。1993年是新一轮外贸体制改革的第三年，在外汇留成方面仍采用1991年国家规定的比例。即实行在外贸部门出口收汇剔除有关费用后，按净收汇金额分成，一般商品20%按官方牌价上缴国家，30%按官方牌价加全国调剂外汇额度加权平均价有偿上缴国家；10%按官方牌价结汇上缴地方政府，40%留给外贸出口企业；机电产品、特定科技产品30%有偿上缴中央，5%上缴地方政府，65%留外贸出口企业。为了改变有偿上缴中央外汇人民币资金不能及时拨补的问题，国务院决定从1993年6月起，有偿上缴中央外汇由人民银行负责收购，这一举措保证了外贸出口企业及时得到了有偿上缴中央外汇的人民币补偿资金。

【出口收汇核销管理】实行出口收汇核销制度，是深化外贸体制改革，加强出口收汇管理的一项重要措施。1993年，我们从清理出口收汇核销情况入手，进一步加强了对出口收汇的监督管理，对各外贸、工贸公司等单位的出口收汇核销情况进行了清理核对，并对清理出的问题提出了处理意见，加强了核销工作各个环节的管理。1993年出口收汇核销单的收单率和核销率均比上年有了明显的提高。全年收单率达99.47%，核销率Ⅰ为91.61%，核销率Ⅱ为92.10%，分别比上年提高19.16、31.72和17.57个百分点。与此同时，我们还配合税务部门利用出口收汇核销数据进行出口退税工作，在出口收汇核销微机管理系统增加了出口退税辅助系统，以保证按时向税务部门提供核销数据，使出口核销和出口退税工作有机地结合了起来，从而增强了出口收汇管理的力度。

【外债管理】1993年，全省的外债余额有新的增长，年底外债余额达20712万美元，比上年增长31.50%，进一步解决了我省建设资金的需要。为了及时反映我省的外债规模和债务结构，我们加强了对外债的统计监测工作，对每一笔债务从借、用、还方面加强管理，并及时反馈信息，为决策机构提供决策依据。

【外汇调剂市场】1993年，全省外汇调剂出现了以下新的情况：一是外汇调剂成交量6250万美元，比上年减少42.07%。主要原因是全省出口创汇下降，留成外汇随之减少，同时外贸企业自营进口使用了部分留成外汇，调剂市场的汇源减少。加之人民币资金紧张，有些单位调剂需求减少。二是调剂外汇价格变动较大。上半年，外汇调剂市场人民币汇价出现了不断下跌的趋势，我省一度跌至1美元兑换10.50元人民币。为了扭转这种局面，国家采取了一系列宏观调控措施，中央银行也积极入市参与调剂，同时，我们进一步改善外汇调剂工作，动员持汇大户入市调剂。从下半年开始，人民币汇价开始回升，达到了1美元兑换人民币8.70元左右较合理的水平，并保持了基本稳定。三是外商投资企业调剂外汇成交量大幅度增加。全年外商投资企业调出外汇296万美元，调入外汇203万美元。与上年相比，调出、调入量分别增加216万美元和162万美元。

【金融机构外汇业务管理】1993年，我们围绕着贯彻落实国家外汇管理局发布的《银行外汇业务管理规定》和《非银行金融机构外汇业务管理规定》及其补充规定，支持我省银行和非银行金融机构开办外汇业务，并加强对其监督管理。一是为适应我省经济、金融和外贸体制改革的需要，我们在批准几家省级专业银行开办外汇业务的基础上，又根据总局下达的设立经营外汇业务的金融机构指标，在对申请开办外汇业务的金融机构进行认真审核的基础上，报请总局批准省投资信托公司和交通银行兰州分行开办外汇业务。与此同时，还批准了各专业银行所属部分地、县机构代办外汇业务。二是对从事外汇业务的银行和非银行金融机构根据总局统一部署，按规定和要求换发和颁发了《经营外汇业务许可证》，其中支行级以上的金融机构14家，分理处、代办处、储蓄所64家。通过换发和颁发许可证，进一步增强了金融机构依法经营外汇业务的观念。

【外汇检查】1993年，根据国家外汇管理局外汇检查工作的精神和要求，结合我省实际，有重点、有步骤地开展了外汇检查。一是贯彻金融机构经营外汇业务管理规定，结合换发《经营外汇业务许可证》，对经营外汇业务的金融机构的经营和对外付汇情况进行了检查；二是贯彻《对公单位现汇帐户管理办法》，结合颁发《现汇帐户使用证》，对231个现汇帐户主要从帐户使用范围、私自买卖外汇等方面进行了检查。三是结合对全省外贸、工贸公司和外商投资企业等出口单位的出口收汇核销情况进行清理，对29个单位进行了重点检查。四是贯彻《关于严厉打击外汇黑市活动的通知》，会同公安、工商行政管理部门，对我省重点地区进行了检查。通过检查发现，绝大多数单位都能按外汇管理政策规定办事，但个别单位仍存在一些问题。对此，我们在查清问题的基础上，及时给予了纠正和处理。

【职工队伍建设】1993年，我局在认真贯彻全国外汇管理局分局长会议精神，做好各项业务工作的同时，积极组织全体职工进行政治业务学习，教育职工干部保持廉洁自律的工作作风，促进干部职工观念转变，为进一步深化外汇管理的改革奠定了思想基础，为更好地开展工作提供了保证。

（国家外汇管理局甘肃分局）

工商银行

努力拓宽财源，提高投资效益，为经济建设服务

甘肃省工商银行，是我省最大的国家专业银行。现有各级分支机构和营业网点886个，职工12037人。全行现已初步形成了资金实力雄厚，业务种类齐全，操作手段先进，服务方便快捷的整体新格局。截至1993年末，全行总资产达到225亿元人民币，各项存、贷款额分别占全省国家专业银行存、贷总额的47.22%和41.82%，有力地支持了国有大中型企业的发展和地方经济建设。

1993年全行系统认真贯彻中央6号文件和7月全国金融工作会议精神，落实宏观调控，整顿金融秩序，转变经营机制，推进业务发展，努力扩大存款，增加资金投入，支持了全省经济的持续、健康发展，各项工作取得了显著成绩。

一、努力扩大资金来源

1993年，我行面对资金供求紧张，社会集资高涨，存款分流严重的严峻形势，认真贯彻“存款第一”、“言必及存”的方针，全行动员，全力以赴大抓存款。各级行处层层建立了存款承包责任制，试行柜员制，坚持储蓄、对公存款两手抓、双并重，以建网点、上手段、增品种、抓服务为主要增存手段，使各项存款保持了较好的增长势头。年末存款余额达到143.3亿元，比年初增加16.1亿元，增长12.65%。其中，储蓄存款余额达到91.6亿元，增加15.3亿元，增长30%创我行储蓄存款增加的历史最好记录；对公存款余额达到51.7亿元，增加0.84亿元，增长1.65%。与此同时，我行在规模、资金日趋紧张的情况下，加强了与总行的情况汇报和资金融通，全年总行为我行的农副产品收购、大中型工商企业、重点技术改造贷款共调剂融通资金14.4亿元，占我行当年新增贷款的62.9%，对缓解我行资金供求矛盾，保证重点贷款及时到位，支持我省经济发展起到了积极作用。

二、适度增加贷款投入

1993年，我行的信贷工作紧紧围绕年初提出的“以效益为中心，以防范风险为重点”的方针。认真贯彻国家产业政策和信贷政策，集中资金保支付、保收购、保重点。年末全行各项贷款余额达到153.8亿元，比年初增加22.94亿元，比上年同期多增加4.55亿元，增长24.74%。全行贷款规模增长适度，信贷结构日趋合理，基本实现了控制总量，搞活存量，优化增量，防范风险的工作目标。其中，流动资金贷款余额达到132.9亿元，比年初增加19.67亿元，重点支持了大中型骨干企业的生产，在我行开户的137户大中型工业企业流动资金贷款增加8.57亿元，占我行全部工业企业贷款增加额的78.2%，比上年提高了1.2个百分点；支持了商业企业合理储备和农副产品收购贷款增加2.5亿元，我行开户的粮食企业在向农民收购粮油中没有出现打“白条”的现象。全年累计发放技术改造贷款4.37亿元，支持了兰州炼油厂、兰化公司、白银公司、酒泉钢铁公司、靖远陶瓷厂等110个技术改造项目。

三、综合业务功能进一步增强

按照把我行逐步转变为国有商业银行的要求，1993年，我行系统进一步深化改革，转换机制，开拓和发

展了新的业务领域和业务种类,相继开办了外汇、信托、信用卡、房地产、信息咨询、证券买卖等新业务。年末我行外汇存款达到1340万美元,外汇贷款达到740万美元;信托业务总资产达到3.3亿元,全年证券交易额1亿多元;住房贷款增加1.2亿元,吸收各类住房基金存款1.3亿元;牡丹卡发卡量达到1.5万张,全年交易额达到2.5亿元。与此同时,我行充分发挥网点遍布全省的优势为工商企业和社会各界提供优良的结算和现金服务。全年累计为客户办理结算业务1721万笔,累计金额达4004亿元;全年累计收付现金365.7亿元,比上年增加96亿元,增长26.3%,对支持企业发展生产,扩大流通,加速社会资金周转,促进全省经济发展做出了应有的贡献。

四、严格执行了"约法三章"的规定

1993年7月之后,我行系统根据中央6号文件精神和全国金融工作会议的要求,认真执行朱镕基副总理提出的"约法三章",整顿金融秩序,严明金融纪律,加强内部管理,重点对违章拆借资金、各种收费的执行标准、自办公司脱钩,以及存贷款利率执行情况进行了全面检查和清理。取消了自定收费项目,公布了统一的收费项目和收费标准,对个别行处利率执行不准的情况进行了认真纠正。

五、电子化建设迈上了新的台阶

1993年,我行继续贯彻科技兴行的方针,按照"加快发展步伐,提高技术档次,不断强化管理,提高应用效益"的指导思想,加强了电子化建设步伐,提高了电子化装备水平。我行"八五"电子化建设重点项目ES/9000大机工程,经过全行上下的共同努力,已完成了机房建设、设备安装和软件调试,基本具备了开机联网运行的条件。临柜网点的电子化履盖率进一步提高,全年新建成电子化网点136个,累计上机网点达到423个,全辖电子化网点履盖率达到42.5%。其中储蓄所上机率达到了60%以上,金昌、白银等城市行达到80%。初步建成了统计四级网,开通了从县支行到省分行的统计数据传输系统。

六、加强队伍建设,不断提高职工素质

始终坚持百年大计,教育为本和教育为业务发展服务的方针,采取多层次、多渠道、多形式的政治、业务、技术、文化教育和岗位培训,坚持两手抓,全面提高职工的政治素质、文化和业务素质。1993年举办各类培训班126期,培训职工5200人次,为培养各类人才,为业务发展,为向商业化银行迈步奠定了基础。

1994年,我行系统要继续认真地贯彻党的十四届三中全会精神和《国务院关于金融体制改革的决定》,按照"深化改革,加强管理,促进发展"的要求,大力扩充资金来源,严格控制信贷总量,深化内部机制改革,继续整顿金融秩序,加快向国有商业银行转变步伐,支持我省经济持续、快速、健康发展。

(中国工商银行
甘肃省分行)

农业银行

1993年甘肃省农村金融工作综述

中国农业银行
甘肃分行行长
罗正亚

1993年,全省农业银行和农村信用社认真学习贯彻党的十四大和江泽民总书记、李鹏总理关于农业问题的重点讲话精神,贯彻中央关于加强宏观调控和开展反腐败斗争的重大决策,大力筹集融通资金,合理安排发放贷款,积极整顿农村金融秩序,推进农村金融改革,加强职工队伍建设,支持全省农业和农村经济的持续全面发展,各项工作取得了新的进展。农行、信用社新增各项存款(剔除信用社缴存准备金、转存银行款)186053万元,比上年增长26.07%,年末余额达到899727万元;新增各项贷款(剔除银行支持信用社款)188532万元,比上年增长21.46%,年末余额达到1066992万元。

纵观1993年全省农村金融工作,主要在以下八个方面,取得明显成效:

一、以支持粮食生产为重点,努力增加对农业的信贷投入

行、社全年累计发放各项农业贷款316901万元,比上年多放65406万元,投量是历史上最多的一年。在投向上,一是适应粮食生产上新台阶的要求,用于支持以粮棉油生产为主的种植业的贷款达158971万元,比上年多放36049万元,其中直接用于粮棉油生产的贷款占35.53%。二是适应发展"两高一优"农业的要求,用于支持农业实用技术推广应用、各类农业星火计划和丰收计划等科技兴农方面的贷款21681万元,比上年多放4832万元;用于支持各类社会化服务体系建设的贷款11002万元,比上年多放5102万元。三是适应全省实施"22274"工程和加快农业综合开发的要求,用于支持开荒、中低产田改造、农田水利建设等农业开发方面的贷款7300万元,比上年增加2009万元。四是适应继续打好以高寒阴湿和少数民族地区为主战场的扶贫攻坚战的要求,行、社全年累计发放各项扶贫贷款26660万元,比上年多放 9638 万元。五是适应畜牧业发展、农副产品转化增殖和增加农民经济收入的要求,用于支持养殖业和各类工副业发展方面的贷款 118604 万元,比上年增加 21956 万元(以上五个方面部分数字重复计算)。

二、高度重视农副产品收购资金的及时足额到位,积极支持农村商品流通

为了扩大粮棉油等主要农副产品收购,切实贯彻落实党中央、国务院关于农副产品收购中不能再给农民打白条的一系列指示精神,全行上下努力做到了"三个到位",一是思想到位。各级行处普遍把 1993 年收购资金的供应工作,不仅作为经济问题,而且作为政治问题认真对待,在思想上比任何一年更为重视。二是领导到位。省、地、县三级行都成立了主管行长负责的收购资金协调机构,收购旺季,各级行长都深入基层,就地研究解决问题。三是资金到位。按时如数发放国家计划安排的 10430 万元粮食预购定金和 2250 万元棉花贴息贷款,及时筹足了当年收购中由农行承担的资金,按规定垫付了未按时到位的企业自筹和财政拨补资金。全年累计发放收购贷款 452894 万元,比上年多放 18677 万元,其中为企业和财政垫付资金 36595 万元。全省没有发生在农行贷款的企业"打白条"问题。与此同时,全行系统发放 344259 万元贷款,用于支持农业生产资料供应、日用工业品下乡和农村市场基础设施等方面的需要,推动了农村市场建设。

三、加大支持力度,促进乡镇企业的快速发展

1993 年,为加大对乡镇企业的支持力度,省农业银行在用足用好新增乡镇企业贷款规模的同时,适当下放乡镇企业贷款项目审批权限,调动了基层行支持发展乡镇企业的积极性,有效地扩大了对乡镇企业的信贷投入。行、社全年累计发放乡镇企业贷款 161299 万元,比上年多放 57951 万元,年末余额达到 140139 万元,比上年增加 37613 万元。在贷款配置上,注意做到"三个倾斜",即:向政府确定的重点县、乡、村和开发小区倾斜,向立足当地资源优势的能源、原材料工业和加工业倾斜:向"双带整推"、科技开发等项目和"名优特新"产品倾斜。

四、大力组织农村存款,积极盘活信贷存量

1993 年,全省农行、信用社面对频繁的直接融资和激烈的同业竞争,紧紧抓住全国农村储蓄存款突破 5000 亿元。国家两次调高利率、整顿金融秩序、省政府批转农行《关于大力组织公存款的报告》等有利时机,组织动员行社职工广泛吸储揽储,扩大公存款。全年行、社各项存款分别增加 116255 万元和 86717 万元,比上年多增加 48745 万元和 37650 万元,年末余额分别达到 603385 万元和 377729 万元,其中行、社储蓄净增 145073 万元,比上年增加 27.47%,增幅之大是前所未有的。与此同时,各级行、社把盘活信贷存量作为解决资金和规模紧张、提高资产质量的重要措施,下大气力清收有问题贷款。全省行、社全年累计收回农贷和乡镇企业贷款 421681 万元,比上年多收 99034 万元。

五、以发展新业务为重点,积极开拓商业性业务

1993 年,全行外汇存、贷款分别比上年增长 1.96 倍和 1.61 倍,建立密押关系的海外银行扩大到 124 家,并在西北首家开通了环球银行间金融电讯网络,国际结算业务得到迅速发展;进一步开拓和规范了信托、证券业务,各项委托、信托存款达到 4343 万元,全年累计融资 122837 万元,信托资产总额增加 9063 万元,年末余额达到 24463 万元;相继在兰州、白银两市开办了信用卡业务,发展特约商号 141 家,受理信用卡业务的营业网点 88 个;省、地两级行以各自的营业部为依托,加大了经营份量,由单纯管理型向经营管理型积极转变。

六、坚决贯彻宏观调控决策,认真整顿农村金融秩序

1993 年 7 月以后,按照中央 6 号文件精神和"约法三章"的要求,全行系统开展了整顿金融秩序、严肃金融纪律工作,坚决停止并清理收回违章拆借资金,规范了行、社正常的融资活动;对行、社所有营业机构执行利率的情况进行全面检查,维护了国家利率政策的严肃性;按规定对自办经济实体进行认真清理整顿,收回对其发放的贷款;在"堵邪门"的同时"开正门",加强对贷款规模和资金的宏观调控,确保存款支付、农业生产和农副产品收购等重点需要,把行、社贷款总规模及各项指令性指标控制在了总行规定的限额之内。全年行、社贷款分别增加 120293 万元和 64971 万元,占年计划的 93.58%和 99.96%。

七、围绕向国有商业银行转变,积极推进农村金融改革

1993 年,为实施新财务会计制度,全行上下层层举办培训班,召开全行会计工作会议,制定下发《关于实施新财会制度中有关问题说明》等一整套制度方法,为新旧财会制度顺利接轨打下了较好的基础;根据农村金融改革和发展的需要,按照精简、效能原则,各级行对其内部机构作了适当调整,部分县、市支行实行了干部聘用制,改进了奖金分配制度,机构、人事、分配制度的改革有了较大进展;进行了综合改革、资产负债比例管理、政策性贷款与商业性贷款分帐核算、信用社股份合作制、实行"贷款证"等方面的试点工作,为深化农村金融改革进行了有益探索;全行电脑业务网点增加到 175 个,兰州、白银、武威三市行同城联机网络初具规模,联行计算机对帐系统正式运行，电子化建设迈出了新的步伐。

八、以反腐倡廉为重点，全面加强队伍建设

党中央、国务院作出了反腐败斗争的重要部署后，全行系统迅速行动，突出抓了县处级以上领导干部和县支行行级干部的自查自纠、经济案件的查处和行业不正之风三件事，取得初步成效。同时，各级行、社组织干部职工认真学习十四大精神、《邓选》三卷和十四届三中全会决定，继续开展“立足本职建功业，我为行徽添光彩”活动，进一步加强和改进了思想政治工作；根据四化方针和德才兼备原则，加强了各级领导班子和后备干部队伍建设；从农村金融改革和发展的现实需要出发，对14450名行、社干部进行了岗位培训，继续开展了大、中专层次的学历教育，农村金融系统职工队伍的整体素质有了进一步提高。

建设银行

奋力开拓的甘肃省建设银行

省建设银行行长

张宗祥

1993年，甘肃建行在省委、省政府和总行的领导下，坚持以党的十四大和十四届三中全会精神为指导，进一步解放思想，转变观念，群策群力，克服了伴随经济过热带来的资金形势紧张、金融秩序混乱等一系列矛盾，坚定不移地以筹资为中心，以支持国家经济建设为已任，以转换信贷机制、经营机制和内部管理机制为重点，深化改革，奋力开拓，全行各项工作在困难大、任务重、头绪多的情况下，取得了较好的成绩，一些业务有了较大发展，千方百计保证了重点建设资金的供应，为支持国家和甘肃经济建设持续、快速、健康地发展做出了积极贡献。

1993年，全省建行一般性存款余额达到58.39亿元，当年新增9.83亿元，是总行下达任务7.8亿元的120.3%。其中：企业存款新增1.05亿元；储蓄存款新增8.78亿元，比1992年多增1.77亿元。

1993年，各项贷款控制在规模之内，年末贷款余额达92.82亿元，当年新增24.58亿元。其中：固定资产贷款新增19.78亿元，流动资金贷款新增4.81亿元，同时累计发放各种临时性贷款5.4亿元。

1993年，全省建行净收回各类到逾期贷款9.6亿元，逾期率控制在9.76%。收回拆出资金1.5亿元。

1993年，全省建行及时拨付财政资金，基建预算支出情况良好。全年财政预算支出11.1亿元，占年度预算的92.5%；并认真履行了财政监督职能，共审查工程预(结)算24.41亿元，审查面为99%，定案率为99%，净核减8290万元。通过参与工程概算，审查工程预结算，严格柜台拨付审查，加强企业财务管理，为各类建设项目提合理化建议等活动，共为国家节约建设资金5.9亿元。

1993年，全省建行顺利完成了新旧财务制度的交接，狠抓了扭亏增盈工作，年末实现利润350万元，完成了总行下达的利润计划。

1993年，甘肃省建设银行从大局出发，不遗余力地大抓存款；加强信贷管理，优化信贷结构；加强资金调控，严肃金融纪律，重点建设项目资金到位率达到100%。

——不遗余力，大抓存款，1993年，省建行始终把广泛筹集资金放在全行工作的首位

全行动员，面向市场，多轮驱动，大抓储蓄：一是引入了激励机制，在全行系统实行多种类型的储蓄承包责任制，充分调动了全行吸存揽储的积极性，二是研究市场，积极开发储蓄新品种，大力推行代发工资，发售大额可转让定期存单，开设多功能所柜，为客户提供结算服务，实行储蓄存款同城通存通取。三是有计划地抓了网点改造和新建、迁建工作。四是不失时机地组织开展吸储活动，于七、八、九三个月抓住国家调整利率的时机，在全省开展了“储蓄百日竞赛”，创月均增储1亿元的好成绩。在抓好储蓄存款的同时，全省建行还狠抓企业存款，拉大户、扩新户，建立依托行业和骨干企业，在紧紧抓住电力、铁路、石油、煤炭、交通、有色等支柱行业的同时，向“建”字号以外的国营、集体、个体、股份制等领域发起攻势，使企业存款取得稳中有增的成绩，广泛筹集了资金，为支持国家重点建设打下了坚实的基础。

——加强信贷管理，优化信贷结构，调整贷款投向

1993年，省建行面对资金供求矛盾突出的情况，在大力组织吸收存款的同时，把管好用好信贷资金作为支持重点建设的大事来抓。全行上下采取了一些行之有效的措施，加强信贷管理，优化信贷结构。一是分行制定印发了《关于转换信贷机制，提高贷款效益的意见》，推行了“三调整、四挂钩”的贷款管理办法。二是积极建立了贷款项目备选库，加强对贷款项目的调查和评估，为贷款决策提供依据。三是坚持先评估后决策、审贷分离和集体审批制度，杜绝个人运用资金，严格按制度和程序发放贷款。四是加强了贷款风险防范管理，除广泛采用第三方担保外，还扩大推行了以产权属已的财产或有价证券作贷款抵押。五是狠抓了清理回收压缩到逾期贷款问题，全年回收各类到逾期贷款9.6亿元。六是调整贷款投向，优先保证了兰新复线建设和石油、电力、有色金属等重点项目资金需求。

——加强宏观管理，强化资金调控力度，树立全行一盘棋的思想

强调资金调度必须无条件地服从分行一个指令，分行每旬召开一次资金调度会，统筹安排，合理调度资金，从而缓解了资金矛盾，有力地支持了重点建设。

由于采取了以上措施，省建行在这不寻常的一年做出了不寻常的业绩，真正为重点建设起到了保驾护航的作用。1993年，是甘肃建行历史上投入贷款最多的一年，全年发放贷款24.5亿元，同时累计发放各种临时性贷款5.4亿元，有力地支持了兰新复线、西北铅锌冶炼厂等16个国家和省列重点项目、大中型项目的建设。

1993年，甘肃省建行在千方百计支持重点建设的同时，从“发展才是硬道理”、“发展的出路在于深化改革”的认识高度出发，在巩固原有阵地，发展传统业务的基础上，不断拓展新领域，力举新业务。

——狠抓资金归集，服务住房改革，房地产金融业务有了新的发展

1993年，全省建行各级房地产信贷部为了配合全省房改的全面起步运转，以筹集住房资为中心，以归集收缴各类住房基金为重点，不断完善房改金融服务功能，做出了新的成绩。截止年末，全行共归集各类政策性住房资金余额达31090万元，经营性资金余额27095万元。其中当年新增政策性存款9031万元，经营性存款11172万元；全行累计为房改单位和个人购建房共发放贷款14200万元。并进一步完善了房改服务措施，加大了宣传力度，房地产金融业务健康发展。

——抓住机遇，拓展了国际金融业务，省建行国际金融业务拓展新天地，取得突破性发展

全行紧紧抓住我省开放搞活、“三资”企业增加较快的极好机遇，迅速建立起了全行的外汇业务网络，各地州市行及时成立了国际业务代办机构，广泛吸收外汇存款，并选准项目开展外汇贷款。全行当年新增外汇存款2965万美元，是1992年新增额的141%，完成总行下达任务的4.2倍，外汇存款余额一举突破5000万美元，实现了外汇存款“保四争五”的目标，省建行外汇存款在全省占31%，仅次于中行，名列全省第二位；全行全年发外汇贷款1082万美元；共办理进出口开证业务和汇出、汇入业务200笔，金额3088万美元，当年实现外汇利润61.6万美元。

——适应市场经济需要，认真抓好证券业务

1993年，省建行从市场经济和建行未来发展需要出发，认真抓了证券发行、交易和代办业务。全行累计发行和代理发行各类有价证券6.04亿元，为地方政府、企业发行投资债券20280万元，证券交易总额达到20986万元。

——积极开办信用卡业务

1993年，省建行加快了信用卡网点布局，加强人员培训，率先在兰州市支行开办了万事达信用卡业务，到年底累计发卡3051张，吸收存款931.6万元，发展特约商户110家，设立指定存取网点46个，自动柜员机4台，交易笔数16629笔，交易金额5299万元。

1993年，全省建行团结奋斗，努力工作，既严格管理政府投资，大力发展储蓄等传统业务、又力举国际金融、信用卡等新业务，千方百计支持了国家重点建设。同时又狠抓了内部管理，对全行171名县以上干部认真进行了自查、自纠，全行全年立案9起，查结5起，其余4起正式移交司法部门审理，全行围绕“约法三章”，狠刹“吃、拿、卡、要”、以权谋私、以贷谋私、以审谋私等行业不正之风。并从适应市场经济、发展商业银行出发，狠抓了干部职工岗位培训和新业务、新知识、新技能的培训，全行共举办各类培训班211期，受培训人员3310人次，使全行整体工作健康、快速、高效地运转。

在新的一年里，甘肃建行将按照国家专业银行向商业银行发展的战略目标和社会主义市场经济建设要求，认真执行国家有关经济、金融方针和政策，广筹资金，力举重点，深化改革，不断探索、奋力开拓，进一步提高投资效益和经营管理水平，为国家和甘肃经济建设做出更大贡献。

中国银行

深化金融体制改革 支持甘肃经济发展

中国银行甘肃省分行行长

平　岳

1993年，我行认真贯彻执行中央、国务院和人民银行有关经济、金融宏观调控一系列方针、政策，认真贯彻执行总行的各项规定、要求和省委、省政府有关指示精神，以整顿金融秩序、严肃金融纪律为工作重心，加强各项管理，积极拓展经营，支持我省经济建设和改革开放事业的发展，各项工作进展比较顺利。年末，各项人民币存款余额达到115800万元，比上年末增加19900万元，增长20.75%；各项外汇存款余额达13967万美元，比上年末增加4865万美元，增长53.4%；各项人民币贷款余额为199060万元，比上年末增加35670万元，增长21.83%；各项外汇贷款余额为14241万美元，比上年末增加6633万美元，增长87.18%；与有关方面协作，支持我省完成出口创汇28000多万美元。

——大抓存款，广辟资金来源

在专业银行商业化走向市场的

过程中，存款多少越来越显示出对于银行具有最重要的意义。我行坚持"存款立行"的思想，全辖通过组织推动、扩大宣传、增加新品种、实行目标管理等措施，有力地推进了我行的存款。其中个人外币存款和储蓄存款增幅较大，分别比上年增长75.8%和34%。在各项存款全面发展中，信用卡吸存呈突进趋势，上半年该项存款余额即突破亿元大关，比上年末增加3663万元，至1993年末，信用卡存款余额占各项人民币存款余额的比率，已上升为8.6%。

——调整信贷结构，优化信贷资产

我行的人民币信贷工作坚持"控制总量，优化结构，面向市场，转换机制，提高效益"的信贷工作总方针，坚持"大外贸"的指导思想，除大力支持外贸进出口企业外，还逐步扩大了对生产企业的贷款范围，向效益好的大中型企业、"三资"企业扩展，使我行的信贷结构有所调整。在流动资金贷款中，外贸贷款比例由上年的82.7%下降到年末的78.9%，省级外贸贷款由59.6%下降到57.8%，出口商品生产企业贷款由5.7%上升到7.86%，外事企业和"三资"企业贷款由4.4%上升到11.88%。地方外汇贷款稳步增长，全年共发放各类地方外汇贷款2805万美元；"三贷"(外国政府贷款、出口买方贷款、混合贷款)发展迅速，全年办理"三贷"项目4个，金额1.16亿美元，重点支持了我省邮电管理局10万门程控电话、金昌化工总厂12万吨磷二铵、长庆石油勘探局安塞油田开发等国家和省上重点项目。"三资"企业信贷业务发展健康，我行重点支持了白银柯登有限公司、深圳兰海电子有限公司和兰州飞乐地毯厂等"三资"企业，同时还支持了长风机器厂、兰光电子有限公司、国营778厂、甘肃无纺织地毯厂等经济效益好的国有大中型企业。

——加大对信贷规模和信贷资金的宏观调控力度

在信贷规模方面贯彻从紧方针，严格控制总量并适时调剂余缺；多次调整全辖信贷指标，使各行的发展趋于合理；进一步理顺信贷工作关系，省分行下划信贷业务，交由企业所在地分、支行管理。在信贷资金方面，对全辖的资金进行综合运筹，制定和完善了辖内存款准备金制度和清理不合理外拆资金的规定等，遵照上级指示，认真整顿金融秩序，从而使信贷资金工作逐步走上灵活调度、合理安排、规范使用、科学管理的轨道。

——积极推进机构网点建设，充分发挥整体优势

1993年新组建了嘉峪关、庆阳、陇南、定西、白银五个分、支行，自此我行的机构延伸至全省除甘南州以外的13个地(州)市，网点总数达85个，增大了我行业务覆盖面，有利于发挥我行整体功能及优势。同时，经过十几年的发展，我行已与世界上50多个国家和地区的100家银行的600多个分、支机构建立了业务往来关系，并培养了一大批既有理论又熟悉国际金融业务的业务骨干。

1994年，是全面推进社会主义市场经济体制改革和具体落实各项改革措施的关键一年。在这一年里，我行要坚持以十四届三中全会精神为指针，稳步推进体制改革，切实加强内部管理，强化经济效益观念，大力发展各项业务，努力把我行办成以外汇外贸业务为重点，本外币业务相匹配，各项业务全面发展的现代化国有商业银行。今年重点要做好以下几方面工作。

——加大改革力度

首先是做好外汇体改相关工作。认真学习贯彻国务院和人民银行的有关政策规定，建好、管好台帐，做好结汇工作，同时方便客户做好售汇工作。在改革中切实加强贷款、结汇、售汇、保值等业务主办部门的协作与配合，以贷款促结算，以结算促收贷，为客户提供一揽子综合性服务。逐步实行贷款限额指导下的资产负债比例管理和风险管理，加大对全辖资金的调控力度。省分行对全辖信贷资金实行集中管理和统一调度，并对全辖资产的流动性及支付能力负全部责任。在向国有商业银行的转化过程中，不断增强效益观念，加强成本核算，重视考核资产利润率、资本回报率和人均效率，努力增收节支，大力提高盈利水平。

——继续抓好存款工作，扩大信贷资金来源

继续坚持实行"放手发展储蓄存款，全面组织企业存款，积极扩大外汇存款，大力开拓信用卡吸存"的方略，使我行的本外币存款有较大幅度的增长。经过积极努力，今年使各项人民币存款新增3.5亿元，力争新增4亿元，各项外币存款新增2000万美元，进一步提高资金自给率。——加强信贷资金管理，提高信贷资产质量。坚持规模和资产相统一的原则。树立"谁经济效益好，贷款风险低，就支持谁"的指导思想，优先支持国家鼓励发展的产业，在落实资金、注重效益的前提下，支持进出口企业、国有大中型企业和外商投资企业的发展，支持能源、交通、通讯、基础原材料等行业的发展，支持轻工、纺织、机电产品、大型成套设备的扩大出口。适应国际国内市场变化和经济体制、金融体制改革带来的变化，不断调整贷款行业结构、客户结构、期限结构、币别结构和改进担保方式。与此同时，切实加强和重视贷款使用的监督和收贷工作。

——加强内部科学管理，提高工作效率

向国有商业银行转变的工作千头万绪，重点是加强内部管理。随着我行机构的增多、业务的扩展、队伍的壮大，要切实转变观念，增强管理意识，采取积极措施，全面加强管理。我们的基本思路是：在改革中找出路，在竞争中求发展，在发展中重管理，在管理中出效率。于此，要坚持不懈地抓好职工队伍建设这个根本措施，不断提高全体职工的政治、业务素质。要在明确职责的前提下，坚持授权有限，相互制约，事后复核的原则，坚持分级负责的制度。要严格各项规章制度，做到令行禁止。通过各项措施的认真落实，大力提高各项工作的科学管理水平。

1994年，我行将继续为社会各界、广大客户提供全方位的良好的金融服务，在国有商业银行的转化中迈出开拓性的一步，为甘肃省加快对外开放和经济发展做出新的贡献。

交通银行

积极发展各项业务不断完善商业银行经营机制

交通银行兰州分行副行长
于淑芬

1993年，是交通银行兰州分行自我完善和继续发展的一年。一年来，我们认真贯彻落实党和国家的各项金融方针、政策，紧紧抓住发展社会主义商业银行这个主题开展工作，坚持把存款工作放在首位，不断壮大资金实力；坚持依法稳健经营，推进各项业务发展；进一步完善经营管理机制，强化风险经营意识，积极开拓综合性业务，完善服务功能，努力为社会各界提供“三个一流”的服务，各项业务有了较快发展，使各项工作取得了新的成绩，提前一个月，超额完成了全年各项计划指标，为促进兰州地区经济发展做出了贡献。截止1993年末，各项存款达85025万元，比上年末增加22618万元，增长36.08%；各项贷款达74111万元，比上年末增加19882万元，增长36.66%；人均创利15万元，居全市各金融机构之首；资本金由建行时的3000万元发展到7000万元；资产总额达137043万元，比上年增加42869万元，增长45.52%。

一、存款是交行的立行之本

在异常困难的情况下，存款工作仍迈上了一个新台阶。作为甘肃省第一家股份制、综合性的社会主义商业银行，我们交通银行兰州分行建立了自主经营、自负盈亏、自担风险、自求平衡、自我约束、自我发展的经营机制。因此，存款是立行之本，是各项业务发展的基本条件，存款的增长直接关系到竞争能力，是保持正常支付，维护银行信誉的可靠保证。我们坚持“存款立行，存款兴行”，始终把组织存款工作放在各项业务工作的首位，千方百计拓宽筹资渠道，采取各种措施调动全行上下大力组织吸收存款的积极性，使存款保持了稳步增长的好势头。到六月底，各项存款比年初增加13133万元，比上年同期多增加1263万元，完成年计划65%，但是，从7月上旬开始，受全国性大气候的影响，存款出现滑坡，到十月底存款余额降至70986万元，较六月底下降1733万元，只完成年计划的43.4%，影响到各项业务的正常进行。为了尽快扭转存款滑坡局面，力争完成全年存款净增2亿元的任务，我们认真分析形势，积极研究对策，于十一月初召开存款会议进行紧急动员，有针对性地提出了十条扭转存款滑坡被动局面的措施和“全行齐动员、大干60天”的口号，在全行掀起了一个组织存款的高潮，由于全行同志的共同努力，存款滑坡的被动局面迅速得到了有效遏制，存款余额迅速增长，十一月份一个月各项存款余额净增11530万元，占年计划的57.7%，提前一个月完成了全年存款任务。

二、积极开拓综合性业务

按照商业银行的发展模式，抓住机遇，使我行的综合性业务积极稳健全面发展：保险业务长足发展并已初具规模，达到了设立中国太平洋保险公司分公司的要求，成为兰州保险市场上一支新的生力军；积极创造条件开办了外汇业务，并办理了外汇存款、贷款、贸易结算和非贸易结算等业务，开始向外向型商业银行发展；证券业务发展加快，向上海、深圳证券交易所申请异地会员单位的请示，已经人民银行甘肃省分行和上交行、深交所批准；还担任了甘肃省首家经国家正式批准、认可，在深交所异地上市交易的国营长风宝安集团股份有限公司股票发行的分承销商。投资、租赁、信托、房地产等业务有了新的发展，投资比例严格控制在规定的比例之内。开办了信用卡。1993年达到了从人民币、放、汇到信托、租赁、委托保险、外汇、投资、咨询等综合性业务，形成了一个传统业务与新兴业务、国内业务与国际业务、金融业务和非银行金融业务并举的新格局，为企业提供了多功能、全功能、全方位的服务。

三、加强资产负债管理，提高资产质量

作为社会主义商业银行，我们紧紧以资金的安全性、流动性、效益性为经营目标、牢固树立风险意识，健全风险防范体系，加强和完善信贷资产监控工作，加强对贷款的审查与风险管理，积极推行抵押贷款和担保贷款制度，增强风险防范能力。我行的逾期贷款，呆滞贷款和呆帐贷款都严格控制在总行规定的比例之内。同时，认真搞好资金情况分析，根据资金来源制约资金的运用，按资产负债比例管理，对资金的运用进行合理、有效配置，使全行的主要经营指标都控制在规定的比例之内，全行资本充足率达到规定的要求，资产质量较好，经济效益进一步提高。1993年全行资本收益比上年有了较大幅度的提高。在贷款工作中，认真贯彻国家产业政策和商业银行信贷管理原则，根据交通银行的经营特点，以市场为导向，以提高资金效益为中心，优化信贷结构，实行重点倾斜，合理发放贷款。据统计，全行80%以上的贷款都用在支持国营大中型骨干企业生产发展和能源、原材料的生产；物资供销企业搞活流通、外贸外事企业扩大出口；农副产品收购以及商业企业时令商品市场供应等合理的资金需求上。

此外，还利用信贷杠杆，促进企业面向市场，开发拳头产品，以及牵线搭桥，促进科研成果转化为生产力，解决企业的资金急需。

四、坚持依法稳健经营

在经营过程中自觉执行“约法三章”，自觉维护金融秩序，巩固和维护了交行在社会上的良好信誉。

1993年上半年全国资金趋紧，金融秩序一度出现比较混乱的情况。在这种情况下，我们交通银行兰州分行严格执行国家的金融方针政策和各项规章制度，坚持在与同行的业务交叉中，做到了不违规、不违纪、文明竞争，依法稳健经营，以优质服务取胜；坚持展业与管理并举，加强服务，做到了不压票、不压汇、不无理退票、保证支付，不擅自提高利率，维护银行信誉；杜绝资金外流炒股票、炒房地产，集中资金保证重点企业、重点项目的资金需求；强化自我约束机制，自觉维护金融秩序、巩固和维护了交行在社会上的良好信誉，七月份始，按照中央的部署和中国人民银行的要求，全行认真开展整顿金融秩序的工作。从认真自查做起。围绕执行“约法三章”，重点做好清理拆借资金等八个方面的清理整顿工作，取得了成效。我行还抓住这次全面整顿金融秩序的机会，狠抓内部管理，整章建制，堵塞漏洞，加强领导班子建设，加强队伍建设，提高员工队伍素质，努力把交通银行办成规范化的商业银行。

保　险

大力发展保险事业
为社会经济发展
创造优良环境

1993年，全省保险业在以业务发展为中心的思想指导下，以改革与发展作为第二次创业的主题，加快内部经营机制转换，抓住时机，积极竞争，使全省保险业务发展又跃上了一个新的台阶。

1. 业务收入持续增长

1993年，全省保险业务收入达到50408.6万元，较上年同期增长33.5%，净增12647.9万元，完成年计划116%。其中，国内业务收入49190.8万元(含储金)，涉外业务收入211万美元，(折合人民币1217.8万元)，分别比上年同期增长33.67%和19.2%。在业务收入中：城市财产保险业务收入为23915.5万元，人身保险业务收入为20169.5万元，农村保险业务收入为5105.8万元，涉外保险业务收入为1217.8万元，分别比上年增长26.91%、39.59%、45.63%和19.61%。

2. 保险经济补偿作用得到发挥

1993年，全省共处理92162起赔付案件，赔付金额达25310万元，比上年增长45.8%，为1804户企事业单位和27052名群众提供了经济补偿。

3. 进一步扩大了服务领域

1993年，全省开办的险种已有财产保险、人身保险、保证保险、责任保险四大类193个险种。与人民群众密切相关的简易人身保险、养老年金保险、住院医疗保险、家庭财产保险、计划生育系列保险等分散性业务大量开办。有8258户企事业参加了财产保险，117万户参加了家庭财产保险，13.3万辆机动车参加了保险；参加各类人身保险的人数达到325万多人，为社会各界提供的风险保障金额已达到664.3亿元。

4. 保险网络遍布全省

到1993年底，保险营业所以上的正式机构达到120个，保险职工2149人；专兼职机构763个，代办人员7803人，其中，专职机构已达456个，专职代办员1133人；专兼职代办业务收入已达到21949万元，占业务总收入的43.54%，其中专职代办业务收入达14739万元，占业务总收入的29.24%。

【城市财产保险】1993年，全省城市财产保险收入23915.5万元(含储金)，比上年净增5071.5万元，增长26.91%，占全省业务总收入的47.4%。其中，城市企财险保费收入为5320.5万元，较上年同期增长17.6%，净增797.6万元，(全省机损险保费收入近1500万元，占全省企财险保费收入的28.1%)；运输工具及责任险保费收入为8981.8万元，较上年同期增长33.3%，净增2245.4万元；货运险保费收入3756万元，较上年同期增长6%，净增213万元，代查勘代理赔案件4835笔，清算资金达37.9万元，清算外省代赔1004笔；家财险业务收入(含储金)5278.6万元，比上年增长41%，净增1533.7万元。承保总额达446.3亿元，比上年增长16.9亿元，增长3.9%，已决赔案50601件，比上年增长87.9%，赔款支出12774.4万元，综合赔付率53.4%。

1993年，根据全省实际开发设计了“矿山企业财产保险及第三者责任保险条款”、“行政事业单位计算机保险”、“科技成果推广保险”、“住房信贷保险”等10多个新险种,推出了城镇家庭财产长效还本综合保险定额保单,增强了城市财险业务发展后劲,不断扩大了保险服务领域,并完成了投资概算为5.5亿元的黄河大峡电站工程的承保工作。其次加强了防灾防损基础工作建设。一方面,根据全省防灾工作现状,制定了各种防灾防损制度,使防灾工作有章可循。另一方面,积极疏通与公安、交管、消防、气象等部门的关系。1993年全省保险系统投入近180万元用于企业隐患改造,增添消防、通讯、交通工具,支持防灾活动和课题研究。其中主要完成了国道312线55处危险路段上安装警示,安全宣传,安全标志,线路指示等标牌。组织各类培训班25起,除防灾理赔人员参加外,各部门企业参加人数约在上万人(次)以上。

【农村保险】1993年,全省农村保险业务取得了新突破。全年农村保险业务收入5105.8万元,比上年净增1599.9万元,增长45.63%。其中,种、养两业险收入886.2万元,(保费收入795.1万元,储金收入91.1万元).较上年增长79%,共处理赔案6757件,赔款504.2万元。种、养两业的发展由于近年不断采取以县统保或多乡连片承包,注重发展经济作物的承保和实行“差额赔付”等措施,赔付率已从1990年的240%下降到1993年的63%;农村企事业财产险保费收入549.9万元,较上年同期增加8.14%,农村家庭财产保险户数为419018户,保险业务收入(含储金)572.4万元,较上年同期增加39.4%,拖拉机承保数量为20557辆,保费收入为216.7万元,较上年年同期增长30.31%,汽车承保数量为22101辆,保费收入2629.2万元,较上年同期增长44.46%。为解决防灾、承保、理赔环节上存在的薄弱问题,全省对大面积、大数量开展两业险的地区提取实收保费的5%为防灾费,同时,先后修订了全省的麦场火灾等14种保险条款,新制定了森林成本火灾等保险条款,并制定部分条款说明,有力地推动了新科技的应用和商品性农业的开发。全年为农村提供的风险保障金额达44.78亿元,比上年净增7.1亿元,全年共处理各类赔案14310起,支付赔款(或给付)2490.7万元,综合赔付率为52%。总之,农村保险业务对促进我省农村市场经济的发展,保障农业生产和农民生活的安定,起到了“稳定器”的作用。

【人身保险】1993年,全省人身保险业务总收入20169.5万元,较上年同期增长39.59%,净增5720.6万元,占全省国内业务总收入的比重为40.01%,其中,养老保险收入4198.2万元,较上年同期增长72.67%,净增1766.9万元,短期人身险收入3018.6万元,较上年同期增长57.51%,净增1102.2万元;储金性人身险收入12952.7万元,较上年同期增长28.23%,净增2851.5万元,上述各项业务收入分别占人险总收入的20.8%、14.9%和64%。

1993年,为适应市场需求,全省引进开发和修改了子女年年康乐保险;美满婚姻保险、生日快乐保险等8个新险种条款与实务,与此同时,各地还自行推出了适合当地实际情况的10多个短期新险种。现在,全省人险业务已开办了50多个险种,有300多万人(次)参加各种人身保险,累计期末有效数达550余万人(次)。全省各种人身保险为16453人给付保险金1008.8万元,比上年增长22.7%。其中,短期意外险给付保险金689.8万元,给付率为22.85%,有效地发挥了保险的经济补偿职能,取得了很好的社会效益。目前,全省人险业务服务体系已形成,对促进生产,安定生活,稳定社会,发展全省经济起了积极作用。

【涉外保险】1993年,全省涉外保险业务取得了新发展。全年承担社会风险保障金额1571526万美元,保险业务收入达到211万美元,较上年同期增长19.2%,其中,水险保费收入为108万美元,与上年同期持平;非水险保费收入为86.7万美元,较上年同期增长33.5%;航空人险保费收入为15.3万美元,与上年同期持平;信用险保费收入为10.6万美元,较上年同期增长了5倍多。全年共处理各类赔案199件,支付各项赔款58.4万美元,综合赔付率为27.8%,较好地发挥了保险的经济补偿作用。

1993年,为适应市场竞争需要,利用“甘肃经贸香港洽谈会”、“甘肃经贸新加坡展销会”、“广交会”、“乌交会”等大型外经贸活动展业,同时,针对出口额下滑,进口额上升的特点,重点做了主要进口代理公司和项目单位工作,使进口业务收入比去年同期增长了26.5%;二是新开办了卖方合同险、邮包运输险、公众责任险、石油开发责任险等,保费收入达10万美元。三是开拓信用保险,为兰化等九家进出口公司投保了出口信用保险,使此项业务保费收入超过了10万美元。四是加快了涉外保险的外拓工作,积极探索,为海外公司提供保险服务方式,与陇汉公司签订保险协议,收取进口货运险保费2.9万美元,较好地支持了全省外经外贸的发展。

(中国人民保险公司
甘肃省分公司)

社会生活

劳动管理

加快培育发展劳动力市场开创劳动体制改革新局面

省劳动局局长

祝晏君

1993年,是甘肃省劳动工作向适应社会主义市场经济体制转变的第一年,也是劳动体制改革全面推进的一年。在这一年中,我省以培育和发展劳动力市场为中心,加强和完善就业服务体系,改进劳动工资宏观调控体系,建立完善社会主义保险体系,加强劳动立法和监督检查体系建设,使劳动领域的各项改革取得了新的进展。

一、劳动工资宏观调控正在有序进行

为使劳动力市场机制健康发育,我省对计划经济体制下的传统管理方法进行了改革,取消了职工人数、工资总额等指令性计划,让企业自主决定招工时间、条件、方式和数量,自主使用和分配应提取的工资总额。与此同时,改进加强了宏观调控措施,积极推行弹性工资计划,通过工资总额间接调控职工人数。

指令性计划取消后,在武威、兰州两地、市试行了动态调控的弹性劳动工资计划管理办法,对酒泉、张掖、嘉峪关、金昌四地(市)实行了工效总挂钩,对白银、陇南、甘南等八地(市、州)实行了工资总额包干管理办法,对省直八个企业集团和公司、十七个厅局也实行了不同形式的工效挂钩和工资总额包干管理。据不完全统计,1993年,全省实行工效挂钩的地方国有企业达900多户,涉及职工54万余人,占地方国有企业职工总数的60%;实行工资总额包干管理的地方国有企业达1800多户,涉及职工27万余人,占地方国有企业职工总数的30%。已经形成了"国家宏观调控,分级分类管理,企业自主用人和自主分配"的劳动工资管理体系。

二、劳动制度改革全面推进,就业工作取得新成绩

劳动制度改革以推行全员劳动合同制为重点,紧紧围绕落实企业用工自主权和劳动者择业自主权,变国家用工主体为企业用工主体,全省85户国有企业实行了全员劳动合同制,80%以上的富余职工得到了妥善安置。到1993年底,全省劳动合同制工人已达到36.6万人,占全民单位职工总数的17.7%。为了落实企业用工自主权,促进企业用工行为法制化和规范化,省上和各地都制定了一批法规文件和办法措施。除征地招工、农转非招工、军队复转人员仍由劳动行政部门协调安置外,其他用工行为均已纳入市场管理并办理有关手续。

为适应市场经济的需要和企业自主用工、劳动者自主择业创造平等竞争的外部条件,我省狠抓了职业介绍中介机构的建设。甘肃省劳务服务中心于1993年4月正式揭牌运转,从而带动和促进了各地、县职业介绍中介机构的建立和发展。截止年底,全省各种职业介绍机构已发展到150多所,登记介绍各类人员达50多万人次。全省已初步形成省、地、县三级职业介绍网络。

劳动争议仲裁工作坚持依法行政,对一些外商投资企业私营企业劳动用工、雇工合同签订、履行等情况进行了检查,维护了企业和劳动者双方的合法权益。1993年,全省共受理劳动争议案件71件,涉及112人;结案65件,涉及106人。企业调解劳动争议94件,调解成功89件。进行劳动合同签证8.7万人(份)。信访工作继续发挥政府同人民群众的桥梁作用,全年处理来信328件,接待来访80多起。

就业工作取得新成效。1993年我省共有城镇待业人员21.19万人,就业形势非常严峻。经过全省上下和各行各业的共同努力,到年底共安置城镇就业11.04万人,其中全民单位安置2.83万,集体单位安置3.05万,其它所有制单位安置0.22万,临时性安置2.7万,自谋个体经营1.19万,非安置性减少1.04万,待业率基本上控制在3.5%左右。为进一步贯彻劳动部关于加强培训中心建设,为企业输送合格劳动者的精神,全年批准新建培训中心14所,使全省培训中心总数达到79所。已建培训中心在抓好规范化管理的同时,开展多种形式的就业培训,全年培训待业人员4.88万人次,推动了全省就业工作。

农村劳务输出工作继续坚持"东进西出"的方针,在巩固原有基地的同时,对新疆、广东劳务站的力量进行了调整充实,在北京、上海等地新建了劳务管理机构。到1993年底,我省在全国50人以上的劳务基地已达7000多个,其中100人以上的其地达3000多个。各级劳务机构在认真贯彻省委、省政府领导批示,加强领导,层层签订责任目标的基础上,深入调查研究,广泛收集劳务信息,狠抓劳务人员的培训和劳务输出、移民工作,为扩大劳务输出创造了较好的条件，有力地推动了劳务输出工作。1993年全省输出农村劳务人员150万人次，劳务总收入12亿元。

三、以岗位技能工资制为主要形式的企业内部分配改革健康发展

企业工资分配制度改革，坚持按劳分配，贯彻效率和公平原则，各级劳动部门积极引导，企业自愿改革，使全省实行岗位技能工资制的地方国有企业发展到120余户，25万职工。从行业和地区情况看，基本形成了条块结合，点面结合，大中型骨干企业与地方中小型企业结合，生产企业与流通企业结合，国有企业与集体企业结合的试点辐射面，正在健康有序发展。与此同时，还调整了煤炭、建材、冶金、石化、林业等艰苦行业的岗位津贴，稳定了这些行业职工队伍的情绪，促进了企业生产经营的发展。为规范集体企业和三资企业的工资管理，加强和指导了这些企业的工资分配。

四、以养老和失业为重点的社会保险制度改革得到新进展

社会保险制度的改革，继续贯彻国务院和劳动部关于加快改革的方针、政策，把养老、失业保险工作作为保险制度改革的重点来抓，采取措施，狠抓落实，使社会保险工作取得了新成绩。全省各地已普遍实现职工个人缴纳基本养老保险金制度，有20户企业开展了补充养老保险，3个县区开展了养老金计发办法改革试点，6个县区开展了外商投资企业中方职工养老保险，11个县区开展了临时工养老保险，6个县区开展了个体劳动者养老保险，由社会保险机构或委托银行直接给离退休人员发放离退休费的县区增加到了62个。省上在认真做好离退休费用省级统筹各项准备工作的同时，制定并向省政府上报了《甘肃省国有企业固定职工离退休费用省级统筹实施办法》，为即将实现的养老保险省级统筹做好准备。失业保险工作认真贯彻国务院《国有企业职工待业保险规定》，进一步扩大保险覆盖面，使原来少数没有参加统筹的国有企业、三资企业和其它所有制形式的企业参加了失业保险，为7000多名失业者发放了救济金300多万元。企业职工大病医疗费用社会统筹和工伤保险改革试点开始起步，7个县区和两个地直系统开展了工伤保险试点，5个县区开展了大病医疗统筹试点，试点工作进展顺利。社会保险基金的收缴、管理和内部审计进一步得到加强，按照劳动部规定，统一实施了社会保险会计制度、统计规定、财务管理规定和保险基金管理办法。到年底，全省共收缴养老保险金4.34亿元，待业保险金3709万元，已为15万多名离退休人员发放离退休退职费用3.26亿元。

五、"一厂两制"集体经济超额完成目标任务

为使"一厂两制"劳动服务集体经济实现新的突破，我省在1993年狠抓了以下几项工作：一是认真落实白银"双带整推"现场会精神，召开全省劳服企业工作会议，制定实施办法，签订责任目标；二是加强对"一厂两制"劳服企业的宏观管理和协调指导，狠抓扭亏增盈，为企业开发新产品，加强销售工作，提供信息服务；三是加强生产调度，三次召开集体经济形势分析会，协助企业解决资金、原料、人才、优惠政策落实等问题，为企业排忧解难；四是适时召集汇报会，交流经验，就地解决集体经济发展中的矛盾和问题。由于全省上下共同努力，"一厂两制"集体经济超额完成了目标任务，1993年实现社会总产值34.36亿元，比上年增长30.67%，其中完成工业总产值24.08亿元，比上年增长21.44%。全年共安置待业青年、富余人员44384人；年末共有企业5549户，其中当年新办604户。

六、职业安全卫生监察工作得到进一步强化

为加强安全生产工作，1993年先后召开了全省第七次安全生产工作会议和安全生产工作紧急电话会，开展了全省安全生产大检查。同时还加强了安全生产宣传教育，组织60多个地区、行业和部门参加了全国安全知识竞赛活动，召开了全省特种作业人员培训站长会议，对60名做出突出成绩的同志给予表彰奖励，有效地防止和控制了重特大恶性事故的发生。

职业安全卫生监察工作以事故预防、监督处理为重点，加强了劳动防护用品的管理和电梯、起重机械等特种设备的监察检测，加强了对工业建设项目的安全审查工作。截止年底，全省劳动防护用品定点企业已增加到78户，共检验电梯136台，培训特种设备检测员51名，审查验收建设项目17个，增补安全卫生措施120项，对6户企业进行了职业安全卫生专项评估，改善了企业劳动环境，为预防重特大事故发生奠定了良好基础。

矿山安全监察工作以重大事故隐患和职业危害为重点，以宣传贯彻《矿山安全法》为中心，强化国家监察，完善监察手段，积极开展现场监察和技术咨询服务，完成了6对矿井的"三同时"设计审查及竣工验收，对38个矿山安全监察科(室)进行了整顿。会同有关部门深入靖远、窑街、阿干等矿区，查处了一些胡挖滥采的无证个体小煤窑，整顿了国有煤田工作秩序，使矿山安全监察工作逐步趋于正规划、法制化。

七、劳动立法、劳动信息、劳动宣传工作也都取得新进展

为加强劳动行政立法，坚持依法行政，根据国家颁布的有关法律、法规，我省集中力量拟定了一批地方性规章，《甘肃省劳动保护监察暂行条例》已经省人大常委会通过并颁布实施，《甘肃省实施＜矿山安全法＞办法》、《甘肃省贯彻＜国有企业富余职工安置规定＞实施办法》、

《甘肃省贯彻<国有企业职工待业保险规定>实施办法》、《甘肃省加强企业工资总额宏观调控实施办法》、《甘肃省劳动监察暂行规定》、《甘肃省<职业技能鉴定>实施办法》等地方性法规、规章已分别多次征求有关部门及企业的意见,可望在1994年出台。1993年,我省还出台了劳动部门实施《全民所有制工业企业转换经营机制条例》的贯彻意见,为企业走向市场,劳动部门进一步转变职能提供了政策依据,奠定了基础。

总之,1993年是我省劳动工作开始转入适应社会主义市场经济新轨道的一年,是积极探索建立新型劳动体制的一年,是劳动体制改革取得较大进展的一年,是各级劳动部门在职能转变上迈出较大步伐的一年。

消　费

维护市场经济秩序 保护消费者的权益

省消费者协会秘书长

赵国文

甘肃省消费者协会,是经甘肃省人民政府批准,依法成立的对商品和服务进行社会监督的保护消费者权益的社会团体。它是全省广大消费者的组织。担负着对商品和服务进行社会监督,保护消费者的合法权益,指导广大群众消费,维护社会经济秩序,促进社会主义市场经济健康发展的历史重任。

甘肃省消费者协会自从1987年11月20日正式成立以来,她经历了一个从无到有、从少到多、从小到大,逐步发展壮大的成长过程。1987年底,包括省消费者协会在内,全省仅有3个消费者协会。1988年起,经过省消费者协会与各级工商行政管理机关的共同努力和各级政府有关部门的积极支持,截止目前,全省已有13个地、州、市和57个县、市、区建立了消费者协会。县以上协会逐步建立起后,又注重抓消费者组织基层网络的延伸工作,在已经建立协会的地县依托工商所建立分会,依托大中型企业建立消费者监督联络站,现全省已建立分会145个,消费者监督联络站134个。组织上取得的这些进展,为我省开展保护消费者权益工作奠定了良好的基础,形成了对商品和服务的全民性社会监督。现在,我省各级消费者协会已经成为党和政府联系群众的一条重要渠道;成为社会监督的一支重要力量;成为反映群众呼声,为消费者办好事、办实事,全心全意为人民服务的重要社会团体。近年来,我省的各级消费者协会在建立和发展社会主义市场经济体制的新形势下,结合我省保护消费者权益工作的实际,不断研究新形势、新情况、新问题,探索保护消费者权益工作的新方法,使保护消费者权益的工作取得了显著成绩。

1.认真受理消费者投诉,释去千家忧,带给万户乐。我省各级消费者协会牢牢遵循"维护广大消费者权益,全心全意为广大消费者服务"的宗旨,认真受理消费者对商品和服务的质量、价格、计量等方面的投诉,为广大消费者排忧解难,对每一件投诉都一抓到底,达到了件件有着落,事事有结果。尤其是近几年来,消费者的投诉大幅度增加,投诉范围不断扩大,增大了各级协会的工作负荷量和受理解决的难度。省消费者协会又适时提出了"认真负责、公正解决、提高效率、取信于消费者"的工作方针,以及采取措施方便消费者投诉,使投诉工作由被动性向主动性转变;抓好投诉热点,使投诉受理工作由一般化向深层次转变;对危害消费者人身健康、安全问题的重大投诉案件,一抓到底,认真予以解决的工作方法。截止1993年底,全省共受理消费者投诉4.34万余件,为消费者挽回经济损失988万余元,接待消费者来访和咨询28万多人次。

2.宣传群众,引导消费,呼起民众的自我保护意识。几年来,甘肃省消费者协会和各地协会认真扎实地抓好宣传教育工作和消费引导工作。一是主动同新闻界取得联系,在各新闻单位的紧密配合下,先后在各地电台、电视台、报刊上开辟了消费宣传新闻专题栏目52个,组织消费教育和消费指导方面的系列专题报道,各地协会的工作人员撰写发表通讯报道文章1800多篇。二是各级消费者协会连年举办丰富多彩的专题宣传活动849次,印发《甘肃省保护消费者合法权益条例》和《中华人民共和国消费者权益保护法》等宣传材料353万多册(份),向广大消费者介绍了国家的有关经济方针和政策,消费者权益保护方面的法律知识、消费知识和商品知识;同时揭露批评了损害消费者利益的种种行为,宣扬了维护消费者权益的先进工商企业。通过大量的宣传工作也呼起了广大消费者的自我保护意识,使广大消费者的消费观念不断更新,自我保护意识不断增强。

3.发挥社会监督作用,查假扫害,净化市场。几年来,我省各级消费者协会不断拓展监督领域,增加监督深度,提高监督水平,广泛深入地开展市场商品质量和服务质量的社会监督。监督的项目和内容有:商品质量、服务质量、商品计量、商品价格、虚假广告、售后服务等。截止1993年底,全省各地协会会同和配合各级工商行政管理机关等政府有关部门开展打假治劣的监督检查活动1720余次,查出了大量的不合格计量器具、劣质家电、自行车、霉烂变质食品与饮料、假劣调味品、假药劣药、假名烟名酒、劣质皮革制品、劣质农药、种子、化肥、地膜等几十个种类的假冒伪劣商品，并对查获的假冒伪劣商品举办展览120余场(次)，有力地打击了制售假冒伪劣商品的违法活动，维护了广大消费者的利益和市场经济秩序。

4.开展消费调查、抓难点、热点问题，反映消费者的呼声。我省各级消费者协会坚持经常性的调查研究，掌握损害消费者权益的倾向性问题，及时反映广大消费者的呼声。一是针对广大消费者反映最集中、最普遍、最强烈的问题进行社会调查，及时解决消费者最关心的问题；二是定期不定期召开不同行业、不同职业、不同文化程度、不同年龄、不同收入的各层次消费者座谈会，广泛征求消费者对市场商品质量、服务质量、价格、卫生及生活消费品供应方面的问题和建议。几年来，我省各级协会有计划、有目的地开展社会专题调查195次，组织召开消费者座谈会409次，为沟通政府、消费者、企业三者之间的联系发挥了桥梁作用。

5.组织"上帝"行使权利，实行全民监督，帮助企业提高商品和服务质量。我省各级消费者协会围绕开展对商品和服务的社会监督，组织广大消费者开展了评议商店、评议商品和服务、商品质量跟踪评议等活动。几年来，共组织评议商品质量活动290次，并评选了维护消费者合法权益的先进企业50家，消费者信得过的商店217家，向广大消费者推荐介绍了名优商品6类64个牌号的产品。消费者的评议活动，有效地促进了企业之间的市场竞争，促使企业不断重视提高商品质量和改善服务质量，在市场经济条件下，真正树立尊重"上帝"、服务于"上帝"的观念。

计划生育

甘肃省计划生育概况

省计生委主任

赖学忠

1993年甘肃省计划生育工作，在党的十四大精神和中央座谈会精神的指引下，省委、省政府高度重视，全省上下进一步统一思想，提高认识，切实加强对计划生育工作的领导，抓基层，打基础，抓重点，促平衡，抓管理，上水平，分类指导，真抓实干，各级党政领导、各部门以及计划生育战线广大同志艰苦努力，基层基础工作逐步加强，管理水平逐步提高，全省计划生育工作取得了新进展，人口过快增长的势头进一步得到控制，完成了国家下达我省的人口计划。

进一步加强了对计划生育工作的领导。各级党委、政府对计划生育工作的认识有了新的提高，党政一把手亲自抓、负总责的要求得到落实。各级党政把计划生育纳入当地经济和社会发展的总体规划之中，层层建立人口计划目标责任制，主要领导亲自抓，主管领导全力抓，有关部门协调配合，齐抓共管，基本形成了全社会重视和支持计划生育工作的局面。

基层计划生育服务网络建设取得较大进展。各地根据省上要求，不断完善县、乡村工作机构，充实工作人员，注意在机构改革中稳定和发展计生工作队伍。1993年底，全省98.5%的乡建立了计划生育工作站，乡级专职工作人员增加到6067人，每个村都有一名专兼职干部，对加强基层、开展经常工作，促进人口计划的科学管理发挥了很好的作用。

各级对计划生育事业费的投入逐步增加。在财力十分困难的情况下，各级想方设法保证对计生经费的投入。1993年全省三级财政投入经费4610万元，人均1.94元，比1992年增加0.26元。兰州、酒泉、嘉峪关、金昌、临夏等地人均计生投入超过2元。

分类指导，集中活动和经常工作相结合收到良好的效果。根据计划生育工作东西部以及少数民族地区不同的情况，在巩固和发展西部地区初步实现"三为主"工作的同时，重点抓困难大、问题多的中、东部和少数民族地区。针对农村计划生育中多胎生育较高的实际，各地普遍抓了几次集中活动，并在集中活动中抓重点、难点，抓后进，促平衡，大力落实各项节育措施，为经常工作创造条件。1993年，全省共做四项手术53.67万例，其中上环26.14万例，结扎20.21万例。

计划生育宣传教育工作和依法管理逐步深入。全省各地认真贯彻执行《婚姻法》、《继承法》、《甘肃省计划生育条例》，依法抓计划生育，计划生育合同公证在全省大部分地区已经开展起来。各级宣传和计生部门，围绕转变群众婚姻、生育观念，开展了"女儿也是传后人"专题讨论和宣传，加强了计划生育与人口知识的宣传教育，开展正确的舆论导向。在基础工作搞得比较好的一些县，把计划生育与农村发展社会主义市场经济相结合、拓宽计生工作路子，取得了初步经验。由于计划生育工作的深入开展和管理水平的不断提高，人口过快增长的势头进一步得到了控制。

人口状况

甘肃省1993年的人口出生率为20.16‰，死亡率为6.84‰，自然增长率为13.32‰，全年自然增长31万人，年末总人口达到2345万人，完成了国家下达我省的人口控制计划，全省14个地、州、市都完成了省上下达的人口控制计划。与1992年人口变动情况抽样调查相比，全省人口出生率上升0.79个千分点，死亡率上升0.20个千分点，自然增长率上升0.59个千分点。主要原因是受第三次生育高峰和全省人口年龄结构年轻化的影响，育龄妇女的群体规模逐年增加，而且处于生育旺盛阶段的育龄妇女的规模也处于最大阶段；1993年全省育龄妇女达到645万人左右，其中20——29岁生育旺盛年龄妇女的规模为275万人左右，占全部育龄妇女的42.63%。因此，目前受全省第三次出生高峰的顶峰阶段的影响，出生率较高。

人口与计划生育目标管理

甘肃省为了加强对计划生育工作的领导，继续推行和完善人口计划生育目标管理责任制，及时加强监督检查。年初省长阎海旺同14个地、州、市的党政领导签订了人口计划责任书；省计生委主任赖学中同14个地、州、市计生委(处)主任(处长)签订了计划生育工作指标。各地也层层签订了人口与计划生育目标管理责任书。年终为检查考核各地、市目标责任制执行的情况，省政府责成省统计局分地区考核人口计划执行情况；由省计生委考核三项指标：工作保证措施具体措施的贯彻落实情况；计划生育工作任务责任指标完成情况，人口与计划生育统计质量指标等。经省上全面考核，省上14个地、州、市都完成了人口计划和计划生育工作指标。省委、省政府将于1994年人代会期间的计划生育工作座谈会上给予表彰奖励。

科学管理基础建卡工作

1992年，省委、省政府在白银召开的全省计划生育基层工作经验交流会上提出：加强、提高科学管理基础工作水平的要求，针对基层对育龄妇女底数不清，统计信息运转不灵的问题，全面推行科学管理工作。在全省范围内。建立了《育龄妇女生育节育卡》，在全省1547个乡(镇)中，已建立《育龄妇女生育节育卡》1516个，占乡镇人数的97.99%，在已建卡的乡(镇)中，能满足统计报表信息需要的有1318个，占85.2%。其中，建立乡村月报表制度的有1297个，占83.84%，已建立月例会制度的有1185个乡镇，占76.60%。由于这项工作的开展，摸清了人口底数，明确了工作重点，对指导甘肃省经常工作的开展，产生了很好的作用。在1993年全省人口与计划生育工作考核中，已发挥了积极作用。

宣传教育工作

一是人口与计划生育基础知识教育进一步普及。二是利用大众传播媒介开展计划生育宣传。

财务工作

一是经费投入有了明显增长。一年来，全省各级政府认真落实中央《决定》，自觉增强投入意识，加大工作力度，将计划生育经费投入列为党政一把手负总责的主要工作目标，有力地保证了计划生育经费的落实。据不完全统计，1993年，全省计划生育事业费的投入总数为4610.18万元，其中中央财政投入424万元，占9.2%，省级财政投入1476万元，占32.02%，地区级财政投入566.8万元，占12.29%，县级投入2142.92万元，占46.48%，县级财政投入比1992年增长43.18%。二是财务管理工作逐渐加强。进一步加强委机关经费的使用管理，重点对业务经费、会议经费、培训经费、电话费、车辆维修费等实行预算包干管理。针对有的县经费到位不及时，截留和挪用的问题，及时组织地区和下属事业单位的财务人员，对天水、平凉、定西三地市计划生育经费使用管理情况进行了重点检查，向全省通报了有关情况，到年底这一问题已全部解决。三是乡统筹款的利用开始引起重视。据统计，截止1993年底，全省乡统筹村提留款的利用由173万元扩大到616万元，在一定程度上缓解了基层计划生育财力不足的矛盾。四是国有资产的清查登记工作，取得了明显效果。1993年，省计生委对委机关和下属事业单位的财产进行了彻底的清查登记。全委共清理出50元以上的各类财产1270件，价值615.7万元，其中帐内财产1043件，价值225.6万元，帐外财产227件，价值360.1万元，清查出有帐无物的财产114件，价值21.6万元(其中丢失54件，0.82万元)；调出未下帐的4件；19.5万元；私人长期占用和借用的56件，1.35万元。甘肃省计生委被国家财政部评为1993年全国国有资产清查先进单位，受到表彰。

信访工作

1993年甘肃省计划生育信访工作，由于各级领导对信访工作的重视，扎扎实实地开展工作，重点抓党员干部、职工违反计划生育政策的问题，收到了明显效果，有力地促进了计划生育工作的顺利进行。全年全省共受理群众来信来访5190件(次)，立案查处231件，结案206件，结案率为85%，其中省计生委受理400件(次)，立案18件，结案率77%。

物　价

1993年甘肃省物价工作综述

省物价委员会主任

尹霖初

1993年，在邓小平同志重要谈话和党的十四大精神指引下，甘肃省价格改革迈出了较大步伐，在加强价格调控和管理、抑制物价过快上涨方面，做了大量工作，取得了一定的成效。

第一，转换价格形成机制取得了新进展。按照国家的统一安排，放开了粮食销售价格，放开了绝大部分统配钢材价格和部分统配煤炭价格，还放开了一部分其他商品价格，使市场机制在价格形成中的范围进一步扩大。据测算，到1993年底，甘肃省生产资料销售收入总额中，市场调节价格的比重达到83%，政府管理的价格只占17%；农副产品收购总额中，市场调节价格的比重达到85%，政府管理的价格只占15%；社会商品零售总额中，市场调节价格的比重达到95%，政府管理的价格只占5%。而且在政府管理的少数商品价格中，有一部分价格管理采取了指导价格的办法，市场调节也发挥着很大作用。显然，市场形成价格已占居主导地位。

第二，价格结构性矛盾进一步得到缓解。根据国家和省上的计划安排，为支持基础产业发展，较大幅度地提高了铁路货运、电力、原油、成品油、铁矿石、工业用盐、计划内铜锌系列产品等价格。这样使市场调节价格在产业大类价格的构成比重上都居于主导地位，有利于资源的优化配置。

第三，价格管理体制发生了新的变化。随着商品价格大部分放开，定价主体由政府向企业转移。中央、省、地、县四级集中把握定价权的格局进一步改变，现在价格管理权限基本上在中央和省两级物价主管部门。目前甘肃省省管价格目录中，农产品中只有粮食、棉花2种，轻工商品中只有中成药1种，重工商品和交通运输中只有9种，行政事业性收费240项、标准3920个。据调查反映，企业定价自主权基本得到落实。

第四，在价格管理调控方面做出了新的努力。为适应建立市场经济体制的需要，针对市场物价涨幅过大，价格秩序比较混乱的情况，控制了调价项目的出台，制定了一些价格管理措施。推动了企业内部价格管理工作，充实了价格监测制度，实施了行政事业性收费年审制度，整顿治理了农村乱收费和行政执法部门的行政事业性收费，房地产价格管理工作开始走上轨道，坚持进行了物价监督检查，使乱涨价、乱收费行为受到了遏制。去年全省分三批向社会公布取消乱收费项目141个，各地取消1165个，减轻企业和群众不合理负担约1.2亿元。此外，价格信息咨询、价格研究、农本调查和物价干部培训，都做了大量工作。

但是，1993年甘肃省物价方面也存在一些不容忽视的突出问题。一是物价总水平上涨幅度过大。1993年全省零售物价总水平上升13%，生活费用价格指数上升15.4%。虽说甘肃的物价总水平是在全国平均水平上下波动，但在西北地区各省中涨幅是最高的。二是对物价工作的重要性和必要性认识不够，对物价管理工作放松了，使物价工作处于薄弱状态，又缺乏价格调控有效手段。三是市场价格秩序比较混乱，乱涨价、乱收费现象仍较严重。这些问题的存在，既有客观因素，也有主观原因；既有历史形成的旧矛盾，也有新体制形成过程中的新问题。这些问题，必须在深化价格改革过程中逐步予以解决。

甘肃省 1993年税收财务物价大检查概况

全省1993年税收财务物价大检查工作，在省政府的直接领导下，以中共中央、国务院关于加强宏观调控的大政方针为指导，认真贯彻落实国务院《通知》和全国大检查工作会议精神，把大检查同整顿金融、财税秩序、增加财政收入，缓解财政困难以及反腐败斗争结合起来，积极开展自查和进行重点检查，取得了一定的成效。对严肃财经法纪，确保财政收支任务的完成，促进企业转换经营机制和全省经济的健康发展起到了积极作用。

截至1993年12月底统计，全省共查出各类违纪资金12198万元，其中应上交财政6510万元，已入库6169万元，入库率94.8%。全省130810户企事业单位和个体工商业户全部进行了自查，其中有违纪问题的11920户，违纪面为9.1%。剔除私营企业和个体工商业户，自查违纪面为11%。自查出各种违纪资金4155万元，占违纪总额的34.1%。全省共重点检查了64273户，检查面达到49%，其中有违纪问题的22235户，违纪面达34.6%，重点检查出各类违纪资金8043万元，占违纪总额的65.9%。

在违纪总额中，按项目分，偷漏工商各税3698万元，占30.3%；违反国家价格法规1360万元，占11.1%；偷漏能源交通重点建设基金和预算调节基金1137万元，占9.3%；国有企业偷漏所得税、调节税及侵占应交利润936万元，占7.7%；违反控制社会集团购买力规定696万元，占5.7%；印制使用各种代币购物券583万元，占4.8%；不按规定用途支用各项财政资金373万元，占3.1%；其他3415万元（其中以前年度查出141万元），占28%。按单位性质分，国营企业查出违纪资金6220万元，占51%；集体企业查出2547万元，占20.9%；行政事业单位查出2995万元，占24.6%；私营企业和个体工商业户290万元，占2.4%；其他单位146万元，占1.1%。按隶属关系和预算级次分，中央在甘单位（受国检办委托重点检查232户）841万元，占6.9%；省级2260万元，占18.5%；地县级9097万元，占74.6%。与上年同期相比，全省查出的违纪资金总额为上年6313万元的193.2%；增长近一倍，应入库、已入库资金也分别上升65.9%、69%，分别增加了2579万元和2519万元。14个地、州、市和省级10个大口中，除外事口略有下降外，其他全部上升。其中：兰州、天水、金昌、嘉峪关、武威、酒泉等8地、州、市和物价、工交、行财等口增幅较大，分别比上年同期增加一倍左右。

全省共抽调11474人，组成2718个工作组和检查组进行督促检查。共查出5——10万元违纪单位104户，10——50万元违纪单位63户，50——100万元违纪单位5户，100万元以上违纪单位2户。全省共有663个单位和191人受到经济处罚，2人受党纪政纪处分，5人移交司法机关立案处理。

(省财政厅大检办　慕　涛)

社会保障

改革发展中的甘肃民政事业

省民政厅厅长

胡培玉

甘肃自然灾害较多、经济基础薄弱的特殊省情决定了甘肃民政工作的极端重要性。1993年，我省民政部门以邓小平同志建设有中国特色社会主义理论为指针，适应建立社会主义市场经济新体制的需要，以社会保障工作为重点，加快民政改革步伐，较好地发挥了维护社会稳定，为全省改革开放和经济建设服务的作用，各项民政工作有了新的进展。

——适应新形势，城乡基层社会保障工作在改革中稳步推进妥善安排灾区群众基本生活，救灾救济工作在维护农村社会稳定和促进农业生产发展中发挥了重要作用。1993年，农作物受灾面积1733万亩，成灾面积1059万亩，受灾人口796.75万人，因灾死亡人口113人，各类灾害造成直接经济损失9.2亿元。在省委、省政府重视、支持和有关部门的配合下，各级民政干部深入基层，了解灾情，摸清底子，保证重点，统筹安排救灾资金和物资。全年下拨救灾款6459.8万元，给重灾民购买粮食2.27亿斤，为3600户灾民重建维修住房1.08万间，发放衣被3.98万件(床)，帮助1.18万灾民医治因灾引起的伤病。组织和发动灾区群众开展以工补农、以秋补夏等生产自救和社会互济互助活动。据不完全统计，全省灾区群众427.47万人参加生活自救活动，收入现金3.87亿元，粮食3.23亿斤；社会捐助资金70.14万元，募集衣物14.97万件(床)。为了加强资金管理，严肃救灾纪律。清理近年来被挤占挪用的救灾款1000多万元，保证了救灾粮、款及时到位。

巩固和发展农村基层“四个一”社会保障网络，加快了多灾贫困地区民政对象脱贫致富奔小康的步伐。扶贫工作坚持生活救济与生产扶持相结合、分户扶持与规模扶持相结合、资金扶持与科技扶持相结合，以兴办经济实体和福利企业为支柱，积极帮助灾民和救济对象开展生产自救，解决温饱。当年新增扶贫2.26万户，脱贫1.36万户，累计扶贫60.87万户，脱贫率达64%。为了增强贫困地区群众自我保障的“造血”功能，积极探索、改革救灾救济办法，大力发展“两会”，“两会”数达9895个，比上年增加525个，增长5.6%，积累资金7474万元，比上年增加1053万元，增长16.4%。全年共投放有偿救灾扶贫资金1194.14万元，扶持91个经济实体和福利企业发展生产，解决了40.92万户重灾民和贫困户生产生活中的实际困难。农村敬老院建设和五保供养向乡镇统筹和集中供养方向发展，基本做到了“供”有来源，“养”能落实。全省敬老院达559所，收养老人2837人，床位利用率50.1%，敬老院覆盖率31.2%。

农村社会养老保险试点工作在困境中艰难发展，农村基层社会保障迈出了新的一步。为了从根本上解决广大农民“老有所养”的问题，根据国务院33号文件精神和省政府关于开展农村社会养老保险试点工作的安排，从我省经济发展水平不均衡的实际出发，充分考虑了农民的经济实力，在农民自愿的基础上，选择敦煌市和西固区进行试点。1993年，酒泉、兰州等地(市)11个县(市、区)开展了农村社会养老保险工作，投保人数3万多人，收取保险费109万元。金昌、张掖、武威、嘉峪关四地市的试点工作正在组织实施。

进一步推进城市社会福利事业的改革开放，扩大了社会服务领域，增强了自身活力。全省24所福利院和精神病院创收184万元，比上年增长40%。以街道和居委会为依托的各种服务设施为网络的城市社区服务体系正在逐步形成，并向产业化、系列化方向发展。全省社区服务中心达46所，各类社区服务设施1249个，便民利民服务网点4641个。

围绕双拥热点，促优抚安置工作难点的突破，增进了军政军民团结，双拥、优抚、安置工作的整体水平有新的提高。创建双拥模范城(县)活动向广度和深度发展，全省已建成34个双拥模范城(县)。配合兰州军区“西部——93”军事演习，全省8个地(州、市)和24个县(市、区)掀起了声势浩大、规模空前的拥军支前热潮，双拥工作深得军心、民心。优抚工作在抓法规建设和优抚事业单位改革的同时，重点解决在乡复员军人“三难”问题。全省60%的县级政府制定颁布了优抚配套法规，优待面达98.5%，户均优抚标准达446.5元，在乡复员军人定补面达81.5%，定补标准提高到23.9元。1993年接收安置退伍义务兵14000名，其中在城镇安置了7600名。军休干部和无军籍职工的安置以及生活待遇得到较好落实，军干所和军供站的服务管理工作有了一定的加强，军地两用人才开发使用率达80%以上。

选准突破口，民政经济继续保

持较好的发展势头按照省委、省政府全省经济发展上新台阶的总体要求，我们坚持把发展社会福利企业和具有民政特色的第三产业(统称民政经济)作为振兴民政事业的突破口，抓住机遇，加快发展。

社会福利企业靠改革生存发展，在激烈的市场竞争中显示出顽强的生命力。1993年福利企业总数达1066个，福利企业总产值达6.7亿元，实现利税5418万元，新增产值1.5亿元，利税644.5万元，分别比上年增长13%，职工总数2.9万人，其中安置残疾人1.1万人。

社会福利有奖募捐持久不衰，成为民政经济的重要支柱。1993年全省销售奖券2366万元，累计达7656万元；筹集福利资金709万元，累计达2454万元。对44个社会福利项目进行资助和扶持，投放资金605万元，解决了一些社会福利企业的困难，资助兴办幸福院、福利院，加深了社会各界和人民群众对募捐工作的认识和理解。

具有民政特色的第三产业蓬勃兴起，活跃了市场，方便了群众，壮大了民政经济。我们把大力发展农村养老保险、假肢科研和生产服务、婚姻和殡葬系列化服务、残疾人康复医疗、城市社区服务等具有民政特色的第三产业作为培育和完善社会保障体系的重要措施，使第三产业在民政经济中的比重增加，其中社会福利企业总产值中第三产业就占20%，达1亿元，形成多门类生产服务体系。婚姻殡葬、福利院、军供站等社会福利事业单位兴办各种形式的第三产业，取得了较好的经济效益和社会效益。

冲破旧模式，基层政权组织民主化进程加快，行政管理法制化水平提高

积极推进基层政权组织民主化进程。在认真贯彻落实《村委会组织法》，总结推广村民自治经验的基础上，重点在13个县(市)、287个乡镇、2461个村委会开展村民自治示范试点活动，增强了群众的民主意识和参与意识。全省17623个村委会中一类班子由30%上升到53%，三类班子由25%下降到4%。全省85%的村通过村民选举配齐了干部，建立健全了村民自治和村规民约。

勘界进展顺利，边界局势基本稳定，行政区划管理逐步走向法制化轨道。全年新勘定省内行政区域界线2847公里，其中，地、州、市内部之间县级界线738公里，地、州、市内部县级界线2109公里，全省累计勘定县界8792公里，约占省内县级界线总长的60%，边界争议调处有一定进展。省内边界争议得到较好解决，恶性事件明显减少。从社会经济的发展需要着眼，适时调整变更了行政区划。

社团、婚姻管理、收遣等行政事务工作坚持管理与服务相结合，各项业务有新的进步。社团活动日趋活跃，较为完备的社团管理机构初步形成，3169个社团组织在社会经济生活中的桥梁纽带作用得到充分发挥。婚姻管理在重点查处违法婚姻，开展争创"无违法婚姻乡镇(街道)"活动的同时，积极开展系列化服务，无违法婚姻乡镇(街道)达338个，殡葬工作在城镇以提高殡仪馆服务质量为主，加强宣传教育，积极推进火葬；在农村以发展经营性土葬公墓为主，教育群众丧事简办，节约耕田，改革土葬。公益性土葬公墓达20143处，火化率有所提高。收容遣送各类流浪乞讨人员近8000人次，全省25所戒毒所收治戒毒人员2807人次。

今后，甘肃民政工作改革和发展的目标是：从本省实际出发，按照市场经济的要求，以保障人民群众基本生活权益为基本任务，充分发挥社会稳定机制作用，以建立完善城乡社会保障制度和社会化服务体系为重点，大力发展民政经济及第三产业，加强民政工作法制化建设，推进民政工作社会化，推进民政事业整体发展。

甘肃民政事业发展具有非常广阔的前景，实现甘肃民政工作改革与发展目标，不仅需要民政部门职员付出艰辛的劳动，同时也需要国内外省内外社会各界人士的鼎力支持。让我们共同努力，通过发展更为广泛、更为实际、更为宏大的社会福利事业，为甘肃的腾飞和振兴作出贡献！

残疾人事业蓬勃发展

残疾人事业是我国社会主义事业的一部分。据1987年全国残疾人抽样调查，甘肃省共有残疾人105.64万，约占总人口的5.1%，略高于全国平均水平。由于历史的原因和生产力水平的限制，残疾人事业仍滞后于社会和经济的发展，残疾人作为一个特殊的群体存在着大量亟待解决的困难和问题。发展残疾人事业，弘扬社会主义人道主义，维护残疾人合法权益，使残疾人同健全人一样以平等的权利和机会参与社会生活，共享社会物质文化成果，对于加速社会主义市场经济体制的建立，促进社会主义精神文明的建设，逐步建立和完善社会保障体系，都具有十分重要的意义。

近几年来，在省委、省政府的领导下，在中国残联的指导下，全省各级残联与各有关部门紧密配合，动员社会各界力量，努力贯彻实施《中华人民共和国残疾人保障法》、《中国残疾事业五年工作纲要》和《中国残疾人事业"八五"计划纲要》，使我省残疾人事业蓬勃发展，残疾人康复、教育、就业、文化、体育等各项工作都取得了显著成绩，残疾人在政治、经济、文化生活等方面的壮况有了一定改善。

【法制建设】1993年11月，第八届省人大常委会第六次会议审议通过并颁布了《甘肃省实施残疾人保障法办法》；自1990年残疾人保障法颁布以来，全省已有7个地(州、市)、31个县(市、区)政府部门制定了扶助残疾人的优惠、减免政策和地方性规章。残疾人保障法列入了全省"二五"普法规划，在全省城乡大张旗鼓地开展"全国助残日"普法宣传和扶残助残活动。省政府制定了《甘肃省残疾人事业五年规划》和《甘肃省残疾人事业"八五"计划》；有关部门联合制定了配套实施方案，将残疾人事业纳入全省国民经济发展计划。1993年12月，成立了甘肃省人民政府残疾人工作协调委员会，综合协调全省残疾人事业方针、政策、规划、计划的制定与实施工作，协调解决残疾人工作中的重大问题；协调完成国务院和中国残联部署的残疾人工作。委员会秘书处设在省残联，具体工作由省残联承担。

【残联组织建设】1993年8月，甘肃省残疾人联合会召开第二次代表大会，163名来自全省各地的残疾人、残疾人亲友和残疾人工作者代表出席了大会，会议选举产生了省残联第二届主席团、执行理事会和各类残疾人专门协会；主席团主席：副省长杨怀孝；执行理事会理事长：景庆云。省残联自1988年成立以来，在全省14个地(州、市)、85个县(市、区)、1690个乡、镇(街道)和一些大型厂矿、企事业单位建立了残联组织，初步形成了残疾人工作体系，为发展残疾人事业奠定了坚实的组织基础。

【残疾预防】有关部门认真贯彻省人大常委会关于预防先天智力残疾的法规，将优生优育、提高人口素质作为计划生育工作的一项重要任务，组织工作组对智残高发区的重度智残人状况进行摸底，深入农户开展残疾预防的宣传教育，为4726名育龄期重度智残人做了绝育手术，占全省育龄期重度智残人总数的34.8%，有效地遏制了先天残疾的发生。

【残疾人康复】各级残联组织在卫生、民政、教育等部门配合下，在全省范围有组织、有计划、有步骤地开展了残疾人三项康复工作。1988——1993五年间，省、地、县各级财政、民政共投入专项资金572万元，用于筹建康复点、购置康复医疗器械及农村手术患者的补助。共为14165名白内障患者作了复明手术，脱盲率达99%，脱残率95%；完成小儿麻痹后遗症矫治手术7846人次，有效率99%，显效率达90%；接受听力语言康复训练的聋儿611人，70%以上的聋儿经训练学会了简单会话，有些已入普通小学学习。

"八五"新开拓的残疾人康复项目在试点基础上逐步展开：

——兰州、平凉等地、市建立了低视力康复站，140名低视力残疾儿童配戴助视器，接受了康复训练。

——全省各地建立了27个社区康复站，同社区服务和管理相结合，为残疾人提供综合康复治疗、训练。——庆阳县政府制定了精神病防治康复试点实施方案，对精神残疾人进行调查摸底；县医院设立精神病防治康复指导中心，在部分卫生院开设专用病床，收治精神残疾患者。天水市也制定了5县2区开展精神病防治康复的试点方案，确定了专项经费。

——天水市、白银市、平凉市在普通小学附设智力残疾儿童康复站，215名智残儿童正在接受康复训练。

——中国残联确定向我省下拨305万元专项贴息贷款，用于扶助残疾人康复、脱贫，其中第一批85万元以永昌、西和、临泽、白银4县、区为康复扶贫试点，制定了方案，完成立项工作，资金到位，已进入实施阶段。

——我省第一座残疾人综合康复设施——省康复培训中心于1993年9月竣工。中心建筑面积6300平方米，内设综合门诊、视力康复、聋儿康复、脑瘫康复、肢体康复、医务人员培训、特教师资培训、残疾人职业培训、残疾人用品用具供应服务等设施，其中综合门诊、聋儿康复和残疾人用品用具供应服务已开展工作。

【残疾人教育】省教委制定了《关于发展我省特殊教育的若干意见》和《甘肃省"八五"期间特教发展计划工作要点》。五年来，全省用于发展特殊教育事业的经费319万元。特教学校由5所增加到10所，普通学校附设特教班41个，在校盲、聋、弱智学生865人；普通小学随班就读的盲、聋、弱智学生达3821人。兰州商学院、省艺术学校分别开办了残疾人财会大专班和聋哑人美术中专班；兰州师专依托兰州市盲聋哑学校建立了省特教师资培训中心。省残联积极配合教育部门做好残疾青年的招生录取工作，共有222名优秀残疾考生被录取到各大、中专院校。杨涛、刘海涛、马中青、唐永强、杜珑林5位残疾青年获得全国高等教育自学考试指导委员会和中国残疾人福利基金会颁发的"1993残疾人自学成才奖"。各级残联与有关单位协作，举办职业培训班45期，1132名残疾人接受了各类职业技术培训。

【残疾人就业】全省城乡社会福利企业发展到1253家，安置残疾职工11481人；各级残联创办经济实体42个，安置残疾人就业283人。成立了"省残疾人劳动就业服务中心"，协助政府和有关部门管理和指导全省残疾人劳动就业服务工作，扶助残疾人发展经济实体。

【残疾人体育】残疾人体育事业得到了各级体委、民政、财政等部门的大力支持。制定了《甘肃省残疾人体育十年发展规划》，全省14个地(州、市)及6个县(市、区)建立了残疾人体育协会；各级各类残疾人体育竞赛活动波及50多个县(市、区)，直接参与体育活动的各类残疾人达数万人次；先后举办了三届全省残疾人运动会、两届残疾人青少年锦标赛和一届智残人运动会。我省运动员被选拔到国家残疾人体育代表团，参加第八届国际伤残人奥运会、第四届夏季特殊奥林匹克运动会、世界青少年伤残运动会、远东及南太平洋伤残人运动会及香港第16届特殊奥运会，两人三次打破两项世界纪录和奥运会纪录；在国内赛场上先后参加了三届全国残疾人运动会、一届智残人运动会和8次乒乓球、蓝球、射击、举重、田径等单项锦标赛、邀请赛，15人27次超全国残疾人运动会最好成绩。在国内外重大体育比赛中，共夺得奖牌140枚，其中金牌73枚、银牌43枚、铜牌24枚。表现了残疾人自强不息的精神，为国家和甘肃省争得了荣誉。19名残疾人运动员分别荣获省“新长征突击手”和“三八红旗手”称号。为残疾人体育事业作出了突出贡献的8个单位、40人次受到省民政厅、省体委、省残联的嘉奖，省残疾人体协连续几年被甘肃省体育总会评为先进集体。两次在全国会议上介绍了经验。

【宣传】建立了省残疾人事业新闻工作者联谊会，形成残疾人事业宣传通讯网络。省残疾联创办了《甘肃残疾人》杂志，甘肃电视台、电台，甘肃日报分别开办了《残疾人园地》、《人生不等式》专题节目和《春天的事业》专栏，拍摄播放了16部反映残疾人生活，宣传残疾人事业的电视专题片、新闻片。

【文艺】举办了全省残疾人美术、书法、摄影作品展览、残疾人文艺调演、残疾人声乐录音比赛及电影《启明星》宣传发行，省残疾人爱心艺术团巡回各地演出受到社会广泛赞誉，并在全国盲聋哑学校文艺调演中获得优异成绩。

【普查、发证】全省大部分地(市、州)进行了残疾人状况普查摸底，发放《残疾人证》，近50万名残疾人凭证享受扶助优惠待遇。

【盲人按摩】全省各地盲人按摩诊所(科、室)已发展到28个，设立了11个按摩联络组，按摩盲人医生78人，著名按摩医师赵振彰《关于颈椎病四要素》的论文在全国盲人按摩学会年会暨北京国际腰腿病学术研讨会上受到专家组高度评价。

【信访】各级残联认真接待办理残疾人来信来访，省残联建立了理事长接待日制度，接待办理残疾人来信来访1650件次，为残疾人解决了康复、就医、教育、婚姻家庭及法律咨询等许多困难和问题，增进了与残疾人及亲属的联系。

【社会募捐】省政府向全省发出了“开展向残疾人事业捐款活动的通知”，省民政、卫生、残联、教委、工、青、妇等11个部门联合发出了倡议书，在社会上得到广泛响应，各界人士踊跃捐款，共募集资金230万元，其中200多万元用于省康复培训中心建设，其余部分用于残疾人三项康复；美国、香港明爱等基金会、慈善机构向我省捐助数万元资金和康复设备；台北曹氏基金会向我省残疾人捐赠了100辆轮椅。

(张海鹰)

什么是三资企业

所谓三资企业是指合资企业、合作企业和外资企业。

合资企业是由一个或几个境外公司、企业或其他经济组织或个人，经我国政府批准，在中华人民共和国境内，同一个或几个中国的公司、企业或其它经济组织，按照平等互利的原则，由合资双方共同投资、共同经营、共负盈亏、共担风险的有限责任企业。

合作企业是指境外的企业和其他经济组织或个人按平等互利原则，同中国的企业或其他经济组织在中国境内共同举办的企业。它是一种契约式的合营，合作双方以各自的法人身份共同签署合作经营合同，在合同中约定投资或合作条件、收益或产品的分配、风险和亏损的分担、经营管理的方式和合作企业终止时财产的归属等各方权利义务。

外资企业是指外国或港澳台地区的投资者(包括海外公司、企业、其他经济组织和个人)按我国法律，经我国政府批准，在我国境内设立的经济实体，企业全部资本为海外投资者所有，独立经营，独立核算，自负盈亏。

无论合资企业、合作企业或外资企业，经我国政府批准和登记后均取得中国法人资格，受我国法律和政府的保护、管理和监督。

民　族

民族工作

1993年甘肃省民族自治地方经济建设综述

省民委副主任

郭长乐

甘肃省民族自治地方包括两州、五县，即：甘南藏族自治州、临夏回族自治州、肃南裕固族自治县、肃北蒙古族自治县、阿克塞哈萨克族自治县、天祝藏族自治县、张家川回族自治县，总人口279万人，占全省总人口的12.4%，主要民族成份有回、藏、东乡、土、裕固、满、保安、蒙古族等10个世居民族。民族自治地方总面积17.58多万平方公里，占全省总面积的38.7%。

1993年，我省民族自治地方各级政府和各族人民在党的十四大路线指引下，认真贯彻党的民族政策和《民族区域自治法》，以建设有中国特色的社会主义理论为指导，进一步解放思想，扩大开放、深化改革，使各自治地方呈现出民族团结、政治稳定、经济发展、欣欣向荣的景象。在各级政府的大力支持下，民族地区各族人民群众继续发扬自力更生、艰苦奋斗的精神，各项建设事业取得了显著的成就。1993年，民族自治地方完成国民生产总值18.1亿元，社会总产值33.59亿元，国民收入15.8亿元，分别比上年增长5.3%、6.6%和12%，自治地方财政收入15198万元，比上年增长29%。

一、农村经济稳中有升，农牧业生产取得较好的收成

1993年，民族自治地方各级政府继续强化农牧业基础，大力推进科技兴农、科技兴牧，在不断建立和完善农牧业综合服务体系的同时，积极引导发展第二、三产业，提高了经济效益，农牧业取得了较好的收成。农业总产值6.04亿元，增长22.5%。其中牧业产值5.35亿元，下降2.5%。

随着农村经济的发展，农牧业机械化程度有了新的提高。1993年，民族自治地方新增机械总动力628224千瓦特，比上年增长3.5%，大中小型拖拉机有1096台，总动力达40438千瓦特，农用载重汽车有1088辆，农用运输车144辆，乡、村办水电站数69个，发电量达2868万千瓦小时，农村用电量达16185万千瓦小时，已有2203个村通了电，占自治地方农村总数的90%以上，农用化肥施用量(按折纯法计算)67400吨，比上年增长258%，有效灌溉面积74.29千公顷，比上年增长36%。

1993年，民族自治地方在战胜局部自然灾害以后仍取得了较好的收成，粮食总产量达到428929吨，比上年增长5.6%，其中小麦、油料等作物增幅较大。

我省是全国六大牧区之一，20个县中有9个县以畜牧业为主。1993年，民族自治地方进一步完善草畜双承包责任制，增加草场建设资金，加强草原管护，注重畜产品的深加工和系列开发，畜产品的商品率和综合经济效率有了一定的提高。大牲畜存栏164.66万头，猪存栏52.63万口，羊存栏331.79万只，分别比上年下降3.1%，增长9.62%和下降10.57%。猪牛羊肉总产量7.32万吨，比上年增长17.90%。

民族自治地方的乡镇企业异军突起，有了突破性的进展。1993年，民族自治地方乡镇企业达41213个，比上年增加3446个，从业人员达17.96万人，比上年增加14514人，完成总收入113966万元，增长40%，纯利润达13979万元，比上年增长112%。乡镇企业的发展，带动了农牧区的进步，显示了民族自治地方的发展潜力和发展后劲。

1993年，民族自治地方农牧区经济总收入达253698万元，比上年增长38%，农村经济纯收入达122527万元，比上年增长23.4%，综合经济实力明显增强。

二、深化改革转换机制，工业有了新进展

1993年，民族自治地方的工业企业在深化改革，转换机制的推动下有了新的发展。各地都注重了立足当地优势，注重资源开发，瞄准市场，加强经营管理，加快技术进步，使民族工业经济效益在各方面的困难条件下有了一定的提高。1993年，工业总产值达156973万元，比上年增长21%。

工业总产值按轻重工业分，轻工业达31533万元，占总产值的20.1%，重工业产值达125440万元，占总产值的79.9%，轻重工业的比重有所调整。

民族自治地方的工业企业以小型企业为主体，在494家企业中，大中型企业仅7家。其中，国有企业108个，集体企业127个，联营企业2个，经济成份向多元化发展。总体看，民族地方工业基础脆弱，规模效益差，经不起市场较大变化的冲击。进一步解放思想，深化改革，扩大开放，多渠道、多方位的招商引资，加快工业发展步伐，是民族地区经济再上新台阶的根本出路。

三、固定资产投资有所增长，投资结构有所调整

1993年，民族自治地方基本建设投资共计16162万元，比上年增长27%，按类别分，第一产业2013万元，占投资总额的12.5%，第二产业5888万元，占投资总额的36.4%，第三产业8261万元，占投资总额的51%；按行业分，农林水牧652万元，减少39%，交通、运输、仓储及邮电通讯业525万元，减少2.4%，卫生、体育和社会福利业1658万元，减少26.4%。投资结构有所调整，第二产业、第三产业的投资比例有所提高，投资结构比较合理，经济效益和社会效益比较明显。

资金来源结构：国家预算内投资1200万元，比上年下降11%，占投资总额的7.4%，国内贷款1170万元，比上年增长64.48%，占投资总额的7.2%，利用外资240万元，比上年增长239%，占投资总额的1.5%，自筹资金5726万元，比上年增长83.53%，占投资总额的35.5%。利用外资和自筹资金比上年有所上升，虽然拓宽了资金来源渠道，但总量仍然偏少。由于民族自治地方自然条件和历史的原因，投资环境相对较差，所以在一定时期内，国家预算内投资和国家银行贷款仍是民族地区主要的建设资金来源。

四、交通运输、邮电通讯等基础建设有了较快的改善

运输、邮电事业是民族地区经济发展的基础条件。1993年，民族自治地方的运输、邮电部门进一步挖掘潜力，积极筹资，改善条件，提高运输和邮电通讯能力。1993年末，公路线路里程达6558公里，比上年增加939公里，民用汽车达9930辆，比上年增加500辆，全年完成公路客运量582.6万人，比上年增长0.8%，完成公路货运量246.42万吨，比上年增长77.11%，横穿甘南、临夏州的212国道兰(兰州)郎(郎木寺)公路改造工程至合作段保质保量地完成了任务，大大改善了两州通往省会兰州的运输条件，提高了运输能力。

1993年，随着经济发展的需要，民族自治地方各族人民强烈要求改善通讯条件，邮电通信业进行了较大的改造和扩容，1993年末，民族自治地方邮电局(所)有148个，邮路及农村投递线路总长度为20018公里，比上年增长30.89%，邮电业务总量1981万元，比上年增长18.55%。合作4000门程控电话和临夏市8000门程控电话工程已全部开通使用，至此，民族自治地方的20个县(市)中除个别县外，全部开通了自动电话，电话机总数有18247部，比上年增长15.9%，其中：市内电话机达15095部，增长19.6%，农村电话机达3152部，增长1.12%，通讯信息落后的状况已得到根本性的转变，方便了和外部的联系。

五、流通领域异常活跃，各类市场发展较快

1993年，民族自治地方商业在全国大气候的影响下，各级领导和各族群众大流通、大市场的观念不断增强，使民族地区的农副产品、矿产资源、劳务、信息等逐渐进入市场领域，形成了以国营、集体商业为主，多种经营成份，多种经营方式、多种流通渠道和多层次的市场体系相交融的开放式流通格局，各种要素市场逐步发展和规范。

1993年民族自治地方纯购进总额达45886万元，增长2.8%，国内纯销售总额达100737万元，增长16.4%，社会商品零售总额达118987万元，比上年增长20.7%。

我省民族自治地方初级产品市场发展较快，张家川龙山镇皮毛市场，广河县祁家集牲畜交易市场，三甲集皮毛综合市场等具有较大规模和较强辐射能力的专业市场的形成和壮大，不仅促进了民族自治地方第二产业的发展和经济结构的调整，拓宽了致富的门路，而且提高了人民群众的商品观念和商品意识。

六、教育、文化等社会事业有了新的发展

到1993年底，民族自治地方有中小学2797所，在校学生达4.03万人，教职员工达2.21万人，都比上年有所增长。1993年民族自治地方考入大中专的学生达8440人，比上年增长5.4%。从1977年恢复高考以来省内外高校共录取我省民族自治地方考生总数147042人，扩大了少数民族干部队伍的来源，加快了少数民族干部的培养。

1993年，民族自治地方有广播电台2座，小功率电视转播台20座，卫星电视地面接收站91个，文艺表演团体18个，图书馆17个，群众艺术馆20个，文化事业的发展促进了民族地区两个文明的建设。

民族自治地方医疗卫生条件逐步改善，卫生队伍不断扩大。1993年，医疗卫生机构发展到523个，专业卫生人员达7102人，医疗病床发展到4084张，群众看病难问题有所缓解，人民的健康水平不断提高。

七、人民生活日益得到改善

民族地区经济和各项社会事业的发展，使人民群众得到了较大的实惠，特别是农村多种经营的发展，农副产品价格的提高和劳务输出等因素，人民群众的收入有了一定的提高。1993年，农牧民人均纯收入达453元，比上年增长14.4%，增加了57元，民族地区贫困人口已由1985年占总人口的65%下降到1993年的30%。民族自治地方职工工资总额36716万元，比上年下降12.7%，其中：国有单位职工工资总额达34118万元，集体单位职工工资总额达2587万元，分别比上年下降8.3%、41.2%，主要是一些企业产品销路不畅，开工不足。1993年，城乡储蓄存款年末余额110577万元，比上年增长22.25%，其中：城镇储蓄89481万元，农户储蓄21096万元，分别比上年增长39.7%、3.4%。

地县概况

兰州市

中共兰州市委书记：李虎林
兰州市人大常委会主任：张官廷
兰州市人民政府市长：柯茂盛
政协兰州市委员会主席：范云龙
中共兰州市纪律检查委员会书记：黄新光

兰州市经济和社会发展概述

【自然概况】兰州位于我国陆域版图几何中心，甘肃省中部。北与武威地区毗邻，西靠青海省，西南接临夏回族自治州，东南和东部与定西地区接壤，东北与白银市相邻。全市总面积1.31万平方公里，占甘肃省总面积的2.9%，东西最长153公里，南北宽130公里，海拔一般为1500～2000米。境内大部分地区属黄土高原丘陵沟壑区，在高山环绕中形成大小不等的多盆地状，地形呈西北高、东南低，全市地貌可分为石质山地、黄土梁峁和盆地、河谷阶地3个类型。城区南北两山对峙，东西黄河穿流，具有带状盆地特征。兰州市大部分地区属温带半干旱气候，温差大，降水少，冬季冷而长，夏季热而短，秋季低温，霜冻较早。年平均气温在10.3℃，年降雨量324.8毫米，日照时间2446小时，无霜期180天。境内除黄河干流外，还有庄浪河、大通河、湟水、苑川河等许多支流。河川径流地表水资源总量337亿立方米，地下水总量约9.6亿立方米，境内黑色金属、有色金属、贵金属、非金属、稀土和能源9大类35个矿种；有野生动植物资源260多种，农作物品种870多个，鱼类资源30多种，林木72种，中药材30多种。

兰州是甘肃省人民政府所在地，是全省政治、经济和文化中心，辖城关、七里河、安宁、西固、红古5区和永登、榆中、皋兰3县。有汉、回、满、藏、裕固、东乡等38个民族。1993年全市总人口261.2万人，非农业人口133.87万人，人口出生率12.98‰，死亡率4.12‰，自然增长率8.86‰。

【名特土产】白兰瓜　兰州黄河北岸的青白石乡是素负盛名的“白兰瓜之乡”。这里生产的白兰瓜是甘肃传统的出口产品之一，其周围的地区是白兰瓜的盛产区。成熟的白兰瓜呈圆球形，个头均匀，每个重1.5～2公斤，白中泛黄，色泽美观，耐贮藏，易携带，瓤厚汁丰，脆而细嫩，含糖量平均在14%左右。这种瓜不仅香甜可口，富有营养，还可以清暑解热，解渴利尿，开胃进食。

黑瓜子　产地多集中在皋兰、永登两县。这种瓜子以其片大，皮薄、板平、口松、肉厚、乌黑发亮、味香隽永、品质优异等特点而著称，是我国传统的出口商品之一。

玫　瑰　永登县苦水乡是著名的“玫瑰之乡”。苦水玫瑰不仅具有抗寒、耐旱、抗病虫害等优良特性，而且花瓣大、肉质厚、色鲜味醇、产花量、含油量和玫瑰油质量都较高。多年来，苦水玫瑰种植面积、株数以及玫瑰花产量，玫瑰油产量均占全国第一。玫瑰除有用途很广、经济价值极高的特点，其花和根还可入药。

百　合　七里河区的西果园、黄峪、铁冶、湖滩、魏岭等山区乡村为兰州市百合的主要产地。兰州百合色泽洁白如玉，形大味甜、肉质肥厚细腻，含有丰富的蛋白质、糖类、矿物盐和果胶，含糖量比驰名南国的宜兴百合、龙东百合还高，而含纤维甚低，是人们馈赠亲友的上等礼品，既能食用，又可入药。

蕨　菜　皋兰北山和榆中南山为主要产地。蕨菜俗名佛手，含有淀粉、蛋白质、脂肪、磷、钙和维生素A、C等，是一种别具风味的野生蔬菜。盐渍蕨菜是甘肃出口产品之一。

桃　安宁区是我国著名的桃乡之一。安宁蜜桃浆汁丰富，果肉柔软粉嫩，甘甜香郁，富含蔗糖、果糖、葡萄糖、麦芽糖、苹果酸、柠檬酸、脂肪、蛋白质、维生素等多种营养成份，被誉为“仙品”、“寿果”，自古闻名，远销各省市和香港地区。

此外，兰州的黄河蜜瓜、西瓜、籽瓜、杏、软儿梨、冬果梨和水烟等土特产品也久负盛名。

【城市建设】1993年，兰州市基础设施建设步伐加快，城市道路、交通、邮电、通讯、供水、供热状况有了较大改善。市区至中川机场高速公路开始建设。邮电通信能力随着城关区3万门程控电话扩容和长途电话5000线工程的完成而明显增强，市话总容量达9.8万门，并发展了一批无线移动电话、磁卡电话和汉字BP机。进行了西水东调二期和雁儿湾污水处理厂工程建设，对市区部分道路排污管道进行修、改、扩建，增加日供水能力6万吨。“蓝天计划”的实施使兰州市环境生态进一步优化。建成煤气管网15.2公里，新发展用户4万户，达到6.4万户；新建、扩建了一批联片供热站(点)，“二热”供热面积达50万平方米；南北两山绿化工程植树1.2万亩，258万株。城市综合开发全面启动，东方红地下广场和金港城项目已开工建设。

【国民经济】兰州市国民经济在上年基础上实现了持续、快速、稳定发展。1993年,全市国内生产总值达到109.6亿元,增长12.6%,兰州已进入全国国内生产总值超百亿元城市之列。第一产业增加值6.54亿元,增长13.2%;第二产业增加值72.11亿元,增长14.7%;第三产业增加值30.91亿元,增长7.9%。

农业随着农村改革的深化和引大入秦工程等农业基本建设的进展,基础地位不断加强,农业条件进一步改善。粮食、油料作物及蔬菜水果等主要产品生产均有较大增长,粮食总产量达到3.49亿公斤,比上年增长5.9%;乡镇企业总产值达到44.84亿元,增长59.1%,实现利税4.55亿元,增长54.6%,上缴税金1.93亿元,增长68.9%。全市已有产值过亿元乡(镇)10个,产值过千万元企业(集团)35个,其中七里河区崔家崖乡和兰州黄河集团公司产值居全市乡镇企业之首。

工业稳步推进企业改革,生产增长,效益改善。全市完成工业增加值64.59亿元,增长16.4%;其中市及市以下工业企业完成增加值18.65亿元,增长32.5%。全市乡及乡以上工业企业实现销售产值152.78亿元,增长8.6%,产销率达到99.5%,其中市及市下乡以上工业企业销售产值34.18亿元,增长17.4%。

1993年,全市流通活跃,市场体系的建立和发展步伐加快。全年社会消费品零售总额60.56亿元,增长22.6%,其中城市56.41亿元,增长40.3%。各种经济类型的商品零售额全面增长。全年共建成不同类型、不同层次的市场77处,总面积17.67万平方米,全市市场达到280处,其中集贸市场156个;交易点101个,生产资料市场10处,生产要素市场13处。年成交额达30.7亿元,其中,年成交额过亿元的市场增长54%以上,达到11个。1993年,全市第三产业发展较快。共完成公路客运量828万人次、货运量1998万吨;完成铁路客运量447万人次,货运量703万吨;完成航空客运量28.6万人次,货运量2966吨。邮电业务总量达到1.71亿元,较上年增长48.3%。银行存款余额144.55亿元,增长18.9%;贷款余额达146.29亿元,增长27.5%。保险业务收入达到1.6亿元,增长27%。生产资料物资购进额29.4亿元。进入市场科技成果1300多项,年成交额4000多万元。有固定门点的商饮服务业网点增加4852个,达到4.1万个,增长23.3%。

【改革开放】1993年,兰州市各项改革不断深化,对外开放取得明显成效。农村改革以稳定家庭联产承包制、完善双层经营为重点,农业"三放开"政策得到较好落实。企业改革以全面贯彻《企业法》和《条例》为重点,促进经营机制的转换,开展了股份制和股份合作制改革试点,采取租赁、拍卖、破产等形式加快企业组织结构调整步伐。全市98.6%的小型商业零售企业、93.7%的粮食企业和全部供销社企业实行了国有民营和社有自营。先后审定批准有限责任公司22户,股份有限公司5户,股本总额7.3亿元;城乡集体企业推行股份合作制64户;宝安长风股份有限公司股票在深、沪两地上市交易。组建企业集团8个,实施兼并、租赁和破产的企业各1户。非国有经济增长迅速,在全部工业增加值中非国有企业占22.1%,达10.58亿元,增长64.2%;个体、私营经济从业人员比上年增加近3万人。全市新办注册外商投资企业426户,合同投资总额4.64亿美元,全市累计外商投资企业达614户,总投资额7.9亿美元,投资范围涉及到房地产、饮食服务、文化娱乐、农产品加工、工业改造、高新科技产业等领域。

内陆开放城市建设的起步工作取得明显成效。根据国务院批准内陆省会城市实行沿海开放城市的政策和省政府下发兰州市对外开放若干政策规定精神,市上先后制订了《关于进一步扩大对外开放的若干规定》、《关于向全省开放的若干政策(10条)》,以及一系列配套政策,促进了全方位的开放。成功地举办了"兰州丝绸之路经贸洽谈交易会",总成交额20.35亿元。组织赴深圳、香港招商活动,签订合同47项、总投资额3.6亿美元,其中利用外资2.7亿美元。全市外贸收购总值20.32亿元,增长7%,出口创汇2.8亿美元。三个开发区坚持"统一规划、合理布局、分片开发、滚动发展"的方针,取得不同程度进展。高新技术开发区完成产业　基地一期场平、科技一条街开始营业,入区企业306户,技工贸总收入3.6亿元;经济技术开发区完成起步区规划工作;连海经济开发区两个年产3万吨电解铝和獐儿沟煤矿扩建工程已基本完成。

【人民生活和精神文明建设】在经济发展的同时,城乡居民生活水平明显提高,精神文明建设不断迈上新的台阶。1993年全市城市居民人均生活费收入2260元,增长21.1%,扣除物价因素增长4.7%;人均消费性支出2029元,增长26.3%;农民人均纯收入723元,增长11.2%,人均生活费支出741元,增长39.5%。城乡居民储蓄存款余额71.6亿元,增长29.2%。城乡居民居住条件继续改善,全年城镇新建住宅66.33万平方米,人均居住面积7.1平方米,农村新建住宅39.53万平方米。

1993年,兰州市突出思想道德和文化科技建设,广泛开展群众性精神文明建设活动。建成精神文明先进县区2个,市政文明小区10个,文明单位标兵120个,其中省级文明单位2个,开展"十星级文明农户"活动的行政村806个。科技工作面向经济建设、市及市以下科研单位，完成科研项目12个，推广新技术、新成果20项，建成科研达标乡镇12个。教育事业稳步发展，学龄儿童入学率达99.5%，初中入学率达95%；职业教育、成人教育也取得好成绩；建成2万平方米教工住宅和50所标准化学校。文化事业进一步繁荣，全年创作新剧目16部，送戏下乡409场；拍摄专题片20部(集)，电视剧8部(集)，市电视台二套节目正式开播；出版发行《兰州日报》。卫生事业继续发展，全年新增医疗卫生机构81个，病床增长7.1%，建标准化卫生院23所，农村医疗条件进一步改善。体育事业创出佳绩，兰州市运动员参加省以上比赛获得奖牌150枚，群众体育活动踊跃开展。

（中共兰州市委政研室：刘挺 刘晓宏）

兰州市城关区经济和社会发展概述

【城关概貌】城关区是甘肃省省会兰州市的中心区，自西汉张骞通西域，一直为古“丝绸之路”必经之路，是省、市党政军机关所在地，是全省政治、经济、科技、金融、交通中心，是发展中的新型内陆开放城区。城关区历史悠久，远在5000年前的新石器时代，这里就有原始先民游牧和居住。殷周时期诸羌聚居，自西魏后，这里一直是郡、州、县治所在地，清康熙五年（公元1666年）陕甘分治后即为全省政治中心。乾隆时始正式成立兰州市，与皋兰县同治于今城关区。建国后为兰州市的县级政区。建国初期几经调整，于1960年底城关区区域范围基本固定，1968年曾改称东风区，1973年8月恢复现名至今。城关区地处兰州市东部，位于东经103°46′——103°59′，北纬35°58′——36°9′之间。东部和东南与榆中县相接，西南和西部与七里河、安宁两区毗连，北部与皋兰县为邻。总面积为215平方公里，其中街区面积41.4平方公里，耕地面积3.93万亩，辖近郊5个乡（共有村民委员会43个，村民小组187个）和20个街道办事处（共有居民委员会305个，家属委员会221个）。城关区地处兰州盆地的东部，依山傍水，南北夹于皋兰、白塔两山之间，滔滔黄河由西向东穿流而过，地形大体分为山、坪、川、滩四类，呈三级阶梯状。南北两山均为黄土山丘，群峰叠嶂、高峻陡峭，海拔多在2000米以上，是兰州市区的天然屏障。黄河自徐家湾入境东流至桑园峡出境，流长18公里，为全区工农业生产和城乡人民生活提供了充裕的水源，也造就了区内天然的风景游览胜地。沿河建成的滨河带状公园，是城市人民游览、休息的良好场所。区内气候属中温带半干旱型，气候干燥，冬无严寒，夏无酷暑，日温差较大，年平均气温9.1℃。最冷月1月，平均－7.3℃，最热月7月，平均22.4℃。年平均无霜期为168天，降水量为331.9毫米，蒸发量为1879毫米，降水偏少且多集中在第三季度，年平均风速为2.3米/秒。温暖宜人的气候与充足的日照，日温差大，适宜于蔬菜瓜果生长，瓜果含糖量高。区内盛产瓜果，素有“瓜果之城”的美誉。全区总户数为19.81万户，总人口为65.69万人。在全区总人口中，非农业人口60.88万人，农业人口4.8万人。在总人口中，男性33.7万人，女性31.98万人。1993年人口自然增长率为3.8‰，城市3.61‰，农村6.63‰。

【经济现状】近年来，随着改革开放和经济建设步伐的进一步加快，经济建设出现了前所未有的发展势头，百业俱兴，前景广阔。1993年，全区工农业总产值达到71833万元，增长31.4%；其中，工业总产值66246万元，增长34.4%；乡镇企业总产值50149万元，增长91.7%；农业总产值为5587万元，增长4.1%；市场成交额25.28亿元；社会消费品零售额17.04亿元。职工人均年收入2552元，农民人均纯收入1230元。

工业，全区乡及乡以上工业总产值40369万元，增长10.8%；工业销售产值31996万元，增长14.8%；按经济类型分，国有经济工业总产值7858万元，增长2.66%，集体经济工业总产值31091万元，增长13.6%，其他经济1419万元，增长0.42%。通过改革、改造、调整，工业结构有了一定的改善。一是坚持产业结构调整。按照宜工则工，宜商则商、工商并举、优势互补、综合经营的原则，优化和调整产业结构。有13户企业实行了转产联营。二是推进产品结构调整。在继续抓好千吨裸线等24项技术改造项目达产达标的基础上，开发了塑料绝缘胶带、钢制住宅分户防盗门、厕所强力消垢剂等83项新产品。三是实施企业组织结构调整。其中联合兼并5户企业，有偿转让2户企业，整体租赁5户企业。全区基本上形成了以食品、服装、印刷、化学、塑料、金属制品、电器等27个行业。

1993年农业总产值为5587万元，增长4.1%。主要农产品产量中，粮食总产量1492吨，增长5%；蔬菜总产量49808吨，增长3.5%；果品产量16841吨，增长3.2%；主要畜产品产量有增有减，猪牛羊肉总产量839吨，增长3.1%；牛奶总产量8044吨，下降2.3%；鲜蛋产量185吨，增长108%。其他农作物产量也较往年有所增加。我们重点抓了上水工程的改造和维修，积极推广节水灌溉技术，提高了水利设施效益。加强了农用土地开发，有计划的改造中低产田，开发荒坡、荒滩、不断扩大农业用地。新开发农业用地550亩，完成“三田”建设1005亩。不断强化科技兴农工作，围绕“菜蓝子”和粮食丰产“111”工程建设，狠抓良种繁育，防虫灭病等农业技术的推广、示范、应用和扩大保护地栽培面积等工作，使全区农业走上了依靠科技发展生产的路子。

近几年我区乡镇企业采取"外引内联、主动出击、创造条件、筑巢引凤"的办法，在资金少、困难多的情况下保持迅猛的发展势头，在规模和档次上开始有所突破。1993年乡镇企业已发展到1461家，较上年增加581家；从业人员19765人，增加9628人；乡镇企业总产值50148万元，增长91.7%；总收入46061万元，增长111.7%；有2个乡实现了产值过亿元，14个村产值过千万元，60个企业产值过百万元。

1993年全区商品总销售20104万元，增长37%；社会消费品零售总额17.04亿元，增长41.0%；商业呈现购销两旺的发展势头。市场建设再掀高潮。新建火车站综合批发市场、阿拉山口边贸一条街、上川生产资料等5个市场；扩建了雁滩建材和光辉布料等4个市场。其中火车站综合批发市场，张苏滩批发市场二部等5个市场已投入营运。旅游资源开发成效显著。以完善兰山公园、雁滩公园、儿童公园景区配套建设为重点，新建了小型高尔夫球场、观览车等4处8个游乐景点。房地产开发稳步发展。九州经济开发试验小区基础设施配套建设正在加快，新型服务业开始起步。

个体私营经济，全区个体工商业22261户，从业人员40694人，销售总额和营业收入21.15亿元。私营企业185户，从业人员3432人，销售总额和营业收入6891万元。全区个体私营企业上缴税费5100万元。财政收支随着经济建设的不断发展，财政收入呈不断增长的趋势。1993年财政收入28570万元，增长20.4%；财政支出10617万元，增长27.1%。

【旅游、交通、邮电】城关区具有丰富的旅游资源，生活环境优美，自然景观宜人。穿城而过的黄河上有著名的"天下黄河第一桥"兰州中山黄河铁桥，黄河北岸有白塔山公园，南岸有南湖公园、儿童公园和滨河风景路，城南有五泉山公园和位于皋兰山之巅的兰山公园。这些景点各具特色，是游览观光的好去处。区内铁路、公路、航空四通八达。兰州火车站是连接陇海、包兰、兰新、兰青四条铁路干线的交汇点，是西北铁路的交通枢纽。还有铁路专线通往重要矿山、工厂。兰州火车站每天有十几列旅客列车始发、几十列客车交汇通往，年客运量740万人(次)，货运量达210多亿吨。闻名中外的"亚欧大陆桥"从这里经过，为我们参与国际经济大循环提供了便利条件。公路有西兰、兰新、甘青、兰包、甘川等25条主干道通往全省各地，并与陕、甘、青、宁、新、川诸省相连，城区内城市和乡村道路布局已形成网络化。西北民航兰州售票处设在区内，每周有百余次航班，可直达香港、北京、上海、广州、乌鲁木齐等25个省、市、自治区。省内还有通往庆阳、天水、敦煌的地方航班，为旅游、经济、技术信息交流提供方便。市区交通十分便利，有公共汽(电)车线路往返循环，小公共汽车、招手停、个体小客运车、出租小汽车迅速发展。兰州港业已建成，黄河水上机动船运输游览项目正在增加，航运前景广阔。

近年来为适应经济发展的要求，电信通讯瞄准高起点高技术，先后引进程控电话等高新技术运用电信通讯业，形成了光纤电缆、微波、传真一体化的四通八达的国内、国外通信网络。目前与300多个国家和地区、1500多个国内城市开通直拨电话。城关区电话总容量4万余门，其中程控电话3万余门，开通了无线移动电话系统，磁卡电话，"160信息台"、"126"汉字数字寻呼系统。普遍开办了邮政、电报昼夜服务，国际国内电报和传真电报业务，国际国内长途电话直拨业务，国际国内函件、包裹业务，以及邮政快件、特快专递、邮政储蓄等业务。

【社会事业】城关区是一个科技人才密集，科技力量雄厚的城区。据不完全统计，区内有各类研究院所(含大专院校)90余所，拥有专业科技人员6万余人。有中科院兰州分院，中科院近物所、化物所、大气所、地质所、冰川所等14个全国性的科研单位。经国务院批准的兰州高新技术产业开发区也在区内。区内还有资料翻译、情报、测试、技术咨询等门类齐全的服务中心。

教育事业，已经形成了比较完整高、中、初等教育网络。区内有兰州大学、兰州医学院、西北民族学院、兰州商学院、甘肃省教育学院等大专院校9所，中专、中技31所，普通中学38所，职业中学4所，小学89所。中小学在校学生85509人，教职工为6662人。幼儿园87所，收托儿童15491人，保教人员1123人。

区内共有各类医疗卫生机构407个，有省、市、区三级人民医院及部队医院、厂矿职工医院、兰州医学院等正规医院16所。医疗设备先进、技术力量雄厚、名老中医汇集，引进各种先进的诊断设备。区属医疗机构42个，拥有病床370张，卫生技术人员694人，开设了"性功能康复中心"，及"中医骨伤科"等特色医疗服务项目。

区内共有影剧院24个，省、市专业文艺团体9个，公共图书馆3个，新华书店8个，画院(画廊)2个，少年宫、青年宫、科学宫、博物馆各1个。文化娱乐场所达到1152个，每年组织开展职工文艺调演及群众文艺演出活动。区内拥有兰州体育馆等大型体育场馆3个，小型运动场10个，足球场5个，蓝球场233个，排球场35个，游泳池3个，体育学校2所，还有射击场、航空运动场、旱冰场等。

【城市建设】就城建风貌而言，城关区是兰州市有代表性的一个分区。

经过多年努力，现在它已成为布局合理、功能齐全、空间层次丰富、基础设施齐全的分区。建国后，城区进行了大规模的建设，街区面积扩大了10余倍，旧城区改造有很大进展，现已建成住宅小区260多个，它们各自的楼群拥有量都在3栋以上，其中标准化配套楼群53个，10栋以上就有6个。小街小巷改造亦达2000多条，建成了张掖路、酒泉路、中山路、庆阳路等商业大街，滨河路、天水路、东岗西路等花园式大街。高楼大厦鳞次栉比，造型各异，其中兰州体育馆、省图书馆、少年宫、科学宫等一大批现代建筑群为城市增添了新的光彩。在公共设施中，城关区拥有兰州市八座广场中的7座，其中以占地45000平方米，可容纳10万人的东方红广场最为著名，它也是兰州第一大广场，广场建筑风格协调，庄严美丽，是全市社会活动的重点场所。新建的兰州火车站占地1.1万平方米，售票、候车大厅宽敞明亮。站前广场占地3.5万平方米，6条线路的公共汽(电)车在此始发。城区路灯数量居全省之首，入夜近6000盏华灯与众多的霓虹灯齐放光芒，似繁星闪烁，构成了闻名西北的美丽夜景。

区内有主次干道73条，小街巷161条，标准化大街12条，它们分别是滨河路、东岗西路、金昌路、平凉路等。73条主次干道110486米，城区市政桥梁达36座，其中最著名的要数清代光绪年间(公元1909)建成的中山桥了。这36座桥梁中有三座跨街人行天桥。它们与其他桥一起，如彩虹高悬于黄河、公路、河道上，构成了城区立体化的交通格局。

现任主要领导：

中共城关区委书记：王振家

城关区人大常委会主任：张志乐

城关区人民政府区长：魏至公

政协城关区委员会主席：杨永旺

(兰州市城关区统计局)

七里河区经济和社会发展概述

【基本情况】七里河区地处兰州市区中南部，位于东经103°50′，北纬36°3′，东接城关区、榆中县，南鞏临洮县，西邻永靖县、西固区，北濒黄河，与安宁区和城关区徐家湾隔河相望。全区总面积397.49平方公里。东西宽21公里，南北长33公里，形如不规则的的手掌。境内梁峁起伏，沟壑纵横。山、坪、沟、滩交错分布，总的地势是南高北低向黄河盆地倾斜。最高点双咀山，海拔3251米，最低点西湖公园，海拔1521米。无霜期110天至180天，年平均降雨量200至500毫米，平均温度9.3℃，气候属大陆性气候。辖区内设有7乡1镇，9个街道，总人口为39万人，居住着汉、回、东乡等29个民族。

七里河区以境内小河流“七里河”而得名。早在新石器时期，这里就有先民生息，商周时为羌戎之地，秦统一六国后属陇西郡，汉三国、西晋时属金城郡，西魏归金城郡子城县，隋隶兰州总管府金城郡、子城县，后改属金城郡兰泉县，唐归兰州金城郡五泉县，北宋属秦凤路兰州兰泉县，清为兰州府皋兰县管辖，民国时期至解放前分属兰州市及皋兰县，1949年8月26日区境解放，成立兰州市第八区区公署，1952年区公署改为区人民政府，1955年开始改名为七里河区，隶属兰州市。

七里河区历史源源流长，史前文化发达，遗存丰富，现已发掘古代文化遗址39处，出土大量文物，是马家窑、半山等文化的发祥地，已经发现的马家窑文化遗址，墓葬有西坡岻、曹家嘴、青岗岔、花寨子、兰工坪等十余处，出土的各种文物1000多种，其中西坡岻的陶石、骨器就达数百件。在本区花寨子村发掘的一处规模较大的半山类型的墓地中，出土各种文物上千件，以32件彩陶壶最具有代表性，充分显示出半山彩陶的特色。名胜古迹有摩云岭、天都山、华林坪、古城坪、石佛沟、后五泉、金天观、握桥、小西湖等，均为史藉所载。曹家嘴、西坡岻遗址和狗牙山、沈家岭的解放战争纪念地，华林山革命烈士纪念塔等五处列为省级文物保护单位。

我区自然资源丰富。水利资源主要为地下水和地表水两部分。地表水有黄河客水(平均年径流量为336亿多立方米)和水磨沟、黄峪沟、西果园沟自产水(年径流量为6000多立方米)地下水蕴藏量约280多万立方米。矿产资源主要有煤、石英石坩泥、石灰石、沙矿、路标石等。植物资源主要农作物以小麦、洋芋、各类蔬菜为主，堪称全国之最的兰州百合就盛产我区，具有鳞茎硕大、瓣厚肉肥，色泽如玉，具有很高的食用、药用和观赏价值。远销香港、澳门、东南亚地区。有驰名省内外的西园冬果梨和苏木梨、苹果等。生长在后山次森林的野生蕨菜，营养丰富，无污染，质地脆嫩，倍受外商青睐，现批量出口日本、南韩、港澳等国家和地区。

电力充足，刘家峡、八盘峡和盐锅峡等水电站电网覆盖全区。交通方便，区内铁路、公路四通八达，兰西火车站是陇海、兰新、兰青、包兰四大铁路干线的重要枢纽，西北最大的铁路货运编组站也在这里。公路是兰州市与省内外各地交流的必经之途，有兰郎、兰宜、兰榆等国道为骨干的公路干线，城区以西津路为主干线，连接本市城关区和西固区，并有45条次干道，新修的滨河路中段道路平坦宽敞，道旁绿树成荫，花坛簇列。有17条公共汽车和无轨电车路线。电信通讯形成完整体系，省级微波通信站电视差转台已开通多年，覆盖率达100%，寻呼电话已形成系统，市话程控装机容量达数万门，直拨电话可接通全国各地及90个国家和地区。

【经济建设】农业，继续稳定和完善以家庭联产承包为主的责任制和统分结合的双层经营体制，坚持科技兴农的方针，推广农业科技成果和农业新技术，发展"一优两高"农业，建立了粮菜良种试验示范场、多种经营试验示范场、畜禽良种试验示范场，38个村建立了科技综合服务站，建立科技示范户1500户，基本形成了乡、村有站(组)，有科技示范户的网络，农村经济全面发展，农村社会总产值达到86469.3万元，比去年同期增长50%，农业总产值达到7804.7万元，比去年同期增长7.53%，粮食总产量再创历史最好水平，达到2071万公斤，比去年同期增长5.94%，蔬菜总产量达到7939万公斤，比去年同期增长26.3%，果品产量达到1241万公斤，比去年同期增长18.87%，百合产量达到434万公斤，比去年同期增长16.09%。农业基础条件继续改善，新增有效灌溉面积2000亩，新增三田面积3056亩，农业机械总动力69804.38万千瓦，比去年同期增长65.45%，大型拖拉机25台，比去年同期增加1台，小型拖拉机1020台，比去年下降2.7%，农用排灌动力机械273台，比去年增加93台，农村用电1289万度，比去年增加16万度，农用化肥施用量4307.2吨，比去年增加906吨，水窖3151眼，比去年增加229眼。林业，为了加快我区绿色工程建设，区林业局率先进行政治体制及人事制度的改革，在保持机关行政职能不变的前提下，机关与财政彻底脱钩，废除了干部职务的终身制，对局属各单位领导实行考评聘任制，在单位内部实行全员劳动合同制，打破了正式职工与农民合同工的界线，层层签订目标责任书，年终考核，奖罚兑现，从而调动了广大职工的积极性，当年造林6523亩，四旁植树10万株。与此同时，他们积极开展种、养、加多种经营，狗牙山造林站建起了两座高效节能温室，种植了黄瓜、生菜等，并引进了美国大青蛙的养殖技术，已繁殖成功，今后每年可提供种蛙3万只，在此基础上，他们已创办了7个经济实体，创收68万元，不仅结束了机关人员吃皇粮的历史，走上了自给自足，自我发展的道路，而且也为我区林业发展、调剂资金做出了贡献。

工业，积极探索各种类型的改革，通过股份制、兼并及租赁等方式，调整组织结构，启动生产，创建了"兰州耐火材料有限公司"，兼并了焊割工具厂、工程塑料厂，租赁了元件二厂、兰州硅厂、兰州锑品厂。工业发展速度明显加快，工业总产值完成31829万元，比去年同期增长24.78%，其中：全民工业完成4321.4万元，比去年同期下降0.9%，集体工业完成27507.8万元，比去年同期增长30.58%，在促生产的同时，大抓技改项目和新产品开发，全年实施技改项目11项，完成9项，完成重点新产品开发20项。

乡镇企业，以推行股份制为突破口，提出了"远学山东莱城，近学天水秦安"的工作方法，并实地考察学习外地先进经验，先后确定了25家企业进行股份制试点，已建成股份制企业1家，股份合作制企业22家，股金总额达到1189万元，全区现有乡镇企业1669个，其中：乡办60个，村办207个，合作36个，个体办1366个，乡镇企业总产值达78664万元，比去年同期增长55.75%，利润总额6226万元，比去年同期增长70.7%，乡镇企业规模继续扩大，现已建成产值双亿元乡1个，亿元乡3个，亿元企业1家，千万元企业5家，百万元以上的企业49家，企业档次、水平不断提高。

外向型经济，在认真分析形势和区情的基础上，我区内陆开放城区和对外开放工作迈出了良好的一步，组织人员赴深、港招商活动，兰交会期间与中外合资签订正式合同11项，总投资21630万元人民币，250万美元，签订意向性协议17项，总投资16910万元人民币，194万美元，在各种展销会上，总成交额878.5万元人民币，参展的项目获银奖1项，优秀奖6项，与此同时，在横向经济联合上，实行多层次多渠道的外引内联，先后与省内外30多个地区、80多个单位建立了友好合作关系，提高了我区在国内外的知名度，为内陆开放城市的早日建成奠定了坚实的基础。

商贸事业，繁荣活跃，遍布城乡的几千家国营、集体和个体商贸网点，起着沟通信息，调剂余缺，繁荣市场，方便人民的作用，以西站、小西湖、文化宫和东西西津路沿街为主的城区商贸网点，经营行业和门店排列有序，以农村供销社和代销店为主的农村商贸也形成了网络，是沟通城乡经济的主渠道，据三产普查资料表明，我区1992年有各种类型(不含个体)三产网点1964个，从业人员62009人，增加值达到4.67亿元，销售税金0.33亿元，分别比上年增长14.12%、6.7%、17.04%、12.55%，在第三产业中，商饮业单位数为875个，从业人员18387人，增加值913.53万元，分别比上年同期增长28.11%、16.83%、19.9%。第三产业个体企业数3946个，比上年增长26%，从业人员8013人，比上年增长38.2%，增加值6370万元，比上年增长49.91%。1993年新建、改建和扩建各类市场21个，占地面积6万多平方米，累计发展各类市场57个，其中：综合性市场20个，批发市场5个，专业市场8个，夜市6个，农村集贸市场3个，交易点7个。市场总占地面积17万平方米，商品成交额2.6亿元，比去年同期增长47%。

【城市建设】坚持"人民城市人民建"的方针，继续实施以"绿化、气化、热化、防尘、型煤"五大工程为主要内容的“蓝天计划”，投资145万元，完成了烟尘处理设施，建成28.9平方公里的烟尘控制区，覆盖率达100%，建成达标区3.97平方公里。

总投资5600万元，建筑面积29500平方米的区文化中心及招待所工程，已完成3000平方米的工程量，改造810米长的光华街，已完成工程量的90%，磨沟沿小区配套建设完成面积7582平方米，占工程总量的85%，中外合资的中港城筹建工作全面展开，西湖公园新建水上娱乐工程，总投资620万元，挖土方24000立方米，“柳荫馆”、“揽秀楼”、“荟真苑”等主体工程建设全部完成，以西津路商贸一条街为主线的黄金大厦等骨干工程突飞猛进，连片发展，已渐成型，近万平方米的住宅小区正在建设之中。

绿化美化工作，本着“巩固、提高、发展”的原则，新增绿地7.5公顷，种植草坪草花85783平方米，绿篱12921米，展摆盆花22600盆，特别是集中抓了滨河西路的重点绿化工程，更换土方2560立方米，完成行道植树1198株，种植草坪草花3940平方米。

环卫基础设施得到改善，新建垃圾台13座，制做果皮箱50个，维修垃圾箱27个。

【社会发展】社会治安和综合治理，坚持“打击和防范并举”、“治标和治本兼顾”的方针，一年内刑事案件发案873起，破获767起，破案率达87.8%，其中：重大案件299起，破获236起，破案率为78.9%，与去年同期相比破案率提高了4.8%，其中：破获毒品案件66起，抓获毒品犯罪分子232名，缴获毒品6635.8克，查处各类犯罪分子1257人，降低了社会不稳定因素。

教育工作全面贯彻党的教育方针，努力深化教育体制改革，办学条件逐年改善，共筹措资金334万元。修缮改造了17所中小学，面积达7854平方米。全区现有2所高等院校，十几所中等专业学校，数十所成人教育学校和职业教育学校，上百所中小学及幼儿园托儿所。职业高中在校人数1411人，高中在校人数2665人，初中在校人数11381人，小学在校人数32032人。科技努力为经济建设服务，促进科技成果向现实生产力转化，围绕开展“科技推广年”活动，引进各类新品种176个，种植试验123项，引进丰产技术50项，建立科技示范户134个，19项工农业科技项目全部完成，“农科教”三教统筹的农村教育体制初步形成。卫生、医疗条件进一步得到改善，区内现有卫生机构50个，其中：地区24个，本区26个。共有医疗床位4217个，卫生技术人员4038人，计划生育工作开始向经常化、科学化、规范化迈进，人口出生率达到12‰，人口自然增长率达到7.2‰，计划生育率为97.6%，农村二孩结扎率为96.78%，一孩放环率为95.18%。

人民生活水平不断提高，全区现有职工人数16022人，工资总额4633万元，人均月工资收入240元，比上年同期增加46元，增长23.7%，农民人均纯收入1024元，比上年增加87元，增长9.28%。

（兰州市七里河区统计局：杨秀玲）

榆中县经济和社会发展概述

【自然概况】榆中县位于甘肃中部，是兰州市的东大门，属兰州市辖三县之一。全县辖3镇25乡，总面积达3300平方公里，总人口40.8万人。榆中县城距兰州市34公里，距被誉为“陇右名山”的国家级自然保护区兴隆山4公里。根据地理环境、自然条件，全县可分为川塬河谷地区，南部高寒二阴山区和北部干旱山区三类不同地区。川塬河谷地区主要是指黄河流经地区和苑川河流域地区，共13个乡镇，这里土地平坦，气候适宜，有丰富的水利资源，是榆中县的主要产粮区，也是工业生产的主要基地，经济比较发达。粮食作物主要是小麦、玉米、豆类和谷物等；经济作物主要是瓜果、蔬菜、烟叶、油料等；来紫堡乡、金崖乡、和平乡是兰州市重要的蔬菜供给基地。北部干旱山区共9个乡，这里干旱少雨，海拔在2000米以上，属传统的旱作农业地带，主要农作物有小麦、豆类、油料、洋芋等，畜牧业比较发达，并有一定储量的矿产资源。南部高寒二阴山区有6个乡，这里气候湿润，雨量充足，畜牧业比较发达。山区有丰富的原始森林，林区面积约5万多亩。因林区野生动、植物资源丰富，有国家二、三类保护动物10余种，名贵中药材100多种，珍奇树木40多种，被列为兴隆山国家级自然保护区。

【经济发展概况】1993年全县经济建设和各项社会事业得到全面发展，取得了较大的成绩。据统计，社会总产值达到8.04亿元，比1992年增长39.9%；国民生产总值达到3.21亿元，比1992年增长21.5%；人均国民收入达到783元，比1992年增长21%；工农业总产值达到5.3亿元，比1992年增长29.69%。其中，农业总产值达到2.03亿元，比1992年增长6.1%；乡以上工业产值完成2.08亿元，比1992年增长35.43%；乡镇企业总产值达到5.32亿元，比1992年增长56.2%；财政收入达到3278.3万元，比1992年增长27.8%。粮食生产和农民人均纯收入保持稳定增长，粮食总产量达到1.21亿公斤，比1992年增长5.73%；农民人均纯收入达到587元，增长8.9%。贫困面持续下降，由1992年的7.4%降低到6.3%。

农村经济，全县农业总产值达到2.03亿元，比去年增长6.1%，其中，种植种植1.37亿元，占67%；畜牧业0.64亿元，占32%。主要农产品中，粮食、油料、烟叶、瓜果、蔬菜等产量均有较大增长。粮食产量达到1.21亿公斤，比去年增长5.73%；油料产量达到632万公斤，比去年增长23.4%；烟叶产量达到435万公斤。

推进“一优双高”农业的发展。在确保粮食总产量增长的前提下，调整粮经比例，由1992年7：3调整为6：4，增大了经济作物的比重，提高了农产品的商品率。经济作物种植面积比去年增加7.3万亩，新发展蔬菜基地2000亩，蔬菜面积累计达到2.39万亩。全县建立了以洋芋、油料、蔬菜、豆类、瓜类、烟叶、甜菜、果品、药材、小杂粮等十个小商品种植基地和以牛、羊、猪、鸡、兔、鸭、鱼等为主的七个养殖业商品基地。十个小商品基地主要分布在城关、和平、青城、金崖等22个乡(镇)。1993年种植总面积达到47.15万亩(含复种)，商品率平均为56.7%。商品收入达到7411.93万元。养殖业商品基地主要分布在城关、青城、来紫堡等北山、南山各乡(镇)。1993年规模养殖业达18村3204户。实现养殖业商品收入2325.4万元。形成了一批具有区域特色的规模经营村。1993年乡镇企业产值达到5.32亿元，发展速度达到56.2%，实现利税6571.5万元，实交财政税收1529万元，占全县财政总收入的46.64%，到1993年底，全县乡镇企业发展到3000多家，从业人员达38600人，占农村总劳力的21%。初步形成了以建材(主要产品为水泥、水泥制品和砖瓦)造纸、水烟、建筑、化工、畜牧六大支柱产业为龙头，工商运建服全方位发展的产业体系。全县各类新、扩、续建和技改项目162项，设计总投资1.16亿元。其中已竣工投产136项，总投资4563.8万元，年新增产值1.4亿元；在建26项，总投资7077.5万元。股份合作制企业达到120多户，股金达1.2亿元。

工商业，全县有国营工交企业5家，国合商业企业8家，17个基层供销社。全县坚持不懈地抓《条例》的贯彻落实，分类指导，因厂制宜，持续推进企业三项制度改革，实行优化组合；进一步简政放权，落实企业经营自主权。先后下放权力16项，为企业创造宽松自主的环境。并按照“双整整推”方针，发展横向联合，兼合并企业3户，拍卖1户。国合商业积极探索“国有民营”和“社有自营”的改革新路，扭转被动局面，初见成效。国营工业完成产值3796万元，比去年增长26.52%；实现销售收入4048.4万元，比去年增长31.9%。城镇集体企业完成产值1836.2万元，比去年增长71.1%；实现销售收入1449.3万元，比上年增长41.7%。完成社会商品零售总额1.51亿元，比去年增长25.6%。同时，加快市场体系建设，多渠道筹资10万元，新建、配套和完善了城关蔬菜肉类市场、城关粮油批发交易市场、和平商贸一条街道等10个专业市场。完成市场成交额1716万元，比去年增长39.1%。第三产业和个体私营经济得到迅速发展。全县第三产业产值占国民生产总值的30.5%，比去年提高4个百分点，新增个体工商户597户，达到2482户。

【基础设施建设】陇海铁路穿越榆中，境内有火车站9个，夏官营车站为中型车站，距县城15公里。两条国道公路(312、309)纵横穿过榆中，即将建成的夏方公路是沿苑川河谷伸向兰州的一条交通要道，为榆中经济的发展起到更大的作用。榆中县邮电局装有两台1000门自动电话交换机，全县11个乡镇4个村开通了自动电话，并与兰州并网，开设国内外直拨电话业务，还配置BP机通话设施，开办“寻呼台”，通讯联络十分方便。全县有高压输电线路1621.84公里，其中，110千伏线路220公里，35～66千伏150公里，3～10千伏1479公里，共有变电所11座，主变18台总容量为48万千伏安，现已投建的“八五”重点建设项目大峡水电站在榆中境内，设计装机容量为30万千瓦，1995年建成后榆中电力资源必具得天独厚的优势。

【资源状况】榆中矿产资源品种较多。储量较为丰富，已探明的矿产品有48种、如铁矿、锰矿、铅锌矿、磺铁矿、砂金矿、石灰岩、白云岩、石英岩、大理岩、白云母、高岭土等。全县有8个水泥厂，年产量达50万吨，轻质碳酸钙化工厂1个，年产轻质碳酸钙1万吨，活性钙2000吨，有规模较大的生产高强度墙地砖建材厂2个。有煤矿1个，年产煤3万吨，发热量3000大卡左右。白云石开采加工量逐年增大，大理岩开采加工已与外商签约，其他矿产有的已小规模开采出售。全县水资源比较丰富，既有大量河谷地表水，黄河提引水，又有较为充分的地下水，地表水主要分布在马衔山国家自然保护区的十条峡谷，常年流量为715万立方米/年，供县城2多人生活用水，并浇灌4万亩良田。黄河流经来紫堡、青城等4个乡镇，60年代起相继建成青电、三电、和电、七电四外提黄引水工程，受益地区有13个乡镇，受益面积22万亩，总设计流量为2亿立方米/年，实际提引为5千立方米/年，其中三电流量最大，为6立方米/秒。地下水资源在部分川塬地带储量充足，正常年景天然补给量为6800万立方米，净储量为19.4亿立方米。一般开挖井深30～80米见水，水量每小时80立方米，全县现有工业、农业用井500多眼。兴隆峡水质为兴隆山山泉重碳酸钙镁型矿泉水质，含有有益于人体健康的锶、锌、溴等矿物质，矿化度为399.6毫升，总硬度不超过12个德国度，是酿酒和生产矿泉饮料的优质水源，现已建成年产5000吨中外合资金立矿泉水公司。远销北京、广州、香港等国内外各大城市。榆中主要的土特产品有水烟、豆类作物、洋芋、中药材;野生植物有蕨菜、发菜、沙棘等。近几年出口产品主要有豆类作物、蕨菜、发菜和名贵中药材。

【社会事业与人民生活】科技工作坚持为经济建设服务的方针,突出中低产田改造,"一优双高"农业发展,新技术引进,新产品开发,企业技术改造,科技乡建设和全民科技素质提高,节温塑料大棚、集流窖、节水灌溉、暖棚养殖、防虫灭病、道路水泥等一批试验、示范推广项目和民办科研项目为经济发展注入新活力。教育工作围绕积极推进普及初等义务教育,改善办学条件,强化教学管理,重视师德教育,入学率、巩固率、毕业率、普及率稳步提高,多方筹资 107.1 万元,排除危房 5860 多平方米。全县普通中学高中在校生 3140 人,初中在校生 6503 人,小学在校生 47721 人,向大中专院校输送新生 691 名;有 2844 人参加自学考试。全县卫生医疗机构 50 所,其中,县级医院 5 所,乡级医院 27 所,医院病床达 435 张,专业卫生技术人员达 801 人,其中,医生 646 人,占 80%。医疗卫生工作重点放在农村,改善医疗条件,开展医德医风教育,提高医疗水平。加强预防保健工作,四苗覆盖率达 98.15%,地方病和传染病得到有效地控制和预防。计划生育工作继续坚持"不松口、不松手、不松劲"的方针,加强服务,依法管理,以"两女户"结扎为突破口,全面落实各项措施。全县完成四项手术 7378 例,计划生育率为 78.9%。人口自然增长率为 9.76‰。

城乡居民收入继续增加,生活水平进一步提高。农民人均占有粮食 619 斤;农民人均纯收入 587 元;职工人均工资收入 2794 元,比上年增加 299 元;城乡储蓄存款余额达 2.13 亿元,其中农村达到 0.89 亿元,比上年分别增长 26.9%和 26.5%;多渠道筹资新建城镇居民住宅 5.68 万平方米,农民建房 11.94 万平方米;山区新建集流窖 3000 眼,累计达到 7100 眼,城乡人民的生活水平有了新的提高。

现任主要领导:

中共榆中县委书记:王恩渭

榆中县人大常委会主任:李得元

榆中县人民政府县长:赵资英

政协榆中县委员会主席:王维烈

中共榆中县纪律检查委员会书记:孙殿福

(中共榆中县委调研室　段琼迪)

永登县经济和社会发展概述

【自然概况】地理位置:永登县位于甘肃省中部,东经 102°36′至 103°46′,北纬 36°12′至 37°07′,东卧秦王川盆地,与皋兰、景泰两县衔接;南临黄河,与西固、红古两区毗邻;西依祁连山,与青海省乐都县为界;北靠乌鞘岭,与天祝藏族自治县犬牙交错。居于古"丝绸之路"要道上,是河西走廊的东部门户。县城距省城兰州 110 多公里。地理位置优越,有利于商品生产的发展。

土地资源:全县总面积 913.55 万亩(6090 平方公里)。其中:耕地面积 138.58 万亩,占 15.17%;水域面积 3.66 万亩,占 0.40%;难利用土地面积 157.51 万亩,占 17.24%。人口密度 77.2 人/平方公里。由于山地、草场未能充分开发利用,人口倍增,耕地减少,人均耕地从 1949 年的 7.43 亩减少到 1993 年的 3.32 亩。计划生育工作虽然卓有成效地降低了了人口自然增长率,但增人减地的总趋势不会逆转,人地生态矛盾日趋尖锐。然而。随着"引大入秦"水利工程的全线贯通,境内将有 70 多万亩的低产田改造为高产田,农作物生产将会在量上有前所未有的巨增,质上有突破性的优化。

气候资源:总的气候特征是:年降水稀少,大部分地区年降水量在 300 毫米以下;热量不富,温差大,耕作区年平均气温在-0.5℃至 9℃之间;无霜期 127--162 天左右;年日照时数为 2659 小时左右;干旱、冰雹严重、霜冻、大风常发生,对农作物生长造成极大危害。

水资源:(1)客水丰富,但水土配合不协调,流经本县的庄浪河和大通河两河流域,年总水量分别为 1.96 亿立方和 28.2 亿立方。全县地表水径流总量为 30.26 亿立方。地下水资源贫缺,全县地下水天然补给总量 8314 万立方米,可开采利用量为 4815 万立方米。且地区分布悬殊,表层水主要集中在庄浪河川区。尤其是龙泉的泉水,量大味甘质优,最宜酿造各种饮料和酒类。(2)水能藏量比较丰富,全县两河流水的天然落差较大,有开发利用价值。经初步计算,水能的理论功率为 38.3 万千瓦,是永登发展工业的潜在优势和后劲。

生物资源丰富,名优特产较多。全县农、林、果、畜、禽、水产、药材等动植物种类多、品种杂。玫瑰、发菜赋有盛名,有广阔的开发利用前景,虹鳟鱼生产已形成西北最大的养殖基地。

矿产资源种类较多,非金属矿产丰富。全县金属矿藏有铜、铅、锌、铁、锰、金等。非金属矿藏有花岗石、大理石、石灰石、石英石、石膏、磷矿石等,其中石灰石、石英石和石膏贮量分别为 2.95 亿吨、3.1 亿吨和 1674 万吨,对发展建材、冶炼等工业具有得天独厚的优势。

【经济发展状况】综合经济指标:1993 年全县农村社会总产值 75838.8 万元,与 1986 年相比,年递增 22.91%。农村社会总产值中,第一、二、三产业所占份额为 28.5%、50.57%、20.93%。工农业总产值(工业只含乡镇办以上企业产值)43617.04 万元,比上年增长 31.36%。工业总产值占工农业总产值的比例为 56.2%。

工业:工业总产值(乡办以上)24510.83万元,比上年增长60.20%。乡办以上固定资产原值17721.9万元,比上年增长15.57%。全员劳动生产率(按增加值计算)6796元/人。

农业:农业总产值19106万元,比上年增长6.71%。按农业人口计算的人均农业总产值457元。农业劳动生产率883元。粮食亩产为108公斤,农业商品率30.99%,人均占有粮食293公斤。林业:全县宜林面积22.46万亩,森林面积37.2万亩,森林覆盖率为6%。天然林主要分布在金嘴、民乐、大有、连城等乡镇,共有31.35万亩;人工林主要分布在八宝川、永登川、秦王川,共有5.89万亩,木材积蓄量227万立方米,1993年,林业产值248.59万元,占农业总产值的1.30%。畜牧业:全县有草山面积565.25万亩。1993年末,大牲畜存栏5.85万头;生猪存栏12.16万头,出栏9.16万头,出栏率为75.3%;羊存栏23.76万只,出栏6.04万只,出栏率为25.4%。畜牧业产值6549.77万元,占农业总产值的34%。1993年猪、鸡、兔防疫密度达95%、85%、90%以上,羊只死亡率在3%以下,1993年底种草面积达7.02万亩,退耕种草达7万亩,草原围栏累计达3.48万亩。渔业:全县养鱼水面累计发展到4412亩,投放鱼苗77万尾、鱼种100万尾,产鲜鱼45万公斤,平均亩产51公斤,总产值185.48万元,占农业总产值的0.97%。

交通运输:县城内已形成四通八达的交通网,铁路、公路、航运齐全,公路里程310.66公里,其中四级以上公路83.96公里。农村运输业总产值9634.5万元,比上年增长41%。按农业人口计算,平均产值231元。农村拥有大中型拖拉机548台。小型拖拉机11551台,按农业人口平均,每万人依次分别拥有13台、276台。

邮电通信:全县市话交换机总容量2000门,市话用户1576户;农话交换点12处,交换机总容量784门,农村电话用户277户;开通了无线寻呼业务,农村投递线路总长度800公里,报刊期发数42786份,邮政储蓄余额950万元,邮电分支机构28处,(其中农村21处)。

商业:社会商品零售总额15330万元,比上年增长3.34%,人均社会商品零售总额326元。

财政金融:全县财政收入6290万元,比上年增长67.6%。全县人均储蓄存款603元。

乡镇企业:全县有乡镇企业724个,其中工业企业574个,从业人员48747人,乡镇企业总产值58646.5万元,比上年增长52%,占农村社会总产值的77%。按农业人口计算,人均占有固定资产原值424元,人均产值1404元。

【引大人秦工程】引大入秦工程是为解决我县秦王川地区干旱缺水问题而兴建的一项大型水利工程。这项跨流域调水的大型自流灌溉工程,将发源于青海的大通河水,从我省天祝县境内的天堂寺引水东调至兰州以北60公里的秦王川地区。总干渠从天祝县的天堂寺到永登县的香炉山,全长86.94公里,其中隧洞33座,总长75.14公里,渡槽9座,倒虹吸2座。盘道岭隧洞长达15.7公里,是目前亚洲第二、国内水工单洞最长的隧洞。总干渠的光明峡桥式倒虹吸工程,水头落差达107米。总干渠到香炉山后设总分水闸,将水分至东一干渠、东二干渠和45条支渠流入灌区。引大入秦工程总设计流量为32秒立方米,灌溉面积86万亩。工程总投资预计为15.7亿元,其中国家投资3600万元,世界银行贷款1.23亿美元(1987年折人民币4.56亿元)。其工程之艰巨,投资之大,堪称“华夏第一渠”。总干渠将于1994年10月建成通水,可灌地20万亩,全部工程于1997年完成。整个灌区按照较优的农、林、牧生产结构分析,农林牧总产值可达3.84亿元,年净增效益2.81亿元,是灌前的五倍多。

【人民生活与社会事业】全县农民人均纯收入551.33万元;全民所有制职工工资总额3354.8万元,人均2916元;集体所有制职工工资总额433.7万元,人均2271元。

科学技术:县上设有科学技术委员会和科学技术协会,22个乡镇都成立了科学技术协会,全县有各类科技人员3699人,平均每万人拥有科技人员78.7人。

教育:全县有师范学校1所,农职业中学5所,职业技术学校1所,幼儿园12所,中小学校548所,在校学生8万人,占全县总人口的17%。1993年小学毕业升学率87.6%、初中升学率26%、高中升学率16%。

卫生:全县有卫生单位30个。县城有县医院、中医院、卫生防疫站、妇幼保健站、卫生学校、药品监督检验所、有农村地区性中心医院3所,乡镇卫生院19所。全县有卫生队伍1197人,其中技术人员1038人,平均每万人有卫生技术人员22人,每万人拥有病床17张。

人口、劳动力及接受教育程度:全县总人口47万人,其中农业人口41.78万人,占总人口的88.89%。现有农村劳动力21.64万人,占农业人口的51.8%,农村劳动力资源丰富,目前农村剩余劳动力在50%,约10.69万人。在役劳动力总体上智能素质偏低,在农村劳动力中,接受过初中以上教育的占39.7%,小学以下的60.3%,劳动力水平接受教育程度5.7年,达不到小学毕业水平。

【城市建设】1993年底,城区总面积达5.2平方公里,已建成面积3.5平方公里,占城区总面积的67.3%,城市总人口3万人(不含五镇),约占全县总人口的0.065%;已建成办公、住宅楼190栋，其中住宅楼118栋，实有房屋建筑面积57万平方米，其中住宅面积35.4万平方米，人均居住面积8.5平方米；城市道路总长18.5公里，面积16.7万平方米，道路硬化面积14.8万平方米；已建青龙山公园，面积32公顷，亭台楼阁八处，建筑面积2050平方米，城市绿地面积98.9公顷，绿地率15%；有全民所有制房地产、公用事业单位8个，城建职工1200多人，集体所有制企业13个，职工2563人。

【永登经济发展战略目标及改革内容】根据党的十四届三中全会作出的《中共中央关于建立社会主义市场经济体制若干问题的决定》和永登实际，永登的总体发展目标是：第一步，已基本实现，即国民生产总值1990年达到（匡算数）44895万元，比1980年的（匡算数）10962万元翻了两番；第二步，从1990年开始到2000年，整个国民经济生产总值再翻一番，达到89790万元，人均实现1800元。全县绝大部分人民生活水平达到小康，农民人均纯收入超过1000元；第三步，从2000年到下世纪中叶，达到中等发达国家水平。要达到上述目标，须从农业、企业、市场、政府、社会保障这五个主要环节和重点领域构建永登社会主义市场经济体系，其目标框架为：构建以"两高一优"为目标的商品农业体系；构建以股份制为主要组织形式的现代企业体系；构建以大县城和小集镇为载体的开放型市场体系；构建以转变政府职能为重点的县级宏观调控体系；构建以社会、单位、个人结合、城乡有别的多层次社会保障体系。

现任主要领导：

中共永登县委书记：郭德清

永登县人大常委会主任：赖全章

永登县人民政府县长：梁增琇

政协永登县委员会主席：蒋灵秀

中共永登县纪律检查委员会书记：索文辉

（中共永登县委研究室：杨兴普　郝德有）

皋兰县经济和社会发展概述

【政区沿革】皋兰县历史悠久，文化灿烂，自然资源丰富，是古丝绸之路上的重镇。早在四、五千年以前就有先民在这里狩猪、放牧和制陶。春秋战国时为羌戎之地，秦统一中国后，归秦。西汉时属金城郡，首置金城县。西、北魏与北周时属子城县，子城县为金城郡治所在。隋初属兰州总管府，废府管郡后，仍属金城郡金城县。唐属五泉县，即现兰州市区所在，亦为金城郡治。唐之后期与五代时为吐蕃辖地。宋、金、元、明具属兰州。几经沿革，开创发展，至清代乾隆六年，因境内有皋兰山而更名皋兰县，此后，一直沿用至今。清代至民国，作为甘肃首县、省会重镇的皋兰，幅员辽阔，广袤数百里，辖今兰州市、白银市的大部分地区。解放初，皋兰县隶属兰州市。1951年8月由省直辖。1956年1月划归定西专区。1958年12月国务院决定撤销皋兰县，行政区域划归白银市。1961年2月恢复皋兰县，归白银市管辖。1963年10月白银市撤销，皋兰县仍隶属定西专区。1970年4月重新划归兰州市管辖至今。县政府驻地几经变迁，解放前原驻兰州市永昌路。1945年迁往盐场堡，翌年迁入市内曹家厅。1955年省人民委员会决定：皋兰县址由兰州市区曹家厅迁往石洞寺。1957年8月迁驻现址。

【自然概况】皋兰县位于甘肃省中部干旱地区，地理坐标是东经103°32′至104°14′，北纬36°05′至36°50′。总面积2556平方公里。全县辖7乡1镇，71个行政村，4个居委会。人口15.7万人，其中农业人口14.81万人。总人口中汉族占99%以上，少数民族有回、土、壮、藏、苗、满等6个民族85人。皋兰县地处陇西黄土高原，黄土丘陵连绵起伏，梁、峁、沟、谷纵横交错。地势呈西北高、东南低，最高海拔2400米，最低为1400米，平均海拔1600米。黄河流经南部什川乡。西南起自桑园峡，东北至于大峡，全长约35公里。境内还有蔡家河、水阜河，河源为地下水，流量很小，含碱较大，两河汇合流入黄河。皋兰县属中温带大陆性季风气候，冬无严寒，夏无酷暑，气候干燥，雨量稀少，日照充足。年平均降水量260毫米，多集中在夏秋两季，年平均蒸发量高达1800多毫米。年平均气温7.2℃，年平均日照2768小时，无霜期144天。全年多北风。

资源，皋兰县水资源贫乏，地下水储量约1830万立方米，过境黄河年平均流量331亿立方米，可供电力提灌；峡谷地带蕴藏比较可观的水能有待开发。全县有耕地面积44万亩，人均2.9亩，其中水浇地20.5万亩，人均1.39亩。草地面积253万亩，林地12.17万亩，村镇、工矿用地面积4.7万亩。全县金属矿点较多，储量可观，金、银、铜、铁、铅、锌等矿均有。非金属矿也较丰富，石英砂储量9600万吨，石灰石1.35亿吨，石英石147万吨，大理石1亿吨，花岗岩数亿吨。皋兰的动植物资源比较贫乏。共有野生动物105种，野生鸟类22种，爬行动物7种，哺乳动物15种，两栖动物21种。共有植物资源98种，其中有各种乔灌木88种。用材林主要有杨、柳、榆、槐等树种，经济林主要有苹果、梨、桃、杏、枣、葡萄等。旅游资源主要有两大景区：一是在被誉为"兰州小江南"的什川乡，有以梨园景色，黄河羊皮筏子，接官厅、骆驼石等古遗迹为中心的自然人文景观。随着什川地区大、小峡电站的建设和各种旅游景点的建成，届时，一年一度的什川"梨花会"将使广大旅游观光者和国内外客商饱览"梨乡"美景，不久的将来，这里将成为兰州地区避暑度假、赏花钓鱼、经贸洽谈的旅游胜地。二是以新建石洞寺为中心的寺庙群体人文景观。石洞寺原名石空寺，始建于清代康熙年间，寺内建筑雕梁画柱，精巧奇妙，别具特色。几经修缮至民国初期，僧众数百，香火缭绕，上香敬佛者络绎不绝，达到鼎盛时期。七十年代，寺庙被毁。近年来，在各级地方政府的帮助下，石洞寺正在恢复新建，目前已具雏形。最近，由省佛教协会组织兴建的兰州市佛学院在石洞寺附近开始动工建设，石洞寺将会重放异彩。

【经济发展现状】皋兰县历为农业之县，原是甘肃省最贫困的地区之一。建国以来，特别是党的十一届三中全会以后，随着改革开放政策的不断落实，极大的解放了农村生产力，农村经济迅速发展，人民生活水平显著提高，社会各项事业长足发展。1989年经国务院"三西办"审定，1990年经兰州市委、市政府验收，皋兰县达到了稳定脱贫标准，提前实现了省委确定的目标，目前，正在向致富奔小康迈进。

农业生产持续增长。1993年粮食总产量达5967万公斤，其中小麦2972.2万公斤；豆类1747万公斤，经济作物面积逐年扩大，油料总产311.4万公斤，瓜类总产2400.8万公斤；黑瓜籽总产量18万公斤；蔬菜总产2000万公斤；种植业总产值为9536万元。全县林地面积12.17万亩，其中经济林7.4万亩，防护林4.77万亩，森林覆盖率3.2%；果品产量达2000万公斤，林果业总产值为2196.53万元。肉类产量343.5万公斤，禽蛋产量104.5万公斤，鲜奶产量2.68万公斤，畜牧业总产值为2272万元。池塘养渔350亩，鲜鱼产量达3万公斤，产值达12万元。

工业生产从无到有，已初具规模。全县现有乡以上工业企业74家，其中县属企业18家，乡办工业56家，从业人员5895人。已初步形成了以化工、建材、冶炼、制造、轻纺、食品为主体，拥有10个行业200多个品种的工业体系。拥有固定资产7490万元，其中县属工业固定资产达2615万元，乡办工业固定资产达4875万元。1993年全县工业总产值达2.89亿元，比上年增长64.2%，其中乡办以上工业产值达1.53亿元，比上年增长65.4%。主要工业产品碳化硅、工业硅、75＃硅铁、针绣产品、脱水菜等已远销美国、日本、韩国及东南亚许多国家和地区，成为皋兰县出口创汇的拳头产品。

乡镇企业蓬勃发展。去年以来，皋兰县正视现实，充分认识到振兴皋兰经济的潜力在乡镇企业，把发展乡镇企业做为振兴皋兰经济的突破口来抓，相继出台了《关于加强横向联合、促进经济发展的规定》、《关于加快乡镇企业发展的若干规定》，使乡镇企业呈现出了超常规、高速度、高效益的发展态势，成为全县经济的"半壁河山"。全县现有乡镇企业420家，从业人员2.32万人，拥有固定资产1.22亿元。1993年完成产值4.28亿元，上交税金554.5万元，占全县工商税收的54%，职工工资总额3380.9万元，农民人均从乡镇企业中所得的劳务收入达223元，占皋兰农民人均纯收入675元的33%。乡镇企业中现有工业企业253家，年产值24276万元；有各类建筑企业37个，完成产值6180万元；有运输业20个，完成产值9740万元；有商饮业110个，完成产值2650万元。全县现有股份制企业63家，拥有股金2826万元，占乡镇企业固定资产总额的20%，完成产值4300万元，占乡镇企业总产值的10%，股份合作制企业作为实现两权分离、改革产权制度的重要举措，将成为皋兰乡镇企业发展的生长点。

近年来，皋兰县商贸流通业不断适应新形势，加大改革力度，调整经营结构，突出网点建设，努力开拓市场，注重发展第三产业，制定了《关于加快发展第三产业的实施意见》，全面加快了第三产业的发展步伐。特别是去年以来，流通领域积极开展了"国有民营"、"社有自营"和发展股份制等改革措施，启动了商贸企业的内部活力，促进了商贸流通业的进一步繁荣。1993年全县商业人员3246人，其中个体1600人，有各类商业网点1024个，完成社会商品零售额5445万元，有城乡集贸市场4处，交易点4处，年成交额达250万元。1993年财政收入1141万元，比上年增长41.2%；财政支出1745万元，比上年增长28.7%。全年出口创汇额515.6万美元，在"三资"企业上实现了零的突破，现有三资企业4家，年产值7348.6万元。

【城乡建设，扶贫工作】县城现有建筑面积30.1万平方米；全县现有水泥沥青路面271.04公里，地设下水道2.15公里，自来水管道32.4公里。县城现有日供水能力7500立方米的输送管道一条和容量分别为8万立方米、10万立方米的水库2座。有11万伏变电所1座。皋兰县具有便利的交通条件，县内有5条县乡骨干公路已经建成开通，县乡村交通四通八达，通车总里程达210公里，包兰铁路，国道109线、省道皋营公路横贯县城。有营运汽车813辆，每170人拥有1辆，年产值近1000万元。全年货运量98.7万吨，客运量82.5万人次。

皋兰县有邮政局(所)7个，邮政网点35个，安装磁石式电话交换机595部，每260拥有1部。为了改善皋兰的邮电通讯条件，目前，设计能力为5000门装机容量的程控电话邮电大楼正在建设中，1994年可建成开通。

扶贫工作，1993年全县参与扶贫的单位78个，扶持贫困户9326户，扶持项目18项，全年投放扶贫资金100多万元，现有2019户已脱贫。今年县上又制定了《皋兰县扶贫攻坚计划》,加紧未脱贫户的脱贫工作,计划在2000年实现无贫困户。

【社会事业】皋兰县现有普通中小学155所,在校学生27770人,教职工1885人。幼儿园18所,儿童入学率为99.7%。有教师进修学校、职业技术学校和农业技术学校10所。已建成标准化学校22所。科技,全县有各种学会、协会、研究会20个,有会员976人,各类获得在职资格的专业技术人员528人。1993年末有49项科研成果获省、市科技成果奖。文化,有各类文化事业机构85个,专业队伍112人,民间成立各种文化社团9个。太平鼓、兰州鼓子、铁芯子是三大独具特色的民间艺术。太平鼓已打遍半个中国,1990年由80名农民组成的《中国·兰州太平鼓》队在十一届亚运会上因精湛表演而享誉国内外,素有"天下第一鼓"之美称。

卫生和计划生育,全县现有医疗机构104个,病床177张,医务人员470人,有高级技术职称的4名,中级职称的45名。现有计生专业队伍60人,县有计生委,乡有计生工作站,村有计生工作室,基层网络健全,计生队伍进一步充实。1993年,全县认真贯彻"三为主"的方针,全面完成了人口控制计划,共完成四项手术3236例,计划生育率为83.9%,人口自然增长率为11.81‰。

体育,有体育设施、场地136个,全年举办群众体育活动600多场,有14000多人参加体育活动。1993年皋兰动员在全国自行车比赛中获金牌1枚,曾为省、市培养出了杨柳霞、魏宏英、李文凯等一批体育优秀人才,被称为兰州市的"体育之乡"。

【名特土产】皋兰县盛产各类瓜果,为兰州瓜果主要产地之一。尤其是白兰瓜、黑瓜籽、冬果梨为本县有名的土特产。黑瓜籽已有数百年的产销历史,遍及全省,其板大肉厚,皮薄口松,形如牛眼,味道醇香,远销东南亚一带,以"兰州大板"蜚声海外。白兰瓜自1944年美国副总统华莱士访问甘肃时带来"蜜露"(白兰瓜)良种在兰州、皋兰试种推广以来,经四十多年栽培,品种不断改良,已成为皋兰传统特产,素有瓜王之称,其色味俱佳,香气四溢,畅销国内市场,近年已打入香港等地,颇负盛名。距县城20公里有远近闻名的万亩果园乡——什川乡,座落在黄河之滨,是皋兰特产香水梨、冬果梨、苹果的集中产地,素有"瓜果之乡"之称。香水梨已有数百年栽培历史,年产200多万公斤,酸甜适口,冬储后又名软儿梨,皮色紫黑,果浆化作一包香水,止咳润肺,老少喜食,独得"瓜果城中第一奇"美誉。冬果梨亦有数百年栽培历史,年产300万公斤,色黄皮薄,汁多味甘。梨腹取核后,装入冰糖封闭煮食,即为香甜可口,兼治咳嗽的名产"热冬果"。苹果则是栽培数十年的后起之秀,良种繁多,色艳味甜,"红元帅"、"红富士"、"新红星"等名优品种相继上市,走俏沿海省市。

现任主要领导:

中共皋兰县委书记:张宗奎

皋兰县人大常委会主任:陈俊卿

皋兰县人民政府县长:张立荣

政协皋兰县委员会主席:杨汉林

中共皋兰县纪律检查委员会书记:高志武

(皋兰县人民政府办公室:王立吉　魏晋文　王道元)

天水市

中共天水市委书记:牟本理

天水市人大常委会主任:牟本理(兼)

天水市人民政府市长:王文华

政协天水市委员会主席:陈　华

中共天水市纪律检察委员会书记:王润康

天水市经济和社会发展概述

【自然概况】天水市位于甘肃省东南部,东临陕西省宝鸡市,南连陇南地区,西与定西地区毗邻,北与平凉地区接壤。陇海铁路从境内通过,是第二条欧亚大陆桥的咽喉,是镶嵌在古"丝绸之路"上的一颗明珠,素有"甘肃小江南"之称。地理座标在东经104°34′——106°43′,北纬34°05′——35°10′之间。东西长195公里,南北宽121公里,总面积14325平方公里。

天水市现辖2区(秦城区、北道区)5县(甘谷、武山、秦安、清水、张家川回族自治县)。共有11个街道办事处、150个乡镇、2964个村委会。

天水市地处六盘山地,陇中黄土高原和秦岭山地之间,跨越渭河(黄河水系)和嘉陵江(长江水系)两大水系,处于暖温带半湿润、半干旱气候的过渡地带。地势西高东低,海拔一般在1000——2100米之间。耕地以山地为主,在全市593.3万亩耕地中,山地549.11万亩,占92.55%,川地只有42.49万亩,塬地仅1.7万亩。渭河横贯中部、渭河及其支流的河谷地带地势平坦、土地肥沃、灌溉方便、农业发达、人口稠密,是全市经济发展水平较高的地区。

环境资源:气候宜人,夏无酷暑,冬无严寒,四季分明,年平均气温10℃左右、平均无霜期185天左右,年降雨量在600毫米左右,森林覆盖率达到总面积的四分之一以上。小陇山、关山、西秦岭三个林区林地总面积达1026.66万亩(包括小陇山林业实验局在外地区的林地)为甘肃省第二大林区。林区树木种类繁多,常见的有235种乔木、337种灌木。林木资源丰富,林区盛产生漆、箭竹、药材、木耳、栓皮栎等多种林副产品。野生动物资源有熊、狼、狐狸、兔、獾等。比较珍贵的野生动物有林麝、毛冠鹿、石貂、水獭、大鲵、兰马鸡等。

自然资源：盛产粮油果菜和其它经济作物。粮食以小麦、玉米为主。其它产量较大的农作物有土豆、蚕豆、大豆、荞、高粱、谷子等。经济作物有油菜、胡麻、甜菜、向日葵等。

矿产资源：已探明的矿产资源有铁、铜、铅、锡、钼、金、银等35种，非金属矿有大理石、白云岩、蛇纹岩等20多种，并得到了有效的开采和利用，地下水资源丰富，水质优良。

【名特产品】以苹果、柿子、梨、桃为主的果类品质优良，其中天水的"花牛"苹果，果形硕大，端正高庄，五角突出，果面洁净，鲜红，皮薄肉脆，含糖份高，香甜可口，享誉国内外市场。仅苹果一项，全市种植面积就达近50万亩，年产苹果8000万公斤以上。为全国十大苹果基地之一；甘谷县的辣椒，以色红肉厚，品质优良在沿海地区及东南亚市场上颇受欢迎；天水出产的猪鬃在国际市场上享有较高知名度；用天水生漆生产的"雕漆产品"一直享受外贸出口免检的特殊对待；秦安县及清水县利用当地野生沙棘资源生产的系列饮品在省内、国内评比中多次获奖；张家川回族自治县是闻名全国的大型皮毛集散地，每年上市皮张约560万张左右，成交金额达亿元以上。

【城市建设】年末市区非农业人口达25.6万人，增长0.4%，建成区面积达25.5平方公里，自来水日产能力16.8万吨，公共交通营运车辆77辆，客运总量1048万人次，集中供热总面积达28万平方米。全年城市综合开发和旧城改造投入资金1.32亿元，开发改造面积38.22万平方米，新开了天水展贸中心、工农路综合展贸商场等一批重点工程建设。年末城市道路总长度达94.5公里，排水管道80.6公里。

【国民经济】1993年全市工业总产值达到34.69亿元，基本形成了以轻纺、电子、电器、机械制造、食品、建材和工艺美术为主的门类比较齐全，多层次、多种类的工业生产体系。有50多种产品出口到欧美、日本、东南亚、独联体等30多个国家和地区。

全市农业经济得到全面发展，初步形成了以农、林、牧、副、渔并举，工、商、贸综合发展的新格局。1993年，全市农业总产值完成12.51亿元，粮食获得全面丰收，全年粮食作物播种面积524.49万亩，总产78.98万吨，再创历史最高水平。农民人均产粮达到592公斤，人均纯收入达到520元。乡镇企业发展迅速，股份合作制企业有突破性进展。全市乡镇企业总数达39070个，实现总产值22.01亿元，增长68.66%，总收入和利税总额分别增长68.63%和54.09%。全市股份合作制乡镇企业达334个，入股资金达1.06亿元。农村扶贫取得新进展，农村贫困面由上年的6%下降到5%。

1993年，全市交通运输条件有了进一步改善，省内第一条高速公路——天北公路已基本建成，定于7月1日正式通车。全市公路总里程达到2811公里，交通部门客运量560万人次，周转量为1946.1万人公里，货运量为32.3万吨，周转量3676.4万吨公里。

邮电通讯业发展迅猛。全年邮电业务总量达3406.7万元，增长29.1%，市内电话机拥有量23746部，增长25.67%；全市五县两区全部进入全国长途自动电话交换网，无线寻呼、移动电话等新业务快速增长，居民安装电话成为新时尚。

全市消费品市场繁荣。全年全社会消费品零售额达14.22亿元，增长16.59%(扣除物价上涨因素后，实际增长5.04%)，其中城市10.59亿元，增长18.2%，农村3.63亿元，增长12.0%。

全市财政收入3.46亿元，增长23.13%；财政支出4.26亿元，增长16.4%。

驻市国家银行各项存款余额21.32亿元，增长16.6%，其中企业存款4.34亿元，下降15.4%；各项贷款余额25.88亿元，增长14.77%，国家银行累计现金收入42.96亿元，增长38.76%，现金支出42.75亿元，增长35.86%，累计回笼2049万元，与上年比多回笼7143万元。

保险事业进一步发展。全市保险系统承保额达47亿元，保费收入5202万元，增长27.75%，赔款支出2389万元，增长46.74%。

【社会事业】1993年，在科教兴市战略实施中，全市共推广科技项目149个，取得科技成果30项，组织开展了科技先导企业的试点、推广成果47项，成功地举办了首届"新技术、新产品、新成果"展示展销会，参展项目2472个，成交额4605万元。全市民办科技机构已达60户，实现产值1826万元。

教育事业全面发展。有高等学校1所，在校学生1850人，中等专业学校12所，在校学生5400人，各类职业中学26所，在校学生6277人，中小学校3607所，在校学生48.77万人，全市学龄儿童入学率、巩固率、普及率分别达到97.75%、97.8%和94.9%，普通高中为高等院校输送新生2474人。

全市共有电影放映单位358个，艺术表演团体8个，文化馆7个，图书馆7所，各类藏书46.9万册。广播电视事业有新的发展，全市共举办、自办电视节目2套，广播节目2套，广播人口覆盖率达80.16%，电视人口覆盖率63.57%，全市有三条广播电视节目获部以上二、三等奖。

卫生事业持续发展。全市共有医疗卫生机构399个，床位数5920张，各类卫生技术人员数8108人，增长2.72%。

体育竞技水平提高。群众性体育运动广泛开展。全市体育健儿在省以上各类竞赛中荣获金牌36枚、银牌41枚、铜牌33枚，三次荣获团体总分第一；有12人达到国家二级运动员标准。全市共有3166所中小学的29.54万名学生达到《国家体育锻炼标准》，体育系统共举办各类运动会65次，参赛人数1.5万人次。群众性体育运动广泛开展。

1993年，全市人口增长得到控制。据公安部门统计，年末全市总人口达304.09万人，比上年末增加3.68万人，非农业人口36.84万人，农业人口267.25万人。据计生部门调查，全市人口出生率19.12‰，人口死亡率5.61‰，人口自然增长率为13.51‰。

1993年末，城镇新增就业11147人，年末城镇待业率为3.0%。

城乡居民储蓄继续增加。年末城乡居民储蓄存款余额达17.08亿元，增长28.81%。

环境保护事业进一步加快发展。全市年环保总投资851万元，增长2.1倍，办成环保实事5件，完成限期治理项目24个，全市废水处理量1839万吨，废气处理量68.63亿标立方米。

（天水市委研究室：刘　勇）

秦城区经济和社会发展概述

【概貌】天水市秦城区位于渭河支流，耤河流域和西汉水上游，在甘肃东南部，居全国腹心。境内西高东低，山峦错综，名胜古迹众多，风光迷人，“莽莽万重山，孤城山谷间”便是对秦城山脉地形的写照。秦城是一座历史悠久的文化古城，是陇上商业贸易重地，故有“拉不完的秦州”之传。从春秋设邽县始至后来各个时期的州、郡、亭、府、县、市等行政区首府均设在这里，是天水市政治、经济、文化中心。

天水市秦城区于1985年7月设立，下辖7个街道办事处，22个乡政府。截止1993年底，全区总面积2442平方公里，城区面积18平方公里，总人口56.2万人，有汉、回、满、蒙、藏、壮、苗、侗、维吾尔、朝鲜等12个民族。全区有耕地面积96.58万亩，其中：山地90.2万亩，川地6.38万亩。农作物主要有小麦、玉米、洋芋、豆类等，核桃、苹果为本区特产，森林覆盖率达到28.5%。水利资源比较丰富，有效灌溉面积可达4.01万亩，有着发展农业生产较好的自然条件，光照充足，气候湿润。辖区内有大小工业企业228个，其中：中央省属17个，区属145个。工业产品风格独特，雕漆制品历史悠久，造型美观，享有外贸出口免验之荣，毛纺织品品种繁多，款式新颖，深受人们的喜爱，地毯是甘肃省重点生产厂家之一，丝毯为西北地区的独家产品，食品、白酒，质美味醇，历来享有盛誉。

【经济建设】1993年全区工农业总产值达到5.6亿元，比上年增长16.5%。农村经济以发展粮食生产、“两高一优”农业和乡镇企业为重点，狠抓各项措施落实，实现了全面丰产丰收和快速增长。农业总产值完成1.97亿元，比上年增长4.7%。粮食生产再创历史最高水平，总产达到2.85亿斤，人均产粮730斤。乡镇企业快速发展，总产值达5.04亿元，比上年增长67.6%，实现利润3820万元，比上年净增1077万元，增长39%。农民人均纯收入达到610元，比上年净增86元。工业生产在资金紧张、原材料价格上涨等困难形势下，基本上实现了产值、销售、利润同步增长，完成产值3.45亿元，比上年增长23.3%，实现销售收入2.1亿元，比上年增长23%，实现利润957.4万元，比上年增长39.4%。商贸流通顺应改革竞争形势，保持了稳定持续发展，全区社会商品零售总额达到3.15亿元，比上年增长5.4%。非公有制经济有了新的发展，城乡个体户和私营企业达到6921户，从业人员16385人，实现产值和营业额分别为1697万元和7170万元。

农村基础设施建设，全区1993年兴修梯田3.23万亩，造林10万亩，并千方百计争取省、市以工代赈投资264.8万元，完成6条区乡公路改造，改线工程64.2公里，乡村公路33条，247公里；完成农田线路13条、30.1公里，修建河堤1500多米，新增保灌面积1000亩。同时，还筹集资金开通了皂郊等5乡自动电话联网。

经济技术开发和城市建设，1993年全区共批准开发项目22项，总投资4.06亿元。其中中外合资项目3项，投资1200万元人民币，已动工建设的有17项，投资3.59亿元，这些项目的建成使用，将进一步改善投资环境，增强城市综合服务能力。

【社会事业】科技工作坚持“面向社会、面向基层、面向经济建设”的方向，强化综合管理，加速科技成果转化，以科技兴农、以科技促工收到了实效。1993年完成各类课题20项，其中省级2项，市列10项，区列8项；科技成果推广应用15项，新增效益1123.52万元，创汇28.72万美元。教育工作贯彻《中国教育改革和发展纲要》精神，深化教育改革，全面实施“2225”教育规划，狠抓基础教育，职业技术教育和高标准脱盲，在农科教结合上做出了新成绩。卫生工作认真落实“预防为主，治防结合”的方针，高标准、高质量地完成了计划免疫任务，多方集资103.5万元，投资24万元，用以改善基层和基础医疗卫生条件。计划生育工作以人口计划为目标，努力加强基础网络建设，开展科学化管理，把经常性工作和突击性活动相结合，抓重抓难，共完成四术任务 11914 例，结扎 3636 例，放环 5774 例，补救 2508 例，人口出生率和自然增长率分别为 18.49‰和 12.86‰，全区年末人口为 56.2 万人。均在市上控制指标之内。

【深化改革，抓主抓重】适应建立社会主义市场经济体制需要，转变农村经济管理办法，加快农村市场经济形成的步伐。按照中央对农业实行“引导、支持、保护、调节”和强化农业基础地位的要求，结合我区实际，在转变政府职能、加强服务的前提下，努力实现三个转变，着重抓了三方面的工作。一是由过去层层下达指令性计划转向宏观指导和项目管理。我们把对全区农村经济有重大影响的四个大类 18 个项目与 22 乡及农口各部门实行项目承包，实施单位又将 18 个项目划分成若干子项目与 215 名行政干部、310 名科技人员及下属单位实行承包，政府负责项目实施中物资供应，资金协调、考核项目进度和质量标准，减少行政干预，强化规划、投资引导的服务职能；二是把直接指挥具体生产活动转向积极引导，提供信息服务；三是由直接行政干预转向典型示范、分类指导。三方面的工作，一是大力发展“两高一优”农业。科技是第一生产力，大力推广实用科学技术是发展农业的动力。去年，我们在稳定 10 万亩地膜玉米、10 万亩洋芋双籽双行垄作、10 万亩小麦丰产小区、10 万亩果园建设的基础上，调整产业结构，优化资源配置，建立支柱产业，发展“两高一优”农业，彻底改变传统农业的耕做方式，加大力度，试验、示范、推广“两高一优”农业的一系列实用科学技术。全区建成“吨粮田”5568 亩，“双千田”6224 亩，“双五百田”7146 亩，高产优质果园 2.5 万亩，为今后我区农业生产向广度、深度和高度发展起到了推动作用。二是认真实施“93366”工程，促进乡镇企业快速发展。我们把加快发展乡镇企业作为振兴全区经济的突破口，作为带动农民致富奔小康的重要途径，经过反复论证，提出实施“93366”工程的战略决策。一年后，9 个重点乡完成产值 3.55 亿元，占全区乡镇企业总产值的 69%，其中 50 万元以上企业新增 11 个，投资达 1000 万元。以地毯加工和电器加工为主的太京和以商贸工为主的七里墩两个开发小区已初见成效。全区 22 乡的企业各有侧重地沿着产品加工、规模养殖、劳务输出、资源开发、建筑建材和第三产业 6 条路子健康发展。发展股份合作制企业 145 个，入股资金 2004.5 万元，45 个企业已投产，完成产值 1589 万元，实现利税 310 万元。同时，我们充分利用近郊和集镇优势，把发展第三产业放在重要位置，去年共发展集体、个体第三产业 1298 个，从业人员 3973 人，在城乡经济流通中发挥了积极作用，已成为全区经济的重要组成部分。三是认真实施温饱工程，巩固温饱成果。我区虽然在面上已越过了温饱线，但还有 6%的 4582 户、23139 人的温饱尚未得到解决，针对这一现状，政府对他们实行了技、财、物的倾斜，为全区贫困户发放贷款 20 万元，以粮食生产为重点，增加收入为目标，制定了一系列措施，狠抓落实，使贫困面下降到 5%。

以市场为导向，从“引、转、让、破”入手，深化企业改革，转换经营机制。“引”，就是积极引进资金、技术和人才，努力开发各类建设项目。一年来，全区工业企业通过各种渠道引进资金 2830 万元，其中中外合资意向性项目 8 个，协议合作资金 1370 万元。同时，积极引进先进适用技术和各类人才，为企业发展注入了活力。“转”，就是按市场经济的要求，转换企业经营机制。一年来，全区企业以贯彻《全民所有制企业转换经营机制条例》和《城镇集体企业条例》为重点，促进企业转轨建制，走向市场。商委、粮食局、供销社对一些小型门店进行“国有民营”、“国有自营”、“社有自营”试点；陇原冷厂与奶牛繁殖场，百纺公司与商业大厦、蔬菜公司先后合并；木器厂与市技术监督局联合创办食品包装材料有限公司、电焊机厂与长城工业公司联合开发节能变压器等产品；刃具厂对轴承分厂的股份合作制改造以及其它企业出租、合资和多种经营等办法的运用，为优势企业的自我发展和困难企业的自我调整，提供了有利条件，收到了初步成效。“让”，就是转变政府职能，还给企业自主权。为了使企业尽快成为独立的经济组织，增强企业活力，区政府在企业干部管理、劳动用工和分配制度上大胆让权，逐步实现所有权管理与行政管理的分离。同时，注意建立健全企业的民主管理制度，使企业的生产积极性空前高涨。“破”，就是对严重资不抵债，扭亏无望的特困企业果断实行破产。针织一厂严重资不抵债，多年来，生产被动局面一直不能改变。经过上下多次讨论，统一认识，按《企业法》和《企业破产法》在全市率先实施破产处理，在改革方面进行了有益尝试。

培育发展市场体系。我们利用现有设施和科技人员，发挥优势，主要抓了四件事：一是巩固提高现有市场的管理水平，完善基础设施，整顿管理秩序，使城乡市场上了一个新层次；二是上下配合，依靠自身力量，狠抓了小百货批发市场、粮油贸易商场的建设；三是完善了劳务市场、科技信息市场，促进了人才交流和劳动力的合理转移，加快了科技成果转化。1993 年全区共输出劳动力 65000 多人，科技信息市场与省内外多家单位建立了信息网，为工业、农业提供了一批新项目，并向各方面提供商情信息 500 多条；四是工农科教结合，完善状大科技服务培训体系。全区共举办各种类型的科技培训班294期，56566人(次)，为建立市场经济体制培养了一大批信息员、推销员和经纪人，在经济建设中起到重大作用。

现任主要领导：

中共秦城区委书记：谢寿璜

秦城区人大常委会主任：魏致中

秦城区人民政府区长：张建祖

政协秦城区委员会主席：贾致谊

中共秦城区纪律检查委员会书记：廖文恺

(秦城区委研究室：杨玉庆　左鸿义　刘祥云)

清水县经济和社会发展概述

【自然概况】清水县位于天水市东北部，东接陕西省陇县、宝鸡市，南连天水市北道区、秦城区，西与秦安县接壤，北同张家川回族自治县毗邻。地处北纬34°32′至34°56′，东经105°45′至106°30′之间，东西长66公里，南北宽47公里，总面积2003平方公里。地势东北高，西南低。最高点海拔2201米，最低海拔1112米，境内平均海拔1500米。河流有大小河流28条。牛头河是全县最大河流，流经8个乡，至北道区注入渭河，全长84.6公里，流域面积达1836平方公里，年最大径流量3.67万立方米。气候属大陆季风性气候，系陇中南中温带半湿润区。雨量适中，夏无酷暑，冬无严寒，气候温凉。年平均气温8.8℃，无霜期为168天左右。年日照时数为2022.7小时，全年降水量约在517～662毫米之间。自然灾害主要有旱灾、冰雹、低温、冻害等。

土地资源较为丰富，全县土地总面积300.49万亩，其中耕地96.71万亩，占土地总面积的32.18%，人均3.6亩；天然草坡地46.81万亩。水资源总量约3.3亿立方米，其中地表水2.3亿立方米，地下水1亿立方米。水能总蕴藏量2.07万千瓦，可采量0.33万千瓦，占总蕴藏量的16%。植物资源种类较多，主要有小麦、玉米、蚕豆、洋芋、高粱、大麻、油料、蔬菜等；林木以恢复的天然次生林为主，树种主要有杨、柳、椿、榆、华山松、白桦、糠椴、漆树、山核桃和灌丛沙棘等；果木有15种，以苹果为主；药材有262种，多为野生。动物有家禽家畜13种，52个品种，；野生动物100多种，其中毛冠鹿、林麝、红腹锦鸡等珍贵动物8种。矿产资源有铁、锰、铜、铅、白云石、大理石、钾长石、辉绿岩等14种。

全县辖1个镇，23个乡，337个村委会，1525个村民小组。全县人口共有55524户，总人口27.52万人，其中男性14.24万人，女性13.28万人；农业人口26.16万人，占总人口的95%。人口密度137人/平方公里。1993年人口自然增长率11.98‰，计划生育率为75.06%，节育总人口达到45782人，节育率为83.27%。全县有汉、回、朝鲜、满、白、藏6个民族成份，少数民族人口为4924人，占全县总人口的1.79%，其中回族有4915人。

【历史沿革】远在新石器时代，就有古人群在清水这块土地上定居。最早为邽戎部族居住。秦武公十年(公元前688年)，置上邽县。秦至汉初，上邽县属陇西郡。汉武帝元鼎二年(公元前115年)，析上邽县至清水县，属天水郡。东汉时清水县并入陇，属汉阳郡。三国初，魏复置清水县，废陇入清水，属广魏郡。晋属略阳郡。北魏置清水郡。隋初废郡，改属天水郡。唐初属邽州，后邽州并于秦州。五代时期为秦州所辖，后为土蕃占据。北宋属秦州府。南宋时为金所据，建炎年间，在今县城北黄门乡王店村卧牛山下另置冶坊县。元朝至元七年(公元1270年)，并冶坊县于清水县，隶秦州。明代因之。清时清水县属秦州直隶州。民国初属渭川道，1936年属甘肃省第四行政督察区。1949年7月31日清水县解放，成立清水县人民政府，属甘肃省天水专区。1953年划出县北部置张家川回族自治县。1958年清水、张家川合并为清水回族自治县，1961年两县分设至今。1985年7月清水县隶属天水市。

【经济发展状况】农业，近年来，县委、县政府立足当地实际，进一步理清经济发展思路，坚持农林牧副渔综合开发，走“两高一优”农业的路子，大抓了苹果、黄牛、油料、大麻、瓜菜、花椒、核桃、沙棘、肉兔等重点产业和项目建设，农业生产有了突破性进展。1993年全县农村社会总产值达到25138.70万元，农业总产值达到14489.05万元，是1978年2989万元的4.8倍，是1985年4995.35万元的2.9倍。种植业，1993年全县种植粮食作物77.21万亩，在遭受严重干旱、冰雹等自然灾害的情况下，粮食总产仍达到10388.34万公斤，创我县历史上最高纪录，农村人均占有粮食达到397公斤。经济作物播种面积趋于合理，总面积11.83万亩，种植大麻1.06万亩，总产44.93万公斤；油料作物10.53万亩，总产643万公斤，其中胡麻6.49万亩，葵花3.11万亩，油菜籽0.57万亩；种植棚膜瓜菜3000亩，总产616.5万公斤。林果业，全县森林面积达46.37万亩，人均1.6亩；其中人工林38.34万亩。1993年造林总面积11万亩。林业总产值952.69万元，占农业总产值的6.6%。经济林木发展较快，已达到10.55万亩。畜牧业，1993年全县有天然草地46.81万亩，人工种草面积24.14万亩，年产鲜草3.27万公斤，载畜量4.84万个羊单位。1993年末，大家畜存栏8.41万头(匹)，比1985年增长21.4%，出栏商品畜5376头(匹)。畜牧业总产值达3600万元，占农业总产值的24.8%。乡镇企业，1993年底，全县乡镇企业已发展到4568个,其中乡办90个,村办165个,联户办194个,户办4119个,从业人员16931人,占全县总劳动力的17.3%,总产值11242.4万元,比1985年增长13倍,占全县农村社会总产值的44.7%。

工业,全县工业企业认真贯彻落实《全民所有制工业企业转换经营机制条例》,深化企业内部三项制度改革,加强经营管理,以提高效益为中心,工业经济在困难中有了新发展。至1993年末,工业总产值3281.41万元,比1985年增长4.4倍,其中全民所有制工业产值2185.32万元,集体所有制工业产值843万元,村及村以下工业产值1290万元,企业拥有固定资产1838.3万元。主要产品有白酒、果酒饮料、水泥、岩棉制品、塑料制品,水泥电杆、大理石板材、针织毛衣裤等。正在加紧建设的县酒厂30吨沙棘籽油生产项目和县办集体企业亚麻脱胶厂麻条生产线,市场前景可观,建成投产后,将成为全县财政扭补支柱项目。

商贸流通,商贸企业积极推行"国有民营"、"社有自营"的改革试点,取得经验后已全面推广铺开。1993年末,全县有国营、集体、商业批发零售机构88个,从业人员928人,个体商业户1564个,从业人员3232人。社会商品零售额4610万元,比1985年的2311.24万元增长99.5%。由于流通格局的变化,全县商业零售额结构也发生了较大变化,1993年与1985年相比,在全县商业零售额中,国营商业所占比重由44.8%下降到42.6%,集体商业所占比重由52.5%下降到46.9%,个体商业的比重由2.7%上升到10.5%,个体商业的发展,弥补了国营、集体商业的不足,起到了拾遗补缺,方便群众,活跃市场的作用。城乡集市贸易空前活跃,有8个市场,3个交易点,其中专业市场2个,市场总面积39666平方米,1993年集市贸易成交额达1120.2万元,是1985年269万元的4.16倍。

财政金融,随着国民经济的发展,财政收入逐年增长。1993年财政收入627万元,比1985年的162.4万元增长2.86倍;财政支出2687万元,比1985年的953.3万元增长1.82倍,但财政困难的问题仍十分突出,影响着各项事业的发展。

人民生活,随着经济的不断发展,全县城乡人民生活水平有较大幅度提高。1993年,全县职工年平均工资收入2503元,较1985年的950元增长1.6倍;农民人均纯收入476元,是1985年172.9元的2.75倍;人均纯收入在500元以上,稳定解决温饱的农户有6839户,占总农户的13%,人均纯收入在300元至500元基本解决温饱的农户有34234户,占总农户的65%,人均纯收入在300元以下的贫困户有11532户,使贫困面由1985年的64%下降至22%。

【基础设施】交通:截止目前,全县共有县乡公路315.61公里=其中县公路194.92公里,乡公路120.69公里;上等级县乡公路183.42公里,占总里程的58.1%;有路面公路里程152.32公里,占总里程的48.3%,24个乡镇全部通公路、通货运汽车,有15个乡(镇)通客运班车。通公路的村250个,占总村数的74.1%,通客运班车的村94个,占总村数的27.9%,乡村道路累计已达到150条,959公里。全县有邮电机构12个,其中邮电支局、所11个,邮路7条,总长296公里,投递线路53条,总长1881公里。有长话电路32路,电报电路1路。1991年开通了自动电话,大大方便了经济建设和群众生活需要。至1993年底,全县电话机拥有量达到747部,其中市话623部,农话124部。全年完成邮电业务总量90.81万元,通信总量77.37万元,邮电业务总收入达到65.71万元。全县有小型水电站4处,装机总容量0.09万千瓦,年生产电154万度,共有35千伏线路115公里,6——10千伏线路703公里,低压线路510公里。

城镇建设,1991年拓宽县城主街道永清路,拆除沿街旧房289间,使长1261米的永清路由过去的7——9米宽,拓宽到22米,并一次铺油。1993年又拓宽了县城西关充国路,建成长290米,宽44米的新街,一改城区面貌。自1990年以来的三年间,多方筹资,创造条件,新建楼房56幢,是解放后前40年的1倍多。新建一处使用面积5000平方米的综合商场,规范了市场行为。在城北牛头河畔,修建了芙蓉公园,建有雷锋塑像、亭阁、高吊灯、60米长的花架走廊和8.4亩的荷花池、5.4亩的人工湖,是群众娱乐消遣的良好场所。自来水供应、街道照明、环境绿化、地下排水及防汛等配套建设一应俱全。

【社会事业】教育,1993年末,全县各类学校总数428所,其中完全中学3所,独立初中20所,完全小学251所,附中6所,职业中学3所,教师进修学校1所,幼儿园2所,在校学生总数达37090人,其中高中1174人,初中6640人,小学29276人;共有教职工1990人,其中民办教职工795人。全县基本普及初等义务教育的乡镇达到18个,占全县乡镇总数的95%,学龄儿童入学率达到95.2%,巩固率为93.4%,毕业率为98.8%,普及率为91.8%。1993年考入各类大学的学生124人,中专99人。

科技,1993年实施农业科技推广项目15项,总面积达30.3万亩,成效显著,新增粮食1800万公斤,新增产值1000多万元,有3项科研项目获年度县级科技进步奖,有6项获县级星火奖,同时申报,推荐1993年度市级奖励科研项目4项。科技队伍不断壮大,至1993年底,全县有农、林、牧、医、气象等14个学会，会员573人，有乡镇科协24个，会员1526人。共有各类专业技术人员2938人，其中高级职称的19人，中级职称的428人，助理级1287人，员级1190人。

广播电视，至1993年末，全县有广播放大站23个，新架设广播线路20杆公里，水泥杆线路达到704杆公里，木杆线路347.6杆公里。通播村达到250个，村通播率75%；全县有卫星地面差转台13个，共有电视接收机13305台（其中彩电826台），电视覆盖率达到24%。

医疗卫生，全县有医疗卫生机构30个，其中县属机构7个，乡卫生院23所。各类医疗卫生人员674人，其中专业技术人员564人，有村卫生站332个，乡村医生203名，卫生员131名，防疫员337名，接生员337名。医院病床总数489张（含省注清疗养院），平均每千人有床位1.7张。1993年县乡医疗单位完成诊疗人次40.7万人次，收治住院病人5484例，治愈率达54.1%，大骨节病、甲状腺肿大等各种急慢性传染病和地方病得到有效预防和控制，发病率逐年降低。

体育，全县有体育机构2个，专职体育干部9名，专职教练员4人，体校1所，有学生40人，等级运动员55人，等级裁判员40人；有灯光球场1座，占地31亩的体育场1处。给省体工队输送运动员2名，给体育学院输送学员30名。

【名特土产】沙棘果酒饮料，采用天然沙棘果为原料，运用先进技术生产而成。果香浓郁，滋味纯正，酸甜适度，营养成份全，VC含量尤高，年产量达4000吨。“上邽牌”系列白酒：产品有充国特曲、头曲、特酿、大曲、散酒等高、中档。以优质高粱为原料，采用传统工艺和新技术成果精制而成，风格独特，窖香浓郁，绵甜爽净，醇厚柔和，入味协调，回味久长，是宴会及馈赠亲友之佳品。“上邽牌”系列白酒年产量达500吨。苹果，清水是驰名中外的“花牛”苹果的主要产区之一。因气候适宜，光照充足，早熟色鲜，果大棱显，含糖量高，质脆耐贮，深受国内外消费者的青睐，苹果被列为全县支柱产业之一，目前已达10万多亩，年产量1000万吨。大麻，栽培历史悠久，分皮麻型和线麻型。麻皮厚而坚韧、纤维柔软细长。耐磨耐水性强；麻籽产量高，粒大饱满。自古为清水特产，名扬关中，远销川、陕，目前种植面积达1万多亩。岩棉制品，县岩棉厂是我国西北首建的年产岩棉制品5000吨的骨干企业。产品已达到国内先进水平，被列为全国16个化工保温材料定点厂家之一。大理石制品，我县大理石矿藏丰富，县大理石厂是以石材加工为主的专业生产厂家。主要产品有花岗石、大理石饰面板、石制工艺、彩石子三大系列，48个品种。庞公石，制作的盆景神形兼备，富贵高雅，质地坚细，翠如碧玉，兼有白黄花纹，堪称中国一绝，属国内外稀世珍品。1992年在中央电视台《祖国各地》栏目中播出后，在国内外引起轰动，不惜花重金购买者络绎不绝。

现任主要领导：

中共清水县委书记：王　义

清水县人大常委会主任：孙有林

清水县人民政府县长：白志家

政协清水县委员会主席：王定成

中共清水县纪律检查委员会书记：韩新华

（中共清水县委研究室：中君明）

（清水县人民政府研究室：蔡俊杰）

秦安县经济和社会发展概述

【历史沿革】秦安县历史悠久，源远流长。远在仰韶文化早期（距今约为7355年），已有人类繁衍生息。县名始于金正隆二年。因“邑故秦州北境，亦名秦”。缀以“安”字以表达人们渴求安宁的愿望而得名。

秦安，相传是伏羲，女娲的出生地，有羲里娲乡之美称。是中华民族的起源地之一。夏、商、西周时为雍州地。西周时期，周孝王封秦非子牧马于秦亭，秦安即为秦亭的一部分。春秋战国时期归陇西郡。西汉时期属天水郡，境域属三县（成纪、陇城、街泉县）一道（略阳道）所辖。东汉时为汉阳郡，境域分属二县（略阳、成纪县）一侯国（寞固侯国）。三国时境内为成纪、显亲和陇城三县所辖，成纪、显亲属天水郡，陇城属广魏郡。西晋时期，境内属成纪、显亲和略阳，临渭4县，分别隶属于天水郡和略阳郡。东晋十六国时期，秦安先后为前赵、后赵、前秦、后秦、前凉、后凉、西秦占据。北魏时属陇城、显亲县，隶属略阳、天水郡。隋、唐时期，境内设成纪、陇东二县，属天水郡。唐宝应元年（公元762年）陷于吐蕃。宋时境域分属三寨（陇城寨、秦寨、鸡川寨）。绍兴十二年，宋割秦州之半于金。金正隆二年（公元1157年），境内设秦安、鸡川、陇城三县，秦安名由此始。元代并陇城，鸡川二县入秦安、属陕西行省之秦州管辖。明时沿用秦安县制，属巩昌府秦州管辖。清属甘肃省巩秦阶道。中华民国时先属渭川道，废道后直属甘肃省。1936年后，属甘肃省第4区行政专员公署。1949年8月4日秦安解放，建立秦安县人民政府，属甘肃省天水地区。1985年归天水市管辖。县人民政府驻地兴国镇。

【自然概况】秦安县地处甘肃省东西部，天水市北部，位于秦岭以北，渭河支流葫芦河下游，东经105°20′至106°02′，北纬34°44′至35°11′之间。东西长63公里，南北宽49公里。东与清水县、张家川回族自治县接壤，南同北道区相邻，西靠通渭县、甘谷县，北邻庄浪县、静宁县，属陇中黄土高原西部梁峁沟壑区，地势西北高而东南低，海拔在1200至2012米之间。县内最大河流为葫芦河，发源于宁夏月亮山,在县境内流长45.2公里,流域面积401.8平方公里,年平均径流量7771万立方米。秦安县属陇中温带半湿润气候,有夏热无酷暑,冬冷无严寒,冬干夏湿的温带大陆性气候特色。年平均气温10.4℃,降雨量为507.3毫米,多集中在7、8、9三个月,年平均蒸发量1457.6毫米,年平均日照时数2208.1小时(日照率50%),无霜期年平均178天。有干旱、暴雨、冰雹、低温、霜冻等自然灾害。全县总土地面积1601.13平方公里,其中耕地面积106万亩,占总土地面积44.2%,耕地面积中,山地101.17万亩,占耕地95.4%,川地4.83万亩,占耕地的4.6%。人均占有耕地2.15亩。本县植被希少,境内无天然植被。仅在郭集乡有一小片残存天然次生林85亩。现有林木均为人工栽植。有86种,果树102种,主要以苹果、桃、梨为主。人工栽培的草类主要有紫花苜蓿、红豆草、沙打旺等。药材资源较为丰富,药用植物有222种,以人工栽培党参为主。野生药物有甘草、冬花、半夏等。矿物类药物有龙骨、石膏等。动物类药物有全蝎。动物类资源,有22科、48种。家畜家禽有15种,野生动物有10种。矿物资源贫乏,除花岗岩、石灰岩储量较为丰富外,还有少量铜、铝等贵重矿藏。全县辖1个镇,21个乡,有515个村委会,1384个村民小组,7个居委会。有汉、回等6个民族,以汉族为主占99.63%,少数民族人口仅占0.37%。全县总户数为102736户(乡村户95501户),总人口517941人(乡村人口493351人)。人口密度323人/平方公里。是全省人口密度最大的县之一。

【经济发展状况】秦安县在改革、开放、搞活的方针指引下,从实践中走出以商促工,以工促农,农工商综合发展的路子,迈开了致富的新步伐,使农业、工业和整个国民经济得到了全面发展。1993年可比价社会总产值达到62041万元,国民生产总值达30640万元,人均国民生产总值586.54元。农村经济,1993年农业总产值22746.1万元,比解放初期增长3.6倍。农业商品产值达9403万元,商品率由1986年的23.3%提高到41.34%。粮食总产量达到11.93万吨,比1949年增长1.4倍,单产由1949年的49公斤提高到126公斤。油料产量达到2484.5吨,比1949年增长9倍,单产由1949年的17公斤提高到45公斤。水果生产在秦安历来占有优势,素有“瓜果之乡”的美誉。从70年代开始,果树发展较快,果园面积由1970年的7273亩发展到1993年的171822.5亩,增长22.6倍;果园面积中,苹果园达149110亩,桃园13517亩.梨园3672亩,葡萄园49亩,杏园72亩,其它(李子)园5400亩。水果产量由1949年的641吨发展到1993年的27279.7吨,增长41.6倍。其中苹果达18361.5吨,桃子6470.2吨,梨1195.4吨,杏子459.6吨,葡萄21吨,其它(李子)771.9吨。全县实有造林面积由1949年的1828亩,增到1993年的464743亩。大家畜1993年末存栏42178头;生猪存栏115033头,比解放初期分别增长77.3%和4.5倍。肉类总产量9370.6吨,人均19公斤。养鸡70.82万只,产蛋2101.6吨。1993年乡镇企业产值达到34055.5万元,比1984年增长15.9倍,占农村社会总产值的比重由1985年的22.3%上升到1993年的61.8%,企业个数由1984年的2793个发展到6446个,从业人员由19948人增加到39194人,占农村劳动力的19.1%,已初步形成了以建筑材料、食品加工、饮食、针织毛纺为主的生产门类。全县各类股份合作企业发展到579家,其中69家骨干企业,股东265人,入股资金3764.5万元,年设计产值17752.4万元。

工业生产,1993年全县共有工业企业2185个,从业人员18199人。实现工业总产值20769.2万元,比解放初期增长631倍,平均递增15.8%。从产值构成看:全民工业产值1675.3万元,占8.07%;集体工业产值2464.7万元,占11.87%;村及村以下工业产值16629.2万元,占80.06%。工业总产值在社会总产值中的比重由1949年的1.1%上升到33.48%。工业产品种类到1993年发展到包括农机修造、建筑材料、皮毛加工、毛睛纺织、地毯、印刷、草编工艺、金属制品、家俱制造等十几个门类,117个品种。1993年生产硬脂酸763.7吨,水泥7500吨,砖3095.4万块,草制工艺品60.5万件,地毯5598平方米,各种线毯2.28万条,沙棘汁167吨,泡化碱418吨,粉条11500吨,冻肉1212吨,其它产品产量也在迅速增加。工业新产品、新工艺不断涌现。草制工艺品和地毯已打入国际市场,沙发布和提花地毯畅销全省各地及青海、西藏等省、市;睛纶毛普鲁创优夺魁,获轻工业部和国家民委颁发的荣誉证书;糖水苹果罐头和糖水梨罐头,在全省同行业产品评比中分别获第一名和第二名;沙棘汁和沙棘浓汁在1986年全国沙棘产品质量评议会上荣获“优质奖”、“新产品开发奖”。生产的“大地湾牌沙棘酱汁”,荣获1988年首届中国食品博览会名、特、优、新产品“银质奖”和“最受消费者欢迎饮料”称号。

基本建设,解放以来,全县累计建设投资9924.57万元,每年平均225.56万元。1978年至1993年,建设投资8400.63万元,占累计投资的84.64%。尤其近六年中,投资额达6041万元,是前38年累计投资的1.56倍,基本建设得到快速发展,县城市容焕然一新。

交通邮电,1993年底,拥有干线公路3条129.5公里,县乡公路21条,213.20公里,乡村公路174条

1127.66公里，公路总里程达1470.28公里，比1949年171.5公里增加7.57倍。共修建大中型桥梁23座，涵洞542道。全县22个乡(镇)，460个村委会通汽车，其中20个乡(镇)，230个自然村通了班车。共有各种客货车辆512车辆(1949年仅有货车1辆)。县属运输企业完成客运量11.2万人次，客运周转量755万人公里，货运量5.2万吨，货运周转量961.3万吨公里。

1993年邮电局、所有19个，拥有职工197人，邮电线路长达2001公里，邮电杆路长度217公里(其中农话杆路204公里)，电报电路3条，长途电路55条。县内市话拥有量1473部，农话307户。电话交换机容量4040部，自动电话1603门。全县22个乡(镇)通电话，14个乡(镇)已自动通话。邮电业务总量达303.7万元。

城乡市场，1993年，全县各种商业网点发展到8926个，从业人员2.2万人。实现社会商品零售总额13379万元。全县共有城乡集市贸易市场23个，年成交额达19489万元。其中县城所在地的秦安小商品市场，自1980年创建以来，更是充满生机，目前已拥有1500多个摊位，从业人员6000多人。形成数百人进货，近千人批发，万余人推销的小商品经营网络。1993年营业额达2亿元以上，上交税费200多万元，经营的商品70%是个体商贩从上海、天津、广州、浙江等地购进的，30%属本地自产商品。通过批量销售给成千上万的货郎担和外来客商，远销青海、宁夏、新疆、内蒙古、西藏等地，甚至销往尼泊尔等国。该市场已成为西北小商品推销的集散地。市场经济进一步促进了财税金融事业的发展。使县级财政收入由1952年的193.42万元增加到1993年的1232.1万元，增长5.4倍，税收由1952年的68.98万元，增加到1993年的1077万元，增长14.6倍。

【社会文化】科学技术，目前，全县有农林、园艺、畜牧。气象等地方性科技机构14个，其中：试验、推广机构13个，管理机构1个。全县形成了县有中心、乡有站，村有技术员，组有示范户的四级农业科技服务网络。有各类农民科技学(协)会及专业研究会676个，有会员7758人，有农民技术员2440人，评定了技术职称的801名，其中技师87名、助理技师188名，技术员526名。参加中国农函大的学员累计达944名。这些科技能人促进了全县农业实用技术的广泛推广应用。

文教、卫生，1993年拥有各类学校653所，其中：初级中学23所，完全中学6所，农职业中学4所，高小368所，初小57所，村学195所。各类学校在校学生达81141人，比解放初期增长20.8倍，教职员工4388人，其中专任教师4156人，比1949年增长10倍。学龄儿童入学率由1949年的30%上升到97.87%，此外，还建立和发展了儿童学前教育，职工专业教育、农民技术教育、电视函授教育等。1977年，恢复高考制度以来，广大教育工作者付出了辛勤的劳动，到1993年共为国家输送大中专学生7365名(每年平均433人)，其中，大学生3182名．中专生4183名。

广播电视，截止1993年，全县22个乡(镇)都有广播放大站，共安装喇叭5万多只。广播电视转播台3个、卫星地面接收站13个(系统内4个)，有电视机3.75万台，广播、电视覆盖面积达1100平方公里，其中广播覆盖率95.6%，电视覆盖率64.9%。

医疗卫生，全县共有医疗卫生机构661个，其中，县及县以上医院3个，乡(镇)卫生院(所)25个，农村卫生站633个。医院病床516张。各级各类卫生技术人员823人。其中：高级医师8人，医师406人，医士131人；个休开业行医人员159人。每千人有医院病床1张。乡乡有卫生院(所)，村村有医疗点。

体育，现有专职体育机构1个，群众性体育协会7个，田径场3个，灯光球场2个。射击青年二级动员2名，等级裁判员83名，专职教练员13名。在省级体育比赛中获金牌2枚，银牌4枚，铜牌3枚。1993年乒乓球获省级比赛团体第三名。一名武术教练员在全国武术邀请赛中获“雄狮奖”。全县有5000多人达到了《国家体育锻炼标准》。

【名特土产】长把梨，唐代曾为贡品。果头隆起，上小下大，故亦名“鸡腿梨”；含糖量达到10%左右，是梨中不可多得的珍品，为唐太宗李世民时期的“贡品”。现共有梨园3672亩，产量1195.4吨。桃，种植历史悠久，品种较多。种植面积已达13517亩，年产桃6470.2吨。西瓜，秦安素有陇南“瓜果之乡”的美称，种植西瓜已有500多年的历史。近10年来，引进新品种中育1号、丰收2号、郑州3号、P2等6个品种，年种植面积4904亩，产量7124.5吨，畅销县内外市场。沙棘汁，沙棘汁和沙棘浓汁，曾荣获全国评比第一、第二名，获省软饮料优良奖和全国“优良奖”、“新产品开发奖”，早畅销省内外，深受用户欢迎。草编，草编是秦安的传统编织工艺品，其中草帽辫曾以“精制轻巧、美观文雅、款式新颖、柔软挺拔”而著名。1974年开始引进天津等地的新工艺并进行了推广和改进。近几年来。创新产品1900多种，港口成交209种，远销英、美、意、日、西德及港、澳等23个国家和地区，出口量曾连续3年居全省第一。

现任主要领导：

中共秦安县委书记：田兴齐

秦安县人大常委会主任：任克基

秦安县人民政府县长：徐　彬

政协秦安县委员会主席：冯文虎

中共秦安县纪律检查委员会书记：杨汉文

（中共秦安县委研究室）

甘谷县经济和社会发展概述

【基本情况】甘谷县位于甘肃省东南部的渭河上游，陇海铁路天兰段、天水市管辖，属黄土高原梁峁沟壑区，东临北道、秦安，南接秦城、礼县，西与武山接壤，北以通渭为邻。南北长60公里，东西宽49公里，总面积1572平方公里，总耕地90万亩，海拔在1230～2716米之间。全县辖20个乡镇，411个村委会，总人口51.85万人。

过去甘谷是一个人多地少、干旱多灾、群众生活困难的贫困县。近几年来，县委、县政府从甘谷实际出发，坚持强化一个基础(粮食)，加快四项建设(基本农田、水利、造林绿化、农村基础设施)、开发八大支柱产业(建筑劳务、乡镇企业、服装加工、农副产品加工、养殖、种植、林果、商贸流通)的思路，使全县人民摆脱了贫困，经济和社会各项事业显现出良好的发展势头。1993年全县国民生产总值达到4.04亿元，工农业总产值达到3.86亿元，粮食总产量达到2.57亿斤，乡镇企业总产值达到4.05亿元，农民人均纯收入达到545.92元，社会商品零售总额达到1.08亿元，集市贸易成交额达到1.21亿元，财政收入2004.6万元，城乡储蓄总额达到2.26亿元。

甘谷是我国历史上建县最早的县之一。夏、商时期属雍州，秦武公十年(公元前668年)伐冀戎，置冀县为甘谷县之始，已有2675年的历史。甘谷历为州、郡、府所治，唐高祖武德三年(620年)改为伏羌县，明、清两代沿用，民国十八年(1929年)改伏羌县为甘谷县，1958年甘谷县并入武山县，1962年1月分治，恢复了甘谷县，沿用至今。

甘谷自古为经济、文化重镇，是古“丝绸之路”的重要通道，文化遗存非常丰富。城西大象山石窟，始建于北魏时期，大佛塑像高23.3米，是国家四大石窟之一，被列为省级重点文物保护单位，境内还有新石器时期的文物古迹11处，古墓葬18座，以及华盖寺石窟、蔡家寺、蜀汉大将军姜维衣冠冢等，初步形成了以城区为中心，渭河为纽带，联结东西南川、南北两山的旅游网络。

甘谷土地广阔，属大陆腹地，为大陆性季风气候，四季分明，气候宜人，光照充足，雨量偏少，夏热而无酷暑，冬冷而无严寒。县内自然资源丰富，有野生动物120多种，其中被列为国家保护的动物有5种，植物资源937种。仅中药材就有270多种，森林覆盖率达18.13%。矿产资源品种较多，储量大。主要矿藏有石灰石、磷、花岗岩、赤铁、煤等20余种，其中花岗岩的储量多达5000万立方米。

【经济建设】甘谷县通过深化农村改革，调整农业经济结构，大搞农业综合开发，逐步形成了以粮、油、菜、药材为基地，林、牧、副、渔全面发展的大农业生产体系。甘谷以盛产粮、油、菜、药材、果、猪、牛、禽而著称于省内外，其中党参、线辣椒以其优良的品质享誉海内外，远销世界各地。全县蔬菜种植面积3万多亩，党参面积2万多亩，辣椒面积6000多亩，以苹果为主的果园面积6万多亩。全县规模养殖发展迅速，有规模养殖村13个，规模养殖户1988户，养殖业已成为农村经济发展的一大支柱。甘谷工业发展迅速。全县有乡以上工业企业120多个，其中省属企业4个，县属国营集体企业32个，乡办工业企业84个，初步形成化工、石棉制品、纺织、机械、建材、食品、包装、印刷、服装、制革等十几个行业，上千种产品，油墨、摩擦密封材料、草编制品、地毯等远销欧美、日本和东南亚许多国家和地区。甘谷乡镇企业异军突起。乡镇企业总数达到4637个，从业人员46126人，乡镇企业以建筑、建材、服装加工为龙头，产供销配套。全县有乡镇水泥厂9个，生产能力达15万吨。建筑业更是一大优势。1989年被国务院确定为建筑劳务基地县。现有三级以上的建筑公司4个，建筑工程队256个，从业3万多人，活跃在广州、上海、兰州、乌鲁木齐、西宁等大中城市和援外建筑工地。得天独厚的条件，改革开放的大潮，推动了甘谷经济持续、快速、协调发展。

甘谷是我国古“丝绸之路”上的商旅重地，早在明代即称为“商旅之家”，改革开放以来，甘谷市场得以迅速发育，商贸更趋繁荣，流通十分活跃。目前，全县有各类市场28个、商场8处，市场面积252.8亩，建筑面积13.48万平方米，可容纳摊位13150个，从业人员1.78万人。位于城北的“冀城大商场”成为容百货、服装、毛皮、药材、建材、禽畜等为一体的专业市场，联结城乡，辐射全国，商贾云集，购销两旺。甘谷对外贸易不断发展，外贸出口额逐年增长，辣椒干、药材、草编、柳编工艺品、羊毛地毯、优质瓜果等工农业产品，远销欧美、日本、东南亚及港澳等20多个国家和地区。

【社会事业】全县有各类小学校337所，普通中学47所，教师进修学校1所，职业大学1所，业余职业体校1所，适龄儿童入学率达99%，在校中小学生达96338人，甘谷连续多年位居全省高考前列。1993年全县共有465人考取了大中专院校，1977年恢复高考以来，甘谷共为高、中等院校输送合格人才5200多人，有近20名志学青年出国深造。同时，办学条件得到了改善，扫盲教育、成人教育取得了可喜的成绩；全县20个乡镇都成立了文化站、广播站，电视差转台在部分乡镇建起，县人民广播电台、有线电视的建成开播又极大地丰富了人民群众的精神文化生活；计划生育、卫生保健、计划免疫、妇幼保健等多项工作发展迅速、成绩显著，各项社会事业得到协调发展。

县乡公路四通八达，交织成网，乡乡通公路、村村通汽车，从福州至兰州的316国道穿越境内45公里，陇海铁路天兰段从东西横贯全县，有6个火车站，连接3镇4乡。邮电通讯发展迅速，新建的邮电大楼已经交付使用，公众传真、电话直拨等先进通讯已广泛应用。电力建设步伐加快，县内现有输变电站4个，总容量达1.24万千伏。农田水利基础建设常抓不懈，全县累计梯田面积达到44.44万亩，新修、恢复水利灌溉工程190处，灌溉面积达到12.84万亩。旧城改造、城姚南北主干道拓宽工程在年内可望竣工，长1850米、宽32米的康庄大街及其临街建设正在加紧进行，将以此形成设施齐全、功能完备的商贸开发区。县城内公用设施建设日新月异，宾馆、饭店、商场、歌厅、舞厅、影院、录像厅、娱乐城、体育场分布于县城，既可以为人们提供生活学习场所、又使娱乐、休息等有着良好去处。

现任主要领导：

中共甘谷县委书记：景云堂

甘谷县人大常委会主任：霍永禄

甘谷县人民政府县长：徐世英

政协甘谷县委员会主席：潘志强

（甘谷县委研究室）

武山县经济和社会发展概述

【概况】武山县地处古“丝绸之路”的咽喉要道。位于甘肃省东南部、天水市西北部，东界甘谷、西毗漳县、南邻礼县、岷县，北与陇西、通渭接壤。介于东经104°34′至105°8′，北纬34°25′至34°57′之间，东西宽51.5公里，南北长59.5公里。地势西高东低、南高北低。全县以渭河、漳河为界分为北部黄土梁峁沟壑山区、南部土石山区和中部河谷川区。北部山区植被稀疏、水土流失严重；南部山区地势陡峭、植被良好；中部河谷川区地势平坦、土壤肥沃、灌溉便利、素有“金腰带”之称。

全县共辖3镇17乡，395个村委会，2个居民委会，1597个村民小组，38.27人，人口密度为190.29人/平方公里，有8个少数民族共224人。

总面积2011平方公里，其中山区1071平方公里，占84.58%，河谷川区310平方公里，占15.42%。耕地面积65.21万亩，其中山地59.14万亩，占90.69%，川地6.07万亩，占9.31%，人均占有耕地1.82亩。海拔在1365米、至3120米之间。属温带大陆性季风气候，四季分明。农业以种植业为主，粮食作物主要有小麦、洋芋、玉米、蚕豆、糜谷、莜麦、荞、豌豆等；经济作物有蔬菜、油料、药材、瓜类、大麻、甜菜、烟叶等；畜禽产品和野生动物资源比较丰富。蔬菜生产已经成为全县经济的一大支柱产业，远销全国10多个省、市、区。

水电资源充裕。渭河及其支流榜沙河、漳河、山丹河、南河和聂河总长约198公里，年平均径流量2.2亿立方米。县内有11万伏双回路变电所1座、3.5万伏变电所5座、小水电站3座，总装机容量达2900千瓦。全县87%以上的行政村已通电。

矿藏资源种类较多。非金属矿藏比较丰富。主要有铅、锌、钼、铜、铬、铁等有色金属和非金属矿藏蛇纹岩（鸳鸯玉）、白云石、石灰石、滑石等：地下热水资源丰富。

交通、通讯较为便利。陇海线穿越县内46.25公里，设有6个火车站。“316国道”纵贯县境，县、乡、村公路四通八达。邮电通讯有2000门自动电话交换机，与国内程控电话并网，还开通了无线寻呼业务。

【经济建设】1993年，全县经济发展较快，国民生产总值达到23142万元（90年不变价），比1992年增长10.4%；国内生产总值22493万元，比1992年增长10.5%；工农业总产值25768.81万元，比1992年增长15.25%。

农业。1993年认真贯彻落实中央关于农村工作的一系列会议精神，坚持以农业为基础的指导思想，把农村工作摆在首位，落实了各项措施，农业总产值达到16043.5万元，较1992年增长5.37%。粮食坚持稳夏增秋、扩大高产、主攻单产、增加总产的思路，实行双轨承包。建立小麦、玉米丰产小区和蚕豆基地，建设“双千田”、“双五百田”和“吨粮田”高效“三田”，推广保护地栽培和优良品种，防治病虫害，粮食生产获得全面丰收。总产量达到85007吨，比1992年增长3.82%。经济作物坚持以市场为导向，科技为动力，合理调整种植业结构，种植面积81418亩，其中油料面积70430亩，产量5307.61吨，分别比1992年增长了5.88%、2.39%和11.68%。蔬菜面积达40715亩，产量87963.59吨，分别比1992年增长6.74%和12.6%。蔬菜品种已由低档大路菜向高档精细菜发展，特别是“高效节能日光温室的发展，使全县蔬菜生产已形成了淡季不淡，旺季不烂，品种齐全，四季有鲜的局面。洛门镇已成为甘肃省最大的细菜批发市场。畜牧业年末大家畜存栏数达到63355头，比1992年增长2.09%。畜产品产量有所提高，猪、牛、羊肉总产量4831.55吨，比1992年增长2.66%。畜牧业产值3427.92万元，比1992年增长3.15%。林业生产，1993年全县果园面积达到33591.9亩，比1992年增长43.46%；水果产量3417.48吨，比上年增长39.79%。造林面积62160.5亩，较上年增长113.7%，林业产值701.13万元，较上年增长81.44%。乡镇企业认真贯彻国务院《关于加快发展中西部地区乡镇企业的决定》，坚持整顿提高与发展扩大相结合。1993年底乡镇企业发展到7004个，完成产值18551.6万元，销售收入17458.8万元，创税396.5万元，分别比上年增长了64.73%、63.7%和35.93%。同时农民生活水平提高，扶贫开发成绩显著，1993农民人均纯收入466.12元，比1992年净增58.43元，增长了14.33%。全县的贫困面由1986年的60%下降到10%以下。农田基本建设在搞好规划的基础上认真落实劳动积累工制度，注重质量，连片治理。全年新修水平梯田16573亩。在抓好现有水利设施的清淤维修的同时，完成了郭槐乡水利示范乡和其他11项水利工程的建设。架设10千伏农电线路31公里，解决了1375户、6875人的生产生活用电；完成人饮病改工程6项，解决了1.09万人和2000头大牲畜的饮水问题。狠抓了县乡两级服务组织和村级组织建设，初步形成了县有中心，乡有站，村有农民技术员，组有技术示范户，上下贯通，纵横相联的服务网络体系。

工业。全县有工业企业3721个，从业人员13292人，其中乡及乡以上工业企业78个，从业人员3912人。1993年全县工业企业进一步贯彻《条例》，转换经营机制，深化"三项"制度改革，推行全员劳动合同制。企业加强内部管理瞄准市场，以产促销，抓住机遇，扩大适销对路产品，提高经济效益。完成工业总产值9725.31万元，占年计划的125.48%，比上年增长29.95%，实现税金190万元，创利353万元，分别比1992年增长了17.66%和49.25%。

城乡建设，1993年共有施工项目21项，完成投资总额9775万元，其中全民投资5065万元，集体投资390万元，城乡居民个人投资4320万元。洛门新区建设吸引投资2394万元，县城供水工程完成322万元，渭河单墩人行桥49万元，南阳水电站109万元。

商贸流通，1993年大力推行国有民营，社有自营的经营方式，14个企业的84个门点已实行了国有民营或社有民营，抽回资金72.2万元。完成社会商品销售额80554万元，社会商品零售总额8703万元，收购农副产品10139万元。

交通、邮电，全县有邮电局所13个，职工169人，邮电业务总量达167.85万元，其中计费项目154.81万元。报刊流转额59.91万元。全县有公路347.23公里，通公路的行政村175个，占全县行政村的44%，通汽车的行政村265个，占全县行政村的67%，完成客运量67万人次，客运周转量14570万人公里，货运量14.7万吨，货运周转量9555万吨公里。

财政、金融和保险业，1993年全县财政、金融和保险业不断发展。财政工作认真落实"控人节钱，以钱生钱，增收节支"，县、乡"分灶吃饭"试点改革和加强税收征管等措施，财政状况有所好转，完成财政收入1503万元，比1992年增长48.2%。金融信贷部门千方百计为各项建设提供资金，为企业深化改革、提高经济效益发挥了很大作用。保险业积极拓展保险业务，开展农业保险，为全县农业生产起到了保驾护航作用。

【社会事业】人口和计划生育。1993年末全县总人口382664人，其中农业人口358979人，非农业人口23685人，人口出生率为19.7‰，死亡率5.7‰，自然增长率14‰。计生队伍不断壮大。1993年在全县20个乡镇设置了计划生育工作站配备了计生专干，实行了计划生育科学化管理，育龄妇女节育率达到83.56%。

文化、教育和体育。1993年在发展完善县乡文化馆室的同时，许多村组建了文化室，藏书4万多册；有"县美术协会"、"县书法协会"、"农民书画协会"等各种文化协会，每逢节庆举办书法、绘画、摄影展览，展出了许多有价值健康向上的作品；县内有电视地面站19座，电视覆盖率80%左右；乡广播站20个，村广播室225个，通广播的行政村262个，占全县行政村的66%，所有这些都为丰富人民文化生活、学习科学技术、促进精神文明建设发挥了很大作用。全县有普通中学17所，在校学生12942人，教职工1036人；小学460所，在校学生46861人；幼儿园6所，在园幼儿1022人，职业中学2所，在校生370人。充实了师资力量，改善了办学条件，提高了教学质量。武山有尚武的传统。近年来由于县委、县政府的高度重视，各乡镇都相继成立了武术协会。1993年武山县被国家体委命名为"全国武术之乡"参加了"首届武术之乡"比赛，并取得了好成绩。

卫生。卫生医疗条件进一步改善，人民健康水平不断提高。全县共有各类医疗机构44个，病床684张，比1992年增长8.4%，各类卫生技术人员874人，比1992年增长8%。

文物古迹。县内有36年仰韶文化、齐家文化遗址，6处省级文物保护单位。其中水帘洞奇峰耸立，风光迷人，有丰富的石窟、壁画、浮雕，具有很高的艺术考古价值；木梯寺石窟开凿在半山之腰，三面为悬崖绝壁，仅一面可攀梯入内，寺内有塑像，壁画和古建筑群；温泉山峦环绕，山花烂漫，绿树丛生，溪流清澈。丰富的矿山温泉水日涌量800吨，水温40℃，水质富含碳酸钠氡，对多种疾病有疗效，建有甘肃省疗养院和兰州铁路疗养院。

【名特土产】建材，有引进德国技术生产的获省优。部优产品奖的"鸳鸯牌"硅酸盐水泥，年产量达70多万吨；有丰富的豪华曲雅的各类玉石，花岗石和大理石板材。农副产品，主要有蚕豆、各类蔬菜、瓜果、"三粉"(粉皮、粉条、粉丝)和"三编"(柳编、竹编、草编)工艺品和生产工具。工艺美术品。有做工精细、造型美观、玲珑别致、晶莹玉润的鸳鸯玉"双龙杯"、"夜光杯"等茶酒具,文房用品和其他各种玉雕工艺品。其次,还有药材当归(属岷当),野生植物沙棘和工业品"金"字牌水烟,毛毯、地毯等。

现任主要领导:

中共武山县委书记:刘宝珍

武山县人大常委会主任:李春发

武山县人民政府县长:王玺玉

政协武山县委员会主席:郭维政

中共武山县纪律检查委员会书记:卢登宝

(武山县委调研室:石磊)

白银市

中共白银市委书记:韩修国

白银市人大常委会主任:韩修国(兼)

白银市人民政府市长:王重国

政协白银市委员会主席:艾立兴

中共白银市纪律检查委员会书记:巨明礼

新兴的工业城市—白银市

白银市是甘肃省省辖市,是国家重要的原材料基地和甘肃省重要的能源基地,农业上是黄河上游百万亩以上的重要的高扬程灌区。她与省会兰州市毗邻,相距80余公里。全市设白银、平川二区,辖会宁、靖远、景泰三县,总人口150多万人,其中城镇人口30万人。全市总面积2.1万平方公里。

白银地名,因历史上盛产金银而得名。据志书记载,明初洪武年间,官方在此设有办机构"白银厂"掘银采金,最盛时人数达三、四千之众,日出斗金。后以"白银厂"成为地名,白银市亦因此得名。白银境内丰富的矿藏得到大规模开发,还是在新中国成立之后。

白银市是新中国成立后逐步发展起来的新兴工业城市,也是一座移民城市。新中国成立后属国家"一五"计划156项重点工程的白银有色金属公司和银光化学材料厂在白银兴建,揭开了白银发展的新篇章。尔后陆续从上海、青岛等地内迁以及后来新建了一批厂矿企业。随着工业的发展,白银市应运而生。1956年成立县级市,1958年发展成为省辖市。但于1963年12月,由于种种原因白银市被撤销。随着改革的深入和经济的发展,1985年8月1日,白银市又恢复成立。白银市成立历史短,但发展迅速,城市的开拓者和建设者们来自全国和全省各地。从这个意义上讲,白银市是一座移民城市。市内工矿企业和科研单位比较集中,目前每万人中受过高等教育的人口比例高于全国平均水平。正是这支由全国和全省各地汇集到白银的开拓者、建设者们经过几十年的艰苦创业,使一片荒塬发生了神奇的变化,一座别具神韵的新兴工业城市已亭亭玉立于陇原之上。1963年3月,邓小平同志视察白银时赞扬说:"你们这里是艰苦奋斗!"。1992年8月,江泽民同志视察白银时,题词勉励白银人民:"艰苦奋斗,振兴白银"。

白银工业的显著特点是原材料和能源工业占主体。市内多种产品的年生产能力居全国或西北地区前列。白银是全国最大的有色金属工业基地,白银公司可年产铜、铝、铅、锌等有色金属量27万吨,目前尚在进一步扩建,扩建后可达年产有色金属40万吨左右。甘肃稀土公司拥有近2万吨氯化稀土生产线,其产量居亚洲之首。银光化学工业公司生产的各类炸药和TDI,白银针布厂生产的弹性针布和金属针布等,其产量均列全国榜首。另外,电线电缆,磷盐产品、氟化盐、硫酸、硫精砂。高强石膏粉及其制品等,可列西北前列。白银市又是甘肃重要的能源基地,靖远矿务局及地方煤矿,年生产煤炭600万吨左右。靖远火电厂一期工程已建成,装机容量80万千瓦,在建的二期工程竣工后可达200万千瓦。黄河上游大峡水电总厂正在建设,总装机容量70万千瓦。另外,白银棉纺厂的棉纱、白银针织厂的针织品、以及地方企业和乡镇企业的建筑陶瓷、水泥、地毯、毛毯、儿童服装等,亦在全省占有相当的比重。

白银是沿黄高扬程灌溉农业的重要开发区。黄河流经白银214公里,沿黄两岸有200多万亩川、塬地可供开发。在国家"三西"和甘肃"两西"的有力支持下,市内先后兴建了景泰川一期、二期和兴堡子川、靖会川、刘川等电灌工程,有效灌溉面积达120多万亩。另有"三田"160多万亩。全市总耕地面积500万亩,基本保证了粮食的稳定生产。全市有养鱼水面5000多亩,水稻种植面积3万多亩。今日黄河两岸,也可称鱼米之乡。农业基本生产条件的改变和"科教兴农"措施的落实,城市的"菜蓝子"基本得到保证。严冬季节,也有本地自产的黄瓜、西红柿、蕃瓜、油菜等新鲜蔬菜满足城乡群众生活需要。

白银市恢复成立以来,改革开放逐步深化,经济发展逐年加快。市委、市政府带领全市各级党政组织和广大干部群众,深入贯彻党的十一届三中全会以来的路线方针政策和党的十四大精神,落实"四项基本市策"(注1),实施"双带整推"战略,坚持"三不三互"原则(注2),围绕经济发展上新台阶的目标,使全市改革开放和经济建设取得了新成就。改革开放步伐加快。以贯彻落实《条例》为重点,积极试点,努力转换国有企业经营机制,对一批企业实行了转产。兼并。商业、供销、粮食、物资系统大力推行"国有民营"、"社有自营”，加快了流通体制改革步伐，城乡市场体系和商品基地建设进展较快，铜城商厦、西区物资交易大厦、靖远蔬菜瓜果批发市场、会宁小杂粮批发市场等一批市场正在加紧建设或投入使用，全市十四个商品基地的建设规模进一步扩大。股份制经济有了较快发展，已发展股份有限公司4家、有限责任公司7家、股份合作制企业68家。个体、私营经济发展加快，全市个体工商户已达1.5万户，私营企业达到125户。从事第三产业的企业发展到1500多户，第三产业在国民生产总值中的比重达到18.50%。城镇住房制度、医疗卫生制度、劳动人事制度、社会保障制度等改革正在全面实施。对外开放进一步扩大，一批引进外资和引进技术项目正在建设之中。经济发展速度明显加快。农业和农村经济贯彻“新三路”(注3)方针，粮食生产稳定增长。1993年，粮食总产量达到38.64万吨，增长8.38%；农村社会总产值达到16.11亿元，增长28.34%；农业总产值达到6.74亿元，增长10.69%；乡镇企业以高速发展，总产值达到10.47亿元，增长45.60%；“畜牧年”活动成效显著，畜禽饲养量和肉类总产量分别增长14.50%和23.41%；农民人均纯收入达到500元，增长15.47%。地方工业生产持续快速发展。1993年，市及市以下工业总产值达到13.68亿元，比上年增长33.41%；城市集体经济发展速度加快，完成社会总产值6.03亿元，增长67.77%，其中工业总产值4.33亿元，增长73.98%；社会商品零售总额完成8.54亿元，增长14.32%。区域经济实力进一步增强。1993年，全市国民生产总值达到26.40亿元，增长14.01%；全部工农业总产值(含中央、省属企业)达到53亿元，增长20.42%；财政收入完成2.48亿元，增长41.13%；全部工农业总产值、市属工业总产值、农业总产值、乡镇企业总产值、农民人均纯收入、社会商品零售额、财政收入等几项主要任务指标提前两年完成“八五”计划。全市经济实力位居全省前列。

坚持两手抓的方针，促进了社会全面进步。市委、市政府坚持两手抓两手都要硬的方针，在抓好改革开放和经济建设的同时，致力于推进社会全面进步，促进了各项事业发展。精神文明建设取得了新成果。以“三项活动”(注4)为重点的群众性精神文明建设活动深入开展，全市命名表彰文明单位标兵59个，文明村标兵9个，继续保持了省辖五城市“精神文明建设先进城市”称号；安定团结的政治局面不断巩固。“依法治市”方案层层得到贯彻落实。依法治市经验在全国性会议上得到肯定并做了交流。以深入开展“严打”斗争为重点，全面落实社会治安综合治理各项措施，全市社会治安局势一直平稳。把反腐败斗争与贯彻“勤俭建市”市策结合起来，反腐败斗争在领导干部廉洁自律、查处大要案、纠正行业不正之风这三方面取得初步成果，党风好转，民主政治建设进一步加强，军政、军民关系密切，我市被省上命名为“双拥模范城”；各项社会事业协调发展。落实“科教兴市”方案，科技教育发展较快。全市已普及了小学教育，农村中小学办学条件逐步改善，教师待遇不断提高。高等院校招生万人录取比例列全省前列。各类职业技术教育和成人教育迅速发展。1993年，完成科研项目168项，经验收鉴定的科技成果16项，其中国内先进1项，省内领先7项，省内先进8项。沿黄农科教一体化试验长廊、示范推广水稻旱育稀植、日光节能温室、70万亩水地、24万亩旱地粮食整乡科技承包等科技兴农措施得到落实，促进了农村经济综合开发，提高了农业整体效益。在科技兴企中，大力推广新技术、新工艺，加快技术改造，提高了经济效益。1993年，全市科技改造投资27572万元，其中市及市以下5960万元，比上年增长48%，全年竣工技改项目17项，开发新产品37个，创省、部优产品25项，优质产品产值率达到14.60%；计划生育工作率先实行科学管理，正在走上科学化、制度化、规范化的轨道，人口自然增长率为14.75‰，较好地完成了计划生育和人口增长控制计划；文化、广播、电视、体育、卫生等各项事业得到了相应发展，广播覆盖率达到91.09%，电视覆盖率达到62.98%，体育活动共参加省级以上比赛26项次，得奖牌52块。

白银市正在成为一座功能齐全的现代化城市。经过多年建设，尤其是白银市恢复成立以来，市委、市政府根据“统一规划、合理布局、综合开发、配套建设”的原则，按照“经济繁荣、服务方便、文明整洁、具有高原丘陵特色的现代化城市”的总体规划要求，加强城市建设和管理，使城市面貌大有改观，城市功能日臻完善。公用基础设施基本配套。金鱼公园的山上平湖和黄河之滨的水中公园及铜花、西山、银光公园，为人们提供了良好的休憩场所；红军会师纪念塔和寿鹿山、铁木山、哈思山、崛吴山、昌林山自然森林，北魏、唐、宋以来的石窟艺术、岩画、古寺及石林，是旅游者的胜地；电影院、剧院、文化宫、俱乐部、歌舞厅等文化娱乐场所遍布市内；市内各种档次的宾馆、饭店、饮食店可满足不同层次客人和消费者的需求；中、西医院遍布城乡，万人人均病床占有率居全国前列；以白银百货大楼、铜城商厦、文化路市场等十几处大型商场为代表的大中小商场、市场、购物中心，保证了群众的生活和消费需要。交通、通讯相当方便。白银以中川飞机场为航空港，市区距机场70多公里，可直航香港、北京、上海、广州等地。兰包、白宝铁路都从境内通过。境内公路有国道3条、省道2条、县乡道路50多条。市邮电程控电话、移动式电话均与全国联网，并可直拨国际长途电话。白银西区开发区建设初具规模。作为黄河上游多民族开发区和甘肃省省级开发小区的白银西区，它的建立使白银得到了难得的发展机遇，东西、南北干道已修通，水库、变电站正在修建，物资交易大厦、住宅区等一批基础设施正在建设之中，一系列小区开发优惠政策和“全程一站式”的服务，使西区具有良好的投资环境。目前，一批国有、集体、私营企业已在这里建成或正在建设，一批“三资”企业也在这里落了户。城市管理和环境保护出现了新局面。《白银市城市总体规划》得到有效实施，城市管理工作日益加强，环境保护、园林绿化和环境卫生管理工作达到了新水平，环境质量明显改善。至1993年底，城市建成面积达到50.5平方公里，城市人均住宅面积8.3平方米，建成区绿地覆盖率达到16.5%。1992年，朱镕基同志视察白银市时称赞：“白银市干净、整洁、卫生，在北方的城市里是很不错的”。

白银境内有比较丰富的自然资源。境内已探明的金属和非金属矿藏达30多种，其中14种在甘肃数一数二。会宁铁木山矿泉水，经国家级鉴定为天然优质饮用矿泉水，正在开发之中。除丰富的土地、水利、矿产、光热资源外，还有一批名土特产品，主要有：滩二毛裘皮。以靖远、景泰所产颇有名气，一般有黑白二色，毛纤长，丰厚美观，富有弹性，保暖防潮，轻便耐用，年产10万多张。大板黑瓜籽和籽瓜。主要产地靖远、景泰、平川和会宁北部。黑瓜籽板大平整、皮薄仁厚、籽饱油足，风味独特。全市年产籽瓜约1亿公斤，黑瓜籽250万公斤。扁豆。尤以会宁扁豆质量最佳。年产量约1200万公斤。发菜。谐音“发财”，是宴请佳宾的高级菜肴，倍受国内外市场欢迎。年产量约20吨左右。大红枣。多产于沿河川地，以靖远石门乡的小口、景泰县五佛乡的车门峡和白银区水川乡的关家沟所产为上乘。年产量约80万公斤。香水梨、冬果梨、苹果。盛产于沿河川灌区，年产量近3000万公斤。

注1【四项基本市策】白银市第三次党代会提出，把“改革强市、科教兴市、依法治市、勤俭建市”作为建设管理全市的四项基本市策。

注2【三不三互】白银市在处理地方政府和企业关系中，提出了“不比大小，互相尊重；不搞分割，互相协作；不分彼此，互相支持”的原则。1992年江泽民总书记视察白银时，称赞“三不三互”是正确处理地企关系的一个创造。

注3【新三路方针】白银市在指导农村经济工作中，根据“三西”建设前十年的“有水走水路，无水走旱路，水旱路不通另找出路”的“三路”方针，针对农村面临的新形势，提出了“坚持走兴水保水之路，大力改变农业生产基本条件；坚持走科教兴农之路，大力发展‘双高一优’商品农业；坚持走农村工业化之路，大力发展乡镇企业和第三产业”的“新三路方针”。

注4【精神文明建设三项活动】白银市在精神文明建设中，坚持在城市开展“三文明一满意”活动，在农村开展“三刹两一建”活动，在窗口服务行业开展“优质服务杯”竞赛活动。

平川区经济和社会发展概述

平川区是1985年10月随白银市恢复而成立的市辖区。现辖五乡（水泉、宝积、共和、种田、复兴）一镇（王家山）三个街道办事处（宝积路、电力路、红会路）31个居委会，51个村委会，297个村民小组。“平川”因濒临黄河面积约5万亩的旱平川而得名。

平川区位于白银市中部偏北，楔插于靖远县中部。南北大部分与靖远县接壤，东北与宁夏回族自治区海原县毗邻，东南与会宁县相接，西北与景泰县相界。平川境内矿产资源丰富，蕴藏着煤炭、沙金、铜、铁、银、陶土、石灰石等。煤炭矿床分布东西长约70公里，南北宽约10公里，总储量11.37亿吨，可采量8.53亿吨。黄河流经境内西北部32公里。境内有靖远矿务局、靖远火力发电厂、靖远陶瓷厂等中央、省、市大中型企业10多家。全区总面积2106.1平方公里，总人口156254人，其中非农业人口67069人。

1993年，在邓小平同志建设有中国特色社会主义理论和党的十四大精神指引下，全区各级党政组织团结和带领广大党员、干部和群众，坚定不移地贯彻执行党的基本路线，紧紧围绕建立社会主义市场经济体制，按照区上年初制定的经济发展上新台阶的奋斗目标，坚持“两手抓，两手都要硬”的方针，坚持“重农、兴工、建城、活商”的发展重点，同心同德，真抓实干，取得了社会秩序基本稳定、各项事业协调发展、经济持续增长、人民生活水平进一步提高的新成果。全区工农业总产值完成8630万元(90年价)，比上年增长26.6%；全区农民人均纯收入达到501元，比上年净增76元；区级财政收入达到1836万元，比上年增长72.5%；全区国内生产总值达到46476万元(90年价)，比上年增长12%。

【农村经济全面发展】全区把农业和农村工作放在首位，不断加强组织领导，狠抓各项基础建设。旱平川电灌一期工程竣工通水。全区新增水地900亩。总灌溉面积7.9万亩。建立健全农村社会化服务体系，建立“科技三村”14个，推广实用科技10项，科技承包面积达13.8万亩，有效地促进了农村经济的全面发展。1993年，农业总产值达到3877万元

(90年价),比上年增长9.4%,粮食总产量达到2190万公斤,比上年增长5.3%,连续五年创历史最高水平,荣获白银市粮食丰收一等奖。乡镇企业总数达到806个,总产值比上年翻了一番,达到1.00亿元。瓜菜、黑瓜籽、羔羊、大枣、渔业等商品基地建设有了新的进展。

【工业生产持续健康发展】在工业企业中,对原有企业进行技术改造,提高经济效益的同时,积极实施"双带整推"战略,坚持把科技帮带、促进科技进步放在首位,下大力继续抓好"双带"项目的落实,全区工业企业总数达到19个(乡及乡以上)。并以提高经济效益为中心,以贯彻《条例》,转换经营机制为重点,不断深化企业改革,加强企业管理,把握市场机遇,调整产业结构,产品质量明显提高,速度和效益同步增长,创造了建　区以来最高经营水平。1993年全区工业总产值达到4748万元(90年价),完成年计划的100.4%,比上年增长45.3%。其中,区办工业完成933万元,比上年增长65%;乡办工业完成1421万元,比上年增长39.5%;村及村以下工业完成2394万元,比上年增长42.2%。预算内国营工业企业经济效益显著提高,产品销售率达到88%,销售收入、实现利税较上年都有较大幅度的提高,保持了速度与效益的同步增长。

【国合商业改革步伐加快,市场建设不断完善】围绕建立适应社会主义市场经济要求的流通运行机制,一手抓商流改革,一手抓市场建设,在深化商流改革方面,积极推行"国有民营"、"社有自营"和承包　经营责任制。全区国营商业企业74个门店、柜组、车间已承包到人,占全门店的85%。供销企业87个门店、柜组实行"社有自营",占全门店的100%。在市场建设方面,建成了宝积路商业一条街、区百货大楼、周家地商场等一批商贸市场,市场体系得到进一步完善,促进了流通。1993全区商品零售总额达到10005万元,比上年增长15.7%。其中消费品零售总额9117万元;集市贸易成交额达到2632万元,比上年增长15.9%。

【交通、通讯事业发展迅速】经过多方努力。国道109线改扩建工程平川段按期完工,区、乡、村公路并网,促进了我区交通运输事业的发展,客运量达104万人次,货运量达到92万吨,分别比上年增长2.9%和41%,全区空分程控长市农合——自动电话由上年的2000门发展到4000门,无线寻呼、移动电话已开通使用。

【城市基础设施建设进一步改善】城建工作以基础设施建设为重点,努力完善城市综合服务功能。充分调动各方面的积极因素,加强城市道路、桥梁、供水供热、绿化等基础设施建设,使市容市貌有了较大改观。利民桥、长征东路非机动车道已开通使用;商业一条街混凝土路面铺修工程、兴平南路改造工程、长征东路罩面维修工程全部结束;长征东路绿化带人行道建设已基本完工;总投资250万元的长征西路大桥主体工程基本完工;中区上水工程铺设供水管道1531米;联片供热锅炉房扩建工程已竣工交付使用。

【科技、教育事业有了较大发展】科技工作按照经济建设依靠科学技术,科学技术面向经济建设的方针,以推广实用技术为重点,不断加快科学技术向生产力转化的步伐。一年来,共组织实施省、市、区科技项目15项。其中农业13项,工业2项;教育工作围绕贯彻《中国教育改革和发展纲要》精神,进一步深化教育改革,实行教育目标管理责任制,有力地促进了全区教育事业的发展。教学质量进一步提高,"四率"得到进一步巩固。全年向大中专院校输送学生304名,比上年增加102名。教学条件不断改善。省、市、区共投入171.5万元(其中:区上49万元,乡村49.5万元),新建、改建、维修校舍2637平方米;平川小学已建成开始招生。教育结构更趋合理,职业教育、成人教育、岗位技术培训不断发展。尊师重教的风尚正在形成。区上在财力十分紧张的情况下,拿出10万元用于教师建房补助;拿出29个农转非指标,优先解决了三十年以上教龄教师家属子女及民办教师农转非问题。

【文化、广播、电视、体育、卫生等事业迅速发展】坚持社会效益第一、服务经济建设的原则,以"热爱平川、建设平川"等系列教育为重点,加强精神文明建设,促进了人民群众思想觉悟。文化素质和健康水平的提高。文化工作以"扫黄"为重点,从严打击和查处贩制淫秽录像书刊等扰乱文化市场的非法行为,加强了文化市场的管理,保证了文化市场的健康发展。文化基础设施建设进一步加强。文化馆已建成投入使用,露天剧场主体工程基本建成,广播电视事业不断发展,开通了中央电视台第三套节目的转播,不断提高平川电视台自办节目的制作质量。全区广播电视覆盖率达到95%以上。体育工作以开展群众性体育活动、提高竞技水平为重点,不断加强学校体育工作和体育队伍建设,广泛开展各种群众性体育活动。卫生工作以传染病、地方病、职业病的防治为重点,狠抓妇幼保健和计划免疫工作。全区儿童计划免疫四苗接种率达到96.2%,覆盖率达到93.78%。医疗条件逐步改善,区人民医院、共和乡卫生院住院部已全面开工建设,水泉乡卫生院门诊部、区鼠防队工作用房已竣工投入使用。

【计划生育的国策得到了进一步贯彻落实】计划生育工作以纯女户结扎为突破口,"二胎平茬"为重点,注重加强表、卡、册科学化管理,通过经常性工作和两次大规模的突击活动,有力地推动了全区计划生育工作。人口自然增长率控制在12.8‰。

之内。

【全区名特土产丰富】1993年总投资105万元，建成了"平川酒厂"。并用境内屈吴山优质矿泉水酿制的"神台"酒已投放市场，年产量达72吨。其它名特土产还有黑瓜籽、黄河蜜瓜、西瓜、二毛裘皮等。黑瓜籽以油足板大而著称，年产40万公斤，主要分布在共和、宝积、水泉3乡。黄河蜜瓜和西瓜以皮薄、水份足、含糖量高、味鲜而颇负盛名，年产分别达到1——2万吨。二毛裘皮，皮板厚实，质地良好，色泽鲜美，毛圈弯曲，素有"九道环"之美称，是传统的出口产品，年产5000张，全区5乡均有生产。

现任主要领导：

中共平川区委书记：

王民强 （兼区人大主任）

平川区人民政府区长：孙晓霖

政协平川区委员会主席：马 凯

中共平川区纪律检查委员会书记：

房全扬

（李家庆 张克诚）

会宁县经济和社会发展概述

【自然概况】会宁县位于甘肃省中部，白银市南端，地处北纬35°33′至36°26′，东经104°31′至105°34′之间。南北长约114公里，北部东西宽约90公里，南部东西宽约40公里，呈倒葫芦状，总面积6439平方公里。

会宁县是陇西黄土高原的组成部分，地势大致由东南向西北倾斜，山脉多南北走向，平均海拔2025米，整个地形大致可分为梁峁山地、河谷川地和北部残原三种类型，可概括为"七川八塬九道梁"。境内矿藏资源贫乏，现已开发利用的只有石灰石、芒硝，正在开发利用的有铁木山优质矿泉水。另外，土高山乡的玻璃石、石膏、杨崖集乡的铝矾土等矿藏，有待进一步勘探，并开采利用。境内有祖厉河水质苦咸，地下水主要集中在南部，是一个水资源非常贫乏的严重缺水县。

会宁县属温带半干旱气候，降水北少南多，北部年平均降水量312.8毫米，南部年平均降水量432.7毫米，且集中在七、八、九这三个月里，占年总降水量的58%左右。而年蒸发量达1800毫米，故干旱是会宁的主要灾害，其次霜灾、冰雹、风灾、洪灾、病虫害也比较突出。

全县辖32个乡，1个镇，350个村(居)民委员会，2638个村(居)民小组。1993年末总户数10.45万户，总人口51.45万人，其中农业人口49.68万人，占总人口的96.6%，全县有汉、回、蒙、满、藏、东乡等6个民族，汉族占96.7%。

会宁县早年在4000多年前的新石器时代就有人类在这里生息繁衍。农牧业生产历史修悠久。可栽培的粮食作物有4科15种，油料作物有4科5种，还可栽培瓜果、蔬菜、大麻、甜菜等多种经济作物。人工种植药材有39种，野生药材有31种。有野生荒山牧草68种，其中优良牧草9种。林业资源有20种32属，85个品种。

会宁境内10余处古遗址出土文物属仰韶半山文化；会宁自古是"丝绸之路"的重镇；1936年10月8日，中国工农红军一、二、四方面军在会宁会师，从此，会宁成了现代中国革命史上的纪念地。

【经济发展概况】1993年，会宁县围绕建立社会主义市场经济体制的总目标，按照县第十次党代会提出的"学习文件换脑筋，狠抓紧粮食保稳定，瞅准项目搞开发，寻计问策抓启动，改革开放活流通，领导牵头鼓实劲"的工作思路，全面实施"1785"区域经济开发工程，即抓好粮食生产这一根本；抓好水、田、电、路、林、市场、城镇设施七项基本建设；抓好优质小杂粮基地、油料基地、畜牧基地，果品基地、瓜菜基地、花椒基地、中药材基地、烤烟基地等八个基地建设；抓好农副产品、加工业、建筑建材业、采矿业、房地产开发业、商流服务业等五大支柱产业。认真落实发展乡镇企业的"3358"工程。全县工农业生产总值完成30739万元，较1992年增长12.78%，其他各项指标都完成了市上下达的计划任务。

农业全面丰收，农村经济稳步发展。1993年，全县粮食总产量达到13050万公斤，占计划的100.38%，比1992年增长17,57%，创历史最高水平。农业总产值达到22509万元，占计划的101.39%，比1992年增长11.98%。全县农民人均纯收入达到405.32元，占计划的100.08%，比1992年净增55.30元，增长15.8%。农业投入也不断增加，全年发放农贷资金3473.8万元，支农资金155.6万元。农业基本条件继续改善，当年新增水地有效面积0.2万亩，新增保灌面积0.1万亩，水地有效面积累计达到23.66万亩；新增"三田"面积4.1万亩，其中百亩以上片13处，1650亩，"三田"面积累计达到97.73万亩；架设6——10千伏农电线路39.9公里，新通电17个村，179个社，6367户，使通电的村累计达276个，通电的社累计达1572个，分别占全县总村、社的78,9%和59.6%。公路建设重点为国道312线改道施工创造一切便利条件，同时大抓了现有公路的养护和上等上级工作。林业建设走生态效益型路子，大力发展果、杏、花椒等经济林，完成造林面积2.08万亩，使森林面积累计达85.51万亩，并集中力量绿化、美化了县城东山和桃花，加强了对铁木山省级自然保护区的建设管理。乡镇企业继续高速发展，总产值首次突破亿元大关，达到10539万元，比1992年增长48.8%，涌现出产值过100万元的村6个，超过300万元的企业6

户。乡镇企业总户数达596个，从业人员1.21万人。

工业生产加快转换经营机制，提高效益，保持了良好的发展态势。全县工业企业393家，其中国有工业企业9家，县属集体工业企业14家，乡镇工业72家，其它村办及个体工业企业297家。列入市、县计划的主要工业产品有：原煤、元明粉、水泥、机制砖、地毯、印刷品及S195油箱等。1993年，县上对工业企业通过强化基础管理，调整产业、产品结构，积极开发新、优、特产品，加快转换经营机制，加强综合管理等措施，企业整体素质明显提高。工业总产值达8230万元，比1992年增长15%，完成销售收入1743.4万元，比1992年增长7.8%，完成利润总额54,5万元，比1992年增长186.8%。绝大多数产品建立在以本县农副产品资源为主要原料的基础上，都够增加市场的有效供给。化学投影仪已列入省级新产品开发项目，刷子系列产品、S1100油箱、消声器、自动卸料拖车、90道机拉洗地毯、杏仁露等6个产品被列入市级新产品开发项目。

市场建设加快，商流逐步活跃。全年共新建和扩建农贸市场5处，全县市场总数达32个，年交易额达3078万元。新堡子农贸市场为省列集镇建设七年规划项目，总投资870万元，建筑面积40000平方米，已完成27000平方米，市场主体已经建成，正式投入使用。国合商业企业积极开展"二次创业"和"重振雄风"活动，大胆改革，推行"国有民营"。"社有自营"，企业内功得到增强。1993年全县完成社会商品零售总额13354万元，比1992年增长14.3%。

【城镇建设进度加快】城镇建设正在有计划、按步骤实施。1000门长、市、农合一自动拨号电话已与全国联网，可以直拨国内外，为发展会宁商品经济创造了条件。全年新增楼房5栋，楼房累计达到100栋。会师路下水工程已经竣工，路面整修、拓宽正在加紧进行。城区卫生状况有了很大改观，全年共筹措落实新建和改建16处公厕资金18万多元，已建成公厕3处。位于县城东南1公里处，国道312线和省道靖天公路交叉路段的桃花山第三产业经济开发区，规模面积40.91公顷，地势平坦。电力。电讯、供水等设施齐全，依托交通，发展第三产业十分便利。目前，开发建设工作进展顺利，报名投资的单位和个人50多家，意向性投资额1800多万元，现有9家开工建设，有的已建成营业。

【各项社会事业迅速发展】教育事业全面发展。全县完成小学招生13203人，初中招生6241人，高中招生1714人，成人招生40人，幼儿招生522人，均达到计划要求。学龄儿童入学率达到98.5%，全县扫除青壮年文盲通过市级验收，提前两年实现了普及初等义务教育，并顺利通过了省级验收。向大中专院校输送新生1143名，首次突破千人大关。全县集资办学的热潮日益高涨，多渠道筹措建设资金366.45万元，新建、改建、扩建校舍49450平方米，使全县学校危房降到了4%以下。学校教学水平和教师素质也有了明显提高。

医疗卫生事业和防疫保健工作不断得到加强，地方病和传染病的暴发流行得到了有效控制。儿童免疫接种率基本普及。全社会集资办医，使农村医疗卫生条件有了进一步改善。

科技工作重点实施"5510"科技承包，旱地春小麦新品种选育、"蓄水覆盖丰产沟"旱农耕作栽培技术、烤烟生产技术研究、引黄灌区高优新果园建设、农业技术综合试验示范乡等五个科研、示范"星火计划"和攻关项目都进度顺利，成果推广较快，为发展全县农村商品经济做出了贡献。全年共培训各类实用技术人才7.98万人，完成科技承包55项(次)，承包总面积达420万亩，累计增产粮食8500万公斤。

计划生育和其他各项社会事业都有了较快发展。特别是计划生育工作，坚持"两个三不"方针，坚持经常性工作与突击活动相结合，全年落实计划生育四项手术12282例，其中结扎5712例，人口出生率为20.58‰，自然增长率为15.84‰，分别比市上下达的控制指标降低了0.42和0.06个千分点。

【名特土产】会宁县的土特产十分丰富。以东南部二阴山区和中北部山塬区为主产区和豌豆、扁豆、莜麦、荞麦、谷糜等多优小杂粮，种植面积达33万亩，总产量达5千万公斤。洋芋年播种面积20万亩以上，总产量约765万多公斤，各种果品年产量696万多公斤，黄豆年产量约500万公斤，大板凤眼黑瓜籽年产量达104.71万公斤，新添堡乡肉牛年存栏6012头，出栏2080头。其他土特产，如杏仁、滩羊皮、发菜，加工产品、如燕麦片、果脯、杏仁露、地毯、亚麻、粉丝等都颇受国内外消费者的青睐。近年发现的铁木山矿泉水，量大质优，年涌出量达7万吨以上，含有对人体有益的多种微量元素，1991年4月通过国家级鉴定，被命名为含锶的硫酸氯化物——钠钙型优质天然矿泉水，属国内少有。

现任主要领导：
中共会宁县委书记：胡永亮
会宁县人大常委会主任：杨恺
会宁县人民政府县长：张廷魁
政协会宁县委员会主席：王价
中共会宁县纪律检查委员会书记：霍歆甲

（中共会宁县县委政研室：周雅昭　杨旭）

靖远县经济和社会发展概述

【自然概况】靖远县地处甘肃中部，位于东经104°18′～105°18′，北纬36°10′～37°15′之间，南北长135公里，东西宽120公里，南部与榆中县、会宁县相连，北部和东北部与宁夏回族自治区中卫县、海原县接壤，西部与白银区、景泰县交界，中间楔插白银市平川区。全县总面积5809.4平方公里。靖远县辖地属黄土高原丘陵沟壑区和干旱草原区，地势大致西低东高，由南向北倾斜，平均海拔1397.8米，最高海拔哈思山主峰大峁槐山海拔3017米。干旱多风降水稀少是该县的主要自然特点，年平均降水量241.5毫米，蒸发量1563.9毫米，年平均气温8.7℃，日照2494.7小时，年无霜期189天左右，作物生长期200天左右。现有耕地113.18万亩，草地30.77万亩，园地2.44万亩，林地17.07万亩，水域11.44万亩。人口密度72.5人/平方公里。矿藏丰富，已探有煤、铜、金、银、锰、铁、石灰石、石膏、稀土、沸石、高岭土、石英石、重金石等资源，尤以煤储量大、品位高、分布广。水资源充裕，黄河流经靖远10乡1镇154公里，流域面积100.49平方公里，水利设施完善，利于发展农业。交通便利，县城距铜城白银市67公里，距省会兰州158公里，铁路、公路纵横，109线国道横穿全境。全县共有1个镇，20个乡，8个居委会，174个村民委员会，1082个合作社。1993年末共有74536户42.15万人，其中农村人口38.62万人，人口自然增长率为15.4‰。有汉、回、满、蒙、藏等18个民族，其中少数民族占总人口的1.1%。县政府驻地城关镇。

【历史沿革】靖远县早在新石器时代就有人类繁衍生息。春秋时为西戎地，秦伐西戎后属北地郡。西汉属安定郡，东汉改为武威郡。三国属魏之域。西晋时前凉因之。苻秦灭前凉后(公元367年)，以鹖阴为平凉郡，自前凉历前秦、后秦、后凉、北凉、南凉到西秦，都属武威郡。西魏时设会州，周武帝保定二年(公元562年)改为会宁防。隋初置会宁镇，大业二年(公元606年)改为凉川县。唐时置西会州，后改为会宁郡、会州。广德(公元763年)至宋初陷于吐蕃，改为汝遮。北宋元符二年(公元1099年)复置会州(州治在今靖远县城)，辖敷文、会川两县，南宋建炎四年(公元1130年)为金所占，改敷文为保川县。贞祐五年(公元1217年)归於西夏，迁州治于会川城，设新会州。金破西夏，收复了旧会州，隶属巩昌都总帅府，明洪武三年(公元1369年)废会州，并保川於会宁，正统二年(公元1437年)，置靖虏卫，属陕西都司；清初未设县治，由卫所单管。雍正八年(公元1730年)改为靖远县，隶巩昌府。后改隶于兰州府。靖远名字的意思为安定边地。民国初隶属于兰州道，北伐后直隶省政府。

解放以后，成立了县人民政府，隶属定西专区，1960年至1963年划归白银市管辖，1964年复归定西专区。1985年8月白银市成立，又划归白银市管辖，同时划出宝积镇和宝积、共和、水泉、种田、复兴五乡，成立平川区。

【发展现状】1993年，靖远县国民经济和社会各项事业都得到全面发展。全县社会总产值达到51415万元，国民收入生产额23069万元，工农业总产值32482.41万元。

农业生产，近年来，县委、县政府针对靖远干旱多灾的实际，按照“因地制宜，分类指导”的原则，紧抓“两西”建设机遇，大搞农田基本建设，兴修了兴堡子川、刘川、三场塬三大水利翻身工程，进一步完善农村家庭联产承包责任制，建立健全农业社会化服务体系，实行科学种田，推动了农村经济的繁荣与活跃。一是农业基本条件得到改善，至1993年底，全县有效灌溉面积增加到45.2万亩，农村人均1.18亩，其中保灌面积37.52万亩，另有砂田14.32万亩，梯田9.94万亩，沟坝地5.89万亩。建成机井139眼，水窖5.68万眼。万亩以上灌区发展到10个，千亩以上灌区发展到38个。二是科学种田水平提高快。地膜覆盖、带状种植、配方施肥等关键性的农业科技措施得到广泛应用，种植业品种优良化已基本达到，水地带套率达100%(除水稻)，地膜覆盖逐步实现由水地向旱地发展、由“白色”向“蓝色”转化，1993年，建成冬暖式日光温室441个254亩，“双千田”8000亩，吨粮田4.2万亩，水稻旱育稀植2万亩。三是区域经济开发成效显著。已建成蔬菜、黑瓜籽、苹果、渔业、水稻、大枣、羔羊、小杂粮等八个商品生产基地。四是农业结构趋于合理。种植业中粮经比例达到8.6∶1.4。1993年全县农作物播种面积达99.02万亩，粮食总产量达12033.14万公斤，创历史最高水平，连续六年获得丰收。农业总产值增加到19077.41万元。在农业总产值中，林牧渔的比重由1978年的30%提高到32.3%，森林面积达17.07万亩，林业产值35.92万元。畜牧业产值5785.86万元；渔业产值96.05万元。

地方工业通过贯彻《条例》、《企业法》，完善各种承包责任措施。企业经营机制日趋完善，内部结构趋向合理。工业部门建设扭补项目，引进技术，更新设备，产品质量、经济效益显著提高。全县工业企业发展到244家(全民、集体)，现有职工2655人，固定资产原值7164万元，净值6522.5万元。1993年投资1326万元，建成硫酸铜、釉面砖、餐巾纸、塑编等10条扭补工业生产线，使全县工业总产值增加到13405万元，实现利润649.4万元，税金完成287.5万元，新增财政收入284.1万元。一个以轻纺、煤炭、建材、建筑、采矿、农副产品加工、运输服务等行业相配套的工业体系初步形成。另外驻靖远的甘肃稀土公司、靖远电厂、二七九厂、靖远矿务局、风雷机械厂、春光厂、磷盐化工厂等中央、省市属企业贯彻“双带整推”的经济战略方针，对本地经济发展起了推动作用。

乡镇企业，1993年，全县乡镇企业发展到804户，从业人员23000人，总产值突破3亿元大关，达到31000万元，总收入达到24903.9万元。产值过千万元的乡有5个，过百万元的村有40个，同时建设了刘川乡镇企业群体开发小区，出现了首家“三资”企业。乡镇企业已成为全县经济的“半壁江山”。

靖远自古以来就是丝绸古道上的“旱码头”。目前，以县城为中心，以年吞吐量亿公斤的大型蔬菜批发市场为龙头，以各类工业品、日用小商品贸易市场为主要内容的流通网络已初步形成。至1993年底，全县商业、饮食业、服务业机构发展到336个，从业人员2507人，城乡个体商业1927户，从业人员2829人。1993年，共投资147万元，建成4个市场5029平方米，使各类市场总数发展到30个92571平方米。国营集体商业普遍实行了国有民营，承包租赁等措施，完善内部管理机制，增设网点，提高了效益。现有批发零售网点336个，完成总购进13200.2万元，总销售17048.9万元。社会商品零售总额完成10548.5万元，外贸出口创汇105万美元。

1993年，县级财政收入完成1373万元，比上年增加368万元，其中工商税收完成1025万元，比上年增加365万元。银行信贷积极为经济建设服务，1993年各类存款累计达21101万元，共发放各类贷款7337.3万元。

人民生活水平显著提高。1993年，职工年人均收入2808.9元，农民人均纯收入540.21元，比上年净增80元。城乡人民群众储蓄总额达13521万元。随着收入的增加，彩电、电风扇、洗衣机等高档消费品涌入千家万户，据统计，全县共有电视机33810台，其中彩电7979台，有录像机226台，收录机35775台，城镇洗衣机、电风扇已得到普及，在农村有洗衣机8151台，冰箱330架，自行车87907辆。

交通邮电，109线靖远段改造工程已经完成，同时建暗门、乌兰两座铁路、公路立交桥，完成投资170多万元。县乡公路已发展到250公里，20个乡，全部通了客车，一个以县城为中心，主线铁路、公路为主体，县乡公路、乡村道路相连接的交通网络已初具规模。电讯服务方便，2000门程控自动电话已开通，住宅电话发展到900多部，每百人拥有电话0.42部。

【社会事业】教育，有中小学校516所，其中：中学47所，在校学生24877人，小学462所，在校学生66074人，农业职中3所，在校学生473人，幼儿园6所，教师进修学校1所。共有教职员工4000人，1993年全县共集资100.7万元，新建、维修改造校舍13994平方米，添置课桌凳3028套，办学条件改善较大。适龄儿童入学率99.37%，巩固率99.21%，普及率99.18%，毕业率98.96%，1986年全县普及了初等义务教育，1993年共向大中专院校输送学生1143人，是恢复高考制度以来最多的一年。

文化广播，现建成广播电台1座，有线电视台1 座，电视差转台12个，卫星地面接收站3座，电视覆盖率达70%。现有文化站(中心)19个，农村电影放影队63个，舞厅5家，县级以上文物保护单位60处，馆藏文物1200件，图书55000余册，1993年共举办群众性的文化活动12次，参加人员约40万人(次)。

卫生单位已发展到365个，其中全民单位28个，卫生技术人员1213人，其中专业卫生技术人员623人，乡村医生、卫生员、接生员725人，个体医生173人，平均每千人有卫生技术人员2.9人。1993年建成县医院住院部大楼1座3919.54平方米，病床增至575张，平均每千人1.41张。

科技，建立健全了县乡村社四级科普网络，成立科普协会20个，专业技术学会、研究会49个，科技示范户发展到5053户，被省、市、县树立的科技村20个。农口有职称的科技人才225人，其中高中级职称的66人，初级职称159人。有乡村农民技术员1064人。1993年共举办科技培训班360期，参加2万多人(次)。1990年至1993年，实施科技示范推广项目46个，已有17个项目通过省市鉴定验收。

【名特土产】哈思梨：产於石门乡哈思堡，果质细腻，味香甜，切开后隔夜不变色。解放前为敬上佳品，但产量甚微。冬果梨：年产40—50万公斤，这种梨果质细嫩，色泽鲜黄，含糖量高。香水梨：年产约250万公斤。此梨存放到入冬后，变甜变软，果色呈深紫色，肉薄汁多，香甜凉爽。大红枣：含糖量在30%以上，年产14万公斤，是益寿健体的滋补品。黑瓜籽：年产约75万公斤，其中以高湾、大芦野糜川出产者最佳，瓣大、油足，远销国内外。羔羊：产于石门、双龙等乡，年产约4万只，尤以石门石山一带所产为佳。发菜：产于五合、北雎等乡，年产2000公斤。黄河蜜瓜：年产约200万公斤，香甜可口，为夏季消暑佳品。

现任主要领导：

中共靖远县委书记：何水清

靖远县人大常委会主任：杜永春

靖远县人民政府县长：赵得琮

政协靖远县委员会主席：杜培灿

中共靖远县纪律检查委员会书记：王美文

(靖远县经济政策研究室)

景泰县经济和社会发展概述

景泰县是甘肃中部18个干旱县之一，位于腾格里沙漠南缘，地处甘、宁、蒙三省交接地带。属典型的温带干旱大陆性气候。总面积5432平方公里，辖12乡2镇，总人口20多万。县境内有大型国营条山农场和65个省、市机关及所属厂矿农场。

1993年，全面完成了确定的目标和任务。完成社会总产值4.2亿元，国民收入1.76亿元，工农业总产值2.79亿元，财政收入2000万元，超额完成了省政府下达的1775万元的扭补收入任务。全县呈现出农业丰收、工业发展、商业活跃、财政超收、社会进步、上下团结的可喜局面。

【景电一二期工程与农业发展】景泰县在总人口20多万中，农业人口就占了90%，是典型的农业县。县境东部虽有黄河过境110公里，但河床低下，人们只能“望河兴叹”。干旱曾使景泰的农业发展有过极其艰难的历史，而今却有着极为丰富的内函。1969年10月，在党中央、国务院的关怀下，在省委、省政府的直接领导下，属全国首例的多级高扬程提灌景电一期工程动工兴建，1974年竣工，实现灌溉面积30万亩，安置移民6.5万人。为景泰的扶贫开发奠定了基础。被称为温饱工程。继景电一期灌区建成后，被称为致富工程的景电二期工程於1984年7月动工修建。经过广大水利工作者和全县人民的艰苦奋斗，1993年主体工程完工。这项工程东西长约130公里，南北宽25公里，从景泰五佛乡盐寺提水后，以平均提水高度460米，流量18立方米/秒，经过30座泵站和100.57公里的总干渠，横跨景泰、古浪两县，实现灌溉面积52万亩(景泰县20万亩、古浪县32万亩)。二期景泰灌区新建2乡1镇，181个行政村，安置移民5.13万人。景电一、二期灌区把袂联臂形成总面积80万亩的灌溉规模，成为目前国内灌溉面积最大的电力提灌工程体系。世界粮食计划署评估团专家称，工程无论是设计施工还是管理效益，都是世界第一流的。

以景电一、二期灌区为主体，中小提灌、井泉灌溉、沿河自流灌溉为补充的灌溉网络，撑起了景泰种植业的基本骨架。灌区内地势平坦，光照时间长，是全国除西藏高原和柴达木盆地以外，光能资源最丰富的地区之一。昼夜温差大，属二季不足，一季有余地区，适宜于各类农作物生长。县上根据本县地理条件，加强宏观调控，按照“规划区域、建立基地、抓好经济支柱产业”的农建方针，加大景电一期灌区间套复带面积和经济作物面积，形成高产、稳产田基地；追加二期灌区有效投入，形成商品粮规模经营基地；培植沿河灌区以高效节能日光温室为代表的瓜果蔬菜基地。景泰在着力建设粮食基地的同时，更注重了科学技术的推广。1993年，全县种植作物品种优良率达90%以上，各类间套复带面积24万亩，由县农技中心牵头进行的21万亩水地整乡科技双向承包和8万亩高效田建设，3万亩小麦、胡麻根腐病综合防治，1万亩苹果幼树早结果，2200亩水稻旱育稀植，573亩高效节能日光温室等实用技术的推广都取得了突破性进展，提高了农业综合开发的能力。粮食总产量达1.79亿斤，人均占有粮食990斤。通过粮食、供销等渠道收购的各种农产品8802万斤，农民实现农业收入4200万元，人均240多元。景泰县的区域性粮食基地建设正走向辉煌。

林业发展方兴未艾。位于腾格里沙漠边缘的景泰县，倍受风沙侵害，县委、县政府制定了“西涵水源，北御风沙，先林后农，以林保农”的建设方针。坚定地走“要种田，先育林”，“农跟水走，林在农先”的林业发展路子。在造林工程中，抓住国家林业部“三北”局将景泰县列为全国5个生态经济型防护林体系重点建设示范区之一的大好机遇，实行国家投苗，农民投劳，机关干部义务植树的有效措施，把全县的植树造林活动进行得既轰轰烈烈又扎扎实实。近几年，由于二期灌区与腾格里沙漠接壤，风灾严重，县上一直把二期灌区的封沙育林放在十分突出的地位。实行政策重心倾斜和资金投入倾斜。完成用材林、经济林3.7万亩，防风林带8万亩。1993年造林总面积累计达到21.4万亩，总产值178万元。荣获国家林业部颁发的“绿色长城”奖。由于灌区农用防护林体系逐步建成，不仅有效地控制了风沙的侵害，而且使本县自然环境、农田小气候得到明显改善。成为省城兰州抵御风沙的重要屏障。

景泰县有三分之二的地区是二阴山区，牧业开发具备得天独厚的优越条件。县委、县政府以“山区养牛养羊，灌区养猪养鸡”为指导思想，千方百计地多渠道扶持养殖户。尤其在山区，养羊已成为广大农户脱贫致富奔小康的有效途径，羊只的多少成为人们视其富裕程度的一个重要标准。二毛裘皮和沙毛裘皮以其板厚毛美成为景泰的主要特产品。1993年羊只存栏达18.8万只，大牲畜2.8万头。在灌区兴办百头猪场16个，规模养殖户2700户，生猪存栏7.3万头，养鸡25万只，总产值达3352万元。畜牧业的蓬勃发展，不仅带来了直接的经济效益，相当数量的积肥又为种植业注入了发展后劲，形成了“以牧养农，以林护农，农、林、牧并举”的经济发展良性循环格局。

【地方工业】景泰的地方工业起步较晚，但发展很快。景泰县有丰富的矿产资源：已探明煤的储量7亿吨，石膏5000万吨，石灰石7000万吨，白盐110万吨，铜217万吨已开发利用。还有一定品位的金、银、铁、锰、锡、铝土等矿产资源，不仅储量丰富，而且品质优良。景泰县有十分便利的交通运输条件。包兰铁路横穿县境数百里，途经13个火车站，使地方大宗的工农业产品通过铁路源源不断地运往各地。省道705（皋兰一银川）公路与铁路平行穿过县境，以县城条山镇为中心，有13条447.6公里的县乡公路，与毗邻的兰州、白银、天祝、古浪、内蒙古的左旗、宁夏的中卫连接贯通。

景泰县委、政府在发展地方工业的问题上依仗丰富的自然资源优势，便利的交通条件和可靠的水电能源保障，始终坚持以“三个有利于”为标准，敢想、敢说、敢创、敢干，积极地跑项目、引资金、抓落实、求效益。短短几年功夫，地方工业迅速崛起。至目前，景泰工业已基本形成了以煤炭开发为主的能源工业体系；以羊毛、皮革、亚麻为原料的轻纺造纸工业体系；以电石、原盐为原料的化工工业体系；以水泥、石膏为龙头的建材工业体系；以农付土特产品为原料的加工工业体系。

景泰县共有国营企业18个，职工3000多人，行业门类齐全，成龙配套并具有一定的技术水平。1993年以“三项制度”改革为重点，全面贯彻落实《条例》，加快了转换企业经营机制的步伐。确立了“干部能上能下，工人能出能进”，分配上“以岗定薪，薪随岗变”等一系列自我约束机制，从而增加了企业活力。年总产值达1.43亿元，利税1199万元。属全国三大石膏基地之一的县石膏矿，产品销往华北、华东、东北等地区，并出口朝鲜和东南亚一些国家。地方国营景泰水泥厂生产的“寿鹿牌”425号硅酸盐水泥，连续6年荣获省优产品称号。县国营高强石膏制品总厂的石膏深加工形成规模，有普通石膏粉、高强混合石膏粉和增强型豪华石膏板三条生产线。尤其是与台商合资建成的增强型豪华石膏板生产线，打开了景泰引进外资的局面。其产品获“全国石膏行检行评优等品优质产品奖第一名”和“省级新产品开发奖”等荣誉，并畅销江西、福建、深圳等沿海城市，成为景泰经济又一个支柱产业。

景泰乡镇企业在全县工农业经济运行中举足轻重，已具备了雄厚的经济实力。仅1993年一年就筹措资金2450万元，在所立116个项目中，续建、新建投产45个，完成技改项目8个，起动停产、半停产企业7个。1993年乡镇企业发展到969家，年产值1.62亿元，占工农业总产值2.79亿元的58%，实现利润564万元。称为“半壁江山”已成定局。

【商贸、城建及社会事业】1993年相继建成了景泰商业大厦、景服批发市场、二轻公司营业楼等一批重点商业项目。在城区3个市场、12个集贸点的基础上，新规划的黄河路个体商业一条街，兴泉、四个山农贸市场等市场设施建设进展顺利。各国营商流企业“国有民营”，“社有自营”的机制转换进行的鸣锣齐鼓。私营企业发展到22户，注册资金335万元。个体工商户如雨后春笋，发展到1955户，从业人员2931人，注册资金900万元，成交额达到1500多万元。全县社会商品零售总额逾亿元。

景泰县城一条山镇，是1969年在景电一期工程指挥部的基础上，从芦阳镇迁址后陆续建设的新型城镇。当年仅是包兰铁路上的一个小火车站和几家零星的商店而已。如今，已拥有2万多城镇居民。楼房鳞次栉比。省县机关、企事业单位星罗棋布。交通四通八达，工商业兴旺繁荣。成为全县政治、经济、文化和景电灌溉农业的指挥中心。1993年，城镇基础设施建设进入高峰年。共完成投资500多万元，建成景泰宾馆等大楼15栋。完成安装城区排水二程管道2776米。投资24万元，配套建成一座景泰浴池。开通四条城区公路。完成城区和部分乡镇程控自动电话安装。整个城镇的水、电、路和通讯、服务设施大为改善。

经济基础的发展促进了上层建筑的发展。1993年全县拥有各类科技人员、教育工作者、医疗工作者共4799人，占全县人口的2.4%。全县各级各类学校295所，形成了一个普及9年制义务教育，教师进修，职业教育以及县乡党校培训各级党政干部的教育体系。全县有各类文化事业单位24个，先后建成了广播电视台、电视差转台、教育电视台和电视卫星地面接收站，电视覆盖率达到88%，有线电视台已在建，局部开通试播。从根本上丰富了城乡人民的文化娱乐活动，促进了精神文明建设。全县建立起了县、乡、村三级医疗和防疫网络，仅县城就有人民医院、中医院等7家保健防疫机构，医务人员401人。普遍开设了门类齐全的诊断医治科室，并拥有了B超、心、脑电图等高科技医疗设备和一定的技术水平，创造了许多高疑难病症医治成功的事例。全县乡村医疗机构已发展到162家，医务人员405名，与县级医疗机构一道组成了庞大的医疗系统。

【条山农场】现有耕地7.26万亩，400多名职工，他们依托肥沃而集中连片的土地优势，致力于农业规模开发，开辟了17520亩的啤酒花、啤酒大麦生产基地，以优质高产受到全国各地用户的欢迎。建成4200亩名优果品生产基地，其“短枝新红星”苹果获农业部农垦司评比第一名。他们顺应市场经济规律，着眼于开发场办企业，建成了年产1000吨优质白酒的“条山酒厂”；年产5万件“泰玉牌”精纺纯羊毛衫厂；年产4.4万吨的水泥厂等一批加工企业。其中，条山酒厂的系列产品“条山玉液”荣获“布鲁塞尔国际名酒最高金奖”和“香港博览会金奖”。“泰玉牌”

高档精纺纯羊毛衫获省优部优。种植业、林果业和场办企业成为条山农场的三大支柱产业。1993年工农业总产值达到4704.8万元,创利税896万元。尤以名优产品取胜形成其开发特色。

现任主要领导:

中共景泰县委书记:王敬文

景泰县人大常委会主任:张有礼

景泰县人民政府县长:梁汝山

政协景泰县委员会主席:蒋崇廉

中共景泰县纪律检查委员会书记:吴隆华

(中共景泰县委政策研究室:张应祯)

金昌市

中共金昌市委书记:赵俊谋

金昌市人大常委会主任:赵敬中

金昌市人民政府市长:赵俊谋

政协金昌市委员会主席:陆佩

金昌市经济和社会发展概述

【自然概况】

位置和面积　金昌是甘肃省的一座新兴的工业城市,被誉为祖国的镍都。始建于1981年,现辖一县一区,即永昌县和金川区,全市总面积9600平方公里,总人口40.10万人,其中非农业人口16.40万人。金昌地处河西走廊东部,祁连山北麓。东连武威,西邻张掖,南托古长城,与肃南裕固族自治县和青海省门源回族自治县毗邻,北靠戈壁滩,同内蒙古自治区阿拉善右旗接壤。东西长140公里,南北宽130公里。

地势　以山地、平原为主、与戈壁沙漠东西展开,相间排列,由西南向东北倾斜,形成三个隆起地带,两个高平原,一块残丘戈壁沙漠区,平均海拔1500米左右。南部祁连山地,山峦起伏,雄伟挺拔,主峰冷龙岭,海拔4442米,终年积雪,为境内最高峰,山间分布天然林,高山草甸,植被覆盖率达75%,为优良林牧区;中部高平原,平均海拔1800米,平坦狭长,素有走廊"蜂腰"之称,亦系平坦狭长的绿洲地带,是主要的农产区;北部山体残散,植被稀疏,海拔1500米左右,为荒漠草原区。

河流　境内主要河流有东大河、西大河,均发源于常年白雪皑皑的祁连山主峰冷龙岭北坡,属石羊河水系,为常年性内陆河。河流产流主要靠大气降水和积雪消融补给.流长80公里,流域面积9000多平方公里。东、西大河的共同特点是径流量年际变化大,年内水量分配不均匀,一般年份,年径流量为5.26亿立方米。另外有金川河、清河和小沟小河,金川河、清河,主要靠地下水补给,小沟小河主要靠降水直接补给。由于气候干旱、蒸发量大、河床渗漏原因,河流流程短,水量季节变化较大。

气候　属温带大陆性气候,空气干燥,风沙大,冬季漫长而严寒,夏季暖热,而无酷暑,春季回春快,秋季降温急。由于地形地热的影响,地区性气候差异明显,自南西北,海拔渐低,使气温北高南低,降水渐少,光照渐强。年均气温4.8℃,年平均降水量173.3毫米,年蒸量平均2300毫米,无霜期134天。年平均日照2878.6小时,日照率65%。自然灾害有大风、干旱、干热风、霜冻、暴雨、冰雹、尤以旱灾为烈。

自然资源　金昌自然资源十分丰富。全市总耕地面积161.45万亩,占总土地面积的11.66%;园地面积3070亩,占0.02%;林地面积56.1万亩,占4.05%;草原面积452.62万亩,占32.6%;荒沟、荒坡、荒地面积400多万亩,适宜农、林、牧生产的发展,创办农副产品加工业有十分优越的条件。矿产资源得天独厚,县矿藏储量大,品种多。全市现已探明的金属非金属矿藏主要有镍、铜、钴、铀、金、银、铁、铝、铅、锌、锑和煤、硫磺、萤石、粘土、石膏、石棉、膨润土、石英石、石灰石、大理石、白云石、石油等45种。矿产地70余处,其中黑色金属矿产地14处,有色金属矿产地21处,非金属矿产地35处。金川多金属共生矿,含有18种有价元素,素有"金娃娃"的美称,已探明镍储量约有553.11万吨,占全国镍金属储量的68%,居世界第二,按现有的生产规模可开采200年。与之伴生的还有铂、钯、锇、铱、钌、铑、硒、碲、铬、硫等10多种矿种,其中铂族金属储量为全国之冠。

【名特土产】

亚　麻　栽培历史悠久,永昌县近年来种植面积保持在10万亩左右。亚麻纤维畅销市场。

胡麻油　为甘肃省优质产品。它既是饮食糕点、糖果等食品工业原料,又是优良的干性油,是制作油漆、肥皂、制革、橡胶等的主要原料。

手工地毯　永昌县地毯厂生产的仿古地毯和波斯地毯,具有质地坚固、图案美观、技术精巧的特色,富有民族风格,产品销往日本、西欧、东南亚等地。

发　菜　由于它的形态和颜色相似头发,故称"发菜"。是具有较高营养价值的野生菌类植物,传统宴席上不可缺少的名肴。分布在荒滩丘陵。

虹鳟鱼　肉质鲜美,营养丰富,被列为高档商品。1984年开始从山西省等地引进。现已成为金昌市一大名特产品。

甜　菜　以茎大、含糖量高畅销省内外。主产于金川区双湾乡。

西　瓜　因本地日照充足,昼夜温差大,所产西瓜个大、汁浓、香甜、含糖量高而享誉河西走廊,远销全国各地,深受消费者欢迎,年总产量在2355.9万公斤以上。

黑瓜子　板大、饱满,远销东南亚。种植面积4329亩,总产量在75

万公斤以上。

【城市建设】1993年，全市城市建设工作认真贯彻党的十四大精神和十四届三中全会《决定》精神，进一步解放思想，深化改革，抓管理，抓规划，抓重点工程建设，完善基础设施建设，全面完成了各项建设任务，实现了1993年城市建设工作奋斗目标，取得了较好的经济效益和社会效益。强化了对基本建设项目的管理，深化了城市规划工作，治理了建设市场，提高了工程设计施工质量。房产市场进一步走向规范轨道，超前进行了道路和供热设施建设，提高了城市市政公用设施的服务功能。在为金昌经济建设和人民生活服务的工作中做出了积极地努力，推进城市建设上了一个新的台阶。

一.基建项目 1993年，全市基本建设项目59项，总投资7371万元，比1992年增加167.76%。其中收尾续建项目31项，投资4555万元；改扩建项目6项，投资772万元；新建项目22项，投资2044万元。

二.城市维护费 1993年，城市维护费计划安排1400万元，调整计划1700万元，其中：煤制气工程安排700万元；安排城市道路建设及改造资金257.3万元。新建工程完成：(1)道路建设：对北京路、天津路等5条路段进行延伸和拓宽建设，共完成延伸和改造路段面积105637.28平方米；铺设人行道7068.84平方米。(2)公园建设：对金川公园的部分设施进行了更新改造，增添了部分游乐设施，为游人提供了更多的游乐服务项目。(3)供热设施建设：进行了三号锅炉房的扩建工程，完成面积929.07平方米，安装4吨锅炉2台，新增供热面积4万平方米，解决了25区供热不足问题。同时，对1号、2号锅炉进行了更换，完成工作量37万元，改造了14区西部供热管网。

三.住宅建设 1993年，商品住宅建设投资1793万元，比上年增长49.4%。

四.环境保护 1993年共完成环境保护实事32件，完成限期治理项目4项，总投资158万元。三废排放量明显减少，省下达的20项控制目标全部完成。

【社会事业】

(一)科技、教育 科技工作取得新成绩。1993年，市列科技项目36项，完成计划项目20项，已有18项通过鉴定验收，实现经济效益1400万元。已建成科技示范乡3个、示范村30个，民办科技实体发展到27家。

教育事业基础设施日渐雄厚。1993年，全市学龄儿童入学率为99.45%，小学在校学生43665名，比上年增长8.2%，普通中学在校生20869名，1993年向全国各地大、中专院校输送新生1040名，比上年增长11.3%。兴办的各类职业中学在校学生1132名，比上年增长12.8%，且开设的专业也逐步趋向实用性、规范性和科学性。

(二)文化、卫生、体育 随着人民生活水平的不断提高，文化生活日趋活跃。全市共有电影放映单位37个；中、短波广播电台1座，人口覆盖率为50.8%；无线电视人口覆盖率达68.5%，并开始筹建有线电视；舞厅、卡拉OK厅及各类群众性文化娱乐活动大量增加，丰富了全市人民的业余文化生活。

医疗卫生条件进一步改善。1993年末，全市共有卫生机构71个，医疗病床1521张，比上年增长7.7%，卫生技术人员1985人，农村医疗点189个。

体育事业蓬勃发展。1993年参加全省比赛获得金牌4枚、银牌3枚、铜牌4枚，为金昌人民争得了荣誉。大、中、小学体育达标率达95%，市、县区举行群众性体育活动72次，参加人数64万人次。

(三)社会治安综合治理 全市社会治安综合治理工作进一步强化。深入开展了“禁毒”、“反盗窃”为重点的专项斗争，认真落实社会治安综合治理的各项措施，确保了社会治安形势的稳定。全市刑事发案685起，破案580起，破案率84.6%，其中重大案件破案率80.3%，刑事破案率比上年有所提高。

(四)民族宗教、民兵、人防、旅游、外事、信访、气象、档案等事业都在发展中取得了新的成绩。

(五)交通、邮电 1993年，全市交通运输能力有较大的提高。市境内公路客运量246.9万人次；公路货运量177.1万吨，货运周转量21722.3公里/吨。

邮电通讯发展迅速。1993年，全年完成邮电业务总量1017.6万元，比上年增长80.5%，全年完成国内函件226.1万件，比上年增长32.6%，长途电话完成120.5万张。市话年末到达户数6686户，农话年末达到978户。万门程控电话的开通，使全市通讯状况较差的局面大为改观。

【国民经济】1993年，在党的十四大和十四届三中全会精神指引下，市委、市政府带领全市各族人民认真学习贯彻党中央、国务院关于加强宏观调控的决策，以经济建设为中心，以建立社会主义市场经济体制为目标，解放思想，克服困难，抓住机遇，深化改革，加快发展，狠抓经济结构调整，努力提高经济效益，全市农村经济稳步增长，城乡企业健康发展，综合实力明显增强，人民生活水平有较大提高。

全市完成国民生产总值21.2亿元(主变价，下同)，比上年增长7.1%；工农业总产值26.66亿元，增长9.94%，其中工业总产值23.99亿元，增长8.98%；地方工农业总产值10.25亿元，增长15.85%，其中农业总产值2.67亿元，增长9.61%，乡及乡以上工业总产值7.59亿元，增长15.8%；乡镇企业总产值

3.97亿元，增长87.66%；粮食总产量17.26万吨，增长11.14%；社会商品零售总额4.36亿元，增长14.52%；农民人均纯收入842元，增加158元，财政收入19982.9万元，比上年增长32.9%，财政支出18979.3万元，比上年增长37.1%；人口自然增长率8.69‰，比计划降低4.81个千分点。

（一）农村经济 市委、市政府认真贯彻党对农村工作的各项政策，坚定不移地把农业放在经济工作的首位，按照市场经济规律的要求，坚持"一手抓粮，一手抓钱"，引导农民及时调整产业结构和种植结构；鼓励农民增加对农业的投入；狠抓科技示范乡和示范村建设，大力发展高产、优质、高效农业；切实减轻农民负担，共清理出各类负担102项，取消不合理项目75项，受到广大农民的欢迎。"渠道年"建设取得显著实效，全年共建干、支、斗渠1238公里，据测算仅此一项每年节约水量2千万立方米，增强了农业发展后劲。粮食生产在播种面积减少、遭遇特大沙尘风暴的不利条件下，仍然夺得了好收成，开创了农业总产值、粮食总产量和乡镇企业产值、收入、利税及农民人均纯收入"四增长"的大好局面。农民人均纯收入比上年增加158元，是改革开放十五年来增长幅度最大的一年。特别是乡镇企业坚持内涵与外延并重的原则，实现了健康发展，新增企业448个，总产值比上年增长87.66%，总收入增长94.2%，利润总额增长97.7%，上缴国家税金增长134.7%，从而为加快农村经济发展和农民致富奔小康步伐奠定了坚实的基础。

（二）工业生产 全市工业企业积极转换经营机制，不断推进技术进步，适应市场经济发展的能力进一步增强，加上投资需要的扩大，加强宏观调控和生产调度，狠抓扭亏增盈，强化企业管理，有力地推动了工业生产的快速发展。特别是集体工业和开发区尤为显著，在地方工业总产值7.59亿元中，城市集体工业完成产值5.84亿元，比上年增长20.1%，工业产品产销率达到96.91%。开发区已累计投入资金近5亿元，批准立项340个，建成投产或试生产的项目208个，实现工业总产值4.5亿元，比上年增长21.07%，销售增长34.3%，产销率达到97.7%。

（三）第三产业 以建设商品市场为重点，大力发展第三产业。已建成各类商品市场25处，占地面积16.54万平方米，建筑面积11.45平方米，累计总投资4204.9万元；个体工商户发展到4465户，从业人员8432人，注册资金2186万元。房地产开发起步良好，建成了一批商品用房；城乡贸易活跃，外贸出口总值完成46万美元。

金川区经济和社会发展概述

【自然概况】位置和面积 金川区位于金昌市东北部，阿拉善台地南缘，龙首山北麓，南与永昌县接壤，东与民勤县毗邻，北和内蒙古自治区阿拉善右旗相连，西与山丹县为邻。地处东经101°23′至102°34′，北纬38°20′至39°00′之间。东西长99公里，南北宽74公里，总面积3770平方公里。地势属残丘平川地带。龙首山由西北向东南缓慢伸延断续渐没于戈壁之中。腾格里沙漠半环东北境内，总趋势是西北高东南低。金川河下游为绿洲，海拔1400米至160米。龙首山成山掌主峰海拔3052米，为区内最高峰。北部草原张家坑海拔1327米，是境内最低地，相对高差1725米。河流主要有永昌县城郊泉水形成的金川河。宁远堡乡的新华、油籽洼、下四分片和双湾乡，以机井提取地下水来补充解决工农业生产、生活用水。由于气候干旱，蒸发量大，河床渗漏等原因，河流流程短，水量季节变化大。

气候属温带大陆性气候。空气干燥，风大沙多，冬无严寒。夏无酷暑，春季回暖迟，秋季降温快，因地形高低悬殊，地区性气候差异较大。无霜期150天，年平均气温7.4℃，最高气温39.5℃，最低气温－27.3℃，年日照2933小时，日照率66%，大于或等于10℃的年积温3127℃，年总辐射每平方厘米138千卡，年平均风速每秒7.9米，最大风速每秒18米，年降水量106毫米，蒸发量是降水量的24倍。主要自然灾害有干旱、风沙、干热风、暴雨、冰暴和霜冻等。

自然资源。1993年全区有耕地10.91万亩，林地1.86万亩，其余荒漠山地和戈壁。矿产资源十分丰富，矿藏储量及品位得天独厚。现已探明主要矿产资源45种，其中以有色金属及贵金属矿产最为丰富，硫化镍储量和品位居世界同类矿床第二位，与铜镍伴生的铂、钯、铱、钌、锇等铂族贵金属储量名列全国首位。非金属矿产中煤炭、硅石、石灰岩、膨润土以及罕见的水晶石、玉髓玛瑙等，储量大，品质好，开发利用前景十分可观。现已建成国家特大型有色冶金化工联合企业——金川有色金属公司。

行政区划及人口 全区域区设街道办事处6个，居民委员会73个；郊区农村设宁远堡和双湾2个乡人民政府，共有村民委员会27个，村民小组164个。全区有45960户，其中，城镇34229户，乡村11731户；总人口16.66万人，其中，农业人口4.6万人，非农业人口12.06万人。

民族 全区有汉、回、满、蒙古、东乡、朝鲜、白、裕固、锡伯、壮、布依、保安、藏、苗、土家、彝、仫佬、门巴、达斡尔、侗等24个民族。其中汉族占总人口的97.79%，少数民族占总人口的2.21%。少数民族中，回族人口最多。

【农业】全区经济工作始终把农业放在首位，积极发展城郊型农业。坚持一手抓农业，一手抓乡镇企业，同时，增加投入，改善农业生产条件，狠抓科技兴农，使农业生产全面丰收。农业总产值6451万元，经济总收入6751.54万元。

种植业。坚持服务城市，富裕农民的指导思想，以市场为导向，大幅度调整内部结构，粮、经作物比例由6：4的单一结构调整为粮、经、林果饲草料作物为4：3：3的复式结构，既丰富了居民"菜篮子"，又增加了农民收入。林业。营造防风林、用材林676万株，新建果园41个，庭院果树开发1200户。共完成造林面积1961亩，比上年增长98.48%。畜牧业。畜牧业生产继续坚持改良品种和提高经济效益并重，并以充足的饲料和优惠的贷款贴息政策为保证，呈现出良好的发展势头。

乡镇企业。以转换机制，提高效益为突破口，促进了乡镇企业的快速发展，实现了速度和效益的同步增长。企业数达319个，比上年增加80个；完成总产值14100万元，增长100.5%，实现了翻番；完成利税1792万元，增长173%。

基础设施建设。建区以来规模最大的"93节水渠道年"成效显著。总投资1549.5万元，共完成渠道建设163.1公里，改造农电线路69.5公里，新打、更新机井101眼，建设条田、低压灌溉田、配套农田36977亩，高速度、高质量地完成了"百公里渠道百眼井，三年工程一年干"的目标，使农业生产的基础条件得到进一步改善。

【工业】全区工业经济持续快速发展，新建项目陆续投产，引进和开发展的多种新产品投向市场，增强了企业的竞争能力，主要产品产量均有较大增加。全区共完成工业总产值5432.6万元，比上年增长53.9%。其中：城市集体工业1058.4万元，比上年增长84.5%，占总产值的比重为19.55%；乡村工业产值4374.2万元，增长47.9%，比重为80.5%。完成工业销售产值4436万元，增长36%。工业产销率83.4%。完成利税737.9万元，增长108.2%。乡及乡以上工业继续保持稳定发展的好势头，经济效益明显好转。全年共完成产值2863.2万元，比上年增长63.6%；完成销售产值2456.5万元，增长57.9%；完成利税464.3万元，增长194.6%。工业经济综合效益指数为101.8；工业产值销售率84.6%；资金利税率为9.5%；工业成本利润率为7.4%；工业增加值率为34.8%；全员劳动生产率为9065.2元/人；营运资金周转率2.43次。

【财贸与固定资产投资】主要以建设综合贸易市场、批发市场为突破口，促进了第三产业的发展。投资2800多万元新建了金川路龙泉市场、18#小区市场、北京路粮油批发市场、西坡大型综合市场等6个市场。新建社区服务网点36个。区属各商业企业共完成社会商品零售总额1497万元，比上年增长2.03%。其中：消费品零售总额854万元，增长4.91%；农业生产零售总额543万元，降低1.53%。

固定资产投资　固定资产投资规模增大，投资结构改善，全年共完成2413万元，比上年增加1461万元，增长153.5%。其中：全民所有制单位投资468万元；集体所有制单位投资1296万元。在总投资中：生产性投资1035万元；非生产性投资998万元。

财政　全区财政收入完成3000.9万元，比年初预算超收540.6万元，比市上下达计划超收640.6万元，比上年实际收入增加了638.3万元，增长了27%。在财政收入中，工商税收增幅较大，占全部增收额的94.5%，其它各项收入均有不同程度的增长。财政支出累计完成28565万元。财政收支相抵后，结转下年使用的专项资金34.3万元。

【人民生活】城乡人民生活水平不断提高。农民人均纯收入首次突破千元，达到1004.9元，比上年净增150.9元。全民所有制单位职工本年度平均工资额为2843元，集体所有制单位职工年平均工资额为2060元。城乡居民住房条件和面积有所改善，农民人均18.72平方米；人均生活消费支出845元，比上年增加47元。

【社会事业】文教、卫生、教育事业稳步发展。普通中学在校学生1799人，比上年下降14.21%；小学在校生6821人，增长8.67%。学龄儿童入学率达99.89%。区属各学校共有教职工648人，其中：专职教师563人，比上年减少15人。办学条件继续改善，教师素质和教学质量有所提高。为种类中等专业学校输送新生51名。

医疗卫生条件进一步提高，城乡新增医疗卫生服务网点5个，改建了8个村级卫生所，乡、村卫生院（所）建设任务已基本完成。年末，全区共有卫生机构6个，医疗病床30张。卫生技术人员52人。农村村设医疗点53个，乡村医生和卫生员62人。

科技　科技在全区经济发展中的作用进一步提高。共实施科技示范推广及星火项目57项。推广高效节能日光温室45个，面积31.5亩；塑料暖棚养猪2760口；花生、枸杞子等引种栽培技术应用收到初步成效。加强了科技工作队伍建设，乡、村科技服务体系日趋完善。

社会治安综合治理　社会治安综合治理工作得以强化。设立了"见义勇为"奖励基金，落实了社会治安综合治理目标管理责任制。全区调解各类民事纠纷362起，共抓获各类犯罪分子194名。破获吸、贩毒案件60起。计划生育　计划生育工作采取抓重点，突难点、带全面的办法，有效遏制了人口增长。全区人口自然增长率和出生率分别为8.7‰和11.5‰，计划生育率达到99.5%，均控制在人口指标以内。

交通邮电 地方道路建设完成下双公路、五营公路、西坡公路等20公里。城区北京路与延安路相通并投入使用。万门程控电话开播。

【名优土产】甜菜。以茎大，含糖量高畅销省内外。种植面积7169亩，总产量2895.2万公斤。西瓜。因个大、香甜、清凉、汁浓而享誉河西走廊，远销东北、上海、北京、广州、武汉等地，深受消费者欢迎。种植面积4642亩，总产量2355.9万公斤。黑瓜籽。板大，饱满，走俏东南亚，种植面积4329亩，总产量75万公斤。苹果梨。肉质细腻，香甜可口，远销广州等地。总产量105.5万公斤。啤酒大麦。种植面积1万亩，总产量554.1万公斤。

现任主要领导：

中共金川区委书记：武时岭

金川区人大常委会主任：曹文光

金川区人民政府区长：任斌相

政协金川区委员会主席：荆长才

中共金川区纪律检查委员会书记：

（金川区委研究室：田尧伦 刘天虎）

嘉峪关市

中共嘉峪关市委书记：李善平

嘉峪关市人大常委会主任：李善平

嘉峪关市人民政府市长：高 复

政协嘉峪关市委员会主席：程万琦

中共嘉峪关市纪律检查委员会书记：

常 江

嘉峪关市经济和社会发展概述

【自然概况】嘉峪关市是甘肃省省辖市之一。位于甘肃省西北部，河西走廊的中段，是以被誉为"天下雄关"的嘉峪关而命名的城市。全市面积1298平方公里，城区面积60平方公里，建成面积27平方公里。人口11万人，城市人口8.7万人。气候干燥，降水量小蒸发量大，年平均气温在6.7℃至7.7℃之间。兰新铁路横贯全境，312国道穿越市区，交通便利。工业基础比较雄厚，已形成以冶金工业为主体，化工、电力、建材、机械、轻纺、食品相配套的工业体系。农村只有3个乡2.3万多人，耕地4.2万亩，基本为水浇地，农业生产条件较好。境内旅游资源丰富，开发前景广阔。名特土产主要有发菜、沙葱、嘉峪关石砚、风雨雕、戈壁石画、夜光杯、骆绒画等。是丝绸之路上一座新兴的工业、旅游城市。

【城市建设】全市共完成固定资产投资44787万元。新建居民住宅22.32万平方米。开通8000门程控电话。建成城市供水工程、南市区下水工程、市第二幼儿园、市图书馆、市中医院。312国道商业街陆续动工，城市面貌大为改观。

【国民经济】1993年，认真贯彻邓小平同志南巡谈话和党的十四大精神，围绕建设社会主义市场经济的总目标，抓住机遇，脚踏实地，加快发展，取得了前所未有的新成绩。全市国民生产总值完成6.2亿元，比上年增长24.8%，其中：第一产业增长6.4%，第二产业增长26.3%，第三产业增长23.8%；国民收入完成5亿元，比上年增长21.2%；工农业总产值完成13.11亿元，比上年增长12.5%。其中地方工农业总产值2.75亿元，比上年增长29.2%。

农村经济全面发展。全年完成农业总产值4309.6万元，较上年增长6.02%；粮食总产量15855.6吨，较上年增长1.76%，夺得了第十一个丰收年；乡镇企业总产值达到4718万元，比上年增长124%；农民从乡镇企业中取得的收入由人均177元增加到210元，增长18.6%。

工业生产形势喜人。全年完成乡及乡以上工业总产值12.68亿元，比上年增长12.78%；完成销售产值11.96亿元，比上年增长12.37%，其中：酒钢工业总产值完成9.48亿元，增长7.48%，销售产值9.04亿元，增长7.87%；地方工业总产值完成2.32亿元，增长34.65%，销售产值2.08亿元，增长31.6%。

商贸旅日趋兴旺。全市社会商品零售额达到2.3亿元，较上年增长28.86%；市场建设新增商业营业面积14834平方米；旅游总收入完成1645万元，较上年增长36.3%。

财政收入大幅度增加，金融形势相对稳定。财政收入达到2.94亿元，比上年增长98.79%，创历史最高水平；财政支出达到7285万元，比上年实际支出数增长48.61%；各项存款余额达到6.94亿元，比上年增长23.96%；各项贷款余额达到10.58亿元，比上年增长19.2%。

人民生活水平稳步提高。城镇居民人均生活费收入达到2690.52元，比上年净增674.96元；农民人均纯收入达到1016元，比上年增加168元；城乡居民储蓄存款余额达到39917.5万元，比上年增长30.93%，人均储蓄额达3575元，较上年增长25.82%。

1993年，全市各级党政组织坚持以经济建设为中心，以科技教育为先导，以转变政府职能和转换企业经营机制为重点，创造性地开展工作。抓思想，转变观念；抓改革，增强活力；抓组织，提供保证；抓环境，奠定基础；抓素质，提供后劲，有力地促进了经济和社会各项事业的发展，全市整体经济实力有了明显地提高，小康建设步伐明显加快。

1、重点发展商贸旅，带动第三产业发展。嘉峪关市作为丝绸之路上的新兴工业、旅游城市，发展商贸旅有许多有利条件，但长期以来，商贸旅发展缓慢，市场发育程度低、第三产业欠发达。根据这种状况，市委、市政府确定商贸旅为全市工作重点。加大商业企业改革力度，将商业企业全部推向市场，实行"五自主"、"四放开"经营，同时制定灵活的政策，帮助企业走"一业为主，多种经营"的新路，提高了企业的竞争能力和应变能力。针对市场体系薄弱的现状，本着"谁投资，谁受益"的原则。千方百计筹集资金，加快市场建设步伐，建成华联商厦、皇都大厦、一得乐商城等一批商业设施，基本上改变了全市商业网点建设不足的局面。旅游业作为全市支柱产业，深挖潜力、大力加强基础设施建设和环境建设，开发出系列旅游新产品，提高了经济效益。利用嘉峪关市得天独厚的气流资源，成功地举办了第二届中国嘉峪关国际滑翔节，扩大了知名度，取得了经济效益和社会效益的双丰收。

2、大力发展农业和乡镇企业，增加农民收入，带领农民致富奔小康。针对我市农村三乡地处近郊，地域狭小，但生产条件好的优势，市委、市政府确立了农村工作"服务城市，富裕农民"的指导思想，坚持以市场为导向，发展城郊型农业。通过采取政策引导、信息服务、推广应用农业科技成果等措施，引导农民根据市场对农产品的需求变化，合理地安排种植计划，调整经济结构，既稳定了粮食产量，推动了菜蓝子工程建设，增加了全市淡季蔬菜的自供量，又提高了农民的种植收益。乡镇企业发展基于起点低、规模小、效益差、农民办乡企热情不足的现状，市委、市政府发挥舆论导向作用，大造声势，积极引导，帮助农民落实资金，筛选论证项目，同时制定了发展乡镇企业的优惠政策，调动了农民兴办乡镇企业的积极性，乡镇企业的发展有了良好的起步。

3、深化企业改革，转换经营机制。为加强对改革的宏观指导，市政府先后研究制定了《嘉峪关市工业试点企业"五自主"放开经营意见》、《嘉峪关市国有企业转换经营机制实施办法》等规范性文件，确保落实企业自主权，扶持企业形成对市场的灵活反应机制和经营机制。各管理部门强化服务意识，按照"简化手续、减少环节、提高效率、方便企业"的原则改进作风，为企业创造宽松的外部环境。各企业根据自身的实际需要，搞活经营，走出一条依托大企业联合经营的新路。嘉峪关市金属制品厂通过加入酒钢集团，缓解了原材料供应紧张的矛盾，效益明显提高。商业、粮食、供销三个系统对符合"三少微亏"(固定资产少、流动资金少、人员少、微利或亏损)条件的24个企业门店实行了国有民营，将私营经济机制引入国有企业，为小型企业改革提供了经验。

4、坚定小康信念，加快小康建设步伐。到本世纪末实现经济发展第二步战略目标，从温饱到小康，是我国人民的既定奋斗目标，在全省率先实现小康是嘉峪关市人民的坚定信念，经过全市人民的艰苦努力和辛勤工作，我市的小康建设已取得重大进展，人均国民生产总值等14项小康考核指标，已达到或基本达到的指标占85.71%，差距较大的指标占14.29%。为早日实现名符其实的小康，市委、市政府针对薄弱环节，制定切实可行的小康规划，不断地增加投入，推动了小康建设步伐。可以确信，经过全市人民的不懈努力，提前三年，到1997年实现小康的目标必然能实现。

【社会事业】科技工作围绕生产建设这个中心，加强新技术、新成果的推广应用，提高了经济效益。教育依靠增加投入，办学条件得到改善，教育质量稳步提高，全市适龄儿童入学率达到99.9%。计划生育工作走上了经常化、科学化、制度化、规范化的管理轨道。全市计划生育率达到100%，人口出生率11.92‰，自然增长率9.22‰。文化事业日趋繁荣，开通了兰州——嘉峪关微波线路，建成有线电视工程，丰富了群众的文化生活。

（中共嘉峪关市委研究室：刘崇鑫）

庆阳地区

中共庆阳地委书记：郭继芳
庆阳地区行政公署专员：黄继祖
中共庆阳地区纪律检查委员会
书记：李翰林

庆阳地区经济和社会发展概述

【自然概况】庆阳地区位于甘肃省东部，习称"陇东"。全区辖七县一市，即正宁、宁县、合水、镇原、环县、华池、庆阳县和西峰市，共144个乡镇。总面积27119平方公里，总人口230万人。本区处于雄浑苍茫的黄土高原上，东有葱郁茂密的子午岭，西临高耸险峻的六盘山，北部高突，梁峁交错(最高海拔2082米)，南部低缓，原面平阔(最低海拔885米)。全区地貌分为中南部黄土高原沟壑区、北部黄土丘陵沟壑区、东部黄土丘陵区。这里高原风貌独特：平原一望无际，梁峁高低起伏，河谷纵横相间，森林层峦叠障。入河谷仰视，是山无疑；上高坡极目，却一马平川。全境有10万亩以上大原12条，面积382万亩。遐迩闻名的董志原总面积136万亩，平畴沃野，广袤无际，土层厚实，质地松散，适宜农作物生长。区内有马莲河、蒲河、洪河、四郎河、葫芦河等5条河流和27条较大的支流纵横贯穿，注入泾河、洛河，最后入黄，东流归海，河流多年平均总流量26.7秒立方米，总径流量8.43亿立方米。境内有41座水库、塘坝，总库容6亿多立方米。其中以巴家咀水库为最，库坝是世界上最大的一座土坝，水库是镶嵌在陇东高原的一颗明珠。庆阳地区属内陆性季风气候，冬寒较短，夏少酷暑，秋季多雨。年平均气温在7°—

10℃之间，日照年平均2250——2600小时。无霜期南部短而北部长，年平均140——180天。降雨量年平均480——660毫米，5——9月，雨量充沛，日照最长，是农作物生长的最佳季节。

【名特土产】区内有种子植物600余种，农作物7大类，320多个品种。粮食作物以冬小麦为主，兼有玉米、高粱、糜子、谷子等145个品种。西峰市什社乡的小米，熬成稀粥，香甜上口，营养颇高；环县有荞麦剁面，食而不胀，自古为人们所称道。经济作物主要有油菜、胡麻、烟叶、黄花菜、白瓜子、大麻等。庆阳黄花菜以色泽黄亮、花苞丰满、质嫩味美、富有营养而驰名国内外，曾获国家经贸部"西北特级金针菜"荣誉证书，评为全国名优产品，年产量约400万公斤。经济林主要有苹果、杏、桃、枣、核桃等，还有沙棘、酸枣等野生果树20多种和丰富的药材资源。宁县的晋枣和黄甘桃以及区内盛产的经济价值很高的苦杏仁，镇原县的杏系列产品久负盛名。子午岭森林是甘肃省主要的水源涵养林，全区活立木总储蓄量为1000多万立方米。畜禽品种共计42个，其中以早胜牛、庆阳驴、环县滩羊出名。环县有羊羔肉，鲜嫩味美，不腻不膻，是待客的上等佳肴。野生动物有金钱豹、野猪、黄鼬、黄羊、扫雪、狐狸、獭、雉等。

【城市建设】1993年全区完成市政公用基础设施投资1391.5万元，比去年增长24%，进一步改善了城市服务功能。城市住宅建设和房地产的发展速度明显加快，1993年全区地县(市)机关单位新建住宅94幢，2076套，建筑面积15.45万平方米，较去年增长21.5%；全区已取得资质证书的14家房地产开发企业当年完成商品住宅投资2890万元，较去年增长62.7%，销售收入900万元，较上年增长35.6%。城市绿化和市容环境卫生工作有了新的发展，去年新植树65万株，植草坪6400平方米，绿化庭院5200平方米，修建小花园(坛)72个、3600平方米，增加了城市公共绿地面积，提高了绿化覆盖率。地委行署所在地的西峰市，自建市以来，8年投资2866.4万元，先后硬化拓宽城市道路13条，总长度达26.5公里，面积53万平方米；城市日供水能力由建市初的2700立方米增加到目前9400立方米，1993年年供水量325万吨；改造原有砖拱暗渠和新修各类排水管道50.7公里，使城市排水管道总长度达到82.75公里；经过几年努力，在城区4条主干道、10条主要街道栽植10多个树种16860多棵，新建小型花坛6处，铺种草坪900平方米，到1993年底，市绿化面积达到100.24公顷，人均公共绿地面积由建市前的0.23平方米提高到1.72平方米，绿化覆盖率由1.3%提高到13.5%，市容面貌发生了较大的变化。

【国民经济】庆阳地区是一个传统的农业地区。建国后，在党和上级政府的亲切关怀下，老区经济不断发展。特别是党的十一届三中全会以来，庆阳地区抓住机遇，深化改革，扩大开放，农村实行"一个工程建设(吨粮田、千斤亩)、四大系列开发(烤烟、林果、羊畜、油料)"，城镇发展"四大主导产业(毛纺、石化、卷烟、食品)"，对外实行"东进西出，外引内联，服务油田，加快发展"的方针，走自己的发展路子。经过十几年的艰苦奋斗，使城乡经济迅速发展，人民生活进一步改善，国民经济开始出现了全面、稳定、持续、协调发展的新局面。1993年，全区国民生产总值完成23.66亿元，增长7%，提前七年实现了翻两番的目标；国民收入19.47亿元，增长4.5%；工农业总产值30.54亿元，增长15.1%。其中：工业总产值11.76亿元，增长23.9%；农业总产值18.78亿元，增长10.1%。从总体看全区经济工作有了新的突破和发展。

——粮油生产创历最好水平。全年粮食总产量17.69亿斤，比上年增长12%，人均产粮862斤，高于全省平均水平。油料总产量达到1.15亿斤，较上年增长15.3%，首次突破亿斤大关。多种经营全面丰收，黄花菜、白瓜籽、瓜菜、中药材等经济作物产量较上年均有大幅度增加。林果生产稳定发展，果品总产量20.36万吨，较上年增长28.2%，产值突破两个亿。畜牧生产出现新的转机，大家畜、猪、羊等主要畜种存栏普遍增加。出栏加快，肉类总产量达到6.19万吨，较上年同期增长15.9%。

——财政收入跨上新的台阶。由于狠抓各项增收节支措施的落实，全区财政收入达到2.3亿元，占年度预测算的124.2%，比上年增长37.52%，增收6310万元。完成财政支出3.7亿元，占调整预算的99.04%，比上年增长18.19%。特别是文教卫生、科教事业、公检法的经费比上年均有增长。

——乡镇企业发展势头强劲。全区新增乡镇企业3568户，新增从业人员2.2万人，累计分别达到41198户和17.46万人，从业人员占劳力总数的20%以上，总产值20.76亿元，总收入17.6亿元，实现利润1.98亿元，上缴税金2795万元，分别比上年增长48.2%、48.85%、27.19%和44.67%。产值利税率达到11.18%。有7个县(市)产值达到亿元以上，其中宁县、西峰市产值分别突破5亿元。46个乡镇产值突破1000万元，274个行政村产值超过100万元，22户企业产值超过300万元，乡镇企业给农民提供的人均收入达到210元，占农民人均总收入的34.88%。

——农民收入增幅较大。1993年农民人均纯收入达到602元，比上年净增71元。其中西峰市农民人均纯收入达到765元。合水县太白乡人均钱粮“双过千”，农民人均纯收入达到1051元。中部特困区、北部半农半牧区和子午岭林缘区3个贫困片，已由基本解决温饱向区域商品经济开发迈进，收入水平有较大幅度的提高。

——金融秩序有所好转。1993年底，各项存款余额17.6亿元，比年初净增2.6亿元。其中城乡储蓄存款达到13.5亿元，比年初增长25%。地县工业企业“三项资金”占用由年初的5049万元降为4900万元，共收回逾期贷款2700万元。各项贷款余额年底达到22.87亿元，比上年增加4.7亿元，增长26%。其中，工商企业流动资金贷款余额12.5亿元，农业贷款余额4.36亿元。

——基础设施建设成绩显著。庆阳、合水烟厂技改项目已先后竣工投产；西峰到镇原330KV、西峰110KV输变电工程已全面完成；西峰8000门程控电话已正式开通。与此同时，盐环定扬黄工程、庆化厂50万吨常减压炼油改造和吴凤公路改建等一批重点工程正在顺利进行；马莲河流域治理项目已经通过评估，于1994年开始实施；平庆地区铁路正在困难中坚持建设；庆阳机场已申请立项。

【社会事业】科技事业迅速发展，成为推动全区经济发展的强大动力。1993年全区重点推广了6个方面35项农业适用技术，实施各级各类农业技术承包项目29项，参加人员5093人，其中技术干部1025人，行政干部846人，农民技术员3222人，总覆盖面积513.8万亩。地区农科所育成“8271”冬小麦良种，通过参加全国北部旱地品种区试，连续两年名列第一，平均亩产226.4公斤，增长15.49%，两年示范面积6.4万亩，增值25万多元。专家们认为，该品种的选育成功是“七五”以来北方旱地小麦品种的新突破。1993年，新增科技达标乡镇54个，累计达到114个，占乡镇总数的78%，其中西峰市、正宁县、合水县全部实现达标。全区146个乡镇全部配齐了科技副乡(镇)长，1350个行政村配上了科技副村长，占乡村总数的91.7%。全区新发展各类民办科技服务组织556个，累计达到2516个，新建立示范村142个，累计达到391个，新建立科技示范户9173户，累计达到31595户。1993年全区开展重点科研项目44项，取得了33项科技新成果，其中达到国内先进水平的4项，省内先进水平的10项。教育事业稳步发展。全区普教入学率、巩固率、毕业率、普及率分别达到94.72%、97.67%、97.41%、96.46%。办起特教班7个，使适龄残疾儿童入学率提高到5.1%。全区共办起幼儿园77所，附设学前班910个，在园(班)幼儿45645名，4—6岁幼儿入园(班)率达到28.9%，比上年提高4.4个百分点。1993年高考被录取人数达1790人，比上年增加588人，创历史最高纪录。高中5科会考成绩合格率均在89.75%以上。职业教育跨入全国先进行列，为农村经济服务的家庭经营专业已在全区推开，有4所学校的5个专业实现了跨县招生，全区职业中学共招生2453人，在校学生达4941人。成人教育，全区共扫除文盲20140名，青壮年文盲率由上年的12.5%下降到10.7%。成人自学考试工作继续得到推进。文化广播电视事业有了新的发展，全区实现了乡镇有文化中心(站)、电影放映队，地县有专业文艺演出团体，全区至1993年年底，有电视台1座，电视转播台95个，卫星地面收转站91个，广播电视覆盖面分别达到87%和67.2%。卫生防疫保健事业持续发展，至1993年底，乡以上医疗卫生机构发展到188个，村卫生所发展到1378个，城乡个体开业诊所发展到1014个，病床总数达到3287张。全区累计建成文明卫生城镇3个，文明卫生单位1770个，文明卫生村744个，文明卫生单位和文明卫生村普及率分别达到63.2%和49.4%。计划生育工作，领导亲自抓，负总责，1993年人口自然增长率控制在13.15‰以内。

（中共庆阳地委研究室）

镇原县经济和社会发展概述

【自然概况】镇原县共辖5镇19乡，269个村委会，2483个村民小组，总人口45.61万人，其中农户9.69万户，农业人口44.15万人。

地理位置：位于甘肃省庆阳地区西南部，介于北纬35°27′至36°16′，东经106°44′至107°36′，东临庆阳，西接宁夏彭阳县，南界泾川，北靠环县。南北长91.2公里，东西宽78.3公里。县城距西峰市75公里，距平凉市区97公里。

自然资源：全县总面积3500平方公里(525万亩)，耕地175万亩，其中山地占68.4%，原地占27.1%，川地占4.5%。有效灌溉面积11万亩，梯条田94.5万亩。境内土壤以黑土类。黄土类为主，土壤肥力较好，可种植多种农作物。土地宽广，总面积中除33.3%的耕地外，有林草地218.5万亩，占总面积的41.26%，发展林牧业具有一定潜力。地下静水量1.112亿立方米/年，动贮量0.003亿立方米/年，可利用水量0.419亿立方米/年。

地形特点：镇原地处陇东黄土高原，地势西北高东南低，自西北向东南逐渐倾斜，属黄河中游黄土高原的沟壑区。海拔1456米，最高海拔1767米。境内有平泉原、屯字原、孟坝原、临泾原、新集原等五条大原，总面积约53.34万亩，耕地面积约40.29万亩，占原面积的75.53%。

气候雨量：气候属于半湿润性大陆温带季风气候，光照充足，年总日照时数平均 2249.7——2437.2 小时，年平均气温 7.5——9.5℃，气温日差 9——15℃；无霜期 140——170 天；历年降雨量平均 450——580 毫米。

水文：境内有茹河、蒲河、洪河、交口河四大河流及黑河、潘杨涧河两小河流一部分过境水系，均属黄河水系的泾河流域上游区。河流总长度 577.6 公里，径流总量 1.389 亿立方米。境内水土流失严重，全县年输沙量 2851 万吨，年平均输沙率 906 吨/秒，年侵蚀模数 8141 吨/平方公里。

【经济综合指标与工农业发展】改革开放以来，全县经济发展迅速，取得了前所未有的好成绩。1993 年全县完成社会总产值 67000 万元；国民生产总值 33918 万元，其中第一产业增加值 26120 万元，第二产业增加值 6060 万元，第三产业增加值 7738 万元；完成国民收入 27657.6 万元；工农业总产值达到 62116 万元，其中农业总产值 35818.5 万元，工业总产值 26297.5 万元；农民人均纯收入 580.89 元。

农业：镇原为甘肃农业大县之一。其格局为“以农为主，农林牧副并举，种栽养加结合”。通行的耕作制是“以麦为主，一年两熟，麦秋轮作，用养结合”。粮食作物主要为小麦、玉米、高粱、糜谷、豆类等。1993 年全县粮食总产量 17,12 万吨，人均产粮 392 公斤。经济作物主要有杏子、水果、黄花、油料、烤烟、药材、花椒、核桃、瓜菜等。全县水果总产量达到 4.48 万吨(其中苹果 1.54 万吨，杏子 2,32 万吨)，油料 1.42 万吨(主要有胡麻、油菜、芸芥、麻子、荏等)，烤烟 11.47 万担，药材 864 吨，核桃 1597 吨，花椒 267 吨。畜牧业以饲养大家畜、羊、猪、鸡、兔为大宗，全县出栏牛 1.87 万头，羊 8.79 万只，猪 11,53 万口，存栏大家畜 15.45 万头(牛 5.63 万头)，羊 21.27 万只，猪 11.25 万口。肉类总产量 13900 吨，奶类总产量 258 吨，羊毛产量 589.95 吨。

乡镇企业：全县乡镇企业总数 7547 个，从业人员 3.21 万人，完成总产值 3.53 亿元，总收入 3.01 亿元，实现利润 3300 万元，入库税金 339 万元。主要产品有杏制品、塑料制品、纺织品、砖瓦等 20 多个门类 120 多个品种。

工业：全县乡镇以上工业产值完成 10888 万元，其中国有企业 4526 万元，城镇集体工业 1561 万元，乡镇工业 4800 万元。生产主要工业产品产量，机制纸 1983 吨，啤酒 11136 吨，发电量 200 万千瓦时，杏制品 11446 吨。目前形成食品加工、轻纺轻化、机械电器、医药化工五大产业和机械、建材、金属制品、医药、造纸、印刷、工艺品、家具电器、文化用品、服装、皮革、纺织、鞋帽、食品等门类生产规模，批量生产的产品达 130 多个品种。造纸厂、啤酒厂、果品厂等企业年产值都在 500 万元以上。

【交通运输、邮电】境内主要有国道兰宜公路和省道郿 肖公路横穿南北，长 141 公里，为国家二、三级公路。县乡公路 17 条，总长 460 公里，全部进入等级路面。全县 22 个乡镇通班车，95%的行政村通汽车。每日出境直达西安、兰州、固原、西峰、平凉、泾川的班车 41 个班次。年末，有各类营运汽车 327 辆，其中货车 299 辆，客车 28 辆，农运两用拖拉机 1770 辆，完成货运量 20.77 万吨，客运量 76.19 人次。

邮政电信：县城自动电话从 1993 年扩容开通后，容量增至 1000 门，电缆出局增至 960 对。县邮电局下设 16 个邮电支局、所，代办所 2 个，邮路总长 764 公里，农村邮路投递总长度 2867 公里。可同全国各省、市、自治区 2000 多个县通邮、通话，并和日本、美国、加拿大、新加坡、西班牙等国家及香港取得了邮政电信联系。邮电业务总量完成 131.85 万元。

【财贸发展】全县现有国营、集体商业网点 330 个，其中国营商业网点 35 个，供销合作社网点 295 个(其中双代点 237 个)。个体工商户 4481 户，从业人员 8821 人，注册资金 741.63 万元。全年社会商品零售总额 11608 万元。集市贸易成交额 3933 万元。国营、集体商业网点收农副产品总值 2087 万元。外贸商品原料主要为冻兔肉、杏仁、黄花等，建起了近 10 家外贸产品的生产企业。全年财政收入总额 3899.2 万元，其中县级财政收入首次突破两千万元大关，达到 2412.5 万元，收入中农业各税 370.8 万元，工商税收 1987 万元。支出总额 4538.1 万元，其中县级包干支出 3869.6 万元。年末，全县各类银行各项存款余额 12285.2 万元，其中储蓄存款 8725.2 万元；各项贷款余额 22527.9 万元。购买国库券 45 万元。

【城镇建设】道路：1984 年以来，全县先后投资 600 多万元，在县城建成一路(南环路)、三巷(兴文、兴武、兴学巷)、六街(东、西、南、中、茹、河、洪河街)，总长度 3824 米。1993 年对主街道进行了拓宽改造，人行与车行分道。给水：县自来水公司始建于 1985 年，累计投资 83.5 万元，建成高位水塔一处，容量 500 立方米，总管道长度 5000 多米，日净化供水 1000 吨。住宅：目前全县共有住宅房屋总面积达 51308 平方米，其中楼房 42444 平方米。仅 1993 年县上鼓励国家、集体、个人进行合作建房、集资建房和开发商品房，投资 1100 多万元，兴建住宅楼 14 栋，建筑面积达 28000 平方米。

【社会事业】教育：全县现有各级各类学校 702 所，其中完全中学 4 所，初级中学 33 所，职业中学 6 所，小学 655 所，幼儿园 5 所，教职工 4369 人，在校学生 72809 人。儿童入学率 98.5%，巩固率 92.84%，毕业率 98.2%，普及率 98.1%。自 1977 年恢复高考制度以来，累计为国家输送大、中专学生6427人。近年来，全县每年考入大中专院校的学生500人左右，1993年达到700多人，名列全区前茅。

科技：1958年始建县科委协和科协，1988年各乡镇都建起了科委和科协，县直部门成立了专业学会、协会、研究会。现有各类科研机构和团体151个，科技人员5000多人，其中授予技术职称的3093人，其中高级职称32人，中级职称742人。授予农民技术职称的855人，其中中级职称的26人。

医疗卫生：全县现有各级医疗卫生机构420个，医疗防保人员562人，乡村赤脚医生、卫生员805人，设置病床549张。三所县级医院设备齐全，技术力量雄厚，可开展肝破裂修补、断臂再植等大型手术项目。肺结核病患者全部投入免费治疗。

广播电视：各乡镇均设有广播放大站，县至乡广播信号为调濒发射。县城电视微波台，装置50瓦米波电视发射机三套，地面接收设备一套，可同时收转三套彩色电视节目。三岔、方山、殷家城、彭阳、寺马电站等川区建有电视插转台。县城建有教育电视台一处。全县电视人口覆盖率达到73.5%，广播入户率达到75%。

文化艺术：全县乡乡有文化站，村村有文化室。县乡共有放映发行单位35个，年均放映11000多场(次)。县城有工人俱乐部、老年活动中心、影剧院、舞厅等公共娱乐场所。县图书馆藏书4.2万册，博物馆收藏各种文物2700件。县乡新华书店7个，年图书发行量180万余册。全县专业秦剧团1个，业余秦剧团4个，演职人员近200人。

社会保障：县保险公司下设10个代理所，1993年承保财产总额6465万元，保险费收入303万元，处理赔案671件，赔款79万元，综合赔付率为42.24%。有乡镇敬老院9所，收养农村孤老29人，集体供养五保户174人，亲邻代耕代种202人。建起集体福利工厂9个，就业残疾人62名。全年县上拨付怃恤金和社会救济费96.81万元。

【名特土产】杏子：在全县林业生产中独占鳌头，也是该县农民收入的主要项目。杏树栽培已有三十多年的历史，现已发展到1000万株，挂果600万株。可加工杏制品20多个品种，年产杏制品8000吨以上。杏仁是我国传统的出口品，年出口杏仁400多吨，居全省第一，全国第三。杏核壳可制作活性炭。

黄花菜：又名金针菜。本县是庆阳黄花菜的主要产区，出产的黄花菜，以其苞长、肉厚、色亮、味美、营养成份高等特点而著称全国，香飘五洲，曾被国家经贸委命名为“镇原黄花”。1993年全县栽培黄花6.08万亩，产商品干菜410.1万公斤。

冻兔肉：县冷冻厂生产，有带骨肉和剔骨肉两种，是低脂肪，高蛋白，肉质细嫩，味道鲜美的上等食品，是国家出口产品，深受国内外消费者的欢迎，外国人称之为“美容肉”。年可产冻兔肉100多吨。

现任主要领导：

中共镇原县委书记：李　峰

镇原县人大常委会主任：赵宝玺

镇原县人民政府县长：王宪峻

政协镇原县委员会主席：白进彩

中共镇原县纪律检查委员会书记：王维东

(中共镇原县委经济部)

合水县经济和社会发展概述

【自然概况】合水县位于庆阳地区东部，隋开皇十六年首置合水县，旧县城原在老合水(现老城镇)，后迁至西华池镇。因位于建水与北岔水交汇处而得名。处于东经107°50′至108°42′，北纬35°36′至36°37′之间，与陕西富县、志丹县和庆阳地区的华池、庆阳、宁县为邻。东西长约138公里，南北宽80公里。全县共辖13个乡，2个镇，96个行政村，695个自然村。总人口14.7万人(含两个国营农林场)，其中农业人口13.3万人(不含农林场)，总农户29941户，劳力42136人。有蒙、回、维吾尔、壮、朝鲜、满、土、裕固等9个少数民族，人口81人。合水县地处陇东黄土高原区，地形以丘陵沟壑为主，山川原相间。子午岭由西北向东南斜贯全境，将全县分为西南、东北两大部分。东北部为子午岭山地丘陵区，地势较高，海拔1458至1682米。面积约2017.4平方公里，占总面积的67.53%。西南部为高原沟壑，海拔1190至1387米，面积970平方公里，占总面积的32.47%。全县总土地面积这2987.4平方公里，折合448.1万亩，其中耕地58.2万亩，占12.99%。园地9.9万亩，占2.2%；林地262.4万亩，占58.57%，牧草地97.6万亩，占21.77%，其它用地8.1万亩，占1.82%，水域2.2万亩，占0.5%。合水县为大陆性气候，西南部气温较高，东北部气温较低。其特点是：春天多雨，干燥多风；夏热伏旱，雹洪为灾；秋凉阴雨，气候湿润；冬干雪少，气候寒冷；春季回暖慢，秋季降温急，全境年降水量为500至800毫米，年平均气温在9.5℃左右，年无霜期平均为110天至180天，绝对无霜期110天，年平均日照时数为2491.8小时，年太阳辐射总量为128.15—131.45千卡/平方厘米，地面平均蒸发量1400至1600毫米。县内以子午岭为界，有属于泾河水系的马莲河、县川河、固城河和属于洛河水系的苗村河、葫芦河等主要河流，年总径流量0.60亿立方米。全县已建成水库4座，库容472万立方米，电机灌溉87处；提灌站95处，已发展水地21590亩。三田面积累计达27.86万亩，人均2.14亩。合水县农作物以冬小麦为主，年均种植面积为18万亩，总产3.9万吨。并盛产玉米、高粱、糜子、稻谷、洋芋。油料、烟叶、药材等。主要农林土特产产品有黄花、木耳、白瓜籽等。县东北部山区盛产秦艽、甘草。麻黄、柴胡、远志、枣仁、鹿茸等150多种中药材。野生动物有豹、狐、黄羊、野猪、狼等。

【经济发展概况】1993年全县改革开放，经济建设，党建工作和各项社会事业建设都有了新的发展和变化，各项经济指标持续增长，全县社会总产值达3.54亿元，较上年增长12.47%；国民生产总值达2.17亿元，较上年增长13.6%；国民收入1.94亿元，较上年增长14.7%；工农业总产值2.59亿元，较上年增长14.9%；其中工业总产值达到0.81亿元，农业总产值达1.78亿元，较上年增长40.4%和6.15%。

农业，全县粮食播种面积完成27.89万亩，总产1.54亿斤，比上年增长8.5%，人均产粮1154斤，再创历史最高纪录。多种经营全面发展，经济作物面积、产量较上年均有大幅度增加。其中白瓜籽种植3.4万亩，总产1439吨，总收入688.4万元。人均收入51.7元；果园面积累计达到11.57万亩，总产量2.1万吨，总收入2103.8万元，人均158元；烤烟种植17536亩，创总产值651.65万元，黄花累计达到19149亩；奶牛存栏705头，油料面积42618亩，总收入722.4万元，人均54.2元。支柱产业总收入达5860.26万元，人均423元，占当年人均纯收入704.6元的60%。造林绿化步伐明显加快，全年完成造林50510亩，新办村级林场17处，机关林场10处，义务植树9.5万株，完成果带栽植1.7万亩。畜牧业生产稳步发展，大家畜、猪、羊存栏分别达5.13万头、5.56万只和11.94万只，分别较上年增长7.32%、3.1%和8.8%，完成黄牛、绵羊和绒山羊改良0.21万头、2.06万只和1.59万只，“三改”良种化程度达到59.3%。全县肉类总产量达到5467吨，畜牧业总收入达到1124.55万元，人均收入69.7元。

全县财政收入完成2530.9万元，占年度预算的103.8%，较上年增长27.9%，完成财政支出3460.4万元，占调整预算的101.5%，较上年增长12.06%。

工业，全县共有工业企业85户，其中中央属企业1户，县属企业19户，乡镇工业企业65户，工业产品有卷烟、食品、乳品、服装、手套、麻纺、地毯、建筑材料、印刷、塑料、砖瓦等8大类30余种，名优产品有远销东欧、日本等国的劳工手套，省优产品有古象牌全脂牛奶粉。全县乡镇以上工业总产值完成4210.25万元，较上年增长18.7%；预算内工业企业完成产品销售收入798.3万元，较上年增长12.5%；实现利润33.6万元，较上年增长10.8%；上缴利税14.4万元，增长94.1%。

金融，年末全县各项存款余额8819.2万元，比年初增长24.8%。其中城乡居民储蓄存款余额达到7393.8万元，比年初增长24.6%。各项贷款余额年底达到16676.4万元，比上年增加1608.3万元，增长10.7%。

基本建设和基础设施建设，公路建设上，顺利完成西合公路10.1公里路面铺油罩面工程；完成了陈铁、罗段、王观公路19公里乡镇公路改线、整修工作，新修县乡三级公路1条，拓宽3条17.9公里。重点养护公路7条139.7公里，县乡公路好路率56%以上。电力建设上，县城至固城35千伏输变电工程建成并投入运行；新建农电线路32.2公里；连家砭35千伏输变电工程前期论证工作已完成。水利建设上，固城二干渠工程峻工并全面发挥效益；县城供水工程已投入正常运行；太白二期水利工程已进入效益区，新增有效灌溉面积1820亩。建成人饮、病改工程6处。市场建设上，建成了陇华商场和老城镇农贸市场，县城商业一条街已打通，劳力和人才市场已经开业，科技服务市场日趋活跃。市政建设上，县城及何家畔自动化改造工程已经完成；建成了县标和12幢营业、科研、办公和住宅楼。

全县新增乡镇企业201户，新增从业人员1053人，累计达到1922户和8800人，从业人员占劳动力总数的21%。总产值完成12808万元，总收入1089万元，分别较上年增长50.4%和47.4%。有4个乡镇产值突破千万元。

【社会事业】年内有9个乡镇实现了科技达标，累计全县15个乡镇全部实现了科技达标任务。推广实用技术30项。取得了16项科技新成果，有7个乡镇分别获得地区科技进步一二三等奖。全县科技综合覆盖率达到85%以上，实现科技增值7160万元，科技对农业的贡献率达到32.9%以上。教育事业在改革中不断发展，办学条件不断改善，教学质量不断提高。年内，全县新建改建校舍4000平方米，添置教学设备829台(件)。全年向大中专院校输送新生196名，其中大专以上98名，创历史最高纪录。计划生育工作完成了四项节育手术有4776例。人口自然增长率控制在12.23‰，全县计划生育率达到70.47%。全县乡镇卫生院消灭了危房，医疗条件明显改观，全县儿童计划免疫接种合格率达到95%，合水电视台、教育电视台的建成开播，电视广播覆盖面不断扩大。群众体育活动得到广泛开展，全县学生体育达标工作获得“第五批全省达标先进县”称号。

现任主要领导：

中共合水县委书记：刘金宝

合水县人大常委会主任：白麟炳

合水县人民政府县长：马达理

政协合水县委员会主席：谢峰

中共合水县纪律检查委员会书记：

杜富前

（合水县委政策研究室：柴小宁）

华池县经济和社会发展概述

华池县位于甘肃庆阳东北部，北与陕西志丹、吴旗、定边三县接壤，西与环县、庆阳相连，东南与合水县毗邻。古属禹雍州，西魏始置县，因二将川河古名华池水而得县名。县辖2镇17乡、24517户、11.5万人，其中农村21778户、10.3万人，总面积3776平方公里，耕地86万亩。境内丘陵起伏，梁峁相间，沟壑纵横，植被较少，气候干燥，年降水量450——550mm，无霜期150——160天，自然条件比较艰苦，是全省十八个干旱困难县之一。粮食作物以冬小麦、糜谷、玉米、豆类为主；经济作物以胡麻面积最大，盛产白瓜籽，且皮薄色艳肉嫩；苹果、杏仁、杏干、木耳、甘草等也形成批量；畜产品羊毛、羊绒、羊皮是本地外贸出口产品，主要工业产品有羊毛服装、各类小农具、沙棘果汁、大小金钱肉罐头等畅销不衰。县内公路总长度440公里，成为连接内外、发展经济的动脉。

【经济发展综述】华池县1934年建立红色革命政权，具有光荣的历史和传统，是全省、全国双拥模范县。十一届三中全会以来，特别是近年来，华池县委、县政府坚持以经济建设为中心，维护社会稳定，强化改革开放，依托资源优势，围绕企业增效、农民增收和财政增长，高度重视农业，突出支柱产业，内引外联，加快发展地方工业，大力发展乡镇企业、二三产业和个体私营经济，促进老区经济和各项社会事业的全面发展。1993年，社会总产值达26778万元，国民收入达到17818万元；工农业总产值达到11815.24万元，比上年增长10.6%，其中乡镇以上工业总产值比上年增长20.2%；农业总产值比上年增长8.14%；乡镇企业总产值达到3751万元，比上年增长53.7%；财政收入达到710.1万元，比上年净增473.7万元，实现了当年翻番；农民人均纯收入达到542.5元，比上年净增63.2元，粮食总产量达到9324.48万斤，比上年增长11.2%，人均产粮904斤。初步形成了农业在不放松粮食生产的同时以乡镇企业和多种经营为主，工业以建筑建材、石油开发和羊毛服装为主，第三产业以饮食和流通为主的经济发展新格局。

【农业发展三特点】(1)支柱产业初具规模。以市场为导向，一手抓粮，一手抓钱，积极探讨在传统农业区发展社会主义市场经济模式，适时调整产业结构，走以经增收的路子，扩大羊、油、果、白瓜籽和黄豆五大支柱产业生产规模，加快开发速度，提高开发效益。全县羊只存栏达到21.37万只，出栏6.5万只，油料种植10万多亩，总产777.3万斤，新建优质果园4000亩，累计达到4.36万亩，果品总产量1500万斤，种植白瓜籽8.2万亩，总产量277.8万斤，种植黄豆13万亩，总产量达到1670万斤，产量均比上年增长20%以上，全县五大支柱产业总收入3462.6万元，人均337元，占农民人均纯收入的62.1%。(2)科技兴农迈上新轨道。以“两高一优”为目标，积极引导农业和农民由计划经济向市场经济转变，由计划管理向项目管理转变，不断改革传统管理形式，重点围绕科技兴农实施项目管理，提高农村经济的管理水平。采取承包、培训、投入三保证，粮食生产、多种经营、扶贫开发三结合的办法。1993年，全县共组织实施农业承包和开发项目28个，落实项目承包面积38万亩，确定承包人员85名，举办各类实用技术培训班181期，培训14168人(次)。改建综合乡镇技术推广站3个，建成科技达标乡镇6个、科技示范村30个、示范点54个，投入农业发展资金和农贷资金353.5万元，各类化肥6139吨，调剂解决各类良种54万公斤。全县仅项目开发就拿回了67.5%的粮食，73.8%的人均纯收入，覆盖了90%以上的贫困面，有1083个贫困户实现了当年脱贫，贫困面由上年的5.6%下降到2.66%。(3)基础建设步伐加快。按照规划、开发、建设三统一，水利、农建、道路三配套，领导、资金、技术三落实，社会、经济、生态效益三兼顾的原则，认真规划，择优先行，加速开发。1993年，全县新修基本农田1.02万亩，累计达到19.43万亩，新增有效灌溉面积700亩，累计达到1.41亩，完成小流域治理8.56平方公里，累计达到80.6平方公里，整修县乡道路356公里，与长庆油田达成830万元悦乔公里基建协议，当年完成路基修筑铺砂任务31.7公里，整修乡村道路133公里，完成朱悦35千伏线路并网，悦阜35千伏线路改造测绘，续架新架10千伏农电线路7条52.6公里，农电入户率由上年的39.9%提高到43.3%。农机总动力达到6334.09千瓦，农机总值达到711.43万元，比上年增长9.3%，农业生产和交通条件进一步改善。

【工商业改革见成效】工业企业以转换经营机制为重点，对销售快、效益好的钢门钢窗、铝合金制品、三沟六行播种机、羊毛服装等重点产品、重点企业，强化服务，重点扶持，整体推进。1993年，全县19户工业企业完成产值1547.5万元，销售收入1306万元，实现利润84.7万元，上交税金57.3万元，分别比上年增长20.2%、57.3%、2.4倍和64.7%。

对外协作。坚持“双带整推”战略，充分利用资源、油田开发和省计委帮扶优势，引进项目资金，促进经济开发。全县共落实省计委帮扶18个项目465万元，以长庆局及二级单位和省民政厅、地矿局为重点，先后确定合作联营项目10个，引进资金近千万元。年内全县共确定的建设项目30个，投资1785.47万元，其中工业建设项目12个496.8万元，均是历史上没有过的。向杭州丝绸厂等4户企业输出劳务124名，收入达345万元。同时还分期分批派出70多名干部到兰州、福建、杭州、上海、陕西、新疆等地考察学习，引进企业管理和技术人才15名。企业在外设立营业窗口17个，其中羊毛服装、甘草粗酸销往兰州、内蒙古、西安等地，三行畜力播种机在区内外均有订货。

商流企业改革有突破。围绕贯彻《条例》，重点对商流企业推行"国有民营"、"社有自营"。1993年，全县106个商业零售门店、柜组实行国有民营或社有自营，占66.3%，抽回资金56.24万元，占应抽资金的47.5%。同时，加快农贸市场建设，新建、扩建、改建市场1884平方米，修建营业用房及服务设施6530平方米，集市贸易成交额达728万元，增长20.1%。积极鼓励和支持干部职工兴办经济实体33个，累计销售收入60.5万元，实现利润4.64万元。

培植地方财源创新路。在抓好税收征管、增收节支等常规措施的同时，突出资源优势，围绕石油化工，着重在建立稳定财源和开发重点财源上下功夫，当年石油开发实现利税50万元，油田在华建设项目增税106.8万元。全县财政收入达到710.1万元，除长庆油田支援地方原油销售收入170万元外，正常财政收入达到540.1万元，比上年净增303.7万元，首次实现当年翻番。

【交通邮电事业】全县国营、集体、个人拥有各种载重汽车142辆，总吨位620吨，完成货物周转量1920万吨公里，客运周转量达2113万人公里。全县邮电局(所)达到17个，邮路长度1814单程公里，邮电业务量61万元，送件21万件，首次开通了县城和悦乐等5个乡镇的千门程控电话，结束了长期使用手摇电话的历史。

【社会事业与人民生活】全县共有中小学335所，各级各类在校学生19211人，教职工1318人，年内向大中专院校输送生员151名，创历史最好水平。此外，还建立和发展了儿童学前教育、农民技术教育、电视函授教育等，使全县人民的科学文化水平有了很大提高。全县共有卫生医疗机构24个，医院病床342张，专业卫生技术人员281人，乡村医生297人，年内完成乡镇卫生院改造3个2280平方米，就医人员达17万多人(次)，使危害人民健康的各种地方病和毒性流行病的发病率大为下降，治愈率明显上升。全县有电影机构24个，专业艺术表演团体1个，文化馆、图书馆、博物馆各1个，建立乡镇文化中心和文化站19个，小型电视差转台和卫星地面接收站49个，电视覆盖率达70%。以业余体校为主体的群众性体育活动蓬勃发展。1993年，在地级比赛中，荣获团体第一名，金银牌各4枚，铜牌3枚，促进了全县人民的精神文明建设。

城乡居民生活。把乡镇企业和个体私营经济作为改善人民生活的主要生长点，坚持多轮齐转，突出重点项目带发展，突出重点产品求质量，突出重点区域带全县。年内共新办乡镇企业100户，新增从业人员500人，乡镇企业总产值与1991年相比实现了翻番，总收入2950万元，实现利税339.2万元，分别增长43%和34.6%。当年新增个体户214个，累计达到781个，全县农民人均纯收入达到542.5元，农民居住条件大为改观，购买力明显增强。1993年全县每百户拥有自行车86辆，收录机、电视机、洗衣机、摩托车等高档商品也步入农户家庭，分别达到3162台、3640台、248台和170辆。

现任主要领导：

中共华池县委书记：王培栋

华池县人大常委会主任：赵秉璋

华池县人民政府县长：王憨群

政协华池县委员会主席：葛登超

中共华池县纪律检查委员会书记：王林虎

(中共华池县委办公室：黄继宗　吕世福　王京林)

环县经济和社会发展概述

【自然概况】环县位于北纬36°01′～37°09′，东经106°21′～107°44′之间。东邻华池县，南连庆阳、镇原县，东北与陕西省定边县接壤，西北同宁夏回族自治区固原、同心、盐池县相连。总面积9236平方公里，其中耕地135.78万亩。属黄土高原丘陵沟壑区，地势西北高，东南低。区内平均海拔为1255.6米，境内多山多沟，有大小山梁859架，沟15960条。最大的河流为环江。境内流长120公里，有大小支流500多条。年平均流量2.16立方/秒米，流经境内6乡镇，流域面积7112平方公里。环县属大陆性季风气候。"风高土燥，秋旱春迟"。年平均温度8.3℃，最高气温37.5℃，最低气温－23.2℃。年平均降水量450mm，蒸发量1800mm。无霜期120天，日照2733小时。全年多风，最大可达9级。干旱、霜冻、冰雹是主要灾害性气候。属甘肃省20个干旱县之一。地下资源有石油、煤等。地表、地下水资源十分贫乏，地下水矿化度高。土地资源丰富，但土壤贫瘠，水土流失和风蚀沙化严重。动、植物资源比较丰富。

全县辖22个乡、3个镇，280个行政村，1802个村民小组。全县人口61750户，30.2万人。其中农业户58181户，28.8万人，非农业户3569户，1.4万人。人口密度为每平方公里32.72人。民族有汉、回、蒙、苗、藏、满、壮、土8个民族，其中汉族占总人口99.7%。

【农业】完成总产值1.81亿元，比上年增长10.4%，其中：种植业11537.17万元，林业612.48万元，牧业5934.14万元，副业9.27万元，分别占总产值的63.76%、3.38%、32.79%、0.07%。农民人均纯收入491.28元，较上年增长16.4%.种植业，粮经比例由上年的82：18调整为81：19.粮食总产量8630.5万公斤，较上年增长22.4%，农民人均产粮301.5公斤，较上年增长20.9%。主要经济作物有油料、蔬菜等。油料总产量1104.5万公斤，比上年增长12.9%；销售992.5万公斤，产销率达82%。

林果业，全年共造林31400亩，累计达到73.6万亩，人均有林2.44亩，木材蓄积量49699万立方米；新建果园17408亩，累计达到89172亩，人均拥有0.31亩。果品总产量1583.7万公斤，较上年增长25.2%；销售1310万公斤，商品率达82.7%.林果业产值较上年增长3%。

畜牧业，主要畜种有牛、驴、骡、马、羊、猪等。年末大家畜存栏11.06万头，羊存栏40.14万只，猪存栏6.44万头，出栏率分别为13.13%、41.3%、82.94%。肉类总产量778.3万公斤，较上年增长9.05%。畜牧业总产值较上年增长11%。

乡镇企业，达到4206户，较上年增长31.4%。其中乡办95户，村办74户，合作52户，个体3985户。从业人员11907人，较上年增长25%，占全县乡村劳动力总数的10.5%。主要有农、工、建筑、交通、运输、商饮服务等产业门类。总产值11600万元，较上年增长51.1%，其中工业产值5368万元，较上年增长42.3%。总收入9405万元，实现利润908万元，完成税金276万元，分别较上年增长51.4%、12.6%、33.1%。

【工交】共有小型工业企业51户，其中全民13户，集体6户，乡镇办32户；职工2024人，其中全民943人，集体174人，乡镇办1007人。完成总产值5539.1万元，较上年增长12.1%，其中全民工业完成2388.4万元，集体工业完成548.7万元，乡镇工业完成2602万元。全县5户预算内工业企业完成产品销售收入679.3万元，较上年增长11.1%。14户预算内企业实现利润69.3万元，较上年增长39.7%。

交通，改建县乡公路3条，15.52公里，新修乡村道路12条，198公里。全县25个乡镇全部通汽车，40%的乡镇通班车，83.6%的行政村通小拖拉机。完成客运量75.84万人次，客运周转量2890万人/公里；贷运量27.81万吨，贷运周转量2015.7万吨/公里。

邮电，共有电信邮政局(所)17个，邮电职工151人。邮路长度3874公里，其中农村投递线路3325公里，电报电路1路，长途电话电路10路，年内安装开通县城1000门长市农自动电话，完成曲子集镇电话自动化改制工程。农话装机总容量达到570门。邮电业务总量90.14万元，较上年增长12.2%。

【财贸】年初分别实行了“国有民营”和“社有自营”提高了企业效益。商业企业完成农副产品收购总值784.8万元，商品纯销售443.5万元，实现利润25.6万元，上缴税金70.6万元；供销企业完成农副产品收购966.9万元，商品总销售4535.6万元，上缴税金104.4万元。

财政收入完成1336.9万元，支出完成3420万元，分别较上年增长81.6%和83.2%。银行存款余额8190万元，贷款余额11307.2万元，分别较上年增长12.2%和0.8%，城乡居民储蓄余额6700.3万元，较上年增长20.5%。税收入库1138.3万元，较上年增长88.1%。

【城区建设】投资143.5万元，安装中街排洪管道780米，排污管道557米，自来水管线2500米，硬化人行道1120平方米，老城道路铺油罩面7600平方米，南城壕改造地13亩。筹资166万元，新建商品住宅楼2幢，总面积5760平方米。增植街道行树97株，初步形成了以红花槐、中槐为主的风景林带。建立花园8座，增加绿地面积3200平方米，硬化庭院9700平方米，涌现出了一批花园式单位。

村镇建设投资1222万元，在曲甜公路沿线6乡镇硬化人行道13000平方米，新修排洪渠道1500米，栽植街道行树1300株，安装路灯15盏，完成街道铺油罩面12600平方米。新建、扩建各类市场13处，新增面积6万平方米。

【社会事业】科技，全县共有各类专业技术人员2008人。其中：自然科学455人，社会科学1553人，获得科学技术职称的1836人。年内完成科研课题3项，推广新技术22项，开发新产品11项。科技达标乡镇11个，累计达到16个。

教育，共有中、小学校770所，在校学生46171名。其中：高中(含职中)4所，在校学生1034名；初中18所，在校学生5983名；小学748所，在校学生39154名。全县学龄儿童入学率达到92%，初等教育普及率达到86%，在校学生巩固率、毕业率分别达到94.5%和97.5%。共向各类大中专院校输送新生285名，是恢复高考制度以来最多的一年。

文化广播电视，共有文化单位27个，从业人员87人。年内制作文艺作品240件。有广播站1个，放大站1个。有线广播线路总长206公里，广播喇叭2900只。有电视卫星地面接收站1个，电视差转台20个，电视节目增加到4套，电视覆盖率达到42.5%。

医疗卫生，共有医疗卫生单位31个，各类卫生人员461人，医院病床365张，每千人平均病床1.2张，每万人平均医务人员15.3人。农村合作医疗站279所，个体诊疗所15个；农村医生280人，农民每万人平均有医生9.7人。

县体育运动委员会和15个业余训练点，共有专业和业余体育工作者72人，其中专业42人。城镇机关篮球普及率为60%，学校排球普及率为20%；机关、学校乒乓球普及率为30%。人均体育事业费0.1元。群众体育活动以篮球、武术为主。县体委年内共举办各种体育比赛活动74场次，参加620人次。

【名特土产】荞麦是本县驰名全国的唯一产品。年产量在600——700万公斤之间。荞面适口性好，具有很高的食用和药用价值；荞麦皮可做枕芯，也是良好的隔音材料。滩羊，环县系本省滩羊重点产区之一.年饲养量26万只左右。年产滩羊毛51.32万公斤，板皮4.57万张。其中：二毛裘皮1.52万张。羊羔肉别具风味，是人所共知的高级佳肴。苦杏仁为蔷薇科植物山杏种子。性温、味辛、苦甘、有小毒。可入药、亦可加工成食用油、食品。年产量33.8万公斤，属国家收购和出口品。甘草，产量居庆阳地区各县之首。年收购量39.6万公斤。豆类，主要有黄豆、绿豆、黑豆、豌豆等。年总产量达4108.5公斤。地毯，手工艺品，系本省优秀产品之一。年产量8334平方米。远销日本、美国、西德等国。

现任主要领导：

中共环县委书记：于树青

环县人大常委会主任：史昌林

环县人民政府县长：卢建敏

政协环县委员会主席：刘尚绪

中共环县纪律检查委员会书记：邓廷信

（中共环县委调查研究室：郭延玉　多辉敌　兴斌）

平凉地区

中共平凉地委书记：丁泽生

平凉行政公署专员：徐拴龙

中共平凉地区纪律检查委员会书记：朱志雄

平凉地区经济和社会发展概述

【自然概况】平凉地区位于甘肃省东部，东邻庆阳，西连定西，北依宁夏，南与天水和陕西接壤。辖一市六县，总面积11141平方公里，人口198.83万人，地区所在地平凉市。

平凉地区属半干旱大陆性气候，年平均气温8.5℃，最高气温37.3℃，最低气温零下22.5℃，年平均降雨量578.5毫米，无霜期169天。中部突起的陇山山脉贯通南北，陇山之东地势由南向东倾斜，纵横交错的泾河水系，把东部地区切割成12条原面，川原之地形成众多的沟壑。陇山之西，地势较高，属黄土丘陵沟壑区。区内主要有泾河、渭河两大水系，共有干、支流17条，年径流量15.28亿立方米。主要河流有8条，以泾河为最大。

全区总面积中，耕地与园林草地占到88.36%以上。矿产资源煤藏量约34.2亿吨，石英砂藏量约4000万吨。水能理论蕴藏量11.19万千瓦。有各种植物资源7个系列1631个品种，动物资源2个系列395种。粮食作物主要有小麦、玉米、豆类、高粱、洋芋等。经济作物以胡麻、烟草、白芸豆、油菜、大麻、白瓜子为主。蔬菜有黄瓜、萝卜、白菜、葱、芹菜等。林木主要有杨、柳、松、柏、榆、槐、椿、桐等。果树有苹果、梨、桃、杏、枣等。已被国务院列为国家级旅游景点的道教名山崆峒山，建于北魏时期的南石窟、王母宫石窟、云崖寺以及柳湖、古灵台、龙泉寺、紫荆山等25处自然和人文景观是主要的旅游资源。

【名特产品】山　药：已有500多年栽培历史，主要分布在泾河川区，尤以平凉市产为佳，年产量50万公斤以上。山药既是上品药材，又是美味佳肴。其状呈鸡腿型，个大皮薄，肉纯白色，质地细密，营养丰富。主要含有粘液汁、胆碱、糖蛋白、多酶氧化酚、甘露多糖、维生素C和17种氨基酸等成份。经测定，粗蛋白含量高达10.27，比全国最有名的河南温县怀山药的粗蛋白含量高出1.34，17种氨基酸含量均优于怀山药。

蕨　菜：名贵山珍之一，有“山菜之王”称誉。主要分布于庄浪、华亭等县阴湿山区，其质脆味美且无污染，含有较高的蕨粉、蛋白质、脂肪等滋补营养素，具有清热利肺，消肿安神之效。全区年出口600吨左右。

沙　棘：是本区主要野生资源之一，主要分布在关山林缘阴湿山区，达21万亩，果质好，无污染，含有大量的果糖、高蛋白、氨基酸、胡萝卜素等，每百克含维生素C达800——850毫克，居干鲜果之冠，且具有补肺、提神、散瘀活血、增食欲之功能。近年在充分保护野生资源的同时，又进行了人工定植，产量逐年增加。

静宁鸡：本省久负盛名的蛋肉型鸡种之一，主产于静宁、庄浪两县，年存栏67万只，活鸡每只重可达3公斤，全净膛出肉率68.71%；每只鸡年产蛋117——218个，蛋均重51.6克。该鸡种抗病性强，适应性好，孵化率高。其加工制作的“静宁烧鸡”弛名西北各省。年出售烧鸡、净光鸡30多万只。

牛心杏：因其外形象牛心而得名，主产于灵台达溪河流域，有150年栽培历史。其果实色泽鲜艳，汁多味浓，甜酸适口，离核甜仁，单果重80克以上，大者可达百余克。其核仁可食可入药，出油率达40%，是本区出口商品之一。牛心杏清末时就弛名陕甘两省，同治年间曾为朝廷贡品。

【城市建设】以宝中铁路建设为契机，动员社会力量，城乡结合，大搞城市基础设施建设，大办城乡市场。全年城市基础设施建设投入资金2400多万元，是建国以来投入最多的一年。平凉市的“两通两达”工程和南环路开拓，结束了平凉城区自古一条街的历史，改变了市危房区连片的旧貌，解决了东西大门交通梗塞的老大难问题。华亭、庄浪县城的改造为全区城市建设创造了新的经验。全年新建各类集贸市场29处，投入资金2138万元。房地产开发投入资金2288万元，建筑面积10万平方米，出售商品房3.2万平方米。地区所在地8000门程控电话开通，使全区邮电通讯事业又向前迈进了一大步，也使平凉的投资环境得到了改善。宝中铁路铺轨进入平凉境内，1994年接轨贯通后，必将对平凉经济带来新的繁荣。

【国民经济】1993年，全区上下从平凉实际出发，坚持以党的十四大精神为指针，按照建立社会主义市场经济体制的总体要求和九十年代全区经济上新台阶的基本思路，进一步解放思想，深化改革，突出重点，加速发展，促使国民经济保持了较好的发展势头，完成了年初确定的主要奋斗目标。全区国民生产总值达到157386万元，比上年增长12.63%；工农业总产值达到259270万元，增长26.57%，其中农业总产值增长7.22%，工业总产值增长29.6%；财政收入达到12903万元，增长46.93%；城乡居民储蓄余额达到92409万元，增长26.74%；农民人均纯收入达到553.68元，增长10.56%；物价上涨幅度控制在7.8%以内。

1993年度经济工作在八个方面有突出发展。

一是不断解放思想，拓宽发展思路，选准推动经济上台阶的突破口。全区进一步明确和细化了实施“双六工程”、建成“四个基地”的发展思路。农村经济提出了以小康村建设总揽全局，发展六大支柱产业，实施“511”工程的发展思路；城市经济以实施三个规划（煤炭“3.5”规划、地直企业发展规划、30个重点财源建设规划）为突破口，落实六项工程，增强后劲，提高效益，增加收入。通过一年的认真实施，全区城乡经济建设取得了显著的成效。全区成功地举办了第二届崆峒旅游节，推动了改革开放的进程。

二是认真落实减轻农民负担的各项政策，继续改革农业基本条件，实施科技兴农，改善粮食购销体制，调动了农民的生产积极性。粮食生产获得了全面丰收，总产量达到69.87万吨，增长8,73%，达到历史最好水平。

三是集中力量狠抓40个重点乡镇，积极推行股份合作制，乡镇企业发展速度加快，总产值达到146200万元，增长58.4%，实现利润和上交税金分别增长30.7%和37.6%。当年新办企业4154户，总投资达到1.07亿元；新办股份合作制企业560户，入股资金4370万元。

四是果品、烤烟两个支柱产业在规模种植、科学管理、系列服务、增产增收方面迈出了新步子。果品、烤烟收入分别达到7000万元和986万元，增长22.8%和40%，上交农林特产税173万元，上交烤烟税327万元。出现了一批种果人均收入过千元、种烟亩均收入过千元的村户，开始发挥绿色企业的富县富民作用。

五是城市经济以打好“三个硬仗”为重点，实现了整体效益的逐步好转。359户国有商业企业和64户基层供销社实行了“国有民营”和“社有自营”改革，遏制了销售、利税下降的局面。37项技术改造达产达标项目新增产值3500万元，新增利税500万元。水泥、煤炭行业分别实现利税1000万元和1240万元，实现了增产增效的目标。预算内国有企业实现利税2933万元，比上年增长18.06%。

六是多渠道筹措资金，加强协调调度，加快前期论证，全社会固定资产投资完成　万元，比上年增长%，形成了新的投资高峰。30个重点在建项目，完成投资7798万元，占计划的100.9%。技改、扭补项目共完成投资6255万元，占年计划的81.7%。全年共建成生产性项目43个，新增煤炭生产能力10万吨、水泥5万吨、棉纱3200锭。30万吨特种水泥厂、煤炭集运站、高性能永久磁、华亭煤矿60万吨洗煤厂、周寨煤矿、平凉纤维板厂、10万吨甲醇、泾川发酵甘油等项目如期完成了前期工程进度。

七是积极发展新的经济增长点，非公有制经济稳步发展。全年新增个体工商户3300户，新办私营企业40户，新建、改组股份制企业7户，新建“引资嫁接”三资企业15户，一批个体、私营加工企业正在兴办，国有企业的资产经营和股份制改革正在推开。小区建设正在起步，已确定建设项目65个，投资总规模12000万元，引进外部资金1500万元。

八是改革财政体制，加强乡级财政建设，强化税收征管，积极为实施新的财税体制做好准备。全区财政收入突破亿元大关。乡级财政有较快发展，收入已占到县级财政收入的35.2%，有16个乡实现上解465万元。行政事业单位创办实体，增收节支，消化增支650万元。

【社会事业】农业科技服务管理体系进一步完善，科技示范网络基本形成。全区1795个行政村全部建立了科技小组，77个乡镇实现科技达标，占乡镇总数的59%。建立农业科技综合示范乡镇10个，示范村68个，示范户8007户。科技成果水平有了显著提高，年内有26项科技成果水平获省、地科技进步、科技星火、科技推广奖。科技市场初具雏型，仅第二届平凉崆峒旅游节技术成果展示交易会上，实现技术成交额391万元。

基础教育取得新的进展，普及程度有了很大提高。学龄儿童入学率、小学和初中毕业生升学率分别达到97.7%、80%和45%；在校学生的巩固率、毕业率、普及率分别为97.67%、97.46%和96.14%；小学、初中毕业生合格率分别达到45.5%和33.8%；除庄浪以外的六县(市)普及了初等义务教育；静宁县被国家树立为全国"教育先进县"；全区1993年向大中专院校输送新生2590人。职业教育和成人教育迅速发展，教育结构趋于合理，全区现有职业中学18所，建立各种培训中心78个，各类职业技术学校与普通高中招生比例达到0.82∶1；通过电大、自学考试等获得大专文凭的1993年累计达到3131人；乡乡办起了农民文化技术学校，扫除文盲18.4万人，5个县(市)达到了"基本扫除文盲单位"标准。

文化事业继续发展。1993年末全区共有艺术表演团体8个，文化馆8个，农村文化站118个，图书馆7个，博物馆8个，调频广播电台6座，中波广播转播台2座，乡镇广播电视站131座，其中标准站41座，广播通播率、喇叭入户率和音响率分别达到94%、83%和85%，电视台1座，电视发射和转播台77座，卫星地面站51座，中央电视台、甘肃电视台、平凉电视台的覆盖率分别达到45%、78%和10%。

卫生事业稳步发展。全区共有县以上医院23所，乡镇卫生院130所，村医疗点2246个。共有病床位4029张，比上年增长9.3%；卫生技术人员5088人，增长2.8%。

计划生育工作圆满完成了各项任务，人口自然增长率为12.47‰。

体育事业取得较好成绩，在省级比赛中获得9枚金牌，5枚银牌；男女自行车队在全省比赛中分获团体第二名；地区体校女子手球队代表甘肃省参加全国比赛，取得第二名的好成绩。群众体育运动蓬勃发展，泾川县被国家体委命名为全国体育先进县；100%的学校推行《国家体育锻炼标准》，94.9%的学生达到合格标准。

灵台县经济和社会发展概述

【自然概况】灵台县地处陇东南部，东南连接陕西省，北接泾川，西北与崇信毗邻。全县东西长78公里，南北宽40公里，总面积1991平方公里，辖16个乡(镇)，227个村，1458个农业生产合作社，39244户，20.12万人。

县境属黄土高原关山支脉泾河流域区，地势西高东低，平均海拔1220米，地貌沟壑纵横，梁峁起伏，山川原兼有，概括为"一条塬两道川和南部山区"地形，即什字原区，达溪河和黑河川区、南部山区。

县内年平均气温8.6℃，年降水量650毫米左右，无霜期159天，属半湿润地区，农作物二年三熟，为典型的旱农耕作区。

县内自然资源丰富，有耕地94.12万亩，其中粮田77.09万亩，宜林荒山189万亩，宜牧草场28万亩，可开发利用滩涂地3800亩。野生中药材资源有8类86种，栽培药材有26种，其中以款冬花品质好，药用价值高而享有盛名，年最高收购量4万斤，远销全国各地及国际市场。

【经济发展战略】我县是传统的"农业大县，工业小县，财政穷县"1993年在 发展经济上，县委、县政府领导全县人民，立足县情，主要采取如下经济发展战略：

1. 坚持从县情出发，按照发展社会主义市场经济体制的要求，进一步解放思想，不断调整发展思路和重点增强了工作上的主动性和针对性。县委、县政府面对市场经济发展趋势，从我县实际出发，在工作实践中形成了今后全县发展经济的总体战略：坚持一个思想，实施"二五"工程，开发三大区域，建设六个小区，振兴灵台经济，实现小康目标。具体说，一个思路即稳农强柱、兴工活商、开放联合、重教兴科；"二五"工程，即加快农村烟、果、牛、药、渔五大支柱产业开发，完善工业化工、制药、肉食、地毯、果品加工五条龙生产线；开发三大区域，即按地理、气候、资源条件和布局，把全县分为什字原区、达溪河、黑河川区和南部山区三大区域实行分类指导，综合开发，形成各具特色的区域经济格局。建设六个小区，即从带动全县经济发展长远角度考虑，拟在交通便利、信息较灵、人口集中、水、电、通讯等基础条件较好的邵寨、独店、什字、朝那、梁原、中台六乡镇创建包括工业、商贸、建筑、建材、运销、房产、服务在内，多门类能辐射带动全县经济的商贸工业小区。以达到振兴灵台经济，实现小康目标。

2. 坚持抓主抓重，抓住关键，突破难点。在全县经济工作上确立了支柱产业和骨干企业两个重点，集中抓了财政收入和农民收入。农村经济注重烟、果、畜三大支柱产业开发，农村服务体系建设和"两高一优"农业的发展，城市经济集中抓了扭亏增盈、达产达标增产增效和国合商业改革。

3. 坚持培养典型，以点带面，推动工作。在1993年的工作中，树立了独店乡发展股份制和股份合作制乡镇企业。中台、什字两镇围绕财政抓经济，邵寨、吊街、新开等乡大力发展烤烟生产，西屯乡发展果园，朝那镇狠抓市场建设的典型，推动了整体工作。

4. 坚持深入实际，务实求真，狠

抓落实。全县经济工作突出了一个"实"字,说实话、办实事、求实效、创实绩,县级领导包支柱产业、包项目责任制、部门包村抓中心、现场会、办公会推动工作,"双文明"示范村建设、小康示范村建设、乡镇企业过百万元村建设、兴一业重点村建设等行之有效的工作方法,使全县工作出现上下齐抓经济的良好局面。

【经济综述】由于我县实行了比较切合县情的经济战略和灵活的工作方法。1993 年全县经济发展较快。全县国民生产总值 17620 万元,比上年增长 12.9%,国民收入达到 14500 万元,增长 9.85%,工农业总产值达到 21687 万元,增长 10.45%,财政收入达到 1046 万元,增长 46.8%,农民人均纯收入达到 580.78 元,增长 10.3%,人口自然增长率控制在 11.33‰以内。

农业基础得到进一步加强,粮食生产获得全面丰收,总产再创历史新水平。全县多渠道对农业投资 2320 万元,亩均投入 33 元,分别比上年增长 23%和 20.81%;完成改土 13060 亩,占任务的 100.5%;推广农业实用技术 27 项,覆盖面积达到 310 多万亩(次);粮食总产 12178.8 万公斤,单产 153 公斤,分别比去年增长 7.2%和 7.7%;农民人均产粮 1200 斤;油料播种面积达到 89501 亩,产量达到 461.1 万公斤,增长 8.9%。烤烟、果树、畜牧三大支柱产业开发步伐加快,已基本形成了规模。围绕农民增收、财政创收这一目标,从强化管理,改进服务入手,组建起了烤烟、果品、畜牧、渔业、药材五大支柱产业开发服务中心(公司),促进了支柱产业的发展。特别是烤烟、果树、畜牧三大支柱产业总产值达到 5026.9 万元,占到了农业总产值的 33.7%,增长 27.25%。畜牧业收入达到 2675 万元,占到了农村总收入的三分之一以上;年末大家畜存栏 98009 头,比上年增长 6.3%。其中牛存栏 89210 头,出栏肉牛 12969 头,产肉 2359 吨,形成了一定规模的"牛经济";生猪存栏 54820 头,出栏 33838 头,产肉 212.49 吨;羊只存栏 58311 只,出栏菜羊 15399 只;产肉 251.12 吨;禽蛋产量 1490 吨,禽肉产量 1322.4 吨。烤烟面积达到 2374 亩,总产达到 2020.46 吨,商品量 1673.68 吨,实现利税 120 万元,比去年有大幅度增长。果园面积 32373 亩,当年新增 10723 亩,其中苹果园面积 26954 亩,产量 2429.45 吨。股份合作制企业发展有了新的突破,乡镇企业整体效益进一步提高。全县新办股份制和股份合作制企业 52 户,入股资金 294.7 万元。乡镇企业总产值达到 11328.9 万元,增长 50.8%,实现利税、上交税金分别比去年增长 41%和 33.3%。新上项目 61 个,其中百万元以上的项目 4 个,完成总投资 849 万元。

全面完成了企业达产达标任务,工业生产基础大大加强。六个达产达标项目新增产值 536.7 万元,利税 42.4 万元,分别占年计划的 109%和 151.4%。实现工业总产值 4977.9 万元,增长 20.4%。

进一步完善了县乡财政分级包干体制,财政收入有了较大幅度增长。全县财政收入首次突破了千万元大关,比预算增收 220 万元。全县 16 个乡镇完成收入 554 万元,占到了县级财政收入的 52.8%。

【城市建设与城乡改革】基本建设进度加快,城乡面貌发生了较大变化。完成固定资产投资 1932 万元,比上年增长 84.2%;35 个在建项目,当年完成投资 395 万元,占计划的 30.6%。城市基本设施建设有了较大突破,县城占地面积 3.01 平方公里,有各种建筑 3000 座,大街 4 条,其中高层建筑从无到有,达到 12.5 万平方米,逐步修复了古灵台,开通硬化了三条主街 4.6 公里,开通了环城路,修建了排污工程,开通了 1000 门自动电话,完成了柳——中 35 千伏输变电工程,投资 78900 元,新建续建市场 4 处,扩大市场面积 24000 平方米,新建家属住宅 113 套,8400 平方米。

城乡改革进一步深入,对外开放迈出了新的步伐。国合商业 170 个门店(柜组)全部推进了"国有民营"和"社有自营",搞活了经营。各行政事业单位多渠道筹措资金 247 万元,创办实体 52 个,实现产值 176 万元,利税 27.2 万元,有效地转变了职能,为机构改革创造了条件。

【社会事业】通过深化教育体制改革,进一步加强基础教育和成人职业技术教育,学校教育质量稳步提高。1993 年高校大专录取 166 人,是我县历史上录取人数最多的一年。科技服务体系建设进一步加强,实用技术推广和科技培训取得了显著成效。年内培训各类农民技术员 46000 人次,有 1700 多名科技人员到生产第一线开展科技项目承包,提供技术服务。县上有广播电台一座,已建成四个标准化乡广播站,建成小型电视差转台 18 个,有 6 个乡 93 个村安装了双向对讲机,广播"三率"达到 90%以上,解决了边远山区群众听广播、看电视难的问题。卫生事业有了很大进步,全县两所县级医院,有先进的 B 超、纤维胃镜、心脏搐控监护仪、自动生化分析仪、超声东普勒等医疗设备,不但能够查清各种疑难病症,胃大部切除手术、针灸等还在全省处于先进地位。16 个乡镇卫生院有门诊病室 11800 平方米,病床 87 张,解决了农村群众看病难的问题。文化、公安、司法、民政、计划生育、侨务、外事、旅游、信访也取得了可喜成果。

【名特土产】我县在发展城乡市场经济的过程中,积极探索提高产品质量的路子,注重企业的达产达标,发展"两高一优"农业,利用本地自然资源,形成了一批具有地方特色的名、优、特、土产品,主要有:

1. 灵台县地毯厂生产的仿古、

京、美彩等各式地毯，图案新颖，做工精细，质地坚韧，洗如锦缎，状似浮雕，既有实用价值，又有观赏价值，产品畅销美国、瑞典、日本、伊朗等国。特别是90道机抽洗欧式地毯为部优产品，供不应求。

2. 灵台县农机修造厂生产的145系列柴油机缸盖，是省优产品，除此外还有2PFX——1型山地水平沟种植播种机，脱粒机，钢门窗畅销西北五省。

3. 灵台县肉联厂生产的冷冻牛肉、鸡肉、兔肉和各种肉制罐头，供不应求。10分体、4分体冷冻牛肉年产500吨，销往前苏联、香港、日本、西德。

4. 灵台杏系嫁接培育而成，俗称“接杏”。平均单果重量80克以上，大者可达百余克，以其果大味美汁浓色鲜闻名遐迩，清时一度成为为朝廷贡品。全县1993年有大杏基地1693亩，年产鲜果529.86吨，商品量达到332.28吨，远销陕、甘、宁、新四省(区)，加工生产的杏脯、罐头，供外贸出口。

5. 灵台甲鱼因其独特的地理、气候条件，成为黄河流域中华甲鱼中的上等品。以它能治疗癌症等疑难杂症和鳖血的高级滋补作用，在全国享有“金鳖”之誉。县甲鱼场进行的甲鱼人工恒温饲养技术课题研究，在西北同类地区遥遥领先，获甘肃省科委科技进步三等奖。

现任主要领导：

中共灵台县委书记：陈全福

灵台县人大常委会主任：李克让

灵台县人民政府县长：胡昌林

政协灵台县委员会主席：张步德

中共灵台县纪律检查委员会书记：彭汉武

（中共灵台县委政策研究室）

华亭县经济和社会发展概述

华亭县位于甘肃东部的关山东麓，北靠平凉市，南邻陕西陇县，西接庄浪和宁夏泾源县，东连崇信县。全县有土地总面积1183.12平方公里。有耕地44万亩，其中山地37.2万亩，占85%；川地6.8万亩，占15%。总人口16.8万人(少数民族1.91万人)，其中农业人口12.4万人，占74%；城镇人口4.4万人，占26%。辖10个乡(含两个少数民族乡)，两个镇，117个行政村，608个合作社。

【自然概况】华亭县属高寒阴湿黄土高塬丘陵沟壑区，境内群山逶迤，梁卯起伏，沟壑纵横，水系密布，草丰林茂。地势自西北向东南逐渐低下，平均海拔1400米。关山支脉三乡、黄甫、双凤、朝那四山呈手指形横贯全境，诸山之内分布着九条较大的河谷川地，形成了由河谷冲积川台区、浅山丘陵沟壑区、中高土石区三个地类组成的地貌特征。六盘山余脉关山横贯在县城西部，既涵养水源，又调节气候，是华亭的绿色屏障和天然水库。气候温凉湿润，年均气温7.9℃，年均降水量615毫米，全年日照总时数2258小时，无霜期168天。水源充裕，年总径流量183亿立方米，水资源总量为2.19亿立方米。矿产资源十分丰富，全县有探明的矿种10个，可供开发利用的7个。煤炭储量为20.7亿吨，占全省储量的47%，占华亭煤田总量的63%。石灰石储量4300万吨，石英砂储量4350万吨，石英石8万吨，陶土24.9万吨，甘泥12.72万吨，铜矿16.64万吨。生物资源有500种左右，其中动物资源两个系列46个品种，植物资源7个系列410个品种。全县有荒坡草地38.3万亩，载畜量可达8万多头。森林面积50.7万亩，森林覆盖率为36.6%。粮食作物以小麦、洋芋、玉米为主，年播种面积在38万亩左右；经济作物以药材、大麻、蔬菜、豆类为主。土特产品有核桃、药材、大麻、蕨菜等12个品种。

【经济发展概况】1993年，全县经济完成了年初确定的各项任务，保持了较好的发展势头，实现了四个突破。全县社会总产值突破4亿元大关，达到4.2亿元，增长10%；乡镇企业产值突破2亿元大关，达到2.3亿元，增长55%，财政收入突破2000万元大关，达到2283万元，增长44.6%；粮食产量突破亿斤大关，总产量达到1.07亿斤，增长10.3%。工农业总产值达到2.9亿元，增长22.7%；农民人均纯收入达到582.4元，比上年增收55元。

【农村经济全面发展】我县始终把发展农村经济放在全县经济工作的首位，强化农业基础，突出粮食生产，开发支柱产业，大办乡镇企业，狠抓扶贫开发，进一步提高农业的综合生产能力，加快了传统农业向高产优质高效农业转化，提高了农业的整体效益。1993年农业总产值达到7960万元，比上年增长5.8%。(1)乡镇企业保持高速发展势头。全县紧紧抓住铁路和矿区建设两大机遇，坚持多轮驱动，多业并举，在投资规模、新上项目、速度效益等方面实现了新的突破。当年投资1338万元，完成乡镇企业技改和新上项目107个，新增各类企业1067户，总户数达到3521户，从业人员达到17585人，发展速度达到了55%。实现利润967.53万元，上缴税金210万元，同比增长31.1%。(2)粮食生产连续八年获得丰收，1993年总产量比上年净增4970吨。(3)药、麻、菜、林、畜等支柱产业开发取得了显著成效。全县种植药材8575亩；大麻13127亩；商品蔬菜1164亩，其中塑料大棚151.7亩；新增造林25251亩，定植经济树种4961亩；大家畜年末存栏5.56万头，肉类总产量达到3050吨；农产品商品率达到13.4%。农业生产条件继续得到改善。当年新增有效灌溉面积1500亩，保灌面积600亩；新修梯田8212

亩，全县梯条田总面积累计达到24.94万亩；新架和整修农电线路18.3杆公里；农用机械和化肥等农资使用量都有一定增长。

【工业生产稳中有增】一是企业管理得到加强。县上首先在管理企业的方式上作了大的调整，开始由依靠行政手段直接管理向运用市场经济手段间接管理过渡，按照《全民所有制企业转换经营机制条例》的要求，还权给企业，让企业根据市场的需求，自主决策经营。企业获得自主权后，加强基层管理工作，不断完善内部经营机制，抓质量，降消耗，以销促产。止年底，完成销售收入8014.9万元，增长6.5%，万元产值综合能耗比上年降低7.4%，16项单耗指标有12项控制在计划之内。二是产品结构得到调整，当年引进和采用新技术、新工艺两项，开发新产品4种，组织生产新产品18种，产值率、利税率分别比上年提高3%和7%。县上对适销产品和骨干行业，从资金、原材料供应、设备、技术方面实行倾斜，使其满负荷生产，规模经营。到年底，全县原煤、水泥、高压电瓷产量分别达到136万吨、3万吨和996吨，同比增长13.3%、56.3%和44.3%。三是技术改造成效显著。当年投资1207.5万元，新上和续建技改项目8项，有5项已建成投产，新增产值451.05万元，利税48.67万元。

【财贸工作取得新成绩】(1)财政收入稳定增长。通过完善财政管理体制，强化税收征管，控制经费支出，培植扩大财源，实现了财政收支平衡，略有贡献的目标，财政收入比上年净增705万元。金融形势进一步好转。各银行认真落实宏观调控措施，整顿金融秩序，积极吸收存款，努力盘活资金，在很大程度上缓解了建设资金的需求矛盾。(2)商品流通更加活跃。通过大力推行"国有民营"、"社有自营"和粮食购销体制改革，使国合商业和粮食企业在流通领域的主渠道作用得到进一步发挥，以个体工商户为补充的流通体系逐步得到完善，全县新增个体户506户，总数达到2155户。社会商品零售总额达到7800万元，市场成交额达到2121万元，比上年增长55%。(3)市场建设跨上新台阶。多方筹措资金857万元，在全县扩建了两个交易中心，新建三个专业市场，开辟了三个农贸市场，新立两个乡村集市，扩大市场用地64.5亩，新增建筑面积3万平方米。(4)第三产业迈出了新的步伐。当年完成商品住宅投资97万元，预售商品住宅40套。开通了三乡程控自动电话，在砚峡、麻庵建起了邮电代办所。县城区供水工程和泾甘公路关山段改道工程通过了省、地验收。围绕支援矿区和铁路建设的服务业也有了大的发展。全县第三产业产值占到国民生产总值的17.27%。

【各项社会事业有了新的发展】教育工作进一步加强了基础教育，加快了实施九年义务教育的步伐。列入当年完成"普九"教育的五乡镇和三个厂矿，办学积极性空前高涨。一方面增加投入，努力改善办学条件，全县共投入建设资金480.6万元，完成了35所中小学、幼儿园的搬迁新建、危房翻建和改扩建任务，另一方面狠抓管理，不断提高教育质量，九项基本指标达到或基本达到了省上"普九"验收标准。科技工作紧紧围绕经济上台阶，组织实施农业生产新技术30项，承担省、地县列科研课题9项，4项通过了鉴定验收，有6个乡镇实现了科技达标。文化体育工作在加强农村文化、育基础建设的同时，积极组织开展了丰富多彩的文体娱乐活动，活跃繁荣了城乡群众文化生活。广播、电视工作抓质量，促发展，开办了华亭电视新闻节目，建成砚峡乡标准广播电视站，全县广播线路通播率、入户率、音响率平均达到90%。卫生工作坚持预防和治疗相结合，狠抓改善医疗条件，提高医疗水平，计划免疫、妇幼保健的各项指标均达到规定标准，地方病发病率明显下降。计划生育工作，从提高整体水平入手，坚持经常性工作与突击活动相结合，当年完成四项节育手术3451例，人口自然增长率和出生率均控制在计划指标以内。坚持专群结合，综合治理，严厉打击了各项刑事犯罪活动，综合治理的各项指标基本完成任务，社会治安秩序进一步好转。

现任主要领导：

中共华亭县委书记：景　泰

华亭县人大常委会主任：杨发录

亭县人民政府县长：张和平

政协华亭县委员会主席：湛文芳

中共华亭县纪律检查委员会书记：田志明

（中共华亭县委调研室
蓝永平　李自长）

陇南地区

成县经济和社会发展概述

【自然概况】成县地处甘肃省东南部，在北纬33°29′至34°02′，东经105°23′至105°57′之间。东北接徽县，西北连西和，南界西汉水与康县相望，东南隅和陕西省略阳县接壤。总土地面积1690.23平方公里。辖16个乡、6个镇、243个行政村、1471个合作社。总户数48596户，总人口22.1万人，总劳动力89486个，其中农业人口20.2万人，占总人口的91.4%，人口密度每平方公里131人。

本县属暖温带半湿润气候区，年平均气温11.7℃，无霜期208天。全县热量资源属一熟有余两熟不足，在低海拔的犀牛江沿岸，热量可满足一年两熟的需要，为发展喜温作物，实行间作套种一年多熟提供了良好的条件。全县平均降水量639毫米；平均日照时数1700.2小时，日照率38%。我县土地总面积253.53万亩，人均11.5亩，其中林地面积118.65万亩，占总面积46.8%，人均5.4亩；草地面积15.5万亩，占总面积6.11%，人均0.7亩；耕地面积83.93万亩，占总面积的33.1%，人均3.8亩，高于全国水平。

县境内铅锌矿藏主要分布点12处，矿体94个，矿石地质储量约10516.16万吨，金属量994万吨。分布在西汉水和东河的砂金总储量3.35吨；分布在宋坪的铁矿地质储量206.45万吨；分布在化垭大坪等地的烟煤，储蓄量约84万吨；分布在二郎、王磨、抛沙等地的大理石总储量约32.6亿立方米。分布广泛的石灰石促进了本县水泥建材的开发。

全县林地中用材林31.83万亩，薪炭林11.14万亩，经济林1.39万亩，人均有林2.0亩，略高于全国水平。其中，有经济树种42种，它们中有较高开发价值的栓皮栎、漆树、黄连木、木本药材杜仲、辛荑等。还有核桃、柿子、花椒、樱桃等果类树种。林木伴生有丰富的野生植物1296种。其中有开发价值的香精饮料植物沙棘、五味子。野生药用植物半夏、天麻等20多种。有蜜源植物298种，有一、二类野生保护动物9种。

【农村经济协调稳定增长】全县以提高粮食单位面积产量为重点，扩大粮食作物播种面积，增加粮食总产，全年粮食总产达到2.09亿斤，比上年增长了4.2个百分点，创历史最高水平，实现了农民人均千斤粮。同时着力改善农业生产基础。兴修梯田1.77万亩，造林6.08万亩，完成水利工程12项，新增水浇地2200亩。以调整作物结构和布局、推广实用技术为重点，全县发展“两高一优”农业，进行农业综合开发，夏秋作物比例由上年的66.7：33.3调整为65：35，粮经比例由上年的90：10调整为87：13；各类作物良种推广面积占作物总面积的91%以上，达到59.21万亩；经济作物面积比上年扩大了9600亩，完成地膜玉米1.03万亩，带状种植6500亩，发展“双千田”5300亩，“吨粮田”700亩；施用磷肥6000标吨。以畜牧、蔬菜、蚕桑、林果、药材及农副产品加工为骨干的多种经营，涌现出一批象苏元、宋坪乡和大垭、广化、卯堡、朱家桥、大营、胡寨、席坪、柏湾、土嵩、黑楼房等村各具特色的示范点和专业基地。全县保护地蔬菜栽培7812亩，地膜大蒜5300亩，种植蔬菜14700亩，新发展经济林果23600亩。1991至1993年累计植桑1030万株，养蚕5230张，产茧27.77万斤，增加农民收入266万元。多种经营总产值达到9810万元，比上年增长15.24%。乡镇企业总产值完成1.51亿元，比上年增长47.2%。比上年计划增长11.9%，涌现出了“一线两点十二乡镇十六村社”的支柱产业和骨干企业大户。其中黄诸、城关、抛沙等十二个重点乡镇的乡镇企业产值占全县乡企总产值的75%以上；九个重点乡镇工业企业的工业产值占全县乡镇工业总产值的54%以上；全县乡镇企业上缴税金586万元，占县级工商税收的34%。乡镇企业的发展成为近几年速度最快的一年。

【工商财税】工业生产和基础设施建设。以建立社会主义市场经济为目标，用改革总揽全局，全县全民工业企业完成利税498.64万元，比上年增长47.96%，新建、扩建重点工业项目14项，完成投资4360万元，已有7个工业项目建成投产，并论证储备建设项目92个。作为全县重点骨干项目的镡河金矿采金船11月中旬出坑进入正常试生产之后，已采金5.5公斤，实现销售收入53万元。全县完成工业产值1.64亿元，比上年增长19.2%，比年计划增长3.2%，其中乡以上工业总产值完成1.15亿元，比上年增长14.8%。社会商品零售总额完成8332万元，比上年增长24.8%，比年计划增长18%，城乡集市贸易成交额达到1.34亿元，比上年翻了一番；城区2000门程控电话开通，邮电业务，通信总量和业务收入达到458.47万元，三项均比上年增长36%以上。晒王公路工程基本完成，镡坝、南康、宋坪三乡输电线工程基本竣工，镡坝代沟口公路桥建成通车。全年投资117.8万元，新建、扩建农贸市场4个，为经济开发和繁荣城乡贸易创造了良好的条件。

财税、金融保持了较好的增长势头。去年，全县财经收入完成2407万元，比上年增长24.65%，比年初地区下达预算数1721万元增长40%，比县上调整预算后收入安排数1923万元增长25%。其中工商税收完成1746万元，城乡各类存款余额达到2.18亿元，比上年增长31%，各项贷款余额达到1.7亿元，比上年增长30%。农业银行存款达6000万元，为全区之首。为了减轻财政压力，我们初步改革了公费医疗办法，全年医药费支出由1992年225万元减到150万元。仅此一项，全年减少支出75万元。在资金十分困难的情况下，财政拿出237万元农业专项资金，农行发放支农贷款723万元，用于对农业的投入，支持农业生产。

各项改革，《条例》赋予企业的14项权利逐步落实，三轮承包工作正在加紧进行，通过转换经营机制，深化企业内部改革，毕家山铅锌矿、红川酒厂、矿业公司、农机厂、水泥厂、面粉厂、活性炭厂、塑料厂等一大批企业活力进一步增强。止去年底，全县已有50个国合商业门店实行了国有民营和社有自营。在深化企业改革上，我们进行了大胆的探索，已批准完成了红川酒厂对食品厂的兼并，二轻供销公司与被服厂的合并。

一年来,我们大力支持鼓励发展个体、私营经济。全县新发展个体工商户1027户,累计达到3459户,从业人员达到5884人,营业额比上年增长67%,有力地促进了非公有制经济的发展。全县机关兴办经济实体已发展到58个,为机构改革,分流人员打下了基础。住房制度改革已有了实质性的进展。

【社会事业】具有成县特色的文化事业,在巩固以往取得较好成绩的基础上水平又有新的提高。文化县城达标活动已通过地区验收。城市建设上,在完成东新街改造工程后,盘旋路一期工程和自来水厂工程正在加紧进行。基础教育稳步发展,教育质量有了新的提高,去年全县为大中专院校输送合格新生246人。农村卫生条件有所改善,医疗水平进一步提高,全县妇幼保健和疫苗接种率在全区评比中居于首位,取得了显著的工作成绩。社会治安、综合治理工作成效明显,保证了全县的社会稳定。计划生育工作全面完成了上级下达的各项指标任务,人口自然增长率控制在13.3‰的控制线以下。

现任主要领导:

中共成县委书记:刘醒初

成县人大常委会主任:者存义

成县人民政府县长:薛治有

政协成县委员会主席:张保华

中共成县纪律检查委员会书记:李志辉

(中共成县委研究室:李志奇)

两当县经济和社会发展概述

【自然概况】两当县位于甘肃省东南,嘉陵江上游,东接秦陇,南通巴蜀。面积1374平方公里,辖14个乡(镇),5万人口。有闻名遐迩"琵琶秋水"、"天门锁云"、"乳洞飞雨"、"镜峰棒日"等八大自然景观,有与九寨沟相媲美的云坪西沟峡、"金滩"张家、"黑河"省级自然保护区,松翠苍柏、奇峰林立、群瀑垂帘,是不可多得的旅游胜地。

两当农业生产条件优越,气候温和,光热水匹配良好,土层肥厚,粮田面积大,可开发利用的荒山荒坡26.4万亩,适宜于各种农作物生长。有林地148万亩,森林覆盖率72%,有国内罕见、面积最大的白皮松林保护区4.48万亩;有蜜源植物144种,有国家保护的羚牛、斑羚、大鲵、金猫、林麝、猕猴、雪豹等珍贵动物。水力资源有一江七河,嘉陵江流经两乡12村85公里,水能理论蕴藏量4.6万千瓦,发展水电事业有广阔的前景。矿产资源已探明的有金、银、铜、铁、铅锌、煤炭、陶土、大理石和优质花岗岩等10多种。

【经济发展】1993年两当县委、县政府在经济建设上总的思路是:粮、多、工并举,富民富县并重"、稳定发展粮食生产,突出发展工业、乡镇企业、多种经营和流通,领导全县人民实现了经济工作战略重点的转移,使全县经济建设保持了持续、快速、健康发展的势头。1993年全县工农业总产值达到5678.57万元,比上年增长8.5%;完成农业总产值3628.07万元,比上年增长4.8%;乡以上工业完成产值2050.50万元,比上年增长15.7%;乡镇企业总产值达到2200.23万元,比上年增长22.2%;粮食总产量达到5385.27万斤,比上年增长2.4%;本级财政收入完成了275万元,比上年增长76.3%;农民人均纯收入达到496.66元,比上年有所增长。

农业,通过改革农业生产条件,推广和实施科教兴农战略,开发"两高一优"农业的区域试点,使粮食产量不断上升,1993年比1992年粮食总产量增长2.4%;特别是以实施"2400"工程为主要内容的多种经营生产,有了较快发展。1993年全县多种经营产值达到1959.89万元,比上年增长11.8%,多种经营在农业总产值的比重达54%,超过了以粮食为主的种植业。1993年全县栽植各类经济林67115亩,达323.26万株,全年完成植树造林21500亩。

工业生产依靠科技和挖潜改造,开发了陶瓷大地砖、IW——65——65——OA供水泵、高压聚合板、果老仙酒、罐头食品等新产品。企业以改革为动力,以提高经济效益为中心,强化管理,提高质量,促进销售,实现了工业发展速度和效益同步增长。1993年全县国有工业企业实现利润32.32万元,占年计划的107.8%。

在乡镇企业发展上提高产品质量,扩大企业规模,积极倡导乡镇企业兼并2户二轻集体企业,推动股份合作制企业试点,通过资金、人才、技术等的生产要素重新流动组合,促进全县乡镇企业大发展。1993年保持了22.2%的高速增长水平。

1993年县委、县政府提出了加快发展个体私营经济的十条意见。为个体私营经济的发展创造良好政策环境。1993年全县个体工商户1163户,比1983年增长3.83倍;人员1771人,比1983年增长4.75倍;私营企业3户,人员67人,个体户投入资金比1983年增长12.5%。

【城区建设】1993年以来,两当县在城区建设上,主要进行了市政基础设施建设和计划投资工程建设。按照县城实施美化新北街、硬化公园路、拓宽东大街、建设环形路近日广场的规划建设方案。从社会集资款筹措73万元用于基本建设。(1)美化新北街工程投资30万元,完成总长390米,宽18米,包括两侧花坛、排水道、人行道和电信、给水、路灯照明等工程建设任务;(2)公园路农贸市场工程投资34万元,完成600平方米钢瓦大棚农贸市场,完成长266米,宽10米的整体混凝土路面及两侧下水道工程和简易货棚安装工程，可提供200摊位，有1073户个体户从事商贸活动；(3)拓宽县城东大街和近日广场环形路工程，计划投资100万元，1993年已组织拆迁准备工作；(4)完成了县城附近窑沟渠北住宅区133米排污和县城西大街18米跨经钢索吊桥建筑安装工程。工程建设，1993年全县有计划投资建设项目8项，总投资246.1万元。本年度工程计划4项，投资125.1万元，完成了县科技服务中心大楼，县教委电教中心楼，劳动服务就业中心楼；另有跨年度工程4项，投资121.1万元，县防疫妇幼保健综合大楼、县看守所、县工商银行职工住宅商品楼、县建设银行营业楼、陇南西坡煤矿2号井矿灯房浴室都在加紧施工建设之中。

【社会事业发展】科技事业，1993年全县科技项目的研究推广取得了显著成绩。省列《栗实害虫寄生蜂应用研究》、《野生板栗高接换优》和地区列《软枣嫁接甜柿子推广》等农业科技项目，都通过了上级业务主管部门的鉴定阶段；县水泵厂“IW——50——50——100B型”水泵新产品获陇南科技进步一等奖；陶瓷系列产品和水泵系列产品，获得了第五届中国西部技术交易会金奖，有10项科研推广项目获县级科技进步一等奖。文教卫生，1993年积极宣传《义务教育法》和《教师法》，提高教师的社会地位。全县有各级各类学校146所，教职工645人，学生9041人，全县小学入学率达到99.2%，巩固率达到98.6%，毕业率达到98.9%，普及率达到98.6%，全县高考有59名高中毕业生考入各类大专院校，两当一中被省政府授予先进集体称号。通过多渠道筹集资金，截止1993年全县新修校舍9804平方米，改建维修校舍15630平方米，全县新建、改建维修校舍面积占现有校舍面积的71.5%，实现一无六有两化三配套的学校已达63所；占全县学校总数的45%。卫生工作，加强了常见病、多发病和地方病的防治。1993年重点加强了基层卫生院基础建设，有4个中心卫生院完成了新建和维修面积566平方米，投入资金10.22万元，并加强了乡村卫生院的专业技术力量。特别是地方病防治、计划免疫和妇幼保健方面，通过采取食用碘硒盐、服药、改水、强化免疫、群众性爱国卫生运动等措施，整体提高了人民的身体健康水平。计划生育，1993年全县人口自然增长率为10.1‰，控制了人口数量，提高了人口质量。邮电通讯，1993年是全县邮电事业发展较快的一年。在县财政困难的情况下，县上筹集55万元资金用于市话改制，1993年底完成了县城1000门自动电话开通工程。县邮电生产办公综合大楼和生产楼附属工程，在1993年8月全部交付投入正常运营。县城市话改制成功后，对外信息交流明显加快，改善了县城的投资环境。广播电视，1993年全县广播电视系统职工队伍壮大稳定。全县广播入户率55.6%，电视覆盖率82.7%，全县14乡(镇)都有广播放大站，开展农村自办节目；全县有31个卫星地面站和差转台，其中地面站15座，差转台16座，有小调频广播转播台1台，全县有线电视目前正在筹备之中。

【名特土产】两当县的名特土产品种较多，形成一定规模和具有名气的产品，主要有以下几种：中外驰名的狼牙蜜年产量50多万公斤；有“水果之王”猕猴桃；干鲜果核桃、板栗、柿子、花椒；各类中药材400多种，主要有杜仲、天麻、厚朴等名贵药材；木耳、银耳、香菇等食用菌数十种；生产香料和清凉饮料的七里香、香草、金银花、啤酒花等。

现任主要领导：

中共两当县委书记：吕国璧

两当县人大常委会主任：王志胜

两当县人民政府县长：李晓华

政协两当县委员会主席：朱玉璋

中共两当县纪律检查委员会书记：

高象全

(中共两当县政研室)

徽县经济和社会发展概述

徽县位于甘肃省东南部，东经105°34′至106°27′，北纬33°33′至34°11′。地处南北秦岭之间的下陷盆地，处于由暖温带向北亚热带的过渡地带，属大陆性季风气候，并具有显著的盆地气候特征。海拔704至2504米，相对高差1800米，年平均气温12℃，无霜期202天，降水量745.8毫米。总面积2722.9平方公里，折合408.4万亩，其中耕地43.48万亩，山旱地占耕地的95.02%，是以旱作农业为主的县。

全县辖18个乡(镇)，249个行政村，1224个合作社，20.2万人，其中农业人口18.3万人。1993年，全县经济和社会各项事业保持了良好的发展态势，社会总产值达到37600万元，比上年增长16.58%；国民生产总值达到19870万元，比上年增长8.2%；工农业总产值完成31989万元，比上年增长11.1%；财政收入2871万元，比上年增收416万元，增长16%。

【农业综合开发成就显著】农业总产值稳定上升。1993年全县农业总产值为17101万元，比上年增长9.2%。其中种植业产值11172万元，增长14.13%；林业产值1618万元，增长45.85%；牧业产值4291万元，增长3.47%；渔业产值20万元，增长27.32%。

粮食生产连续获得丰收。1993年粮食播种面积56.08万亩，总产1.315亿公斤，比上年增产5.43%；商品量达到0.3亿公斤，占总产量的23%；粮食亩产234公斤，比上年228公斤增长2.63%，全县人均占有粮食722.5公斤，进入全国先进行列。

支柱产业开发初具规模。一是商品畜基地建设稳步发展。1993年全县生猪存栏9.42万头，出栏8.63万头，出栏率91.5%；牛存栏4.98万头，出栏商品牛6100头，出栏率12.2%；鸡存栏22万只，出栏13万只，出栏率60%；全县养猪5头以上的饲养大户达1845户，户均养牛4头的饲养大户270户，户均养鸡86只的饲养大户210户。二是林果基地建设长足发展。全县果树面积达到2.69万亩，242.49万株，水果总产量255万公斤，总产值229万元。其中雪梨面积8300亩，39.96万株，产量达25.17万公斤。累计完成板栗高接换优47.2万株，人工建园1300多亩；银杏人工建园累计达1300亩，结果树97株，产量5000公斤，产值达15万元。三是蚕桑基地建设出现稳步发展势头。全县植桑32万株，桑园面积达3403亩；1993年养蚕1400张，产鲜茧3.2万公斤，蚕农收入32万元，分别比上年增长8.9%，22.5%和25%；制种1.45万张，共育小蚕1400张，共育率达100%。四是蔬菜基地建设取得突破性进展。蔬菜生产以稀、缺、早、优为方向，以外销为目标，1993年全县蔬菜种植面积1.8万亩，比上年增长54%。其中地膜栽培面积3300亩，小拱棚栽培370亩，新建塑料大棚125个，80.5亩，日光节能温室5个，2.5亩，总产量2500万公斤，产值712万元，分别比上年增长22%和51%。全县西瓜种植面积发展到8000亩，比1992年的5000亩增长60%，总产量超过2000万公斤，直接经济收入达400万元以上。五是食用菌开发迈上新台阶。1993年全县点种黑木耳2.8万架，累计保存5.21万架，总产11.29万公斤，比上年增长85.5%；香菇袋料栽培6万筒，平菇5万袋，共收鲜菇8万公斤。同时全县培育黑木耳菌种47.6万袋(瓶)，菇类菌种1.95万袋，形成了以黑木耳为主，袋料香菇、平菇多种食用菌共同发展的新格局。

种植业结构逐渐趋于合理。全县以“469”耕作改制效益计划为方向，采取压夏扩秋，压粮扩经，压低产作物扩高产作物，压劣质品种扩优质品种等措施，1993年秋播小麦22.6万亩，比上年减少6%；冬油菜3.7万亩，比上年扩大33%；复种黄豆11.26万亩，比上年增加13.6%；复种玉米4.17万亩，比上年增长6%。

农业社会化服务体系逐步加强，农业生产基本条件得到进一步改善。一是1993年分配的20多名农业院校毕业的大中专学生，全部分配到乡一级服务体系工作，同时转正了原招聘的69名农民技术员。目前18个乡镇服务体系基本健全，有人员221人。全县有农民专业技术协会(研究会)79个，会员1859人，服务网络延伸到村、社、农户。二是兴修水平梯田6310亩，占任务的126.2%；植树造林1.5万亩，比上年增加近1万亩；治理水土流失面积20767亩，占任务11400亩的182.2%。三是完成了一批河堤及沟头治理新建工程，新增灌溉面积1400亩，恢复灌溉面积12600亩；新修防汛河堤3811米，检查维修重险堤5处650米，加固了3处156米，保护耕地2666亩，保护村庄5个，3100多人。四是抓了秸杆还田、绿肥压青、苜蓿种植翻压和圈所改造、精肥上山等有机投入，改善了土壤结构，增强了农业发展后劲。五是抓种子基地建设，落实改粮中单2号、掖单13号玉米制种田5000亩，制种41万多公斤；繁育小麦新品种1515亩，40万公斤，

农民生活逐步改善。1993年全县农民家庭人均纯收入610.98元，比上年净增38.77元，增长6.75%；农村居民储蓄5501.2万元，比上年4727.4万元增长16.4%；农民人均住房面积达到15.5平方米，比上年增加1.1平方米。

【乡镇企业发展进入快车道】1993年，全县筹措资金1868.9万元，新发展各类乡镇企业1062个，其中乡办12个，个体私营1009户，股份合作制41个，全县乡镇企业累计发展到6014户，比上年4952户增长21.4%；从业人员15912人，比年初增加4098人。乡镇企业总产值达到12101万元，首次突破亿元大关，比上年增长32.57%。其中工业总产值6665.05万元，增长29.03%；乡以上工业产值2706万元，增长40.07%。总收入11173.07万元，比上年增长36.4%；利润1213.6万元，增长39.93%；上交税金434.4万，增长36.83%。

【工业生产稳步发展】工业上围绕白酒、丝绸、豆制品、矿产品开发“四条龙”配套建设，以提高效益为中心，狠抓了挖潜改造和现有企业的达产达标、减亏、扭亏及重点项目建设。1993年全县完成工业总产值14887万元，比上年同期净增774.3万元，增长7.6%；完成销售收入9453.7万元，比上年增长17.5%。随着企业经营机制的转换，产品结构得到了进一步调整，产品质量不断提高，双特陇南春获得首届中国食品博览会金奖，陇南春酒被商业部列入国家名酒调拨行列。豆浆晶厂研制开发的五个系列产品，在西交会上获得金奖。

【商贸流通渠道不断拓宽】全县商业系统有4户企业的34个门店实行“国有民营”，分别占企业和门店数的50%和66.7%，八个月完成销售额123万元，比上年同期增长29.2%，实现利润3.2万元，比上年增加2.8万元。供销系统有1个公司和8个基层单位的103个门店实行“社有自营”，分别占企业和门店数的60%和60%，八个月上缴承包费36.8万元，城乡社会购买力显著增长，全年社会商品零售总额约10222万元，比上年6001万元增长70.3%。

在商业网点建设上，完成了立项修建金徽商场4200多平方米，自筹资金修建百货公司北街营业楼1200多平方米，修建饮食公司旅社楼800多平方米等一批工程，总投资400多万元。在市场建设上，新开辟两处农贸市场，交易面积3400平方米；投资11万元新建了永宁农贸市场；完成了"陇南蔬菜批发市场"一期工程；征地28546平方米，完成了"城关综合农贸市场"前期建设工程的各项准备工作。一年来，全县共投入市场建设资金187.7万元（县财政投入136万元），占历年累计投资的66.37%，使全县农贸市场和专业市场达到12处，交易面积由上年的6.3万平方米增加到9.8万平方米；市场成交额由上年的5300万元，增长到1993年的6300多万元，净增1000万元，增长18.8%。

【基础设施建设速度加快】徽谈公路续建工程已完成工程量530万元，路基工程7.8公里，铁路下立交桥一处，黄沙河大桥一座。县乡公路民工建勤的四项养护指标全面完成，好路率比1992年有所上升，提高了通行能力。电力建设上架设了10千伏农电线路10条13公里，解决了三个乡6个行政村642户村民的生产生活用电，投资近百万元的大河变电工程已基本完成，电力局受到了电力部门表彰，被评为"三为"服务达标单位。通讯上开通了县城及柳林、伏镇、江洛等7个乡镇的自动电话，为经济开发奠定了良好的基础。

【社会各项事业蓬勃发展】教、科、文、卫、体等事业有了新的发展，具有地方特色的机关文化、校园文化、企业文化健康发展。特别是文化长廊建设，寓教于乐，把丰富多彩的文化活动同推广科技、改善环境、发展经济融为一体，发挥了积极作用。人才开发工作有了新起色，全县1993年参加学历教育的485人，其中向高校选送紧缺专业委培生80人，职工各类技术培训6期（次）188人。社会治安综合治理工作进一步加强。计划生育工作也有新的进展，全县人口自然增长率控制在地区下达的计划以内。民兵建设和双拥工作得到了加强巩固。以劳养武取得了新经验，县人武部被省、地军事机关评为先进单位，多次受到表彰。行政执法检查工作成绩显著，得到了陇南行署的肯定，并以正式文件下发全区学习交流，其他各个方面的工作也都有了进展。

现任主要领导：

中共徽县委书记：肖兴学

徽县人大常委会主任：温恩仲

徽县人民政府县长：蒋　雁

政协徽县委员会主席：汪作藩

中共徽县纪律检查委员会书记：李鸿启

（中共徽县委研究室：周立钧）

西和县经济和社会发展概述

【自然概况】西和县位于甘肃省东南部，东临徽、成县，南濒武都、康县，西北与礼县为邻，东北于天水接壤。全县管辖24个乡镇，487个行政村，33.5万人。境内北高南低，西高东低，中间高，南北低。海拔在986——2543米之间，年平均气温8.4℃，无霜期149——214天，降雨量550——600毫米。总面积1861平方公里，人均耕地1.8亩，土壤瘠薄，矿产药材资源比较丰富。主要金属矿藏有铅、锌、锑、铜、金、铁等，其中以铅锌矿和锑矿蕴藏量最多，分别属全国第二大铅锌矿带和第三大锑矿带，金矿处于陕、甘、川"金三角"地带，全县盛产名药材半夏，也是花椒、苹果、洋芋、玉米的盛产地。同时，大面积种植当归，党参、黄芪、山朱萸等中药材。但由于人多地少，地貌复杂，"冬干、春寒、夏旱、秋涝"等自然灾害发生濒繁，是一个典型的"一山有四季，十里不同天"的复杂多样的小气候区。加之交通不便，文化落后，社会发展程度低等诸多因素的影响，长期以来是一个"吃粮靠返销，花钱靠救济，财政靠补贴"的"三靠县"。党的十一届三中全会以来，随着改革的不断深入，县委、政府带领全县人民为了早日摘掉贫穷的帽子，经过长期的实践，探索出了"依靠人才，依托资源，依赖市场，发展地方工业，强化农业基础，狠抓粮食生产，打好扶贫攻坚战"的经济发展思路，经过全县人民的共同努力，各项事业都取得了前所未有的好成绩，全县经济稳定发展，综合实力明显增强，人民生活也有了很大提高。

【经济发展现状简述】1993年，是全面贯彻党的十四大精神，建立社会主义市场经济的第一年，全县人民在县委、县政府的领导下，抓住机遇，努力拼博，真抓实干，改革开放，经济建设和各个方面的工作都取得了可喜的成绩。全县国民生产总值达到13319万元；工农业总产值达到24024万元，比1985年净增19324万元；财政收入达到993万元，比1985年净增235万元，城乡人民的生活进一步得到改善和提高。

农业发展：西和是个农业大县，县上把发展农业始终放在各项工作的首位，常抓不懈，"以农为本"是总的指导思想。全县农村社会总产值达到23479万元，比1985年增长260%。粮食生产按照"一手抓粮，一手抓钱"的方针，在"坚持一个稳定"（稳定粮田面积），抓好"两个建设"（加强种子建设和肥料建设），落实"三个提高"（提高地膜玉米规范化种植水平，提高科学种田覆盖率，提高土地利用率），实现"四个扩大"（扩大配方施肥面积，扩大良种面积，扩大新修梯田当年不减产的示范推广面积，扩大病虫害防治面积）等主要措施的落实下，粮食产量达到20304万斤，比1985年净增

9034.2万斤，首次突破两亿斤大关，实现了“122”奋斗目标的要求；完成长防长治造林面积13.73万亩，新修梯田2万亩，当年完成小流域治理面积88.6平方公里；畜牧业生产的结构也在发生着变化，大家畜存栏6.07万头，比1992年有所减少，但鸡、猪、羊等的饲养量有所上升；异军突起的乡镇企业，在改革开放的大潮中蓬勃发展，全县共有乡镇企业54411个，全年实现总产值10078万元，比1985年净增产值9342万元，比1992年增长30.57%；扶贫开发在进行“四个一”建设，实行规模扶持和区域开发的基础上，拓展在创办扶贫经济实体，积累滚动发展资金的轨道上来。1993年各类扶贫经济实体创产值1115.4万元，实现利润214.9万元，从业人员3065人，其中带农村贫困户2650人，人均收入在1200元以上，全县贫困面由1992年的40.3%，下降到34.6%，农业生产条件和生态环境逐步得到改善。

工业运行：在邓小平同志南巡谈话和党的十四大精神指引下，县级领导联系企业，企业领导以主人翁的责任感抓住机遇，真抓实干，金融部门大力支持企业，解决流动资金“放水养鱼”，使我县工业生产在克服各种困难的情况下，仍然保持了稳定发展的势头。1993年全县完成工业总产值10360万元，比1985年增加产值9804万元，比1992年增长27%，其中：乡及乡以上工业总产值达到6975万元，比1992年增长36.5%。1993年西和工业经济发展有以下特点：一是企业转换经营机制工作有了突破性进展，《条例》得到充分落实。二是重点骨干企业走出了低谷，经济效益稳定增长，八户正在投产的国有企业，有六户全面完成和超额完成全年任务，各项指标与上年同期相比，销售收入增长48%，实现利润增长107%，上交税金增长73%，全员劳动生产率增长40%。三是矿管工作经过整顿逐步纳入法制轨道，乱挖乱采得到有效遏制，四是石油、煤炭企业在激烈的市场竞争中仍然发挥着主渠道作用。五是安全生产工作进一步加强，国有企业年内无一例事故发生，工业企业事故起数比上年降低50%，死亡人数降低75%。

交通能源和邮电通讯建设：在交通建设上；晒王公路和周花公路全面峻工，全长45公里，小南路改造工程完成3公里，使公路有效的服务于经济建设。电力建设，历时二年的草关至石峡35千伏送变电工程全面峻工并投入使用，架通综化厂、六巷黄金矿、陇南磨沟矿等工业专线。同时实现全县24个乡镇全部通电，乡至村通电率达到76.2%，村至户通电率达到61.4%。在通讯建设上，实现程控自动电话并网联网和国内长途自动直拨，有四个乡已接通农用电话。在市场建设上，全县共有各类集贸市场12个，1993在进一步完善城北农贸市场和城乡集镇的同时，新开辟了规模较大的城南市场和城北食品公司商业街。

【社会事业发展情况】一是顺应市场需求加快人才开发。县委、政府就如何加快人才开发，服务于经济建设，人尽其力，物尽其用，使西和这样贫困的“三靠县”早日实现经济腾飞，制定了《关于加强和发展横向经济联合的优惠办法》和《引进人才、技术、项目、资金的优惠政策》，先后聘请了西北矿冶研究院、白银公司、兰州有色冶金设计院、安徽泗县化工厂、江苏邗县技术改造办公室、上海京华化工厂等单位的30多名科技人员，到我县矿山，化工企业进行长期技术合作，并取得了一定成效。尖崖沟铅锌矿，通过科技人员的技术攻关，重新设计了矿山开采方案，可延长矿山服务年限两年，铅锌矿品位和回收率分别提高了7.51%和6.6%，二氧化硅由原来的8%下降到4%以下。他们联合攻关研制的《新型降硅抑制剂——PPS》已获成果，并已申请国家专利，论文还入选西北五省(区)第二届选矿技术交流会交流论文。仅几家矿山企业聘请科技人员进行技术服务，每年可增收100多万元。与此同时，我县还收编了《西和籍在外工作人员名录》，同西和100多名在外的有一技之长的工作人员取得联系，建立了“人才库”开展了人人服务家乡，发展家乡的“献智兴乡”活动。面对沿海、大中城市激烈的人才市场竞争，为了在我们这样贫困偏辟的县城留住人才，县上在制定优惠政策的同时，一方面“筑剿引凤”，另一方面与各大专院校联系，选拨一批进行专业培训，县上也开办了“财会”、“英语”、“党政管理”等各类大专班、中专班，共培训各类人才100多名。这类人才因由本县选送，给予优惠，他们能够扎根于本地，为我县的经济建设服务。二是计划生育工作取得新进展。1993年，我县计划生育工作，坚持党政一把手总负责的原则，始终按照年初提出的“四抓，四坚持，实现四个突破，达到三个一”的总思路进行，通过办“三栏一箱”(即县上评比栏，乡上评茬栏，村上监督栏，举报箱)评比活动，使我县计划生育达到预期的目的。1993年全县完成结扎4457例，占任务的99%，放环3841例，占任务的101%；三是教育工作协调发展，形势喜人。教育为我县的经济振兴与繁荣培训了一大批德才兼备的各类人才。1993年全县入选的大、中专学生达到244名。比1992年增加37名，其中大学录取90名，创近几年来最好成绩。全县小学双科合格率地区统考达到36.4%，比1992年增长5.3%，初中六科合格率达到29.5%，比1992年增长6.4%。全县有152所学校完成“一无六有两化三配套”。12所学校达到标准化，南关小学普及了电化教育。1993年全县多方筹资215.38万元，新建、扩建校舍5055平方米，新修三幢教学楼，为全县师生提供了良好的教学环境；四是社会治安进一步加强，社会秩序不断好转。1993年县上认真落实了各项综治措施，全年共发现和受理各类刑事案件54起，其中重大案件14起，比1992年全案减少3起，重大案件减少3起，受理各类治安案件75件，查处75件，调处治安纠纷155件，交通事故4起，共摧毁各类犯罪团伙17个，88人，与1992年相比，各类案件发案率降低，案件破获率上升。

【名优土特产】以经济建设为中心，以农业生产为基础，立足资源优势，发展多种经营，是我县发展生产力、脱贫致富的基本思想和出发点。近年来全县人民依靠资源优势，发展一乡一业，一村一品的新经济格局已逐步形成。

我县地处陇南山区，气候湿润凉爽，是适宜于洋芋生长的良好地区。我县洋芋资源十分丰富，历年来播种面积稳定在15万亩左右，1993洋芋总产量4.2亿公斤，50%的用于淀粉、粉条加工，创造增值收入1000多万元。以洋芋为原料的加工业已在我县发展到千家万户，是当前农民较为可靠的收入来源。

目前，全县除洋芋加工外，草编、地毯的加工也在日益扩大。近年来，我县与兰州飞天地毯厂联合办起西和飞天地毯分厂，现有职工100多人，通过辐射带动发展了23个乡村地毯加工点，从业人员795人，1993年共收入地毯加工费78.6万元，人均近1000元。

县编织工艺厂已有20年的历史，产品拥有七大类180个品种，曾荣获国家经贸部颁发的“出口商品生产基地”荣誉证书。草编生产创产值120万元，创汇24万元，产品远销美、日、英、法等30多个国家和地区，是我县妇女就业的一条好致富门路。我县盛产玉米，每年有着500万斤的玉米皮资源，充分利用这些资源，以县编织工艺厂为龙头，带动乡村千家万户，把全县办成辐射所有农户的无围墙草编工艺品出口基地。

现任主要领导：

中共西和县委书记：张兴民

西和县人大常委会主任：高孔岗

西和县人民政府县长：魏安民

政协西和县委员会主席：艾继贤

中共西和县纪律检查委员会书记：姜文珍

（中共西和县政研室：赵冕）

康县经济和社会发展概述

【自然概况与历史沿革】康县位于甘肃省东南部，嘉陵江上游，西汉水之滨，是甘、陕、川交界处的山区县，东经105°18′～105°58′，北纬32°53′～33°39′。全县辖1区8镇20乡，350村，19.6万人，总面积2958.46平方公里，耕地36万亩，林地235.57万亩，草地115.56万亩。由于地处秦巴山区亚热带和温暖带过渡区，境内气候温和，夏无酷署，冬无严寒，年平均气温11℃，雨量充沛，年平均降雨807.5毫米，日照时数年平均1715.7小时，无霜期212天。境内主要山脉为牛头山和万家大梁，这两座山呈东西走向，横亘在中部地区南北两侧，将全县划分为南、中、北三个地理景观迥然不同的地理区，在三个区域内，气候、水文、植被等地理要素有明显差异。独特的气候和地形使康县山青水秀，景色宜人，是旅游渡假的好地方，同时为发展多种经营提供了自然条件和自然资源，素有万宝山之称。

地上地下自然资源丰富。一是林木资源多，全县森林覆盖率达46%，木材蓄积685万立方米，有野生植物1200余种，其中珍稀树种28种，有水杉、银杏等活化石树种。有被列入国家重点保护的金丝猴、金猫、羚牛、麝、大鲵等14种珍贵动物，有银耳、黑木耳、猴头、香菇、灵芝等96种菌类植物。有天麻、杜仲、麝香、黄连、猪苓、厚补等440多种野生药材。二是地下有储量丰富、品质优良的金、银、铜、铁、大理石、水晶石、石灰石等矿产资源20多种。三是有丰富的名特土产品。县内有国家挂牌收购的300多种。木耳、杜仲、核桃已被林业部列为名、优、特产品。核桃产量名列全国第六位，是全国基地县之一，出口东南亚、西欧、北美等地，质量荣获经贸部优质产品证书。蚕桑、茶叶、天麻、板栗、棕片等产品在全县经济中占有重要地位，还有丰富的肉、禽、蛋。四是水利资源丰富，全县境内有1江（犀牛江）14河，总储量29.33万千瓦，目前仅开发0.1196万千瓦，发展潜力很大。五是有丰富的旅游资源。康县是陇南山区的绿宝地，不但与毗邻各地旅游风景点连成旅游网点，而且县内还有与九寨沟相媲美的梅园沟，清河、阳坝既可供旅游疗养，又是生物实习考察之地。县城还有闻名遐迩的白云洞、白云观及白云山公园，这些都是旅游的好地方。

康县历史悠久，早在4000多年前，已有先民生息繁衍。夏商州三代属雍州，春秋至秦，属秦辖地，为氐人住地，汉设平乐道，北魏置平落县，从西汉八辖武都郡至唐昭宗景福元年。此后一直为阶州之一部。1929年正式建县，县址白马关（今云台镇政府驻地），1944年县址迁往岸门口。康县解放后划入武都专区，1957年县址迁至嘴台，1958年，康县并入武都县，1961年恢复康县，1985年，康县归属陇南地区。现在县内有两大民族，即回族和汉族。

【经济建设】1993年，全县人民在县委、政府的领导下，各个领域，各个方面都取得了显著成绩，大的方面主要有：

粮食丰收，农村经济持续发展。全县主要粮食作物推广良种21.24

万亩，良种覆盖率达98%。增施磷肥2100吨，施磷肥面积达19.64万亩，完成玉米营养钵栽培0.21万亩，地膜玉米1.63万亩，带状种植3.1万亩，间作套种9.3万亩，兴修梯田6532亩，中南部石砍梯田3550亩，长防造林7000亩，长治工程造林54100亩，扶贫造林7900亩，营造规模经济林带4处共89871亩，新增水浇地2600亩。康南食用菌，康北花椒、蚕桑、核桃。全县范围内的"四小"种植园，养殖户，家庭加工业和庭院经济等有了较快发展。全县1993年粮食总产量达到1.12亿斤，接近历史最高水平；多种经营产值5752万元，比上年增长4%；农业总产值达到9143.9万元，比上年增长4.7%；农民人均纯收入达到298元，比上年净增3元；农村贫困面下降4.8个百分点。农村各项经济指标均超额完成了任务。其中，涉及国家整体投资的"长防"工程赢得了省地好评，"长治"工程一期顺利通过国家验收。

工业增长，经济效益有所回升。针对我县工业基础差，包袱重和面临新的市场挑战的情况下，1993年，我们以深化企业改革，贯彻落实《条例》，转换经营机制，强化管理，苦练内功，提高企业整体素质为重点，紧紧围绕提高效益，狠抓了现有企业的达产达标，扭亏增盈和促产促销工作。在重点企业实行了全员劳动合同制，工效挂钩分配制和风险金抵押制度。推行了"五自主"、"四放开"，进行了三项制度改革试点，取得了阳坝铜矿改革试点的新经验；按照以大带小，以强带弱的原则，进行企业组织结构调整的大胆探索，兼并了三官水泥厂、县农机厂；狠抓了企业班子建设，调整充实了四户企业的领导班子；加强了人才培训，采取多形式、多层次培训各类企业管理人才26名，提高了企业的管理水平。同时还重点抓了扭亏增盈和重点企业的达产达标，根据存在的症结，进行整顿，实行一厂一策，取得了明显效果。实现扭亏一户，减亏两户，减亏0.61万元。阳坝铜矿，王坝金矿实现了达产达标，创造了较好的经济效益。大部分企业超额完成了各项经济技术指标，基本实现了产值、利润、税金三个增长。1993年，全县乡以上工业总产值完成3580万元，比上年增长10.02%，完成销售收入1073.17万元，比上年增长61.9%，实现利润140.75万元，比上年增长9.4%，实现税金82.21万元，比上年增长0.8%。

乡镇企业异军渐起。1993年，我县紧紧抓住国家发展中西部乡镇企业和全省第二次乡镇企业发展浪潮的良好机遇，充实调整了县乡镇企业领导小组，开展了三次全县范围内的乡企工作大检查，整顿了29户现有企业，论证开发了一批符合区域实际的新项目，并按照因地制宜，分类指导的原则，把重点放在交通便利，能源动力充足的乡镇，把工作重点放在启动各个阶层的能人大户上，把项目开发重点放在以当地资源为基础的采矿、建材、轻纺、酿造、农、林、副产品加工、绿色企业以饮食、服务业等第三产业上，重点在打破所有制结构，改变资金投入方式上下功夫，按照多轮驱动、多轨运行、多渠道发展的原则，积极鼓励乡镇、村社和个人独办、联办工业，大力发展股份制合作企业。1993年全县新发展各类乡镇企业853户，其中股份制企业11户，企业总数达到5159户，比上年增长17.6%，从业人员8355人，占全县农村劳动力总数的9.7%，完成总产值5623万元，比上年增长25.7%，实现利润513.6万元，比上年增长30.4%。不仅规模扩大，速度加快，而且效益比较明显。

商贸繁荣、市场日趋活跃。为了全面促进经济工作转轨变型，使之尽快适应社会主义市场经济体制的要求，1993年，我县把流通工作当作振兴康县经济的一件大事来抓。首先，面对市场，进行商业、供销、粮食系统的体制改革，出台并实施了三个系统的改革方案，组建了集团公司，实行管理、经营职能并存，以经营为主，国有民营、社有自营、承包经营、租赁经营并存，以承包、租赁经营为主的体制和劳动合同制、干部聘用制、内部待业制、效益工资制、风险抵押制并存的运行机制，使企业在商品市场的大潮中，逐步走向了平等竞争、自主经营、自我约束、自我发展的道路。其次，按照社会主义市场经济的要求和"谁建设，谁管理，谁投资，谁受益"的原则，大抓了市场建设。兴建了三个市场，扩建了两个市场，恢复了七个交易点，使全县逐步形成了布局合理，功能健全的市场网络。第三，转换观念，提高认识，放手发动个体私营经济。1993年，我县把发展非公有制经济放在与国有经济同等重要的位置，列入各级政府工作的重要议事日程，作为繁荣经济增加财政收入的一项重要措施来抓。全年新发展个体工商户1617户，实现了年初的奋斗目标。注册资金达209.73万元，当年实现商品零售额1701万元，为财政上缴税金79.10万元。

财政收入明显增长，金融形势有所好转。由于受全国大气候的影响，1993年我县财政、金融部门出现了前所未有的困难局面，拖欠职工工资长达两个半月之久，针对这种情况，县委、政府采取了"一改二收三要四节约"的刚性措施。一是改革财政管理体制和县直单位财政供给办法。对乡财政实行分灶吃饭、划定基数、超支不补、超收分成；对县直有收入的事业单位，由全额拨款转向差额拨款。并鼓励县乡党政机关兴办各类经济实体53个，年内创收50多万元。二是在大力发展工农业生产的同时，狠抓了各项收入。由于各级领导重视，广大税务干部的艰辛努力和多方配合，争取抓大户，抓零散、抓大检、抓清欠等各种措施，共完成财政收入617万元，比上年增收119万元，增长23.9%。查出和收缴各种违纪资金27.4万元，清收历年税欠款11.93万元，为财政加大了收入。三是强化预算刚性，严格控制支出。牢固树立“勒紧裤带、过紧日子”的思想，重点对人、车、会、房、水、电、医疗、旅差费、奖金、社会集团购买力等支出进行了严格的控制，紧缩了开支，保证了运转。四是多方争取，积极向省地争取超汇近百万元，缓解了部分供需矛盾。由于狠抓了以上措施的落实，保证了1993年职工工资的发放和各项工作的正常运转。

在金融方面，通过贯彻中央6号文件精神，整顿金融秩序，严肃结算纪律，清收逾期贷款和违章拆借资金，盘活了资金存量，加速了资金流转。1993年年末存款余额4650.7万元，比1992年净增363.1万元，各项贷款余额4961.9万元，比1992年净增240.7万元。金融形势由资金紧张逐步转向存贷两增。

基础设施得到加强，基本条件进一步改善。1993年在交通方面，坚持修养并举的方针，新上云台环城公路改建、店子寺坝公路桥和长坝、托河、铜钱人行吊桥工程，维修了两座吊桥，完成了9处水毁工程，进行了全县公路养护整修584公里，保持标准化养路91公里，实现优良里程84.08公里，使公路通行能力大为提高。在能源建设上，架通了两个乡镇10千伏农电线路55.75公里，完成了城关至阳坝35千伏输变电工程测设、定位、分坑，杆塔二次运输等前期工作，并新建小型水电站3处总容量12千瓦。同时，还抓了电网的延伸，架通村社10千伏线路23公里，使全县通电率由1992年的11.5%上升到1993年的17.3%。在通讯建设上，完成了阳坝、岸门口自动电话和市话二期工程，使通讯手段大为改进。

【社会事业】科技工作紧紧围绕七大支柱产业，强化科技承包服务、培训各类人员2000多人(次)，推广新技术5项。黑木耳丰产栽培通过省地验收，为我县农村产业开发提供了较好的服务。教育工作以九年制义务教育实施为重点，以提高教育质量为中心，加强督导评估，强化管理，取得了较好的效果。1993年，考入大专19人，中专100人，打破了历年来最高纪录。文化工作主要抓了28个文化长廊重点村建设，进一步整顿了文化市场，注重了文学艺术生产，群专结合，开展了丰富多彩的文娱活动，为繁荣城乡文化生活做出了积极的努力。卫生工作以抓基层卫生院建设、卫生执法、儿童计划免疫和地方病防治为重点。维修改造基层卫生院43间，增设医疗网点15个，查处各种假冒伪劣药品124种，四苗接种率达97.1%，小儿麻痹糖丸投服率达99.2%，麻风、甲状腺肿大等地方病得到了有效的控制。计划生育工作“三术”超额完成，人口自增率控制在8.29‰以内。广播电视工作紧紧围绕宣传和自我发展，较好地开办了县内电视新闻，县内自办的广播节目每天分三次传送到每个乡镇，每日报道和转播全县重大活动和先进人物，部分村社恢复了有线广播，扩大了电视和广播的覆盖面。城市建设1993年总规模为1180.52万元，施工面积27915.81平方米。在城区基础设施上，一是拆除了有碍市容美观的树基栏杆，补铺水泥砖500平方米；二是重新修建了综、琉璃瓦式的白云山公园大门；三是补栽了街道行道树和公园风景树500余株；四是设立了“白云山公园风景保护区”，立了三个界碑、一个标志碑；五是对570株城区行道树进行了修剪和防虫；六是维修了城区垃圾台、果皮箱13个，使城区垃圾及时得到清运，城区卫生每日临晨环卫工人全部清扫干净。

现任主要领导：

中共康县委书记：杨伯福

康县人大常委会主任：高玉峰

康县人民政府县长：任晓祥

政协康县委员会主席：沈　青

中共康县纪律检查委员会书记：张清堂

（康县县委研究室　梁新荣　张玉忠）

武都县经济和社会发展概述

【自然概况】武都县位于陇南山区腹地，处在岷山山脉与秦巴山地的结合部；地势西北高，东南低，海拔高度在667米至3600米之间；属亚热带向暖温带过渡气候，年日照时数1900小时，平均气温14.6℃，年均降雨量480毫米，适宜小麦、水稻、玉米、洋芋、豆类等各种农作物的生长，素有“陇上江南”之称誉。境内总面积4683平方公里，有耕地71.5万亩，林地189.7万亩，草场121.4万亩。辖1区6镇38乡，人口48.6万人。

【1993年经济发展概况】该县是一个“七山二林一分田”的山区农业县，经济基础比较薄弱。近年，县委、县政府根据县情，提出了“立足山区资源，抓命脉，强基础，建基地，推科技，种养加综合经营，贸工农一体发展，城乡一体化，整体推动全县经济建设”的指导思想，使经济建设和各项社会事业取得了较快的发展。1993年，全县工农业总产值28886万元，比上年增长8.0%，财政收入1416.8万元，比上年增长33.2%，农民人均纯收入377元，比上年提高10元。

农业。通过大兴农田水利建设和推广农业实用技术，农业基本生产条件逐步改善。1993年，全县种植粮食作物88.6万亩，产粮9181万公斤，人均有粮188.9公斤。

地方国有工业。县属国有企业16家，有职工2804人，固定资产5016万元；1993年实现工业总产值

2660万元，上交利税441万元。

国合商业。国营、合作商业企业56家，从业人员2260人，固定资产2931万元；1993年国内纯购进959万元，总销售额5502万元，上交利税100万元。

乡镇企业。有乡镇企业4570家（个体工商户4215家），从业人员1.6万人；1993年总收入9578万元，上交税金308万元，占全县财政收入的22%；行业涉及建筑材料、交通运输、轻纺化工、农林产品加工、商业流通、饮食服务等；达到全省A级乡镇企业标准的企业7个，省优质产品3种；有18人获省、地、县“农民企业家”称号，84人取得各种专业技术职称。

【多种经营】武都山川交错，地貌复杂，“一山有四季，十里不同天”；多样型的自然环境，给多种生物创造了宜于生长繁衍的条件。近年，县委、县政府在开发多种经营生产上，提出了重点发展的6个支柱产业。(1)、中药材。武都有“千年药乡”之称，境内中药材资源丰富，已发现的有1300多种，红芪、纹党、当归、大黄、黄连等药材，量多质优。1993年，各类药材人工种植面积达3.24万亩，年产量456.1万公斤，收入2638万元。“八五”期间，着重发展“六木”（杜仲、枣皮、厚朴、辛荑、黄柏、吴芋）、“五草”（红芪、半夏、纹党、大黄、黄连）等中药材，积极开发白果、古槐、西洋参等后续药材。(2)、花椒。以“大红袍”为代表的武都花椒，以色鲜、油重、麻辣香味久长，饮誉川陕等地。1993年，全县有花椒树3300万株，产量65.4万公斤，产值816.9万元。“八五”末，计划花椒树发展到3900万株，产量130万公斤。(3)、油橄榄。1987年引进种植，1993年有油橄榄树3万株，产鲜果2500公斤，收入1万元。经国家计委、轻工部科研机构和有关专家鉴定，单株产量和果品质量居全国之首。国家计委将武都县确定为全国油橄榄重点建设基地，投资建成了年产50吨橄榄油的综合加工厂1座。计划到“八五”末，全县油橄榄发展到50万株，年产鲜果5000吨，产橄榄油500吨。(4)、蚕桑、县内三分之二的地方适宜种桑养蚕。1993年有桑园9800亩，产丝7740公斤，产值8万元。“八五”末，桑园将达4万亩，养蚕4万张，产茧1000吨。(5)、林果。武都林果资源丰富，种类繁多，柑桔、梨、苹果、核桃等已初具规模。1993年干鲜果品产量473万公斤，产值534万元。“八五”期间，大抓荒坡建园，林果将发展到30万亩，产量2000万公斤。(6)、食品。有粮油、酒类、饮料、调味品、肉奶蛋、茶叶等10多种食品加工业，初步形成多家经营、联合发展的食品工业体系。1993年，全县食品加工业收入近千万元。今后以县食品厂、面粉厂、浸出油厂、冷库、罐头厂、饮料厂等企业为龙头，抓好粮油、食用菌、蔬菜、肉奶蛋、果露、黄白酒等系列产品的开发；建设魔芋、蕨根加工厂，开发魔芋精粉、魔芋干、蕨根粉丝等产品。

1993年，全县多种经营总收入达到4732万元，比上年增长2.8%，成为增加群众收入的主要来源。

【城区建设】武都城是一座有悠久历史的古老山城。现有常住人口5.7万（城镇户口4.4万）人。在上级有关部门的支持下，八十年代建成了长4148米的堤路结合城防工程，成为抵御城南白龙江和城西北峪河水患的坚固防线，同时可遇环甘川公路和缓解城区车辆交通紧张状况。近年，地县提出了城东教场坝以房地产为主、城西钟楼滩以第三产业为主、白龙江南岸以农林果菜郊区经济为主的三个小区开发计划，从总体上加快了城区建设。1993年，建成了总投资264万元的供水工程；筹资15万元，加宽过水渠道39米，提高街面8000平方米，解决了旧城区中心地段新市街与人民街交汇的低洼排水问题；开拓铺设了新城区东西走向的一号路路面977.5米，加宽垫高了南北走向的二号路面474米，一、二号路交汇处的圆盘街心花园也已具雏型；在城区主要街道地段，更新安装了三代光源钠灯141盏；城区文化、体育、卫生设施，以及住宅、绿化等生活环境，也都有了较大的改观。

【社会事业】交通能源。(1)、公路建设。截止1993年底，全县过境国道1条，省道3条，县乡公路17条，乡村公路137条，平均每百平方公里有公路32.5公里；(2)、邮电通讯。由城到乡逐步向现代化发展。在原有自动电话2000门，长途程控设备72路的基础上，1993年，从西班牙引进的5000门数字程控电话和960路数字微波传输设备，投入使用；(3)、电力开发。县内有中、小型水电站16座，装机容量2.5万千瓦。1993年建成投产的白鹤桥水电站，装机8000千瓦，缓解了城区用电紧张状况。自文县碧口到洛塘镇的48.7公里35千伏输变电线路的建成，为开发1700平方公里的洛塘山区，创造了先决条件。

科教卫生。(1)、科技。有各类科技人员732名，科研机构2个，科技推广机构10个。农业科技人员在推广农作物地膜覆盖、带状间作种植、蔬菜瓜果丰产栽培方面，成效显著；(2)、教育。有中小学720所（中学23所），教师2697人（中学教师460人），在校学生5.7万人（中学9100人）。学龄儿童入学率93%，巩固率92.7%，毕业率97%，普及率82.5%；(3)、文化。有文化机构52个，电视地面接收站38座，小片广播548个。1993年广播、电视覆盖率分别为41%和62%，比上年上升6个百分点和1个百分点；(4)、卫生。有各类医疗机构689个，医务人员1409名。1993年，儿童基础免疫“四苗”接种率为88%。武都县被世界银行列入结核病控制县，对历年查出的158例菌阳病人，通过免费化疗，已治愈120人，治愈率为84%。

计划生育。严格执行政策，落实各项节育措施，人口得到控制。1993年，绝育结扎5643例，放环5460例，人流引产1271例。当年出生9462人，出生率为19.4‰，净增人口6556人，人口自然增长率为13.45‰。

【名特土产】“大红袍”花椒：粒大肉厚，色泽红艳，麻辣郁香，含油量高，是深受云贵川陕等地欢迎的调味品。“武都蜜桔”：个大色鲜，汁甜无核，有养胃润肺之功效。现有桔园1.6万亩，产量150万公斤。无花果：皮薄瓤细，甘甜香馥，宜于鲜食和多种加工，白龙江沿岸多有种植。橄榄油：是一种既可食用，又可药用和作化妆品配料的植物油。武都所产橄榄果和橄榄油，有效成份超过地中海等原产地。“阶州毛峰”茶：以“墨绿有光泽，条索紧结，稍勾曲”的外形，“香高持久”的香气，“黄绿明亮”的汤色，“鲜浓”的滋味和“嫩绿匀齐”的叶底，在陇南茶叶评审会上荣膺第一。茶区地处深山密林，无污染源。面积3100亩，产量8万公斤。黑木耳：朵大色正，肉厚味鲜，化痰清淤，适口性好。主要产于洛塘林区，年产量2万公斤。香菇菌类：洛塘山区特产，无污染，肉厚盖圆，醇香美味。主要品种有花菇、平菇、凤尾菇等；野生的有羊肚菌等。年产量5万公斤。“米仓红芪”：名贵中药材，也可加工饮料。糖份充沛，含硒量高，颇受港、台及东南亚客商欢迎。年产量50万公斤。武都黄连：有效成份小檗碱含量达10.62%，超过国家药典规定的标准，年产量1万公斤。杜仲、枣皮、天麻、半夏等中药材，均以上乘的质量和丰富的资源，取信于市场。

现任主要领导：

中共武都县委书记：肖庆平

武都县人大常委会主任：蔡廷彦

武都县人民政府县长：唐志敏

政协武都县委员会主席：刘志义

中共武都县纪律检查委员会书记：杨允忠

（武都县委政研室：王　贤）

宕昌县经济和社会发展概述

宕昌县位于甘肃南部，东接礼县，南连武都，西邻舟曲、迭部，北靠岷县。总面积3331平方公里，辖31个乡镇，有行政村333个，总人口27.54万人，其中农业人口26.35万人，占总人口的95%。1992年全县农民人均占有粮156公斤，人均纯收入279.8元，全县5.46万户农户中，近2.5万户没有解决温饱，是一个典型的以农业生产为主的贫困县。

1993年，较好地完成县十届人代会确定的工作任务，保持了经济稳定发展的势头。全年完成工农业总产值13646.8万元，比1992年增长9%；农业总产值达到11366万元，比1992年增长12%，农民人均纯收入达到283元，比1992年增长0.82%；财政收入达到438万元，比1992年增长36%。这些成绩的取得，是在全面搞好经济工作的同时，突出抓农业生产的结果。

【农业】我县属于高寒阴湿山区，土地瘠薄，44.70万亩耕地中有90%是山地，川地只占10%。气候复杂，自然条件差，灾害性天气多，不利于农作物的生长。为了适应发展社会主义市场经济的新形势，去年县上放开了种植计划，但仍然把农业适用技术的推广作为硬任务来抓，精心组织和实施了科技兴农战略。一是按照“推广科技，增加收入，主攻单产，提高总产”的思路，继续推广四大作物的八项适用技术，全年共完成四大作物良种推广27万亩，小麦条播6.7万亩，地膜玉米和地膜洋芋1.46万亩，洋芋坑种垄作5.9万亩，洋芋蚕豆带状种植1.8万亩，药剂拌种10万亩，配方施肥10万亩，化肥深施1.41万亩，土壤消毒1.88万亩。由于落实了科技增产措施，及粮食生产在多灾的情况下仍有所增长，总产达到4316.4万公斤，比1992年增长5.8%。二是按照在岷江、白龙江沿岸7乡镇25村建立高产、优质、高效农业示范区的思想，突出抓了以地膜和塑料大棚种植蔬菜为主的“两高一优”农业，并且开展了6个乡镇的科技达标活动。新建春、秋塑料大棚133个，44亩.冬暖棚8个，3亩；复种大白菜728亩，推广西瓜、蔬菜优质丰产栽培710亩，促进了蔬菜生产向专业化、基地化发展。三是狠抓药材、经济林果基地建设。宕昌素有“千年药乡”的美称，当归、红芪、大黄、党参，是出口的传统土特产，曾荣获国家出口荣誉证书。唐代《新修本草》称：“当归以宕州者最佳”。享誉中外的“岷归”产区集中在我县的阿坞，哈达铺、理川、车拉等乡镇，目前产量达400万公斤。其它野生药物资源品种也很多，岷江两岸林区盛产猪岑、杜仲、黄连、细辛等。为了促进药材这一支柱型产业的发展，1993年全县完成当归防麻口病9150亩，引进桔梗、宁夏枸杞等药材新品种11个，试种10亩；在哈达铺、好梯、竹院等地推广半夏种植64亩。1993年全县种植药材达44003亩，产量达5307吨。近年来，大面积种植红芪、天麻、党参取得了显著成绩。与此同时，有关部门充分发动群众在条件好的荒山荒坡和田间块头，房前屋后大规模栽种优质林果树，已初具规模，全县果园面积达10562亩。1993年县上对3.7万株果树进行了综合管理，水果产量达到了2640吨，比1992年增加1962吨。

1993年省、地、县多方投资，在畜牧业上重点抓了畜种改良，科学饲养和防疫灭病工作，全县的牧业产值达到3634.06万元，比1992年的3425.73万元，增长3.1%，年末大家畜存栏9.11万头，比1992年增长1.33%，年末猪存栏9.87万头，比1992年增长1.54%，年末羊存栏8.71万只，比1992年下降3.11%。全县共完成黄牛改良3757头，小尾寒羊引进、推广、扩繁182只，推广瘦肉型杂交猪1138头，推广良种鸡1.56万只，引进父母代艾维茵鸡400套。注射丁猪瘟、鸡瘟、牛出败、猪肺疫等疫苗，免疫密度均达80%以上。检疫畜禽1.8万头（只），肉品21.09万公斤。仅扶贫部门就投放15.2万元，用于扶持贫困户发展养殖业。

我县山大沟深，由于长期过度垦殖，植被遭到严重破坏，许多地方沟壑纵横，山体岩石裸露，水土流失严重，全县水土流失面积达2365.01平方公里，占总土地面积的71%，年平均侵蚀摸数每平方公里高达3000吨。自1989年我县被列为长江上游重点防治区内后，县上十分重视"长治"、"长防"工程建设，以工程造林为中心，开展区域内的综合治理，仅1993年就完成"长防"造林1.75万亩，占年计划的103%，其中经济林7800亩，用材防护林9700亩；育苗1000亩，容器育苗20万袋，封山育林3.5万亩，零星植树105万株。重点开辟了南阳区和岷江沿岸两个战场，建设了8个骨干工程，其中千亩以上工程造林6处，7500亩。县上结合"长治"工程建设，重点抓了农田水利建设，全年安排水利工程20项，完成13项，新增有效灌溉面积2747亩，完成人畜引水工程4处，解决了4村2512人和600多头大家畜的饮水问题。同时，完成坡改梯8900亩，低产田改造2.6万亩，"长治"造林6.06万亩，发展经济林2.21万亩，果园5320亩，种草1.5万亩。

1993年，宕昌县成立了由县长挂帅的乡镇企业协调领导小组，做出了进一步加快发展乡镇企业的决定，制定优惠政策，动员和吸引各类人才流向乡镇企业，到年底全县乡镇企业总数达4106个，比1992年增加了465个；从业人员达10754人，比1992年增加513人；总产值达4708万元，比1992年增长23.7%；总收入达3922万元，比上年增长11.4%；上缴税金156万元，比1992年增长3.8%；实现利润507万元，比1992年增长4.6%。县上新建的城关锑品厂铜浮选生产线，理川机砖厂，新寨地毯厂乡镇企业，生产规模较大，生产能力明显提高。乡镇企业通过整顿，增加了企业内部活力和自身发展能力，促进了全县乡镇企业向更高水平发展。

我县的扶贫工作已开展了八年，取得了较大的成绩，但农村中的贫困面仍然很大，全县仍有49%的农户生活处在温饱线以下。1993年，县上确定了"内抓扶贫开发，外抓劳务移民"两条腿走路的工作思路，把劳务输出和移民当做一个重要产业来抓，精心组织，进行了整户迁移的尝试。到年底，全县输出劳务3.1万多人次，总收入1643万元，人均530元；向新疆农八师移民257户819人，这项工作得到了省、地的肯定，也为我县群众脱贫致富探索了一条有效途径。

扶贫工作由救济型转变为扶持开发型，在项目建设上有了一定规模。1993年，投放省上下达的老困资金551.8万元，用于科技种植业、养殖业、工副业、农电线路等方面的开发；"两西"水利资金投放158.6万元，开展工程8项，已完成工程量的80%以上。

【国有企业】从加强企业领导班子，强化内部管理，积极开拓市场入手，狠抓了现有企业的整顿提高和扭亏增盈工作。县财政在十分困难的情况下，拨付省地安排的技改资金130万元，对印刷厂等企业进行了技术改造。但是由于资金紧缺，原材料涨价，市场不景气等原因，全县的工业企业效益仍有所下降。1993年，全年工业总产值2281万元，比1992年下降3.84%，与此同时，利税也不同程度的减少。

国合商业企业重点对零售门点进行了以"国有民营"、"社有自营"为主要内容的改革，着重解决了长期困扰企业的劳动纪律松驰，服务质量差，经济效益低下等问题。粮食部门顺应市场经济的新形势，把企业推上市场，保证了粮油的正常供应。

【城市建设与社会事业】1993年，在交通建设上，县上组织力量，发动群众开展了大规模的民工建勤活动，对全县12条县乡公路进行了维修，确保了干线公路畅通。同时，狠抓交通运输能力的提高。仅县车队当年就创经济收入达127万元，实现客运量132.5万人。在能源建设上，重点抓了沙湾至城关35千伏输变电工程，并架设10千伏农电线路13条，25.3公里，低压配套线路4.5公里，新建小水电站3处。通讯事业建设上，1993年，全县已发展自动电话用户614户，并开通了无线寻呼业务，邮电业务总量完成69.47万元，比上年增长22.44%。这一切都为我县的经济起飞注入了新的活力。为了美化环境，以更新更好的姿态迎接国内外各界朋友来我县进行贸易洽谈活动，县政府重点抓了城区绿化工作，共栽植长青树12万株，规范绿化街道3条，3100米，并整顿充实了环卫队伍，狠抓环境卫生，基本上杜绝了脏乱差，取得了良好的效果。

1993年，全县高考开学率创历史最好水平，高考人均分名列全区第三，小学毕业统考，双科平均分名列全区第二。通过实施"希望工程"，教学条件有了进一步的改善，适龄儿童入学率达到86.1%，巩固率达到90.4%，都比上年有所提高。文化、广播电视事业上，县上成功地举办了"百名将军墨迹展览"活动，建成了宕昌有线电视台，开通了七套节目，新建了两处地面接收站，电视覆盖率达到68.5%。对全县文化教育事业的繁荣起到了很大的促进作用。

宕昌县历史悠久，具有光荣的革命传统。宕昌县是历史上有名的宕昌国国址所在地。我县山色秀丽，景色迷人，主要名胜游览地有哈达铺长征纪念馆和大河坝风景区。到宕昌可饱览“花源晓月，江崖夕照，阳海三城，桥头古刹，南山积翠，壮岭烟云，锁龙阁桥，楼寺晨钟”八大景观。

哈达铺盛产驰名中外的当归，而且还是毛泽东等老一辈无产阶级革命家领导中国工农红军住过的地方，哈达铺被誉为红军长征的加油站。宕昌县蕴藏着较大的旅游开发潜力，只要注重开发建设，定会为我县带来可观的旅游收入的。

现任主要领导：

中共宕昌县委书记：袁怀贵

宕昌县人大常委会主任：朱宗贤

宕昌县人民政府县长：蒋正礼

政协宕昌县委员会主席：王永忠

中共宕昌县纪律检查委员会书记（暂缺）

（宕昌县委研究室：王　平）

定西地区

中共定西地委书记：刘生荣

定西地区行政公署专员：顾　军

中共定西地区纪律检查委员会书记：

赵国义

定西地区经济和社会发展概述

【自然概况】

位置　定西地区位于甘肃省中部，北与兰州、白银两市相连，东与平凉地区、天水市毗邻，南与陇南地区接壤，西与甘南藏族自治州、临夏回族自治州交界。全区总面积为2.03万平方公里，占全省总面积的4.5%。

地势　全区大致由南向北倾斜。南部为秦岭石质山区，南起岷县大拉梁、岷峨山、北至渭河以南，为秦岭山脉向西北延伸部分，山峦重叠，河谷深切，山地坡度25—35度以上，海拔2000—3000米，渭源县与漳县交界处的露骨山高达3941米。西中部为河谷阶地，分布在洮河、渭河、漳河流经区，海拔一般在1600—1800米，河谷盆地相间，光热条件较好，是农业发达地区。中北部为黄土丘陵沟壑区，自渭河以北到定西县白碌乡、临洮县马衔山及七道梁以南，约占全区总面积60%以上，海拔1800—2200米，黄土覆盖深厚，但地形破碎，沟壑纵横，水土流失严重。

河流　全区境内河流大多属黄河水系。主要河流有：洮河，流经岷县西北部和渭源县西部边境，并从南到北纵贯临洮县西部，迭藏河、漫坝河、东峪沟河为其主要支流，年径流量3.63亿立方米，流域面积占全区总面积的30%；渭河，发源于渭源县，流经陇西县，主要支流有清源河、莲峰河、漳河、龙川河、榜沙河、牛谷河等，年径流量7.93亿立方米，流域面积占全区总面积的50.4%；祖厉河水系，在定西县境，支流有关川河、西巩河，年径流量6585万立方米，流域面积占全区总面积的19.2%。此外，发源于岷县的燕子河（又名湫山河），属长江流域西汉水水系，年径流量4280万立方米，流域面积占全区总面积的1.1%。

气候　全区属南温带半湿润——中温带半干旱区。光能较多，热量不足，降水少，变率大，蒸发快，大陆性季风气候特征显著。气候南北差异较大，渭河以北气温较高但少雨干旱，渭河以南降水较多但高寒温低。全年日照时数2239.5—2500.1小时，年平均气温5.7—7.7℃，积温2597.6—3211.2℃，持续日照122.5—155.9天，无霜期122—158天。年降水量北部定西县为425.1毫米，南部岷县为589.5毫米，呈北多南之状。年蒸发量1192.2—1526.2毫米，降水集中在夏末秋初，占年降水量的49.0—54.0%。

资源　全区共有耕地776.17万亩，85%以上为山地。种植业以粮食作物为主，粮食作物有小麦、豆类、洋芋和玉米、谷、糜等10余种；经济作物有油料、药材、蔬菜、瓜果等；中药材资源有313种，其中当归及红芪、黄芪、党参远近闻名，岷县当归更是驰名中外，素有“千年药乡”称誉。野生植物120多种，主要有沙棘、蕨菜、山杏、野百合等。野生动物有野猪、狐狸、山羊、狼、鹿、獐、旱獭等，还有国家重点保护的雪鸡、锦鸡、蓝马鸡、穿山甲、苏门羚、毛冠鹿、麝等10余种珍禽异兽。家畜家禽有牛、马、驴、骡、猪、羊、鸡、兔等。森林面积416.25万亩，林木资源上百种，主要有杉、松、柏、杨、柳、榆、桦和苹果、梨、杏等。水资源总量62.82立方米，可利用15.38立方米。水力资源总蕴藏量87.73万千瓦，可利用35.40万千瓦。已探明的矿产资源有井盐、大理石、石灰石、红柱石及金属矿点，其中井盐、大理石、红柱石储量丰富。

区划　全区辖定西、临洮、渭源、岷县、漳县、陇西、通渭等7县，有11个镇、167个乡、2038个村民委员会、54个居民委员会。

人口　全区1993年总人口为267.65万人，其中男性为138.49万人、女性129.16万人。人口出生率为19.13%，死亡率为5.74%，自然增长率为13.39‰。农业人口为万人。

民族　全区共有汉、回、藏、满、东乡、蒙古等18个民族成份。汉族人口占总人口数的98.93%,少数民族人口占1.07%。

【名特土产】豆类,扁豆——含蛋白质25.7%、淀粉55.4%、脂肪2.12%、赖氨酸2.29%,具有和中下气、清热消暑、止泄解毒作用,又是加工粉条、粉面的理想原料,产于定西、通渭、陇西等县。大量出口换汇。蚕豆——含蛋白质30%,并含有维生素A、B、C,茎、叶、花均可入药,有健脾除湿、通经凉血之功能,主要产于渭源、漳县、岷县,系传统出口贸易产品。豌豆——含蛋白质20.6%、淀粉52.7%、脂肪3.15%、碳水化合物58%,幼嫩荚果含有多种维生素,为出口商品,国内外已在食品、酿造、轻化、医疗工业上广泛应用。各县均有出产。

麦类,莜麦——各县种植,营养丰富,含蛋白质15%以上、脂肪8.51%,并含维生素、钙、磷、铁等矿物质,由于含有大量豆油酸,其食品对动脉粥样硬化、冠心病、糖尿病和肠胃病均有一定疗效。荞麦——各县山区种植,含蛋白质10.8%、脂肪2.4%、糖水化合物64—75%、精氨酸12.7%、赖氨酸1%,经常食用有防止贫血、胃炎、胃溃疡等疾病的作用。

薯类,主要是洋芋,各县种植,营养价值高,每市斤含蛋白质10.1克、糖73克、脂肪3.1克、粗纤维3.5克,并含有钙、磷、铁和多种维生素,既是菜又是粮食,还有和胃、调中、健脾、益气之功效,加工后可制作各种食品及营养品、医用品。

油料类,主要是胡麻,籽实中含油脂35—47%,每50公斤可榨油15—17公斤,营养丰富,食味清香,在化工部门亦有广泛用途。油渣可作饲料和肥料,麻皮可作优质纺织原料,麻宵可制作多种纸板。

山珍类,以渭源等地蕨菜为最有名,肉质肥厚,美味可口,享誉中外,对外出口。遍布全区的沙棘亦很有名,其果含多种维生素、营养素,可制作饮料和食品。其种子还可制作珍贵的药用油。

花卉类,以陇西、临洮花卉最有名,主要有牡丹、芍药、菊花、大丽花、唐蒲菖、月季等,为全国唐蒲菖良种繁育生产基地。

中药材,当归——产于岷、漳、渭源3县,年产量占全国需要量的80%以上,"岷归"个头大、枝条粗、茬粉白、含有19种氨基酸和13种微量元素,在中药配方中有"十方九归"之说,系血家圣药,《本草纲目》称其"质佳"。产品行销全国,并打入国际市场。党参——全区种植,为全国党参主要产地之一,尤以岷县白条党参最佳,为药用营养滋补品,产品行销全国,也是出口重要商品。红、黄芪——产于岷、漳、渭源3县,亦以岷芪为最佳,主治贫血虚弱、消化不良等症,有健胃补脾之功能。亦为重要出口商品。贝母——亦以岷县贝最驰名,同浙贝、川贝、伊贝并列,在国内外市场享有盛誉。

食品,陇西"四肴"——火腿、腊羊肉、金钱肉、腌驴肉甲于天下。漳县"三宝"——红元帅苹果、漳盐、秦岭细鳞鲑鱼名扬全国。岷县松花蜜亦很有名。

手工艺品,洮砚——全国四大名砚之一,系砚中珍品,出自岷县洮河岸。地毯——各县制作,产量占全省三分之一,以临洮仿古地毯和定西、通渭美术地毯为最有名。草编——盛产于通渭,年代久远,工艺精湛,产品销往全国并出口。卫生香——临洮出产,制作悠久,气味芳香,畅销全国各地。

新型产品,无纺织针刺地毯——由甘肃无纺织地毯厂生产,为引进当今世界生产线中最先进的机器设备所产,产量、质量、销量占全国第一。活塞环——定西活塞环厂生产,产品质量稳定,产品型号多样,获部优产品称号。复合软包装——陇西复合软包装材料厂生产,拥有从日本引进的现代化生产线,为当代第一流包装材料。味精——通渭味精厂生产,为省优产品,质量可靠,产品行销省内外。贞芪扶正冲剂——定西制药厂生产,可提高人体免疫功能,并配合手术促进正常功能恢复,为国家中医药管理局优秀产品。

【城市建设】城镇设置,目前全区7个县的县城均为建制镇,另外还有定西县内官营镇、渭源县会川镇、陇西县文峰镇等3个建制镇。

基础设施,到1993年,全区各县城都有了自来水设施,目前基本可以满足工业生产和居民生活用水。经过多年建设、拓宽、取直、造面,城区道路状况不断改善,如定西中华路几经改造,已形成机动车道、自行车道、人行道、并栽有行道树的高级道路。进入八十年代,各城区照明有很大改观,路灯数量增加,照明度提高,照明时间延长。通讯正向现代化发展,各县城市话改造全部竣工,定西县城区8000门程控电话顺利开通。各县对城市绿化、园林建设都很重视,每年都有新的进展。

住宅建设,进入八十年代以来,各县城住宅基本上都是4层以上楼房,水暖配设施配套,设计合理,万平方米以上住宅小区已有多处,居民居住条件显著改善,仅1993年新建改建城镇居民住宅121.83万平方米。

城市规划与建设,全区7个县城的总体规划已于1989年全部完成,城市建设已基本纳入规划的渠道。在总体规划的指导下,各县城建部门已全面开始详细规划的编制工作。到1993年底,全区已完成城区道路拓宽12124米,总面积达62700平方米。全区旧城改造共投资3550万元。定西筹资454.6万元,将原老街改造成商业一条街,占地2万平方米,修建起多座综合营业楼,面积达3120平方米。临洮多方筹资4000多万元,新建起84栋3层以上楼房和133栋平房,总面积达4万多平方米，一次性改造了东、西两条最繁华的街道。漳县投资340万元，建成商贸一条街，并搞成“十大建筑”，使城区面貌大为改观。通渭、渭源、岷县及陇西主要街段建设也都取得突破性进展。城区上水工程又有新的成就，年内共完成投资412万元，主要有定西城区二期上水、漳县及通渭城区上水、陇西县文峰镇上水等工程，定西城区二期上水工程已于去年10月完成，日增水能力8500吨，缓解了城区供水矛盾，方便了居民生活，促进了工业生产及各行各业的发展。

城市管理，各县都设有城市建设的专门管理机构，加强了对城市的行政管理。并根据国家和省上制订颁布的各项法规和条例，陆续制定出了地方性法规和办法，使城市管理逐步走上了法制轨道，大大促进了城市建设。

【国民经济】1993年，全区国民生产总值达到16.4亿元，比上年增长15.5%。国民收入14.1亿元，增长13.7%。工农业总产值23.17亿元，增长17.02%。

农业，1993年，全区农业总产值达到13.07亿元，比上年增长9.88%。其中农业产值8.60亿元，增长10.43%；林业产值0.42亿元，增长30.87%；牧业产值4.04亿元，增长6.97%；渔业产值0.08亿元，增长6.99%。粮食产量创历史最好纪录，为第11个丰收年，达到470430吨，比上年增长9.75%。农村经济总体实力增强，农村经济总收入达23.13亿元，比上年增长25.80%，其中农、林、牧、渔业收入12.51亿元，增长12.03%。实现农村社会总产值22.30亿元(现价，下同)其中第一产业产值12.91亿元，比重为57.88%，下降6.77个百分点；第二产业产值6.11亿元，比重为27.39%，上升3.29个百分点；第三产业产值3.28亿元，比重为14.73%，上升3.48个百分点。林业建设稳步发展，全年完成造林面积20.03万亩，比上年增加0.48万亩，年末累计森林保存面积达到545.83万亩。畜牧业生产持续增长，大牲畜、生猪、羊只年末存栏数分别达70.57万头、97.45万头、96.12万只，分别比上年增长2.17%、2.52%、0.46%；肉类总产量达6.91万吨，增长12.95%；禽蛋总产量达到1.01万吨，增长2.84%。乡镇企业高速发展，总数达到4.18万个，增加0.6万个；从业人数达到16.21万人，增加2.35万人；总产值达到11.43亿元、总收入达到9.53亿元、上缴税金达到0.34亿元，分别增长58.60%、54.90%和62.0%。

工业，1993年全区实现工业总产值15.43亿元，比上年增长19.23%，其中地县工业总产值10.11亿元，增长27.87%；地县工业中乡及乡以上工业总产值6.59亿元，增长15.67%。国有企业完成总产值3.57亿元，增长8.18%；集体企业完成总产值3.02亿元，增长25.97%，其中乡办企业完成总产值1.35亿元，增长29.09%。轻重工业结构调整又有新的进步，轻工业总产值4.61亿元，增长9.88%；重工业总产值1.98亿元，增长31.80%。全社会工业增加值为3.16亿元，地县工业增加值2.45亿元，其中国有企业1.34亿元、集体企业1.11亿元、轻工业1.52亿元、重工业0.93亿元。工业经济效益有所提高，其综合指数由上年的59.70%提高到70.05%。工业企业技术进步取得可喜成绩，全年完成技术改造项目11项，在建技术项目32项，其中省级11项、地区级21项。

交通，1993年全区国有交通运输业再现活力，私营运输业迅猛发展。全区机动车辆拥有1.23万辆、2.57万吨位，比上年增加0.24万辆、0.49万吨位。其中营运车辆6090辆，增加578辆。在营运车辆中客车拥有1734辆，增加262辆；货车拥有4356辆，增加316辆。在营运车辆中个体运输户拥有客车246辆、货车793辆。

邮电，邮电通讯业适应市场经济的能力进一步增强，1993年完成邮电业务总量1421万元，比上年增长5.08%。邮电业务收入1217万元，增长22.11%。年末市内用户达7923户，增长28.18%。市内电话交换机总容量12000门，增长41.18%。报刊、杂志全年定销累计份数达1736.9万份，增长1.03%。

投资，固定资产投资高速增长，1993年全社会完成固定资产投资3.16亿元，比上年增长47.52%。其中地县完成固定资产投资2.65亿元，增长23.58%。在全社会固定资产投资中，国有单位完成投资1.37亿元，增长29.01%；集体单位投资0.42亿元，增长100%；城乡居民个人投资1.42亿元，增长56.28%。在国有单位投资中，基本建设投资0.85亿元，增长12.55%；更新改造投资0.38亿元，增长61.15%；商品房建设投资0.04亿元，增长20.58%；其他投资0.05亿元。

财贸，1993年，全区财政收入首次突破亿元大关，达到11150.7万元，比上年增长33.83%。全区完成社会商品零售总额8.01亿元，增长15.25%，扣除价格因素，实际增长2.95%。其中农业生产资料零售额1.38亿元，增长16.95%，扣除价格因素下降2.57%；消费品零售额6.63亿元，增长14.90%，扣除价格因素实际增长2.59%。全年外贸出口收购额3757万元，“三资”企业实现零的突破，创办合资企业7家。

【社会事业】科技，全区1993年科技成果大量涌现，全年鉴定科技成果36项，获省科技进步奖4项、省星火奖1项，获地区科技进步奖13项，当年推广26项。

文化，全区文化艺术事业稳步发展，1993年有艺术团体7个；电影放映队177个，城镇全年放映8300

场次;文化事业单位305个;图书馆7个,藏书40.8万册;县乡广播站164个,广播覆盖率85.09%;电视转播台40座,卫星电视地面站42座,电视覆盖率56.1%。

教育,全区教育事业有了新的发展,1993年有大专院校1所,在校学生364人,比上年增长30.47%;中等专业学校5所,在校学生2941人;中学(包括农、职中)188所,在校学生9.25万人;小学2884所,在校学生为26.43万人;幼儿园30所,在园幼儿3.02万人,增长8.58%。小学巩固率92.97%,小学毕业率95.48%,小学升学率78.46%。考入高等院校学生1668名,比上年增加524人,为历年之冠。成人高等院校从本区录取本、专科学生960人。成人高等自学考试全年报考6268人次,有2909人次获4739门单科合格证书,120人获取大专毕业证书。全年共脱盲5.71万人。

卫生,全区卫生事业稳步发展,共有各类医疗卫生机构305所,病床4042张,专业卫生技术人员5179人,增长1.69%,其中医生2671人,增长5.61%;护理人员1158人,增长3.76%。农村医疗点2690个,乡村医生2261人,卫生员1465人。

体育,全区体育事业取得新的成绩,1993年全区承办全省1项1次比赛,参加运动员42人;举办地级6项5次比赛,参加运动员680人。在省内外各项比赛中,获全省团体第一名4个、第二名2个、第三名1个,个人获金牌11枚、银牌9枚、铜牌6枚。有4人1队7次改写了3项地区田径纪录,17人达国家级运动员标准,9人代表省参加全国性比赛,获国家级金牌4枚、银牌3枚、铜牌1枚。全国残疾人比赛获3枚金牌、1枚银牌。陇西县被评为全省体育先进县。

保险 全区保险事业有较大发展,1993年全区共积累财产、人身保险各类保险责任准备金901万元,保户储金900万元。全区有277户企业、69213户居民参加了财产保险,23.67万人参加了人身保险。共处理各类财产赔案4827起,支付已决赔款715万元,人身险给付6610人(件),给付金额384.5万元。

(中共定西地委政策研究室:陈述德)

通渭县经济和社会发展概述

通渭县属于黄河流域开发较早地区,汉武帝元鼎三年(公元前114年)在境内设置平襄县,宋代改为通渭县至今,已有2015年的历史。

【自然概况】地理位置,通渭位于甘肃省东南部,定西地区东部。地处东经104°48′至105°39′,北纬34°55′至35°30′。东南、西南分别与秦安、甘谷县接壤;西南、西分别与武山、陇西县相邻;西北、北、东北分别与定西、会宁和静宁毗连。东西长78公里,南北宽64公里。县城距省会兰州和定西地区所在地定西县分别为170公里和70公里。

地形与气候,通渭属于黄土丘陵沟壑区域。海拔在2000——2200米之间,地势大致由西北向东南倾斜,最高为境内西北蟾姆山海拔2521米,最低为东南青石峡海拔1420米,相对高差1100米。属温带半湿润向半干旱过渡的温带大陆性季风气候类型。年平均气温6.6℃,极端最低和最高气温分别为零下26.9℃和33.7℃。年日照时数为2200——2430小时,无霜期为140——160天,降水量390——510毫米。全县地表水资源9540万立方米,地下水资源1478万立方米,除去重复外,全县水资源总量为9690万立方米。

资源,矿藏资源有辉铁、铝矾土、莹石、石英石、石灰石、蜡石、大理石、石膏、硝、花岗石、辉钼等。境内还有丰富的动植物资源。

政区划分与人口土地,全县辖1镇、22乡、332个行政村、2440个农业合作社,1个居民委员会。全县总户数77373户,总人口41.4万人(男性21.2万人,女性20.2万人),其中农业人口39.9万人,有劳动力17.5万人。全县土地总面积2912.7平方公里,耕地185.28亩,其中旱川地11.75万亩。林地57.28万亩,草地91.48万亩,未利用地73.19万亩。人口密度142.25人/平方公里。

【经济发展概况】农业,1993年通渭县农村经济蓬勃发展。一是生产条件得到极大改善,1993年,全县兴修水平梯田和条田96.94万亩。兴修水利工程10项,已发挥效益的8项。完成小流域治理面积22平方公里。农业机械总动力达到44752千瓦,拥有各类动力机械2226台(辆),半机械化农具5496台(件)。全县100%的乡和76%的村通了电,农业年用电量830万度。粮油加工和农村运输基本实现机械化和半机械化。二是农村产业结构得到较大调整。1993年全县农村个体、私营经济和乡镇企业迅速发展,粮食获得全面丰收。农经比达到87:13,农村产业结构渐趋合理。全县农业总产值达到19960.5万元,占工农业总产值的74%。粮食总产量达到11746.5万公斤,人均产粮295公斤。经济作物以胡麻为主,总产量达到10452.65吨,蔬菜产量达到427万公斤。全县森林面积达到54.9万亩,森林覆盖率由解放初的0.19%提高到13.1%,林木总蓄积32.5万立方米,年林木采伐量3236.4立方米。森林面积中经济林面积1.14万亩,1993年经济林果产量3012吨。林业总产值达到423.19万元。种草面积47.96万亩。畜牧业已发展成为一大支柱产业,1993年产值达到5543.94万元,其中商品产值3061.23万元,占总产值55%。大家畜由1949年的5.47万头增加到12.1万头。羊存栏8.98万只,猪存栏14.08

万头，肉类总产量达到10752.07吨。农村副业产值达到1222.54万元。农业商品经济产值达到6049.16万元，占农业总产值的30%，农民人均纯收入487元。

工业，建国后特别是党的十一届三中全会后，全县工业快速发展。先后建成了毛纺织、印刷、农机制造、建筑建材、食品、服装加工、木器加工、地毯、淀粉、粉丝、味精、草编、铝盐、卷烟纸等行业和企业。1993年底全县工业企业总数达到1148户，其中全民所有制企业9户，集体所有制企业41户，县办工业企业职工人数3131人。工业总产值达到7000.3万元，占工农业总产值的26%，完成销售收入4612.9万元。县办工业企业实现税金200万元。全县工业企业拥有固定资产原值3454.2万元，全员劳动生产率达到3480元/人。产品结构已形成毛纺织、食品、机械、化工、草编织五大系列50余种。其中味精、粉丝先后获省部优，亚麻油、脱粒机、地毯、塑料包装袋、农膜、淀粉先后获省优。优质产品产值达到3627万元，占工业总产值的52%。十几年来，先后有地毯厂晋升为省一级企业，粮油加工厂、粉丝厂、味精厂晋升为省二级企业。

乡镇企业，自党的十四大后，通渭乡镇企业迅猛发展，已成为全县经济的"半壁江山"。1993年底乡镇企业数达到3078户，从业人员12704人，实现总产值6507万元，总收入5700万元，利税460万元。主要产品有味精、粉条、地毯、童鞋、酱油、糕点、草编、服装、铁制及木制农具和建材等10多种。

交通运输，解放后，通渭交通运输事业发展迅速。1993年底，全县有省属公路3条，全长131.16公里；县乡公路10条，全长400公里；乡村公路77条，全长646公里。境内23个乡(镇)和87%的行政村通了汽车。全县共有运输汽车369辆，其中机关、事业单位253辆，专业运输公司30辆，个体运输汽车86辆。年客运量50.6万人，客运周转量1660.6万人/公里；年货运量11.37万吨，货运周转量947.6吨/公里。营运收入433.3万元，税金12.8万元。

商供贸易，1993年全县共有商业、供销网点217个，其中商业28个，供销189个，职工1210人。城乡个体工商户达到2267户，从业人员3197人。完成社会商品零售总额7933万元。全县共有农村集贸市场51处，年集贸市场成交额达到4600万元。

邮电通讯，1993年，兴建县邮电通信大楼一座，并完成了长途电话进网工程。马营乡建成了自动电话。目前，县邮电局下设19个邮电所，邮电服务网点20处，干线邮路6条，里程310公里，农村邮路105条，里程4867公里，全县23个乡镇和332个行政村全部通邮。电讯电路有长途电话线路28条，电报电路3条，市话线路13.295杆公里，农话线路274.56杆公里。电信设备有市话交换机1套，容量1000门，市话单机624部；农话交换机20部，容量750门，农话单机225部。电话普及率达到0.2部/百人。年邮电通信总量93.3万元，邮电业务总量121万元，邮电业务收入99.4万元。

财税金融，1993年，全县完成财政收入852万元，财政支出2517万元。全县完成各种税收713.4万元。金融机构45个，其中乡营业所12个，农村信用社22个。职工350人，其中营业所56人，农村信用社108人。城乡个人储蓄存款5613.5万元，其中城镇3515.6万元，农村2107.9万元。人均存款达到135.48元。

【社会事业】教育，1993年底，全县普通高中7所，初中16所，教职工3762人，其中中学1237人，小学2525人。在校学生61498人，其中高中2860人，初中11391人，小学44811人。学龄儿童入学率96%，教育普及率达95%。幼儿园2所，在园幼儿322人，教职工29人。农职业中学4所，学生792人，教职工117人。教师进修学校1所，学员40人，教职工16人。私人办学5所，学生151人。自1977年恢复高考制度以来，共向全国各大专院校输送学生4588人，其中1993年输送505人，大专263人，中专242人，成人教育上电大132人，函授125人，参加自学考试257人。40年来教学条件大为改善，全县公办中小学校舍建筑面积增加到17.9万平方米，教学设备总额达到318.2万元。

科技，到1993年底，全县有科级管理机构24个，群众性学术团体县直10个，会员790人。乡(镇)科协23个，会员305人。全县科技人员中获得高级职称的22人，中级职称的423人，初级职称1901人。农民获得技术职称的293人。

文化艺术，随着国民经济和社会事业的不断发展，文化艺术事业日益繁荣。1993年底，全县共有秦剧团6个，从业200人。民间皮影戏班8个。电影放影队19个，从业40人，其中个体放映队11个，年放影5000场(次)。县图书馆藏书6700万册，年借阅量10000人(次)。县文化馆下设文化站和文化中心15个，从业17人。文化馆藏文物有新石器时代、战国、秦国、秦、汉、宋、明、清代陶器、石器、铜器以及明清书画、各代货币等1260件，革命文物110件，其中国家一级文物4件。新华书店有门市部3个，代销点13个，年读书发行量119万册，销售收入217万元。全县有业余文艺创作者24人，书画爱好者656人。剪纸能手125人，业余摄影210人。有5件作品获得省级以上奖励。1993年12月，通渭县被中央文化部命名为"书画艺术之乡"。

医疗卫生，全县有乡以上医院

26个，有县人民医院、温泉医院、中医院各1所，乡镇卫生院23所。医院床位总数477个，医务人员657人，其中技术人员566人，获得高中级职称的114人。村医疗站477个，医生656人。全县每万人拥有病床11张，拥有医生16人，基本形成了县、乡、村三级医疗卫生网络。

广播电视，1993年底，以通渭县人民广播电台为中心，县到乡实现了调频广播，23个乡镇全部建成了广播放大站，全县广播覆盖率达到79%。通渭电视事业起步晚，发展快。1993年建成了有线电视台，全县共有卫星地面接收站8个，电视差转台14个，电视发射机14台，功率0.096千瓦，能接收3个频道的节目。电视覆盖半径15平方公里，覆盖率达到32%。

社会保障，1993年底，全县有保险公司1家，保险业务代办所1处。开办了机动车辆、人身、财产、牲畜、劳动等保险业务，共有干部职工25人。1993年，全县承保财产总额达到3938.8万元，保险费收入60万元，全年处理赔案47件，赔款29万元。全县有乡镇敬老院2所，收养农村孤老3人。集体供养五保户309人，集体办福利工厂7家，就业盲、聋、哑、残79人。1993年财政拨怃恤和社会福利救济费29.7万元。

计划生育，1993年底，全县总人口达到41.4335万人，比地区计划数41.47万人少370人，完成人口计划指标。年共内出生7233人，出生率为17.58‰；自然增长率13.03‰。全年完成四项节育手术10774例，计划生育率达到69.39%。

【土特产品】通渭土特名优产品有莜麦、荞麦、豌豆、胡麻、洋芋、杏、苹果、草编织品、味精和粉丝。

现任主要领导：

中共通渭县委书记：邵　昕

通渭县人大常委会主任：敬根年

通渭县人民政府县长：张　鹤

政协通渭县委员会主席：孙毓业

中共通渭县纪律检查委员会书记：田东良

（中共通渭县委政研室：王绍博）

陇西县经济和社会发展概述

【基本情况和自然概况】陇西县地处甘肃省东南部，定西地区中部。东接通渭，南连武山、漳县，西邻渭源，北靠定西，面积2400平方公里，系中部18个干旱县之一。全县地形西北高，东南低，南北山均向渭河、大咸河倾斜，海拔1612——2778米，构成南山、城川、北山三块条件明显差异的自然区域。属典型的黄土梁峁地貌，土壤以黄绵土、黑垆土为主。气候属温带大陆性季风气候，多属温和半干旱区，兼有温寒半湿润区，年均气温7.7℃，年日照时数2292小时，年均降水量为445.8mm，年蒸发量1440mm，年均无霜期146天。可利用水资源总量1.78亿立方米，人均416立方米。渭河境内流长46.1公里，水质好，宜于灌溉。适宜种植的粮食作物有10多种（小麦、扁豆、豌豆、蚕豆、玉米、洋芋、谷等），小麦种植面积最大，约占粮食面积的40%以上。经济作物主要有胡麻、油菜、药材、大麻等，党参、当归已形成地方拳头产品。蔬菜、水果种类多，产量高。有林木100多种，花卉650余种。

陇海铁路纵贯东西，境内有8个火车站，走行长度75公里，与境内3条干线公路和16条县乡公路联网，形成较好的交通条件；境内有330千伏变电站1座，110千伏变电站2座，35千伏变电站9座，总装机容量17.13万千伏安，电力供应充足。

全县现辖2个镇，23个乡，279个村民委员会和23个居民委员会，总人口44.7万人，其中农业人口39.58万人。耕地122万亩，农业人口人均占有耕地3.1亩。

【经济发展概况】1993年，全县经济和社会发展各方面都取得了新的成绩。国民生产总值达到38489万元，比上年增长10.4%；实现国民收入30714万元，比上年增长12%；工农业总产值达到32068万元，比上年增长16.7%；财政收入达到3292万元，比上年增长30.9%。

一是农业基础条件有了新的改善，人民生活水平明显提高。兴修梯田2.21万亩，累计达到49.76万亩；治渭工程完成砂堤700米，维修新建护坡268米，治渭总长达到24.7公里；7.6公里的陇渭渠延长工程基本完成；完成小水利工程28项；完成河道险段加固工程9处，保护良田3925亩，新增有效灌溉面积2750亩，恢复有效灌溉面积1750亩，使水浇地发展到13.65万亩。架设农电线路37.69公里，累计达到1006.26公里，村通电率达到92.8%。粮食总产量创历史最高水平，达到10526.7公斤，比上年增长17.8%，人均占有粮食266公斤；农业总产值达到19865.74万元，比上年增长11.5%，其中畜牧业产值5778.11万元，林业产值447.93万元；农民人均纯收入达到558元，比上年增加64元，增长12.9%，农民居住条件大为改善，大部分人家新瓦房代替了土房土窑，人均住房面积显著增大；家用电器等耐用消费品不断进入普通农家。

二是工业生产稳定发展。1993年，通过实行“一厂一策”措施，狠抓工业企业扭亏增盈和达产达标，有5个县属企业退出亏损行列；洗衣粉、太空棉、第二粉丝厂等新项目相继投产；一批县属重点企业实现达产达标和完成技改计划。全县工业总产值达到12202.28万元，比上年增长26.12%，实现利润200.53万元。现有的28个（全民14个，集体14个）县属工业企业，固定资产原值达6385万元。主要产品有液压件、机制纸、复合包装材料、洗衣粉、机制砖瓦、水泥、电石、大理石板材及工艺品、硫酸、磷肥、地毯、服装、粉丝、配合饲料、食品、中药浸膏等20余种。土特产品金钱肉、口条、火腿被誉为陇原三绝。

三是乡镇企业迅速发展。县上把乡镇企业作为振兴农村经济的突破口来抓，制订优惠政策，扶持鼓励发展。1993年总产值达23100万元，比上年增长66.2%，总收入达17500万元，比上年增长68.8%。乡镇企业总产值和从业人员分别占农村社会总产值和农村总劳动力的54%、16%。特别是股份合作制企业的发展成为乡镇企业发展的新热点，全县现有7552个乡镇企业、31210人从业人员中，股份合作制企业达81家，从业人员1747人，完成产值2179万元，入股农户245户，入股资金750万元。

四是商贸流通进一步活跃。随着流通体制改革的深入，适应社会主义市场经济体制的流通领域全面放开，多种经济成份共同发展，平等竞争的流通格局已经形成，活跃了城乡商品市场。1993年，国合商业商品销售总额达9030.2万元；社会商品零售总额达到20001万元；集市贸易年成交额12600万元；首次突破亿元大关；市场建设出现全民动员，全社会兴办的热潮，成为经济建设的新热点，1993年新增市场8处，总数达38处；个体、私营经济增长速度分别达到16.94%、28.94%。

【各项社会事业取得新进展】科学技术工作立足试验和示范，加强科技推广服务体系建设，积极推广了科技成果和先进适用技术。重点以12项重点农业科技项目集团承包为先导，试验、示范、推广种类农业科技70余项，农业生产的科技含量进一步增强。现有各类专业技术人员3460人，初步形成县、乡科委，村农科主任，社农科组长的科技管理体系和县有中心、乡有站、村有组、社有户的科技推广应用体系。

教育工作以农村教育综合改革为动力，“三教”都有新发展：初等教育“四率”不断巩固提高，“普九”稳步推进；中等教育质量稳步提高，1993年被各类大、中专院校录取598人(其中大专以上396人)；职业技术教育由初级向高层次发展，县办三所职校全部达到C级标准，甘工大、甘农大机械设计与制造、种养加综合技术陇西大专班招生123人；已有22个乡镇基本扫除文盲，南安等15个乡镇已经县政府验收合格，青壮年文盲率下降到10%；现有各级各类学校398所，在校学生72353人，教职工3909人，校舍建筑面积17.4万平方米。

卫生工作在医疗、保健、防疫、管理等各方面都有新的改善，新建的妇幼保健站服务大楼投入使用；县二院住院楼开工建设；19个乡镇卫生院改革管理体制，移交乡镇政府管理，现有妇幼保健站、卫生防疫站各1个，县级医院3个，中心卫生院5个，乡卫生院19个，村医疗站276个，个体医疗诊所191个，卫生技术人员810人。形成了乡乡有卫生院，村村有医疗点的农村三级医疗网。

群众性体育活动在全县城乡蓬勃发展，成功地举办了全国男篮甲级队陇西邀请赛和全省无线电测向比赛，陇西今年还被省体委命名为全省体育先进县。

广播电视充分发挥了喉舌和媒体作用，兴建了云田和马河两个电视收转台，成立了定西电视台陇西记者站，积极筹建了陇西有线电视台。目前有2个电视差转台、3个卫星地面接收站、1个调频广播电台、1个教育电视台，开通了定西电视站微波传输，电视覆盖率甘肃台达59%，其他台49%，调频广播覆盖率达74%。

基础服务设施进一步改善，市政建设完成了对北城路东段、文巩路东段、建新路、西城路丁字口以南东侧道路四处主要交通路段的改造拓建，市容市貌明显改观；整修县乡公路80.5公里；续建文峰水厂，城区供水容量进一步扩大；自动电话扩容2446门，实现了国际国内直拨，目前电话容量为3728门，电话机2804部。

现任主要领导：

中共陇西县委书记：王志诚

陇西县人大常委会主任：曹宗周

陇西县人民政府县长：朱同心

政协陇西县委员会主席：史　祯

中共陇西县纪律检查委员会书记：张继文

(中共陇西县委办公室：马万才　王鉴)

渭源县经济和社会发展概述

【自然特点】渭源县地处甘肃省定西地区南部，东经103°44′—104°24′和北纬34°55′—35°45′之间。土地总面积为2034平方公里。全县有20个乡(镇)，216个行政村，1509个村民小组，31.57万人，其中农业人口占96.94%。有耕地80.15万亩，其中山地占84%。自然环境总的特点是：①海拔高，平均海拔2311米，最高3941米。②无霜期短，平均不到126天。③气温低，年平均气温在4——7℃之间。④自然灾害多，北部干旱少雨，南部高寒阴湿。自古就有“南山丰收北山旱，北山丰收南山烂”的说法。

【农业】1993年，渭源县委、县政府全面贯彻定西地委、行署提出的“一手抓粮、一手抓钱、以钱为主、抓钱促粮、全面发展”的农业指导方针，农村经济保持了良好的发展势头。全县农业总产值为1.58亿元，比上年增长11.3%。粮食总产量达到9.2万吨，比上年增长4.82%，创历史最好水平。呈现出六个特点：一是种植业结构得到调整，开始走上适应社会主义市场经济发展的路子，粮食作物播种面积由上年的66.99万亩压缩到62.84万亩；经济作物面积由上年的11.69万亩增加到16.46万亩，粮经比由上年的8.4：1.5调整到7.8：2.1。二是开发支柱产业，发展区域经济初见成效。1993年初，县委、县政府从发挥资源优势出发，制定了“强化农业基础，开发中药材、畜牧业、淀粉、林果、建筑、建材五大支柱产业，建设中药材、肉牛和细毛羊、豆类、经济林、亚麻、油菜六大商品基地”的经济发展新思路，并按照“五个一”(每个支柱产业由一名县级领导负责。有一个好的发展规划，有一支较强的技术队伍，有一个龙头企业，有一个依托牵头单位)的要求，把基地建设和发展“两高一优”农业结合起来，不断扩大豆类、洋芋、药材、油料等名优特产种植面积，豆类、中药材、洋芋、亚麻和油料、畜牧业、林果业基地基本形成。年底五大支柱产业共完成产值1.10亿元，占农业总产值的70%，比上年增长24.7%。三是狠抓科技兴农，全县科技覆盖率达到80%以上，科技入户率达到95%以上。四是农业生产基本条件大幅度改善。①石门水库北干渠主干渠工程全部竣工，冬灌面积8000亩。②完成小水利工程10项，新增有效灌溉面积2900亩。配套面积5200亩。③新修梯田13387亩。④完成小流域治理14.17平方公里。⑤架设农电线路33.4杆公里，新增通电8个村，12个社。⑥新增农用机动大小拖拉机、三轮车249台(辆)，新增三行播种机125台(架)。五是乡镇企业异军突起，农村经济“半壁河山”的格局初步形成。县里采取硬逼硬上快发展的方针，乡镇企业总数达到6252个，比上年净增1421个；实现利润496万元，上缴税金137万元，分别比上年增长34.2%和61.2%；农民人均从乡镇企业中收入达到199元，比上年增加89元，增长80.9%。六是劳务输出已成为农村剩余劳动力的主要出路和部分农民的主要经济来源。1993年全县劳务输出2.2万人，比上年增长30.9%，已占全县总劳力的15%。劳务收入达到1111.7万元，比上年增长21.1%。

【工业、交通、邮电】1993年，全县工业在全面贯彻落实《企业法》和转换经营机制《条例》，狠抓三项制度改革的同时，集中人力、物力、财力，对县水泥厂等5个企业进行了技术改造和扩建，建成2个技术项目。实现工业总产值2412万元，比上年增长12%。完成销售1835.9万元，比上年增长34.7%。公路运输快速发展，运输条件得到极大改善。1993年完成定渭公路北寨大桥主体工程和4条境内县县、县乡公路，并投入使用。全年客运量27.26万人次，比上年增长113.9%；旅客周转量831.8万人公里，比上年增长83.3%。完成货物运输量23.99万吨，比上年增长89.2%；货物周转量784.12万吨公里，比上年增长18.3%。

邮电通讯事业发展迅速。1993年新开通了会川等4个乡(镇)的自动电话。全年完成邮电业务总量9784万元，比上年增长41.92%；邮电业务收入76.80万元，比上年增长43.22%；年末城市市内电话机拥有量625户，比上年增长24%；市内交换机容量1000门。报刊发行量134.6万份，比上年增长1.95%。

【商业】商贸、供销等企业，按照社会主义市场经济的要求，在保证国有资产所有权的前提下，实行“国有民营”、“社有自营”使全县商业、供销市场繁荣，企业效益明显提高。全年社会商品零售总额6310万元，比上年增长8.33%。全县共筹资666.4万元，建成集贸市场20处，其中专业市场8处。全县个体工商业户达到2139户，突破两千户大关，比上年增长13%。集贸市场成交额达到2741.2万元，比上年增长39%。

【科技文化、卫生、体育】科技工作紧紧围绕经济建设，开展技术引进，新技术推广、示范、试验、科研成果转化和科技攻关。通过省地鉴定验收的省、地列科技项目有《粮食作物综合增产整乡双轨科技承包》等9项，其中《定西南部阴湿区优质油菜丰产技术示范》达到国内领先水平。

教育事业发展较快。全年投入排危建校资金120万元，共维修、改建教室4520平方米，基本排除了一级危房。全县有中等专业学校1所，在校学生60人，比上年增长一23%；中学(包括农中、职中)22所，在校学生10427人，比上年增长一14.5%；小学354所，在校学生32643人，比上年增长0.3%；幼儿园3所，在园幼儿309人，比上年增长8.5%。1993年完成了2个乡的普及初等教育，初等义务教育普及率92%，儿童入学率98%。1993年为大中专院校输送学生316名，首次突破300名大关。全县参加自学考试的人员达121人。1993年取得中专以上毕业证书有7人。

文化艺术事业快速发展。全县有艺术团体1个，42人；电影事业单位3个，13人，城镇全年放映223场次；文化事业单位4个，全年共举办集体性群众文化活动9场(次)，有图书馆1个，藏书3.43万册；广播站20个，广播覆盖率55%；1993年新开通中央3台和云贵台，建成1个差转台和3个地面接收站，使全县拥有电视差转台6座，卫星地面接收站9座，电视覆盖率80%。

医疗卫生条件大幅度改善。全县共有各类医疗卫生机构26所，专业卫生技术人员228人。计划免疫建卡率达100%。

【人民生活与人口】县委、县政府以1992年12月省委、省政府渭源扶贫现场办公会议精神为动力，1993年共落实扶贫资金4500万元，用于17个扶贫项目开发。同时，坚持干部、党员帮扶责任制，全县共有1975名干部和1426名党团员，帮扶贫困户3926户，其中有1815户群众到年底解决了温饱。全县温饱面由1992年的65.5%上升到1993年的71%，300元以下的贫困户由1992年的23203户减少到1993年的19880户。全县农民人均纯收入达到469.31元，比上年增加52.16元。人均占有粮达到302公斤，比上年净增10.4公斤。200元以下的贫困户(不含社救对象)下降到2742户，占全县总农户的4%。

全年共完成财政收入580万元，占年度预算的116%，比上年增长39.8%。

1993年共出生人口5561人，出生率为17.74‰，低于控制指标2.46个千分点。人口自然增长率为11.97‰，低于控制指标1.73个千分点，年末全县人口为315673人。

现任主要领导：

中共渭源县委书记：秦素梅

渭源县人大常委会主任：田　龙

渭源县人民政府县长：周志祥

政协渭源县委员会主席：王国祯

中共渭源县纪律检查委员会书记：马　敬

(中共渭源县委政研室：张学恩　周英)

临洮县经济和社会发展概述

【自然概况】临洮县位于甘肃中部，地处洮河下游，东经103°29′至104°19′，北纬36°04′至35°57′，在陇西盆地的西缘，青藏高原的东边。东临定西县，西与临夏回族自治州的东乡、广河、康乐三县接壤，南连渭源县，北接省城兰州市。全县地势，由东向西北倾斜。总土地面积2867平方公里，耕地面积113.13万亩。南北长103公里，东西宽78公里。海拔中部河谷区在1730至2100米之间，边缘山区多在3000米以上。气温，夏季最高温度33.9℃，冬季最低温度－29.6℃；年平均温度7.0℃。年平均降雨量427.7毫米。洮河水纵贯南北115公里，是全县最大的水利电力资源，可灌川区及台坪耕地40多万亩。

【历史沿革】临洮县是中华民族和中国古代文化的发祥地之一，早在公元前三千多年的母系氏族公社制时期，人类祖先就在这块土地上繁衍生息。公元前384年秦献公始设狄道。公元前287年秦昭王灭戎后，设陇西郡。西汉时期建临洮县，至晋朝分建狄道郡。南北朝时期改称临洮郡。唐代乾元初设狄道州。宋代设岷州、熙州、和政郡。元代初称岷州。金代皇统二年至明代、清初为临洮府。当时经济、文化呈复兴之势。清代乾隆五年复称狄道州。辛亥革命后废州设县，辖境分为洮沙、临洮两县。1949年8月16日，全县解放。新中国建立初期及六十年代初曾两度设临洮专区，其余时期一直为定西地区所辖。现有5镇29乡，人口48.7万人。

【经济发展概况】1993年全县农村工作按照省上提出的农业实行“四放开”；地提出的“二十字”方针和县上提出的“紧盯总目标，狠抓两收入”的指导思想，以市场为导向，以科技为先导，以效益为重点，以致富奔小康为目标，放手发展农业生产，走“两高一优”的路子，走贸工农、种养加一体化的路子；大搞农田水利基本建设，使农业生产增强了发展后劲。农业总产值达到26013.2万元，占计划的100%，比1992年增长11.5%。粮食总产量达到7695.34万公斤；单产达到171.6公斤，人均占有粮食332.6公斤；农民人均纯收入达到544元；比1992年净增62元。全县乡镇企业总产值突破4亿元大关；完成总收入35658万元，比上年增长52.5%；实现利润1437万元，比上年增长60.2%；上缴税金1237万元，比上年增长76.2%。

1993年全县工业、商贸企业转换经营机制，深化内部改革，克服由计划经济旧体制转入市场经济新体制过程中存在的各种困难和问题，千方百计发展生产，群策群力开发引进新项目。全县乡以上工业完成产值7867万元，比上年增长8.8%。其中：县办工业企业完成产值4905万元；完成产品销售收入4073万元；上缴利税104万元。国合商业企业，积极推行“国有民营”和“社有自营”，全年完成销售额997.5万元，上缴利税183万元。1993年，县委、县政府以建设市场入手，积极鼓励支持全县大办个体私营企业和第三产业，全县新建和完善各类市场53个，其中专业市场24个，综合市场29个，交易点50个，总面积15万平方米，集市贸易成交额突破亿元大关，达10139万元，比1992增长36.2%。全县新发展个体户1426户。个体户总数累计达到4650户，从业人员7075人，注册资金1324万元，实现总产值1565万元，营业额4809万元，分别比1992年增长90.5%和39.8%；新发展私营企业6户，缴纳税、费近300万元，为安置待业青年，闲散人员和转移农村剩余劳动力开辟了新的道路。全县财政收入完成1385万元。其中：工商税完成911.8万元。金融系统，积极筹措资金，为经济建设服务。全县存款余额达22345万元，比上年增长29.5%，贷款14972万元，比上年增长19.5%。

【社会事业】1993年，全县共承担省、地、县列各类科技项目36项，完成21项。农业高新增产技术，高效节能日光温室等项目得到了推广。省列名贵花卉郁金香引种繁殖项目达到全省先进水平，全县已初步形成了以大丽花、唐菖蒲、郁金香为主的花卉基地，面积达200多亩，年收入80多万元。同时，通过科普宣传、科普培训、乡镇科技达标、科技示范、发展民办科技组织，使科学技术是第一生产力的理论深入人心。

教育事业，1993 年向省内外大中专院校输送新生 588 名，比上年增加了 109 名。成人教育、职业教育为经济建设培养适用技术人才 1735 人；以发展校园经济为主的勤工俭学活动取得了成绩，纯收入达到 35 万元；全县捐资办学继续保持了良好的发展势头，征收教育附加 145 万元，群众捐资 17 万元，新建、改建教学楼舍 4244 平方米。新增"六配套"标准学校 150 所；教师队伍建设得到重视和加强，有 34 个集体和 27 名个人分别受到国家、省、地的表彰奖励。

体育事业，全县有 67 名动员参加了国家级、省级、地级各类比赛，夺得金牌 15 枚、银牌 13 枚、铜牌 10 枚，经运动学校、体育院校输送优秀动员 34 名。县体委、临洮二中、体育中学先后受到全国七运会、国家体委、省体委的表彰奖励，临洮县被省委评为全省体育达标先进县。

卫生计生工作，投资 6 万元整建了两个卫生院，投资 8.2 万元给基层卫生院增添医疗设备。继续开展了计划免疫工作，组织实施了全国消灭脊髓灰质炎强化免疫活动，实施了世行贷款结核病控制项目及农村改水项目。成立了临洮县红十安会，发展团体会员 247 人。计划生育工作始终坚持了国策教育，坚持经济要上，人口要降的原则。全年结扎 4493 例；放环 6411 例；人流 1411 例；引产 1334 例；分别占任务的 107%、102%、101%和 95.3%。计划生育率为 57.7%。

全县架设农电线路 40 公里，使全县 34 个乡镇 85%的农户通了电。同时，县电力部门实现了安全供电 2000 天，保证了全县工农业生产、乡镇企业和城镇建设的顺利发展。洮河三甲电站重点工程建设，在资金困难的情况下，进展顺利，按计划第一台机组 1994 年建成发电。兰郎公路的改扩建共伐除树木 10420 棵，拆迁房屋 563 户 3385 间，挖运土石方 20 万立方，征用土地 49.8 亩。拓宽了中铺、太石、辛店、巴下、康家崖 5 个集镇的街道。多方争取资金新上马投资 480 万元的刘排子坪万亩电灌工程，世行贷款农村改水项目进入实施阶段，完成了投资 5.6 万元的西坪阎吴家村小型水厂。洮阳水厂正在积极筹建，投资 130 万元开工兴建东二十铺大桥，1994 年可建成通车。

【城区建设】临洮县城是陇上文化名城，建治已有 2300 多年，城内有东、西、南、北 4 条大街和 37 条小街、巷道。解放后在党和人民政府的领导下，城区建设虽有发展，改善和兴建了许多公用事业。但仍然不适应经济发展的需要。为了改变这种落后状况，县委、县政府 把改造旧城作为一个硬仗来打。广泛动员，多方投资兴建，经过两年的努力，旧建改造已初具规模。完成了东大街、北大街、粮食市 3 条主街道 279 户、19847 平方米的拆迁任务，有 45 个机关单位和 245 户居民投资约 3900 多万元，新建了 4 万多平方米楼房和平房。工贸大厦、临洮商城、东方宾馆、购物中心建成开业、农行综合大楼、城建综合大楼、建行办公楼、洮阳镇办公楼、临洮电信大楼、二轻总公司综合大楼等一批骨干工程，即将峻工。建成标准化的道路 520 米，整修了几条小巷道。集中供热工程，已进入安装阶段。投资 50 万元，完成了洮湖公园的设计和围栏修建。开通了自动电话全国长途直拨联网和 BP 机无线寻呼业务。

【名特土产】地毯：临洮仿古地毯的生产，已有几百年的历史。县地毯厂生产的地毯以龙凤呈祥，红花绿叶为图案，色彩艳丽，具有传统的民族特色和古老的艺术风格。1980 年 90 道被评为全国质量第一，1981 年荣获中国工艺美术品质优产品百花奖，1982 年又获全省仿古地毯质量第一名。产品远销美国、日本、西欧、东南亚及港澳等 10 多个国家和地区。卫生香：制作历史悠久，清代"贡香"就出自临洮"王真人"之手。县化工厂生产的卫生香畅销全国 16 个省、市。所产"飞天牌"蚊香，被评为部优产品，当归香、檀香博得外商的欢迎，已打入国际市场。洮河鱼：洮河鱼类繁多，品种多样，而以金片鱼、双重嘴鱼最为著称。洮河鱼膘厚肉鲜，刺少质嫩，含蛋白质高，具有独特风味。烹成菜肴，滋味腴美，上口柔糯，非其它食品所能及。花卉：临洮素有"陇上花圃"之称。现已形成大丽花、唐菖蒲、郁金香为主要产品的球根花卉生产基地，造就了实力雄厚的花卉专业科技队伍。1988 年经全国花卉专家鉴定，认为培育的 136 个大丽花品种花大、色艳、株矮、为全国先进水平。在 1989 年"第二届中国花卉博览会"上，我县参展的大丽花荣获良种选育一等奖，郁金香荣获引进栽培三等奖，唐菖蒲获良种繁育科技进步奖。

现任主要领导：

中共临洮县委书记：阎尚人

临洮县人大常委会主任：雷 炯

临洮县人民政府县长：田得如

政协临洮县委员会主席：张 勋

中共临洮县纪律检查委员会书记：尤天佑

（中共临洮县委政研室）

武威地区

中共武威地委书记：王国文

武威地区行政公署专员：杨兴昌

中共武威地区纪律检查委员会书记：毛如针

武威地区经济和社会发展概述

【自然概况】武威，亦称凉州，地处甘

肃省中部，河西走廊东端，祁连山北麓，是古丝绸之路上的要冲。东靠景泰、永登县，南倚祁连山与青海省为邻，西与肃南县、永昌县接壤，北邻巴丹吉林和腾格里大沙漠与内蒙古自治区相连。全区辖武威市、天祝藏族自治县、古浪县和民勤县，总面积3.3万平方公里，占全省总面积的7.4%，有174万人口，聚居着汉、藏、回、蒙、满、土等26个民族。工业初具规模，已形成了以冶金、煤炭、建材、化工、机械、造纸、制糖、酿造、纺织、制药、印刷、制革、食品、粮油加工等行业为主体的门类齐全的工业体系。有国营、集体、乡镇、个体、私营、"三资"企业4300多户，产品有原煤、水泥、硅铁、地毯、白酒、化肥、皮革、花岗岩板材等2000多种。凉州皇台酒、凉州古酒、雷台酒、冬虫夏草酒、葡萄干白(红)酒屡次在国际博览会获金、银奖，享誉海内外；硅铁、锰铁、铬铁、地毯、熏醋、工业酒精、祖师麻膏药等61种产品分别获国优、部优、省优产品称号。

矿产资源种类多、储量大、品位高，现已发现的矿种25个，矿点120多处，探明储量的矿种15个。钛铁、石墨矿国内特大型矿床，非金属矿和能源燃料资源在省内占居优势。钛、锰、铁、铜、金、煤炭、石墨、重晶石、花岗岩、石灰岩等矿产品的开发前景极为广阔。

农业资源：高山细毛羊繁育基地，农畜土特产品分布广、品种多、品质优，粮食、油料、甜菜、肉类、亚麻、瓜果、蔬菜、葵花籽、黑瓜籽、小茴香、红枣、沙棘、发菜等已形成批量，无壳瓜籽、白牦牛为世所仅有，金冠苹果获全国名优奖，大板黑瓜籽走俏国内外市场，中药材多达250多种。以农畜土特产品为原料的粮油加工、脱水蔬菜、玉米淀粉、精制白糖、食用酒精、甘草甜素、皮毛制品、亚麻制品、蕃茄酱、中成药，以及甜果类、沙棘饮料等系列产品开发和深度加工增值十分诱人。

旅游资源：悠久的历史文化，留下了丰富的文物古迹；独特的地理环境，造就了绮丽的自然风光。境内有出土文物3万多件，文物保护点543处，出土于武威雷台汉墓的铜奔马，是驰名中外的稀世珍宝，被定为中国旅游标志；举世无双的"西夏碑"被列为国家重点保护文物；建于明正统四年、气势辉宏、清幽秀丽、号称陇右之冠的武威文庙，明清造就、古朴庄严的丝路名刹海藏寺，历经千百年风蚀雨浸的古长城遗址，以及古钟楼、罗什寺塔、弘化公主墓和汉代简牍等大量文物古迹向世人开放。始建于十六国时期、规模宏大、堪称石窟之祖的天梯山石窟，已经国家立项批准，正在加紧修复；建于元代的凉州白塔寺，是元朝统一全国的历史进程中，蒙古西凉王阔端与西藏宗教领袖萨加·班智达·贡噶坚赞举行著名的凉州会商的遗址，是西藏正式纳入中国版图、回归祖国的历史见证，现正在重建之中。此外，还有野驴、野马、野骆驼、雪鸡等珍稀野生动物18种，为全省之最。现已开通旅游专线4条，开辟景点13处，古朴典雅的海藏公园、具有现代气息的西郊公园、世界少有的沙漠公园、举世闻名的沙生植物园、沙漠水库和全国最大的濒危野生动物繁育中心，已成为人们观光旅游的胜地。

环境资源：这里交通便利，兰新、干武铁路穿越境内，312国道横贯三县市，地方道路纵横交错、四通八达。邮电通讯基础较好，通往全国各地的光缆通信、8000门程控电话，已并入国际国内自动交换网。电力、煤炭等能源供应充足。商贸发达，各类专业批发市场和集贸市场沟通城乡、连接内外，成为河西有名的商品集散中心。金融、保险、科技、文化、教育、卫生、体育等各项社会事业日益进步，均有了较大发展。

【国民经济】全区完成国民生产总值16.35亿元，比上年增长14.5%；工农业总产值20.17亿元(1990年不变价)，增长14.7%。全区呈现出经济稳定增长、改革不断深化、政治稳定、民族团结、人民生活不断提高、各项事业协调发展的可喜局面。

——农村经济稳定发展。全区以发展"两高一优"农业为重点，调整农业结构，狠抓科技兴农，完善社会化服务，战胜了风沙、干旱、冰雹等多种自然灾害，农业生产喜获丰收。全年农业增加值达7.21亿元，比上年增长13.1%；农业总产值12.19亿元(1990年不变价)，比上年增长12%；粮食总产量达到6.78亿公斤，比上年增长4.3%，创历史最好水平。乡镇企业快速发展，乡镇企业达到16384个，比上年增加3225个，增长24.5%；从业人数112478人，增加11506人，增长11.4%；总产值达到7.73亿元，比上年增长50.2%；总收入7.15亿元，增长52.9%；实现利税6138.6万元，增长41.9%。

——工业生产稳定增长。全区认真贯彻《条例》，加快企业"三项制度"改革，企业经营机制转换和结构调整步伐加快，市场机制作用逐步增强，效益逐步回升。地县属完成工业总产值7.98亿元，比上年增长19.2%，其中乡及乡以上工业总产值完成6.54亿元，比上年增长13.6%；完成工业增加值1.69亿元，增长25.6%，工业增加值中轻重工业之比为64.8：35.2，国有工业占59.7%，集体工业占40.3%；工业销售产值完成6.95亿元，增长45.6%；工业经济效益综合指数为63.6，比上年增高10.91个百分点；盈利企业盈利额1184万元，比上年增长35.9%；开发省地级新产品43项，产值达0.83亿元，比上年增长66.5%。

——商贸流通稳中见旺。全年社会商业商品纯购进9.66亿元，比上年增长19.93%，纯销售11.89亿元，增长10.98%；实现社会商品零售总额10.81亿元，比上年增长13.6%，其中消费品零售额8.21亿元，增长13.6%，农业生产资料销售额2.59亿元，增长13.6%；集市贸易成交额达到3.85亿元，增长106.1%；集贸市场达到73个，占地面积67.7万平方米，建筑面积22.2万平方米；全年完成外贸收购总值1.08亿元，比上年增长1.14倍。

——财政收入增加，银行存款余额上升。全区财政收入达到1.26亿元，比上年增长25.2%，其中工商税收完成9664万元，增长22.59%。银行各项存款年末余额达到14.19亿元，比上年末增长22.2%；贷款余额16.4亿元，增长21.3%。

——城乡居民收入增加，生活水平有所提高。全区职工工资总额达到3.08亿元，比上年增长9.4%，职工平均工资2738元，增长10.7%，其中地县属职工工资总额2.25亿元，比上年增长15.2%，平均工资2594元，增长10.9%；城市居民人均月生活费收入124.5元，增长13.1%；农民人均纯收入达到564元，比上年增长11.2%；城乡居民个人储蓄存款余额13.66亿元，增长30.9%；城乡居住条件有所改善，1993年城镇新建住宅7.63万平方米，农村新建住房58.76万平方米。

【社会事业】科技、教育、文化、卫生、体育、计划生育等都取得了新的成绩。全区实施科研项目50项，其中地列项目25项，当年验收鉴定科技成果28项，荣获省科技进步奖2项，省星火科技奖5项，评出地区科技进步奖20项。全区招收中等专业学校学生1606人，普通中学在校学生6.88万人，农职业中学在校学生3203人，小学在校学生19.86万人，学龄儿童入学率由上年的99.4%提高到99.5%。广播人口覆盖率为88.29%；电视人口覆盖率为87.42%。全区有各类医疗卫生机构294个，各类卫生技术人员4605人；人口自然增长率为11.93‰。全区有6名运动员参加了全国性体育比赛，获金牌4枚、银牌1枚；有58名运动员参加了省上的多项比赛，共获金牌16枚、银牌17枚、铜牌16枚，并有1人2次打破省记录。精神文明建设不断发展，社会治安稳定、秩序较好，这就为改革和发展创造了良好的社会环境。

【改革开放】大力推行企业内部"三项制度"改革，全面贯彻落实《条例》。全区进行三项制度改革和单项制度改革的企业94户，占全区127户企业的74%。流通企业全面推行以国有民营、社有自营为主要形式的改革，有88.9%的商业小型零售企业实行了国有民营，有80%以上的供销企业实行了社有自营，有32%的粮食企业实行了国有民营。对外开发进一步扩大，地县市主要领导走出去选项目、引资金、搞协作；层层聘请经济技术顾问单位18个、高级经济技术顾问19人；先后在北京、天津、乌鲁木齐、深圳、广州等地建立13个办事机构；与山东青岛市、天津河北区、新疆乌鲁木齐市、江苏无锡市等15个地市建立了友好地市关系；与江苏、四川、新疆、陕西、天津、上海等28个经济发达省市区建立了技术协作关系；与42家大专院校、科研单位建立了联系。对外经济联合有了实质性的进展，引进协作项目48个、资金2695万元，三资企业发展12户，利用外资640万美元。

（中共武威地委研究室：张勋元）

民勤县经济和社会发展概述

【自然概况】民勤县地处河西走廊东北部，石羊河流域下游。位于东经102°03′至104°02′，北纬38°05′至39°06′之间。南邻武威市，西南与金昌市毗连，西北和东南面分别与内蒙古自治区的阿拉善右旗和阿拉善左旗接壤。东西长203公里，南北宽150公里，总面积1.6万平方公里，占全省总面积的3.6%。地势自西南向东北缓倾，地面纵坡为1‰，平均海拔1350米。地形以高平原为主，间有低山、残丘、盆地。按自然地理特征，可分为三个区域和一块盆地；西部西沙窝，属巴丹吉林沙漠东缘，面积约800平方公里，是境内主要放牧区；中部绿洲，属石羊河下游冲积、湖积平原，面积约2400平方公里，为本县主要农耕区；东部东沙窝，系腾格里沙漠南缘，面积约5500平方公里，为境内第二牧区；北部北亭海，属内陆半封闭湖盆，海拔降至1000米，为境内最低凹地。河流属石羊河水系。上游主要支流有古浪河、黄羊河、杂木河、金塔河、西营河、东大河等，靠祁连山降雨和冰雪融水补给，出山后被上游灌区截引，潜入地下的水在中游出露，汇集成红水河、白塔河、清水河等，与县境南诸河汇合，流入红崖山水库，年径流量50年代初为5.88亿立方米，80年代为2.2亿立方米，进入90年代减少到1.5亿立方米。气候属于蒙新区干燥性沙漠气候。其显著特点是：日照时数长(年均3028小时)，光辐射强(137.22千卡/平方米)，昼夜温差大(年均日较差15.2℃)，降水量少(年均115毫米)，蒸发量大(年均2644毫米)，风大沙多(年大于8级的大风日27.8天，沙暴37.3天)。年均气温7.7℃，无霜期162天。经常性灾害天气有大风、沙暴、霜冻、干旱和干热风。现有耕地93万亩，荒地135万亩。矿产资源有煤炭、芒硝、石灰石、石墨、石棉、食盐等。地下水在现状条件下补给量为3.4亿立方米/年。农作物主要有小麦、大麦、糜子、谷子、玉米、洋芋、黑瓜籽、甜菜、油料、葵花、西瓜、白兰瓜、黄河蜜瓜、小茴香等。天然林和人工林树种有22科、23属、50种，草场植物有36科、115属、152种。野生珍贵动物有石貂、盘羊、鹅候鸽、天鹅等。全县辖5镇，18个乡，242个村民委员会，4个居民委员会，1699个村民小组。人口有64218户，27.2万人，其中农业人口25.1万人；非农业人口2.1万人，每平方公里人口密度为17人。县境内有汉、蒙、回、藏、彝、满、土、维吾尔等民族成份，汉族占总人口的99.97%。

【经济概况】1993年农业总产值达到25640万元，粮食总产量达到1.33亿公斤，亩产达到348公斤，提供商品粮6343万公斤，粮食商品率达47.6%。通过调整种植业结构，经济作物总面积达到45万亩，粮经比例达到1:1。全年油料产量554万公斤，甜菜产量7860万公斤，皮棉产量22万公斤，黑瓜籽产量694万公斤，瓜类产量3411万公斤，蔬菜产量1183万公斤，主要经济作物商品率达95%以上。林业生产逐步由单一的生态型向生态、经济、效益型发展，全县累计造林面积88.3万亩，人均3.25万亩，形成60多条防护林带，长达250公里，治理了180余处风沙口道。经济林总面积达到3.5万亩，苹果、苹果梨、红枣等果品总产量149万公斤。林木总蓄积量达到241万立方米。林业产值达到771万元，占农业总产值的3%。畜牧业生产向着优化畜种、规模养殖的方向发展，年末大牲畜存栏7.84万头，羊只存栏19.31万只，出栏6.27万只，生猪存栏10.51万口，出栏8.82万口，肉类总产量达到674万公斤，驼羊毛总产量达23.9万公斤，畜牧业总产值完成4949万元，占农业总产值的19.3%。

工业现有煤炭、食糖、酒精、化工、地毯、针织、印刷、农机修造、酿酒、粮油加工、饲料加工、白铁加工、食品加工、缝纫加工等工业企业61个，职工1650人，工业产值达5746万元，占全县工农业总产值的18.3%。在工业产值中，全民企业2390万元，占41.6%；集体企业1046万元，占18.2%；乡镇工业2300万元，占40%。主要工业产品品种达到35种，其中，唐家沟煤矿生产的长烟煤，热量达6500大卡，是工业生产和家庭取暖的良好燃料；县地毯厂生产的高级仿古地毯，自1983年以来连获甘肃省地毯质量第一名，1990年荣获全国质量评比优秀奖，远销日本、美国等十多个国家和地区；县酒厂生产的“腾格里酒”、“景苏春”系列酒，质量均达到国家优级和一级标准，堪称塞外佳酿；县糖厂生产的白砂糖，达到省优级标准，远销台湾等地。

全县乡镇企业发展至4110个，就业人数达16968人，完成总产值1.01亿元，实现利润975万元，上交税金278万元，固定资产原值达到5007万元。民勤县三雷针织厂生产的绣花圆领、春秋衫等产品远销俄罗斯等地，该厂被树为“甘肃省乡镇明星企业”。民勤县烟花爆竹总公司生产的70余个花色品种的花炮，畅销省内外。

县城新建、扩建了广场市场、东郊市场、西关市场、工贸市场、文化夜市等五处商品交易市场，农村建起了20处集贸市场，全年集市贸易成交额2400万元，社会商品零售总额达1.88亿元。个体工商户累计发展到2529户。县境内交通以公路为主，有6条干线，长达500公里。邮电通讯业在继电报进入全国自动转报网后，实现了市话自动化，进入了国际国内直拨网。目前市内安装开通了874门自动电话，有15个乡镇实现了农话自动交换。

全年财政收入1582万元，税收总额1424万元。全县农民总收入2.34亿元，净收入1.58亿元，人均纯收入630元。职工年均工资2557元。全县城乡储蓄总额2亿元，人均772元。

【城市建设】1993年，城市建设投资总额4458万元，累计完成3层以上建筑38幢，建筑总面积达到72万平方米。城区有主街道4条，全长4.5公里；次街道8条，长4公里；巷道51条；环城公路逐步接通并拓宽，全长已达7公里。主要街道架设了自控路灯。给水工程累计投资197万元，铺设管网73900米，年供水能力达到32.5万立方米，供水户2583户，供水人口13360人，占城区居民的98%。排水工程于1993年4月破土动工，现已铺设主管道5923米，预计1994年可投入使用。住房从1985年到1993年，城区个人建房投入3948万元，建成住宅20.49万平方米，有2134户居民靠自己的力量解决了住房问题。1992年以来，建成商品住宅楼8幢，建筑面积11000平方米。

【社会事业】1993年，全县共有学校301所，其中中等专业学校1所，普通中学23所，职业中学4所。小学273所。校舍总面积达23.1万平方米，教职工3194人，在校学生40378人。适龄儿童入学率达99.55%，巩固率达97.51%，普及率达98.9%，毕业率达99.79%。1993年高中毕业1474人，考入各类大专院校的429人、中专学校的47人，占毕业生总数的32%；初中毕业生2989人，升入高中1210人，升入中专160人，分别占毕业生总数的40%和5%；全县每万人中有59个大学生。城区幼儿园4所，入园儿童262名。

科技，全县共有11个学会，各类科技人员4057人。其中，高级工程师31人，工程师540人，助理工程师1507人，技术员673人。共建立科普协会31个，发展会员796人。1980年以来，共取得各类科研成果113项，其中5个项目荣获国家奖励，52个项目获省、地奖励。

县内有6个科级卫生医疗单位，职工及医务人员264人；乡属医疗单位20个，职工及医务人员312人；村属医疗单位243个，医务人员492人。县属医院设有床位196张，乡属医院设有床位186张。全县每千人平均床位1.4张，每千人平均医务人员2.1人。主要地方病得到有效控制，高氟区的饮水标准达到了国家规定标准。

广播电视，全县建成广播放大站21个，有线广播线路总长达2258杆公里，广播喇叭入户率达91.6%。建成电视地面卫星接收站5座，电视覆盖率达98%。

体育，全县有体校1所，体育场地面积13.69万平方米，人均有体育活动场地0.32平方米。现有等级运动员252人，等级裁判员50人，专业和业余体育工作者280人。体育运动的主要项目是蓝球、足球、田径。民勤一中是全国体育运动传统项目先进学校。建国以来，全县先后有120名运动员参加全国、全省性的体育比赛，共夺得金牌11枚、银牌11枚、铜牌68枚。

【名特土产】黑瓜籽，民勤黑瓜籽板片大，无翘板，无麻板，色泽分明，片形均匀，籽多粒饱，壳薄肉厚；全县年总产量800万公斤左右，产品主要销往台湾、香港等地，并远销新加坡等东南亚国家和地区。小茴香，民勤县是我国小茴香重点产区，广泛应用于医学、食品加工及化妆工业，也是主要的调味品。年产量500万公斤左右。胡麻油又称亚麻油，系干性油类，是特造熟油、油漆、油墨、油布、肥皂等工业产品的优质原料，1988年获首届中国食品博览会金奖。民勤黄河蜜瓜品质优良，皮薄瓤厚，色纯肉嫩，汁多，气味芳香，含糖量高，年产量6000万公斤左右，畅销国内外，在全省优质瓜类评比会上被评为优质农产品。苹果梨皮色亮黄，向阳面略带红色。果肉纯白细脆，汁多味甜，营养丰富，品质上乘，极耐贮藏。年总产量500万公斤，产品畅销北京、江苏等地。红枣已有200多年的栽培历史。年总产量35万公斤左右。甘草为中药处方中应用最普遍的调味剂，也是制作烟草、酱油的辅助香料。民勤境内乌拉尔红皮甘草分布极广，年产量4万公斤，产品远销欧洲等地。沙樱桃是白刺的果实，因有樱桃之色，形、味而称"沙樱桃"。民勤境内白刺面积14万公顷，年产沙樱桃1485万公斤，具有很大的开发潜力。锁阳为锁阳科植物，表皮棕色或棕褐色。用于治疗腰膝痿软，阳萎滑精，肠燥便秘等疾病效果极佳。多生于广漠内的白茨、红柳丛中，年产量25万公斤。麻黄为麻黄科植物，绿色。用于发汗散寒，宣肺平喘，利水消肿。年产量1.4万公斤。

现任主要领导：

中共民勤县委书记：祁子湘

民勤县人大常委会主任：何立臻

民勤县人民政府县长：王世茂

政协民勤县委员会主席：汤希忠

中共民勤县纪律检查委员会书记：李峰德

（民勤县委经济部：李禄仁 谢宏杰）

古浪县经济和社会发展概述

【自然概况、历史沿革】古浪县地处河西走廊东端，乌鞘岭、毛毛山北麓。东倚景泰县，南枕天祝藏族自治县，西与西北同武威接壤，北邻腾格里沙漠。毗连内蒙古阿拉善左旗。县城南蜿蜒数里的古浪峡，两山相峙，形势险要，是古丝绸之路的险隘，被古人喻为"驿路通三辅，峡门控五凉"的咽喉。历史上，又名苍松。早在四千多年前这里就有人类繁衍生息。战国及秦属月氏，汉初为匈奴休屠王牧地，汉元狩二年，武帝开始拓疆土，置河西四郡，在今县境内设苍松、楫次、朴劁三县，属武威郡；三国西晋时期，设苍松、楫次二县，属武威郡；从东晋到明初，在近千年中，统治者不断更替，这块地方几经置郡设县，县名更变复用频繁，以苍松、昌松居多。明洪武十年，千户江亭依水名改为古浪（"古浪"是藏语音译，意思是"黄羊沟"），筑古浪城，先属庄浪卫，后改设古浪千户所属陕西行都指挥使司。清雍正二年改古浪所为古浪县，隶属凉州府。民国初属甘凉道。1927年属甘肃第六行政督察区。1949年9月13日古浪解放，属武威专区。1955年属合并的张掖专区。1961年又归属分设后的武威专区。其间，1958年12月20日并入天祝藏族自治县，1962年12月25日恢复古浪县。现辖3镇，223个村委会，1579个村民小组，至1993年底总人口为35.3万人，其中，农业人口33.8万人。有汉、回、土、藏、满等民族。如今县境内交通便利，兰新、干武两条铁路纵横穿越县境，甘新公路跨县城而过。县、乡公路10条、290公里，初步形成了交通网络。全县总面积5587平方公里，南北长68公里，东西宽88公里，地势南高北低。南部山区群山耸立，多有林草分布，是古浪县主要水源地；中部地势平坦，土壤肥沃，是古浪农业的主要产区；北部荒漠区沙生杂草遍布，宜于放牧。古浪县属典型的大陆干旱气候，光照资源充足，昼夜温差悬殊，区域性差异较大。年平均降水量为360毫米左右，年平均蒸发量为2292毫米，年平均气温5.75℃，无霜期167天。

全县以种植小麦为主，辅助粮食作物有大麦、豌豆、糜子、洋芋等；经济作物有胡麻、油菜、甜菜、啤酒大麦、蔬菜、瓜果及少量的烟叶、葵花等。有草原面积24.2万亩，木材蓄积量为20.63万立方米。全县水资源多年平均为1.16亿立方米；水能蕴藏量7379千瓦，可开发量为2922千瓦。野生动物主要有狐狸、狼、鹿、麝、旱獭、野兔、野猪、石羊、黄羊等10余种。药材有麻黄、芍药、羌活、甘草、荆芥、大黄、大戟、蒲公英、鹿茸、麝香等。

矿产资源已经发现和探明的有铁、铜、石膏、石灰石（3亿多吨）、高岭土、水粘土、陶瓷粘土等。目前，依靠资源优势，兴办了水泥厂、化工厂、制药厂、电石厂、榨油厂等一批地方工业。

【经济建设】改革开放以来，全县人民立足县情，在上级政府的大力支持下，艰苦创业，经济面貌发生了很大变化。农业生产基本条件有了很大改善。景电二期工程已基本建成，新增水地25万亩；河灌区通过逐年改造，水的利用率提高，保灌面积达19万亩；农业小片开发成效显著，建成了6万亩的新型井灌区。全县保灌面积达到50万亩，农民人均占有水地近1.5亩。地方工业发展迅速，初步形成了建材、化工和农副产品加工的主导产业。全县经济开始步入一个持续、快速发展的新阶段。1993年，全县工农业总产值达到21511万元，比1992年增长21.1%。其中工业总产值5137万元，增长25.2%；农业总产值16374万元，增长19.8%。乡镇企业总产值8898万元，比1992年增长42.6%。财政收入809.6万元，比1992年增长39.6%。粮食总产量1.12亿公斤，增长15.5%。农民人均纯收入428元，比上年净增73元。按“双三百”的标准，农村贫困面由1985年的62%下降到16.7%。

【名优特产】金冠苹果，是古浪县北部腾格里沙漠边缘一带盛产的名特产品，个头大，成熟后表面金黄色中透出红晕，皮薄无锈斑，光泽鲜，内质细密，汁液丰满，味浓醇香，甜酸爽口。1993年举行的泰国曼谷中国优质农产品及科技成果展览会上获银奖，同年参加全国优质水果鉴评会，获全国金冠苹果第二名。麻黄，生于古浪北部沙漠沿线，具有发汗解表、宣肺平喘、利水等功效。生长面积约10万亩左右，年收购量在20万公斤左右，并有部分出口创汇。胡麻，是古浪的主要油料作物之一，遍产全县各地，年产200至300多万公斤。驼毛是古浪的畜产品之一，出产量大，是高级毛织品的上等原料。西瓜(红优2号、P2)，瓜体呈椭圆形，外形瓜面呈绿白条状，单瓜重3——5公斤，1993年全县种植面积4964亩，产量达3100吨。苹果梨，其主要产于古浪北部沙漠边缘地区。1985年甘肃省农业厅举办的全省优质苹果梨鉴评会上，获全省苹果梨第二名。甜菜，是古浪近几年发展起来的主要经济作物之一，我县是黄羊镇糖厂的主要原料基地。古浪的甜菜，含糖量均在16%以上，最高的达到21——22%，可为上等食糖原料。亩产在3000公斤以上，最高的可达6000公斤左右。1993年全县种植面积2.76万亩，总产达66407吨。啤酒大麦，是古浪近两年发展起来的主要经济作物之一。具有成色好、颗粒大、质量好、栽培技术简单、成本低、产量高、经济效益好等优点，很适应古浪的自然条件。亩产在400——500公斤，最高可达650公斤左右。一些外地啤酒厂家争先来古浪抢购，形成了畅销不衰的发展势头。1993年全县种植面积3.6万亩，总产量1249万公斤。发菜，自古以来就是古浪的名优特产，以其丝路正、弹性好、均匀色正、净洁度高等特点享誉海内外，曾应邀参加了广交会，产品远销广州、深圳、天津、宁夏、兰州等十多个省市，并通过外贸销往海外。目前，已形成了以古浪大靖为中心的发菜交易市场——全国最大的发菜集散地之一。年采集量约50吨左右，成交额达1000万元以上。

【城区建设】古浪的城区建设近几年变化较大，总面积由原来的1.67平方公里，发展到现在的2.5平方公里，具体建设项目发展也很快。经省城建局、计委列项，于1988年7月动工修建县城上水工程。总投资213.38万元。省上拨款162万元，地县自筹51.38万元。共完成水厂、水塔等主体土建工程999平方米、输水管网2.1公里，至1993年已基本竣工验收；排水工程(地区批准立项)于1993年9月动工修建。工程总概算406.92万元，计划分三期完成。一期工程总造价285.82万元，至1993年12月底完成输水管道3000平方米，投入资金71万元，其余部分计划于1994年6月底完工。二、三期工程根据资金到位情况，逐步实施。古浪宾馆，于1992年8月动工，1993年9月竣工，总投资350万元，建筑面积5300平方米。古浪城关市场，占地面积5446平方米。于1992年5月至1993年12月建成。总投资140万元，建筑面积1500平方米。

社会事业进一步发展。1993年新建妇幼站大楼，投资68万元，建筑面积1200平方米，于1993年4月动工，预计到1994年6月竣工。新建大墩滩乡卫生院560平方米，投资19万元。扩建泗水、土门、黄花滩、永丰滩四乡(镇)门诊1500平方米，投资40万元；黄灌区新建小学7所，扩建2所，总投资44.5万元，建筑面积2501平方米；投资22万元，修建了黄花滩、冰草湾、定宁、干城、新堡五个乡的敬老院，总建筑面积为1300平方米；此外，多方筹集资金，于1992年10月动工修建文化商业综合楼，预算资金26万元(不包括水暖电)，建筑面积1000平方米，计划到1994年8月竣工。

现任主要领导：

中共古浪县委书记：柴尔俐

古浪县人大常委会主任：他玉璞

古浪县人民政府县长：苏　喜

政协古浪县委员会主席：王志勇

中共古浪县纪律检查委员会书记：苟三启

(中共古浪县委政策研究室 李顺年 张有聪)

天祝藏族自治县经济和社会发展概述

【自然概况】天祝藏族自治县位于甘肃省武威地区南部，青藏、黄土和内蒙古三大高原交汇处，东临景泰，南接永登，西靠青海，北连古浪和武威。境内祁连山冷龙岭东延山脉横亘东西，兰新铁路与312国道线纵贯南北；山脉与交通线相交处的乌鞘岭耸天矗立，是地扼东西、势控河西的咽喉孔道。地理位置十分重要，素有“河西走廊门户”之称，而今又是欧亚大陆桥的必经之路。天祝地势呈西高东低，海拔4874米至2040米之间，总面积为7150平方公里。境内居住着藏、汉、土、回、蒙古、苗、壮、满、侗、土家、东乡、保安、裕固、撒拉、瑶、白等16个少数民族，是一个以藏族为主体的多民族聚居的民族自治县，总人口21.4万人，少数民族占总人口的31%。全县辖5镇17乡194个村民委员会和6个居民委员会。自治县首府设在华藏寺镇。由于天祝所处的纬度较高，加之地势高隆，远离海洋，因此，境内气候主要是呈大陆性高原寒冷半湿润和寒冷半干旱两种特征。日照时数年均2500至2700小时，年均气温气温－1℃左右，无绝对无霜期，年均降水量265至632毫米，本区域气候复杂多变，常有冰雹、干旱、霜冻和春季风雪等自然灾害。天祝县地域辽阔，矿产资源丰富，现已探明的有煤炭、石膏、硅石、重晶石、磷、金、银、铜、铁等12种，煤炭和石膏储量分别达2.5亿吨和2亿吨，黄金的储量也占一定比例。目前，黄（黄金）、白（石膏）、黑（煤炭）的开采已成为天祝经济发展的三大支柱产业，全县共有开采矿点130多个。

境内大山连绵起伏，沟谷鳞次栉比，森林资源丰富，现有天然森林262万亩，占祁连山东端森林面积的98%，森林覆盖率为26.8%。有松、柏、桦、云衫、白杨等27个乔木树种和柳、杜鹃 、枇杷、黄刺等十多个灌木品种，木材蓄积量达346万立方米。在森林和草原中栖息着麝、鹿、猞猁、雪豹、岩羊、兰马鸡等数十种珍稀野生动物。盛产鹿茸、麝香、羌活、秦艽、柴胡等数百种名贵药材。

境内大部分地方属河源区，河流纵横、水势湍急，地表水和地下水资源丰富。主要河流有金强河、石门河、哈溪河、毛藏河、冰沟河等数十条，全县河流年径流量约为8亿立方米，武威、民勤、古浪、永登等县的大部分土地靠这些河流灌溉。由于这些河流落差大、水能资源也较丰富，可开发利用3.5万千瓦。

【悠久的草原畜牧】天祝是我省主要牧区之一，有着悠久的放牧历史，早在《宋史》中就有“凉州畜牧甲天下”的记载，遥远的古代，藏族人民就在这里过着潼酪、衣皮革，被毡裘、住穹店的狩猎、游牧生活。辛勤地开发和建设着这块地方，在长期的生产活动中积累了丰富的经验，为发展现代畜牧业开拓了美好的前景。天祝境内既有广袤秀丽的抓喜秀龙滩、宽广平坦的松山滩等大片草原，又有沟谷、河滩、山峁、林间的小片草场，天然草原总面积达700万亩，可利用面积587万亩，围栏草原40万亩，优质人工饲草料地4万亩，抗灾保畜育草基地3万亩，为发展畜牧业提供了良好的自然条件。在美丽富饶的草原上，牧草葳蕤，牛羊肥壮，稀有珍贵的天祝白牦牛、遐迩闻名的岔口驿马、甘肃高山细毛羊、俗称天祝“三宝”。1980年以来，天祝先后被甘肃省、国家农业部列为“百万只高山细毛羊生产基地县”，改良后的细毛羊，产毛量较土种羊提高了2至3倍，是毛纺工业比较理想的细毛原料。1993年末，全县大小畜存栏55.54万头（只），出产绒毛878吨，肉类总产量近6000吨，牛羊皮5万多张。

【天祝经济和各项事业】1993年，天祝县以社会主义市场经济为导向，深化农村牧区改革，强化基础建设，坚持“三个大办”（大办工业、大办乡镇企业、大办第三产业）和“两高一优”农业，狠抓经济效益，在农业大面积遭受严重自然灾害的情况下，仍然取得了较好的成绩，农业总产值达7813.37万元，粮食总产完成3173.07万公斤，工业总产值实现6202.5万元，乡镇企业总产值突破8000万大关，达到8091.5万元。国民生产总值达到14169.3万元，农牧民人均纯收入452元。民族工业和乡镇企业迅速崛起。全县工业企业已达到十多个行业，80余家，基本形成了电力、煤炭、采矿、冶炼、农林牧副业产品加工、农牧机具修造、食品加工、酿洒等地方工业体系。工业产品不仅有传统的原煤、石膏、红砖，还开发了硅铁、硅锰、焦炭、网围栏、低芥酸菜籽油、配合饲料、白酒等十几个新品种。民族贸易繁荣兴旺，市场活跃，私营企业、股份制企业和个体经济不断发展。1993年底全县有私营企业19家，从业人员468人；股份制企业28家，从业人员534人；个体工商户1289户，从业人员1922人。农电建设发展迅速，截止1993年末，全县已有164个行政村通电，覆盖率达84.5%，解决了大部分地区群众生产生活用电问题。

天祝东临省会兰州，西靠丝路重镇武威，延伸欧亚大陆桥口岸新疆。经济信息灵、科技辐射快、商品交流活。312国道和兰新铁路穿境而过，县内公路通车里程达460多公里，基本实现了乡乡通客车，村村能行车。1993年客运周转量达159717万人公里，邮电通讯已实现县城和五乡镇电话自动化，市话总容量已达1000门，并安装开通了无线电寻呼系统，长途电话也进入了国内自动网。

科教文卫事业，近年来，全县科技队伍不断壮大，科技交流与协作日益增加，现有各类科技人才500多人，每年实施科技项目30多项。全县有中专和各类中小学329所，在校学生30860人。民族教育已形成由民族师范、民族中学、小学为主体的藏语文教学体系，每年为国家输送大中专生100多人。电视事业有了较快的发展，已建成电视差转台10个，地面卫星收转站27座，电视覆盖率达到47.9%。文化市场初具规模。医疗卫生条件日臻完善，城乡卫生网基本形成，1993年末，有医疗卫生机构31所，病床357张，缺医少药的状况明显改变。群众性体育活动活跃，民族体育传统项目摔跤、赛马、爬山、打梭等成为群众喜爱的活动。

【旅游业前景】天祝有悠久的历史，灿烂的文化，瑰丽的山川和名刹古寺、旅游景观。闻名遐迩的千年古刹天堂寺，为全县十四寺院之首，初建于唐宪宗年间，座落在依山膀水的天堂乡大通河东岸。景色迷人的"天祝三峡"——朱岔峡、金沙峡、光明峡是难得的旅游胜地。这里层峦叠翠，古树参天，峰岭如画，曲径通幽，潺潺流水穿峡过，啾啾鸣呜绕山林，每个景点都有神话般的传说，令人神驰，令人陶醉。天祝首府华藏寺，自1983年经国务院批准作为县府所在地后，经数年建设，已成为以林木畜产品加工及冶炼为主的，具有牧区风貌和民族特色的新兴高原城镇。

现任主要领导：

中共天祝县委书记：苏　鸿

天祝县人大常委会主任：

李桑吉(藏族)

天祝县人民政府县长：

王全文(藏族)

政协天祝县委员会主席：

任有琪(藏族)

中共天祝县纪律检查委员会

书记：任锡美(藏族)

(天祝县委政策研究室：王元林 吴才生)

张掖地区

中共张掖地委书记：马西林

张掖地区行政公署专员：毛郁生

中共张掖地区纪律检查委员会书记：陆　瑜

张掖地区经济和社会发展概述

【自然概况】素以"塞上江南"著称的"金张掖"，位于甘肃省西部，河西走廊中段。这里东连镍都金昌，西接古郡酒泉，南邻青海草原，北依瀚海居延。东西长210～465公里，南北宽30～165公里，总面积4.19万平方公里。辖张掖市和临泽、高台、山丹、民乐、肃南裕固族自治县一市五县，总人口117万人，其中裕固族8000多人，为甘肃独有民族。

张掖又称"甘州"，"甘肃"省名首字即源于此。西汉初以"张国臂掖，以通西域"而得名。自丝绸之路开通，张掖就成为中原通往西域的经济、商贸、文化交流重镇。"金张掖"亦以其华实蔽野、黍稷盈畴蜚声中外。在几千年的历史长河中，张掖几度辉煌，几经沧桑。虽朝代更易，归属变迁，其兴衰际遇都与祖国的命运息息相关。今天，随着社会主义市场经济体制的建立和国家经济建设战略重点的西移，张掖将以重要的地理位置，丰富的资源优势，发达的交通通讯网络，绚丽多姿的名胜风光，开放的优惠政策和条件，成为大西北开发的新热点和联接内地与边疆，沟通我国与西亚、东欧各国经济贸易、文化交流的纽带和桥梁，"金张掖"必将再度辉煌。1992年8月12日，中共中央总书记江泽民视察张掖时，兴奋地挥毫题写了"金张掖"三个大字，赋予我区改革开放新的时代内涵。

土地资源。张掖系绿州灌溉农业，地势平坦，光热同期，土质肥沃，水源充沛。全区土地总面积6321万亩，有耕地280万亩，其中保灌面积186.56万亩。有可垦荒地470万亩，其中宜农地200万亩，宜林地148万亩。耕地在土壤类型构成上，水浇地主要是灌耕土，为高产稳产良田。全区有草原面积2631万亩，占总面积的40.25%。森林面积728万亩，其中人工林138万亩，木材蓄积量1297万立方米，森林平均覆盖率为8.7%。有水域60.78万亩。

水文资源。区内共有大小河流26条，年径流量24.6亿立方米，地下水储量1.15亿立方米。现有中小型水库42座，总库容1.83亿立方米。冰川是养育张掖人民的天然"固体水库"，祁连山在张掖境内的冰川面积408.68平方公里，总储量达159亿立方米。水质好，适宜工农业生产用水。

黑河干流从牛脖颈至莺落峡95公里，总落差为941米，可建12个梯级电站，装机容量可达到52万千瓦。其中，在张掖境内能建6座电站，总装机容量34万千瓦，年发电量19.84亿度。

气候资源。张掖地区属大陆性中温带干旱气候。光照充足，年日照总时数3000小时以上，年太阳总辐射量为133.36～148.42千卡/平方厘米，属太阳辐射高值区。年平均气温6—8摄氏度。年平均降水量214.3毫米，蒸发量2000～2700毫米，具有日照时间长、昼夜温差大的特点，有利于植物的光合作用，成为我区一大宝贵资源。

生物资源。我区地域辽阔，生物资源比较丰富。农作物共有11类，76种，508个品种。其中粮食作物主要有小麦、玉米、洋芋、糜子、谷子、蚕豆、豌豆、大豆、青稞、水稻等，小麦占65%。经济作物以油菜、胡麻、甜菜、啤酒大麦、葵花、瓜子、蔬菜为主，品种多、品质好。畜禽品种有山丹马、河西马、黑白花牛、河西黄牛、肃南牦牛、河西驴、民乐猪、河西双峰驼、肃南藏羊、河西山羊、三黄鸡、土种鸡、本地白鹅、鸭等20多个品种的原始畜禽种。现有树种110多种，其中属杨、柳、松、柏、槐、白腊、槭、椿、桦等乔木60多种。得天独厚的自然环境中，繁衍生息着270余种野生动物，其中属于国家保护的一、二类野生兽类有雪豹、野驴、白唇鹿、马熊、水獭、野耗牛、荒漠猫、马麝、鹅喉羚、草原斑猫、猞猁、白臀鹿、盘羊、岩羊等17种；属于国家保护的一、二类野生珍贵鸟类有黑鹳、白肩雕、白尾海雕、藏雪鸡、天鹅等38种，并有候鸟61种。区内有世界最大、中国唯一的蓝马鸡养护中心。境内盛产麻黄、秦艽、羌活、甘草、黄芪、鹿茸、麝香、熊胆、豹骨等动、植、矿物性中药材80余种，年产量达300多万公斤。

矿产资源。区内矿产资源丰富。现已探明的矿产资源达32种，有的储量名列全省前茅。以花岗岩、煤、铁、石灰石为最多，其次有石膏、粘土、高岭土、白云石、硅石、芒硝、萤石、滑石，此外还有金、银、铜、铅、锌、铬、锑、铀、钴、镍、水晶石等多种有色金属矿藏。原煤储量10.6亿吨，石灰石、石膏、粘土均在3亿吨以上。

旅游资源。张掖历史悠久，文化灿烂，风光独特，是1986年国务院审定的国家历史文化名城。这里有全国最大的创建于西夏时期的室内泥塑卧佛；有开凿于北凉时期的金塔寺，窟内有国内独一无二的高肉雕彩塑飞天；藏传佛教胜地马蹄寺，独特的三十三天洞窟为国内罕见。境内还有雄伟壮观的汉明长城、烽燧、古墓和以"黑水国"、骆驼城为代表的众多古城遗址；有风光旖旎的祁连山自然保护区（国家级）和河西名山焉支山、影视外景拍摄基地窟窿峡；有建于西汉时期、现为世界第一的山丹军马场；有高耸入云的雪山冰川和风蚀岩奇观；有高台、临泽红西路军烈士陵园和山丹路易·艾黎捐赠文物陈列馆等。这些文物古迹和自然景观为开展文化交流、发展旅游事业提供了优越条件。

【国民经济】改革开放以来，张掖人民在党的路线、方针、政策指引下，坚持以经济建设为中心，充分发挥自身优势，积极开拓进取，加快了经济建设和各项事业发展的步伐。1993年，全区国民生产总值达到19.39亿元，比上年增长12.96%；工农业总产值达到26.5亿元，比上年增长19.6%。国民经济获得了新的成就：

1.农村经济全面发展。1993年，全区农村社会总产值达到25.14亿元，比上年增长41.63%；农业总产值达到14.15亿元，比上年增长7.87%；农业生产获得第12个丰收年，粮食总产量达到8.09亿公斤，比上年增长3.8%；乡镇企业总产值达到12.01亿元，比上年增长72.6%。在全区280万亩耕地中，有效灌溉面积达214.56万亩，已建成吨粮田23.2万亩，小麦千斤田24.6万亩，双千田3.6万亩，农业商品率达到58%以上，是国家的商品粮生产基地之一，也是甘肃的"粮仓"全区种植的蔬菜品种达70多个，产量达36万吨，果品产量4万多吨。张掖市南关批发市场被国家国内贸易部列为五大蔬菜批发市场之一，蔬菜销往全国23个省市区的120多个城市。经济林主要有苹果梨、苹果、红枣、杏等，农区果园面积已达到33.85万亩。民乐苹果梨先后四次获省优、两次获部优称号，号称"中国一代梨王"。1993年大家畜、生猪、羊只、鸡饲养量均比上年增加，肉类总产量达4.18万吨。全区已形成粮、油、肉、糖、菜、瓜、果、皮、毛、草十大农副产品优势，油料、甜菜、瓜菜、水稻、棉花、啤酒大麦、大蒜、苹果梨、红枣、奶肉牛、瘦肉猪、细毛羊、蛋肉鸡、淡水鱼等14个农副产品基地已初具规模，商品率已达到70%以上。

2.工业生产持续增长。1993年，全区乡及乡以上工业产值完成8.4亿元，比上年增长18.8%；城市工业销售收入完成5.7亿元，比上年增长35.7%；工业产品销售率达到102.5%。目前，全区在29个工业行业中，已有18个初步形成具有地方特色的工业体系，以农副产品为原料的轻工业占绝对优势，产值占70%以上。食糖、淀粉、酿酒、建材、煤炭、化工、食品为主要行业，有48种地方产品获省优、部优称号，有的远销国外。张掖丝路春酒厂的45度丝路春特曲在31届世界精品评选会上荣获布鲁塞尔金奖。民乐县滨河酒厂的"滨河御液"获得首届新加坡国际名优产品博览会金奖。

3.第三产业发展速度加快，城乡市场繁荣稳定。1993年全区社会商品零售总额达到9.59亿元，比上年增长8.03%。外贸出口收购总值达到5773万元，比上年增长28.91%，完成调拨总值5649.64万元，比上年增长19.98%。全区商业网点发展到10030个，从业人员达29600人。全区已建成各类市场140处，1993年集市贸易成交额达到3.24亿元，比上年增长21%，有近千个农民运销组织和8万农民进入流通领域，在全区初步形成了以专业批发市场为重点、综合贸易市场为主体、集贸交易点为补充的市场网络。

同时，我区旅游事业也已步入大发展阶段。1992、1993两年成功地举办了两届金张掖梨花会和马蹄寺旅游观光节，现已开通张掖商城一日游、马蹄寺一日游、山丹一日游、军马场一日游、高台、临泽一日游等五条旅游线路，开发旅游产品10多个系列、200多个品种。1993年接待游客76万人（次），其中接待了10多个国家的外宾和国内12个省市的宾客，外宾达1200多人，实现收入823万元，洽谈经济项目68项，协议资金3692万元。为广交朋友，宣传张掖，促进对外开放发挥了重要作用。

4.交通、通讯、能源等基础设施日臻完善，对外开放取得新的进展。区内交通方便，兰新铁路、甘新公路、甘青公路贯穿全境，县、乡公路四通八达。区内有军用飞机场一个可起降波音737以下大型客机，欧亚航线在此经过。兰新铁路复线将于1994年建成通车，全长10.7公里的张火高速公路已完成路基，计划于1995年建成通车。区内六县市已实现城镇、城郊电话程控化和国内电话直拨，张掖市8000门程控电话将于1994年下半年开通，进入国内、国际长途电话自动交换网。目前市内已开办无线寻呼电话业务，各县市邮电部门全部进入自动转报网，并开设了传真业务。

区内能源充足。刘家峡电网覆盖全区城乡，有火电站1座，小水电11座与之并网。农村能源以煤为主，太阳能、风能发展前景广阔。

与此同时，城市建设取得重大进展。张掖市城区规划面积26平方公里，已建成面积12.17平方公里，绿化面积达123公顷。城区供电可靠率可达99.8%，供排水设施完善，旧城改造已见成效，文化娱乐设施更趋健全，城市的辐射功能日益增强。

基础设施的不断配套完善，促进了外向型经济的发展。全区共签订意向性协议254项，落实146项，协议资金5亿多元，落实引进1.01亿元，引进各类人才289人。"三资"企业从无到有，已建成3家，达成协议正在落实的5家。

【社会事业】全区拥有科研所5个，各类专业技术人员14570人；有各级各类学校944所，在校学生总数达到173603人；有各种卫生机构229个，卫生技术人员4249人，拥有病床2571张。1993年全区人口自然增长率控制在7.35‰以下。区内文化馆、影剧院、博物馆、群艺馆、体育馆、新华书店设施齐全，群众文化活跃。1993年，全区有81名运动员参加了省级以上比赛，获金牌15枚、银牌16枚、铜牌7枚。全区社会就业保险、民政优抚、社会治安等各个方面都迈出了新的步伐。

【城乡人民生活】1993年，城镇居民平均消费水平为1697元，比上年增长13%；职工平均工资2769元，增长12.5%；农民人均纯收入达到852元，比上年增加100元。全区城乡居民储蓄存款余额9.79亿元，比上年增长22.86%。城乡居住条件进一步改善。城市居民人均住房面积7.4平方米，农村人均21平方米。目前，以解决城镇居民"困难户、危房户、无房户"为重点的"安居工程"已经启动，农村小康建设已全面实施，张掖人民已从温饱型向富裕的小康型全面迈进。

（中共张掖地委研究室：何成才）

高台县经济和社会发展概述

【地理位置和基本情况】高台县位于河西走廊中部，黑河中游下段。位于北纬39°03′至39°59′，东经58°57′至100°06′之间，东靠临泽县，西与酒泉市、金塔县和肃南县明花区相连，南同肃南县大河区接壤，北依合黎山与内蒙古自治区阿拉右旗相邻。全境地势由东南向西北倾斜，海拔在1260——2630米之间，除南部祁连山北麓洪积倾斜平原高差较大，北部干燥剥蚀残山有起伏外，大部分地区地势平坦，土壤肥沃，灌溉较方便。

气候属大陆沙漠干旱型，冬季寒冷干燥，夏季干热，春季多风，全年无霜期160多天，年降雨量100毫米左右，年蒸发量2000毫米左右，平均气温为摄氏7.4度，年日照3100多小时，光照充足，昼夜温差大，适宜于各类农作物生长。

全县总面积4312平方公里，折合646万亩。现有耕地31.9万亩，人均2.5亩。有宜垦荒地95万亩，其中宜农荒地21万亩，宜林荒地21.5万亩，宜牧荒地52.6万亩。县境内有6条河流，建成中小型水库和塘坝26座，年蓄水量3100多万立方米，打机井3000多眼，基本可保证现有土地的灌溉。兰新铁路和312国道横贯全境。主要农产品有小麦、玉米、水稻、蚕豆、黄豆、胡麻、洋芋、瓜菜、桃、梨、杏、苹果、苹果梨等；主要矿产品有芒硝、萤石、原盐等十几种，其中芒硝地质储量3000万吨，占全省芒硝储量的一半以上，原盐储量1168万吨，为全省最大产盐地，萤石储量170万吨。

全县共辖12个乡(镇)，132个行政村，932个村民小组，36973户，14.97万人，其中农业人口13.35万人。有16个基层党委，17个党总支，374个党支部(农村支部132个)。党员7282名，其中农村党员5487名。

【经济发展概述】1993年，全县各级党政组织和广大人民群众认真学习贯彻党的十四大和邓小平同志南巡重要谈话精神，解放思想，深化改革，集中精力抓经济建设，使全县各项工作都有了新的发展。全县工农业总产值完成33498.2万元，比上年增加5383.4万元，增长19.15%，其中工业产值12505.8万元，农业产值20992万元(90年不变价)；粮食总产量达到14897万公斤，比上年增加4.07万公斤，亩产平均640公斤；乡镇企业总产值完成21270万元，比上年增加7470万元，增长54.13%；财政总收入1705.2万元，比上年增加501.3万元，增长41.5%；农民人均纯收入981元，比上年增加91元，增长10.2%；人口自然增长率7.15‰，比上年下降0.55‰。

【改革不断深化】农村改革紧紧围绕建立社会主义市场经济体制的总目标，县上在继续稳定家庭承包、完善双层经营的同时，取消了指令性种植计划，指导性地提出了农村经济发展的总量调控指标，农民种什么、养什么，根据市场需求由农民自己决定，各级政府和有关部门提供信息、生产、技术、产品销售等方面的服务，引导帮助农民发展市场农业。

城市改革，以转换企业经营机制为重点，在所有工商企业内部继续深化“三项制度”改革，推行“国有民营”、“社有自营”，全面落实企业自主权，积极推进城镇住房制度改革。一是采取“利税递层包干，包死上交，超额全留，欠收用风险金抵顶”的办法，完善了19户工商企业的第三轮承包。二是商业系统的29个小型网点实行了个体承包经营形式，供销系统38个门点实行了一人牵头、集体承包的经营形式，强化了盈亏责任。三是全县225个行政、企事业单位，按照“提高租金，发放补贴”的办法，实施了新的房改制度。四是加快政府职能转变，全县有49个涉农部门和专业经济组织创办经济实体55个，减轻财政开支，壮大服务实力。

【农业产业结构趋于合理】一是按照市场需求，调整了种植业内部结构，发展“两高一优”农业。粮食面积和经济作物面积的比例由上年的78：22调整到了72：28。二是发展商品畜牧业，继续推广“双推五改”养猪和“青贮氨化”养牛新技术措施，全县生猪饲养量达到18.89万头，出栏9.3万头；牛饲养量达2.07万头，羊饲养量13.1万只，畜牧业产值达6228万元，占农业总产值的29.7%，比上年提高了1个百分点。三是发展林果业，全县共完成造林33474亩，其中经济林25858亩。经济林累计面积61869亩，建成百亩以上的果园68个，千亩果园村10个，万亩果园乡1个。

【城市经济发展加快】一是抓技术改造，新上骨干项目。建成了县农机厂年产8000吨焊管生产线和100台搅拌机装配线，萤石矿四工段井下开拓延伸和6000吨石英砂生产线，选矿厂1万吨铜选车间、精细化学厂200吨洗衣粉生产线，无纺布厂120吨薄型无纺布生产线，食盐1000吨无机盐车间，综合食品厂年产100吨甘草霜和县白酒厂、盐化公司西大池改造等项目。二是强化管理，降低成本，提高质量，扩大销售，提高效益。全县工业企业年实现利润194.6万元，上交税金297万元，创历史最高水平。三是拓宽市场，搞活流通。全县社会商品零售总额11549万元，比上年增加1630万元，增长16.4%。多方筹资700万元，共建了县城华联购物中心、悦民饭店、生资公司和食盐购销站营业大楼，招商市场，启发和完善了规模较大的巷道乡蔬菜批发市场和南华乡农贸综合市场。巷道蔬菜批发市场，销售旺季日成交蔬菜20万公斤左右，使县内大部分蔬菜远销金昌、嘉峪关、乌鲁木齐等地。南华农贸综合市场增加商业网点103家，饮食门点23家，加油站4座，新建了综合营业楼五幢，吸引了大量过往商客。全县个体工商户达到1930户，比上年增加了519户。

【乡镇企业快速发展】去年在资金十分困难的情况下，经过多方争取，多渠道筹资，先后投入2603万元资金，新建了黄豆油厂、新坝高新皮革厂和红砖厂、南华晶硅熔炼厂、合黎石英砂厂、黑泉皮革厂和电线电缆厂等11个规模较大的项目；完成了新坝水泥扩建、南华预制件厂、巷道元钉厂铅丝生产线等8个技术改造项目。止年底，全县乡镇企业总数累计达2027个，其中乡办83，村办96个，个体联户办1848个；从业人员18370人，完成总产值21270万元，总收入12111万元，实现利润1017.5万元，税金900万元，分别比上年增长54.13%、64.7%、45%和45.9%。并积极推行股份合作制，止年底，全县改组、改造和新建股份合作制企业64家，入股资金984.7万元。

【加强基础设施建设】在通讯建设上，继年初城区千门自动电话开通后，又投资50万元，完成了巷道、合黎、南华、盐池四乡农村电话与县城市话并网，加快了信息传递速度。在电力建设上，投资340万元，完成了县城110千伏安变电站、2万千伏安增容工程建设，盐池乡2000千伏安变电站，骆驼城变电站增容和骆驼城至南华10千伏线路架设，使城区、盐池和骆驼城供电能力有了很大提高。在交通建设上，除积极支持兰新复线建设外，投资150万元，完成了罗城至盐池乡40公里的路基改造和13公里的油路铺设，全县12个乡(镇)除骆驼城乡外，其他11个乡(镇)乡乡通油路，132个村村村通汽车。在城市建设上，投资近2000万元，新建了23座营业楼和住宅楼，完成了县城人民西路和县府两条主街道2.6公里油路铺设，完成了东关拓宽拆迁和月牙湖公园的部分设施建设。

【社会事业进一步发展】教育事业紧紧围绕普及九年义务教育，结合本县实际，调整了中小学布局，优化教育结构，全面推行“四制”改革，增强了教师责任感，提高了教学质量。全县有中小学150所，其中完全中学3所，职业高中1所，初中12所，小学134所，在校学生21229名，其中高中生1098名，初中生5477名，小学生14654名。1993年向省内外大中专学校输送新生162名，其中本科生15名。高考名列张掖地区第二。县上建有电视差转台，罗城、盐池、新坝三乡设有电视卫星地面接收站，电视人口覆盖率达到100%，全县村村通广播，入户率达90%，音响率达95%；县城有文化馆、图书馆、博物馆，12个乡(镇)有文化站。卫生防疫工作成效明显，传染病、地方病得到了有效防治，全面完成了全县儿童计划免疫。计划生育工作的科学化、规范化、制度化的水平进一步提高，1993年再次荣获“全国计划生育工作先进县”称号。社会治安综合治理措施得到落实，“二五”普法教育逐步广泛深入地开展，社会治安好转，万人刑事案件率为万分之四点三。

现任主要领导：

中共高台县委书记：郭尚俊

高台县人大常委会主任：周国康

高台县人民政府县长：张兴龙

政协高台县委员会主席：晁吉祥

中共高台县纪律检查委员会书记：雷　训

（中共高台县委研究室：孙维新）

酒泉地区

金塔县经济和社会发展概述

【自然概况】金塔县位于酒泉地区东北部，地处北纬39°47′至41°00′，东经97°至10°20′之间。东与高台县毗邻，西和玉门市相连，南邻酒泉、嘉峪关市，北界内蒙古额济纳旗。东西长190公里，南北宽120公里，总面积1.88万平方公里，占全省总面积的4%。总面积中耕地占0.98%，草原占5.58%，林地占1.2%，宜农荒地占5.1%，沙漠占5.6%，城镇建设和街道用地占0.02%，戈壁、丘陵及其它占81.5%。地势从西南向东北逐渐由高变低，三面环山。北有鸡心和大红山等，属马鬃山山地东南部的低山地带，海拔在1400至1900米之间；南有夹山，主峰1481米；东南有合黎山，主峰1816米；中部为金塔盆地，地势低平，海拔在1100至1200米之间，有肥沃的金塔绿洲和鼎新绿洲。东部有黑河流经鼎新片4个乡（镇），境内流长124公里，流域面积310平方公里，最大洪水量每秒1900立方米。气候属典型的大陆性气候，昼夜温差大，四季分明。年均温度8℃，最高的7月份平均23.6℃，最低的1月份平均零下10℃。全年无霜期141天。年均降雨量59.9毫米，蒸发量2538.6毫米。年日照时数3193.2小时。主要自然灾害有风沙、干热风、霜冻、冰雹。全县有耕地27.67万亩，林地33.7万亩，草原157.65万亩，宜农荒地143.1万亩。地面水和地下水较丰富，黑河年入境水量10.9亿立方米，讨赖河年流入鸳鸯池水库3.63亿立方米，可开采利用的地下水储量2.69亿立方米。野生动物主要有黄羊、青羊、羚羊、沙鸡等。野生植物主要有胡杨、梭梭、红柳、白刺、甘草、锁阳、丛蓉等。矿产资源有煤、铁、铜、芒硝、铅、滑石、石膏等。光热资源充足，年总辐射为每平方厘米153千卡。

全县辖9个乡，3个镇，有118个村民委员会，670个村民小组，4个街道办事处。1993年全县有34574户，13万人，其中男性占51.5%，女性占48.5%。农业户28515户，占总户数的82.5%，非农户6032户，占17.5%。农业人口11.4万人，占总人口87.7%，非农业人口15987人，占总人口12.3%。全县人口自然增长率为7.29‰。民族有汉、回、蒙古、满、藏、维吾尔、裕固族7个民族成份，汉族占总人口的99.95%。

【历史沿革】金塔县系原金塔、鼎新两县合署。原金塔县昔名王子庄，因北凉国王长子曾在今中东地方建立牧庄而得名。民国2年（1913年）以县城东南之古塔取名金塔县。原鼎新县昔名毛目，因地沿黑河，呈眉毛状，故名毛目。民国17年（1928年）又按双树墩、毛目城和天仓三足鼎立之势，改称鼎新县。

金塔县在春秋、秦初为乌孙王领地，后为月氏国属地。西汉置会水县（地域包括金塔、鼎新全境），属酒泉郡。三国、两晋袭前制。南北朝时北魏废会水县，王子庄并入酒泉，隶敦煌镇，毛目并入张掖，隶凉州。隋置福禄县（包括酒泉、王子庄、高台、毛目），隶张掖郡。唐代王子庄属酒泉县，毛目属福禄县，隶肃州。“安史之乱”后，先后为吐蕃、回鹘所据。宋属西夏国，王子庄属蕃禾郡，毛目属镇夷郡。元代王子庄属肃州路，毛目属甘州路。明在王子庄设威虏卫，在毛目设威远卫。清初袭前制，雍正3年（1725年）将高台、镇夷、毛目等地合置高台县，属甘州。雍正7年增设肃州直隶州王子庄州同，雍正13年设“毛目城屯田县丞”，又称高台县毛目县丞。民国2年（1913年）改王子庄州同为金塔县，改毛目县丞为毛目县，肃安肃道。民国17年改毛目县为鼎新县。民国24年改安肃道为第七行政督察区，金塔、鼎新均属之。

1949年9月金塔、鼎新两县和平解放，均属酒泉地区专署管辖。1956年3月鼎新县并入金塔县，属张掖专区。1959年1月金塔、酒泉合并为酒泉市。1962年金塔县恢复建制，属酒泉专署。

【农业】农村社会总产值达30433.93万元，比上年增长11.42%。农业总产值达20383.62万元，比上年增长7.8%。农村经济总收入达31420.61万元，比上年增长19.6%。农村经济纯收入达14776.25万元，比上年增长7.8%。全县农作物播种面积34.76万亩，粮食作物占63.23%，经济作物占36.77%。全县粮食总产达10.97万吨，棉花总产达3000.18吨，油料总产达2287.19吨，蔬菜总产达37738吨。农业产值达15000.95万元，比上年增长6.5%。森林面积达19.5万亩，其中人工林18.83万亩。果园面积35591亩，其中当年新植777亩。水果总产达5613.6吨，比上年增长35.4%。当年造林面积达11778亩，比上年增长6%。当年零星义务植树58.6万株，比上年增长28.7%。树木采伐4060.7立方米。林业产值达559.17万元，比上年增长32.7%。大牲畜年末存栏27461头，猪年末存栏54584头，羊年末存栏92286只，鸡存栏53.91万只，养兔7.17万只。当年出栏肉猪66024头，比上年增长15.9%；当年出售菜羊48099只,比上年增长16.2%;当年出栏肉鸡68.69万只,比上年增长8.5%。肉类总产量达5693.4吨,比上年增长13.3%。禽业产量达2028.43吨,牛奶产量达90.2吨,比上年增长65.4%。牧业产值达4871.39万元,比上年增长9.9%。全县乡镇企业总数已达2981个,比上年增加990个。从业人员达16461人,比上年增加2525人。乡镇企业产值达15293.05万元,比上年增长34.2%,乡镇企业总收入达13194.7万元,比上年增长34.4%。同时农业生产的基本条件继续改善。全县农机总动力达81658.03千瓦,比上年增加8110.29千瓦。其中大中型拖拉机408台,小型拖拉机3034台。排灌动力机械达1497台,农用汽车73辆,农用机井1203眼,保灌面积达282992亩。农用化肥施用(折纯量)达7600吨,比上年增加874吨。

【工交、基建】全县工业企业总数达751个,比上年增加190个。其中:全民工业17个,比上年增加2个。集体工业83个,比上年增加8个。村办工业94个,比上年增加20个。个体办521个,增加124个。全县工业总产值达13738.8万元,比上年增长31.1%。工业销售产值达12525.6万元,比上年增长37.8%。主要工业产品产量大幅度增长。全县原煤产量达74400吨,比上年增长54.9%;水泥产量达17300吨,比上年增长22%;铜金属产量达1884吨,比上年增长71.7%;发电量达1254万度,比上年增长12%。绵白糖产量达7482吨,砖产量达3500万块。工业企业经济效益不断提高,独立核算工业企业工业产品销售率达94.1%,工业资金利税率达10.7%,全员劳动生产率达7939元/人,流动资金周转次数为1.5次。

基本建设,全县计划内基本建设投资达1839万元,比上年增加1197万元,增长65.1%。完成了县糖厂扩建、陶瓷厂筹建、县医院制剂室、大墩门引水枢纽工程等建设项目。计划外基本建设投资额达1473万元,比上年增加353万元,增长24%。完成县供销社住宅楼、金兰食品添加剂车间、农行住宅楼、金塔宾馆、棉花公司轧花车间等建设项目18项。

交通邮电:县境内有省级公路3条,长257公里。县乡公路长987.2公里.其中铺路面长124.5公里。有汽车579辆,比上年增加175辆,其中客车257辆,比上年增加183辆,货车322辆。全县11个农村乡镇全部通公路、通汽车,75%的村通汽车。客运量达86.3万人,比上年增加48.9万人;货运量达24.5万吨,比上年增加1.1万吨。全县有邮电局(所)6个,1993年改建、扩建并完成了2000门程控电话交换系统和数字、汉字寻呼系统的建设,基本实现了自动通话。全县11个农村乡镇和118个村民委员会全部通邮,33个村通电话,年完成邮电业务总量112万元,比上年增长19.7%。

财贸:1993年,有批发贸易机构7个,网点108个,人员817人。有零售贸易业机构13个,网点55个,人员342人。社会商品零售总额达11772万元,比上年增长12.8%。社会商品购进总额14172.9万元,比上年增长7.3%。商品销售总额达17223万元,比上年增长15.6%。农产品收购总额达6621万元。财政总收入达1469万元,比上年增长20.4%,财政总支出达2580万元。税收总额达1248万元,比上年增长23.5%。全县城乡个体工商业户达1403户,比上年增加111户,增长7.9%,从业人员达2019人,比上年增加123人,增长6.1%,营业额达1404.6万元,比上年增加330.9万元,增长23.5%。

【人民生活与社会事业】农民人均纯收入达1142.2元,比上年增长10.2%,职工年平均工资达2371元,比上年增长9.3%。城镇储蓄存款9610万元,人均6011元,比上年增长53.8%,农户储蓄存款达4745万元,人均416元,比上年增长12.1%。农村共有住房面积462.33万平方米,人均40.53平方米。城镇居民全部用上了自来水,有71%的村和65%的人口用上了自来水,94%的农户通上了电。全县农村有电视机18615台,普及率达65.3%,电冰箱73台,洗衣机9497台,收录机14104台,录像机64台,摩托车1086辆,自行车39282辆。

教育文化:全县有普通中学14所,在校学生6774人,农职业中学1所,在校学生208人。小学131所,在校学生12170人,其中农村小学126所,在校学生10020人。学龄儿童入学率达100%,在校学生巩固率达99.88%,毕业率达99.9%。全县有文化机构795个,人数386人。县城建有文化馆、电影院、艺术团、图书馆、广播站,农村有乡电影放映站12个,文化站8个,文化中心3个,乡村文化俱乐部767个,群众业余演出队151个。全年演出场次达101场,观众达45万人次。放映电影204场,观众达24363人次。图书流通册数达48389册次。

卫生、体育:全县有卫生机构19个,其中县城8个,农村11个。共有医务人员323人,共有床位285张。全年共举办运动会146次,参加运动会的运动员达33945人。

【名特土产】黑瓜籽:种植面积达7800亩,总产达2200吨,商品率在90%以上。以粮食为主要原料用传统手工艺方法酿造制作的黑醋、面筋、粉皮子等特色产品,年产量达100万公斤以上。

现任主要领导:

中共金塔县委书记:张俊明

金塔县人大常委会主任:李万春

金塔县人民政府县长:张世汉

政协金塔县委员会主席:李春江

中共金塔县纪律检查委员会书记:

孙占寿

(金塔县委研究室:卢永春 金玉萍)

玉门市经济和社会发展概述

【概况】玉门市地处河西走廊西部,是我国石油工业的摇蓝。总面积1.35万平方公里,总人口18.4万人。市区座落在祁连山北麓的石油河畔,建城面积18平方公里。市内中央、省、地属大中型企业居多,具有一定的工业基础,是一座新型工业城市。市辖三镇六乡和市区三个街道办事处,全市农村人口6.7万,总耕地面积2.5万公顷,森林覆盖面积3.7万公顷,草原24万公顷,发展农、林、牧业有广阔的前景。

全市属大陆性中温带干旱气候。年均降水量农区61.8毫米,无霜期134天,主要农作物有小麦、蚕豆、玉米、青稞、豌豆、胡麻、蔬菜等。其中,官庄子的韭菜、玉门镇的大葱、花海的辣椒,还有普遍种植的西瓜、甜瓜、葱头等素负盛名,深受省内外欢迎。近年来,新开发的甘草、孜然、大麦、啤酒花等作物有较高的经济价值。

1993年,全社会工农业总产值135598万元,国民生产总值59925万元,比上年增长22.54%,国内生产总值60617万元,比上年增长19.43%。第一产业6848万元,占11.30%,第二产业42816万元,占70.63%,第三产业10953万元,占18.07%,人均国民生产总值6741元。剔除中央、省属企业外,市属工农业总产值30980.74万元,比上年增长17.96%。

【农业】以小康为目标,以市场为导向,强化农业基础建设,大力调整产业结构,突出乡镇企业提高经济效益,推动农村经济全面发展。1993年,市属农业总产值12656万元,比上年增加3.3%。

种植业上,依靠科技调整,大力发展两高一优农业,在稳定发展粮食生产的前提下,按照市场需求,调整种植结构,粮经比例由上年79∶21调整到73∶27,经济作物提高了6个百分点。两高一优农业突出了蔬菜生产,建成了适合玉门气候特点的"玉门Ⅰ型"、"玉门Ⅱ型"高效节能日光温室,1993年试种温棚蔬菜258亩,春节前后,各类自产的新鲜蔬菜上市,打破了玉门冬季不能生产蔬菜的传统历史。同时开发种植了啤酒花、大麦、孜然、甘草等高效经济作物。粮食生产狠抓了各项科技增产措施的落实,单产增加20公斤,达到516公斤,总产接近上年,取得了显著的经济效益。

林业:坚持"提高质量、加快发展、连片定植、规模经营"的原则,突出重点抓基地,集体建园办企业。1993年全市已建成集体果园179个,0.82万亩,其中千亩果园5个,并推广了滴灌、地下管道灌溉新技术。当年造林面积5008亩,比上年增加15.2%,成林抚育面积21367亩。

畜牧业:优化畜禽品种,大力发展草食动物,以规模养殖为重点,饲养、存栏、出栏一起抓,良种、良法、良料一起上,在稳定发展养猪、养鸡的基础上,大力发展养牛、养羊、养兔基地,引导农民养鸽、鹅、鸭、蛇和银狐、乌骨鸡等特优珍稀品种。应用温棚养殖和饲料青贮氨化等新技术,促进了养殖业发展。1993年肉类总产量达4539.78吨,鲜蛋奶2679吨,比上年增长4.1%和14.3%。畜牧养殖业收入达4200万元,占农村经济总收入的18.8%。

乡镇企业有了新的突破。产值和效益同步高速度增长。1993年底,全市乡镇企业达2692个,比上年增加1081个,企业人数14622人,增加2977人;乡镇企业总产值19532万元,比上年增长58.4%;总收入10714万元,增长60%;实现利润1127万元,增长52.3%。1993年,全市上下进一步解放思想,转变观念,采取了强硬的改革性措施,开创了大办乡镇企业的新局面。一是引资筹资,市委、市政府于8月份作出了《进一步加速发展乡镇企业的决定》,采取扣发奖励工资,市级领导带头引资,包村部门帮办企业等措施,加速发展乡镇企业。止去年底,全市共引进资金2611万元;二是学习万丰村,大办股份合作制企业。市上出台了股份合作制企业的《实施意见》,先后发展股份合作制企业48户,入股资金1714.5万元。三是逐步完善企业经营机制,租赁承包,对部分效益较差的乡村小型企业进行了拍卖、兼并,增强了企业活力。四是双带整推,走城乡发展的路子。与周边大企业和省内外30多家科研单位进行合作,引进资金1370多万元,引进人才30人,开发新产品18项25种,共同创办乡镇企业22户。五是多轮驱动、多轨运行、多层次发展乡镇企业,多渠道增加农民收入。

【工商业发展】1993年,工业企业以贯彻《条例》为突破口,加快深化改革步伐,抓好机制转换,落实了劳动、工资、人事三项制度改革及14项自主权,克服了缺水、缺电、缺资金等方面的困难,完成了年度计划。市属工业实现产值18324.5万元,比上年增加30.8%,其中全民所有制企业完成产值7490.4万元,增长7.1%,集体工业完成产值10649.1万元,增长23.7%。其间采取的主要措施:一是城市工业挖内潜、练内功,瞄准市场,以销促产。效益速度同步增长。市农机修造厂利税创千万元大关,成为全区二个利税大户之一。二是加强基础建设,加大科技投入。工业系统全年投资1300万元,完成技术改造项目16项。工业系统整体实力大大增强。三是二轻系统面向市场,调整产业结构,拓宽服务领域,实现了经济效益的高速增长,产值达到814.44万元,增长

43.1%,利税 54.64 万元,增长 52.5%。

商业:以转变观念、深化改革、拓展经营范围,扩大新的增值点为动力,转换经营机制,68%的门点实现了国有民营,商品销售总额和上交利税有了大幅度增长,既满足了市场需求,又提高了职工收入。1993 年商贸流通企业完成商品销售总额 30783.4 万元,比上年增加 13.24%。

【社会事业】科技工作有了新进步,1993 年市属科研部门推广科技成果 23 项,培训基层技术人员 5048 人次,为两高一优农业和乡镇企业发展做出了新的贡献。教育事业,城乡九年制义务教育普及,学校教育质量不断提高,各类成人教育和职业技术教育得到了加强。学龄儿童入学率达到 100%,1993 年市属中学为各类大中专院校输送新生 243 人。市上先后投资 198.4 万元,改善了教学条件,还引进香港知名人士邵逸夫先生资金 50 万港元,正在修建逸夫小学。文化事业,完善加强了基础设施,市区建成文化中心、博物馆、图书馆、文化馆,农村健全了三级文化网络。各类群众性的文化娱乐活动丰富多彩。卫生事业,医疗条件得到改善,爱国卫生取得新成绩。1993 年,全市有卫生机构 64 个,卫生技术人员 1679 人,病床 1067 张,每千人拥有医疗技术人员 9 人。体育事业,各种群众性活动普遍开展,1993 年市级举办各种运动会 19 次,参加 4550 人。《国家体育锻炼标准》达标人数 11492 人,已建成可容纳近万人的综合体育场一座。交通运输,交通设备有所改善,运输能力不断增强。1993 年,完成货运量 184 万吨,完成客运量 62 万人次。城市交通发展迅速,仅市区内的"招手停"就达 68 车辆。1993 年,完成邮电业务总量 442.64 万元,增长了 30.56%,年末拥有电话机 8144 部。建成 4000 门程控电话交换网,兰乌光缆通讯玉门段已开始建设。玉门镇赤金镇农话并入程控电话网。旅游业,已建成铁人故居和事迹陈列馆,进一步开发老君庙。规划、引进资金开发火烧沟文化遗址,修复红山古寺,开辟玉门镇——塔尔湾——花海边墙井——干海子候鸟保护区为重点的旅游景点。另外人民生活水平不断改善,居民收入增加。1993 年农民人均纯收入 1177 元,比上年增加 108 元。城镇居民人均年收入达 2151 元。城乡居民年末储蓄存款余额 43752 万元,增长 15.63%。

【油城建设与开发区发展】随着玉门石油管理局开发建设吐哈油田的转移,玉门经济开发区的优势越来越突出,城市建设的基本思路是完善配套老油城,重点建设开发区。1993 年,在市区中心地带北坪修建了综合贸易大楼,在新市区修建了蔬菜批零市场,进一步增强了城市服务功能。同时加快住房建设和住房制度改革。1993 年共投资 680 万元修建了 14400 平方米的住宅楼,出售了 22 套商品房,房改售房 786 套,加快了住房制度改革,改善了城市居民的居住生活条件。

玉门镇距市区 77 公里,集镇面积 3 平方公里,现有城镇人口 0.8 万人,历史上是玉门县的政治、经济、文化、教育中心,发挥着联系周围 4 乡镇的经济文化纽带作用。市政府的农口部门均设在该镇,是全市农业经济管理的中心,教育、卫生、文化设施完备。横跨兰新铁路和国道 312 线,交通方便。1992 年,经省政府批准,玉门镇被定为经济开发区,将为玉门市经济振兴发挥巨大作用。1993 年市上共投资 680 万元,建成了 4.8 公里长的一级公路,架通了水、电等基础设施,今年将引进资金 5000 多万元,建设 30 多幢楼房。商业网点、综合市场、游乐中心、生活服务设施。拟建中的铁路立交桥、新、旧城区的贯通玉门镇汽车站,新区管委会办公大楼,邮电通讯大楼,居民住宅楼已开工建设,一个新型城市的雏形即将形成。

现任主要领导:

中共玉门市委书记:赵　林

玉门市人大常委会主任:郭富才

玉门市人民政府市长:李全寿

政协玉门市委员会主席:罗福智

中共玉门市纪律检查委员会书记:李宏道

(玉门市委调研室)

敦煌市经济和社会发展概述

【自然概况】敦煌市位于甘肃省河西走廊最西端,全市辖 2 镇 10 乡 78 个村。总人口 12.01 万,其中农业人口 9.7 万。汉族占 99%,另有回、东乡、蒙古、满、哈萨克、维吾尔、土家、裕固、土等 10 个少数民族。土地肥沃,资源丰富,更有很多星罗棋布的名胜古迹。全市总面积有 3.12 万平方公里,其中绿洲面积 1397 平方公里,平均海拔 1138 米。年日照时数 3200 小时,年平均气温 9.4℃,年平均降水量 39.9 毫米,而蒸发量高达 2400 毫米,平均无霜期 150 天,属典型的暖温带内陆干旱性气候。

【城乡经济取得新的成绩】"发展才是硬道理"。全市坚持以改革总揽全局,以贯彻落实《条例》为重点,在改革中求发展,靠改革促发展,使全市城乡经济取得了新成绩。全市国民生产总值达到 27013 万元,比上年增长 9.67%;工农业总产值完成 44520 万元,其中工业总产值达到 28881 万元,分别比上年增长 13.1%和 31.58%,农业总产值达到 15639 万元,比上年下降 8.91%。在战胜了冰雹、病虫等自然灾害后,粮食总产量达到 7753 万公斤,比上年减产 352 万公斤,亩产占 511.3 公斤,比上年增加 3.5 公斤;棉花总产达到 606.42 万公斤,比上年减产 148.5 万公斤;瓜菜总产量达到

6344.6万公斤，比上年增加320.8万公斤；水果总产量达到991.44万公斤，比上年增加49.89万公斤；肉类总产达到446万公斤，比上年增长4.3%。特别是在乡镇企业的发展上，采取领导抓，部门帮，能人带，股份推等办法，坚持上规模、上项目、上水平、上效益、上台阶，取得了突破性进展。全市新上项目90个，其中建成100万元以上企业8个，20万元以上企业34个，20万元以下企业48个；个体私营企业达到2944个，产值占全市乡镇企业总产值的38.2%。全市乡镇企业总产值达到30105.8万元，总收入15735万元，实现利润1017.3万元，分别比上年增长53.9%、45.9%和32.9%；通过积极鼓励和扶持农民大办二、三产业，千方百计地增加农民收入，全市农村向二、三产业转移劳动力14349个，占农村总劳动力33765的42.5%，农民人均纯收入达到1331元，比上年增加121元；农村经济总收入完成32163万元，比上年增长21.56%；全市社会商品零售总额完成22433万元，比上年增长19.49%；围绕旅游业积极兴起的手工地毯、刺绣、夜光杯、水晶石眼镜的加工业和敦煌书画、彩塑、工艺美术陶瓷等旅游产品以及石棉、芒硝、食盐、磷钒共生矿的开发都在不断地上规模、上档次、上批量，促进了经济的全面发展。1993年，全市旅游接待总人数48万人(次)，比上年增长6.67%，其中外宾3.7万人(次)，比上年下降2.6%；旅游接待收入2330万元，增长22.63%；创汇1356.1万元外汇人民币，增长12.8%；实现利润492.6万元，增长23.2%。全市财政收入达到2738.2万元，完成预算的125.47%，比上年净增793万元，增长40.78%。

【以旅游开发为重点的市镇建设取得了新进展】自1992年4月敦煌被省政府批准为旅游开发区以后，在省地的正确领导和有关部门的大力支持下，市委、市政府坚持“对外大宣传，对内大发动，全面大开放，全力大发展”的方针，使旅游开发为重点的市镇建设取得了新进展、新变化。一是市上先后投资200多万元完善了市区、景区的卫生设施，整修了集贸批发市场，修建了东城门牌楼，改造了城市饮用水源，完成了敦煌公园假山堆筑，人工湖开挖和门楼修建等项工程。与此同时，投资115万元完成了水厂扩建工程，日供水能力由3000吨提高到6000吨。丁字路的延伸工程也完成了拆迁、土方开挖等前期准备工作。投资600多万元的南湖店电站已建成投入使用，沙枣墩梁电站也已开工修建。二是在一年多的时间里，全部完成和正在开工建设的项目达122项，投资总额45587.7万元。其中花岗石板材股份有限公司、七里镇粮油加工厂、敦煌高登地膜有限公司、敦煌酒厂等已建成投入使用。投资1000多万元兴建的金山宾馆、莫高酒楼、西域宾馆、悬泉宾馆、九色鹿宾馆等五家宾馆已竣工，新增床位800多张，大大提高了综合接待能力。敦煌山庄、敦煌国际大酒店、敦煌宾馆贵宾楼、沙州大酒店，敦煌石窟保护研究中心、敦煌商城、金叶大厦、矿泉水饮料公司等一批骨干项目正在加紧施工，将于1994年陆续投入使用。三是千方百计筹措资金，动员全社会的力量，使投资95.2万元的鸣山公路拓宽工程当年投入使用。计划投资1600万元的第三产业开发区阳关西路拓宽工程，第一期按计划完成了800万元的建设规模，已油铺和开通长5.2公里，宽20米的机动车主干道。从而大大缓解了旅游旺季市区至机场、莫高窟、鸣沙山月牙泉、电影城、渥洼池等路段交通不畅的矛盾，也为第三产业开发区的建设奠定了良好的基础。投资3亿元的敦煌机场扩建工程完成了国家专家组的最后论证，目前正在积极争取国家审批。投资千万元开通了5000门程控直拨电话，通讯条件大为改善。

【两高一优农业的发展初具规模】发展农村经济，增加农民收入，重要的一条是发展两高一优农业。对此，我们坚持面向市场，调整农业内部结构，依靠科技大力发展区域化、基地化、集约化农业，取得了显著的效果。以棉花、葡萄、李广杏、鸣山大枣、瓜类、蔬菜、畜牧养殖等七个农业商品基地建设已初具规模，总面积达到11.4万亩，总收入达到8000多万元，占了农村经济总收入的30%。规模最大的棉花基地面积已达到8.5万亩，总产达到606.4万公斤，收入4000多万元，已成为敦煌农民奔小康的支柱产业之一。效益好的蔬菜基地，面积已发展到1.5万亩，其中温室大棚蔬菜面积2000亩，蔬菜总收入达1000多万元，具有敦煌特色的葡萄基地已发展到5000多亩，年产鲜葡萄350万公斤，不但满足了周边城市市场的需求，而且成为农民致富的有效途径。其它基地也已初具规模并逐年增大，基本形成了具有敦煌特色的批量产品。

【社会各项事业全面进步】在集中精力搞好旅游开发、推动经济发展的同时，市上坚持“两手抓，两手都要硬”的方针，紧紧围绕经济建设这个中心，统筹兼顾，狠抓了精神文明建设和各项社会事业的发展。一是突出思想教育。全市党员群众普遍进行了党的基本路线、三热爱、三兼顾、民主法制和科技文化教育，使人们的思想观念不断更新，价值观念，效益观念和市场经济观念不断树立，成为各级干部和广大群众发展经济的强大动力。二是突出“双基”教育。全市现有11所初级中学，2所完全中学，1所职业中学，84所小学，1所幼儿园，另有为成人教育设置的教育培训中心、电大工作站、教师进修学校。有教师1300多名。近年来，市上把发展职业教育和成人教育作为重点，努力改革管理制度，促进了教育的发展。1993年的120多人考入大中专院校，成为历史上最多的一年。市幼儿园首次开办了聋哑儿童特教班，填补了我市空白。三是卫生工作积极为经济建设服务。全市现有医院2所，中心卫生院4所，乡卫生院7所，医疗站75个，共有病床350张。在保障人民身体健康等方面做出了新成绩。1993年，敦煌市医院被评为国家二级甲医院，防疫站被评为全国计划免疫先进单位，同时，敦煌市被评为计划免疫先进市。四是计划生育工作按照三不放松(政策上不放松、领导上不放手、工作上不松劲)的要求，坚持三为主(宣传教育为主、避孕节育为主、经常工作为主)的工作方针，实行科学管理，并通过"突击月"活动促落实。1993年，全市人口出生率为15.87‰，人口自然增长率为10.01‰，被评为全国计划生育工作先进单位，受到国务院的表彰奖励。五是政法部门从普法教育、抓要案、建制度、群防群治等为重点的综合治理深入开展，为改革和经济建设创造了良好的内外部环境。

现任主要领导：

中共敦煌市委书记：李济民

敦煌市人大常务委员会主任：王成业

敦煌市人民政府市长：肖洪才

政协敦煌市委员会主席：湛国德

中共敦煌市纪律检查委员会书记：赵加固

（中共敦煌市委政研室：李跃祖　姚建军）

临夏回族自治州

中共临夏回族自治州委书记：马尚英

临夏回族自治州人大常委会主任：马尚英

临夏回族自治州人民政府州长：敏　政

政协临夏回族自治州委员会主席：李效祖

中共临夏回族自治州纪律检查委员会书记：惠全鹰

临夏回族自治州经济和社会发展概述

【自然概况】地理位置：临夏回族自治州位于黄河上游，甘肃省中部西南面。地处北纬34°57′—36°12′，东经102°41′—103°40′之间。东临洮河与定西地区相连，西倚积石山与青海省毗邻，南靠太子山与甘南藏族自治州为界，北濒湟水与兰州接壤。

地势河流：临夏地处青藏高原和黄土高原丘陵沟壑区的过渡地带。境内有大山163座、大中沟8150条、大川16道、大原15处。西南部是积石山、太子山脉，东北部是马衔山、巴米山、雾宿山脉。积石山脉从西部向西南延伸，在西南部横亘着五台山、雷积山、达里加山、太子山等海拔均在3000米以上的山峰，形成全州地势西南部高、东北部低的倾斜盆地状态。平均海拔2000米，最高山峰达里加山海拔4636.6米，最低盐锅峡附近黄河沿岸海拔1580米。境内黄河自西部积石关入境，横贯北部，过境流长103公里；洮河流贯临夏东部，长约100公里；大夏河自西南向东北，贯穿中部，长约150多公里。

气候：临夏属内陆性气候，年平均气温6.3℃，最高32.5℃，最低零下22.3℃。年平均降雨量537毫米，多集中在夏末秋初。年平均日照时数2467小时，无霜期157天。

自然资源：临夏州自然资源比较丰富，主要有：① 土地资源。全州总面积8169.38平方公里，人口密度每平方公里208人。总耕地223.55万亩，占总面积的18.24%；荒地面积285万亩，占23.26%；林地面积252.8万亩，占20.03%；水域面积108.6万亩，占8.86%。农民人均耕地1.44亩。在总耕地中，川地43.42万亩、原地19.24万亩、山地163.14万亩。② 水资源。全州水资源总量12.15亿立方米，其中地表水11.3立方米、地下水0.85亿立方米。年过境径流量324亿立方米。初步勘测，水力蕴藏量191万千瓦，已开发161.5万千瓦，主要是刘家峡、盐锅峡水电厂占160万千瓦。小水力资源12万千瓦，已开发和正在开发的2万千瓦。③ 植物资源。种植业作物中，粮食有小麦、青禾、玉米、洋芋、蚕豆、米谷；油料有芥子、胡麻。另外，还有大麻、甜菜、瓜果、花椒、药材等经济作物。野生植物主要有松、桦、青岗、毛竹及当参、大黄、甘草等数百种药材。④ 矿产资源。初步探明的有大理石、花岗岩、石灰石、石膏、铁、锑等。其中，大理石蕴藏量丰富，质地优良，仅在和政、临夏两县境内分布面积约有60平方公里，总藏量达22亿立方米。

行政区划、人口：现辖临夏市、临夏县、永靖县、和政县、广河县、康乐县和东乡族自治县、积石山保安族东乡族撒拉族自治县。有132个农村乡镇、6个城市街道办事处、1144个行政村、11101个经济合作组。到1993年底，全州总人口为1697757人，其中汉族757444人，占总人口的44.61%；少数民族940313人，占55.39%。在少数民族中，回族574532人，占总人口的33.84%。在总人口中农业人口1551761人，占总人口的91.4%。

【名特产品】蚕　豆：蚕豆是临夏的传统优势作物，粒大味美，营养丰富，蛋白质含量高达25%以上，现年播种面积近30万亩，总产6万多吨。在国际市场上享有很高的声誉，是我州大宗的主要出口商品，年出口在4万吨以上。

大　麻:大麻是临夏的主要经济作物之一,种植历史悠久,所产大麻柔软、质白、细长,产量高,比誉为“陇上名产”。

药　材:种类繁多,野生和家种药材达300多种,其中100多种成为全国传统通用的中药材,部分已载入《甘肃中药材手册》,当归、当参、黄芪、大黄、甘草被誉为甘肃的五大宝,驰名全国,远销世界。

蕨　菜:资源丰富,质地脆嫩,色味俱佳,是出口的主要山珍,远销日本等国,年出口566吨左右。

桃　杏:盛产于东乡唐汪川的桃杏,誉满遐迩,其果形桃,色红,瓤厚汁多,甜酸适度,是我国优良的杏种,远销香港等地。另外,盛产于积石山县大河家的鸡蛋皮核桃、冬果梨、永靖县刘、盐两峡和唐汪川的红枣、黑瓜子、西瓜也在省内外享有很高的名气。

黄　酒:临夏酿造黄酒的历史悠久,技术精湛,年产1000多吨,临夏县黄酒厂生产的《五山池》黄酒,在全国黄酒类评选中名列第7位。

保安腰刀:保安腰刀是保安族人民传统的手工艺品,有3大类、14个品种,其中以什样绵腰刀为上品。年产约10多万把,远销国内青海、西藏、云南、宁夏、内蒙等地和国外的尼泊尔、印度、巴基斯坦等国家。

【城市建设】全州城市建设,特别是基础设施建设发展比较快。现建成水厂7座,供水能力21900吨/日,城镇人口用水率达68%;建成城市道路面积0.91平方公里,占城市总体规划的55.5%;城市主街道架设路灯1516盏,装置率达到60%;城市园林绿化覆盖率达到7.2%;城市新建住宅面积52216平方米,人均达到7.6平方米。

【国民经济】1993年,全州各级党政组织,以邓小平建设有中国特色社会主义理论为指针,全面贯彻党的十四大精神,围绕建立社会主义市场经济体制的总目标,竭尽全力维护社会稳定,集中精力搞好经济建设,深化改革,扩大开放,促进工农业生产稳定发展,全州呈现民族团结,社会安定,经济发展,市场繁荣的良好局面。全年完成国民生产总值84566万元(现行价),按可比口径(下同),比上年增长4%,比1980年增长3倍;工农业总产值118030万元,比上年增长20.18%,比1980年增长3.5倍;社会商品零售总额61217万元,比上年增长15.36%,比1980年增长3.3倍;财政收入6362万元,比上年增长25%,比1980年增长3.9倍;农民人均纯收入383.44元,比上年增长7.9%,比1980年增长5倍多。农民人均纯收入200元以下的贫困面由1986年的44%下降到16.08%。如果按人均纯收入不到300元温饱线标准计算,贫困面仍占42.37%。

农业:全州农林牧副渔全面发展。全年完成农业增加值46377.16万元,比上年增长21.69%;农业总产值64522.4万元,比上年增长13.65%;乡镇企业总产值86979.8万元,增长55.34%。粮食总产量405981吨,比上年增长13.06%;平均亩产200公斤,比上年增长26公斤;农民人均占有粮266公斤,比上年增加28公斤。林业当年完成造林面积16.24万亩,其中经济林5.14万亩。森林覆盖率11.66%。牧业生产发展良好。大牲畜年末存栏35.9万头,比上年增长2.37%;羊存栏89.03万只,增长4.54%;猪存栏27.22万口.增长4.73%。肉类总产量达到28679吨,增长9.42%。绵羊毛产量1594吨,增长11.16%。奶类产量6538吨,增长31.79%。

农业生产条件有所改善。农业机械总动力达到39.18万千瓦,增长3.65%。大中小型拖拉机14370台,增长9.77%。农用汽车467辆,减少4.5%。有效灌溉面积达到71.13万亩,新增4200亩;保灌面积64.23万亩,新增2400亩;梯田83.49万亩,新增51700亩。

工业、建筑业:工业生产稳步发展。全年完成工业总产值53508万元(不包括中央、省属在临工业),比上年增长29.12%。其中乡及乡以上工业完成产值20353万元,增长0.51%;村及村以下工业完成产值33155万元,增长56.46%。在工业总产值中,国有企业完成11983万元,下降6.91%;集体企业完成7740万元,增长13.82%;个体企业完成17481万元,增长59.19%。全民、集体建筑业13个,从业3629人,完成施工产值3392.2万元。全年完成固定资产投资15711万元(不包括中央、省属在临单位),比上年增长53.16%。其中个体投资9459万元,比上年增长83.49%,占总投资的60.2%。

交通、邮电:交通运输业不断发展。全年完成客运量410.07万人,客运周转量15839.21万人公里,分别比上年增长20.59%和7.44%。完成货运量87.82万吨,货运周转量11692.84万吨公里,分别比上年增长21.84%和32.74%。

邮电通讯事业进一步发展。全年完成邮电业务总量达到1052万元,比上年增长20.6%,邮电业务收入达到817万元,比上年增长22.5%。报刊发行为12.99万份,市话交换机总容量达到14592门,其中程控10192门。

商贸、物价:全州城乡市场繁荣。在全年社会商品零售总额中,社会消费品零售总额52996万元,增长13.22%。全州城乡市场109处,集市贸易成交额34476万元,比上年增长136.83%。

市场物价上涨幅度较大。据临夏市调查,全年零售物价指数上涨11.6%,职工生活费用价格指数上涨13.1%,服务项目价格指数上涨24.4%。

财政、金融:地方财政收入增长

较快，全年完成财政收入 6362 万元，比上年增长 25%。其中，工商税收入 5249 万元，比上年增长 21.67%，占财政总收入的 82.5%。财政支出 23497 万元，比上年增长 18.01%。

金融运行相对平稳。全州国家银行各项存款余额达 66493 万元，比上年末增加 12745 万元，增长 19.3%。银行各项贷款达 71081 万元，比上年末净增 7865 万元，增长 12.44%。城乡居民储蓄余额 59873 万元，比上年末增长 37.23%。

【社会事业】全州教育、科技、文化、卫生、体育等各项社会事业稳步发展。教育方面，全州有各级各类学校 1295 所，其中，普通中学 73 所、职业学校 7 所、中专 8 所、小学 1169 所、幼儿园 38 所。普通中学在校学生 39569 人，其中少数民族学生占 34.01%；小学在校学生 149323 人，其中少数民族学生占 46.02%；职业中学在校学生 994 人。小学适龄儿童入学率为 81.17%。教师队伍进一步扩大，专任教师总数达 9234 人，比上年增长 7.21%。科技方面，现有各类科研机构 7 所，专业科技人员 12565 名，其中高级职称的 218 人、中级 2044 人。全州有县级的各种学会、协会 122 个，民间研究会 118 个，会员 3492 人。全年共取得科技成果 35 项，科技进步在经济增长中的含量达到 37%。文化方面，全州新闻单位有民族报社、周二报，年发行 18000 份。有广播台、电视台，广播覆盖率 70%、电视覆盖率为 71%。电影放映单位 81 个、艺术表演团体 2 个、群众艺术馆 1 个、博物馆 1 个、文化馆 8 个、图书馆 7 个。卫生方面，全州乡以上医疗单位 42 个，医院病床 2273 张，比上年末增长 7.83%，专业卫生技术人员达到 3141 人，比上年末增长 6.11%。农村 村级医疗卫生单位 998 个，乡村医生 1075 人，卫生员 425 人。体育方面，全州有体育机构 25 个，体育工作者 101 人。标准化场地 8 个。参加体育锻炼的 57.6 万人，占总人口的 35%。全年共举办各种类型的比赛 596 次，参加运动员 13.8 万人(次)。在全省田径、射击、无线电测向三个项目的比赛中，获个人第一名 7 个，第二名 4 个，1 人平 1 项省纪录，二人达二级运动员标准。

（中共临夏回族自治州委政策研究室：张顺成　王才中　张佩荟）

临夏市经济和社会发展概述

【市情梗概】临夏市是一个环境优美、历史悠久、多民族合睦聚居的城市。是一个生活习俗、宗教信仰、地方经济以伊斯兰民族为特色的文化古城。是临夏回族自治州州委及州政府所在地，亦是全州政治、经济、文化、交通的中心。面积 88.50 平方公里，人口 17.3 万人，有 18 个民族，其中少数民族和汉族人口各占一半，回族人口占全市总人口的 47.5%。

人类的地质史，留给临夏人的是东南两座山，北面一块塬，中间夹着一道川的地貌特征，人多地少，矿产资源贫乏，工业基础薄弱，长期以来困扰着民族经济的发展。临夏民族经济的发展，有着优越的客观条件。第一，临夏市地处青藏牧区与内地农区的交汇地带，历史上曾是丝绸南路和唐蕃古道的重镇，是有名的“茶马互市”，多少年来群众有着经商的传统和才干，形成西北重要的商品集散地，从而为临夏民族工业的发展提供了非常丰富的市场条件。第二，党的十一届三中全会特别是党的十四大以来，民族地方的农业、林业及牧业有了全面发展，民族地方的工业以多形式、多元化、多方位稳步全面展开。同时市委、市政府又提出“东进西出，内营外联的战略思路，活跃了市场，扩大了贸易。第三，临夏市素有西部“小麦加”之称，这不仅在国内，即在国际上也有一定的影响。而临夏市归侨和侨属同中东、西亚、东南亚 20 多个国家和地区的临夏侨民有特殊联系，同世界其它穆斯林群众有密切往来。1993 年底以来世界上已有 20 多个国家和地区的伊斯兰团体和个人访问过临夏，这对加强临夏同这些国家及地区的经济往来有不可低估的作用。第四，水作为临夏这一得天独厚的自然资源，有很大潜力。水给临夏工农业生产及人畜生活用水提供了来源，水为临夏电力事业的发展提供了充分的电力资源，临夏市是全国首批实现电气化的城市之一，是被国家爱卫会命名的全国县级卫生城市。第五，临夏作为国家乙级开放城市，境内有众多的名胜古迹和富有民族特色的人文景观，素有“彩陶之乡”、“花儿故乡”的美誉，旅游资源相当丰富。

改革开放以来，临夏人民，在市委和市政府的领导下，从实际出发，扬长避短，充分发挥自身优势，坚持以流通为先导，走以贸促工、以贸促农，贸工农一体化建设的路子，使民族经济得到了迅速发展。1992 年 7 月临夏市被甘肃省人民政府批准为民族经济开发试验小区，享有甘肃黄河上游经济开发试验区的各种优惠政策，使临夏民族经济发展步入了一个新的阶段。

1993 年，全市实现国民生产总值 21690 万元，人均 1275 元，比上年增长 12.70%，工农业总产值 19290 万元，比上年增长 26.20%；商品零售总额完成 21274.9 万元；零售物价指数为 106.7%；完成财政收入 1981.73 万元，比上年增长 18.2%；全市职工工资总额 2749.5 万元，比上年增长 15.5%，职工平均月工资 195 元，比上年增长 8.3%；农民人均纯收入 638.52 元，比上年增加 67.68 元；城市待业率由上年的 7%下降到 6%。

【自然概况】临夏位于甘肃省中部，东经 103°6′至 103°16′，北纬 35°31′至 35°39′之间，东面与东乡族自治县邻界，南西北 三面与临夏县接壤。东西长 20 公里，南北宽 4 公里，平均海拔 1917 米，形成周山中川的地貌特征，因地处内陆，中温带大陆性气候较为典型，具有日照较长，但热量不足，干湿分明，但冷暖悬殊的特点。年平均气温 7.3℃，年降水量 500 毫米左右，无霜期 149 天，平均风速 1 米/秒。全市土地面积为 88.50 平方公里，城市规划区 13 平方公里，已建城区面积 7 平方公里，可供开发土地 7116 亩，农村耕地 5.17 万亩，人均耕地 0.59 亩。全市水流总量 10.87 亿立方米，地下水储量 0.63 亿立方米，日开采量为 13520 吨。电力蕴藏量为 19980 千瓦。临夏市境内及附近地区有众多的名胜古迹和具有浓郁民族特色的人文景观，如独具地方民族特色，融古典建筑、花卉、动物园、游乐场为一体的人民公园，具有园林风光、花卉齐备的东郊公园；富有回族建筑风格和艺术特色，堪称"三陇一绝"的东宫馆，以及周围的炳灵寺、刘家峡水库、拉不愣寺院、桑科草原、莲花山等重点游览区，是旅游度假的好地方。

【历史沿革】临夏市建制历代不同，辖境各异，名号亦多次更迭。夏朝属雍州之域，春秋战国为西羌之地。西汉建立枹罕县，归属陇西郡。东晋时始建河州，元时归附河州路，明后一直称渭河州。1913 年更名导河县。1928 年改为临夏县至解放。

1949 年 8 月 22 日临夏解放后，行政区域和称号又几经返复。1959 年 2 月在城区设临夏市；1958 年底将永靖、临夏县并入临夏市.1961 年复分为永靖、临夏县和临夏市；1973 年 12 月临夏市并入临夏县；1981 年 9 月从临夏县分出大河家等 16 乡，成立积石山保安族、东乡族、撒拉族自治县；1983 年 8 月，经国务院批准，再次将临夏县市分设，恢复了临夏市。

【经济发展现状】农业，临夏市地少人多，人均耕地只有 0.59 亩，农作物以小麦、玉米为主，经济作物主要是油菜籽、大麻和甜菜。城市东西郊区为大麻、商品蔬菜等经济作物的集中产区，所产蔬菜主要满足城市居民所需，随着水利建设的发展和农业机械化程度的提高，耕作条件不断改善，生产能力大大提高，生产结构日趋合理，乡镇企业蓬勃发展。1993 年农业总产值达到 6703.09 万元，比上年增长 16.9%；乡镇企业总产值 22140.9 万元；比上年增长 53.6%；粮食总产量达 21746.62 吨，比去年增长 3.4%；蔬菜总产量达到 51814.6 吨，比去年增长 11.3%；肉类总产量达到 390.36 吨，比去年增长 3.4%；蛋奶产量分别比去年增长 51%和 11.1%。1993 年营林面积 3577 亩，四旁植树 86.88 万株，封山造林 4472 亩，育苗面积 210 亩，森林覆盖率达 9.4%。

工业，党的十四大以来，临夏民族工业有了迅猛发展。1993 年实现工业总产值 12587 万元，比上年增长 14%。其中，全民企业完成产值 4870 万元，比上年增长 4.3%；集体企业完成产值 4032 万元，比上年增长 13.4%；乡镇企业完成产值 3685.4 万元，比上年增长 18.6%；目前，临夏已形成皮毛加工、家俱制作、棉麻造纸、铸造包装、刺绣服装、文化用品、民族特需、工艺美术等门类齐全的工业体系，一些企业和产品在省级部级评比中获得好荣誉，受到上级的好评。

财政，1993 年临夏市国民生产总值达到 21690 万元，比 1992 年增长 12.7%；工农业总产值，乡镇企业总产值和社会商品零售额比上年增长 26.2%、18.6%和 14.7%；财政收入、农民人均纯收入也分别比上年增长 18.24%和 11.6%。

商业，历史上的临夏是中原与西北少数民族地区进行商品交易的重要贸易集散地。这里大部分回族群众有很长的经商历史，过往客商不断。目前临夏市已形成多层次、多成份、布局合理方便群众的商业服务体系。1993 年完成社会商品零售总额 21274.9 万元。城乡集市贸易成交额达到 11201 万元，比上年增长 67%。交纳税金占所有工商税总额 64.01%。

【社会事业】文教卫生，文化教育事业发展很快，全市各级各类学校、职业技术学校、成办阿语学校各 1 所，独立初中 6 所，小学 49 所，公办幼儿园 4 所，城乡幼儿入园率达到 61.3%；青壮年文盲率下降到 9.2%，被国家教委评为"全国扫盲先进单位"。全市共有医疗卫生单位 11 个，床位 199 张，卫生技术人员 358 人，有个体诊所 53 个，药店 16 个，41 个村有卫生所(室)61 个，全年完成门诊量 26 万人次。计划免疫四苗覆盖率、新生接生率、传染病报告率、食品卫生合格率均达标准要求。城市卫生设施和公共环境卫生得到明显改善，是国家爱卫会命名的全国县级卫生城市。

科技事业已形成一个面向生产、面向基层、引进试验、推广新技术、新品种、新工艺的科技体制。1978 年成立了市科委，1979 年成立了市科协，全市各类科研、设计机构 7 个，社会科技人员 1460 人，自然科学人员 1690 人。由于科学技术的广泛推广，许多新的技术如地膜覆盖、小带田、吨粮田、高效节能温室种植蔬菜新技术等，得到广泛应用。全市共有电影院 6 座，图书馆、文管所、文化馆、乡文化中心等文化团体 8 个，主要文化遗址 12 处；农村有线广播覆盖率由 14%上升到 16%。

城市建设，全年完成固定资产投资 2107 万元，新增产值 3685.4 万元；城镇集体所有制完成建筑业总产值 758 万元，增长 18.6%；城乡私人建房投资额为 1530 万元，建筑面积为86554平方米，分别比上年增长12.3%和26.2%；新建城市居民住宅26800平方米，安置住房353户；集资近50多万元，硬化路面40000万平方米。截止1993年底，全市房屋建筑总面积已达186万平方米，其中住宅面积56万平方米，人均居住面积7平方米；硬化道路16公里，路面4万平方米；安置自来水管6310米，年供水50多万吨。66%的居民已使用自来水和电炊。

体育，全市共有各项等级裁判员220多人，等级运动员370多人；全年举办各项运动会10余次，连续两年被省上命名为“群众体育运动先进县(市)。

现任主要领导：

中共临夏市委书记：马光明

临夏市人大常委会主任：

马光明(兼)

临夏市人民政府市长：王世杰

政协临夏市委员会主席：党仁德

中共临夏市纪律检查委员会书记：

马成荣

（临夏市委政研室：丁建涛）

永靖县经济和社会发展概述

【概况】永靖县位于甘肃中部西南，东北与省城兰州紧邻，南隔黄河与东乡县、临夏县、积石山县相望，东南与定西地区临洮县接壤，西靠青海省民和县。全县辖刘家峡、盐锅峡2个镇和17个山川塬区乡，共139个行政村。总人口18.8万人，其中农业人口16.3万人，少数民族人口2.56万人。全县总面积1863.6平方公里，海拔在1580——2850米之间。黄河流经县城107公里，被誉为黄河明珠的刘家峡、盐锅峡两个水电站均在境内，建有刘家峡、盐锅峡、八盘峡三大水库，高峡平湖形成黄土高原独特的景观。刘家峡水库水域面积131平方公里，水产品有鲤鱼、鲢鱼、草鱼、鲫鱼等，其中黄河鲤鱼以肉味鲜嫩而闻名。这里是甘肃重要的水产品养殖基地之一。境内有驰名中外的国家重点保护文物炳灵寺石窟，有巴咪山、抱龙山原始林区。还有刘家峡化工总厂、盐锅峡化工总厂、水电四部刘家峡分局等中央、省属企业10多家。盛产红枣、苹果、梨、桃、杏、葡萄、西瓜、籽瓜、香瓜等。矿产资源主要有锰、铜、金、蛇纹岩、白云岩、大理岩、石灰岩、石膏、岩棉矿等。县城刘家峡距兰州72公里。公路有国道309线、213线和刘白环线，县乡公路与此相接。水路有刘家峡水库航运线，直通炳灵寺和临夏。铁路有刘兰铁路专用线，县内交通十分方便。

【经济建设】1993年，永靖县经济全面发展，工农业总产值完成15394万元，乡镇企业总产值13711万元，财政收入2190万元，农民人均纯收入336元，比上年净增25.8元，农村贫困面下降了3.5个百分点。全县粮食总产量登上了一亿斤台阶，达到10391万斤，比上年增长30.8%，创我县历史最好水平；油料总产达335.6万斤，比上年增长33.1%；当年完成造林2.4万亩，比上年增长40.1%。大牲畜年末存栏4.21万头，羊年末存栏15.52万只，猪年末存栏6.35万口，分别比上年增长1.69%、4.27%和5.64%，肉类总产量达686万斤，比上年增长4.9%。全县农业总产值6704万元，比上年增长14.5%。1993年，乡镇企业继续坚持多轮驱动、多轨运行，乡办、村办、联户办、个体办、股份合作制等多种经济成份一齐上的原则，年内乡镇企业有了突破性的发展。年末全县乡镇企业已达1792个，当年新增100个，产值首次登上了亿元大关，比上年增长了50%。1993年，工业生产以市场为导向，进一步深化各项改革，产销同步增长，综合经济效益有了较大提高。全县完成工业总产值8690.3万元，比上年增长39.1%，其中乡及乡以上工业产值3055万元，比上年增长7.1%。销售收入2015.5万元，比上年增长41.6%。商贸企业及时组织适销对路商品，千方百计拓展销售渠道，市场流通呈现出淡季不淡，购销两旺的新局面。全县完成国内纯购进4194万元，比上年增长25.9%；国内纯销售5978万元，比上年增长3.12%。商业系统90%的企业实行了“国有民营”，供销系统93%的企业实行了“社有自营”。个体私营经济发展势头强劲，年末个体工商户达到2230户，注册资金431万元，从业人员达4034人，年营业额达2321万元。个体私营经济成份在整个市场商品交易中已成为繁荣市场的一支中坚力量。

1993年，交通运输业完成货运量2.5万吨，比上年增长18.5%；完成货运周转量48.95万吨公里，比上年增长23%；完成客运量73万人次，比上年增加0.3%；客运周转量876.86万人公里；营业收入达194.1万元，比上年增长9.3%。电话在全省率先开通1000门国内直拨电话的基础上，进行了盐锅峡地区的扩容改造，调整安装了农话线路设备，延伸了市话电缆，使全县通讯条件进一步改善，新兴业务有了大幅度增长。

【社会事业】去年，全县计划生育工作在“四平茬”的基础上，建立健全了一表、九卡、十册、十制度，并进入正常运转。去年，共结扎1486例，其中纯女户116例；一孩放环1672人，人流336例，引产98例。人口自然增长率为10.05‰，比计划控制指标多降低3.45个千分点，年末人口总数比计划减少1414人。教育事业，全县考入大中专院校学生397名，创我县历史最高水平。学龄儿童入学率达93.2%，比上年提高1.3个百分点；巩固率97%，毕业率92.2%，普及率75%。卫生事业不断深化管理体制改革，14所乡镇卫生院移交给乡(镇)政府管理;投入资金40.7万元,完成5所卫生院1744平方米的危房改造。

现任主要领导:

中共永靖县委书记:孙矿生

永靖县人大常委会主任:金永歆

永靖县人民政府县长:吴家白

政协永靖县委员会主席:张延辉

中共永靖县纪律检查委员会书记:孔德平

(永靖县委政策研究室:陈贵辉)

东乡族自治县经济和社会发展概述

【自然概况】东乡县是一个以东乡族为主,回、汉民族杂居的地区。1950年9月25日成立东乡自治区(县级),1955年改为东乡族自治县。全县辖25个乡镇,227个行政村,1892个合作社。1993年全县共有39865户,23.3万人,其中,东乡族占77.8%,回族占7.7%,汉族占14.6%,农业人口占97.6%,总劳力8.64万人。全县总面积1510平方公里,其中陆地面积1462平方公里,总耕地面积37.66万亩,占总面积的17.2%,其中山地32.87万亩,占总耕地面积的87.3%,川塬地4.79万亩,占12.7%。

东乡县地处甘肃省中部,境内山大沟深,土地支离破碎,最高海拔2664米,最低海拔1735米,年降水量350毫米左右,多集中在秋季;年蒸发量1387毫米,是全省二十个干旱贫困县之一。农作物主要有春小麦、马铃薯、玉米、豆类,经济林主要有杏、梨、桃、苹果、花椒等。目前,探明可采的矿产只有石英石,属甲级品位,储量较大。

【经济发展状况】1993年,全县工农业总产值达到8416.21万元,比上年增长9.08%;完成地方财政收入137万元;乡镇企业总产值达到7645万元;农民人均纯收入282元。农业,全县粮食总产量达到50022吨,比上年增长6.4%;平均亩产达到141公斤,增长8.6公斤。林业,完成植树造林2.3万亩,144万株,占任务的109.5%,其中营造用材林0.22万亩,防护林0.68万亩,薪炭林0.23万亩,经济林1.17万亩,育苗0.12万亩,义务植树150万株,林木覆盖率达到7.4%。畜牧业,一是狠抓北部12个乡小尾寒羊基地建设。小尾寒羊已辐射到全县25个乡镇,存栏达到2.55万只,比1992年增长25.6%;全县山绵羊存栏17.6万只,增长2.09%。二是努力提高畜牧业商品率。全县牲畜存栏总数达到9.4万头(只),比1992年增长10.8%;肉类总产量达到3266.48吨,增长9.9%;牛羊商品率达到58.4%。工业,完成工业总产值1121万元,比上年增长32.8%,其中县属工业企业完成产值542万元,增长22.4%;乡以上工业企业完成产值645万元,增长28%;实现利税62万元。商贸,全县有集贸市场17处,占地面积1.6万平方米。商贸企业185户,从业人员7384人,集市贸易成交额620万元。商贸企业完成国内纯购进785万元,比1992年增长22.5%;完成国内纯销售2629万元,增长11.4%;社会商品零售额达到2888万元。乡镇企业,各类乡镇企业达到1250个,其中乡以下建筑企业105个,乡镇企业完成总产值7645万元(按90年不变价格计算),比1992年增长45.4%。全县输转劳务2.96万人,比上年增长3.6%;实现劳务总收入1738.95万元,增长47%。同时,狠抓了两个小区开发建设,建成食品、商业企业6个,建材加工等企业4个,正在筹建的15个。全县完成地方财政收入137万元,比上年增长9%,其中,完成工商税收105.4万元,增长10%。全年地方财政支出1933万元,增长12.09%,其中,生产性支出317万元,占总支出的16%,非生产性支出1616万元,占总支出的84%。当年财政赤字达134万元,滚存赤字达520万元。全县金融运行相对平稳,银行各项存款余额达2031万元,增长40.55%;其中企业存款372万元,比上年下降47.5%。各项贷款余额2314万元,增长5.86%;其中农业贷款 余额553万元,比上年减少23.7%。"两西"建设,一是狠抓基础设施建设。那勒寺35千伏变电所基本完成;董岭人饮工程完成管道延伸12.2公里,建成35千伏输电线路30公里;新修人工和机械化梯田1万亩,新增耕地136亩。二是扶贫工作效益显著,当年解决温饱3430户,19831人,农民人均收入达到282元,比1992年增加25元。贫困面由1992年的20%下降到17.3%。三是移民工作进展顺利。小金湾东乡族移民基地已形成1207户、6005人的规模,完成了乡级建制;建立了景电二期古浪东乡族移民工作站,安置移民134户、556人。

【社会事业】全县有普通中学7所(其中初中4所),在校学生3431人,其中少数民族学生1464人,占总数的42.7%。小学154所,在校学生17420人,其中少数民族学生13331人,占总数的76.5%,适龄儿童入学率达60.3%,比1992年上升0.3个百分点。全县专职教师1204人,其中小学822人,分别比1992年增长4.7%和-7.1%,学生巩固率、毕业率、合格率、普及率分别达到90%、95%、38.9%、36%,当年向大中专院校输送189人。当年全县共实施科技项目9项,其中部级1项,省级6项,州级1项,在全部科技项目中,农业科技项目占总项目的77.8%,其中6项通过鉴定验收,部分项目达到省内和州内先进水平。全县乡以上医疗机构26个,医务人员170人,其中护士45人。医院病床数达到119张,比1992年增长13.3%。计划生育工作取得显著成效，全县25个乡镇中已有8个乡实现平茬。当年完成四术7394例，其中结扎1644例，纯女户结扎105例；上环5631例；人流82例。引产39例。全县计划生育率达到61.7%，人口出生率为18.1‰，自然增长率为13.7‰，人口增长控制在计划指标以内。社会福利事业，当年修建敬老院1所，有27名乡村五保老人安度晚年。全县有各类福利企业10个，安置残疾人72人，总投资200万元，创产值140万元，实现利润23万元。当年安置城乡退伍军人6名，解决救灾粮50万公斤，救灾款34.31万元，保障了重灾民、特困户、五保户的生活。修建了一所长年戒烟所。邮电通讯事业，全年邮电业务总量达到51.21万元，比1992年增长20.6%；报刊期发份数7529份，增长16.3%；市话交换机总容量达到1000门，乡镇自动交换机不断开通。

【名特土产】马铃署(本地称洋芋)。当年总产量达15081.62吨，是当地群众喜爱的主粮。畅销本地各大市场，近销临夏、兰州，远销甘南、青海、宁夏、广州等地，年销售量达6千多吨。大接杏，唐汪大接杏曾被评为全省优质农产品，以其果实大、味甜多汁、富有芳香、品质极佳而驰名国内外，有四百多年历史。1988年被省上列为基地建设项目后，发展迅速。1993年补栽1000亩，1.3万株，优种改良嫁接1.6万株，累计达到1.27万亩，17.8万株，产量达到82.5万公斤，产值66万元。早酥梨，自1976年引入我县，初步试植推广。1993年底，早酥梨茎地扩展到7个乡镇，定植0.77万亩、21.68万株，累计达到261万亩，产量达44万公斤，销售收入88万元。花椒，自1988年以来，县上将发展花椒基地作为北部干旱12个乡脱贫致富的主要措施来抓，现已形成一定规模。1993年定植0.21万亩、17万株，全县累计达到0.83万亩、167万株，当年产量5.25万公斤，经济收入105万元。

现任主要领导：

中共东乡县委书记：

马进龙(东乡族)

东乡县人大常委会主任：

马维清　(回族)

东乡县人民政府县长：

马成武　(东乡族)

政协东乡县委员会主席：唐占明

中共东乡县纪律检查委员会书记：

马永魁(东乡族)

(东乡县委政研室)

甘南藏族自治州

中共甘南藏族自治州委书记：

郝洪涛

甘南藏族自治州人大常委会主任：

贡卜扎西(藏族)

甘南藏族自治州人民政府州长：

杨镇刚(藏族)

政协甘南藏族自治州委员会主席：

丹正嘉(藏族)

中共甘南藏族自治州委纪律检查委员会书记：董怀德(藏族)

甘南藏族自治州经济和社会发展概述

【自然概况】甘南藏族自治州是一个以藏族为主体的多民族聚居地区，位于青藏高原与黄土高原结合部的甘肃省西南部地区，地理座标东经100°46′—104°44′，北纬33°06′—36°10′之间。西与青海省黄南、果洛州接壤，南和四川省阿坝州毗邻，东北分别跟本省定西、陇南地区、临夏回族自治区相连。总面积4.5万平方公里，平均海拔3000米以上。地貌为侵蚀构造的高原山地景观，地势西高东低，地形复杂，可分为高山草原区，是天然的优良牧场，草地面积4084.88万亩，亩产鲜草300公斤左右；高山森林区，森林茂密，沟壑纵横，是本省的主要林区，林地面积1326.28万亩，木材蓄积量占全省的45%；丘陵低山区，山峦起伏，沟浅谷宽，是发展饲养业和种植业的主要地区，耕地面积181.49万亩。山脉主要有岷山、西倾山、积石山等，均属昆仑山系，呈西北东南走向，主峰多在3500—5400米之间，本州分属长江、黄河两大流域，主要河流有黄河、白龙江、洮河、大夏河等。气候特点为高寒湿润，气温年较差小、日较差大，雨热同季，垂直气候差异显著等，年平均气温西部1.1—2.6℃，东部3.2—6.7℃，年降雨量450—800毫米。

全州辖7个县，即夏河县、临潭县、卓尼县、舟曲县、迭部、碌曲县、玛曲县，102个乡，6个镇。1993年全州总人口60.73万人，其中藏族29.07万人，回等其他少数民族3.94万人。

【名土特产】河曲马：　亦称乔科马，是我国著名的地方优良马种，以地处黄河首曲部的玛曲曼尔玛、采尔玛、欧拉、阿万仓及河曲马场所产的最为有名，全州约有6万多匹。该种马体形结构匀称，四肢关节筋腱发育壮实。繁殖性能好、遗传性稳定，性情温顺，气质稳静，对高寒多变的气候有极强的适应能力，在海拔4000米以上的高山骑乘，行走自如，特别以善走沼泽草地而著称。

藏　羊：　较著名的品种有：甘加羊，主要分布在夏河县甘加地区，现有约20余万只，其毛光泽好，净毛率高，是优良的地毯用毛；欧拉羊，主要分布在玛曲县，现有30万只左右，其体大、膘肥、肉多，成年羊屠宰率50.18%，胴体重38.18公斤；黑紫羔羊，系山谷型藏羊的一种优良的裘皮用羊，羔皮名贵，产于临潭、卓尼部分地区。

牦　牛　是青藏高原特有的畜

种，对高寒草原有极强的适应性能。全州七县均有分布。其乳营养丰富，肉鲜嫩味美，皮毛骨是重要的工业原料，又是草原上骑乘和驮运的役畜，享有"高原之舟"的美称。

合作猪： 因喜食蕨麻，又称蕨麻猪。是一种高寒农牧区放牧饲养的小型原始猪种，中心产区在夏河、卓尼、碌曲。其鬃长质优，肉质细嫩，瘦肉较多，肥瘦相间，味粘而不腻，除鲜食外，群众多作腊肉，系地方佳肴之中上品。

花 椒： 古称"西固椒"，集中产于舟曲县。该花椒颗粒饱满，色泽鲜艳，香味醇浓，尤以早熟品六月椒—"大红袍"为上品，现有椒树160多万株，年产量6万多公斤。

蕨 麻： 学名鹅绒萎陵菜，紫红色，味甘富含淀粉，可食用和酿酒，人称长寿果。食之甘美异常，实为山珍之属。蕨麻全株可提炼栲胶，根可入药。广布于州内海拔3000米上下的河谷和湿草地。

狼 肚： 学名羊肚菌，属囊菌类。州内卓尼、临潭、舟曲、迭部县针叶林内多有分布。富含蛋白质，又含19种氨基酸和多种维生素，营养丰富，味极佳美，有"素中之荤"的美称，是著名的山珍，又兼药用。

洮 砚： 于卓尼洮砚乡境内，早在秦、汉以来，就已开采制砚。与端、歙二砚齐名，是中国三大名砚之一。

蕨 菜： 除玛曲县外，其余6县均有分布，是滋养食品，含淀粉36.5%。嫩茎盐渍后可长期存放或运输。现出口日本等国。

药 材： 州境内植物药材异常丰富，栽培药材主要是当归(统称岷归)，产量高、品质好。野生药材有党参、贝母、秦艽、黄芪、红芪、丹参、半夏、羌活、甘松等。稀缺名贵药材有冬虫夏草、雪莲、鹿茸、麝香、牛黄等。

【国民经济】1993年全州实现国民生产总值6.5亿元，比上年增长5.2%，国农收入4.4亿元，增长5.3%，实现工农业总产值5.7亿元，增长9.1%。

1.农业：1993年农业总产值35289万元，比上年增长5.9%。粮食总产达91936吨，增长5.3%，油料7990吨，增长13.7%，中药材252吨，水果2406吨。畜牧业各类牲畜年末存栏282.87万头(只)，其中大牲畜106.59万头，绵羊160.77万只，猪15.51万口。总增率23.7%，出栏率27.1%，商品率19.9%。主要畜产品产量：肉29224吨，奶48537吨，羊毛951吨。1993年乡镇企业达9739户，从业人员24572人，完成总产值16960万元，比上年增长24.3%，实现利税2650万元，增长20.08%。农业机械总动力100477千瓦，比上年增长4.2%，农村用电量2351千瓦小时，增长40.7%。

2.工业：全州已建立起拥有食品制造、纺织、皮革制品、印刷、木材采伐、建材、机械、采矿等28个行业的民族工业体系。1993年全州乡及乡以上工业企业已达258家，其中全民所有制企业81家，城镇集体所有制企业134家，工业总产值达21850万元，比上年增长14.6%。全地区主要工业品产量：原煤15200吨，发电量11558万千瓦小时，水泥44700吨，木材23.5万立方米，鞣制皮革(折合牛皮)15330张，洗净毛171.53万公斤，皮鞋9.81万双，地毯6562平方米，乳制品843吨，服装5.64万件，畜肉制品4984吨，黄金223千克，铁合金1492吨。

3.交通、通信：全州通车里程达2870公里，其中国道231.5公里，省道595公里，县乡公路2044公里。全州社会运输换算周转量完成6062.3万吨公里，货运量29.84万吨，客运量56.67万人。现有大小公共汽车站20多处，客运线路44条，5500公里。现有州县邮电局8处，邮电支局、所51处，邮电职工2695人，1993年全年完成邮电业务总量627万元，比上年增长17.6%，市话用户3884户，增加608户，农话用户598户，增加26户邮电通信业务收入553万元，增长20.7%。市话交换机总容量9200门。农牧村投递邮路82条。程控交换设备已在全州采用，公众电报全部由人工改为电传，并直接进入了全国自动交换网，绝大部分县镇实现市话自动化，并开通了国内国际长途直拨电话，合作开通4000门程控电话。

4.商业贸易：全州现有商业机构4466个，职工9235人，1993年实现社会商品零售总额25519万元，比上年增长4.26%。国际贸易，全州出口商品5大类20个品种，主要有粮油、蚕豆、食品、蕨菜、冻牛肉、绵羊肠衣、羊肚菌、骨粒、地毯、大黄、羊皮、兰湿革等，1993年外贸收购总值465.8万元。

5.财政金融：1993年全州财政收入5395万元，比上年增长37.3%，财政支出19098万元。全社会固定资产投资完成14586万元，比上年增长52%，其中国有单位投资11592万元，增长34.3%，集体所有制单位投资452万元，增长11%，居民个人投资2542万元，是上年的4.56倍。有金融机构229个，1993年银行各项存款余额47025万元，比上年增长11.89%，各项贷款余额37366万元，增长12.6%，城乡居民储蓄存款31245万元，增长22.01%。保险系统承保金额53949万元，增长38.4%，全年参加保险的企业219户，参加财产保险的居民家庭3955户，51937人参加了人身保险，全年处理国内财产险赔案540件，支付赔款161万元。

【社会事业】

1.教育：全州有各类学校740所，其中：小学698所，中学29所，中等专业学校4所，高等师范专科学校1所。各级各类学校在校学生67076人，其中：少数民族学生

38688 人，占 58%，藏族学生 31610 人。小学在校学生 50157 人，学龄儿童入学率 76.43%，巩固率 93.27%，毕业率 92.5%。共有教职工 5216 人。至 1993 年底，牧区创办寄宿制学校 56 所，其中：中学 6 所，小学 50 所，学生达 12000 多名。

2. 科技：全州已建立科研机构 7 个，共有职工 206 名，其中研究人员占 54.8%。建立技术推广机构 214 个，专业技术人员 996 人。在科技人员中，获得各种专业任职资格的 8540 人，其中副高以上 220 人，中级 2020 人，初级 6300 人。1993 年，组织鉴定科技成果 23 项，达到国内先进水平有 4 项，省内领先水平 3 项，省内先进水平 6 项，州内领先水平 2 项，州内先进水平 8 项。这些科技成果共投入总经费 91.2 万元，创直接经济效益达 3284.8 万元。

3. 文化：全州共有电影事业机构 72 个，艺术表演团体 5 个，文化馆(站)、艺术馆 37 个，公共图书馆 7 个，广播电台 1 座，有线广播站 7 个，广播人口覆盖率 42.5%，电视收转台(站)205 个，电视人口覆盖率 60.7%。新建甘南电视台正式开播，出版发行藏汉两文报纸 171.6 万份，杂志公开发行 4500 册。

4. 卫生：1993 年全州共有医疗卫生机构 200 个，农牧村村级医疗点 488 个，乡村医生和卫生人员 819 人。年末全州医院病床 1182 张，各类专业卫生技术人员 2234 人，其中：医生 1412 人，护理人员 435 人。儿童计划免疫四苗覆盖率 97.7%。

5. 体育：1993 年，全州运动员在参加全省两个项目的的比赛中，获金牌 1 枚，银牌 3 枚，铜牌 1 枚。群众性体育事业蓬勃发展。30185 名学生达到《国家体育锻炼标准》，达标率 91.6%。

【人民生活】1993 年州、县全部职工人数 33792 人，职工年平均工资 3364 元，扣除价格因素实际增长 3.7%，农牧民家庭人均纯收入 493 元，200 元以下的贫困户由 11493 户下降到 10455 户。城镇待业率 6.5%。城镇居民住房面积增加 35609 平方米，农牧民住房面积增加 156216 平方米。

(甘南藏族自治州委政策研究室)

临潭县经济和社会发展概述

【基本情况】临潭县位于甘肃南部，东距合作 75 公里，总面积 1557.68 平方公里，境内山大沟深，地势自西北向东南倾斜，海拔约在 2209 米至 3926 米之间，多在 2500 米以上，县城海拔 2800 米。气候为高寒半湿润地区，县城平均气温 3.2℃，最冷月(1 月)平均气温－8.4℃、最热月(7 月)平均气温 13.3℃，年降水量在 383 至 668 毫米之间；年日照时数平均为 2242 小时，年相对无霜期 84 天左右，绝对无霜期 9——11 天，风力最大 8 级，灾害性天气主要有冰雹、霜冻、干旱等。

全县现辖 1 镇 18 乡，141 个村委会，723 个村民小组，1 个居委会。截止 1993 年底全县总户数 49475 户 13.8 万人，其中农业户 27545 户，农业人口 12.8 万人，占总人口的 93.9%，少数民族 34599 人，以回族和藏族为主，占全县总人口的 25.1%。

全县现有耕地 26 万亩，森林面积 56 万亩，草地面积 123 万亩。矿藏资源已发现的有锑、石膏等 9 种，有 200 多种中药材和珍贵的动物资源。经济以农业为主，主要作物有小麦、青稞、蚕豆、洋芋、油菜等，主要畜种有牛、马、羊、猪等。工业主要有食品、建材、机械维修、金属制品、电力等。国营商业有民贸、食品等 48 个单位，集体商业主要有供销社、手联社等 108 个单位。

全县现有中学 6 所，在校学生 2777 人；小学 145 所，在校学生 10967 人，适龄儿童入学率 82.52%；全县有教职工 980 人，专任教师 866 人。县内有新华书店 2 个，个体书店 2 个，图书馆 1 个(不包括学校和科研单位图书馆)，文化馆 1 个、乡文化站 10 个；近年来累计修建电视差转台、卫星地面接收站 18 处，覆盖面占总人口的 68.5%，电影录像放映队(室)发展到 34 个。全县有医院 21 所，并设有防疫站、妇幼保健站、计划生育指导站，现有医务人员 276 人，病床 172 张。

县内有干线公路 1 条，全长 121.5 公里，县道 7 条，乡道 4 条，全长 242 公里，全县有大小机动车辆 913 辆(台)，其中汽车 380 辆、拖拉机 533 台、摩托车 126 辆。19 个乡镇 133 个村委会通了汽车。

县内已架通了刘家峡 10 千伏输变电线路 271.6 公里，中型变电所 2 座，容量 5755 千伏安，全县有小水电站 7 座，装机容量 2575 千瓦。全县设有农技推广站、种籽管理站、林业技术工作站、畜牧兽医站、草原站、农业机械推广站、气象站等科技机构，有各级技术员 1094 人。

【经济建设】1993 年，全县在县委、县政府的正确领导下，以十四大精神为指针，坚持改革开放，推进经济社会发展，使各项事业保持了良好的发展势头，完成了确定的计划任务。工农业总产值达到 6102 万元，比上年增长 6.29%，其中农业总产值 4663 万元，增长 6.29%；工业总产值 1439 万元，增长 21.64%；粮食总产 2592 万公斤，增长 4.75%；油料总产 240 万公斤；乡镇企业总产值 2358 万元，比上年增长 26.30%；财政收入完成 204 万元，占年度预算的 122.15%，财政支出 1936 万元，占预算的 105.3%；商业、医药、供销完成国内纯销售 1335.4 万元，占计划的 86.4%，国内纯购进 464 万元，占计划的 136.4%；农牧民人均纯收入达到 370.15 元，比上年增加 23.15 元；人口自然增长率为 13.08‰、出生率19.63‰、计生率68.71%、多胎率6.21%、节育率80%。

农业生产，完成粮食作物整乡承包面积12.7万亩，粮食亩产达到129.5公斤；完成粮油丰产栽培面积7.1万亩；病虫害防治15.4万亩，配方施肥4300亩，良种率达到74%，拌种率81.3%；投入种植业贷款77.6万元，施用化肥1272.1吨，农药9146公斤、农作物粮种6.6万公斤。年末各类牲畜存栏194813头（匹、只），总增率、出栏率、商品率分别达到27.05%、43.70%、31.49%，牧业总产值完成1602.24万元，比上年增长2.45%，占农业总产值的34.36%。林业完成造林面积8564亩，完成林业产值86.74万元。乡镇企业个数达到3139个，从业人员8117人，分别比上年增长17.43%、15.04%。扶贫工作全年实际到位资金546.7万元，先后从9个行业进行了扶持，使300元以下的贫困面由1992年的60%下降到1993年底的57%。

城镇经济把发展社会主义市场作为核心，以贯彻《条例》深化改革为重点，以提高效益为目的，通过深化改革，落实扭亏增盈措施，增收节支等方面的工作效益有了好转。在工业企业方面，认真贯彻落实《条例》和甘肃省《实施办法》，县上放权，企业用权，基本上落实了《条例》规定的十四项主权。全县6户全民所有制独立核算工业企业在深化内部改革、转换经营机制方面，都进行了大胆尝试；在商业企业方面，着重开展了“国有民营”工作；工商企业在认真总结一、二轮承包的经验教训，在承包人选定，指标测算、合作管理、奖惩制度等方面进行了进一步完善，为第三轮承包合同的签订做好了准备工作。同时，增收节支、缓解财政压力。一方面大力“开源”，强化税收征管；另一方面严格“节流”，从严控制一切非生产性经费支出。

基本建设和邮电等事业有了新的发展。基本建设共安排新建、续建项目16项，计划投资388万元，年内累计完成工程量351.5万元，加强了施工管理，保证了工程质量；邮电事业，在县政府和邮电部门筹集资金，对县城电话进行了自动化改造、改善了我县的通讯条件。

【社会事业】教育工作：一是基础教育得到了加强，学龄儿童入学率、巩固率、毕业率分别达到82.5%、91.4%、98%。二是改善了办学条件投入17万元，维修、修建了13所学校的校舍1860平方米，投入4万元，制作配发了584套课桌凳、121套办公桌。三是加强了农村教育附加费的征、管、用工作。四是加强了教师队伍建设。科技工作：结合“星火计划”，利用多种形式举办各类实用技术学习班218期、印发各类科普资料2285份（册）、近54000人（次）群众受到了不同程度的教育。科技队伍不断壮大，社会化服务体系不断健全和完善。医疗卫生事业以预防为主，抓了乡卫生院建设、预防保健、地方病防治、卫生执法、医德医风教育等方面的工作。全县儿童四苗接种率、建卡率、入保率均达到100%。计划生育工作狠抓了节育措施的落实和科学管理等工作。一年中共完成节育手术2542例，其中结扎1351例、放环1069例，分别占年任务的90.10%、42.7%；人流100例、引产22例，完成了人口年度计划。

【十项重点工作】一是新增、恢复水浇地2000亩的任务。年内完成新增水浇地485亩，恢复水浇地846亩，合计完成1331亩。二是以沟坝地为主的“三田”建设2290亩的任务。共完成2033.2亩，占任务的88.7%。三是县城引水工程任务。一期工程已通过初验，已有3000人用上了自来水，二期工作计划已上报有关部门，待投资落实后即可施工。四是县城公路改线任务。积极动员干部职工和广大群众大搞义务劳动，民工建勤，共投入1万多个工日，搬运土方4万多立方米，完成了城关2.62公里的路基改建任务。县政府筹资18万元用于征地搬迁，贷款19.5万元，新建路基护堤1400米。五是青石山电站的前期论证审批和立项任务。已由有关部门负责同志和有关专家对工程现场实地考查论证后，召开了青石山电站可行性咨询评估会，进行了充分的分析评估。六是独山电站增加机组和尾水改造工程任务已完成了初设报告。七是地毯厂的整顿和扩大任务。年初由县政府与有关部门和乡（镇）签订了责任书，解决资金5万元，缓解了资金困难的矛盾。到年底，实有上岗职工790人，占任务总数的60%，完成2.19万平方英尺，占任务总数的78%，实现产值83.4万元。八是奶牛基地建设任务。在五个乡实施，重点在术布、卓洛两乡，共投资53.78万元，两个重点乡安排了152户群众，购进奶牛213头，育肥牛100头。九是市场建设任务。完成了城关新桥市场扩建，新建了新城东街中心商场和新城生猪市场，新辟了店子集贸市场，共11680平方米，建筑面积4050平方米。修建单层铺面300余间，安排摊位300多个，为全县个体私营经济和第三产业发展创造了有利条件。十是企业扭亏增盈任务。经过有关部门和领导及企业职工的努力，使6户全民所有制工业企业中盈利4户，持平1户，亏损1户。医药、物资、煤炭、电影企业中盈利2户，亏损2户。

现任主要领导：

中共临潭县委书记：刘志民

临潭县人大常委会主任：单秉忠

临潭县人民政府县长：刘登福

政协临潭县委员会主席：张福海

中共临潭县纪律检查委员会书记：王录贤

（中共临潭县委调研室：马炳宏）

玛曲县经济和社会发展概述

【**自然概况**】玛曲县位于甘南藏族自治州西南部，地处甘、青、川三省交界地带，地理座标东经 100°46′～102°29′，北纬 33°06′～34°33′。东北与碌曲县接壤，东南与四川若尔盖、阿坝两县相邻，西南、西北分别与青海省久治县、甘德县、玛沁县相连，北邻青海省河南蒙古族自治县。全县地势西北高，东南低，由西北向东南递减。阿尼玛卿山(积石山)横贯全境，其最高峰乔木格日海拔为 4806 米，全县平均海拔为 3700 米。黄河干流由南向东折而向西环绕县境而过，形成了闻名于世的九曲黄河第一弯曲部，境内流程 433 公里，流域面积 8850 平方公里。气候高寒湿润，受大气环流和高原地貌影响，全年无明显四季之分，冷季长，暖季短，秋季降温快，春季升温慢，夏秋多雷雹，无绝对无霜期。年平均气温 1.1℃，平均降雨量为 615.5 毫米，平均日照时数为 2583.9 小时。全县土地总面积为 10190.80 平方公里，约占甘南藏族自治州总面积的四分之一。活野广袤，物产丰富。可利用草场面积为 1288.02 万亩，植被良好，草质丰美，是得天独厚的天然牧场，也是全州主要的畜牧业基地。现辖尼玛、欧拉、曼日玛、采日玛、齐哈玛、阿万仓、木西合、欧拉秀玛 8 个乡，36 个村民委员会，1 个畜牧试验站和 1 个大鹿养殖场。全县共有 6746 户，31259 人。其中：男 16031 人，女 15228 人；藏族 27580 人，汉族 3246 人，回族 393 人，满族 15 人，蒙古族 13 人，撒拉族 8 人，东乡族 2 人，土族 2 人。

【**1993 年经济发展概况**】玛曲县是一个以畜牧业生产为主的纯牧业县，畜牧业经济是全县国民经济的主导和支柱。1993 年，县委、县政府紧紧围绕州委提出的“维护稳定，加快发展，在稳定中求发展，以发展促稳定”的基本思想，坚持以牧为主，牧工商并举和“抓基层，打基础，求发展，奔小康”的工作方针，以市场经济为导向，积极引导牧民群众解放思想，更新观念，狠抓草原围栏、牧民建房、牲畜棚圈、人畜饮水工程、服务体系牧业五大配套建设，全县社会政治安定，经济稳步发展，民族团结和睦，人民安居乐业。1993 年全县工农业总产值完成 8782.8 万元，比上年增长 11.6%。其中牧业总产值完成 6018.8 万元，比上年增加 138.8 万元，增长 2.36%；工业总产值完成 2643 万元，比上年增长 40.8%；农业总产值完成 121 万元。乡镇企业总产值完成 1232 万元，比上年增长 34.3%。财政收入达到 255 万元，比上年增长 11.8%。社会商品销售总额完成 1964 万元，其中零售总额完成 1881 万元；国内商品纯购进完成 1417.2 万元，纯销售完成 1455.6 万元。牧民人均纯收入 902 元，比上年净增 33 元，各类牲畜总增 14.18 万头，总增率为 23.3%；各类牲畜商品数为 11.23 万头，商品率为 18.46%；出栏各类牲畜 14.19 万头，出栏率为 23.31%。年末各类牲畜存栏 60.87 万头。加强牲畜疫病防治和抗灾保畜工作，重点开展“五号病”、牛出败、羊四联等疫病防治和牲畜驱虫工作，各类疫苗注射覆盖密度在 95%以上，牲畜驱虫 35 万头；种植当年生牧草 265 万公斤，割贮饲草 1315 万公斤，加工贮备饲料 25 万公斤。发电量完成 88 万度；水泥预制品完成 1328 平方米；黄金产量完成 200 公斤，比上年增加 150 公斤，增长 300%；铁制小农具、木制家俱、肉、奶等产品产量均比上年有所增加。

【**社会事业**】民族教育：全县共有各级各类学校、幼儿园 17 所，其中：完全中学 2 所，小学 13 所，幼儿园 2 所。共有教职工 222 人。1993 年，玛曲县针对教育工作中存在的入学率较低，学生宿舍等基础设施较差的困难和问题，发起捐资助学活动，全县共有 46 个单位，2017 人积极响应，共捐资 8.98 万元，使全县教育基础设施有了一定的改善，入学率亦有了较大幅度的提高。全年小学毕业 118 名，初中毕业 77 名，高中毕业 17 名；小学招生 313 名，初中招生 110 名，高中招生 44 名；全县共有在校学生 2133 名，其中：高中生 103 名，初中生 311 名，小学生 1719 名，幼儿园及学前班儿童 150 名。入学率为 53.3%，巩固率为 90.3%。

医疗卫生：全县共有县、乡医疗卫生机构 14 个，其中县级 5 个，乡级 9 个；共有业务技术人员 146 人，其中大专以上的 18 人，中专 121 人。1993 年着重开展了医务人员培训和基层医疗队伍建设，使全县医疗水平有所提高，医风医德明显好转，牧民群众看病难的状况有所改善，全县儿童入保率虽没有达到指标，但四苗覆盖率达 96.6%。

交通运输：玛曲县公路交通起步较晚，建政初期与外界无公路相通，物资仍然用牦牛驮运。1956 年修通了郎木寺至玛曲的公路。1976 年实现了乡乡通公路。1986 年建成尕海至玛曲等级公路。现有养护路线 6 条，营业里程 520.78 公里。1993 年采取“民办公助，民工建勤”等办法和措施，加强乡级公路养护，改变了便道公路通车能力低的状况，保证了公路四季畅通。

邮电通信：全县共设邮电营业所 7 个，乡级邮路总长 330 公里，电话线路总长 288(线对)公里，电话总机容量 330 门。1993 年邮电业务总量完成 32.90 万元；通信业务总量完成 23.3 万元；报刊流转额完成 11.78 万元。加快通信自动化建设，多方筹资，加紧施工，使千门长话市话自动电话于年末在我县建成并投入运行，极大地方便了用户，为玛曲的经济建设和对外交往、信息传递发挥了积极的作用。

【城镇建设】玛曲县政府机关驻地美都塘，原为一片荒草滩，建政初期只有几顶帐篷，后修建了一些简易房屋。五十年代末六十年代初，开始修建了一些土木结构的房舍。党的十一届三中全会以后，随着改革的不断深入和发展，玛曲县的市政建设逐步走上了正轨，高层建筑如雨后春笋，在昔日荒原拔地而起，如今已形成东西长2公里，南北宽1.5公里的新型草原城镇，成为全县政治、经济、文化中心。1993年4月成立了玛曲县城乡建设环境保护局。市政建设按照《玛曲县城区总体规划》要求，本着"谁建、谁管、谁受益"的原则，全年投资123.2万元，新建铺面202间，建筑面积5897平方米。集资50万元，修建了占地3500平方米的牧民商贸中心。

【名特土产】牦牛：本地牦牛属高寒草地型，是我国青藏高原的特有牛种。所产肉、乳、皮、毛等畜产品，是牧民群众的主要生产、生活资料。也是骑乘和驮载的重要役畜，素有"高原之舟"的美称，在本县牧业经济中占有重要地位。1993年全县年末牦牛存栏27.95万头。藏羊：本县藏羊是当地牧民群众长期驯养选育而形成的地方原始品种，属草地型藏系绵羊，为肉毛兼用种，是牧民群众的主要生产、生活资料，本县食品公司冷库加工生产的冻绵羊肉和冻去骨绵羊肉，远销省内外和科威特、沙特阿拉伯等国家和地区。羊毛、羊皮、羊肠衣等畜产品，又是重要的轻工原料和出口换汇物资。1993年全县年末藏羊存栏29.05万只。

河曲马：河曲马俗称乔科马，是我国优良的地方马种之一，属挽乘兼用型，平均体高132至143厘米，体长144至151厘米，体重350至370公斤，素以能爬越高山，善走沼泽地而享名于国内外。1993年全县年末河曲马存栏38649匹。

虹鳟鱼：原产于美国加利福尼亚州，是一种驰名世界的名贵鱼种，玛曲鱼场于1974年建立了大水虹鳟鱼养殖场，经过多年试养，使虹鳟鱼在玛曲草原安家，现年产2万公斤以上。

【自然资源】玛曲县幅员辽阔，地形地貌多样，植被类型较多，在诸生态因子的共同作用下，形成了适应高寒气候特征的野生动物区系。境内经济价值较高，属国家保护的珍贵动物有雪豹、猞猁、藏原羚、麝、马鹿、白唇鹿、梅花鹿(饲养)、棕熊、水獭、天鹅、雪鸡、蓝马鸡等10余种。玛曲县是野生中药材的宝库，境内种类繁多的野生药用植物分属39科，100属，151种。分布广，数量多，经济价值高的名贵药材有冬虫夏草、烈香杜鹃、裂叶羌活、水母雪莲花、唐古特大黄、甘青乌头、裸蕊乌头，甘肃贝母、麻花艽、多花黄芪、异叶青兰、狼毒、独一味、甘松香、密花香薷、箭叶橐吾、绿绒蒿等20余种。玛曲县地大物博，矿产资源较为丰富，主要有金、银、铜、铅、钨、煤、泥炭等，开发利用的潜力很大，近几年来，金矿资源的勘测开采已初具规模，1993年生产黄金200公斤，收入960万元。水力、风力、太阳能资源也很丰富，有着广阔的开发前景。

现任主要领导：

中共玛曲县委书记：

旦智塔(藏族)

玛曲县人大常委会主任：

阿　老(藏族)

玛曲县人民政府县长：

尕　考(藏族)

政协玛曲县委员会主席：

德合拉(藏族)

中共玛曲县纪律检查委员会书记：

华尔旦(藏族)

(中共玛曲县委调查室：宁小平　李瑛)

甘肃的自然保护区

甘肃自然保护区现有18个，分为森林植物群落及自然景观和珍奇动物栖息环境两大类。最著名的有陇南地区的白水江自然保护区、河西走廊的祁连山保护区、临夏州的莲花山保护区和武威濒临危绝野生动物保护区等。白水江自然保护区，是国宝大熊猫主要栖息繁殖地之一。这里还生栖着金丝猴、羚羊、绿尾虹雉、毛冠鹿、岩羊、木麝、红腹锦雉、金鸡、兰马鸡、大鲵等我国珍稀动物和一级保护动物。保护区所属铁楼大熊猫繁殖场是一个以科研为主的训养场，现已对外开放，可供游人参观。

甘肃的野生动物资源十分丰富，在上述保护区内及其它一些高山草原上生栖的上千种野生动物中，除原国家禁止捕猎的被保护的稀有珍贵动物外，可以进行有计划地捕猎。因此，甘肃具有开展专项狩猎旅游的条件。

甘肅省石油總公司

總經理：王新權 Director: Wang Xin Quan

簡介

甘肅省石油總公司是我省經營成品石油的大型銷售企業和主渠道。下轄14個地、州、市公司，78個縣、區、市公司，連同直屬各單位共100余戶分支企業，有職工7000余人。全系統有配套齊全的經營設施和銷售網絡，有121座油庫，總庫容量30余萬立方米；有373座加油站，318個經營網點；鐵路自備槽車150余輛，油罐汽車300余輛。固定資產1.8億元。

地址：蘭州市互助巷60號
電話：8464913—344
郵編：730030
Add: No.60 Huzhu lane, Lanzhou
Tel: 464913 · 344
Post Code: 730030

GANSU OIL COMPANY

The company is a large-scale selling enterprise and the main channel managing end-productoil. The company is composed of 14 district, prefecture, city companies and 78 county, region, city companies with each unit directly under the company, total 100 branch enterprises. It hasover 7000 staff and workers. The whole system has the management instruments and sellingnetworks with complete set, 121 oil depots, over 300000 m3 capacity, 373 filling stations, 318management networks, over 150 railway trough vehicles, over 300 oil cars, 1.8 hundred millionyuan flxed assets.

甘肅省石油總公司

總公司領導班子成員 Leading members

甘肃省石油總公司

總公司辦公大樓 Office building

武威油庫

武威油庫 Wuwei oil depot

甘肅省石油總公司

東崗加油站 Donggang filling station

化驗室 Laboratory

微機室 Microcomputer Room

自備鉄路油槽車 Oil trough vehicles provided for itself.

小高爾夫球場 Small golf course

天水自動化油庫 Tianshui automatic oil depot

甘肅省冶金工業廳

GANSU METALLURGICAL INDUSTRY DEPARTMENT

廳長：柳宏克同志 Director: Liu Hong Ke

簡介

甘肅冶金工業從"一五"起步，在36年的歷程中，相繼建成了9戶大中型企業和200余家地縣中小冶金企業。生產的主要產品有：鐵礦石、生鐵、鋼、鋼材、焦炭、鐵合金、炭素制品、鋁、銻、鎂、黃金、耐火材料等二十多種，年總產量可達760多萬噸。全行業共有職工7萬多人。1993年，全省鋼產量首次突破100萬噸，完成工業總產值23億多元，實現利稅7.1億元，創歷史最好水平。冶金工業已成為全省國民經濟的重要支柱產業之一。

地址：蘭州市平涼路186-206號
電話：8417901
郵編：730000
Add: No. 186-206 Pingliang Road, Lanzhou.
Tel: 8417901
Post Coad: 730000

GANSU METALLURGICAL INDUSTRY DEPARTMENT

Gansu metallurgical industry started form the first five-year plan. During the course of 36years, 9 large or medium scale enterprises and over 200 medium or small scale metallurgicalenterprises of the regions, counties have been built in succession. The main products includeiron ore, pig iron, steel, steel material, coke, ferroalloy, carbon products, aluminium, antimony, magnesium, gold, refractory, etc. The annual production capacity reaches over 7600000tons. The department has over 70000 staff and workers. In 1993, The provincial steel outputtopped 1 million tons for the first time. It completed over 23 hundred million yuan of thetotal industry output value, realized 7.1 hundred million yuan profit tax. and was an all- timegood. Metallurgical industry has become one of the key pillar estates for the national economyin Gansu.

廳領導班子在一起研究工作

The department leaders are studying the work.

柳宏克廳長在蘭鋼調查研究

Director Liu Hong Ke is investigating and researching in Lanzhou Steel Plant.

西北鐵合金廠

簡介

西北鉄合金廠是國家大型鉄合金骨干企業之一。現有職工6000余人，擁有固定資產3.34億元，形成鉄合金年生產能力10萬余噸。主要產品硅鉄1986年獲省出口產品自檢認可證書和出口產品商檢權。1989年榮獲國家最高質量獎。此外還生產硅粉、橡塑、水泥、碳化硅、石英砂等產品。

THE NORTHWEST FERROALLOY PLANT

The plant is one of the largest−scale key ferroalloy enterprises in China, with over 60000staff and workers, 3.34 hundred million yuan of fixed assets, the annual production capacity of over 100000 tons ferroalloy Ferrosilicon‥ the main product won the self− examination approvedcertificate of the provincial export products and the commodity inspecting power of export products in 1986. It also won the highest quality prize of the state in 1989. The plant also producessilicon powder, rubber plastic, cement, carborundum, quartz sand, etc.

上圖：工廠全貌鳥瞰
Full view of the Plant
中圖：75%硅鉄榮獲國家優質獎
75% ferrosilicon has won the good quality prize of the state
下圖：生產車間一角
A corner of the workshop

THE NORTHWEST FERROALLOY PLANT

地址：甘肅永登連城鎮
電話：8417596 8418998 (09460) 22502 22602
郵編：730334

Add: Liancheng Town, Yongdeng, Gansu
Tel: 8417596 8418998 (09460) 22502 22602
Post Code: 730334

甘肅省白龍江金礦

BAILONG RIVER GOLD ORE IN GANSU

1991 年 6 月，省委副書記閻海旺視察工作。(左一)為刁家喜礦長。
Vice-secretary Yan Hai Wang of Gansu Province Party Committee was in specting in June, 1991 Director Diao Jia Xi (the left one)

簡介

甘肅省白龍江金礦位于文縣碧口，是我省首家以股份制形式投資建成的國營大型黃金礦。該礦擁有目前我國最大的兩艘 300 升超挖深采金船，總建設規模為年采礦砂量 248 萬立方米，年產黃金 652kg。屬我省"七五"重點建設項目。

地址：甘肅文縣碧口鎮
郵編：746412
電話：3227
電掛：6855

BAILONG RIVER GOLD ORE IN GANSU

The gold ore, lying in Bikou, Wen county, is the first large-scale, state gold ore investedand built in the form of stock in Gansu. The ore now has the two biggest, deeply overdigging, pitting gold ships of 300l in China. The total building scale is the annual pitting ore sandvolume of 2480000 m2, the annual production gold is 652kg. It's the key building item duringthe period of the seventh five-year plan.

Add:Bikou Town, Wen County, Gansu
Post Code:746412
Tel:3227

金錠 Gold tablet

300 升采金船全貌 300l pitting gold ship

甘肅省烟草專賣局(公司)

簡介

甘肅省烟草專賣局(公司)于 1984 年 3 月成立。全省烟草系統現有 4 戶烟廠、10 個分局(公司)、55 個縣(市、區)局(公司),大多數單位的經營設施已基本完成。

省局(公司)成立以來,堅持技術進步, 共投資 19593 萬元,進行了大規模的技術改造,使全省卷烟生產能力由原來的 20 萬箱擴大到 50 萬箱。

同時注重調整產品結構,全省卷烟產品初步形成了等級、品種、類型、規格比較齊全,結構趨于合理的新局面。目前,全省共生產 44 個牌號的卷烟,6 個牌號的雪茄烟。烤烟型甲級烟嘴海洋、奔馬,乙級烟嘴蘭州、鳳壺等 4 個牌號被評為省優產品。

GANSU TOBACCO MONOPOLY BUREAU

The bureau, set up in March, 1984, now has 4 tobacco plants, 10 branch bureaus, 55 county (city, region) bureaus. The management equipments of most units have basically completed.

Since setting up, the company has carried out a large-scale technical reform with 195. 93 million yuan assets. The capacity producing cigarettes has enlarged from 200000 boxes to 500000 boxes. Meanwhile the company pays attention to adjust product structure, and the cigarette products has preliminary formed a new prospect of reasonable structure and full grades, kinds, types and standards. Now the bureau total produces 44 brands of cigarettes, 6 brands of cigars. Flue-cured tobacco of Grade A cigarette holder Haiyang and Benma and Grade B cigarette holder Lanzhou and Fenghu have been elected as the provincial good products.

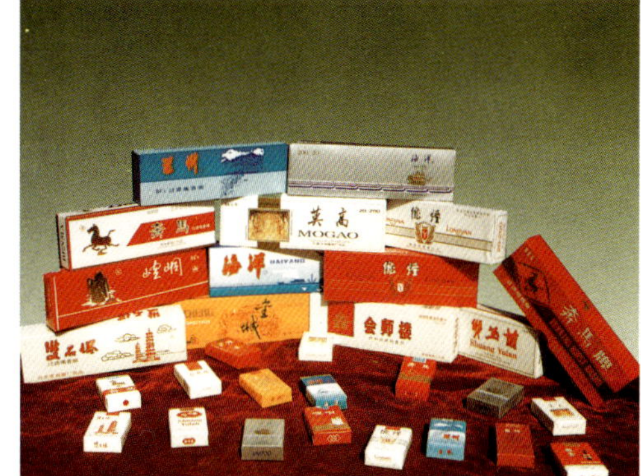

甘肅省主要卷烟產品 Main cigarette products in Gansu

地址: 蘭州市東崗西路 229 號
電話: 8881311-2908
郵編: 730000
Add:No.229, Donggang West Road, Lanzhou
Tel: 8881311· 2908
Post Code: 730000

蘭州卷烟廠引進的英國 MOLINS 公司生產的"長城"卷接機組

"The Great Wall" rolling and joining unit imported from MOLINS company of the UnitedStates

甘肅省烟草專賣局(公司)辦公大樓 Office Building

GANSU TOBACCO MONOPOLY BUREAU

GANSU TAX BUREAU

局領導班子研究稅務工作 The bureau is studying tax work.

甘肅省稅務局

簡介

甘肅省稅務局是管理全省稅收事業的職能部門，受甘肅省人民政府和國家稅務總局的雙重領導，負責全省稅收政策的解釋、稅政業務及全省國營、集體、私營企業、外資企業、個體工商業戶的稅款征收管理等工作。下設流轉稅處、地方稅處、所得稅處、征管處、稽查處、出口退稅處、涉外稅處、計會處、辦公室、人事處、政策研究室、稅務檢察室等處室及系統工會、機關黨委等職能部門。稅務系統實行省以下垂直管理，全省稅務部門共有 12000 多名干部職工，下設 1 所稅務學校，14 個地州市稅務局，86 個縣市區稅務局，900 多個基層稅務所、隊、站。

地址：蘭州市皋蘭路 76 號（統辦 3 號樓）
電話：8415318
郵編：730000
Add: No.76 Gaolan Road, Lanzhou.
Tel: 8415318
Post Code: 730000

GANSU TAX BUREAU

The bureau is the function department managing the provincial tax undertakens. Under theleadership of Gansu People's Government and China Tax Bureau, it is in charge of the provincialtax policy explanation, tax policy business, managing taxation imposed of state, collective, private enterprises, foreign fund enterprises, individual industry and commerce consumers. Thebureau includes Circulation tax department, Local tax department, Income tax department, Collecting and managing department, Checking department, Export drawback department, Foreignnational tax department, Plan and accounting department, Office, Personnel division, Policyresearch office, Tax inspected office, System trade union, Office Party committee, etc. The taxsystem carries out verticle management under the province. The provincial tax department hasover 12000 cadres and workers, one tax college, 14 region, prefecture, city tax bureaus, 86county, city, district tax bureaus, over 900 basic tax institutions, teams and stations.

1993年9月被國家稅務局、人事部授予"全國稅務系統先進集體"

In Sep. 1993, the bureau was elected as advanced collective of China Tax System by ChinaTax Bureau and Personnel Division

蘭州市稅務局城關一分局東部市場稅務所

East Market Tax Institution of Lanzhou Chengguan Tax Branch.

基層稅務所納稅大廳

Pay taxes hall of the basic tax institutions.

我省各級稅務部門始終將促產增收、培養稅源列為重要議事日程，積極開展各種形式的"支、幫、促"活動。圖為定西地區稅務局領導在甘肅省無紡織地毯廠了解機制地毯的生產與管理情況。

Promoting production, increasing income, training tax source are all along placed on theimportant agenda by the various-grade tax departments in Gansu. They actively develop variousactivities of supporting, helping, promoting. The picture is that Dingxi Tax Bureau leaders areunderstanding the productive and managing conditions of machine-made carpets in Gansu Adhesive-Bonded Carpet Works.

《甘肅稅務》是由甘肅省稅務局、甘肅省稅務學會聯合主辦的稅務專業性雜志。1992 年 7 月，在由甘肅省新聞出版局、甘肅省出版工作者協會組織的首屆內部優秀期刊評選活動中，獲得"優秀內部期刊獎"。現發行量已居全省內刊之首，在指導全省稅收工作、傳播稅法知識等方面發揮了積極作用。

Gansu Tax is a specialized tax magazine sponsored by Gansu Tax Bureau and Gansu TaxInstitute. It won Excellent Internal Periodical Prize of the first internal excellentperiodical choosing activity organized by Gansu News Publishing Bureau and Gansu PublishingWorkers Society in July, 1992. The publishing volume is the first of Gansu internal publication. It has played the active role of guiding the provincial tax work and spreading tax policyknowledges.

甘肅省建築工程總公司

GANSU CONSTRUCTION ENGINEERING CORPORATION

簡介

甘肅省建築工程總公司系由原建築工程部第七工程局和原甘肅省建築工程局幾經遷沿合并而成，第二名稱為甘肅華隴建築總公司。是甘肅省規模最大的國有建築施工企業。經營範圍為建築安裝施工，房地產開發，建築機械，建築制品，建築材料，高新技術開發以及商業、貿易等。現有各類大中型企業和事業單位54家，其中具有國家一級資質的建築安裝施工企業13家，中型工業、運輸、供銷、商貿企業8家，房地產開發、工程承包、技術開發企業9家，外經企業和境外企業9家，并設有與施工生產相配套的科研、設計、大中專院校、職工醫院和生產服務體系。職工5萬多人，各類專業人員8000多人，高級專業技術人員300多人。年總產值10億元，竣工面積100多萬平方米。

本公司堅持"建築、工業、貿易、房地產開發一體化，省內、省外、國外一體化，施工總承包、項目總承包和設計、施工、設備供應總承包一體化"的經營方針，技術力量雄厚，施工經驗豐富，機械裝備先進，服務體系齊全。組建四十多年來轉戰東北、華東、華北、中南和西北地區，承建過大批重點工程和大中型項目，涉及石油、化工、機械、冶金、電力、電子、輕工、紡織、建材、核工業、兵器、航空、航天、醫藥、食品、旅游、商業、教育、衛生、科研等各行各業。先後參與施工或建成蘭州化學工業公司、蘭州煉油化工總廠、蘭州鋁廠、蘭州鋼廠、蘭州石油化工機器廠、白銀銀光廠、四0四廠、五0四廠、酒泉衛星發射中心、甘肅光學儀器廠、劉家峽化肥廠、連城電廠、蘭州第二熱電廠、靖遠電廠、蘭州煤制氣廠、蘭州中川飛機場、蘭州電訊樞紐、甘肅省人民政府大樓、蘭州飯店、金城賓館、敦煌賓館、甘肅省博物館、蘭州體育館、蘭州大學、西北師範大學、西北民族學院、甘肅農業大學、青海拖拉機廠、寧夏化工廠、西北軸承廠、拉薩啤酒廠、上海教育會堂等數百個大型項目。現在施工隊伍遍布全省各地，并在陝西、青海、寧夏、河南、貴陽、上海、深圳、珠海、海南、廈門等省市承建工程和設立分支機構。

總經理：崔志英
Manager: Cui Zhi Ying

GANSU CONSTRUCTION ENGINEERING CORPORATION

Gansu Construction Engineering Corporation (GCEC), grew out of the former No.7 ConstructionEngineering Bureau of The Ministry of Construction and Gansu Construction Engineering Bureau, named Gansu Hualong Construction Corporation as well, is the largest state-owned constructionenterprise in Gansu province. GCEC's business scope is: construction and installation, development of real estate, construction machinery, building products and building materials, development of high technology, commerce and trade. GCEC has 54 large and medium sizeenterprises and institutions of various kinds, including 13 construction and installationenterprises with the first-grade qualifications, 8 of industries of medium size, transportations, supply and sales, business and trades, 9 of development of real estate, construction projectscontracting, development of high technologies, 1 foreigh-oriented and 8 enterprises abroad withnecessary scientific research & design institutions, a college and a secondary school, ahospital and other service facilities for construction. GCEC possesses 50000 employees, including 8000 technical and managerial personnel, 300 senior engineers. Its annual output is1 billion yuan (RMB) of value and completed areas of more than 1 million square metres.

GCEC, with large technical force, rich experience and fully equipped services, carrys thebusiness policies of unified construction industry, trade and development of real estate, ofunified construction projects contracting design, construction and equipment supply. For more than 40 years, GCEC has undertaken many large, medium sized key projects in thefields of petroleum, chemical machinery, metallurgy, power, electronic, light industry, textile, building materials, nuclear industry, weaponry, aviation, space, medicine, food, tour, commerce, education, sanitary, scientific research in northeast China, east China, north China southchina and northwest China. It has completed hundreds of large projects, such as: LanzhouChemical Industry Corporartion, Lanzhou Oil Refinery, Lanzhou Aluminium Plant, Lanzhou SteelPlant, Lanzhou Petrochemical Machinery Works, Lanzhou General Machinery Works, Lanzhou WaterWorks, Lanzhou Plant Glass Factory, Lanzhou Third Woollen Textile Mill, The Northwest SyntheticPharmacentic Factory, Baiyin Yinguang Chemical Works, No. 404 Works, No. 504 Works, JiuquanArtificial Sattelite Launching Centre, Gansu Optical Instrument Works, Liujiaxia NitrogenFertilizer Factory, Liancheng Power Plant, Lanzhou Second Power Plant, Jingyuan Power Plant, Lanzhou Coal Gas Works, Lanzhou Zhongchuan Airport, Lanzhou Telecommunication Hub, The OfficeBuilding of Gansu People's Government, Lanzhou Hotel, Jincheng Hotel, Dunhuang Hotel, GansuMusenum, Lanzhou Gymnasium, Lanzhou University, Northwestern Teachers' University, NorthwesternNational Minority College, Gansu Agriculture University, Qinghai Tractor Factory, NingxiaChemical Works, The Northwestern Bearing Factory, Lasa Brewery, Shanghai Educational Hall, etc. GCEC now can be found all over Gansu province, it is undertaking projects as well is theprovinces and cities of Shanxi, Qinghai, Ningxia, Henan, Hainan, Guiyang , Shanghai, Shenzhen, Zhuhai, and Xiamen where branches have been established.

甘肅省建築工程總公司

蘭州大廈 Lanzhou Mansion

多哥人民聯盟之家工程榮獲的國際墨丘利和平金像獎獎杯

The project of Togo People's Alliance Home won the cup of International Moqiuli Peace GoldStatue Prize.

蘭州電訊樞紐 Lanzhou telecommunication hub

GANSU CONSTRUCTION ENGINEERING CORPORATION

津巴布韋國家體育場 The national stadium of Zimbabwe

地址：中國蘭州市西津東路 253 號 Add: No. 253 Xijin East Road, Lanzhou China.
郵編：730050 Post Code: 730050
電話：(0931) 2336981 Tel: (0931) 2336981
傳真：(0931) 2338644 Fax: (0931) 2338644

加固後的麥積山北崖棧道
North cliff plank road of Maiji Mountains after reinforced

敦煌機場候機樓
Waiting Building of Dunhuang Airport

甘肅省第一安裝工程公司

THE FIRST INSTALLATION ENGINEERING COMPANG IN GANSU

甘肅省第一安裝工程公司經理：柏成盛
Manager: Bai Cheng Sheng

地址：蘭州市合水東路 37 號
郵編：730060
電話：(0931) 7556252
Add: No. 37 Heshui East Road, Lanzhou
Post Code: 730060
Tel: (0931) 7556252

簡介

甘肅省第一安裝工程公司是國家一級資質施工企業，現隸屬甘肅省建總公司。組建四十多年來，先後承擔石油、化工、冶金、機械、建材、水電、輕紡、食品、國防、科研等行業的國家和省重點大中型工程項目 40 多個。

現有職工 2800 多名，其中施工生產技術工人 2300 多名，各類技術人員 289 人(高級工程師 12 人，工程師 51 人，會計師 14 人，經濟師 28 人)。擁有固定資產凈值 1596 萬元，流動資金 769 萬元。各類施工機械及檢測設備 800 臺。技術裝備率 2408 元／人。安裝施工基本實現機械化作業。施工技術實力雄厚，現具有省勞動局頒發的 B 級鍋爐安裝和修理改造許可證、ⅠⅡ類壓力容器制作安裝許可證，建設部頒發的客貨電梯安裝維修許可證。公司下屬八個綜合施工工程處，以及機械廠、動力站、試驗調整隊等 11 個生產單位，可承擔各類大中型工業生產裝置和高級民用工程的成套設備安裝工程。年建安產值 1 億元以上。

THE FIRST INSTALLATION ENGINEERING COMPANG IN GANSU

The company, under the command of Gansu Construction Company, is the first-classqualifications and quality construction enterprise in China. For 40 years, it has undertakenover 40 large-medium scale key engineering items in the state and Gansu province such as oil, chemical industry, metallurgy, machinery, building materials, water and electron, light. industry and textile, food, national defence, scientifical research, etc.

Now, it has over 2800 staff and workers among whom there are over 2300 technical workers ofconstruction and production and 289 various specialized technical personnel including 12 seniorengineers, 51 engineers, 14 accounters, 28 economists with 15. 96 million yuan net value offixed assets, 7.69 million yuan circulating fund, 800 various construction machineries andinspection equipments. The rate of technical installation is 2408 yuan／person. Its installationconstruction has basically accomplished mechanical operation. The construction skill is withstrong strength. Now it has the licences of Grade B boiler installation and rebuilding and type Ⅰ Ⅱ pressure containers making and installation issued by Gansu Labour Bureau, the licence ofpassenger-cargo lifts installation and repairing. The company includes 8 synthetic constructionengineering departments, as well as 11 productive units such as the Machinery Factory, thePower Station, the Test and Adjustment Team, etc. They can undertaken various large-medium scaleindustrial production installation and complete sets of equipment installation works of seniorcivil engineering. The annual production value of building and installation is over 1 hundredmillion yuan.

甘肅省第一安裝工程公司

八0五廠電站機組
The electric station unit of Factory No. 805.

八0五廠 TDI 工程氣體凈化裝置
TDI works gas purifying installation of Factory No. 805.

四零四廠鈦白粉工程轉窰
The titanium white project rotary kiln of Factory No, 404.

甘肅省商檢局

簡介

中華人民共和國甘肅進出口商品檢驗局(簡稱甘肅商檢局)成立于 1957 年，它是中華人民共和國國家進出口商品檢驗局(簡稱國家商檢局)設立在甘肅省的直屬商檢機構，負責全省進出口商品的檢驗、監管和鑒定業務。

甘肅商檢局內設 11 個處(室)，下屬天水、平凉、酒泉 3 個地(市)商檢局，現有職工 140 多名，其中具有大學、大專、中專學歷和授于各類專業技術職稱的人員分別占職工總人數的 87%和 72%以上，形成了一支訓練有素的多學科、多門類、多層次的技術隊伍。局系統有二級實驗室 2 個，三級實驗室 6 個，配有液相色譜、氣相色譜、原子吸收、紫外分光光度計等一批較先進的儀器設備 100 多臺(件)。能夠獨立、準確、快速地完成本省進出口商品檢驗和社會委托的檢驗鑒定業務。適應外貿事業發展的需要。局內還設有圖書資料室，收藏國內外各類檢驗標準 1960 多冊，資料 320 多冊，圖書 950 多冊，期刊 1080 多冊，可以保證檢驗、鑒定工作的需要。

地址：蘭州市城關區大雁灘 75—1 號
郵編：730000
電話：8414092
傳真：(0931) 8414064
電掛：2914

甘肅商檢局局長：陳　鵬
Director: Chen Peng

GANSU COMMODITY INSPECTION BUREAU

Gansu Import and Export Commodity Inspection Bureau of the People's Republic of China, setup in 1957, is the commodity unit in Gansu directly under the State Import and Export CommodityInspection Bureau. It is in charge of inspection, control and appraisal of import and exportcommodity in Gansu.

The bureau is composed of 11 offices, 3 city commodity inspection bureaus of Tianshui, Pingliang, Jiuquan, with over 140 staff and workers, among whom the staff with diploma and thetitle of a technical separately makes up 87 and 72 per cent of the total personnel. It hasformed a well-trained technology team with various subjects, various department and variousadministrative levels. The bureau has two second- class laboratories, six third- classlaboratories with over 100 advanced equipments of liquid chromatogram, gas chromatogram, atomabsorption, etc. It can independently, exactly, quickly complete import and export commodityinspection and inspection, appraisal business trusted by society in Gansu, can suit the needsof foreign trade cause devoloping. It also has books and reference room with over 1960 variousinspection standard books at home and abroad, 320 reference books, 950 books, 1080 periodicals. and can ensure the needs of inspection and appraisal.

Add : No.75--1 Dayantan,Chengguan, Lanzhou
Post Code: 730000
Tel: 8414092
Fax: (0931) 8414064
Cable: 2914

GANSU COMMODITY INSPECTION BUREAU

二級農副食品實驗室
Second-class farming and side-line food laboratory

二級金屬化礦實驗室
Second-class metal chemistry ore laboratory

商檢人員檢驗長風牌出口電冰箱
The staff is inspecting Changfen refrigerator for export.

甘肅省郵電管理局

GANSU POST AND TELECOMMUNICATIONS MANAGEMENT OFFICE

局長：姚學禮　Director: Yao Xue Li

簡介

改革開放以來，甘肅郵電部門在郵電部和省委、省政府的領導下，以發展通信為中心，堅持改革開放，加快通信建設，在困難的環境和條件下，奮發進取，努力工作，在物質文明和精神文明建設中取得了顯著的成績，開創了郵電通信事業加快發展的新局面。

到目前為止，一個以蘭州為中心，聯結全省城鄉，溝通國內外的郵電通信網逐步形成，為甘肅的經濟和社會發展，做出了應有的貢獻。

GANSU POST AND TELECOMMUNICATIONS MANAGEMENT OFFICE

Under the Leadership of Posts and Telecommunications Ministry, Gansu Provicial Committeeand Provicial Government, the office sets the heart of developing communication aboveeverything else, insists on reform and open, speeds up signal construction since reform andopen. Under the difficult environment and conditions, the office exerts itsself and keepsforging ahead, works hard. In the construction of material and culture civilization, the officeachieves remarkable results and initiates a new aspect of speeding up post andtelecommunication business development.

By now, a post and telecommunication network of setting the centre in Lanzhou, joining theprovincial town and country, linking up home and abroad, has generally formed. It has made adue contribution for Gansu economical and social development.

特快專遞以優化的作業組織，由專人、專車傳遞郵件，其最大特點是：迅速、安全、準確。

Express transmitting delivers post with special person, special car. Its supremecharacteristics is quick, safe and exact.

蘭州郵政樞紐樓

Lanzhou postal hub building

地址：蘭州市平涼路 371 號
電話：8417990
郵編：730000
Add: No.371 Pingliang Road, Lanzhou
Tel:8417990

全省有 283 處郵電局(所)受理個人人民幣儲蓄業務。圖爲郵政儲蓄營業人員上門服務。
283 post offices in Gansu accept adividual RMB saving business The office business persons service to the doorstep

草原鴻雁
Grassland swan goose

商業信函處理中心
The commercial letter handling centre

蘭州電信樞紐樓
Lanzhou post and telecommunication hub building

GANSU POST AND TELECOMMUNICATIONS MANAGEMENT OFFICE

移動電話具有機動、靈活、使用方便等特點。類型：車載式、便携式、手提式，已開通移動電話業務的有蘭州市、白銀市
Moving telephone has the characteristics of motorized, elastic, convenient, etc. Thekinds include car-load type, convenient-carry type and hand-carry type. Lanzhou and Baiyin havehad moving telephone business.

"127"自動無綫尋呼臺機房
"127" automatic wireless seeking call generator

無綫尋呼機，又稱 BP 機，可分數字和漢字顯示兩種，既可人工呼叫又可自動尋呼，是手持移動電話機的好伴侶。
Wireless seeking call trigger, also named BP trigger, divided into two kinds of figure andChinese character shows, not only man-made call, but also automatic seeking call, is a goodpartner of hand-moving telephone.

程控電話除用于一般電話通信外，還有多種服務性功能。如：縮位撥號 熱綫服務 呼叫等待 三方通話 轉移呼叫 鬧鐘服務 呼出限制 遇忙回叫 免打擾服務 缺席用戶服務 追查惡意呼叫圖為程控電話機房。
Programme control telephone not only uses in general telephone signal, but also has many servicefunctions such as reduced-place dialing number, heat ray service, call waiting, tripartiteconversation, transferation call, clock service, calling out linit, meeting busy and recalling, not troubled service, absent consumer service, tracing malice call The picture is Programme control telephone generator

甘肅省郵電管理局

少數民族地區電信通信能力有了較大增強

The post–telecommunication signal capacity has cosiderably strengthen in the minoritynationality areas.

喜讀禮儀電報

Happily reading rite telegram

一卡在手，撥通全球。圖爲 使用街頭磁卡電話

A card in hand, putting through all over the world

The above picture is using magnet card telephone in the street

公用分組交換數據網(CHINAPAC)是郵電部門經營和管理的全國性分組交換數據網絡。該網具有高速率、高質量、接續時間短、響應快等特點。爲實現不同速率、不同類型終端之間的互通及數據庫資源共享提供高質量、低成本的國際及國內數據通信服務。

Public group exchange data network (CHINAPAC) is the state group exchange data networkmanaged and controlled by Ministry of Posts and Telecommunication

The network has the characteristics of high speed rate, high quality, short putting throughand conversation time, quick respond, etc. It provides international and internal data signelservice of high quality and low cost in order to realize conversing each other between thedifferent speed rate and types ends, and enjoy date base resources.

鐵道部第一勘測設計院

簡介

鐵道部第一勘測設計院是國家大型綜合性勘測設計單位，成立于 1953 年 1 月 1 日。該院持有國家頒發的工程勘察甲級證書、工程設計甲級證書、環境影響評價甲級證書、工程建設監理甲級證書和工程總承包甲級資格證書、擁有外經貿部批準的對外經濟技術合作權。主要從事工程勘察設計、技術咨詢、工程總承包和工程建設監理業務。

40 多年來，該院在國內 20 多個省、市、自治區承擔了鉄路工程、公路工程、市政工程、岩土工程、環境工程、機電工程、通信工程和地鉄輕軌，城市規劃、工業與民用建築、橋梁隧道、道路與立交、采暖通風、燃氣熱力、計算機與自動控制、有綫電視等各類工程項目的測繪、勘探、咨詢、設計、監理和總承包業務。

該院擁有職工近 6500 人，其中，工程技術人員 3400 多名，含高級工程師 579 名，工程師、經濟師 1200 多名。設有 40 多個專業，技術力量雄厚。該院在烏魯木齊、西寧、蘭州、西安、上海、廈門、太原、海口、北海等市設置 9 個分院，在廣州、南京、濟南、北京、銀川、塔城、南陽等地設立 9 個勘測設計處（辦事處）。

該院注冊資金 1.6 億元，實力雄厚，裝備齊全，技術先進。擁有 GPS 衛星定位儀、全站型速測儀、數字解析攝影測量系統、大地電磁測深儀、計算機網絡工作站等高新技術裝備及其他設備 3000 臺件。目前，主要勘測設計生產環節的硬件環境達到國際八十年代末期水平，設計 CAD 成圖率已達 40%以上。

該院歷年來獲得國家、省、部級優秀勘察設計、標準設計、計算機軟件項目獎和科技進步獎 75 項。1992 年，該院被評為中國勘察設計單位綜合實力百強第二十七名。

地址：甘肅省蘭州市和政路 75 號
郵編：730000
電話：8825673
傳真：8829070

THE FIRST PROSPECTING AND DESIGNING INSTITUTE OF THE RAILWRY MINISTRY

The institute, set up on Jan. 1, 1953, is a large-scale, synthetic, state prospectingand designing unit with the state project prospecting certificate of Grade A, project designcertificate of Grade A, environment influence appraising certificate of Grade A, projectconstruction control certificate of Grade A, project contracting certificate of Grade A, foreign economic and technical cooperation power of the Foreign Economic and Trade Department. The institute mainly undertakes project prospecting and designing, technical consultation, project contracting, project construction control business.

The institute has undertaken mapping, prospecting, consulting, designing, controlling andcontracting of railway projects, highway projects municipal works, rock works, environmentprojects, mechanical and eletric works, communication works, underground railway, city plan, industrial and civil construction, bridges and tunnels, highway and crossing, heating andventilation, burning gas and heating power, computers and automatic control, wire televisions, etc.

The institute has near 6500 staff and workers among whom there are over 3400 engineeringtechnicians including 579 senior engineers, over 1200 engineers and economists with more than 40specialities, strong technical power. The institute has set up 9 parts in Wulumuqi, Xinin, Lanzhou, Xian Shanghai, Xiamen, Taiyuan, Haikou, Beihai, etc. 9 prospecting and designingoffices in Guangzhou, Nanjing, Jinan, Beijing, Yinchuan, Tacheng, Nanyang, etc.

The institute has registered funds of 1.6 hundred million yuan with strong strength,complete equipment,advanced technology,3000 senior and new technical equipments and otherequipments of GPS satellite positioner, rapid surveying equipment of complete station numeralanalysis, film and messure system, earth electromagnetism fathometer, the work station ofcomputer networks. Now, the hardware envioronment of mainly prospecting, designing andproduction link has reached the international level of the end of the eighties. The existingmaps rate of designing CAD has reached over to 40 percent.

The institute has won 75 excellent prospecting and designing, standard design, computersoftware item prizes and scientific and technical progress prizes. In 1992, the insititute waselected as the twenty-seventh of hundred synthetic force of China Prospecting and DesigningUnites.

Add: No.75 Hezheng Road, Lanzhou, Gansu
Post Code: 730000
Tel: 8825673
Fax: 8829070

通過騰格里大沙漠邊緣的包蘭鉄路，幾十年來，治沙成績顯著，多次得到鉄道部和國家獎勵，而且信譽世界，被稱為世界第一流治沙工程。

Baolan Railway through the side of the Tenggeli Desert has been awarded by the RailwayMinistry and China for its harnessing sand well and has been the first–class harnessing worksin the world

我國西北地區最大的鉄路編組站一蘭州西編組站 獲國家優秀設計獎

Lanzhou West Marshalling sta-·tion·· the largest marshalling station in the Northwest, China, has won the state, excellent design prize.

雄據南京鬧市區的張府園小區高層建築群，獲鉄道部優秀設計獎、江蘇省優質工程獎

The small district, high–storey building groups of Zhangfuyuan in Nanjing busy streets haswon the excellent design prize of the Railway Ministry excellent quality works prize ofJiangshu.

鐵道部第一勘測設計院

阿拉山口國境站站房風格別致，氣度不凡，充分體現了莊重雄偉的"國門"形象，獲鉄道部QC小組成果一等獎，新疆自治區優秀設計二等獎。國境站綜合設計(含站房)獲新疆自治區優秀設計一等獎及國家優秀設計銀質獎。

The station house of Alashankou boundary station with unique style and no ordinary bearing, fully embodies the image of the serious and grand "State Gate". It has won the first prize, for QC group achievement of the Railway Ministry the second prize for Xinjiang excellentdesign. The synthetic design of the boundary station has won the first prize for Xinjiangexcellent design and the silver prize for the state excellent design.

隴海鉄路寶天段葡萄園渭河特大橋，全長1831.8米，避免了滑坡等灾害，保證了隴海綫的暢通無阻。同類型的新(鄉)荷(澤)鉄路跨京廣綫立交特大橋獲國家優質工程銀質獎。

The Putaoyuan Weihete Bridge of Baotian section of Longhai railway with 1831. 8m length, avoids the calamity of landslip, etc. ensures Longhai line opening. The Xinhe

寶蘭、寶成綫采用框架式棚洞，解决了坡面流泥落石及塌方的灾害。Baolan, Baocheng Lines uses frame shed-hole, solves the diseases of slope shifting putly, dropping stones and landslip.

電算技術廣泛應用于各類工程的勘測設計和管理中，近年來研制開發的軟件，有15項獲部、院級科技進步獎，2項獲國家優秀軟件二等獎。

Electronic computers are widely applied in prospecting, designing and managing of variousworks. The softwares have been developed in recent years. 15 of them have won the Ministry and. Institute prizes for scientific and technical progress. 2 of them has won the second prizefor the state excellent softwares.

GPS衛星定位儀，全站型速測儀，大地電磁測深儀等一大批具有世界先進水平的新設備、新技術廣泛應用于勘測設計中

A great of new equipments and new technology, such as GPS satellite positioner, rapidsurveying equipment of complete station, earth electromagnetism fathometer with the worldadvanced level, are widely applied in prospecting and designing.

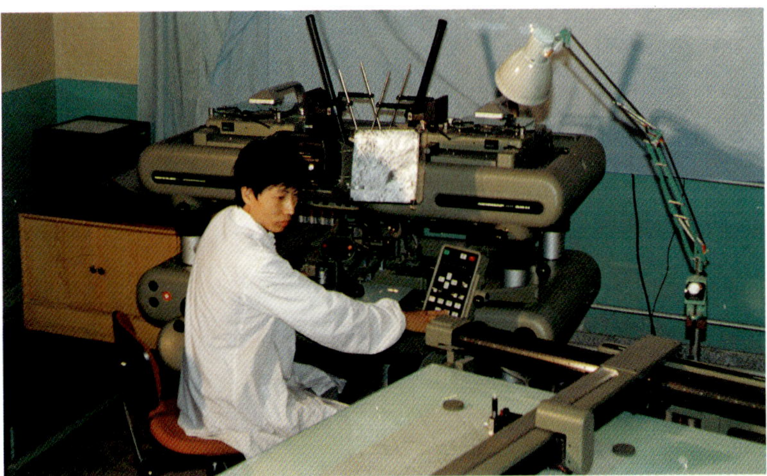

先進的BC2解析測圖儀，配合航測遙感進行數字圖像處理。

Advanced BC2 analysis mapping equipment is engaging in numeral picture handled supportingaerial survey and remote sensing.

按“整舊如舊”的原則，對舉世聞名的敦煌莫高窟進行了加固工程設計。獲甘肅省優秀設計獎

According to the principle of ″Repairing it old and making it as good as old ″, theinsititute engaged in reinforcing works design for Dunhuang Mogao Grottoes·· be famous for theworld. The design has won the

甘肅省煤炭工業總公司

甘肅省煤炭工業局

省煤炭工業局局長、省煤炭工業總公司經理苗宗杰。

Director and manager Miao Zong Jie is working

簡介

甘肅省煤炭工業局，是省人民政府的煤炭工業主管部門，對全省煤炭行業實行統一歸口管理，對全省煤炭工業實施“規劃、協調、監督、服務”的職責。甘肅省煤炭工業總公司，是全民所有制的企業組織，為獨立核算的經濟實體單位，現有直屬企事業單位 24 個，職工 7 萬多人。經過 40 多年的開發建設，甘肅煤炭工業有了很大發展，已累計生產原煤 2 億多噸，為全省國民經濟的發展做出了巨大貢獻。

地址：蘭州市天水路 219 號
電話：8822888
郵編：730000

GANSU COAL INDUSTRY BUREAU
GANSU COAL INDUSTRY COMPANY

The bureau is in charge of the coal industry of Gansu People's Government, practises unitedmanagement of Gansu coal trade, carries out the duty of "Plan, coordination, supervise, service" to Gansu coal industry. The company is a state-owned enterprise organization, aneconomic entity unit of independent accounting with 24 enterprises and institutions, over 70000 staff and workers. After 40 years of developing and building, Gansu coal industry has a great development, total produced over 2 hundred millon tons of raw coal, made a great contribution to Gansu national economy.

Add: No. 219 Tianshui Road, Lanzhou
Tel:8822888
Post Code:730000

源源不斷的“烏金”運出礦區。
"Black Gold" flows out of the mining area in a steady stream.

省煤炭工業局黨委書記、省煤炭工業總公司黨委書記張景春同志在礦井下與工人親切交談。Party secretary Zhang Jing Chun is talking with the workers in the mine.

礦區全景
The full view of the mine

煤礦井下機械化采煤的情景
The view of mechanical coal mining in the mine

甘肅省交通廳

省交通廳廳長胡國斌同志在中川高速公路檢查施工情況
The director Hu Guo Bin of Gansu Traffic Office is checking the construction inZhongchuan Speed Highway

概 況

甘肅省交通廳是省政府對全省公路、水路交通實行組織領導和宏觀調控，歸口進行行業管理的職能部門。主要負責：擬定全省公路、水路交通運輸行業發展戰略和方針、政策，編制全省公路、水路交通運輸中遠期發展規劃；全省公路、主要汽車站點、重點港口碼頭等基本建設和技術改造項目；全省公路的養護與管理及航道、航標、港口設施的維護管理和監督，交通規費的征收、管理與使用；全省公路、水路客貨運輸的組織協調；交通行業的外資利用與技術引進；廳屬二級局、處有公路局、運管局、征稽處、水運處、工程處、質監站等。下轄13個公路總段，分布在除嘉峪關市外的13個地、州、市。還有公路規劃設計院、交通學校、監理公司、貨運中心、駝鈴客車廠、物資公司、汽車運用研究所等事、企業單位。擁有直屬職工15000多人，行業職工5萬多人。1993年底，全省公路里程34875公里，其中二級公路2115公里，三級公路8931公里。全省民用汽車保有量12萬多輛，公路貨運量16900萬噸，貨物周轉量88億噸公里，客運量8540萬人，旅客周轉量45.6億人公里。

地址：甘肅省蘭州市翠英門47號　電話：總機8461216　傳真：8464035　郵編：730030

GANSU COMMUNICATION OFFICE

The office is a function department of Gansu Government instituting organic leading and macroregulating to the provincial highway, waterway, and instituting trade management. It is mainly in charge of drafting the development strategy general and specific polices and workingout medium-far development plan of the provincial highway, waterway traffic transportation trade. The capital construction and technical reform items of the provincial highway, main bus stops,key ports and docks, etc. Maintenance and management the provincial highway and defence,management, supervision of the channel, navigation mark, port installation, collection, management and using of traffic set fees.Organic coordination of the provincial highway and waterway passenger-cargo transportation,foreign money utilization and import technology of traffic trade. The office is under the leadership of the second-grade bureau the department has Highway Bureau, Transportation and, Management Bureau, Collection and Checking Department Water Transportation Department,Engineering Department, Quality Control Station, etc. 13 general highway sections which spreadin 13 regions, prefectures, cities except Jiayuguan city, are under the leadership of the office. It also includes some institutions and business unites such as Highway Plan Designing Institute, Communication College, Control and, Management Company, Cargo Transportation Centre, Tuoling Bus Factory, Goods and Materials Company, CarWielding Research Institute. The office has over 15000 staff and workers directly under it, By the end of 1993, the provincial highway mileage is 34875km among whom there are 2115 km second grade highway, 8931 km third- grade highway. The provincial civil car possession volume is over 120000 cars, the highway goods transported volume is 16.9 hundred million tons, the rotation volume of goods transport is 88 hundred million ton / km, the passenger transported volume is 8.54 hundred million persons, therotation volume of passenger transport is 45.6 hundred million persons / km.

Add: No. 47 Cuiyingmen, Lanzhou, Gansu　Tel: 8461216　Fax: 8464035　Post Code:730030

西蘭公路蘭州太平溝高填土雙面加筋土擋牆工程，是我省公路跨越黃土冲溝的典型構造物。

Highly filling earth, double sides of reinforced earth retaining wall project of LanzhouTaipinggou of Xilan Highway is the model tectonic material of our provincial highway crossingthe loess stormed crack.

1993年8月竣工的蘭郎公路蘭州至合作段改造工程全綫按GBM工程標準實施。
The total line of Lanzhou to Hezuo rebuilt project of Lanlang Highway, finished in Aug,1993, was carried out according to GBM projects atndard.

全省公路運輸支持保障系統進一步完善。圖為已建成的白銀汽車站。
The transportation supporting and ensuring system of the provincial highway is beingperfected. The picture is Baiyin Bus Stop.

全省公路養路費征收工作實現了微機程序管理化作業
The collecting road toll work of the provincial highway has realized microcomputerprogram running work.

依靠自力更生精神，用10個月時間，于1992年8月建成了蘭州至敦煌1112公里河西千里窗口路。
1112 km Hexi thousand li "window" road of Lanzhou to Dunhuang was finished in Aug, 1992. The projected was just lasted for ten months depending on self-reliance.

甘肅省環保局

GANSU ENVIRONMENTAL PROTECTION BUREAU

省環境保護局黨組成員經常召開碰頭會，對全省環保工作的開展作出重大决策。左起副局長石敏媛、陳天華、局長張坤、副局長吴仁銘、田炳申。

The Party orgnization members often have brief meetings and make the key policies of theenvironmental protection work in Gansu. Vice director Shi Min Yuan, Chen Tian Hua, DirectorZhang Kun, Vice director Wu Ren Ming, Tian Bing Shen. (form left to right)

河西自然生態、環境狀況進行考察，深切關注酒泉沙生植物、人工種植甘草生長情况。

In Aug. 1993, Herkom and his party of the United Nations organization in China accompaniedby Chairman Qiugeben of the Environmental Resources Committee of the National People's Congressand Director Zhangkun of Gansu Environmental Protection Bureau, were inspecting the naturalecology, environmental conditions in Hexi, dearly following with interest of the developingsituation of sand plants, artificially planting licorice root in Jiuquan.

1993年4月22日，"地球日"蘭州市百名兒童五十米長卷揮毫作畫，表達對地球環境的愛心。

"Earth Day"·· Apr.22, 1993 Lanzhou hundred children were drawing apicture of fifty meters, expressing their love to the earth environment.

甘肅省白銀市環境警察在進行環境監察活動。

Environmental police of Bai Yin conducting environmental control activity

地址：蘭州市皋蘭路 123 號
電話：8418240
郵編：730030
Add: No.123 Gaolan Road, Lanzhou
Tel: 8418240
Post Code: 730030

蘭州第三毛紡織廠

圖為五千錠引進紡紗生產綫。

The pictureis to import textile productive line of 5000 spindles.

圖為計算機控制中心

The picture is Computer Control Centre.

圖為樣品室一角

The picture is a corner of Sample Room.

簡介

蘭州第三毛紡織廠是亞太地區最大的毛精紡全能綜合企業，始建于1972年。現有職工7000多人，固定資產原值1.6億元，具有年產精紡呢絨500萬米、針織絨800噸、羊毛衫20萬件、服裝15萬件和價值500萬元的紡專器材的生產能力。主導產品有精紡呢絨、針織絨、羊毛衫、服裝和紡專器材五大類。產品行銷全國，遠銷歐美、日本、新加坡、香港等二十多個國家和地區。

1989年精紡呢絨和服裝同時獲得國際羊毛局頒發的純羊毛和毛混紡標志等四個使用特許執照

蘭州第三毛紡織廠法人代表：任俊亭

地址：蘭州市西固區玉門街82號

郵編：730060

電話：7556841

THE THIRD WOOLLEN MILL IN LANZHOU

The mill; set up in 1972, is the largest, all-round, synthetical worsted spinningenterprise in Aisan and the Pacific areas with over 7000 staff and workers, 1.6 hundred millionyuan of fixed assets, also with the annual productive capacity of 5 million m of worstedspinning woollen goods, 800 tons of knit flannel, 20 thousand woollen sweaters, 15 thousandclothes, 5 million yuan value of textile specialized equipments.

Its main products has five kinds of worsted spinning woollen goods, kint flannel, woollensweaters, clothing and textile specialized equipments. The products are selling well throughoutChina and exported to over 20 countries and regions such as Europe, America, Japan, Singapore, Hongkong, etc.

In 1989 worsted spinning woollen goods and clothing won four using special permit with netwoollen and woollen blending sign issued by the International Woollen Bureau.

Legal person: Ren Jun Ting

Add: No.82 Yumen Street, Xigu District, Lanzhou.

Post Code: 730060

Tel: 7556841

白龍江林管局迭部林業局

局長：張浩
Director: Zhang Hao

中國創業者評價中心和國務院發展研究中心中國企業家調查系統授予張浩局長的"中國 500 名企業創業者"的證書。
The certificate of 500 China enterprise builders was awarded to Director Zhang Hao by Chinaenterpriser inspecting system of China builder apprasing centre and the State Councildevelopment research centre.

簡介

白龍江林管局迭部林業局始建于 1969 年，下設益哇、旺藏、安子溝、達拉、阿夏、水泊溝、洛大、臘子口 8 個生產經營林場和纖維板廠等 24 個生產經營及附屬單位，現有職工 5248 人，擁有各類林業生產機械設備 317 臺(套)，固定資產原值 9415 萬元、凈值 7852 萬元，注冊資金 4559 萬元，年生產木材能力 13.73 萬立方米，硬質纖維板 0.3 萬立方米，是甘肅省最大的國營大中型森工企業。

該局主要森工產品有：特級原木、針葉樹加工用原木等，營林產品有：雲杉苗、冷杉苗和油松營養袋苗等，木材加工產品有：鋸材、纖維板、家俱、鋸沫炭棒和紡織配件等，其它產品有：蕨菜、黑木耳、當歸、水泥空心磚和三氧化二砷等。目前，迭部林業局正在進行 5 萬立方米中密度纖維板的考察論證工作，該項目是白龍江林管局和甘南州"九五"期間重點聯建項目。

1993 年，全局共生產木材 13.72 萬立方米，清理回收材 1.06 萬立方米，生產纖維板 0.2 萬立方米，木制家俱 1 萬件，實現不變價工業總產值 6930 萬元，銷售收入 13322 萬元，利潤 4348 萬元，上繳稅金 1463 萬元，人均實現利稅費 12389 元，多次受到上級政府和有關部門的嘉獎。

1993 年，被列為"中國行業 50 家最大工業企業第 46 名"，"中國行業 50 家最佳經濟效益工業企業第 8 名"，"甘肅省 50 家最大工業企業第 43 名"，"甘肅省 50 家最佳經濟效益工業企業第 15 名"。

地址：甘肅省迭部縣白雲新村
郵編：747401
電話：(09418)、22296
聯系人：雒恆煊

DEIBU FORESTRY BUREAU

Diebu Forestry Bureau of Bailong River Forestry Administrative Bureau, set up in 1969, has8 productive management forestry centres such as Yiwa, Wangzang, Anzigou, Dala, Axia, Shuibogou, Luoda, Lazikou and fibreboard, etc. 24 productive management and its subsidiary units with 5248staff and workers, 317 various forestry mechanical equipments, 94.15 million yuan of fix assets, 78.52 million yuan of net value, 45.59 million yuan of registered funds, the annual productioncapacity of 13.73 thousand m2 wood, 0.3 thousand m3 of hard fibreboard. It is the largest, state large-medium scale forestry enterprise in Gansu.

Its main forest productive products include superfine log, conifer processing log, etc. Itsmanaging forestry products include dragon spruce seedling, fir seedling, Chinese pine nutritiveseedling, etc. Its wood processing products include sawwood, fibreboard, furniture, sawdustcharcoal stick and textile fittings, etc. Its other products include brake food, black ediblefungus, Chinese angelica, cement hollow brick, arsenic trioxide, etc. Now, the bureau is makinginvestigation and proof of 50000 m2 medium density fibreboard. The item is the key jointbuilding item of Bailong River Forestry Administrative Bureau and Gannan prefecture during theperiod of the 9th five-year plan.

In 1993, the bureau producted 13.72 thousand m3 wood, 0.2 thousand m3 fibreboard, 10000wood furnitures, checked up and recovered 1.06 thousand m3 wood, and realized 6930 thousand yuanof fixed price industry value, 133.22 million yuan of sales income, 4348 thousand yuan of profit, 1463 thousand yuan of the tax turned over to the state, 123.89 million yuan of profit and taxdues per capita. The bureau was cited for many times by the higher government and thedepartment concerned.

In 1993, the bureau is elected as the forty-sixth of the 50 largest industry enterprises inChina trades, the 8th of the 50 best economy benefit in China trades, the forty-third of the 50largest industry enterprises in Gansu, the fifteenth of the 50 best economy benefit in Gansu.

迭部林業局獲得的部分榮譽稱號之銅匾

Copper silk banners of some honour titles were won by Diebu Forestry Bureau.

Add: Baiyunxincun, Diebu County, Gansu.
Post Code: 747401
Tel(09418) 22296
Contact Person: Luo Heng Xuan

DEIBU FORESTRY BUREAU

該局標準化苗圃一角

A corner of the standard nursery

白龍江林管局迭部林業局

伐區采伐迹地
Cutover in the cutting area

郁閉的人工林
Closing man-made forest

人工伐區更新造林
Reforestation in the man-made cutting area

用戶生產的長 22 米，小頭直徑 64 公分的特級松原木
Superfine log of 22 m long and 64 cm minor diameter produced for users.

DEIBU FORESTRY BUREAU

白龍江林管局迭部林業局

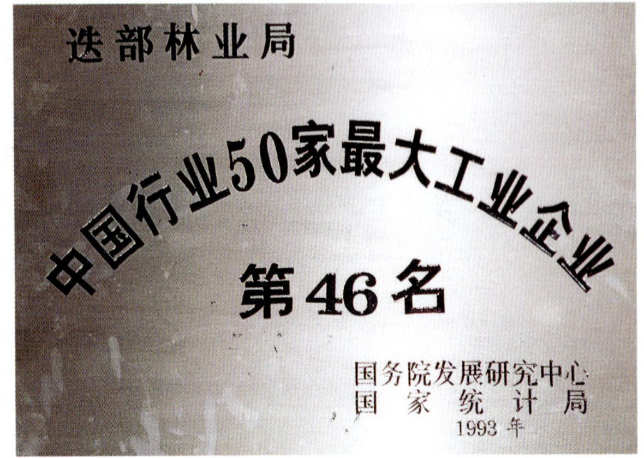

質量檢驗人員對纖維板進行抽查
The check persons are conducting spot test of fibreboard.

該局業余文工藝術團為林區職工群眾表演節目
Amateur art ensemble is give a performance to the mass and workers of the cutting area.

該林業局養鷄廠一角 A corner of chicken farm

職工子弟學校課間操活動 Setting-up exercises during the break of Children School of the workers.

甘肅省財政廳

GANSU FINANCIAL OFFICE

廳長：張文啟 Director: Zhang Wen Qi

地址：蘭州市東崗西路340號
電話：8821914
傳真：8829756
郵編：730000

甘肅省財政廳

簡介

甘肅省財政廳是甘肅省政府直接領導下的綜合經濟管理部門。其主要職能是貫徹執行黨和國家財政經濟方面的方針、政策，遵照國務院、財政部的指示精神，擬訂我省財政、預算、稅收、財務、會計等方面的補充規定和實施辦法，掌握全省財政收支情況，幷對一切財務活動進行財政監督和管理。

甘肅省財政廳內設：預算處、綜合計劃處、工交企業財務處、商貿企業財務處、中央企業財務處、農業財務處、行政事業財務處、會計管理處、控制社會集團購買力辦公室、支援經濟不發達地區發展資金辦公室等處室；下設財政科研所、甘肅省投資信托公司、國債服務中心、甘肅省職工財經學院、甘肅省財政學校。

GANSU FINANCIAL OFFICE

The office is a synthetic economy management department under Gansu Provincial Government. Its main function is to obey the indicator spirit of the State Council and the FinancialMinistry implementing the Party's and state's policy about financial economy, drafting theadditional regulations and implementation means of Gansu finance, budget, tax revenue, financial affairs, accounting, etc. mastering Gansu financial balance condition, inspecting andmanaging all financial activities.

The office has Budget Office, Synthetic Plan Office, Financial Office of Industrial andTraffic Enterprise, Financial Office of Commercial and Trade Enterprise, Financial Office ofthe Central Committee, Financial Office of Agriculture Financial Office of AdministrativeUtilities, Accounting Management Office, Control Social Group's Purchasing Power Office, SupplyDevelopment Funds to Indeveloped Economic Regions Office, etc. Financial Scientific ResearchInstitute, Gansu Investment Trust Company, National Debt Service Centre, Gansu Labour Financialand Economic College, Gansu Financial School are under the office.

甘肅省投資信托公司

GANSU INVESTMENT TRUST COMPANY

簡介

甘肅省投資信托公司成立于1980年2月，是甘肅省唯一的省級地方性非銀行金融機構。公司現有資本金3.5億元，其中外匯資本金750萬美元，資產總額7.2億元人民幣。公司成立以來，累計發放各種貸款10.04億元.實現利稅1億元。

公司現有職工70人，高級經濟師3人，經濟師19人，會計師3人，工程師2人。下設五部一室、三個子公司、三個交易廳

公司股票交易廳位于蘭州東方紅廣場科學宮內，營業場地面積980平方米，內設貴賓室、大戶室、散戶室。交易廳用衛星技術接收上海、深圳證券交易所的股市行情，采用大型彩色顯示屏及最快的股市行情顯示和先進的乾隆分析系統，為投資者提供一流的服務。

GANSU INVESTMENT TRUST COMPANY

The company, set up in February, 1980, is the only one nonbank financial organ of the provincial-grade locality. Now, it has 3.5 hundred million yuan of capital including 7.5million $, 7.2 hundred million yuan of total capital volume. Since its setting up, the company has total granded 10.04 gundred million yuan of various credits, realized 1 hundred million yuan of profits tax.

The company now has 70 staff and workers among whom there are 3 senior economists, 19 economists, 3 bookkeepers, 2 engineers, also with 5 departments, 1 office, 3 companies, 3 exchange halls under it.

Its stock exchange hall lies in the Scientific Palace of Dongfanghong Square in Lanzhou. Ithas 980 m2 business area with Honoured Room, Large Family Room, Bulk Family Room in it. Theexchange hall recieves the quotations on the stock market of Shanghai, Shenzhen Stock Exchangewith satellite technology. It provides the first- class service to investers with large-scale colour show screen, the fastest quotation shows and advanced Qianlong analysis system.

地址：蘭州市小北街
總經理：王志杰
副經理：楊宏光
電話：8417236 8419253
郵編：730000
Add: Gansu Investment Company, Xiaobei Street, Lanzhou
General manager: Wang Zhi Jie
Vice-amnager: Yang Hong Guang
Tel: 8417236 8419253 Post Code: 730000

大戶室
Large Family Room

甘肅省投資信托公司

甘肅省投資信托公司證券營業部
Stock business Department of the company

股票交易廳營業櫃臺
Business counter of the Stock Exchange Hall

電腦室
Electric Brain Room

大型彩色顯示屏
Large-scale colour show screen

GANSU BROADCASTING TELEVISION OFFICE

甘肃省廣播電視廳

廳長：楊德儒 Director: Tang De Ru

簡介

甘肃省廣播電視廳是中共甘肃省委領導下的宣傳機構，也是甘肃省人民政府管理全省廣播電視事業的行政機關。

廳機關設 11 個縣級部門。廳屬地級事業單位 2 個：甘肃人民廣播電臺、甘肃電視臺，縣級事業單位 9 個：甘肃有綫電視臺、無綫電臺管理處、微波臺管理處、生活管理服務中心、甘肃省廣播電視學校、甘肃廣播電視報社、甘肃省音像出版社、甘肃省音像資料館，甘肃省廣播電視器材供應站

GANSU BROADCASTING TELEVISION OFFICE

The office is a propaganda organ under the leadership of Gansu Provincial Committee and anadministrative organization of Gansu Provincial People's Government managing the provincialbroadcasting television business.

The office organization has 11 county departments, 2 prefecture institutions of GansuPeople's Broadcasting Station and Gansu Television Station, 9 county institutions of Gansu WireTelevision Station, Management Department of Radio Station, Management Department of MicrowaveStation, Service Centre of Living Management, Gansu Broadcasting Television School, GansuBroadcasting Television Newspaper Office, Gansu Sound and Videotape Publishing House, GansuSound and Videotape Reference Centre, Gansu Supply Station of Broadcasting Television Equipment.

地址：蘭州市東崗西路 146 號
郵編 730000
電掛：4997
傳眞：(0931) 8825832
Add: No.146 Donggang West Road, Lanzhou
Post Code: 730000 Cable: 4997
Fax: (0931) 8825832

龍尾山 687 臺發射機房外景。
Outdoor view of the launching generator of 687 station.

龍尾山687臺的機務人員在機房巡視設備運行狀況。
The maintenance personnel is inspecting the condition of the equipment working in thegenerator of 687 station at Longwei Mountains.

由日本秋田電視株式會社牽綫搭橋，甘肅電視臺與韓國江陵文化放送就節目交換、人員互訪、合拍電視節目等內容，在蘭州簽定友好合作協議。

Pill wires and build a bridge by Zhushi Society of Japan Qiutian Television, GansuTelevision Station signed friendy coopratiye agreement in Lanzhou with Jianglin Culturalbroadcasting about changing programmes, visiting each other, shooting television programmescooperatively, etc.

甘肅省廣播電視廳

1989 年新安裝的電視播控中心設備
Television broadcasting and controlling center equipments newly fixed in 1989.

甘肅電視臺

簡介

甘肅電視臺創建于 1970 年 10 月 3 日。目前自辦兩套節目，開設 34 個欄目，日平均播出節目 8.18 小時，節目內容豐富多彩，形式多樣，生動活潑，弘揚民族文化，突出地方特色，做廣大觀衆的忠實朋友，盼望得到社會各界和海內外朋友的大力支持

GANSU TELEVISION STATION

The station set up on Oct. 3, 1970. Now it has run two sets of programmes, opened 34columns, broadcast programmes for 8.18 nours per day. The programme contents are rich andvaried, various forms, lively, enlarge national culture, stick out local characteristics arefaithful friends to vast viewers, The station looks forward to getting energetic support ofthe friends, of various circles.

甘肅人民廣播電臺

概況

甘肅人民廣播電臺創辦于 1949 年 9 月 7 日，全臺現有編制 174 人，具有各類專業技術職稱的 120 人。設新聞部、農村部、專題部、科教部、通采部、文藝部、播出部、辦公室八個縣級部門，在全省 14 個地、州、市、個別大企業和廣東惠州設有 17 個記者站，派有常住記者。

目前，本臺辦有中波、調頻和調頻立體聲廣播節目三套，每天播出 34 小時 40 分，廣播人口省內覆蓋率達到 65%。

GANSU PEOPLE'S BROADCASTING STATION

The station set up on Sep. 7, 1949 with 174 staff and workers among whom there are 120persons with various specialized technical title. It has 8 county-grade departments ofInformation Service, Countryside Department, Special Subject Department, Popular ScienceDepartment, General Collect Office, Literary and Art Office, Broadcasting Office, Office. Thereare 17 reporter stations with resident correspondents in 14 regions, prefectures, cities, individual enterprises and Huizhou of Guangdong.

Now, the station runs three sets of medium wave, frequency modulation, frequency modulationstereophony stereo broadcasting programmes. It opens for 34 hours and 40 minutes per day. Thecovered rate of the broadcasting population in Gansu reaches 65 per cent.

甘肅人民廣播電臺"5.20"廣播輿論監督日投訴現場。

GANSU COMPANY OF CHINA NONFERROUS METAL IMPORT AND EXPORT CORPORATION

總經理：海春旺 Manager: Hai Chun Wang

銅及銅材
Copper and copper material

中國有色金屬進出口甘肅公司

簡介

甘肅公司是中國有色金屬進出口總公司在甘肅省的專業公司，具有獨立的法人資格。它以多個大型聯合企業和重點科研所為依托，擁有雄厚的經濟和技術實力。

甘肅公司于1984年4月正式成立，是工貿一體、技貿結合的對外貿易實體。連續幾年被評為省外貿系統的先進集體，多次受到有色金屬進出口總公司、省經貿委和蘭州公司等有關部門的表彰和嘉獎。

公司主營產品：銅、鋁、鉛、鋅、鎳、鈷、鎘、銻、錳、硒、碲及有色金屬加工材；鉑、鈀、鋨、銥、釕等貴金屬；氧化鈷、氧化鎳、硫酸銅、硫酸鎳等氧化物和鹽類；金屬硅、碳化硅、硅錳、硅鐵、鉻鐵等鐵合金；鎢砂、鉛精礦、鋅精礦等礦產品；氟化鹽、選礦藥劑、硫化鹼等化工產品，稀土及單一的稀土氧化物 及礦產品， 以及機械設備、備品備件等。

兼營：儀器儀表的進口、金屬制品及合金的進出口、代理進出口業務、承辦來樣、來料加工、補償貿易、合資、合作項目及有色金屬冶金設備的進出口業務。經營轉口貿易、國內貿易。

隨着公司業務的不斷擴大，產品遠銷西歐及東南亞等國家和地區，貿易遍及全國和世界各地。

甘肅公司願意與各界朋友協手合作、共同發展甘肅的對外經濟貿易！熱忱歡迎與甘肅有色公司洽談各種業務。

地址：甘肅省蘭州市底巷子15號
電話：(0931) 8412563 8412171
傳真：(0931) 8412197

GANSU COMPANY OF CHINA NONFERROUS METAL IMPORT AND EXPORT CORPORATION

Gansu company is a specialized company with independent corporation qualifications in Gansuof China Nonferrous Metal Import and Export Corporation. It has a rich economy and technologystrength depending on its large– scale integrated complexes and key scientific researchinstitutions.

Gansu company, set up in April, 1984 , is an external trade entity of industry with tradeand technology with trade. The company has continuously been an advanced collective of GansuForeign Trade System. and has been cited for many times by Gansu Economic and Trade Committee, Lanzhou Company, etc.

Its main products include copper, aluminnium, lead, zinc, nickel, cobalt, cadmium, antimony, manganese, selenium, tellurium, nonferrous metal processing material, platinum, palladium, osmium, iridium, ruthenium, etc. oxidizing cobalt, oxidizing nickel, cupric sulphate, nickelsulphate, metal silicon carborundum, silico manganese, ferrosilicon, flatiron, tungsten , ore, lead concentratc, zinc concentratc, salt fluoride, ore dressing drug, alkali sulphide, rareearth, single rare–earth oxide, mechanical installation, machine parts, spare parts, etc.

Also managing: importation of instruments, importation and exportation of metal productsand alloy, acting import and export business, undertaking incoming sample, incoming materialprocessing, compensation trade, combined funds cooperative items, importation and exportationof nonferrous metallurgy equipments, Managing entrepot trade, domestic trade.

With continuously extending of the company's business, the products have been exported toWest Europe, Southeast Asia and other countries and regions. Its trade has spread all overChina and world.

The company likes to cooperate with all friends, together develops Gansu foreign economytrade. Welcome to talk various business with us warmheartedly.

Add: No. 15 Di Lane, Lanzhou, Gansu
Tel: (0931) 8412563 8412171
Fax: (0931) 8412197

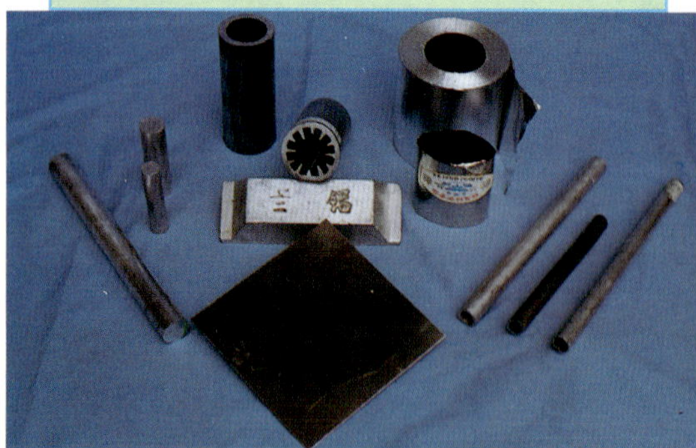
鋁及鋁材
Aluminium and aluminium material

稀土礦產品及單一氧化物，化工產品
Rare–earth minerals, single oxide and chemical and industria products.

蘭州長津電機廠

地址：中國甘肅省蘭州市火車站東路 18 號
郵編：730000
電話：8821721 轉廠辦
Add: No. 18 Huochezhan East Road, Lanzhou, Gansu
Post Code: 730000
Tel: 8821721

廠長：劉新昆 Director: Liu Xin Kun4

LANZHOU CHANGJIN ELECTRIC MOTOR FACTORY

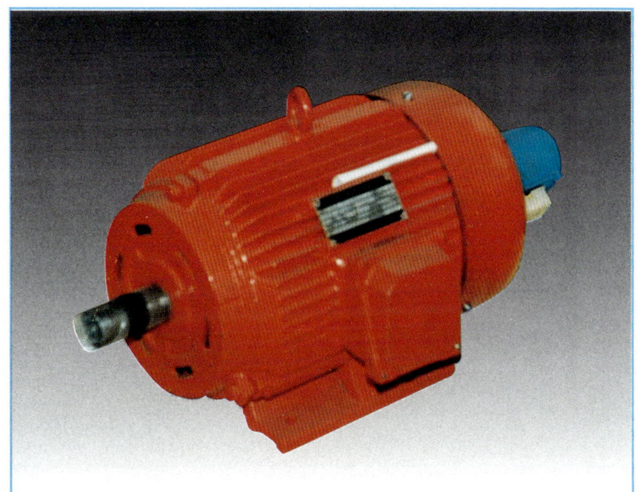

我廠生產的調速電機
The governing electric motor is produced by the factory

冶金及起重用三相异步電動機
The three phase asynchronous motor by metallurgy and lifting

簡介

蘭州長津電機廠是機電部重點企業，是西北地區定點生產三相异步電動機的專業廠家、西北地區電梯生產的重點企業、鉄道部内燃機車電機大修定點廠家。1965 年由天津内遷來蘭，地處蘭州火車站東路，占地 8.3 萬平方米，固定資產原值 2347 萬元，職工 1300 人。工廠擁有各類設備 528 臺，1993 年產值達 2601.8 萬元。主要生產二大系列、49 個品種、183 個規格的電機產品，6 個系列、60 個規格的電梯產品。其中 Y 系列 132、200 三相异步電動機為甘肅省優質產品，1990 年榮獲國家建設部頒發的售後服務優秀奬（電梯）。

LANZHOU CHANGJIN ELECTRIC MOTOR FACTORY

The factory is a key enterprise of Machinery and Electronics Ministry, a specializationfactory designated to produce three phase asynchronous motors in the Northwest, a keyenterprise to make lifts in the northwest China and a factory to carry out the heavy repair ofmotors of diesel locomotives of Railway Ministry. The factory was migrated to Lanzhou fromTianjin in 1965. It is located in the east road of Lanzhou Railway Station, occupies 83, 000square meters, with 23,470,000 yuan original value of the fixed assets, 1300 staff and workers, 528 various sets. The annual output value reached 26,018,000 yuan in 1993. It mainly producestwo series of motor products with 49 species and 183 specifications, and six series of liftproducts with 60 specifications. Among them, the 132 and 200 three phase asynchronous motors inthe Y series is the provincial high quality products. It owned the excellent prize for exsaleservice confered by Construction Ministry.

蘭州電力修造廠

LANZHOU POWER BUILDING FACTORY

簡介

蘭州電力修造廠是電力部具有較強科研、設計力量及電站輔機設備和備品配件的定點生產廠家，也是我國最大的電除塵器生產廠。可承擔電除塵器的科研、試驗、設計、制造、調試、安裝、運行等一系列服務。所研制的LD牌RWD／KFH型電除塵器爲燃煤電廠鍋爐及大型工業鍋爐的專用除塵設備，產品和技術榮獲國家優質產品金質獎和科學技術進步二等獎，產品銷往全國的60多家新建和擴建電廠，并出口印尼等國。同時還可提供制造各類鍛造鋼球，電站管道支吊架，高壓管道連接法蘭，PND—32型烟道飛灰采樣管及各類大型鍛件等。

地址：甘肅省蘭州市七里河區光華街31號
法人代表：耿現珊
電話：(0931) 2336931 2334626
電報掛號：3000　　郵編：730050

LANZHOU POWER BUILDING FACTORY

The factory, with stronger scientific research and designed power, is a fixed factoryproducing auxiliary machine equipments and equipment fittings of power station of The PowerDepartment, also the biggest factory producing eletrostatic precipitator in our country. It canundertake a series of eletrostatic precipitator service of scientific research, test, designing, building, debugging, installing, moving, etc. Its LD Brand-RWD／KFH eletrostatic precipitator is thespecilized boiler dust remover of burned coal power factory and large- scale industry. Itsproduct and technology have been awarded gold prize of good quality products by state and thesecond-grade prize of science and technology. Its products are selling well to more than 60newly built and rebuilt electric factories in China and exported to Indonesia and othercountries. Meanwhile it can provide and produce various forging steel balls, piping prop hangersof power stations, high-pressure piping connected Falan, PND--32 flue dust sampling tube andvarious, larg-scale forgings, etc.

300MW 機組配套電除塵器正在運行
300MW unit conveyance eletrostatic precipitator is working.

RWD／KFH 型高壓靜電除塵器榮獲國家優質產品金質獎
RWD／KFH high voltage eletrostatic precipitator has been awarded the gold prize of the stateexcellent quality products.

甘肅省畜牧廳　蘭州正大有限公司

四色旗廠辦公大樓外景
Outdoor view of the office building of four-colour banner plant.

LANZHOU ZHENGDA LIMITED COMPANY

簡介

蘭州正大有限公司是甘肅省畜牧廳與泰國正大集團合作興辦的現代化農牧企業，成立于1991年7月。公司建有年產18萬噸的飼料廠，總投資4000多萬元，引進世界一流自動生產綫和泰國正大集團科學配方，可加工生產粉料、顆粒料兩大類，濃縮料、全價配合料兩大系列，數十種優質飼料，產品銷往西北五省區，深受廣大客戶歡迎。公司續建的現代化父母代種鷄場，總投資近2000萬元，年可提供600萬只高產優質肉鷄苗。

蘭州正大公司以"質量第一、信譽第一、客戶第一"為宗旨，竭誠為飼養界服務。

LANZHOU ZHENGDA LIMITED COMPANY

The company, set up in July, 1991, is a modern farming and animal husbandry enterprisecooperatively initiated by Gansu Animal Office and Thailand Zhengda Group. It has a feed plantwith the annual production of 180000 tons The total investment is over 40 million yuan. The companyhas imported the first-class, world automatic production line and scientific directions ofThailand Zhengda Group. It can produce two kinds of powder material and granulated material, two series of enriched material and total price mixed material, over the kinds of good qualityfeed. Its products are selling well throughout five provinces and autonomous regions of theNorthwest. and welcomed by vast customers. The modern seed chicken farm of parents generation istotal invested for near 20 million yuan by the company. It can provide 6 million meat chickenseedlings of high production and excellent quality " Quality first, Credit first, Customersfirst" is the main policy pursued by the company. It likes to serve feed circles wholeheartedly.

地址：甘肅省蘭州市皋蘭縣城
郵編：730200
電話：(0931) 8464677 8883669 8883673
傳真：(0931) 8466317 8883672
電掛：1089
Add: Gaolan town, Lanzhou, Gansu
Post Code: 730200
Tel: (0931) 8464677 8883669 8883673
Fax: (0931) 8466317 8883672
Cable: 1089

飼料廠全景　Full view of the feed farm

LANZHOU ZHENGDA LIMITED COMPANY

LANZHOU PETROLEUM AND CHEMICAL MACHINERY WORKS

廠長: 王永森 Director: Wang Yong Sen

蘭州石油化工機器總廠

簡介

蘭州石油化工機器總廠是國家大型一檔企業，是國內最大的石油鑽采機械和煉油化工設備制造基地。建廠40年來，為我國石化工業提供了85萬余噸技術裝備。工廠占地面積140萬平方米，擁有職工11000余人，主要設備2300臺。具有設計制造從1800—8000米系列的陸地和海洋石油鑽機、成套煉油化工設備、高壓聚乙烯反應器以及各種通用機械的能力。測試手段完善，質量保證體系健全，各種產品暢銷國內，部分產品還遠銷美國、加拿大、日本、菲律賓、印度等十多個國家和地區。

地址: 中國甘肅蘭州市西津西路112號
郵編: 730050
電話: 2335911　2336911
電報: 4258
電傳: 72114 LPECH CN
傳眞: (0931) 8487458

LANZHOU PETROLEUM AND CHEMICAL MACHINERY WORKS

The works is a large-scale, first-grade enterprise and the largest base making the machinesof drilling and extracting oil and the equipments of oil refining and chemical industry inChina. It has been 40 years since the works set up, it has supplied China petroleum and chemicalindustry with over 850000 tons of technical installment. It has 1. 4 million m2 areas, over11000 staff and workers, 2300 major equipments and the capacity of designing and making drillingrigs of lands and seas from 1800 to 8000 m series, complete sets of oil refining and chemicalindustry equipments, high pressure polythene reactor and various universal machinery. It alsohas perfect test means and amplify quality ensurance system. Its various products are sellingwell throughtout China, some has been exported to over 10 countries and regions, such as theUnited States, Canada, Japan, the Philippines, India, etc .

Add: No. 112, Xijin West Road, Lanzhou, Gansu, China.
Post Code: 730030
Tel: 2335911　2336911
Cable: 4285
Telex: 72114 LPECH CN
Fax: (0931) 487458

LANZHOU PETROLEUM AND CHEMICAL MACHINERY WORKS

ZJ60L鑽機是蘭石總廠90年代自行設計，制造的新型6000米機械驅動鑽機，適用于沙漠邊緣或其它陸地石油和天然氣的勘探與開發。

ZJ60L rig is a new mechanical rig of 6000m made and designed by Lanzhou Petroleum andChemical Machinery Works itself in the nineties. It is suitable for explorating and developingoil and natural gas on the border of desert and other lands.

蘭州石油化工機器總廠

壁厚0.09米，筒長14米，內徑2.1米的熱壁加氫反應器。蘭石總廠生產的高壓容器主要有加氫反應器、尿素合成塔、氨合成塔、高壓氮氣瓶、高壓球型氣瓶、高壓釜、高壓聚乙烯反應器等。

The overlayed hydroreactor with 0.09m thick, 14m long, 2.1m internal dia.

Its high-pressure containers mainly include hydroreactor, urea synthetic tower, ammoniasynthetic tower, high-pressure nitrogen air bottle, high- pressure ball air bottle, high-pressure cauldron, high-pressure polythene reactor, etc.

Φ400——Φ530 的系列軋鋼機主機

The main engine of Φ400· Φ530 seriers of rolling mills.

新一代產品105平方米氨冷式套管結晶機
A new generation product·· 105 m2 cold ammonia casting crystalline machine.

LANZHOU PETROLEUM AND CHEMICAL MACHINERY WORKS

用于硫酸等強腐蝕行業的板式換熱器
The plate changed heat machine being suitable for sulphuric acid and other etching trades.

甘肅福樂實業總公司

甘肅福樂實業總公司總經理：馮全福先生 General manager: Feng Quan Fu

簡介

甘肅福樂實業總公司是直屬于省鄉鎮企業管理局的全民所有制企業，現有員工 152 名，擁有固定資產 840 萬元，流動資金 500 多萬元，1993 年完成產值 1500 多萬元，實現利稅 160 多萬元。總公司先後創辦了甘肅省福樂塑料廠；甘肅福樂食品公司；甘肅福樂機械制造公司；甘肅福樂銷售公司；甘肅福樂實業總公司蘭州經營部、新疆分公司等，現已成為跨行業的綜合性企業。形成了生產(PE)塑料農用棚、地膜，工業包裝膜；建築阻燃穿綫管；以(BOPP)為主要原料的塑料彩印復合軟包裝；(EPS)塑料發泡成型一次性衛生餐具系列；以及福樂牌(保健八寶蓋碗茶)、(蘭州風味牛肉面)和申報國家專利的塑料發泡成型機等深受用戶及消費者歡迎的產品體系。

總公司全體員工發揚“團結、奉獻、勤奮、務實”的企業精神，以“予用戶一切權力、盡我們一切義務”為宗旨，以強烈的社會責任感開拓進取，以優良的產品、溫馨的服務奉獻給用戶一片愛心。

地址：中國·甘肅蘭州市七里河區工林路 2—1 號
郵編：730050
電掛：9631
傳眞：(0931) 2334211
電話：(0931) 2336497 2338466
業務詢呼：8413488－23

GANSU FULE INDUSTRY COMPANY

The company, with 152 staff and workers, 8.4 million yuan of fixed assets, over 5 millionyuan of circulating funds is a ownership enterprise by the whole pecple under Gansu, TownsEnterprise Management Bureau. In 1993, it completed over 15 million yuan of output value, realized over 1.6 million yuan of profit tax.

The company has built Gansu Fule Plastic Plant, Gansu Fule Food Company, Gansu Fule MechanicalMaking Company, Gansu Fule Sales Company, Lanzhou Business Department of Gansu Fule IndustryCompany, Xinjiang Branch Company, etc. Now it has become transtrade, synthetic enterprise. Ithas formed product system welcomed by consumers producing (PE) plastic farming sheds, earth film, industrial packing film, thread wire tubes of building hindering burned Compound soft packingof plastic colour printed mainly with the raw material·· BOPP, once sanitary tableware seriesof EPS plastic foaming forming, Fule keep–fit Babao lid bowl tea, Lanzhou typical local beefnoodles, plastic foaming forming machine reporting patent to the state, etc.

The staff and workers carries forward the enterprise's spirit of "Be united, contribution, diligent, dealing with concrete matters relating to work. Its mein police is "Give consumer allpowers, fulfil our duty". The company will open up and keep forging ahead with strong socialduty sense, present a love heart to consumers with excellent products and warm service.

GANSU FULE INDUSTRY COMPANY

Add: No.2· 1 Gonglin Road, Qilihe, Lanzhou, Gansu
Post Code: 730050
Cable: 9631
Fax: (0931) 2334211
Tel: (0931) 2336497 2338466
Legal Person: Zhong Kun Hou
Business inquiring call: 8413488－23

福樂塑料廠彩印復合車間 YA6650 六色凹印機組 車間

YA 6650 six–colour concave printing unit of colour printing compound workshop of FulePlastic Plant.

甘肅福樂實業總公司

甘肅福樂塑料廠吹膜車間SG－65× 30−FM1600和SG－65×28−MCST−1000吹膜機組
SG－65× 30－FM1600, SG－65× 28－MCST−1000 blow film unit of the blow film workshop ofGansu Fule Plastic Plant

GANSU FULE INDUSTRY COMPANY

甘肅福樂塑料廠衛生餐具車間 SC－A 系列衛生餐具生產設備局部
Sanitary tableware workshop of Gansu Fule Plastic Plant Part of SC · A series of sanitarytableware productive equipments Mark of Gansu Fule Industry Company

甘肅福樂實業總公司直屬生產企業部分產品
Part products of the productive enrerprises under the company.

甘肅省構件工程公司

簡介

我公司創建于 1955 年，發展至今已成為集生產建築混凝土構件、粉煤灰加氣混凝土制品、水泥、菱鎂系列建築配件制品，多功能建築膠等建工、建材產品和建築安裝施工為一體的中型企業。現有職工 1478 人，其中，各類專業技術人員占職工總數的 12%。公司屬主要經營單位有：混凝土制品廠、硅酸鹽制品廠、機械運輸處、土建工程處、水電安裝處，此外，還有聯營企業蘭州祁連山水泥粉磨站和永登建川水泥廠。

在改革開放的新形勢下，我們銳意深化企業內部的改革工作，使企業實力大大增強，1992 年擠身于甘肅省大中型企業經濟效益 50 強中的第 29 位，榮獲 1993 年度甘肅省“質量效益型先進企業稱號”。

地址：蘭州市西固區環行中路 161 號
郵編：730060
電話：(0931) 7556623
企業法人代表：鐘坤厚

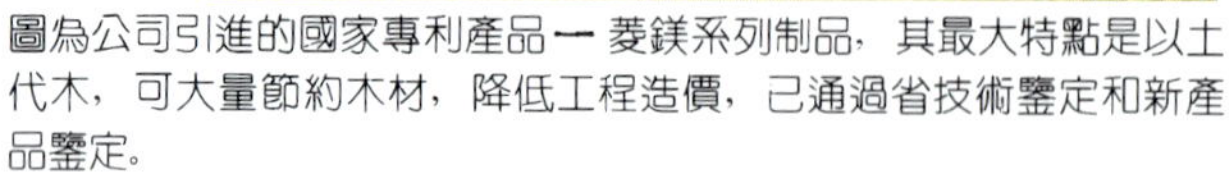
圖為公司引進的國家專利產品一菱鎂系列制品，其最大特點是以土代木，可大量節約木材，降低工程造價，已通過省技術鑒定和新產品鑒定。

The picture is the state patented products imported by the company Lingmeiseries ofproducts. Its characteristics are to rely upon earth instead of wood, to save a great deal ofwood, to reduce the projects'cost. It has been through Gansu provincial: technical appraisaland new product appraisal.

公司下屬硅酸鹽制品廠，是全國加氣行業重點骨干廠家。其生產的 06 級粉煤灰加氣砼砌塊連續三年經國家行檢獲優等品和一等品，從 1992 年開始進行技術改造後，產量達 20 萬立方。超過設計能力的一倍，圖為車間一角。

The Silicate product plant under the company is the state key enterprise of air entrainingtrade. Its 06 grade powder coal ash aerocrete bricks has continuously won exce; lent product andthe first-class product in China for three years. After technical refom 1992, the outputreaches 200000 cube and surpasses redoubled design function. The picture is a corner of theworkshop.

由我公司一處承建的“慶陽大廈”工程，位于蘭州市高新技術開發區，建築面積 11177 平方米，圖為工程外景。

Qingyang mansion with 11177 m2 building areas built by the first office of the company liesin the high, new technical develop areas of Lanzhou. The picture is the outdoor view of theproject.

我公司獲得的全國加氣混凝土協會頒發的"設備管理"獎杯
The company won the cup of equipment management awarded by the State Aerocrete Society.

GANSU COMPONENT ENGINEERING COMPANY

GANSU COMPONENT ENGINEERING COMPANY

The company, set up in 1955, has developed into a medium-scale enterprise with concretecomponent of productive construction, aerocete prosucts of powder coal has, cement, magnesiteseries of building fittings prosucts, building hum with many functions, etc. and buildinginstallation construction together. Now it has 1478 staff and workers among whom variousspecialized technical personnel makes up 12 per cent of the total numbers. Its main managementunits include Concrete product plant, Silicate Product plant, Mechanical Transport Office, LandBuilding project Office, Water and Elevtric Installation Office, and Lanzhou Qilianshan CementPowder Station, Yongden Jianchuan Lement Plant as well.

Under the new situation of reform and open, we deepen restricted enterprise's reformstrengthen the enterprise's strength. In 1992 the company become the 29th of 50 best, Large-medium enterprise economic benefit. In 1993, it won the advanced enterprise title of qualitybenefit.

Add: No.161 HuanXing Central Road, Xigu, Lanzhou
Post Code: 730060
Tel: (0931) 7556623

公司屬混凝土制品廠是西北地區最大的生產混凝土予制構件的廠家。在經營上，走"人無我有，人有我精"的路子，形成了自己的一些拳頭產品。成為蘭煉、蘭化等大中型企業的指定產品。圖為省優產品一 大型屋面板。圖三為暢銷蘭州地區的混凝土方樁。

The concrete product plant under the company is the largest plant producing concreteprefabricated components in the Northwest area. They walk the managenent road of "Others havenot, We have; others have, ours are superior" Now it has formed some fist products of itselfand has become the assignment products of Lanzhou Oil Refining Company and Lanzhou ChemicalIndustry Company, etc. The second picture is the provincial excellent product· large-scale roof board.The third picure is concrete square pile sold well in Lanzhou.

蘭州化學工業公司

簡介

蘭州化學工業公司，是我國"一五"期間重點引進、最早建成的化工骨干企業之一，現已發展成為一個特大型石油化工聯合企業。

蘭州化學工業公司，現擁有職工 42000 人，固定資產原值 26.4 億元，主要生產裝置 44 套，中間試驗裝置和環保裝置 65 套；下設生產建設、科研設計、設備制造、文教衛生、後勤服務和集體經濟等二級單位 30 個；生產各類石化產品 110 種，系我國石化行業品種最多的企業之一。

投產 36 年來，蘭州化學工業公司作為我國第一個石油化工基地，在產品、技術、人才、經驗等方面，發揮了重要的先導作用，被稱為中國開拓石油化工技術、造就石油化工人才的搖藍。

經理：郭錫廉（高級工程師）
Manager: Guo Xi Lian (Senior engineer)
黨委書記：朱廉寶（高級工程師）
Party Secretary: Zhu Lian Bao (Senior engineer)

LANZHOU CHEMICAL INDUSTRY COMPANY

The company is one of the state key chemical industry enterprises built earliest andintroduced during the first five-year plan. Now it has developed into a large- scale oil andchemical inaustry enterprise.

The company has 42000 staff and workers, 26.4 hundred million yuan of fixed assets, 44 setsof major productive installation, 65 sets of middce test installation and enviornmentprotection installation. There are 30 second- grade units under it, such as productiveconstruction, scientific research design, equipments making, culture and education and health, logistics service, collective economy, etc. The company can produce 110 kinds of various oiland chemical products It's one of the enterprises with the most varieties in China oil andchemical trade.

As the first oil and chemical industry base in our country, the company has flayed theguide part in products, technology, qualified personnel, experience, etc. for 36 years. It'salso named the cradle of opening up oil and chemical industry technology, electing qualifiedpersonnel of oil and chemical industry in China.

Add: Fuli Road, Xigu, Lanzhou, Gansu
Post Code: 730060
Tel: 7555321
Telx: 72107 LROUC CN
Fax: (0931) 7555851

江澤民總書記視察蘭化
General Secretary Jiang Ze Min is Visiting the company.

地址：甘肅省蘭州市西固區福利路
郵編：730060
電話：7555321
電傳：72107 LYOUC CN
傳眞：(0931) 7555851

苯乙烯生產裝置
The productive installation of styrene

LANZHOU CHEMICAL INDUSTRY COMPANY

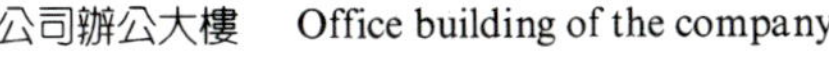
公司辦公大樓　Office building of the company

毫秒爐裂解裝置
Splitting installation of millisecond stove

蘭州化學工業公司

跨黃河管橋提取地下水
Recover groundwater across the tube bridge of the Yellow River

化肥廠廠景 View of the Chemical Fertilizer Plant

LANZHOU CHEMICAL INDUSTRY COMPANY

福利區一角
A Corner of the welfare area
大型塔器安裝
Installation of large–scale tower equipment
蘭化公司全景
Whole View of Lanzhou Chemical Industry Company

蘭州佛慈製藥有限公司

FECI PHARMACEUTICAL FACTORY IN LANZHOU

FECI PHARMACEUTICAL FACTORY IN LANZHOU

In 1929, Mr Yuhuiguan built the factory named Feci in Shanghai, meanwhile advanced the mainpolicy of "Scientifically refine, improve state medicine". It became the earliest Chinese pillmedicine factory producing new drug form·· enriched pills adopting "Recover technology, usenew equipments and new management means. In 1956, the factory was moved to Lanzhou in order toutilize Gansu provincial rich medicinal resources.

Now, Its 11 kinds such as Jinkuishenqi pill, Danggui extract tablet, Liuweidi yellow pillspeparately won excellent product titles of the state, the ministry and the province. Itsproducts are selling well in 28 provinces, cities and autonomous regions in China. Over 10kinds of its products have been exported to Japan, Singapore, Thailand, Malaysia, Indonesia, the United States, Canada, Australia, etc, as well as Hongkong, Aomen regions. In 1991, thefactory promoted to the second-class state enterprise.

In Dep. 1993, the factory cooperaterd with Meiweihang Trade Company in the United Statesand built "Feci Pharmaceutical Limited Company in Lanzhou". It has laid a solid fundation so asto make traditional Chinese pill medicine to rush out of Asia and advance towards the world. The company likes to serve patients wholeheartedly under the guidance of good quality, highefficiency, clear, civilization.

地址：蘭州市鹽場路 336 號
郵編：730046
電掛：0154
傳真：8418945
電話：8413890
Add: No.336 Yanchang Road, Lanzhou
Post Code: 730046
Cable: 0154
Fax: 8418945
Tel: 8413890

公司董事長兼總經理：何光明
Director and the general manager: He Guang Ming

簡 介

1929 年，玉慧觀先生在上海建藥廠，取名(佛慈)，同時提出"科學提煉，改良國藥"的建廠宗旨，成為全國最早采用提取工藝，使用新設備、新的管理方法生產新劑型— 濃縮丸的中成藥廠。1956 年為利用甘肅省豐富的藥材資源，遷到蘭州市。

目前企業生產的金匱腎氣丸、當歸浸膏片、六味地黃丸等 11 個品種分別榮膺國家級、部級、省級優質產品稱號，產品暢銷全國 28 個省、市、自治區，有數十種產品遠銷日本、新加坡、泰國、馬來西亞、印尼、美國、加拿大、澳大利亞等國及港澳地區，1991 年晉升為國家二級企業。

1993 年 12 月，該廠與美國美威行貿易公司全面合作，成立"蘭州佛慈制藥有限公司"，為傳統的中成藥冲出亞州，走嚮世界奠定了堅實的基礎，公司將一如既往地在"優質、高效、清潔、文明"的方針指引下，竭誠為廣大患者的健康服務。

獲得省優產品獎的杞菊地黃丸
Qijudi yellow pill won the prize of the provincial excellent products.

甘肅電力變壓器廠

原蘭州電器廠

簡介

該廠是甘肅省最大的變壓器生產廠，是電力工業部西北變壓器檢修中心，技術力量雄厚，擁有國際先進的專用設備。新近該廠生產的 S720-500KVA/6-10KV 節能變壓器被甘肅省質量局確認為省優質產品。

熱誠為廣大用戶提供國內一流的H型110KV電力變壓器。S7、S8各種規格的節能電力變壓器 10-63000KVA/6-110KV。各種型號的電爐變壓器。SN7、SN8農用變壓器。各種型號的電流電壓互感器。高壓硅整流設備。高低壓配電屏櫃。

LANZHOU POWER TRANSFORMER PLANT

The plant is the largest plant producing transformers in Gansu, also the northwest centrerepairing transformers of the Power Industrial ministry with rich technical power andinternational advanced special equipments. Its S7 20-5000KVA /6- 10KV transformer with savingenergy is elected as Gansu good quality product by Gansu Quality Bureau.

The plant supplies vast consumers whloeheartedly with the first-class H type of 110KV powertransforer in China, S7 S8 various standards of power transformer 10- 63000KVA / 6- 110KV withsaving energy, various types of electric transformers, SN, SN * farming transformers, varioustypes of current voltage mutual inductance equipment, pressure silicon rectifier installation, high or low-pressure distribution screen cupboard.

地址：蘭州市城關區鹽場路 276 號
電話：8827951
電掛：0702
郵編：730030
Add: No.276 Yanchang Road, Chenghuan, Lanzhou
Tel: 8827951
Cable: 0702
Post Code: 730020

LANZHOU POWER TRANSFORMER PLANT

甘肅省林業廳

甘肅省林業廳廳長：朱耀光
Director of Gansu Forest Office: Zhu Yao Guang

地址：蘭州市秦安路 1 號
電話：8823911 轉
郵編：730030
Add: No.1 Qinan Road, Lanzhou
Tel: 8823911
Post Code: 730030

簡介

甘肅省林業廳下設 13 個處(室)，21 個廳直企事業單位，2.2 萬多職工。10 年累計人工造林 2857 萬畝，占建國 44 年造林總面積的 53%；森林覆蓋率達到 8.42%，增長了1.14%；活立木總蓄積量達到 1.924 億立方米，林木年總生長量 381 萬立方米，實現了森林覆蓋率和面積雙增長。

GANSU FOREST OFFICE

The office, with 22000 staff and workers, has 13 departments (offices), 21 enterprises andinstitutions under it. It has added up 28.57 million mu of man-made afforestation for the yearswhich makes up 53 per cent of the total area of founding the state for 44 years. The forestcovered rate reaches 8.42 per cent, increases 1.14 per cent. The store volume of living treesreaches 1.924 hundred million m3, the total annual growth volume of forest is 3.81 million m3. It has realized double increasing of forest covered rate and area.

截止 1993 年底，我省經濟林面積已達 600 萬畝，年產果品 70 多萬噸，農民人均增收 130 多元。圖為禮縣石橋鄉的苹果林
By the end of 1993, the economic forest area of our province reached 6 million mu, the annual productive fruit is over 700000 ton, the peasants per capita increased over 130 yuanincome. The picture is the apple forest of Shiqiao village, Li county.

我省長防林工程建設卓有成效，五年已完成 306 萬畝，占一期工程計劃的 74%。這是西和縣洞山長防林工程。
Good results have been atlained in building the long shelter-forest project. 3.06 millionmu has been fulfilled for five years and makes up 74 per cent of the first-project-plan. The picture is the long shelter-forest project of Xihe county.

“三北”和治治工程的建設，有效地控制了風沙等自然灾害的危害程度，促進了農業和農村經濟的穩步增長。

The construction of ″three–north″ and ″adouble harnessing- project has effectivelycontrolled harmful degree of wind, sand and other narual calamity, and promoted stedadincreasing of agriculture and farming forest economy.

我省速生豐産林已有長足的發展。圖為生長茂盛的小隴山林業實驗局黨川林場日本落葉松。

The quick–growth high yield forest has made considerable develop. The picture isluxuriant Japanese larch of Dangchuan Forestry Centre, Small Longshan Forest Laboratory Bureau.

林業公安人員積極開展專項打擊和重點整治工作，維護了林區治安，保障了林業生產建設順利進行。圖為林警在林區巡邏的情景。

The Forest policemen actively launch special atlack and key management. It has saftguardedpublic order of the forest area, ensured forest productive construction. The picture is thepatrol view of the forest policemen. in the forest area.

地處武威的甘肅野生動物繁育中心在保護珍貴的野生動植物資源，保護自然生態環境方面做了有針對性的研究，成功地飼養了普氏野馬、野驢、野駱駝、金絲猴和鵝喉羚等。

Gansu Wild Animal Breed Centre has made no mistaking research in protecting the resourcesof valuable wild animal and plant and natural ecology environment, and successfully raisedPushi wild horses, wild donkeys, wild camels, golden monkeys and ehou antelopes, etc.

甘肅省慶陽石油化工廠

廠址：甘肅省慶陽縣三十里鋪鎮
郵編：745115
電掛：0553
電話：(09441) 22362 22236
Add: Sanshilipu Town, Qingyang County, Gansu.
Post Code: 745115
Cable: 0553
Tel: (09441) 22362 22236

甘肅省慶陽石油化工廠廠長：班 文 Director: Ban Wen

簡介

甘肅省慶陽石油化工廠是1971年隨着長慶油田的開發和建設而創建的一個省屬中型綜合性石油化工企業。現有職工1800多人，固定資產1.2億元。主要生產裝置三套：20萬噸/年常壓煉油、5萬噸/年催化裂化、2.2萬噸/年硝酸銨。主要產品有70#、90#車用汽油；0#、-10#輕柴油；燈用煤油；石油液化氣和農用硝酸銨等。輔產品有多元素高效復合肥；"83"增抗劑；高級洗發護發香波及系列清洗劑等。

1993年銷售收入突破兩億元，利稅超過2000萬元；列省利稅50強第32位，銷售30強第12位。

為了增強企業發展後勁和適應市場應變能力，企業組建了甘肅省慶陽石油化工廠銷售總公司，分支機構遍布甘肅、陝西、寧夏、山西等省區，并在海南設有辦事機構。企業第三產業的經營範圍已涉及到交通運輸、印刷、商品流通、房地產開發和服務等多種領域。一個綜合、開放、外嚮、高速、高效的現代化企業正在健康成長。熱誠歡迎社會各界人士前往考察，投資，洽談合作項目。

QINGYANG OIL AND CHEMICAL INDUSTRY PLANT

The plant, set up in 1971 with the development and construction of Changqing Oil Field, isa medium-scale synthetic oil and chemical enterprise. Now it has over 1800 staff and workers, 1.2 hundred million yuan of fixed assets, three sets of major productive installations ·· 200000 ton / year normal pressure oil refining, 50000 ton / yuar catalytic cracking, 22000 ton / yearammonium nitrate. Main products include 70# vihicle petrol, 0#, -10# light diesel, lamp kerosene, liquefied petroleum gas, farming ammonium nitrate, etc. It auxiliary products include higheffective compound fertilizer with many elements, "83 " increased resistant agent, highshampoo and hair conditioncr and series of washing agent.

It 1993 sales income topped 2 hundred million yuan, profit tax exceeded 20 million yuan. Itwas rated as thirty-second of the first 50 profit tax ehterprises, twelfth of the first 30sales enterprises in Gansu.

In order to strengthen the development aftereffect of the enterprise and suit courtesycapacity of the market, the enterprise has set up the Sales Company of Gansu Qingyang Oil andIndustry Plant. Its branch organs spread in Gansu, Shanxi, Ningxia, Shanxi, etc. It has alsoset up a working body in Hainan. The management scopes of its third estate have involvedtraffic transportation, printing, commodity circulation, development of real estete and service, etc. A modern enterprise with synthetics, open, extrocersion, high seeking, high effection ishealthly growing up. Welcome personalities of various circles here to inspect, invest andcooperate wholeheartedly.

廠領導班子研討長遠規劃
The leader group is discussing the long-term plan.

煉油分廠催化裂化裝置
The catalytic cracking installations of the branch refinery.

廠辦公大樓
Office building

核工業甘肅礦冶局

GABSU ORE SMELTING BUREAU OF CHINA NUCLEAR INDUSTRY CORPORATION

簡介

核工業甘肅礦冶局領導核工業在甘的七九二礦、七九六礦、二七九廠、甘肅昆侖工業公司和在陝西的七九四礦。目前已建成了硅鉄、純碱、冰晶石、黄金、玉米澱粉、檸檬酸、膨潤土、人造金剛石等生產綫，其中硅鉄、檸檬酸已打入國際市場，"雪晶"牌玉米澱粉獲省優、部優稱號，產品供不應求。二七九廠黄金生產綫采用先進工藝生產的黄金純度可達 99.99%。回收率達到國內先進水平，其黄金為中國工商銀行免檢產品。該局的目標是，通過今後五年的滚動發展，成為技工貿相結合的大型企業集團，為甘肅經濟發展作出新的貢獻。

核工業甘肅礦冶局局長、黨組書記劉中厚
Director and Party Secretary: Liu Zhong Hou

地址：蘭州市 19 號信箱
郵編：730050
電話：2334178 2336991 轉 278
Add: No.19 Mailbox, Lanzhou
Post Code: 730050
Tel: 2334178 2336991-278
法人代表：劉中厚 Legal person: Liu Zhong Hou

GABSU ORE SMELTING BUREAU OF CHINA NUCLEAR INDUSTRY CORPORATION

The bureau leads No.792 Ore, No.796 Ore, No.279 Factory in Gansu, Gansu Kunlun IndustryCompany, No.794 Ore in Shanxi of China Nuclear Industry Corporation. Now it has built theproductive lines of ferrosilicon, soda ash, cryolite, gold, corn starch citric acid, bulk moistearth, man-made diamond, etc. among whom ferrosilicon and citric acid has entered internationalmarkets, Xuejing corn starch has won the excellent titles of the province and ministry. Itsproducts have supplied falls short of demand. The gold purity of No. 279 Factory adoptingadvanced technical production line reaches 99.99 per cent. Its recovery rate has reached thenational advanced level. Its gold is the product without examination of China Industrial andCommercial Bank. The purpose of the bureau is to become a large-scale enterprise group withtechnology, industry, trade together through rolling development in the next five years. and tomake new contribution for Gansu economic development.

國營七九二礦

簡介

國營七九二礦系中國核工業總公司下屬的鈾金屬采、冶中型聯合企業。擁有固定資產原值 1.24 億元，現有固定職工 1800 余人。

本企業除已開發出人造金剛石、硅鐵等民用產品投放市場外，還擬在"八五"末至"九五"初，利用國家軍工三綫調整政策、調動企業自身優勢，積極爭取外部合作，异地新建一批中小型企業，為國家和地方經濟發展作出更大貢獻。

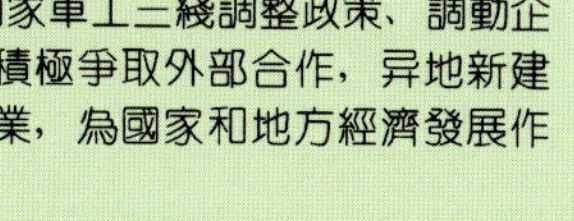

NO. 792 ORE

The No.792 Ore is a state-run medium scale integrated complex mining and smelting uraniummetal under China Nuclear Industry Corporation: Now it has over 1800 fixed staff and workers, 1.24 hundred million yuan of fixed assets.

The enterprise has not only developed some civil products such as man- made diamond, ferrosilicon, ete. and has put them on the market, but also drawn up using state war three-line, adjusting the policy, arousing its superiority, actively striving for outside cooperation, newly building some medium and small enterprises, making more contribution for the state andlocal economic development from the end of the 8th five-year plan to the beginning of the 9thfive-year lpan.

NO. 792 ORE

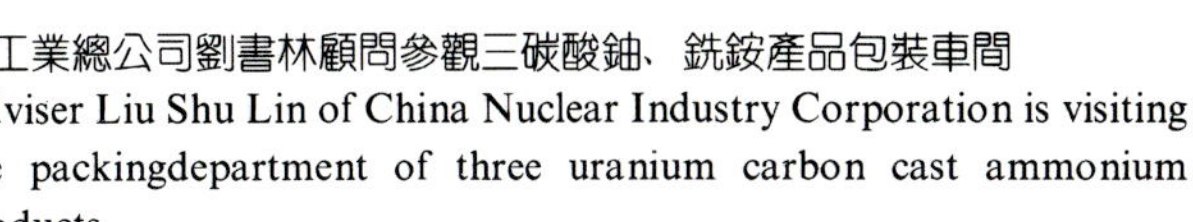

工業總公司劉書林顧問參觀三碳酸鈾、銑銨產品包裝車間
dviser Liu Shu Lin of China Nuclear Industry Corporation is visiting e packingdepartment of three uranium carbon cast ammonium oducts.

企業法人：陳石安
Legal person: Chen Shi An
地址：甘肅省甘南藏族自治州迭部縣 3 號信箱
郵編：747400
電話：09418——22235
Add: No.3 Mailbox, Diebu County, Gansu Prefecture.
Post Code: 747400
Tel: 09418——22235

國營二七九廠

CHINA NUCLEAR INDUSTRY CORPORATION
NO.279 FACTORY

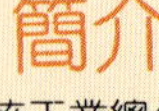

簡介

國營二七九廠是中國核工業總公司下屬的一個生產多種化工產品的綜合性企業。主要生產純碱、人造冰晶石、氟化鋁、硅鐵等產品。本企業由軍工生產轉為民品生產，經過二十多年的建設和發展，工藝先進，設備精良，技術力量雄厚，現有職工 1400 余人，其中各類專業技術人員 280 余人。

廠內有鉄路專用綫與蘭包鉄路干綫相接，包蘭公路從廠前穿過，交通極為便利。

本廠產品質量優質、可靠，受到國內外各界用戶的信賴和好評；熱情歡迎各界用戶繼續與本企業眞誠合作。

CHINA NUCLEAR INDUSTRY CORPORATION NO.279 FACTORY

The No.279 Factory is a state–run comprehensive enterprise under the China Nuclear IndustryCorporation. It produces various chemical products, including soda ash, artificial cryolite, aluminium fluoride, ferrosilicon, etc. The No. 279 Factory has changed it′s productionorientation from military to civilian. It has a history of construction and development morethan 20 years. It has outstanding technology and equipments. It has more than 1400 high. skilledworkers in their respective fields and of which more than 280 technicians in various fields.

The No.279 Factory is located in Jingyuan county, Baiyin city, Gansu province, that 150kmto Lanzhou wicth is the capital of Gansu province. It′s communication is very convenient. Thereis special railway linked to the main railway from Lanzhou to Baotou in the factory. Thehighway from Baotou to Lanzhou is pass by it.

The products of the No.279 factory have won high compliments and trust for it′s highquality and trustworthy.

All our user are welcome to cooperate with the No.279 Factory honestly.

廠長：張華安
Mr. Zhang Hua An, director of No.279 factory

廠址：中國·甘肅·靖遠
電話：09467–21279 22279
郵編：730621
電掛：8800
Add: Jingyuan, Gansu China
Tel: 09467–21279 22279
Post Code: 730621
Cable: 8800

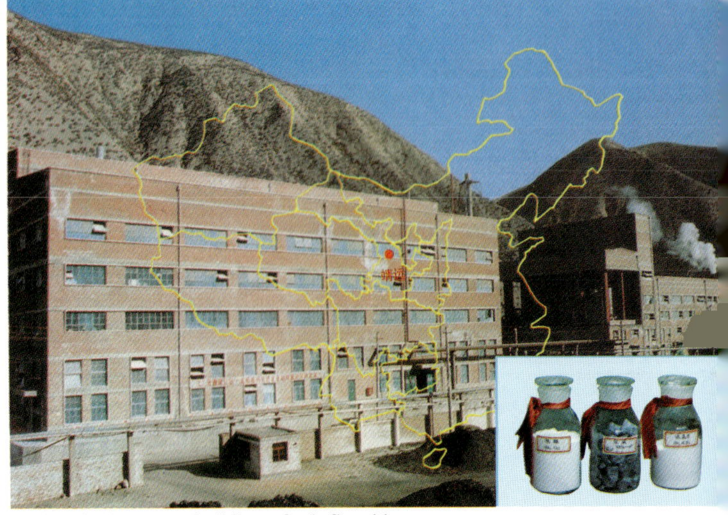

氟化鹽廠房 Factory building of salt fluoride

统 计 资 料

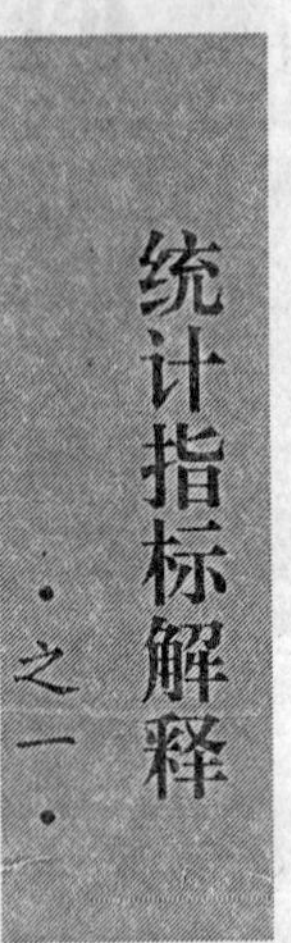

【森林面积、木材蓄积量】森林面积包括人工经营的和天然的森林面积，不包括灌木林地和疏林地。木材蓄积量包括有林地上的幼龄林、中龄林、成熟林、过熟林、枯立木等的全部积蓄量。

【草原面积】草原面积包括天然草原和人工种植的、改良的草场总面积，但不包括农区草山、草坡。

【年径流量】年径流量是指陆地上某个区域一年中从地表、地下排出的水流的体积。年径流量通常按水文站河岸流域计算。

【总产出】核算期内全部生产活动的总成果，包括本期生产的已出售可供出售的物质产品和服务、在建工程以及自产自用消费品和自制固定资产价值。总产出等于中间投入与增加值之和，一般按生产者价格计算。

【中间投入】在生产过程中消耗或转换的物质产品和服务价值。记入中间投入必须具备两个条件，一是与总产出相对应的生产过程所消耗或转换的物质产品和服务；二是本期消耗的不属于固定资产的非耐用品。中间投入分为物质产品投入和服务投入。

【物质产品投入】生产过程中消耗或转换的物质产品。物质产品投入包括货物和物质性服务（货运、邮电通讯、商业和饮食等服务）的消耗，不包括固定资产消耗。

【服务投入】在生产过程中消耗的除物质性服务以外的各种服务。包括金融保险、文化教育、科学研究、医疗卫生、行政管理等。

【增加值】生产过程中的产出价值扣除中间投入的价值后的余额，反映生产单位或部门对国内生产总值的贡献。增加值包括固定资产折旧、劳动者报酬、生产税净额、营业盈余。

【固定资产折旧】核算期内为补偿生产活动中所耗用的固定资产而提取的价值，反映固定资产存量在生产过程中损耗或转移的价值。包括基本折旧和大修理折旧，行政事业单位的办公用房及其他固定资产折旧和居民住房折旧参照一定折旧率虚拟计算。

【劳动者报酬】常住单位在生产过程支付给劳动者的全部报酬。包括三部分：一是货币工资，生产单位直接支付给劳动者的各种工资、奖金、津贴、补贴等；二是实物工资，即生产单位以免费或低于成本价提供给劳动者的各种物品和服务，以及居民自产自用的消费品等；三是社会保险，指单位为劳动者直接向政府和保险部门支付的待业、退休、养老、人身、医疗、家庭财产等保险金，这些支付款不论何时实际支付给劳动者，都应记入本期的劳动者报酬。

【生产税净额】各部门向政府支付的生产税与政府向各部门支付的生产补贴相抵之后差额。

1—1 行政区划

(1993年)　　单位:个

地名	地级单位	县级					乡镇级					
		合计	县	自治县	市	市辖区	合计	县辖区	镇	乡	民族乡	街道办事处
全省	14	86	60	7	8	11	1 689	8	191	1 321	40	129
兰州市	1	8	3			5	132		13	77		42
天水市	1	7	4	1		2	160		12	137		11
白银市	1	5	3			2	84		5	74	1	4
金昌市	1	2	1			1	23		4	8		11
嘉峪关市	1	1				1	9			3		6
庆阳地区	1	8	7		1		148		26	119	1	2
平凉地区	1	7	6		1		134		17	103	11	3
陇南地区	1	9	9				244	2	39	196	7	
定西地区	1	7	7				169		14	154	1	
武威地区	1	4	2	1	1		126		21	93	1	11
张掖地区	1	6	4	1	1		112	6	8	80	7	11
酒泉地区	1	7	2	2	3		102		19	59	2	22
临夏回族自治州	1	8	5	2	1		138		9	119	4	6
甘南藏族自治州	1	7	7				108		4	99	5	

1—2 甘肃省地(市、州)所在地和邮编

地名	所在地及邮编	地名	所在地及邮编
兰州市	城关区(730030)	陇南地区	武都县(746000)
天水市	秦城区(741000)	定西地区	定西县(743000)
白银市	白银区(730900)	武威地区	武威市(733000)
金昌市	金川区(737100)	张掖地区	张掖市(734000)
嘉峪关市	嘉峪关区(735100)	酒泉地区	酒泉市(735000)
庆阳地区	西峰市(745000)	临复回族自治州	临夏市(731100)
平凉地区	平凉市(744000)	甘南藏族自治州	合作镇(747000)

1—3 各部门基层单位数和人数

指　　标	机构数(个)		1993年为1992年%	人数(万人)		1993年为1992年%
	1992年	1993年		1992年	1993年	
一.农业基层单位						
乡政府	1 365	1 528	111.94			
镇府	163	166	101.84			
村民委员会	17 675	17 708	100.19			
农户数(万户)	399.29	407.88	102.15			
国营农林牧渔场	723	341	47.16			
#农场	343					
农技站	1 318.00	1 355.00	102.81			
乡镇企业数	239 472	274 658	114.69			
二.工业企业单位						
国有经济	1 624	1 489	91.69	88.29	89.63	101.52
集体经济	5 235	4 843	92.51	22.85	33.49	146.56
三.公路运输单位						
国有经济	83	83	100	4.71	4.89	103.82
集体经济	10	10	100	0.78	0.82	105.13
四.建筑业施工单位						
国有经济	83	84	101.20	13.48	14.08	104.46
集体经济	3 180	3 199	100.60	6.50	6.21	95.45
农村建筑队	7 791					
五.批发零售贸易和餐饮业						
国有经济	7 979	8 096	101.47	7.92	8.13	102.65
集体经济	19 330	19 430	100.52	10.73	11.24	104.75
私营经济	1	7	700.00	7 421.00	7 799.00	105.09
个体经济	178 619	189 021	105.82	27.72	28.13	101.48
六.自然科学研究和开发机构						
中央	48	48				
地方	121	121				
七.教育						
高等教育	17	17	100.00	3.45	4.17	120.87
中等教育	37.50			12.50	15.01	120.08
小学	25 320	23 887	94.34	247.12	250.00	101.17
成人学校	25	25		82.46		
幼儿园	568	574	101.06			
盲聋哑学校	8	9	112.50	236.00	247.00	104.66
八.文化事业机构						
电影事业机构	2 843	2 473	86.99	0.76	0.70	92.11
艺术表演团体	83	80	96.39	0.49	0.47	95.92
图书馆	86	86	100.00	0.09	0.09	100.00
广播电视	39	41	105.13	0.99	1.21	122.22
九.卫生事业机构						
医院	1 561	1 637	104.87	7.63	6.32	82.83
疗养院.所	9	9	100.00	0.01	0.01	100
十.保险业						
(一)省级公司	1	1	100.00	0.02	0.02	100.00
(二)地.市级公司	14	14	100.00	0.05	0.06	120.00
(三)县支公司	78	77	98.72	0.08	0.09	112.50
(四)市辖办事处	17	12	70.59	0.04	0.05	125.00
(五)县以下营业所	15	16	106.67	0.005	0.01	200.00

1—4 土地状况

(1993年)

项　　目	面积 (平方公里)	占总面积 (%)
总面积	454 430.00	100.00
1.按地形分		
山地	118 014.00	25.97
高原	134 049.00	29.50
川地	134 549.00	29.61
戈壁.沙漠	68 115.00	14.99
2.按地高分		
海拔1000米以下	34 890.00	7.68
海拔1000—2000米	233 878.00	51.47
海拔2000—3000米	93 524.00	20.58
海拔3000米以上	91 708.00	20.18
3.按特征分(万亩)		
耕地	5 221.73	7.66
森林	6 069.66	8.90
水面	765.07	1.12
草原	25 369.46	37.21

1—5 河流基本情况

(1993年)

名　称	流域面积 (万平方公里)	河流长度 (公里)	年径流量 (亿立方米)
长江	3.80	1 116.40	106.00
#白龙江	1.90	454.10	62.80
黄河	14.50	533.50	135.00
#洮河	2.50	673.10	51.50
内陆河	27.10	1 274.70	58.00
#疏勒河	15.20	622.00	10.00
黑河	5.60	527.00	22.00

1—6 国民经济主要指标

指标	单位	1978年	1980年	1985年	1990年	1993年
一.年末人口数	万人	1 870.05	1 918.43	2 041.29	2 229.91	2 318.57
自然增长率	‰	12.22	10.90	12.86	14.48	13.32
二.从业人员数	万人	694.00	796.00	1 081.00	1 293.00	1 417.80
#国有单位职工人数	万人	144.00	157.00	175.00	195.00	207.00
三.国内生产总值(当年价)	万元	647 328	739 025	1 233 875	2 339 584	3 583 363
四.农业						
1.农业总产值(当年价)	万元	224 533	273 886	527 217	1 030 526	1 404 213
2.主要农产品产量						
粮食	万吨	491.00	492.50	530.55	686.20	750.26
棉花	万吨	0.33	0.27	0.51	0.79	1.28
油料	万吨	8.59	13.95	22.65	33.65	37.53
种草面积	万亩			627.42	394.26	375.47
大牲畜	万头	366.08	392.38	507.88	584.04	596.38
生猪	万头	474.99	423.94	546.51	594.74	645.10
羊只	万头	1 043.22	1 187.50	912.76	1 109.83	1 025.58
五.工业						
1.工业总产值(当年价)	万元	772 945	770 887	1 264 052	2 746 265	5 052 478
#轻工业	万元	141 153	153 457	326 147	781 582	1 148 377
重工业	万元	631 792	617 430	937 905	1 964 683	3 904 101
2.主要工业产品产量						
布	万米	5 883.00	6 210.00	5 806.00	6 781.00	3 769.39
呢绒	万米	425.24	476.86	769.00	978.62	685.99
卷烟	万箱	10.97	13.60	15.47	27.96	30.40
发电量	亿千瓦小时	114.48	119.48	147.34	171.39	227.91
原油	万吨	81.97	135.51	156.45	146.11	148.19
原煤	万吨	980.34	766.23	1 184.53	1 564.11	1 805.58
钢	万吨	15.39	16.99	29.39	66.93	106.45
水泥	万吨	155.66	179.35	292.76	358.38	543.11
3.国有单位独立核算工业企业全员劳动生产率	元	11 306	12 319	14 045	16 085	29 398
六.全社会固定资产投资总额	万元	92 978	126 451	338 964	593 470	1 220 812
#国有单位固定资产投资额	万元	92 575	125 653	259 740	492 667	957 031
#基本建设投资额	万元	92 575	101 582	162 443	294 760	570 006
基建竣工住宅面积	万平方米	59.97	143.20	162.79	95.82	124.57
国有单位建筑企业全员劳动生产率	元	3 531	3 941	7 575	13 568.00	22 069.00
七.运输.邮电						
1.铁路货运周转量	亿吨公里	163.97	158.16	219.83	286.71	318.02
公路货运周转量	万吨公里	115 549	87 594	105 395	563 117	810 653
2.铁路客运周转量(境内)	万人公里	355 100	462 433	758 260	727 603	914 261
公路客运周转量	万人公里	101 700	137 295	252 570	348 802	344 746
3.邮电业务总量(当年价)	万元	2 322	2 547	4 794	10193	37 036
八.国内商业						

1—6续

指　标	单位	1978年	1980年	1985年	1990年	1993年
1.社会消费品零售总额	万元	207 222	264 779	518 104	961640	1 561 087
2.主要商品零售量						
粮食	万吨	87.50	120.52	123.32	147.83	106.55
食用植物油	万吨	1.11	1.47	4.25	4.14	9.65
肥猪	万头	136.08	136.92	124.80	154.39	1 428.93
棉布	万米	14 215	12 806	9 284	3 680	938.80
九.对外贸易						
出口额	万美元	3 454	3 927	7 098	18 574	28 347
进口额	万美元			2 906	1 647	20 088
进出口总额	万美元	3 454	3 927	10 004	20 221	48 435
十.财政						
财政收入	万元	205 280	149 348	164 837	342 605	521 132
财政支出	万元	143 429	123 045	240 787	459 395	631 676
十一.科技教育						
1.各类专业技术人员	人			198 470	312 423	331 030
2.在校学生数	万人	447.88	420.02	376.66	351.04	354.06
#高等学校	万人	1.39	1.84	2.72	3.39	4.05
中等专业学校	万人	1.94	2.68	3.61	4.97	5.52
普通中学	万人	104.70	96.77	100.04	96.49	87.28
小学	万人	339.85	318.73	270.29	241.69	249.97
十二.文化						
1.报刊出版数	万份	9 524	10 300	17 593	20 568	24 986
2.杂志出版数	万册	87	671	3 217	3 274	5 522
3.图书出版数	万册	5 041	5 776	6 935	7 235	6 136
十三.卫生						
1.卫生医疗机构	个	3 536	3 675	4 007	4 132	4 141
2.卫生床位数	张	33 676	36 071	40 931	48 988	54 845
3.卫生技术人员	人	45 733	48 861	60 144	71 071	77 807
#医生	人	22 298	24 102	25 660	33 019	35 751
十四.人民生活						
1.农民人均纯收入	元	101.00	151.00	257.00	431.00	550.83
2.职工年平均生活费收入	元		360.00	641.00	1 245.00	1 839.00
3.职工年工资总额	万元	114 123.60	145 396.70	268 017.00	548860.00	858 851.80
4.职工年平均工资	元	708.00	875.00	1 363.00	2 407.00	3 422.00
5.城乡居民储蓄存款余额	万元	36 719	62 543	252 024	1 005 759	2 039 573
#城镇	万元	30 537	51 756	200 101	841 532	1 730 088
农村	万元	6 182	10 787	51 923	167 227	309 485
十五.物价总指数						
(1952年=100)						
1.零售物价总指数	%	113.60	120.40	93.60	227.30	284.30
2.职工生活费用价格总指数	%	114.50	125.10	151.80	255.70	334.70
3.农副产品收购价格总指数	%	145.20	187.90	233.60	358.30	418.60
4.农村工业品零售价总指数	%	92.60	93.60	103.00	158.70	

注:公路货运周转量90年、93年包括非交通系统

1—7 国民经济主要指标发展速度

单位:%

指　　标	1993年为下列年份的%					1978—1993年平均增长%
	1978年	1980年	1985年	1990年	1992年	
一. 年末人口	123.98	120.86	113.58	103.98	101.33	1.44
二. 从业人员数	204.29	178.12	131.16	109.65	108.56	4.88
#国有单位职工人数	143.75	131.85	118.29	106.15	100.98	2.45
三. 国内生产总值	335.85	303.61	205.82	130.36	111.58	8.41
四. 工农业总产值						
农业总产值	244.76	234.96	159.96	119.24	108.64	6.15
工业总产值	280.51	320.07	317.78	139.95	109.99	7.12
#轻工业	368.52	439.33	286.81	114.36	99.59	9.08
重工业	261.53	288.20	328.30	138.90	113.59	6.62
五. 主要农产品产量						
粮食	146.95	152.34	141.41	109.34	108.86	2.60
棉花	376.47	474.07	250.98	162.03	73.14	9.24
油料	436.40	269.03	165.70	111.53	102.88	10.32
大牲畜	162.91	151.99	117.43	102.11	100.96	3.31
生猪	135.81	152.17	118.04	108.47	102.89	2.06
羊只	98.31	86.36	112.36	92.41	101.32	−0.11
六. 主要工业品产量						
布	64.07	60.69	64.92	55.58	80.98	−2.92
呢绒	161.32	143.86	89.21	39.44	82.39	3.24
卷烟	277.12	223.53	196.51	108.73	103.05	7.03
发电量	199.08	190.75	154.68	132.98	113.77	4.70
原油	180.79	109.36	94.72	101.42	74.81	4.03
原煤	184.18	235.64	152.43	115.44	117.07	4.16
钢	691.68	626.55	362.20	159.05	113.97	13.76
水泥	348.91	302.82	185.51	151.54	110.93	8.69
七. 国有单位独立核算工业企业全员劳动生产率	170.58	156.56	137.32	119.91	104.37	3.62
八. 全社会固定资产投资总额	1 312.69	965.06	360.12	205.70	143.40	18.73
#国有单位基本建设投资	615.55	561.02	350.99	193.35	144.27	12.88
基建竣工住宅面积	207.72	86.99	76.52	130.00	103.52	4.99

1—7 续 单位:%

指标	1993 年为下列年份的%					1978—1993 年平均增长%
	1978 年	1980 年	1985 年	1990 年	1992 年	
九. 运输. 邮电						
铁路货运周转量	193.95	201.07	144.67	110.92	101.68	4.52
公路货运周转量	701.57	925.47	769.16	143.96	101.17	13.87
铁路客运周转量	257.47	197.71	120.57	125.65	109.40	6.51
公路客运周转量	338.98	251.10	136.50	98.84	94.23	8.48
邮电业务总量	668.01	636.28	455.15	214.06	137.31	13.50
十. 社会消费品零售总额	753.34	589.58	301.31	162.34	108.28	14.41
十一. 主要商品零售量						
粮食	121.77	88.41	86.40	72.08	61.41	1.32
食用植物油	869.37	656.46	227.06	233.09	172.94	15.51
肥猪	1 050.07	1 043.62	1 144.98	925.53	735.16	16.97
棉布	6.60	7.33	10.11	25.51	46.04	—16.57
十二. 对外贸易						
出口额	820.70	721.85	399.37	152.62	80.58	15.07
进口额			691.26	1 219.67	313.24	
十三. 财政						
财政收入	253.86	348.94	316.15	152.11	130.37	6.41
财政支出	440.41	513.37	262.34	137.50	118.12	10.39
十四. 科技教育						
各类专业技术人员			166.79	105.96	104.67	
高等学校在校学生数	291.37	220.11	148.90	119.47	117.05	7.39
中等专业学校在校学生数	284.54	205.97	152.91	111.07	106.98	7.22
十五. 文化						
报纸出版数量	262.35	242.58	142.02	121.48	93.29	6.64
杂志出版数量	6 347.13	822.95	171.65	168.66	110.79	31.88
图书出版数量	121.72	106.23	88.48	84.81	76.82	1.32
十六. 卫生						
卫生医疗机构数	113.92	112.68	103.34	100.22	98.78	0.87
卫生床位数	162.86	152.05	133.99	111.96	104.64	3.30
卫生技术人员	170.13	159.24	129.37	109.48	102.04	3.61

1—8 货币流通增长速度同相关指标增长速度的比率

（以货币流通增长速度为 1）

年　份	国内生产总值	国民收入	工业总产值	社会消费品零售总额	社会农副产品收购总额
1978	0.05	0.31	0.26	0.20	
1980	0.29	0.24	0.17	0.54	1.12
1985	0.42	0.48	0.58	0.92	0.66
1990	0.18	0.16	0.24		0.41
1991	0.21	0.21	0.23	0.33	0.15
1992	0.31	0.32	0.40	0.67	0.84
1993	0.37	0.47	0.32	0.26	

1—9 国民经济主要指标之间的比例

单位：%

年　份	财政收入占国内生产总值的比重	财政收入占国民收入的比重	工业增加值占国内生产总值的比重	国有单位固定资产投资占国内生产总值的比重	基建拨款占财政支出的比重
1978	31.71	37.58	53.55	16.20	28.92
1980	20.21	24.60	47.70	17.00	21.72
1985	13.36	16.20	40.96	21.05	17.15
1990	14.62	16.50	35.86	21.06	8.40
1991	15.65	17.70	38.05	22.32	7.97
1992	13.17	14.94	36.54	18.94	7.69
1993	14.54	16.36	43.76	26.71	7.03

1—10 国民经济主要指标占全国比重

(1992 年)

指 标	单位	全国	甘肃	甘肃省占全国%
一. 人口				
年底总人口	万人	117 171.00	2 288.12	1.95
二. 劳动力(年底数)				
劳动力资源人数	万人	72 120.00	1 647.70	2.28
社会从业人员数	万人	59 432.00	1 306.40	2.19
#职工人数	万人	14 792.00	252.00	1.70
三. 国民生产总值	亿元	24 036.00	301.64	1.25
四. 国民收入	亿元	19 845.00	265.78	1.34
五. 工农业总产值	亿元	46 151.00	491.97	1.07
六. 全社会固定资产投资	亿元	7 854.98	85.13	1.08
国有单位固定资产投资	亿元	5 273.64	71.76	1.36
#基本建设投资	亿元	3 012.65	39.51	1.31
更新改造投资	亿元	1 754.91	21.61	1.23
七. 财政				
1. 财政收入	亿元	4 153.10	39.97	0.96
2. 财政支出	亿元	4 389.70	53.48	1.22
八. 物价总指数(上年=100)				
1. 农副产品收购价格总指数	%	103.40	108.80	+5.40 百分点
2. 零售物价总指数	%	105.40	105.70	+0.30 百分点
3. 职工生活费用价格总指数	%	108.60	107.30	−1.30 百分点
九. 工资				
1. 职工工资总额	亿元	3 939.20	72.29	1.84
2. 职工平均工资	元	2 711.00	2 902.00	+191.00 元
十. 居民消费水平	元	935.00	689.00	− 246.00 元
1. 农民	元	648.00	452.00	− 196.00 元
2. 非农业居民	元	1 983.00	1 855.00	− 128.00 元
十一. 农业				
1. 农业总产值	亿元	9 085.00	122.70	1.35
2. 主要农产品产量				
粮食	万吨	44 266.00	689.18	1.56
棉花	万吨	450.80	1.75	0.39
油料	万吨	1 641.20	36.48	2.22
甜菜	万吨	1 506.90	94.22	6.25
水果	万吨	2 440.10	47.12	1.93
猪牛羊肉	万吨	2 940.60	44.51	1.51

1—10 续 1　　(1992 年)

指　标	单位	全国	甘肃	甘肃省占全国%
十二. 工业				
1. 工业总产值	亿元	37 066.00	369.27	1.00
2. 主要工业产品产量				
布	亿米	190.70	0.47	0.25
机制纸及纸板	万吨	1 725.00	12.68	0.74
糖	万吨	829.00	10.72	1.29
自行车	万辆	4 083.60	2.69	0.07
家用电冰箱	万台	485.80	4.80	0.99
电视机	万台	2 867.82	14.41	0.50
# 彩色电视机	万台	1 333.08	8.81	0.66
家用洗衣机	万台	707.93	22.20	3.14
录放音机	万台	3 231.80	19.11	0.59
照相机	万架	526.48	10.20	1.94
原煤	亿吨	11.16	0.15	1.34
原油	万吨	14 210.00	198.09	1.39
发电量	亿千瓦小时	7 539.00	200.32	2.66
钢	万吨	8 094.00	93.40	1.15
成品钢材	万吨	6 697.00	64.54	0.96
水泥	万吨	30 822.00	489.59	1.59
3. 国有独立核算工业企业主要财务指标				
年底固定资产原值	亿元	15 669.80	345.67	2.21
资金总额	亿元	16 094.70	392.92	2.44
年底固定资产净值	亿元	10 982.60	228.60	2.08
定额流动资金年平均余额	亿元	5 112.00	97.93	1.92
利润和税金总额	亿元	1 944.10	36.43	1.64
十三. 运输邮电				
1. 货物周转量	亿吨公里	29 218.00	391.40	1.34
铁路	亿吨公里	11 576.00	312.76	2.70
公路	亿吨公里	3 755.00	78.61	2.09
空运	亿吨公里	13.00	0.03	0.23
2. 旅客周转量	亿人公里	6 949.00	130.51	1.88
铁路	亿人公里	3 152.00	83.57	2.65
公路	亿人公里	3 [illegible]3.00	44.03	1.38
空运	亿人公里	406.00	2.91	0.72
3. 邮电业务总量(90 年不变价)	亿元	290.94	2.68	0.92
4. 函件	亿件	57.18	0.88	1.53
5. 报刊期发数	万份	25 104.00	433.60	1.73

1—10续2 (1992年)

指 标	单位	全国	甘肃	甘肃省占全国%
十四.能源生产与消费(标准煤)				
能源生产总量	万吨	107 256.00	1 712.09	1.60
能源消费总量	万吨	108 900.00	2 348.56	2.16
十五.国内商业				
1.社会商品购进总额	亿元	10 653.70	125.45	1.18
2.社会商品零售总额	亿元	10 993.70	144.17	1.31
3.主要消费品零售量				
粮食	万吨	9 774.70	173.50	1.77
食用植物油	万吨	519.90	5.58	1.07
猪肉	万吨	1 448.70	29.13	2.01
食糖	万吨	602.70	1.84	0.31
布	亿米	125.00	0.20	0.16
缝纫机	万架	501.20	8.77	1.75
自行车	万辆	3 243.40	25.30	0.78
电视机	万台	2 137.80	12.73	0.60
洗衣机	万台	1 091.00	5.52	0.51
电冰箱	万台	472.10	3.69	0.78
4.农业生产资料销售量				
化学肥料(标准量)	万吨	10 119.40	178.36	1.76
化学农药	万吨	53.80	0.20	0.37
农用动力机械	万千瓦	1 154.70	5.92	0.51
十六.对外贸易				
进出口总额	亿美元	1 656.10	4.16	0.25
进口额	亿美元	806.10	0.64	0.08
出口额	亿美元	850.00	3.52	0.41
十七.教育文化				
1.在校学生数				
高等学校	万人	218.40	3.46	1.58
中等专业学校	万人	240.80	5.16	2.14
普通中学	万人	4 770.80	94.01	1.97
小学	万人	12 201.30	247.12	2.03
2.出版数量				
图书	亿册	63.40	0.80	1.26
杂志	亿册	23.60	0.50	2.12
报纸	亿份	189.10	2.68	1.42
十八.卫生				
医院床位数	万张	274.40	5.24	1.91
卫生技术人员数	万人	407.40	7.63	1.87
#医生	万人	180.80	3.86	2.13

注:本表价值指标均按当年价格计算。

1—11 按经济类型分的国民经济主要比例关系

单位：%

指　　标	1978年	1980年	1985年	1990年	1993年
1.从业人数比例					
国有单位	20.81	19.42	16.15	15.06	14.60
集体单位	2.18	2.14	2.41	2.86	3.29
其他单位			0.01	0.02	0.15
城镇个体劳动者	0.13	0.14	0.93	0.64	1.08
乡村劳动力	76.88	78.30	80.50	81.42	80.88
2.全社会固定资产投资额比例					
国有单位	99.57	99.37	73.63	83.01	78.39
集体单位	0.43	0.63	11.66	5.15	11.61
城乡个人			11.71	11.84	10.00
3.工业总产值比例					
国有经济	90.84	92.18	88.25	77.96	83.59
集体经济	9.16	7.82	10.64	17.90	15.67
私营经济					0.01
联营经济					0.18
其他经济			1.11	4.14	0.55
4.社会消费品零售总额					
国有经济				46.61	40.47
集体经济				24.60	20.81
私营经济					0.84
个体经济				18.87	25.41
其他经济				9.92	12.47

1—12 甘肃的一天

指标	单位	1978年	1980年	1985年	1990年	1993年
每天创造的财富						
工农业总产值(当年价)	万元	2 790	2 904	4 799	10 459	17 689
农业总产值(当年价)	万元	615	791	1 444	2 823	3 847
工业总产值(当年价)	万元	2 175	2 112	3 354	7 636	13 842
国内生产总值(当年价)	万元	1 774	2 025	3 380	6 410	9 817
财政收入	万元	562	409	452	937	1 428
布	万米	16.12	17.00	15.90	18.58	10.33
原油	吨	2 246	3 713	4 286	4 003	4 060
原煤	吨	26 804	20 993	32 453	42 852	49 468
发电量	万千瓦小时	3 136	3 273	4 037	4 696	6 244
卷烟	箱	301	373	424	766	833
毛毯	条	2 265	2 571	5 093	4 526	3 186
呢绒	万米	1.2	1.3	2.1	2.7	1.8
粮食	万吨	0.24	1.35	1.45	1.88	2.06
油料	吨	235	382	721	843	1 028
一天消费量						
城乡居民消费额	万元	735	931	1 674	3 340	5 075
每人消费额	元	0.40	0.49	0.82	1.49	2.20
粮食	万吨	1.12	1.07	1.12	1.29	1.32
食用植物油	吨	74.00	92.00	170.00	271.00	387.91
猪肉	吨	244.00	313.00	349.00	523.00	761.45
鲜蛋	吨			85.00	89.61	278.53
食糖	吨			99.00	123.51	71.02
棉布	万米	37.05	38.43	25.64	12.16	31.04
自行车	辆			1 072.00	875.00	1 414.84
缝纫机	架			295.00	228.00	171.38
电冰箱	台				76.00	296.61
电视机	台			623.00	427.00	704.22
洗衣机	台				174.00	261.25
其他经济活动						
住宅竣工活动	平方米	1 778	3 923	4 460	3 572	4 133
函件	万件	16.82	18.67	24.28	28.63	25.57
电报	万份	1.03	0.94	1.18	1.48	1.45
出版报纸	万份	26.09	28.22	48.20	56.36	68.45
人口变动和婚姻						
出生	人		741	1 023	1 268	1 281
死亡	人		273	305	380	434
结婚	对			411.6	488.8	426.0
离婚	对			7.2	10.3	5.5

1—13 按人口平均计算的国民经济主要指标

指标	单位	1978年	1980年	1985年	1990年	1993年
1.国内生产总值(当年价)	元	348.26	387.71	608.28	1 063.28	1 555.72
第一产业	元	71.06	86.33	163.08	291.11	379.60
第二产业	元	210.03	209.08	289.95	446.89	694.47
第三产业	元	67.18	92.31	154.87	325.27	481.65
2.工农业总产值(当年价)	元	547.85	556.06	863.46	1 734.95	2 803.17
农业总产值	元	120.80	147.35	240.28	468.35	609.64
工业总产值	元	427.06	412.37	623.17	1 266.61	2 193.53
轻工业产值	元	78.30	87.12	158.23	365.35	498.57
重工业产值	元	348.76	325.25	464.94	901.26	1 694.97
3.财政收入	元	110.44	78.35	81.26	155.46	226.25
财政支出	元	77.16	64.55	118.70	208.78	274.24
4.基本建设投资	元	49.80	53.29	80.08	133.96	247.47
5.社会消费品零售总额	元	138.69	159.60	288.17	498.03	677.75
6.主要工农业产品产量						
粮食	公斤	274.67	257.20	261.55	311.86	325.73
棉花	公斤	0.18	0.14	0.25	0.43	0.56
油料	公斤	4.63	7.32	11.17	15.29	16.29
生猪	头	0.26	0.22	0.27	0.27	0.28
棉布	米	3.17	3.26	2.86	3.08	1.64
呢绒	米	0.23	0.25	0.38	0.45	0.30
毛毯	条	0.04	0.05	0.09	0.08	0.05
发电量	度	615.92	626.85	726.37	778.92	989.47
7.主要消费品社会零售量						
粮食	公斤	47.07	63.23	60.40	66.10	46.26
食用植物油	公斤	0.60	0.77	2.20	1.90	4.15
猪和猪肉	头	0.07	0.07	0.10	0.10	
棉布	米	7.65	6.72	4.60	1.70	0.41
8.在校学生数(每万人)	人	2 409.56	2 203.55	1 845.20	1 569.20	1 505.72
高等学校(每万人)	人	7.48	9.65	13.30	15.20	17.58
9.专业卫生技术人员数(每万人)	人	25.57	25.63	29.50	32.00	33.78
卫生床位数(每万人)	张	18.12	18.92	20.10	21.90	23.81

注:平均人中按公安年报中的户籍计算。

1—14 国内生产总值、指数和构成

年 份	国内生产总值	第一产业	第二产业	第三产业	人均国内生产总值(元)
一. 绝对值(万元)					
1978	647 328	132 075	390 389	124 864	348
1979	675 161	128 918	409 803	136 440	359
1980	739 025	164 552	398 522	175 951	388
1981	708 850	176 297	353 039	179 514	367
1982	768 755	196 749	385 376	186 630	393
1983	914 998	276 518	429 207	209 273	462
1984	1 031 714	278 278	499 874	253 562	515
1985	1 233 875	330 796	588 139	314 940	608
1986	1 407 404	380 184	652 682	374 538	684
1987	1 595 231	452 675	684 075	458 481	764
1988	1 918 432	527 668	813 345	577 419	905
1989	2 168 392	590 122	917 864	660 406	1 007
1990	2 339 584	640 554	983 323	715 707	1 046
1991	2 554 565	665 470	1 119 149	769 946	1 133
1992	3 016 371	742 031	1 286 594	987 746	1 314
1993	3 583 363	874 343	1 599 602	1 109 418	1 540
二. 指数(1978 年为 100)					
1978	100.00	100.00	100.00	100.00	100.00
1979	101.41	87.43	104.89	108.88	103.16
1980	110.62	108.26	102.78	139.27	109.77
1981	101.29	101.57	88.29	143.16	104.60
1982	110.33	117.96	95.58	148.02	112.07
1983	126.72	144.67	108.14	163.01	131.61
1984	140.16	160.84	122.10	193.42	147.13
1985	163.18	173.91	138.60	228.62	173.56
1986	181.17	185.88	147.13	285.45	195.40
1987	197.33	198.03	150.59	348.23	218.39
1988	224.27	213.16	171.57	410.36	258.33
1989	243.90	225.95	188.21	448.52	287.93
1990	257.63	237.17	198.39	477.55	304.31
1991	274.38	240.96	216.25	513.84	325.57
1992	300.99	254.94	238.31	578.58	377.58
1993	335.85	277.37	270.70	642.63	442.52

1—14 续

年份	国内生产总值	第一产业	第二产业	第三产业	人均国内生产总值（元）
指数(以上年为 100)					
1978					
1979	101.41	87.43	104.89	108.88	103.16
1980	109.09	123.82	98.00	127.91	106.41
1981	91.56	93.83	85.90	102.79	95.29
1982	108.92	116.13	108.25	103.40	107.14
1983	114.86	122.64	113.14	110.13	147.44
1984	113.76	111.18	112.91	118.66	111.79
1985	113.19	108.13	113.51	118.20	117.96
1986	111.03	106.88	106.16	124.86	112.58
1987	108.92	106.54	102.41	122.05	111.77
1988	113.65	107.64	103.94	117.84	118.29
1989	108.75	105.99	109.75	109.32	111.46
1990	105.63	104.97	105.36	106.44	105.69
1991	106.50	101.60	109.00	107.60	106.99
1992	109.70	105.80	110.20	112.60	115.98
1993	111.58	108.80	113.59	111.07	117.20
三. 构成(%)					
1978	100.00	20.40	60.31	19.29	
1979	100.00	19.09	60.70	20.21	
1980	100.00	22.27	53.92	23.81	
1981	100.00	24.87	49.80	25.33	
1982	100.00	25.59	50.13	24.28	
1983	100.00	30.22	46.91	22.87	
1984	100.00	26.97	48.45	24.58	
1985	100.00	26.81	47.67	25.52	
1986	100.00	27.01	46.38	26.61	
1987	100.00	28.38	42.88	28.74	
1988	100.00	27.51	42.40	30.09	
1989	100.00	27.21	42.33	30.46	
1990	100.00	27.38	42.03	30.59	
1991	100.00	26.05	43.81	30.14	
1992	100.00	24.60	42.65	30.75	
1993	100.00	24.40	44.64	30.96	

1—15 国民经济主要指标分类比例关系

指　　标	1978年	1980年	1985年	1990年	1993年
一.国内生产总值	100.00	100.00	100.00	100.00	100.00
第一产业	20.40	22.27	26.81	27.38	24.40
第二产业	60.31	53.92	47.67	42.03	44.64
第三产业	19.29	23.81	25.52	30.59	30.96
二.工农业总产值	100.00	100.00	100.00	100.00	100.00
农业	22.05	25.84	28.69	26.99	21.75
工业	77.95	74.16	71.31	73.01	78.25
轻工业(工业＝100)	18.33	21.13	25.51	28.84	22.73
重工业	81.67	78.87	74.49	71.16	77.27
三.农业总产值	100.00	100.00	100.00	100.00	100.00
农作物种植业	70.45	71.96	60.12	65.61	64.85
林业	2.30	2.26	6.83	3.17	3.37
牧业	16.85	16.20	19.12	25.54	25.72
副业	10.40	9.57	13.92	5.47	5.76
渔业		0.01	0.01	0.21	0.30
四.基本建设投资中(国有)					100.00
第一产业					5.04
第二第业					40.40
第三产业					40.65
五.基本建设投资中	100.00	100.00	100.00	100.00	100.00
农业	13.90	15.10	9.19	9.71	1.38
工业	54.22	51.20	54.70	66.73	48.42
轻工业	3.13	3.40	5.68	2.90	6.38
重工业	51.09	47.80	49.02	63.83	42.04
六.财政收入占国民收入比例	37.58	24.60	16.20	16.50	16.36
七.基本建设支出占财政支出比例	28.92	21.72	17.21	8.40	7.03
八.文教卫生科学事业费占财政支出比例	14.49	21.58	23.79	24.01	23.50

1—16 劳动生产率、消费水平和平均工资增长速度

年　份	全社会劳动生产率（元/人）	全社会劳动生产率增长速度（%）	居民消费水平增长速度（%）	国有独立核算工业企业劳动生产率增长速度（%）	工业企业职工平均工资增长速度（%）
1978	933		7.60	−0.91	3.95
1980	928	−2.30	4.70	2.96	5.05
1981	921	−5.31	5.10	−9.71	−1.60
1982	884	−3.59	4.80	4.78	1.35
1983	921	0.50	9.70	6.73	2.66
1984	995	5.99	6.50	5.73	24.46
1985	1 142	11.71	9.20	9.33	1.15
1986	1 281	9.20	10.00	−0.15	8.87
1987	1 400	7.33	7.70	6.22	−0.35
1988	1 627	7.53	7.50	4.07	−3.94
1989	1 786	5.59	−1.00	2.20	−3.89
1990	1 810	−0.77	−3.05	1.52	7.78
1991	1 961	5.68	1.40	7.27	6.28
1992	2 310	9.52	6.06	7.10	9.98
1993	2 529	2.79	6.00	4.37	19.8

注：全社会劳动生产率是平均每一个社会劳动者创造的国内生产总值表示的。

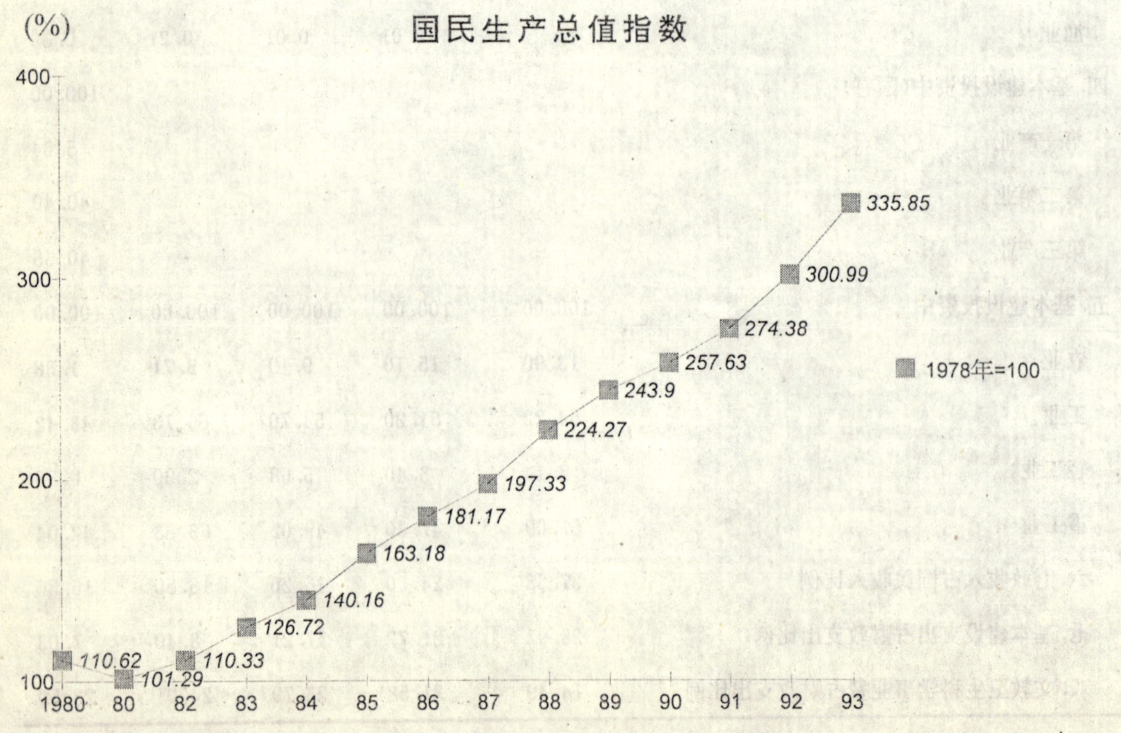

1—17 甘肃省股份制企业一览表

(1993年)

企业名称	批准日期	法人代表	注册资金(万元)	经营范围
兰州连海铝业进出口公司	93.8.27	王传圣	2000.00	本企业自产产品及相关技术出口,本地生产科研所需原辅材料,机械设备,仪器仪表、零配件及相关技术的进口.
甘肃省蓝天广告艺术有限公司	93.9.18	张世奇	16.00	设计、制作、发国内广告,组织策划、举办展览,装璜及设计,摄影,摄像,信息咨询.
兰州金鼎旅游服务有限公司	93.11.1	刘兰平	250.00	住宿.房屋出租
白银铜城商厦股份有限公司	93.11.1	魏兴毅	5000.00	农副产品、建筑材料、金属材料、化工产品、汽车配件、机电产品、普通机械、五金交电
兰州涌泉精细化工有限公司	93.11.6	李少强	50.00	装饰材料、建筑材料、室内装饰。
甘肃省租赁有限公司	93.4.3	张升吉	3300	动产、不动产的租赁、转租赁、回租、委托租赁;向金融机构借款,及其它融资;特定项下信托资金业务;租赁;闲置设备的转租赁;租赁项下的短期流动资金贷款;担保;经济咨询;代理业务;经人民银行批准发行债券及其它金融业务。
甘肃金川冶金股份有限公司	93.4.15	何焕华	5000	电解铜,金属深加工。
甘肃三星石化股份有限公司	93.11.18	韩大可	4528	石油化工产品,仪器仪表,电子计算机,金属材料,建筑材料。
甘肃医药集团天威药业有限公司	93.10.22	梁兰珍	80	化学药制剂,中成药,医疗器械。
甘肃八达交通商务有限公司	93.2.26	范汝勤	58	公路及附属设施开发,建筑材料。

注:工商局提供

1—17 续 1

企业名称	批准日期	法人代表	股本总额（万元）	经营范围
白银有色工贸股份有限公司	93.1.2		5000.00	金属材料、矿产品、有色金属加工材料
兰州华都聚氨酯制品有限公司	93.1.11	张新华	60.00	生产经营聚氨酯原料及模塑制品
兰州永合机电设备有限公司	93.1.30	于志文	70.00	机电产品、机电设备成套、安装调试
甘肃长风宝安实业股份有限公司	93.3.18		12250.00	家用电器、视像产品、通讯设备
甘肃电子大厦股份有限公司	93.3.31		5000.00	电子电器产品的开发、销售、成果推广应用
甘肃金厦建筑安装有限责任公司	93.6.4	陈立华	200.00	工业、民用建筑施工、装饰、装璜、房地产
甘肃三佳稀土有限责任公司	93.6.14	尉锦昌	1764.50	氯化稀土和其他稀土化合物
甘肃科弘实业发展有限公司	93.6.21	王德存	50.00	高新技术产品开发、引进生产、销售、咨询、培训
甘肃省农垦实业有限公司	93.6.21		100.00	混凝土制品、塑料制品、食品加工
甘肃北荣技术实业有限公司	93.7.12	朱怀安	48.00	新产品、新技术开发、培训、咨询服务
甘肃振兴冶化有限公司	93.7.16		120.00	净水剂、纸品、铝锭、EPS 轻型包装材料
白银氟化盐有限公司	93.8.7		1519.00	铝冶炼熔剂氟化盐系列产品、化工产品、有色金属及矿产品的生产、销售
甘肃证券研究设计中心	93.9.3		1 000.00	证券交易、咨询、培训、证券编辑
兰州黄河实业股份有限公司	93.9.21		8680.00	生产经营"兰乐"牌啤酒及系列产品
甘肃省兰桦工贸有限责任公司	93.10.4	何玉梅	300.00	轮胎.化工材料.汽车及配件等

注：体改委提供

1—17续2

(单位:万元)

企业名称	批准时间	股本总额	股权结构		
			国家股	法人股	个人股
兰州百货大楼股份有限公司	93.3.26	3 000.00	1 050.00	1 650.00	300.00
兰州工贸商场股份有限公司	93.3.26	2 000.00	800.00	1 000.00	200.00
星宇有限公司	93.1.30	890.00		740.00	150.00
永昌建材工业有限公司		585.00	175.50	120.08	289.42
甘肃陇海实业有限公司	93.2.6	500.00		400.00	100.00
永昌县水电局皇城电业有限公司		430.91	130.00	90.00	210.91
海嘉经济技术开发有限公司	93.2.27	1 000.00		1 000.00	
向阳湖砖瓦有限公司	93.3.2	200.00		45.00	155.00
深酒贸易有限公司	93.3.3	40.00		40.00	
酒泉富达工贸实业有限公司	93.3.4	50.00		40.00	10.00
陇宝房地产有限公司	93.3.12	50.00		50.00	
兰州康灵生物工程开发有限公司	93.3.12	1 632.00		1 632.00	
徽县铅锌开发有限公司	93.3.20	200.00		200.00	
景泰陇盛实业开发有有限责任公司	93.3.30	916.80		916.80	
敦煌茂源有限公司	93.3	42.00		34.00	8.00
酒泉恒达矿业有限公司	93.4.2	50.00		30.50	19.50
酒泉市物运有限责任公司	93.4.2	65.00		65.00	
农行临夏州中心支行房地产开发有限责任公司	93.4.6	600.00	300.00	290.00	10.00
兰州文达贸易有限公司	93.4.10	50.00		50.00	
陇东特种水产开发有限公司	93.4.23	310.00		310.00	
景泰宇龙肉鸽有限责任公司	93.4.26	321.50		321.50	
白银长通企业有限公司	93.4.28	500.00		150.00	350.00
鸣沙山矿泉水有限公司	93.4	600.00		600.00	
甘肃白银市联合运输有限公司	93.5.4	100.00		100.00	
甘肃省陇南地区石油有限公司	93.5.5	50.00		20.00	30.00

1—17 续 3 (单位:万元)

企业名称	批准时间	股本总额	股权结构		
			国家股	法人股	个人股
华油腾达实业有限公司	93.5.6	25.00			
天水宏露饮料食品有限公司	93.5.16	50.00		40.00	10.00
白银金世界珠宝有限公司	93.5.17	60.00		40.00	
甘肃平凉三星高技术开发有限公司	93.5.21	11.40	5.00	5.00	1.40
甘肃美高鞋业集团有限公司	93.6.12	300.50		300.50	
兰州原子印章有限公司	93.6.16	98.07		87.57	10.50
兰州耐火材料有责任公司	93.6.16	300.00		285.41	14.59
嘉峪关市石野开发有限公司	93.6.16				
甘肃省庆阳地区华龙食品有限公司	93.6.26				
兰州双飞精细化工有限公司	93.7.17	110.00		110.00	
西北二轻供销有限公司	93.7.27	50.00		50.00	
兰州三晶有限责任公司	93.11.5	160.00		160.00	
兰州苏皇医药保健品有限公司	93.12.2	100.00		100.00	
兰州文捷电力印刷有限公司	93.12.2	61.00		21.69	39.31
省企业股份制咨询策划有限公司	93.12.3	30.00		10.00	20.00
敦煌肃州房地产有限公司	93.	300.00		300.00	
兰州科达实业有限公司	93.9.3	50.00		50.00	
兰州江文发展有限公司	93.10.4	50.00		50.00	
兰州海洋卷烟材料有限公司	93.10.14	60.00		60.00	
敦煌花岗石板材有限公司	93.	350.00		350.00	
安西柳园水泥有限公司	93.	39.00		39.00	
兰州荣达实业有限公司	93.10.16	98.00		30.00	
天水鑫鑫食品包装有限公司	93.10.25	70.00		65.00	5.00
平凉钢铁有限公司	93.12.23	1 000.00		1 000.00	
天华实业有限公司	93.2.18	165.00		150.00	15.00
兰州房地产开发集团股份有限公司	93.2.15	5 114.00	800.00	4 314.00	

注:省体改委提供。

二. 人口与劳动力

统计指标解释

·之二·

【生产税】政府向各部门征收的有关生产、销售、购买、使用货物和服务的税金,记入各部门生产费用。生产税有四种形式,一是含在货物和服务价格中的,由生产者直接向政府缴纳的税金,如产品税、营业税、增值税、农牧业税、车船使用税、房产税、屠宰税等;二是不含在货物和服务价格中而由购买者直接缴纳并由生产者代征的税金,如牲畜交易税、集市交易税、关税、进口税、特别消费税;三是从专营专卖活动所获得的利润中上缴政府的专项收入和利润,如烟、酒等商品的专项收入;四是依照规定向政府支付的有关规费。

【生产补贴】政府为控制价格和扶持生产而对生产部门提供的补助,包括价格补贴和亏损补贴。

【营业盈余】增加值减去固定资产折旧、劳动者报酬和生产税净额后的余额。

【国内生产总值】一国所有常住单位在核算期内生产活动的最终成果。从生产角度它等于各部门增加值之和;从收入角度它等于固定资产折旧、劳动者报酬、生产税净额和营业盈余之和;从支出角度它等于总消费、总投资和净出口之和。

【物质产品净值】物质生产部门总产出减去物质产品投入和固定资产折旧后的余额。

【来自国外的劳动者报酬净额】常住居民从非常住单位获得的劳动者报酬与非常住居民从常住单位获得的劳动者报酬相抵后的差额。

【来自国外的财产收入净额】常住单位从非常住单位获得的财产收入与非常住单位从常住单位获得的财产收入相抵后的差额。

【国民生产总值】核算期内的国内生产总值与来自国外的劳动者报酬净额和来自国外的财产收入净额之和。

【财产收入】因使用其他部门的金融资产、土地,以及版权和专利权等无形资产而引起的收入转移。包括利息、红利、土地租金、特许权使用费和虚拟保险财产收益。

【初次分配收入】通过生产所得到的初次收入(营业盈余、劳动者报酬或生产税净额)经过财产收入分配后的余额,各部门的初次分配收入之和等于国民生产净值。

【收入税】各部门支付给政府的除生产税之外的税金。包括所得税、调节税、奖金税、个人收入所得税、收入调节税等。

【经常转移】部门之间以实物和资金方式实现的收入转移,其转移来自支付者的收入,并构成接受者的收入。包括社会保险、社会补助和其它经常转移,经常转移在国内各部门汇总时将被抵消,国民帐户仅反映与国外部门的经常转移净额。

2—1 人口数及构成

年份	总人口（万人）	按性别分				按城乡分			
		男		女		城镇人口		乡村人口	
		人口数（万人）	比重（%）	人口数（万人）	比重（%）	人口数（万人）	比重（%）	人口数（万人）	比重（%）
1952	1 064.69	553.64	52.00	511.05	48.00	102.22	9.60	962.47	90.40
1957	1 255.06	651.26	51.89	603.80	48.11	169.42	13.50	1085.64	86.50
1965	1 345.44	698.89	51.95	649.55	48.04	212.50	15.79	1132.94	84.21
1970	1 585.66	819.47	51.68	766.19	48.32	229.23	14.46	1356.43	85.54
1975	1 804.02	931.96	51.66	872.06	48.34	265.04	14.69	1538.98	85.31
1978	1 870.05	965.88	51.65	904.17	48.35	269.44	14.41	1600.61	85.59
1980	1 918.43	989.75	51.59	928.68	48.41	290.65	15.15	1627.78	84.85
1981	1 941.40	1 004.31	51.73	937.09	48.27	304.70	15.69	1636.70	84.31
1982	1 974.88	1 021.33	51.17	953.55	48.23	305.83	15.49	1669.05	84.51
1983	1 987.50	1 028.07	51.72	959.43	48.28	372.83	18.76	1614.67	81.24
1984	2 015.60	1 042.19	51.71	973.41	48.29	414.57	20.57	1601.03	79.43
1985	2 041.29	1 057.09	51.79	984.20	48.21	771.24	37.78	1270.05	62.22
1986	2 071.08	1 070.97	51.71	1 001.11	48.29	813.56	39.28	1 257.52	60.72
1987	2 103.41	1 087.04	51.68	1 016.37	48.32	869.00	40.32	1 255.25	59.68
1988	2 135.69	1 103.98	51.69	1 036.71	48.31	869.00	40.69	1 266.69	59.31
1989	2 170.78	1 121.54	51.66	1 049.23	48.34	890.16	41.01	1 280.62	58.99
1990	2 229.91	1 153.15	51.71	1 076.76	48.29	914.32	41.00	1 315.59	59.00
1991	2 258.01	1 166.98	51.68	1 091.03	48.32	1 026.70	45.47	1 231.32	54.53
1992	2 288.12	1 183.99	51.75	1 104.13	48.25	945.19	41.31	1 342.93	58.69
1993	2 318.57	1 200.11	51.76	1 118.46	48.24	970.45	41.86	1 348.12	58.14

2—2 人口出生率. 死亡率. 自然增长率

单位:‰

年 份	出 生 率	死 亡 率	自然增长率
1952	33.30	11.00	22.30
1957	33.00	11.33	21.67
1965	45.30	12.30	33.00
1970	39.43	7.92	31.51
1975	20.96	7.42	13.54
1978	17.77	5.58	12.19
1980	16.53	5.15	11.38
1981	20.12	5.72	14.40
1982	19.30	5.63	13.67
1983	19.79	6.76	13.03
1984	19.78	6.01	13.77
1985	18.31	5.46	12.85
1986	21.14	5.91	15.23
1987	20.55	5.71	14.84
1988	20.41	5.06	15.35
1989	22.57	5.60	16.97
1990	20.68	6.20	14.48
1991	19.38	6.05	13.33
1992	19.37	6.64	12.73
1993	20.16	6.84	13.32

2—3 人　口

指　标	单位	户籍数			人口变动情况抽样调查数		
		1990 年	1992 年	1993 年	1990 年	1992 年	1993 年
总人口	万人	2 229.91	2 288.12	2 318.57	2 254.67	2 314.19	2345.23
女性	万人	1 076.76	1 104.13	1 118.46			
男性	万人	1 153.15	1 183.99	1 200.11			
性别比(女性=100)	%	107.09	107.23	107.30			
出生率	‰				20.68	19.37	20.16
死亡率	‰				6.20	6.64	6.84
自然增长率	‰				14.48	12.73	13.32
在总人口中:							
城镇人口	万人	914.32	945.13	970.45			
乡村人口	万人	1 315.59	1 342.93	1 348.12			
在总人口中:							
农业人口	万人	1 868.25	1 905.84	1 926.13			
非农业人口	万人	361.66	382.28	392.44			
未落常住户口的人	万人	9.37	8.11	9.10			

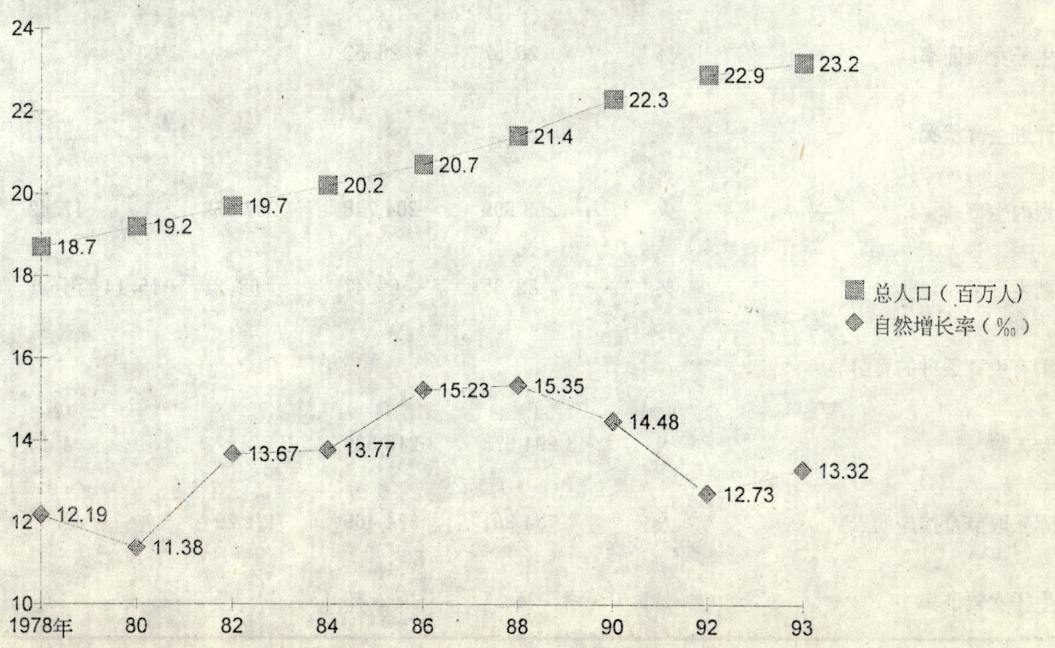

2—4 计划生育状况

项目	单位	1990年	1992年	1993年	1993年比1990年(±)%
全省计划生育状况					
计划内生育	人	339 566	238 591	287 476	−15.34
计划生育率	%	85.42	72.34	71.42	−14.00百分点
已婚有生育条件的育龄妇女人数	人	4 516 328	4 611 766	4 741990	5
实际采取节育措施的人数	人	967 463	513 960	574 673	−40.60
独生子女领证率	%	10.23	9.57	8.05	−2.18百分点
城市计划生育状况					
计划内生育	人	85 667	33 843	17 673	−79.37
计划生育率	%	92.19	70.71	99.97	7.78百分点
已婚有生育条件的育龄妇女人数	人	1 221 355	1 372 997	1 310718	7.32
实际采取节育措施的人数	人	233 162	139 491	153 379	−34.22
独生子女领证率	%	26.57	26.52		
农村计划生育状况					
计划内生育	人	253 899	204 748	209 672	−17.42
计划生育率	%	83.35	69.47	68.21	−15.14百分点
已婚有生育条件的育龄妇女人数	人	3 294 973	3 213 330	3 431272	4.14
实际采取节育措施的人数	人	734 301	374 469	421 294	−42.63
独生子女领证率	%	4.17	2.33		

2—5 劳动力资源和劳动力

年 份	劳 动 力 资 源		从 业 人 员		
	人数（万人）	占总人口比重(%)	人数（万人）	占总人口比重(%)	占劳动力资源比重(%)
1952	480.00	45.00	415.00	37.00	86.00
1957	573.00	46.00	488.00	39.00	85.00
1965	635.00	47.20	585.00	43.50	92.10
1970	754.00	47.50	648.00	40.80	85.90
1975	828.00	45.80	666.00	36.90	80.40
1978	875.00	46.70	694.00	37.10	79.30
1980	942.00	49.10	796.00	41.50	84.50
1981	1 002.00	51.60	769.80	39.70	76.80
1982	1 019.00	52.00	870.00	44.00	85.00
1983	1 147.00	58.00	994.00	50.00	87.00
1984	1 206.00	60.00	1 047.00	52.00	87.00
1985	1 272.00	62.00	1 081.00	53.00	85.00
1986	1 273.00	62.00	1 099.00	53.00	86.00
1987	1 372.00	65.00	1 140.00	54.00	83.00
1988	1 420.00	68.00	1 179.00	56.00	83.00
1989	1 474.00	68.00	1 214.00	56.00	82.00
1990	1 517.00	68.00	1 293.00	58.00	85.00
1991	1 520.10	67.32	1 302.40	57.68	85.68
1992	1 521.20	65.73	1 305.90	56.00	86.00
1993	1 647.70	71.06	1 417.80	61.00	86.00

2—6 从业人员数

单位:万人

年 份	从业人数合计	职工				城镇私营企业及个体劳动者	乡村劳动者
			国有单位	集体单位	其他单位		
1952	415.00	18.60	18.10	0.50		16.80	379.60
1957	488.00	56.20	48.50	7.70		1.50	430.30
1965	585.00	77.10	69.20	7.90		0.80	507.10
1970	648.00	107.00	98.60	8.40			541.00
1975	666.00	132.20	120.60	11.60			533.80
1978	694.00	159.50	144.40	15.10		0.90	533.60
1980	796.00	171.60	154.60	17.00		1.10	623.10
1981	842.00	179.90	161.20	18.70		2.20	659.70
1982	870.00	184.10	164.60	19.50		2.70	683.20
1983	993.80	185.80	166.30	19.50		5.20	802.80
1984	1 047.00	195.20	169.50	25.70		10.20	841.70
1985	1 081.40	201.20	174.80	26.30	0.10	10.10	870.10
1986	1 098.90	208.20	179.10	29.00	0.10	12.80	877.90
1987	1 139.70	215.00	184.50	30.40	0.10	16.20	908.50
1988	1 178.80	220.30	188.30	31.80	0.20	16.00	942.50
1989	1 214.00	223.70	190.10	33.40	0.20	13.60	976.70
1990	1 292.40	231.90	194.60	37.00	0.30	8.30	1 052.20
1991	1 302.40	247.40	202.80	44.30	0.30	9.70	1 045.30
1992	1 305.90	252.00	204.70	46.20	1.10	12.10	1 041.80
1993	1 417.80	255.80	207.00	46.60	2.20	15.30	1 146.70

2—7 分产业和部类从业人员数

项目	1992年			1993年		
	合计	城市	农村	合计	城市	农村
从业人员数(万人)	1 306.40	264.60	1 041.80	1 417.76	271.06	1 146.70
一.按产业分						
第一产业	898.00	7.10	890.90	973.94	8.64	965.30
第二产业	205.40	134.20	71.20	232.26	135.06	97.28
第三产业	203.00	123.30	79.70	211.56	127.36	84.20
二.按部类分						
物质生产部门	1 192.00	198.20	993.80	1 291.35	199.65	1 091.70
非物资生产部门	114.40	66.40	48.00	126.41	71.41	55.00
构成(%)						
一.按产业分						
第一产业	68.70	2.70	85.50	68.70	3.19	84.18
第二产业	15.70	50.70	6.80	16.38	49.83	8.48
第三产业	15.60	46.60	7.70	14.92	46.98	7.34
二.按部类分						
物质生产部门	91.20	74.90	95.40	91.05	73.66	95.20
非物质生产部门	8.80	25.10	4.60	8.92	26.34	4.80

从业人员数构成

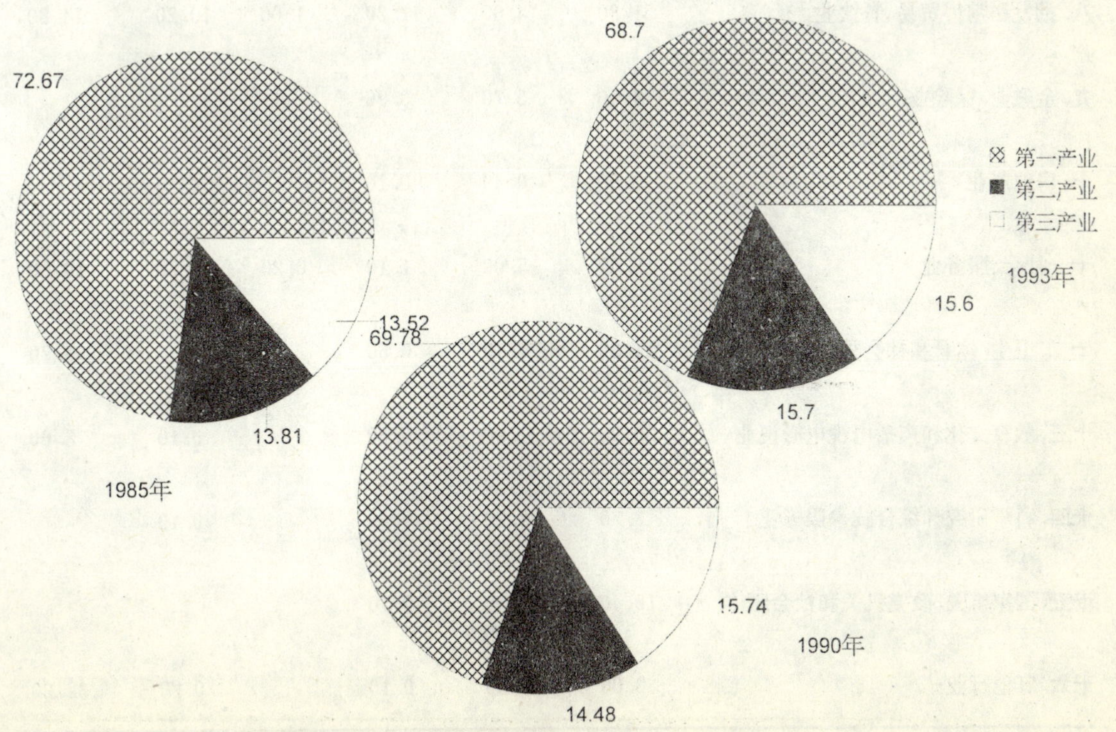

2—8分行业从业员数

(1993年末)　　　　单位:万人

行　业	合计	国有经济单位	城镇集体经济单位	其他各种经济单位	城镇私营企业和个体劳动者	农村劳动者
总　计	1 417.80	207.00	46.60	2.20	15.30	1 146.70
一.农.林.牧.渔业	977.90	12.10	0.50			965.30
二.采掘业	35.2	19.20	1.30		0.10	14.60
三.制造业	130.00	63.90	19.80	0.90	2.20	44.00
四.电力.煤气及水的生产和供应业	4.40	4.40				
五.建筑业	61.90	13.80	9.30		0.20	38.60
六.地质勘查业.水利管理业	5.40	5.30	0.10			
七.交通运输及邮电通信业	29.50	13.60	0.90	0.10	0.50	14.40
八.批发和零售贸易.餐饮业	51.80	14.60	11.20	1.00	10.20	14.80
九.金融业.保险业	4.60	3.70	0.90			
十.房地产业	0.50	0.40	0.10			
十一社会、服务业	18.50	5.00	1.10	0.20	1.70	10.50
十二.卫生.体育和社会福利业	11.30	7.10	0.50			3.70
十三.教育文化和广播电视电影视业	30.90	21.90	0.30		0.10	8.60
十四.科学研究和综合技术服务业	3.70	3.20	0.40		0.10	
十五.国家机关.政党机关和社会团体	18.40	18.30	0.10			
十六.其他行业	33.00	0.50	0.10		0.20	32.20

2—9 城镇从业人员及城镇职工工资

(1993年末)

行　　业	年末人数(万人)	平均人数(人)	城镇职工年工资总额(万元)	城镇职工年人均工资(元)
全省总计	2 710 598	2 662 039	858 851.80	3 422
一.农.林.牧.渔业	125 784	125 370	32 421.40	2 586
1.农业	48 617	48 504	11 478.70	2 367
2.林业	28 682	28 595	8 456.90	2 957
3.畜牧业	8 674	8 614	2 241.80	2 603
4.渔业	453	440	154.70	3 516
5.农.林.牧.渔.服务业	39 358	39 217	10 089.30	2 573
二.采掘业	205 958	202 626	85 608.40	4 241
1.煤炭采选业	84 230	82 589	30 747.60	3 734
2.石油天然气开采业	59 322	58 681	30 021.20	5 116
3.黑色金属矿采选业	6 989	7 029	3 251.70	4 626
4.有色金属矿采选业	21 875	21 859	10 081.00	4 612
三.制造业	867 916	866 456	306 166.50	3 623
1.化学工业	131 781	131 939	52 811.10	4 003
2.建筑材料及其他非金属矿物制品业	45 967	46 125	16 983.60	3 682
3.黑色金属冶炼及压延加工业	53 557	55 222	24 389.20	4 417
4.有色金属冶炼及压延加工业	129 355	129 980	62 294.00	4 793
5.机械.电气.电子设备制造业	267 831	266 723	88 715.80	3 326
6.其他制造业	239 425	236 467	60 972.80	2 578
四.电力.煤气及水的生产和供应业	43 848	42 036	17 200.50	4 092
1.电力.蒸汽.热水的生产和供应业	37 329	35 552	15 038.10	4 229
2.煤气生产和供应业	2 433	2 417	719.00	2 975
3.自来水的生产和供应业	4 086	4 067	1 443.40	3 549
五.建筑业	232 948	214 401	71 799.60	3 376
1.土.木工程建筑业	193 739	174 776	56 587.40	3 238
2.线路.管道和设备安装业	36 022	36 627	14 794.80	4 161
3.建筑物的装修装饰业	3 184	2 998	417.40	1 775
六.地质勘查业.水利管理业	54 420	54 785	18 299.80	3 340
1.地质勘查业	32 152	31 825	11 637.10	3 657
2.水利管理业	22 268	22 960	6 662.70	2 902
七.交通运输.仓储及邮电通信业	150 328	142 546	60 727.30	4 414
1.铁路运输业	67 239	65 876	32 192.90	4 887
2.公路运输业	39 015	35 171	9 618.80	3 185
3.管道运输业				
4.水上运输业				
5.航空运输业	3 251	3 242	1 842.20	5 682
6.交通运输辅助业	15 111	13 757	4 379.30	3 183
7.其他交通运输业	294	298	101.30	3 399
8.仓储业	4 817	4 761	1 411.10	2 964
9.邮电通信业	20 601	19 441	11 181.70	5 752
八.批发和零售贸易.餐饮业	369 707	367 090	66 678.80	2 517
1.食品.饮料.烟草和家庭用品批发商业	78 378	77 822	22 690.60	2 916
2.能源.材料和机械电子设备批发业	30 788	30 117	7 585.30	2 519
3.其他批发业	20 477	19 859	4 798.80	2 416
4.零售业	227 587	227 144	28 895.00	2 298
5.商业经纪与代理业	177	175	69.20	3 954
6.餐饮业	12 300	11 973	1 038.00	925

2—9续

(1993年末)

行　业	年末人数（万人）	平均人数（人）	城镇职工年工资总额（万元）	城镇职工年人均工资（元）
九.金融保险业	45 585	44 327	15 606.00	3 521
1.金融业	43 527	42 290	14 739.00	3 485
2.保险业	2 058	2 037	867.00	4 256
十.房地产业	4 828	4 735	1 550.10	3 274
1.房地产开发与经营业	1 502	1 460	435.90	2 986
2.房地产管理业	3 304	3 253	1 103.40	3 392
3.房地产代理与经纪业	22	22	10.80	4 909
十一.社会服务业	80 758	76 055	16 577.30	2 799
1.公共服务业	24 269	23 259	7 105.40	3 055
2.居民服务业	27 942	26 915	2 253.10	2 235
3.旅馆业	19 276	17 506	4 943.30	2 824
4.租凭服务业	338	338	140.30	4 151
5.旅行社	2 097	1 935	659.70	3 409
6.娱乐服务业	638	546	138.20	2 531
7.信息.咨询服务业	2 904	2 668	635.70	2 383
8.计算机应用服务业	316	300	99.70	3 323
9.其他社会服务业	2 978	2 588	601.90	2 326
十二.卫生.体育和社会福利业	76 145	74 978	22 536.80	3 006
1.卫生	70 805	69 774	20 990.40	3 008
2.体育	2 072	2 038	590.40	2 897
3.社会福利保障业	3 268	3 166	956.00	3 019
十三.教育.文化艺术和广播电影电视业	222 808	220 306	69 953.30	3 189
1.教育	200 549	198 642	63 072.50	3 175
#(1)普通高等学校	19 195	18 586	6 495.40	3 495
(2)普通中学	70 610	69 938	21 507.70	3 075
(3)小学校	109 644	109 038	33 020.80	3 028
2.文化艺术业	13 048	13 410	4 136.50	3 085
3.广播电影电视业	9 211	8 254	2 744.30	3 325
十四.科学研究和综合技术服务业	37 358	36 861	11 125.40	3 133
1.科学研究业	22 592	22 592	7 300.50	3 231
(1)自然科学研究	19 558	19 587	6 165.90	3 148
(2)社会科学研究	2 010	2 003	760.50	3 797
(3)综合科学研究	1 024	1 002	374.10	3 734
2.综合技术服务业	14 766	14 269	3 824.90	2 960
(1)气象	1 985	1 999	693.40	3 469
(2)地震	1 521	1 415	538.40	3 805
(3)测绘	627	620	227.50	3 669
(4)技术监督	1 715	1 688	537.50	3 184
(5)海洋环境				
(6)环境保护	1 005	974	305.50	3 137
(7)技术推广和科技交流服务业	1 058	1 039	274.50	2 642
(8)其他综合技术服务业	6 855	6 534	1 248.10	2 405
十五.国家机关.政党机关和社会团体	184 437	181 821	60 882.80	3 349
其中:国家机关	165 869	167 324	55 747.10	3 332
政党机关	13 317	13 079	4 493.90	3 436
十六.其他行业	7 770	7 646	1 717.80	3 085

2—10 分行业职工人数

(1993年末)

行业	全部职工	国有单位	集体单位	其他各种合营单位	在全部职工中合同制职工
绝对值(人)					
全省总计	2 558 298	2 070 228	465 957	22 113	438 953
一.按行业分					
1.农林.牧.渔业	125 784	120 710	5 074		31 508
2.采掘业	205 172	192 264	12 765	143	45 095
3.制造业	846 424	639 114	198 370	8 940	182 593
4.电力.煤气及水的生产和供应业	43 848	43 826	22		11496
5.建筑业	231 231	137 867	93 364		29 147
6.地质勘查业.水利管理业	54 420	53 531	889		8 278
7.交通运输.仓储及邮电通信业	145 359	135 915	8 887	557	25 575
8.批发和零售贸易.餐饮业	267 551	146 169	111 512	9 870	56 444
9.金融.保险业	45 585	36 548	9 037		5 929
10.房地产业	4 828	4 135	659	34	722
11.社会服务业	63 923	50 421	11 029	2 473	12 997
12.卫生.体育和社会福利业	76 145	71 183	4 962		6447
13.教育.文化和广播电影电视业	221 885	218 552	3 333		6794
14.科学研究和综合技术服务业	36 013	31 586	4 331	96	3 601
15.国家机关.政党机关和社会团体	184 437	183 480	957		11660
16.其他行业	5 693	4 927	766		667
二.按三次产业					
第一产业	86 426	82 230	4 196		24 775
第二产业	1 326 675	1 013 071	304 521	9 083	268331
第三产业	1 145 197	974 927	157 240	13 030	145 847
构成(%)					
一.按行业分					
1.农.林.牧.渔业	4.90	5.80	1.10		7.20
2.采掘业	8.00	9.30	2.70	0.70	10.30
3.制造业	33.10	30.90	42.60	40.40	41.60
4.电力.煤气及水的生产和供应业	1.70	2.10			2.60
5.建筑业	9.00	6.70	20.00		6.60
6.地质勘查业.水利管理业	2.10	2.60	0.20		1.90
7.交通运输.仓储及邮电通讯业	5.70	6.60	1.90	2.50	5.80
8.批发和零售贸易.餐饮业	10.50	7.10	23.90	44.60	12.80
9.金融业.保险业	1.80	1.80	1.90		1.40
10.房地产业	0.20	0.20	0.20	0.20	0.20
11.社会服务业	2.50	2.40	2.40	11.20	2.90
12.卫生.体育和社会福利业	3.00	3.40	1.10		1.50
13.教育.文化和广播电影.电视业	8.70	10.50	0.70		1.50
14.科学研究和综合技术服务业	1.40	1.50	0.90	0.40	0.80
15.国家机关.政党机关和社会团体	7.20	8.90	0.20		2.70
16.其他行业	0.20	0.20	0.20		0.20
二.按三次产业分					
第一产业	3.40	4.00	0.90		5.60
第二产业	51.90	48.90	65.40	41.10	61.10
第三产业	44.70	47.10	33.70	58.90	33.20

2—11 国有单位固定职工.合同制职工增减情况

单位:人

项目	1992年			1993年		
	合计	中央	地方	合计	中央	地方
净增人数	16 534	—150	16 684	10 501	.2 107	8 394
一.增加人数	85 974	22 997	62 977	119 188	29 078	90 110
从农村招收	7 508	2 122	5 386	14 994	3 442	11 552
从城镇招收	24 927	4 676	20 251	22 691	3 607	19 084
录用的复员转业军人	6 834	2 923	3 911	7 426	3 457	3 969
录用的大.中专.技校毕业生	33 453	10 146	23 307	31 012	10 745	20267
调入	5 092	1 928	3 164	35 537	5 107	30 430
#由外省区调入	3 073	1 039	2 034	2 166	974	1 192
其他	8 160	1 202	6 958	7 528	2 720	4 808
二.减少人数	69 440	23 147	46 293	108 687	26 971	81 716
离休.退休.退职	39 603	11 634	27 969	37 432	12 328	25 104
开除.除名.辞退	4 610	1 620	2 990	6 510	1 055	5 455
终止解除合同	2 720	203	2 517	5 334	570	4 764
调出	9 681	5 387	4 294	42 911	7 761	35 150
#调至外省.区.市	7 335	4 814	2 521	5 442	2 945	2 497
其他	12 826	4 303	8 523	16 500	5 257	11 243

2—12 城镇新增就业人员

单位:人

项目	1990年	1992年	1993年
总计	73 914	155 103	139 777
国有	82 681	87 206	83 651
集体	43 484	37 160	22 284
其他	749	7 815	3 434
个体	—53 000	22 922	30 408

2—13 城镇就业人员主要来源及安置去向

单位:人

项目	1985 年	1990 年	1992 年	1993 年
总计	89 741	73 914	155 103	139 777
一.就业人员主要来源				
城镇劳动力	34 227	11 723	77 990	31 337
农村劳动力	16 469	19 043	19 966	26 437
大学.中专.技校毕业生	17 128	34 598	34 381	32 357
其他	21 917	9 000	22 766	49 646
二.就业人员安置去向				
国有单位	74 172	82 681	87 206	83 651
城镇集体单位	16 054	43 484	37 160	22 284
各种合营单位	403	749	7 815	3 434
城镇个体劳动者	— 888	—53 000	22 922	30 408

2—14 城镇待业人员及待业率

年 份	城镇待业人员(万人)	#青年人数	#女青年	青年待业人员占总待业人员的(%)	待业率(%)
1980	8.60	5.40		62.80	4.80
1981	10.80	8.20		75.90	5.60
1982	9.00	6.00		66.70	4.60
1983	5.10	3.70		72.50	2.60
1984	4.30	3.90		90.70	2.10
1985	7.20	6.30		87.50	3.30
1986	7.10	7.00	4.20	98.60	3.10
1987	10.80	9.50	6.10	88.00	4.50
1988	12.00	10.80	6.60	90.00	4.80
1989	13.70	11.10	6.90	81.00	5.50
1990	12.50	11.60	6.80	92.80	4.90
1991	11.30	10.50	6.30	92.70	4.20
1992	9.50	8.80	5.80	92.90	3.50
1993	10.12	9.35	5.29	92.39	3.59

2—15 农村劳动力转移情况

(1993 年)　　　　单位:%

指　标	构　成	指　标	构　成
一.当年移动的劳动力	100.00	(二)行业分布	100.00
(一)素质情况		1.转向工业	14.94
按性别分组	100.00	2.转向建筑业	37.87
1.男劳动力	76.61	3.转向交通运输邮电业	7.86
(1)整劳动力	74.95	4.转向商业 饮食服务业	17.69
(2)半劳动力	1.66	5.转向教育文化艺术和广播事业	0.87
2.女劳动力	23.39	6.转向卫生体育和社会福利事业	1.38
(1)整劳动力	22.15	7.转向其他非农业	19.39
(2)半劳动力	1.24	(三)地域分布	100.00
按文化程度分组	100.00	1.本省内转移	86.44
1.文盲和半文盲	15.99	#转向城市	58.73
2.小学程度	33.41	2.转向外省	13.56
3.初中程度	34.38	(1)转向东部地区	5.88
4.高中程度	16.13	#转向城市	3.35
5.中专程度	0.05	(2)转向中部地区	1.33
6.大专及以上程度	0.05	#转向城市	0.64
按是否受对专业培训分组	100.00	(3)转向西部地区	6.35
1.受过各种专业培训的劳动力	10.02	#转向城市	2.57
2.无受过各种专业培训的劳动力	89.98	二.当年返回农业的劳动力	55.06
按有无特殊分组	100.00	(一)由本省返回	46.51
1.有残疾的劳动力	2.89	#由城市返回	28.49
2.无残疾的劳动力	97.11	(二)由外省返回	8.55
		#由城市返回	4.14

三·固定资产投资

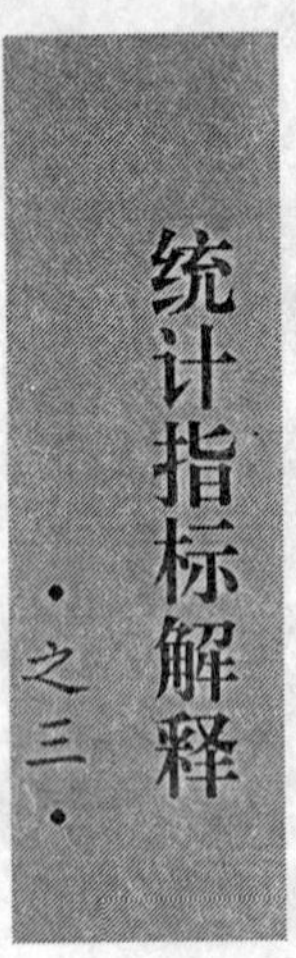

【来自国外的经常转移净额】常住单位与非常住单位之间单方面收入转移相抵后的差额。包括与国际组织来往、无偿援助的捐赠、侨汇以及征收或交纳国外收入税等。

【可支配收入】各部门经过初次分配和转移收支之后可用于消费与投资的收入，反映最终分配的结果。国民可支配收入等于国内生产净值、来自国外的劳动者报酬和财产收入净额及来自国外的经常转移净额之和。

【总消费】常住单位在核算期内对物质产品和服务的消费支出合计。由居民消费和社会消费组成。

【居民消费】常住居民在国内和国外的全部消费品和生活服务支出合计。它等于常住居民和非常住居民在国内市场的全部消费支出，加上常住居民在国外市场的消费支出减去非常住居民在国内市场的消费支出。消费支出包括居民直接购买的耐用和非耐用消费品支出、各种生活服务支出。还包括居民以实物工资获得的各种物品和服务的消费，以及居民自有住房和虚拟房租消费等。

【社会消费】包括政府消费支出和集体消费支出。政府消费支出指政府部门总产出减去其销售收入后的余额。集体消费支出指行政、事业、企业单位和农村集体对物质产品和服务的最终消费支出。

【储蓄】可支配收入和扣除用于最终消费支出后可用于投资的部分。储蓄不包括固定资产折旧，总储蓄包括固定资产折旧。

【资本转移】部门之间以实物和资金方式实现的资本转移，其转移来自支付者的储蓄或资产，并增加接受者的投资来源。包括部门之间的资产无偿调拨、政府的投资拨款以及遗产税等。国内各部门之间的资本转移在汇总时将被抵消，国民帐户仅反映与国外部门的资本转移净额。

【来自国外的资本转移净额】常住单位与非常住单位之间单方面资本转移相抵后的差额。包括对外往来中非经常性(不规则)的所有无偿转移。

【总投资】常住单位在核算期内对固定资产和库存的投资支出合计，包括固定资产形成和库存增加。

【固定资产】社会生产的，能在长时期内发挥作用的耐用生产资料。一般应同时具备两个条件，即使用限期在一年以上和单位价值在规定限额以上。包括各类房屋、建筑物、机器设备、役畜种畜、多年生经济林木和在建工程等。固定资产不包括居民拥有的耐用消费品和作为纯军事目的而使用的耐用品。

3—1 主要年份固定资产投资

单位:万元

年份	全社会固定资产投资	国有单位固定资产投资	基本建设投资	#地方投资	更新改造投资	其他投资
1953	19 739	19 739	19 739	2 021		
1957	76 299	76 299	76 299	13 544		
1965	68 733	68 733	68 733	15 837		
1970	103 249	103 249	103 249	31 544		
1975	109 781	109 781	109 781	79 786		
1978	92 978	92 575	92 575	43 280		
1980	126 451	125 653	101 582	51 979	24 071	
1981	141 023	117 326	80 627	36 480	36 699	
1982	156 855	133 568	92 696	46 412	40 872	
1983	189 053	164 159	99 485	42 170	51 107	13 567
1984	245 050	199 823	133 176	64 132	52 941	13 706
1985	338 964	259 740	162 443	80 863	80 092	17 205
1986	404 246	310 899	191 230	97 232	108 718	10 951
1987	479 055	383 870	236 146	110 347	134 593	12 131
1988	595 397	469 973	293 498	119 288	154 647	21 828
1989	511 920	406 488	266 259	164 088	119 635	20 594
1990	593 470	492 667	294 760	47 352	151 525	46 382
1991	685 897	570 272	342 927	143 450	159 779	67 566
1992	851 286	717 578	395 142	181 686	216 126	106 310
1993	1 220 812	957 031	570 006	231 559	276 493	110 532

3—2 全社会固定资产投资额

单位:万元

项　目	1992年			1993年		
	合计	中央	地方	合计	中央	地方
全社会固定资产投资额	851 286	387 466	463 820	1 220 812	545 955	674 857
一.国有单位	717 578	386 067	331 511	957 031	542 781	414 250
基本建设	395 142	213 456	181 686	570 006	338 447	231 559
更新改造	216 126	105 924	110 202	276 493	144 386	132 107
国有其他	70 084	66 577	3 507	61 947	58 239	3 708
商品房	29 524	110	29 414	48 585	1 709	46 876
零星	6 702		6 702			
二.集体经济	44 453	1 399	43 054	141 721	3 174	138 547
城镇	12 326	1 399	10 927	78 601	3 174	75 427
农村	32 127		32 127	63 120		63 120
三.私人经济	89 255		89 255	122 060		122 060
城镇	9 227		9 227	16 086		16 086
农村	80 028		80 028	105 974		105 974

3—3 国有单位固定资产投资资金

单位:万元

项　目	拨款额			拨款额中基本建设财务拨款额		
	合计	中央	地方	合计	中央	地方
一.上年末结余资金	44 787	16 128	38 659	20 725	6 916	13 809
二.本年拨.贷款	953 884	496 462	457 422	563 827	293 108	270 719
国家预算内资金	85 121	46 463	38 658	78 335	42 853	35 482
国内贷款	268 884	139 804	129 080	191 322	116 940	74 382
利用外资	24 492	9 128	15 364	20 373	7 791	12 582
自筹资金	443 451	245 056	198 395	190 089	84 344	105 745
其它资金	131 936	56 011	75 925	83 708	41 180	42 528

3—4 固定资产投资额

单位:万元

项目	1992年			1993年		
	合计	中央	地方	合计	中央	地方
投资额	851 286	387 466	463 820	1 220 812	545 955	674 857
一.按构成分						
建筑安装工程	525 759	213 855	311 904	824 705	339 451	485 254
设备.工器具购置	246 619	130 647	115 972	263 136	114 652	148 484
其他	78 908	42 964	35 944	132 971	91 852	41 119
二.按用途分						
第一产业	82 702			65 982	2 948	63 034
第二产业	515 292			566 044	319 840	246 204
第三产业	99 512			354 155	178 837	175 318
住宅	153 780	34 676	119 094	234 631	44 330	190 301
三.按建设性质分						
新建	280 415	63 485	216 930	622 161	206 230	415 931
改建	502 859	317 702	185 157	172 609	67 801	104 808
扩建				372 647	255 868	116 779
生活设施	20 903	4 670	16 233	39 140	15 230	23 910
购置设备	5 834	913	4 922	1 559	70	1 489
四.按建设规模分						
基本建设投资大中型项目	202 809	146 147	56 662	313 129	251 944	61185
基本建设投资小型项目	192 333	67 309	125 024	256 877	113 181	143696
限额以上更改措施项目	21 443	17 204	4 239	18 217	12 912	5305
更新改造措施投资小型项目	194 683	88 720	105 963	258 276	131474	126 802
五.按所有制分						
国有	717 578	386 067	331 511	957 031	542 781	414 250
集体	44 453	1 399	43 054	141 721	3 174	138 547

3—5 基本建设投资主要指标

单位:万元

项目	1992年			1993年		
	合计	中央	地方	合计	中央	地方
基本建设投资额	395 142	213 456	181 686	570 006	338 447	231 559
一.按构成分						
建筑安装工程	257 162	119 450	137 712	149 219	221 911	197 308
设备.工器具购置	81 205	61 060	20 145	65 112	60 232	4 880
其他	52 341	28 512	23 829	85 675	56 304	29 371
二.按用途分						
第一产业				28 703		28 703
第二产业				230 269	192 943	37 326
第三产业				231 709	109 989	121 720
住宅				79 325	35 509	43 816
三.按建设性质分						
新建	154 973	61 975	92 998	192 796	67 688	125 108
改建				31 235	7 774	23 461
扩建				200 170	143 015	57 155
生活设施	18 164	4 567	13 597	33 158	14 877	18 281
购置设备	856	49	807	312	70	242
四.按建设规模分						
大中型项目	202 809	146 147	56 662	307 692	267 515	40 177
小型项目	192 333	67 309	125 024	262 314	70 932	191 382
五.按所有制形式分						
国有	395 142	213 456	181 686	570 006	338 447	231 559
集体						
六.按工农业分						
工业投资	247 938	176 362	71 576	275 979	202 985	72 994
#重工业	233 526	175 156	58 370	239 623	200 266	39 357
农业投资	38 415	141	38 274	7 884		7 884
七.房屋建设面积						
施工房屋面积(平方米)	5 790 300			5 758 386		
#住宅	2 731 400			2 792 000		
竣工房屋面积(平方米)	2 432 755			2 419 395		
#住宅	1 203 400			1 245 700		
峻工房屋价值(万元)	99 400			114 934		
峻工房屋造价(元/平方米)	409			499		

3—6 分行业基本建设投资额

(1993 年)　　　　单位:万元

行　业	合计			按建设性质分	
		中央	地方	新建	扩建
总　计	570 006	338 447	231 559	294 272	201 236
一.农.林.牧.渔业	11 228		11 228	9 514	1 294
农业	7 884		7 884	7 884	
林业	985		985	119	856
畜牧业	400		400	235	35
农林.牧.渔服务业	1 959		1 959	1 276	403
二.采选业	24 663	18 010	6 653	12 433	12 120
煤炭采选业	13 156	15 674	4 985	10 228	2 928
石油和天然气开采业	1 025	1 000	25	25	1 000
黑色金属矿采选业	330	330			330
有色金属矿采选业	8 363	7 503	860	590	7 683
非金属矿采选业	1 378	1 006	372	1 202	156
木材及竹材采选业	411		411	388	23
三.制造业	156 434	117 814	38 620	31 010	107 769
食品加工业	5 376		5 376	4 211	480
食品制造业	421		421	398	
饮料制造业	343		343	243	
烟草加工业	328	215	113	113	
纺织业	645		645	85	327
服装及其他纤维制品制造业	230		230	29	
皮革.毛皮.羽绒及其制品业	45		45		
木材加工及竹藤.棕.草制品业	232		232		232
家具制造业	417		417	67	50
造纸及纸制品业	633		633	483	11
印刷业.记录媒介	341		341	130	171
文教体育用品制造业	40		40		
石油加工及炼焦业	28 183	28 183		11 476	16 707
化学原料及化学	12 762	2 227	10 535	7 763	3 775
医药制造业	2 874	2 504	370	330	50
塑料制造业	50		50	50	
非金属矿物制品业	6 413	1 273	5 140	178	4 033

3—6 续　　(1993 年)　　单位:万元

行　　业	合计	中央	地方	按建设性质分	
				新建	扩建
黑色金属冶炼及压延加工业	11 239	11 239		5 233	6 006
有色金属冶炼业及压延加工业	68 072	66 281	1 791	90	67 982
金属制品业	266		266	33	83
普通机械制造业	3 809	513	3 296	61	280
专用设备制造业	2 900		2 900	37	160
交通运输设备制造业	4 492	4 362	130		3 997
电气机械及器材制造业	2 471	1 017	1 454		1 247
电子及通信设备制造业	1 674		1 674		
仪器仪表及文化办公用机械制造业	2 178		2 178		2 178
四. 电力. 煤气及水的生产和供应业	94 882	67 161	27 721	65 311	29571
五. 建筑业	12 015	5 425	6 590	8 069	1 887
六. 地质勘查业. 仓储及邮电通信业	41 274	4 070	37 204	29 748	6432
七. 交通运输. 仓储及邮电通信业	121 974	106 257	15 717	96 297	9 083
交通业	96 749	81 480	15 269	92 434	410
邮电通讯业	8 793	8 345	448	2 462	4 403
八. 批发和零售贸易. 餐饮业	17 109	1 095	16 014	8 936	4 660
九. 金融. 保险业	8 610	7 618	992	3 881	1 924
金融业	7 858	6 917	941	3 548	1 794
保险业	752	701	51	333	130
十. 房地产业	2 713	237	2 476	1 076	194
十一. 社会服务业	13 542	50	13 492	7 687	1 787
十二. 卫生. 体育和社会福利业	5 539		5 539	1 962	2 193
卫生事业	4 084		4 084	1 491	1 858
体育事业	832		832	137	255
社会福利保险业	623		623	334	80
十三. 教育. 文化艺术及广播电影电视业	22 237	6 557	15 680	5 825	8 979
教育事业	17 723	6 492	11 231	4 375	7 345
文化艺术业	2 001		2 001	1 010	746
广播电影电视业	2 513		2 513	440	888
十四. 科学研究和综合技术服务业	3 430	2 043	1 387	625	2 219
十五. 国家机关. 政党机关和社会团体	28 937	1 736	27 201	9 214	8708
十六. 其他行业	5 419	374	5 045	2 684	2 416

3—7 分行业按用途分的基本建设投资

(1993 年)　　　　单位:万元

行　业	投资额	按用途分			
		第一产业	第二产业	第三产业	住宅
总计	570 006	28 703	230 269	231 709	79 325
一.农.林.牧.渔业	11 228	9 781		738	709
农业	7 884	7 770		5	109
林业	985	915			70
畜牧业	400	210		40	150
农林.牧.渔服务业	1 959	886		693	380
二.采选业	24 663	240	17 775	2 799	3 849
煤炭采选业	13 156	220	7 843	2 799	2 294
石油和天然气开采业	1 025	20			1 005
黑色金属矿采选业	330		330		
有色金属矿采选业	8 363		8 151		212
非金属矿采选业	1 378		1 062		316
木材及竹材林采选业	411		389		22
三.制造业	156 434	5 789	128 417	657	215 771
食品加工业	5 376		4 276		1 100
食品制造业	421		166		255
饮料制造业	343	243			100
烟草加工业	328		113		215
纺织业	645		327		318
服装及其他纤维制品制造业	230		217	13	
皮革.毛皮.羽绒及其制品业	45				45
木材加工及竹藤.棕.草制品业	232			6	226
家具制造业	417		50		367
造纸及纸制品业	633		494		139
印刷业.记录媒介	341		253	18	70
文教体育用品制造业	40		25		15
石油加工及炼焦业	28 183		25 031		3 152
化学原料及化学	12 762	50	7 371	271	5 070
医药制造业	2 874		2 794		80
塑料制造业	50		50		
非金属矿物制品业	6 413	5 496	419		498
黑色金属冶炼及压延加工业	11 239		11 239		

3—7 续　　　　　　　　　　(1993 年)　　　　　　　　　　单位:万元

行　业	投资额	按　用　途　分			
		第一产业	第二产业	第三产业	住宅
有色金属冶炼业及压延加工业	68 072		65 289		2 783
金属制品业	266		104	5	157
普通机械制造业	3 809		2 518	89	1 202
专用设备制造业	2 900		1 489	155	1 256
交通运输设备制造业	4 492		3 156		1 336
电气机械及器材制造业	2 471		606	100	1 765
电子及通信设备制造业	1 674		1 460		214
仪器仪表及文化办公用机械制造业	2 178		970		1 208
四. 电力. 煤气及水的生产和供应业	94 882	7 198	83 530	1 231	2923
五. 建筑业	12 015	130	120	9 635	2 130
六. 地质勘查业. 水利管理业	41 274	5 230	30	33 302	2 712
七. 交通运输. 仓储及邮电通信业	121 974		10	110 970	10 994
交通业	96 749		10	89 504	7 235
邮电通讯业	8 793			6 545	2 248
八. 批发和零售贸易. 餐饮业	17 109		24	14 774	2 311
九. 金融. 保险业	8 610		5	4 741	3 864
金融业	7 858		5	4 290	3 563
保险业	752			451	301
十. 房地产业	2 713		80	851	1 782
十一. 社会服务业	13 542			11 445	2 097
十二. 卫生. 体育和社会福利业	5 539		83	3 991	1 465
卫生事业	4 084		43	2 658	1 383
体育事业	832			832	
社会福利保险业	623		40	501	82
十三. 教育. 文化艺术及广播电影电视业	22 237			14 272	7 965
教育事业	17 723			11 266	6 457
文化艺术业	2 001			1 791	210
广播电影电视业	2 513			1 215	1 298
十四. 科学研究和综合技术服务业	3 430	40	20	2 179	1 191
十五. 国家机关. 政党机关和社会团体	28 937	295	175	17 365	11 102
十六. 其他行业	5 419			2 759	2 660

3—8 全社会固定资产投资额及新增固定资产

单位:万元

项　目	1992年			1993年		
	合计	中央	地方	合计	中央	地方
固定资产投资额	851 286	387 466	463 820	1 220 812	545 955	674 857
国有单位	717 578	386 067	331 511	957 031	542 781	414 250
集体单位	44 453	1 399	43 054	141 721	3 174	138 547
个人	89 255		89 255	122 060		122 060
新增固定资产	664 632	313 330	351 302	830 217	336 265	493 952
国有单位	537 466	313 066	224 400	604 767	335 661	269 106
集体单位	37 911	264	37 647	103 390	604	102 786
个人	89 255		89 255	122 060		122 060

3—9 基本建设投资额及新增固定资产

单位:万元

项　目	1992年			1993年		
	合计	中央	地方	合计	中央	地方
基本建设投资额	395 142	213 456	181 686	570 006	338 447	231 559
新增固定资产	376 664	169 011	107 653	216 960	73 947	143 013

3—10 基本建设固定资产交付使用率和项目投产率

项　目	单位	1992年			1993年		
		合计	中央	地方	合计	中央	地方
施工项目	个	1 629	232	1 397	1 693	269	1 424
#新开工项目	个	876	100	776	960	151	809
全部建成投产项目	个	844	90	754	852	114	738
新增固定资产	万元	276 664	169 011	107 653	216 960	73947	143 013
固定资产交付使用率	%	70.02	79.18	59.25	38.06	21.85	61.76
建成项目投产率	%	51.82	38.79	53.97	50.32	42.86	51.83

3—11 分行业基本建设施工投产项目个数和新增固定资产

(1993 年)

行　　业	施工项目(个)	#新开工	全部建成投产项目(个)	项目建成投产率(%)	新增固定资产(万元)	固定资产交付使用率(%)
总　　计	1 693	960	852	50.32	216 960	38.06
一.农.林.牧.渔业	72	42	45	62.50	9 257	82.45
农业	9	6	6	66.67	7 784	98.73
林业	9	6	7	77.78	203	20.61
畜牧业	6	3	3	50.00	192	48.00
农林.牧.渔服务业	48	27	29	60.42	1 078	55.03
二.采掘业	43	17	12	27.91	11 460	46.47
煤炭采选业	25	5	4	16.00	7 097	34.35
石油和天然气开采业	3	2	1	33.33	1 015	99.02
黑色金属矿采选业	1	1				
有色金属矿采选业	8	6	3	37.50	2 217	26.51
非金属矿采选业	3	2	2	66.67	392	28.45
木材及竹材采选业	3	1	2	66.67	739	179.80
三.制造业	169	83	62	36.69	59 987	38.35
食品加工业	16	10	6	37.50	5 714	106.30
食品制造业	3	3	1	33.33	143	33.97
饮料制造业	2	1	1	50.00	243	70.85
烟草加工业	2		1	50.00	325	99.09
纺织业	5	1	2	40.00	3 424	531.85
服装及其他纤维制品制造业	4	4	4	100.00	230	100.00
皮革.毛皮.羽绒及其制品业	1					
木材加工及竹藤.棕.草制品业	2	1	2	100.00	237	102.20
家具制造业	3	1	2	66.67	737	176.70
造纸及纸制品业	4	2	1	25.00		
印刷业.记录媒介	5	4	2	40.00	82	24.05
文教体育用品制造业	1		1	100.00	120	300.00
石油加工及炼焦业	4	1			4 448	15.78
化学原料及化学	24	16	7	29.17	11 283	88.41
医药制造业	4	2	1	25.00	212	7.38
塑料制造业	1	1	1	100.00	50	100.00
非金属矿物制品业	12	7	6	50.00	1 801	28.08
黑色金属冶炼及压延加工业	3	3	1	33.33	4 150	36.92
有色金属冶炼业及压延加工业	7	1			13 004	19.10

3—11 续 (1993 年)

行业	施工项目(个)	#新开工	全部建成投产项目(个)	项目建成投产率(%)	新增固定资产(万元)	固定资产交付使用率(%)
金属制品业	4	3	3	75.00	160	60.15
普通机械制造业	20	7	8	40.00	911	23.92
专用设备制造业	8	3	4	50.00	1 073	37.00
交通运输设备制造业	7	3	1	14.29	6 142	136.70
电气机械及器材制造业	21	8	6	28.57	890	117.00
电子及通信设备制造业	3		1	33.38	977	44.86
仪器仪表及文化办公用机械制造业	3	1			1 631	97.43
四.电力.煤气及水的生产和供应业	110	47	47	42.73	21 511	22.67
五.建筑业	29	14	8	27.59	7 268	60.49
六.地质勘查业.水利管理业	57	9	22	38.60	23 420	56.74
七.交通运输.仓储及邮电通信业	115	82	59	51.30	1 840	12.17
交通业	17	13	7	41.18	563	0.58
邮电通讯业	45	34	26	57.78	9 017	102.50
八.批发和零售贸易.餐饮业	116	102	75	64.66	11 459	66.98
九.金融.保险业	121	89	56	46.28	4 613	53.58
金融业	106	77	50	47.17	4 323	55.01
保险业	15	12	6	40.00	290	38.56
十.房地产业	24	15	10	41.67	1 333	49.13
十一.社会服务业	84	48	40	47.62	4 822	35.61
十二.卫生.体育和社会福利业	83	43	43	51.81	3 023	54.58
卫生事业	68	33	35	51.47	2 392	58.57
体育事业	7	4	4	57.14	365	43.87
社会福利保险业	8	6	4	50.00	266	44.48
十三.教育.文化艺术及广播电影电视业	224	106	94	41.96	14 288	64.25
教育事业	181	80	76	41.99	11 841	66.81
文化艺术业	26	16	13	50.00	1 410	70.46
广播电影电视业	17	10	5	29.41	1 037	42.36
十四.科学研究和综合技术服务业	33	13	14	42.42	1 663	48.48
十五.国家机关.政党机关和社会团体	377	226	242	64.19	24 766	85.59
十六.其他行业	36	24	23	63.89	3 250	59.97

3—12 更新改造投资主要指标

指　标	1992年	1993年
一.投资总额(万元)	216 126.00	276 493.00
1.按资金来源分		
预算内投资	8 968.00	6 528.00
国内贷款	76 146.00	67 507.00
利用外资	270.00	2 920.00
自筹投资	113 778.00	180 115.00
其他投资	16 964.00	18 423.00
2.按构成分		
建设安装工程	108 555.00	147 090.00
设备.工具.器具购置	92 887.00	112 354.00
其他费用	14 684.00	17 049.00
3.按建设性质分		
#新建	9 549.00	7 896.00
扩建	68 483.00	119 601.00
改建	131 468.00	144 005.00
4.按用途分		
增产	54 465.00	90 981.00
节约能源	8 939.00	8 758.00
增加品种	35 998.00	41 219.00
提高产品质量	14 048.00	14 565.00
三废治理	2 934.00	4 417.00
其他	62 295.00	116 553.00
二.新增固定资产(万元)	173 515.00	218 322.00
三.房屋建设面积(万平方米)		
施工面积	189.92	180.03
#住宅	78.13	71.21
竣工面积	93.95	84.33
#住宅	40.26	34.27
竣工房屋价值(万元)	39 400.00	38 884.00
竣工房屋造价(元/平方米)	419.00	461.00

3—13 分行业按用途和建设性质分的更新改造投资

(1993 年)

行　业	投资额	按用途分				按建设性质分	
		第一产业	第二产业	第三产业	住宅	新建	改建和扩建
全省总计	276 493	206	195 152	61 089	20 046	7 896	263 606
中央	144 386		90 113	44 213	10 060		
地方	132 107	206	105 039	16 876	9 986		
按国民经济行业分							
一.农.林.牧.渔业	117	35		82			117
二.采掘业	24 294		21 375	1 793	1 126		23 971
三制造业	165 651	171	148 676	2 700	14 104	2 354	160 300
四.电力.煤气及水的生产和供应业	25 731		24 862	150	719	4 100	21181
五.建筑业	618		194		424		131
六.地质勘查业.水利管理业							
七.交通运输.仓储及邮电通信业	44 390		45	42 512	1 833	583	43576
八.批发和零售贸易.餐饮业	6 681			6 030	651	484	6 034
九.金融.保险业	4 343			4 155	188	150	4 088
十.房地产业							
十一.社会服务业	3 904			3 129	775	142	3 702
十二.卫生.体育和社会福利业	121			26	95		26
十三.教育.文化艺术及广播电影电视业	294			294			294
十四.科研和综合技术服务业	81			81			81
十五.国家机关.政党机关和社会团体	228			137	91	83	105
十六.其他行业	40				40		

3—14 分行业更新改造施工.投产项目个数和新增固定资产

(1993年)

行 业	施工项目(个)	全部建成投产项目(个)	项目建成投产率(%)	投资额(万元)	新增固定资产(万元)	固定资产交付使用率(%)
总 计	1 421	545	38.40	276 493	218 322	79.00
一.农.林.牧.渔业	5	4	80.00	117	82	70.10
二.采掘业	74	55	74.30	24 294	20 447	84.20
三制造业	957	308	32.20	165 651	140 792	85.00
四.电力.煤气及水的生产和供应业	70	20	28.60	25 731	19 096	74.20
五.建筑业	8	4	50.00	618	463	74.90
六.地质勘查业.水利管理业						
七.交通运输.仓储及邮电通信业	195	79	40.50	44 390	27 964	63.00
八.批发和零售贸易.餐饮业	66	49	74.20	6 681	3 614	54.10
九.金融.保险业	14	8	57.10	4 343	4 058	93.40
十.房地产业						
十一.社会服务业	15	7	46.70	3 904	1 268	32.50
十二.卫生.体育和社会福利业	2			121		
十三.教育.文化艺术及广播电影电视业	5	3	60.00	294	133	45.20
十四.科研和综合技术服务业	2	1	50.00	81	10	12.30
十五.国家机关.政党机关和社会团体	7	6	85.70	228	355	155.70
十六.其他行业	1	1	100.00	40	40	100.00

3—15 基本建设和更新改造措施主要新增生产能力

指　标	单位	1992 年		1993 年	
		基本建设	更新改造	基本建设	更新改造
锌冶炼	万吨	5.00		5.00	
镍采矿	万吨				17.00
铝加工	万吨				3.00
水泥	万吨	7.00	7.00		15.00
合成氨	万吨		0.50		0.80
电石	万吨			1.80	
化学农药	吨				2 500.00
塑料树脂及芳聚物	万吨				1.00
拖拉机制造	台		5 000.00		500.00
化学纤维	吨				4 000.00
饼干	吨				1 075.00
白酒	吨				4 200.00
合成洗涤剂	吨			3 000.00	
汽车购置	辆		171.00	3.00	89.00
新建公路	公里	6.94	0.61	47.00	
市内电话自动交换机	门	5 000.00	51 596.00	2 500.00	83 300.00
长途自动电话交换设备	路端			296.00	9 342.00
有效灌溉面积	万亩	41.18		19.00	
粮食仓库	万公斤	2 885.00	3 845.05	2 501.00	275.00
	平方米			9 444.00	954.00
商业饮食服务网点	处	85.00	40.00	184.00	29.00
	平方米			89 312.00	17 725.00
中等学校学生席位	个	17 479.00		8 113.00	
小学校学生席位	个	8 903.00		5 955.00	
其他学校学生席位	个			1 830.00	
影剧院座席	个			1 064.00	
医院病床床位	张	956.00		2 575.00	
宾馆.旅馆.招待所客房数	间			30.00	5 743.00
城市自来水管理长度	公里	6.00		64.00	
城市道路扩建面积	万平方米			5 616.00	3.00
发电机但容量	万千瓦	47.48		1.00	10.00
钛白粉	万吨				1.50
钢材热轧钢材	万吨			2.00	
炼钢	万吨				4.00
石油加工:裂化设备	万吨				2.00
铜选矿:处理原矿	万吨			2.00	
铅锌选矿:处理原矿	万吨				3.00
输电线路(11 万伏及以上)	公里	266.00		253.00	
变电设备能力 (11 万伏及以上)	万千伏安			30.00	
磷肥	吨			881.00	
机制甜菜糖	吨			7 750.00	

表3-16 城镇集体单位建设项目完成投资情况

(1993年)

行业	施工项目个数(个)	完成投资合计(万元)	第一产业	第二产业	第三产业	住宅
总　计	222	38 871	90	11 915	10 967	15 899
一.农.林.牧.渔业	2	59	58			
二.采掘业	3	281		281		
三制造业	95	10 217	32	6 295	2 238	1 652
四.电力.煤气及水的生产和供应业	2	3 720		3 648	72	
五.建筑业	9	722		140	128	454
六.地质勘查业.水利管理业						
七.交通运输.仓储及邮电通信业	1	62			62	
八.批发和零售贸易.餐饮业	48	6 108		400	4 953	755
九.金融.保险业	1	9			9	
十.房地产业	43	15 810			2 795	13 015
十一.社会服务业	10	587			577	10
十二.卫生.体育和社会福利业	1	7				7
十三.教育.文化艺术及广播电影电视业	2	73			73	
十四.科研和综合技术服务业						
十五.国家机关.政党机关和社会团体	2	60			60	
十六.其他行业	3	1 156		1 151		5

3—17 城镇集体单位新增固定资产

(1993年)

行　业	投资额(万元)	新增固定资产(万元)	固定资产交付使用率(%)
总　　计	38 871	25 905	66.60
一.农.林.牧.渔业	59	59	100.00
二.采掘业	281	216	76.90
三制造业	10 217	9 861	96.50
四.电力.煤气及水的生产和供应业	3 720		
五.建筑业	722	605	83.80
六.地质勘查业.水利管理业			
七.交通运输.仓储及邮电通信业	62		
八.批发和零售贸易.餐饮业	6 108	4 970	81.40
九.金融.保险业	9	9	100.00
十.房地产业	15 810	9 617	60.80
十一.社会服务业	587	443	75.50
十二.卫生.体育和社会福利业	7	7	100.00
十三.教育.文化艺术及广播电影电视业	73	73	100.00
十四.科研和综合技术服务业			
十五.国家机关.政党机关和社会团体	60	45	75.00
十六.其他行业	1 156		

3—18 农村集体固定资产投资

(1993年)

行业	施工项目(个)	完成投资(万元)	本年新增固定资产(万元)	房屋建筑面积(万平方米)	
				施工面积	竣工面积
总计	1 586	63 120	55 175	115.53	103.09
一.按建设性质分					
新建	1 153	44 623	39 153	90.95	79.73
扩建	301	13 340	11 432	17.91	17.16
改建	100	4 181	3 749	6.30	5.84
其他	32	976	841	0.37	0.36
二.按国民经济行业分					
农林牧渔业	140	3 426	2 700	4.76	4.32
煤炭采选业	61	2 523	2 289	0.80	0.68
黑色金属矿采选业	3	276	276	0.05	0.05
有色金属矿采选业	17	1 015	943	0.99	0.29
非金属矿采选业	92	2 626	2 447	2.21	2.12
食品加工业	71	1 491	1 400	11.63	11.56
食品制造业	72	2 104	2 029	7.43	6.81
纺织业	18	850	829	1.56	1.26
家具制造业	7	463	430	0.46	0.23
造纸及纸制品业	16	1 287	1 236	3.87	3.82
石油加工及炼焦业	15	2 745	2 121	1.31	1.31
化学原料及化学制品制造业	41	2 739	2 560	1.50	0.89
医药制造业	12	224	199	0.61	0.61
黑色金属冶炼及压延加工业	37	3 331	3 037	5.26	5.21
有色金属冶炼及压延加工业	4	627	401	0.24	0.08
金属制品业	22	424	326	0.77	0.77
其他工业	359	17 826	16 363	21.69	19.70
建筑业	42	1 463	1 128	1.49	1.44
地质勘查业.水利管理业	37	762	731	0.19	0.18
交通运输.仓储及邮电通信业	13	429	170	0.06	0.06
批发零售贸易.餐饮业	174	9 916	7 548	23.79	18.93
金融.保险业	1	10	10	0.03	0.03
房地产业	5	243	75	0.84	0.77
社会服务业	27	1 037	1 008	2.63	2.28
卫生体育和社会福利业	80	928	862	4.76	4.35
教育文化艺术及广播电影电视业	125	1 594	1 327	8.30	7.69
科学研究和综合技术服务业					
国家机关.党政机关和社会团体	73	1 933	1 901	5.02	4.40
其他行业	22	829	829	3.28	3.25

四. 能源原材料消费与库存

【固定资产形成】常住单位在核算期内通过购置、转入或为自用而生产所获得的固定资产扣除销售或转出的固定资产后的价值。固定资产形成包括四个部分；一是基本建设投资新形成的固定资产价值；二是由更新改造投资增加的固定资产价值；三是通过大修理增加的固定资产价值；四是由其他资金支出形成的固定资产价值。

【库存】生产单位拥有的原材料、燃料、产成品、在制品、半成品以及种籽、饲料、幼禽畜、育肥禽畜、低值易耗品等；流通领域库存，包括商业物资供销单位期末库存商品和物资；国家物资储备，包括生产资料和生活消费品。

【库存增加】常住单位在核算期内库存的实物量变动的市场价值。购入库存产品的变化按本期购买者价格估价，产出库存产品的变化按本期生产者价格估价。期初与期末差额为正值表示库存增加，负值表示库存减少。库存产品包括生产单位从其他单位购买的原材料、燃料和各种储备物资等，也包括生产单位产出的各种产成品、在制品、半成品等。

【其他非金融资产】其他非金融资产指非金融资产中除固定资产和库存以外的部分，它包括土地和无形非金融资产。土地包括土地本身和位于其上的森林与河流，以及土地下面的天然资源，，但不包括位于土地之上的房屋及其建筑物。无形资产是指国家或法律所赋的生产某些特殊货物或服务、从事某些特殊活动、销售、购买某些货物或资产的特殊权力。无形资产的例子有版权、专利权、商标权等等。大多数无形资产能够为他的所有者带来财产收入。

【其他非金融资产购买净额】包括土地购买净额和无形资产购买净额，但国外部门投资帐户中的其他非金融资产购买净额仅包括无形资产购买净额，不含土地购买净额。土地购买净额指购买的所有土地的价值与销售的所有土地的价值之差；无形资产购买净额是指无形资产的购买价值减去他的销售价值。

【净出口】等于出口减去进口。进口是指常住单位从非常住单位购买或无偿得到的物质产品和服务总值；出口是指常住单位向非常住单位出售或无偿转让的物质产品和服务价值。出口大于进口为正数，反之为负数。

【资金余缺】某部门的储蓄、固定资产折旧及资本转移收入净额之和与固定资产形成总额、库存增加和其他非金融资产购买净额之和之间关系额。反映一个部门全部资金来源与运用的平衡状况。

4—1 主要原材料消费与库存

（1993 年）

项　　目	单位	年初库存量	本年消费量			乡镇建筑企业施工消费量	年末库存量
			合计	主营活动用	附营活动用		
一. 原材料							
生铁	吨	47 310	1 108 579	1 099 017	9 562	328	45 160
钢材	吨	268 763	967 948	862 697	105 251	34 881	476 086
#铁道用钢材	吨	3 189	85 021	82 998	2 023	112	9 417
普通大型钢材	吨	8 851	17 254	14 137	3 117	793	12 888
普通中型钢材	吨	22 087	59 010	52 467	6 543	2 514	40 546
普通小型钢材	吨	41 524	188 291	163 528	24 763	8 046	93 250
钢带	吨	3 025	14 595	13 668	927	204	3 411
线材	吨	18 397	135 491	119 607	15 884	14 273	33 971
特厚钢板	吨	2 408	5 143	5 103	40	67	2 805
中厚钢板	吨	44 794	110 097	95 622	14 475	1 587	63 580
薄钢板	吨	21 778	81 493	77 062	4 431	580	35 821
硅钢片	吨	853	10 584	10 522	62	2	1 248
优质钢型材	吨	26 303	53 671	51 241	2 430	375	27 641
无缝钢管	吨	49 340	96 268	81 130	15 138	945	57 542
焊接钢管	吨	17 244	49 413	41 298	8 115	1 777	28 613
铜	吨	1 896	19 155	19 097	58		5 898
铝	吨	770	25 191	25 190	1	2	8 186
铅	吨	575	3 470	3 468	2	3	1 398
锌	吨	1 421	5 507	5 487	20		2 286
锡	吨	2 026	1 585	1 583	2		534
铜材	吨	2 399	5 123	4 759	364	175	2 602
铝材	吨	1 598	7 225	7 185	40	92	2 775
硫酸	吨	15 894	251 124	249 418	1 706		79 549
烧碱	吨	11 559	45 594	45 514	80		4 400
纯碱	吨	7 789	87 108	83 285	3 823		12 499
天然橡胶	吨	160	1 439	1 409	30		263
合成橡胶	吨	759	1 750	1 732	18	263	655
水泥	吨	164 007	1 626 580	1 411 576	215 004	139 625	1 079 146
平板玻璃	重量箱	54 239	236 371	217 050	19 321	15 429	118 268
原木	立方米	85 669	209 547	188 211	21 336	14 484	108 600
#原本直接消费	立方米		107 601	88 977	18 624	6 353	
锯材	立方米	23 475	86 876	80 377	6 499	2 755	31 497
润滑油	吨	17 636	20 557	20 461	96	99	56 540
二. 能源							
煤炭	万吨	195	1 783	1 732	52	13	400
焦炭	吨	154 374	1 304 829	1 255 451	49 378	16 879	248 514
焦炉煤气	万立方米		12 405	12 405			
其他煤气	万立方米		1 036	1 036			
原油	吨	193 558	5 455 594	5 455 594			188 005
汽油	吨	64 271	326 131	300 484	25 647	276	141 215
煤油	吨	12 051	22 284	21 854	430	231	32 347
柴油	吨	28 947	230 892	191 059	39 833	249	77 456
燃料油	吨	106 543	464 002	453 951	10 051	42 083	120 731
液化石油气	吨		23 260	23 176	84		
炼厂干气	吨		103 614	103 614			
天然气	万立方米		4 689	4 689			
热力	万百万千焦		4 199	4 140	59		
电力	亿千瓦小时		200	195	5		

4—2 分行业主要原材料消费与存库

(1993 年)

项　目	单位	本年消费量						
		农业	工业	建筑业	运输邮电业	批零贸易餐饮业	服务业	行政事业
一. 原材料								
生铁	吨		592 305	5 090	4 370	31	1 216	818
钢材	吨	136	592 305	279 265	70 241	7 448	4 490	14 063
#铁道用钢材	吨		8 003	22 660	54 325			33
普通大型钢材	吨		11 637	5 381	28	158	28	22
普通中型钢材	吨	38	34 374	21 939	1 250	524	586	299
普通小型钢材	吨		77 665	94 480	6 790	2 840	1 066	5450
钢带	吨		13 070	1 120	1	20	302	82
线材	吨	53	63 038	63 175	2 251	1 390	818	4 766
特厚钢板	吨		4 384	715				44
中厚钢板	吨		81 650	26 514	1 024	248	204	457
薄钢板	吨	7	72 465	6 088	2 035	463	129	306
硅钢片	吨		10 536		43			5
优质钢型材	吨		50 707	1 073	1 255	1	458	177
无缝钢管	吨		76 372	18 404	103	263	446	680
焊接钢管	吨	7	29 788	16 538	1 071	737	95	1 184
铜	吨		18 160	162		817	12	4
铝	吨		25 129	47			12	3
铅	吨		3 417	20			28	5
锌	吨		5 184	302			19	2
锡	吨		1 582	3				
铜材	吨		4 624	464		11		23
铝材	吨		2 134	5 054		2	22	13
硫酸	吨	432	249 812	652	6	2	162	58
烧碱	吨		39 037	6 468	5		69	15

4—2 续 1　　　　　　　　(1993 年)

项　　目	单位	本年消费量						
		农业	工业	建筑业	运输邮电业	批零贸易餐饮业	服务业	行政事业
纯碱	吨		86 788	22	112	54	96	36
天然橡胶	吨		1 437		2			
合成橡胶	吨		1 195		4	550	1	
水泥	吨	1 422	775 199	742 164	912	9 205	9 027	88 651
平板玻璃	重量箱		116 087	110 113	136	4 314	2 321	3 400
原木	立方米	199	137 097	54 824	182	6 313	1 016	9 916
#原木直接消费	立方米	55	85 028	17 690		327	248	4 253
锯材	立方米		45 366	39 392	51	167	72	1 828
润滑油	吨	31	141	17 544	168	94	83	2 496
二. 能源								
煤炭	万吨	5	1 647	8	42	15	21	45
焦炭	吨	847	1 277 636	1 928	2 173	17 798	920	3 527
焦炉煤气	万立方米		12 205					
其他煤气	万立方米		908	50	60			
原油	吨		5 454 871		723			
汽油	吨	3 715	112 364	14 953	57 006	53 934	18 813	65 346
煤油	吨	209	3 849	635	15 116	1 953	42	480
柴油	吨	2 351	89 152	6 860	106 513	17 184	1 989	6 843
燃料油	吨	9	460 399	206	2 110	1 043	147	88
液化石油气	吨	2	22 950			58	67	183
炼厂干气	吨		103 607					7
天然气	万立方米		4 689					
热力	万百万千焦		4 182	4	7	2	2	2
电力	亿千瓦小时	10	175	2	6	1	1	4

4—2续2

(1993年)

项目	单位	乡镇建筑企业施工消费量							
		合计	农业	工业	建筑业	运输邮电业	批零贸易餐饮业	服务业	行政事业
一. 原材料									
生铁	吨	328		52			4	100	172
钢材	吨	34 881		21 075		369	2 262	1 304	9 871
#铁道用钢材	吨	112		97					15
普通大型钢材	吨	793		42					751
普通中型钢材	吨	2 514		1 924			369		221
普通小型钢材	吨	8 046		5 027		110	125	366	2 418
钢带	吨	204		54					150
线材	吨	14 273		7 479		209	1 363	449	4 773
特厚钢板	吨	67							67
中厚钢板	吨	1 587		1 202			173	101	111
薄钢板	吨	580		549			7	8	16
硅钢片	吨	2		2					
优质钢钢型材	吨	375		360				2	13
无缝钢管	吨	945		745			15	12	173
焊接钢管	吨	1 777		486		50	191	89	961
铜	吨								
铝	吨	2							2
铅	吨	3		3					
锌	吨								
锡	吨								
铜材	吨	175		11				164	
铝材	吨	92		10		10		72	
硫酸	吨								
烧碱	吨								
纯碱	吨								
天然橡胶	吨								
合成橡胶	吨	263		1			110		152
水泥	吨	139 625		71 571		1 368	7 751	5 050	53 885
平板玻璃	重量箱	15 429		5 662		90	264	537	8 876
原木	立方米	14 484		5 159		207	1 993	598	6 527
#原木直接消费	立方米	6 353		2 891		10	630	51	2 771
锯材	立方米	2 755		2 266			43	138	308
润滑油	吨	99		1			88		10
二. 能源									
煤炭	吨	129 638		128 302		10	81	3	1 242
焦炭	吨	16 879		16 808			7	9	55
焦炉煤气	万立方米								
其他煤气	万立方米								
原油	吨								
汽油	吨	276		119		15	3	44	95
煤油	吨	231		230					1
柴油	吨	249		33				5	211
燃料油	吨	42 083		42 083					
液化石油气	吨								
炼厂干气	吨								
天然气	吨								

4—2 续 3　　　　　　　　(1993 年)

项目	单位	年末库存量				
		合计	农业	工业	建筑业	运输邮电业
一. 原材料:	吨	45 160		39 495	290	805
生铁	吨	476 086	8	279 414	51 159	10 735
钢材	吨	9 417		2 374	1 991	4 731
#铁道用钢材	吨	12 888		10 867	1 222	23
普通大型钢材	吨	40 546	6	23 144	5 692	674
普通中型钢材	吨	93 250		27 500	18 598	1 959
普通小型钢材	吨	3 411		2 775	136	2
钢带	吨	33 971		9 296	6 363	330
线材	吨	2 805		2 407	79	
特厚钢板	吨	63 580		41 945	7 454	829
中厚钢板	吨	35 821	1	16 333	1 232	587
薄钢板	吨	1 248		1 202	14	
硅钢片	吨	27 641		25 025	339	618
优质钢型材	吨	57 542	1	49 587	3 440	177
无缝钢管	吨	28 613		10 860	4 055	804
焊接钢管	吨	5 898		2 905	511	
铜	吨	8 186		897	1	
铝	吨	1 398		416	10	
铅	吨	2 286		276	2	
锌	吨	534		498	1	
锡	吨	2 602		1 923	110	
铜材	吨	2 775		1 405	84	
铝材	吨	79 549		21 919	1	2
硫酸	吨	4 400		1 877	1	
烧碱	吨	12 499		5 405	1	12
纯碱	吨	263		94		
天然橡胶	吨	655		153		
合成橡胶	吨	1 079 146	55	204 227	21 953	390
水泥	吨	118 268		25 151	9 557	20
平板玻璃	重量箱	108 600	39	46 559	5 491	24
原木	立方米					
#原木直接消费	立方米	31 497		14 582	5 662	18
锯材	立方米	56 540		33	124	10
润滑油	吨					
二. 能源:						
煤炭	万吨	400		173	1	1
焦炭	吨	248 514		158 396	512	
焦炉煤气	万立方米					
其他煤气	万立方米					
原油	吨	188 005		175 805		
汽油	吨	141 215	40	49 977	627	1 755
煤油	吨	32 347	8	10 226	33	164
柴油	吨	77 456	9	25 930	318	384
燃料油	吨	120 731		94 481	71	
液化石油气	吨					
炼厂干气	吨					
天然气	万立方米					
热力	万百万千焦					
电力	亿千瓦小时					

4—2 续 4

项目	单位	年末库存量					
		批零贸易餐饮业	服务业	行政事业	工业企业产品库存	附营生产单位产品库存	批零贸易企业经营商品库存
一.原材料:	吨	964		579	1 200		1 827
生铁	吨	9 875	1 214	6 254	21 700		95 727
钢材	吨			2			319
#铁道用钢材	吨	60		32			684
普通大型钢材	吨	810	5	248			9 967
普通中型钢材	吨	3 936	31	997	13 600		26 629
普通小型钢材	吨	18					480
钢带	吨	278	289	877	5 100		11 438
线材	吨	33		24			262
特厚钢板	吨	763	686	1 673			10 230
中厚钢板	吨	1 120	30	347	2 800		13 371
薄钢板	吨			5			27
硅钢片	吨	74	24	455			1 106
优质钢型材	吨	43	26	852			3 416
无缝钢管	吨	2 104	8	657	200		9 925
焊接钢管	吨			4	1 753		725
铜	吨	9	5	2	6 317		955
铝	吨	2		4	609		357
铅	吨				1 487		521
锌	吨						35
锡	吨	4	2	208	224		131
铜材	吨		1	70	1 197		18
铝材	吨	14			57 500		113
硫酸	吨	84			2 400		38
烧碱	吨	88		4	5 100		1 889
纯碱	吨						169
天然橡胶	吨	6	1		463		32
合成橡胶	吨	2 283	240	2 838	811 000		36 160
水泥	吨	7 423		989	47 000		28 128
平板玻璃	重量箱	14 239	39	1 355	6 300		34 554
原木	立方米						
#原木自接消费	立方米	478		269	6 400		4 088
锯材	立方米	90	7	486	24 700		31 090
润滑油	吨						
二.能源:							
煤炭	万吨	4		4	161		56
焦炭	吨	2 646	1	555	86 400		4
焦炉煤气	万立方米						
其他煤气	万立方米						
原油	吨				12 200		
汽油	吨	1 687	89	642	43 100	43 298	
煤油	吨	622		11	5 600	15 683	
柴油	吨	372	7	291	21 600	28 545	
燃料油	吨	106		373	25 700		
液化石油气	吨						
炼厂干气	吨						
天然气	万立方米						
热力	万百万千焦						
电力	亿千瓦小时						

4—3 原材料消费与库存总值

（1993 年）　　　　单位：万元

项　目	企业单位数(个)	年初库存总值	本年消费总值 合计	本年消费总值 主营活动用	本年消费总值 附营活动用	本年乡镇建筑企业施工消费总值	年末库存总值
总　计	4 105	328 674	1 477 389	1 408 216	69 173	22 315	404 824
一. 按类值分							
1. 黑金属材料类	1 619	102 964	451 097	410 299	40 798	10 370	140572
2. 有色金属材料类	587	41 415	249 432	248 734	698	1 137	63 072
3. 化工类	1 052	28 906	189 090	185 540	3 550	113	34 345
4. 建材类	1 311	22 002	121 363	111 878	9 485	6 639	17 966
5. 木材类	1 146	6 576	28 328	26 723	1 605	1 879	10 300
6. 一次转移价值的机电产品类	887	51 048	134 946	125 967	8 979	861	64 641
7. 其他类	2 517	75 763	303 133	299 075	4 058	1 316	73 928
二. 按隶属关系分							
中央企业	1 163	137 722	618 582	566 151	52 431	5 361	199 451
地方企业	4 462	190 952	858 807	842 065	16 742	16 954	205 373
#县属企业		40 272	248 841	244 706	4 135	13 860	34 205
三. 按经济类型分							
国有经济		289 218	1 257 064	1 189 888	67 176	20 601	375 646
集体经济		37 219	213 829	211 832	1 997	1 649	28 159
私营经济							
联营经济		11	127	127			13
股份制经济		43	384	384			382
外商投资经济		2 118	5 871	5 871			601
港. 澳. 台. 投资经济		65	114	114		65	23
其他经济							
四. 按国民经济行业分							
(一). 农林牧渔业		178	1 918	1 852	66	344	192
(二). 工业		266 014	1 186 839	1 126 006	60 832	5 065	349 556
采掘业		41 049	120 951	95 660	25 291	4 837	62 074
制造业		217 253	1 049 721	1 014 815	34 905	7 301	275 817
(三). 交通运输仓储及邮电通信业		5 223	40 721	40 495	226	547	5642
#交通运输业		5 143	40 554	40 328	226	453	1 757
(四). 批发和零售贸易. 餐饮业		21 312	5 261	4 630	631	1 607	12299
(五). 房地产管理. 公用事业居民服务和咨询业		1 156	3 399	3 335	64	1 273	1 359
(六). 卫生. 体育和社会福利事业		170	836	833	3	859	120
(七). 教育. 文化. 艺术及广播影视		377	3 509	3 447	62	530	505
(八). 科学研究和综合技术服务业		2 335	34 946	34 921	25	1	2864
(九). 国家. 政党机关和社会团体		966	3 474	3 240	234	3 585	229
(十). 其他行业		56	404	404		199	23

4—4 能源消费与库存总值

(1993年) 单位:万元

指标	企业单位数(个)	年初库存总值	本年消费总值			本年乡镇建筑企业施工消费总值	年末库存总值
			合计	主营活动	附营活动用		
总计	26 456	742 853	14 994 436	14 730 405	264 031	450 327	915 060
一.按隶属关系分							
中央企业	1 170	529 015	6 330 620	6 164 403	166 217	432100	652 312
地方企业	25 286	213 838	8 663 816	8 566 002	97 814	18227	262 748
#县属企业	14 895	60 100	5 740 652	5 728 555	12 097	4614	75 125
二.按经济类型分							
国有经济	18 343	735 647	14 190 271	13 931 201	259 070	449143	906 614
集体经济	8 012	7 198	715 147	710 277	4 870	1 184	8 104
私营经济	30		100	100			
联营经济	22	1	1 857	1 857			6
股份制经济	16		48 295	48 295			249
外商投资经济							
港.澳.台投资经济	2	1	38	14	24		
其他经济	3		26	26			
三.按国民经济行业分							
(一)农.林.牧.渔业	1 406	1 141	25 594	24 383	1 211	128	475
(二)工业	6 132	658 633	13 542 122	13 308 410	233 712	443 830	855692
轻工业							
重工业							
采掘业	749	56 794	749 282	647 018	102 264	1 137	70 116
制造业	5 207	597 389	12 266 085	12 134 852	131 233	442 693	737518
(三)交通运输仓储及邮电通信业	438	32 432	500 359	498 149	2210	400	35 639
#交通运输业	364	27 763	430 210	428 011	2 199	398	35 602
(四)批发和零售贸易.餐饮业	4 486	11 205	341 240	332 895	8 345	2675	8 975
(五)房地产管理.公用事业.居民服务咨询业	1 032	18 499	237 865	236415	1 450	203	3 703
(六)卫生.体育和社会福利事业	1 646	633	21 827	21 403	424	18	209
(七)教育.文化艺术及广播影视	3 145	3 128	46 323	44 272	2051	69	2 445
(八)科学研究和综合技术服务业	564	2 704	17 208	16 780	428		1 434
(九)其他行业	162	43	3 348	3 330	18	43	41

4—5 分行业主要原材料消费量

(1993)

行业分类	本年消费量				
	钢材(吨)	铜材(吨)	铝材(吨)	原木直接消费立方米	锯材立方米
一. 农. 林. 牧. 渔业	623			2 242	54
二. 工业					
采掘业	123 656	44	19	40 921	5 461
制造业	461 601	4 521	2 062	43 884	39 301
三. 交通运输. 仓储及邮电通信业	71 186			263	161
#交通运输业	804			230	103
四. 批发和零售贸易. 餐饮业	7 448	11	2	327	167
五. 房地产管理. 公用事业居民服务咨询业	2 066		4	125	30
六. 卫生. 体育和社会福利事业	256			211	
七. 教育. 文化. 艺术及广播电影电视业	3 076			162	320
八. 科学研究和综合技术服务业	939	14	12	121	125
九. 其他行业	259			26	

4—5 续 (1993)

行业分类	其中:主营活动用				
	钢材(吨)	铜材(吨)	铝材(吨)	原木直接消费立方米	锯材立方米
一. 农. 林. 牧. 渔业	574			2 198	31
二. 工业					
采掘业	86 692	29	16	33 163	3 149
制造业	405 696	4 178	2 031	35 135	35 635
三. 交通运输. 仓储及邮电通信业	71 076			263	151
#交通运输业	767			230	103
四. 批发和零售贸易. 餐饮业	6 824	11	2	327	45
五. 房地产管理. 公用事业居民服务咨询业	2 044		4	125	30
六. 卫生. 体育和社会福利事业	254			211	
七. 教育. 文化艺术及广播影视业	2 906			162	320
八. 科学研究和综合技术服务业	878	14	12	121	125
九. 其他行业	259			26	

4—6 分行业主要能源消费量

(1993)

行业分类	本年消费量						
	煤炭(吨)	焦炭(吨)	焦炉煤气(万立方米)	高炉煤气(万立方米)	原油(吨)	汽油(吨)	煤油(吨)
一.农.林.牧.渔业	51 304	847				3 715	209
二.工业	16 469 274	1 277 636	12 205	908	5 454 871	112 364	3849
采掘业	1 039 845	10 727			1 475 379	33 822	603
制造业	15 429 429	1 266 909	12 205	908	3 979 492	78 542	3246
三.交通运输仓储及邮电通信业	423 682	2 173		60	723	57 006	15 116
#交通运输业	417 842	2 173		60	723	56 459	15 112
四.批发和零售贸易.餐饮业	153 220	17 798	18			53 934	1 953
五.房地产管理.公用事业.居民服务和咨询业	177 085	801		18		14 072	26
六.卫生.体育和社会福利事业	56 290	5				1 395	1
七.教育文化艺术及广播影视业	155 138	2 473	5			3 793	21
八.科学研究和综合技术服务业	38 878	127				7 337	313
九.其他行业	4 568					560	

4—6 续

(1993)

行业分类	本年消费量						
	柴油(吨)	燃料油(吨)	液化石油气(吨)	炼厂干气(吨)	天然气(万立方米)	热力(百万千焦)	电力(万千瓦时)
一.农.林.牧.渔业	2 351	9	2				106 201
二.工业	89 152	460 399	22 950	103 607	4 689	41 823 071	1 750 403
采掘业	27 950	72 844	2 169	4 722	4 689	10 381 100	78 508
制造业	61 202	387 555	20 781	98 885		31 441 971	1 671 895
三.交通运输.仓储及邮电通信业	106 513	2 110				73 630	62 655
#交通运输业	106 478	2 110				73 630	60 609
四.批发和零售贸易.餐饮业	17 184	1 043	58			20 062	10 980
五.房地产管理.公用事业.居民服务和咨询业	1 864	47	21			4 188	14 094
六.卫生.体育和社会福利事业	4 213		16			1 368	4 024
七.教育.文化艺术及广播影视业	319	2	117			1 257	7 382
八.科学研究和综合技术服务业	67	1				420	5 462
九.其他行业	36						259

五· 财政税收

统计指标解释

·之五·

【**金融资产(负债)**】金融资产是指一部门拥有的对另一部门的债权;金融负债是指一部门对另一部门的债务。具体分为国内金融资产(负债)、国外金融资产(负债)和储备资产。国内金融资产(负债)包括通货、存款、贷款、证券和其他;国外金融资产(负债)包括长期资本来往、短期资本来往;储备资产包括黄金储备、外汇储备、特别提款权、在基金组织的储备头寸对基金信贷的使用。

【**国内金融往来**】常住单位间进行的各金融交易,根据金融交易的不同形式特点,可分为通货、存款、证券、贷款、政府借款和其他金融往来。

【**通货**】以现金形式存在于流通领域中的货币,是中央银行的负债,持有通货者的资产,包括居民手持现金和企业现金库存等。

【**存款**】各部门存入金融部门的货币和支票,是存款人的资产,金融部门的负债。包括活期存款和定期存款。

【**活期存款**】存款期限没有约定、随时可提用的存款,活期存款是货币供应量的主要组成部分,包括居民活期存款、企业结算户存款、机关团体存款等。

【**定期存款**】存款期限有时间约定的存款。包括居民定期存款、单位定期存款和企业自筹基建存款等。

【**债券**】政府和其他部门以票据形式为筹集资金而发行的,承诺按一定利率付息或按盈利状况分红的书面债务证书。是发行者的负债,持有者的资产。分为政府债券和其他债券及集资。

【**政府债券**】政府发行的有价证券。包括国库券、国家重点建设债券、国家建设债券、保值公债等。

【**其他债券**】政府以外各部门发行的各种债券和股票。如金融债券、企业债券和企业短期融资券等。

【**贷款**】金融部门对各部门所需资金的贷出款项,是金融部门的资产,其他部门的负债。包括短期贷款和长期贷款等。

【**短期贷款**】金融部门对所需资金部门的期限在一年以内的贷款。如对占用原材料、在产品、成品及结算资金提供的贷款。

【**长期贷款**】金融部门对所需资金部门的期限在一年以上的贷款。如对固定资产维修、更新、改造和扩建等资金提供的贷款。

【**财政借款**】中央银行以透支、借款形式对财政预算提供的信贷,即财政借款和透支抵减财政预算存款后的额。是财政部门的负债,金融部门的资产。

上或未规定借贷期限的资本往来。包括直接投资,证券投资,国际组织贷款,外国政府贷款,银行借款,地方、部门借款,延期付款,延期收款,加工装配、补偿贸易中应付客商作价设备款,租赁,对外贷款和其他。

5—1 地方财政收支总额及指数

单位:万元

年 份	收 入	支 出	收支差额	指数(上年=100)	
				收入	支出
1952	11 163	6 421	4 742	136.72	174.44
1957	20 407	24 581	—4 174	111.47	87.83
1965	37 795	41 889	—4 094	114.53	124.80
1970	59 930	65 575	—5 645	128.49	144.44
1975	171 708	106 394	65 314	106.50	95.94
1978	205 280	143 429	61 851	119.31	129.10
1980	149 348	123 045	26 303	80.90	86.77
1981	129 859	111 955	17 904	86.95	90.99
1982	124 713	127 857	—3 144	96.04	114.20
1983	109 003	155 256	—46 253	87.40	121.43
1984	132 339	211 510	—79 171	121.41	136.23
1985	164 837	240 787	—75 950	124.56	113.84
1986	197 635	300 125	— 102 490	119.90	124.64
1987	225 831	317 747	—91 916	114.27	105.87
1988	249 786	303 835	— 114 049	110.61	114.50
1989	315 242	412 645	—97 403	126.20	113.42
1990	342 065	459 395	— 117 330	108.51	111.33
1991	399 801	513 188	— 113 387	116.88	111.71
1992	399 736	534 786	— 137 447	106.78	104.21
1993	521 132	631 676	— 110 544	130.37	118.12
恢复时期	24 219	11 993	12 226		
"一五"时期	80 562	90 596	—10 034	12.82	30.80
"二五"时期	230 583	316 185	—85 602	4.21	—1.06
1963—1965 年	100 688	102 506	—1 818	14.64	21.59
"三五"时期	213 031	223 458	—10 427	9.66	9.38
"四五"时期	765 821	477 195	288 626	23.43	10.16
"五五"时期	891 459	631 599	259 860	—2.75	2.95
"六五"时期	660 751	847 365	— 186 614	1.99	14.37
"七五"时期	1 330 559	1 853 747	— 523 188	15.72	13.79

5—2 财政分部门收入

单位:万元

年　份	工业			农业	商业	交通运输业	建筑业
		轻工业	重工业				
1985	16 943	988	15 955	— 810	— 243	—4 733	938
1986	18 410	1 317	17 093	— 819	2 792	99	822
1987	24 083	1 492	22 591	— 892	1 736	162	926
1988	21 106	1 606	19 500	— 961	—74	217	1 057
1989	20 979	1 923	1 750	— 955	— 206	556	307
1990	16 868	2 870	13 998	— 915	—1 096	253	204
1991	18 778	2 881	15 897	— 951	— 114	213	142
1992	15 942	2 244	13 698	— 997	972	143	604
1993	16 119	2 290	13 829	— 771	2 859	—6	27

5—3 财政分项目收入

单位:万元

年　份	工商税收收入	企业收入				其他
			#工业	#商业	#交通运输	
1985	153 907	—24 103	—1 157	—4 733	— 243	35 033
1986	171 985	15 839	18 410	2 792	99	9 811
1987	190 098	24 057	24 083	1 736	162	11 676
1988	216 172	13 398	21 106	—74	217	20 216
1989	265 310	6 104	20 979	— 206	183	43 828
1990	295 300	—2 582	16 868	—1 096	253	49 347
1991	312 619	10 892	18 778	— 114	213	76 290
1992	345 183	9 361	15 942	972	143	45 192
1993	472 218	7 409	16 119	2 859	—6	41 505

5—4 各项税收

单位:万元

年份	各项税收合计	#工商税收	#盐税	#农牧业税	#建筑税
1978					
1980	78 911	75 859	59	2 993	
1981	74 562	71 022	121	3 419	
1982	83 707	78 924	106	3 312	
1983	92 004	84 859	84	4 117	
1984	114 322	100 801	87	3 544	2 573
1985	189 057	153 907	83	5 549	3 762
1986	210 832	171 985	119	6 314	3 709
1987	235 215	190 098	66	7 181	4 211
1988	267 766	216 172	86	9 016	3 213
1989	317 768	265 310	145	11 316	3 340
1990	341 541	295 300	192	11 459	3 144
1991	359 225	312 619	173	11 770	1 262
1992	393 208	345 183	183	11 394	42
1993	520 393	472 218	260	11 308	

5—5 财政分项目支出

单位:万元

年份	基本建设支出	企业挖潜改造资金	支援农村生产支出类	行政管理费	文教卫生事业费	价格补贴支出	其他支出
1985	41 292	17 238	10 017	30 634	57 095	15 698	68 813
1986	51 287	12 443	11 948	37 103	67 987	30 949	88 408
1987	47 706	8 320	12 841	37 064	69 273	36 857	105 686
1988	41 498	18 372	17 753	40 309	82 241	42 498	61 164
1989	40 157	12 134	19 913	44 895	93 638	48 901	153 007
1990	38 579	18 479	24 599	52 019	105 246	49 242	171 231
1991	40 914	18 428	24 422	59 802	110 889	51 498	207 235
1992	41 102	18 939	27 397	73 524	130 374	44 302	199 148
1993	44 414	28 185	28 237	83 641	148 441	27 593	271 165

5—6 预算外资金收入

单位:万元

年份	预算外收入	地方财政.预算外资金	行政事业单位预算外资金	国营企业和主管部门预算外资金
1985	155 313	8 251	34 654	112 407
1986	179 779	6 222	48 788	124 768
1987	198 207	4 596	53 793	169 819
1988	232 191	4 948	64 272	162 971
1989	250 375	6 609	72 642	171 124
1990	246 894	6 654	85 563	154 676
1991	268 881	5 492	89 534	173 855
1992	298 726	6 370	96 564	195 783
1993	147 370	10 145	137 225	

注:1993 年预算外收入中不含国营企业和主管部门预算外资金

5—7 预算外资金支出

单位:万元

项　　目	1992 年	1993 年	1993 年比 1992 年(±)%
固定资产投资支出	14 731	14 235	—3.40
养路费支出	25 071	36 796	46.70
城市维护支出	2 469	5 583	126.10
福利奖励支出	5 183	5 295	2.20
行政事业支出	32 645	51 238	56.90
转作抵支收入		2 046	
上交国家能交基金	6 243	3 472	—44.40
上交国家预算调节基金	4 200	4 029	—4.10
奖金税	15	28	86.60
投资方向调节税	60	476	776.00
其他支出	14 137	26 364	86.50

5—8 财政价格补贴

单位:万元

年　份	价格补贴	粮.棉.油价格补贴	调整.调价增加补贴	其他价格补贴
1978				
1980	8 201	7 517		684
1985	15 698	11 000	4 669	29
1990	49 242	34 277	11 434	3 531
1992	44 302	21 394		22 908
1993	27 592	13 469		14 123

六·物　价

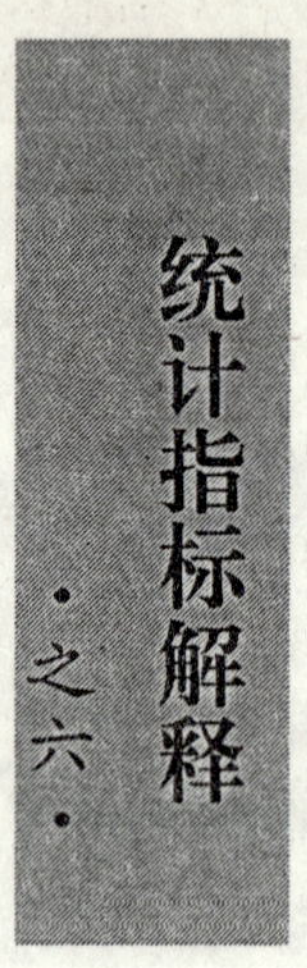

统计指标解释

·之六·

【短期资本往来】借贷期限在一年或一年以下的资本往来。包括银行借款、地方、部门借款，延期付款，延期收款和其他。

【储备资产】一国拥有的可以直接对国外支付的黄金储备、外汇储备、特别提款权、在基金组织的储备头寸以及对基金信贷的使用等。

【国内生产总值】是按市场价格计算的国内生产总值的简称。它是一个国家(地区)所有常住单位在一定时期内生产活动的最终成果。国内生产总值有三种表现形态，即价值形态、收入形态和产品形态。从价值形态看，它是所有常住单位在一定时期内所生产的全部货物和服务价值超过同期投入的全部非固定资产货物和服务价值的差额，即所有常住单位的增加值之和；从收入形态看，它是所有常住单位在一定时期内所创造并分配给常住单位和非常住单位的初次分配收入之和；从产品形态看，它是最终使用的货物和服务减去进口货物和服务。在实际核算中，国内生产总值的三种形态表现为三种计算方法、即生产法收入法和支出法。三种方法分别从不同的方面反映国内生产总值及其构成。

【国有经济单位】指生产资料归国家所有的各种企业、事业单位，以及各级国家机关、人民团体等单位。

【集体经济单位】指生产资料归公民集体所有的各种企业、事业单位。包括农村各种经济组织经营的农、林、牧、副、渔业，乡、村经营的企业、事业单位；城市、县、镇以及街道举办的集体经济性质的企业、事业单位。

【平均每年增长速度】《年鉴》内所列的年平均增长速度，都是用于“水平法”计算的。从某年到某年平均增长速度的年份，均不包括基年在内。如建国 34 年的平均增长速度是以 1949 年为基期计算的，则写为 1950——1984 年的平均增长速度其余类推。

【人口数】人口数指一定时点、一定地区范围内的有生命的个人的总和。年度统计的年末人口数是指每年 12 月 31 日 24 时的人口数。

【出生率(又称粗出生率)】指在一定时期内(通常为一年内)平均每千人所出生的人数的比率，一般用千分率表示。计算公式：

出生率＝年出生人数÷年平均人数×1000‰

出生人数是指活产婴儿，即胎儿脱离母体时(不管怀孕月数)，有过呼吸或其他生命现象。年平均人数是年初、年末人口数的平均数，也可用年中人口数代替。

【死亡率】指在一定时期内(通常为一年内)一定地区的死亡人数与同期平均人数(或期中人数)之比，一般用于千分率表示。计算公式：

死亡率＝年死亡人数÷年平均人数×1000‰

6—1 各种物价总指数

年 份	零售物价总指数	职工生活费用价格总指数	农副产品收购价格总指数	农村工业品零售价格总指数	工农业商品综合比价指数	
					以农副产品收购价格总指数为100	以农村工业品零售价格总指数为100
(上年=100)						
1985	108.50	110.60	105.70	103.00	97.40	102.60
1986	106.00	107.00	107.40	103.30	96.20	103.90
1987	107.40	108.40	111.90	105.60	94.40	105.90
1988	118.60	120.60	118.80	113.90	95.90	104.30
1989	116.40	118.20	110.20	116.30	105.50	94.80
1990	103.40	101.90	97.50	106.70	109.40	91.40
1991	104.60	105.70	100.00	104.80	104.80	95.40
1992	105.80	107.30	108.80	104.30	95.90	104.30
1993	113.00	115.20	107.40			
(1952年=100)						
1957	101.50	99.80	111.70	98.70	88.40	113.20
1965	116.40	116.70	124.50	96.80	77.80	128.60
1970	113.30	113.60	129.10	92.60	71.70	139.40
1975	113.20	114.00	139.90	91.70	65.50	152.60
1978	113.60	114.50	145.20	92.60	63.80	156.80
1980	120.40	125.10	187.90	93.60	49.80	200.70
1981	122.80	128.40	202.40	93.70	46.30	216.00
1982	124.50	131.30	200.00	95.10	47.60	210.30
1983	125.10	132.80	218.60	96.70	44.20	226.10
1984	128.90	137.20	221.00	100.00	45.20	221.00
1985	139.90	151.80	233.60	103.00	44.10	122.80
1986	148.20	162.40	250.80	106.40	42.40	235.70
1987	159.20	176.00	280.70	112.30	40.40	250.00
1988	188.80	212.30	333.50	127.90	38.40	260.80
1989	219.80	250.90	367.50	148.70	40.40	247.10
1990	227.30	255.70	358.30	158.70	44.30	225.80
1991	237.80	270.30	358.30	166.30	46.40	215.50
1992	251.60	290.00	389.80	173.50	44.50	224.60
1993	284.30	334.70	418.60			

6—2 全省零售物价细分类指数

（上年=100）

年份	总指数	一、消费品	#1. 食品类	#(1) 副食品	#蔬菜	#肉禽蛋	#水产品	#食糖
1979	100.80	101.10	101.40	103.60	110.20	105.70	101.60	100.00
1980	104.10	104.20	107.00	113.80	108.80	124.20	131.10	100.00
1981	101.60	101.70	102.80	104.00	109.40	99.40	104.00	100.00
1982	101.20	101.10	102.00	100.10	98.40	100.10	106.20	100.00
1983	100.60	100.20	101.00	100.60	97.40	100.10	134.50	100.00
1984	103.00	101.90	103.30	105.80	111.70	102.80	114.20	100.00
1985	108.50	109.20	114.90	119.80	144.40	117.70	140.70	100.00
1986	106.00	106.70	109.00	113.50	110.00	116.70	128.00	100.00
1987	107.40	107.80	111.60	116.00	128.10	116.10	133.80	100.00
1988	118.60	119.00	121.50	130.30	131.80	135.20	131.30	147.20
1989	116.40	116.80	113.80	114.30	108.80	115.70	142.10	103.50
1990	103.40	102.20	101.30	103.20	105.40	98.70	94.80	100.30
1991	104.60	104.60	106.10	107.40	110.90	102.00	101.90	125.60
1992	105.80	105.70	108.20	106.20	104.10	105.20	96.70	86.90
1993	113.00	112.40	111.20	110.70	113.00	105.20	109.20	114.10

6—2 续表 1.

年份	#(2) 烟酒茶	#烟	#酒	#茶	#(3) 其他食品	#鲜果	#糖果	#糕点	#奶及奶制品
1979	99.50	99.50	100.00	100.00	102.60	100.00	100.00	103.40	101.00
1980	102.30	102.80	100.60	101.80	104.20	107.30	100.40	105.00	103.20
1981	103.50	104.50	102.50	100.40	103.30	111.30	100.00	100.00	100.80
1982	115.20	121.70	107.90	101.00	101.00	103.50	100.00	100.00	101.80
1983	100.20	99.80	98.00	111.80	103.60	111.00	100.00	100.20	99.80
1984	100.20	99.00	100.20	103.40	101.60	102.90	99.90	100.00	100.10
1985	101.50	101.40	101.20	103.30	116.40	134.10	101.10	106.10	101.10
1986	102.00	100.50	104.50	101.30	110.80	119.90	100.10	101.00	106.10
1987	105.50	99.80	109.30	112.70	113.80	123.50	101.30	104.10	111.60
1988	111.00	110.40	111.80	111.60	119.90	122.50	115.30	124.40	117.90
1989	111.90	108.10	117.70	110.90	117.90	112.30	118.70	125.40	112.30
1990	100.30	99.00	99.50	106.30	99.30	94.60	105.60	103.50	103.90
1991	101.80	100.20	102.60	104.40	106.90	93.30	107.40	110.70	105.50
1992	103.50	104.50	100.90	106.10	102.30	93.50	105.70	108.20	104.40
1993	104.60	103.30	106.30	105.20	112.90	123.10	113.30	109.80	103.40

6—2 续表 2.

年份	#2 衣着类	#棉布	#化纤布	#呢绒	#绸缎	#针纺织品	#服装
1979	100.10	100.00	102.50	100.00	100.00	99.40	
1980	100.10	100.00	99.90	100.20	100.60	100.10	
1981	99.40	100.00	97.70	99.80	100.00	99.50	
1982	99.20	100.00	95.80	99.70	100.00	100.20	
1983	97.40	120.00	82.60	89.50	99.90	104.10	92.40
1984	100.00	99.90	99.90	100.30	100.00	100.20	96.40
1985	101.50	99.80	100.30	103.90	101.40	100.90	102.00
1986	102.50	101.20	100.60	107.40	103.00	101.90	102.40
1987	103.10	103.50	100.80	106.40	107.60	104.90	101.20
1988	114.90	117.20	107.40	122.80	119.20	117.40	112.20
1989	118.70	135.00	108.40	124.40	116.80	124.50	116.10
1990	106.10	109.50	111.10	100.50	107.40	104.10	105.00
1991	105.50	108.80	106.30	98.70	105.50	104.80	103.90
1992	101.50	102.00	103.30	99.90	101.50	102.60	101.20
1993	111.60	103.00	106.00	104.40	105.00	108.60	122.90

6—2 续表 3.

年份	#鞋	#其他衣着	#3 日用品类	#一般日 用品	#日用机电 消费品	#家俱	#日用杂品
1979	99.70	99.80	101.20	100.20		102.90	100.10
1980	100.00	99.70	101.70	99.70		101.30	106.50
1981	99.80	100.00	100.10	100.00	99.80	101.20	100.70
1982	99.90	100.30	99.00	99.90	94.00	101.90	102.20
1983	99.40	96.90	100.00	100.20	97.50	107.10	100.10
1984	101.10	104.30	99.80	100.30	97.90	101.10	102.60
1985	105.30	101.80	103.70	104.70	99.90	104.80	110.70
1986	101.80	102.90	105.10	103.40	106.90	102.20	107.70
1987	101.80	106.10	107.30	106.00	109.40	102.90	110.90
1988	112.30	131.50	113.30	119.70	108.20	115.80	119.80
1989	112 10	125.90	116.00	123.10	111.50	113.70	123.90
1990	107.10	98.60	101.60	107.20	96.00	101.60	109.50
1991	104.40	101.90	101.20	103.70	99.50	99.90	102.00
1992	101.70	99.50	102.10	103.30	101.60	101.30	102.30
1993	118.40	100.00	111.40	112.70	109.40	112.90	110.30

6—2 续表 4.

年份	#4.文化娱乐用品类	#纸张文具	#文娱用机电消费品	#其他文娱用品	#5.书报杂志表
1979	103.40	104.90		100.00	
1980	100.90	101.20		100.10	
1981	100.50	100.10		101.10	
1982	99.20	100.00		97.30	
1983	97.50	100.20	96.10	95.00	
1984	99.90	100.00	100.00	99.60	100.00
1985	101.20	102.60	100.10	105.50	131.60
1986	101.40	104.20	100.70	102.30	112.30
1987	100.80	108.40	98.50	106.40	101.40
1988	127.20	111.40	131.50	106.00	109.30
1989	110.40	113.30	109.70	115.20	191.20
1990	95.30	108.30	91.70	102.90	108.00
1991	95.50	106.30	92.20	102.70	99.00
1992	98.20	104.20	95.80	101.50	105.90
1993	102.30	111.50	98.20	109.70	110.00

6—2 续表 5.

年份	#6.药及医疗用品类	#中药	#西药及医疗用品	#7.建筑材料类	#8.燃料类	二.农业生产资料
1979	102.10	106.00	99.60		99.10	100.20
1980	102.40	105.20	100.80		100.00	100.20
1981	103.20	108.30	100.00		100.80	99.80
1982	102.10	105.40	99.90		100.60	101.30
1983	104.40	107.10	101.70		100.50	104.40
1984	104.90	107.90	101.70		101.40	108.30
1985	108.00	115.80	103.10		106.30	104.60
1986	105.60	109.10	102.00		110.10	100.60
1987	106.10	104.10	108.20		105.70	104.80
1988	124.60	131.30	120.00	116.60	108.20	114.30
1989	124.80	117.60	129.40	120.10	134.50	113.70
1990	98.40	91.40	103.00	101.40	107.60	111.20
1991	100.70	103.20	99.50	100.10	115.40	104.50
1992	111.10	121.50	104.50	102.80	107.10	106.70
1993	116.60	123.00	112.60	137.20	131.10	120.10

6—3 全省零售物价分类指数

(1952 年=100)

年份	总指数	#食品类	#衣着类	#日用品类	#文化娱乐用品类	#药及医疗用品类	#燃料类	农业生产资料
1957	101.50	107.40	98.60	92.90	79.60	111.60	103.40	99.60
1965	116.40	118.10	101.00	96.00	80.90	95.60	102.50	98.40
1970	113.30	117.90	99.50	89.50	77.50	66.80	103.20	88.60
1975	113.20	119.40	99.40	93.50	72.70	63.50	97.90	83.90
1978	113.60	118.90	100.40	94.60	73.90	64.90	99.40	84.10
1980	120.40	129.00	100.60	97.40	77.20	67.90	98.50	84.40
1981	122.80	132.60	100.00	97.40	77.50	70.10	99.30	83.50
1982	124.50	135.30	99.20	96.40	76.90	71.60	99.90	84.60
1983	125.10	136.60	96.60	96.40	74.90	74.80	100.40	88.30
1984	128.90	141.10	96.60	96.20	74.90	78.40	101.80	95.70
1985	139.90	162.20	98.10	99.80	75.80	84.70	108.20	100.10
1986	148.20	176.80	100.50	104.90	76.90	89.40	119.10	100.70
1987	159.20	197.30	103.60	112.60	77.50	94.90	125.90	105.50
1988	188.80	239.70	119.10	127.50	98.60	118.20	136.30	120.60
1989	219.80	272.70	141.40	147.90	108.80	147.60	183.30	137.10
1990	227.30	276.30	150.00	150.30	103.70	145.20	197.20	152.50
1991	237.80	293.10	158.20	152.10	99.00	146.20	227.60	159.30
1992	251.60	317.10	160.60	155.30	97.20	162.40	243.80	169.90
1993	284.30	352.60	179.20	173.00	99.40	189.40	319.60	204.00

6－4 全省零售物价细分类指数

(1993 年)

项　目	1978 年＝100	1980 年＝100	1990 年＝100	1992 年＝100
总指数	250.10	236.10	125.10	113.00
一. 消费品零售价格指数	245.20	232.80	124.30	112.40
1. 食品类	296.70	273.40	127.60	111.20
(1)粮食	259.80	259.50	169.90	122.80
细粮	236.10	235.90	165.80	120.60
粗粮	410.60	410.60	203.50	139.10
(2)副食品	399.80	339.20	126.30	110.70
食用植物油	264.90	264.90	152.60	102.90
鲜菜	563.40	469.80	130.40	113.00
干菜	458.40	423.80	122.10	108.80
肉禽蛋	373.60	284.60	112.90	105.20
水产品	1 036.30	778.10	107.60	109.20
调味品	319.70	311.30	148.20	116.60
食糖	190.30	190.30	124.50	114.10
(3)烟酒类	182.70	179.50	110.20	104.60
烟	167.00	163.30	108.20	103.30
酒	181.90	180.90	110.00	106.30
茶叶	215.80	211.90	116.60	105.20
(4)其他食品	298.60	279.30	123.50	112.90
鲜果	391.80	365.10	107.30	123.10
干果	359.10	308.40	139.80	113.10
糖果	191.10	190.30	128.60	113.30
糕点	257.70	237.40	131.50	109.80
奶及奶制品	200.40	192.20	113.80	103.40
罐头			102.70	105.20
2. 衣着类	178.40	178.10	119.50	111.60
棉布	248.10	248.10	114.30	103.00
化纤布	121.00	118.30	116.40	106.00

6—4续

(1993年)

项 目	1978年=100	1980年=100	1990年=100	1992年=100
呢绒	167.90	167.60	102.90	104.40
绸缎	189.80	188.80	112.40	105.00
针纺织品	198.30	199.30	116.70	108.60
服装			129.20	122.90
鞋	184.70	185.30	125.70	118.40
其他衣着	185.50	186.50	101.40	100.00
3.日用品类	182.90	177.80	115.10	111.40
一般日用品	219.50	219.80	120.70	112.70
日用机电消费品		134.00	110.60	109.40
家 具	196.10	188.10	114.20	112.90
日用杂品	278.70	261.40	115.00	110.30
4.文化娱乐用品类	134.50	129.00	95.90	102.30
纸张文具	208.30	196.20	123.50	111.50
文娱用机电消费品			86.70	98.20
其他文娱用品	153.70	153.60	114.30	109.70
5.书报杂志类			115.30	110.00
6.药及医疗用品类	291.40	278.70	130.50	116.60
中药	421.00	377.60	154.20	123.00
西药及医疗用品	221.00	220.10	117.10	112.60
7.建筑装璜材料类			141.20	137.20
8.燃料类	321.40	324.30	162.00	131.10
二.服务项目价格指数			179.40	141.00
房租			229.90	199.40
水电费			116.10	108.60
交通费			151.20	120.70
邮电费			200.80	142.50
医疗保健费			172.30	166.30
学杂、保育费			253.60	165.00
文娱费			245.70	155.70
修理及其他服务费			144.50	119.90

6—5 全社会及国有商业零售物价指数

(上年=100)

商品类别	全社会			国有		
	全省	城镇	农村	全省	城镇	农村
零售物价指数	113.00	112.30	114.50	114.10	112.40	114.50
一.消费品价格指数	112.40	112.30	112.60	112.90	112.40	112.60
(一)食品类	111.20	111.30	111.00	110.60	110.50	111.00
1.粮食	122.80	120.90	130.70	125.80	123.70	130.70
细粮	120.60	120.40	122.20	122.60	123.00	122.20
粗粮	139.10	129.70	151.70	150.30	143.40	151.70
2.副食品	110.70	108.70	112.60	109.80	107.10	112.60
食用植物油	102.90	102.20	105.40	103.50	102.20	105.40
鲜菜	113.00	113.00		113.00	113.00	
干菜	108.80	106.00	113.80	113.40	110.10	113.80
肉禽蛋	105.20	105.00	110.60	107.60	105.30	110.60
水产品	109.20	108.40	110.50	107.70	107.40	110.50
调味品	116.60	113.70	118.30	116.90	114.80	118.30
食糖	114.10	114.60	113.80	114.10	114.60	113.80
3.烟酒茶	104.60	106.10	102.40	104.60	106.10	102.40
烟	103.30	104.70	101.80	103.30	104.70	101.80
酒	106.30	108.20	103.50	106.30	108.20	103.50
茶	105.20	109.60	101.90	105.90	109.80	101.90
4.其他食品	112.90	114.50	107.60	108.10	108.60	107.60
鲜果	123.10	123.60	94.20	102.20	110.10	94.20
干果	113.10	109.90	121.60	113.10	109.90	121.60
糖果	113.30	118.90	106.40	113.30	118.90	106.40
糕点	109.80	111.10	104.20	109.80	111.10	104.20
奶及奶品	103.40	102.80	106.00	103.40	102.80	106.00
罐头	105.20	105.80	104.10	105.20	105.80	104.10
饮料	106.80	106.30	112.60	108.00	106.30	112.60
(二)衣着类	111.60	114.30	106.30	111.60	114.30	106.30
1.棉布	103.00	105.00	101.90	103.00	105.00	101.90
2.棉花化纤混纺布	100.60	105.20	98.70	100.60	105.20	98.70
3.化纤布	106.00	111.00	102.10	106.00	111.00	102.10

6—5续　　　　　　　　　　　　(上年=100)

商品类别	全社会			国有		
	全省	城镇	农村	全省	城镇	农村
4.呢绒	104.40	104.60	103.80	104.40	104.60	103.80
5.绸缎	105.00	106.70	102.50	105.00	106.70	102.50
6.针纺织品	108.60	109.80	106.20	108.60	109.80	106.20
7.服装	122.90	123.40	116.00	122.90	123.40	116.00
8.鞋	118.40	121.40	110.80	118.40	121.40	110.80
9.其他衣着	100.00	99.30	103.30	100.00	99.30	103.30
(三)日用品类	111.40	113.30	107.00	111.40	113.30	107.00
1.一般日用品	112.70	114.00	108.40	112.70	114.00	108.40
2.日用机电消费品	109.40	110.70	106.40	109.40	110.70	106.40
3.家俱	112.90	117.10	104.10	112.90	117.10	104.10
4.日用杂品	110.30	109.40	112.10	110.30	109.40	112.10
(四)文化娱乐用品类	102.30	102.60	101.30	102.30	102.60	101.30
1.纸张文具	111.50	111.90	110.00	111.50	111.90	110.00
2.文娱用机电消费品	98.20	98.40	97.50	98.20	98.40	97.50
3.其他文娱用品	109.70	110.30	104.70	109.70	110.30	104.70
(五)书报杂志类	110.00	109.00	110.40	110.00	109.00	110.40
(六)药及医疗用品类	116.60	115.50	118.10	116.60	115.50	118.10
1.中药	123.00	123.00	122.90	123.00	123.00	122.90
2.西药及医疗用品类	112.60	110.10	115.20	112.60	110.10	115.20
(七)建筑材料类	137.20	143.30	134.60	137.20	143.30	134.60
(八)燃料类	131.10	134.50	129.50	131.10	134.50	129.50
二.农业生产资料价格指数	120.10		120.10	120.10		120.10
1.小农具	131.40		131.40	131.40		131.40
铁制小农具	145.60		145.60	145.60		145.60
竹木制小农具	101.30		101.30	101.30		101.30
2.半机械化农具	126.40		126.40	126.40		126.40
3.机械化农具	113.40		113.40	113.40		113.40
4.化学肥料	117.50		117.50	117.50		117.50
5.农药及农药械	108.80		108.80	108.80		108.80
化学农药	112.10		112.10	112.10		112.10
农药械	103.30		103.30	103.30		103.30
6.农机用油	170.50		170.50	170.50		170.50
7.其他	105.90		105.90	105.90		105.90

6—6 服务项目价格指数

(上年=100)

年份	服务项目价格指数	房租	水电费	交通费	邮电费	医疗保健费	学杂保育费	文娱费	修理及其他服务费
1982	100.00	100.00	100.00	100.00	100.00	100.00		100.00	100.00
1983	106.60	100.00	100.00	100.00	125.70	138.60		100.00	102.50
1984	108.40	103.20	100.00	121.30	134.10	104.20		100.00	108.30
1985	109.50	113.70	100.30	102.60	100.00	116.60	107.70	132.50	110.40
1986	105.80	103.60	100.0	101.3	100.0	105.1	118.2	109.6	107.0
1987	106.60	102.9	100.0	102.9	100.0	118.7	110.4	116.6	118.3
1988	120.20	103.0	100.0	123.2	102.2	120.5	140.3	127.4	118.0
1989	129.60	106.4	100.6	117.5	100.0	105.2	188.2	126.4	113.7
1990	111.90	102.10	101.60	138.20	142.30	100.1	109.90	106.80	105.70
1991	107.2	100.1	101.5	102.2	135.9	100.3	110.2	128.1	107.4
1992	118.70	115.20	105.30	122.60	103.70	103.3	139.50	123.20	112.20
1993	141.00	199.40	108.60	120.70	142.50	166.30	165.00	155.70	119.90

6—7 居民生活费用价格指数

(上年=100)

年份	总指数		消费品		服务项目	
	城镇	农村	城镇	农村	城镇	农村
1985	110.60	107.10	110.70	107.00	109.80	109.10
1986	107.00	106.00	107.20	106.00	105.40	106.50
1987	108.40	106.50	108.70	106.40	105.20	109.00
1988	120.60	116.00	120.80	115.30	118.30	124.70
1989	118.20	117.60	115.90	117.70	140.20	116.40
1990	101.90	104.70	100.60	104.00	113.60	110.10
1991	105.70	104.50	105.20	104.40	110.70	105.40
1992	107.30	106.40	106.10	104.70	116.70	119.60
1993	115.20	115.80	112.30	112.60	137.10	141.60

6—8 1993 年农副产品收购价格分类指数

(1992 年=100)

商品类别	指数	商品类别	指数
总指数	107.40	3. 皮张	135.60
一. 粮食类	105.90	4. 鬃毛	117.60
二. 经济作物类	105.80	5. 其它畜产品	135.90
1. 食用植物油及油料	108.80	五. 蚕茧蚕丝类	99.80
2. 棉花	107.80	六. 干鲜果类	88.70
3. 麻	132.30	1. 瓜果	65.30
4. 烟叶	128.50	2. 干果	128.00
5. 糖料	100.70	七. 干鲜菜及调味品类	109.90
6. 茶叶	55.50	1. 鲜菜	166.10
三. 工业用油漆类	117.30	2. 干菜	107.00
四. 畜禽产品类	118.70	3. 调味品	88.30
1. 肉畜	116.10	八. 药材类	134.20
2. 禽蛋	118.40	九. 土副产品类	105.10

七. 人民生活

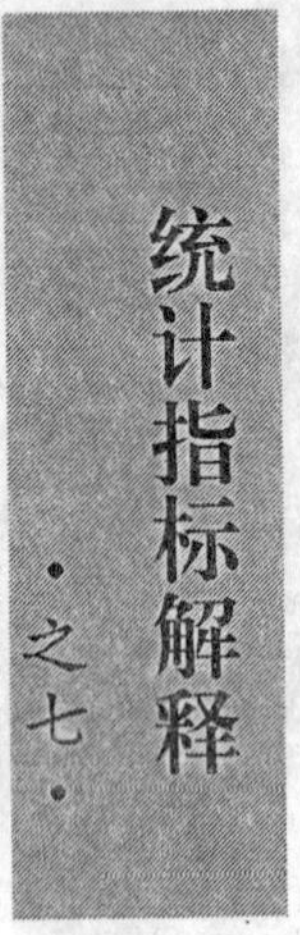

【人口自然增长率】在一定时期(通常为一年内)人口自然增加数(出生人数减死亡人数)与平均人数(或其中人数)之比,一般用千分率表示。计算公式为:

人口自然增长率=本年出生人口数—本年死亡人口数÷年平均人数×1000‰

【性别比】反映两性人口间比例的指标,指在总人口中或各年龄组人口中,男性人数与女性人数之比。通常以每100个女性人口相对应的男性人口数。计算公式:

性别比=男性人口÷女性人口×100

【从业人员】指从事一定社会劳动并取得劳动报酬或经营收入的全部劳动力。包括:1.全部职工

2.城镇私营企业从业人员

3.城镇个体劳动者

4.农村社会劳动者

5.其他社会劳动者

【职工】指在国有经济,城镇的集体经济、联营经济、股份制经济、外商和港、澳、台投资经济、其他经济单位及其附属机构工作,并由其支付工资的各类人员。不包括城镇私营企业和乡镇企业从业人员。

【城镇个体劳动者】指经工商行政管理部门核准登记,领取营业执照,参加生产经营活动,户口在城镇的全部人员。

【城镇待业人员】一般指劳动年龄以内,有劳动能力无业而要求就业并在城镇基层政权组织进行登记的人员。包括城镇年满16岁至25岁的初高中毕业生未能升学、参军的社会青年和年龄在25岁至男50岁、女45岁以下的其他待业人员。

【城镇待业率】是反映城镇劳动者就业程度的指标。它的计算公式:

城镇待业率=城镇待业人员÷(城镇社会劳动者+城镇待业人员)×100%

【职工工资总额】指各单位在一定时期内直接支付给本单位全部职工的劳动报酬总额。包括计时工资、计件工资、奖金、津贴和补贴、加班加点工资和其他工资。

【职工平均工资】指企业、事业、机关单位的职工在一定时期内平均每人所得的货币工资额。它表明了一定时期职工工资收入的高低程度,是反映职工工资水平的主要指标。计算公式为:

职工平均工资=报告期实际支付的全部职工工资总额÷报告期全部职工平均人数

【职工平均实际工资】扣除物价变动因素后的职工平均工资。计算公式为:

职工平均实际工资=报告期职工平均工资÷报告期职工生活费价格指数

7—1 人民物质文化生活提高情况

项 目	单位	1978年	1985年	1990年	1993年
一.就业					
每一农村劳动力负担人数	人	2.42	1.75	1.67	1.67
每一城镇就业者负担人数	人		1.83	1.88	1.73
城镇就业率	%		96.70	95.10	96.30
二.收入					
农民家庭人均纯收入	元	100.93	257.00	430.99	550.83
城镇居民家庭人均生活费收入	元		640.80	1 245.49	1 839.40
职工年平均工资	元	708.00	1 363.00	2 407.00	3 422.90
三.消费水平					
全体居民消费水平	元	143.00	299.00	552.00	799.00
农民	元	99.00	210.00	382.00	527.00
非农业居民	元	419.00	780.00	1 402.00	2 116.00
四.储蓄					
城乡居民年底储蓄存款余额	亿元	3.67	25.20	100.58	204.00
平均每人储蓄余额	元	19.74	125.00	457.11	879.85
五.住房					
农村平均每人住房面积	平方米		13.24	11.88	13.77
城市平均每人居住面积	平方米		7.44	8.86	8.96
六.零售商业.饮食业.服务业网点					
每万人口拥有营业点(包括个体)	个		71.00	76.00	84.00
每万人口拥有人员数(包括人体)	个		160.00	168.00	187.00
七.交通					
每百人拥自行车	辆		11.05	18.23	61.36
城市每万人拥有公共车辆	辆		1.64	1.71	1.53
八.城市公用事业					
自来水普及率	%			44.78	48.80
煤气、液化气普及率	%			15.06	16.10
每万人拥有绿地	公倾			788.00	716.00
九.文化					
每百人拥有电视机	台		0.77	5.41	6.61
每百人拥有收音机	台		8.30	8.92	10.80
每百人每天有报纸	份		2.40	2.55	2.74
每百人每年有图书.杂志	册		1 825.00	1 716.00	1 817.00
十.教育					
学龄儿童入学率	%	91.00	89.40	94.40	95.76
每万人口有大学生数	人	7.00	13.30	15.13	17.24
十一.卫生					
每万人拥有医院病床数	张	17.61	20.05	21.90	23.65
每万人拥有医生数	人	11.90	12.57	14.76	36.00

7—2 居民消费水平

单位:元/人

年　份	全体居民	农民	非农业居民	工农消费水平对比(以农民为 1)
1978	143	99	419	1:4.23
1980	177	121	509	1:4.21
1985	299	210	780	1:3.71
1990	552	382	1 402	1:3.67
1991	588	405	1 501	1:3.71
1992	698	456	1 888	1:4.14
1993	799	527	2 116	1:4.02

7—3 居民消费水平指数

单位:%

年　份	全体居民(上年=100)	农业居民	非农业居民	全体居民(1978 年=100)	农业居民	非农业居民
1978	107.64	108.08	105.83	100.00	100.00	100.00
1980	104.73	101.68	107.16	123.08	121.21	120.05
1985	109.21	112.18	103.18	209.09	212.20	186.16
1990	96.95	95.77	95.77	386.01	385.86	334.61
1991	101.45	101.31	101.42	411.19	409.09	358.23
1992	106.06	103.09	109.32	481.82	456.57	442.72
1993	106.05	103.00	107.82	441.26	416.17	401.43

7—4 居民消费水平平均每年增长速度

单位:%

时期	全体居民	农民	非农业居民	时期	全体居民	农民	非农业居民
"一五"时期	11.96	10.14	10.78	"五五"时期	8.71	8.69	7.26
"二五"时期	0.91		2.65	"六五"时期	7.10	7.70	4.90
1963—1965年	8.38	13.17	—1.38	"七五"时期	12.06	12.91	10.31
"三五"时期	3.26	5.51	0.61	1985—1993年	15.47	14.74	13.28
"四五"时期	4.43	2.49	5.85	1978—1993年	13.24	14.23	12.38

7—5 职工工资总额和平均工资

指　　标	1978年	1980年	1985年	1990年	1993年
一.工资总额(万元)	114 123.60	145 396.70	268 016.90	548 859.50	858 851.80
国有单位	106 040.40	134 617.50	239 442.50	487 412.50	745 044.00
集体单位	8 083.20	10 779.20	28 461.40	60 834.00	107 257.70
其他			113.00	613.00	6 550.10
二.平均工资(元/人)	708.00	875.00	1 363.00	2 407.00	3 422.00
国有单位	751.00	896.00	1 400.00	2 546.00	3 627.00
集体单位	437.00	676.00	1 116.00	1 675.00	2 457.00
其他			1 640.00	2 058.00	3 415.00
三.平均工资增长速度(%)					
国有单位	100.00	19.30	86.40	239.00	382.96
集体单位	100.00	54.70	155.40	283.30	462.24

7—6 国有单位职工工资总额

单位:万元

指标	1980年	1985年	1990年	1992年	1993年	1993年为1980年(倍)
工资总额	134 617.50	233 989.70	487 412.50	624 950.80	745 044.00	5.53
1.记件标准工资和计时工资	101 781.20	166 633.60	283 575.90	346531.20	370179.80	3.64
2.奖金和计件超额工资	10 269.80	28 967.00	69 890.80	109 560.80	131403.00	12.79
3.津贴和补贴	18 047.60	31 396.50	120 419.10	154 697.40	167931.00	9.30
4.其他	4 518.90	6 992.60	13 526.70	14 161.40	75530.20	16.71

7—7 国有单位职工工资总额增长因素

指标	1993年比1980年		1993年比1985年		1993年比1992年	
	增加额(万元)	占增加额的比重(%)	增加额(万元)	占增加额的比重(%)	增加额	占增加额的比重(%)
工资总额	724 234.30	100.00	624 862.10	100.00	233 901.00	100.00
1.由于增加计时工资和计件标准工资	330 000.10	45.60	265 147.70	42.40	85 250.10	36.50
2.由于增加奖金和计件超额工资	137 006.40	18.90	118 309.20	18.90	37715.40	16.10
3.由于增津贴和补贴	175 763.20	24.30	162 414.30	26.00	39 113.40	16.70
4.由于其他增资因素	81 464.60	11.20	78 990.90	12.70	71 822.10	30.70

7—8 国民经济各部门职工工资总额和平均工资

行业	1992年合计	#国有单位	#城镇集体单位	1993年合计	#国有单位	#城镇集体单位
工资总额(万元)	722 894.40	624 950.80	95 716.00	858 851.80	745 044.00	107257.70
一.农.林.牧.渔业	22 157.70	21 730.40	427.30	32 421.40	31 371.90	1 049.50
二.采掘业	68 136.00	61 316.50	6 561.10	85 608.40	83 455.40	2113.80
三.制造业	248 150.40	206 037.30	40 733.40	306 166.50	247 843.70	55252.80
四.电力.煤气及水的生产供应业	14 278.80	14 052.50	226.30	17 200.50	17 195.60	4.90
五.建筑业	59 095.20	44 307.90	14 619.20	71 799.60	56 444.80	15354.80
六.地质勘查业.水利和管理业	15 910.40	15 865.80	44.60	18 299.80	18146.00	153.80
七.交通运输.仓储及邮电通信业	53 540.80	51 221.10	2 254.70	60727.30	59 461.40	1 248.10
八.批发和零售贸易.餐饮业	61 716.60	37 577.90	23 854.70	66 678.80	37 619.40	26 184.50
九.金融.保险业	12 748.80	10 475.90	2 272.90	15 606.00	13 652.40	1 953.60
十.房地产业	1 056.10	833.60	218.80	1 550.10	1 449.10	96.50
十一.社会服务业	12 460.80	10 014.80	2 377.30	16 577.30	14700.60	1 351.70
十二.卫生.体育和社会福利业	18 851.40	18 394.20	457.20	22 536.80	21689.40	847.40
十三.教育.文.艺和广播影视业	64 077.10	63 794.50	282.60	69953.30	69 368.10	585.20
十四.科研和综合技术服务业	10 134.90	9 664.30	470.60	11 125.40	10 366.60	740.10
十五.国家.政党机关和社会团体	56 725.40	56 047.70	677.70	60882.80	60 700.10	182.70
十六.其他行业	3 854.00	3 616.40	237.60	1 717.80	1579.50	138.30
平均工资(元/人)	2 902.00	3 077.00	2 127.00	3 422.00	3627.00	2 457.00
一.农.林.牧.渔业	2 302.00	2 311.00	1 914.00	2 586.00	2608.00	2 071.00
二.采掘业	3 581.00	3 780.00	2 449.00	4 241.00	4 354.00	2109.00
三.制造业	2 830.00	3 057.00	2 079.00	3 623.00	3 903.00	2731.00
四.电力.煤气及水的生产供应业	3 569.00	3 608.00	2 131.00	4092.00	4 093.00	2 579.00
五.建筑业	3 021.00	3 347.00	2 343.00	3 376.00	3 886.00	2277.00
六.地质勘查业.水利管理业	3 123.00	3 129.00	1 742.00	3 340.00	3 354.00	2 235.00
七.交通运输.仓储及邮电通信业	3 433.00	3 526.00	2 147.00	4414.00	4 592.00	1 556.00
八.批发和零售贸易餐饮业	2 262.00	2 464.00	1 998.00	2 517.00	2609.00	2 361.00
九.金融.保险业	3 015.00	3 124.00	2 597.00	3 521.00	3 851.00	2 201.00
十.房地产业	2 691.00	2 585.00	3 213.00	3 274.00	3 546.00	1522.00
十一.社会服务业	2 341.00	2 475.00	1 881.00	2 799.00	2988.00	1 582.00
十二.卫生.体育和社会福利业	2 789.00	2 817.00	1 993.00	3 006.00	3 098.00	1 704.00
十三.教育.文.艺和广播影视业	3 093.00	3 100.00	2 020.00	3189.00	3 210.00	1 785.00
十四.科研和综合技术服务业	3 096.00	3 149.00	2 292.00	3133.00	3 302.00	1 822.00
十五.国家.政党机关和社会团体	2 910.00	2 909.00	2 441.00	3349.00	3 356.00	1 911.00
十六.其他行业	3 522.00	3 761.00	1 789.00	3 085.00	3 237.00	2 004.00

7—9 职工平均工资及指数

年份	全部职工			国有单位			城镇集体单位		
	平均工资(元)	指数(1978年=100)		平均工资(元)	指数(1978年=100)		平均工资(元)	指数(1978年=100)	
		货币工资	实际工资		货币工资	实际工资		货币工资	实际工资
1978	708	100.00	100.00	751	100.00	100.00	437	100.00	100.00
1980	857	123.60	113.20	896	119.30	109.20	676	154.70	141.70
1985	1 363	192.50	145.30	1 400	186.40	140.70	1116	255.40	192.80
1986	1 555	219.60	154.90	1 630	217.00	153.00	1090	249.40	175.90
1987	1 680	237.30	154.40	1 761	234.50	152.60	1188	271.90	176.90
1988	1 949	275.30	148.50	2 040	271.60	146.50	1400	320.40	172.80
1989	2 207	311.70	142.30	2 317	308.50	140.80	1577	360.90	164.70
1990	2 407	340.00	152.30	2 546	339.00	151.90	1675	383.30	171.70
1991	2 566	362.40	153.60	2 706	360.30	152.70	1918	438.90	186.00
1992	2 902	409.90	161.90	3 077	409.70	161.80	2127	486.70	192.20
1993	3 422	483.30	165.70	3 627	482.90	165.50	2457	562.20	192.70

7—10 职工及离休.退休.退职人员保险福利费用构成情况

单位:万元

指标	1978年	1985年	1990年	1993年	1993年为下列年份%	
					1978年	1992年
总计	13 421.50	64 819.20	135 475.80	251 092.50	1 870.80	123.50
为工资总额的%	12.70	24.90	24.70	29.20	229.90	103.90
总计中:公费医疗费	5 997.20	12 505.80	34 524.50	56 220.30	937.40	111.70
职工保险福利费			65 758.00	111 205.33		115.80
一.国有单位合计	13 421.50	60 233.10	126 051.80	229 356.80	1708.90	122.70
#公费医疗费	5 997.20	11 927.10	32 431.40	52401.10	873.80	111.70
职工保险福利费			60 781.90	99 835.40		114.00
二.城镇集体单位合计		4 581.20	9 382.90	20 814.50		127.10
#公费医疗费		578.00	2 077.70	3 571.80		105.80
职工保险福利费			4 935.50	10 719.30		128.10
三.其他单位合计		4.90	41.10	921.20		1 029.30
#公费医疗费		0.70	15.40	247.40		649.30
职工保险福利费			40.60	650.60		738.50

7—11 国有单位在职职工分行业保险福利费

(1993年) 单位:万元

行业	费用总额	医疗卫生费	职工生活困难补助费	职工及直亲属丧葬救济费	文娱体育宣传费	集体福利事业补贴费
总　计	99 835.36	38 117.72	1 752.72	2 096.75	2 785.55	9 176.06
一.农.林.牧.渔业	3 652.73	1 019.23	89.38	100.12	99.00	315.32
二.采掘业	6 124.79	2 276.90	139.77	257.15	131.80	383.00
三.制造业	28 886.18	12 750.55	446.16	537.34	868.89	3 214.39
四.电力.煤气及水的生产供应业	3 096.92	1 440.40	44.54	38.95	99.21	268.41
五.建筑业	8 130.81	3 063.06	119.48	300.50	253.97	993.02
六.地质勘查业.水利管理业	2 741.48	1 105.67	45.07	76.57	104.34	273.71
七.交通运输.仓储及邮电通讯业	6 908.41	1929.59	163.01	113.13	253.27	519.65
八.批发零售贸易餐饮业	6 161.59	2 250.25	92.72	93.70	106.84	320.34
九.金融.保险业	2 519.07	872.63	36.20	36.80	117.40	123.70
十.房地产业	248.51	94.66	7.30	2.49	5.60	15.49
十一.社会服务业	2 285.23	579.13	26.88	26.36	40.48	120.28
十二.卫生.体育和社会福利业	4 183.79	1 858.02	65.63	52.26	86.65	384.92
十三.教育.文化和广播影视业	8 919.48	2892.00	188.04	172.96	262.18	799.82
十四.科研和综合技术服务业	2 583.37	957.32	17.74	33.24	53.92	291.90
十五.国家.政党机关和社会团体	10 898.21	4185.90	242.16	216.61	222.32	839.27
十六.其他行业	2 494.79	812.41	28.64	38.57	79.68	312.84

7—11 续　　(1993年)　　单位:万元

行　　业	集体福利设施费	计划生育补贴	交通费补贴	洗澡.理发卫生费	其他
总　计	8 307.83	1 667.54	5 738.05	15 765.37	14 427.77
一.农.林.牧.渔业	334.81	51.09	261.90	718.84	663.04
二.采掘业	860.80	62.81	402.00	809.96	800.60
三.制造业	2 615.52	570.98	910.54	4 096.44	2 875.37
四.电力.煤气及水的生产和供应业	350.50	45.10	61.08	457.51	291.22
五.建筑业	687.86	124.59	491.38	837.41	1 259.54
六.地质勘查业.水利管理业	223.60	36.77	116.97	396.08	362.70
七.交通运输.仓储及邮电通讯业	711.50	162.46	286.43	1 253.69	1 515.68
八.批发零售贸易.餐饮业	502.56	119.67	412.11	1 228.90	1 034.50
九.金融.保险业	116.10	66.13	371.21	436.82	342.08
十.房地产业	6.30	3.51	27.30	48.48	37.38
十一.社会服务业	281.02	43.18	136.40	372.07	659.43
十二.卫生.体育和社会福利业	169.15	58.72	324.68	629.07	554.69
十三.教育.文化和广播电影电视业	369.60	97.72	723.51	1 967.04	1446.61
十四.科学研究和综合技术服务业	285.23	35.66	147.26	323.88	407.22
十五.国家.政党机关和社会团体	499.18	143.10	890.55	1 835.26	1823.86
十六.其他行业	294.10	46.05	174.73	353.92	653.85

7—12 城镇居民家庭人口情况

（1993年）

指　　标	单位	全省平均	城市平均	#最高收入户	#最低收入户	县城平均	#最高收入户	#最低收入户
调查户数	户	880.00	830.00	83.00	83.00	50.00	5.00	5.00
一. 平均每户家庭人口数	人	3.36	3.33	2.66	3.79	3.41	3.07	4.20
(一.)平均每户有收入者人数	人	2.21	2.24	2.24	2.04	2.15	2.27	1.60
1. 平均就业人口数	人	1.94	1.92	1.70	1.72	1.99	2.07	1.40
(1)全民所有制职工人数	人	1.67	1.66	1.54	1.29	1.69	1.87	1.20
(2)集体单位工人数	人	0.24	0.23	0.11	0.40	0.26	0.20	0.20
(3)其他单位工人数	人							
(4)个体经营者人数	人	0.02	0.02		0.02	0.02		
(5)离退休再就业人数	人	0.01	0.02	0.05	0.01			
(6)其他就业人数	人							
2. 离退休人员数	人	0.26	0.30	0.53	0.25	0.16	0.20	0.20
3. 其他有收入者人数	人	0.01	0.01	0.01	0.07			
(二)平均每户无收入者人数	人	1.15	1.10	0.42	1.75	1.26	0.80	2.60
二. 平均每户期末家庭人口数	人	3.35	3.32	2.63	3.80	3.42	3.00	4.20

职工平均工资增长速度

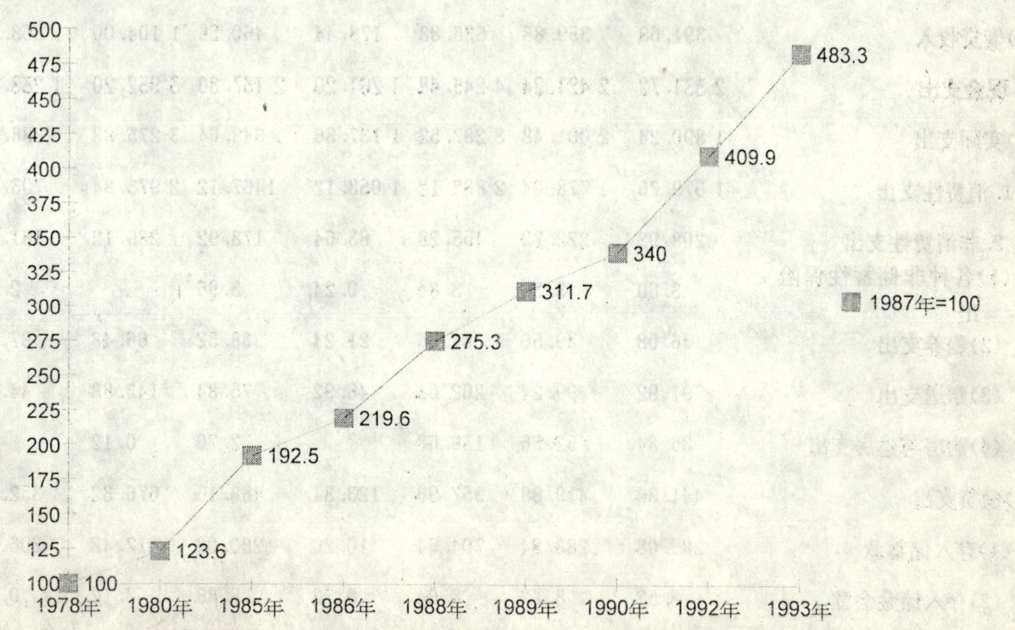

7—13 城镇居民家庭平均每人全年现金收支情况

（1993 年）　　　　单位:元

指　　标	全省平均	城市平均	#最高收入户	#最低收入户	县城平均	#最高收入户	#最低收入户
一. 现金收入	2 395.92	2 489.52	4 376.16	1 291.80	2 193.48	4049.52	1 239.36
(一)实际收入	2 004.24	2 129.64	3 740.28	1 113.36	1 732.92	2 945.52	870.72
#生活费收入	1 839.36	1 952.16	3 420.00	1 025.16	1 595.28	2 695.68	711.84
1. 国有单位职工工资	1 398.24	1 451.40	2 270.04	657.48	1283.28	1 901.52	734.52
2. 集体单位职工工资	119.40	123.36	96.72	136.08	110.88	66.24	39.36
3. 其他单位职工全部收入	0.60	0.84	0.96	0.12			
4. 职工从单位得到其他收入	87.72	101.04	183.72	42.24	59.04	83.04	12.72
5. 个体经营者的净收益	11.28	14.28	0.12	19.32	4.56		
6. 个体被雇者收入	0.72	0.48			0.96		
7. 离退休再就业人员收入	4.32	6.24	20.64	0.60			
8. 其它就业者收入	0.12	0.12					
9. 其它劳动收入	19.68	21.72	80.28	20.64	15.24	21.48	
10. 财产性收入	21.24	15.48	75.60	0.84	33.84	130.80	8.28
11. 转移性收入	340.32	393.84	1 012.20	234.96	224.64	724.44	75.84
12. 家庭副业生产收入	0.72	0.81		0.96	0.60		
(二)借贷收入	391.68	359.88	635.88	178.44	460.56	1 104.00	368.64
二. 现金支出	2 331.72	2 421.24	4 245.48	1 261.20	2 137.80	3 952.20	1 238.64
(一)实际支出	1 890.24	2 001.48	3 287.52	1 137.36	1 649.64	3 275.88	886.56
#1. 消费性支出	1 679.76	1 778.04	2 832.12	1 053.12	1467.12	2 973.84	703.56
2. 非消费性支出	208.92	222.72	455.28	83.64	178.92	285.12	181.56
#(1)各种非储蓄性保险支出	3.60	3.36	3.84	0.24	3.96		2.64
(2)赡养支出	46.08	49.56	81.96	21.24	38.52	66.48	97.32
(3)赠送支出	91.92	99.24	202.08	46.92	75.84	143.88	44.64
(4)购房与建房支出	36.84	52.56	136.68		2.76	0.12	
(二)借贷支出	441.36	419.88	957.96	123.84	488.16	676.32	352.08
#(1)存入储蓄款	286.08	288.84	704.64	10.20	280.08	417.48	206.76
(2)存入储金会款	8.52	8.40	8.04	0.72	8.88	3.12	0.48
(3)购买有价证券	20.04	24.48	94.92	3.96	10.68	26.04	

7—14 城镇居民家庭平均每人全年消费支出情况

(1993 年) 单位:元

指标	全省平均	城市平均	#最高收入户	#最低收入户	县城平均	#最高收入户	#最低收入户
消费性支出	1 679.76	1 778.04	2 832.12	1 053.12	1 467.12	2973.84	703.56
一.食品	851.76	907.92	1 357.92	607.44	730.08	1 278.84	370.92
#(一)粮食	122.88	127.32	172.56	117.00	113.40	139.92	50.04
(二)油脂类	34.68	33.12	42.00	31.20	38.04	45.12	32.28
(三)肉禽及制品	157.44	169.56	247.80	102.48	131.04	202.32	85.44
#猪肉	87.84	90.60	125.04	65.28	81.96	142.68	67.32
(四)蛋类	32.88	34.08	49.92	24.00	30.36	32.16	23.76
(五)水产品类	2.22	27.00	55.92	14.88	11.64	16.20	9.84
(六)菜类	99.48	108.48	141.12	84.48	80.16	96.24	51.48
(七)烟草类	81.00	81.96	141.96	44.04	79.08	241.08	5.76
(八)酒和饮料	61.44	63.24	107.52	38.40	57.48	124.80	27.48
(九)干鲜瓜果类	59.88	63.24	91.44	36.96	52.68	96.24	32.40
(十)糕点类	17.04	19.32	8.88	25.20	12.36	23.88	3.84
(十一)奶及奶制品	19.44	22.20	37.56	13.08	13.56	15.60	4.32
(十二)其它食品	20.64	21.96	28.80	11.04	17.52	21.84	5.04
二.衣着支出	283.56	301.08	474.24	134.88	245.88	370.08	107.76
#(一)服装	150.48	163.56	269.64	70.32	122.16	176.28	42.36
(二)衣着材料	62.52	62.64	94.44	25.32	62.16	105.96	30.84
(三)鞋袜帽及其它	59.64	63.36	93.72	34.80	51.84	74.88	30.00
三.设备用品及服务	135.48	137.40	263.88	47.16	131.04	460.32	19.68
(一)耐用消费品	79.08	76.68	153.60	19.44	84.24	358.44	6.24
(二)室内装饰品	8.16	8.04	20.64	1.80	8.52	31.68	
(三)床上用品	10.68	10.68	18.36	4.68	10.68	7.56	2.04
(四)家庭日用杂品	29.64	30.84	53.88	18.24	27.00	62.64	11.28
(五)家具材料	3.12	4.56	7.92	1.92			
(六)家庭服务	4.80	6.72	9.48	1.08	0.72		0.12
四.医疗保健	61.32	58.20	84.00	40.08	68.16	231.48	55.32

7—14续　　(1993年)　　单位:元

指　标	全省平均	城市平均	#最高收入户	#最低收入户	县城平均	#最高收入户	#最低收入户
#(一)医药费	50.64	48.24	69.72	31.80	55.92	212.40	46.32
(二)滋补药品	1.56	1.92	2.76	1.44	0.60	6.00	
五. 交通和通讯	44.76	47.52	94.92	16.92	39.00	22.80	11.88
(一)交通	31.56	32.04	45.24	15.12	30.36	22.32	11.52
#交通费	13.80	14.16	19.20	5.16	12.84	20.40	11.28
(二)通讯	13.32	15.48	49.68	1.68	8.64	0.48	0.36
六. 娱乐. 文教服务	144.84	154.68	208.32	108.24	123.36	438.24	101.64
(一)耐用消费品	41.04	35.52	71.76	10.32	52.80	394.20	3.96
(二)教育	72.12	80.76	69.12	82.32	53.28	16.20	91.68
#学杂费	54.96	59.64	45.24	60.72	44.76	16.20	90.12
托幼费	6.00	6.96	3.84	7.20	3.72		
(三)文化娱乐	31.68	38.40	67.44	15.48	17.28	27.96	6.00
#书报杂志	11.16	12.48	21.60	4.80	8.52	7.08	2.76
文娱费	9.00	12.60	23.40	5.28	1.20	0.60	0.24
七. 居住	67.92	78.24	140.16	59.64	45.60	93.52	13.32
(一)住房	26.04	31.56	74.40	16.32	14.04	34.44	7.56
#房租	16.92	18.84	24.96	11.46	12.60	24.00	7.56
(二)水电燃料及其他	41.88	46.56	65.76	43.32	31.56	55.08	5.76
#水费	3.36	3.60	5.28	2.52	2.64	4.08	1.56
电费	13.68	14.76	24.00	10.80	11.40	3.60	16.32
八. 杂项商品和服务	90.12	93.00	208.56	38.88	84.00	82.68	23.04
(一)个人消费	67.20	69.24	129.48	28.20	62.52	59.76	17.64
#个人用品	24.96	24.48	45.84	7.56	26.16	14.28	4.80
理发美容用品	9.36	10.08	19.32	3.12	7.68	9.72	3.96
旅游	23.04	25.56	47.76	10.44	17.40	2.40	17.52
(二)其他商品	13.32	12.36	20.88	6.24	15.36	14.52	3.72
(三)其他服务	9.60	11.28	58.08	4.44	6.12	8.52	1.68

7—15 城镇居民家庭消费支出构成情况

(1993年)

单位:%

指　标	全省平均	城市平均	#最高收入户	#最低收入户	县城平均	#最高收入户	#最低收入户
消费性支出	100.00	100.00	100.00	100.00	100.00	100.00	100.00
一.食品	50.70	51.06	47.95	57.68	49.76	43.00	52.73
#(一)粮食	7.32	7.16	4.09	11.11	7.73	4.71	7.12
(二)油脂类	2.07	1.87	1.48	2.96	2.59	1.52	4.59
(三)肉禽及制品	9.37	9.54	8.75	9.74	8.93	6.80	12.15
#猪肉	5.23	5.09	4.42	6.19	5.59	4.80	9.57
(四)蛋类	1.96	1.92	1.76	2.27	2.07	1.08	3.37
(五)水产品类	1.32	1.52	1.97	1.41	0.79	0.54	1.39
(六)菜类	5.92	6.10	4.98	8.24	5.47	3.24	7.32
(七)烟草类	4.83	4.61	5.01	4.18	5.39	8.11	0.81
(八)酒和饮料	3.66	3.56	3.80	3.64	3.92	4.20	3.90
(九)干鲜瓜果类	3.57	3.56	3.23	3.51	3.59	3.24	4.60
(十)糕点类	1.02	1.08	0.89	0.84	0.84	0.80	0.54
(十一)奶及奶制品	1.16	1.25	1.33	1.24	0.93	0.52	0.62
(十二)其他食品	1.23	1.24	1.02	1.05	1.20	0.74	0.71
二.衣着支出	16.88	16.93	16.75	12.81	16.76	12.44	15.31
#(一)服装	8.96	9.20	9.52	6.68	8.33	5.93	6.02
(二)衣着材料	3.72	3.52	3.34	2.40	4.24	3.56	4.39
(三)鞋袜帽及其他	3.55	3.56	3.31	3.31	3.53	2.52	4.26
三.设备用品及服务	8.06	7.73	9.32	4.47	8.94	15.48	2.79
(一)耐用消费品	4.71	4.31	5.43	1.85	5.74	12.05	0.88
(二)室内装饰品	0.49	0.45	0.73	0.17	0.58	1.07	
(三)床上用品	0.63	0.60	0.65	0.44	0.73	0.25	0.29
(四)家庭日用杂品	1.77	1.74	1.90	1.73	1.84	2.11	1.60
(五)家具材料	0.18	0.26	0.28	0.18			
(六)家庭服务	0.28	0.38	0.33	0.10	0.05		0.02
四.医疗保健	3.65	3.27	2.96	3.81	4.65	7.78	7.87

7—15 续 (1993年) 单位:%

指　标	全省平均	城市平均	#最高收入户	#最低收入户	县城平均	#最高收入户	#最低收入户
#(一)医药费	3.01	2.71	2.46	3.02	3.81	7.14	6.59
(二)滋补药品	0.09	0.11	0.10	0.14	0.04		
五.交通和通讯	2.67	2.67	3.35	1.60	2.56	0.77	1.68
(一)交通	1.88	1.80	1.60	1.44	2.07	0.75	1.63
#交通费	0.82	0.80	0.68	0.49	0.88	0.69	1.60
(二)通讯	0.79	0.87	1.75	0.16	0.59	0.01	0.05
六.娱乐.文教服务	8.62	8.70	7.36	10.28	8.41	14.74	14.45
(一)耐用消费品	2.44	2.00	2.53	0.98	3.60	13.25	0.56
(二)教育	4.29	4.54	2.44	7.82	3.63	0.54	13.03
#学杂费	3.27	3.35	1.60	5.76	3.05	0.54	12.81
托幼费	0.36	0.39	0.14	0.68	0.25		
(三)文化娱乐	1.89	2.16	2.38	1.47	1.18	0.94	0.86
#书报杂费	0.67	0.70	0.76	0.46	0.58	0.24	0.39
文娱费	0.53	0.71	0.82	0.50	0.08	0.01	0.08
七.居住	4.04	4.40	4.95	5.66	3.11	3.01	1.89
(一)住房	1.55	1.78	2.63	1.55	0.95	1.16	1.07
#房租	1.01	1.06	0.88	1.11	0.86	0.81	1.07
(二)水.电燃料及其他	2.49	2.62	2.32	4.11	2.15	1.85	0.82
#水费	0.20	0.21	0.19	0.24	0.18	0.14	0.22
电费	0.82	0.83	0.85	1.03	0.78	0.55	0.51
八.杂项商品和服务	5.37	5.23	7.36	3.69	5.73	2.78	3.28
(一)个人消费	4.00	3.90	4.57	2.67	4.26	2.01	2.51
#个人用品	1.49	1.38	1.62	0.72	1.78	0.48	0.69
理发美容用品	0.56	0.57	0.68	0.30	0.52	0.33	0.57
旅游	1.37	1.44	1.69	0.99	1.18	0.59	0.34
(二)其他商品	0.79	0.70	0.74	0.59	1.05	0.49	0.53
(三)其他服务	0.57	0.64	2.05	0.43	0.41	0.29	0.24

7—16 城镇居民家庭平均每人全年购买商品数量

(1993年)

指标	单位	全省平均	城市平均	#最高收入户	#最低收入户	县城平均	#最高收入户	#最低收入户
一.粮食	千克	130.32	100.68	130.56	96.60	194.52	236.04	83.88
1.细粮	千克	128.64	99.36	128.40	95.28	192.00	231.48	83.04
2.粗粮	千克	1.68	1.32	2.16	1.20	2.52	4.56	0.84
二.油脂类	千克	10.56	7.20	9.12	6.72	17.64	19.20	13.08
#1.菜籽油	千克	6.00	4.68	7.20	3.60	8.76	10.68	4.92
2.芝麻油	千克		0.12	0.12				
3.其它植物油	千克	4.08	2.28	1.44	2.88	7.92	8.40	7.92
三.肉禽类								
#1.猪肉	千克	21.36	13.68	21.12	12.00	30.72	55.08	25.68
2.牛肉	千克	1.44	1.68	2.16	0.96	1.20	1.08	0.12
3.羊肉	千克	1.08	1.32	2.40	0.60	0.48	0.24	
4.其它禽及制品	千克	4.92	4.68	4.32	1.68	5.64	7.20	2.88
四.蛋类	千克	9.24	7.08	10.56	4.91	13.92	14.40	12.12
五.水产类								
#1.黄花鱼	千克		0.12	0.12				
2.带鱼	千克	1.44	1.56	3.24	0.84	1.08	0.84	1.32
3.鲤鱼	千克	0.48	0.48	0.84	0.12	0.48	0.36	0.24
4.其它鱼及制品	千克	0.84	96.72	1.08	0.48	1.08	2.52	1.56
六.菜类	千克	138.00	114.96	139.68	99.36	188.04	214.92	138.24
1.鲜菜	千克	136.68	113.76	138.00	98.64	186.48	213.24	137.76
#(1)白菜	千克	13.56	14.76	18.00	12.48	11.16	12.12	0.48
(2)芹菜	千克	5.76	4.80	5.88	4.56	7.80	9.48	2.64
(3)韭菜	千克	5.64	3.96	4.92	3.36	9.12	7.32	7.56
(4)菜花	千克	3.96	3.12	3.72	3.36	5.76	9.12	3.48
(5)萝卜	千克	8.88	6.96	9.48	6.72	13.20	4.68	17.04
(6)胡萝卜	千克	2.64	2.64	3.12	2.52	2.76	1.44	1.68
(7)蒜苔	千克	3.60	3.00	3.60	2.16	4.92	7.68	1.80
(8)黄瓜	千克	5.64	5.40	7.56	3.60	6.12	8.16	3.24
(9)西红柿	千克	10.56	9.24	10.20	7.44	13.68	17.40	10.80
(10)茄子	千克	5.52	4.56	5.88	3.96	7.68	9.60	4.32
(11)青椒	千克	11.40	8.52	10.24	6.24	17.88	17.28	13.80
(12)豆角	千克	3.36	4.08	4.56	2.88	2.04	4.20	0.48
(13)其它鲜菜	千克	15.48	13.80	15.96	12.60	19.08	25.68	16.44
2.干菜	千克	0.36	0.36	0.48	0.36	0.36	0.60	
#(1)黄花菜	千克					0.12	0.12	
(2)黑木耳	千克							
(3)香菇	千克	0.12	0.24	0.24	0.24			
七.糖类								
1.食糖	千克	1.56	1.32	1.92	1.32	1.80	1.68	1.32
2.糖果	千克	0.96	0.60	0.84	0.36	1.92	4.44	1.32
八.烟草类								

7—16 续 (1993 年)

指标	单位	全省平均	城市平均	#最高收入户	#最低收入户	县城平均	#最高收入户	#最低收入户
#卷烟	盒	45.36	42.96	61.44	28.08	50.28	132.84	5.40
九.酒饮类								
#1.白酒	千克	2.88	2.28	6.24	1.44	4.44	8.40	2.28
2.啤酒	千克	2.76	2.64	4.56	1.80	2.28	4.08	3.00
3.汽水.可乐	千克	0.36	0.48	0.60	0.24	0.24		0.12
4.咖啡.可可粉	千克							
十.干鲜瓜果类	千克	64.44	50.76	72.72	33.12	91.56	160.20	49.20
#1.苹果	千克	16.08	11.76	13.56	7.80	25.56	37.68	20.76
2.桔子	千克	4.56	3.24	4.68	1.68	1.32	7.56	3.48
3.桃子	千克	5.04	4.68	6.00	2.88	5.88	10.68	2.52
4.梨	千克	5.88	5.40	10.32	3.36	6.96	13.92	0.84
5.西瓜	千克	19.32	16.68	23.64	11.28	24.84	41.54	3.84
十一.糕点类	千克	3.24	2.64	3.84	1.44	4.56	9.36	1.44
十二.奶类								
#1.鲜乳品	千克	8.52	9.36	17.52	5.40	6.72	4.56	1.92
2.奶粉	千克	0.84	0.60	0.96	0.48	1.44	1.80	0.36
十三.衣着类								
1.服装	件	4.56	4.58	6.31	2.44	4.51	5.15	3.10
(1)男士服装	件	1.71	1.58	2.26	0.88	1.98	2.02	1.81
(2)女士服装	件	2.17	2.31	3.05	1.19	1.88	2.48	1.05
(3)各式童装	件	0.69	0.70	1.00	0.37	0.66	0.65	0.24
2.衣着材料	米							
(1)棉布	米	0.87	0.78	1.71	0.49	1.07	3.11	0.54
(2)棉化纤混纺布	米	0.31	0.22	0.39	0.09	0.50	1.50	0.30
(3)化纤布	米	2.01	1.71	1.80	0.82	2.68	5.74	2.51
(4)呢绒	米	0.31	0.38	0.59	0.07	0.15		0.05
(5)绸缎	米	0.35	0.39	1.25	0.11	0.27		0.38
3.鞋帽袜								
#(1)皮鞋	双	0.80	0.83	1.16	0.47	0.74	1.17	0.14
(2)雨鞋	双							
(3)旅游鞋	双	0.13	0.13	0.17	0.13	0.13	0.13	0.33
(4)布鞋	双	0.70	0.55	0.62	0.50	1.04	0.65	1.33
(5)各种袜子	双	1.62	1.65	2.03	1.03	1.56	1.24	1.67
(6)各种帽子	顶	0.09	0.08	0.14	0.03	0.12		0.05
十四.日用品及燃料								
#1.肥皂	块	1.52	2.02	2.55	1.38	0.43	0.13	0.19
2.洗衣粉	千克	0.99	1.00	1.51	0.84	0.96	0.26	1.43
3.水	吨	11.77	13.91	22.22	8.71	7.13	13.37	3.82
4.电	度	64.75	70.16	114.22	45.35	53.02	78.34	17.67
5.煤炭	千克	117.07	126.22	176.71	176.99	97.27	185.91	
6.液化石油气	千克	7.24	9.32	9.83	8.21	2.75	2.94	1.43

7—17 城镇居民家庭主要消费品平均每百户拥有量

(1993年)

指　　标	单位	全省平均	城市平均	#最高收入户	#最低收入户	县城平均	#最高收入户	#最低收入户
毛皮大衣	件	51.00	48.80	67.47	44.58	56.00	80.00	80.00
呢大衣	件	211.74	213.69	272.29	174.70	168.00	260.00	80.00
组合家具	套	34.92	38.07	48.19	27.71	28.00	40.00	
沙发床	个	42.29	41.57	48.19	22.89	44.00	40.00	60.00
沙发	个	242.86	245.30	319.28	169.88	238.00	380.00	220.00
摩托车	辆	2.16	3.13	6.02	1.20			
自行车	辆	205.92	212.41	201.20	175.90	192.00	220.00	200.00
缝纫机	台	54.15	55.18	55.42	53.01	52.00	80.00	80.00
洗衣机	台	90.07	94.70	98.80	84.34	80.00	120.00	60.00
电风扇	台	35.38	48.67	67.47	31.33			
电冰箱	台	40.31	49.50	66.27	31.33	20.00	20.00	20.00
黑白电视机	台	22.18	20.48	10.84	32.53	26.00	20.00	40.00
彩色电视机	台	83.68	89.04	89.16	68.67	72.00	140.00	40.00
录放像机	台	6.22	7.23	10.84				
游戏机	台	10.33	14.10	16.87	4.82	2.00		
组合音响	套	5.02	6.39	14.46	6.02	2.00	20.00	
立体声收录机	台	33.80	35.54	39.76	18.07	30.00	20.00	40.00
普通收录机	台	36.24	38.19	33.73	38.55	32.00	40.00	80.00
照相机	架	21.69	26.99	38.55	13.25			
电炊具	台	19.83	28.80	44.58	10.84			
淋浴热水器	台	11.57	14.10	21.69	7.23	6.00		20.00
脱排油烟机	台	12.03	13.68	25.30	2.41			
吸尘器	台	4.19	5.18	6.02	3.61			

7—18 城镇居民家庭主要消费品平均每百人拥有量

（1993年）

指　　标	单位	全省平均	城市平均	#最高收入户	#最低收入户	县城平均	#最高收入户
毛皮大衣	件	15.20	14.64	25.35	11.77	16.41	26.09
呢大衣	件	63.09	69.50	102.29	46.13	49.22	84.80
组合家具	套	10.40	11.42	18.11	7.32	8.20	13.05
沙发床	个	12.60	12.47	18.11	6.04	12.89	13.05
沙发	个	72.36	73.58	119.95	44.86	69.73	123.94
摩托车	辆	0.64	0.94	2.26			
自行车	辆	61.36	63.71	75.59	46.45	56.25	71.75
缝纫机	台	16.14	16.55	20.82	14.00	15.23	26.09
洗衣机	台	26.84	28.41	37.12	22.27	23.44	39.14
电风扇	台	10.54	14.60	25.35	8.27	1.73	
电冰箱	台	12.01	14.85	24.89	8.27	5.86	6.52
黑白电视机	台	6.61	6.14	4.07	8.59	7.62	6.52
彩色电视机	台	24.93	26.71	33.49	18.13	21.09	45.66
录放像机	台	1.85	2.17	4.07			
游戏机	台	3.08	4.23	6.34	1.27	0.59	
组合音响	套	1.50	1.92	5.43	1.59	0.59	6.52
立体声收录机	台	10.07	10.66	14.94	4.77	8.79	6.52
普通收录机	台	10.80	11.46	12.67	10.18	9.38	13.05
照相机	架	6.46	8.10	14.48	3.50	2.93	
电炊具	台	5.91	8.64	16.75	2.86		
淋浴热水器	台	3.45	4.23	8.15	1.91	1.76	
脱排油烟机	台	3.58	4.16	9.51	0.64	2.34	
吸尘器	台	1.25	1.55	2.26	0.95	0.59	

7—19 城镇居民家庭生活基本情况

指　　标	单位	1990年	1992年	1993年	1993年比1992年(±)%
调查户数	户	880	880	880	
平均每户家庭人口数	人	3.77	3.40	3.36	-1.18
平均每户就业人口数	人	2.01	1.94	1.94	
平均每一就业者负担人数	人	1.87	1.75	1.73	-1.14
平均每人每月全部收入	元	108.65	142.57	167.02	17.15
平均每人每月生活费收入	元	99.73	130.60	153.28	17.36
平均每人每月实际支出	元	94.21	136.42	157.52	15.47
平均每人每月生活费支出	元	85.88	121.45	139.98	15.26
平均每人居住面积	平方米	8.86	8.99	8.96	-0.33

7—20 城镇居民家庭生活基本情况

(1993年按城市规模分组)

指　　标	单位	全省	大城市	中等城市	小城市	县城
调查户数	户	880	300	100	430	50
平均每户家庭人口数	人	3.36	3.20	3.28	3.44	3.41
平均每户就业人口数	人	1.94	1.84	2.21	1.91	1.99
平均每户就业面	%	57.74	57.50	67.38	55.52	58.36
平均每一就业者负担人数(包括就业者本人)	人	1.73	1.73	1.48	1.80	1.71
平均每人年全部收入	元	2 004.24	2 462.58	1 905.22	1 963.79	1732.92
平均每人年生活费收入	元	1 839.36	2 280.34	1 700.71	1 795.34	1 595.28
平均每人年生活费支出	元	1 679.76	2 029.25	1 562.13	1 663.12	1 467.12

7—21 城镇居民家庭生活基本情况

（1993 年按收入等级分组）

指　标	单位	总平均	最低收入户	低收入户	中等收入户	高收入户	#最高收入户
调查户数	户	880	88	88	528	88	88
平均每户家庭人口数	人	3.36	3.91	3.90	3.28	3.22	2.79
平均每户就业人口数	人	1.94	1.62	2.03	1.97	2.14	1.81
平均每户就业面	%	57.74	41.43	52.05	60.06	66.46	64.87
平均每一就业者负担人数（包括就业者本人）	人	1.73	2.41	1.92	1.66	1.50	1.54
平均每人年全部收入	元	2 004.24	1 032.36	1 348.92	1 996.61	2758.80	3 468.36
平均每人年生活费收入	元	1 839.36	920.64	1 233.24	1 831.87	2582.28	3 172.20
平均每人年生活费支出	元	1 679.76	936.48	1 156.44	1 687.97	2126.88	2 880.60

7—22 城镇居民家庭生活基本情况

（1993 年按平均每户每月生活费收入水平分组）

指　标	单位	50 元及以下	50—60 元	60—70 元	70—80 元	80—90 元	90—100 元	100—110 元	110—120 元	120—130 元
调查户数	户	12	8	17	26	21	51	53	65	73
平均每户家庭人口数	人	3.98	5.43	3.58	3.97	3.84	3.82	3.77	3.71	3.33
平均每户就业人口数	人	1.22	1.51	1.52	1.53	1.74	2.12	2.02	2.23	2.04
平均每户就业面	%	30.65	27.81	42.46	38.54	45.31	55.50	53.58	60.11	61.26
平均每劳负担人数（包括本人）	人	3.26	3.60	2.36	2.59	2.21	1.80	1.87	1.66	1.63
平均每人年收入	元	622.56	795.00	852.72	1 038.36	1 083.60	1228.08	1 380.36	1 505.16	1 639.80
平均每人年生活费收入	元	485.04	667.20	787.08	902.40	1 012.68	1134.96	1 262.88	1 376.76	1 497.48
平均每人年生活费支出	元	680.40	653.52	696.24	891.36	1 148.76	1214.64	1 113.84	1 381.92	1 393.68

7—22 续

指　　标	单位	130—150元	140—150元	150—160元	160—170元	170—180元	180—190元	190元以上
调查户数	户	65	67	43	54	36	50	239
户均家庭人口数	人	3.23	3.26	3.40	3.11	3.05	3.03	3.08
户均就业人口数	人	1.89	1.99	1.92	1.80	1.87	1.73	2.01
平均每户就业面	%	58.51	61.04	56.47	57.88	61.31	57.10	65.26
平均每劳者负担人数(包括本人)	人	1.71	1.64	1.77	1.73	1.63	1.75	1.53
平均每人年收入	元	1 766.04	1 894.92	2 050.68	2 186.16	2260.08	2 377.92	3 089.64
人均年生活费收入	元	1 617.96	1 739.04	1 862.04	1 989.12	2 102.52	2 219.16	2 848.68
人均年生活费支出	元	1 519.56	1 636.92	1 714.68	1 749.84	1 939.92	2 129.16	2 466.96

7—23 历年城镇居民家庭生活基本情况

年　　份	每一城镇就业者负担人数(人)	城镇居民人均生活费收入(元)	城镇居民人均生活费支出(元)	#食品	人均居住面积(平方米)
1980	2.64	403.44	399.00	211.88	
1981	1.80	447.73	433.38	238.20	5.60
1982	1.75	473.52	447.40	252.36	6.01
1983	1.74	490.62	482.30	273.84	6.74
1984	1.70	571.89	552.16	310.44	7.11
1985	1.83	640.77	625.21	316.32	7.44
1986	1.83	776.76	737.11	375.66	7.51
1987	1.82	870.52	828.94	430.83	7.65
1988	1.84	978.92	1 026.53	501.71	8.29
1989	1.82	1 132.70	1 065.36	586.45	8.55
1990	1.87	1 196.72	1 030.54	556.73	8.86
1991	1.85	1 368.80	1 234.86	665.77	9.09
1992	1.75	1 567.21	1 457.40	765.22	8.99
1993	1.73	1 839.37	1 679.74	851.76	8.96

7—24 城市居民家庭平均每人全年购买主要商品数量

指　标	单位	1985年	1990年	1992年	1993年	1993年比1992年(±)%
粮　食	公斤	128.40	133.93	152.78	100.68	—34.10
鲜　菜	公斤	134.52	142.01	140.84	113.76	—19.23
食用植物油	公斤	7.80	6.43	8.03	7.08	—11.83
猪　肉	公斤	12.72	14.64	17.57	16.92	—3.70
牛羊肉	公斤	3.84	3.78	4.36	3.12	—28.44
家　禽	公斤	1.08	1.51	1.23	0.96	—20.33
鲜　蛋	公斤	7.56	5.22	9.05	6.84	—24.42
食　糖	公斤	2.04	1.86	1.62	1.32	—18.52
卷　烟	盒	48.12	46.08	44.49	42.96	—3.44
酒	公斤	4.32	4.83	5.42	5.40	—0.37
棉　布	米	2.14	1.40	0.68	0.78	14.71
化　纤　布	米	1.65	2.03	1.74	1.71	—1.72
呢　绒	米	0.63	0.39	0.44	0.38	—13.64
绸　缎	米	0.71	0.42	0.27	0.39	44.44
布制服装	件	0.33	1.60			
化纤布服装	件	1.47	0.16			
呢绒服装	件	0.25	0.06			
针织服装	件	1.30	0.90			
皮　鞋	双	0.70	0.62	0.79	0.83	5.06
肥　皂	块	4.52	2.32	1.76	2.02	14.77
煤　炭	公斤	233.59	192.09	103.57	126.22	21.87

7—25 城市居民家庭平均每百户拥有耐用消费品数量

指　标	单位	1985年	1990年	1992年	1993年	1993年比1992年(±)%
自行车	辆	170.52	209.28	209.28	212.41	1.50
缝纫机	架	62.74	70.00	56.63	55.18	-2.56
电风扇	只	4.14	39.64	45.18	48.67	7.72
洗衣机	台	57.93	86.75	88.43	94.70	7.09
电冰箱	台	2.41	29.88	40.48	49.52	22.33
彩色电视机	架	19.48	72.41	87.35	89.04	1.93
黑白电视机	架	68.97	38.19	24.46	20.48	-16.27
立体声收录机	架	24.48	39.04	37.35	35.54	-4.85
照相机	架	10.34	20.84	27.11	26.99	-0.44

7—26 农村住户人口状况

单位:人

指　标	1993年	指　标	1993年
一.常住人口	9 260	二.常住人口中职工人数	74
#1.整半劳动力	5 545	三.常住人口中乡村企业从业人员	65
(1)整劳动力	4 906	四.常住人口中外出劳动人数	167
(2)半劳动力	639	五.劳动力文化程度	5 545
2.学龄前人数	973	1.文盲或半文盲人数	1 756
3.6—11岁人口	1 162	2.小学程度人数	1 717
#在校人口	892	3.初中程度人数	1 517
4.12—14岁人口	447	4.高中程度人数	513
#在校人口	400	5.中专程度人数	25
5.15—17岁人口	285	6.大专以上人数	17
#在校人口	251		

7—27 农村住户总收入纯收入和总支出

单位:元

指　　标	1993年	指　　标	1993年
总　收　入		**总支出**	
一.全年总收入	839.91	一.全年总支出	833.26
1.劳动者的报酬收入	73.97	1.家庭经营费用支出	239.78
(1)在集体组织中劳动的报酬收入	5.32	(1)种植业生产支出	169.96
(2)在企业劳动得到的报酬收入	52.80	(2)林业生产支出	3.88
(3)在其他单位劳动得到报酬收入	15.85	(3)牧业生产支出	35.34
2.家庭经营收入	735.80	(4)渔业生产支出	
(1)种植业收入	492.95	(5)手工业生产支出	1.74
(2)林业收入	23.43	(6)工业生产支出	4.42
(3)牧业收入	103.53	(7)建筑业生产支出	1.80
(4)渔业收入		(8)运输业支出	10.85
(5)手工业收入	4.01	(9)商业支出	3.47
(6)采集捕猎收入	5.75	(10)饮食业支出	1.01
(7)工业收入	9.85	(11)服务业支出	3.07
(8)建筑业收放	12.72	(12)其他经营支出	4.22
(9)运输业收入	20.83	2.购生产用固定资产支出	22.78
(10)商业收入	8.36	3.缴纳税金	10.01
(11)饮食业收入	2.34	4.上交集体承包任务	6.10
(12)服务业收入	9.18	5.集体提留和摊派	6.87
(13)其他家庭经营收入	42.86	6.生活消费支出	537.76
二.转移性收入	28.25	7.其他非借贷性支出	9.95
三.财产性收入	1.86		
平均每人纯收入	550.83		

7—28 农民家庭平均每人主要消费品消费量

指　标	单位	1985年	1990年	1992年	1993年
粮　食(原粮)	公斤	242.11	247.30	234.80	262.68
细　粮	公斤	199.28	244.32	233.79	234.76
蔬　菜	公斤	45.24	43.74	45.19	29.36
食　油	公斤	2.91	3.86	4.18	3.64
肉　类	公斤	6.24	8.30	9.07	5.59
家　禽	公斤	0.12	0.15	0.23	0.16
蛋　类	公斤	0.82	1.02	1.30	0.92
食　糖	公斤	5.15	0.48	0.58	0.80
酒	公斤	1.03	0.96	1.09	1.49
棉　布	米	2.95	0.85	0.67	0.35
棉　花	公斤	0.16	0.07	0.17	
化纤布	米	1.95	1.15	1.34	1.38
呢　绒	米	0.15	0.04	0.05	0.10
绸　缎	米	0.19	0.06	0.06	0.01
毛线及毛织品	公斤	0.03	0.51	0.69	0.13
胶鞋.球鞋.皮鞋	双	1.08	0.45	0.54	0.44

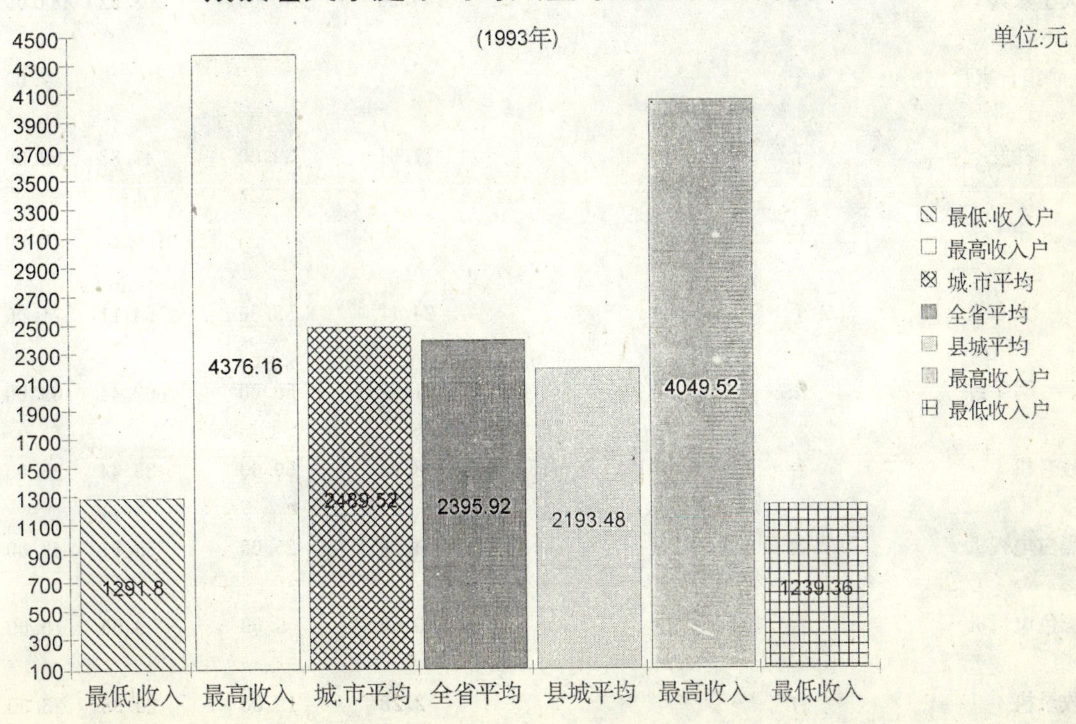

7—29 农民家庭平均每百户耐用消费品年末拥有量

项 目	单位	1978年	1980年	1985年	1990年	1992年	1993年
自行车	辆	30.66	40.56	64.28	102.00	104.67	117.00
缝纫机	架	12.32	18.89	39.44	59.00	58.00	65.00
钟	只	26.93	48.05	137.22	43.00	37.78	53.00
手表	只	8.30	23.61	108.72	193.00	186.61	201.00
#电子表	只				81.00	77.06	106.00
电风扇	台			0.22	1.00	0.94	2.00
洗衣机	台			1.06	6.00	8.61	9.00
电冰箱	台					0.11	20.00
摩托车	辆			0.06		0.50	1.00
大型家具	件			149.56	240.00	268.22	444.00
#组合家具	个						7.00
沙发	个			11.61	39.00	47.83	59.00
床	只						26.00
大衣柜	个			24.17	53.00	64.11	71.00
写字台	张			31.22	50.00	62.44	69.00
收音机	台	5.10	15.56	48.28	50.00	35.44	35.00
黑白电视机	台			4.00	25.00	35.61	43.00
彩色电视机	台			0.50	5.00	9.50	10.00
收录机	台			2.28	19.00	20.38	25.00

7—30 农民家庭平均每人生活费支出

单位:元

指　标	1985年	1990年	1992年	1993年
生活消费支出	125.54	339.24	419.68	537.76
(一)生活消费品支出	121.94	315.86	383.48	
按生活消费类别分				
1.食品	81.35	205.22	247.76	297.70
主食	60.29	125.88	141.34	170.54
副食	20.92	54.67	75.10	74.27
其他		22.23	28.74	43.85
2.衣着	16.85	30.35	35.47	39.53
3.住房	8.99	23.79	29.50	103.45
4.家庭设备.用品及服务				27.59
5.医疗保健				21.56
#医药卫生用品				
6.交通和通讯				8.70
7.文化教育娱乐用品及服务				32.36
文化娱乐用品				13.07
书报杂志				19.29
8.其他商品和服务				6.87
(1)商品性支出				0.80
(2)服务支出				6.07

7—31 农村住户建房和居住情况

指　　标	单位	数量	指　　标	单位	数量
一. 建房情况:(户均)			2. 年末住房面积	平方米	70.84
年内新建房屋间数	间	0.21	#砖木结构面积	平方米	10.02
年内新建房屋面积	平方米	2.74	钢筋混凝土结构面积	平方米	0.25
#砖木结构面积	平方米	0.65	3. 年末住房价值	元	2 833.24
钢筋混凝土结构面积	平方米	0.05	三. 人均指标		
年内新建房屋价值	元	178.93	平均每户年末住房单数	间	7.90
新建房屋占用耕地面积	市亩	0.04	平均每人年末住房面积	平方米	13.77
新建生活用房面积	平方米	2.42	平均每户本年新建房屋	平方米	2.74
新建楼房面积	平方米	0.02	平均每人年内新建房屋面积	平方米	0.53
二. 居住情况			平均每户新建楼房面积	平方米	0.02
1. 年末住房间数	间	7.90			

7—32 农民家庭生活基本情况

年份	每个农村劳动力负担人数(人)	人均纯收入(元)	人均生活费支出(元)	#食品	人均居住面积(平方米)
1978	2.42	100.93	88.18	65.98	
1979	2.36	111.57	96.69	69.69	
1980	2.32	153.41	125.54	81.35	13.87
1981	2.25	158.63	135.23	92.99	12.75
1982	2.14	174.16	141.05	95.65	13.53
1983	1.15	213.06	162.68	103.62	12.95
1984	1.95	221.05	178.39	113.01	12.96
1985	1.75	257.00	204.61	123.52	13.24
1986	1.73	282.89	232.79	137.84	13.44
1987	1.73	302.82	252.84	144.42	13.93
1988	1.70	345.14	276.98	152.24	14.32
1989	1.69	375.80	296.38	163.80	14.67
1990	1.67	430.99	339.24	205.22	11.88
1991	1.68	446.42	403.41	238.21	12.85
1992	1.69	489.47	419.68	247.76	13.13
1993	1.67	550.83	537.76	297.20	13.77

八. 城市概况

【固定资产投资总额】固定资产是对固定资产进行更新和扩大再生产的重要手段。通过建造和购置固定资产的活动，国民经济不断采用先进技术装备，进一步调整经济结构和生产力的地区分布。增强经济实力，这对实现我国社会主义现代化建设具有重要意义。

固定资产投资总额是以货币表现的建设和购置固定资产活动的工作量，它是反映固定资产投资规模和使用方向的综合性指标。按现行统计制度，全民所有制单位固定资产投资总额分为基本建设，更新改造措施和其他固定资产投资三个部分。全社会固定资产投资总额还包括城乡集体所有制单位投资和城乡个人建房投资。

全民所有制单位固定资产投资总额按资金来源分为国家预算内投资，地方、部门和企业自筹投资，国内贷款等，按工程的用途分为生产性建设和非生产性建设。

【基本建设投资额】基本建设是指国民经济各部门新建、扩建、改建和恢复工程以及设备等的购置活动。包括工厂、矿山、铁路、桥梁、港口、农田水利、商店、住宅、学校、医院等工程的建设和机械设备、车辆、船舶、飞机的购置。

基本建设投资额是以货币表现的基本建设完成的工作量，是反映一定时期内基本建设规模和建设进度的综合性指标，它是根据工程的实际进度按预算价格（预算价格是编制施工图预算时所用的价格）计算的工作量。没有形成工程实体的建筑材料和没有开始安装设备，都不计算投产完成额。

基本建设投资完成额与财政上的基本建设拨款是两个含义不同和指标，基本建设投资完成额中按预算的工作量；基本建设拨款的实际拨款数，使用时应加以区别。

【更新改造措施投资】更新改造措施是指现有的全民所有制企业、事业单位对其固定资产进行更新改造的工程和购置（不包括大修理和维修工程）更新改造措施投资是以货币表现的更新改造工作量。根据我国现行制度，基本建设和更新改造措施的划分是：(1)列入基本建设计划项目的投资作为基本建设投资，列入更新改造措施计划项目作为更新改造措施投资；(2)计划外项目则根据工程项目的性质而定，属于新建、扩建、的作为基本建设投资，属于改建或更新改造以及迁建、恢复的作为更新改造措施投资。

【其他固定资产投资】指按照国家规定不纳入基本建设和更新改造计划管理的全民所有制单位其他固定资产投资，这些投资主要是用于维持简单再生产资金安排工程、简易建筑以及零星固定资产投资和购置等。

8—1 城市社会经济主要指标在甘肃省所占比重

(1993年13个城市)

指　标	单位	甘肃省总计	全省城市合计		占甘肃省比重(%)	
			地区	市区	地区	市区
1.年底人口数	万人	2 318.57	1 052.76	615.70	45.40	26.56
#非农业人口	万人	392.44	295.62	265.15	75.33	67.56
年未劳动力资源总数	万人	1 647.70	636.88	396.59	38.65	24.07
2.土地面积	平立公里	454 430	120 638	74 801	26.54	16.46
3.农业总产值(当年价格)	万元	1 404 213	587 006.	366 059	41.80	26.06
农业总产值(90年不变价)	万元	1 345 057	519 664	309 101	38.64	22.97
乡村劳动力	万人	857.53	395.28	178.25	46.10	20.79
主要农产品产量						
粮食	万吨	750.26	224.10	119.23	29.87	15.89
水果	吨	596 617.23	271 937	182 561	45.57	30.61
猪肉	吨		160 621	91 644		
牛羊肉	吨		26 200	16 036		
水产品	吨		3 180	1 834		
4.工业企业单位数	个	7 010	3 912	2 774	55.81	39.57
#国有单位	个	1 639	920	729	56.13	44.48
集体单位	个	5 294	2 934	1 999	55.42	37.76
工业总产值(当年价格)	万元	5 052 478	4 148 662	3 725529	82.11	73.74
轻工业	万元	1 148 377	680 473	619 289	59.26	53.93
重工业	万元	3 904 101	3 106 116	2 805 688	79.56	71.87
工业总产值(90年不变价)	万元	4 165 066	3 368 947	2 976572	80.88	71.47
独立核算工业企业财务指标						
产品销售收入	万元	4 489 124	3 715 712	3 316 303	82.77	73.87
利税总额	万元	479 660	153 853	122 217	32.06	25.47
资金总额	万元		3 755 186	3 743 012		
固定资产原值	万元	3 582 610	3 128 877	270 045	87.34	75.38
每百元资金提供利税	元		3.59	26.27		
每百元固定资产原值实现的产值	元		102.14	1 085		
5.客运量(发送)	万人	9 580.00	7 069.80	6 199.43	73.80	64.71
货运量(发送)	万吨	19 193.30	6 124.89	5 428.23	31.91	28.28
年底邮电局所数	个	1 164	481	303	41.32	26.03

8—1 续

(1993 年 13 个城市)

指　　标	单位	甘肃省总计	全省城市合计		占甘肃省比重(%)	
			地区	市区	地区	市区
邮电业务总量(90 年不变价)	万元		37 340	26 601		
年末电话机数	部		250 358	232 616		
全年用电量	万千瓦小时		1 843 121	1 578 298		
6. 固定资产投资总额	万元	1 220 812	720 911	635 496	59.05	52.06
#住宅	万元		133 563	125 536	56.95	53.50
#国有单位	万元	957 031	635 455	555 678	66.40	58.06
城镇集体	万元	141 721	19 880	14 865	14.03	10.49
国有单位新增固定资产	万元	604 767	334 853	283 517	55.37	46.88
城镇集体单位新增固定资产	万元	103 390	11 943	7 244	11.55	7.01
7. 社会消费品零售总额	万元	1 561 087	1 201 395	1 009 069	76.96	64.63
批零贸易业.餐饮业机构数	个	1 493 178	140 061	106 880	72.50	55.33
批零贸易业.餐饮业人员数	人	901 604	387 132	303 748	42.94	33.69
8. 实际利用外资金额	万美元	5 610.00	2 194.80	1 944.80	39.12	34.67
旅游外汇收入总额	外汇券万元		5 605			
9. (在校生数)普通高等学校	人	40 514	39 779	39 779	98.19	98.19
中等专业学校	人	55 156	45 137	42 684	81.84	77.39
普通中学	万人	87.28	4 766.00	28.68	54.61	32.86
农业.职业中学	人	43 377	27 889	20 648	64.29	47.60
技工学校	人	27 983	21 806	20 556	77.93	73.46
小学	万人	249.97	122.31	66.96	48.93	26.79
成人高等学校	人		18 872	18 872		
自然科技人员数	人		174 636	150 935		
#中级技术职称以上人员	人		52 354	46 826		
卫生机构数	个	4 141	2 428	1 967	58.63	47.50
#医院	个	1 637	600	372	36.65	22.72
医院床位数	张	54 845	31 952	26 732	58.26	48.74
卫生技术人员	人	77 807	51 127	42 872	65.71	55.10
#医生	人	35 751	21 524	17 579	60.21	49.17
10. 职工工资总额	万元	858 852.80	599 622	549 701	69.81	64
城乡储蓄存款余额	万元	2 039 573	1 486 963	669 491	72.91	32.83

8—2 城市土地面积

(1993年)

单位:平方公里

城市名称	土地面积		建城区土地面积(市.区)	城市名称	土地面积		建城区土地面积(市.区)
	地区	市区			地区	市区	
合计	120 638	74 801	391	平凉市	1 936	1 936	8
兰州市	13 806	1 632	163	临夏市	89	89	7
嘉峪关市	1 329	1 329	30	武威市	5 081	5 081	12
金昌市	9 600	2 080	36	张掖市	4 240	4 240	13
白银市	21 158	3 478	51	酒泉市	3 386	3 386	18
天水市	14 325	5 862	26	西峰市	996	996	8
玉门市	13 492	13 492	17	敦煌市	31 200	31 200	2

8—3 城市人口

(1993年包括市辖县)

城市名称	市区人口年未数(万人)	#非农业人口	市区人口密度(平方公里)	城市名称	市区人口年未数(万人)	#非农业人口	市区人口密度(平方公里)
合计	1 052.76	295.62	87.27	平凉市	39.86	9.99	205.88
兰州市	261.21	133.87	189.20	临夏市	17.73	8.58	1 947.19
嘉峪关市	11.40	9.10	85.78	武威市	90.51	14.41	178.13
金昌市	40.09	16.39	41.76	张掖市	43.84	9.16	103.40
白银市	152.71	29.20	72.18	酒泉市	30.73	7.85	90.76
天水市	304.09	36.84	212.28	西峰市	28.36	5.60	284.74
玉门市	20.22	12.26	15.06	敦煌市	12.01	2.37	3.85

8—4 国内生产总值

(1993年) 单位:万元

城市名称	国内生产总值	第一产业	第二产业	第三产业
合计	2 555 270	353 535	1 517 827	683 908
兰州市	1 099 485	65 391	721 643	312 451
嘉峪关市	111 430	3 323	93 026	15 081
金昌市	216 534	15 363	150 615	50 556
白银市	264 160	41 872	173 418	48 870
天水市	373 528	76 934	174 004	122 590
玉门市	113 359	8 180	93 681	11 498
平凉市	39 755	12 233	13 682	13 840
临夏市	19 263	6 799	6 100	6 364
武威市	102 137	39 450	28 950	33 737
张掖市	85 566	33 197	22 273	30 096
酒泉市	65 307	23 705	21 513	20 089
西峰市	37 798	11 146	14 411	12 241
敦煌市	26 948	15 942	4 511	6 495

8—5 乡村劳动力

(1993年) 单位:万人

城市名称	乡村劳动力		城市名称	乡村劳动力	
	地区	市区		地区	市区
合计	395.28	178.25	平凉市	12.42	12.42
兰州市	64.69	16.96	临夏市	4.20	4.20
嘉峪关市	1.19	1.19	武威市	43.66	43.66
金昌市	12.21	2.78	张掖市	22.14	22.14
白银市	66.60	8.60	酒泉市	11.53	11.53
天水市	139.70	38.40	西峰市	8.78	8.78
玉门市	4.25	4.25	敦煌市	3.91	3.91

8—6 城市农业总产值和农业商品产值(包括市辖县)

(1993 年)　　单位:万元

城市名称	农业商品产值		农业总产值	
	地区	市区	地区	市区
合　　　计	587 006	366 059	29 630	208 729
兰　州　市	98 266	42 122	48 883	28 832
嘉 峪 关 市	5 084	5 084	3 124	3 124
金　昌　市	30 065	7 483	17 279	4 591
白　银　市	70 049	13 869	28 595	8 232
天　水　市	130 953	44 912	52 519	18 048
玉　门　市	15 410	15 410	8 730	8 730
平　凉　市	17 789	17 789	7 047	7 047
临　夏　市	8 838	8 839	5 874	5 874
武　威　市	73 571	73 571	45 175	45 175
张　掖　市	55 685	55 685	32 420	32 420
酒　泉　市	40 309	40 309	24 037	24 037
西　峰　市	23 107	23 107	12 257	12 257
敦　煌　市	17 880	17 880	10 326	10 326

8—7 工业企业单位数和职工人数

(1993 年)

城市名称	企业单位数(个)		全部独立核算工业企业全部职工人数(万人)	
	地区	市区	地区	市区
合　　　计	3 912	2 774	95.17	83.48
兰　州　市	1 307	940	41.01	36.48
嘉 峪 关 市	69	69	4.27	4.27
金　昌　市	224	80	6.96	5.31
白　银　市	369	115	14.64	12.02
天　水　市	777	404	11.60	8.71
玉　门　市	99	99	4.75	4.75
平　凉　市	170	170	2.77	2.77
临　夏　市	112	112	1.00	1.00
武　威　市	223	223	3.02	3.02
张　掖　市	167	167	1.78	1.78
酒　泉　市	180	180	1.74	1.74
西　峰　市	115	115	1.20	1.20
敦　煌　市	100	100	0.43	0.43

8—8 工业总产值

(1993年) 单位:万元

城市名称	工业总产值		轻工业		重工业	
	地区	市区	地区	市区	地区	市区
合计	4 148 662	3 725 529	680 473	619 289	3 106 116	2 805 688
兰州市	2 136 700	1 938 100	362 000	345 200	1 606 100	1 424300
嘉峪关市	219 784	219 784	13 656	13 656	203 516	203 516
金昌市	269 386	228 457	9 123	2 516	252 852	222 660
白银市	550 199	472 869	27 749	17 312	502 620	448 058
天水市	377 627	271 353	92 981	65 641	199 370	165 496
玉门市	243 107	243 107	3 732	3 732	234 838	234 838
平凉市	59 437	59 437	17 062	17 062	26 133	26 133
临夏市	22 332	22 332	10 717	10 717	4 926	4 926
武威市	68 605	68 605	45 246	45 246	16 119	16 119
张掖市	69 614	69 614	33 729	33 729	18 950	18 950
酒泉市	72 098	72 098	38 328	38 328	23 639	23 639
西峰市	39 791	39 791	16 923	16 923	6 298	6 298
敦煌市	19 982	19 982	9 227	9 227	10 755	10 755

8—8续表 (1993年) 单位:万元

城市名称	全部独立核算工业企业		#国有单位工业企业	
	地区	市区	地区	市区
合计	3 755 406	3 407 772	3 196 001	2 929 994
兰州市	1 958 300	1 759 800	1 721 800	1 569 700
嘉峪关市	216 238	216 238	194 337	194 337
金昌市	261 975	222 172	202 480	180 302
白银市	530 369	465 370	450 313	400 676
天水市	286 622	231 137	231 916	189 824
玉门市	236 905	236 905	223 190	223 190
平凉市	43 195	43 195	31 793	31 793
临夏市	13 491	13 491	3 639	3 639
武威市	53 454	53 454	42 280	42 280
张掖市	51 578	51 578	30 400	30 400
酒泉市	60 469	60 469	39 216	39 216
西峰市	22 828	22 828	19 234	19 234
敦煌市	19 982	19 982	5 403	5 403

8—9 国有单位独立核算工业企业固定资产和资金总额

(1993年包括市辖县)　　单位:万元

城市名称	年末固定资产原值	资金总额	定额流动资产平均金额	年末固定资产净值
合　计	2 856 715	3 755 186	1 841 432	1 672 403
兰州市	1 260 700	1 698 100	906 000	792 100
嘉峪关市	198 425	249 697	119 928	129 769
金昌市	192 332	264 614	132 089	132 525
白银市	656 178	817 334	303 857	513 477
天水市	212 847	350 079	207 115	142 964
玉门市	193 555	152 925	79 013	73 921
平凉市	40 798	60 339	26 854	33 485
临夏市	2 713	4 855	2 895	1 960
武威市	32 383	53 398	31 053	22 345
张掖市	26 958	33 733	12 757	20 976
酒泉市	25 344	42 866	25 019	17 847
西峰市	11 290	19 641	11 710	7 931
敦煌市	3 192	7 596	4 755	2 841

8—10 工业增加值

(1993年)　　单位:万元

城市名称	全部独立核算工业企业增加值		#国有单位工业企业增加值	
	地区	市区	地区	市区
合　计	1 267 741	1 155 008	1 032 229	961 985
兰州市	592 300	535 400	487 800	451 200
嘉峪关市	86 816	86 816	72 690	72 690
金昌市	127 510	113 599	106 681	100 529
白银市	158 272	141 876	131 068	121 945
天水市	122 500	96 974	95 988	77 619
玉门市	97 114	97 114	85 934	85 934
平凉市	14 495	14 495	12 689	12 689
临夏市	3 912	3 912	1 054	1 054
武威市	16 740	16 740	10 700	10 700
张掖市	16 484	16 484	9 728	9 728
酒泉市	15 630	15 630	9 197	9 197
西峰市	8 517	8 517	75 534	75 534
敦煌市	7 451	7 451	1 146	1 146

8—11 国有单位基本建设投资

（1993年） 单位：万元

城市名称	投资额		#住宅建设	
	地区	市区	地区	市区
合计	372 731	307 202	59 531	55 368
兰州市	143 458	107 495	32 402	30 434
嘉峪关市	17 362	17 362	1 466	1 466
金昌市	57 645	44 321	4 578	4 043
白银市	79 999	72 069	4 388	4 012
天水市	29 347	21 035	6 056	4 772
玉门市	1 356	1 356	1 000	1 000
平凉市	5 975	5 975	1 665	1 665
临夏市	1 800	1 800	717	717
武威市	11 250	11 250	4 020	4 020
张掖市	11 480	11 480	1 385	1 385
酒泉市	6 679	6 679	1 094	1 094
西峰市	6 197	6 197	700	700
敦煌市	183	183	60	60

8—12 全社会固定资产投资

（1993年） 单位：万元

城市名称	投资额		#住宅建设	
	地区	市区	地区	市区
合计	53 888	48 604	7 296	4 856
兰州市	5 652	5 627	3 420	1 573
嘉峪关市	1 377	1 377	25	25
金昌市	6 686	3 120	258	
白银市	6 075	5 117	150	150
天水市	2 406	1 671	940	605
玉门市	28 565	28 565	1 752	1 752
平凉市	225	225	38	38
临夏市	189	189		
武威市	1 195	1 195	150	150
张掖市	972	972	420	420
酒泉市	333	333	85	85
西峰市	213	213	58	58
敦煌市				

8—13 批发零售贸易业商品购进与销售额

(1993 年)　　单位:元

城市名称	批发零售贸易业商品购进总额		批发零售贸易业商品销售总额	
	地区	市区	地区	市区
合　计	2 539 075	2 048 622	2 896 243	2 333 163
兰州市	1 568 027	1 189 388	1 745 098	1 305 466
嘉峪关市	46 152	46 152	58 814	58 814
金昌市	48 722	29 233	61 765	37 058
白银市	98 501	60 818	106 376	62 701
天水市	199 787	145 145	223 933	168 867
玉门市	22 900	22 900	28 046	28 046
平凉市	30 275	30 275	34 823	34 823
临夏市	19 905	19 905	24 011	24 011
武威市	76 535	76 535	82 871	82 871
张掖市	51 633	51 633	61 477	61 477
酒泉市	88 825	88 825	96 229	96 229
西峰市	47 569	47 569	53 124	53 124
敦煌市	240 244	20 244	319 676	319 676

8—14 城市批发零售贸易业.餐饮业网点人员数

(1993 年)

城市名称	网点数(个)		人员数(人)	
	地区	市区	地区	市区
合　计	140 061	106 880	387 132	303 748
兰州市	48 918	43 048	178 383	156 977
嘉峪关市	2 000	2 000	4 319	4 319
金昌市	5 835	3 676	9 760	6 149
白银市	12 156	5 376	24 469	10 956
天水市	33 276	14 904	80 911	36 057
玉门市	1 226	1 226	2 462	2 462
平凉市	6 965	6 965	15 420	15 420
临夏市	2 701	2 701	5 960	5 960
武威市	11 270	11 270	27 083	27 083
张掖市	5 237	5 237	14 117	14 117
酒泉市	3 471	3 471	9 615	9 615
西峰市	4 031	4 031	10 826	10 826
敦煌市	2 975	2 975	4 077	4 077

8—15 社会消费品零售总额

(1993年)

单位:万元

城市名称	社会消费品零售总额		市名称	社会消费品零售总额	
	地区	市区		地区	市区
合　　计	1 201 395	1 009 069	平　凉　市	32 792	32 792
兰　州　市	662 806	589 885	临　夏　市	21 089	21 089
嘉 峪 关 市	28 202	28 202	武　威　市	30 079	30 079
金　昌　市	62 792	37 675	张　掖　市	40 040	40 040
白　银　市	80 579	28 525	酒　泉　市	31 470	31 470
天　水　市	142 225	99 991	西　峰　市	21 947	21 947
玉　门　市	24 936	24 936	敦　煌　市	22 438	22 438

8—16 外　贸.旅　游

(1993年)

城市名称	外贸收购总额(万元)	实际利用外资总额(万美元)	协议(合同)外资金额(万美元)	旅游人数(人)	旅游外汇收入(外汇券万元)
合　　计	228 713	2 195	29 859	102 076	5 605
兰　州　市	204 800	1 063	24 503	34 678	3 507
嘉 峪 关 市	1 300			14 326	456
金　昌　市	165				
白　银　市	3 600	200	889		
天　水　市	3 247	328	1 433	1 952	81
玉　门　市					
平　凉　市	5 484			462	11
临　夏　市	1 379			10 000	1
武　威　市	100			1 500	27
张　掖　市	2 596			1 235	11
酒　泉　市	4 808	67	284	856	154
西　峰　市	1 234	537	537	67	1
敦　煌　市			2 213	37 000	1 356

8—17 财 政 收 支

(1993 年)　　单位:万元

城市名称	地方财政预算内收入		地方财政预算内支出	
	地区	市区	地区	市区
合　计	308 247	283 383	245 219	200 594
兰州市	147 391	136 660	91 550	78 322
嘉峪关市	29 396	29 396	7 285	7 285
金昌市	19 982	15 965	18 808	14 003
白银市	24 845	20 634	26 557	16 441
天水市	34 622	28 717	42 633	26 157
玉门市	6 939	6 939	4 316	4 316
平凉市	4 826	4 826	6 038	6 038
临夏市	2 670	2 670	3 220	3 220
武威市	8 730	8 730	8 617	8 617
张掖市	7 250	7 250	6 471	6 471
酒泉市	10 027	10 027	12 952	12 952
西峰市	8 831	8 831	12 997	12 997
敦煌市	2 738	2 738	3 775	3 775

8—18 交 通

(1993 年)

城市名称	客运发送总量(万人)		货运发送总量(万吨)	
	地区	市区	地区	市区
合　计	7 069.80	6 199.43	6 124.89	5 428.23
兰州市	1 303.32	928.32	2 730.66	2 538.00
嘉峪关市	152.49	152.49	533.03	533.03
金昌市	275.88	173.20	334.00	110.00
白银市	700.00	516.01	954.00	690.00
天水市	1 139.00	930.30	290.00	274.00
玉门市	657.00	657.10	173.00	173.00
平凉市	603.00	603.00	396.00	396.00
临夏市	199.80	199.80	50.00	50.00
武威市	335.50	335.50	179.00	179.00
张掖市	460.71	460.71	161.00	161.00
酒泉市	440.61	440.61	179.00	179.00
西峰市	429.39	429.39	144.00	144.00
敦煌市	373.00	373.00	1.20	1.20

8—19 邮电

(1993年)

城市名称	本年邮电业务总量(万元)		本年末电话机数(部)	
	地区	市区	地区	市区
合计	37 340	26 601	250 358	232 616
兰州市	17 077	16 346	150 367	144 327
嘉峪关市	715	715	9 741	9 741
金昌市	9 434	837	6 686	5 847
白银市	1 884	1 349	19 990	15 777
天水市	3 407	2 531	25 648	18 998
玉门市	443	443	8 144	8 144
平凉市	603	603	4 409	4 409
临夏市	463	463	3 565	3 565
武威市	820	820	6 258	6 258
张掖市	688	688	4 068	4 068
酒泉市	829	829	5 273	5 273
西峰市	528	528	3 528	3 528
敦煌市	449	449	2 681	2 681

8—20 教育

(1993年)　　单位:人

城市名称	高等学校在校学生数		成人高等学校在校学生数	
	地区	市区	地区	市区
合计	39 779	39 779	18 872	18 872
兰州市	34 250	34 250	10 532	10 532
嘉峪关市			820	820
金昌市			150	150
白银市			748	748
天水市	1 957	1 957	371	371
玉门市				
平凉市	25	25	2 859	2 859
临夏市				
武威市			2 300	2 300
张掖市	1 620	1 620	486	486
酒泉市			179	179
西峰市	1 927	1 927	427	427
敦煌市				

8—21 科技人员

(1993年)　　单位:人

城市名称	自然科技方面的人员		中级技术职称以上的人员	
	地区	市区	地区	市区
合计	174 636	150 935	51 631	46 104
兰州市	105 842	98 433	33 772	31 478
嘉峪关市	4 301	4 301	2 203	2 203
金昌市	25	25		
白银市	20 666	16 073	3 487	2 712
天水市	23 491	11 792	5 222	2 767
玉门市	1 986	1 986	723	723
平凉市	3 911	3 911	1 322	1 322
临夏市	2 933	2 933	900	900
武威市	2 500	2 500	750	750
张掖市	4 043	4 043	1 226	1 226
酒泉市	3 914	3 914	1 529	1 529
西峰市	2 251	2 251	693	693
敦煌市	769	769	527	527

8—22 卫生

(1993年)

城市名称	医院(个)		医院床位数(张)		医生(人)	
	地区	市区	地区	市区	地区	市区
合计	600	372	31 952	26 732	21 524	17 579
兰州市	151	87	12 974	11 542	9 159	8 164
嘉峪关市	2	2	701	701	444	444
金昌市	16	7	1 444	940	742	481
白银市	100	27	4 021	2 596	2 199	1 231
天水市	148	66	4 861	3 002	4 007	2 286
玉门市	13	13	974	974	621	621
平凉市	24	24	1 154	1 154	620	620
临夏市	11	11	640	640	498	498
武威市	72	72	2 052	2 052	1 242	1 242
张掖市	26	26	1 006	1 006	822	822
酒泉市	23	23	1 010	1 010	595	595
西峰市	12	12	815	815	429	429
敦煌市	2	2	300	300	146	146

8—23 社会治安

(1993年不包括市辖县)

城市名称	刑事案件发案数(件)	犯罪人数(人)	青少年数(人)(25岁以下)	城市名称	刑事案件发案数(件)	犯罪人数(人)	青少年数(人)(25岁以下)
合计	11 273	10 043	6 060	平凉市	501	258	93
兰州市	5 527	4 881	2 876	临夏市	302	109	62
嘉峪关市	390	355	232	武威市	950	580	395
金昌市	685	756	452	张掖市	421	441	210
白银市	691	845	548	酒泉市	455	458	297
天水市	711	755	510	西峰市	203	103	35
玉门市	208	285	197	敦煌市	229	217	153

8—24 城市公用事业

1.园林绿地(不包括市辖县)

城市名称	施工住宅建筑面积(包括商品房)(万平方米)	竣工住宅建筑面积(包括商品房)(万方米)	年末实有住宅居住面积(万平方米)	园林绿地面积(公顷)
合计	458.24	284.24	1 916.75	4 204.00
兰州市	235.13	91.63	891.00	2 185.00
嘉峪关市	24.47	22.94	76.10	113.00
金昌市	14.57	4.28	99.50	246.00
白银市	47.07	22.88	182.80	442.00
天水市	54.45	20.49	180.00	176.00
玉门市	5.70	5.70	74.20	114.00
平凉市	9.60	5.20	76.40	420.00
临夏市	3.03	1.42	61.40	62.00
武威市	32.95	95.06	113.40	78.00
张掖市	13.12	5.40	64.95	108.00
酒泉市	17.47	8.56	61.00	223.00
西峰市	0.68	0.68	36.00	37.00
敦煌市				

8—25 城市公用事业

2.自来水(不包括市辖县)

城市名称	年末城市自来水厂生产能力(万吨/日)	年末供水管道总产度(公里)	全年供水总量(万吨)	#生产用量	#生活用量
合计	263.70	1 905.00	73 322.00	52 083.00	21 239.00
兰州市	134.00	421.00	35 642.00	21 794.00	13 848.00
嘉峪关市	31.00	84.00	8 063.00	7 513.00	550.00
金昌市	18.00	196.00	6 300.00	5 055.00	1 245.00
白银市	26.00	334.00	7 440.00	6 030.00	1 410.00
天水市	20.10	102.00	5 525.00	3 421.00	2 104.00
玉门市	7.00	263.00	3 306.00	2 941.00	365.00
平凉市	4.00	49.00	1 136.00	430.00	706.00
临夏市	2.00	150.00	610.00	440.00	170.00
武威市	4.00	48.00	1 368.00	1 048.00	320.00
张掖市	7.00	100.00	2 229.00	1 641.00	588.00
酒泉市	6.60	37.00	1 227.00	963.00	264.00
西峰市	1.00	95.00	386.00	136.00	250.00
敦煌市	3.00	26.00	90.00	35.00	55.00

8—26 城市公共汽(电)车.出租汽车

(1993 年不包括市.辖县)

城市名称	年末实有公共汽(电)车营运车辆(辆)	全年公共汽(电)车客运总数(万人次)	年末实有出租汽车数(辆)	每万人拥有出租汽车(辆)
合计	944	31 474.13	2 941	37.57
兰州市	626	28 799.00	2 226	1.43
嘉峪关市	9	68.00	58	5.09
金昌市	59	175.00	10	0.60
白银市	33	490.00	21	0.54
天水市	77	1 048.00	60	0.56
玉门市	24	620.00	145	7.17
平凉市	94	501.60	3	0.08
临夏市			80	4.51
武威市			56	0.62
张掖市	20	214.23	12	0.27
酒泉市			114	3.71
西峰市	2	9.30		
敦煌市			156	12.99

8—27 城市市政工程

(1993 年不包括市辖县)

城市名称	建成区绿化覆盖面积(公顷)	年末实有铺装道路面积(万平方米)	城市下水道总长度(公里)	城市工业废水自处理能力(万吨)
合计	2 682	1 419.20	1 232	66.83
兰州市	479	521.00	566	21.74
嘉峪关市	113	79.00	26	27.79
金昌市	417	85.00	69	5.22
白银市	555	151.00	146	6.41
天水市	210	78.00	81	0.65
玉门市	119	47.90	25	0.08
平凉市	200	23.00	25	0.72
临夏市	62	50.00	23	0.08
武威市	22	63.20	62	0.45
张掖市	47	45.00	34	2.49
酒泉市	342	56.00	67	1.18
西峰市	85	186.10	36	0.02
敦煌市	31	34.00	72	

8—28 城市设施水平

(1993 年不包括市辖县)

城市名称	人均居住面积(平方米/人)	城市人口用水普及率(%)	城市燃气普及率(%)	每万人拥有公共汽(电)车(台)	人均拥有铺装道路面积(平方米)	人均园林绿地面积(平方米)
合计	7.42	48.80	16.10	1.53	2.30	7.16
兰州市	7.11	97.34	35.38	3.97	3.31	13.86
嘉峪关市	8.46	100.00	74.56	0.79	6.93	9.91
金昌市	6.72	97.84	63.62	3.54	5.10	14.77
白银市	8.16	56.04	4.63	0.85	3.88	11.36
天水市	7.02	27.80	3.35	0.71	0.72	1.63
玉门市	6.42	57.12	51.78	1.19	2.37	5.64
平凉市	7.49	20.32		2.35	0.58	10.54
临夏市	6.90	52.45			2.82	3.50
武威市	9.04	14.31	1.10		0.70	0.86
张掖市	8.65	24.40	5.75	0.46	1.03	2.46
酒泉市	8.13	24.41	12.72		1.82	7.25
西峰市	6.58	23.27	3.10	0.07	6.56	7.30
敦煌市	15.65	19.15	0.75		2.83	3.08

8—29 全省"三废"排放、处理及综合利用情况

项　目	单位	1985 年	1990 年	1992 年	1993 年
一. 废水					
废水排放总量	万吨	44 586	47 363	46 928	45 120
工业废水	万吨	37 234	38 585	37 562	36 298
经过处理的	万吨	10 294	12 128	24 126	25 455
经过处理达标的	万吨	5 467	6 072	5 499	16 245
二. 废气					
废气排放总量	亿标立方米	1 664	1 788	2 505	2 463
燃料燃烧过程中排放量	亿标立方米	867	1 048	1 540	1 196
经过消烟除尘的	亿标立方米	603	847	963	1 065
生产工艺过程中废气排放量	亿标立方米	797	740	924	995
经过净化处理的	亿标立方米	374	359	524	559
废气中：二氧化硫	吨	329 267	361 980	354 162	337 805
烟尘	吨	176 076	227 335	135 997	149 103
三. 工业粉情况					
工业粉尘排放量	万吨	14	17	11	14
工业粉尘回收量	万吨	33	45	38	78
四. 工业固体废物产生.排放及处理利用情况					
工业固体废物产生量	万吨	918	1 131	1 214	1 287
工业固体废物处置量	万吨		717	118	314
工业固体废物综合利用量	万吨	130	214	313	363
工业固体废物排放量	万吨	728	138	69	83
工业固体废物堆存总量	万吨	10 397	13 274	15 068	15 139
工业固体废物占地面积	万平方米	1 490	2 143	2 053	2 006
占耕地面积	万平方米		9	14	6
"三废"综合利用产品产值	万元		11 962	23 564	24 732
"三废"综合利用利润	万元		1 697	2 527	1 504
五. 企事业污染治理资金来源合计	万元	5 290	7 180	8 648	11 645
1. 基本建设资金	万元	2 757	2 672	2 457	4 401
2. 更新改造资金	万元	1 051	2 545	3 821	3 433
3. 综合利用利润留成	万元	23	43	13	133
4. 环境保护补助资金	万元	828	881	1 560	1 617
#贷款	万元	461	445	455	521
5. 其他	万元	170	594	797	2 062
六. 企事业污染治理资金使用合计	万元	5 290	7 180	8 648	11 645
1. 治理废水	万元	1 045	2 451	3 598	4 070
2. 治理废气	万元	3 009	3 274	3 248	4 048
3. 治理固体废物	万元	817	615	811	2 844
4. 治理噪声	万元	96	269	176	253
5. 其他	万元	323	571	816	430
七. 交纳排污费单位	个	931	2 482	2 898	3 632
本年征收排污费数	万元	1 514	2 500	3 177	3 951
环境保护补助资金支出数	万元	1 148	1 373	1 973	2 213
污染事故	万元	11	21	33	39
污染赔款总额	万元	22	39	38	90
污染罚款总额	万元	15	21	11	23

九·农　业

统计指标解释

·之九·

【新增固定资产】新增固定资产，是指通过基本建设、更新改造等投资建成投入生产或交付使用的建筑物和达到固定资产标准的设备、工具、器具价值，以及应摊入固定资产的其他费用。在固定资产投资完成额中，购置不够固定资产标准的设备、工具、器具价值，生产人员培训费，施工机构转移费，报废工程的投资，以及其他核销费用，都不计算在新增固定资产的价值内。新增固定资产与投资额的比例称为固定资产交付使用率。

【自行完成施工产值】指建筑业企业或附属建筑业施工单位自行完成的按工程进度计算的建筑安装总价值。它包括建筑工程产值、设备安装工程产值、房屋、构筑物修理产值、非标准设备制造产值。

【竣工产值】指在报告期内，按照设计所规定的工程内容全部完成，达到了设计规定的交工条件，经有关部门检查验收鉴定合格的单位工程价值之和。

【房屋建筑施工面积】指在报告期内施工的全部房屋建筑面积。包括本期内新开工的、上期施工跨入本期继续施工、上期停建本期复工的房屋建筑面积；不包括上期开工后又停工，本期未施工的房屋建筑面积。

【房屋建筑竣工面积】指在报告期内，按照设计所规定的工程内容全部完成，达到设计规定的交工条件，经有关部门检查验收鉴定合格的房屋建筑面积。

【住宅竣工面积】指房屋建筑竣工面积中的供居住用的房屋建筑竣工面积。

【能源生产总量】指一定时期内全国（地区）一次能源生产量的总和。一次能源生产量包括原煤、原油、天然气、水电及其它动力能发电量，如风能、地热能等。不包括生物质能、太阳能等的利用和由一次能源加工转换而成的二次能源产量。能源生产总量是观察全国（地区）能源生产水平、规模、构成和发展速度的总量指标。

【能源生产弹性指数】是研究能源生产量的增长与国民经济增长之间的指标，其计算公式为：

能源生产弹性系数＝能源生产总量年平均增长速度÷国民经济年平均增长速度

国民经济年平均增长速度，可根据不同的目的或需要，用国民生产总值、国民收入等指标来计算，本资料是采用国民收入指标计算的。

【电力生产弹性系数】是研究电力生产量的增长与国民经济增长之间的关系的指标。一般来说，电力的发展应当快于国民经济的发展，也就是说电力应超前发展。其计算公式为：

电力生产弹性系数＝电力生产量年平均增长速度/国民经济年平均增长速度

9—1 甘肃省农村基层组织情况

项　目	单位	1991 年	1992 年	1993 年
一. 农村基层组织				
1. 乡镇政府	个	1 527	1 528	1 528
# 乡镇政府	个	159	163	166
民族政府	个	50	50	49
2. 村民委员会	个	17 658	17 675	17 708
3. 村民小组	个	100 671	100 735	100 868
二. 乡村户口	万户	392.43	399.29	407.58
三. 乡村人口	万人	1 871.51	1 890.48	1 911.46
四. 乡村劳动力	万人	834.45	848.45	857.53
1. 按性别分				
男劳动力	万人	440.95	447.60	452.09
女劳动力	万人	393.50	400.85	405.44
2. 按行业分				
农林牧副渔业	万人	690.21	696.57	678.90
工业	万人	24.65	25.78	30.22
建筑业	万人	25.34	27.30	31.02
交通运输和邮电业	万人	11.52	12.67	13.66
商业. 饮食业	万人	11.26	12.48	14.28
服务业	万人	4.20	4.48	5.34
文化艺术和教育事业	万人	5.79	5.78	5.66
卫生体育和社会福利事业	万人	2.86	2.77	2.97
科学研究事业	万人	0.11	0.20	0.17
乡(镇)务管理	万人	0.89	0.92	0.86
金融保险业	万人	0.21	0.23	0.20
其他	万人	57.41	59.27	74.25

9—2 甘肃省农村社会发展情况

项目	单位	1991年	1992年	1993年
一. 村镇建设				
1. 村镇现有房屋	万平方米	43 535.80	44 201.22	45 184.43
#居民生活用房	万平方米	37 206.23	37 640.25	38 629.21
2. 自来水受益村	个	2 954	3 208	3 450
3. 通电的村数	个	13 742	14 222	14 705
4. 通公路的乡镇数	个	1 481	1 484	1 510
二. 农村文化				
1. 有线广播喇叭数	万只	103.79	105.61	103.44
2. 电影放映机数	部	2 805	2 755	3 341
3. 电视机数	万台	103.32	121.40	141.67
#彩电数	万台	20.20	25.97	33.32
4. 录音机	万台	82.34	92.49	104.25
5. 录放像机	台	3 333	3 603	7 461
三. 农村教育				
小学数	所	23 129	22 935	22 779
中学数	所	1 378	1 395	1 412
#职业中学数	所	118	107	104
四. 农村科技				
科技服务站	个	1 029	1 046	1 118
农业技术人员	个	22 259	26 826	34 035
五. 福利事业				
1. 敬老院单位数	个	444	465	490
2. 敬老院收养人数	人	2 263	2 283	2 347

9—3 甘肃省农业生产条件

指　标	单位	1978 年	1992 年	1993 年	1993 年比下列年份(±)%	
					1978 年	1992 年
一. 耕地面积	**万亩**	5 343.33	5 223.55	5 221.73	−2.28	−0.03
#山地	万亩	3 461.07	3 376.21	3 370.31	−2.62	−0.17
川地	万亩	1 467.83	1 450.42	1 459.02	−0.60	0.59
塬地	万亩	414.43	396.92	392.40	−5.32	−1.14
二. 主要农机拥有量						
1. 农业机械总动力	千瓦	211 825	6 341 143	6 637355	206.98	4.67
2. 大中型拖拉机	台	13 719	19 254	17 415	26.94	−9.55
3. 小型拖拉机	台	38 308	243 798	260 634	580.36	6.91
4. 大中型机引农具	部	25 154	21 344	19 310	−23.23	−9.53
5. 粮食加工机械	部	63 066	87 237	87 470	38.70	0.27
6. 饲料加工机械	部	44 566	46 886	47 013	5.49	0.27
7. 农用排灌动力机械动力	亿瓦特	14.31	9.97	9.87	−0.31	−1.00
8. 农用水泵	台		43 375	44 462		2.51
9. 喷灌机械	套		1 468	1 764		20.16
10. 联合收割机	台	173	406	407	135.26	0.25
11. 机动脱粒机	台	18 923	12 658	12 947	−31.58	2.28
12. 农用载重汽车	辆	1 594	11 847	11 552	624.72	−2.49
13. 畜力胶轮车	万辆	4.53	4.98	4.89	7.95	−1.81
三. 有效灌溉面积	**万亩**	1 273.12	1 327.37	1 349.70	6.10	1.68
四. 农业劳动力	**万人**	534.80	696.57	678.90	26.95	−2.54
#种植业	万人		614.85	642.12		4.44
林业	万人		4.36	5.41		24.08
牧业	万人		28.31	30.63		8.19
副业	万人		48.87			
渔业	万人		0.18	0.74		311.11
五. 农村固定资产原值	**亿元**		141.75	150.44		6.13
#生产性固定资产原值	亿元		68.24	74.19		8.72

9—4 农业现代化

指标	单位	1978年	1992年	1993年	1993年比下列年份(±)%	
					1978年	1992年
一.农业机械化						
当年机耕地面积	万亩	1 402.63	1 574.62	1 629.24	6.16	3.47
占耕地面积	%	26.25	30.15	31.20	18.86	3.48
当年机播面积	万亩	239.81	974.54	907.93	278.60	−6.84
占总播面积	%	4.56	17.74	16.63	264.69	−6.26
二.农业水利化						
有效灌溉面积	万亩	1 273.12	1 327.37	1 349.70	6.02	1.68
占总播种面积	%	24.21	24.17	24.73	2.18	2.32
水平梯田面积	万亩	808.29	1 472.33	1 562.36	93.29	6.15
条田面积	万亩	946.56	1 070.48	1 111.89	18.31	4.62
三.农业电气化						
农村用电量	万千瓦时	76 804.05	203 821.54	218 360.69	184.31	7.13
#农村生产用电	万千瓦时		162 552.43	172 386.48		106.05
农民生活用电	万千瓦时		41 269.11	45 974.21		11.40
农村水电站	个	53	300	282	432.08	−6.00
#村及村以下办水电站	个	676	179	182	−73.08	1.68
已通电的村	个	7 082	14 222	14 705	107.64	3.40
占全省总数	%	47.48	80.46	83.04	74.90	3.21
四.农业化学化						
农用化肥施用量(实物量)	万吨	7.56	139.01	153.94	1 036.24	10.74
农用化肥施用量(折纯量)	万吨		40.02	43.35		108.32
农药施用量	吨		7 522.34	555.07		−26.21
农用塑料薄膜使用量	吨		20 954.53	28 293.07		35.02

9—5 生产性固定资产情况

指标	单位	1990年	1992年	1993年	1993年为1992年(%)
一.年末生产性固定资产原值(户均)		1 262.51	1 543.31	1 607.18	104.14
1.役畜.产品畜	元	496.86	502.80	567.73	129.91
2.大中型铁木农具	元	115.70	112.14	133.54	119.08
3.农林牧渔业机械	元	205.73	343.11	353.37	102.99
4.工业机械	元	61.95	60.72	42.54	70.06
5.运输机械	元	174.91	263.11	288.02	109.47
6.生产用房	元	170.09	200.29	221.98	110.83
7.其他	元	37.26	61.14		
二.年末主要生产性资产拥有量(百户平均)					
1.汽车	辆		1.00	0.17	17.00
2.大中型拖拉机	台	0.33	0.50	1.00	200.00
3.小型和手扶拖拉机	台	8.00	8.90	11.50	129.21
4.机动脱粒机	台	1.00	0.40	0.89	222.50
5.胶轮大车	辆	4.00	1.80	1.94	107.78
6.胶轮手推车	辆	25.00	64.90	75.78	116.76
7.抽水机	台	0.10	0.10	0.17	170.00
8.水泵	台	0.10	0.30	0.28	93.33

9—6 主要年份农.林.牧.副.渔.业产值和发展速度

年 份	总计	农业	林业	牧业	副业	渔业
一.绝对数(万元)						
(按1970年不变价计算)						
1978	214 378	162 588	5 297	38 882	7 600	11
1980	223 350	171 510	5 400	38 629	7 800	11
(按1980年不变价计算)						
1980	286 945	217 383	13 734	48 004	7 800	24
1985	421 501	276 869	31 460	88 052	25 052	68
1990	565 362	365 546	20 875	128 017	50 498	426
(按1990年不变价计算)						
1990	1 128 045	710 576	45 134	316 215	54 681	1439
1992	1 238 032	764 391	49 281	350 325	72 162	1873
1993	1 345 057	841 186	51 476	374 711	75 511	2173
(按当年价格计算)						
1980	272 886	212 176	6 509	47 379	6 800	22
1985	488 182	320 726	36 296	104 545	26 525	90
1990	1 030 526	676 084	32 679	263 228	56 380	2156
1992	1 227 042	795 132	41 310	311 061	76 227	3312
1993	1 404 213	910 626	47 260	361 135	80 974	4218
二.构成(以农业总产值为100)						
1978年	100.00	75.84	2.47	18.14	3.55	
1980年	100.00	75.76	4.79	16.73	2.72	
1985年	100.00	65.69	7.46	20.89	5.94	0.02
1990年	100.00	62.99	4	28.03	4.85	0.13
1992年	100.00	61.74	3.98	28.30	5.83	0.15
1993年	100.00	62.54	3.83	27.86	5.61	0.16
三.发展速度(1978年=100)						
1979年	93.30	91.50	88.70	101.30	93.40	118.20
1980年	104.20	105.50	101.90	99.40	102.60	100.00
1985年	153.00	134.40	233.50	182.20	329.60	283.30
1990年	205.20	177.40	155.00	264.90	664.40	1 775.00
1992年	222.10	190.80	169.20	293.50	876.80	2 312.30
1993年	244.76	209.99	176.72	313.96	917.56	2 680.39
平均年增长速度						
"七五"时期	6.05	5.71	—7.88	15.05	15.05	44.34
1992—1993年	8.64	10.05	4.46	6.96	4.64	16.02

9—7 主要年份农村社会总产值构成和发展速度

单位:万元

年 份	农村社会总产值	农业总产值	.工业总产值	建筑业总产值	交通运输业产值	商业饮食业产值
一.绝对数(现行价)						
1980	323 415	273 886	30 623	5 660	3 239	10007
1985	677 502	488 182	74 644	57 768	19 277	37 631
1990	1 697 138	1 030 526	367 555	78 085	112199	108 773
1992	2 240 051	1 227 042	564 479	114 387	170168	163 975
1993	2 989 682	1 404 213	902 229	146 126	258016	279 098
二.构成(%)						
1980	100.00	84.70	9.50	1.70	1.00	3.10
1985	100.00	72.10	11.00	8.50	2.80	5.60
1990	100.00	60.70	21.70	4.60	6.60	6.40
1992	100.00	54.80	25.20	5.10	7.60	7.30
1993	100.00	46.97	30.18	4.88	8.63	9.34
三.发展速度(1980年=100)						
1985	209.50	178.20	243.80	1 020.60	595.20	376.00
1990	524.80	376.30	1 200.30	1 379.60	3 464.00	1 086.90
1992	692.60	448.00	1 843.30	2 021.00	5 253.70	1 638.60
1993	924.41	512.70	2 946.25	2 581.73	7 965.92	2 788.03
平均年增长速度(%)						
"七五"时期	20.20	15.10	37.60	6.20	42.20	23.70
1992—1993年	33.46	14.44	59.84	27.71	51.59	70.18

9—8 甘肃省农业分项产值

指标	绝对数(万元)		构成(%)		指数
	1992年	1993年	1992年	1993年	93年为92年%
农业总产值	1 227 042.02	1 404 212.88	100.00	100.00	108.64
一.种植业产值	795 131.54	910 625.61	64.80	64.85	110.05
(一)农作物主要产品产值	715 524.36	824 217.48	90.00	90.51	110.61
1.粮食作物	411 313.18	471 725.68	57.48	57.23	108.67
2.经济作物	148 782.44	173 801.32	20.79	21.09	115.76
3.蔬菜.瓜果	91 138.04	109 366.01	12.74	13.27	104.31
4.茶桑水果	50 758.62	55 958.73	7.09	6.79	125.80
5.饲料绿肥作物	13 070.69	12 907.17	1.83	1.57	94.60
6.其他农作物	461.39	458.57	0.07	0.05	107.22
(二)农作物副产品产值	79 607.18	86 408.13	10.00	9.49	104.99
1.粮食作物	72 370.30	78 488.75	90.91	90.83	105.21
2.经济作物	7 236.88	7 919.38	9.09	9.17	102.20
二.林业产值	41 310.45	47 259.76	3.37	3.36	104.46
1.林木产值	23 546.51	24 681.91	57.00	52.23	98.62
2.林产品	11 203.88	15 147.70	27.12	32.05	122.31
3.竹木采伐	6 560.06	7 430.15	15.88	15.72	105.29
三.牧业产值	311 061.16	361 135.33	25.35	25.73	107.03
1.大小家畜	208 983.20	248 215.92	67.18	68.73	110.31
2.家禽饲养	35 242.06	37 102.63	11.33	10.28	86.16
3.活的畜禽产品	65 413.46	74 476.62	21.03	20.62	105.59
4.其他动物饲养	1 421.55	1 340.46	0.46	0.37	91.77
四.副业产值	76 227.31	80 973.73	6.21	5.73	112.21
1.采集	16 159.28	18 147.74	21.20	22.41	104.25
2.捕猎	67.63	160.41	0.09	0.20	366.68
3.农民家庭兼营手工业	60 000.40	62 665.58	78.71	77.39	104.44
五.渔业产值	3 311.56	4 218.45	0.27	0.30	116.01
1.捕捞	81.99	108.76	2.48	2.58	120.82
2.养殖	3 229.57	4 109.69	97.52	97.42	115.77

9—9 农业净产值

单位:万元

指　标	1985年	1990年	1992年	1993年	1993年比1990年净增加额
净产值合计	301 416	638 928	744 923	854 425	215 497
种植业	195 043	407 035	466 151	528 214	121 179
林　业	24 333	25 788	26 810	31 415	6 627
牧　业	63 588	163 469	190 116	228 780	65 311
副　业	18 397	41 808	59 079	62 350	20 542
渔　业	55	1 828	2 767	3 666	1 838

9—10 农业商品产值

指　标	1990年	1992年	1993年	1993年比1992年(±)%
农业商品产值	420 948.28	559 284.94	676 830.63	21.02
种植业	224 660.37	302 577.33	372 585.26	23.14
林　业	8 739.21	11 413.41	15 169.49	32.91
牧　业	137 407.52	175 357.34	215 368.51	22.82
副　业	48 463.83	67 421.30	70 392.70	4.41
渔　业	1 677.35	2 515.56	3 314.67	31.77

9—11 农业生产基本情况

年　　份	耕地面积（万亩）	机耕面积占耕地面积的比重（%）	有效灌溉面积占耕地面积的比重（%）	每亩化肥施用量（公斤）	农业机械总动力（万千瓦）
1978	5 343	26.25	23.83	14.00	211 825
1980	5 331	18.30	23.97	11.50	356 169
1985	5 236	15.98	23.82	13.88	439 381
1990	5 215	27.13	24.58	24.46	568 116
1992	5 224	30.14	25.41	26.61	6 341 143
1993	5 222	31.20	25.85	29.48	6 637 355

9—12 农作物播种面积

单位:万亩

指　　标	1978年	1990年	1992年	1993年	1993年比下列年份(±)%	
					1978年	1992年
总播种面积	5 258.68	5 417.02	5 492.39	5 458.09	3.79	—0.62
粮食作物	4 493.93	4 312.73	4 340.31	4 269.04	—5.00	—1.64
#小麦	2 140.52	2 187.37	2 077.82	2 105.34	—1.64	1.32
玉米	449.66	450.59	480.58	463.43	3.06	—3.57
大豆	44.82	91.47	105.42	129.00	187.82	22.37
经济作物	339.45	578.24	635.68	688.49	102.83	8.31
#棉花	16.02	8.93	18.83	18.16	13.36	—3.56
油料	250.26	453.53	463.10	463.03	85.02	—0.02
甜菜	14.48	28.95	31.99	36.56	152.49	14.29
其他农作物	425.30	526.05	516.40	500.56	1.09	—3.07
#蔬菜	67.74	95.43	112.84	116.77	72.38	3.48

9—13 主要年份农作物产量

单位:万吨

指 标	1978年	1985年	1990年	1992年	1993年
粮 食	510.55	530.55	686.20	689.18	750.26
#谷 物	458.13	479.49	585.68	582.74	633.54
豆 类	5.37	6.37	39.44	39.24	52.36
薯 类	47.05	44.69	61.08	67.20	64.36
棉 花	0.34	0.51	0.79	1.75	1.28
油 料	8.60	22.65	33.65	36.48	37.53
甜 菜	5.81	61.62	72.35	94.22	104.62
大 麻	0.36	0.36	0.27	0.25	0.28
烟 叶	0.48	1.01	2.73	5.13	5.32
#烤 烟	0.18	0.38	2.22	4.33	4.53
药 材	1.28	3.23	2.64	3.23	5.29
蔬 菜		116.20	204.58	232.50	249.40
水 果	11.69	19.91	38.49	47.12	59.66

9—14 主要年份农作物产量增长速度

指 标	1993年为下列年份的%				1978年—1993年平均增长%
	1978年	1985年	1990年	1992年	
粮 食	146.95	141.41	109.34	108.86	2.60
#谷 物	138.29	132.13	108.17	108.72	2.18
豆 类	975.05	821.98	13.11	133.44	16.40
薯 类	136.79	144.01	105.37	95.78	2.11
棉 花	376.47	250.98	162.03	73.14	9.24
油 料	436.40	165.70	111.53	102.88	10.32
甜 菜	1 800.69	169.78	144.60	111.04	21.25
大 麻	77.78	77.78	103.70	112.00	-1.67
烟 叶	1 108.33	526.73	194.87	103.70	17.39
#烤 烟	2 516.67	1 192.11	204.05	104.62	23.99
药 材	413.28	163.78	200.38	163.78	9.92
蔬 菜	18.00	214.63	121.91	107.27	10.02
水 果	510.35	299.65	155.00	126.61	11.48

9—15 按人口计算的粮·棉·油占有量和亩产量

年　份	按人口计算的占有量(公斤/人)			平均亩产量(公斤/亩)		
	粮食	棉花	油料	粮食	棉花	油料
一.绝对数						
1978	273.00	0.18	4.50	113.50	21.00	34.00
1980	255.60	0.14	7.30	111.50	32.00	48.00
1985	259.90	0.30	11.20	127.50	59.00	66.00
1986	266.00	0.20	12.60	133.00	47.00	70.00
1987	251.70	0.24	12.70	125.00	70.00	68.00
1988	277.70	0.23	14.30	142.00	71.00	67.00
1989	294.50	0.24	14.00	151.00	78.00	69.00
1990	307.70	0.35	15.00	159.00	89.00	74.00
1991	290.70	0.55	14.90	155.00	103.00	70.00
1992	305.40	0.77	15.98	161.00	93.00	79.00
1993	323.53	0.55	16.19	176.30	70.00	81.00
二.发展速度						
(1978年=100)						
1980	93.63	77.78	162.22	98.24	152.38	141.18
1985	95.20	166.67	248.89	112.35	280.59	194.12
1986	97.44	111.11	280.00	117.18	223.81	205.88
1987	93.20	133.33	282.22	110.13	333.33	200.00
1988	101.72	127.78	317.78	125.11	338.10	197.06
1989	107.88	133.33	311.11	133.04	371.43	202.94
1990	112.71	194.44	333.33	140.09	423.81	217.65
1991	106.48	305.55	331.11	136.56	490.48	205.88
1992	111.87	427.78	355.11	141.85	442.86	232.35
1993	118.51	305.55	359.78	155.33	333.33	238.24

9—16 主要农产品商品量及商品率

指　标	单位	1990 年	1992 年	1993 年	1993 年比 1992 年(±)%
商品粮数量	吨	1 315 496.00	1 434 517.00	1 702 674.27	18.69
商品率	%	19.20	20.60	22.82	10.78
商品棉数量	吨	7 794.00	16 809.00	12 037.50	—28.39
商品率	%	98.30	95.90	93.83	—2.16
商品油数量	吨	151 720.00	149 755.00	160 665.69	7.29
商品率	%	45.10	41.10	42.81	4.16
出售猪头数	万头	249.00	211.00	303.34	43.76
商品率	%	53.30	75.90	56.22	—25.93
绵羊毛出售量	吨	11 861.00	11 599.00	11 812.14	1.84
商品率	%	76.30	78.10	76.65	—1.86
鲜蛋出售量	吨	56 440.00	65 631.00	68 713.59	4.70
商品率	%	66.30	67.30	67.33	1.00

9—17 水果生产

指　标	单位	1978 年	1990 年	1992 年	1993 年	1993 年比 1992 年(±)%
水果产量	吨	116 860.00	384 879.35	471 214.29	596 617.23	26.61
#苹果	吨	42 877.20	174 530.60	226 085.86	315 177.89	39.41
梨	吨	33 731.05	63 298.29	93 630.71	115 808.59	23.69
葡萄	吨	331.15	6 839.24	7 473.52	6 035.44	—19.24
红枣	吨	4 483.65	12 378.92	8 158.71	7 543.01	—7.55
柿子	吨	17 650.85	13 477.34	12 535.82	9 803.29	—21.81
杏子	吨			71 311.55	81 490.85	14.27
果园面积	万亩	52.61	246.86	278.52	325.83	16.99
#苹果园	万亩		172.50	189.61	226.65	19.54
梨园	万亩		37.73	46.76	53.98	15.44

9—18 主要年份牲畜年末存栏数和肉蛋鱼产量

年　份	存栏数(万头.万只.头.只)			产量(万吨.公斤)				
	大牲畜	猪	羊	牛肉产量	猪肉产量	羊肉产量	禽蛋	鱼产量(吨)
一.总产量								
1978	366.08	474.99	1 043.22	0.37	11.32	1.20		
1980	392.38	423.94	1 187.50	0.47	12.26	1.22		
1985	507.88	546.51	912.76	1.33	25.80	2.29	5.01	
1986	538.93	574.68	976.61	1.96	24.84	2.52	6.04	
1987	556.14	529.48	1 018.76	2.64	24.76	3.15	6.81	
1988	569.35	548.93	1 096.08	3.13	26.69	2.94	7.45	
1989	577.80	574.00	1 128.70	3.00	27.90	3.30	7.78	
1990	584.04	594.74	1 109.83	3.49	30.15	3.83	8.52	
1991	585.23	596.97	1 019.81	4.15	32.20	5.12	9.41	4 292.32
1992	590.69	626.96	1 012.18	5.21	34.87	4.43	9.75	4 845.89
1993	596.38	645.10	1 025.58	5.61	38.20	5.30	10.21	5 271.64
二.人均占有量								
1978	0.20	0.25	0.56					
1980	0.21	0.22	0.62	0.25	6.39	0.64		
1985	0.25	0.28	0.45	0.65	12.65	1.12	2.45	0.03
1986	0.26	0.28	0.47	0.95	11.99	1.52	2.92	0.06
1987	0.26	0.25	0.48	1.26	11.77	1.50	3.24	0.09
1988	0.27	0.26	0.51	1.47	12.50	1.38	3.49	0.10
1989	0.24	0.26	0.52	1.38	12.80	1.52	3.58	0.14
1990	0.26	0.27	0.50	1.57	13.52	2.30	3.82	0.16
1991	0.26	0.26	0.45	2.31	15.44	1.96	4.17	0.19
1992	0.26	0.28	0.44	2.28	15.27	1.94	4.27	0.21
1993	0.26	0.28	0.44	2.42	16.48	2.29	4.40	0.23
三.人均占有量增长速度								
(1978年=100)								
1980	0.05	−0.12	0.11					
1985	0.25	0.12	−0.20					
1986	0.30	0.12	−0.16					
1987	0.30		−0.14					
1988	0.35	0.04	−0.09					
1989	0.20	0.04	−0.08					
1990	0.30	0.08	−0.11					
1991	0.30	0.04	−0.20					
1992	0.30	0.12	−0.20					
1993	0.30	0.12	−0.21					

9—19 林业生产

指　　标	单位	1978年	1985年	1990年	1992年	1993年
一.当年造林面积	万亩	75.44	345.73	210.87	233.06	248.25
#防护林	万亩		104.28	71.72	79.69	76.07
用材林	万亩		195.69	76.25	74.99	72.78
经济林	万亩		45.45	40.50	49.35	68.46
二.幼林抚育实际面积	万亩		243.25	217.66	227.43	200.46
三.成林抚育面积	万亩		77.95	98.62	178.70	141.87
四.迹地更新	万亩	11.43	9.53	5.30	2.72	5.90
五.当年零星(四旁)植树	万株	20 494.14	16 384.58	11 476.64	10743.92	10 265.32
六.年末实有育苗面积	万亩	11.63	46.56	11.97	13.47	11.29
#本年新育面积	万亩	1.17	23.37	6.22	7.95	6.99
七.林产品产量						
#油桐籽	吨		395.89	339.89	489.32	952.08
核　桃	吨		7 937.85	13 003.36	15 702.10	18 836.88
毛　栗	吨		155.70	392.30	436.39	281.96
花　椒	吨		1 421.25	2 858.10	2 920.57	3 352.04
木　耳	吨		176.25	251.74	266.61	309.77
八.集体和个人采伐的木材	万立方米		19.16	17.24		

9—20 种 草

单位:万亩

指 标	1985 年	1990 年	1992 年	1993 年
一.种草面积	1 168.72	1 143.45	1 095.20	1 055.60
#当年种植	627.42	394.26	375.47	346.88
耕地种草	569.46	506.64	450.12	417.12
三荒地种草	408.61	527.32	550.16	547.00
退耕地种草	190.65	109.49	94.92	91.48
二.草原建设				
草原围栏面积	101.82	306.85	282.37	307.60
草原补播改良面积	15.52	23.36	20.31	20.31

9—21 受灾面积和成灾面积

单位:千公顷

年份	受灾面积	成灾面积	成灾面积占受灾面积%	水灾			旱灾		
				受灾面积	成灾面积	成灾面积占受灾面积%	受灾面积	成灾面积	成灾面积占受灾面积%
1978	1 583.06	1 276.61	80.60	123.25			780.05		
1979	2 407.09	2 005.96	83.30	188.38			1 312.60		
1980	1 543.09	1 328.82	86.10	92.86			876.07		
1981	2 750.85	238 102.00	86.50	230.76			1 761.92		
1982	2 500.22	2 126.91	85.10	43.74			1 895.75		
1983	1 425.44	1 165.91	81.80	140.54			347.30		
1984	1 789.05	1 453.11	81.20	473.53			177.00		
1985	1 878.39	1 572.56	83.70	150.01			262.67		
1986	1 979.17	1 545.05	78.10	128.44			921.74		
1987	2 454.32	2 008.38	81.80	59.84			1 727.35		
1988	1 938.67	1 421.04	73.30	226.00			704.49		
1989									
1990									
1991	2 697.03	1 919.03	71.20	104.49	69.48	66.50	1591.99	1 212.44	76.20
1992	2 311.45	1 759.20	76.10	230.74	161.98	70.20	1535.93	1 210.35	78.80
1993	1 042.97	678.47	65.05	79.76	53.30	66.83	243.75	176.98	72.61

9—22 乡镇企业基本情况

指　　标	单位	1985年	1990年	1992年	1993年
一.企业数	个	84 640	211 451	239 472	274 658
1.按隶属关系分					
乡办	个	5 708	6 700	6 441	7 242
村办	个	6 555	6 314	6 923	8 047
合作	个	8 659	9 554	8 430	8 567
个体	个	63 718	188 883	217 678	250 802
2.按行业分					
农业	个	1 664	1 931	2 302	2 754
工业	个	5 879	76 121	83 483	92 486
建筑业	个	1 949	7 719	7 791	9 331
交通运输业	个	1 061	54 484	63 775	72 015
批发.零售.餐饮业	个	799	56 312	66 062	79 241
#餐饮业	个				20 985
服务业	个	518	10 898	12 420	14 866
其他	个	393	3 986	3 639	3 965
二.职工人数		68.34	129.37	143 164.00	166.46
1.按隶属关系分					
乡办	万人	26.91	33.57	36.66	41.41
村办	万人	15.03	17.01	18.48	21.04
合作	万人	10.12	14.59	14.09	15.95

9—22 续 1

指　　标	单位	1985 年	1990 年	1992 年	1993 年
个体	万人	16.28	64.20	74.41	88.06
2. 按行业分					
农业	万人	0.95	1.49	1.93	2.28
工业	万人	17.16	54.68	60.03	69.05
建筑业	万人	21.12	35.34	38.25	44.39
交通运输业	万人	1.49	17.25	20.13	22.80
批发.零售.餐饮业	万人	0.43	13.78	16.98	21.46
#餐饮业	万人	0.35	9.90	12.43	5.58
服务业	万人	0.53	3.33	3.18	3.76
其他	万人	0.26	3.50	3.14	2.72
三. 总产值(1990 年价计算)	万元	193 453.87	740 803.31	1 119 029.64	1 772 242.26
1. 按隶属关系分					
乡办	万元	97 807.91	247 240.95	375 787.26	565 925.47
村办	万元	42 021.59	110 280.17	160 855.54	260 173.41
合作	万元	21 771.88	83 236.72	104 336.97	170 705.85
个体	万元	31 852.49	300 045.47	478 049.87	775 437.53
2. 按行业分					
农业	万元	1 526.10	7 589.87	10 311.97	18 204.05
工业	万元	69 839.31	383 903.73	580 201.82	889 857.21
建筑业	万元	57 768.35	146 308.47	214 641.33	347 238.82

9—22 续 2

指　标	单位	1985 年	1990 年	1992 年	1993 年
交通运输业	万元	4 738.78	112 199.49	170 168.09	258 016.17
批发.零售.餐饮业	万元	2 724.44	90 801.75	143 706.43	258 926.01
#餐饮业	万元				59 732.38
服务业	万元	1 642.65			
其他	万元	984.83			
四.总产值(按当年价计算)	万元	124 541.52	723 354.10	1 103 251.28	1 784 435.13
1.按隶属关系分					
乡办	万元	87 450.88	229 075.42	362 580.31	568 754.00
村办	万元	37 090.64	105 857.90	156 028.47	262 318.62
合作	万元		86 703.25	105 291.93	173 158.41
个体	万元		301 717.53	479 350.57	780 204.10
2.按行业分					
农业	万元	1 281.39	6 486.51	10 256.01	18 025.40
工业	万元	55 395.89	367 557.88	564 479.42	902 228.73
建筑业	万元	57 768.35	1 463 081.47	214 641.33	347 238.82
交通运输业	万元	4 738.78	112 199.49	170 168.09	258 016.17
批发.零售.餐饮业	万元	2 724.44	90 801.75	143 706.43	258 926.01
#餐饮业	万元				59 732.38
服务业	万元	1 642.65			
其他	万元	984.83			

9—23 乡镇企业主要财务指标

单位:万元

指标	1985年	1990年	1992年	1993年
总收入	144 575.19	622 907.68	981 754.36	1 554 076.00
费用支出	122 447.55	540 368.06	858 655.15	515 474.94 *
生产费用		458 342.02	707 728.10	36 487.67 *
利润总额		58 793.99	87 774.56	132 497.00
实际上交国家税金	5 959.15	20 624.14	31 419.54	48 373.00
纯利润	16 168.49	53 051.82	78 086.54	107 855.08
工资总额	44 034.37	127 198.35	172 737.38	231 562.03
固定资产原值		278 191.72	377 826.01	506 288.19
本年提取折旧		20 869.70	29 046.60	25 283.59 *
年未占有流动资金		144 429.66	232 155.80	277 328.39 *
定额流动资金平均余额		82 797.12	144 063.01	232 382.65 *
自有流动资金		56 868.00	92 588.10	
本年银行贷款总额		56 610.88	86 731.59	108 010.84 *
本年银行贷款余额		66 154.86	87 058.96	95 439.67 *
利息支出		8 206.34	10 235.08	8 288.11 *
亏损企业(个)		367.00	250.00	204.00
亏损金额		1 626.68	1 204.64	1 404.68

注:“*”口经为乡村两级。

十、工　业

统计指标解释

·之十·

【国家财政总支出】是国家政权为行使其职能,对筹集的财政资金进行有计划的分配使用的总称。国家财政总支出,体现政府的活动范围和方向,反映财政资金的分配关系。财政总支出主要包括基本建设支出、增拨企业流动资金、企业挖潜改造资金、新产品试制费、地质勘探费、工交商部门事业费、支援农村生产支出和各项农业事业费、文教科学卫生事业费、抚恤和社会救济费、国防费、行政管理费及债务支出。

1. 基本建设支出:是指国家预算内的基本建设拨款,不包括国家预算外自筹的各种基本建设资金。为加强基本建设投资规模的控制,提高这部分财政资金的使用效益,从1985年起,对预算内基本建设拨款实行拨款改贷款的新管理办法,即由原来直接无偿的拨给建设单位,改为拨给建设银行视同信贷基金管理,建设银行根据国家预算安排的基建项目,给予有偿贷款,用投产后新增利润还本付息。从1988年起,为了进一步提高投资效益,使投资活动的管理符合发展市场经济的要求,并保证重点建设有稳定的资金来源,国家建立了中央基本建设基金制,实行专款专用,每年在国家预算内列收列支。基本建设基金分为经营性的和非经营性的两部分。各专业投资公司对经营性建设项目执行基本建设基金贷款,各主管部门对非经营性建设项目执行基本建设基金拨款。

2. 增拨企业流动资金:是指国家预算增拨各部门所属国有企业的流动资金和增拨银行的信贷资金。

3. 企业挖潜改造资金　是指国家预算安排用于企业挖潜、革新、改造方面的资金。企业用于挖潜、革新、改造方面的资金,主要来自企业的更新改造资金、大修理基金等自有资金及银行贷款,国家预算安排的挖潜、革新、改造资金主要用于支持重点行业的技术改造。

4. 文教、科学、卫生事业费:是指国家预算用于科学、文化、教育、卫生、公费医疗、体育、通讯和广播、地震、海洋、文物、计划生育等方面的事业费。

【能源消费弹性系数】是反映能源消费增长速度与国民经济增长速度之间比例关系的指标。其计算公式为:

能源消费弹性系数＝电力生产量年平均增长速度÷国民经济年平均增长速度

【电力消费弹性系数】是反映电力消费增长速度与国民经济增长速度之间比例关系的指标。其计算公式为:

电力消费弹性系数＝电力消费量年平均增长速度÷国民经济年平均增长速度

【保险金额】指的是保险对象的投保价值,也是保险承担经济补偿或给付的最高金额。

10—1 工业企业单位个数

单位:个

指　标	1990年	1991年	1992年	1993年	1993年为下列年份的%	
					1990年	1992年
总　计	12 768	14 684	14 991	14 768	115.66	98.51
一.国有经济	1 613	1 630	1 624	1 639	101.61	100.92
中央企业	105	99	104	102	97.14	98.08
地方企业	1 508	1 531	1 520	1 537	101.92	101.12
二.集体经济	5 063	5 182	5 235	5 294	104.56	101.13
#县(市.区)属企业	721	725	708	1 149	159.36	162.29
三.私营经济				10		
四.联营经济	12	6	7	27	225.00	385.71
五.股份制经济				15		
六.外商投资经济		4	6	12		200.00
中外合资经营企业				11		
中外合作经营企业		4	6	1		16.67
外资企业						
七.港.澳.台投资经济	7	2	2	13	185.71	650.00
与大陆合资经营企业				12		
与大陆合作经营企业	7	2	2			
港.澳.台独资企业				1		
八.其他经济	2		2			
在总计中:轻工业	9 075	11 182	10 936	10 229	112.72	93.54
重工业	3 693	3 502	4 055	4 539	122.91	111.94
在总计中:大型企业	65	66	60	65	100.00	108.33
中型企业	105	103	126	122	116.19	96.83
小型企业	12 598	14 515	14 805	14 581	115.74	98.49
附:城镇联营工业和个体工业	6 071	7 860	8 114	7 758	127.79	95.61
#城镇个体工业	5 735	7 675	7 759	7 489	130.58	96.52
村及村以下工业	70 645	75 383	79 117	81 790	115.78	103.38

10—2 主要年份全部工业总产值

单位:万元

年　份	工业总产值	按经济类型分			按轻重工业分	
		国有工业	集体工业	其他	轻工业	重工业
1952	24 169	8 807	226	15 136	15 637	8 532
1957	63 471	47 662	12 313	3 496	25 784	37 687
1965	201 417	193 718	7 699		40 452	160 965
1970	422 769	409 068	13 701		82 318	340 451
1975	631 304	597 758	33 546		128 444	502 860
1978	772 945	724 456	48 489		141 153	631 792
1980	770 887	723 953	46 904	30	153 457	617 430
1981	731 567	685 550	45 717	300	170 092	561 475
1982	795 448	745 932	49 145	371	185 493	609 955
1983	862 177	807 348	54 257	572	197 783	664 394
1984	994 081	887 941	103 103	3 037	220 644	773 437
1985	1 264 052	1 115 500	104 100	44 452	326 147	937 905
1986	1 440 020	1 245 000	130 400	64 620	372 234	1 067 786
1987	1 608 060	1 358 494	161 778	87 788	447 064	1 160 996
1988	2 039 004	1 672 003	225 146	141 855	604 812	1 434 192
1989	2 500 223	1 995 519	294 429	210 275	746 203	1 754 020
1990	2 746 265	2 172 728	369 945	195 971	781 582	1 964 683
1991	3 131 728	2 436 569	556 300	138 859	859 414	2 272 314
1992	3 692 666	2 794 511	523 152	375 003	1 001 683	2 690983
1993	5 052 478	3 748 559	703 766	600 153	1 148 377	3 904101

注:1.本表按当年价格计算。　2.工业总产值口经为全部工业包含村及村以下工业。

10－3 工业总产值指数

年份	工业总产值	按经济类型分		按轻重工业分	
		国有工业	集体工业	轻工业	重工业
一.(1952 年＝100)					
1957	242.97	507.31	4 847.64	160.32	394.44
1965	771.03	2 061.93	3 031.10	251.52	1 684.79
1970	1 618.44	4 354.04	5 385.84	511.85	3 646.35
1975	2 814.18	7 443.13	13 581.38	911.66	6 157.22
1978	3 343.77	8 486.81	27 750.44	1 095.62	7 464.06
1980	3 671.60	9 457.07	25 960.73	1 192.39	8 028.10
1981	3 426.07	8 766.67	26 000.88	1 263.87	7 388.84
1982	3 714.08	9 512.38	27 881.42	1 376.02	7 999.17
1983	4 054.06	10 374.37	30 642.48	1 479.01	8 773.46
1984	4 501.00	11 382.12	37 367.26	1 659.67	9 708.44
1985	5 314.29	13 057.62	52 492.36	2 160.15	10 859.66
1986	5 767.60	13 781.96	68 138.55	2 413.48	11 663.11
1987	6 296.17	14 642.27	81 978.31	2 815.81	12 409.70
1988	7 224.07	16 024.49	110 476.30	3 383.64	13 966.69
1989	7 810.25	17 006.08	130 049.80	3 716.41	14 996.39
1990	8 397.63	17 571.97	153 742.97	4 028.11	16 065.87
1991	8 998.06	18 657.92	167 810.45	4 197.29	17 408.98
1992	8 997.36	18 712.54	128 725.22	3 597.69	18 893.59
1993	11 751.30	21 921.44	199 091.71	3 938.63	26 069.95
二.(上年＝100)					
1952	120.59	157.44	113.00	111.69	141.21
1957	117.68	120.13	117.75	119.52	116.94
1965	128.08	128.17	128.75	140.68	125.26
1970	134.99	135.00	134.80	167.14	129.00
1975	115.82	115.06	131.48	112.81	116.62
1978	108.24	108.02	110.52	104.13	105.73
1980	105.18	106.16	94.78	107.52	104.59
1981	93.31	92.70	100.17	105.98	90.06
1982	108.41	108.51	107.23	108.87	108.26
1983	109.15	109.06	109.90	107.48	109.68
1984	111.02	109.71	121.95	112.22	110.66
1985	118.07	114.72	140.51	130.17	114.30
1986	108.53	105.55	129.81	117.73	107.40
1987	109.16	106.24	120.31	116.67	106.40
1988	114.74	109.44	134.76	120.16	112.55
1989	108.11	106.13	117.72	109.84	107.34
1990	107.52	103.62	118.22	108.39	107.13
1991	107.15	106.18	109.15	104.20	108.36
1992	114.39	110.12	123.90	114.03	114.53
1993	114.18	106.38	124.83	109.44	116.04

注：指标口经为全部工业，包含村及村以下工业。

10—4 工业总产值

单位:万元

指标	按1990年不变价格计算		按当年价格计算	
	1992年	1993年	1992年	1993年
总计(含村及村以下)	3 647 769	4 165 066	3 692 666	5 052 478
(不含村及村以下)	3 306 893	3 637 376	3 352 945	4 516 317
一.国有经济	2 732 516	2 906 914	2 794 511	3 748 559
中央	1 349 652	1 475 199	1 420 976	2 051 006
地方	1 382 864	1 431 715	1 373 536	1 697 553
二.集体经济	540 339	674 506	523 152	703 766
#县(市.区)属企业	95 063	143 540	89 116	145 703
三.私营经济		436		440
四.联营经济	2 374	5 157	3 007	8 285
五.股份制经济		6 011		7 224
六.外商投资经济	10 510	10 363	11 534	13 187
中外合资经营企业		10 122		12 927
中外合作经营企业	10 037	241	10 256	260
外资企业	473		1 278	
七.港.澳.台投资经济	1 791	3 992	1 478	4 377
与大陆合资经营企业		3 381		2 778
与大陆合作经营企业	1 791		1 478	
港.澳.台独资企业		611		1 599
八.其他经济	109		74	
在总计中:乡属企业	228 644	277 141	214 215	281 428
在总计中:轻工业	849 099	845 631	823 620	864 747
重工业	2 457 794	2 791 745	2 529 325	3 651 570
在总计中:大型工业	1 783 255	1 925 149	1 843 197	2 610 537
中型工业	474 040	506 607	484 667	611 386
小型工业	1 049 598	1 205 620	1 025 081	1 294 394
附:城镇联营工业和个体工业	19 255	29 997	19 190	30 479
#城镇个体工业	15 160	22 114	15 109	22 469
村及村以下办工业	340 876	527 690	339 721	536 161

10—5 工业总产值发展速度

指　　标	1993年为下列年份的%				1978年—1993年平均年增长速度%	1990年—1993年平均年增长速度%
	1985年	1990年	1991年	1992年		
总　　计	317.78	139.95	123.65	109.99	7.12	9.91
一.国有经济	280.32	124.39	117.15	106.38	6.04	7.55
中央	278.08	136.51	128.17	109.30	13.74	10.93
地方	282.67	113.97	107.62	103.53	2.48	4.46
二.集体经济	655.50	172.04	154.66	124.83	14.30	8.99
#县(市.区)属企业	355.30	181.24	270.81	150.99	10.02	21.92
三.私营经济						
四.联营经济	1 031.40	416.56	273.15	217.33		60.90
五.股份制经济						
六.外商投资经济		111.39	111.32	98.60		
中外合资经营企业						
中外合作经营企业	9.64	2.59	2.59	2.40		1.37
外资企业						
七.港.澳.台投资经济			286.78		222.89	
与大陆合资经营企业						
与大陆合作经营企业						
港.澳.台独资企业						
八.其他经济						
在总计中:乡属企业				121.21		
在总计中:轻工业	286.81	114.36	109.48	99.59	9.08	9.1
重工业	328.30	138.90	128.69	113.59	6.62	12.93
在总计中:大型企业	349.46	142.95	134.42	107.96	6.59	12.65
中型企业	190.17	112.91	108.66	106.87	5.36	4.13
小型企业	361.06	126.38	115.55	114.87	9.11	13.65
附:城镇联营和个体工业	1 725.94	210.42	257.62	155.79		28.14
#城镇个体工业	1 272.38	223.46	262.39	145.87		31.43
村及村以下办工业	1 325.39	232.68	213.44	154.80	22.25	32.51

注:本表口经为乡级以上发展速度。

10—6 主要年份按轻重工业分工业总产值构成和发展速度

年　份	轻工业	以农产品为原料	以非农产品为原料	重工业	采掘工业	原材料工业	制造业
一.绝对数(万元)							
按现行价格计算							
1978	144 450	91 267	53 183	628 528	57 310	401518	169 700
1980	156 696	103 241	53 455	612 525	57 652	415059	139 814
1985	306 000	211 700	94 300	916 500	117 500	488900	310 100
1990	670 021	487 372	182 649	1 880 273	212 823	1 144 367	523 083
1992	807 422	577 886	229 536	2 526 333	294 888	1 558 117	673 327
1993	838 289	593 531	244 758	3 647 549	564 526	2 237 545	845 478
二.构成(%)							
(总产值=100)							
1978	100.00	63.18	36.87	100.00	9.13	63.88	26.99
1980	100.00	65.89	34.11	100.00	9.41	67.76	22.83
1985	100.00	69.18	30.82	100.00	12.82	53.34	33.84
1990	100.00	72.74	27.26	100.00	11.32	60.86	27.82
1992	100.00	71.57	28.43	100.00	11.67	61.68	26.65
1993	100.00	70.80	29.30	100.00	15.48	61.34	23.18
三.平均年增长速度(%)							
"一五"时期	9.90			31.58			
"二五"时期	12.38			17.86			
1963—1965年	7.56			13.43			
"三五"时期	15.27			16.16			
"四五"时期	12.66	9.99	9.05	11.46	7.66	17.80	1.90
"五五"时期	5.52	6.80	3.33	5.45	4.92	8.07	—0.31
"六五"时期	13.15	13.48	12.53	6.07	11.69	1.42	14.39
"七五"时期	13.27	15.08	9.33	8.15	8.85	8.27	7.69
1978—1993年	9.08	9.32	7.84	6.62	6.64	5.64	9.56
1992—1993年	—0.41	—1.97	—0.63	13.59	15.65	14.50	9.87

注:本表口经为乡级乡以上。

10—7 主要年份分行业工业总产值构成和发展速度

行　业	工业总产值(万元)(当年价格计算)		构成(全部工业总产值=100)		1993 年为下列年份的%	
	1978 年	1993 年	1978 年	1993 年	1978 年	1992 年
总　计	772 978	4 485 838	100.00	100.00	580.33	134.56
煤炭采选业	16 743	86 335	2.17	1.93	515.65	130.33
石油和天然气开采业	31 230	381 169	4.04	8.50	1 220.52	251.38
黑色金属矿采选业	287	2 879	0.04	0.07	1 003.14	187.43
有色金属矿采选业	518	39 755	0.07	0.89	7 674.71	121.92
非金属矿采选业	2 468	36 315	0.32	0.81	1 471.43	122.73
其他矿采选业		100		0.01		
木材及竹材采运业	3 406	20 664	0.44	0.46	606.69	142.89
食品加工业	20 107	132 323	2.60	2.95	658.09	98.28
食品制造业	8 055	53 013	1.04	1.18	658.14	104.99
饮料制造业	1 010	60 913	0.13	1.36	6 030.99	126.84
烟草加工业	6 457	53 513	0.84	1.19	828.76	98.66
纺织业	25 116	118 286	3.25	2.64	470.96	96.18
服装及其他纤维制品制造业	9 673	31 140	1.25	0.69	321.93	133.71
皮革.毛皮.羽绒及其制品业	4 101	18 276	0.53	0.41	445.65	74.26
木材加工及竹藤.棕.草制造业	4 871	11 343	0.63	0.25	232.87	109.80
家具制造业		13 299		0.30		115.02
造纸及纸制品业	2 305	31 011	0.30	0.69	1 345.38	112.17
印刷业.记录媒介的复制		25 243		0.56		92.76
文教体育用品制造业	2 067	2 847	0.27	0.06	137.74	91.57
石油加工及炼焦业	68 478	462 449	8.86	10.31	675.32	151.17
化学原料肪化学制品制造业	80 692	401 128	10.44	8.94	497.11	125.87
医药制造业	4 505	52 703	0.58	1.17	1 169.88	118.73
化学纤维制造业	5 176	19 010	0.67	0.42	367.27	117.31
橡胶制品业	3 319	19 443	0.43	0.43	585.81	102.40
塑料制品业	6 821	35 192	0.88	0.79	515.94	76.44
非金属矿物制品业	32 537	255 236	4.21	5.69	784.45	147.84
黑色金属冶炼及压延加工业	15 807	347 945	2.05	7.76	2201.21	175.97
有色金属冶炼及压延加工业	97 256	814 163	12.58	18.14	837.13	140.36
金属制品业	29 491	103 914	3.82	2.33	352.36	148.79
普通机械制造业	74 186	113 462	9.60	2.53	152.94	114.72
专用设备制造业	92 788	141 911	12.00	3.16	152.94	114.73
交通运输设备制造业	9 078	74 521	1.17	1.67	820.90	123.84
武器弹药制造业		9 562		0.21		
电气机械及器材制造业		167 826		3.74		144.86
电子及通信设备制造业	15 588	56 737	2.02	1.26	363.98	68.27
仪器仪表及文化办公用机械制造业		26 555		0.59		200.02
其它制造业	29 089	30 889	3.75	0.68	106.19	93.48
电力.蒸汽.热水的生产和供应业	69 753	222 057	9.02	4.95	318.35	115.63
煤气生产和供应业		1 847		0.04		
自来水的生产和供应业		10 864		0.24		121.51

10—8 主要工业产品生产销售库存总量

(1993年)

产品名称	单位	生产量	销售量	库存量
原煤	万吨	1 805.58	1 707.28	160.69
原油	万吨	148.19	149.27	1.22
天然气	万立方米	0.13		
铁矿石原矿量	万吨	387.65	20.81	25.71
铁矿石成品量	万吨	158.54		4.94
锰矿石原矿量	万吨	4.78	1.93	2.85
锰矿石成品量	万吨	0.35	0.17	0.18
石灰石	万吨	132.33	100.17	16.26
耐火粘土成品矿	万吨	1.75	1.25	0.64
硫铁矿生产量	万吨	28.84	26.47	6.14
铳铁矿运出量	万吨	26.87	26.47	0.40
原盐	万吨	7.43	7.06	2.49
石棉	万吨	8.87	7.88	1.23
石膏	万吨	28.74	20.00	22.46
木材(全社会木材)	万立方米	53.93	53.74	0.72
小麦粉	万吨	204.99	155.36	38.45
混合饲料	万吨	3.28	3.09	5.38
食用植物油	万吨	10.77	10.54	1.11
冻畜肉	万吨	2.21	2.26	0.36
畜肉制品	万吨	1.51	1.71	
糖果	万吨	1.37	3.00	0.07
糕点	吨	11 242.00	9 695.00	1 673.00
乳制品	吨	2 030.00	2 226.00	290.00
罐头	万吨	1.44	1.26	0.44
味精	吨	497.00	353.00	266.00
饮料酒	万吨	15.67	15.55	2.23
#白酒	万吨	2.88	2.15	1.35
啤酒	万吨	12.54	13.15	0.81
卷烟	万箱	30.40	31.68	0.28
纱	吨	15 738.00	12 017.00	717.00
布	万米	3 769.39	4 429.26	526.55
印染布	万米	725.00	698.00	468.00
毛线	吨	5 260.00	4 986.00	1 251.00
呢绒	万米	685.99	746.01	696.91
毛毯	万条	116.30	124.40	42.87
丝织品	万米	39.38	44.83	15.45
服装	万件	1 303.06	1 043.10	473.12
缝制帽	万顶	98.56	66.31	66.98
皮鞋	万双	92.86	98.88	95.28
轻革	万平方米	54.46	55.68	16.98
重革	吨	233.42	230.03	30.16

10—8 续 1

(1993 年)

产品名称	单位	生产量	销售量	库存量
锯材	万立方米	6.02	5.85	0.64
人造板	万立方米	0.59	0.73	0.26
家具	万件	221.18	205.09	69.09
机制纸及纸板	万吨	15.68	14.80	3.46
#机制纸	万吨	9.17	8.90	2.59
原油加工量	万吨	496.25	495.64	9.06
汽油	万吨	110.99	103.17	4.31
煤油	万吨	29.56	30.11	0.56
柴油	万吨	111.14	103.59	2.12
燃料油	万吨	76.62	66.99	2.57
焦炭	万吨	90.32	13.44	8.64
硫酸	万吨	34.73	35.72	5.75
浓硝酸	万吨	11.53	10.03	0.28
电石	万吨	9.44	7.53	0.30
合成氨	万吨	37.31	29.15	4.76
农用化肥	万吨	26.57	26.38	2.45
#氮肥	万吨	21.70	21.71	0.45
磷肥	万吨	4.87	4.67	2.00
化学农药	万吨	0.17	0.20	0.07
乙烯	吨	68 353.00		
丙烯	吨	26 337.00		
油漆	吨	29 667.00	28 982.00	3 665.00
油墨	吨	3 948.00	4 061.00	504.00
合成橡胶	吨	46 829.00	46 857.00	455.00
火柴	万件	72.46	71.93	25.94
中成药	吨	2 708.53	2 792.73	696.29
合成纤维	万吨	1.85	1.96	0.06
轮胎外胎	万条	17.40	17.34	3.09
轮胎内胎	万条	17.00	16.00	4.00
塑料制品	吨	46 326.64	42 527.88	10 678.43
#塑料薄膜	吨	18 568.10	19 273.25	2 551.61
水泥	万吨	543.11	574.06	81.10
砖	亿块	58.61	487.92	243.72
瓦	亿片	4.92	4.94	0.81
平板玻璃	万重箱	250.70	241.90	4.71
保温瓶	万个	367.66	362.69	16.57
日用陶瓷	万件	1 537.64	1 594.91	509.94
生铁	万吨	111.59	44.42	0.12
钢	万吨	106.45	15.43	0.87
成品钢材	万吨	79.10	80.04	2.17

10—8续2　　　　　　　　　　(1993年)

产品名称	单位	生产量	销售量	库存量
铁合金	万吨	16.29	15.20	2.94
铜	吨	69 582.00	30 511.00	1 505.00
镍	吨	26 478.00	24 454.00	27.00
铝	吨	210 209.00	208 126.00	6 317.00
日用搪瓷制品	吨	1 625.00	1 609.00	266.00
日用精铝制品	吨	535.95	601.18	131.67
工业锅炉	台	825.50	789.00	222.00
内燃机	万千瓦	8.33	8.23	1.13
金属切削机床	台	923.00	751.00	251.00
轴承	万套	758.83	757.07	618.23
高中压阀门	吨	370.70	357.60	192.00
石油钻采设备	吨	13 235.00	15 678.00	4 601.00
缝纫机	万架	0.26	0.15	0.17
小型拖拉机	万台	0.65	0.66	0.04
中小农具	万件	485.95	351.54	123.06
汽车	辆	155.00	101.00	109.00
改装汽车	辆	777.00	686.00	324.00
自行车	万辆	1.92	2.52	1.25
发电设备	台(组)	150.00	120.00	30.00
交流电动机	台	21 739.70	21 254.00	6 686.10
电线	万公里	7 608.21	5 871.28	3 950.93
原电池	亿只	0.33	0.29	0.03
家用洗衣机	万台	24.95	25.04	1.13
吸尘器	万台	0.01	0.28	0.61
家用电冰箱	万台	2.47	2.78	0.79
灯泡	万只	4 297.02	4 111.84	1 693.97
灯具	万只	54.13	56.09	8.05
电话单机	万部	7.32	7.31	1.04
电子元件	万只	5 632.91	5 462.14	10 304.95
电视机	万台	10.38	10.75	1.14
#彩色电视机	万台	5.29	5.27	1.08
照相机	万架	13.32	21.97	15.21
发电量	亿千瓦小时	227.91	213.53	0.02
#水电	亿千瓦小时	102.11	101.89	0.02
煤气生产量	万立方米	30 628.00	13 913.00	
自来水供应量	万吨	57 446.22	53 598.20	1 087.10

10—9 主要工业产品产量

产品名称	单位	1978年	1990年	1992年	1993年	1993年比下列年份(±)%	
						1978年	1992年
原煤	万吨	980.34	1 564.11	1 542.36	1 805.58	84.18	17.07
原煤(标准煤量)	万吨	700.26	1 117.24	1 101.71			
原油	万吨	81.97	146.11	198.09	148.19	80.79	—25.19
全部木材	万立方米	69.35	53.91	46.63	53.93	—22.24	15.66
发电量总计	万度	1 144 848	1 713 900	2 003 200	2 279100	99.07	13.77
自来承(供应量)	万吨		43 358.98	50 525.94	57 446.22		13.70
小麦粉	万吨		110.76	343.07	204.99		—40.25
食用植物油	万吨	2.70	8.68	8.89	10.77	298.89	21.15
糖	吨	2 970.00	65 100.00	107 200.00	94 000.00	3 064.98	12.31
卷烟	万箱	10.97	27.96	29.50	30.40	177.12	3.05
化学纤维	吨	6 636.00	13 400.00	18 600.00	18 500.00	178.78	—0.54
针锦织折用纱线	万吨	0.30	0.46	0.38	0.28	—6.67	—26.32
纱总计	万吨	10 125.00	18 118.00	19 889.00	15 738.01	55.44	—20.87
布总计(长度)	万米	5 883.23	6 781.48	4 653.68	3 769.39	—35.93	—19.00
(面积)	万平方米	35 161.77	6 508.61	4 682.08	3 649.68	—29.29	—21.55
毛绒	吨	1 916.86	6 371.00	7 356.00	5 259.59	174.39	—28.50
呢绒	万米	425.24	978.62	852.59	685.99	61.32	—19.54
机制纸及纸板	吨	23 571.00	102 300.00	126 800.00	156 800.00	565.22	23.66
地毯	万平方米		210.61	237.00	329.77		39.14
汽油	万吨	42.00	66.69	100.34	110.99	164.26	10.61
煤油	万吨	26.89	27.90	31.71	29.56	9.93	—6.78
柴油	万吨	45.50	89.21	109.81	111.14	144.26	1.21
农用化肥总计	万吨	18.31	26.67	32.87	26.57	45.11	—19.17
化学农药	万吨	0.25	0.24	0.25	0.17	0.16	—36.00
水泥	万吨	155.66	358.38	489.59	543.11	248.91	10.93
平板玻璃	万重量箱	67.56	251.85	291.29	250.70	271.08	13.93
钢	万吨	15.39	66.93	93.40	106.45	591.68	13.97
生铁	万吨	46.58	48.93	101.96	111.59	139.57	9.44
缝纫机	万架		0.03		0.26		
照相机	架		51 160.00	102 020.00	133 240.00		30.60
自行车	辆	55.00	86 500.00	26 900.00	19 200.00	34 809.09	—28.62
家用电冰箱	万台		3.00	4.80	2.47		—48.54
家用洗衣机	万台		34.88	22.20	24.95		12.39
吸尘器	台		12 479.00		100.00		
电视机	万台	0.21	25.46	14.41	10.38	48.43	—27.97
彩色电视	万台		15.21	8.81	5.29		—39.95
录音机	万台		9.20	19.11			

10—10 独立核算工业企业全员劳动生产率

单位:元/人

指　　标	1990 年	1992 年	1993 年	1993 年为 1992 年的%
全　省	22 747	27 018	28 889	106.93
国有经济	26 885	30 888	32 237	104.37
中央企业	39 130	43 595	44 324	101.67
地方企业	21 129	23 958	25 116	104.83
# 县属企业	18 553	20 085	20 146	100.30
在总计中:轻工业	20 780	23 400	25 026	106.95
重工业	23 539	28 483	30 246	106.19
在总计中:大型企业	35 547	38 011	38 532	101.37
中型企业	21 521	28 437	30 988	108.97
小型企业	14 950	17 268	19 900	115.24
集体经济	11 266	15 916	19 719	123.89

10—11 全部独立核算工业企业主要经济指标

单位:万元

指标	企业单位数(个)	#亏损企业	工业总产值(当年价)	工业增加值	成品产销存生产价值
总 计	6 390	777	4 452 438	1 635 524	4 106 911
在总计中:国有经济	1 489	352	3 731 159	1 275 216	3 488 872
中央企业	92	18	2 048 606	643 510	1 873 037
地方企业	1 397	334	1 682 553	631 706	1 615 835
#县(旗)属企业	939	182	292 724	154 890	296 839
集体经济	4 843	415	689 166	341 516	588 050
#县(旗)属企业	818	144	134 503	73 891	107 354
私营经济	7		440	432	429
联营经济	14	1	6 885	5 857	6 710
股份制经济	13	3	7 224	3 230	7 140
外商投资经济	11	4	13 187	6 557	11 354
中外合资经营企业	10	4	12 927	6 413	11 231
中外合作经营企业	1		260	144	123
港、澳、台投资经济	13	2	4 377	2 716	4 356
与大陆合资经营企业	12	2	2 778	1 117	2 757
港、澳、台独资企业	1		1 599	1 599	1 599
在总计中:乡属工业	2 892	107	279 428	142 859	240 746
在总计中:轻工业	3 097	476	823 089	378 850	787 211
重工业	3 293	301	3 629 349	1 256 674	3 319 700
在总计中:大型企业	65	14	2 610 537	778 186	2 422 780
中型企业	122	35	611 386	241 765	582 606
小型企业	6 203	728	1 230 515	615 573	1 101 525
按行业分:					
煤炭采选业	241	19	86 335	48 343	77 250
石油和天然气开采业	4	1	381 169	147 698	380 681
黑色金属矿采选业	33		2 879	1 447	2 876
有色金属矿采选业	136	5	37 155	26 728	31 121
非金属矿采选业	341	19	36 215	22 334	31 438
木材及竹材采运业	5		18 164	14 653	18 594
食品加工业	471	63	126 623	66 202	108 914
食品制造业	397	67	51 313	22 721	46 682
饮料制造业	111	24	60 813	29 182	47 260

10—11 续1

单位:万元

指　　标	成品产销存		工业中间投入合计	本年应付工资	本年应付福利费
	销售价值	年末库存价值			
烟草加工业	14	2	53 213	27 780	51 708
纺织业	196	56	117 186	45 936	111 044
服装及其他纤维制品制造业	201	40	30 940	14 209	24 346
皮革、毛皮、羽绒及其制品业	119	18	17 176	8 050	16 209
木材加工及竹、藤、棕、草制品业	123	13	10 143	4 492	8 564
家具制造业	167	14	12 699	6 745	10 403
造纸及纸制品业	146	29	30 911	13 830	25 782
印刷业、记录媒介的复制	153	22	24 843	15 343	16 756
文教体育用品制造业	53	3	2 847	1 494	3 347
石油加工及炼焦业	39	4	462 349	83 586	459 929
化学原料及化学制品制造业	349	61	400 928	126 567	385 206
医药制造业	66	13	52 403	29 242	47 393
化学纤维制造业	5		19 010	4 138	18 947
橡胶制品业	40	5	19 443	7 150	18 171
塑料制品业	150	33	34 792	17 267	28 241
非金属矿物制品业	903	52	251 336	130 113	228 379
黑色金属冶炼及压延加工业	83	16	347 845	89 067	338 836
有色金属冶炼及压延加工业	61	14	814 163	243 786	655 271
金属制品业	544	30	102 514	47 389	143 724
普通机械制造业	164	18	111 062	41 698	97 937
专用设备制造业	257	26	139 011	43 451	124 846
交通运输设备制造业	132	35	73 921	26 645	55 652
武器弹药制造业	2		9 562	8 291	7 048
电气机械及器材制造业	131	10	167 326	55 865	155 570
电子及通信设备制造业	19	5	56 737	19 805	53 658
仪器仪表及文化、办公用机械制造业	28	7	26 355	9 572	24 824
其他制造业	329	36	29 389	15 774	27 096
电力、蒸汽、热水的生产和供应业	132	8	220 957	111 798	211 550
煤气生产和供应业	2		1 847	1 392	1 525
自来水的生产和供应业	43	9	10 864	5 741	10 133

10—11续2

单位:万元

	成品产销存		工业中间投入合计	本年应付工资	本年应付福利费
	销售价值	年末库存价值			
总　　计	3 887 222	472 566	2 817 155	391 686	43 916
在总计中:国有经济	3 307 063	344 422	2 456 008	318 344	35 679
中央企业	1 653 285	85 371	1 405 098	151 066	16 193
地方企业	1 653 778	259 051	1 050 910	167 278	19 486
#县(旗)属企业	300 413	62 270	137 878	27 411	2 645
集体经济	551 318	124 004	347 827	67 296	7 432
#县(旗)属企业	112 927	35 615	60 641	11 749	1 354
私营经济	310	450	8	33	7
联营经济	6 488	220	1 027	146	9
股份制经济	5 825	1 517	3 996	4 961	689
外商投资经济	12 788	415	6 630	433	42
中外合资经营企业	12 653	356	6 514	432	42
中外合作经营企业	135	59	116	1	
港、澳、台投资经济	3 430	1 538	1 659	473	58
与大陆合资经营企业	2 051	1 461	1 659	434	45
港、澳、台独资企业	1 379	77		39	13
在总计中:乡属工业	210 067	42 557	136 675	20 437	1 881
在总计中:轻工业	795 191	171 909	444 358	64 507	8 369
重工业	3 092 031	300 657	2 372 797	327 179	35 547
在总计中:大型企业	2 176 551	178 197	1 832 354	219 159	23 416
中型企业	617 514	74 435	369 627	51 012	6 665
小型企业	1 093 157	219 934	615 174	121 515	13 835
按行业分:					
煤炭采选业	76 565	8 188	38 003	31 391	2 192
石油和天然气开采业	381 447	14 291	233 471	58 090	5 599
黑色金属矿采选业	2 740	391	1 431	528	77
有色金属矿采选业	32 652	5 270	10 435	3 211	425
非金属矿采选业	27 202	9 259	13 898	3 094	303
木材及竹材采运业	17 932	733	3 511	3 115	481
食品加工业	121 085	16 959	60 439	4 743	500
食品制造业	44 257	7 409	28 599	3 424	323

10—11 续 3

单位:万元

指　　标	成品产销存		工业中间投入合计	本年应付工资	本年应付福利费
	销售价值	年末库存价值			
饮料制造业	45 710	14 900	31 633	2 653	392
烟草加工业	52 296	819	25 435	1 362	160
纺织业	113 356	42 621	71 259	14 259	2 273
服装及其他纤维制品制造业	22 255	7 405	16 730	3 435	435
皮革、毛皮、羽绒及其制品业	16 519	7 961	9 129	1 614	171
木材加工及竹、藤、棕、草制品业	7 930	1 627	5 648	1 233	225
家具制造业	16 401	2 206	5 972	1 172	98
造纸及纸制品业	24 518	6 471	17 084	2 613	313
印刷业、记录媒介的复制	16 630	2 329	9 507	2 886	334
文教体育用品制造业	2 942	1 268	1 359	301	29
石油加工及炼焦业	59 013	18 728	378 768	10 273	1 543
化学原料及化学制品制造业	390 252	33 522	274 377	18 412	1 958
医药制造业	46 542	9 315	23 158	3 536	394
化学纤维制造业	18 797	584	14 871	1 144	109
橡胶制品业	17 904	3 418	12 297	1 443	165
塑料制品业	27 636	7 060	17 539	2 125	338
非金属矿物制品业	228 208	30 536	121 257	30 223	3 102
黑色金属冶炼及压延加工业	346 784	15 965	258 781	23 855	2 560
有色金属冶炼及压延加工业	669 694	52 012	570 384	68 507	7 905
金属制品业	138 314	23 104	55 136	7 073	873
普通机械制造业	98 439	21 820	69 371	16 401	1 655
专用设备制造业	124 899	31 842	95 555	12 348	1 432
交通运输设备制造业	53 820	14 636	47 284	11 291	1 354
武器弹药制造业	8 633	898	1 272	1 652	304
电气机械及器材制造业	153 045	28 108	111 472	11 471	1 713
电子及通信设备制造业	55 115	11 375	36 934	5 881	924
仪器仪表及文化、办公用机械制造业	23 479	11 172	16 786	5 363	518
其他制造业	25 328	7 743	13 628	3 652	383
电力、蒸汽、热水的生产和供应业	367 139	424	109 161	16 036	1 994
煤气生产和供应业	1 477	197	455	117	8
自来水的生产和供应业	10 267		5 126	1 759	354

10—11 续 4　　　　单位:万元

	全部职工年平均人数(人)	资本金合计	国家	法人	个人
总　　计	1 237 282	2 422 867	2 152 635	228 212	17 780
在总计中:国有经济	896 315	2 142 070	2 078 192	46 118	5 958
中央企业	332 278	1 203 026	1 192 386	10 641	
地方企业	564 037	939 044	885 806	35 477	5 958
#县(旗)属企业	133 780	160 691	142 757	14 674	488
集体经济	334 864	255 291	71 238	163 223	11 647
#县(旗)属企业	70 179	61 867	32 291	25 578	2 167
私营经济	253	128		32	96
联营经济	631	860	721	115	24
股份制经济	1 408	16 844	354	16 436	55
外商投资经济	1 354	4 468	2 130	216	
中外合资经营企业	1 321	4 369	2 061	216	
中外合作经营企业	33	99	69		
港、澳、台投资经济	2 457	3 206		2 072	
与大陆合资经营企业	2 331	3 030		2 072	
港、澳、台独资企业	126	176			
在总计中:乡属工业	138 638	79 885	22 163	46 251	6 766
在总计中:轻工业	321 660	363 856	286 112	62 986	5 643
重工业	915 622	2 059 011	1 866 523	165 226	12 137
在总计中:大型企业	499 625	1 579 723	1 512 873	55 662	4 638
中型企业	163 486	289 270	277 890	7 211	700
小型企业	574 171	553 874	361 872	165 339	12 442
按行业分:					
煤炭采选业	95 717	103 048	96 753	4 824	414
石油和天然气开采业	91 524	299 525	294 675	4 850	
黑色金属矿采选业	1 229	773	304	346	118
有色金属矿采选业	17 547	17 144	14 882	2 027	119
非金属矿采选业	17 426	8 024	5 565	1 537	401
木材及竹材采运业	9 249	8 840	8 840		
食品加工业	25 866	49 458	40 720	6 745	745
食品制造业	23 717	25 442	18 590	5 101	316
饮料制造业	13 663	39 346	28 574	9 328	143

10—11 续5

单位:万元

指标	全部职工年平均人数(人)	资本金合计	国家	法人	个人
烟草加工业	3 962	13 454	13 175	266	13
纺织业	62 906	54 793	45 084	5 852	590
服装及其他纤维制品制造业	16 812	12 247	8 493	3 217	393
皮革、毛皮、羽绒及其制品业	10 028	7 896	5 504	1 445	759
木材加工及竹、藤、棕、草制品业	6 302	4 535	3 223	1 116	102
家具制造业	8 139	3 917	2 293	1 314	166
造纸及纸制品业	18 258	13 091	9 476	3 109	413
印刷业、记录媒介的复制	12 835	12 534	10 655	1 708	165
文教体育用品制造业	1 749	1 187	631	454	41
石油加工及炼焦业	26 905	109 027	87 765	18 836	721
化学原料及化学制品制造业	83 424	235 093	219 003	14 228	1 078
医药制造业	10 711	17 030	15 000	1 859	53
化学纤维制造业	3 804	12 407	12 378	29	
橡胶制品业	6 153	7 148	5 381	1 378	367
塑料制品业	13 771	15 673	7 053	7 844	418
非金属矿物制品业	114 092	110 921	85 756	21 893	2 428
黑色金属冶炼及压延加工业	58 327	202 835	188 572	9 683	465
有色金属冶炼及压延加工业	154 640	352 003	292 122	55 799	75
金属制品业	35 848	28 603	15 523	11 751	846
普通机械制造业	46 929	52 482	43 924	7 955	130
专用设备制造业	58 110	84 829	77 581	6 141	588
交通运输设备制造业	39 575	56 232	53 559	2 524	108
武器弹药制造业	4 744	6 938	6 938		
电气机械及器材制造业	38 696	50 079	43 318	5 969	583
电子及通信设备制造业	14 421	56 390	48 851	2 939	4 600
仪器仪表及文化、办公用机械制造业	18 770	15 312	14 413	804	96
其他制造业	32 081	11 588	6 353	4 554	308
电力、蒸汽、热水的生产和供应业	34 217	300 063	298 918	617	18
煤气生产和供应业	519	463	413	50	
自来水的生产和供应业	4 616	22 497	22 377	120	

10—11 续6

单位:万元

指标	外商	年末资产负债及所有者权益			
		流动资产合计	#货币资金	#存货	#产成品
总　　计	12 996	3 194 669	213 769	1 569 323	456 316
在总计中:国有经济	5 380	2 721 948	168 056	1 338 980	347 444
中央企业		1 234 261	79 571	608 798	109 600
地方企业	5 380	1 487 687	88 485	730 182	237 844
#县(旗)属企业	2	230 425	19 562	105 133	47 576
集体经济	4 361	428 357	41 863	218 538	105 555
#县(旗)属企业	135	99 540	7 668	58 461	33 699
私营经济		528	169	359	217
联营经济		601	63	465	388
股份制经济		26 914	1 535	3 925	546
外商投资经济	2 121	11 228	327	4 744	1 140
中外合资经营企业	2 091	11 108	327	4 664	1 081
中外合作经营企业	30	120		80	59
港、澳、台投资经济	1 134	5 093	1 756	2 312	1 026
与大陆合资经营企业	958	4 095	1 756	1 529	949
港、澳、台独资企业	176	998		783	77
在总计中:乡属工业	1 984	122 734	14 755	58 939	29 288
在总计中:轻工业	2 917	658 663	45 106	326 875	131 559
重工业	10 079	2 536 006	168 663	1 242 448	324 757
在总计中:大型企业	3 605	1 810 180	112 641	914 540	186 722
中型企业	3 422	472 862	24 029	235 778	76 115
小型企业	5 969	911 627	77 099	419 005	193 479
按行业分:					
煤炭采选业		72 467	7 108	24 699	6 049
石油和天然气开采业		220 383	24 923	124 935	23 013
黑色金属矿采选业		1 748	371	525	175
有色金属矿采选业		23 823	2 067	12 278	8 709
非金属矿采选业		17 958	1 850	6 696	3 736
木材及竹材采运业		12 467	2 305	3 549	341
食品加工业	20	58 807	7 236	24 619	8 924
食品制造业	1 186	41 708	3 647	18 749	8 338
饮料制造业	1 150	49 387	1 878	25 164	9 778

10—11 续7 单位:万元

指标	外商	年末资产负债及所有者权益 流动资产合计	货币资金	存货	产成品
烟草加工业		43 593	2 102	18 552	1 196
纺织业		127 152	4 221	70 404	29 322
服装及其他纤维制品制造业		26 933	1 814	15 349	6 263
皮革、毛皮、羽绒及其制品业	129	21 735	1 231	11 462	6 736
木材加工及竹、藤、棕、草制品业		9 339	705	4 223	2 079
家具制造业	24	7 475	674	4 160	2 247
造纸及纸制品业		25 475	1 507	11 101	5 078
印刷业、记录媒介的复制		23 141	3 343	12 361	7 369
文教体育用品制造业		1 886	198	835	386
石油加工及炼焦业	1 649	97 378	12 365	52 830	13 284
化学原料及化学制品制造业	107	234 073	12 197	120 970	40 421
医药制造业	2	37 091	1 668	21 885	6 260
化学纤维制造业		17 995	504	8 235	925
橡胶制品业		14 911	834	8 136	3 388
塑料制品业	183	26 470	1 669	12 522	6 582
非金属矿物制品业	40	157 022	11 065	72 560	25 791
黑色金属冶炼及压延加工业	3 972	245 304	16 533	119 195	33 440
有色金属冶炼及压延加工业	3 912	614 552	20 172	319 434	58 337
金属制品业	23	65 056	6 079	32 091	14 875
普通机械制造业	443	124 011	5 617	70 188	21 388
专用设备制造业		173 124	4 826	104 893	32 205
交通运输设备制造业	40	78 628	4 709	43 317	14 594
武器弹药制造业		11 811	412	7 352	3 864
电气机械及器材制造业		130 798	5 186	88 223	29 120
电子及通信设备制造业		90 742	11 685	40 426	9 809
仪器仪表及文化、办公用机械制造业		49 917	1 589	18 329	6 279
其他制造业	116	20 078	2 517	9 976	4 523
电力、蒸汽、热水的生产和供应业		213 188	25 118	28 138	1 137
煤气生产和供应业		622	22	285	208
自来水的生产和供应业		6 421	1 822	677	147

10—11 续 8

单位:万元

指　　标	年末资产负债及所有者权益				年末资产负债及所有者权益
	长期投资合计	固定资产合计	固定资产原价合计	累计折旧	固定资产净值合计
总　　计	286 510	3 582 610	4 551 030	1 529 052	3 022 192
在总计中:国有经济	247 390	3 275 141	4 201 961	1 447 444	2 754558
中央企业	175 148	2 000 463	2 705 900	997 759	1 708 148
地方企业	72 242	1 274 678	1 496 061	449 685	1 046 410
#县(旗)属企业	5 202	216 652	233 650	48 732	184 934
集体经济	35 490	294 830	331 634	79 315	252 492
#县(旗)属企业	2 548	58 308	69 746	21 028	48 746
私营经济		66	66	4	61
联营经济	3	715	827	124	704
股份制经济	5	821	3 266	704	2 563
外商投资经济	3 622	9 268	10 439	1 117	9 321
中外合资经营企业	3 622	9 142	10 313	1 066	9 246
中外合作经营企业		126	126	51	75
港、澳、台投资经济		1 769	2 837	344	2 493
与大陆合资经营企业		1 504	2 531	303	2 228
港、澳、台独资企业		265	306	41	265
在总计中:乡属工业	13 570	108 615	123 330	28 852	94 596
在总计中:轻工业	32 925	486 580	547 470	147 375	400 193
重工业	253 585	3 096 030	4 003 560	1 381 677	2 621 999
在总计中:大型企业	195 288	2 509 922	3 345 043	1 190 713	2 154330
中型企业	24 679	395 132	430 571	138 637	291 940
小型企业	66 543	677 556	775 416	199 702	575 922
按行业分:					
煤炭采选业	9 762	144 384	191 722	52 932	138 803
石油和天然气开采业	6 558	621 537	718 788	267 235	451 554
黑色金属矿采选业	251	1 456	1 484	208	1 276
有色金属矿采选业	5 308	21 395	30 454	11 352	19 103
非金属矿采选业	4 592	11 560	13 187	3 699	9 509
木材及竹材采运业	2 635	11 262	12 770	3 070	9 700
食品加工业	1 815	53 299	59 216	13 632	45 608
食品制造业	1 077	34 899	38 738	7 048	31 690
饮料制造业	5 043	50 759	46 715	8 680	38 037

10—11 续 9 单位:万元

指　标	年末资产负债及所有者权益				年末资产负债及所有者权益
	长期投资合计	固定资产合计	固定资产原价合计	累计折旧	固定资产净值合计
烟草加工业	326	18 800	17 883	1 773	16 110
纺织业	1 663	98 552	108 298	29 465	78 838
服装及其他纤维制品制造业	641	9 620	14 498	6 523	7 983
皮革、毛皮、羽绒及其制品业	956	8 817	11 445	3 392	8 063
木材加工及竹、藤、棕、草制品业	364	4 847	5 909	1 538	4 373
家具制造业	651	4 190	5 500	2 095	3 410
造纸及纸制品业	377	24 987	29 811	7 492	22 321
印刷业、记录媒介的复制	10 299	16 025	20 871	7 063	13 816
文教体育用品制造业	53	1 202	1 398	349	1 051
石油加工及炼焦业	8 737	148 283	209 914	75 097	134 817
化学原料及化学制品制造业	11 222	382 357	465 134	145 421	319 701
医药制造业	494	28 330	26 820	7 949	18 873
化学纤维制造业	190	16 856	21 719	7 032	14 686
橡胶制品业	236	6 780	9 855	3 201	6 659
塑料制品业	3 788	21 470	23 002	6 432	16 580
非金属矿物制品业	9 294	157 547	194 644	58 475	136 203
黑色金属冶炼及压延加工业	14 747	245 904	285 054	89 609	195 451
有色金属冶炼及压延加工业	59 918	510 052	664 091	218 380	445 707
金属制品业	2 540	32 195	37 404	10 986	26 451
普通机械制造业	2 073	65 282	80 806	26 917	53 892
专用设备制造业	4 038	84 561	120 462	50 383	70 078
交通运输设备制造业	1 112	60 465	76 244	27 237	49 008
武器弹药制造业	204	7 731	8 385	3 041	5 345
电气机械及器材制造业	3 185	62 205	69 414	22 444	46 976
电子及通信设备制造业	3 682	40 055	50 373	16 137	34 236
仪器仪表及文化、办公用机械制造业	1 473	25 445	28 791	10 928	17865
其他制造业	402	12 999	15 388	3 882	11 520
电力、蒸汽、热水的生产和供应业	105 693	512 956	800 303	305 754	494 555
煤气生产和供应业	76	754	977	275	701
自来水的生产和供应业	1 035	22 792	33 563	11 926	21 643

10－11续10　　单位:万元

指　　标	年未资产负债及所有者权益				
	无形及递延资产合计	其他长期资产合计	流动负债合计	#未交税金	长期负债合计
总　　计	128 192	49 281	2 872 105	102 419	1 705 735
在总计中:国有经济	118 596	37 907	2 490 927	88 282	1 571 729
中央企业	37 657	24 197	1 112 265	53 378	962 130
地方企业	80 939	13 710	1 378 662	34 904	609 599
#县(旗)属企业	7 237	8 337	208 181	9 236	109 276
集体经济	9 119	9 172	355 952	13 969	118 778
#县(旗)属企业	2 804	3 286	77 252	2 788	31 050
私营经济			177	22	
联营经济	75		307	84	197
股份制经济	207		10 278	34	2 708
外商投资经济	52	2 202	9 743	26	12 115
中外合资经营企业	52	2 202	9 669	25	12 115
中外合作经营企业			74	1	
港、澳、台投资经济	143		4 721	2	208
与大陆合资经营企业	143		3 855	2	208
港、澳、台独资企业			866		
在总计中:乡属工业	3 033	3 783	98 529	4 096	55 427
在总计中:轻工业	43 893	8 394	619 179	19 316	261 926
重工业	84 299	40 887	2 252 926	83 103	1 443 809
在总计中:大型企业	73 398	26 498	1 648 982	62 044	1 219 129
中型企业	24 923	2 838	440 192	11 413	151 824
小型企业	29 871	19 945	782 931	28 962	334 782
按行业分:					
煤炭采选业	4 271	79	63 738	1 374	68 966
石油和天然气开采业	6 725		218 298	2 012	275 713
黑色金属矿采选业	12	166	961	51	442
有色金属矿采选业	165	725	16 294	592	13 666
非金属矿采选业	324	425	13 786	737	5 794
木材及竹材采运业	199		11 163	829	945
食品加工业	3 887	1 788	52 437	1 870	30 650
食品制造业	1 294	1 596	39 587	1 021	20 882
饮料制造业	3 254	317	49 311	2 102	35 870

10—11 续 11

单位:万元

	年末资产负债及所有者权益				
	无形及递延资产合计	其他长期资产合计	流动负债合计	#未交税金	长期负债合计
烟草加工业	1 130	2	41 079	1 241	8 646
纺织业	13 415	1 359	139 673	5 577	61 225
服装及其他纤维制品制造业	636	1 727	21 901	433	5 875
皮革、毛皮、羽绒及其制品业	1 184	122	18 984	371	6 187
木材加工及竹、藤、棕、草制品业	146	8	7 528	172	2 026
家具制造业	341	54	6 184	212	2 186
造纸及纸制品业	1 765	129	26 554	1 157	15 365
印刷业、记录媒介的复制	1 622	54	22 194	370	7 199
文教体育用品制造业	23	21	1 170	55	656
石油加工及炼焦业	426	70	88 664	2 604	53 588
化学原料及化学制品制造业	25 132	3 057	229 381	6 749	190 868
医药制造业	1 385	163	33 907	699	8 434
化学纤维制造业	4 581		18 300	256	8 959
橡胶制品业	821		12 621	476	3 383
塑料制品业	1 362	245	21 911	311	10 610
非金属矿物制品业	5 210	3 573	132 640	6 356	74 887
黑色金属冶炼及压延加工业	2 945	97	216 450	3 847	79 277
有色金属冶炼及压延加工业	6 786	24 644	548 742	10 888	347 555
金属制品业	1 387	298	54 449	1 586	13 369
普通机械制造业	6 595	382	112 853	2 827	28 743
专用设备制造业	8 841	1 823	159 396	1 972	30 789
交通运输设备制造业	2 289	3 257	70 717	1 786	19 150
武器弹药制造业			10 099	210	583
电气机械及器材制造业	3 668	53	107 589	3 477	31 215
电子及通信设备制造业	7 652		67 383	477	20 958
仪器仪表及文化、办公用机械制造业	5 481	15	47 621	947	18 752
其他制造业	1 733	742	17 459	708	7 210
电力、蒸汽、热水的生产和供应业	1 469	2 212	166 870	36 024	193 314
煤气生产和供应业	7		488	12	409
自来水的生产和供应业	29	78	3 723	31	1 389

10—11 续12 单位:万元

指标	年末资产负债及所有者权益		损益及分配		
	所有者数益合计	#股本	产品销售收入	#产品销售税金及附加	#产品销售利润
总计	2 527 258	50 292	4 489 124	345 918	502 129
在总计中:国有经济	2 289 635	27 788	3 889 412	315 011	439 955
中央企业	1 429 483		2 112 707	199 831	182 010
地方企业	860 152	27 788	1 776 705	115 180	257 945
#县(旗)属企业	138 863	3 061	255 626	17 848	30 844
集体经济	217 346	7 779	568 533	29 691	60 441
#县(旗)属企业	44 070	513	103 146	5 641	9 527
私营经济	239	19	385	14	53
联营经济	771	30	1 267	81	153
股份制经济	15 091	14 580	11 710	159	— 332
外商投资经济	4 171	96	13 112	771	838
中外合资经营企业	4 072		12 931	764	806
中外合作经营企业	99	96	181	7	32
港、澳、台投资经济	5		4 705	191	1 021
与大陆合资经营企业	5		2 792	94	720
港、澳、台独资企业			1 913	97	301
在总计中:乡属工业	74 218	3 337	204 131	11 027	23 927
在总计中:轻工业	305 219	3 535	781 340	69 645	77 851
重工业	2 222 039	46 757	3 707 784	276 273	424 278
在总计中:大型企业	1 732 765	12 250	2 795 008	223 614	304 152
中型企业	296 161	5 928	600 886	61 179	83 532
小型企业	498 332	32 114	1 093 230	61 125	114 445
按行业分:					
煤炭采选业	57 796	963	97 079	3 204	4 534
石油和天然气开采业	361 362		382 126	16 847	2 087
黑色金属矿采选业	1 229	194	2 445	100	449
有色金属矿采选业	20 496	721	27 840	2 460	5 159
非金属矿采选业	8 054	42	19 649	1 473	2 696
木材及竹材采运业	23 410		14 263	1 446	6 336
食品加工业	28 821	136	103 841	2 523	7 963
食品制造业	16 486	—92	45 944	1 856	4 030
饮料制造业	24 649	910	51 110	7 786	5 963

10—11续13

单位:万元

指　　标	年末资产负债及所有者权益		损益及分配		
	所有者数益合计	#股本	产品销售收入	#产品销售税金及附加	#产品销售利润
烟草加工业	13 649	11	66 207	28 690	3 211
纺织业	40 846	193	127 480	8 974	7 798
服装及其他纤维制品制造业	9 648	87	30 043	878	3 019
皮革、毛皮、羽绒及其制品业	5 511	481	15 705	651	1 149
木材加工及竹、藤、棕、草制品业	3 565	23	8 263	359	956
家具制造业	3 550	47	9 532	511	1 044
造纸及纸制品业	10 379	307	27 764	1 525	2 301
印刷业、记录媒介的复制	12 116	46	26 707	898	3 136
文教体育用品制造业	1 250	10	2 521	125	422
石油加工及炼焦业	112 663	1 511	494 159	40 251	52 949
化学原料及化学制品制造业	240 232	4 970	385 885	31 647	41 282
医药制造业	24 777	403	40 875	2 611	9 050
化学纤维制造业	12 365		18 160	1 341	1 926
橡胶制品业	7 355	905	20 595	1 732	2 407
塑料制品业	14 923	131	28 321	991	3 226
非金属矿物制品业	106 793	2 149	218 166	15 491	38 090
黑色金属冶炼及压延加工业	209 576	83	425 094	39 544	79 129
有色金属冶炼及压延加工业	347 156	14 954	730 475	55 165	81 962
金属制品业	29 213	2 939	93 936	3 580	9 542
普通机械制造业	50 585	— 176	115 949	5 008	19 838
专用设备制造业	76 775	455	143 772	4 366	16 003
交通运输设备制造业	55 395	4 502	74 666	2 374	4 807
武器弹药制造业	7 475		6 888	120	830
电气机械及器材制造业	55 047	730	157 317	10 038	27 564
电子及通信设备制造业	48 989	12 250	54 262	2 000	8 868
仪器仪表及文化、办公用机械制造业	12 257		37 325	570	4 573
其他制造业	8 575	—36	20 976	1 097	1 935
电力、蒸汽、热水的生产和供应业	440 651	431	351 080	47 133	30 988
煤气生产和供应业	562		1 781	187	289
自来水的生产和供应业	23 077	12	10 923	366	4 618

10—11 续14

单位:万元

指 标	损益及分配				
	其他业务利润	营业利润	利润总额	亏损企业亏损总额	利税总额
总 计	28 881	149 364	133 705	92 932	479 660
在总计中:国有经济	25 615	126 277	110 080	85 041	425 082
中央企业	11 357	57 390	48 397	29 956	248 221
地方企业	14 258	68 887	61 683	55 085	176 861
#县(旗)属企业	2 715	10 538	22 740	4 547	40 589
集体经济	2 965	24 258	24 427	5 888	54 166
#县(旗)属企业	475	1 335	1 393	1 880	7 015
私营经济		38	38		51
联营经济	2	127	119	31	199
股份制经济	24	—1 039	—1 061	1 100	— 901
外商投资经济	207	— 715	— 751	842	19
中外合资经营企业	207	— 726	— 762	842	1
中外合作经营企业		11	11		18
港、澳、台投资经济	68	418	853	30	1 044
与大陆合资经营企业	40	292	678	30	772
港、澳、台独资企业	28	126	175		272
在总计中:乡属工业	1 012	13 554	13 508	1 158	24 586
在总计中:轻工业	4 464	10 872	19 575	23 729	89 253
重工业	24 417	138 492	114 130	69 203	390 407
在总计中:大型企业	11 875	84 571	66 296	48 804	289 904
中型企业	8 393	33 710	26 945	13 302	88 125
小型企业	8 613	31 083	40 464	30 826	101 631
按行业分:					
煤炭采选业	1 949	—11 287	—15 232	18 057	—12 035
石油和天然气开采业	3 551	—16 008	—19 799	21 915	—2 952
黑色金属矿采选业	12	282	290		385
有色金属矿采选业	347	1 896	2 207	335	4 671
非金属矿采选业	390	1 188	1 101	271	2 582
木材及竹材采运业	1 425	6 072	4 708		6 154
食品加工业	514	1 340	1 100	1 687	3 623
食品制造业	281	279	210	1 298	2 065
饮料制造业	568	1 617	1 541	815	9 330

10—11 续 15

单位:万元

指标	损益及分配				
	其他业务利润	营业利润	利润总额	亏损企业亏损总额	利税总额
烟草加工业	12	712	710	155	29 401
纺织业	511	−7 642	−8 742	11 440	245
服装及其他纤维制品制造业	203	579	413	522	1 289
皮革、毛皮、羽绒及其制品业	170	− 866	− 921	1 548	− 263
木材加工及竹、藤、棕、草制品业	145	398	328	97	690
家具制造业	49	254	243	43	760
造纸及纸制品业	286	−77	− 199	1 752	1 334
印刷业、记录媒介的复制	342	957	844	116	1 731
文教体育用品制造业	14	167	159	5	289
石油加工及炼焦业	38	17 778	17 494	217	57 742
化学原料及化学制品制造业	3 013	11 509	8 351	3 721	39 994
医药制造业	207	5 037	17 704	852	20 313
化学纤维制造业	24	368	153		1 496
橡胶制品业	46	835	765	89	2 502
塑料制品业	305	628	513	549	1 491
非金属矿物制品业	1 203	20 475	18 651	890	34 142
黑色金属冶炼及压延加工业	1 460	38 132	35 539	4 694	75 079
有色金属冶炼及压延加工业	2 400	28 610	25 087	3 386	80 255
金属制品业	466	3 053	2 703	885	6 287
普通机械制造业	1 089	4 306	3 118	2 007	8 125
专用设备制造业	3 844	1 427	− 623	4 442	3 746
交通运输设备制造业	760	−5 953	−2 878	4 796	− 499
武器弹药制造业	1 359	1 175	633		753
电气机械及器材制造业	1 159	9 419	8 118	181	18 159
电子及通信设备制造业	49	2 394	1 877	209	3 876
仪器仪表及文化、办公用机械制造业	187	− 827	−1 673	2 151	−1100
其他制造业	91	7	32	501	1 139
电力、蒸汽、热水的生产和供应业	346	27 506	25 742	3 260	72 872
煤气生产和供应业	6	163	150		338
自来水的生产和供应业	60	3 461	3 288	46	3 651

10—12 重点行业实物劳动生产率

指　　标	单位	1978 年	1990 年	1992 年	1993 年
一. 冶金工业					
炼铁工人	吨/人		513.00	1 252.00	1 426.00
顶吹转炉	吨/人.年	86.98	239.70	352.33	417.87
炼钢工人					
电炉炼钢工人	吨/人.年	108.36	132.01	135.59	125.44
铁矿选矿工人	吨/人.年		1 880.00	3 221.19	3 529.00
铁矿井下采矿工人	吨/人.年		635.00	1 248.00	1 281.00
二. 煤炭工业					
原煤全员效率	吨/工	0.70	0.88	0.94	1.04
回采工效率	吨/工		4.15	4.71	5.22
掘进工效率	米/工		0.11	0.11	0.13
三. 化学工业					
硫酸工人	吨/人		205.64	248.67	236.52
合成氨工人	吨/人	141.00	250.52	234.50	233.12
四. 森林工业					
木材采运工人	立方米/人	55.50	61.30	63.00	63.00
五. 轻工业					
卷烟工人	箱/人		172.00	167.40	158.50
六. 石油工人					
炼油工人	吨/人		944.36	698.00	1 120.95

10—13 部门分行业产品质量指标

指　标	单位	1978年	1990年	1992年	1993年
一.冶金工业					
生铁合格率	%	98.14	99.83	100.00	100.00
烧结矿合格率	%	66.59	86.15	89.54	95.40
电炉钢锭合格率	%	96.42	98.28	99.22	99.47
轧钢材合格率	%	94.71	95.58	97.86	98.24
铁精矿品位(弱磁)	%		56.68	55.72	55.75
二.煤炭工业					
商品煤灰粉	%	16.85	12.86	13.75	13.29
商品煤含矸率	%	0.87	0.32	0.22	0.19
三.石油工业					
原油商品率	%		97.25	96.04	
石油产品质量合格率	%	99.98	100.00	100.00	100.00
四.化学工业					
尿素合格率	%	100.00	99.94	100.00	100.00
精甲醇合格率	%	100.00	100.00	100.00	100.00
烧碱合格率	%				
(89年起为离子膜碱)	%	98.26	100.00	100.00	100.00
轮胎外胎合格率	%		99.48	99.62	99.65
五.机械工业					
铸铁件综合废品率	%	13.33	11.48	18.49	15.42
机械加工件综合废品率	%	2.64	1.90	1.51	1.21
六.建筑材料工业					
水泥熟料平均标号	号	660.00	597.20	581.16	575.42
出厂水泥合格率	%	99.50	100.00	100.00	100.00
平板玻璃一级品率(垂直引上工艺)	%	62.91	84.16	88.06	87.05
七.森林工业					
锯材一等品率	%	82.00	65.96	58.13	58.43
八.纺织工业					
合成纤维正品率(混合)	%	75.11	99.70	99.69	99.89
棉纱一等一级品率	%	98.64	100.00	99.99	100.00
毛线入库一等品率	%	93.08	93.00	94.54	94.78
粗纺毛织品入库一等品率	%	93.93	86.37	88.60	90.48
精纺毛织品入库一等品率	%	86.86	93.60	93.97	94.00
毛毯入库一等品率	%	84.45	88.20	89.62	92.96
纺织品(成品绸)入库一等品率	%		76.50	92.00	97.96
九.轻工业					
普通灯泡综合合格率	%	86.73	87.50	88.78	88.14
机制纸及纸板成品率	%	95.10	92.16	91.94	91.24
卷烟合格率	%	98.69	99.60	87.20	99.40
内销皮鞋正品率(合格率)	%	98.10	99.89	99.60	99.11
日用普通陶瓷制品一级品率	%	64.13	64.82	70.01	70.33
轻革合格率	%	92.13	97.38	97.14	98.27
重革合格率	%	97.20	99.52	98.90	100.00
铝锅一级品率	%	68.50	75.06	72.07	79.58
五号保温瓶胆一级品率	%	59.87	80.05	82.35	83.67
啤酒合格率	%		99.89	100.00	99.81
木家具板材利用率	%		59.66	66.40	62.34

10—14 村办工业企业主要指标

(1993年)

行业	企业单位数(个)	工业总产值(当年价)(万元)	年末全部从业人员(人)	产品销售收入(万元)
总计	**4 026**	**183 453**	**125 970**	**132 083**
轻工业	1 608	75 371	43 112	44 598
重工业	2 418	108 082	82 858	87 485
按行业分:				
煤炭采选业	216	12 014	10 132	9 260
石油和天然气开采业	1	29	17	9
黑色金属矿采选业	27	596	569	411
有色金属矿采先业	56	3 811	2 197	2 801
非金属矿采选业	290	7 996	7 854	5 005
其他矿采选业	53	974	1 103	716
木材及竹材采用业	2	28	13	19
食品加工业	425	16 180	4 739	11 260
食品制造业	326	7 682	5 324	5 568
饮料制造业	19	643	253	523
烟草加工业	22	1 259	893	969
纺织业	51	4 744	2 077	3 982
服装及其他纤维制品制造业	37	5 860	3 600	5 278
皮革.毛皮.羽绒及其制品业	38	3 676	1 137	1 779
木材加工及竹.藤.棕.草制品业	90	2 470	2 639	1 931
家俱制造业	50	1 316	707	982
造纸及纸制品业	68	4 260	2 471	4 048
印刷业.记录媒草的复制	36	1 375	686	1 246
文教体育用品制造业	10	149	223	95
石油加工及炼焦业	34	4 914	919	4 329
化学原料及化学制品制造业	85	8 418	2 030	6 394
医药制造业	30	1 152	855	776
化学纤维制造业	7	136	161	83
橡胶制品业	2	116	146	111
塑料制品业	76	5 250	2 564	4 299
非金属矿物制品业	847	34 857	38 985	18 492
黑色金属冶炼及延加工业	86	9 012	3 862	6 074
有色金属冶炼及压延加工业	22	2 009	705	1 793
金属制品业	181	9 604	3 768	7 601
普通机械制造业	95	9 402	3 537	7 606
交通运输设备制造业	11	2 094	755	2 426
电气机械及器材制造业	17	1 731	575	1 167
电子及通份设备制造业	31	350	938	240
其他制造业	633	18 771	19 306	14 241
电力.煤气.及水的生产和供应业	45	433	156	443
煤气生产和供应业	7	142	74	126

10—14 续　　　　　　　　　(1993年)

行　　业	产品销售税金及附加(万元)	应交所得税(万元)	利润总额(万元)	固定资产原价年末数(万元)	流动资产年末数(万元)
总　计	7 315	13 895	12 067	61 114	58 666
轻工业	2 816	12 468	4 066	20 183	23 771
重工业	4 499	1 427	8 001	40 931	34 895
按行业分：					
煤炭采选业	437	5 186	1 008	4 203	2 814
石油和天然气开采业				3	3
黑色金属矿采选业	16	8	58	348	276
有色金属故采先业	137	46	179	1 436	1 200
非金属矿采选业	267	77	479	2 133	2 855
其他矿采选业	31	16	106	326	215
木材及竹材采用业	1	2	1	10	6
食品加工业	411	65	853	4 051	8 599
食品制造业	201	74	546	1 882	2 213
饮料制造业	19	5	37	259	261
烟草加工业	283	3	48	206	269
纺织业	80	45	359	2 593	1 862
服装及其他纤维制品制造业	654	4	185	735	921
皮革.毛皮.羽绒及其制品业	87	20	193	862	1 705
木材加工及竹.藤.棕.草制品业	80	27	159	685	507
家俱制造业	60	12	89	482	324
造纸及纸制品业	142	28	262	2 336	1 317
印刷业.记录媒草的复制	61	23	142	449	358
文教体育用品制造业	5	10	17	55	35
石油加工及炼焦业	190	53	300	1 849	1 671
化学原料及化学制品制造业	319	48	392	2 124	1 913
医药制造业	39	12	66	349	312
化学纤维制造业	5	7	9	81	56
橡胶制品业	2	1	15	13	7
塑料制品业	171	104	369	1 675	1 223
非金属矿物制品业	1 672	402	2 657	16 241	11 944
黑色金属冶炼及延加工业	340	139	552	3 625	3 815
有色金属冶炼及压延加工业	73	28	176	498	455
金属制品业	357	95	674	2 335	2 700
普通机械制造业	368	112	865	1 863	2 895
交通运输设备制造业	134	29	137	197	127
电气机械及器材制造业	54	12	99	593	481
电子及通份设备制造业	7	3	35	195	33
其他制造业	592	7 176	983	6 109	5 138
电力.煤气.及水的生产和供应业	7	1	14	273	97
煤气生产和供应业	13	5	3	40	59

10—15 城乡联营工业和城乡个体工业主要经济指标

(1993 年)

指　标	户数(个)	从业人数(个)	工业总产值(当年价格)(万元)	上交税金(万元)	自有资金(万元)
一.城镇联营工业总计	269	5 097	8 010	355	1 207
在总计中:					
轻工业	192	3 559	7 005	321	980
重工业	77	1 538	1 005	34	227
二.农村联营工业总计	4 761	76 881	90 453	2 264	13 738
在总计中:					
轻工业	2 455	36 309	45 569	1 077	8 119
重工业	2 306	40 572	44 884	1 187	5 619
三.城镇个体工业总计	7 489	20 515	22 469	784	5 035
在总计中:					
轻工业	6 583	17 832	19 453	643	4 276
重工业	906	2 683	3 016	111	759
四.农村个体工业总计	73 003	272 005	262 255	10 847	37 9171
在总计中:					
轻工业	53 866	182 576	162 690	7 572	25 478
重工业	19 137	89 429	99 565	3 275	12 439

工业总产值构成

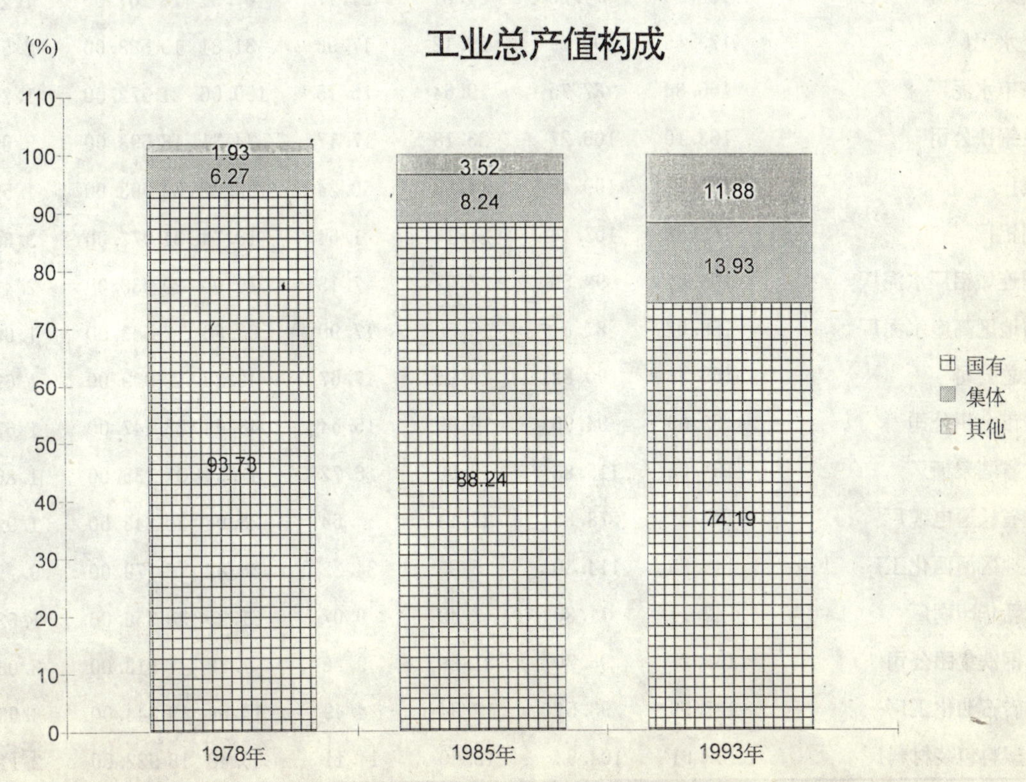

10—16 1993年全省大中型工业企业经济效益30强

企业名称	综合指数(%)	产销率(%)	资金利税率(%)	成本利润率(%)	净产值率(%)	劳动生产率(%)	资金周转次数(次)
天水卷烟厂	477.04	99.67	112.25	2.22	53.05	102 395.00	2.37
天水供电局	468.07	514.71	42.56	110.91	78.09	21 055.00	3.29
兰州卷烟厂	410.57	100.52	65.76	3.63	54.55	126 722.00	1.83
兰州平板玻璃厂	328.05	86.69	62.64	33.82	51.23	31 534.00	4.32
卫生部兰州生物制品研究所	320.65	87.55	28.14	65.47	64.00	58743.00	1.04
白龙江林业管理局迭部林业局	302.97	98.18	39.25	68.01	82.04	20282.00	1.71
甘肃省电力工业局	279.39	20.26	8.55	5.12	54.21	130 614.00	1.74
中国石化兰州炼油化工总厂	236.06	—	37.25	3.75	14.58	34 255.00	7.93
兰州市自来水公司	230.62	100.00	19.12	59.81	51.19	16 847.00	1.96
武山水泥厂	204.77	96.73	31.12	15.37	68.34	31 433.00	1.77
兰州佛慈制药厂	188.88	99.25	15.05	15.53	71.88	45 735.00	1.29
丝路春酒厂	188.53	61.52	32.35	14.72	59.15	27 071.00	1.57
平凉地区印刷机械厂	187.39	96.74	24.98	8.33	35.81	7 011.00	7.20
首钢跃进机械厂	182.26	71.26	21.31	32.17	67.31	18 261.00	1.29
永登水泥厂	173.45	99.69	25.12	17.93	31.81	19 588.00	2.56
平凉市水泥厂	166.86	87.75	19.64	15.15	100.00	21 672.00	1.23
酒泉钢铁公司	163.10	106.27	23.18	17.17	34.31	18 693.00	2.09
甘绒厂	161.72	109.48	14.63	0.24	92.32	38 993.00	1.59
兰州铝厂	160.88	103.15	21.14	1.64	19.74	31 977.00	3.38
兰州连城铝厂水泥厂	156.41	99.56	27.92	7.13	16.90	20 930.00	2.47
定西地区高崖水泥厂	156.07	87.81	18.88	17.90	63.86	17 653.00	1.68
矿业总公司	155.43	90.82	25.94	17.67	42.26	12 079.00	1.69
金昌市金川公司	152.69	94.95	16.99	15.54	48.45	23 447.00	1.67
甘肃省酒泉糖厂	151.05	115.83	12.08	6.72	41.54	37 135.00	1.86
甘肃省长通电缆厂	147.27	78.85	22.14	4.64	23.08	30 345.00	1.92
酒泉地区河西化工厂	143.35	114.30	15.95	34.32	36.82	5 179.00	0.75
兰州新华印刷厂	142.11	11.80	7.49	9.07	81.25	38 356.00	1.62
兰州钢铁集团公司	138.29	96.70	31.38	9.78	1.78	1 513.00	3.06
甘肃省石油化工厂	137.98	93.51	17.94	4.49	14.54	19 344.00	3.63
兰州塑料包装材料厂	137.61	104.62	13.80	14.11	35.48	18 922.00	2.11

10—17 全省大中型企业一览表

企业名称	邮政编码	电话	主要产品	工业增加值（万元）
四零四厂	732 850	417584	元明粉	3 942
兰州钢铁集团公司	730 020	498811	钢	1 857
中国石化总公司兰化公司	730 060	555981	化学肥料	66 405
中国石化兰州炼油化工总厂	730 060	556011	汽.煤.柴.润滑油	58 668
国营长风机器厂	730 070	667111	洗衣机	1 972
兰州市自来水公司	730 060	556954	自来水	4 439
甘肃省兰州阀门厂	730 046	8416744	低压阀门	5
中国人民解放军七三二三工厂	730 020	496013	火炮修理	595
兰州油泵油嘴厂	730 020	498018	高压油泵总成	1 599
兰州制药厂	730 046	8822951	片剂	1 340
甘肃省电力工业局兰州电器厂	730 046	8827951	电力变压器	605
中国人民解放军第七二一九工厂	730 000	8825210	书刊排字	2 080
卫生部兰州生物制品研究所	730 046	8823511	乙肝疫苗	10 039
甘肃省兰州客车厂	730 046	8827611	长途客车	474
兰州灯泡	730 000	8829411	普光	720
解放军七四三七工厂(金兰汽车厂)	730 020	498111	汽车修理	512
兰州柴油机厂	730 000	8417971	柴油机	123
兰州卷烟厂	730 030	465311	卷烟	15 207
甘肃省纺织机械厂	730 046	8821911	SYZ－4A 四梭塑料编机	340
兰州日用化工厂	730 046	8826328	肥皂	1 369
兰州市第二毛纺织厂	730 046	8824421	粗纺呢绒	376
解放军第六四一三工厂	730 020	498229	工程机械修理	109
解放军三五一二工厂	730 046	8824114	皮大衣	1 954
兰州佛慈制药厂	730 046	8413889	金匮肾气丸	2 881
兰州厨房设备总厂	730 046	8826827	煤气灶	372
国营华兴电子机器厂	730 046	666305	淋浴器	3 271
兰州水泵总厂	730 000	8829221	工业泵	2 082
兰州电力修造厂	730 050	334626	电站备品配件	237
兰州电机厂	730 050	336951	大中型交直流电机	12 659
兰州玻璃厂	730 050	336611	瓶罐	259
兰州通用机器厂	730 000	333921	采油机械设备	742
铁道部兰州机车工厂	730 050	333490	铁路运输设备修理	3 048
兰州新华印刷厂	730 050	335821	书刊印刷	3 813
兰州真空设备厂	730 050	336011	真空获得设备	955
兰州轴承厂	730 050	336941	工业轴承	2 360
兰州石油化工机器厂	730 050	335595	钻采设备	11 169
兰州锅炉厂	730 060	555074	工业锅炉	532
国营四七一厂	730 065	523311	锅炉产品	693
西北合成药厂	730 060	555691	咖啡因	1 750
省第一建筑机械制造厂	730 060	555521	JZC350 搅拌机	658
兰州塑料包装材料厂	730 060	555355	塑料包装箱	700
省建筑木材加工厂	730 060	555266	锯材	610
兰州铝厂	730 060	556533	普通铝锭	11 426
兰州维尼纶厂	730 094	557455	聚乙烯醇	4 081
兰州高压阀门厂	730 060	556711	高中压阀门	1 738
兰州平板玻璃厂	730 060	556702	平板玻璃	12 450
兰州棉纺织印染厂	730 060	556434	纱	1 295
兰州第三毛纺织厂	730 060	556841	精纺尼绒	5 592
甘肃省建筑构件工程公司	730 060	556611	加气砼	2 000
国营和平化工厂	730 094	523217	硝胺炸药	982
兰州三叶公司	730 060	558954	聚丙烯	8 270
兰州专用汽车制造厂	730 070	668411	轻客及轻客底盘	523
兰州沙井驿建筑材料公司	730 079	667411	红砖	1 035
兰州长新电表厂	730 070	666441	电度表	574
兰州汽车齿轮厂	730 079	666454	汽车齿轮	1 903
甘肃省兰州机床厂	730 070	666227	普通车床	2 432
兰州市窑街水泥厂	730 080	311666	普通硅酸盐水泥	1 566
兰州炭素厂	730 084	8417837	石墨电极类	8 977
窑街矿务局	730 080	311311	原煤	11 757

10—17 续 1

企业名称	邮政编码	电话	主要产品	工业增加值（万元）
兰州连城铝厂	730 335	483409	铝锭	12 303
西北铁合金厂	730 334	418998	铁合金	1 694
定西地区高崖水泥厂	730 113	09440	硅酸盐水泥	3 165
酒泉钢铁公司	735 100	713132	生铁	58 317
金川镍都实业公司	737 104	812385	铜线	10 215
七九六矿	737 111	9455	黄金	85
金昌市金川公司	737 104	812230	电镍	77 524
金昌化工总厂	737 000	321223	纯碱	5 825
甘肃(国营第八零五厂)	730 900	222470	梯恩梯	3 362
甘肃矿用化工厂	730 913	23791	炸药	938
甘肃省白银棉纺厂	730 900	222993	棉纱线	777
甘肃省白银针织厂	730 900	222884	针织内衣	108
白银纺织机械针布厂	730 900	222760	金属针布	165
甘肃稀土公司	730 922	416821	氯化稀土	8 157
甘肃省白银磷盐化工厂	730 600	22083	黄磷	213
甘肃省长通电缆厂	730 900	221656	裸电线	4 931
靖远矿务局	730 913	22991	原煤	14 663
白银有色金属公司	730 900	222560	电铜	63 130
国营风雷机械厂	730 600	22312	四道平磨机	654
国营二七九厂	730 621	22279	纯碱	121
景泰县石膏矿	730 400	22307	石膏	514
天水塑料厂	741 000	214855	聚乙烯农地膜	504
甘棉厂	741 024	236677	棉纱	797
天水海林轴承厂	741 018	212174	轴承	2 206
天水啤酒厂	741 022	236191	啤酒	1
天水铁路信号厂	741 001	214920	色灯信号机	203
甘绒厂	741 024	236753	毛线	12 139
天水电缆厂	741 000	212629	信号电缆	1 490
天水卷烟厂	741 020	236767	卷烟	9 687
甘肃长成电器工业公司	741 018	212873	高低压电器元件	10 333
天光集成电路厂	741 000	211317	ECL 集成电路	2 188
天水长城精密电表厂	741 000	212915	教学表	218
天水 213 机床电器厂	741 001	212171	机床电器	2 217
6913 厂	741 002	212936	理疗器	535
天水红山试验机厂	741 001	212330	试验机	1 070
天水新华印刷厂	741 001	212922	报刊印刷	2 105
首钢岷山机械厂	741 018	212914	枪械	7 696
天水长成电工仪器厂	741 001	212796	自动化仪表	421
天水轴承仪器厂	741 000	212811	轴承仪器	626
天水风动工具厂	741 020	236732	凿岩机	1 778
5722 工厂	741 025	236023	歼击机大修	614
天水星火机床厂	741 024	236973	切割机床	1 127
天水拖拉机厂	741 020	236389	小四轮拖拉机	33
天水锻压机床厂	741 020	236873	折弯机	1 430
国营庆华仪器厂	741 605	522069	电子仪器	2 033
国营永红器材厂	741 606	52237	半导体分离器件	1 784
甘肃省摩擦密封材料厂	741 200	621006	石棉制品	1 451
甘谷油墨厂	741 200	622006	油墨	2 307
武山水泥厂	741 316	21521	水泥	5 963
矿产部西北探矿机械厂	741 300	21553	XY－4 岩心钻机	－3 535
甘肃毛纺织厂	741 300	21537	毛毯	5
酒泉地区河西化工厂	735 201	222	硫酸	600
甘肃省酒泉糖厂	735 009	4363	白砂糖	5 240
玉门石油管理局	735 200	22555	原油	80 508
玉门市化工厂	735 200	44577	元明粉	162
矿业总公司	736 200	23165	石棉	289
张掖糖厂	734 000	3114	白砂糖	1 065
张掖地区造纸厂	734 027	3939	箱板纸	574
甘肃省轻工机械厂	734 000	4097	塑料编制袋	1 123

10—17 续 2

企业名称	邮政编码	电话	主要产品	工业增加值（万元）
丝路春酒厂	734 000	2489	白酒	2 171
国营高台盐化公司	734 300	21592	粉洗精盐	68
甘肃山丹焦化厂	734 100	21249	焦炭	2 987
甘肃黄羊糖厂	733 006	217930	白糖	1 139
甘肃凉州皇台酒厂	733 000	212830	凉州皇台酒	1 564
西北铝加工厂	748 111	22830	铝材	5 990
西北有色冶金机械厂	748 112	66104	矿山设备	794
陇西酒精厂	748 000	88321	酒精	2 264
国营敬东机器厂	743 000	2088	电视机配件	9 869
徽县陇南春酒厂	742 308	21888	金徽酒	1 750
国营红峰机械厂	744 000	3492	疏水阀系列	2 171
首钢胜利机械厂	744 101	3102	冶金机械备件产品	1 009
首钢跃进机械厂	744 027	4566	冶金备品备件	2 182
首钢前进机械厂	744 101	9334770	冶金备件	2 220
国营虹光电子管厂	744 000	3801	超高频电子管	1 352
国营丰收机械厂	744 000	4711	彩板门窗	697
华亭矿务局	744 100	21511	原煤	1 426
平凉地区印刷机械厂	744 000	4831	电脑切纸机	761
华亭县安口陶瓷厂	744 103		日用陶瓷器	390
甘肃省石油化工厂	745 115	22362	汽油	2 758
长庆石油勘探局	745 100	2221	原油	57 461
甘光仪器公司	731 100	212810	照相机	1 056
盐化总厂	731 601	32672	烧碱	3 162
刘化总厂	731 603	32693	合成氨	3 554
白龙江林业管理局迭部林业局	747 401		木材	10 267
国营七九二矿	747 000	22235	采矿	486
甘肃省电力工业局	730 050	334311	电力	—98 786
核工业总公司五0四厂	730 065	556932	有色金属压延加工业	4 938
航天工业部万里机电厂	730 070	666451	工业缝纫机	1 912
兰州飞控仪器总厂	730 070	666131	四梭园织机	3 890
农业部兰州生物药厂	730 046	8823516	牲畜菌疫苗	772
兰州手扶拖拉机厂	730 050	334721	手扶拖拉机	2 421
甘肃省铝业公司	730 079	555921	铝锭	10 441
西北油漆厂	730 020	497111	油漆	1 840
甘肃省轮胎厂	730 000	8821127	普通载重汽车轮胎	1 558
兰州煤矿机械厂	730 050	333136	单体液压支柱	239
甘肃省金城机械厂	730 316	22577	雪花炸药系列产品	
兰州第一毛纺织厂	730 050	336961	精纺呢绒	3 200
兰州毛条厂	730 050	335961	毛条	1 837
国营兰新无线电厂	730 020	497615	抛物面天线	1 386
甘肃电视机厂	730 000	8418616	彩色电视机	2
永登水泥厂	730 301	22597	水泥	5 673
兰州啤酒厂	730 050	334506	啤酒制造业	2 170
兰州(原兰州热水瓶厂)	730 050	334427	玻璃保温容器	899
兰州第四毛纺织厂	730 030	466626	人造毛皮	53
兰州皮革厂	730 020	498418	牛面革	36
兰州市肉类联合加工厂	730 050	334511	猪油	2 704
兰州建筑通用机械总厂	730 000	8825221	砼搅拌机	1 132
兰州量具刃具厂	730 000	8820931	刃具	1 098
兰州长津电机厂	730 000	8821721	电动机制造	1 136
兰州长虹电焊条厂	730 000	461016	电焊条	681
兰州塑料厂	730 050	334326	聚氨乙烯板管异型材	684
兰州机械制造公司	730 050	333611	机械配件	1 121
省天祝建材厂	733 204		石膏	391
平凉市水泥厂	744 000	2481	硅酸盐水泥	2 527

10—17 续 3

企业名称	销售收入（万元）	全部资金（万元）	生产用固定资产（万元）	职工人数（万人）
四零四厂	16 452	62 541	28 054	9 908
兰州钢铁集团公司	127 944	70 392	26 653	12 274
中国石化总公司兰化公司	188 198	236 707	207 614	27 104
中国石化兰州炼油化工总厂	436 713	138 443	145 726	17 127
国营长风机器厂	28 154	60 700	15 346	1 820
兰州市自来水公司	8 672	17 604	23 938	2 635
甘肃省兰州阀门厂	830	1 765	646	535
中国人民解放军七三二三工厂	2 029	2 912	1 189	942
兰州油泵油嘴厂	2 166	3 175	1 253	1 228
兰州制药厂	4 667	4 384	1 666	1 109
甘肃省电力工业局兰州电器厂	1 977	3 421	1 976	614
中国人民解放军第七二一九工厂	2 398	3 535	1 372	1 033
卫生部兰州生物制品研究所	10 050	15 944	6 959	1 709
甘肃省兰州客车厂	2 320	4 978	1 480	722
兰州灯泡	2 764	2 514	1 124	1 441
(金兰汽车厂)	1 752	3 091	1 325	1 272
兰州柴油机厂	1 784	5 028	94	1 466
兰州卷烟厂	32 102	24 050	6 589	1 200
甘肃省纺织机械厂	1 624	3 405	550	1 042
兰州日用化工厂	6 978	4 723	1 657	672
兰州市第二毛纺织厂	3 093	8 737	2 775	2 166
中国人民解放军第六四一三工厂	1 564	1 969	922	503
中国人民解放军三五一二工厂	15 108	11 007	3 267	2 084
兰州佛慈制药厂	3 979	4 650	2 340	630
兰州厨房设备总厂	715	2 258	880	566
国营华兴电子机器厂	3 858	5 882	1 864	1 258
兰州水泵总厂	2 826	3 080	989	1 125
兰州电力修造厂	12 890	22 266	5 374	1 764
兰州电机厂	34 192	31 823	12 629	5 858
兰州玻璃厂	1 837	1 966	1 147	784
兰州通用机器厂	15 676	25 986	7 605	4 989
铁道部兰州机车工厂	6 713	17 176	7 872	6 332
兰州新华印刷厂	1 940	3 249	2 587	994
兰州真空设备厂	3 781	5 335	1 717	852
兰州轴承厂	5 841	13 514	3 865	3 335
兰州石油化工机器厂	30 132	96 675	31 822	11 058
兰州锅炉厂	2 096	2 390	926	515
国营四七一厂	4 140	6 965	2 524	1 490
西北合成药厂	6 541	6 234	2 130	1 297
甘肃省第一建筑机械制造厂	1 485	1 486	516	683
兰州塑料包装材料厂	2 064	2 128	1 465	370
甘肃省建筑木材加工厂	2 095	3 385	712	992
兰州铝厂	62 438	30 792	13 633	3 573
兰州维尼纶厂	18 049	29 777	20 075	3 770
兰州高压阀门厂	4 689	6 519	2 174	2 021
兰州平板玻璃厂	21 234	11 123	6 824	3 948
兰州棉纺织印染厂	14 761	19 715	9 415	5 908
兰州第三毛纺织厂	15 497	22 168	8 335	5 288
甘肃省建筑构件工程公司	3 691	3 087	1 812	1 498
国营和平化工厂	3 038	3 715	1 450	871
兰州三叶公司	22 073	25 596	12 279	5 182
兰州专用汽车制造厂	1 760	5 685	1 887	1 453
兰州沙井驿建筑材料工业公司	3 673	5 845	2 636	2 846
兰州长新电表厂	3 519	4 042	855	1 048
兰州汽车齿轮厂	7 382	6 006	2 534	1 879
甘肃省兰州机床厂	3 754	5 950	1 419	1 505
兰州市窑街水泥厂	1 668	3 235	1 321	1 429

10—17 续 4

企业名称	销售收入（万元）	全部资金（万元）	生产用固定资产（万元）	职工人数（万人）
兰州炭素厂	31 473	57 261	34 278	6 342
窑街矿务局	31 652	46 767	28 387	20 272
兰州连城铝厂	77 364	43 526	16 875	5 878
西北铁合金厂	46 213	58 583	25 757	4 864
定西地区高崖水泥厂	4 154	5 481	818	1 793
酒泉钢铁公司	220 254	223 129	150 398	31 198
金川镍都实业公司	41 370	71 248	20 228	17 513
七九六矿	397	220	342	649
金昌市金川公司	158 039	218 283	132 157	33 064
金昌化工总厂	13 475	17 263	11 176	2 805
甘肃(国营第八零五厂)	28 324	77 494	35 914	7 501
甘肃矿用化工厂	2 843	2 193	1 182	724
甘肃省白银棉纺厂	4 577	6 388	2 990	2 369
甘肃省白银针织厂	2 769	10 113	4 440	2 279
国营白银纺织机械针布厂	2 445	7 064	3 624	1 476
甘肃稀土公司	22 824	27 235	9 854	2 811
甘肃省白银磷盐化工厂	5 550	7 323	2 056	1 140
甘肃省长通电缆厂	18 003	12 849	4 327	1 625
靖远矿务局	28 926	97 700	78 000	23 442
白银有色金属公司	185 814	265 721	180 726	40 119
国营风雷机械厂	1 227	2 874	682	1 026
国营二七九厂	3 684	6 852	4 194	1 264
景泰县石膏矿	1 256	1 971	1 156	502
天水塑料厂	3 046	3 701	1 092	385
甘棉厂	5 117	8 468	4 160	2 903
天水海林轴承厂	14 705	16 658	4 064	4 894
天水啤酒厂	1 821	3 206	1 620	537
天水铁路信号厂	3 156	4 695	1 107	1 320
甘绒厂	15 014	16 093	3 599	3 113
天水电缆厂	10 461	8 555	2 874	1 455
天水卷烟厂	19 487	8 492	2 559	946
甘肃长成电器工业公司	35 097	34 933	10 603	8 397
天光集成电路厂	1 779	8 490	4 115	1 616
天水长城精密电表厂	572	4 866	1 110	1 207
天水 213 机床电器厂	6 010	6 045	1 154	1 146
6913 厂	2 762	3 084	767	585
天水红山试验机厂	3 866	6 409	2 168	1 977
天水新华印刷厂	742	2 006	1 551	679
首钢岷山机械厂	4 859	13 441	2 286	3 802
天水长成电工仪器厂	537	3 660	1 265	1 256
天水轴承仪器厂	1 053	4 648	628	1 387
天水风动工具厂	10 568	10 428	4 454	3 037
5722 工厂	2 041	5 680	2 998	1 648
天水星火机庆厂	5 012	7 213	4 287	2 080
天水拖拉机厂	4 396	10 058	2 914	1 721
天水锻压机床厂	5 381	5 918	1 302	1 325
国营庆华仪器厂	2 401	5 648	3 420	1 850
国营永红器材厂	2 028	5 026	2 056	1 594
甘肃省摩擦密封材料厂	2 723	3 587	1 708	1 207
甘谷油墨厂	7 090	6 502	1 336	1 874
武山水泥厂	5 054	2 849	6 696	1 897
地质矿产部西北探矿机械厂	5 144	3 986	2 117	1 246
甘肃毛纺织厂	1 956	4 664	2 409	1 725
酒泉地区河西化工厂	3 630	7 003	3 684	1 159
甘肃省酒泉糖厂	14 609	13 450	7 998	1 411
玉门石油管理局	190 209	146 227	151 292	36 602
玉门市化工厂	793	5 074	2 834	625
矿业总公司	622	510	220	239
张掖糖厂	12 876	11 984	7 020	1 395

10—17 续 5

企业名称	销售收入（万元）	全部资金（万元）	生产用固定资产（万元）	职工人数（万人）
张掖地区造纸厂	1 732	2 703	1 455	1 245
甘肃省轻工机械厂	4 461	6 073	2 557	934
丝路春酒厂	4 687	4 216	1 673	802
国营高台盐化公司	721	3 270	1 517	416
甘肃山丹焦化厂	5 379	8 119	4 118	1 075
甘肃黄羊糖厂	11 563	11 745	3 667	1 269
甘肃凉州皇台酒厂	2 133	13 906	10 264	916
西北铝加工厂	17 050	39 385	21 420	5 061
西北有色冶金机械厂	7 724	9 484	4 826	2 750
陇西酒精厂	5 294	5 851	888	733
国营敬东机器厂	115	41	49	1 968
徽县陇南春酒厂	5 598	8 552	3 127	1 573
国营红峰机械厂	1 906	6 135	2 334	1 843
首钢胜利机械厂	2 825	11 560	3 618	2 425
首钢跃进机械厂	1 466	2 907	1 989	1 195
首钢前进机械厂	915	6 142	915	1 568
国营虹光电子管厂	2 454	10 451	5 856	2 071
国营丰收机械厂	1 510	2 797	313	1 543
华亭矿务局	3 999	11 000	9 038	6 846
平凉地区印刷机械厂	1 441	850	1 093	1 086
华亭县安口陶瓷厂	1 006	1 347	1 168	1 016
甘肃省石油化工厂	17 738	11 050	8 887	1 426
长庆石油勘探局	175 298	614 137	390 866	54 494
甘光仪器公司	6 915	18 003	8 401	3 694
盐化总厂	11 228	17 761	10 096	2 205
刘化总厂	11 397	12 241	14 528	2 729
白龙江林业管理局迭部林业局	10 096	12 350	6 790	5 062
国营七九二矿	1 722	7 919	10 869	1 896
甘肃省电力工业局	306 355	650 619	694 520	937
中国核工业总公司五0四厂	18 741	27 317	49 077	5 150
航空航天工业部万里机电厂	4 854	10 419	5 901	5 295
兰州飞控仪器总厂	8 848	15 510	5 974	3 918
农业部兰州生物药厂	1 314	2 276	1 419	680
兰州手扶拖拉机厂	14 836	9 407	1 297	2 117
甘肃省铝业公司	44 991	55 488	27 950	3 575
西北油漆厂	19 429	12 661	6 625	1 630
甘肃省轮胎厂	9 432	10 218	2 745	1 092
兰州煤矿机械厂	2 538	4 330	1 637	1 056
甘肃省金城机械厂	354	1 430	559	670
兰州第一毛纺织厂	11 021	21 213	4 355	6 061
兰州毛条厂	2 595	2 684	2 590	1 455
国营兰新无线电厂	2 403	7 044	2 699	1 588
甘肃电视机厂	8 003	8 064	1 531	1 064
永登水泥厂	17 009	15 539	19 456	2 896
兰州啤酒厂	3 757	8 402	5 616	847
兰州(原兰州热水瓶厂)	4 575	3 246	1 523	1 540
兰州第四毛纺织厂	1 154	2 834	1 409	778
兰州皮革厂	1 824	3 221	1 071	668
兰州市肉类联合加工厂	3 016	3 527	2 024	1 382
兰州建筑通用机械总厂	5 001	4 027	779	901
兰州量具刃具厂	4 867	4 947	756	1 152
兰州长津电机厂	3 158	5 166	1 767	1 372
兰州长虹电焊条厂	9 337	5 132	1 220	682
兰州塑料厂	4 072	4 360	2 086	1 135
兰州机械制造公司	2 510	3 469	1 113	959
省天祝建材厂	1 288	2 403	1 157	650
平凉市水泥厂	2 452	1 416	2 206	1 166

十一.建筑业

统计指标解释

·之十一·

【**能源加工转换效率**】指一定时期内能源经过转换加工后，产出的各种能源产品的数量与同期内投入加工转换的各种能源数量的比率。它是观察能源加工转换装置和生产度世先进与落后、管理水平高低等重要指标。计算公式为：

能源加工转换效率＝加工转换产出量÷加工转换投入量×100％

【**国家财政总收入**】是国家通过财政各个环节筹集的财政资金的总称，它是保证国家行使其职能不可缺少的财力。主要包括：各项税收、企业收入、债务收入及其他收入。

1. 各项税收：是国家按法律规定对经济单位和个人无偿征收的实物和货币，是财政收入的主要来源。我国现行的税收主要有工商税收，包括产品税、增值税、营业税、所得税、城市维护建设税、房产税、车船使用税、资源税、印花税、建筑税、盐税、烧油特别税等；关税，包括关税和进口调节税；农牧业税和耕地占用税；国有企业所得税；国有企业调节税。

2. 企业收入：包括各部门所属国有企业及事业单位上交国家的利润和事业收入。1985年实行国有企业第二步利改税办法，企业利润主要以税收形式上交后，只有尚未实行利改税办法的企业和少数实行利润包干企业上交的收入。

3. 债务收入：包括国外借款，国内公债收入、国库券收入以及专业银行购买财政专项债券等。

4. 其他收入：包括专款收入、基本建设贷款归还收入、国家能源交通重点建设基金收入等。

【**中央财政和地方财政**】财政是国家为了实现其职能，凭借政治权力，对一部分社会产品进行分配和再分配的经济活动，中央财政和地方财政，是指财政体制上划分中央政府和地方政府以及地方各级政府之间财政管理权限的一项根本制度。它是经济管理体制的重要组成部分，它在财政管理体制中居于主导地位。它具体规定了各级政府筹集资金、支配使用资金的权力、范围和责任，使各级政府在财政管理上有责有权。这对于正确处理中央和地方之间，以及地方各级之间的分配关系，充分发挥各级政府的积极性，更好地完成国家财政收支任务，促进社会主义建设的发展有着极其重要的意义。中央财政收入和地方财政收入，是指中央和地方各级负责组织征收的收入，不是按财政体制计算的收入分成数。其收入中还包括了国外借款。

【**现金投放**】“现金回笼”的对称。中央银行在一定时期内，根据国家批准计划，而投入流动领域的现钞。它是国家银行根据市场现金流通状况，有计划地通过工资发放、商品采购、贷款等渠道，将现金投入市场。

11—1 按行业分建筑业企业产值及增加值

(1993年)　　单位:万元

项　目	建筑业总产值	建筑工程	安装工程
总　计	410 029.60	334 364.10	61 913.30
土木工程建筑业	321 803.30	295 360.40	19 563.40
#房屋建筑业	248 278.00	227 606.10	13 932.00
矿山建筑业	8 979.60	8 043.10	884.80
铁路公路.隧道桥梁建筑业	47 753.50	43 607.20	4 146.30
堤坝电站码头建筑业	686.00	636.00	40.00
其他土木工程建筑业	16 106.20	15 468.00	560.30
线路管道设备安装业	86 840.90	37 806.20	42 279.90
#线路管道安装业	48 197.30	32 359.10	14 860.50
设备安装业	38 643.60	5 447.10	27 419.40
建筑物装修装饰业	1 385.40	1 197.50	70.00

11—1 续1　　(1993年)　　单位:万元

项　目	房屋构筑物修理	非标准设备制造	建筑业增加值	竣工产值
总　计	2 689.70	11 062.50	126 559.80	278 909.30
土木工程建筑业	2 418.40	4 461.10	96 866.30	200 875.40
房屋建筑业	2 357.80	4 382.10	73 701.00	165 629.20
矿山建筑业	6.70	45.00	4 586.30	4 070.00
铁路公路.隧道桥梁建筑业			11 879.60	24 446.20
堤坝电站码头建筑业	10.00		125.70	200.00
其他土木工程建筑业	43.90	34.00	6 573.70	6 530.00
线路管道设备安装业	191.40	6 563.40	29 076.50	76 117.60
#线路管道安装业	191.40	786.30	15 494.10	53 163.50
设备安装业		5 777.10	13 582.40	22 954.10
建筑物装修装饰业	79.90	38.00	617.00	1 916.30

11—2 按经济类型分的建筑业企业产值及增加值

(1993 年)　　单位:万元

项　目	建筑业总产值	建筑工程	安装工程
总　计	410 029.60	334 364.10	61 913.30
国有经济	310 730.30	248 730.30	50 957.70
#中央企业	142 620.20	99 460.20	35 000.30
地方企业	168 110.10	149 270.10	15 957.40
大中型	267 293.20	209 709.50	47 192.40
城镇集体经济	99 299.30	85 633.80	10 955.60
大中型	29 511.80	23 807.80	5 375.00
城镇私营经济			
联营经济			
股份制经济			
外商投资经济			
港澳台投资经济			
其他经济			

11—2 续 1　　(1993 年)　　单位:万元

项　目	房屋构筑物修理	非标准设备制造	建筑业增加值	竣工产值
总计	2 689.70	11 062.50	127 787.40	278 909.30
国有经济	447.10	10 595.20	102 144.60	208 141.70
#中央企业	99.90	8 059.80	44 696.60	101 145.70
地方企业	347.20	2 535.40	57 448.00	106 996.00
大中型	34.70	10 356.60	88 748.80	178 033.70
城镇集体经济	2 242.60	467.30	25 642.80	70 767.60
大中型		329.00	6 676.00	23 615.00
城镇私营经济				
联营经济				
股份制经济				
外商投资经济				
港澳台投资经济				
其他经济				

11—3 建筑施工企业机械设备

(1993 年)

项 目	自有机械设备年末总台数(台)	自有机械设备年末总功率(万千瓦)	#施工机械功率(万千瓦)	自有机械设备净值(万元)
总 计	39 584	69.59	45.11	51 323.80
国有经济	23 491	50.14	31.11	42 551.70
#地央企业	9 668	23.25	16.37	23 387.00
地方企业	13 823	26.89	14.74	19 164.70
大中型	17 119	41.19	25.03	36 959.30
城镇集体经济	16 093	19.45	14.01	8 772.10
#大中型	1 778	3.71	1.66	2 277.30
城镇私营经济				
联营经济				
股份制经济				
外商投资经济				
港澳台投资经济				
其他经济				

11—4 建筑业企业施工及竣工情况

(1993 年)

项 目	单位工程施工个数(个)	单位工程竣工个数(个)	单位工程优良品率(%)	房屋建筑竣工面积(万平方米)	房屋建筑竣工面积优良品率(%)
总 计	7 246	5 035	36.00	329.25	34.64
土木工程建筑业	5 481	3 540	31.13	314.97	35.35
#房屋建筑业	4 220	2 721	19.88	303.39	35.47
矿业建筑业	295	109	23.85	5.61	20.14
铁路公路隧道桥梁建筑业	699	523	86.43	3.02	68.33
堤坝电站码头建筑业	16	2	50.00	0.54	42.60
其他土木工程建筑业	251	185	44.32	2.40	13.75
线路管道设备安装业	1 664	1 401	50.25	11.35	23.88
#线路管道安装业	428	395	36.46	8.58	23.19
设备安装业	1 236	1 006	55.67	2.76	26.09
建筑物装修装饰业	101	94	6.38	2.93	

11—5 建筑业劳动生产率、工程成本降低率及资金利税率

(1993 年)　　单位:元/人、%

项　目	总产值劳动生产率	增加值劳动生产率	工程成本降低率	流动资产利润率
总　计	20 208.46	6 298.50		1.05
国有经济	22 068.91	7 254.59		1.06
#中央企业	28 467.11	8 921.48		2.15
地方企业	18 534.73	6 333.85		0.28
大中型	24 455.01	8 119.74		1.20
城镇集体经济	15 990.23	4 129.28		1.02
#大中型	28 376.73	6 419.23		1.00
城镇私营经济				
联营经济				
股份制经济				
外商投资经济				
港澳台投资经济				
其他经济				

11—6 建筑施工企业财务及经济效益

指　标	单位	1992 年			1993 年		
		合计	国有	集体	合计	国有	集体
资金总额	万元	187 228	172 283	14 945.00			
固定资产原值	万元	147 930	129 820	18 110.00	164 101.60	141256.70	22 844.90
固定资产净值	万元	101 721	88 742	12 979.00	118 247.90	101583.30	16 664.60
固定资产年平均净值	万元	102 321	90 347	11 974.00	109 984.45	95 162.65	14 821.80
流动资金年未数	万元						
利润总额	万元	4 133	3 519	614.00	3 294.20	2440.40	853.80
利税总额	万元	12 709	10 085	2 624	15 193.10	11 254.30	3 938.80
百元资金实现利润	元/百元	2.20	2.03	—0.00			
百元产值占用资金	元/百元	59.40	68.06	23.45			
百元产值占有流动资金	元/百元	27.29	33.30	2.33			

11－7 建筑业企业财务状况

(1993年)　　单位:万元

指　标	资本金合计	国家资金	法人资金	个人资本金	外商资本金
总　计	123 222.20	106 440.00	16 096.80	343.40	
国有经济	100 429.00	95 594.20	4 566.80		
#中央企业	57 691.40	56 375.90	1 315.50		
地方企业	42 737.60	39 218.30	3 251.30		
大中型	86 207.60	83 734.40	2 473.20		
城镇集体经济	22 793.20	10 845.80	11 530.00	343.40	
#大中型	4 235.20	3 641.00	527.00	67.20	
城镇私营经济					
联营经济					
股份制经济					
外商投资经济					
港澳台投资经济					
其他经济					

11－7 续1　　(1993年)　　单位:万元

指　标	流动资产年末合计	#货币资金	存货	#在建工程	长期投资年末合计
总　计	314 337.00	19 350.80	122 277.90	46 767.50	8 118.30
国有经济	230 807.40	15 354.40	92 580.20	28 217.50	7 005.30
#中央企业	95 565.90	7 787.80	45 542.80	14 630.90	4 680.50
地方企业	135 241.50	7 566.60	47 037.40	13 586.60	2 324.80
大中型	19 313.00	13 049.20	80 465.20	22 786.60	6 651.50
城镇集体经济	83 529.60	3 996.40	29 697.70	18 550.00	1 113.00
#大中型	19 687.60	1 100.30	12 235.30	8 736.30	97.10
城镇私营经济					
联营经济					
股份制经济					
外商投资经济					
港澳台投资经济					
其他经济					

11—7 续 2 (1993年) 单位:万元

指标	固定资产年末合计	固定资产原价年末合计	#生产经营用	本年提取折旧	专项工程年末合计	无形及递延资产年末合计
总计	122 085.60	164 101.60	95 986.40	7 150.50	9 706.50	6 558.20
国有经济	106 204.70	141 256.70	80 644.40	5 979.30	8 981.50	5599.40
#中央企业	63 995.00	82 266.20	45 068.90	3 347.30	7160.10	812.70
地方企业	42 209.70	58 990.50	35 575.50	2 632.00	1 821.40	4 786.70
大中型	93 687.10	123 898.50	70 898.10	5 096.00	8 240.20	5016.50
城镇集体经济	15 880.90	22 844.90	15 342.00	1 171.20	725.00	958.80
大中型	3 133.60	5 670.10	3 963.80	307.90	323.90	500.00
城镇私营经济						
联营经济						
股份制经济						
外商投资经济						
港澳台投资经济						
其他经济						

11—7 续 3 (1993年) 单位:万元

指标	其他资产年末合计	资产年末总计	流动负债年末合计	长期负债年末合计	所有者权益年末合计	#股本
总计	2 735.70	463 541.30	263 631.30	45 721.40	113 593.60	2 251.20
国有经济	1 842.00	360 440.30	213 951.80	41 495.50	92 539.70	2174.10
#中央企业	528.60	172 742.80	86 170.10	19 640.20	49 915.00	
地方企业	1 313.40	187 697.50	127 781.70	21 855.30	42 624.70	2 174.10
大中型	1 442.80	307 351.10	180 358.00	37 158.20	78 578.90	2174.10
城镇集体经济	893.70	103 101.00	49 679.50	4 225.90	21 053.90	77.10
大中型	15.60	23 757.80	18 653.00	1 186.00	6 894.40	67.20
城镇私营经济						
联营经济						
股份制经济						
外商投资经济						
港澳台投资经济						
其他经济						

十二. 交通运输邮电通讯业

统计指标解释

·之十二·

【预算外资金】是指不纳入国家财政预算，由各地方、各部门、各企业、事业、行政单位，按国家规定范围自行筹集和使用的资金。它是国家财政预算内资金的补充财力。其收入来源，主要包括地方财政机关掌握使用的自筹资金，如工商税附加、农业税附加、城市公用事业附加等；部门、企业单位管理的专用基金，如更新改造资金、企业利润留成、企业福利基金等；事业行政单位自收自支和以收抵支未纳入预算管理的各项资金，如养路费、学杂费等。这些资金一般都有特定用途，主要是：基本建设或更新改造固定资产投资，增加流动资金，简历建筑、大修理、科技三项费用，支付养路费、城市维护费，职工福利和奖励支出，补充事业、行政经费，上交财政能源交通重点建设基金、预算调节基金等。预算外资金的使用，也要纳入计划管理的轨道，不得擅自扩大使用范围。

【现金回笼】"现金投放"的对称。它是中央银行在一定时期内。吸回流通中的现钞。它是国家银行根据市场现金流通状况，有计划地通过出售商品、提供劳务、吸收储蓄、收回贷款，向居民个人征收税款，组织市场多余现金，流回国家银行。

【保费收入】

1. 保险费收入：指投保人或被保险人为获得保险保障而付给保险人的代价。

2. 储金收入：指投保人为取得经济保障而存入保险公司的存款，保险期满，保险公司连同部分利息退还投保人。

【赔偿支出】

1. 赔款：财产保险在被保险财产发生保险合同规定的损失后，保险公司按实际损失给予的经济补偿金额。

2. 给付：人身保险在保险责任发生的意外伤害或事故及返还性保险期满，保险公司给保险人支付的款项。

【赔案件数、赔付率】赔案件数指的是保险公司已经支出赔款（给付）的业务笔数。财产险按立案件数统计，人身险按人数统计。赔付率指的是保险公司支付的赔款金额占同期保费收入（不包括储金）总额的百分比。

【职工家庭全部收入】职工家庭全部收入是指调查户的全部实际的现金收入，包括家庭人口的劳动收入（如固定职工和临时工的工资，奖金、津贴、个体劳动者的净收入），退休金、交通补助、定期性困难补助、赡养费、抚恤费、助学金等各项经常性的收入以及退职金、复员费、转业费、发明创造一次性奖金、稿费等一次性的收入。不包括周期性收入，如提取银行存款，向亲友借入款，收回借出款以及其他各种暂行款。

12－1 主要年份省内运输线路长度

单位:公里

年　份	铁路通车里程	公路通车里程	民航线路里程
1952	50.40	4 042.00	
1957	715.40	11 372.00	
1965	2 016.60	22 003.00	523.00
1970	2 133.10	27 155.00	
1975	1 911.00	33 694.00	718.00
1978	1 906.70	34 521.00	24 093.00
1980	1 909.00	33 632.00	1 118.00
1985	2 221.00	32 531.00	6 099.00
1986	1 885.00	33 574.00	2 166.00
1987	1 884.00	34 187.00	2 166.00
1988	1 884.00	34 354.00	2 166.00
1989	1 884.00	34 613.00	2 166.00
1990	1 884.00	34 708.00	2 166.00
1991	1 884.00	34 776.00	2 166.00
1992	1 884.00	34 822.00	2 166.00
1993	1 884.00	34 875.00	2 166.00

12—2 主要年份运输车辆

年　份	铁路机车数（台）	铁路客车数（辆）	民用汽车数（辆）	#载贷	#载客
1952			2 294	1 971	262
1957	160	227	8 109	6 860	957
1965	335	471	10 799	8 758	1 536
1970	389	455	14 122	11 366	1 901
1975	487	601	25 988	19 593	4 404
1978	538	616	35 632	26 343	6 265
1980	538	678	45 049	33 233	8 082
1985	603	906	65 951	44 395	17 518
1986	637	1 002	73 196	48 517	20 286
1987	660	1 102	80 858	53 172	23 252
1988	696	1 154	93 312	60 879	27 592
1989	739	1 232	97 449	63 036	29 139
1990	804	1 293	104 930	67 848	31 463
1991	846	1 346	115 292	74 105	35 091
1992	905	1 438	122 259	76 016	39 860
1993	862	1 453	132 374	79 194	46 574

12—3 主要年份客运量和客运周转量

年　份	客运量合计(万人)	铁路	公路	民航	客运周转量合计（万人公里）	铁路	公路	民航
1952	38.00		37.00	0.59	5 291		4 719	571.60
1957	947.00	576.00	371.00	0.93	124 385	96 170	27 032.00	1182.60
1965	1 222.00	684.00	534.00	3.63	243 012	213 920	26 512.00	2580.40
1970	1 466.00	597.00	865.00	3.34	332 388	287 310	42 569.00	2509.40
1975	2 526.00	671.00	1 840.00	15.60	475 474	379 850	83 144.00	12 480.10
1978	3 038.00	686.00	2 324.00	27.70	517 244	394 470	101 700.00	21 074.40
1980	3 865.00	789.00	3 038.00	38.00	615 282	462 433	137 295.00	15 554.00
1981	3 882.00	751.00	3 123.00	8.00	630 667	456 567	156 107.00	17 993.00
1982	4 387.00	883.00	3 494.00	10.00	671 083	491 181	170 374.00	9 528.00
1983	4 871.00	893.00	3 974.00	4.00	747 147	551 551	192 306.00	3 290.00
1984	5 526.00	1 026.00	4 496.00	4.00	846 471	622 656	220324.00	3 491.00
1985	6 067.00	1 094.00	4 968.00	5.00	1 014 687	758 260	252570.00	3 857.00
1986	6 738.00	1 131.00	5 595.00	12.00	1 121 994	817 713	297297.00	6 984.00
1987	7 511.00	1 173.00	6 320.00	18.00	1 207 468	837 559	349657.00	20 252.00
1988	8 135.00	1 244.00	6 871.00	20.00	1 336 615	937 992	373109.00	25 514.00
1989	8 146.00	1 083.00	7 046.00	17.00	128 042	877 921	382245.00	19 876.00
1990	7 505.00	860.00	6 625.00	20.00	1 099 397	727 603	348802.00	22 992.00
1991	7 468.00	850.00	6 593.00	25.03	1 211 874	799 460	384311.00	28 103.00
1992	7 170.00	874.00	6 270.00	26.00	1 230 676	835 667	365870.00	29 139.00
1993	6 822.00	883.00	5 910.00	29.00	1 293 153	914 261	344746.00	34 146.00

注:公路中未包括非交通运输系统。

12—4 主要年份铁路.公路货物运输量和周转量

年 份	铁路货物运输量(万吨)	公路货物运输量(万吨)	#交通运输部门	铁路货物周转量(万吨公里)	公路货物周转量(万吨公里)	#交通运输部门
1952		221	219		8 031	7 968
1957	328	1 243	972	243 590	28 241	24 343
1965	757	762	656	896 150	29 985	27 941
1970	1 161	994	766	1 345 510	48 982	46 324
1975	1 845	2 132	1 126	1 877 900	99 271	80 511
1978	2 216	2 206	1 052	2 248 923	114 514	83 672
1980	2 059	1 742	532	1 581 640	87 594	60 720
1981	1 867	1 317	439	1 401 651	69 182	46 460
1982	1 904	1 484	497	1 546 783	82 556	59 041
1983	2 051	1 403	581	1 756 788	87 535	65 633
1984	2 192	1 691	631	1 965 203	100 862	71 337
1985	2 414	1 856	604	2 198 316	105 395	67 978
1986	2 384	2 139	551	2 321 373	122 453	65 417
1987	2 373	2 432	554	2 467 467	146 394	68 651
1988	2 361	2 622	551	2 671 064	169 740	72 171
1989	2 397	2 732	520	2 822 220	200 447	71 925
1990	2 386	3 225	515	2 867 147	221 758	65 785
1991	2 426	3 612	458	3 033 640	230 641	57 965
1992	2 501	4 149	395	3 127 573	243 982	47 764
1993	2 571	4 496	321	3 180 172	263 918	37 468

12—5 运输量和周转量

项目	1992年	1993年	1993年比1992年增长%
一. 货运			
货运总量(万吨)	17 144.30	19 193.30	11.00
铁路	2 501.00	2 571.00	2.81
#发送量	2 501.00	2 571.00	2.80
公路	14 642.00	16 622.00	13.50
交通运输系统	395.00	321.00	—23.05
非交通运输系统	14 248.00	16 301.00	14.40
民航	0.30	0.30	
货物周转总量(万吨公里)	3 913 987.00	3 991 162.00	2.00
铁路	3 127 573.00	3 180 172.00	1.68
公路	786 101.00	810 653.00	3.10
交通运输系统	47 764.00	37 468.00	—27.48
非交通运输系统	738 337.00	773 185.00	4.70
民航	313.00	337.00	7.67
二. 客运			
客运量总计(万人)	9 108.00	9 580.00	5.18
铁路	874.00	883.00	1.03
公路	8 208.00	8 668.00	5.60
交通运输系统	6 270.00	5 910.00	—6.09
非交通运输系统	1 938.00	2 758.00	42.31
民航	26.00	29.00	11.54
客运周转量总计(万人公里)	1 305 117.00	1 407 127.00	7.82
铁路	835 667.00	914 261.00	9.40
公路	440 311.00	458 720.00	4.18
交通运输系统	365 870.00	344 746.00	—6.13
非交通运输系统	74 441.00	113 974.00	53.11
民航	29 139.00	34 146.00	17.72

12—6 全省独立核算运输企业民用车辆拥有量

指　标	单位	总计	独立核标运输企业	#交通部门系统	附营运输单位	个体及联户
一. 民用汽车	辆	9 542	7 592	6 161	1 950	
载客量	客位	113 613	105 515	99 343	8 098	
载重量	吨位	30 165	21 265	14 915	8 900	
1. 载客汽车	辆	3 280	3 018	2 816	262	
2. 普通载货汽车	辆	5 735	4 128	3 071	1 551	
3. 专用载货汽车	辆	217	80	21	137	
4. 其他专用汽车	辆	232	232	199		
5. 特种汽车	辆	78	78	54		
二. 轮胎式拖拉机	辆	14 339	14 339	14 339		
三. 摩托车	辆	72	72	585		
四. 其他机动车	辆	212	26	18	186	
五. 载货挂车	辆	866	866	794		

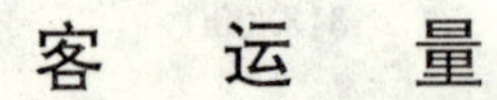

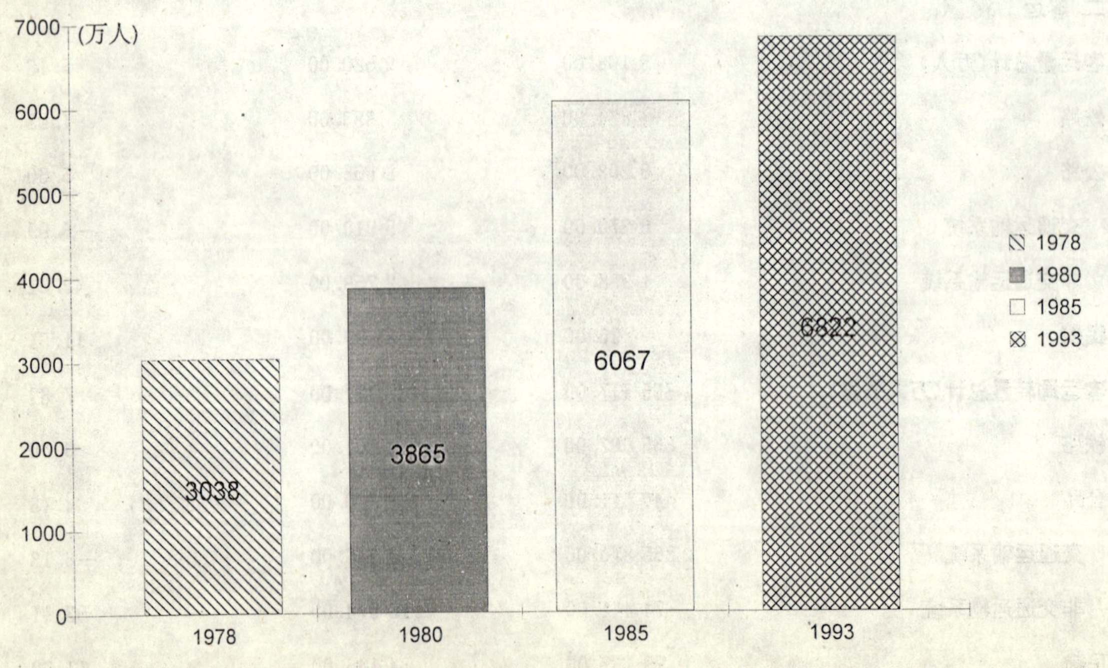

12—7 独立核算交通运输企业财务状况

单位:万元

指　标	总计	按经济类型分			按专业类型分		
		国有经济	集体经济	其他经济	公路运输	水上运输	港口
企业个数(个)	209	157	50	2	182		
#亏损企业	70	60	10		56		
资本金合计	6 981 216	6 944 479	35 506	1 231	92 538		
#国家资本金	6 940 019	6 938 734	1 285		51 626		
法人资本金	4 018	981	1 847	1 190	3 829		
个人资本金	421	11	369	41	418		
外商资本金							
流动资产年末合计	1 150 535	1 072 067	78 125	342	1 389 692		
#货币资金	307 547	257 189	50 290	68	65 873		
存货	203 088	195 597	7 457	34	29 669		
长期投资年末合计	35 104	11 319	23 615	170	29 063		
固定资产年末合计	1 620 678	1 572 692	46 755	1 231	301 144		
固定资产原价	9 955 165	9 884 067	70 707	391	361 449		
累计折旧	1 040 074	1 017 264	22 779	30	62 699		
无形及递延资产年末合计	617	582	35		617		
其他资产年末合计	19 547	1 426	18 121		18 365		
流动负债年末合计	461 816	428 611	33 190	15	59 243		
长期负债年末合计	2 034 677	2 032 160	2 516		13 678		
#未交税金	48 237	47 016	1 221		2 449		
所有者权益年末合计	7 095 169	7 006 809	88 359		135 466		
#股东	1 644	1 605	39		1 644		
主营业务收入	2 052 638	1 966 705	81 889	4 045	303 421		
营业成本	1 963 012	1 886 931	75 747	334	253 907		
营业税金及附加	77 526	75 785	1 588	152	3 440		
主营业务利润	−66 455	−70 053	3 389	209	19 982		
其他业务利润	172 349	166 945	5 384	20	8 026		
管理费用	461 617	451 558	10 041	18	16 382		
财务费用	100 512	100 377	−67	202	872		
营业利润	−456 235	−455 043	−1 200	9	10 754		
补贴收入	1		1		1		
投资收益	19	18	1		18		
营业外收入	10 768	6 765	4 003		7 979		
营业外支出	143 913	141 978	1 935		8 653		
利润总额	−589 359	−590 238	871	9	10 100		
亏损企业亏损额	612 518	611 872	646		2 466		
应交所得税	254	92	162		246		
应交特种基金	7 046	7 042	4		56		
转作奖金的利润	365	13	2	350	365		
应付利润	436	163	273		347		
本年应付工资	172 048	160 891	10 648	509	74 326		
本年应付福利费	120 111	119 507	404	200	10 639		

12—8 邮电通讯网

年份	邮电局所合计(个)	#在乡村	邮路总长度(公里)	长途电话业务电路(路)	电报业务电路(路)
1952	843	8	221 858	91	120
1957	887	497	55 524	143	196
1965	806	561	83 172	175	225
1970	892	640	99 057	324	214
1975	1 067	826	149 835	454	261
1978	1 131	929	153 675	494	289
1980	1 094	919	139 007	549	288
1981	1 088	910	139 762	587	286
1982	1 093	910	136 971	606	294
1983	1 096	894	139 494	639	300
1984	1 115	928	138 304	668	303
1985	1 133	941	140 151	769	311
1986	1 118	943	137 792	842	325
1987	1 113	857	138 166	1 025	324
1988	1 113	933	147 302	1 142	354
1989	1 111	930	151 763	1 467	338
1990	1 116	932	152 669	1 564	348
1991	1 122	851	154 723	1 945	343
1992	1 122	935	162 427	3 049	356
1993	1 164	960	164 406	4 126	357

12—9 邮电通信现代化水平

年份	市话交换机总容量(门)	省会至地县平均长途电话(路)		特快专递(件)	邮政快件(万件)	邮政储蓄年末余额(万元)
		省会至地(市)	省会至县(市)			
1985	54 220	9.20				
1986	58 150	11.10				513.20
1987	73 420	12.50				4 005.30
1988	77 820	14.20	1.30	7 046	98.20	6 571.70
1989	88 000	21.50	1.30	11 862	374.30	10 717.90
1990	105 920	21.70	1.50	19 320	625.00	19 164.90
1991	125 130	36.30	2.20	22 076	602.50	30 783.60
1992	164 144	47.80	3.80	36 301	666.70	42 151.80
1993	242 360	71.70	5.70	74 381	712.50	55 921.90

邮电业务总量

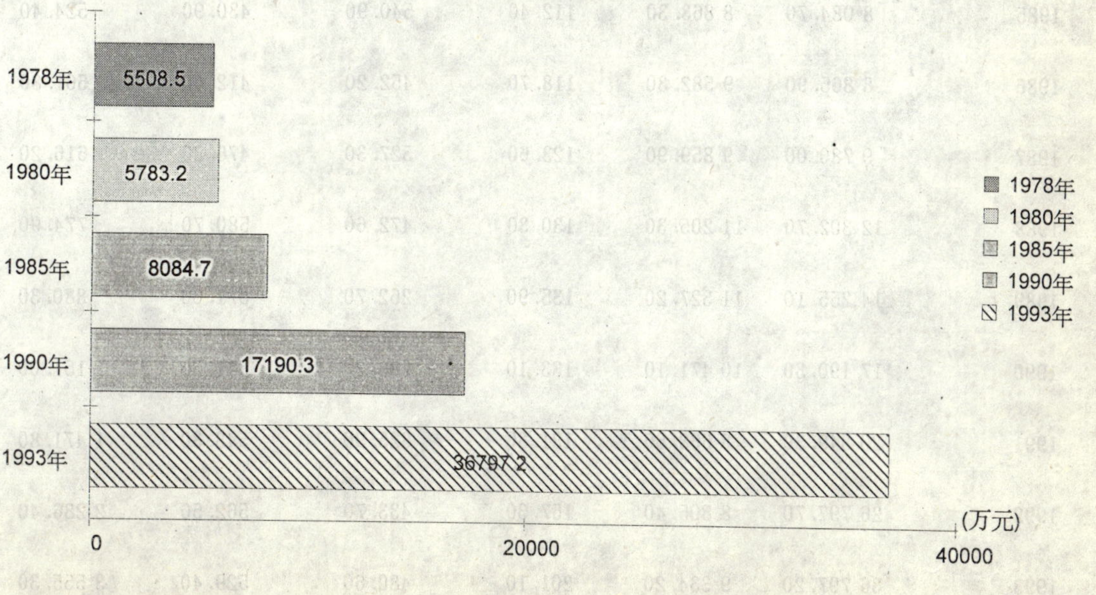

12—10 邮电业务量

年　份	邮电业务总量（90年不变价格）（万元）	函件（万元）	包件（万件）	报刊期发数（万份）	电报（万份）	长途电话（万张）
1952	367.30	676.00	14.50	16.60	26.40	24.90
1957	1 309.00	2 879.00	48.00	68.70	46.30	51.20
1965	2 731.10	3 790.80	49.00	86.10	152.20	160.80
1970	3 180.90	4 818.20	127.70	60.90	254.00	175.20
1975	4 643.60	5 825.20	124.50	150.20	356.10	332.60
1978	5 508.50	6 140.40	121.40	205.60	377.60	372.40
1980	5 783.20	6 815.20	108.20	278.50	344.20	361.60
1981	5 806.60	6 773.40	105.40	196.10	378.70	348.10
1982	6 003.90	6 797.90	99.20	298.40	377.80	373.90
1983	6 353.00	6 833.30	102.10	352.40	404.30	398.10
1984	7 063.90	7 590.10	104.80	426.60	379.10	476.80
1985	8 084.70	8 863.30	112.40	540.90	430.90	524.40
1986	8 865.90	9 582.30	118.70	452.20	412.00	561.80
1987	9 780.00	9 859.90	123.60	527.30	476.30	616.20
1988	12 302.70	11 205.30	130.30	472.60	580.70	774.90
1989	14 255.10	11 327.20	135.90	262.70	571.60	880.30
1990	17 190.30	10 471.10	133.10	286.20	541.50	1 151.00
1991	20 849.30	8 668.60	131.30	325.90	543.30	1 471.80
1992	26 797.70	8 805.40	157.30	433.70	562.50	2 286.40
1993	36 797.20	9 334.20	201.10	480.60	529.40	3 555.30

十三.批发零售贸易和餐饮业

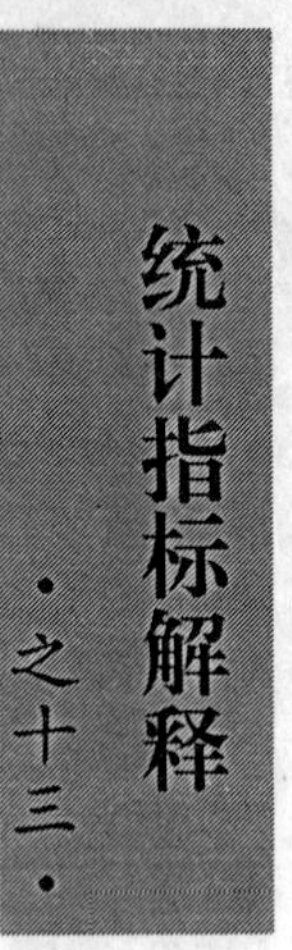

【各种物价总指数】各种物价总指数,包括零售物价总指数,职工生活费用价格总指数,农副产品收购价格总指数和农村工业品零售价格总指数等。

我国的商品价格有多种,除全民所有制商业部门的各种价格外,还有集市贸易价格。故除计算全民所有制商业各项目指数外,还要计算包括全民所有制商业和集市贸易价格的零售物价总指数和职工生活费用价格总指数。在计算这些指数时使用各种价格的实际购、销金额作为权数加权汇总。

1. 零售物价指数是采用加权算数平均公式计算的。每年根据实际零售资料调整一次权数。历年计算指数的市场和所选商品逐步增加。1988 年全国有 195 个市、203 个县作为基层填报单位。城市指数所选商品有 285 种左右,县城指数所选商品有 377 种左右,每种商品的指数采用代表规格品平均价格计算。

2. 职工生活费用价格指数,1952 年以前采用固定数量加权综合法(即总值法)计算,1953 年至 1956 年采用加权算数平均公式计算,1957 年以后根据消费品零售物价指数与服务项目价格指数汇编职工生活费用价格指数。目前计算指数所选商品和服务项目约 314 种。

3. 农副产品收购价格指数,是采用加权倒数平均公式(即按报告期实际收购金额加权综合法)计算的。目前计算指数所选的商品有 11 个大类,25 个小类,包括 250 多种农副土特产品。

4. 主要农产品与工业品交换比价是由农产品收购价格和农村工业品零售价格计算的。

【职工家庭可用于生活费的收入】职工家庭可用于生活费的收入是指家庭全部收入中能用于安排家庭日常生活的实际收入,即全部收入中扣除对亲友的“赡养、赠送支出”。

平均每人生活费收入是用家庭生活费收入除以家庭人口数。

【农民家庭总收入】总收入是指农民家庭在调查期内从各种来源得到的全部实际收入。包括:1. 从各级集体经济中得到的收入,如从统一核算单位得到的分配收入。从乡(社)村(队)企业中得到的工资、奖金、各种补贴收入;从公益金中得到的补助救济收入,从集体得到的奖励和其他收入等;2. 从经济联合体得到的劳动报酬、奖金、各种补贴和入股分红收入;3. 农民家庭经营农、林、牧、渔业和手工业、商业、饮食业、服务业、运输业、建筑业 4. 其他非借款性收入(如在外人口寄回和带回、职工工资、亲友赠送、国家财政发放、存款利息等)。

总收入是反映农民家庭实际收入水平,收入来源和构成变化的总量指标。

13—1 批发零售贸易餐饮业机构和人员数

(1993年) 单位:个.人

项目	合计			市		
	机构	网点	人员	机构	网点	人员
总计	193 178	35 080	901 604	52 363	14 018	469 108
一.批发贸易业	1 935	8 662	119 183	1 027	3 789	70 007
1.独立核算国内批发商业	1 209	6 461	74 099	513	2 526	46 324
2.独立核算对外贸易批发业	73	92	4 267	53	73	3 892
3.独立核算物资供销批发业	300	1 297	12 115	192	919	8 703
4.附营批发贸易单位		812	28 235		271	10 780
5.乡镇企业管理的批发贸易业						
6.个体批发商业	353		467	269		308
二.零售贸易业	151 271	23 171	675 473	34 911	8 631	354 220
1.独立核算零售贸易业	2 474	16 722	91 604	773	7 606	49 253
2.附营零售贸易业单位		1 826	301 796		1 025	251 926
3.乡镇企业局管理的零售贸易业		4 623	44 624			
4.个体零售商业	148 797		237 449	34 138		53 041
三.餐饮业	39 972	3 247	106 948	16 425	1 598	44 881
1.独立核算餐饮业	101	1 672	8 066	59	1 564	7 232
2.附营餐饮业		34	791		34	791
3.乡镇企业局管理的餐饮业		1 541	16 365			
4.个体餐饮业	39 871		81 726	16 366		36 858

13—1续 (1993年) 单位:个.人

项 目	县			县以下		
	机构	网点	人员	机构	网点	人员
总 计	49 334	11 664	234 445	91 481	9 398	198 051
一.批发贸易业	650	3 919	43 781	258	954	5 395
1.独立核算国内批发商业	465	3 001	22 579	231	934	5 196
2.独立核算对外贸易批发业	19	18	358	1	1	17
3.独立核算物资供销批发业	99	364	3 286	9	14	126
4.附营批发贸易单位		536	17 434		5	21
5.乡镇企业管理的批发贸易业						
6.个体批发商业	67		124	17		35
二.零售贸易业	40 121	6 901	164 073	76 239	7 639	157 180
1.独立核算零售贸易业	753	3 875	23 770	948	5 241	18 581
2.附营零售贸易业单位		798	49 858		3	12
3.乡镇企业局管理的零售贸易业		2 228	24 374		2 395	20 250
4.个体零售商业	39 368		66 071	75 291		118 337
三.餐饮业	8 563	844	26 591	14 984	805	35 476
1.独立核算餐饮业	42	108	834			
2.附营餐饮业						
3.乡镇企业局管理的餐饮业		736	8 979		805	7 386
4.个体餐饮业	8 521		16 778	14 984		28 090

13—2 批发贸易业分类型机构和人员数

(1993年)　　单位:个.人

项　目	合计			市		
	机构	网点	人员	机构	网点	人员
总　计	1 935	8 662	119 183	835	3 789	70 007
一.独立核算国内批发商业	1 209	6 461	74 099	513	2 526	46 324
国有经济	776	3 621	50 019	276	1 313	30 737
集体经济	427	2 829	24 010	233	1 205	15 535
私营经济	4	8	52	4	8	52
联营经济	1	3	18			
股份制经济						
其他经济	1					
二.独立核算对外贸易批发业	73	92	4 267	53	73	3 892
国有经济	70	89	4 187	53	73	3 892
集体经济	3	3	80			
三.独立核算物资供销批发业	300	1 297	12 115	192	919	8 703
国有经济	250	1 173	10 325	157	841	7 501
集体经济	48	122	1 766	33	76	1 178
联营经济	1	2	9	1	2	9
其他经济	1		15	1		15
四.附营批发贸易单位		812	28 235		271	10 780
国有经济		801	28 129		267	10 737
集体经济		11	106		4	43
五.乡镇企业管理的批发贸易业						
六.个体批发商业	353		467	269		308

13—2续　　(1993年)　　单位:个.人

项　目	县			县以下		
	机构	网点	人员	机构	网点	人员
总　计	650	3 919	43 781	258	954	5 395
一.独立核算国内批发商业	465	3 001	22 579	231	934	5 196
国有经济	324	1 902	15 695	176	406	3 587
集体经济	139	1 096	6 866	55	528	1 609
私营经济						
联营经济	1	3	18			
股份制经济						
其他经济	1					
二.独立核算对外贸易批发业	19	18	358	1	1	17
国有经济	16	15	278	1	1	17
集体经济	3	3	80			
三.独立核算物资供销批发业	99	364	3 286	9	14	126
国有经济	85	319	2 709	8	13	115
集体经济	14	45	577	1	1	11
联营经济						
其他经济						
四.附营批发贸易单位		536	17 434		5	21
国有经济		530	17 381		4	11
集体经济		6	53		1	10
五.乡镇企业管理的批发贸易业						
六.个体批发商业	67		124	17		35

13—3 零售贸易业分经济类型机构和人员

(1993年)　　单位:个.人

项　目	合计			市		
	机构	网点	人员	机构	网点	人员
总　计	151 271	23 171	675 473	34 911	8 631	354 220
一.独立核算零售贸易企业	2 474	16 722	91 604	773	7 606	49 253
国有经济	1 136	3 962	44 865	265	1 184	23 900
集体经济	1 323	7 758	38 326	499	1 780	17 455
私营经济	7	4 982	7 799	3	4 631	7 315
联营经济	1	4	10			
股份制经济	3	9	484	3	9	484
其他经济	4	7	120	3	2	99
二.附营零售贸易业单位		1 826	301 796		1 025	251 926
国有经济		794	57 445		258	34 059
集体经济		1 032	244 351		767	217 867
三.乡镇企业局管理的零售贸易业		4 623	44 624			
四.个体零售商业	148 797		237 449	34 138		53 041

13—3 续　　(1993年)　　单位:个.人

项　目	县			县以下		
	机构	网点	人员	机构	网点	人员
总　计	40 121	6 901	164 073	76 239	7 639	157 180
一.独立核算零售贸易企业	753	3 875	23 770	948	5 241	18 581
国有经济	504	2 212	16 520	367	566	4 445
集体经济	243	1 303	6 735	581	4 675	14 136
私营经济	4	351	484			
联营经济	1	4	10			
股份制经济						
其他经济	1	5	21			
二.附营零售贸易业单位		798	49 858		3	12
国有经济		535	23 383		1	3
集体经济		263	26 475		2	9
三.乡镇企业局管理的零售贸易业		2 228	24 374		2 395	20 250
四.个体零售商业	39 368		66 071	75 291		118 337

13—4 餐饮业分经济类型机构和人员

(1993年) 单位:个.人

项目	合计			市		
	机构	网点	人员	机构	网点	人员
总计	39 972	3 247	106 948	16 425	1 598	44 881
一.独立核算餐饮业	101	1 672	8 066	59	1 564	7 232
国有经济	50	290	4 502	20	207	3 846
集体经济	49	1 382	3 564	37	1 357	3 386
私营经济	2			2		
二.附营餐饮业		34	791		34	791
三.乡镇企业局管理的餐饮业		1 541	16 365			
四.个体餐饮业	39 871		81 726	16 366		36 858

13—4续 (1993年) 单位:个.人

项目	县			县以下		
	机构	网点	人员	机构	网点	人员
总计	8 563	844	26 591	14 984	805	35 476
一.独立核算餐饮业	42	108	834			
国有经济	30	83	656			
集体经济	12	25	178			
私营经济						
二.附营餐饮业						
三.乡镇企业局管理的餐饮业		736	8 979		805	7 386
四.个体餐饮业	8 521		16 778	14 984		28 090

13—5 批发零售贸易业商品购进、销售、库存总额

(1993年)　　　　单位:万元

项　目	合计	国内商业	对外贸易业	物资供销业	附营商业
一. 商品购进总额	2 591 332	1 771 522	144 418	626 167	49 225
1. 从生产者购进	1 409 876	848 491	114 044	423 330	24 011
#农副产品购进	253 823	195 506	48 674	6 982	2 661
2. 从批发零售贸易业购进	1 054 530	849 914	2 747	178 595	23 274
3. 进口	38 591	13 872	22 498	2 203	18
4. 其他	88 335	59 245	5 129	22 039	1 922
二. 商品销售总额	3 018 890	2 074 399	151 440	730 832	62 219
1. 批发合计	2 171 571	1 353 802	145 607	640 706	31 456
对生产经营者批发	807 179	352 102	8 632	436 681	9 764
#对农民农业生产资料销售	145 105	121 806	180	21 713	1 406
对批发零售贸易业批发	1 230 721	998 817	10 619	204 025	17 260
出口	133 671	2 883	126 356		4 432
2. 对居民和社会集团商品零售额	847 319	720 597	5 833	90 126	30 763
三. 年末库存额	766 239	606 414	35 006	104 668	20 151

批发零售贸易业商品购进与销售构成

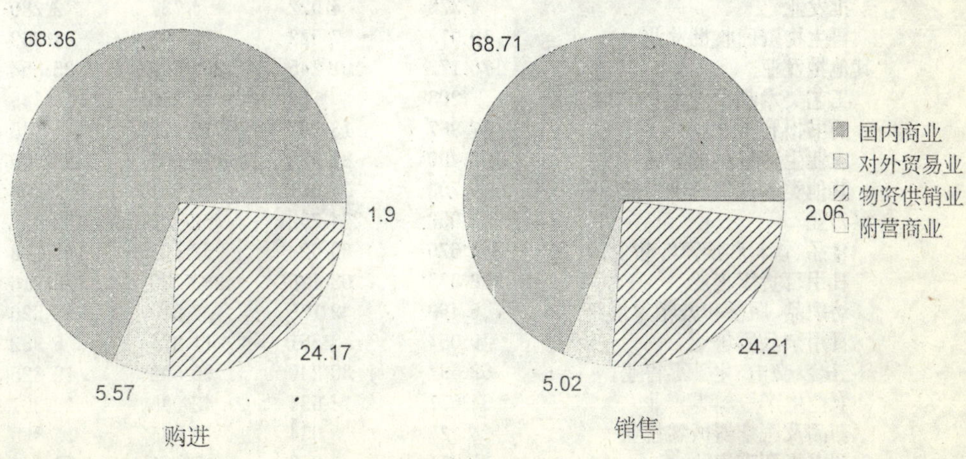

13—6 批发零售贸易业商品购.销.存总额(国内商业)

(1993年) 单位:万元

项　目	商品购进总额	#从生产者购进	商品销售总额	#消费品零售额	年末库存额
总　额	1 816 146	870 511	2 128 003	749 117	622 161
一.独立核算的国内商业	1 771 522	848 491	2 074 399	720 597	606 414
(一)按经济类型分					
国有经济	1 211 321	618 379	1 410 452	516 962	403 223
集体经济	540 360	224 024	642 624	186 721	197 324
私营经济	12 419	3 987	13 171	12 828	3 879
联营经济	124	7	142	33	19
股份制经济	4 863	1 493	4 975	3 048	539
其他经济	2 435	601	3 035	1 005	1 430
(二)按国民经济行业分					
食品.饮料.烟草和家庭用品批发商业	799 186	384 048	927 880	201 054	281 827
食品.饮料.烟草批发业	403 057	182 400	449 851	54 795	106 087
棉.麻.土畜产品批发业	85 895	31 436	105 290	11 593	19 643
纺织品.服装和鞋帽批发业	8 828	6 717	9 924	1 279	6 257
日用百货批发业	106 821	56 245	130 594	41 492	46 495
日用杂品批发业	35 767	19 341	42 221	12 036	26 407
五金.交电.化工批发业	85 897	48 655	99 141	31 166	37 724
药品及医疗器械批发业	72 921	39 254	90 859	48 693	39 214
能源.材料和机械电子设备批发业	154 110	88 436	167 801	51 562	31 665
能源批发业	102 303	61 215	105 876	40 321	19 642
化工材料批发业	1 587	1 409	877	226	134
木材批发业	1 560	1 560	1 137	31	844
建筑材料批发业	2 657	1 943	3 539	473	415
矿产品批发业	2 958	2 943	3 161	37	168
金属材料批发业	9 751	2 174	12 161	549	1 060
机械.电子设备批发业	9 908	6 138	12 522	3 370	1 603
汽车.摩托车及零配件批发业	4 373	4 022	4 737	2 286	2683
再生物资回收批发业	19 013	7 032	23 791	4 269	5 116
其他批发业	175 173	101 245	209 526	35 554	43 068
工艺美术品批发业	203	169	215	45	120
图书报刊批发业	17 867	13 207	19 529	4 145	3 140
农业生产资料批发业	150 400	82 968	179 091	29 606	37 415
其他类未包括的批发业	6 703	4 901	10 691	1 758	2 393
零售业	643 053	274 762	769 192	432 427	249 854
食品.饮料和烟草零售业	204 676	80 624	262 101	136 178	82 433
日用百货零售业	238 833	103 126	283 233	179 716	104 910
纺织品.服装和鞋帽零售业	6 459	2 175	7 810	5 526	3 565
日用杂品零售业	9 054	3 561	11 875	6 932	4 124
五金.交电.化工零售业	58 697	35 240	66 520	19 825	16 778
农业生产资料零售业	34 557	14 634	42 036	12 301	11 209
药品及医疗器械零售业	24 325	5 054	19 935	15 859	14 484
图书报刊零售业	15 851	5 253	15 181	14 446	3 886
其他零售业	50 601	25 095	60 501	41 644	8 465
二.附营国内商业	44 624	22 020	53 604	28 520	15 747

13—7 批发零售贸易业商品购.销.存总额(对外贸易业)

(1993年)　　　　单位:万元

项目	商品购进总额	#从生产者购进	商品销售总额	#消费品零售额	年末库存额
总　额	146 425	114 677	155 387	6 239	38 151
一.独立核算对外贸易业	144 418	114 044	151 440	5 833	35 006
(一)按经济类型分:					
国有经济	142 902	112 612	149 576	5 555	34 786
集体经济	1 516	1 432	1 864	278	220
(二)按国民经济行业分:					
食品.饮料.烟草和家庭用品批发业	118 602	100 379	110 724	5 464	24875
食品.饮料.烟草批发业	38 214	25 391	27 234	316	5 265
棉.麻.土畜产品批发业	31 163	29 173	28 903	5 135	2 150
纺织品.服装和鞋帽批发业	36 789	34 711	37 614		8 442
日用百货批发业					
日用杂品批发业	102	101	169		90
五金.交电.化工批发业	422	75	798	13	59
药品及医疗器械批发业	11 912	10 928	16 006		8 869
能源.材料和机械电子设备批发业	17 030	10 525	27 998	89	7 755
能源批发业	135	135	135		160
化工材料批发业	3 693	3 693	5 884		399
木材批发业					
建筑材料批发业					
矿产品批发业	5 762	3 516	8 605		5 403
金属材料批发业	3 243	1 227	6 127		1 550
机械.电子设备批发业	4 197	1 954	7 247	89	243
汽车,摩托车及零配件批发业					
再生物资回收批发业					
其他批发业	8 307	2 931	12 205	256	2 263
工艺美术品批发业	2 819	1 287	7 489	35	899
图书报刊批发业					
农业生产资料批发业					
其他类末包括的批发业	5 488	1 644	4 716	221	1 364
零售业	479	209	513	24	113
食品.饮料和烟草零售业			2	2	
日用百货零售业			2	2	
纺织品.服装和鞋帽零售业					
日用杂品零售业					
五金.交电.化工零售业					
农业生产资料零售业					
药品及医疗器械零售业	479	209	509	20	113
图书报刊零售业					
其他零售业					
二.附营对外贸易业	1 007	633	3 947	406	3 145

13—8 批发零售贸易业商品购.销.存总额(物资供销业)

(1993年) 单位:万元

项　　目	商品购进总额	#从生产者购进	商品销售总额	#消费品零售额	年末库存额
总　　额	629 761	424 688	735 500	91 963	105 927
一.独立核算物资供销业	626 167	423 330	730 832	90 126	104 668
(一)按经济类型分					
国有经济	570 399	400 054	634 836	71 112	88 525
集体经济	54 213	21 951	93 665	18 941	16 065
联营经济	304	74	358	10	15
其他经济	1 251	1 251	1 973	63	63
(二)按国民经济行业分					
食品.饮料.烟草和家庭用品批发业	4 540	2 714	5 565	1 364	3 180
食品.饮料.烟草批发业	154	87	170	2	57
棉.麻.土畜产品批发业	1 535	1 201	2 162	1 316	508
纺织品.服装和鞋帽批发业					
日用百货批发业					
日用杂品批发业					
五金.交电.化工批发业	2 851	1 426	3 233	46	2 615
药品及医疗器械批发业					
能源.材料和机械电子设备批发业	567 819	391 646	657 788	62 641	82484
能源批发业	19 906	16 620	21 188	12 785	1 186
化工材料批发业	44 156	35 467	51 383	47	3 659
木材批发业	20 032	11 091	22 458	3 010	3 515
建筑材料批发业	58 481	46 664	61 663	4 525	7 373
矿产品批发业	5 509	2 365	5 434	6	505
金属材料批发业	310 309	193 106	385 951	18 409	42 735
机械.电子设备批发业	74 163	63 469	72 297	6 688	13 588
汽车.摩托车及零配件批发业	23 532	20 182	24 750	17 019	8628
再生物资回收批发业	11 731	2 682	12 664	152	1 295
其他批发业	17 031	11 918	23 592	5 374	4 248
工艺美术品批发业					
图书报刊批发生					
农业生产资料批发业	15 148	10 665	21 437	5 327	3 919
其他类未包括的批发业	1 883	1 253	2 155	47	329
零售业	36 777	17 052	43 887	20 747	14 756
食品.饮料和烟草零售业	675	225	987	572	2 331
日用百贷零售业	5 247	2 267	6 716	2 749	2 336
纺织品.服装和鞋帽零售业					
日用杂品零售业	5 296	2 266	7 810	4 488	2 103
五金.交电.化工零售业	371	85	462	162	161
农业生产资料零售业	21 137	9 615	22 886	9 509	6 197
药品及医疗器械零售业					
图书报刊零售业					
其他零售业	4 051	2 594	5 026	3 267	1 628
二.附营单位	3 594	1 358	4 668	1 837	1 259

13—9 批发零售贸易企业商品销售.库存数量(国内商业)

(1993年)

指　标	单位	批　发				零售	年末库存
		合计	对生产经营单位批发	对批发零售贸易业批发	出口		
粮食	吨	2 037 721	186 568	1 848 930	2 223	1 048 532	2 486 682
食用植物油	吨	83 926	1 906	82 020		95 580	31 806
猪和猪肉	吨	19 093	47	19 046		12 838	3 161
牛和牛肉	吨	7 832	5 986	1 846		2 003	2 199
羊和羊肉	吨	4 896	1 511	3 385		1 784	1 153
鲜蛋	吨	1 440		1 440		499	70
水产品	吨	1 245	57	1 188		5 871	2 361
盐	吨	267 973	116 723	151 250		30 781	100 923
食糖	吨	20 546	5 299	15 247		8 717	3 396
卷烟	箱	766 896	75 201	691 695		434 411	215 539
酒	吨	51 390	6 421	44 834	135	15 624	15 334
茶叶	吨	2 206	325	1 881		2 656	2 948
棉花	吨	4 235	175	4 060		624	3 444
布	百米	209 056	17 342	191 714		104 553	259 413
#棉布	百米	127 256	11 858	115 398		88 504	134 985
呢绒	百米	22 644	15 507	7 137		20 925	21 850
绸缎	百米	50 012	1 797	48 215		35 474	52 763
服装	百件	69 255	967	68 288		2 108 646	247 634
针织内衣裤	百件	196 808	22 252	174 556		1 623 851	809 349
鞋	百双	349 400	6 195	343 205		1 475 652	705 386
#皮鞋	百双	42 923	1 095	41 828		134 283	104 422
合成洗衣粉	吨	11 645	674	10 971		3 919	3 595
黄金饰品	千元	15 753		15 753		156 165	39 952
自行车	辆	351 596	47 386	304 210		203 920	114 754
摩托车	辆	2 142	254	1 888		2 690	1 178
电视机	台	181 714	28 366	153 348		104 284	59 253
#彩色电视机	台	89 280	15 094	74 186		58 181	27 205
录音机	台	131 464	29 373	102 091		61 270	61 555

13—9 续 (1993 年)

指标	单位	批发				零售	年末库存
		合计	对生产经营单位批发	对批发零售贸易业批发	出口		
录像机	台	5 095	651	4 444		3 857	1 710
照相机	架	5 627	1 807	3 820		15 411	8 375
家用电风扇	台	33 535	4 556	28 979		30 073	42 203
家用洗衣机	台	65 890	6 430	59 460		52 022	22 511
家用电冰箱	台	29 162	7 460	21 699	3	40 275	12 099
房间空调器	台	2 502	1 345	1 157		395	1 986
抽油烟机	台	14 215	3 741	10 474		23 027	15 474
化学肥料	吨	1 283 967	133 275	1 150 692		577 131	243 887
化学农药	吨	26 356	720	25 636		26 019	50 887
农用塑料薄膜	吨	7 817	1 558	6 259		8 677	17 518
农用动力机械	台	5 242	2 255	2 987		9 380	4 138
汽车	辆	65		65		1 124	1 057
#载货汽车	辆	15		15		441	35
生铁	吨	7 351		7 351		2 007	186
钢材	吨	10 097		10 097		8 225	2 451
铜	吨					383	15
铝	吨					267	65
铅	吨					30	8
锌	吨	2		2		3	
铜材	吨	4		4			
烧碱	吨					4	1
纯碱	吨	6 016		6 016		630	702
水泥	吨	19 229		19 229		585	3 245
平板玻璃	重量箱	16 117		16 117		2 550	4 622
原木	立方米	1 077		1 077		7 653	126
锯材	立方米	100		100			147
润滑油	吨	30 309	13 472	16 837		13 411	5 896
煤炭	吨	492 674	180 892	311 782		1 781 352	506 107
汽油	吨	189 913	36 833	153 080		162 061	39 602
柴油	吨	167 979	40 550	127 429		91 713	26 746
煤油	吨	14 057	3 485	10 572		64 874	14 878
燃料油	吨					205 000	15 000

13—10 批发零售贸易企业商品销售.库存数量(对外贸易业)

(1993年)

指标	单位	批发				零售	年末库存
		合计	对生产经营单位批发	对批零贸易业批发	出口		
粮食	吨	73 558	11 008	34 102	28 448	9 969	15 036
食用植物油	吨					73	
猪和猪肉	吨	225		225			4
牛和牛肉	吨	1		1			1
羊和羊肉	吨	35		35		3	
卷烟	箱					31	58
酒	吨					2	
棉花	吨	4	4			38	
布	百米	315 176		30 384	284 792	37	16 284
#棉布	百米	110 309		8 838	101 471	5	11 175
呢绒	百米	124			124		
服装	百件	65 135		28 774	36 361	3 261	5 187
针织内衣裤	百件	206 354		169 328	37 026		1 077
鞋	百双	157 559		157 559			
皮鞋	百双	146 369		146 369			
录音机	台	82 412		52 444	29 968		
照相机	架	65 500		65 500			
家用电风扇	台	62 879		62 879			
家用洗衣机	台	840		840			
化学肥料	吨	120	120			144	
铝	吨	1 522		1 522			239
铅	吨	1 567		1 567			48
锌	吨	900		900			
铜材	吨						94
铝材	吨	6		6			
烧碱	吨	200			200		
纯碱	吨	1 550			1 550		
润滑油	吨	124			124		
煤炭	吨	40 190		40 190			16 044

13—11 批发零售贸易企业商品销售.库存数量(物资供销业)

(1993年)

指 标	单位	批 发				零售	年末库存
		合计	对生产经单位批发	对批发零售贸易业批发	出口		
粮食	吨	13 935	6	13 929		7 032	10 070
盐	吨	14		14		2 500	309
食糖	吨	94		94		446	145
卷烟	箱	4 468	1	4 467		23 355	9 629
酒	吨	407	1	406		705	466
茶叶	吨	268		267		143	100
棉花	吨	53		53		112	53
布	万米	83	35	48		817	677
棉布	万米	45	9	36		537	423
呢绒	万米	7	1	6		32	31
绸缎	万米	20		20		80	45
服装	百件	9 580	2 746	6 834		7 647	5 752
针织内衣裤	百件	23 185	8 991	14 194		19 692	13 439
鞋	百双	3 000		3 000		32 489	13 530
#皮鞋	百双	1 132		1 132		2 547	1 282
合成洗衣粉	吨	128	4	124		251	116
自行车	辆	1 605		1 605		7 494	1 327
摩托车	辆	91	3	88		803	51
电视机	台	911		911		3 017	1 440
#彩色电视机	台	479		479		1 690	889
录音机	台	292		292		2 687	1 097
录像机	台	6		6		95	1
照相机	架					3	25
家用电风扇	台	111		111		437	316
家用洗衣机	台	585		585		2 019	1 189
家用电冰箱	台	63		63		150	77

13—11 续

(1993年)

指标	单位	批发				零售	年末库存
		合计	对生产经单位批发	对批发零售贸易业批发	出口		
抽油烟机	台	43		43		713	615
化学肥料	吨	102 124	8 755	93 369		55 806	29 159
化学农药	吨	109	3	106		9 073	1 357
农用塑料薄膜	吨	26 360	226	26 134		552	95
农用动力机械	台	3 481	865	2 616		2 249	1 374
汽车	辆	3 521	1 410	2 111		3 570	1 319
#载货汽车	辆	2 409	828	1 581		1 471	1 046
生铁	吨	73 828	66 293	7 535		5 549	1 641
钢材	吨	582 425	330 318	251 920	187	99 942	93 343
铜	吨	7 594	4 688	2 906		81	713
铝	吨	28 777	16 248	12 529		93	641
铅	吨	1 444	979	465		10	301
锌	吨	5 907	3 381	2 526			521
锡	吨	107	46	61			35
铜材	吨	84	40	44			37
铝材	吨	178	45	133		6	18
硫酸	吨	671	510	161		312	169
烧碱	吨	1 519	1 133	386		19	37
纯碱	吨	11 729	9 948	1 781		221	1 187
天然橡胶	吨	3 134	2 433	701			169
合成橡胶	吨	8 207	3 761	4 446		3	28
水泥	吨	412 159	240 160	171 999		17 330	32 945
平板玻璃	重量箱	317 231	107 482	209 749		35 138	23 626
原木	立方米	135 704	74 880	60 824		31 759	34 750
锯材	立方米	19 772	14 071	5 701		3 824	3 946
润滑油	吨	83 972	81 154	2 818		581	24 206
汽油	吨	20 451	6 453	13 998		30 666	4 028
柴油	吨	12 704	4 384	8 320		50 804	1 932
煤油	吨	1 422	602	820		34 917	1 944

13—12 社会消费品零售总额

(1993 年)　　单位:万元

项目	1990 年	1991 年	1992 年	1993 年	1993 年为下列年份的%	
					1990 年	1992 年
社会消费品零售总额	961 640	1 061 667	1 282 631	1 561087	172.29	121.71
一. 按销售地区分						
市的零售额	576 403	645 920	798 889	1 055 232	183.07	131.09
县的零售额	192 667	199 421	233 439	291 352	151.22	124.81
县以下的零售额	192 570	216 326	250 303	214 503	111.39	85.70
二. 按经济类型分						
国有经济	448 210	525 839	602 854	631 833	162.32	104.81
集体经济	236 578	241 017	277 101	324 793	137.29	117.21
私营经济				13 112		
个体经济	181 439	196 704	286 164	396 674	218.63	138.62
联营经济	2		374	165		44.12
股份制经济				30 113		
外商投资经济				6		
港澳台投资经济						
其他经济	95 411	98 107	116 138	164 391	172.30	141.55
三. 按行业分						
批发零售贸易业	720 232	801 564	972 441	1 177 823	176.82	121.12
餐饮业	59 668	61 210	85 286	103 508	173.47	121.37
制造业	62 403	76 604	83 257	106 676	170.95	128.13
其他	23 926	24 182	25 509	9 976	41.70	39.11
农民对非农业居民零售	95 411	98 107	116 138	163 104	170.95	140.44

13—13 批发零售贸易企业财务状况(国内商业)

(1993年)　　单位:万元

项　目	资本金合计	国家	法人	个人	外商
独立核算的国内商业	381 108	301 667	35 479	18 934	1 153
(一)按经济类型分					
国有经济	262 581	241 320	6 975	9 355	
集体经济	115 765	59 650	28 357	7 694	1 153
私营经济	1 952		54	1 865	
联营经济	55		35	20	
股份制经济	537	479	58		
其他经济	218	218			
(二)按国民经济行业分:					
食品.饮料.烟草和家庭用品批发业	135 835	123 306	6 756	1489	137
食品.饮料.烟草批发业	83 377	78 104	1 698	193	
棉.麻.土畜产品批发业	11 377	9 139	1 986	192	
纺织品.服装和鞋帽批发业	773	631	125	17	
日用百货批业	15 745	12 797	1 814	338	137
日用杂品批发业	5 568	4 742	316	509	
五金.交电.化工批发业	11 572	10 696	616	216	
药品及医疗器械批发业	7 423	7 197	201	24	
能源.材料和机械电子设备批发业	24 133	20 502	1 603	1 503	513
能源批发业	15 242	14 953	278		
化工材料批发业	83	39	44		
木材批发业	1 098	1 098			
建筑材料批发业	340	270	62	8	
矿产品批发业	170	76		94	
金属材料批发业	1 209	346	181	682	
机械.电子设备批发业	818	218	529	71	
汽车.摩托车及零配件批发业	1 176	1 131	45		
再生物资回收批发业	3 997	2 371	464	648	513
其他批发业	23 944	18 803	3 364	1 157	277
工艺美术品批发业	103	103			
图书报刊批发业	1 064	893	170		
农业生产资料批发业	20 316	15 681	2 989	1 099	205
其他类未包括的批发业	2 461	2 126	205	58	72
零售业	197 196	139 056	23 756	14 785	226
食品.饮料和烟草零售业	42 221	39 153	1 948	86	
日用百货零售业	59 725	27 869	15 536	13 492	198
纺织品.服装和鞋帽零售业	1 905	1 322	203	159	
日用杂品零售业	2 463	1 811	486	127	
五金.交电.化工零售业	6 275	5 025	1 019	120	
农业生产资料零售业	22 973	4 058	3 161	704	6
药品及医疗器械零售业	2 448	2 158	246	2	
图书报刊零售业	48 813	48 616	178	17	
其他零售业	10 373	9 044	979	78	22

13—13 续 1

单位:万元

项　　目	年末资产负债				
	流动资产合计	货币资金	存货	长期投资合计	固定资产合计
独立核算的国内商业	1 349 700	112 774	668 251	33 522	210 328
(一)按经济类型分					
国有经济	934 887	79 821	511 957	13 956	150 929
集体经济	410 242	32 747	152 853	17 636	58 747
私营经济	295	58	236	1 865	6
联营经济	43	20	19		14
股份制经济	2 056	44	1 679	63	543
其他经济	2 177	84	1 507	2	89
(二)按国民经济行业分:					
食品.饮料.烟草和家庭用品批发业	541 550	48 439	277 254	18 457	77 725
食品.饮料.烟草批发业	264 585	32 515	129 819	5 102	31 950
棉.麻.土畜产品批发业	62 448	6 909	22 506	2 006	8 403
纺织品.服装和鞋帽批发业	8 651	179	6 264	123	999
日用百货批业	76 155	1 578	42 945	9 695	12 966
日用杂品批发业	23 074	1 719	12 387	397	2 946
五金.交电.化工批发业	57 535	3 378	34 126	980	13 367
药品及医疗器械批发业	49 102	2 161	29 207	154	7 094
能源.材料和机械电子设备批发业	81 108	6 296	25 466	1 841	16563
能源批发业	54 720	4 468	14 168	948	12 313
化工材料批发业	595	12	238	255	32
木材批发业	1 100	174	863	16	68
建筑材料批发业	3 930	304	318	1	163
矿产品批发业	1 003	2	44	434	122
金属材料批发业	2 230	223	734		359
机械.电子设备批发业	3 433	320	1 287	18	187
汽车.摩托车及零配件批发业	3 696	89	2 811	3	331
再生物资回收批发业	10 401	704	5 003	166	2 988
其他批发业	104 247	8 352	38 079	5 241	15 033
工艺美术品批发业	308	10	165		59
图书报刊批发业	4 902	1 379	598	612	771
农业生产资料批发业	80 129	5 648	32 253	2 584	10 868
其他类未包括的批发业	18 908	1 315	5 063	2 045	3 335
零售业	622 795	49 687	327 452	7 983	101 007
食品.饮料和烟草零售业	195 131	20 792	110 039	759	27 313
日用百贷零售业	242 855	12 544	83 463	4 728	40 098
纺织品.服装和鞋帽零售业	5 128	380	2 949	161	892
日用杂品零售业	7 432	403	4 226	168	1 736
五金.交电.化工零售业	17 773	1 135	11 805	305	4 737
农业生产资料零售业	20 210	2 443	11 013	666	3 218
药品及医疗器械零售业	11 123	667	5 116	79	1 819
图书报刊零售业	101 676	8 686	91 194	127	12 354
其他零售业	21 467	2 637	7 647	990	8 840

13—13 续 2　　　　单位:万元

项　　目	年末资产负债					
	未交税金	固定资产原价	累计折旧	无形及递延资产合计	其他长期资产合计	流动负债合计
独立核算的国内商业	311 453	94 250	16 439	31 043	1 058 495	9 655
(一)按经济类型分						
国有经济	237 248	71 981	11 064	7 630	788 651	6 809
集体经济	73 390	22 079	4 941	23 413	266 350	2 838
私营经济	6	1			206	
联营经济	20	6	1		57	
股份制经济	613	96	433		1 940	8
其他经济	176	87			1 291	
(二)按国民经济行业分						
食品.饮料.烟草和家庭用品批发业	104 926	35 297	3 811	25506	476 500	4 289
食品.饮料.烟草批发业	50 749	18 971	750	4 474	212 961	2125
棉.麻.土畜产品批发业	10 826	3 504	457	18 817	70 316	391
纺织品.服装和鞋帽批发业	1 162	176	90		8 730	17
日用百货批发业	15 116	5 597	674	21	61 780	1 154
日用杂品批发业	4 509	1 683	211	1 994	19 233	123
五金.交电.化工批发业	14 366	3 017	1 545		60 807	215
药品及医疗器械批发业	8 198	2 349	84	200	42 673	264
能源.材料和机械电子设备批发业	22 293	5 498	508	222	76 880	774
能源批发业	17 196	4 029	288	3	56 518	435
化工材料批发业	52	20		219	271	11
木材批发业	71	3	53		141	8
建筑材料批发业	132	43	9		3 552	11
矿产品批发业	75	24	1		926	2
金属材料批发业	480	123	14		1 197	109
机械.电子设备批发业	252	39	17		2 932	21
汽车.摩托车及零配件批发业	374	84	11		3 009	50
再生物资回收批发业	3 661	1 133	115		8 334	127
其他批发业	17 862	5 059	2 020	1 902	90 338	364
工艺美术品批发业	73	13		20	199	1
图书报刊批发业	1 453	373	9		5 288	14
农业生产资料批发业	12 652	4 062	1 393	1 882	66 340	247
其他类未包括的批发业	3 684	611	618		18 511	102
零售业	166 372	48 396	10 100	3 413	414 777	4 228
食品.饮料和烟草零售业	32 941	10 190	430	2 558	139 762	1482
日用百货零售业	37 504	9 768	8 233	651	95 399	1 987
纺织品.服装和鞋帽零售业	1 309	395	53		4 189	66
日用杂品零售业	2 194	586	229	20	4 811	37
五金.交电.化工零售业	4 964	1 355	742	9	24 983	180
农业生产资料零售业	4 434	1 392	212	36	16 591	63
药品及医疗器械零售业	3 551	1 950	13		10 314	11
图书报刊零售业	69 724	20 182	1		100 771	51
其他零售业	9 751	2 578	187	139	17 957	351

13—13 续 3

项目	年末资产负债			损益及分配	
	长期负债合计	所有者权益合计	#股本	商品销售收入（营业收入）	商品销售收入净额
独立核算的国内商业	184 539	299 843	21 416	2 425 580	2 221 697
(一)按经济类型分					
国有经济	132 832	214 858	11 736	1 766 313	1 622 999
集体经济	50 691	83 807	9 143	645 354	585 118
私营经济		3		7 072	6 740
联营经济		9		142	142
股份制经济	152	1 001	537	3 974	3 974
其他经济	864	165		2 725	2 724
(二)按国民经济待业分					
食品.饮料.烟草和家庭用品批发业	65 373	86 590	1 057	924782	864 526
食.饮料.烟草批发业	33 920	40 641	125	455 694	419 333
棉.麻.土畜产品批发业	5 255	10 269	208	108 218	101 087
纺织品.服装和鞋帽批发业	34	749	17	9 224	9 212
日用百货批发业	12 721	12 258	572	124 240	117 598
日用杂品批发业	4 323	4 680	325	43 458	41 397
五金.交电.化工批发业	3 427	9 867	86	107 500	100 954
药品及医疗器械批发业	5 693	8 126	— 276	76 448	74 945
能源.材料和机械电子设备批发业	6 533	20 551	1 388	179 445	168578
能源批发业	2 970	13 775		125 322	120 509
化工材料批发业	113	153		439	389
木材批发业		923		1 140	207
建筑材料批发业	148	276		3 101	2 608
矿产品批发业	433	186		1926	1 926
金属材料批发业	226	942	668	10 116	10 048
机械.电子设备批发业	279	321		8 403	6 350
汽车.摩托车及零配件批发业	646	252	74	5 240	4 281
再生物资回收批发业	1 718	3 723	646	23 758	22 260
其他批发业	10 588	24 844	1 380	255 390	239 513
工艺美术品批发业		123		180	180
图书报刊批发业		1 234		18 627	14 940
农业生产资料批发业	7 306	20 396	1 328	201 099	192 506
其他类未包括的批发业	3 282	3 091	52	35 484	31 887
零售业	102 045	167 858	17 591	1 065 963	949 080
食品.饮料和烟草零售业	30 072	34 700	—41	247 855	219 226
日用百货零售业	23 888	52 466	15 642	282 194	255 791
纺织品.服装和鞋帽零售业	626	1 311	79	22 695	5 182
日用杂品零售业	2 288	2 384	250	10 922	9 766
五金.交电.化工零售业	2 013	5 438	516	62 374	57 120
农业生产资料零售业	3 263	8 465	1 526	44 826	43 289
药品及医疗器械零售业	1 376	1 279	— 538	31 462	16 848
图书报刊零售业	35 880	52 308	38	304 767	289 128
其他零售业	2 639	9 507	119	55 868	52 730

13—13 续 4

项　　目	损益及分配				
	商品销售成本（营业成本）	经营费用（营业费用）	商品销售税金及附加费	商品销售利润	代购代销收入
独立核算的国内商业	2 061 837	132 131	44 845	110 944	742
（一）按经济类型分					
国有经济	1 495 487	90 908	36 938	90 684	632
集体经济	559 892	40 873	7 806	20 060	110
私营经济	234	28	4	6	
联营经济	128	5	2	6	
股份制经济	3 433	224	89	226	
其他经济	2 663	93	6	—38	
（二）按国民经济待业分					
食品.饮料.烟草和家庭用品批发业	816 993	45 870	10 683	30809	178
食.饮料.烟草批发业	413 722	19 608	3 819	10 060	39
棉.麻.土畜产品批发业	94 149	6 367	743	2 021	22
纺织品.服装和鞋帽批发业	8 261	243	107	603	
日用百货批发业	105 599	6 142	2 142	5 928	—1
日用杂品批发业	37 797	3 029	651	955	6
五金.交电.化工批发业	93 553	5 223	1 795	6 395	108
药品及医疗器械批发业	63 912	5 258	1 426	4 846	4
能源.材料和机械电子设备批发业	151 363	12 451	3 270	12 135	109
能源批发业	105 151	8 959	2 483	8 705	23
化工材料批发业	312	56	13	58	
木材批发业	828	147	37	129	1
建筑材料批发业	2 583	120	34	225	83
矿产品批发业	1 795	32	3	96	
金属材料批发业	8 810	486	121	650	
机械.电子设备批发业	7 529	338	82	449	
汽车.摩托车及零配件批发业	4 194	320	127	599	
再生物资回收批发业	20 161	1 993	370	1 225	3
其他批发业	225 217	13 740	2 275	9 192	6
工艺美术品批发业	140	13	6	21	
图书报刊批发业	12 742	781	331	1 087	
农业生产资料批发业	180 759	11 744	1 101	6 331	
其他类未包括的批发业	31 576	1 202	837	1 754	6
零售业	868 264	60 070	28 617	58 808	449
食品.饮料和烟草零售业	226 624	19 012	2 405	—4 329	—102
日用百货零售业	233 860	14 757	7 080	12 993	477
纺织品.服装和鞋帽零售业	4 670	376	177	369	—2
日用杂品零售业	9 386	862	189	368	
五金.交电.化工零售业	54 687	2 758	1 028	3 377	17
农业生产资料零售业	40 137	2 623	394	1 549	55
药品及医疗器械零售业	22 772	3 238	828	659	
图书报刊零售业	229 515	11 092	14 633	39 654	1
其他零售业	46 613	5 352	1 883	4 168	3

13－13 续 5

项　目	损益及分配				其他	
	主营业务利润	其他业务利润	营业利润	利润总额	本年应付工资	本年应付福利费
独立核算的国内商业	111 685	4 739	－17 029	1 338	102 860	28 812
(一)按经济类型分						
国有经济	91 315	3 403	－14 802	3 567	79 856	7 010
集体经济	20 170	1 335	－2 154	－2 232	22 229	21 750
私营经济	6		5	5	604	
联营经济	6		2	2	5	1
股份制经济	226	1	147	122	140	47
其他经济	－38		－227	－126	26	4
(二)按国民经济行业分						
食品.饮料.烟草和家庭用品批发业	30 987	1 387	－12 647	－5995	30 998	23 096
食品.饮料.烟草批发业	10 099	865	－12 264	－5 893	23 405	2 263
棉.麻.土畜产品批发业	2 043	－13	－2 101	－1825	876	20 052
纺织品.服装和鞋帽批发业	603		－8	－8	132	7
日用百货批发业	5 928	83	－119	－95	2 299	251
日用杂品批发业	961	－15	－677	－645	795	110
五金.交电.化工批发业	6 503	455	1 222	1 268	1 703	184
药品及医疗器械批发业	4 850	12	1 300	1 188	1 788	229
能源.材料和机械电子设备批发业	12 244	378	2 897	2 696	4284	391
能源批发业	8 728	282	2 170	2 093	1 796	224
化工材料批发业	58	－1	24	24	15	2
木材批发业	129		59	59	29	1
建筑材料批发业	308	6	169	164	59	5
矿产品批发业	96	36	53	57	15	3
金属材料批发业	650	11	40	28	57	9
机械.电子设备批发业	449	15	133	107	1 732	13
汽车.摩托车及零配件批发业	599	20	149	128	112	14
再生物资回收批发业	1 227	10	101	37	469	120
其他批发业	9 198	1 008	2 475	2 089	6 982	360
工艺美术品批发业	21	3	－5	－5	11	1
图书报刊批发业	1 087	9	253	250	163	30
农业生产资料批发业	6 331	394	1 551	1 325	6 572	266
其他类未包括的批发业	1 760	602	676	519	236	64
零售业	59 256	1 966	－9 754	2 548	60 596	4 965
食品.饮料和烟草零售业	－4 431	665	－19 864	－9 345	11206	1 118
日用百货零售业	13 470	271	1 354	1 301	8 629	843
纺织品.服装和鞋帽零售业	368	15	－159	－168	1191	203
日用杂品零售业	368	6	－314	－276	408	160
五金.交电.化工零售业	3 394	39	310	364	904	149
农业生产资料零售业	1 604	118	145	343	1 036	108
药品及医疗器械零售业	659	571	216	176	19 090	172
图书报刊零售业	39 655	127	7 519	9 066	12 900	1 758
其他零售业	4 169	154	1 039	1 094	5 232	454

13—14 批发零售贸易业企业财务状况(对外贸易业)

单位:万元

项　目	资本金合计	国家	法人	个人	外商
独立核算的对外贸易业	11 982	11 237	737	8	
(一)按经济类型分:					
国有经济	11 770	11 161	607	1	
集体经济	212	76	129	7	
(二)按国民经济行业分					
食品.饮料.烟草和家庭用品批发业	8 632	8 201	425	6	
食品.饮料.烟草批发业	2 066	1 824	237	5	
棉.麻.土畜产品批发业	2 571	2 469	102		
纺织品.服装和鞋帽批发业	2 644	2 562	80	1	
日用百货批发业					
日用杂品批发业	23	23			
五金.交电.化工批发业	20	20			
药品及医疗器械批发业	1 308	1 303	5		
能源.材料和机械电子设备批发业	2 105	1 942	163		
能源批发业	23	23			
化工材料批发业	322	314	8		
木材批发业					
建筑材料批发业					
矿产品批发业	789	634	155		
金属材料发业	468	468			
机械.电子设备批发业	503	503			
汽车.摩托车及零配件批发业					
再生物资回收批发业					
其他批发业	1 007	1 005	2		
工艺美术品批发业	302	300	2		
图书报刊批发业					
农业生产资料批发业					
其他类未包括的批发业	705	705			
零售业	238	89	147	2	
食品.饮料和烟草零售业	17		17		
日用百货零售业	35	34	1		
纺织品.服装和鞋帽零售业					
日用杂品零售业					
五金.交电.化工零售业					
农业生产资料零售业					
药品及医疗器械零售业	186	55	129	2	
图书报刊零售业					
其他零售业					

13—14 续1

单位:万元

项目	年末资产负债				
	流动资产合计	货币资金	存货	长期投资合计	固定资产合计
独立核算的对外贸易业	151 346	12 507	51 163	3 947	7 381
(一)按经济类型分:					
国有经济	150 824	12 429	50 918	3 939	7 217
集体经济	522	78	245	8	164
(二)按国民经济行业分					
食品.饮料.烟草和家庭用品批发业	96 024	3 586	35 400	2 973	5422
食品.饮料.烟草批发业	22 692	1 522	8 500	73	1 403
棉.麻.土畜产品批发业	23 319	1 174	6 957	34	3 009
纺织品.服装和鞋帽批发业	38 493	717	10 618	2 860	933
日用百货批发业					
日用杂品批发业	155	13	87		3
五金.交电.化工批发业	277	41	82		13
药品及医疗器械批发业	11 088	119	9 156	6	61
能源.材料和机械电子设备批发业	45 761	8 162	12 900	645	1 405
能源批发业	526	261		70	24
化工材料批发业	7 937	88	638	48	320
木材批发业					
建筑材料批发业					
矿产品批发业	20 496	2 933	7 003	212	622
金属材料发业	4 118	457	2 061	170	175
机械.电子设备批发业	12 684	4 423	3 198	145	264
汽车.摩托车及零配件批发业					
再生物资回收批发业					
其他批发业	9 166	704	2 739	314	416
工艺美术品批发业	4 540	547	1 238	15	214
图书报刊批发业					
农业生产资料批发业					
其他类未包括的批发业	4 626	157	1 501	299	202
零售业	395	55	124	15	138
食品.饮料和烟草零售业	10	3	1		3
日用百货零售业	67	5	1	13	20
纺织品.服装和鞋帽零售业					
日用杂品零售业					
五金.交电.化工零售业					
农业生产资料零售业					
药品及医疗器械零售业	318	47	122	2	115
图书报刊零售业					
其他零售业					

13—14 续 2 单位:万元

项目	年末资产负债					
	未交税金	固定资产原价	累计折旧	无形及递资产合计	其他长期资产合计	流动负债合计
独立核算的对外贸易业	11 811	3 484	18	26	169 978	618
(一)按经济类型分:						
国有经济	11 627	3 463	17	26	169 399	616
集体经济	184	21	1		578	2
(二)按国民经济行业分						
食品.饮料.烟草和家庭用品批发业	9 123	2 781	9		115 280	75
食品.饮料.烟草批发业	1 975	588			24 579	16
棉.麻.土畜产品批发业	2 374	780	8		39 861	13
纺织品.服装和鞋帽批发业	3 175	892			39 944	44
日用百货批发业						
日用杂品批发业	4				154	
五金.交电.化工批发业	29	16			349	
药品及医疗器械批发业	1 566	505	1	26	10 393	2
能源.材料和机械电子设备批发业	1 753	418	6		44 532	371
能源批发业	26	2			582	3
化工材料批发业	323	166			10 443	
木材批发业						
建筑材料批发业						
矿产品批发业	779	197	6		23 000	137
金属材料批发业	190	15			3 758	183
机械.电子设备批发业	435	38			6 749	48
汽车.摩托车及零配件批发业						
再生物资回收批发业						
其他批发业	731	219			9 508	172
工艺.美术品批发业	327	103			4 849	3
图书报刊批发业						
农业生产资料批发业						
其他类未包括的批发业	404	116			4 659	169
零售业	204	66	3		658	
食品.饮料和烟草零售业	5	1	3			
日用百货零售业	39	19			100	
纺织品.服装和鞋帽零售业						
日用杂品零售业						
五金.交电.化工零售业						
农业生产资料零售业						
药品及医疗器械零售业	160	46			558	
图书报刊零售业						
其他零售业						

13—14 续3

项　目	年末资产负债			损益及分配	
	长期负债合计	所有者权益合计	#股本	商品销售收入（营业收入）	商品销售收入净额
独立核算的对外贸易业	33 190	25 798	— 844	151 167	124 063
(一)按经济类型分					
国有经济	33 185	25 685	— 840	149 618	123 758
集体经济	5	113	—4	1 549	305
(二)按国民经济行业分					
食品.饮料.烟草和家许用品批发业	32 869	21 521	— 630	98 472	79714
食品.饮料.烟草批发业	20	818	— 333	22 342	13 300
棉.麻.土畜产品批发业	29 090	14 116	— 238	31 264	25 629
纺织品.服装和鞋帽批发业	3 664	4 953		34 582	30 940
日用百货批发业					
日用杂品批发业		5		111	111
五金.交电.化工批发业		—58	—59	53	53
药品及医疗器械批发业	95	1 687		10 120	9 681
能源.材料和机械电子设备批发业	175	3 634	—13	36 983	34 521
能源批发业		4		158	
化工材料批发业	60	15		4 647	4 647
木材批发业					
建筑材料批发业					
矿产品批发业	85	2 461	—13	18 969	18 649
金属材料批发业		717		2 504	2 184
机械.电子设备批发业	30	437		10 705	9 041
汽车.摩托车及零配件批发业					
再生物资回收批发业					
其他批发业	173	773		13 209	7 644
工艺美术品批发业	73	85		7 863	6 524
图书报刊批发业					
农业生产资料批发业					
其他类未包括的批发业	100	688		5 346	1 120
零售业	—27	— 130	— 201	2 503	2 184
食品.饮料和烟草零售业				8	
日用百货零售业	—32			1 980	1 980
纺织品.服装和鞋帽零售业					
日用杂品零售业					
五金.交电.化工零售业					
农业生产资料零售业					
药品及医疗器械零售业	5	— 130	— 201	515	204
图书报刊零售业					
其他零售业					

13—14 续 4

项　　目	损益及分配				
	商品销售成本（营业成本）	经营费用（营业费用）	商品销售税金及附加费	商品销售利润	代购代销收入
独立核算的对外贸易业	143 371	13 299	1 021	—20 427	708
(一)按经济类型分					
国有经济	141 958	13 199	1 020	—20 458	708
集体经济	1 413	100	1	31	
(二)按国民经济行业分					
食品.饮料.烟草和家许用品批发业	93 875	8 324	330	—14 576	485
食品.饮料.烟草批发业	21 751	2 017	120	—4 535	10
棉.麻.土畜产品批发业	29 117	3 727	178	—5 706	404
纺织品.服装和鞋帽批发业	34 389	1 623	32	—5 030	71
日用百货批发业					
日用杂品批发业	111	15		—20	
五金.交电.化工批发业	48	8	1	—4	
药品及医疗器械批发业	8 459	934	—1	719	
能源.材料和机械电子设备批发业	35 041	4 067	649	—4 534	195
能源批发业	135	8	3	12	
化工材料批发业	4 560	620	46	— 579	47
木材批发业					
建筑材料批发业					
矿产品批发业	17 793	1 602	541	—1 060	114
金属材料批发业	2 007	960	34	— 498	9
机械:电子设备批发业	10 546	877	25	—2 409	25
汽车.摩托车及零配件批发业					
再生物资回收批发业					
其他批发业	12 069	855	41	—1 373	28
工艺美术品批发业	7 540	433	18	—1 743	28
图书报刊批发业					
农业生产资料批发业					
其他类未包括的批发业	4 529	422	23	370	
零售业	2 386	53	1	56	
食品.饮料和烟草零售业	9			—8	
日用百货零售业	1 949	1		30	
纺织品.服装和鞋帽零售业					
日用杂品零售业					
五金.交电.化工零售业					
农业生产资料零售业					
药品及医疗器械零售业	428	52	1	34	
图书报刊零售业					
其他零售业					

13—14 续 5

项　目	损益及分配				其他	
	主营业务利润	其他业务利润	营业利润	利润总额	本年应付工资	本年应付福利费
独立核算的对外贸易业	－19 719	24 090	－9 866	－6 967	824	158
(一)按经济类型分						
国有经济	－19 750	24 090	－9 846	－6 949	777	147
集体经济	31		－20	－18	47	11
(二)按国民经济行业分						
食品.饮料.烟草和家庭用品批发业	－14 091	71 013	－7 804	－5428	489	73
食品.饮料.烟草批发业	－4 525	4 456	－2 792	－ 818	172	42
棉.麻.土畜产品批发业	－5 302	3 227	－4 942	－4 859	180	18
纺织品.服装和鞋帽批发业	－4 959	9 076	－ 245	109	48	8
日用百货批发业						
日用杂品批发业	－20		－25	－25	1	
五金.交电.化工批发业	－4	2	－18	－23	63	
药品及医疗器械批发业	719	252	218	188	25	5
能源.材料和机械电子设备批发业	－4 339	5 424	－1 614	－1183	251	71
能源批发业	12	20	2	2		
化工材料批发业	－ 532	41	－1 422	－1 427	70	3
木材批发业						
建筑材料批发业						
矿产品批发业	－ 946	1 908	86	53	88	10
金属材料批发业	－ 489	928	33	33	31	50
机械.电子设备批发业	－2 384	2 528	－ 313	156	62	8
汽车.摩托车及零配件批发业						
再生物资回收批发业						
其他批发业	－1 345	1 653	－ 425	－ 336	54	10
工艺美术品批发业	－1 715	1 649	－ 387	－ 389	43	3
图书报刊批发业						
农业生产资料批发业						
其他类未包括的批发业	370	4	－38	53	11	7
零售业	56		－23	－20	30	4
食品.饮料和烟草零售业	－8		－8	－8	2	
日用百货零售业	30		5	5	9	2
纺织品.服装和鞋帽零售业						
日用杂品零售业						
五金.交电.化工零售业						
农业生产资料零售业						
药品及医疗器械零售业	34		－20	－17	19	2
图书报刊零售业						
其他零售业						

13—15 批发零售贸易业企业财务状况(物资供销业)

单位:万元

项目	资本金合计	国家	法人	个人	外商
独立核算物资供销业	70 769	60 598	4 163	515	
(一)按经济类型分					
国有经济	60 106	53 385	1 657	11	
集体经济	10 271	7 172	2 155	504	
联营经济					
其他经济	392	41	351		
(二)按国民经济行业分					
食品.饮料.烟草和家庭用品批发业	809	667	122	20	
食品.饮料.烟草批发业	23	23			
棉.麻.土畜产品批发业	290	270		20	
纺织品.服装和鞋帽批发业					
日用百货批发业					
日用杂品批发业					
五金.交电.化工批发业	496	374	122		
药品及医疗器械批发业					
能源.材料和机械电子设备批发业	60 588	52 331	2 737	120	
能源批发业	2 173	1 795	378		
化工材料批发业	2 727	2 727			
木材批发业	2 551	2 505	38		
建筑材料批发业	3 796	3 537	140	12	
矿产品批发业	940	667	273		
金属材料批发业	26 721	19 816	1 909	32	
机械.电子设备批发业	3 865	3 865			
汽车.摩托车及零配件批发业	1 951	1 951			
再生物资回收批发业	15 864	15 468		76	
其他批发业	2 006	1 536	395	74	
工艺美术品批发业					
图书报刊批发业					
农业生产资料批发业	1 631	1 284	271	74	
其他类未包括的批发业	375	252	124		
零售业	7 366	6 065	908	301	
食品.饮料和烟草零售业	312	312			
日用百货零售业	1 342	1 140	109	84	
纺织品.服装和鞋帽零售业					
日用杂品零售业	1 227	687	406	126	
五金.交电.化工零售业	264	121	115	28	
农业生产资料零售业	3 559	3 159	262	63	
药品及医疗器械零售业					
图书报刊零售业					
其他零售业	663	646	16		

13—15 续1

单位:万元

项　目	年末资产负债				
	流动资产合计	货币资金	存货	长期投资合计	固定资产合计
独立核算物资供销业	370 736	23 473	11 586	15 517	31 715
(一)按经济类型分					
国有经济	342 705	20 612	99 985	14 171	27 150
集体经济	27 204	2 371	15 536	1 346	4 517
联营经济					
其他经济	827	490	65		48
(二)按国民经济行业分					
食品.饮料.烟草和家庭用品批发业	3 145	310	1 322	27	513
食品.饮料.烟草批发业	70	—4	54		22
棉.麻.土畜产品批发业	1 464	146	488	22	252
纺织品.服装和鞋帽批发业					
日用百货批发业					
日用杂品批发业					
五金.交电.化工批发业	1 611	168	880	5	239
药品及医疗器械批发业					
能源.材料和机械电子设备批发业	337 368	21 063	97 872	15 075	26454
能源批发业	8 850	522	1 103	2	2 453
化工材料批发业	15 217	1 457	5 010	1 865	1 934
木材批发业	9 999	606	4 717	269	1 285
建筑材料批发业	17 616	2 868	6 296	1 772	3 243
矿产品批发业	1 946	317	547	439	685
金属材料批发业	107 020	10 955	48 569	10 202	9 130
机械.电子设备批发业	22 527	2 770	14 024	487	1 519
汽车.摩托车及零配件批发业	132 551	837	8 135	17	1 269
再生物资回收批发业	21 642	731	9 471	22	4 936
其他批发业	9 449	848	4 511	52	1 606
工艺美术品批发业					
图书报刊批发业					
农业生产资料批发业	8 066	736	4 026	38	1 294
其他类未包括的批发业	1 383	112	485	14	312
零售业	20 775	1 252	11 881	364	3 142
食品.饮料和烟草零售业	523	13	396	9	102
日用百货零售业	4 056	259	2 133	152	518
纺织品.服装和鞋帽零售业					
日用杂品零售业	3 039	149	2 131	114	484
五金.交电.化工零售业	1 109	122	358	3	69
农业生产资料零售业	9 551	583	5 623	73	1 407
药品及医疗器械零售业					
图书报刊零售业					
其他零售业	2 497	127	1 250	13	562

13－15 续 2 单位:万元

项　目	年末资产负债					
	未交税金	固定资产原价	累计折旧	无形及递资产合计	其他长期资产合计	流动负债合计
独立核算物资供销业	70 898	11 093	1 151	1 313	193 687	1 330
(一)按经济类型分						
国有经济	64 879	9 291	813	1 214	176 608	1 018
集体经济	5 962	1 792	338	99	16 688	312
联营经济						
其他经济	57	10			391	
(二)按国民经济行业分						
食品.饮料.烟草和家庭用品批发业	935	137	10		2 011	10
食品.饮料.烟草批发业	22	7			59	
棉.麻.土畜产品批发业	280	40	2		1 162	5
纺织品.服装和鞋帽批发业						
日用百货批发业						
日用杂品批发业						
五金.交电.化工批发业	633	90	8		790	5
药品及医疗器械批发业						
能源.材料和机械电子设备批发业	63 876	9 132	648	1 215	170 984	1 144
能源批发业	2 472	668	1		10 023	28
化工材料批发业	1 902	729	2	1	14 111	83
木材批发业	2 271	666	161	44	4 890	74
建筑材料批发业	4 100	1 283	96	448	14 184	131
矿产品批发业	913	183	12		1 625	198
金属材料批发业	43 486	4 031	279	706	86 868	504
机械.电子设备批发业	1 818	579	4	16	19 780	17
汽车.摩托车及零配件批发业	1 485	427	77		13 084	66
再生物资回收批发业	5 429	566	16		3 419	43
其他批发业	1 715	449	141		6 063	36
工艺美术品批发业						
图书报刊批发业						
农业生产资料批发业	1 491	394	133		4 772	19
其他类未包括的批发业	224	55	8		1 291	17
零售业	4 372	1 375	353	99	14 629	140
食品.饮料和烟草零售业	152	34			457	2
日用百货零售业	750	228	111	7	2 207	37
纺织品.服装和鞋帽零售业						
日用杂品零售业	775	304	29	36	1 914	16
五金.交电.化工零售业	187	48	21	45	1 126	5
农业生产资料零售业	1 944	602	58	5	6 857	72
药品及医疗器械零售业						
图书报刊零售业						
其他零售业	563	159	134	6	2 068	8

13—15 续 3

项　　目	年末资产负债			损益及分配	
	长期负债合计	所有者权益合计	#股本	商品销售收入（营业收入）	商品销售收入净额
独立核算物资供销业	22 226	52 659	599	731 068	644 469
（一）按经济类型分					
国有经济	16 497	40 642	— 186	666 319	589 992
集体经济	5 729	11 533	785	62 713	52 441
联营经济					
其他经济		484		2 036	2 036
（二）按国民经济行业分					
食品.饮料.烟草和家庭用品批发	228	1 068	10	5 981	5 286
食品.饮料.烟草批发业	2	24		174	174
棉.麻.土畜产品批发业	98	443	10	2 187	2 187
纺织品.服装和鞋帽批发业					
日用百货批发业					
日用杂品批发业					
五金.交电.化工批发业	128	601		3 620	2 925
药品及医疗器械批发业					
能源.材料和机械电子设备批发业	16 476	43 021	— 156	657 615	582206
能源批发业	110	2 239		21 723	21 723
化工材料批发业	440	4 429		58 783	58 580
木材批发业	196	2 243	—70	23 017	21 471
建筑材料批发业	4 366	5 182	113	65 933	50 761
矿产品批发业	117	1 204		5 607	5 407
金属材料批发业	9 493	23 645	— 201	369 759	322 803
机械.电子设备批发业	689	1 571		73 772	62 969
汽车.摩托车及零配件批业	290	2 083		25 637	25 542
再生物资回收批发业	775	425	3	13 387	12 950
其他批发业	2 803	2 057	76	22 562	18 883
工艺美术品批发业					
图书报刊批发业					
农业生产资料批发业	2 638	1 721	76	19 933	17 184
其他类未包括的批发业	165	336		2 629	1 699
零售业	2 718	6 514	669	44 911	38 093
食品.饮料和烟草零售业	1	250	16	940	767
日用百货零售业	933	1 227	114	6 780	5 401
纺织品.服装和鞋帽零售业					
日用杂品零售业	691	1 009	158	6 392	4 219
五金.交电.化工零售业	1	299	37	2 204	2 194
农业生产资料零售业	642	3 017	343	24 161	21 479
药品及医疗器械零售业					
图书报刊零售业					
其他零售业	450	712	2	4 434	4 033

13—15 续 4

项 目	损益及分配				
	商品销售成本（营业成本）	经营费用（营业费用）	商品销售税金及附加费	商品销售利润	代购代销收入
独立核算物资供销业	**656 895**	**24 887**	**6 398**	**30 142**	**113**
(一)按经济类型分					
国有经济	608 373	19 545	5 674	28 053	79
集体经济	46 745	5 291	693	1 911	34
联营经济					
其他经济	1 777	51	31	178	
(二)按国民经济行业分					
食品. 饮料. 烟草和家庭用品批发	5 129	458	98	208	31
食品. 饮料. 烟草批发业	158	8	2	7	
棉. 麻. 土畜产品批发业	1 793	258	48	31	31
纺织品. 服装和鞋帽批发业					
日用百货批发业					
日用杂品批发业					
五金. 交电. 化工批发业	3 178	192	48	170	
药品及医疗器械批发业					
能源. 材料和机械电子设备批发业	596 808	19 151	5 612	26 854	63
能源批发业	18 656	1 135	558	1 374	
化工材料批发业	54 639	1 355	418	2 165	
木材批发业	20 393	761	232	1 197	
建筑材料批发业	57 528	4 633	453	2 836	1
矿产品批发业	4 265	223	109	199	
金属材料批发业	344 941	7 298	2 554	14 230	52
机械. 电子设备批发业	68 990	1 352	599	2 675	
汽车. 摩托车及零配件批业	22 336	1 536	471	1 283	10
再生物资回收批发业	5 060	858	218	895	
其他批发业	15 830	2 821	153	1 120	1
工艺美术品批发业					
图书报刊批发业					
农业生产资料批发业	13 552	2 745	119	880	
其他类未包括的批发业	2 278	76	34	240	1
零售业	39 128	2 458	534	1 960	18
食品. 饮料和烟草零售业	818	60	14	38	
日用百货零售业	6 053	344	99	240	
纺织品. 服装和鞋帽零售业					
日用杂品零售业	5 603	411	81	198	2
五金. 交电. 化工零售业	1 992	112	25	76	
农业生产资料零售业	21 663	1 143	221	1 040	16
药品及医疗器械零售业					
图书报刊零售业					
其他零售业	2 999	388	94	368	

13—15 续 5

项 目	损益及分配				其他	
	主营业务利润	其他业务利润	营业利润	利润总额	本年应付工资	本年应付福利费
独立核算物资供销业	30 254	5 990	8 651	9 768	35 496	1 229
(一)按经济类型分						
国有经济	28 131	5 873	8 586	9 673	18 859	1 113
集体经济	1 945	117	23	8	16 632	115
联营经济						
其他经济	178		42	87	5	1
(二)按国民经济行业分						
食品.饮料.烟草和家庭用品批发业	240	61	53	39	173	26
食品.饮料.烟草批发业	7					
棉.麻.土畜产品批发业	62	34	7	—5	125	19
纺织品.服装产品批发业						
日用百货批发业						
日用杂品批发业						
五金.交电.化工批发业	170	27	46	44	48	7
药品及医疗器械批发业						
能源.材料和机械电子设备批发业	26 917	5 735	8 169	9 297	21022	1 070
能源批发业	1 374	27	406	441	19	8
化工材料批发业	2 165	44	397	275	12 765	19
木材批发业	1 197	170	82	— 153	960	79
建筑材料批发业	2 838	126	525	584	749	76
矿产品批发业	199	87	84	83	61	9
金属材料批发业	14 281	583	2 106	2 564	4 478	407
机械.电子设备批发业	2 675	119	919	885	341	103
汽车.摩托车及零配件发业	1 293	25	216	176	80	33
再生物资回收批发业	895	4 554	3 434	4 442	1 569	336
其他批发业	1 120	82	363	337	242	39
工艺美术品批发业						
图书报刊批发业						
农业生产资料批发业	880	80	325	298	190	39
其他类未包括的批发业	240	2	38	39	52	
零售业	1 977	112	66	95	14 059	94
食品.饮料和烟草零售业	38	119	—11	—11	26	1
日用百货零售业	240	8	—5	—15	5 563	6
纺织品.服装和鞋帽零售业						
日用杂品零售业	200	6	—83	—90	126	19
五金.交电.化工零售业	76		—19	—11	48	4
农业生产资料零售业	1 055	—8	148	185	8 155	49
药品及医疗器械零售业						
图书报刊零售业						
其他零售业	368	—13	36	37	141	15

13—16 餐饮业财务状况

（1993 年）　　　　　　　　　　　　单位：万元

项　　目	资本金合计	国家	法人	个人	外商	年未资产负债 流动资产合计	货币资金	存货
一. 餐饮业总计	4 844	4 138	401	125		5 739	1 202	2 525
按经济类型分								
国有经济	3 644	3 267	187	19		3 737	920	1 531
集体经济	1 187	871	202	105		1 972	278	981
私营经济	13		12	1		30	4	13
其他经济								
二. 按行业分：								
餐饮业	4 844	4 138	401	125		5 739	1 202	2 525
正餐	4 586	3 993	389	24		5 543	1 164	2 400
快餐	5		5			5	4	
其他餐饮业	253	145	7	101		191	34	125
三. 按企业规模分：								
大型餐饮业								
中型餐饮业	2 409	2 192	57			2 567	609	1 035
小型餐饮业	2 435	1 946	344	125		3 172	593	1 490

13—16 续 1　　　　　　　　　　　　单位：万元

项　　目	年未资产负债 长期投资合计	固定资产合计	固定资产原价	累计折旧	无形及递延资产合计	其他长期资产合计	流动负债合计	未交税金
一. 餐饮业总计	572	5 749	6 740	1 971	120	928	5 227	88
按经济类型分					81			
国有经济	239	4 497	5 269	1 686	39	878	3 405	69
集体经济	333	1 250	1 376	284			1 818	19
私营经济		2	95	1		50	4	
其他经济								
二. 按行业分：								
餐饮业	572	5 749	6 740	1 971	120	928	5 227	88
正餐	498	5 556	6 578	1 890	117	928	5 060	87
快餐								
其他餐饮业	74	193	162	81	3		167	1
三. 按企业规模分：								
大型餐饮业								
中型餐饮业	180	2 675	3 427	1 002	33	878	2 025	64
小型餐饮业	392	3 074	3 313	969	87	50	3 202	24

13—16 续 2

单位:万元

项　目	年未资产负债			损益及分配				
	长期负债合计	所有者权益合计	股本	商品销售收(营业收入)	商品销售收入净额	商品销售成本(营业成本)	经营费用(营业费用)	商品销售税金及附加费
一. 餐饮业总计	1 795	5 002	93	13 711	6 855	7 969	3 364	607
按经济类型分								
国有经济	1 124	3 946		10 714	4 378	6 190	2 618	468
集体经济	671	1 056	93	2 887	2 477	1 716	703	133
私营经济				110		63	43	6
其他经济								
二. 按行业分:								
餐饮业	1 795	5 002	93	13 711	6 855	7 969	3 364	607
正餐	1 750	4 803	—5	12 876	6 118	7 421	3215	573
快餐		4		5	5	4	1	
其他餐饮业	45	195	98	830	732	544	148	34
三. 按企业规模分:								
1. 大型企业								
2. 中型企业	1 151	2 390		7 925	2 162	4 550	1 960	374
3. 小型企业	644	2 612	93	5 786	4 693	3 419	1 404	233

13—16 续 3

单位:万元

项　目	损益及分配						其他	
	商品销售利润	代购代销收入	主营业务利润	其他业务利润	营业利润	利润总额	本年应付工资	本年应付福利费
一. 餐饮业总计	1 581	50	1 630	98	620	581	1 546	129
按经济类型分								
国有经济	1 316	48	1 364	68	526	510	1 191	96
集体经济	266	2	267	28	97	74	342	33
私营经济	—1		—1	2	—3	—3	13	
其他经济								
二. 按行业分:								
餐饮业	1 581	50	1 630	98	620	581	1 546	129
正餐	1 482	50	1 531	97	581	557	1 500	125
快餐								
其他餐饮业	99		99	1	39	24	46	4
三. 按企业规模分:								
1. 大型企业								
2. 中型企业	971	48	1 018	27	384	422	929	72
3. 小型企业	610	2	612	71	236	159	617	57

13－17 国合商业和供销合作社经济效益主要指标

单位:万元

指标	1978年	1992年	1993年	1993年为下列年份的%	
				1978年	1992年
商品销售总额	982 533	2 060 982	2 223 764	226.33	107.90
商业厅	377 064	564 184	623 224	165.28	110.47
供销社	269 465	561 206	629 832	233.73	112.23
粮食局	185 813	423 677	405 171	218.05	95.63
商品销售毛利	79 665	200 594	226 354	284.13	112.84
商业厅	32 847	67 261	79 148	240.96	117.67
供销社	28 281	57 383	64 671	228.67	112.70
粮食局	938	8 639	10 919	1 164.07	126.39
商品流通费	63 586	202 925	235 354	370.13	115.98
商业厅	20 924	47 362	62 917	300.69	132.84
供销社	19 199	50 425	62 562	325.86	124.07
粮食局	12 419	59 417	60 820	489.73	102.36
商品经营利润	8 237	－26 821	－32 035		119.44
商业厅	8 158	9 466	3 288	40.30	34.73
供销社	5 978	1 701	－4 361		
粮食局	－11 041	－52 175	－50 696	459.16	97.95
全部企业利润总额(补贴前)	7 687	－32 626	－40 331		123.62
商业厅	7 601	6 475	5 522	72.65	85.28
供销社	5 223	－ 113	－5 423		4 799.12
粮食局	－9 243	－49 694	－51 815	560.59	104.27
利税总额	20 988	43 862	41 702	198.69	95.08
商业厅	10 421	17 083	17 573	168.63	102.87
供销社	5 679	7 557	2 314	40.75	30.62
粮食局	1 404	7 370	2 032	144.73	27.57
全部企业全部流动资金平均占用额	420 184	1 106 564	1 113620	265.03	100.64
商业厅	133 994	261 457	348 450	260.05	133.27
供销社	125 291	268 233	307 055	245.07	114.47
粮食局	107 603	412 543	434 195	403.52	105.25
全部企业年末固定资产原值	127 762	288 116	339 544	265.76	117.85
商业厅	45 901	103 970	120 715	262.99	116.11
供销社	26 438	27 646	76 802	290.50	133.23
粮食局	36 041	75 085	85 523	237.29	113.90
商业企业职工平均人数	130 416	128 285	187 945	144.11	146.51
商业厅	45 862	50 297	71 555	156.02	142.26
供销社	43 592	57 261	57 619	132.18	100.63
粮食局	22 025	44 194	36 765	166.92	83.19

13—18 集市贸易成交额和成交量

品名	单位	全省		城镇		农村	
		1992 年	1993 年	1992 年	1993 年	1992 年	1993 年
成交总额	万元	444 016	702 733	309 753	471 540	134 263	231 193
粮食	万元	7 798	13 270	1 912	3 334	5 886	9 936
#大米	吨	6 310	12 096	1 788	3 873	4 522	8 223
玉米	吨	18 820	26 049	3 677	3 567	15 143	22 482
小麦	吨	37 219	56 923	8 689	13 517	28 530	43 406
油脂油料	万元	6 267	11 486	1 686	5 149	4 581	6 337
棉烟麻	万元	1 869	3 261	711	1 397	1 158	1 864
肉食禽蛋	吨	56 120	88 195	34 330	58 653	21 790	29 542
猪肉	吨	52 391	76 345	33 320	52 756	19 071	23 589
牛肉	吨	9 385	13 564	5 854	8 587	3 531	4 977
羊肉	吨	8 990	13 184	4 931	7 886	4 059	5 298
鸡蛋	吨	22 195	29 826	13 117	19 229	9 078	10 597
鸡.鸭.鹅	吨	7 284	9 715	2 925	4 204	4 359	5 511
水产品	万元	5 982	11 195	5 726	10 540	256	655
蔬菜	万元	63 066	94 435	46 982	70 888	16 084	23 547
鲜菜	吨	505 254	1 276 308	333 844	839 859	171 410	436 449
干鲜果	万元	45 819	344 661	36 850	214 991	87 146	129 670
鲜瓜果	吨	292 549		205 403			
日用杂品	万元	1 736	3 146	737	2 184	999	962
家畜	万元	9 026	12 442	1 661	2 142	7 365	10 300
仔猪	吨	15 322	39 611	1 685	2 405	13 637	37 206
工业品	万元	172 713	265 161	136 883	197 018	35 830	68 143
其他	万元	55 180	104 820	34 589	55 344	20 591	49 476

13—19 城. 乡集贸市场贸易情况

指　　标	1978 年	1992 年	1993 年	1993 年为下列年份%	
				1978 年	1992 年
一. 集市数(个)	481	1 564	1 682	349.69	107.54
城市		455	528		116.04
乡村	481	1 109	1 154	239.92	104.06
在总计中批发市场		39	49		125.64
城市		23	25		108.70
乡村		16	24		150.00
二. 集市成交额(万元)	10 001	444 016	702 733	7 026.63	158.27
城市		309 753	471 540		152.23
乡村	10 001	134 263	231 193	2 311.70	172.19
在总计中批发市场		137 208	171 502		124.99
城市		124 672	143 220		114.88
乡村		12 536	28 282		225.61

社会消费品零售指数

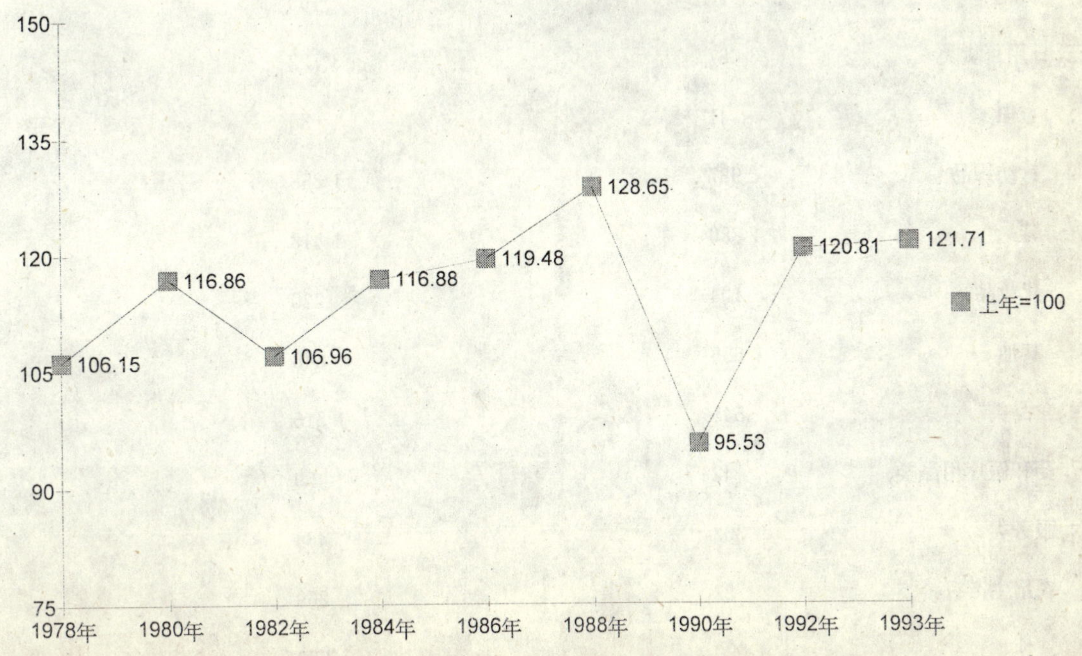

13—20 消费者投诉处理

单位:件

指标	1992年			1993年		
	投拆件数	解决件数	解决率%	投拆件数	解决件数	解决率%
总计	6 852	6 703	97.83	8 114	8 016	98.79
一.家用电子电器类	808			763		
电视机	235			191		
电冰箱	241			216		
洗衣机	35			63		
收录机(音响)	114			115		
其他	183			178		
二.家用机械类	315			649		
照相机	32			30		
自行车	61			144		
摩托车	14			28		
钟表	135			279		
其他	73			168		
三.日用百货类	3 667			3 722		
家俱	41			85		
针纺织品	987			1 358		
鞋	1 880			1 413		
化妆品	104			220		
其他	655			646		
四.食品类	545			1 315		
五.药和医疗用品类	42			59		
六.服务类	363			484		
七.农用生产资料类	22			269		
八.其他类	1 090			853		

13－21 全省十大百货商场主要经济效益指标

(1993 年)

商场名称	商品销售额		销售百元商品的毛利		销售百元商品开支的费用	
	绝对数(万元)	位次	绝对数(万元)	位次	绝对数(万元)	位次
全省合计	77 747		15.80		4.24	
兰州民主西路百货大楼	27 065	1	16.42	5	3.30	7
兰州百货大楼	12 968	3	14.44	9	3.09	8
兰州工贸商场	20 689	2	14.84	8	4.81	4
兰州飞天商场	3 412	4	19.49	1	4.22	6
白银市百货大楼	3 372	5	15.07	7	4.60	5
兰州妇女儿童用品商店	2 480	6	17.76	3	7.81	2
天水市第一百货大楼	1 944	8	17.06	4	6.98	3
兰州市永昌路百货大楼	2 148	7	18.30	2	13.13	1
酒泉市百货大楼	1 800	10	16.20	6	2.71	9
玉门市玉门百货商场	1 869	9	14.38	10	2.54	10

13－21 续

商 场 名 称	销售百元商品实现的利润		实现利润总额		平均每一职工销售总额	
	绝对数(元)	位次	绝对数(元)	位次	绝对数(元)	位次
全省合计	7.43		2 198.00		1 116	
兰州民主西路百货大楼	8.78	3	1 200.00	1	347	10
兰州百货大楼	7.40	5	223.00	3	572	8
兰州工贸商场	5.72	8	525.00	2	437	9
兰州飞天商场	11.54	1	50.00	6	917	4
白银市百货大楼	7.44	4	30.00	7	1 254	3
兰州妇女儿童用品商店	5.55	9	26.00	9	887	5
天水市第一百货大楼	5.85	7	－32.00	10	1 528	1
兰州市永昌路百货大楼	2.79	10	32.00	8	1 266	2
酒泉市百货大楼	9.08	2	91.00	4	717	7
玉门市玉门百货商场	7.31	6	53.00	5	749	6

13—22 全省大中型流通企业一览表

企业名称	经营范围	企业地址	邮政编码
靖远县物资局	黑色化工建材木材	靖远县	730 600
玉门市供销联社	商品销售	玉门市玉门镇	735 211
省建筑工程材料公司	建材批发	中山林 47 号	730 030
省供销合作联社果菜副食批发总公司	果品蔬菜肉食水产	焦家湾 78 号	730 020
省日用杂品公司	日用杂品	东岗西路 358 号	730 000
甘肃省百货公司	纺织百货	兰州民主东路	730 000
省畜产公司	皮革及其制品	天水路 343 号	730 000
省五交化总公司	五金交电	一只船北 1 号	730 000
甘肃省物资再生利用公司	钢材	城关区旧大路 56 号	730 000
甘肃省物资贸易中心	钢材	城关区滨河路 495 号	730 030
省农业生产资料总公司	农资	一只船南 12	730 000
省水利物资供应公司	农资	平凉路 24 号	730 000
省电力工业局物资供应公司	三材及电力设备	西津东路 306 号	730 050
省民族贸易总公司	丝绸,民族特需用品	中山路 272 号	730 030
省建筑材料供销公司	建筑材料	平凉路 252 号	730 000
省再生资源回收公司	废旧物资收购	天水路 2 号	730 000
省飞天工贸总公司	其它日用百货	东岗东路 1093 号	730 020
省物资配套承包供应公司	建材	城关区白银路街道办事处 95 号	730 030
省工矿设备配件供应公司	工矿设备配件	中山路 360 号	730 030
省两西物资供应公司	黑色金属材料	宋路 180 号	730 030
甘肃建筑材料总公司	建筑材料	城关区永昌路 244 号	730 030
省汽车工业总公司	汕及配件	中山路 360 号	730 030
省轻纺工业供销总公司	化工材料批发	平凉路 174 号	730 000
省物资作资源开发公司	黑色金属	兰州城关区	730 030
省烟草公司卷烟销售公司	烟草及其制品	和政东路 32 号	730 000
省化工轻工材料总公司	化工轻工材料	城关区陇西路	730 030
省石油化学工业供销公司	化工材料批发	滨河东路 261 号	730 030
省石油总公司	石油及制品批发	互助巷 60 号	730 030
中国烟草总公司甘肃省兰州分公司	卷烟	天水路 339 号	730 000
省农业机械总公司	农业生产资料	滨河东路 209 号	730 030
省煤炭物资供应公司	黑金材料	上西园 119 号	730 050
省印刷物资公司	印刷物资	小沟头 89 号	730 030
中国有色金属兰州供销运输公司	有色金属材料	旧大路 8 号	730 000
省机械工业供销总公司	黑色金属批发	中山路 360 号	730 030
甘肃省有色金属材料总公司	有色金属	城关区旧大路 56 号	730 000
省供销合作联社果品食杂公司	肉,禽,蛋及其制品	天水路 6 号	730 000
省木材总公司	木材制品	七里河区土门 258 号	730 050
省烟草商贸总公司	烟草,五金交电	和政东街 32 号	730 000
省进出口贸易公司	粮油食品.农副产品	城关定西路 188 号	730 000
省商业对外贸易公司	农副,粮油等	天水路 343 号	730 000

13—22 续 1

企业名称	经营范围	企业地址	邮政编码
省物资进出口公司	金属材料	城关区南城巷 113 号	730 000
省化工进出口公司	对外贸易业	城关区定西路 188 号	730 000
甘肃省医药保健品进出口公司	中西药材及医疗器械	城关焦家湾 393#	730 020
省邮电器材公司	机电,建材	晏家坪北路 5 号	730 050
白银铜城商厦股份有限公司	五金交电化工零售	人民路街道五一街 8 号	730 900
兰州百货采购供应站	日用百货	张家园 23 号	730 000
省兰州交电采购供应站	交电,家用电器	城关区皋兰路 3 号	730 000
兰州市冶金工业供销公司	黑色金属材料	红山根西村 252 号	730 000
兰州市百货公司	日用百货	中山路 87 号	730 030
兰州糖酒副食公司综合经营公司	副食糖烟酒小食品	兰州市城关区中山路 31#	730 030
兰州有色金属开发公司	有色金属批发	安西路 177 号	730 000
兰州市石油公司	石油产品	柏道路 52 号	730 030
兰州友谊旅游侨汇商品经营部	百货零售业	天水路 9 号	730 000
兰州轻工业资源开发公司	黑色金属材料	五泉西路 2 号	730 000
兰州民主西路百货大楼	综合经营	城关区民主西 7 号	730 000
省医药总公司新药物药采购供应站	西药批发	秦安路 100 号	730 030
省友谊公司经营部	糖酒食品批发	天水路 341 号	730 000
省供销联社棉麻公司	棉麻	天水路 2 号	730 000
省供销合作联社土产公司	土特产品	天水路 2 号	730 000
省器械化玻采购供应站	医疗器械	一只船北街 1 号	730 000
省医药集团兰州采购供应站	西药批发	酒泉路 202 号	730 030
省食品公司	农副土特产品	一只船北街 1 号	730 000
省医药集团兰州药材采购供应站	中草药及其制品	井儿街 50 号	730 030
省糖酒副食公司经营部	糕点糖果饮料批发	天水路 339 号	730 000
兰州市七里河区物资总公司	黑色金属材料批发业	七里河区安西路 156 号	730 050
兰州兰石商场	百货零售业	七里河区建兰路 68 号	730 050
兰州广东产品总汇	百货零售业	七里河西津西路 54 号	730 050
兰州市七里河区五金交电化工公司	五金交电化产品	七里河西站西路 64 号	730 050
兰州市七里河区糖业烟酒副食品公司	其他食品饮料烟零售	七里河区西津西路 54 号	730 050
兰州市七里河区糖业烟酒公司	其他食品饮料烟批发	七里河硷沟沿 118 号	730 050
兰州敦煌商场	百货零售业	七里河西津西路 52 号	730 050
西固新城加油站	石油制品	西固新城	730 094
兰州平板玻璃厂蓝天实业公司	玻璃批零	西固区先锋路 49 号	730 060
兰州市安宁区供销经理部	玻璃批零	十里店南 23 号	730 070
兰州市安宁区物资部公司	金属材料,木材建材	十里店南 23 号	730 070
榆中县物资局	金属材料,木材建材	榆中县栖云北路 54 号	730 100
榆中县经贸服务公司	金属材料	榆中县兴隆路 77 号	730 100
嘉峪关市对外经济贸易公司	建筑材料	嘉峪关市新华南路	735 100
嘉峪关市百货公司	土畜工艺品	嘉峪关市中心什字 1 号	735 100

13—22 续 2

企业名称	经营范围	企业地址	邮政编码
嘉峪关市糖烟酒公司	百货.纺织.文化	嘉峪关市	735 100
嘉峪关市五交化公司	糖.烟.酒食品	嘉峪关市新华北路 26 号	735 100
省酒泉地区金属材料公司	五金.交电	嘉峪关市文化街 1 号	735 100
嘉峪关市饮食公司	金属材料	嘉峪关市	735 100
嘉峪关市医药公司	饮食	嘉峪关市新华南路 72 号	735 100
嘉峪关市石油公司	药品类药材类	嘉峪关市机场路 1 号	735 100
省烟草公司酒泉分公司	汽油.煤油	嘉峪关市雄关西路	735 100
嘉峪关市五交化采购供应站	卷烟	嘉峪关市雄关西路	735 100
省百货公司嘉峪关采购供应站	五金化工家电	嘉峪关市兰新路 31 号	735 100
嘉峪关市五金站联营公司	百货.五交化	嘉峪关市新华北路 31 号	735 100
省糖酒付食公司嘉峪关采购站	五金.交电	嘉峪关市雄关西路	735 100
嘉峪关市物资总公司	糖.酒.小食品	嘉峪关市雄关西路 27 号	735 100
嘉峪关市粮油食品供应公司	黑色金属	嘉峪关市富强西路 4 号	735 100
金昌市再生资源回收公司	粮油食品	金昌市	737 100
金昌市农付公司	再生资源回收批发业	金昌市金川区金川路	737 100
金昌市物资局	农业生产资料批发业	金川区延安路 15 区 14 栋	737 100
省石油总公司金昌市公司	农资石油制品批发业	永昌县河西堡镇	737 109
金昌市百货公司	百货零售	金川区金川路	737 100
省盐业公司河西堡购销站	原盐.精细盐	永昌县河西堡镇车站路 45 号	737 000
金昌市工业品综合批发公司	五金交电化工	金昌市金川路 166 号	737 100
省白银市农业机械公司	农机配件零售	公园路街道兰包东路	730 900
白银市乡镇企业供销公司	有色金属批发业	兰包新路	730 900
白银市百货大楼	日用百货零售	友好路 77 号	730 900
白银市医药公司	药品及医疗器械零售	人民路街道人民路 4 号	730 900
白银市粮食储运公司	粮食食用油批发业	东台村	730 900
省烟草公司白银分公司	烟卷批发业	人民路街道工岘西路 37 号	730 900
省石油总公司白银市分公司	石油及制品批发业	工农路街道新建路 22 号	730 900
白银市对外经济贸易公司	矿产品批发业	红星街	730 900
白银市物资总公司	黑色金属材料批发业	人民路街道水川路 27 号	730 900
白银市西区物资供销公司	黑色金属材料批发业	工农路街道	730 900
白银市白银区百货公司	日用百货零售	四龙路街道四龙路 172 号	730 900
白银市白银区再生资源回收公司	再生物资回收批发业	公园路	730 900
白银市白银区贸易中心	五金交电化工零售	公园路街道公园路 1 号	730 900
白银市白银区蔬菜公司	副食品零售	人民路街道纺织路 2 号	730 900
白银市白银区糖业烟酒公司	食品饮料烟酒零售	人民路街道纺织路 2 号	730 900
白银市白银区乡镇企业供销公司	轻质建筑材料批发	公园路街道公园路 7 号	730 900
白银市白银区物资总公司	黑色金属材料批发业	人民路街道人民路 23 号	730 900
白银市白银区粮食仓库	粮油零售	工农路 88 号	730 900
白银市白银区粮油供应公司	粮油零售	人民路街道中心街 69 号	730 900

13—22 续 3

企业名称	经营范围	企业地址	邮政编码
白银华银商城	日用百货零售	人民路街道人民路 11 号	730 900
白银市平川区百货公司	百货，针织零售	平川区积路 384 号	730 913
平川区物资公司	机电，化工批发	宝积路 176 号	730 913
白银市石油公司平川分公司	石油产品零售	宝积路	730 913
会宁县物资供应公司	其他零售	会师镇东关南路 18 号	743 200
省石油总公司景泰县公司	石油制品零售业	景泰县一条山镇	730 400
省景泰县农业机械公司	农机及配件零售业	景泰县一条山镇	730400
景泰县物资局	农业生产资料零售业	景泰县一条山镇 705 路 7 号	730 400
天水百货采购供应站	日用百货批发	二马路东 11 号	741 020
甘肃省天水市百货公司	付食百货，交电，钟表	民主东路 61 号	741 000
市金属材料公司	有色金属材料	秦城区新华东路 51 号	741 000
天水市物资贸易中心	建筑五金	秦城新华东路 51 号	741 000
天水五金交电化工批发业	五金化批发业	一马路东 23 号	741 020
天水市石油公司	石油	社棠 45 号	741 020
天水市燃料总公司	煤炭沥青	新华路 8 号	741 000
天水糖酒付食采购供应站	糕点，糖果，饮料，酒	桥南花牛 12 号	741 020
烟草公司天水分公司	卷烟，	分路口	741 020
天水土特产品公司	棉麻，烟茶，工业品	二马路东 42 号	741 020
天水市食品公司	猪牛羊，水产品	环城路西段	741 000
天水市第一粮库	粮食油	秦城岷山路 65 号	741 018
天水市化工轻工公司	化工轻工	新华路 5 号	741 000
天水华西大厦	另售批发	秦城民主西路 10 号	741 000
天水市物资供销公司	钢材，机电供销	北道渭滨北路东 1 号	741 020
天水市农副产品公司	农业生产资料零售业	解放路 176 号	741 000
天水市糖业烟酒公司	仪器饮料，烟草零售业	解放路 106 号	741 000
天水商业大厦	百货零售业	大众路	741 000
天水市五金交电公司	五金交电，化工零售业	解放路 7 号	741 000
天水市蔬菜食杂公司	副食品零售业	伏牺路 23 号	741 000
甘肃省石油总公司泰城区公司	石油制品零售业	人民西路张家窑 2 号	741 000
北道区石油公司	汽油零售	北道区滨南路 37 号	741 020
省医药集团天水医药采购供应站	医药批发	北道区前时北路 30 号	741 020
天水市北道区饮食服务公司	正餐	北道区渭河南路 4 号	741 020
天水市北道区北道粮油供应公司	粮油零售	北道区道献街前进南路 6 号	741 020
天水市北道区粮油储运公司	粮油零售	北道区社棠路火车站	741 024
天水市北道区五金公司	五交化家电零售	北道区一马路东 19 号	741 020
天水市北道区糖业烟酒公司	糖烟酒批发	北道区渭河南路 7 号	741 020
天水市北道区百货公司	百货零售	北道区解放路东 1 号	741 020
省盐业公司天水购销站	仪器烟草饮料批发业	北道渭河南路 57 号	741 020
天水供销大厦	日用工业品零售	北道区二马路东 14 号	741 020

13—22 续 4

企业名称	经营范围	企业地址	邮政编码
天水市北道区农副公司	农副产品批发	北道区二马路东 14 号	741 600
秦安县生产资料公司	生产资料类	兴国镇解放路	741 600
秦安县物资供应公司	钢材,木材,水泥	兴国镇解放路 71 号	741 600
秦安县农付公司	农付日杂类	兴国镇解放路 9 号	741 200
甘谷县石油公司	石油产品	甘谷新兴 86 号	741 200
甘谷县五金交电公司	五金,交电	甘谷西巷 2 号	741 200
甘谷县姚庄粮油仓库	粮油及副产品	甘谷新兴道北 5 号	741 300
省烟草公司武山县公司	烟草及制品批发业	城关镇富强路 39 号	741 300
省石总公司武山县公司	石油制品零售业	城关镇陈家六村	741 300
武山县生产资料公司	农业生产资料零售业	城关镇陈家门村	741 300
省武山县洛门供销社	百货零售业	洛门镇东街村	741 306
省石油总公司酒泉地区公司	石油及制品批发	酒泉市祁连路 1 号	735 000
省供销合作联社酒泉工贸公司	日用杂品批发	酒泉市东大街 46 号	735 000
省医药集团酒泉医药公司	西药批发	酒泉市东大街 3 号	735 000
玉门市五金交化公司	五金销售	玉门市北坪	735 200
玉门市百货公司	百货批发零售	玉门市北坪	735 200
玉门市糖酒副食公司	糖酒副食销售	玉六诎解放路	735 200
玉门市物资总公司	黑色金属批发	玉门市新市区	735 200
玉门市煤炭运销公司	煤炭销售	玉门市和坪街五村	735 200
酒泉农垦物资供应站	物资供销	玉门市玉门镇	735 200
玉门市粮食局	粮油销售	平门市解放门	735 200
玉门市饮食服务业公司	饮食业	玉门市北坪	735 200
省酒泉地区百货批发总公司	百货批发	酒泉市南大街 2 号	735 000
省酒泉糖烟酒食品总公司	糕点.糖果和饮料批发	酒泉市东大街 119 号	735 000
省酒泉地区酒泉市蔬菜果品公司	副食品零售	酒泉市解放路 29 号	735 000
省酒泉地区酒泉市饮食服务公司系统	正餐	酒泉市西文化街 1 号	735 000
省酒泉地区酒泉市商业综合公司	副食品零售	酒泉市东大街 44 号	735 000
酒泉综合贸易公司	棉.麻.土畜产品批发	酒泉市南环西路 12 号	735 000
酒泉市农杂生资公司	棉.麻.土畜产品批发	酒泉市东大街 74 号	735 000
省酒泉地区酒泉市物资总公司	黑色金属材料批发	酒泉市南后街 5 号	735 000
安西县物资局	黑色金属材料批发	安西县县府街 89 号	736 100
安西县农副公司	农业生产资料批发业	安西县志大街 19 号	736 100
省石油总公司安西县分公司	石油制品批发零售业	安西县老城西门外	736 100
安西县水电物资公司	建筑材料批发业	安西县祁连街 60 号	736 100
张掖百货站	日用百货批发	张掖火车站西路 29 号	734 012
张掖五金站	五金交电批发	火车站	734 000
张掖石油公司	石油批发	张掖市	734 012
张掖医药站	西药批发	张掖市火车站南路 74 号	734 000
烟草分公司	烟草批发	北街 38 号	734 000

13—22 续 5

企业名称	经营范围	企业地址	邮政编码
张掖土特产品公司	棉麻土畜产品批发	张掖市火车站南路 81 号	734 012
张掖物资经销总公司	黑色金属材料批发	张掖县府街 94 号	734 000
糖酒副食公司	糕点糖果批发	北街 43 号	734 000
百货公司	百货	西街 15 号	734 000
医药公司	药品医疗器械零售业	西街 43 号	734 000
蔬菜果品公司	食品饮料零售定	青年街 64 号	734 000
农机公司	农业机械零售业	东街 42 号	734 000
生产资料服务公司	黑色金属批发业	新建街 289 号	734 000
机电建化公司	建筑材料批发业	新建街 289 号	734 000
金属材料公司	黑色金属批发业	新建街 289 号	734 000
商业综合公司	百货零售	北街 22 号	734 000
生产资料公司	化肥农药薄膜批发业	西街 1 号	734 000
日用杂品公司	百货零售业	南街 24 号	734 000
小满供销社	百货零售业	小满	734 000
河西大厦	日杂零售业	南街 22 号	734 000
沙井供销社	日用百货零售业	沙井	734 023
临泽县商业总公司商业贸易公司	百货零售业	沙河街 26 号	734 200
临泽县板桥供销合作社	百货零售业	板桥乡	734 207
临泽县粮油工贸总公司	粮油	沙河街 328 号	734 200
高台县农业机械公司	农业生产资料零售业	解放南路 48 号	734 300
省石油总公司高台县公司	石油产品零售	解放南路 11 号	734 300
石油公司	石油制品零售	光荣新村 49 号	734 100
农机公司	农业生产资料零售	山红路 2 号	734 100
省武威地区农业机械化服务公司	农业生产资料批发业	武威	733 300
省供销社武威土特产品公司	棉麻批发业	武威	733 000
武威地区金属材料公司	黑色金属批发业	武威	733 000
省武威地区机电设备公司	汽车摩托车配件批发	武威	733 300
省石油公司武威地区公司	石油及制品批发业	武威	733 000
医药集团武威地区医药公司	医疗器械批发业	武威	733 000
省糖酒付食公司武威采购供应站	糕点糖果批发业	武威	733 000
省武威地区物资再生利用公司	其他未包括的批发业	武威	733 300
省烟草公司武威分公司	烟草及制品批发业	武威	73 000
武威地区物资总公司地区物资局	黑色金属批发业	武威	733 300
武威地区建材化轻公司	建筑材料批发业	武威	733 300
武威市医药公司	药品吸医疗器械	西大街 56 号	733 000
武威市百货公司	百货批发	建国街 74 号	733 000
武威市五金交电化工公司	五金交化水暖	北大街 15 号	733 000
武威市糖酒副食贸易公司	糖酒副食	西大街 181 号	733 000

13—22 续 6

企业名称	经营范围	企业地址	邮政编码
武威市饮食服务公司	饮食服务	东大街 69 号	733 000
武威市石油公司	石油销售	南关街西路 20 号	733 000
武威市农业生产资料公司	农业生产资料	南关西路 18 号	733 000
武威市农副产品公司	棉麻土畜产品	建国街新青年巷 23 号	733 000
省武威新华书店	图书报刊零售业	武威	733 000
武威市综合贸易中心	日用杂品	东大街 73 号	733 000
武威市黄羊物资公司	木材批发	黄羊镇新镇路 9 号	733 006
武威市木材公司	木材批发	建设北路 12 号	733 000
武威市金属材料公司	黑色金属材料	西南小区 2 号	733 000
武威市物资交易中心	黑色金属材料	火车站建设北路 11 号	733 000
武威市物资公司	木材批发	建设北路 14 号	733 000
武威市机电设备公司	机电设备批发	火车站建设北路 12 号	733 000
武威市建材化轻公司	建筑材料	建设北路 12 号	733 000
古浪县木材建材公司	木材批发业	古浪	733 100
古浪县木材公司	木材批发业	古浪	733 100
古浪县金属机电公司	金属批发业	古浪	733 100
古浪县物资公司	金属批发业	古浪	733 100
天祝藏族自治县工业品贸易公司	百货零售业	天祝	733 200
天祝藏族自治县民族贸易公司	百货零售业	天祝	733 200
天祝藏族自治县煤炭公司	煤炭零售业	天祝	733 200
天祝藏族自治县物资总公司	黑色金属材料批发业	天祝	733 200
陇西土特产品公司	其食品.饮料.烟草	文峰	748 000
省陇西物资贸易储运总公司	黑色金属材料批发业	东郊	748 112
石油总公司定西地区分公司	成品石油	焦家坡新村 4 号	743 000
定西汽车配件公司	汽车摩托车配件产品等	交通路 183 号	743 000
定西地区物资总公司	金属.木材	中华路 72 号	743 000
城关粮油供应站	粮油	中华路 40 号	743 000
定西县陇中商贸公司	百货零售	城关解放路 26 号	743 000
定西县农业机械公司	农业服务业	中华路 125 号	734 000
石油总公司定西县公司	汽油等	交通路 436 号	743 000
省定西县物资公司	金属机电	交通路 467 号	743 000
定西烟草公司	烟批发	交通路	743 000
定西县供销大楼	工业品批零业	城关中华路 13 号	743 000
省石油总公司通渭县公司	石油制品零售业	平襄镇北街 46 号	743 300
省通渭县物资总公司	黑色金属	平襄北街街 50 号	743 300
省烟草公司定西分公司	烟草及其制品批发业	文峰	748 000
陇西县煤炭销公司	煤炭零售业	文峰	748 000
陇西县文峰粮食管理所	粮油零售业	文峰	748 000

13—22 续 7

企业名称	经营范围	企业地址	邮政编码
陇西县石油公司	石油制品零售业	城关	748 100
陇西县医药公司	药品医疗器械零售业	巩昌	748 100
陇西县文峰供销社	农业生产资料零售业	文峰	748 000
陇西县农业生产资料公司	农业生产资料批发业	文峰	748 000
陇西县物资公司	建筑材料批发业	文峰自由路 5 号	748 000
渭源县物资公司	建材,化工品购销	渭源县清源镇	748 200
省渭源县供销贪图总公司会川公司	综合性商业	渭源县会川镇西大街	748 201
省渭源县供销售团总公司	综合性商业	渭源县清源镇下集 224 号	748 200
省临洮县物资公司	黑色金属材料批发业	洮阳镇纸坊 85 号	730 500
省漳县物资公司	黑色金属批发业	定西漳县城关	748 300
岷县烟草公司	烟草制品	新民街广场后院	748 400
陇南地区烟草分公司	烟草	陇南琥都县南桥路 130 号	746 000
武都县糖酒付食公司	食口付食批发零售业	陇南地区琥城关	746 000
礼县物资局	建筑材料销售	城关镇	742 200
平凉烟草公司	烟草	平凉东大街 45 号	744 000
华亭县物资局	金属材料批发业	华亭县安口镇	744 103
华县乡镇企业物资供销公司	机械设备批发	华亭县东华镇	744 100
静宁县金属机电化轻公司	黑色金属批发业	静宁县城关镇南关什字 5 号	743 400
宁县木材建材公司	木材批发业	静宁县城关镇南关什字 5 号	743 400
省石油总公司庆阳地区公司	成品油批发	西大街 2 号	745 000
省供销合作联社庆阳土特产品公司	土特产批发	南大街 24 号	745 000
省百货公司庆阳地区分公司	百货零售	北大街 22 号	745 000
省烟草公司庆阳分公司	卷烟批发	南二路	745 000
省烟草公司正宁县公司	烟草及其制品批发业	正宁北街	745 300
庆阳地区医药公司	西药批发	南大街 35 号	745 000
省烟草公司西峰市烟叶公司	烟草批发	南街办三里庙旅社	745 000
西峰市粮油供应公司	粮油仪器零售业	南街办南大街 14 号	745 000
宁县物资公司	金属材料批发	新宁镇	745 200
省石油总公司临夏州公司	石油批发	市民主西路 29—2 号	731 100
糖业烟酒公司	糖烟酒批发	红园新村 82	731 100
临夏县物资公司	黑色金属材料批发业	临夏市东关街滨河西路 2 号	731 100
永靖县民族贸易公司	百货零售业	永靖县川东路 85 号	731 600
永靖县农业生产资料公司	农业生产资料零售业	永靖县古城路 362 号	731 600
永靖县粮食局古城仓库	粮油仪器零售业	永靖县古城路 59 号	731 602
州糖烟酒公司	糖烟酒.小食品	甘南合作	747 000
甘南州合作粮油公司	粮食制品食用植物油	甘南合作	747 000
州石油公司	石油制品零售业	甘南合作	747 000
秦安县水利局物资站	50	兴国镇解放路水电巷 18 号	741 600

企业名称	经营范围	企业地址	邮政编码
肃南县皇城煤炭购销公司	煤炭零售	肃南县铧尖乡	733 014
省西峰市物资公司	金属材料批发	南街办合水巷 7 号	745 000
省五金矿产进出口公司	有色.黑色金属进出口	城关定西路 188	730 000
省纺织品进出口公司	各类服装纺织品类	城关区南昌路 289 号	730 000
省农垦农工商联合总公司	综合性	平凉路 4 号	730 000
省农副产品进出口公司	农副产品	天水路 2 号	730 000
兰州邮政局	书报杂志	民主东路 32 号	730 000
省糖酒副食公司第二经营部	副食批发	庆阳路 62 号	730 030
省糖酒副食公司副食商场	副食批发	东岗西路 209 号	730 000
省糖酒副食公司经营部	糕点，糖果和饮料	东岗西路 209 号	730 000
省供销合作联社联发贸易公司	农副产品	天水路 343 号	730 000
省供销联社兰山商场	五金，交电，化工	天水路 2 号	730 000
贸易信托公司	五金交化	天水路 2 号	730 000
省轻工业物资公司	黑色金属材料	东岗西路 267 号	730 000
省电子工业物资供销公司	黑色金属材料	东岗西路 254 号	730 000
甘肃省机电设备总公司	机械电器设备	城关区旧大路 56 号	730 000
甘肃省黑色材料总公司	钢材	市城关区旧大路 56 号	730 000
兰州市医药公司	医药用品	皋兰路 3 号	730 000
兰州农业机械总公司	农业机械	西津西路 224 号	730 050
兰州木材总公司	木材及其加工	西津西路 356 号	730 050
兰州金属材料总公司	黑色金属材料	民主西路 31 号	730 000
兰州机电设备总公司	机械电子设备	民主西路 31 号	730 000
兰州化工轻工总公司	化工轻工产品建材	民主西路 31 号	730 000
兰州建筑材料总公司	建筑材料	萃英门 25 号	730 030
兰州物资贸易中心	黑色金属材料	萃英门 25 号	730 030
兰州物资协作开发总公司	黑色金属材料	安定门外 10 号	730 030
兰州市轻纺工业局供销公司	黑色金属材料	靖远路 193 号	730 046
兰州市机械工业供销总公司	黑色金属材料	红山根西村 100 号	730 000
永登县供销联社	农业生产资料	永登县城关镇	730 300
兰州市红古区供销联社	农业生产资料	红古区海石湾	730 084
兰州市七里河区供销联社	农业生产资料	西津东路 76 号	730 050
兰州市城关区供销联社	农业生产资料	小沟头 102 号	730 030
兰州市农副土产日用杂品公司	日用杂品批发	中山路 100 号	730 030
兰州市果品茶叶公司	果品批发	酒泉路 268 号	730 030
兰州市土产公司	土特产品	中山路 7 号	730 030
兰州市回收公司	再生物资回收	小西湖东街 1 号	730 050
兰州市农业生产资料公司	农业生产资料	武都路 163 号	730 030
兰州粮油总公司城关购销公司	粮油，食品	庆阳路 265 号	730 030

13—22 续 9

企业名称	经营范围	企业地址	邮政编码
兰州粮油总公司西郊购销公司	粮油食品	合水路 23 号	730 060
兰州粮油总公司七里河购销公司	粮油食品	王家堡 117 号	730 050
兰州粮油总公司	粮油食品	十里店 82 号	730 070
兰州市红古区粮油购销公司	粮油食品	海石湾	730 084
兰州市粮油贸易总公司	粮油食品	民主东路 158 号	730 000
兰州花庄粮库	粮油	花庄	730 086
兰州市小西坪粮泪总公司	粮油	建西东路 125 号	730 050
兰州市土门墩国家粮食储备库	粮油	西津西路 649 号	730 050
兰州市焦家湾粮食仓库	粮油	排洪南路 40 号	730 000
兰州新兰面粉厂粮食储运站	粮油食品	土门墩 745 号	730 050
兰州油脂加工厂综合服务公司	粮油食品	建兰路工家堡 1 号	730 050
兰州市粮食局汽车队贸易公司	粮油食品	吴家园 156 号	730 050
榆中县粮油供应公司	粮油食品	城关光陇路 57 号	730 100
皋兰县粮油供应公司	粮油食品	城关镇	730 200
永登县粮油购销公司	粮油食品	城关镇民主 18 号	730 300
兰州市煤炭工业总公司	煤炭购销	一支船北街 79 号	730 000
兰州市煤炭工业总公司城关一公司	煤炭购销	城关区贡元巷黄家园九号	730 030
兰州百货大楼	日用,百货,家电,副食	城关区庆阳路 275 号	730 030
兰州工贸商场	综合经营	城关区皋兰路 1 号	730 000
兰州化工采购供应站	化工	庆阳路 106 号	730 030
兰州五金机械总公司	五金,化工	天水路一只船北街 1 号	730 000
兰州针纺织品采购供应站	针纺织品	城关区柏道路 48 号	730 030
兰州文化用品采购供应站	文化用品	城关区张家园 23 号	730 000
兰州市五金交电化工公司	五金,家电	中山路 69 号	730 030
兰州市糖酒副食公司	糖酒副食	酒泉路 212 号	730 030
兰州市食品公司	肉食禽蛋水产品	畅家巷 9 号	730 030
兰州市蔬菜公司	蔬菜瓜果副食糖烟酒	仲山路 41 号	730 030
兰州市饮食公司	饮食住宿	武都路 166 号	730 030
省兰州市红古区商业局	糖酒副食	海石镇	730 084
永登县商业局	糖酒副食	城关缜合作街 1 号	730 300
西固北滩石油库加油站	汽油柴油	西固环形路 2 号	730 060
玉门市医药公司	药品销售	玉门市北坪	735 200
甘肃安西粮油贸易总公司	粮油食品零售业	安西县府衔 80 号	736 100
岷县粮油总公司	粮油产品零售业	人民街	748 400
白银市白银区农副日杂公司	日用杂品零售	工农路街道工农路 154 号	730 900
天水市七里墩综合商店	日用百货零售业	七里墩	741 000
天水市再生资源回收公司	其它未包括的零售业	环城路 20 号	741 000
天水市工商行政管理局秦城局	其它未包括的零售业	滨河西路 23 号	741 000

企业名称	经营范围	企业地址	邮政编码
武山县粮食局城关粮站	粮油食品零售业	城关镇富强路 33 号	741 300
省国营酒泉农垦贸易中心	五金.交电.化工批发	酒泉市东大街 79 号	735 000
省酒泉地区五交化批发总公司	五金.交电.化工批发	酒泉西环北路 2 号	735 000
省酒泉地区轻工业供销公司	黑色金属材料批发	酒泉市东环南路 5 号	735 000
省酒泉地区农机总公司	农业生产资料批发	酒泉市南环东路 21 号	735 000
省酒泉地区煤炭运销公司	煤炭零售	酒泉市北市街 32 号	735 000
酒泉市粮食局系统	粮食.食用油批发	酒泉市西大街 22 号	735 000
金塔县百货公司	百货零售业	金塔县金塔镇新华街 249 号	735 300
省石油总公司金塔县公司	石油制品零售	金塔县金塔镇解放路 65 号	735 300
金塔县个体工商协会	百货零售业	金塔县解放路 302 号	735 300
金塔县城乡集市贸易管理所	副食品零售	金塔县解放路	735 300
金塔县供销社	农业生产资料批发	金塔县西城街 6 号	735 300
鼓楼商场	百货零售业	东街 3 号	734 000
武威地区木材公司	木材批发业	武威	733 000
武威地区物资贸易中心	黑色金属批发业	武威	733 000
武威友谊贸易公司	百货批发业	武威	733 000
武威地区对外贸易总公司	棉麻批发业	武威	733 000
民勤县物资供应公司	黑色金属材料批发业	民勤	733 300
民勤县物资局农建公司	黑色金属材料批发业	民勤	733 300
省石油总公司天祝藏族自治县公司	石油制品零售业	天祝	733 200
岷县医药公司	药品零售业	城关	748 400
岷县物资公司	建筑材料	中华街 83 号	748 400
百货公司	百货	成县城关	742 500
石油公司	石油	成县城关	742 500
烟草公司	烟	成县城关	742 500
平凉地区五金交化公司	五金交化	东大街 52 号	74 000
平凉地区石油公司	石油类	平凉市新生巷	74 000
平凉土特产品公司	农业生产资料购销	平凉市宝塔路 10 号	74 000
酒泉市供销合作社系统	黑色化工建材木材	靖远县	735 000

十四. 对外经济贸易和旅游业

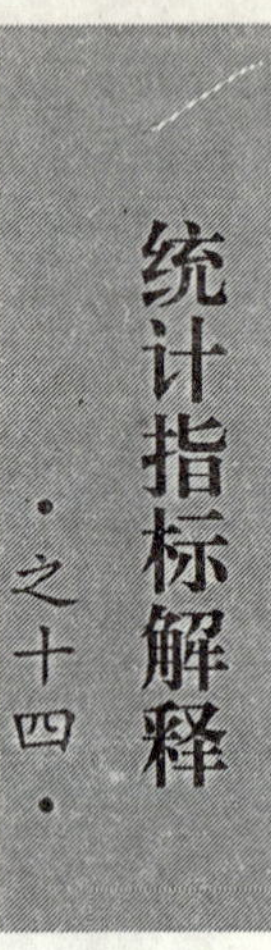

【农民纯收入】农民纯收入是指农民家庭调查期内总收入中扣除家庭经营费用支出，上交集体承包任务和缴纳税款以及生活用固定资产折旧等支出后，可以直接支配用于扩大再生产和生活费用的那一部分收入。它是反映农民真实收入水平和经济效益的主要指标，其计算公式为：

纯收入＝总收入－（家庭经营费用支出＋缴纳税款＋生产性固定资产折旧＋上交集体的承包任务＋调查户补贴）

每人平均纯收入，是农民家庭纯收入与家庭常住人口相比较的结果，是衡量全体农民收入、生活水平高低的主要依据，其计算公式是：

每人平均纯收入＝家庭纯收入÷家庭常住人口

【农村社会总产值】是指在农村中生产的社会总产值。根据我国目前农村经济现状，农村社会总产值的统计范围暂定为：乡、村及村以下各种合作经济组织和农户从事农业、工业、建筑业、运输业、商业、饮食业活动所生产的产值和国营农场的农业总产值两部分的产值。凡是在农村的国营工业、建筑业、运输业、商业、饮食业所生产的产值均不计算在内。国营农场及县镇的工业、建筑业、运输业、商业、饮食业和产值也不计算在内。集体和国营联合的企业凡场址在农村，利用农村劳动力、土地或生产用房进行生产的联合企业，其产值应计入农村社会总产值中。

【农业总产值】农业总产值是以货币表现的一定时间（通常是一年）的农业产品总量指标。它反映全年农业生产的总成果。农业总产值的计算通常是以行政区划为范围的。凡是在本行政区划范围内各种经济类型当年生产的全部农产品产值，都应包括在内。既要包括辖区内从事农业生产的全民所有制、集体所有制其它经营单位、农户所生产的全部农产品，又要包括非农业生产单位所生产的全部农产品。但不包括农业科研单位专门用作试验研究的非生产部分，也不包括军事部门的军马。

【农业商品产值】农业商品产值是指报告期内全部农业生产单位的农产品总量中实际出售的商品量的价值。农业商品产值理论上应按各种农产品的生产年度来计算，但考虑到在正常年景的情况下各种农产品的商品量大部分都收获农产品的日历年度内出售，跨年度出售的数量只占少部分。因此，为了便于计算并及时报送资料，现行统计制度规定，统一按农业生产单位在日历年度内实际出售的商品量的价值来计算。

14—1 进出口总额

单位:万元.万美元

指标	1978年		1992年		1993年	
	人民币	美元	人民币	美元	人民币	美元
进出口总额(经贸口径)	5 941	3 454	231 656	41 590	275 937	48 435
进口额			35 720	6 413	114 359	20 088
出口额	5 941	3 454	195 936	35 177	161 578	28 347
差额(十顺差,一逆差)	5 941	3 454	160 215	28 764	47 219	8 259
进出口总额(海关口径)			465 730	83 614	90 767	15 924
进口额			315 691	56 677	65 254	11 448
出口额			150 039	26 937	25 513	4 476
差额(十顺差,一逆差)			－165 652	－29 740	－39 740	－6 972

14－2 主要年份进出口贸易总额

单位:万美元

年份	进出口总额	进口总额	出口总额	差额(十顺差,一逆差)
1971	108		108	
1975	1 324		1 324	
1978	3 454		3 454	3 454
1980	3 927		3 927	3 927
1981	5 129	793	4 336	3 543
1982	5 069	739	4 330	3 591
1983	5 695	1 083	4 612	3 529
1984	6 631	2 058	4 573	2 515
1985	10 004	2 906	7 098	4 192
1986	13 648	3 541	10 107	6 566
1987	15 504	2 844	12 660	9 816
1988	16 624	1 419	15 205	13 786
1989	18 674	3 336	15 338	12 002
1990	20 221	1 647	18 574	16 927
1991	27 649	2 365	25 284	22 919
1992	41 590	6 413	35 177	28 764
1993	48 435	20 088	28 347	8 259

14—3 主要年份进出口贸易总额

单位:万元人民币

年份	进出口总额	进口总额	出口总额	差额 (十顺差,一逆差)
1971	280		280	
1975	2 608		2 608	
1978	5 941		5 941	5 941
1980	5 883		5 883	5 883
1981	8 871	1 188	7 683	6 495
1982	8 850	1 107	7 743	6 636
1983	10 151	1 622	8 529	6 907
1984	20 638	4 789	15 849	11 060
1985	37 917	8 535	29 382	20 847
1986	59 353	12 227	47 126	34 899
1987	68 291	10 585	57 706	47 121
1988	67 085	5 248	61 837	56 589
1989	103 668	15 713	87 955	72 242
1990	102 965	7 759	95 208	87 451
1991	144 052	12 322	131 730	119 408
1992	231 656	35 720	195 936	160 215
1993	275 937	114 359	161 578	47 129

14—4 进出口贸易总额

单位:万美元

名 称	1979年		1992年		1993年	
	贸易额	比重(%)	贸易额	比重(%)	贸易额	比重(%)
进口商品总额			6 413		20 088	
1. 工贸公司			2 576		1 534	
2. 有经营权的企业					424	
3. 三资企业出口					12 059	
4. 易货贸易(含边贸)					1 355	
5. 专业公司			3 837	100.00	4 716	100.00
粮油食品类			12	0.31		
土畜产品类			306	7.97	1 978	41.94
纺织品类			592	15.43	231	4.90
轻工产品类			159	4.14	30	0.64
工艺品类			80	2.08	29	0.61
五金矿产类			529	13.80	1 051	22.20
化工类			1 730	45.09	145	3.07
医药保健类			235	6.12	163	3.46
机械设备类			194	5.06	1 089	23.09
出口商品总额	3 972	100.00	35 177	100.00	28 364	100.00
粮油食品类	67	1.69	4 449	12.65	4 060	14.31
土畜产品类	3 040	76.53	5 480	15.58	3 429	12.09
纺织品类	51	1.29	8 495	24.15	6 884	24.27
轻工产品类			2 656	7.55	1 772	6.25
工艺品类			462	1.31	224	0.79
五金矿产类	381	9.59	7 064	20.08	6 598	23.26
化工类	433	10.90	4 456	12.67	2 680	9.45
医药保健类			603	1.71	630	2.22
机械设备类			1 449	4.12	1 754	6.18
原料加工工缴费总值			63	0.18	333	1.18
进出口贸易差额	3 972		28 764		8 301	

注:此数字为经贸委口经。

14—5 主要商品出口量

商品名称	单位	1978年		1992年		1993年	
		数量	金额（万美元）	数量	金额（万美元）	数量	金额（万美元）
荞 麦	吨			2 759	57	2 495	47.00
蚕 豆	吨			18 489	434	30 468	467.00
豌 豆	吨			1 837	32	2 779	56.00
芸 豆	吨			2 224	78	2 293	78.00
扁 豆	吨			9 572	273	12 345	288.00
葵花籽	吨			190	9	55	0.82
大麻籽	吨			680	15	1 302	28.00
活 牛	吨			354	12	501	14.00
冻兔肉	吨			228	62	18	5.50
苹 果	吨	561		189	11	90	1.40
哈蜜瓜	吨	5		176	4		
核桃仁	吨			474	114	433	123.00
苦杏仁	吨			354	45	838	120.00
黑瓜子	吨	247		8 096	826	8 118	689.00
大 蒜	吨			300	15		
腌咸菜	吨			2 206	202	1 970	205.00
咸蕨菜	吨			2 169	196	1 729	180.00
辣椒干	吨			230	33		
金针菜	吨	177		489	63	206	30.00
蜂 蜜	吨			386	24	144	13.00
甜菜粕	吨			18 837	233	22 786	253.00
亚麻籽饼	吨			15 389	175	14 420	176.00
小回香	吨			1 681	84	1 281	60.00
猪 警	箱	4 838		3 431	83	2 012	35.00
猪肠衣	桶			200	11	845	36.00
羊革皮	张	260 000		87 143	45		
皮裤子	条			31 584	36	1 010	1.60
当 归	吨	627		1 450	531	608	193.00
棉 布	万米			1 029	632	1 127	571.00
地 毯	万平方米	36 099		401 328	2 604	473 964	1 677.00
电风扇	台			122 685	281	55 405	128.00
电冰箱	台			8 334	97	6 298	63.00
洗衣机	台			27 235	178	10 442	57.00
彩色电视机	台			3 307	67	26 416	141.00
黑白电视机	台			7 850	54		
水 泥	吨			61 546	244		
无明粉	吨			58 714	578	19 204	143.00
冰晶粉	吨			4 178	254	470	29.00
工业轴承	万套			976 379	128	109	138.00
煤	吨			33 311	114	40 190	123.00

14—6 外汇收支情况

(1993年) 单位:万美元

月 份	收 入	支 出
合 计	18 579	11 909
元 月	1 463	575
二 月	2 356	1 079
元至二月止累计	3 819	1 654
三 月	2 063	1 422
元至三月止累计	5 882	3 076
四 月	1 289	974
元至四月止累计	7 171	4 050
五 月	1 222	730
元至五月止累计	8 393	4 780
六 月	1 402	1 033
元至六月止累计	9 795	5 813
七 月	1 661	755
元至七月止累计	11 456	6 568
八 月	1 325	579
元至八月止累计	12 781	7 147
九 月	1 523	218
元至九月止累计	14 304	7 365
十 月	1 397	481
元至十月止累计	15 701	7 846
十 一 月	1 565	853
元至十一月止累计	17 266	8 699
十 二 月	1 313	3 210

14—7 外商投资企业现状分类情况

(1993年)

项　目	单位	合计		合资经营企业		合作经营企业		外资企业	
		累计	#本年	累计	#本年	累计	#本年	累计	#本年
一. 批准外商投资企业	个	823	556	576	372	33	18	214	166
#产品出口企业	个	19	7	7	4	6	2	6	3
外商出资额	万美元	47 700	29 253	33 043	19 297	3 757	1776	10 900	8 180
二. 已建成投产									
(开业)企业	个	178	121	125	81	7	4	46	36
销售(经营)收入	万元								
三. 正在投资建设企业	个	503	342	352	228	20	12	131	102
实际投入外资	万美元								
四. 已撤销企业	个	6	6	2	2			4	4
合同外资金额	万美元	250	250	44	44			206	206
五. 未开工企业	个	142	134	90	82	15	15	37	37

14—8 实际利用外资情况

年　份	合同个数(个)	合同投资总金额(万美元)	实际利用外资金额(万美元)
1980	3	238.00	155.42
1981			
1982	3	1 786.56	1 424.55
1983	2	222.00	222.00
1984	4	338.97	196.50
1985	10	657.20	323.45
1986	5	764.79	585.85
1987	9	792.56	543.40
1988	17	3 670.25	865.80
1989	12	7 058.15	17.00
1990	19	2 787.00	471.52
1991	14	1 883.00	56.00
1992	174	12 688.00	4 740.00
1993	556	63 015.00	5 610.00

14—9 对外承包工程和劳务合作

年　份	签定合同数(个)	合同金额(万美元)	完成营业额(万美元)
一.对外承包工程	110	37 008	26 666
1980	1	17	616
1981			580
1982	3	1 244	737
1983	1	14	580
1984	8	4 615	943
1985	8	1 382	1 451
1986	8	734	1 971
1987	12	649	2 149
1988	16	3 339	1 697
1989	8	16 413	2 615
1990	7	1 352	3 183
1991	14	4 162	3 854
1992	13	1 246	2 690
1993	11	1 841	3 600
二.对外劳务合作	51	1 847	1 304
1983	1	842	210
1984			325
1985	1	37	344
1986	5	54	39
1987	8	35	43
1988	13	128	35
1989	5	513	1
1990	3	2	10
1991	8	149	119
1992	5	23	125
1993	2	64	53

14--10 甘肃省、兰州市与外国结成友好城市(地区)一览表

国　别	城市(地区)	缔结日期	缔结省(市)
日本	秋田县	1982 年 8 月 5 日	甘肃省
日本	秋田县	1982 年 8 月 5 日	兰州市
新西兰	克赖斯特彻奇市	1984 年 4 月 22 日	甘肃省
美国	俄克拉荷马州	1986 年 6 月 15 日	甘肃省
土库曼斯坦	土库曼斯坦阿什哈巴德市	1992 年 5 月 1 日	兰州市
澳大利亚	澳大利亚本迪戈市	1993 年 4 月 10 日	天水市
哈萨克斯坦	哈萨克斯坦奇姆肯特市	1993 年 5 月 15 日	白银市

14—11　1993 年止甘肃省海外企业一览表

企业名称	所在国别.地区	合作项目	中方合作者	外方合作者
华陇建筑有限公司	津巴布韦	建筑业	省建筑总公司	政府单位
中城莫桑比亚项目组	莫桑比亚	建筑业	省建筑总公司	政府单位
甘肃省国际公司纳米比亚有限公司	纳米比亚	建筑业	省建筑总公司	政府单位
华陇建筑南非有限公司	南非	建筑业	省建筑总公司	政府单位
中建加纳有限公司	加纳	建筑业	省建筑总公司	政府单位
多哥联门之家技术合作组	多哥	建筑业	省建筑总公司	政府单位
甘肃几内亚建馆组	几内亚	建筑业	省建筑总公司	政府单位
陇亚建筑私人有限公司	巴布亚新几内亚	建筑业	省建筑总公司	政府单位
甘肃国际公司乍得有限公司	乍得	建筑业	省建筑总公司	政府单位
中建利比亚有限公司	利比亚	建筑业	省建筑总公司	政府单位
陇波建筑工程私人有限公司	巴布亚新几内亚		国际公司	
甘肃国际公司住津巴布韦国际经理部	津巴布韦		国际公司	
甘肃国际公司乍得国际经理部	乍得		国际公司	

14—12 接待港澳·侨胞和外国旅游人数

指　标	1979 年	1990 年	1992 年	1993 年
一.旅游人数(人次)	2 485	32 834	109 807	103 949
华侨		168	619	131
港澳台同胞		8 135	31 607	23 428
外国人	2 485	24 531	77 581	80 390
#日本人	1 011	12 769	42 246	38 949
菲律宾人			87	178
新加坡人		324	2 937	2 870
泰国人		474	923	380
印尼人	2		310	
美国人	124	1 448	4 855	4 592
加拿大人			897	952
英国人	96	1 277	4 298	3 175
西德人	128	1 699	5 210	7 733
法国人	74	1 583	5 904	6 034
意大利人	181		1 841	1 994
瑞士人	52		1 056	1 087
瑞典人	325		432	532
荷兰人			873	783
比利时人			341	
西班牙人			735	
奥地利人			458	
澳大利亚人	13	322	1 032	1 046
新西兰人	24		358	200
俄罗斯	1		128	
其他	455		2 788	9 885
二.旅游外汇收入总额(万美元)	20	805	1 188	1 210

14—13 甘肃省外商投资企业一览表

名　　称	合作方式	合同总投资额(万美元)	合作中方
兰州森基米尔作作公司	合作经营	200	兰州钢厂
兰州春晖卫生巾厂	合资经营	22	省轻工科研所综合实验厂
西北彩色胶袋有限公司	合资经营	40	国营金城机械厂
新华西服有限公司	合资经营	70	新时代技术开发公司
陇港彩塑袋有限公司	合资经营	30	崇信县印刷厂
兰州华凯工程公司	合资经营	100	中国石化国际事业公司
兰曙电器有限公司	合资经营	48	兰州电热电器总厂
兰博教育器材有限公司	合资经营	70	甘肃光学仪器工业公司
兰港毛衫有限公司	合资经营	285	兰州毛针织厂,纺织品进出
兰德塑料有限公司	合资经营	231	甘肃省纺织品进出口公司轻
飞天大酒店有限公司	合资经营	2 500	省飞天贸易公司
兰港进口汽车维修中心	合作经营	34	甘肃驼铃客车厂
兴飞地毯有限公司	合资经营	50	甘肃飞天地毯企业集团公司
兰康电子有限公司	合资经营	300	兰新无线电厂
广州兰星工程有限公司	合资经营	403	兰州兰洋工程公司
甘肃武港纸制品厂	合资经营	112	武威市羊下坝造纸厂
甘肃金德纺织有限公司	合资经营	988	金昌市毛纺织厂
甘肃金江再生革有限公司	合资经营	108	金昌市劳动服务公司
兰州金港五金厂	合资经营	320	甘肃省铝业公司
加源兰州林歌农付土特产 CO	外资企业	40	
甘肃金联药业有限公司	合资经营	30	省医药保健品进出口公司
兰州康尔乐生化有限公司	合资经营	11	兰州助剂厂
兰州金港湾饮食服有限公司	合资经营	97	甘肃省经济协作商贸公司
甘肃华阳农产品有限公司	合资经营	44	省供销社庆阳土特产品公司
甘肃金立矿泉饮料有限公司	合资经营	446	甘肃金圳科技工贸公司
兰州台新化学工业有限公司	合资经营	39	甘肃化工新技术有限公司
黄河进口汽车维修中心	合资经营	75	黄河啤酒厂
兰州正林农垦食品有限公司	外资企业	101	无
兰州金夏利酒店有限公司	合资经营	20	金城宾馆
兰州正大有限公司	合作经营	687	甘肃省牧工商联合总公司
兰州宝来皮革制品有限公司	合资经营	22	兰州皮革厂
兰州蓝星—BC 清洗技术 LTD	合资经营	52	蓝星化学清洗集团有限公司
兰州万陇铜制品有限公司	合资经营	450	兰州长津电机厂
甘肃兰澳电器有限公司	合资经营	22	兰州自动控制器件厂
兰州大得利有限公司	外资企业	32	无
兰州金台土特产有限公司	合资经营	61	省土畜产品进出口公司
兰州台联实业有限公司	合资经营	30	杭州振兴灯具厂兰州经销部
兰州天园大酒楼有限公司	外资企业	377	
兰州金百合有限公司	合作经营	60	省进出口贸易公司
甘肃华兴铝业有限公司	合资经营	965	甘肃省铝业公司
兰州新亚电力电子有限公司	合资经营	140	兰州仪表厂新技术开发公司
甘肃穆斯林华侨有限公司	合资经营	7	省乡镇进出口公司监潭公司
兰州云峰快餐娱乐中心	合资经营	48	甘肃省经济协作商贸公司
兰州金族木业有限公司	外资企业	20	
甘肃兰恒塑料有限公司	合资经营	80	兰州塑料包容器材料厂
兰州南北药业有限公司	合作经营	113	兰州佛慈制药厂
兰州台通电脑有限公司	合资经营	57	甘肃华侨企业总公司汽修司

14—13 续 1

名　　称	合作方式	合同总投资额(万美元)	合作中方
姚氏(兰州)艺术品有限公司	外资企业	39	
兰州科文办公自动化有限公司	合资经营	23	兰州办公自动化设备公司
甘肃金隆铁合金有限公司	合资经营	55	甘肃榆中金属硅厂
甘肃陇兴铁合金有限公司	合资经营	183	甘肃电力股份有限公司
甘肃新陇铁合金有限公司	合资经营	81	省电力局八盘峡水电厂
兰州辰光电子有限公司	合资经营	13	兰州计算机工程公司
兰州天河有限公司	合作经营	909	省乡镇第三产业公司
甘肃玉祥化工有限公司	合资经营	79	甘肃玉门化工厂
兰州陇金酒楼有限公司	合作经营	35	省金城工贸公司
兰州云峰清洗设备有限公司	合资经营	30	经协商贸,市服务,省进出口
兰州敦煌饮食有限公司	外资企业	55	
甘肃隆恒房地产开发LTD	合资经营	182	兰州商业网点改造开发公司
甘肃众志房地产开发LTD	外资企业	91	
甘肃省金鑫房屋开发LTD	合资经营	298	省三鑫企业总公司
甘肃金鑫高岭土有限公司	合资经营	245	省三鑫企业总公司
甘肃兰特五金制品有限公司	合资经营	30	兰州厨房设备总厂
甘肃天港工业自动化LTD	合资经营	18	天水长城电工仪器厂
兰州钰盛技术有限公司	外资企业	10	
甘肃金亿彩印有限公司	合资经营	70	兰州针纺采购供应站
甘肃兰瑞珠宝有限公司	合资经营	91	兰州矿业集团
甘肃嘉峰冶金有限公司	合资经营	257	酒泉钢铁公司
兰州金实添加剂有限公司	合资经营	28	省医药保健品进出口公司
兰州大地房地产开发LTD	外资企业	490	
兰州万利达塑胶制品LTD	合资经营	40	兰州糖果厂
兰州云峰机动车维修配件CO	合资经营	27	省经济协作商贸公司
兰州泛菱玻璃器皿有限公司	合资经营	239	兰州兴华玻璃厂
兰州兰泰环境保护有限公司	合资经营	42	兰州市五里铺农工商企业C
平凉亚源皮革制品有限公司	合资经营	66	平凉白坡工业公司福利制革
兰州净晶清洗有限公司	合作经营	14	兰州西北宾馆第一经营部
兰州金岛汽车维修有限公司	合资经营	40	海南省经济特区发展总公司
兰州胜利仪器有限公司	合资经营	9	兰州无线电厂
甘肃金星消毒制品有限公司	合资经营	11	中国兰州大通实业有限公司
甘肃晶景装饰工程有限公司	外资企业	96	
兰州先合塑料有限公司	合资经营	30	省华侨企业总公司气修公司
金昌金港房地产开发LTD	合资经营	436	金昌市开发区金海房地产开
兰州金合节能技术有限公司	合资经营	11	中国甘肃冶金物资供销公司
金昌京源房地产开发有限CO	外资企业	182	
兰州大翔典当有限公司	合资经营	122	兰州保安服务总公司兰州兰
甘肃海兰游乐汽运有限公司	合资经营	130	外贸开发公司
兰州丝路复式住宅有限公司	合资经营	36	建行甘肃分行房地产开发CO
兰州百思特农产品有限公司	外资企业	10	
甘肃华纬建材有限公司	合资经营	800	甘肃省国营屯沟湾石英矿
陇港(兰州)有限公司	外资企业	10	
兰州锦秀有限公司	合资经营	135	基地甘肃分公司
金昌金安铜制品有限公司	合资经营	18	金昌东区工贸公司
兰州明达商业咨询有限公司	外资企业	12	

14—13 续 2

名　称	合作方式	合同总投资额(万美元)	合作中方
兰州文成塑料有限公司	外资企业	24	
兰州华德生态制品有限公司	合资经营	55	甘肃省微孔膜科学技术开发
兰州大地绿化有限公司	合资经营	23	兰州南北两山绿化开发公司
兰州澳普工艺品有限公司	外资企业	20	
兰州云峰房地产开发 LTD	合资经营	636	省经协商贸 C,省体育开发 C
兰州恒达交通设施有限公司	合资经营	51	省公路局劳动服力 C,深圳 C
甘肃金鹏电子有限公司	合资经营	59	兰州仪表标准件厂
兰州天丰卫生材料有限公司	合资经营	60	兰空后勤部科技开发中心
新银兰州房地产开发有限 CO	合资经营	546	建行兰州市房地产开发公司
兰州广通地产开发有限公司	合资经营	600	甘肃广厦房地产开发公司
甘肃威华葡萄酒业有限公司	合资经营	30	黄羊河农场
兰州美升鞋业有限公司	合资经营	16	兰州美高皮鞋厂
兰州大西北水泵配件有限 CO	合资经营	25	兰州水泵总厂配件分厂
兰州京源房地产开发 LTD	合资经营	182	七里河区城市建设开发公司
兰州金优电子技术有限公司	合资经营	55	甘肃经济技术资源开发中心
B&K(兰州)网络系统开发 LTD	外资企业	30	
甘肃美佳节能设备有限公司	外资企业	36	
甘肃隆治皮革制品有限公司	合资经营	91	康乐县虎关乡吴坪加工厂
甘肃永新药业有限公司	合资经营	26	省器化站,兰州制药厂
甘肃南威食品厂有限公司	合资经营	81	省料油进出口武威分公司
兰州丽景服装有限公司	合资经营	36	兰州民主西路百货大楼
甘肃新雅食品有限公司	合作经营	60	甘肃省进出口贸公司
甘肃华威机械有限公司	合资经营	100	甘肃化工机械厂
甘肃金来合金线材有限公司	合资经营	154	金川特种焊条厂
兰州兰阿什有限公司	合资经营	15	兰州塑料三厂
兰州东方国际旅游服务 LTD	合资经营	36	兰州市胜利宾馆
甘肃中亚货柜运输有限公司	合资经营	406	甘肃省公路运输服务中心
甘肃龙腾汽车有限公司	合资经营	873	省华侨企业 CO 汽车维修公司
兰州地安矿产勘查发展 LTD	合作经营	34	甘肃省地质工程总公司
兰州露斯嘉霍美容有限公司	外资企业	18	
兰州利民机械配件有限公司	外资企业	6	
兰州金城宾馆有限公司	合作经营	329	兰州金城宾馆
甘肃陇明型材有限公司	合作经营	1 250	兰州钢铁集团公司
兰州意德通讯设备有限公司	合资经营	10	兰州通讯技术公司
兰州金凯彩扩维修有限公司	合资经营	50	兰州市服务公司延安照相馆
甘肃兰台农付产品加工 LTD	合资经营	55	兰山商业集团公司
兰州欧亚建材有限公司	合资经营	34	兰州钢管厂
兰州天业中药材加工 LTD	外资企业	67	
甘肃陇昌饮片有限公司	合资经营	91	宕昌县工业公司
兰州天马美食娱乐有限公司	合资经营	82	
兰州富士山服装有限公司	合资经营	40	兰州轴承厂劳动服务公司
兰州兴业有限公司	外资企业	55	
兰州三叶化工有限公司	合资经营	51	兰州精化新产品开发 LTD
甘肃兰星电脑刺绣有限公司	合资经营	24	兰州第三服装厂
甘肃长丰喷胶棉有限公司	合资经营	114	庆阳平庆地方铁路总公司
兰州卡利亚针织有限公司	合资经营	148	兰州针织厂
兰州银信房地产开发有限 CO	合资经营	200	兰州电脑公司

14—13续3

名　称	合作方式	合同总投资额(万美元)	合作中方
康易达(兰州)美容保健LTD	外资企业	13	
兰州荣利物业有限公司	合资经营	128	甘肃建设开发公司
兰州黄河实业有限公司	合资经营	185	兰州雁滩房地产开发公司
甘肃兆慧发展有限公司	合资经营	130	庆阳地区汽车修配厂
敦煌国际大酒店	合资经营	510	中旅敦煌公社,中旅集团
甘肃兰凯机械技术有限公司	合资经营	11	兰凯科技开发公司
兰诚机械制造有限公司	合资经营	100	兰州三叶公司
甘肃金赢毛纺有限公司	合资经营	813	兰州第一毛纺厂
甘肃金夏华侨房地产有限CO	合资经营	130	甘肃华侨经济发展公司
兰州台兰电脑绣花有限公司	外资企业	50	
兰州金源农副产品加工	外资企业	50	
甘肃宏宝房地产开发有限CO	合资经营	241	深宏宝实业,甘肃矿产工业
甘肃大力神有限公司	合资经营	127	庆阳长庆综合贸易公司
甘肃金龙装饰有限公司	合资经营	38	省建七公司
甘肃腾达异型钢管有限公司	合资经营	46	兰州钢厂管带公厂小轧管厂
甘肃金果土特产品有限公司	合资经营	49	甘肃果品食杂公司
兰州金源农付产品加工LTD	外资企业	15	
甘肃信通房地产开发LTD	合资经营	185	省建行房地产开发公司
兰州黄河悦利印务有限公司	合资经营	80	兰州黄河集团公司
兰州天蓝环保有限公司	合资经营	17	兰州石进出口公司
兰州金都有限公司	合资经营	44	兰州饭店
兰州敦记超硬材料有限公司	外资企业	10	
优达(兰州)实业有限公司	合资经营	210	省旅游实业发展公司
甘肃龙海矿泉饮料有限公司	合资经营	100	甘肃榆中县二建公司
宕昌县民亿中药材有限公司	合资经营	55	宕昌穆斯林中药材加工厂
兰州森美服装有限公司	外资企业	26	
兰州沙海石油工程有限公司	合资经营	30	兰州油田油气水工程公司
白银千里鞋业有限公司	合资经营	65	白银羊毛衫厂
兰州真龙真空机械设备	合资经营	100	兰州真空设备厂
兰州罗林电子技术有限公司	外资企业	18	
甘肃翘适装饰工程有限公司	合资经营	22	兰州工业设计公司
兰州金狮化工有限公司	合资经营	856	兰化有机厂
兰州百乐有限公司	外资企业	19	
兰州精工汽车修理有限公司	合作经营	50	兰州钢厂
瑞龙(兰州)生物工程有限CO	外资企业	19	
甘肃奥夏生化制品有限公司	合资经营	250	甘肃省夏河县生化制品厂
兰州金港影帝楼有限公司	合资经营	125	兰州上海照相馆
隆基兰州计算机软件CO,LTD	外资企业	19	
兰州正昌实业有限公司	外资企业	130	
兰州贝祥包装材料有限公司	合资经营	71	石化厅锅炉压力容器检测站
甘肃伟利医药有限公司	合资经营	18	甘肃伟康新技术开发应用CO
天水天港房地产开发LTD	合资经营	90	天水秦城伏龙多种经营公司
兰州天龙针织品有限公司	合资经营	150	国际公司实业CO,兰棉厂
甘肃惠发房地产开发有限CO	合资经营	109	科技物资供销公司电力局建
兰州金港娱乐有限公司	合资经营	85	兰州三晋实业有限公司
兰州纬迪黄金首饰有限公司	合资经营	210	兰州市长津电机厂
兰州顺达饮食娱乐有限公司	外资企业	15	

14—13续4

名　　称	合作方式	合同总投资额(万美元)	合作中方
甘肃兰临宝来皮革有限公司	合资经营	74	临夏兰临皮革总厂
甘肃兰普卡玫瑰有限公司	合资经营	14	兰州玫瑰公司
兰州赛特自动化工程LTD	合资经营	60	兰州同位素仪表研究所
优达医业保健塑料制品LTD	合资经营	119	甘肃医保品科贸开展公司
甘肃陇赢家具有限公司	合资经营	45	小陇山林业局贮木场
甘肃华兴铝兴有限公司(II)	合资经营	2 050	甘肃铝业公司
甘肃兰美印务有限公司	合资经营	120	兰州八.一印刷厂
甘肃嘉联家具有限公司	合资经营	53	嘉峪关棉纺织厂
甘肃环球节能技术开发CO	合资经营	38	甘肃环球能源开发设计所
甘肃盛达包装印刷有限公司	合资经营	77	中国包装进出口甘肃印刷厂
甘肃金盛化工有限公司	合资经营	702	甘肃亚盛化工有限公司
兰州咏三食品厂有限公司	合资经营	191	省粮油食品进出口公司
甘肃新陇电脑针织时装有限	合作经营	400	平凉市羊毛衫厂
甘肃昌运房地产开发LTD	合资经营	182	西北实业总公司
兰州天乐城娱乐有限公司	合资经营	1 849	兰州市西固工人具乐部
平凉新雅廊房地产开发CO	合资经营	105	平凉白坡工业公司
甘肃信宜毛纺有限公司	合资经营	995	庆阳平庆地方铁路总公司
兰州澳亚皮毛有限公司	合资经营	30	兰州皮毛厂
兰州宝峰 皮革有限公司	合资经营	43	兰州皮革厂
兰康皮革有限公司有限公司	合资经营	995	省轻工业品进出口公司
兰州嘉兴汽车配件有限公司	外资企业	38	
兰州金煌绿色农产品LTD	合资经营	7	兰州金谷科技实业公司
甘肃永林汽车维修配件LTD	外资企业	30	
旭日发展(甘肃)饮料LTD	合资经营	120	甘肃泾川啤酒厂
兰州信宇装饰工程有限公司	合资经营	22	兰州消防工程公司
甘肃新陇电脑印花制衣LTD	合作经营	200	平凉第一针织厂
甘肃兰峰机械维修有限公司	合资经营	28	省水利厅机械施工队
兰州美达同源工艺有限公司	合资经营	12	兰州同源陶瓷厂
兰州国茂珠宝有限公司	合资经营	20	甘肃珠宝公司
兰州樱花影印有限公司	合资经营	35	甘肃省送变电工程公司
兰州艺宝有限公司	外资企业	19	
兰州宝佳添加剂有限公司	合资经营	45	甘肃省工研究院
兰州合发农付产品加工LTD	外资企业	50	
兰州阿里山轧钢有限公司	外资企业	15	
东方瑰宝(兰州)艺术品LTD	外资企业	40	
兰州兰蓝天玻璃制品LTD	合资经营	24	兰州平板玻璃厂
甘肃威驼客车有限公司	合资经营	1 823	甘肃驼铃客车厂
甘肃金力房地产有限公司	合资经营	499	省进出口贸公司
甘肃卓祥制革有限公司	合资经营	51	甘肃广河建材厂
甘肃德胜卫生用品有限公司	合资经营	86	兰州饮料添加剂厂
甘肃西宝国药开发有限公司	外资企业	30	
华洋兰州实业有限公司	外资企业	110	
兰州兴陇房地产开发LTD	合资经营	714	省工会建筑安装工程公司
兰州夏威夷餐饮娱乐有限CO	合资经营	20	兰州夏威夷西餐歌舞厅
兰州鸿西实业有限公司	合资经营	172	省工矿设备配件供应公司
兰州星通化工有限公司	合资经营	20	兰炼三星公司
甘肃西菱汽车有限公司	合资经营	172	陇西机械集团公司

14—13续5

名　称	合作方式	合同总投资额(万美元)	合作中方
甘肃金兰建筑装饰工程LTD	合资经营	24	甘肃金城化工科技开发公司
兰州星通电脑有限公司	合资经营	20	兰炼三星公司
兰州科文宏莲家俱装饰用品	合资经营	32	兰州金利来家俱厂等
甘肃嘉怡工艺有限公司	合资经营	59	甘肃进境贸易嘉峪关公司
兰州鑫成激光技术有限公司	合资经营	31	兰州西固汽车配件供应站
兰州华源太阳能有限公司	合资经营	44	甘肃格耐用光电公司
兰州瑞达电有限公司	合资经营	49	兰州电子实业公司
裕濠兰州装饰工程有限公司	外资企业	30	
甘肃永毅电子技术有限公司	合资经营	36	兰州科技产品总公司
甘肃金盛装饰有限公司	外资企业	21	
兰州金威小汽车修配LTD	合资经营	84	兰州小汽车修配厂
兰州美叶油品包装有限公司	合资经营	120	兰州三叶公司
甘肃金城装饰有限公司	外资企业	120	
康易达(兰州)冷冻食品LTD	合资经营	17	铁道设计院文化冷饮食品厂
甘肃兰雅房地产开发LTD	合资经营	120	西固物资供应站,市保安CO
甘肃友连建筑装饰设计LTD	合资经营	34	连铝连海综合开发总公司
甘肃加荣塑料有限公司	合资经营	27	敦煌市塑料制品厂
甘肃银港化工有限公司	合资经营	52	甘肃化工新技术有限公司
兰州兰宇房地产开发CO.LTD	合资经营	85	兰州市房屋开发公司
兰州弘利房地产开发有限CO	合资经营	51	兰州弘杨太极实业公司
兰州黄河啤酒有限公司	合资经营	1 660	兰州黄河集团公司
兰州宝佳装饰纺织品LTD	合资经营	19	兰州新兰服装厂新兰商场
甘肃金城锑品有限公司	合资经营	268	甘肃锑厂
兰州百利大实业有限公司	外资企业	52	
甘肃澳威房地产开发CO.LTD	合资经营	170	武威房地产开发有限公司
兰州陇祥汽车服务有限公司	合资经营	35	甘肃省扶贫开发集团公司
兰州陇祥绗棉制品有限公司	合资经营	25	甘肃扶贫开发集团公司
兰州旭华电子通讯工程LTD	外资企业	30	
甘肃鑫源冶金有限公司	合资经营	34	兰州石油 工贸易公司
甘肃银鼎塑胶制品有限公司	合资经营	80	国营黄羊河农场
甘肃大龙农产品有限公司	合资经营	34	省供销社华陇综合服务贸易
甘肃光华房屋开发有限公司	合资经营	169	甘肃联合大学实业公司
甘肃扶贫抽纱工贸有限公司	合资经营	51	甘肃省扶贫基金会/汕头抽
甘肃银意皮革有限公司	合资经营	200	甘肃白银西区经济开发LTD
甘肃兰利达制衣有限公司	合资经营	20	甘肃利得经贸公司
兰州福星餐饮娱乐有限公司	合资经营	48	兰州大福楼餐饮娱乐公司
甘肃泰州美容保健有限公司	外资企业	52	
张掖皇嘉娱乐有限公司	合资经营	104	张掖市商业综合公司
甘肃鑫宝金属矿业有限公司	外资企业	100	
金马(甘肃)实业有限公司	合资经营	52	甘肃土地综合开发总公司
兰州胜利机电设备有限公司	合资经营	39	兰州铝厂永达商场
甘肃鹏祥装饰工程有限公司	外资企业	50	
兰州雅豪装饰工程有限公司	合资经营	36	深圳源丰机电工程有限公司
金昌力行大世界文化中心	合资经营	166	金昌东区经济开试验公司
甘肃港桥化矿有限公司	合资经营	66	甘肃陆桥实业公司
兰州多德天然保健饮品有限	合资经营	36	甘肃省科技实业发展公司
兰州三星餐饮娱乐有限公司	外资企业	15	

14—13 续 6

名　称	合作方式	合同总投资额(万美元)	合作中方
兰州三友应用软件开发 LTD	合资经营	20	中国石化兰州炼油总厂
甘肃华通电子设备有限公司	合作经营	52	甘肃省酒泉地区工商银行
兰州华澳娱乐有限公司	合资经营	192	金城宾馆康乐部，省建行工
甘肃永盛装饰有限公司	外资企业	26	
兰州享乐食品有限公司	合资经营	52	兰州肉食水产冷冻厂
甘肃旅游航空服务有限公司	合资经营	35	甘肃省海外旅游包机公司
晶晶特种晶体(甘肃)有限 CO	外资企业	30	
兰州金丰餐饮娱乐有限公司	外资企业	33	
兰州金泰饮食娱乐有限公司	合资经营	48	甘肃靖远矿务局兰州招待所
甘肃新夏房地产开发有限 CO	合资经营	207	甘肃省新夏房地产开发公司
兰州新地机械有限公司	外资企业	98	
甘肃滨河酒业有限公司	合资经营	79	甘肃滨河酒厂
甘肃天德装饰有程有限公司	外资企业	19	
甘肃永安地毯有限公司	合资经营	289	庆阳地区地毯厂
兰州金力农副产品有限公司	外资企业	19	
兰州美新装饰建设有限公司	外资企业	10	
天水天新艺术有限公司	合资经营	52	宁夏文化开发总公司
永昌天富矿泉水有限公司	合资经营	161	永昌实业开发 CO，省建一司
兰州可里山土畜产有限公司	外资企业	33	
兰州佳美装饰工程有限公司	外资企业	33	
张掖绿色食品有限公司	合资经营	86	国营张掖农场
甘肃侨港旅游娱乐有限公司	合资经营	55	甘肃省华侨旅游侨汇服务司
兰州津田计算机有限公司	外资企业	38	
甘肃天府景设计装饰有限 CO	外资企业	15	
兰州宝丰大酒楼有限公司	合资经营	45	甘肃省食品总公司
甘肃广兰运输有限公司	合作经营	39	甘肃省供销社茶叶公司
甘肃金铠添加剂有限公司	合资经营	20	兰州市西固开然植物制品厂
甘肃泰安装饰有限公司	外资企业	83	
兰州天福工程有限公司	外资企业	120	
兰州威斯顿电子技术 LTD	合资经营	20	兰州意达经济发展公司
白银银红灯饰有限公司	合资经营	50	甘肃省白银市工业发展公司
兰州通达汽车发展有限公司	合资经营	140	中国外运甘肃公司，省扶贫
兰州钟兰木制品有限公司	合资经营	18	基地工艺地板厂
兰州三宝饮食娱乐有限公司	合资经营	52	兰州市友谊公司
甘肃兰雅花卉有限公司	合资经营	26	兰州兰花研究开发公司
兰州陇集食品有限公司	合资经营	68	甘肃陇中通达实业公司
陇源(兰州)有限公司	外资企业	58	
兰州联谊轻工有限公司	合资经营	32	兰州联发工业品经销公司
兰州多利亚食品有限公司	外资企业	14	
兰州金运有限公司	外资企业	20	
甘肃港昌食品有限公司	合资经营	88	永昌县油脂化工厂
兰州大富豪酒楼有限公司	外资企业	60	
甘肃天宝电脑针织时装 LTD	合资经营	400	甘肃绒线厂
甘肃福隆电子有限公司	外资企业	10	
兰州汇宝冶金有限公司	合资经营	44	皋兰县工业硅有限公司
兰州迅发食品有限公司	合资经营	26	兰州经济新技术发展公司
甘肃三元物业开发有限公司	合资经营	86	庆阳三元实业开发公司

14—13续7

名　称	合作方式	合同总投资额(万美元)	合作中方
白银侨力通讯设备有限公司	合资经营	135	白银区机关服务公司
甘肃金龙港有限公司	合资经营	80	兰州金海文化娱乐中心
兰州标佳生物技术有限公司	合资经营	55	兰州生物试剂实验研究所
兰州旭日汽车服务有限公司	合资经营	207	兰州友谊饭店
甘肃美源设计装饰工程有限	外资企业	21	
甘肃蓝星—赛克技术LTD	合资经营	100	中国蓝星化学清洗集团公司
甘肃碌洋食品有限公司	合资经营	220	甘肃省碌洋食品公司
兰州达祥宾馆用具有限公司	外资企业	27	
兰州远通电子有限公司	合资经营	48	省科技实业发展公司
兰州陇洋国际物业有限公司	合资经营	620	甘肃经贸陇粤贸易公司
甘肃兰港农付产品有限公司	合资经营	33	省供销社科学技术研究所
甘肃协和镁业有限公司	合资经营	900	兰州镁厂
甘肃信誉建材有限公司	合资经营	19	景泰县喜龙建材厂
甘肃武港食品有限公司	合资经营	60	兰州黄河新技术开发研究所
甘肃永合皮革有限公司	合资经营	210	兰州市针织品采购供应站
兰州金力房地产有限公司	合资经营	498	省进出口贸易公司
兰州佳利医疗保健品有限公司	合资经营	35	甘肃医药集团公司
兰州台龙塑胶机械有限公司	合资经营	50	兰州三叶公司
兰州隆台化工有限公司	合资经营	17	榆中县寺隆油脂化工厂
甘肃百利大锌冶炼厂有限公司	合资经营	209	甘肃兴百科技开发公司
甘肃星火轻工有限公司	合作经营	71	甘肃省少数民族用品工业公
甘肃金山房地产开发有限公司	合资经营	190	甘肃省乡镇矿业物资经销部
兰州乌麻园农副土特产品加	外资企业	70	
甘肃河桥碳化有限公司	合资经营	72	甘肃永登河桥碳化硅厂
兰州亿展再生物资加工有限公司	外资企业	200	
甘肃陇康药业有限公司	外资企业	34	
兰州巨信晨光实业有限公司	外资企业	27	
甘肃华港化工有限公司	合资经营	76	甘肃省机械进出口公司
兰州三意给水设备有限公司	外资企业	12	
甘肃银源旅游文化娱乐LTD	合资经营	800	甘肃白银铜城商厦股份LTD
兰州润安饮食娱乐有限公司	外资企业	58	
兰州金鼎工程材料有限公司	合资经营	220	甘肃省农垦工业公司
兰州维多利亚餐饮娱乐LTD	合资经营	35	兰德服务公司
兰州红叶摄影冲印有限公司	合资经营	17	甘肃智达实业公司
兰州三毛欧亚服饰有限公司	合资经营	245	兰州第三毛纺织厂
兰州瑞尔帝食品有限公司	合资经营	60	甘肃省粮油工业公司
甘肃省新星泉时装有限公司	合资经营	380	甘肃省暖泉工业公司
兰州时运美食娱乐城有限公司	外资企业	21	
兰州华德建筑装饰工程LTD	外资企业	17	
兰州永盛食品有限公司	合资经营	43	兰州市西固区蔬菜公司
甘肃鑫利铝型材有限公司	合资经营	110	甘肃铝椅公司
兰州中川山庄有限公司	合资经营	670	民航甘肃省管理局
甘肃陇源工艺品有限公司	合资经营	36	甘肃省工艺进口公司
甘肃交运汽车配件有限公司	合资经营	51	甘肃省交通物资供应公司
兰州海兰德特种工艺设备厂	合资经营	10	兰州磁性器研究所
达祥(兰州)房地产开发有限	外资企业	132	
兰州世业装饰设计工程有限	外资企业	10	

14—13 续 8

名　称	合作方式	合同总投资额(万美元)	合作中方
甘肃民基房地产开发有限 CO	合资经营	281	甘肃鑫冠科技发展公司
兰州新世纪电子有限公司	合资经营	52	中国工商银行兰州市支行
甘肃兰新包装用品有限公司	合资经营	31	甘肃省粮食局陈官营仓库
兰州凯迪实业有限公司	合资经营	172	甘肃金在实业发展中心
甘肃陇东纽匪尔能源 LTD	合资经营	118	丝路穆斯林经济平凉分公司
兰州全非实业有限公司	外资企业	78	
甘肃陇耀汽车货运有限公司	合资经营	430	兰州第一汽车运输公司
易达倍(兰州)有限公司	外资企业	35	易达倍(兰州)有限公司
甘肃金鹰工艺美术厂 LTD	合资经营	37	甘肃滨源多种经营公司
甘肃金属工艺美术厂有限公	合资经营	36	甘肃滨源多种经营公司
兰州龙飞聚酯制品有限公司	合资经营	46	甘肃省聚酯工业公司
兰州摩登家私制造有限公司	外资企业	31	
兰州摩登装饰工程有限公司	外资企业	14	
甘肃银宝电脑印花有限公司	合作经营	200	甘肃白银针纬编厂
兰州大得利生物化学制药有	外资企业	55	
兰州兰澳娱乐有限公司	合资经营	62	
兰州兰澳房地产开发有限公	合资经营	172	兰州市住宅建设开发公司
永昌天福矿泉水有限公司	合资经营	161	甘肃永昌实业开发总公司
兰州星光电子有限公司	合资经营	34	兰州星光电子器材厂
兰州古海电子有限公司	合资经营	200	甘肃电视机厂
甘肃康达教科文有限公司	合资经营	17	甘肃教科文实业公司
甘肃中林实业有限公司	合资经营	35	兰州市中林汽车修理厂
武威企鸿建筑装璜有限公司	合资经营	28	甘肃武威市蔬菜副食品公司
酒泉兴达塑料制品 LTD	合资经营	76	酒泉市长城塑料厂
鑫基兰州计算机周边设备有	合资经营	86	兰州炼油化工总厂安装公司
甘肃港酒房地产开发 LTD	合资经营	500	酒泉地区房地产开发公司
甘肃甘霖房地产开发有限公	合资经营	310	兰州市网点开发经营服务公
兰州黄河精细化工有限公司	合资经营	54	兰州黄河集团公司
甘肃金宇装饰工程有限公司	合资经营	13	甘肃省广播电视实业公司
兰州万国摩托车服务有限司	合资经营	52	兰州市保安服务总公司
隆基兰州计算机系统工程研	合资经营	34	兰州化学工业公司化工研究
甘肃永嘉工艺品有限公司	外资企业	30	
甘肃安利达仪器有限公司	合资经营	20	甘肃省对外经济技术合作实
甘肃三台配电照明设备有限	合资经营	65	兰州特种灯具成套电控厂
白银柯登五金化工工业有限	合资经营	640	中国有色金属工业第二十一
兰州宝源房地产开发公司	合资经营	150	甘肃省工艺品进口公司
西峰新三菱汽车运输 LTD	合资经营	1 053	西峰市第三汽车运输公司
兰州恒力磁器件有限公司	合资经营	10	兰州磁性器件研究
兰州通力焊接设备有限公司	合资经营	21	兰州通力技术有限公司
兰州伊斯兰饮食有限公司	合资经营	52	兰州伊斯兰大餐厅枯食
兰州工达石油化工有限公司	合资经营	86	兰化职工技协服务中心
兰州金港汽车自动清洗保养	合资经营	52	省机电设备总公司
兰州石金天然保健食品	合资经营	50	万里机电厂企业公司
兰州必科新房地产开发 LTD	合资经营	151	兰州新亚贸易开发公司
成盛(兰州)音频电子公司	外资企业	50	
兰州金泰房地产有限公司	合资经营	257	兰州市九州房地产开发公司
甘肃税源印刷有限公司	合资经营	34	甘肃省税务局计算机维修部

14—13 续 9

名　　称	合作方式	合同总投资额(万美元)	合作中方
兰州新星机械化工程LTD	合资经营	17	兰州市西固区联合建筑工程
兰州百利福电子有限公司	外资企业	52	
临洮鑫源中药材有限公司	合资经营	86	甘肃临洮县医药公司
兰州兰敦建材有限公司	合资经营	48	兰州兰盾实业有限公司
兰州津田机械有限公司	外资企业	60	
甘肃天元建筑装饰工程有限	合资经营	78	甘肃天元现代装饰工程公司
兰州中侨清洁洗涤有限公司	合资经营	50	广州市中桥贸易公司兰州分
甘肃兰华机械有限公司	合资经营	22	省机械工业设备公司
甘肃基隆房地产开发有限司	合资经营	310	甘肃振兴房地产开发公司
甘肃美兰清洁剂有限公司	合资经营	52	甘肃国纺工业供销公司
甘肃澳亚稀土材料有限公司	合资经营	54	甘肃稀土实业公司
兰州东宝晶体产为有限公司	外资企业	10	
临夏利民汽车服务有限公司	合资经营	19	临夏市利民汽车修理厂
甘肃大达摩托车有限公司	合资经营	897	甘肃省华侨实业公司
华基兰州计算机软件的限公	合资经营	17	兰州石油化工机械总厂
金昌力行电讯有限公司	合资经营	258	金昌东区试验小区
兰州索立得化学有限公司	合资经营	50	甘肃省科技实业发展公司
兰州陇台玻璃有限公司	合资经营	35	兰州利华玻璃厂
甘肃陇辰房地产开发LTD	合资经营	351	甘肃省水利水电对外公司
甘肃华鑫化工有限公司	合资经营	40	省供销合作联社土产公司
兰州加宝金属制品有限公司	合资经营	145	兰州铝丝厂
甘肃华泰食品有限公司	合资经营	100	省供销合作联社生产公司
酒泉金利木制品有限公司	合资经营	35	酒泉金果宾馆
甘肃嘉丽装饰工程有限公司	外资企业	38	
兰州得顺大酒楼有限公司	合资经营	66	甘肃省华科工贸公司
甘肃新星泉时装有限公司	合作经营	380	甘肃省暖泉工业公司
甘肃金洲房地产开发LTD	合资经营	245	甘肃省经济贸公司
兰州星达新型建材有限公司	合资经营	44	甘肃润达实业开发,高阀服
甘肃康发电子有限公司	合资经营	50	中国西北同位素仪表集团
兰州金驼药业有限公司	合作经营	34	兰州中药饮片厂
甘肃永发电子有限公司	合资经营	50	中国西北同位素仪表集团公
甘肃银光皮革有限公司	合资经营	200	甘肃白银西区经济开发总司
兰州华夏婚礼影视服务有限	合资经营	13	甘肃省物资进口公司兰州大
武威市铮锋建筑工程公司	合资经营	50	武威高坝建筑工程公司
兰州始乐冷冻仪器有限公司	外资企业	60	
兰州环球力车配件有限公司	外资企业	19	
泰基兰州电子设备有限公司	合资经营	34	兰州石油化工机器总厂
惠基兰州电子有限公司	合资经营	52	国营长风机器厂
兰州九龙装饰工程有限公司	外资企业	13	
兰州兴达房地产有限公司	合资经营	172	甘肃自控成套有限公司
兰州三友电子仪表有限公司	合资经营	83	兰州海河办公器材公司
兰州永恒喷镀铝箔材料有限	合资经营	862	兰州铝厂永达实业开发总司
兰州美兰科技发展中心有限	合资经营	10	兰州科讯公司
兰州锦宇建筑装饰工程公司	合资经营	17	兰州寰寓建筑装饰工程有限
兰州东安汽车清洗有限公司	合资经营	50	兰州华安总公司
兰州桑尼保税仓库有限公司	合作经营	50	兰州市进口汽车办公用品保
甘肃宏港化工有限公司	合资经营	80	甘肃靖远宏光化工厂

名　称	合作方式	合同总投资额(万美元)	合作中方
兰州菊金娱乐有限公司	外资企业	15	
甘肃陇大聚氨酯制品有限公司	合资经营	31	甘肃聚酯产品销售中心
兰州俊业摩托车维修有限公司	合资经营	51	兰州台湾工贸公司
兰州金美汽车修理有限公司	合资经营	20	甘肃金桥经济技术开发公司
兰州贝琪乐食品有限公司	外资企业	150	
玉门黎明特种防腐工程公司	合资经营	600	玉门市化工厂
兰州必可电子有限公司	合资经营	200	兰州市交电采购供应站
兰州金光工程材料有限公司	合资经营	220	甘肃省农垦工业公司
甘肃松本实业有限公司	外资企业	9	
天水天龙再生皮革有限公司	合资经营	83	天水秦城天龙实业开发公司
兰州金泉塑料有限公司	合资经营	21	兰州小西坪粮库
兰州黄河金属制品有限公司	合资经营	173	兰州黄河集团公司
平凉欣澳冶金有限公司	合资经营	103	平凉市自坡工业公司
兰州捷辉ABC系统工程有限	外资企业	15	
兰州恒星纺织有限公司	外资企业	31	
甘肃爱士达国际物业有限司	外资企业	100	
金英甘肃有限公司	外资企业	26	
兰州名律石油化工有限公司	外资企业	33	
兰州兰新百利达电子有限公司	合资经营	48	国营兰新无线电厂
兰州东方旅游服务有限公司	合资经营	36	兰州胜利宾馆
兰州金鹰计算机系统工程有	合资经营	40	兰化兰达公司
兰州膨美聚氨酯有限公司	合资经营	35	兰州白云海棉厂
甘肃天宝装饰材料有限公司	合资经营	27	兰州金城标牌厂
兰州兰荣无纺布有限公司	合资经营	100	兰州兴隆造纸厂
甘肃龙宇水利机械设备有限	合资经营	98	甘肃省水利物资实业公司
兰州金威电子有限公司	合资经营	140	甘肃省水利物资实业公司
兰州欧亚医械有限公司	合资经营	38	兰州新技术药械研究所
甘肃双鸿基房地产开发有限	合资经营	172	甘肃省建筑基础工程公司
甘肃三益蜡制品有限公司	合资经营	32	兰州市三叶公司机械仪器厂
兰州鸿运食品有限公司	合资经营	40	兰州罐头食品厂
兰州中兴国际实业发展LTD	外资企业	188	
兰州天宝大酒店有限公司	合资经营	50	兰州建兰饭店
兰州威科化学品有限公司	合资经营	190	甘肃民政工业高新技术公司
兰州美亚果菜仪器有限公司	外资企业	17	
兰州金秦装饰有限公司	合资经营	52	省轻工业品进出口公司
兰州益华饮食娱乐有限公司	合资经营	83	甘肃益华有限公司
甘州金泰装饰有限公司	合资经营	52	甘州消防安全装修联营公司
兰州海菱电器有限公司	合资经营	57	兰州金碧豪保健食品饮料公
陇石丰泽园酒楼(兰州)有限	外资企业	21	
兰州金瑞房地产有限公司	外资企业	513	
甘肃干酪素有限公司	合资经营	87	甘肃甘酪素厂省轻纺供公司
兰州凯利汽车修配有限公司	合资经营	31	中国凯利实业兰州公司

14—13续11

名　称	合作方式	合同总投资额(万美元)	合作中方
兰州广州大酒家有限公司	合资经营	70	兰州广州大酒家
嘉峪关宾馆有限公司	合资经营	500	嘉峪关宾馆
兰州黄河麦芽有限公司	合资经营	218	兰州黄河集团公司
兰州黄河宏达房地产开发有	合资经营	351	兰州黄河集团公司
甘肃莹华刻花玻璃制品公司	外资企业	58	
甘肃瑞骐皮革制品有限公司	外资企业	20	
嘉峪关星宇钢材工程有限司	合资经营	175	嘉峪关星宇钢材有限公司
甘肃金麦运输有限公司	合资经营	181	张掖市外贸总公司
兰州港昌食品有限公司	合资经营	88	永昌县油脂化工厂
甘肃兰科恒昌装饰有限公司	合资经营	52	兰州楼宇清洗技术总公司
威成(兰州)音频电子有限公	合资经营	50	兰州利威音频电子有限公司
兰州佑群饮食乐有限公司	合资经营	60	兰州市医药公司
甘肃金鸿家俱装饰有限公司	合资经营	66	甘肃三利实业公司
兰州澳特珠宝工艺有限公司	外资企业	30	
兰州奈茨泵业有限公司	合资经营	340	兰州水泵总厂
兰州金茂超硬材有限公司	合资经营	17	甘肃矿产应用开发研究所
金昌台积机电有限公司	合资经营	86	金昌东区经济开发试验小区
甘肃天盛钢铁有限公司	合资经营	228	兰州钢铁集团
甘肃西美金属材料有限公司	合资经营	42	甘肃省定西车辆厂
甘肃兰台联合机械化工业工	合资经营	150	甘肃工商矿产贸易公司
甘肃顺达农副产品有限公司	外资企业	35	
兰州百汇精品有限公司	合资经营	19	兰州百货大楼
兰州利富兰房地产开发有限	合资经营	439	兰州市城市建筑综合开发公
甘肃陇东通远竹木有限公司	合作经营	66	西峰市通达竹木有限公司
兰州天时橡塑电子有限公司	合资经营	25	兰州天城贸易有限公司
甘肃瑞兰建筑装饰工程玻璃	外资企业	19	
兰州悦心酒楼有限公司	合资经营	13	
兰州陇辉实业有限公司	合资经营	175	兰州九州经济开发总公司
兰州绿峰园艺有限公司	合资经营	12	兰州花木公司
兰州金格隆铝制品有限公司	合资经营	150	兰州铝制品厂
兰州云峰机电发展有限公司	合资经营	69	兰州市徽型汽车维修中心
兰州陇金建筑装饰工程公司	外资企业	128	
甘肃天宇建化有限公司	合资经营	86	甘肃物资资源开发经销公司
兰州金誉房地产开发有限司	合资经营	172	兰州经济技术开发区开发总
甘肃兰雅土特产品开发有限	合作经营	44	甘肃省供销合作联社工业品
兰州华港金属门窗有限公司	合资经营	34	兰州华明金属门窗结构厂
天水远运木业有限公司	外资企业	13	
兰州嘉丽国际娱乐有限公司	合资经营	61	兰州赛特综合公司
甘肃杰达餐饮娱乐有限公司	合资经营	31	省科达科技开发公司
兰州鸿达纸业有限公司	外资企业	38	
十荣企业(兰州)轻工代工有	合资经营	86	甘肃省工矿材料总公司
甘肃永林建筑工程装饰有限	外资企业	140	
甘肃华泰万春酿造有限公司	合资经营	93	甘肃徽县建新有限公司
兰州方园娱乐有限公司	外资企业	32	
兰州金城房地产开发有限公	合资经营	175	兰州九州经济开发总公司
兰州陇德工业技术咨询有限	外资企业	13	

14—13 续 12

名称	合作方式	合同总投资额(万美元)	合作中方
兰州金海湾房地产有限公司	外资企业	682	
兰州正上宾馆有限公司	外资企业	100	
甘肃辉全文具油墨印刷发展	合资经营	154	兰州市智利塑料文具厂
甘肃新大方石羊鞋业LTD	合资经营	168	甘肃新大方石羊鞋业LTD
兰州兰港餐饮娱乐有限公司	合资经营	50	兰州市农工商公司
甘肃陇江机械有限公司	合资经营	60	省商业物资贸易公司
甘肃来可乐娱乐有限公司	合资经营	42	甘肃省五交化公司
兰州现代保安设施有限公司	外资企业	21	
兰州昌宏汽车配件有限公司	外资企业	38	
平凉港龙汽车修理有限公司	合资经营	26	中国人民解放军84855部队
甘肃金波特装饰有限公司	外资企业	26	
甘肃陇泰土物产品有限公司	合资经营	52	陇南地区对外经贸总公司
甘肃丽新建筑装饰有限公司	合资经营	50	省果品食杂公司
兰州文鑫房地产开发有限公	外资企业	80	
甘肃箕失电子娱乐有限公司	合资经营	50	省歌剧团汽车修理部
兰州华宇物业发展有限公司	合资经营	263	兰州市外贸贸易公司
甘肃盛翔装饰工程有限公司	外资企业	53	
张掖华通电力开发有限公司	合资经营	310	甘肃省张掖电力公司
甘肃大港设计咨询有限公司	合资经营	22	兰州采色冶金设计研究院
兰州联波塑料制品有限公司	外资企业	10	
兰州山本商务翻译咨询有限公司	外资企业	5	
兰州飞天阁牛肉拉面有限公司	合资经营	49	兰州市饮食公司
兰州蕾宝诺移印刷制品有限公司	合资经营	200	国营风雷机械厂
兰州陇安汽车维修有限公司	合资经营	49	甘肃陇安实业总公司
兰州万顺化工实业有限公司	合资经营	88	兰州金泉化工厂
兰州中良西服有限公司	合资经营	89	温州永达纺织品公司
兰州金龙房地产开发经营有限公司	合资经营	246	兰州市糖酒副食公司
甘肃荣陆石化有限公司	外资企业	38	
兰州宁港实业有限公司	合资经营	263	兰州宁卧庄宾馆
兰州永新涂料有限公司	合资经营	105	西北油漆厂
兰州强华电子有限公司	外资企业	50	
兰州金海化工有限公司	合资经营	50	省地方煤矿公司
兰科恒昌装饰有限公司	合资经营	52	兰科楼宇清洗公司
兰州恒裕房地产开发有限公司	合资经营	175	兰州市土地房屋综合开发公
兰州金泰装饰有限公司	合资经营	52	兰州消防安全装修配套联营
兰州港银房地产开发有限公司	合资经营	103	中国人民银行兰州分行
甘肃玉港汽车维修有限公司	合资经营	35	玉门市交通局
兰州煜达展鉴装饰有限公司	合资经营	69	甘肃对外展览公司
甘肃金顺工艺饰品有限公司	合资经营	37	中国旅游服务公司甘肃分司
甘肃兰华旅游服务公司	合资经营	14	省商贸旅游实业公司
甘肃穗鑫印刷发展公司	外资企业	70	
甘肃丝绸之路旅游服务有限公司	合资经营	126	甘肃丝绸之路旅行社
甘肃辉文原子印章公司	外资企业	35	西峰市南一路东段
甘肃珍宝食品有限公司	外资企业	24	
兰州港星装饰建设有限公司	合资经营	30	中国蓝星化学清洗总公司
兰州港合石油化工有限公司	合资经营	18	兰州西固石油化工厂
甘肃百利达家用电器有限公司	合资经营	50	甘肃兰州地产新品精品展销

14—13续13

名　　称	合作方式	合同总投资额(万美元)	合作中方
天水长城饭店有限公司	外资企业	18	
甘肃金宁铁合金有限公司	合资经营	88	甘肃省进出口贸易公司等
兰州云峰金城娱乐有限公司	合资经营	20	甘肃省经济协作商贸公司
兰州亨利来娱乐有限公司	外资企业	10	
甘肃捷成针织品有限公司	合资经营	97	白银针织厂
兰州金健装饰工程有限公司	合资经营	35	兰州体育经济技术发展总公
兰州天慈医药保健品有限CO	合资经营	15	兰州天慈医药保健品公司
兰州永兴农业新技术开发CO	外资企业	13	
兰州辉达机电有限公司	外资企业	26	
兰州国贸大厦有限公司	合资经营	862	兰州五金交电化工公司
甘肃明兴制革有限公司	合资经营	35	广河县祁家集第一皮革厂
镇原艾波瑞珂果品有限公司	合资经营	37	镇原县果品厂
兰州金恒鞋业有限公司	合资经营	120	兰州三信鞋业总公司(兰胶)
甘肃港龙皮件制造有限公司	合资经营	50	甘肃平凉地区制革厂
兰州华宜大酒店有限公司	合作经营	1 319	兰州友谊饭店
兰州工府饮食娱乐有限公司	外资企业	52	
武威荣华包装印刷有限公司	合资经营	300	甘肃省武威荣华工贸总公司
甘肃中保电子有限公司	合资经营	18	中保甘肃分公司
兰州维纳斯电子有限公司	合资经营	25	兰高新技开区管委开发公司
兰州力行电讯器材有限公司	外资企业	18	
甘肃恒通纺织品有限公司	外资企业	20	
兰州天都饮食娱乐有限公司	外资企业	20	
甘肃金临食品有限公司	合作经营	20	甘肃省进出口贸易公司
兰州时代体育健身有限公司	合资经营	20	兰州阳光实业有限公司
兰州格林食品有限公司	合资经营	12	西北同位素仪表集团公司
兰州润大天然饮料有限公司	合作经营	1 263	兰州金星机械厂
兰州兰远装饰工程有限公司	合资经营	50	兰州五十铃汽车配件供应站
兰州黎兰州磁电技术有限CO	合资经营	30	兰州磁性器件集团公司
兰州鸿达电脑印刷有限公司	外资企业	50	
甘肃奥侨汽车服务有限公司	合作经营	35	甘肃中侨汽车修配公司
兰州金灵木制品有限公司	合资经营	100	兰州吉华木地板公司,省基
兰州像家楼酒店有限公司	外资企业	50	
甘肃中业科技有限公司	合资经营	42	甘肃迅达商务代理公司
甘肃星光房地产开发有限CO	合资经营	175	甘肃扶贫开发集团公司
甘肃朝阳土畜产品有限公司	合资经营	32	甘肃临洮县皮毛厂
兰州特力丝蔓化纺有限公司	合资经营	450	兰高技产业开发经济发展CO
兰州利丰电子有限公司	合资经营	53	中国电子科技开发珠海公司
甘肃顺安机动车服务有限CO	合资经营	70	甘肃交通安全报社
兰州西格拉特娱乐有限公司	合资经营	49	甘肃机械集团润达公司
兰州金泰仪器仪表工程LTD	外资企业	37	
甘肃戴氏乐器有限公司	外资企业	25	
兰州华纬汽车服务有限公司	外资企业	26	
兰州陇峰房地产开发LTD	合资经营	105	甘肃省城乡房地产开发公司
兰州蓝星清洗剂有限公司	合资经营	211	中国蓝星化学清洗总公司
兰州华西豪华装饰玻璃有限	合资经营	72	兰州簇绒地毯厂
甘肃澳银汽车修理有限公司	合资经营	18	甘肃稀土公司职工医院劳服

14—13 续 14

名　称	合作方式	合同总投资额(万美元)	合作中方
兰州兰歌娱乐有限公司	合资经营	52	兰州兰歌实业公司
兰州香山娱乐有限公司	外资企业	86	
兰州永泰丰食品有限公司	外资企业	60	
力源(甘肃)杨氏食品有限 CO	合资经营	129	甘肃省甜菜糖业研究所
兰州天天乐有限公司	外资企业	48	
甘肃天龙艺术设计装饰工程	外资企业	10	
兰州泉顺啤酒有限公司	合资经营	139	兰州啤酒厂
甘肃迅益水化工科技工程 CO	合资经营	38	甘肃四方高科技工程系统 CO
甘肃利华塑料制品有限公司	合资经营	50	兰州维尼纶厂
兰州海业电机有限公司	合作经营	140	万里机电厂/广东外贸投资
甘肃肇丰皮革有限公司	合资经营	263	广河县土畜产工贸公司
兰州香港大酒店有限公司	合资经营	84	中国航空油料兰州贸总公司
甘肃东方明珠铝塑有限公司	外资企业	140	
兰州金港洪涛装饰设计 LTD	合资经营	21	兰州天鹏装饰艺术广告公司
兰州兰景房地产开 LTD	合资经营	517	兰州市建设综合开发公司
兰州黄河娱乐有限公司	合资经营	141	兰州市保安器材设备 LTD
兰州通达塑料制品有限公司	合资经营	28	中国有色金属兰州供销公司
天水兴田橡机械有限公司	合资经营	63	天水轴承仪器厂
甘肃陇桑粮油食品有限公司	合资经营	30	定西地区对外经济贸易总司
兰州安达机电设备有限公司	外资企业	50	
兰州可尔得食品有限公司	合资经营	32	兰州可尔得食品公司
兰州活性碳纤维制品有限 CO	合资经营	35	化工机械研究院新技术开发
甘肃鸿兴农业技术有限公司	外资企业	17	
兰州恒通电器有限公司	外资企业	33	
兰州捷达装饰工程有限公司	外资企业	45	
天水台联寿龄矿业有限公司	合资经营	103	甘肃省长龄北道选矿厂
甘肃敦煌山庄股份有限公司	合资经营	865	甘肃广达实业总公司
兰州润琪电子技术有限公司	外资企业	35	
甘肃省大公房地产开发 LTD	合资经营	123	兰州住友建筑装饰工程公司
天地人(兰州)商务咨询 LTD	外资企业	25	
酒泉凯方汽车维修有限公司	合资经营	28	酒泉市汽修厂
兰州文鑫餐饮娱乐有限公司	外资企业	17	
甘肃兰太工业技术咨询 LTD	合资经营	14	甘肃兰东科技设计咨询总 CO
兰州兰太工业技术咨询 LTD	合资经营	14	甘肃兰东科技设计咨询 CO
兰州海外城酒楼有限公司	外资企业	22	
兰州潮汕大酒楼有限公司	合资经营	60	甘肃省五金矿产进出口公司
兰州科文计算机技术有限 CO	合资经营	26	兰州办公自动化设备公司
兰州开泰装饰有限公司	合资经营	19	兰州开泰实业公司
兰州深兰精雅珠宝首饰 LTD	合资经营	35	兰州工贸商场
兰州富力美食娱乐有限公司	外资企业	21	
敦煌高登地膜有限公司	合资经营	44	敦煌市政府招待所
兰州金泰保温有限公司	外资企业	50	
兰州永通房屋开发有限公司	合资经营	86	兰州市房地产开发公司
信辉(兰州)电器有限公司	外资企业	10	
甘肃永达冶金有限公司	外资企业	345	
兰州东方国际房地产有限 CO	合资经营	225	深圳市珠宝城企业有限公司

14—13 续 15

名　称	合作方式	合同总投资额(万美元)	合作中方
兰州科文泰吉利娱乐饮食	合资经营	26	兰州办公自动化设备公司
兰州新龙和洋酒有限公司	合资经营	500	
甘肃金纬旅游服务有限公司	合资经营	51	甘肃金城旅行社
兰州先科立体摄影有限公司	合资经营	46	兰州先科摄影有限公司
甘肃馨业绿色食品有限公司	合资经营	103	张掖地区对外经贸公司
兰州金鑫娱乐发展有限公司	合资经营	48	兰州百货公司
甘肃泰兴利五矿有限公司	合资经营	35	兰州凯茂硅业有限公司
甘肃天鹰脱水蔬菜有限公司	合资经营	259	甘肃天水食品公司
甘肃天鹰肉制品有限公司	合资经营	336	甘肃天水市食品公司
兰州华西宝饮料有限公司	合资经营	35	甘肃省土畜产品进出品公司
金昌天池农副产品有限公司	合资经营	76	金昌市农林特产有限公司
甘肃兰特植物化学有限公司	合资经营	29	兰州医药科技公司
甘南特兴粮油食品有限公司	合资经营	28	甘南州粮油食品进出口公司
甘肃恒达化工有限公司	合作经营	350	甘肃甘谷油墨厂
甘肃龙登合金铸管有限公司	合资经营	525	海南飞龙贸易公司
甘肃金海马家俱装饰有限 CO	合资经营	66	甘肃三力，军区，新新糖酒
兰州宏兴五金有限公司	外资企业	51	
兰州富昌卫生用品有限公司	合资经营	22	兰州富昌种植养殖场
兰州豪美大酒店有限公司	合资经营	49	甘肃先科旅游实业有限公司
兰州蓝星－马卡耶夫清洗	合资经营	55	蓝星化学清洗总公司
兰州美鑫工艺有限公司	外资企业	30	
甘肃鑫达农付产品有限公司	外资企业	35	
甘肃科苑粮油土畜产品 LTD	外资企业	30	
兰州金联服装有限公司	外资企业	50	
甘肃陇原食品添加剂有限 CO	合资经营	103	兰州陇丰添加剂厂
万隆装饰工程(甘肃)LTD,CO	合资经营	48	
甘肃新世界装饰工程 LTD,CO	外资企业	26	
庆阳庆港生化制品有限公司	合资经营	17	甘肃省华池县经济开发公司
兰州宏发汽车维修有限公司	外资企业	80	
兰州华兰仪表有限公司	合资经营	70	兰炼智能仪表厂
兰州宝珍珠宝有限公司	合资经营	52	兰州大众工贸公司
兰州天元防腐保鲜有限公司	合资经营	412	甘肃天元防腐保鲜集团公司
武威十院 CT 医学检查中心	合作经营	21	陆军十院，军区总院
兰州飞亚纸制品有限公司	外资企业	21	
甘肃宏源娱乐有限公司	外资企业	14	
兰州辰光房地产开发 LTD,CO	外资企业	121	
兰州万达彩色制版印刷 LTD	合资经营	31	甘肃省经济开发公司
兰州金名特种涂料有限公司	合资经营	26	甘肃省残联物资公司
兰州不夜城饮食娱乐有限 CO	合资经营	53	兰州市西固区四川豆花饭庄
酒泉曼哈顿卡拉 OK 娱乐 LTD	外资企业	17	
兰州泉威扎啤有限公司	合资经营	100	兰州啤酒厂沈阳祥胜电器
兰州威如汽车服务有限公司	外资企业	14	
甘肃天岳蔬黍食品有限公司	合资经营	200	甘肃天岳实业有限公司
兰州意德电子技术有限公司	合资经营	38	中科院近物所科印厂
兰州金海有限公司	合资经营	862	甘肃金海实业公司

14—13续16

名　称	合作方式	合同总投资额(万美元)	合作中方
甘肃北方旺族装修工程LTD	外资企业	19	
兰州吉海电子有限公司	合资经营	200	甘肃电视机厂
甘肃隆治实业有限公司	外资企业	86	
甘肃港桥化矿有限公司	合资经营	66	甘肃陆桥实业公司
兰州泰和功能材料有限公司	外资企业	16	
兰州宝川铝业有限公司	合资经营	4 311	甘肃宝川铝业有限公司
兰州先特电子有限公司	外资企业	52	
兰州泰昌服装精品有限公司	外资企业	13	
兰州福尔摩沙服饰有限公司	外资企业	52	
兰州宏宇珠宝工艺制品LTD	外资企业	95	
甘肃银河机械工程有限公司	合资经营	232	甘肃银河实业开发公司
北兴(兰州)肠衣有限公司	外资企业	30	
甘肃华利特种紧固件LTD	合资经营	180	甘肃化工机械厂
武威企鸿酒店娱乐有限公司	外资企业	43	
甘肃华盛木制品有限公司	合资经营	50	甘肃徽县嘉陵镇
临夏裕泰塑料制品有限公司	合资经营	117	临夏州工程塑料厂
甘肃精龙农产品有限公司	外资企业	78	
甘肃艾中珠宝饰品有限公司	合资经营	38	甘肃电建实业公司
白银时来有色金属有限公司	合资经营	517	甘肃银城实业总公司
兰州香通房地开发LTD	外资企业	182	
兰州改涛饮食娱乐有限公司	外资企业	30	
兰州三动工具有限公司	合资经营	52	兰州三动工具批发部
甘肃华美农副产品有限公司	合资经营	18	甘肃省民乐县食品公司
兰州新兴家具有限公司	外资企业	64	
甘肃香君化妆品有限公司	外资企业	69	
兰州国泰服装有限公司	外资企业	90	
甘肃金粮油食品有限公司	合资经营	25	甘肃省农付产品进出口公司
甘肃靖银油脂化工有限公司	合资经营	155	白银工业公司化工厂
兰州金源房地产开发LTD	外资企业	207	
甘肃德隆土畜产品有限公司	外资企业	39	
酒泉金通农产品开发LTD	合资经营	86	酒泉客运贸易有限公司
兰州国轩食品有限公司	外资企业	53	
兰州华丰塑料制品有限公司	外资企业	50	
甘肃亨通化学工业有限公司	合资经营	394	甘肃省陇中农药厂
金昌福海石油树脂有限公司	合资经营	91	金昌石油树脂厂
甘肃鸿峰土特产品加工LTD	外资企业	20	
兰州金叶塑胶管件有限公司	合资经营	150	甘肃省农垦工业公司
甘肃中山广告装饰工程LTD	合资经营	61	兰州中山装饰广告美术公司
甘肃巨龙装饰工程有限公司	外资企业	28	
甘肃金龙稀土有限公司	合资经营	50	甘肃省工业科技公司
兰州距丰雨具有限公司	外资企业	55	
兰州精工工业仪表有限公司	外资企业	51	
甘肃合和家私制品有限公司	外资企业	43	
甘肃通兴祥纺织有限公司	合资经营	26	甘肃外贸毛纱厂
兰州大同装饰材料有限公司	外资企业	54	
金昌天池农付产品有限公司	合资经营	76	金昌市农材特产有限公司

14—13 续17

名　称	合作方式	合同总投资额(万美元)	合作中方
兰州吉圣化工有限公司	外资企业	50	
兰州龙琪制鞋有限公司	外资企业	54	
甘肃泰龙涂料有限公司	合资经营	21	天水兰天建筑安装工程公司
甘肃兰泰保温防腐塑料LTD	外资企业	50	
甘肃万隆娱乐饮食有限公司	合资经营	48	甘肃省万隆经贸发展LTD
兰州富友食品工业有限公司	合资经营	78	甘肃省友谊公司
白银鑫光金属有限公司	合作经营	48	白银有色金属公司铝厂
甘肃金源房地产开发有限司	外资企业	138	
兰州俊皓装饰工程有限公司	外资企业	17	
兰州开实办公设备有限公司	外资企业	60	
甘肃腾龙日讯电讯有限公司	合资经营	86	甘肃省电信器材厂
兰州金樽食品有限公司	合资经营	124	兰州保健营养食品厂
兰州金美食品有限公司	合资经营	35	兰州维力宝饮料厂
兰州天强化工有限公司	合资经营	35	兰州炼油化工总厂三星公司
兰州通达娱乐服务有限公司	合资经营	31	兰州金城科贸实业总公司
甘肃联丰制衣玩具有限公司	外资企业	32	
甘肃东方机电设备有限公司	合资经营	18	兰州工程机械配件公司
兰州兴达建筑装饰材料LTD	合资经营	21	兰州成达服务公司
兰州金冠铁合金有限公司	合作经营	86	兰州市榆中县三电电石厂
兰州恒丰食品有限公司	合资经营	70	兰州罐头食品厂
甘肃兰塔时装有限公司	合资经营	19	甘肃省建四方企业发展公司
甘肃金磊电子有限公司	外资企业	11	
甘肃臻城房地产开发LTD	合资经营	175	甘肃长城房地产开发总公司
甘肃中雅家具装饰有限公司	合资经营	49	兰州中雅企业有限公司
兰州宏侨食品有限公司	合资经营	382	兰州宏达经济服务发展公司
兰州金冠农业发展有限公司	合资经营	70	兰州市农业技术引进开发所
兰州泰南宝树脂有限公司	外资企业	50	
兰州国鸿制袜有限公司	外资企业	50	
兰州荣泰木器制品有限公司	外资企业	50	
兰州实泰五金制品有限公司	外资企业	50	
兰州华新橡胶工业股份LTD	外资企业	50	
兰州天宇装潢设计工程LTD	合资经营	22	兰雨建筑装饰材料公司
甘肃华茂塑料有限公司	合资经营	48	兰化石油化工厂塑料加工厂
甘肃新津房地产开发LTD	合资经营	241	甘肃新型建筑材料房屋开发
甘肃宏远电子实业有限公司	合资经营	52	甘肃省转业军官实业总公司
兰州金鑫电子技术有限公司	合作经营	49	兰州黄河电子服务中心

14—14 人民币对主要外币年平均汇价

外币名称	外币单位	1990年		1992年		1993年	
		买价（人民币元）	卖价（人民币元）	买价（人民币元）	卖价（人民币元）	买价（人民币元）	卖价（人民币元）
澳大利亚元	100	372.68	374.55	404.64	406.67	391.51	393.47
奥地利先令	100	42.14	42.36	50.17	50.42	47.42	47.66
加拿大元	100	408.44	410.19	456.16	458.45	432.58	434.74
瑞士法郎	100	345.71	347.44	392.68	394.65	390.52	392.48
德国马克	100	296.42	297.90	353.27	355.04	334.91	336.59
丹麦克朗	100	77.35	77.74	91.36	91.82	85.88	86.32
芬兰马克	100	124.98	125.60	123.44	124.06	101.33	101.83
法国法郎	100	88.00	88.44	104.17	104.69	98.63	99.13
荷兰盾	100	263.02	264.34	313.58	315.15	299.15	300.65
挪威克朗	100	76.41	76.79	88.78	89.22	77.82	78.22
新加坡元	100	263.59	264.92	337.41	339.10	362.58	364.40
瑞典克朗	100	80.77	81.17	94.86	95.33	69.41	69.75
英镑	100	852.32	856.59	971.71	976.58	854.52	858.80
美元	100	477.18	479.57	550.11	552.87	578.55	581.45
港元	100	61.24	61.54	71.06	71.42	74.90	75.28
意大利里拉	10 000	39.96	40.15	44.87	45.06	33.97	34.15
日元	100 000	3 314.97	3 331.59	4 349.87	4 371.67	5 195.08	5 221.12
比利时法郎	10 000	1 433.07	1 440.24	1 715.45	1 724.05	1612.01	1 620.09

十五、金融、保险

统计指标解释

·之十五·

【工业总产值】我国的工业包括:1.对于自然的开采,如采矿、晒盐、森林采伐等(但不包括擎兽捕猎和水产捕捞);2.对农副产品的加工,如碾米、磨粉、酿酒、榨油、轧花、缫丝、屠宰、药材加工等;3.对工业品的加工,如炼钢、炼铁、轧钢、炼焦、化工生产、机器制造、木材加工、纺织、印染、服装加工、造纸等;4.对工业品的修理,如修理机械设备、交通运输工具等;5.自来水、煤气的生产和电力的生产及供应。

工业总产值是以货币表现的工业企业生产的产品总量,反映一定时期工业生产的总成果和总规模。工业总产值目前采用"工厂法"计算,包括各工业企业生产的符合产品质量标准的入库成品价值(无论自备原料的产成品或来料加工的产品都按全价计算)和对外承作的工业性作业价值。一个企业内部自产自用的产品、半成品不允许重复计算产值,但企业间存在着重复计算。

1958年及以后工业总产值中,将农村人民公社工业的轧花、碾米、磨粉、屠宰、缝纫等作业,由按产品全值计算。改为按加工费计算,并将机械捕渔和生产大队、生产队办的工业产值划归农业总产值。从1984年以后把村办工业产值划归工业总产值。

【轻工业】轻工业一般是指提供生活消费品的工业。包括以下两类工业:1.以农产品为主要原料的轻工业。包括棉、毛麻、丝纺织和缝纫、皮革及其制品、纸浆和造纸、食品工业等等。这类工业主要以农产品为基础原料。2.以非农产品为主要原料的轻工业。包括日用金属制品、生活用机械制造、生活用电子和电气用具、日用化工品、化学纤维及其织品、制盐、日用玻璃、日用陶瓷、生活用燃料加工等等。

【重工业】重工业一般是指生产生产资料工业,它为国民经济各部门提供物质技术基础。包括下列两类工业:1.采掘(伐)工业是指石油开采、煤炭开采、金属矿开采、非金属矿开采和木材采伐工业。2.制造工业是指重工业中心的加工工业,包括金属冶炼及加工,炼焦及焦炭化学化工原料,建筑材料等原料工业;电力、石油和煤炭加工等动力燃料工业;为装备国民经济各部门的机械设备制造工业;以及化肥、农药等农业生产资料工业等。

根据上述划分原则,修理业中修理作业对象是重工业的划为重工业,否则划为轻工业。各工业部门总产值的划分也是按"工厂法"计算的,即一个工业企业在正常情况下生产的主要产品性质属于轻工业,则该企业的全部总产值作为轻工业总产值;一个工业企业生产的主要产品的性质属于重工业,则该企业的全部总产值作为重工业总产值。

15—1 银行存款余额

单位:万元

年　份	存款余额	#企业存款	#农村存款	#城镇储蓄存款
1978	208 319	72 303	25 792	30 367
1980	312 790	123 415	30 635	62 543
1985	652 540	286 202	59 380	200 101
1986	823 538	350 120	66 856	280 191
1987	1 001 528	400 456	81 050	379 113
1988	1 049 884	389 972	86 543	456 046
1989	1 615 633	395 958	83 556	612 283
1990	1 615 633	509 519	84 396	835 624
1991	2 038 471	671 585	84 721	1 070 164
1992	2 570 641	908 302	92 772	1 347 861
1993	3 033 791	924 392	114 801	1 708 193

15—2 银行贷款余额

单位:万元

年　份	贷款余额	#工业贷款	#农村贷款	#商业贷款
1978	293 344	82 014	30 939	170 573
1980	324 061	86 665	46 324	184 931
1985	757 922	211 414	89 810	316 923
1986	1 008 851	302 806	104 309	377 135
1987	1 220 324	362 104	118 218	431 446
1988	1 399 103	408 640	93 485	506 180
1989	1 620 819	491 089	102 572	582 811
1990	2 053 293	646 343	114 023	703 817
1991	2 573 642	777 804	128 787	807 481
1992	3 021 261	898 551	147 931	958 084
1993	3 678 296	1 092 088	168 281	1 101 078

15—3 国家银行信贷资金平衡表(资金来源)

(年末余额)　　单位:万元

项　目	1990年	1992年	1993年
资金来源合计	2 113 666	3 149 116	3 804 443
各项存款	1 615 633	2 570 641	3 033 791
企业存款	509 519	908 302	924 392
财政存款	18 561	15 016	37 876
基本建设存款			
机关团体存款	100 765	112 774	119 832
城镇储蓄存款	835 624	1 347 861	1 708 193
农村存款	86 439	92 772	114 801
信托存款	3 418	1 584	2 360
其他存款	61 307	92 332	126 337
金融债券	12 368	13 730	7 039
对国际金融机构负债			
流通中货币			
银行自有资金			
当年结益	27 074	26 741	3 873
其他	458 591	538 004	759 740

15—4 国家银行信贷资金平衡表(资金运用)

(年末余额)　　单位:万元

项　目	1990年	1992年	1993年
资金运用合计	2 113 666	3 149 116	3 804 443
各项贷款	2 053 293	3 021 261	3 678 296
工业贷款	646 343	898 551	1 092 088
商业企业贷款	703 807	958 084	1 101 078
建筑企业贷款	60 133	72 147	83 622
乡镇企业贷款	48 259	64 524	84 351
个体工商业贷款	5 244	4 895	6 282
农业贷款	114 023	147 931	168 281
固定资产贷款	432 814	767 512	1 008 970
其他贷款	42 670	107 617	133 624
金银占款	483	1 877	8 504
外汇占款	7 824	463	—11 145
在国际金融机构资产			
财政借款			
其他支出	52 066	125 515	128 788

15—5 金融机构信贷资金平衡表

（期末余额） 单位:万元

项 目	1992年	1993年
资金来源合计	3 509 171	4 297 046
各项存款	3 032 309	3 606 387
企业存款	978 927	1 003 082
财政存款	15 016	37 876
基本建设存款		
机关团体存款	112 774	119 832
城镇储蓄存款	1 361 803	1 730 088
农村存款	62 758	86 222
其他存款	239 927	302 516
(金融)债券	14 111	7 641
发行基金往来	227 543	205 266
自有资金	236 965	286 451
当年结益	33 101	6 426
其他	—34 858	184 875
资金运用合计	3 509 171	4 297 046
流动资金贷款	2 079 847	2 475 182
工业贷款	924 979	1 122 234
商业贷款	983 812	1 140 578
建筑企业贷款	76 323	89 608
个体工商业贷款	30 209	38 411
乡镇企业贷款	64 524	84 351
农业贷款	289 269	377 857
固定资产贷款	767 512	1 008 970
其他贷款	229 424	296 127
购买债券	67 173	73 826
金银库存占款	1 877	8 504
外汇占款	463	—11 145
现金	21 429	30 261
其他	341 446	415 321

15—6 银行现金投放回笼差额

单位:万元

年　份	现金收入	现金支出	净投放	净回笼
1952				
1957	118 264	117 522		742
1965	115 717	121 508	5 791	
1970	150 871	151 193	322	
1975	195 595	202 920	7 305	
1978	226 340	233 991	7 651	
1980	329 710	346 271	16 561	
1981	366 503	376 471	9 968	
1982	410 917	420 156	9 239	
1983	485 953	504 688	18 735	
1984	595 344	644 862	49 518	
1985	794 412	830 103	35 691	
1986	949 269	1 000 329	51 060	
1987	1 236 539	1 280 075	43 536	
1988	1 680 491	1 817 567	137 076	
1989	1 881 051	1 926 671	45 620	
1990	2 097 577	2 165 931	68 354	
1991	2 447 670	2 590 503	142 833	
1992	3 277 098	3 499 825	222 727	
1993	4 835 103	5 026 269	191 166	

15—7 银行现金收入

单位:万元

项　目	1985年	1990年	1992年	1993年
收入总计	794 412	2 097 577	3 277 097	4 835 103
商品销售收入	408 285	740 920	958 782	1 183 943
服务事业收入	49 346	129 914	190 567	242 673
税款收入	3 210	12 291	18 767	24 614
农村信用社收入	42 034	98 547	123 499	146 525
乡镇企事业收入	6 624	20 553	30 584	43 821
个体经营收入	12 215	29 213	44 321	64 522
储蓄存款收入	214 505	858 426	1 506 082	2 508 795
其他金融机构收入		34 251	81 513	125 266
汇兑收入	24 440	67 257	88 488	117 751
其他收入	33 753	95 748	198 810	322 345
债券收入		10 457	35 684	54 848

15—8 银行现金支出

单位:万元

项　目	1985年	1990年	1992年	1993年
支出总计	830 103	2 165 931	3 499 825	5 026 269
工资及对个人其他支出	330 037	723 318	1 008 240	1 236 203
农副产品采购支出	101 403	213 187	271 986	279 025
工矿产品收购支出	4 517	13 708	20 322	39 899
行政企业管理费支出	55 924	125 481	206 480	309 991
农村信用社支出	100 679	148 978	222 617	247 458
乡镇企事业支出	14 802	42 093	65 193	81 343
个体经营支出	16 621	38 841	60 800	82 377
储蓄存款支出	165 503	695 614	1 360 203	2 331 839
其他金融机构支出		25 053	54 715	87 195
汇兑支出	16 336	49 690	74 079	100 338
其他支出	24 281	80 605	130 312	218 370
债券支出		9 363	24 877	12 232

15—9 货币流量表

指标	1985年	1990年	1992年	1993年	1993年为1992年的%
一. 货币流通量(万元)	131 000	296 000	480 000	630 000	131.25
# 城乡居民手持现金	88 102	241 200	297 200	430000	144.68
# 城镇居民	23 432	58 200	71 600	100 000	139.66
农民	64 670	143 300	225 600	250 000	110.82
二. 平均每人持币量(元/人)	43.12	133.94	130.75	186.68	142.78
# 城镇居民	73.45	160.77	184.54	187.93	101.84
农民	37.51	77.80	118.24	185.80	157.14

15—10 每元货币流通量拥有库存量

指标	单位	1985年	1990年	1992年	1993年	1993年为1992年的%
一. 年末货币流通量	万元	131 000	296 000	480 000	630 000	131.25
二. 年平均货币流通量	万元	124 000	282 300	420 000	555000	132.14
社会消费品零售总额	万元	518 104	961 640	1 282 631	1 561087	121.71
每元货币流通拥有库存量	元	4.71	3.41	3.05	2.81	92.13

15—11 保险业务主要经济指标

项　　目	单位	1990年	1992年	1993年
一.国内业务				
(一)承保金额	千元	40 645 418	54 833 662	57 367 320
1.企财险	千元	19 515 699	27 429 089	28 059 346
2.运输工具险	千元	3 790 004	5 283 867	7 189 761
3.货运险	千元	11 234 275	11 238 834	9 735 985
4.家财险	千元	1 434 721	2 551 786	2 275 333
5.农业险	千元	64 098	217 934	377 169
6.其它财产险	千元	304 357	1 081 748	1 472 347
7.短期人身险	千元	3 295 031	4 657 117	6 411 335
8.储金性人身险	千元	1 007 233	2 373 287	1 846 044
(二)保费业务收入(包括储金收入)	千元	196 709	367 988	491 908
1.企财险	千元	34 996	50 314	58 704
2.运输工具险	千元	62 681	87 591	119 091
3.货物运输险	千元	35 263	36 108	38 564
4.家财险	千元	5 829	41 555	58 510
5.农业险	千元	1 462	4 248	8 862
6.其它财产险	千元	549	3 683	6 482
7.养老金险	千元	9 597	24 313	41 982
8.短期人身险	千元	13 326	19 164	30 186
9.储金性人身险	千元	33 006	101 012	129 527
(三)赔付案件数	件数	149 391	58 992	91 963
(四)保险业务支出	千元	73 859	142 704	212 614
1.企财险	千元	13 540	19 860	30 903
2.运输工具险	千元	30 900	54 041	65 042
3.货运险	千元	8 551	10 490	9 119
4.家财险	千元	1 509	5 780	41 210

15—11 续

项　　目	单位	1990 年	1992 年	1993 年
5. 农业险	千元	3 504	979	971
6. 其它财产险	千元	118	6 615	5 406
7. 养老金险	千元	1 277	3 095	12 707
8. 短期人身险	千元	3 055	6 157	6 898
9. 储金性人身险	千元	11 405	35 687	40 358
二. 国外业务				
(二)承保金额	千元	4 161 956	8 924 947	9 067 709
(二)保费	千元	6 423	10 181	12 178
(三)赔案件数	千元	311	221	199
(四)赔款金额	千元	2 052	2 577	3 376
三. 计划完成情况	%	118.73	125.88	116
(一)国内业务	%	119.22	126.71	116
(二)国外业务	%	106.57	132.29	101
四. 赔付率	%	40.06	48.20	42.18
(一)国内业务	%	40.41	49.35	51.05
(二)国外业务	%	31.95	25.31	27.72
五. 年内平均职工人数	人	1 329	1 703	1 996
六. 年末实有职工人数	人	1 329	1 867	2 149
七. 年内费用支出	千元	30 409	52 531	71 721
八. 增加值	千元	9 443	15 621	19 190
九. 机构数	个	112	118	120
(一)省级公司	个	1	1	1
(二)地. 市级公司	个	14	14	14
(三)县支公司	个	87	89	89
#市辖区办事处	个	11	12	12
(四)县以下营业所	个	10	14	16

15—12 主要存款项目利率表

(1990年—1993年) 单位:年利率%

项目	1990年1月1日	1990年4月15日	1990年8月21日	1991年	1993年	
					5月5日	7月11日
一.城乡居民储蓄存款						
(一)活期	2.88	2.88	2.16	1.80	2.16	3.15
(二)定期						
1.整存整取						
三个月	7.56	6.30	4.32	3.24	4.86	6.66
半年	9.00	7.74	6.48	5.40	7.20	9.00
一年	11.34	10.08	8.64	7.56	9.18	10.98
二年	12.24	10.98	9.36	7.92	9.90	11.70
三年	13.14	11.88	10.08	8.28	10.80	12.24
五年	14.94	16.20	13.68	10.08	12.06	13.86
八年及八年以上	17.64	16.20	13.68	10.08	14.58	17.10
2.零存整取,整存零取						
存本取息						
一年	9.54	8.28	7.20	6.12	7.20	9.00
三年	11.34	10.08	8.64	6.84	9.18	10.98
五年	13.14	11.88	10.08	7.56	10.80	12.24
3.定活两便	按同期定期整存整取储蓄存利率打九折计息	同前	同前	同前	按同期定期整存整取利率打六折执行	同前
二.华侨人民币储蓄存款						
一年	13.14	11.88	10.08	8.28	10.80	12.24
三年	14.94	13.68	11.52	9.00	12.06	13.86
五年	16.74	15.48	13.68	9.90	14.58	17.10
三.单位(企事业单位,机关团体)						
个体工商户存款						
(一)活期	2.88	2.88	2.16	1.80	2.16	3.15
(二)定期						
三个月	7.56	6.30	4.32	3.24	4.86	6.66
半年	9.00	7.74	6.48	5.40	7.20	9.00
一年	11.34	10.08	8.64	7.56	9.18	10.98
二年	12.24	10.98	9.36	7.92	9.90	11.70
三年	13.14	11.88	10.08	8.28	10.80	12.24
五年	14.94	13.68	11.52	9.00	12.06	13.86
八年及八年以上	17.64	16.20	13.68	10.80	14.58	17.10

15—13 主要贷款项目利率表

(1990年—1993年)　　　　单位:年利率%

项目	1990年 1月1日	1990年 4月15日	1990年 8月21日	1991年	1993年 5月5日	1993年 7月11日
一.一般流动资金						
三个月	11.34	7.92	7.92			
六个月	11.34	9.00	8.64	8.10	8.82	9.00
一年	11.34	10.08	9.36	8.64	9.36	10.98
二.个体工商户贷款	在1.34%基础上上浮30%	在10.08%基础上上浮20%	在9.36%基础上上浮20%	在8.64%基础上上浮20%		
三.技术改造贷款	同基本建设贷款利率	10.08	9.36	8.64	9.18	10.98
四.基本建设贷款						
一年以内(含一年)	11.34	10.08	9.36	8.46	9.18	10.98
一年以上至三年(含三年)	12.78	10.80	10.08	9.00	10.80	12.24
三年以上至五年(含五年)	14.40	11.52	10.80	9.54	12.06	13.86
五年以上至十年(含十年)	19.26	11.88	11.16	9.72	12.24	14.04
十年以上	按一年期	11.88	11.16			

15—14 优惠贷款利率表

(1990年—1993年)　　　　单位:年利率%

项目	1990年 1月1日	1990年 4月15日	1990年 8月21日	1991年	1993年 5月5日	1993年 7月11日
1.粮.棉.油贷款	10.08	9.00	8.28	7.74	8.46	10.08
2.外贸出口产品收购贷款	9.00	7.92—9.00	7.92—9.00	7.74	8.46	10.08
3.老少边区地区发展经济贷款	7.02	5.76	5.76	5.76	6.48	8.10
4.贫困县办工业贷款	7.02	5.76	5.76	5.76	6.48	8.10
5.民族贸易及民族用品生产贷款	8.46	7.20	6.48	5.76	6.48	8.10
6.扶贫贴息专项贷款(含牧区)	2.88	2.88	2.88	2.88	2.88	2.88
7.特区.开发区差别利率开发贷款						
五年期以下	2.88	2.88	2.88	2.88		
五年期以上	4.32	4.32	4.32	4.32		

十六、教育、科技及文化事业

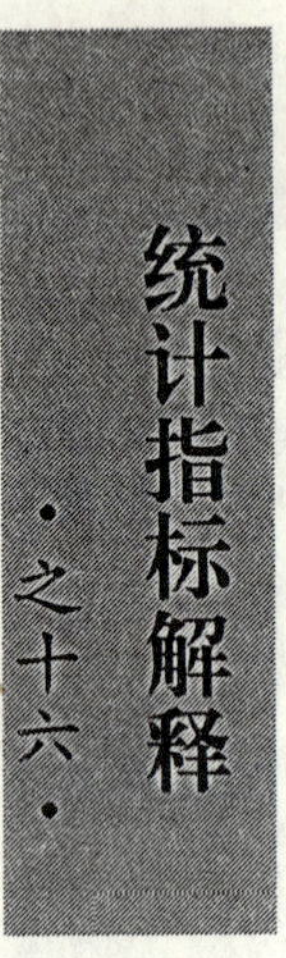

【独立核算工业企业】工业企业按其行政和财务是否独立，分为独立核算工业企业和非独立核算工业企业。

独立核算工业企业，应同时具备下列三个条件：

1.行政上有独立组织形式；2.独立核算盈亏，编制独立的资金平衡表；3.有权与其他单位签订合同，并在银行设立独立户头。独立核算工业企业不论是单一生产或联合性生产的企业，均以整个企业作为一个基层单位进行统计。

【大、中、小型企业】大、中、小型企业的划分标准有下列两类：

1.按企业产品的年生产能力划分。如钢铁联合企业，年产钢100万吨以上的为大型，10万吨以上、100万吨以下的为中型，10万吨以下的为小型。棉纺织厂，拥有棉纺锭10万枚及以上的为大型，5万枚以上，10万枚以下的为中型，5万枚以下的为小型等。对不同产品的企业分别规定有不同的划分标准。

2。凡不按产品的年生产能力为划分标准的企业，则以企业拥有固定资产原值为划分大、中、小型的标准。

【资本金】资本金，通俗地讲就是办企业的本钱。根据财政部颁布的《企业财务通则》规定，资本金是指企业在工商行政管理部门登记的注册资金。

资本金构成：

资本金按照投资主体一般分为四种：

1.国家资本金：是指有权代表国家投资的政府部门或机关以国有资产投入企业形成的资本金。不论企业的资本金是哪个政府部门或机构投入的，只要是以国家资金进行投资的，均作为国家资本金。

2.法人资本金：是指其他法人单位投入本企业形成的资本金。

3.个人资本金：是指社会个人或者本企业内部职工以个人合法财产投入企业形成的资本金。

4.外商资本金：是指外国投资者以及我国香港、澳门和台湾地区投资者投入企业形成的资本金。

资本金在一般情况下是相对稳定的，企业增加或减少注册资金数额，必须向原登记机关申请办理变更登记。

资本金指标的资料来源

资本金的本年实际数，根据企业在工商行政管理部门的注册资金登记数或者会计师事务所出具的验资报告中的数据填列（工业企业可以直接从资产负债表的补充资料中取得数据）。当企业增加或减少注册资本金时，应按企业资本金变更登记后的数字填列。

16—1 各类学校基本情况

单位:所.人

指　标	学校数		教职员工		#专任教师	
	1992年	1993年	1992年	1993年	1992年	1993年
总　计	26 059	25 895		251 286	206 988	208 291
高等学校	17	17	15 632	15 759	5 835	5 882
#地方	12	12	7 894	8 111	3 062	3 137
中等职业技术教育	375	380	24 025	23 930	12 602	12 529
中等专业学校	115	115	12 592	12 747	5 994	6 053
技工学校	71	74	5 990	5 673	2 993	2 883
职(农)业学校	189	191	5 443	5 510	3 615	3 593
普通高中	471				14 032	13 368
城镇	304				10 300	9 853
农村	167				3 732	3 515
义务教育	25 187				174 348	176 294
初中	1 124				48 275	48 715
城镇	139				16 585	16 984
农村	985				31 690	31 731
小学	24 063	23 887	133 231	134 520	126 073	127 579
城镇	994	1 154	26 418	26 948	23 673	24 373
农村	23 069	22 733	106 813	107 572	102 400	103 206
特殊教育	9	11	255	298	171	218
工读学校						
盲聋哑学校(班)	8	9	236	247	154	168
弱智儿童辅读学校	1	2	8	31	8	30

16—1续 单位:人

指标	毕业生数		招生数		在校学生数	
	1992年	1993年	1992年	1993年	1992年	1993年
总　计	638 101	635 296	815 689	829 086	3 571 546	3 540 587
高等学校	10 371	9 395	12 065	15 391	34 591	40 514
#地方	5 931	5 668	6 918	8 661	18 892	21 839
中等职业技术学校	39 540	40 672	48 418	51 278	124 684	126 516
中等专业学校	15 773	16 269	17 832	20 067	51 596	55 156
技工学校	8 370	9 755	10 016	10 185	27 124	27 983
职(农)业学校	15 397	14 648	21 020	21 026	45 964	43 377
普通高中	66 659	66 495	58 267	55 621	184 684	156 570
城镇	48 795	47 804	42 753	42 207	134 651	118 141
农村	17 864	18 691	15 514	13 414	50 033	38 429
义务教育	521 469	518 609	696 790	706 556	3 226 615	3 215 960
初中	215 094	211 327	254 799	251 826	755 369	716 260
城镇	71 701	73 159	79 657	76 174	242 393	233 781
农村	143 393	138 168	175 142	175 652	512 976	482 479
小学	306 375	307 282	441 991	454 730	2 471 246	2 499 700
城镇	68 487	65 997	78 413	86 589	429 155	455 336
农村	237 888	241 285	363 578	368 141	2 042 091	2 044 364
特殊教育	62	125	149	240	972	1 027
工读学校						
盲聋哑学校	61	95	108	158	731	760
弱智儿童辅读学校	1		11	13	49	83

16—2 各级各类学校女学生和女教师

单位:人

指　标	1985年	1990年	1992年	1993年
一. 女学生数	1 458 010	1 465 453	1 539 981	1 539 558
高等学校	7 935	10 378	11 654	13 332
中等专业学校	12 383	18 760	19 975	21 859
普通中学	357 700	360 268	382 183	362 064
职业学校	10 492	18 195	19 161	20 362
技工学校		9 589	11 203	10 515
小学校	1 069 500	1 048 263	1 095 805	1 111 426
二. 女学生占学生总数(%)	38.20	41.46	43.13	43.48
高等学校	28.11	30.68	32.54	32.26
中等专业学校	34.35	37.83	38.71	39.63
普通中学	35.76	37.34	40.66	41.48
职业学校	30.88	40.44	41.69	46.94
技工学校		39.02	41.30	37.58
小学校	39.57	43.37	44.34	44.46
三. 女教师数	42 397	51 381	55 835	58 341
高等学校	1 327	1 582	1 653	1 707
中等专业学校	971	1 848	1 967	1 996
普通中学	10 310	13 143	15 020	15 320
职业学校	174	654	786	854
技工学校				
小学校	29 615	34 154	36 409	38 464
四. 女教师占教师总数(%)	23.54	25.52	27	28.43
高等学校	25.15	27.02	26.53	29.02
中等专业学校	25.82	31.44	32.82	32.98
普通中学	21.27	22.22	24.11	24.68
职业学校	11.56	19.22	21.70	23.77
技工学校				
小学校	24.80	27.43	28.88	30.15

16—3 高 等 学 校 情 况

(1993年)　　单位:所.人

各类学校	校数	毕业生数	招生数	在校学生数	教职员工数	#专任教师
总　　计	17	9 395	15 391	40 514	15 759	5 882
综合文学	1	1 086	2 203	6 687	3 062	1 052
理工院校	3	1 611	2 901	7 605	3 196	1 071
农业院校	1	632	862	2 355	1 485	496
林业院校						
医药院校	2	765	1 006	3 609	1 287	482
师范院校	6	3 863	5 523	13 611	4 599	1 871
语文院校						
财经院校	1	427	1 050	2 435	717	286
政法院校	1	144	440	776	306	131
体育院校						
艺术院校						
民族院校	1	603	1 036	2 731	996	443
短期职业大学	1	264	370	705	111	50

16—4 高等学校分科学生数

单位:人

学科	毕业生数		招生数		在校学生数	
	1992年	1993年	1992年	1993年	1992年	1993年
总　计	10 371	9 395	12 065	15 391	34 591	40 514
工　科	1 845	1 623	2 293	3 271	6 450	8 313
农　科	643	592	690	714	2 160	2 017
林　科	70	29	91	50	199	222
医　药	740	808	955	1 074	3 615	3 872
师　范	3 997	3 853	4 398	4 725	11 663	12 506
文　科	802	748	925	1 255	2 841	3 341
理　科	975	667	982	1 249	3 436	4 008
财　经	995	829	1 179	2 155	3 216	4 572
政　法	205	179	372	517	732	1 071
体　育	33	28	56	57	84	113
艺　术	66	39	124	324	195	479

16—5 中等专业学校基本情况

(1993 年)　　单位:所,人

项　目	校数	毕业生数	招生数	在校学生数	教职员工数	#专任教师
总　计	115	16 269	20 067	55 156	12 747	6 053
一.中等技术学校	93	10 982	15 074	40 109	10 350	4 734
工　业	31	4 605	6 491	16 517	4 694	1 941
农　业	13	1 415	1 979	5 898	1 550	670
林　业	2	334	425	1 177	244	118
医　药	14	1 922	2 472	7 200	1 496	810
财　经	14	1 559	2 228	4 954	1 091	527
政　法	2	200	335	647	198	84
体　育	10	368	390	1 554	568	319
艺　术	2	79	89	261	154	92
其　他	5	500	665	1 901	355	173
二.中等师范学校	22	5 287	4 993	15 074	2 397	1 319
#幼儿师范	1	126	180	519	80	50

16—6 各级成人教育在校学生数

单位:人

项　目	1980 年	1985 年	1990 年	1992 年	1993 年
总　计	41 197	91 725	519 295	824 648	1 109 746
一.成人高等教育	9 026	17 271	12 824	8 630	11 948
广播电视大学	6 975	11 109	8 643	4 319	5 900
职工大学	953	4 465	2 105	2 654	3 362
其他	1 098	1 697	2 076	1 657	2 686
二.成人中等教育	15 271	23 991	29 658	32 077	33 970
中等专业学校	7 671	16 883	28 910	31 350	33 431
# 小学教师进修学校	1 871	1 412	2 343	3 434	1 612
成人中学	7 600	7 108	748	727	539
三.成人初等教育	16 900	50 030	316 399	341 035	365 018
#小学班	6 900		9 009	13 463	7 957
扫盲班	10 000	49 861	288 619	327 547	357 031
四.成人技术培训学校			160 414	442 906	698 810

16—7 高等教育自学考试情况

(1993年)

指　　标	报考人数（人）	报考科次（科）	单科合格（人次）	专科毕业（人）	本科毕业（人）
本年数	128 569	310 255	92 561	3 162	75
至本年累计	763 852	1 774 620	468 768	14 401	134

16—8 高等教育自学考试分专业毕业生

单位:人

学科分类	专科毕业人数		本科毕业人数	
	1993年	至1993年累计	1993年	至1993年累计
总　　计	3 162	12 508	75	134
中　文	1 042	3 852	21	59
数　学	163	193		1
基础英语	321	1 556	6	14
哲　学				
法　律	279	522		
价格学				
财　会	212	1 098		
工业与民用建筑	34	251		
新　闻	95	1 972		
中　医	311	428		
商业经济				
农　学				
统　计	24	578		
财　政	28	140		
行政管理	64	185		
工业企业管理	36	443		
税　收	30	246		
政治管理	119	234		
经济管理				
农业经济管理	37			
园　林	115	156		
水利建筑工程				
农　学	140	248		
果　树	29	29		
政治理论			7	20
卫电高师数学	4	16		
卫电高师英语	29	176		
卫电高师汉语言	50	61	41	41
机电一体化		124		

16—9 学龄儿童入学率

年 份	学龄儿童 (万人)	在校学龄儿童 (万人)	入学率 (%)
1978	273.10	248.60	91.00
1980	274.10	230.10	83.90
1985	193.40	172.50	89.20
1986	182.20	166.50	91.40
1987	178.60	164.80	92.30
1988	178.40	166.30	93.20
1989	179.80	168.90	93.90
1990	191.30	171.20	94.40
1991	211.00	199.40	94.50
1992	213.10	203.10	95.30
1993	219.50	210.19	95.76

16—10 平均每万人口在校学生数

单位:人

指 标	1990 年	1992 年	1993 年
大学生	15.10	15.10	17.26
中等职业教育	53.50	54.50	53.95
普通中学	311.60	410.80	372.21
小学	1 083.90	1 080.00	1 065.97

16—11 平均每一专任教师负担学生数

单位:人

指 标	1990 年	1992 年	1993 年
大学生	5.80	5.90	6.89
中等职业教育	10.10	9.90	10.10
普通中学	11.80	15.10	14.06
小学	19.40	19.60	19.59

16—12 各类专业技术人员

单位:人

指　　标	1985年	1990年	1992年	1993年
总　　计	198 470	312 423	316 256	331 030
工程技术人员	33 143	50 747	50 642	51 658
农业技术人员	9 807	11 843	11 017	12 155
科学研究人员	2 684	1 863	1 906	1 941
卫生技术人员	33 029	39 378	41 162	42 485
教学人员	95 583	135 871	148 462	153 222
船舶.飞行技术人员		2		
会计人员	14 462	21 788	18 440	20 032
统计人员	2 893	4 917	3 614	3 666
经济人员	1 717	35 364	26 047	27 452
新闻.出版人员	910	1 897	1 860	2 070
播音人员		142	133	152
翻译人员	154	406	432	392
体育教练人员	422	573	541	534
工艺美术人员	74	384	315	343
律师.公证人员		702	438	571
图书.档案资料人员	552	3 812	3 543	3 801
艺术人员	3 040	2 734	2 268	2 534
政工人员			5 436	8 022

16—13 重大技术研究成果及发明奖

单位:项

指　　标	1980年	1985年	1990年	1992年	1993年
获省部级奖励	21	30	272	18	138

16—14 国有企事业单位专业技术人员数

(1993 年)　　　　单位:人

指　　标	合计	按专业技术职务分			
		高级	中级	初级	未被聘用
总　计	331 030	11 377	78 324	201 102	40 227
工程技术人员	51 658	3 190	13 222	29 127	6 119
农业技术人员	12 155	359	2 737	6 816	2 243
卫生技术人员	42 485	1 465	10 332	26 917	3 771
科学研究人员	1 941	324	741	701	175
教学人员	153 222	4 792	35 315	93 010	20 105
经济人员	27 452	217	6 272	17 795	3 168
财会人员	20 032	62	2 898	14 577	2 495
统计人员	3 666	14	450	2 878	324
编辑.记者.播音员	2 222	188	785	809	440
翻译人员	392	10	72	173	137
艺术人员	2 534	177	1 063	960	334
其他	13 271	579	4 437	7 339	916

16—15 国有企事业单位分行业.专业技术人员数

(1993 年)　　　　单位:人

指标	合计	按国民经济行业分				
		农林牧渔水利业	工业	地质勘查和勘探	建筑业	交通运输邮电通讯业
总　计	331 030	24 252	56 104	715	10 532	4 728
工程技术人员	51 658	8 567	27 095	424	5 971	1 817
农业技术人员	12 155	11 047	81	41	25	3
卫生技术人员	42 485	479	2 444	22	521	156
科学研究人员	1 941	58	4			
教学人员	153 222	900	2 830	50	327	122
经济人员	27 452	655	10 357	52	1 559	867
财会人员	20 032	1 698	6 130	52	1 051	930
统计人员	3 666	192	2 056	5	154	224
编辑.记者.播音员	2 222	3	41		31	7
翻译人员	392	8	72		4	3
艺术人员	2 534	1	11			
其他	13 271	644	4 983	69	889	599

16—15续　　　　　　　　(1993年)　　　　　　　　单位:人

指标	按国民经济行业分						
	商业公共饮食投资运输和仓储业	房地产管理公共事业居民服务和咨询业	卫生体育和社会福利事业	教育文化事业和广播电视业	科学研究和综合技术服务事业	金融保险业	其他行业
总　计	21 312	4 262	38 802	160 138	6 425	222	3 538
工程技术人员	1 878	1 546	133	1 568	2 741	21	397
农业技术人员	126	74	17	88	625		28
卫生技术人员	613	108	36 633	357	534		318
科学研究人员	4	1	14	369	1 416		75
教学人员	57	70	302	148 353	36	1	174
经济人员	11 022	889	200	769	298	85	699
财会人员	6 073	700	852	1 213	349	111	873
统计人员	557	108	62	76	61	1	170
编辑.记者.播音员	14	7	12	1 794	51		262
翻译人员	16	195	2	34	37		21
艺术人员		1	7	2 509	3		2
其他	1 452	563	568	2 708	274	3	519

16—16 大.中型工业企业

指　标	单位	1985年	1990年	1992年	1993年
工业企业数	个	160	170	186	187
大型工业企业	个	61	66	60	65
中型工业企业	个	99	104	126	122
全部职工年末人数	人	568 237	621 980	637 661	863 111
#工程技术人员	人	7 551	42 336	43 561	
全年工业总产值	千元	9 363 940	16 615 540	23 279 682	3 221 923
#新产品	千元	523 590	1 502 898	2 832 482	
产品销售收入	千元	9 419 640	14 702 640	21 858 761	3 395 894
#新产品	千元	435 960	1 116 346	2 671 784	1 745 530
出口产品	千元	186 110	468 274	455 347	
#新产品	千元	29 150	100 776	76 775	97 486
全年实现利税额	千元		2 520 372	2 874 361	315 928
#新产品	千元		121 627	597 226	303 376
企业办技术开发机构数	个	104	132	166	162
大型	个	66	76	81	89
中型	个	38	56	85	73

16—17 大.中型工业企业从事技术开发人员

单位:人

指　标	1985年		1992年		1993年		技术开发人员比例比上年(±%)
	绝对数	占全部企业技术人员比例%	绝对数	比例%	绝对数	比例%	
技术开发人员数	21 026	100.00	26 797	100.00	29 586	100.00	10.41
#技术开发机构中的人员	7 741	36.82	10 638	39.70	9 124	30.83	−14.23
#具有中.高级职称(务)人员			3 601	13.44	9 384	31.71	160.59
工程技术人员	7 551	35.91	14 655	54.69	19 307	65.26	31.74

16—18 大.中型工业企业技术开发项目及经费情况

指　标	单位	1986年	1990年	1992年	1993年
一.技术开发项目数	项	1 276	1 000	1 172	1 048
#上级计划项目	项	476	434	597	427
市场需要自选项目	项	56	30	31	52
其他单位委托项目	项	744	536	544	569
二.技术开发经费筹集总额	千元	354 410	264 764	299 200	469 650
#上级拨款	千元	45 390	28 984	58 691	55 296
专项贷款	千元	186 070	38 744	22 159	77 633
企业自筹	千元	116 980	167 442	202 064	247 470
三.技术开发经费支出总额	千元	325 570	256 776	273 390	373 972
#]开发新产品用款	千元	72 320	107 749	76 884	107 783
四.技术改造支出总额	千元	596 570	708 684	1 213 039	1 824 614
五.技术引进支出总额	千元	161 340	90 869	125 491	143 894
六.用于消化吸收的经费	千元	37 720	61 207	6 653	15 148

16—19 科技成果情况

(1993年)

指标	单位	合计	科研机构	大专学校	企业	集体.个体.民间	其他
一.基本情况							
鉴定项目	个	632	113	112	210	26	171
省.部级登记项目数	个	243	72	46	53	3	69
省.部级奖励项目数	个	138	67	12	32	3	24
二.成果水平							
国际首创/领先	个	2	1	1			
国际先进	个	3	2	1			
国内首创/领先	个	45	15	13	10		7
国内先进	个	97	23	21	29	2	22
省.部级先进	个	96	31	10	14	1	40
三.应用领域							
工业(交通/邮电/建筑/地质)	个	102	28	16	50	3	5
农业(林/牧/渔/水利)	个	89	34	18			37
四.已应用项目数	个	184	56	23	47	2	56
五.经济效益							
新增产值	千元	472 860	93 034	42 411	140 576	4 113	192 726
#新增利税	千元	61 375	12 041	6 303	28 031	340	14 660
节支	千元	26 111	4 817	3 835	6 717	109	10 633

16—20 大中型工业企业技术开发成果情况

(1993 年)

指　标	技术开发成果获奖数（项）	#国家级	#省部级	科学论文（篇）	科技著作（种）	专利申请（件）	专利授权（件）
总　计	365	6	133	474	16	41	25
国有企业	365	6	133	474	16	41	25
集体企业							
中央属企业	84		49	310	2	26	15
地方属企业	281	6	84	164	14	15	10
大型企业	128	1	89	379	14	30	16
中型企业	237	5	44	95	2	11	9

16—21 各类技术合同鉴定及执行情况

(1993 年)

单位:项.千元

指　标	合同数	合同金额		实现金额	
	合计	合计	#技术交易额	合计	#技术交易额
合　计	1 237	22 582.50	16 598.10	13 367.80	9 768.30
技术开发合同	213	8 174.90	7 275.60	4 237.60	3 126.80
技术转让合同	581	8 378.10	5 479.30	6 110.40	3 641.20
技术咨询合同	152	2 326.00	2 311.10	2 112.30	2 100.10
技术服务合同	291	3 703.50	1 532.10	907.40	900.30

16—22 技 术 交 易 会 情 况

年　份	次数(次)	展出技术项数(项)	成交技术合同数(项)	成交金额(千元)
1990	8	1 521	112	8 456.00
1991	7	985	63	4 750.00
1992	4	9 284	478	211 752.10
1993	21	46 831	1 237	22 582.50

16—23 文化事业机构和职工人数

指　标	机构数(个)			职工人数(人)		
	1978年	1992年	1993年	1978年	1992年	1993年
一.电影事业	2 746	2 843	2 473	8 103	7 595	6 991
电影制版厂	1	1	1	32	60	56
电影发行管理机构	90	94	94	1 040	1 236	1 196
电影放映单位	2 640	2 745	2 373	6 933	6 258	5 714
#影院	53	136	100	701	1 196	1 224
影剧院	33	27	19	442	273	194
开放礼堂俱乐部	57	90	94	690	993	953
二.艺术事业	136	136	149	6 316	5 643	5 722
创作机构	4		13	29		114
表演团体	98	83	80	6 038	4 874	4 698
#话剧	1	1	1	127	109	104
歌舞剧	7	2	2	888	217	213
艺术表演场所	34	53	50	249	769	713
研究机构			1			20
艺术展览机构			1			12
其他			4			165
三.图书馆事业	39	86	86	363	900	897
四.群众文化事业	240	1 334	1 341	1 273	2 637	2 650
#文化馆	85	83	83	932	948	955
五.文物事业	15	76	80	353	1 123	1 182
#博物馆	8	49	50	172	626	644

16—24 广播电视事业

指　标	单位	1990年	1992年	1993年
一. 广播				
1. 广播电台	座	20	27	29
2. 广播发射台及转播台	座	21	23	24
3. 县市有线广播站	个	68	63	62
4. 乡有线广播放大站	个	1 380	1 422	1 421
5. 广播喇叭总数	万只	136	151.72	140.77
6. 喇叭入户率	%	33.00	36.95	35.34
7. 广播发射机总功率	千瓦	655.00	672.10	674.10
	架	39	44	
8. 广播人口覆盖率	%	61.80	63.30	65
二. 电视				
1. 电视台	座	8	12	12
2. 电视发射台及转播台	座	788	1 000	1 049
3. 电视发射机总功率	千瓦	120.40	129.84	152.09
	架	928	1 195	
#系统内电视发射机总功率	架	97.70	106.01	126.79
	架	488	702	
4. 电视人口覆盖率	%	66.50	68.40	70

16—25 电视台和节目

指　标	单位	1985年	1990年	1992年	1993年
一.基本情况					
电视台	座	1		12	12
发射台	座			1 000	1049
节目	套	1	8	12	14
平均每周播出时间	小时	62.30	177.30	353.40	435.30
电视人口覆盖率	%	55	66.50	68.40	70.00
二.制作电视节目	83	88	103		
新闻节目	小时	52.10	312.00	541.43	506.32
文艺节目	小时	114.10	332.10	451.28	532.20
专题节目	小时	42.50	99.00	226.34	460.16
教育节目	小时	2.50	4.50	28.59	13.45
服务性节目	小时	33.10	156.10	42.46	629.48

16—26 出版 事业

项　目	单位	1985年	1990年	1992年	1993年
一.图书出版					
1.种数	种	403	755	1 206	1 183
#新出版	种	100	591	629	657
2.总印数	万册	6 935.50	7 234.51	7 787.23	6 136.02
3.总印张	千印张	283 061.00	268 837.00	303 025.00	247 070.25
二.杂志出版					
1.种数	种	83	88	103	107
2.总印数	万册	3 216.50	3 274.10	4 985.86	5 521.85
3.总印张	千印张	94 343.00	95 441.00	143 907.00	162 441.37
三.报纸出版					
1.种数	种	43	46	55	57
2.总印数	万份	17 592.00	20 568.00	26 784.00	24 986.00
3.总印张	千印张	163 013.00	151 998.00	184 358.00	223 274.00

十七、体育、卫生及其他事业

统计指标解释

·之十七·

【资产】所谓资产，是指企业拥有或控制的能以货币计量的经济资源，包括各种财产、债权和其他权利。

财务会计改革之前，企业资产主要是按照其特点和用途分类的，即分为固定资产，流动资产和专项资产，新的会计制度对企业资产按其流动性划分为：流动资产、长期投资、固定资产、无形资产、递延资产和其他资产。所谓流动性是指企业资产的变现能力和支付能力。财务状况统计表中的资产分类是按照新的会计制度中的上述分类列示的：

1. 流动资产：是指可以在一年内或者超过一年的一个生产周期内变现或者耗用的资产，流动资产可以按变现能力（程度）划分，包括现金及各种存款、短期投资、应收及预付款项、存货等。

2. 长期投资：是指不可能或者不准备在一年内变现的投资。

3. 固定资产：是指使用年限在一年以上，单位价值在规定标准以上，并在使用过程中保持原有物质形态的资产，包括房屋及建筑物、机器设备、运输设备、工具器具等。

4. 无形资产：是指企业长期使用而没有实物形态的资产，包括专利权、非专利技术、商标权、著作权。土地使用权、商誉等。

5. 递延资产：是指不能全部计入当年损益，应当在以后年度内分期摊销的各项费用，包括开办费、租入固定资产的改良及大修理支出等。

6. 其他资产：是指除以上各项之外的资产，如特种储备资产、银行冻结存款、冻结物资、涉及诉讼中的财产等。

【负债】负债是指企业所承担的能以货币计量，将以资产或劳务偿付的债务。其偿还形式可以用货币，也可以用资产或提供劳务的方式进行偿还。负债一般按其偿还期长短分为流动负债和长期负债。

流动负债：是指在一年内或超过一年的一个营业周期内偿还的债务，其中包括短期借款、应付款项、预付

贷款、应付工资、应交税金和应交利润等。

长期负债：是指偿还期在一年以上或者超过一年的一个营业周期以上的债务，其中包括长期借款、应付债务、长期应付款项等。

【所有者权益】所有者权益是企业投资人对企业净资产的所有权，企业净资产等于企业全部资产减去全部负债后的余额，其中包括企业投资人对企业的最初投入以及资本公积金、盈余公积金和未分配利润。对股份制企业，所有者权益即为股东权益。

股本：是指企业（公司）在发行股票时按股票面值收到的股票本金。

17—1《国家体育锻炼（标准）》达标学生数

（1993年）　　单位：人

项　目	合计	普通高校	中专中技	初中	小学
总计	1 943 569	2 415	20 168	764 259	1 156 727
及格级	988 404	1 298	9 460	380 554	597 092
良好级	651 357	774	7 275	254 056	389 252
优秀级	303 808	343	3 433	139 649	170 383

17—2 体育活动场所

单位：个

项　目	1991年	1992年	1993年
体　育　场	12	12	34
体　育　馆	5	5	5
游　泳　池	29	30	10
有固定看台灯光球场	69	69	24

17—3 甘肃省运动员破记录情况

单位：项.人.次

项　目	项数	#女子	人数	#女子	次数	#女子
破全国纪录						
1949—1993年累计	20	2	36	2	29	2
破全省纪录						
1991年	53	30	62	31	82	45
1992年	31	17	22	8	35	19
1993年	13	1	15	1	19	1
1949—1993年累计	1 738	646	2 099	774	2 226	767

17—4 甘肃省共青团和少先队组织情况

年份	基层团支部（个）	共青团员（万人）	#女团员	青年团干部（人）	少先队员数（人）	辅导员数（人）
1978	35 722	89.62	32.41	2 648		
1980	39 156	81.90	30.02	3 049		
1985	47 797	81.48	29.43	3 400	217.11	68 312
1990	17 683	89.88	32.55	3 900	216.71	75 910
1991	50 209	98.55	33.88	4 108	216.72	
1992	50 431	102.42	29.85	3 229	225.20	77 858
1993	51 972	109.21	38.35	3 764	216.00	70 783

17—5 甘肃省妇联组织及干部基本情况

指　标	单位	1990年	1992年	1993年
全省妇联组织	个	1 706	1 736	1 720
妇联干部	人	2 212	2 274	2 306
#正副主任	人	1 334	1 110	1 235
在干部中少数民族干部数	人	260	169	271
占干部总数	%	11.80	7.40	11.75

17—6 甘肃省各党派党员(成员)数

项目	单位	1979年	1985年	1990年	1992年	1993年
中国共产党	万人	71	78	90	95	98
中国国民党革命委员会	人	124	949	1 375	1 407	1 468
中国民主同盟	人	870	2 056	3 297	3 414	3 529
中国民主建国会	人	380	587	978	1 045	1 102
中国民主促进会	人	13	438	1 072	1 124	1 172
中国农工民主党	人	11	137	390	432	475
九三学社	人	72	280	1 061	1 124	1 191

17—7 甘肃省工会组织情况

年份	工会基层组织数(个)	在建立工会的基层单位的职工和会员人数(人)				工会专职工作人员数(人)
		职工人数	#女职工	会员人数	#女会员	
1980		1 260 126	374 901	1 047 394	296 055	
1985	7 938	1 589 835	488 125	1 395 792	433 178	4 900
1990	11 545	179 377	614 243	1 611 368	556 042	9 903
1991	12 082	1 868 746	652 945	1 686 774	594 315	11 042
1992	12 198	1 869 733	644 884	1 702 642	573 787	10 341
1993	12 300	1 853 574	633 995	1 680 940	559 254	10 299

17—8 医疗卫生机构基本情况

项目	单位	绝对数		构成(%)	
		1992年	1993年	1992年	1993年
一. 卫生事业机构	个	4 192	4 141	100.00	100.00
#医院合计	个	1 561	1 637	37.20	39.53
门诊部.所	个	2 222	2 071	53.00	50.01
疗养院.所	个	9	9	0.20	0.22
卫生防疫站	个	103	106	2.50	2.56
妇幼保健所.站	个	94	93	2.20	2.25
二. 床位	张	52 412	54 845	100.00	100.00
# 医院合计	张	49 119	51 293	93.70	93.52
门诊部.所	张	4 569	1 469	3.00	2.68
疗养院.所	张	1 017	1 127	1.90	2.05
平均每千人拥有医院床位	张	2.20	2.37		
三. 卫生技术人员	人	76 254	77 807	100.00	100.00
中医师	人	4 899	5 030	6.40	6.46
西医师	人	19 306	19 857	25.30	25.52
中医士	人	2 753	2 801	3.60	3.60
西医士	人	6 164	5 739	8.10	7.38
药师	人	2 594	2 764	3.40	3.56
检验师	人	1 413	1 444	1.90	1.86
助产士	人	506	459	0.70	0.59
药剂士	人	2 325	2 245	3.00	2.89
平均每千人拥有中西医师	人	1.10	1.28		
平均每千人拥有中西医师(士)	人	1.40	1.43		
护士(师)	人	2 325	17 386	22.00	22.35

17—9 城乡医院基本情况

医院类别	医院数(个)	床位数(张)	职工人数(人)	卫生技术人员	中医师	西医师
总 计	1 637	51 293	63 166	51 947	3 354	12 754
县及县以上医院	352	39 724	49 790	39 681	2 020	10 314
市	164	24 518	32 610	25 555	1 170	7 083
县	188	15 206	17 180	14 126	850	3 231
区.乡(镇)卫生院	1 283	11 509	13 346	12 242	1 329	2 439
其他医院	2	60	30	24	5	1
在县及县以上医院中						
综合医院	260	32 154	40 135	32 015	1 056	8 819
中医医院	71	3 797	5 081	4 178	871	359
传染病院						
精神病院	5	743	529	384	7	68
结核病院	1	244	265	193	1	48
妇幼保健院	5	445	905	699	12	237
肿瘤医院	1	300	245	217	4	88
康复医院	2	190	119	58	3	6
口腔医院	1	21	98	79		28

17—9 续

医院类别	中医士	西医士	药师	检验师	助产士	护师(士)
总 计	1 504	3 087	2 071	959	374	14 791
县及县以上医院	588	1 443	1 872	926	240	13 361
市	245	673	1 327	679	160	9 322
县	313	770	545	247	80	4 039
区.乡(镇)卫生院	846	1 644	197	32	134	1 426
其他医院			2	1		4
在县及县以上医院中						
综合医院	258	1 267	1 544	755	209	11 080
中医医院	249	110	179	54	21	900
传染病院						
精神病院	4	25	10	2		180
结合病院	1	4	74	77	2	662
妇幼保健院	3	15	25	19	8	287
肿瘤医院	1	9	11	9		69
康复医院	1		3	1		7
口腔医院		3	4	1		20

17—10 卫生防疫站

项目	合计		县卫生防疫站	
	1992年	1993年	1992年	1993年
一.机构数(个)	103	106	66	66
二.卫生技术人员(人)	3 327	3 407	1 480	1 508
# 中医师	56	130	44	44
西医师	1 398	1 434	576	594
中医士	32	29	22	24
西医士	508	552	235	245
药剂士	17	16	13	14
检验师	347	314	98	93
检验士	234	172	97	75
护师	44	56	23	31
护士	63	59	40	38

17—11 专科防治所、站

项目	合计		结核病防治站.所		职业病防治站.所	
	1992年	1993年	1992年	1993年	1992年	1993年
一.机构数(个)	30	28	6	5	1	2
二.卫生技术人员(人)	572	367	61	55	43	52
#中医师	11	15	2	2	19	
西医师	216	135	25	28		26
中医士	1	1	1	1		
西医士	56	43	1			
护师	18	14	8	8		1
护士	13	20	4	4		
检验师	64	31	5	5	13	17
检验士	17	7	2	1	6	2
药师	3	3	1	1		2
药剂士	2	1			1	
助产士	8					

17—12 社会福利企业单位情况

项目	单位	1992年	1993年	1993年比1992年增长%
一.民政部门办福利企业				
单位数	个	224	284	26.80
职工人数	人	10 418	11 138	6.90
四残职工	人	3 696	4 052	9.60
固定资产	万元	8 948	11 991.60	34.00
总产值	万元	22 187	28 043.50	26.40
利税	万元	1 172	1 468.20	25.30
二.社会办福利企业				
单位数	个	678	782.00	15.30
职工人数	人	15 841	18 618	17.50
四残职工	人	6 232	7 062	13.30
固定资产	万元			
总产值	万元	30 578	39 168.00	28.10
利税	万元	3 602	3 950.30	9.70

17—13 社会福利事业单位基本情况

(1993年)

项目	院数(个)	工作人员(人)	床位(张)	收养人数(人)	床位利用率(%)
全省合计	587	1 365	7 357	4 031	54.80
一.优抚事业单位	4	42	168	51	30.30
复退军人精神病院	1	28	50	31	62.00
国家办光荣院	3	14	118	20	16.90
二.社会福利事业单位	24	563	1 526	1 143	74.90
社会福利院	19	271	940	610	64.90
儿童福利院	2	75	200	190	95.00
社会福利精神病院	3	217	386	343	88.90
三.城镇.乡村集体办敬老院	559	760	5 663	2 837	50.10

17—14 全省主要民政对象情况

单位:人

项目	1992年	1993年	1993年比1992年增长%
全省合计	3 062 434	3 078 280	0.50
一.优抚对象	670 081	654 924	—2.30
1.烈属	19 395	18 213	—6.10
2.牺牲病故军人家属	8 296	8 118	—2.10
3.现役军人家属	320 486	305 273	—4.70
4.革命伤残人员	9 487	9 540	0.60
5.在乡复员军人	41 069	38 933	—5.20
6.在乡退伍军人	270 736	274 285	1.30
7.在乡退伍红军老战士	612	562	—8.20
二.社会主要救济对象	2 390 382	2 421 224	1.30
1.社会困难户	2 352 432	2 384 015	1.30
2.社会散居孤.老.残.幼	37 950	37 209	—1.90
三.离退休.退职人员	1 971	2 132	8.20
1.军队干部	477	461	—3.40
2.军队职工	425	633	48.90
3.地方人员	1 069	1 038	—2.90

17—15 优抚救济对象得到国家抚恤、补助、救济人员情况

单位:人

项 目	1992年	1993年	1993年比1992年增长%
一.抚恤人数	13 058	13 096	0.29
1.烈属定期抚恤人数	2 055	1 995	—2.92
2.牺牲病故定期抚恤人数	1 516	1 561	2.97
3.革命伤残人员抚恤人数	9 487	9 540	0.56
二.优抚对象定补人数	34 415	35 951	4.46
1.在乡复员军人	30 916	31 722	2.61
占在乡复员军人总人数%	75.30	81.50	
2.在乡退伍军人	2 807	2 999	6.84
占在乡退伍军人总人数%	1.04	1.09	
3.其他人员	692	1 230	77.75
三.社会救济人员情况	19 098	17 860	—6.48
1.社会困难户定救人数	6 056	4 693	—22.50
占困难户总人数%	0.26	0.19	
2.社会散居孤老.残.幼定救人员	6 826	7 227	5.87
占社会散居孤老.残.幼总人数%	17.99	19.42	
3.精减退职老职工救济人数	6 216	5 940	—4.44
(1).享受40%救济	3 915	3 819	—2.45
(2).享受定救	2 301	2 121	—7.82
四.自然灾害救济人次数(人次)	3 784 529	3 491 850	—7.73

17—16 婚姻登记和离婚情况

年份	准予登记结婚(对)	初婚(人)	再婚(人)	离婚(对)	离婚率(%)
1985	150 254	295 234	5 274	2 636	1.80
1990	178 413	349 171	7 655	3 768	2.10
1991	164 313	318 712	9 914	4 234	2.60
1992	188 227	368 528	7 926	4 039	2.10
1993	155 478	302 896	8 060	3 997	2.60

十八. 少数民族

统计指标解释·之十八·

【货(客)运量】指运输业实际运送的货物量(旅客)数量。货运按吨计算,客运按人计算。货物不论运输距离长短。货物类别,均按实际重量统计,旅客不论行程远近或票价多少,均按一人一次作为客运量统计。半票价、小孩也按一人统计。货(客)运量是反映运输业为国民经济和人民生活服务的数量指标,也是制定和检查运输生活计划,研究运输发展规模和速度的重要指标。

货物(旅客)数量与其相应运输距离的乘积之总和。通常以吨公里和人公里为计算单位。计算货物周转量通常按发出站与到达站之间的最短距离,也就是计费距离计算它是反映运输业生活总成果的重要指标,也是编制和检查运输生活计划,计算运输效率、劳动生产率以及核算运输单位成本的主要基础资料。

【邮电业务总量】指以货币表现的邮电部门为用户传递信息和其他邮电服务的总量,它由各种邮电分类业务量,如涵件件数、电报份数、长话张数、市内电话和农村电话的年均户数、订销报刊累计份数等,分别乘以相应的平均单价(不变价),加总后再加上出租电路和设备的收入、代用户维护电话交换机和线路等设备收入,其他业务收入求得。邮电业务总量综合反映了一定时期邮电工作的总成果,是研究邮电业务量构成和发展趋势的重要指标。

【商品购进总额】指从本企业以外的单位和个人购进(包括从国外直接进口)作为转卖或加工后转卖的商品。本指标由从生产者购进额、从批发零售贸易业购进额、进口额和其他项目组成。这个指标反映批发零售贸易企业从国内、国外市场上购进商品的总量。

【商品销售总额】指对本企业以外的单位和个人出售(包括对国(境)外直接出口)的商品(包括售给本单位消费用的商品),本指标由对生产经营单位批发额、对批发零售贸易业批发额、出口额和对居民和社会集团商品零售额项目组成。这个指标反映批发零售贸易企业在国内市场上销售商品以及出口商品的总量。商品销售总额包括:

1 售给城乡居民和社会集团消费用的商品;

2. 售给工业、农业、建筑业、运输邮电业、批发零售贸易业、餐饮业、服务业、公用事业等作为生产、经营使用的商品;

3. 售给批发零售贸易业作为转卖或加工后转卖的商品;

4. 对国(境)外直接出口的商品。

【社会消费品零售额】指各种经济类型的批发零售贸易业、餐饮业、制造业和其他行业对城乡居民和社会集团的消费品零售额和农民对非农业居民零售额的总和。

18—1 民族自治地方年末人口数与人口自然变动情况

单位:人.‰

年份	总人口	城镇人口	乡村人口	在总人口中		出生率	死亡率	自然增长率
				农业人口	非农业人口			
1949	1 129 159	95 320	1 033 839	1 036 473	92 686			
1952	1 209 564	101 427	1 108 137	1 126 013	83 551			
1957	1 484 962	109 381	1 375 581	1 388 786	96 176	28.19	3.98	24.21
1962	1 443 604	120 967	1 322 637	1 338 334	105 270	34.94	9.59	25.35
1965	1 565 927	134 138	1 431 789	1 431 721	134 206	51.90	15.93	35.97
1970	1 585 660	229 230	1 356 430			39.43	7.92	31.35
1975	2 116 521	173 146	1 943 375	1 944 934	171 587	28.94	11.21	17.73
1978	2 219 322	155 843	2 063 479	2 042 409	176 913	21.59	6.89	14.70
1980	2 283 227	162 275	2 120 952	2 085 822	197 405	15.61	5.43	10.18
1981	2 312 165	173 321	2 138 844	2 113 248	198 917	17.08	5.96	11.12
1982	2 375 625	181 391	2 194 234	2 171 922	203 703	19.22	6.00	13.22
1983	2 393 451	182 644	2 210 807	2 174 941	218 510	15.60	5.65	9.95
1984	2 441 023	199 968	2 241 055	2 211 050	229 973	16.68	5.24	11.44
1985	2 471 624	302 533	2 169 091	2 236 419	235 205	15.06	4.93	10.13
1986	2 505 786	515 522	1 990 264	2 263 023	242 758	15.94	4.69	11.25
1987	2 543 844	526 733	2 017 111	2 292 589	251 255	51.49	4.76	11.73
1988	2 583 012	537 299	2 045 713	2 325 302	257 710	15.74	4.87	10.90
1989	2 626 062	548 952	2 077 110	2 360 441	265 621	17.61	4.97	12.64
1990	2 726 312	577 619	2 148 693	2 452 043	274 269	30.58	5.74	24.84
1991	2 757 251	587 906	2 169 345	2 477 247	280 004	16.89	5.11	11.78
1992	2 790 679	597 021	2 193 658	2 504 620	286 059	16.48	4.99	11.49
1993	2 838 884	613 511	2 225 373	2 542 518	296 366	17.38	5.13	12.25

18—2 民族自治地方年末人口构成

单位:%

年 份	总人口	城镇人口	乡村人口	在总人口中 农业人口	在总人口中 非农业人口
1978	100.00	7.02	92.98	92.03	7.97
1980	100.00	7.11	92.89	91.35	8.65
1985	100.00	12.24	87.76	90.48	9.52
1986	100.00	20.57	79.41	90.31	9.69
1987	100.00	20.71	79.29	90.12	9.88
1988	100.00	20.80	79.20	90.02	9.98
1989	100.00	20.90	79.10	89.89	10.11
1990	100.00	21.19	78.81	89.94	10.06
1991	100.00	21.32	78.68	89.84	10.16
1992	100.00	21.39	78.61	89.75	10.25
1993	100.00	21.61	78.39	89.56	10.44

18—3 民族自治州、县职工人数

单位:人

年份	临夏回族自治州	甘南藏族自治州	肃北蒙古族自治县	阿克塞哈萨克族自治县	肃南裕固族自治县	天祝藏族自治县	张家川回族自治县
1978	27 180	21 002	1 062	776	2 443	4 407	2 575
1980	26 981	21 803	1 235	849	2 578	3 795	2 998
1985	32 177	30 833	1 263	1 175	2 808	4 713	3 823
1986	49 379	43 512	1 567	1 149	3 172	5 203	4 590
1987	49 852	43 420	1 726	1 055	3 388	5 526	4 221
1988	52 126	44 504	1 054	1 105	3 309	5 657	5 227
1989	55 375	44 134	1 459	1 057	3 861	5 751	5 276
1990	57 044	45 096	1 757	1 095	3 891	6 502	4 665
1991	58 630	46 130	2 257	1 675	4 100	6 838	4 875
1992	61 327	47 669	1 942	1 828	5 276	6 771	5 804
1993	45 216	47 059	2 188	1 280	3 936	7 116	6 400

18—4 历年民族自治地方农、林、牧、副、渔业产值

单位:万元

年份	总计	农业	林业	牧业	副业	渔业
(按1952年不变价格计算)						
1953	8 144	4 577	116	2 978	473	
1954	8 798	5 125	148	2 991	534	
1955	10 133	6 229	210	3 110	584	
1956	11 716	7 038	523	3 493	662	
1957	12 644	7 741	582	3 666	655	
(按1957年不变价格计算)						
1957	12 742	7 857	584	3 579	722	
1958	14 087	8 380	976	3 908	822	1
1959	13 256	7 564	830	4 078	784	1
1960	11 180	6 251	462	3 720	746	1
1961	9 368	4 932	154	3 511	770	1
1962	9 296	4 613	192	3 725	764	2
1963	12 719	7 587	163	4 129	837	3
1964	14 408	8 365	213	4 942	885	3
1965	16 141	9 706	289	5 280	862	4
1966	14 515	8 083	319	5 243	866	4
1967	16 403	9 834	287	5 298	980	4
1968	15 297	9 643	244	5 482	924	4
1969	16 769	9 698	282	5 762	1 022	5
1970	21 214	12 665	555	6 886	1 103	5
1971	20 964	12 925	362	6 621	1 051	5

18—4续

单位:万元

年份	总计	农业	林业	牧业	副业	渔业
(按1970年不变价格计算)						
1971	23 280	13 979	411	7 607	1 277	6
1972	25 189	17 580	879	5 096	1 623	11
1973	23 344	16 436	1 101	4 830	967	10
1974	26 510	16 234	1 083	7 820	1360	13
1975	28 060	17 659	1 469	6 979	1948	5
1976	26 375	16 134	1 228	7 736	1274	3
1977	25 571	16 011	824	7 130	1 598	8
1978	270 62	15 308	698	9 098	1 949	9
1979	24 824	13 822	573	9 238	1 185	6
1980	28 312	16 490	345	10 040	1 431	6
1981	26 745	15 023	352	9 949	1 417	4
(按1980年不变价格计算)						
1981	33 211	19 070	797	11 198	2 138	8
1982	36 234	20 445	1 328	12 889	1566	6
1983	37 488	21 665	1 762	11 796	2260	5
1984	39 664	19 615	3 214	13 688	3141	6
1985	43 299	21 767	2 301	15 908	3244	9
1986	45 877	23 070	2 760	17 777	2256	14
1987	46 408	21 443	2 873	18 963	3107	22
1988	48 493	23 422	2 394	19 094	3553	30
1989	47 366	22 535	2 089	19 546	3172	24
1990	51 740	25 169	2 068	20 651	3809	43
(按1990年不变价格计算)						
1990	108 957	49 731	4 765	49 622	4693	146
1991	109 929	47 466	4 348	53 009	4934	172
1992	114 970	49 314	5 032	54 617	5834	172
1993	125 115	55 175	4 968	58 328	6454	190

18—5 民族自治地方农牧业生产基本情况

指　标	单位	1985年	1990年	1992年	1993年	1993年为1992年%
一. 农业总产值	万元	91 036.00	108 956.80	114 970.10	125 115.20	108.82
（按1990年不变价计算）						
农业	万元	45 837.00	49 730.50	49 314.40	55 174.90	111.88
林业	万元	4 843.00	4 764.70	5 032.30	4 968.40	98.73
牧业	万元	33 501.00	49 621.70	54 617.20	58 327.70	106.79
副业	万元	6 828.00	4 693.20	5 834.60	6 454.30	110.62
渔业	万元	27.00	146.80	171.70	190.00	110.66
二. 耕地面积	万亩	431.90	427.30	427.30	427.10	99.05
#有效灌溉面积	万亩	90.60	87.80	89.00	89.50	99.44
三. 总播种面积	万亩	422.10	432.50	438.60	438.40	99.95
#粮食作物	万亩	347.10	352.80	358.20	355.10	99.13
四. 主要农作物产量						
粮食	万吨	47.60	57.10	56.20	60.70	108.01
油料	百吨	275.90	274.10	297.30	323.30	108.75
甜菜	吨	345.90	4 002.90	4 905.70	2 588.50	52.77
五. 畜牧业产品产量						
猪肉产量	万吨	1.45	2.02	2.35	3.01	128.09
牛肉产量	万吨	1.07	1.72	2.29	2.40	104.80
羊肉产量	万吨	1.09	1.41	1.56	1.74	111.54
牛奶产量	万吨	2.91	5.13	4.94	5.82	117.81
羊毛产量	百吨	462.40	552.20	548.70	591.03	107.71
六. 造林情况						
当年造林面积	万亩	29.50	26.80	23.45	22.60	96.38
#迹地更新面积	万亩	0.70	0.50	0.30	0.18	60.00
七. 农机、用电、化肥						
农业机械总动力	万瓦特	38 444.80	57 949.10	62 622.30	64803.30	103.48
农村用电量	万千瓦小时	10 101.70	13 491.20	16 146.40	16314.50	101.04
化肥施用量						
按实物量计算	万吨	5.20	[illegible].20	6.80	7.80	114.71
按折纯量计算	万吨	1.20	1.60	1.90	4.60	242.11

18－6 民族自治地方农、林、牧、副、渔业产值构成

单位：%

年份	总计	农业	林业	牧业	副业	渔业
1978	100	56.57	2.58	33.62	7.20	0.03
1980	100	58.24	1.22	35.46	5.05	0.02
1981	100	57.42	2.40	33.72	6.44	0.02
1982	100	56.42	3.67	35.57	4.32	0.02
1983	100	57.79	4.70	31.47	6.03	0.01
1984	100	49.45	8.10	34.51	7.92	0.02
1985	100	50.35	5.32	36.80	7.50	0.02
1986	100	50.29	6.02	38.75	4.92	0.03
1987	100	46.12	6.18	40.79	6.68	0.05
1988	100	48.30	4.94	39.37	7.33	0.06
1989	100	47.58	4.41	41.27	6.70	0.05
1990	100	48.65	4.00	39.91	7.36	0.08
1991	100	43.18	3.96	48.22	4.49	0.16
1992	100	42.89	4.38	47.51	5.07	0.15
1993	100	44.10	3.97	46.62	5.16	0.15

18－7 民族自治地方农、林、牧、渔业增加值

（1993 年）

单位：万元

地　县	农.林.牧渔业增加值	农业	林业	牧业	渔业
民族自治地方合计	92 925	41 097	3 993	47 561	275
临夏回族自治州	46 377	27 340	2 886	15 955	196
甘南藏族自治州	31 048	8 746	944	21 283	76
肃北蒙古族自治县	876	107	25	744	
阿克塞哈萨克族自治县	577			577	
肃南裕固族自治县	5 331	968	8	4 355	
天祝藏族自治县	4 785	1 349	20	3 413	3
张家川回族自治县	3 931	2 587	110	123	

18—8 民族自治地方牲畜头数

单位:百头.百只

年份	大牲畜年末数	牛	马	驴	骡	骆驼	羊年末数		猪年末数
							山羊	绵羊	
1953	6 762	4 555	993	983	182	49	3 354	15 415	953
1957	9 060	6 640	1 084	1 071	211	55	4 760	16 532	1 802
1965	8 786	7 099	823	632	153	80	6 317	19 033	2 523
1970	10 130	8 121	1 084	632	188	105	6 231	19 426	3 127
1975	11 445	9 048	1 353	661	240	143	6 732	25 239	3 431
1978	11 838	9 459	1 302	654	265	158	6 443	28 081	3 557
1980	13 070	10 468	1 352	818	280	152	6 421	29 952	3 398
1981	13 543	10 867	1 414	822	282	158	6 420	29 928	3 389
1982	13 838	11 034	1 447	897	304	157	6 297	29 134	3 609
1983	14 269	11 521	1 427	860	321	141	6 450	27 980	3 480
1984	14 983	12 214	1 434	863	345	128	5 998	28 882	3 607
1985	15 867	13 067	1 451	856	387	106	5 969	29 598	4 037
1986	16 361	13 418	1 466	933	442	102	5 970	29 799	4 064
1987	16 616	13 617	1 453	942	501	103	6 160	29 930	3 916
1988	16 766	13 744	1 435	943	536	108	6 570	30 252	4 108
1989	16 900	13 840	1 410	960	630	60	6 910	30 970	4 317
1990	17 009	13 949	1 379	932	628	121	7 166	30 920	4 474
1991	16 887	13 864	1 353	920	641	109	7 179	29 405	4 575
1992	16 994	13 917	1 359	940	684	94	7 410	29 754	4 802
1993	16 954	13 862	1 367	938	707	80	7 578	29 915	5 048

18—9 民族自治地方牲畜增长率

单位:%

	大牲畜	牛	马	驴	骡	骆驼	羊		猪
							山羊	绵羊	
"一五"时期	7.40	9.13	3.79	2.67	4.79	3.19	11.03	3.99	15.28
"二五"时期	−6.59	−4.89	−10.63	−15.96	−6.35	0.36	−3.50	0.04	−8.50
1963—1965年	11.60	11.73	11.08	13.80	0.33	10.94	18.10	15.06	−23.51
"三五"时期	2.89	2.73	5.66	0	4.21	5.59	−0.27	0.41	4.39
"四五"时期	2.47	2.19	4.53	0.90	5.01	6.37	1.56	5.38	1.87
"五五"时期	2.69	2.96	−0.01	4.35	3.13	1.23	−0.94	3.48	−0.19
"六五"时期	3.95	4.54	1.42	0.91	6.69	−6.96	−1.45	−0.24	3.51
"七五"时期	1.40	1.31	−1.01	1.72	10.17	2.68	3.73	0.88	2.08
1978—1993年	2.42	2.58	0.33	2.43	6.76	−4.44	1.09	0.42	2.36
1992—1993年	−0.23	−0.40	0.59	−0.21	3.30	−14.89	2.27	0.54	5.12

18—10 民族自治地方牲畜存栏及畜产品产量占全省比重

单位:%

年份	存栏数			畜产品产量		
	大牲畜	羊	猪	牛肉	羊肉	猪肉
1978	32.34	33.09	7.49			
1980	33.31	30.63	8.02	90.03	63.38	7.56
1985	31.24	38.97	7.39	75.19	52.40	5.81
1986	30.36	36.63	7.07	67.86	48.81	7.00
1987	29.88	35.43	7.40	53.41	42.86	7.43
1988	29.45	33.59	7.48	52.40	44.22	6.89
1989	32.64	33.56	7.52	50.67	38.18	6.88
1990	29.12	34.32	7.52	49.28	36.81	6.70
1991	28.86	35.87	7.66	47.47	33.40	6.52
1992	28.77	36.72	7.66	43.95	35.21	6.74
1993	28.43	36.56	7.83	42.78	32.83	7.88

18—11 历年民族自治地方工业总产值

单位:万元

年份	工业总产值	国有经济	#州(县)属工业	集体经济	在工业总产值中	
					轻工业	重工业
(按1952年不变价格计算)						
1953	565	192	52	84	250	315
1954	814	305	110	89	331	483
1955	1 402	606	433	150	712	690
1956	1 522	1 161	422	362	771	751
1957	1 808	1 341	603	392	747	1 061
(按1957年不变价格计算)						
1957	1 968	1 446	649	439	789	1 179
1958	4 463	3 511	2 107	952	1 315	3148
1959	7 601	5 284	3 778	2 317	2391	5 210
1960	7 677	5 907	4 182	1 770	2788	4 889
1961	2 094	1 753	1 040	341	1 071	1023
1962	2 665	2 509	635	156	681	1 984
1963	2 966	2 844	560	122	594	2 372
1964	3 337	3 155	603	182	675	2 662
1965	5 797	5 561	962	236	1 105	4 692
1966	9 460	9 120	1 371	340	1 472	7988
1967	9 395	8 705	1 287	329	1 318	8077
1968	9 440	9 192	492	248	1 286	8 154
1969	12 200	11 885	594	315	1 473	10 727
1970	18 667	18 288	918	379	1 775	16 892
1971	25 206	24 604	1 309	602	2 778	22428

18—11续　　　　　　　　　　　　　　　　　　　　　　　　　　　单位:万元

年份	工业总产值	国有经济	#州(县)属工业	集体经济	在工业总产值中	
					轻工业	重工业
(按1970年不变价格计算)						
1971	25 908	25 273	1 417	624	2 961	22947
1972	29 438	28 733	1 709	705	3 586	25852
1973	41 180	40 118	2 050	662	4 610	36570
1974	48 048	47 275	2 267	714	4 395	43653
1975	78 403	77 145	3 524	1 168	5823	72 580
1976	57 450	55 782	3 935	1 567	6384	51 066
1977	58 666	56 378	4 059	2 206	6608	52 058
1978	54 670	52 318	3 949	2 208	6265	48 405
1979	58 740	56 544	3 540	2 067	7514	51 226
1980	55 104	52 936	3 232	2 034	6307	48 797
1981	55 847	53 828	3 197	1 807	5049	50 798
(按1980年不变价格计算)						
1981	57 440	54 969	3 423	1 921	5331	52 109
1982	66 570	64 365	4 425	1 932	6653	59 917
1983	70 897	68 737	5 138	1 953	8181	62 716
1984	72 029	69 364	5 707	2 529	9202	62 827
1985	74 627	59 907	7 350	3 541	10701	63 926
1986	68 913	59 907	18 841	5 096	11794	35 226
1987	65 343	51 650	18 092	7 933	13388	46 230
1988	71 285	51 609	22 381	10 017	17319	44 979
1989	87 754	67 753	25 688	11 231	17547	62 261
1990	97 532	65 097	39 490	13 802	19414	67 142
(按1990年不变价格计算)						
1990	155 503	119 104	49 143	19 262	37708	117 795
1991	155 862	118 222	63 662	20 415	41232	114 630
1992	168 960	102 209	49 456	51 779	50625	118 336
1993	202 375	131 487	70 56	32 423	59 005	143 370

18—12 民族自治地方工业总产值及主要产品产量

指标	单位	1985年	1990年	1992年	1993年	1993年为下列年份%	
						1985年	1992年
一.工业企业单位数	个	505	762	798	713	89.35	141.19
二.工业总产值	万元	118 885	155 503	168 960	202 375	17 023	119.78
(按1990年不变价计算)							
#轻工业	万元	18 785	37 708	50 625	59 005	314.11	116.55
重工业	万元	100 200	11 795	118 336	143370	143.08	121.16
#国有经济	万元	129 605	119 104	102 209			
三.主要工业产品产量							
原煤	万吨	30	68	71	46	153.33	64.79
发电量	万千瓦小时	737 596	792 705	621 075	766 372	103.90	123.39
木材	立方米	271 457	268 276	261 255	243 200	89.59	93.09
水泥	吨	65 929	112 380	152 500	185200	280.91	121.44

18—13 民族自治地方工业企业总产值及增加值

(1993年)

地县	工业总产值	轻工业	重工业	在工业总产值中		工业增加值
				国有经济	集体经济	
临夏回族自治州	88 241	14 626	73 615	79 977	8 115	57 749
甘南藏族自治州	35 975	8 680	27 295	29 865	6 048	17 664
肃北蒙古族自治县	3 995	105	3 890	2 262	1 733	1 898
阿克塞哈萨克族自治县	7 741	191	7 550	1 145	6 596	3 419
肃南裕固族自治县	3 494	450	3 044	1 376	2 118	3 677
天祝藏族自治县	12 637	2 375	1 0262	8 401	4 236	3 677
张家川回族自治县	3 809	3 347	462	769	3 040	3 766

18—14 民族自治地方交通、邮电情况

指　　标	单位	1985年	1990年	1992年	1993年
一、交通					
年末公路线路里程	公里	8 025	8 554	7 818	6 558
年末实有民用汽车	辆	3 862	8 596	9 430	
全年公路客运量	万人	455	579	539	583
全年公路货运量	万吨	29	128	139	246
二、邮电					
邮电局.所数	处	158	159	160	148
#设在农村数	处	135	135	135	124
邮路及农村投递线路总长度	公里	18 763	16 037	15 295	
电话机	部	7 147	12 170	15 744	

18—15 民族自治地方社会消费品零售总额

(1993年)

单位:万元

地　　县	社会消费品零售总额	农民对非农业居民零售额	按销售地区分		
			市的零售额	县的零售额	县以下零售额
民族自治地方合计	98 345	10 465	23 904	50 412	24 029
临夏回族自治州	52 587	7 718	23 904	17 899	10 784
甘南藏族自治州	23 186	1 161		18 608	4 578
肃北蒙古族自治县	1 722	366		1 398	324
阿克塞哈萨克族自治县	913	16		833	80
肃南裕固族自治县	5 869	159		1 984	3 885
天祝藏族自治县	11 384	1 014		7 707	3 677
张家川回族自治县	2 684	31		1 983	701

18—16 民族自治地方财政金融

单位:万元

指　标	1985 年	1990 年	1992 年	1993 年
一、财政				
地方财政收入	5 193	10 282	11 710	16 320
#工商税收	4 155	9 324	10 087	13 704
农牧业税	507	749	906	1 215
地方财政支出	23 439	40 199	45 722	53 299
#基本建设支出	2 234	2 110	1 775	1 935
支援农业生产支出	1 276	2 162	2 228	2 104
农林.水利气象等部门事业啊	1 788	2 806	3 689	4 187
文教.科学.卫生事业费	6 560	11 247	14 144	16 137
二、金融				
银行存款余额	38 328	98 062	13 525	158 610
银行贷款余额	35 645	96 976	128 487	150 773
城乡居民储蓄存款	14 456	58 011	90 455	110 577

18—17 民族自治地方医疗卫生情况

指　标	单位	1985 年	1990 年	1992 年	1993 年
卫生技术人员	人	5 109	5 685	6 527	6 643
#少数民族	人	838	886	1 774	1 927
#中医	人	865	955	969	936
西医	人	673	1 438	1 622	1 771
西医士	人	1 267	775	1 027	989
中西医结合高级医师	人	6	18	10	14
卫生机构数	人	528	483	534	534
#卫生部门	人	317	349	377	369
卫生床位数	张	3 869	3 696	1 426	4 471
#卫生部门	张	2 894	3 055	3 505	3 787

18—18 民族自治地方文化、教育与人民生活

指 标	单位	1985 年	1990 年	1992 年	1993 年
一、文化					
图书杂志出版					
种类	种	3	3	3	3
印数	万册	3.80	3.80	2.70	1.3
报纸出版					
种类	种	2	4	4	3
印数	万册	190.55	404.08	401.60	379.60
二、教育					
高等学校所数	所	1	1	1	1
专任教师数	人	12	80	96	98
在校学生数	人	114	483	622	715
中等学校所数	所	9	9	10	11
专任教师数	人	260	408	416	427
在校学生数	人	3 103	3 355	3 518	3 528
普通中学数	所	123	118	140	145
专任教师数	人	3 712	4 761	4 832	4 864
在校学生数	万人	6.97	7.54	7.52	6.76
小学校所数	所	2 611	2 591	2 512	2 486
专任教师数	人	12 220	12 983	12 900	12 800
在校学生数	万人	26	25.02	25.96	25.62

十九.分地县主要指标

统计指标解释

·之十九·

【出口】海关按经营单位统计的本地区出口总值，扣除来料加工装配贸易，境外驻本地区外交机构的出口总值、本地区出口商品退货总值和本地区代理外地区出口、加上外地区代理本地区出口后的总值。

【进口】海关按经营单位统计的本地区进口总值，扣除来料加工装配贸易、境外驻本地区外交机构的进口总值、本地区进口商品退货总值和本地区代理外地区进口、加上外地区代理本地区进口后的总值。

【旅游人数】指来我国参观、访问、旅行、探亲、访友、休养、考察、参加会议和从事经济、科技、文化、教育、体育、宗教等活动的外国人、华侨、港澳和台湾同胞的人数。

【旅游外汇收入】指国内各部门为来我国旅游的外国人、华侨、港澳和台湾同胞提供商品和劳务而获得的外汇收入。

【小学学龄儿童入学率】指调查范围内已入小学学习的学龄儿童占校内外学龄儿童总数(包括弱智儿童在内，但不包括聋哑儿童)的比重。计算公式是：

小学学龄儿童入学率＝已入学的小学学龄儿童数÷校内外小学学龄儿童总数×100％

【自然科学技术人员】自然科学技术人员是指下列各类人员：

1. 已取得科学技术职称或大学、中专的理、工、农、医科系毕业，以及国民经济各部门从工农群众中提拔，从事理、工、农、医等自然科学方面的科学研究、教学工作、生产(事业)技术三个基本方面的科学技术人员。

2. 已取得科学技术职称或大学、中专的理、工、农、医科系毕业在机关、企业、事业中从事科学技术业务管理工作的人员。

【医院】指名称为医院，设有固定床位能收容病人住院并能为病人提供医疗、护理服务的医疗机构。包括县及县以上医院，农村卫生院，其他医院三部分。按属性分为卫生部门、工业及其他部门、集体所有制三类。其中县及县以上医院按业务性质分为综合医院和专科医院。

【卫生技术人员】指卫生事业机构支付工资的全部固定职工和合同制职工中现任职务为卫生技术工作的人员。包括中医师、西医师、中西医结合高级医师、护师中药师、西医师、其他技师、中医士、西医士、护士、助产士。中药剂士、西药剂员检验员。其他初级卫生技术人员。

【等级运动员】指经考核正式批准授予等级运动员称号的人数。运动员等级分为国际级运动健将、运动健将、一级运动员、二级运动员、三级运动员、少年级运动员。

19—1 分地区国内生产总值

(1993年)　　　　单位:万元

地区	国内生产总值	第一产业	第二产业	第三产业	位次	
					国内生产总值	第三产业
兰州市	1 099 485	65 391	721 643	312 451	1	1
天水市	373 528	76 934	174 004	122 590	2	2
白银市	264 160	41 872	173 418	48 870	4	7
金昌市	216 534	15 363	150 615	50 556	6	6
嘉峪关市	111 430	3 323	93 026	15 081	12	14
定西地区	161 657	82 002	38 216	41 439	10	10
庆阳地区	244 970	90 582	102 834	51 554	5	5
平凉地区	156 139	69 025	48 686	38 428	11	11
陇南地区	167 392	75 992	43 792	47 608	8	8
武威地区	163 474	72 159	44 754	46 561	9	9
张掖地区	192 974	91 421	46 307	55 246	7	4
酒泉地区	267 090	68 151	125 329	73 610	3	3
临夏回族自治州	101 207	46 377	30 942	23 888	13	12
甘南藏族自治州	65 000	28 056	19 855	17 089	14	13

19—2 分地区人均国内生产总值及排序

(1993年)　　　　单位:元

地区	人均国内生产总值		人均第一产业		人均第二产业		人均第三产业	
	绝对数	位次	绝对数	位次	绝对数	位次	绝对数	位次
兰州市	4 232	3	252	14	2 778	3	1 202	3
天水市	1 236	7	255	13	576	6	405	6
白银市	1 749	5	277	11	1 148	5	324	7
金昌市	5 401	2	383	6	3 757	2	1 261	2
嘉峪关市	9 979	1	297	10	8 328	1	1 350	1
定西地区	608	13	308	8	144	14	156	13
庆阳地区	1 085	8	401	5	456	7	228	10
平凉地区	789	11	349	7	246	11	194	11
陇南地区	677	12	307	9	177	13	193	12
武威地区	943	10	416	4	258	10	269	9
张掖地区	1 649	6	781	2	396	8	472	5
酒泉地区	3 142	4	802	1	1 474	4	866	4
临夏回族自治州	601	14	275	12	184	12	142	14
甘南藏族自治州	1 079	9	466	3	330	9	283	8

19—3 分地区国内生产总值发展速度

（上年=100）　　单位:%

地区	国内生产总值	第一产业	第二产业	第三产业	人均国内生产总值
兰州市	111.80	114.00	115.00	108.10	110.50
天水市	123.60	77.40	141.40	153.70	121.90
白银市	114.00	105.40	117.00	113.10	111.70
金昌市	106.30	107.50	104.90	110.30	103.10
嘉峪关市	138.80	103.30	134.60	185.00	133.30
定西地区	115.80	109.20	123.30	124.20	114.10
庆阳地区	107.10	86.50	150.70	102.90	105.50
平凉地区	109.10	104.60	117.90	107.00	107.90
陇南地区	107.50	103.00	115.60	107.80	106.00
武威地区	114.50	113.10	114.70	116.40	113.00
张掖地区	113.60	107.90	123.10	116.40	112.60
酒泉地区	116.50	90.30	139.40	115.10	115.10
临夏回族自治州	111.30	117.60	101.40	108.40	108.60
甘南藏族自治州	105.20	106.10	104.80	104.20	103.70

19—4 分地区国内生产总值的构成

（1993年）　　单位:%

地区	国内生产总值	第一产业	第二产业	第三产业
兰州市	100.00	6.00	65.60	28.40
天水市	100.00	20.60	46.60	32.80
白银市	100.00	15.90	65.60	18.50
金昌市	100.00	7.00	69.50	23.50
嘉峪关市	100.00	3.00	83.50	13.50
定西地区	100.00	54.30	21.60	24.10
庆阳地区	100.00	37.00	42.00	21.00
平凉地区	100.00	44.20	31.20	24.60
陇南地区	100.00	45.40	26.20	28.40
武威地区	100.00	44.10	27.40	28.50
张掖地区	100.00	47.40	24.00	28.60
酒泉地区	100.00	25.50	46.90	27.60
临夏回族自治州	100.00	45.80	30.60	23.60
甘南藏族自治州	100.00	43.20	30.50	26.30

19—5 分县国内生产总值

单位:万元

地　县	国内生产总值	第一产业	第二产业	第三产业	人均国内生产总值(元)
兰州市	1 099 485	65 391	721 643	312 451	4 232
榆中县					
永登县					
皋兰县					
城关区					
七里河区					
西固区					
安宁区					
红古区					
天水市	373 528	76 934	174 004	122 590	1 236
清水县	14 259	8 565	2 530	3 164	518
秦安县	29 674	14 786	5 118	9 770	577
甘谷县	37 190	15 100	11 881	10 209	715
武山县	23 868	10 915	8 069	4 884	628
张川县					
秦城区	91 091	14 409	51 749	24 933	1 635
北道区	80 072	14 012	45 993	20 067	1 557
白银市	264 160	41 872	173 418	48 870	1 749
会宁县	24 195	17 040	2 503	4 652	474
靖远县	36 163	13 820	14 908	7 435	865
景泰县	19 936	8 643	5 805	5 488	987
白银区	167 511	6 535	132 721	28 255	
平川区	53 532	2 364	45 240	5 928	3 478
金昌市	216 534	15 363	150 615	50 556	5 401
永昌县					
金川区					
嘉峪关市	111 430	3 323	93 026	15 081	9 979
嘉峪关区	111 430	3 323	93 026	15 081	9 979
庆阳地区	244 970	90 582	102 834	51 554	1 085
西峰市	37 798	11 146	14 411	12 241	1 333
庆阳县	76 754	8 463	57 023	11 268	2 608
镇原县	35 761	19 609	8 277	7 875	806
宁县	32 864	17 522	10 314	5 028	707
正宁县	14 298	9 171	2 899	2 228	681

19—5续1

单位:万元

地县	国内生产总值	第一产业	第二产业	第三产业	人均国内生产总值(元)
合水县	16 795	8 694	4 461	3 640	1 128
华池县	12 883	5 397	4 431	3 055	1 128
环县	21 425	11 404	3 802	6 219	714
平凉地区	**156 139**	**69 025**	**48 686**	**38 428**	**789**
平凉市	39 755	12 233	13 682	13 840	995
泾川县	27 644	15 635	5 472	6 537	918
灵台县	18 290	11 620	2 841	3 829	851
崇信县	8 498	3 962	2 920	1 616	965
华亭县	21 136	5 112	12 688	3 336	1 268
庄浪县	16 535	9 752	3 527	3 256	436
静宁县	24 128	10 711	7 556	5 861	562
陇南地区	**167 392**	**75 992**	**43 792**	**47 608**	**677**
成县	28 021	13 675	6 106	8 240	1 223
两当县	3 814	2 299	548	967	768
徽县	23 143	10 167	7 527	5 449	1 151
西和县	17 871	8 670	4 862	4 339	531
礼县	18 796	11 147	2 633	5 016	403
康县	11 729	5 713	2 098	3 918	598
武都县	26 383	17 241	2 536	6 606	545
文县	24 176	9 583	9 314	5 279	1 063
宕昌县	13 211	8 082	1 590	3 539	482
定西地区	**161 657**	**82 002**	**38 216**	**41 439**	**608**
定西县	35 877	18 855	8 125	8 897	839
通渭县	26 993	20 264	2 573	4 156	656
陇西县	36 341	10 318	18 724	7 299	820
渭源县	15 760	9 843	1 878	4 039	499
临洮县	30 010	14 157	8 138	7 715	617
漳县	10 932	7 045	1 775	2 112	647
岷县	14 005	9 215	2 911	1 879	343
武威地区	**163 474**	**72 159**	**44 754**	**46 561**	**269**
武威市	102 137	39 450	28 950	33 737	1 136
民勤县	23 978	14 411	3 076	6 491	882
古浪县	18 811	11 249	3 129	4 433	540
天祝县	14 169	5 263	3 966	4 940	663

19—5续2

单位:万元

地 县	国内生产总值	第一产业	第二产业	第三产业	人均国内生产总值(元)
张掖地区	192 974	91 421	46 307	55 246	472
张掖市	85 566	33 197	22 273	30 096	1 883
肃南市	10 210	5 330	2 393	2 487	2 900
民乐县	24 690	16 084	4 314	4 292	1 107
临泽县	22 662	12 132	4 294	6 236	1 635
高台县	24 168	14 631	4 151	5 386	1 617
山丹县	25 678	10 047	8 882	6 749	1 373
酒泉地区	267 090	68 151	125 329	73 610	866
酒泉市	65 307	23 705	21 513	20 089	2 164
金塔县	22 152	13 344	3 982	4 826	1 703
玉门市	113 359	8 180	93 681	11 498	6 194
安西县	16 871	7 068	4 276	5 527	2 438
敦煌市	26 948	15 942	4 511	6 495	2 253
肃北县	3 444	967	1 617	860	3 164
阿克塞县	3 016	514	1 620	882	3 973
临夏回族自治州	101 207	46 377	30 942	23 888	601
临夏市	19 263	6 799	6 100	6 364	1 092
临夏县	21 159	11 499	4 668	4 992	635
康乐县	11 097	6 534	1 456	3 107	534
永靖县	10 982	3 923	4 301	2 758	639
广河县	11 521	4 439	3 193	3 889	678
和政县	7 327	3 482	1 511	2 334	423
东乡族自治县	6 617	4 329	340	1 948	288
积石山保安族东乡族撒拉族自治县	2 613	1 400	484	729	335
甘南藏族自治州	65 000	28 056	19 855	17 089	1 079
临潭县	6 098	3 011	1 074	2 013	445
单尼县	9 140	4 538	3 339	1 263	989
舟曲县	6 829	2 980	2 250	1 599	556
迭部县	18 479	3 056	14 490	933	3 513
玛曲县	7 372	4 618	2 401	353	2 385
碌曲县	4 077	2 608	251	1 218	1 510
夏河县	13 973	8 224	2 729	3 020	1 275

19—6 分县人口

单位:人

地　县	年末人口	#女性	城镇人口	农村人口	非农业人口
兰州市	2 612 071	1 260 088	1 813 705	798 366	1 338 654
城关区	656 912	319 868	656 912		608 798
七里河区	377 339	178 665	377 339		275 123
西固区	289 844	139 581	289 844		212 713
安宁区	130 851	61 946	130 851		89 387
红古区	121 031	56 349	121 031		67 267
榆中县	409 130	198 064	65 400	343 730	24 334
永登县	470 003	228 183	165 074	304 929	52 167
皋兰县	156 961	77 432	7 254	149 707	8 865
天水市	3 040 943	1 474 289	1 408 448	1 632 495	368 419
秦城区	562 248	271 469	562 248		166 599
北道区	516 525	250 769	516 525		97 711
清水县	275 286	132 870	20 712	254 574	13 680
秦安县	517 941	253 039	35 856	482 085	24 590
甘谷县	518 485	252 364	152 133	366 352	29 873
武山县	382 592	183 270	77 364	305 228	23 685
张家川回族自治县	267 866	130 508	43 610	224 256	12 281
白银市	1 527 055	738 362	483 782	1 043 273	292 037
白银区	232 700	109 458	232 700		157 167
平川区	156 254	71 079	156 254		67 069
会宁县	514 490	251 009	11 700	502 790	17 683
靖远县	421 471	206 164	22 897	398 574	28 443
景泰县	202 140	100 652	60 231	141 909	21 675
金昌市	400 925	191 560	304 316	96 609	163 981
金川区	166 595	78 883	166 595		120 626
永昌县	234 330	112 677	137 721	96 609	43 355
嘉峪关市	113 991	51 617	113 991		91 034
嘉峪关区	113 991	51 617	113 991		91 034
庆阳地区	2 275 879	1 092 525	922 624	1 353 255	219 522
西峰市	283 554	134 674	283 554		59 954
庆阳县	291 717	140 498	143 529	148 188	67 265
镇原县	456 283	219 833	137 340	318 943	15 314
宁县	467 812	226 423	166 755	301 057	24 343

19—6 续 1 单位：人

地 县	年末人口	#女性	城镇人口	农村人口	非农业人口
正宁县	209 504	99 579	86 779	122 725	12 055
合水县	149 900	72 346	33 588	116 312	14 361
华池县	115 049	55 171	23 262	91 787	11 955
环县	302 060	144 001	47 817	254 243	14 275
平凉地区	**1 988 318**	**949 624**	**735 927**	**1 252 391**	**204 940**
平凉市	398 586	190 895	398 586		99 893
泾川县	304 970	144 733	63 087	241 883	15 256
灵台县	216 362	101 058	53 337	163 025	11 180
崇信县	88 063	42 038	24 554	63 509	8 653
华亭县	166 653	79 896	68 152	98 501	41 510
庄浪县	381 341	182 352	62 992	318 349	11 903
静宁县	432 343	208 652	65 219	367 124	16 545
陇南地区	**2 473 692**	**1 185 542**	**623 472**	**1 850 220**	**179 596**
成县	231 110	110 600	100 627	130 483	22 226
两当县	49 637	23 068	8 865	40 772	8 409
徽县	201 977	96 879	89 559	112 418	18 323
西和县	338 008	164 521	37 678	300 330	19 514
礼县	468 269	223 374	49 716	418 553	21 176
康县	195 736	91 947	80 383	115 353	10 207
武都县	486 189	232 938	129 142	357 047	44 048
文县	227 380	109 970	40 606	186 774	23 810
宕昌县	275 386	132 245	86 896	188 490	11 883
定西地区	**2 676 534**	**1 291 621**	**468 784**	**2 207 750**	**192 464**
定西县	430 642	205 756	98 035	332 607	53 183
通渭县	414 364	201 951	37 671	376 693	15 599
陇西县	446 963	215 032	85 893	361 070	50 822
渭源县	315 483	148 885	62 983	252 500	9 909
临洮县	490 234	238 055	145 770	344 464	29 114
漳县	170 239	83 299	15 532	154 707	9 140
岷县	408 609	198 643	22 900	385 709	24 697
武威地区	**1 743 935**	**849 770**	**1 170 974**	**572 961**	**205 397**
武威市	905 049	442 001	905 049		144 134
民勤县	271 923	134 553	87 905	184 018	20 761
古浪县	353 005	171 974	80 495	272 510	15 154
天祝藏族自治县	213 958	101 242	97 525	116 433	25 348

19—6 续 2

单位:人

地　县	年末人口	#女性	城镇人口	农村人口	非农业人口
张掖地区	**1 173 614**	**566 713**	**495 258**	**678 356**	**156 743**
张掖市	438 353	211 175	438 353		91 589
肃南裕固族自治县	35 218	17 426	6 112	29 106	7 729
民乐县	224 649	107 215	7 579	217 070	10 300
临泽县	138 145	67 426	10 435	127 710	12 414
高台县	149 731	72 896	12 108	137 623	13 215
山丹县	187 518	90 575	20 671	166 847	21 496
酒泉地区	**855 373**	**412 157**	**705 368**	**150 005**	**268 108**
酒泉市	307 273	150 097	307 273		78 539
金塔县	130 062	63 063	36 740	93 322	15 987
玉门市	202 229	94 475	202 229		122 617
安西县	77 167	36 544	30 626	46 541	19 731
敦煌市	120 132	59 049	120 132		23 692
肃北蒙古族自治县	10 960	5 241	5 070	5 890	4 371
哈萨克族自治县	7 550	3 688	3 298	4 252	3 171
临夏回族自治州	**1 695 986**	**824 678**	**372 758**	**1 323 228**	**145 212**
临夏市	177 297	87 500	177 297		85 752
临夏县	338 097	163 310	15 908	322 189	6 066
康乐县	210 521	102 276	21 398	189 123	7 100
永靖县	187 986	89 501	46 048	141 938	24 857
广河县	171 513	85 368	61 243	110 270	5 217
和政县	174 755	85 377	22 081	152 674	6 224
东乡族自治县	233 264	114 242	15 521	217 743	5 659
积石山保安族东乡族撒拉族自治县	202 553	97 104	13 262	189 291	4 337
甘南藏族自治州	**607 346**	**296 007**	**85 138**	**522 208**	**98 254**
临潭县	137 856	65 894	20 263	117 593	8 955
卓尼县	91 443	44 855	14 789	76 654	8 888
舟曲县	122 894	61 114		122 894	11 990
迭部县	52 599	24 934		52 599	16 062
玛曲县	31 260	15 229		31 260	4 015
碌曲县	27 662	13 918		27 662	4 445
夏河县	143 632	70 063	50 086	93 546	43 899

19—7 分地区国有单位职工人数

（1993年末）　　　　　　　　　　　　　　　　　　　　　　　　　　单位：人

地　　区	职工人数	农.林.牧渔业	采掘业	制造业	电力.煤气及水的生产和供应业	建筑业	交通运输仓储及邮电通讯业	批发和零售贸易餐饮业
兰　州　市	647 757	6 469	28 585	277 306	19 853	76 633	16 181	55 305
天　水　市	184 353	11 825	909	80 620	2 712	7 577	6 989	14 739
白　银　市	157 748	3 190	24 355	73 099	4 367	11 019	3 285	6653
金　昌　市	77 355	5 356	1 785	40 018	2 919	12 226	1 203	3935
嘉 峪 关 市	47 784	154		36 952	936	4 149	148	1 476
定 西 地 区	88 505	4 155	878	22 176	3 276	732	3 966	8 788
庆 阳 地 区	120 465	6 281	34 381	16 842	2 131	958	3 620	9 446
平 凉 地 区	100 911	3 178	11 013	29 220	2 001	2 156	4 511	7769
陇 南 地 区	83 174	4 886	6 332	8 321	3 120	1 083	3 998	8 787
武 威 地 区	89 289	7 850	5 889	17 377	1 137	3 364	3 783	8500
张 掖 地 区	77 714	3 111	3 847	18 859	1 663	1 631	3 276	8864
酒 泉 地 区	124 261	2 741	40 132	30 012	1 719	2 624	4 090	9368
临夏回族自治州	62 501	2 155	28	14 676	3 297	1 790	2 774	4 362
甘南藏族自治州	45 955	1 730	13 153	3 481	1 054	423	2 262	2 320

19—8 分地区集体单位职工人数

（1993年末）　　　　　　　　　　　　　　　　　　　　　　　　　　单位：人

地　　区	集体单位职工人数	农.林.牧渔业	采掘业	制造业	电力.煤气及水的生产和供应业	建筑业	交通运输仓储及邮电通讯业	批发和零售贸易餐饮业
兰　州　市	171 841	675		84 550		30 573	6 253	35 689
天　水　市	47 233	98	114	19 310		10 774	425	14 056
白　银　市	33 680		2 658	27 759		593		3 973
金　昌　市	25 190	65	40	20 411		1 229	70	1 517
嘉 峪 关 市	8 971		18	5 576		1 985	52	894
定 西 地 区	20 395	120		9 425		4 024	15	5 408
庆 阳 地 区	15 405		1 958	4 313	39	2 670	181	5 205
平 凉 地 区	19 028			8 881		4 617	463	4 273
陇 南 地 区	18 546	405	2 529	3 736	273	3 086	498	6 382
武 威 地 区	26 130	152	966	10 308		1 738	693	10 264
张 掖 地 区	11 848		404	4 795		538	429	4 407
酒 泉 地 区	11 886	58	317	4 926		1 328	58	4 192
临夏回族自治州	8 693			2 933		2 205	26	2 675
甘南藏族自治州	2 533			975		156	64	1 029

注：各地区数据均采用各地正式上报年报数，各地区数据相加不等于全省总计数。

19—9 全社会固定资产投资

(1993年)　　单位:万元

地区	本年完成投资				本年新增固定资产			
	合计	国有	个体	集体	合计	国有	集体	个体
合计	1 220 812	957 031	141 721	122 060	830 217	604 767	10 339	12 206
兰州市	501 269	418 286	72 354	10 629	351 323	198 026	52 669	10 629
天水市	69 876	43 624	10 315	15 937	44 535	23 258	5 340	15937
白银市	139 770	116 008	13 906	9 856	69 046	53 481	5 709	9856
金昌市	88 934	80 669	6 423	1 842	53 950	46 179	5 929	1842
嘉峪关市	46 876	44 368	1 702	806	30 340	28 066	1 468	806
定西地区	30 316	12 021	4 064	14 231	24 087	4 750	5 106	14231
庆阳地区	93 683	74 303	1 775	17 605	91 757	72 567	1 585	17605
平凉地区	43 528	26 012	7 872	9 644	29 363	13 750	5 969	9644
陇南地区	21 419	13 469	1 559	6 391	14 943	7 419	1 133	3691
武威地区	31 857	21 211	4 239	6 407	27 198	17 258	3 532	6407
张掖地区	51 233	30 129	9 350	1 754	29 726	10 008	7 964	11754
酒泉地区	63 136	52 804	5 607	4 725	33 028	23 239	5 064	4725
临夏回族自治州	24 064	12 502	2 103	9 459	20 992	9 974	1559	9 459
甘南藏族自治州	14 851	11 625	452	2 774	9 929	6 792	363	2774

19—10 按用途分固定资产投资

(1993年)　　单位:万元

地区	全社会固定资产投资额				基本建设投资			
	合计	第一产业	第二产业	第三产业	合计	第一产业	第二产业	第三产业
合计	1 220 812	65 982	566 044	354 155	570 006	28 703	230 269	231 709
兰州市	501 269	2 596	186 971	229 293	204 524	966	44 583	158 975
天水市	69 876	7 244	17 658	18 919	29 337	4 867	6 396	11979
白银市	139 770	5 753	95 445	21 693	79 999	45	60 735	14 831
金昌市	88 934	11 815	58 921	10 707	57 645	7 644	37 714	7709
嘉峪关市	46 876	206	28 649	8 256	17 001		12 400	3 128
定西地区	30 316	2 514	8 744	6 129	8 511	528	4 905	1 751
庆阳地区	93 683	12 074	55 591	7 714	18 661	8 585	1 133	5165
平凉地区	43 528	2 049	14 919	12 050	1 846	693	6 108	7 390
陇南地区	21 419	3 087	5 085	5 674	7 480	1 282	747	3 470
武威地区	31 857	3 622	11 173	5 411	10 998	502	4 561	2 888
张掖地区	51 233	8 273	22 266	8 037	16 919	1 556	5 874	4589
酒泉地区	63 136	4 284	44 047	7 223	86 458	1 670	39 894	3809
临夏回族自治州	24 064	1 958	11 832	6 198	4 893	182	1 712	1 675
甘南藏族自治州	14 851	507	4 743	6 851	9 034	183	3 507	4350

19—11 分地区全社会房屋建筑面积

单位:万平方米

地区	本年施工房屋面积				本年竣工房屋面积			
	合计	国有	集体	个体	合计	国有	集体	个体
合计	2 053.05	916.97	221.40	914.68	1 449.60	391.49	143.44	914.67
兰州市	526.17	382.79	92.81	50.57	230.70	132.41	47.72	50.57
天水市	216.42	96.50	19.09	100.83	147.62	39.09	7.70	100.83
白银市	151.10	88.36	11.98	50.76	92.38	36.09	5.53	50.76
金昌市	73.81	54.76	7.31	11.74	45.35	26.60	7.01	11.74
嘉峪关市	46.83	41.63	2.26	2.94	34.60	29.79	1.87	2.94
定西地区	153.35	20.89	2.28	130.18	139.41	7.32	1.91	130.18
庆阳地区	195.48	23.43	5.19	166.86	184.74	14.42	3.46	166.86
平凉地区	139.38	40.23	14.84	84.31	114.89	19.29	11.29	84.31
陇南地区	83.25	27.45	3.99	51.81	64.67	10.70	2.16	51.81
武威地区	121.79	33.02	20.61	68.16	106.43	20.76	17.51	68.16
张掖地区	131.72	33.12	25.13	73.47	110.66	15.12	22.09	73.47
酒泉地区	70.87	36.33	7.47	27.07	57.54	23.00	7.48	27.06
临夏回族自治州	106.64	22.31	7.54	76.79	91.14	7.36	6.98	76.79
甘南藏族自治州	36.24	16.15	0.90	19.19	29.48	9.54	0.75	19.19

19—12 分地区耕地面积

单位:万亩

地区	合计	山地	川地	塬地
兰州市	328.69	175.58	147.23	5.88
天水市	588.54	544.92	41.98	1.64
白银市	452.33	253.64	172.27	26.42
金昌市	68.81		68.81	
嘉峪关市	4.46		4.46	
定西地区	786.34	686.23	91.39	8.72
庆阳地区	667.75	384.03	37.36	246.36
平凉地区	611.68	473.84	55.23	52.61
陇南地区	448.77	410.39	38.38	
武威地区	388.09	99.14	288.95	
张掖地区	320.43	87.48	232.95	
酒泉地区	166.95	0.07	166.88	
临夏回族自治州	223.55	162.93	41.21	19.41
甘南藏族自治州	102.98	87.86	15.12	

19—13 分县农作物播种面积

（1993年）　　　　　　　　　　　　　　　　　　　　单位:万亩

地　县	农作物播种总面积	粮食作物播种面积	经济作物播种面积	其他农作物播种面积
甘肃省	5 458.09	4 269.04	688.49	500.56
兰州市	318.50	263.34	28.14	27.02
榆中县	114.69	95.53	12.23	6.93
永登县	128.22	113.85	9.43	4.94
皋兰县	39.90	33.00	3.88	3.02
城关区	3.50	0.85	0.01	2.64
七里河	15.63	11.70	1.67	2.26
西固区	6.34	3.24	0.38	2.72
安宁区	1.68	0.17	0.01	1.50
红古区	8.54	5.00	0.53	3.01
嘉峪关市	4.46	3.22	0.65	0.59
金昌市	60.06	45.85	9.11	5.10
永昌县	48.60	38.80	6.87	2.93
金川区	11.46	7.05	2.24	2.17
白银市	394.84	329.36	44.52	20.96
会宁县	193.26	161.31	22.40	9.55
靖远县	99.01	85.04	8.75	5.22
景泰县	62.11	49.76	9.31	3.04
白银区	15.53	12.65	1.21	1.67
平川区	24.93	20.60	2.85	1.48
天水市	663.31	526.79	58.80	77.72
清水县	105.82	77.21	11.83	16.78
秦安县	119.53	94.56	7.34	17.63
甘谷县	102.31	79.90	9.22	13.19
武山县	74.64	61.39	8.14	5.11
张川县	63.78	51.90	4.43	7.45
秦城区	106.73	85.94	11.40	9.39
北道区	90.50	75.89	6.44	8.17
市直				
酒泉地区	187.82	118.60	38.98	30.24
酒泉市	73.16	46.04	10.49	16.63
金塔县	34.76	21.98	7.57	5.21
玉门市	28.24	19.83	5.52	2.89
安西县	23.45	14.71	6.63	2.11

地　县	农作物播种总面积	粮食作物播种面积	经济作物播种面积	其他农作物播种面积
敦煌市	27.09	15.16	8.59	3.34
肃北县	0.91	0.72	0.17	0.02
阿克塞	0.21	0.16	0.01	0.04
张掖地区	**310.12**	**211.24**	**67.39**	**31.49**
张掖市	92.08	56.98	11.75	23.35
肃南县	3.82	2.86	0.74	0.22
民乐县	79.02	61.15	15.69	2.18
临泽县	24.68	18.23	4.97	1.48
高台县	29.70	23.26	3.84	2.60
山丹县	42.02	30.29	11.50	0.23
军马管理局	38.80	18.47	18.90	1.43
武威地区	**327.40**	**249.47**	**58.41**	**19.52**
武威地区	148.75	113.57	25.20	9.98
民勤县	58.53	38.21	15.64	4.68
古浪县	87.51	72.53	13.13	1.85
天祝县	32.61	25.16	4.44	3.01
定西地区	**789.22**	**603.54**	**110.21**	**75.47**
定西县	181.70	138.08	19.05	24.57
通渭县	187.20	132.12	20.89	34.19
陇西县	124.25	93.92	19.39	10.94
渭源县	80.10	62.84	16.46	0.80
临洮县	109.11	89.13	15.49	4.49
漳县	46.17	38.02	7.99	0.16
岷县	60.69	49.43	10.94	0.32
陇南地区	**526.77**	**476.04**	**35.46**	**15.27**
成县	59.21	54.99	2.65	1.57
两当县	14.82	14.02	0.51	0.29
徽县	62.23	56.08	3.63	2.52
西和县	62.94	56.13	2.91	3.90
礼县	100.98	88.64	8.91	3.43
康县	47.61	46.34	0.52	0.75
武都县	88.64	80.49	6.55	1.60
文县	43.70	40.06	2.92	0.72
宕昌县	46.64	39.29	6.86	0.49
平凉地区	**693.40**	**514.68**	**66.63**	**112.09**
平凉市	114.03	89.01	11.57	13.45

地　县	农作物播种总面积	粮食作物播种面积	经济作物播种面积	其他农作物播种面积
泾川县	112.52	79.14	9.78	23.60
灵台县	106.86	79.54	12.39	14.93
崇信县	47.25	33.33	4.54	9.38
华亭县	49.24	41.66	4.99	2.59
庄浪县	103.44	75.01	8.77	19.66
静宁县	160.06	116.99	14.59	28.48
庆阳地区	800.83	622.70	125.74	52.39
西峰市	79.86	61.50	12.42	5.94
庆阳县	94.54	79.89	10.96	3.69
镇原县	202.02	158.73	31.25	12.04
宁县	123.77	99.36	18.87	5.54
正宁县	55.32	41.09	11.11	3.12
合水县	50.03	38.05	10.07	1.91
华池县	50.88	36.90	6.22	7.76
环县	142.73	106.62	23.72	12.39
林业处	1.68	0.56	1.12	
临夏回族自治州	240.49	203.34	20.26	16.89
临夏市	6.99	4.63	0.04	2.32
临夏县	46.00	37.85	2.95	5.20
康乐县	34.73	30.23	4.32	0.18
永靖县	36.31	30.62	2.42	3.27
广河县	23.55	18.15	2.24	3.16
和政县	23.77	20.36	3.25	0.16
东乡县	40.17	36.85	1.50	1.82
积石山	28.97	24.65	3.54	0.78
甘南藏族自治州	96.59	70.96	13.14	12.49
临潭县	26.19	20.02	3.86	2.31
卓尼县	15.41	10.62	2.51	2.28
舟曲县	19.01	18.17	0.68	0.16
迭部县	8.64	7.98	0.47	0.19
玛曲县				
碌曲县	3.65	1.66	0.56	1.43
夏河县	23.48	12.46	4.90	6.12
州级	0.21	0.05	0.16	
省农垦公司	42.16	28.18	10.85	3.13
省劳改局	2.12	1.73	0.20	0.19

19—14 分地县农业总产值

（按1990年不变价计算）　　　　单位:万元

地县	农业总产值	农业	林业	牧业	渔业
甘肃省	1 345 057.14	916 463.94	51 476.05	374 943.96	2 173.19
兰州市	87 924.87	63 013.60	1 361.41	23 191.69	358.17
榆中县	20 387.89	13 665.65	178.00	6 467.41	76.83
永登县	18 947.43	12 122.21	250.18	6 389.55	185.49
皋兰县	12 004.32	9 536.23	182.01	2 273.71	12.37
城关区	5 581.72	4 214.06	200.11	1 164.25	3.30
七里河	8 479.47	6 719.92	99.11	1 657.43	3.01
西固区	8 623.44	5 077.50	119.41	3 358.10	68.43
安宁区	4 000.26	3 491.10	41.49	467.67	
红古区	9 900.34	8 186.93	291.10	1 413.57	8.74
嘉峪关市	4 309.62	3 142.09	58.12	1 095.81	13.60
金昌市	26 660.99	19 577.95	166.48	6 838.65	77.91
永昌县	20 212.28	14 544.40	111.89	5 478.08	77.91
金川区	6 448.71	5 033.55	54.59	1 360.57	
白银市	67 356.31	42 923.06	1 410.97	22 657.89	364.39
会宁县	22 881.45	12 721.14	670.41	9 489.90	
靖远县	19 077.41	12 836.28	359.22	5 785.86	96.05
景泰县	13 630.99	9 879.41	178.17	3 552.39	21.02
白银区	7 889.41	4 936.71	145.59	2 564.32	242.79
平川区	3 877.05	2 549.52	57.58	1 265.42	4.53
天水市	125 084.12	90 130.59	6 012.56	28 786.41	154.56
清水县	14 669.93	10 446.75	952.69	3 258.12	12.37
秦安县	22 557.92	16 328.93	675.41	5 552.01	1.57
甘谷县	20 244.85	15 105.57	575.47	4 537.22	26.59
武山县	16 152.06	11 869.56	701.13	3 536.48	44.89
张川县	8 781.50	6 001.82	370.44	2 409.24	
秦城区	19 647.91	15 224.51	922.62	3 468.38	32.40
北道区	22 015.00	15 153.45	799.85	6 024.96	36.74
市直	1 014.95		1 014.95		
酒泉地区	102 425.25	74 998.63	2 110.02	25 107.11	209.49
酒泉市	38 664.08	28 645.17	551.56	9 349.50	117.85
金塔县	18 985.81	14 189.60	559.81	4 211.01	25.39
玉门市	13 690.12	9 634.94	207.97	3 823.30	23.91
安西县	12 764.39	9 880.25	380.47	2 474.77	28.90

19—14续1 (按1990年不变价计算) 单位:万元

地 县	农业总产值	农业	林业	牧业	渔业
敦煌市	15 630.75	12 304.97	379.25	2 933.09	13.44
肃北县	1 957.71	295.44	30.93	1 631.34	
阿克塞	732.39	48.26	0.03	684.10	
张掖地区	146 721.37	99 688.86	2 901.22	43 909.20	222.09
张掖市	57 153.30	37 615.87	1 861.96	17 598.06	77.41
肃南县	6 019.39	1 202.16	14.38	4 802.85	
民乐县	24 525.00	18 549.51	159.17	5 816.32	
临泽县	18 613.43	12 205.60	508.69	5 804.96	94.18
高台县	20 997.96	14 424.13	289.68	6 234.68	49.47
山丹县	14 149.54	10 769.32	65.14	3 314.05	1.03
军马管理局	5 262.75	4 922.27	2.20	338.28	
武威地区	121 898.74	85 398.40	1 545.06	34 937.97	17.31
武威市	72 071.09	50 046.59	849.88	21 174.62	
民勤县	25 640.05	20 260.62	413.23	4 949.71	16.49
古浪县	16 374.23	12 174.38	222.23	3 977.62	
天祝县	7 813.37	2 916.81	59.72	4 836.02	0.82
定西地区	130 673.51	85 976.99	4 235.67	40 379.32	81.53
定西县	25 026.15	16 543.95	446.30	8 034.11	1.79
通渭县	19 960.81	13 001.42	496.65	6 462.74	
陇西县	19 865.74	13 629.81	447.93	5 778.11	9.89
渭源县	15 798.47	10 778.39	419.87	4 591.56	8.65
临洮县	26 013.22	16 518.91	1 501.10	7 951.17	42.04
漳县	10 665.78	6 954.07	477.24	3 219.84	14.63
岷县	13 343.34	8 550.44	446.58	4 341.79	4.53
陇南地区	120 338.10	74 170.73	13 328.55	32 676.81	162.01
成县	16 473.75	11 042.53	1 484.89	3 929.43	16.90
两当县	3 628.07	2 116.42	486.71	1 012.51	12.43
徽县	17 103.21	11 424.51	1 370.88	4 288.20	19.42
西和县	13 664.18	8 471.90	1 221.77	3 951.96	18.55
礼县	17 486.71	11 059.51	1 403.48	5 016.51	7.21
康县	9 142.43	4 938.73	2 106.58	2 084.10	13.02
武都县	20 813.53	11 997.71	2 838.32	5 940.40	37.10
文县	10 660.42	6 239.79	1 563.81	2 819.64	37.18
宕昌县	11 365.80	6 879.63	852.11	3 634.06	
平凉地区	107 058.91	74 826.32	5 145.44	26 860.64	226.51
平凉市	17 882.13	12 950.07	723.57	4 111.63	96.86

19—14 续 2　　(按 1990 年不变价计算)　　单位:万元

地　县	农业总产值	农业	林业	牧业	渔业
泾川县	22 366.99	16 101.23	1 209.87	4 976.75	79.14
灵台县	16 709.20	11 976.09	1 045.60	3 642.13	45.38
崇信县	5 913.35	4 233.08	375.74	1 301.13	3.40
华亭县	7 869.05	5 059.73	712.87	2 095.96	0.49
庄浪县	16 545.75	11 511.03	643.82	4 390.90	
静宁县	19 772.44	12 995.09	433.97	6 342.14	1.24
庆阳地区	187 811.80	136 688.22	8 260.67	42 780.56	82.35
西锋市	25 481.65	20 195.05	612.90	4 660.51	13.19
庆阳县	18 114.75	12 655.35	720.48	4 737.68	1.24
镇原县	35 814.85	25 428.83	1 430.76	8 945.78	9.48
宁县	42 804.68	33 581.57	1 791.16	7 412.87	19.08
正宁县	18 931.03	14 157.10	731.71	4 029.85	12.37
合水县	17 828.56	12 428.81	1 344.37	4 043.43	11.95
华池县	9 647.34	6 462.09	220.13	2 959.35	5.77
环县	18 093.06	11 537.17	612.48	5 934.14	9.27
林业处	1 095.88	242.25	796.68	56.95	
临夏回族自治州	64 522.40	39 047.94	3 509.41	21 823.06	141.99
临夏市	6 703.09	3 751.78	278.56	2 665.54	7.21
临夏县	14 440.13	8 103.84	592.59	5 737.06	6.64
康乐县	9 393.14	6 471.58	542.51	2 377.73	1.32
永靖县	6 704.17	4 129.62	248.23	2 225.05	101.27
广河县	6 772.94	4 172.34	622.57	1 978.03	
和政县	6 576.27	3 692.92	218.65	2 661.81	2.89
东乡县	7 295.21	4 765.55	573.52	1 936.36	19.78
积石山	6 637.45	3 960.31	432.78	2 241.48	2.88
甘南藏族自治州	35 288.58	12 099.09	983.50	22 158.74	47.25
临潭县	4 663.33	2 974.35	86.74	1 602.24	
卓尼县	4 953.36	1 992.29	58.71	2 902.36	
舟曲县	4 019.21	2 231.33	453.85	1 334.03	
迭部县	3 110.41	1 701.02	240.55	1 168.84	
玛曲县	6 139.76	100.44		6 039.32	
碌曲县	3 077.39	353.30	81.06	2 643.03	
夏河县	8 730.60	2 724.52	57.14	5 948.94	
州级	594.52	21.84	5.45	519.98	47.25
省农垦公司	15 496.65	13 538.55	441.30	1 504.38	12.42
省劳改局	1 485.92	1 242.92	5.67	235.72	1.61

19—15 分地县农业商品产值

单位:万元

地 县	农业商品产值	农业	林业	牧业	渔业
甘肃省	676 830.63	442 827.05	15 169.49	215 519.42	3 314.67
兰州市	48 883.09	35 828.65	152.35	12 510.15	391.94
榆中县	7 332.90	4 613.35	6.15	2 629.98	83.42
永登县	6 042.52	3 343.86	37.64	2 438.68	222.34
皋兰县	6 676.07	5 699.92		961.75	14.40
城关区	4 244.79	3 058.78		1 180.76	5.25
七里河	8 096.25	6 597.57		1 494.84	3.84
西固区	6 984.10	4 328.12	17.63	2 586.75	51.60
安宁区	3 104.37	2 778.31		320.06	
红古区	6 402.09	5 408.74	90.93	891.33	11.09
嘉峪关市	3 124.37	2 500.01	18.81	556.05	49.50
金昌市	17 279.77	13 033.59	13.23	3 978.55	254.40
永昌县	12 688.81	9 443.00		2 991.41	254.40
金川区	4 590.96	3 590.59	13.23	987.14	
白银市	28 595.18	17 601.18	297.24	10 053.48	643.28
会宁县	8 114.27	4 036.52	138.87	3 938.88	
靖远县	6 973.52	4 533.29	16.87	2 259.49	163.87
景泰县	5 275.41	3 490.72	52.50	1 702.44	29.75
白银区	6 869.76	4 652.72	84.00	1 692.18	440.86
平川区	1 362.22	887.93	5.00	460.49	8.80
天水市	52 519.09	37 931.11	1 021.45	13 357.25	209.28
清水县	5 185.94	3 552.77	72.77	1 545.90	14.50
秦安县	9 401.02	6 599.15	335.73	2 464.70	1.44
甘谷县	8 863.27	6 630.59	72.16	2 114.57	45.95
武山县	8 216.32	6 574.07		1 587.40	54.85
张川县	2 804.26	1 684.92	21.36	1 097.98	
秦城区	8 934.40	6 800.55	16.62	2 067.38	49.85
北道区	9 113.88	6 089.06	502.81	2 479.32	42.69
市直					
酒泉地区	64 227.68	45 210.98	280.99	18 252.20	483.51
酒泉市	24 069.45	16 998.52	60.15	6 748.10	262.68
金塔县	11 649.72	8 515.84	60.23	3 012.05	61.60
玉门市	8 733.40	6 317.32	9.21	2 348.87	58.00
安西县	7 613.29	5 824.96	38.04	1 701.22	49.07

单位:万元

地　县	农业商品产值	农业	林业	牧业	渔业
敦煌市	10 409.82	7 432.41	110.96	2 814.29	52.16
肃北县	1 166.50	113.66	2.40	1 050.44	
阿克塞	585.50	8.27		577.23	
张掖地区	88 025.72	62 286.88	299.26	25 151.46	288.12
张掖市	32 956.00	22 844.45	151.25	9 825.98	134.32
肃南县	4 048.24	746.18		3 302.06	
民乐县	15 461.35	11 898.19	54.60	3 508.56	
临泽县	10 912.36	8 136.19	88.20	2 620.37	67.60
高台县	12 154.98	8 580.36	5.21	3 484.11	85.30
山丹县	7 968.99	5 830.34		2 137.75	0.90
军马管理局	4 523.80	4 251.17		272.63	
武威地区	66 294.56	42 830.50	45.22	23 402.04	16.80
武威市	45 174.61	29 393.28		15 781.33	
民勤县	11 773.35	9 290.42	30.82	2 440.11	12.00
古浪县	5 905.31	3 728.32	10.40	2 166.59	
天祝县	3 441.29	418.48	4.00	3 014.01	4.80
定西地区	50 054.32	27 172.66	1 149.38	21 625.13	107.15
定西县	9 652.25	5 529.26	34.56	4 088.43	
通渭县	6 050.56	2 906.00	81.93	3 062.63	
陇西县	7 132.16	4 069.88	44.57	3 001.61	16.10
渭源县	5 175.09	2 658.06	29.07	2 475.16	12.80
临洮县	10 802.20	5 271.33	859.77	4 621.60	49.50
漳县	3 986.04	2 270.82	20.41	1 672.77	22.04
岷县	7 256.02	4 467.31	79.07	2 702.93	6.71
陇南地区	54 250.67	32 939.78	6 428.81	14 634.90	247.18
成县	11 288.97	8 393.13	832.32	2 046.18	17.34
两当县	1 496.25	859.69	213.36	408.86	14.34
徽县	9 481.43	5 944.25	1 117.29	2 392.83	27.06
西和县	4 136.49	2 097.32	169.31	1 849.36	20.50
礼县	5 060.35	3 213.25	232.40	1 601.90	12.80
康县	2 548.29	754.94	1 195.96	585.93	11.46
武都县	9 437.79	5 096.62	1 829.31	2 430.86	81.00
文县	5 772.39	2 876.22	675.90	2 157.59	62.68
宕昌县	5 028.71	3 704.36	162.96	1 161.39	
平凉地区	43 740.49	25 105.48	894.28	17 485.82	254.91
平凉市	7 047.11	3 555.94	134.98	3 289.87	66.32

19—15 续 2 单位:万元

地　县	农业商品产值	农业	林业	牧业	渔业
泾川县	11 694.09	6 926.50	456.82	4 185.97	124.80
灵台县	7 261.78	4 459.42	70.30	2 674.66	57.40
崇信县	2 349.68	1 525.02	75.52	745.22	3.92
华亭县	2 799.54	1 735.10	109.27	954.45	0.72
庄浪县	7 027.28	4 411.99	31.32	2 583.97	
静宁县	5 561.01	2 491.51	16.07	3 051.68	1.75
庆阳地区	**96 128.11**	**67 295.39**	**3 390.07**	**25 334.34**	**108.31**
西锋市	12 262.47	9 039.99	290.87	2 913.69	17.92
庆阳县	8 753.13	6 357.55	89.92	2 304.01	1.65
镇原县	18 766.14	12 077.42	787.47	5 887.45	13.80
宁县	26 538.93	20 538.77	941.90	5 032.80	25.46
正宁县	9 948.80	7 171.14	329.85	2 433.81	14.00
合水县	9 395.57	6 340.22	863.92	2 174.03	17.40
华池县	4 356.54	2 760.91	51.30	1 538.63	5.70
环县处	5 837.83	2 756.77	29.28	3 039.40	12.38
林业处	268.70	252.62	5.56	10.52	
临夏回族自治州	**28 284.23**	**13 551.31**	**597.35**	**13 943.33**	**192.24**
临夏市	5 869.63	3 664.69	12.47	2 180.71	11.76
临夏县	7 113.59	2 165.73	174.17	4 764.93	8.76
康乐县	3 567.02	2 559.73	44.84	961.03	1.42
永靖县	1 499.00	400.50	30.72	924.24	143.54
广河县	2 896.32	1 302.26	27.19	1 566.87	
和政县	2 562.83	1 510.41	38.00	1 010.19	4.23
东乡县	2 616.96	1 135.74	124.41	1 337.41	19.40
积石山	2 158.88	812.25	145.55	1 197.95	3.13
甘南藏族自治州	**17 405.96**	**2 803.10**	**489.65**	**14 077.41**	**35.80**
临潭县	1 661.57	800.09		861.48	
卓尼县	2 110.85	512.62	12.40	1 585.83	
舟曲县	1 170.46	469.92	398.49	302.05	
迭部县	952.40	365.05	21.26	566.09	
玛曲县	4 790.15	32.51		4 757.64	
碌曲县	1 724.27	103.69	20.00	1 600.58	
夏河县	4 629.00	501.20	37.50	4 090.30	
州级	367.26	18.02		313.44	35.80
省农垦公司	16 882.10	15 816.57	90.84	944.04	30.65
省劳改局	1 135.29	919.86	0.56	213.27	1.60

19—16 分地县农业总产值增长速度

(1992年=100) 单位:%

地 县	农业	农业	林业	牧业	渔业
甘肃省	8.64	9.56	4.46	7.01	16.01
兰州市	6.64	7.29	4.10	4.05	1.63
榆中县	7.52	11.47	—39.37	2.15	—0.43
永登县	5.80	7.62	6.51	2.53	4.51
皋兰县	5.64	6.15	15.53	3.02	—18.89
城关区	—0.39	2.15	20.88	—10.88	—48.68
七里河	7.91	8.14	76.32	4.61	
西固区	9.35	8.60	7.98	10.60	6.91
安宁区	3.88	3.01	68.11	7.01	
红古区	7.03	4.66	9.98	22.44	—3.64
嘉峪关市	6.01	8.52	0.97	—0.76	65.05
金昌市	9.61	10.24	—2.26	7.56	117.26
永昌县	8.07	10.15	—5.00	2.51	117.26
金川区	14.72	10.51	3.88	34.18	
白银市	10.69	5.15	—15.34	25.63	11.69
会宁县	13.84	11.59	—27.71	22.09	
靖远县	8.12	2.00	5.21	24.42	41.23
景泰县	9.41	1.89	—2.46	38.86	—6.41
白银区	11.09	4.45	—14.78	29.98	4.80
平川区	9.44	5.63	30.15	17.11	9.95
天水市	9.92	9.48	6.97	11.97	9.55
清水县	10.43	12.14	95.72	—6.13	20.10
秦安县	22.53	21.66	—6.04	30.11	—36.44
甘谷县	7.11	10.90	—25.32	1.23	1.95
武山县	8.59	6.75	81.44	6.38	—0.36
张川县	9.96	12.11	—20.21	11.11	
秦城区	4.70	5.37	—7.42	5.12	54.14
北道区	7.19	0.70	5.39	28.32	4.61
市直	—2.24		—2.24		
酒泉地区	1.48	2.11	17.46	—1.71	47.03
酒泉市	1.80	3.70	13.67	—4.62	71.52
金塔县	4.61	5.78	14.42	—0.28	13.65
玉门市	3.99	5.89	1.89	—0.61	56.79
安西县	8.57	6.50	90.82	9.66	22.41

19—16 续 1　　(1992 年=100)　　单位:%

地　县	农业	农业	林业	牧业	渔业
敦煌市	−8.97	−9.45	−3.87	−7.71	33.07
肃北县	−2.94	−27.20	75.44	2.37	
阿克塞	6.16	26.73	−99.52	6.38	
张掖地区	8.04	6.23	−10.15	13.84	40.35
张掖市	5.22	2.22	−0.84	12.96	25.20
肃南县	12.16	−7.27	−52.70	18.89	
民乐县	6.38	6.48	−1.57	6.32	
临泽县	5.20	2.61	−30.17	15.82	62.63
高台县	9.56	8.69	−17.37	13.22	33.34
山丹县	22.63	21.49	−13.16	27.60	
军马管理局	12.78	14.56	−57.69	−7.21	
武威地区	12.00	12.06	−25.30	14.40	−6.63
武威市	16.57	16.76	−29.80	19.26	
民勤县	4.64	4.49	24.01	8.74	−6.94
古浪县	19.85	25.62	−5.40	6.46	
天祝县	−11.63	−31.59	−24.50	7.52	
定西地区	9.89	10.43	30.87	6.97	6.99
定西县	7.03	12.27	3.64	−2.19	3.47
通渭县	6.51	6.60	0.28	6.83	
陇西县	11.55	18.75	0.35	−1.66	0.30
渭源县	10.93	11.36	0.15	10.97	39.07
临洮县	11.52	8.95	122.60	6.77	1.47
漳县	16.53	4.71	32.86	50.49	16.39
岷县	8.79	7.37	8.49	11.73	3.19
陇南地区	7.70	12.95	13.53	−4.39	8.10
成县	10.52	21.04	9.03	−10.79	6.49
两当县	5.38	0.72	44.59	1.83	18.83
徽县	9.76	11.37	22.52	2.39	16.44
西和县	−3.91	4.14	−35.27	−5.48	15.36
礼县	16.24	21.99	10.54	6.70	9.24
康县	11.06	8.44	31.64	1.03	−8.18
武都县	5.28	14.30	40.05	−17.61	7.13
文县	1.09	2.46	10.64	−6.24	6.11
宕昌县	13.71	17.72	17.48	6.08	
平凉地区	7.22	7.91	10.12	4.84	5.49
平凉市	2.[illegible]	1.55	−5.05	9.13	0.78

19—16 续 2　　(1992 年=100)　　单位:%

地　县	农业	农业	林业	牧业	渔业
泾川县	11.54	11.22	—3.61	17.13	9.70
灵台县	7.79	6.46	40.67	4.91	23.11
崇信县	5.31	9.77	—1.80	—5.24	8.28
华亭县	4.58	4.05	22.50	0.81	
庄浪县	5.89	9.92	23.22	—5.18	
静宁县	8.93	11.35	2.16	4.83	—79.26
庆阳地区	10.18	13.68	—6.99	3.66	24.10
西锋市	11.79	14.69	—16.38	4.81	99.85
庆阳县	19.73	26.46	19.02	4.90	51.22
镇原县	10.29	12.81	8.62	3.92	27.76
宁县	13.41	17.68	2.56	—0.40	8.90
正宁县	5.89	7.58	—11.44	3.80	20.10
合水县	6.15	—1.01	75.70	16.58	61.05
华池县	8.14	16.13	18.71	—3.97	52.24
环县	10.35	15.11	2.34	2.88	32.24
林业处	—52.88	—1.58	—60.53	2.95	—100.00
临夏回族自治州	13.65	18.89	1.08	7.34	12.98
临夏市	16.88	24.29	3.46	9.10	71.67
临夏县	15.88	23.53	—0.48	8.20	118.42
康乐县	10.30	10.25	—5.33	14.78	6.45
永靖县	14.43	23.22	23.28	0.70	4.99
广河县	21.39	22.36	—8.83	33.03	
和政县	6.95	11.20	—22.26	4.61	39.61
东乡县	7.15	13.81	9.03	—6.85	23.09
积石山	17.16	26.67	26.31	2.18	10.77
甘南藏族自治州	5.98	10.72	2.16	3.72	10.68
临潭县	6.31	6.93	130.51	2.23	
卓尼县	2.26	6.08	—28.22	0.64	
舟曲县	9.37	8.84	14.38	8.62	
迭部县	4.85	4.33	—13.43	10.46	
玛曲县	1.74	4.83		10.69	
碌曲县	9.36	22.02	—15.70	8.84	
夏河县	8.76	24.51	—18.45	3.12	
州级	8.41	57.01	128.03	6.25	10.68
省农垦公司	6.41	6.94	12.75	0.37	—8.00
省劳改局	28.43	35.88	—22.86	0.84	43.75

19—17 分县粮食产量

单位:吨

地　县	粮食	#小麦	#玉米	#薯类	人均粮食占有量(公斤)	
					绝对数	位次
兰州市	349 430.80	216 681.70	22 038.00	39 796.30	133.78	14
榆中县	118 810.90	73 380.70	9 753.80	11 999.00	290.42	39
永登县	122 515.00	86 078.50	718.10	11 638.40	260.67	49
皋兰县	59 670.00	29 850.00	4 954.00	5 342.00	380.06	24
城关区	1 492.50	943.20	90.00	321.10	2.27	83
七里河区	20 582.40	12 025.70	350.10	5 818.70	54.55	80
西固区	6 876.30	4 566.60	279.60	1 354.10	23.73	82
安宁区	90.50	90.50			0.69	84
红古区	19 393.20	9 746.50	5 892.40	3 323.00	160.27	72
天水市	789 845.50	344 432.00	231 383.40	112 591.20	259.74	9
清水县	103 883.40	33 714.90	51 007.70	8 544.60	377.48	25
秦安县	119 344.00	64 451.50	20 174.40	19 512.60	230.44	60
甘谷县	128 322.00	60 081.60	25 373.10	24 569.00	247.49	56
武山县	85 007.20	33 282.00	9 464.10	19 886.90	222.18	62
张川县	67 587.80	30 182.80	14 892.60	12 440.60	252.29	54
秦城区	142 381.00	56 988.90	55 251.30	19 166.70	253.26	53
北道区	143 320.10	65 730.30	55 220.20	8 470.80	277.48	45
白银市	386 252.90	190 040.70	64 282.00	22 093.00	252.94	10
会宁县	130 651.10	60 493.30	20 201.40	12 225.60	253.94	52
靖远县	120 000.00	57 290.40	24 324.40	5 496.50	284.70	43
景泰县	89 400.00	46 382.00	9 974.00	3 522.30	442.36	19
白银区	24 220.20	13 500.00	8 762.20	263.60	104.08	78
平川区	21 981.60	12 375.00	1 020.00	585.00	140.64	75
金昌市	169 761.50	114 184.50	5 436.50	4 557.40	423.42	3
永昌县	144 992.60	98 283.00	3 780.00	3 175.00	618.83	10
金川区	24 768.90	15 901.50	1 656.50	1 382.40	148.67	74
嘉峪关市	15 851.60	11 866.20	3 063.50		139.06	13
嘉峪关区						
庆阳地区	884 452.30	519 906.30	143 910.70	40 477.20	388.62	5
西峰市	131 671.90	80 010.90	29 166.00	5 071.20	464.29	16
庆阳县	83 701.90	55 061.50	6 153.20	5 032.20	286.95	40
镇原县	171 234.70	105 881.50	29 879.10	8 151.80	375.27	27
宁县	200 672.00	133 123.30	24 185.50	5 400.00	428.97	23

地　县	粮食	#小麦	#玉米	#薯类	人均粮食占有量(公斤)	
					绝对数	位次
正宁县	86 550.20	40 467.00	29 029.60	3 859.70	439.78	21
合水县	76 864.60	40 986.50	13 874.50	2 553.20	286.95	41
华池县	46 622.40	21 329.50	7 299.60	5 337.00	366.04	28
环县	86 405.10	42 988.60	3 882.90	5 056.10	286.01	42
平凉地区	734 023.10	387 263.50	149 652.10	57 418.50	369.17	6
平凉市	140 240.90	76 978.40	28 488.90	9 925.70	351.83	29
泾川县	132 994.10	79 042.20	30 081.30	1 651.10	436.05	22
灵台县	125 812.30	66 943.00	34 987.20	1 870.00	581.39	11
崇信县	38 924.30	19 394.80	12 235.10	766.10	441.82	20
华亭县	53 686.40	22 924.40	19 008.90	5 419.70	322.05	31
庄浪县	97 622.20	49 734.00	11 812.80	21 101.80	256.02	51
静宁县	144 742.90	72 246.70	13 037.90	16 684.10	334.82	30
陇南地区	722 946.90	288 994.20	238 782.70	95 140.10	292.25	7
成县	107 375.00	52 490.60	44 641.40	5 564.60	464.63	15
两当县	24 206.80	10 540.00	11 402.80		488.04	12
徽县	133 499.80	49 933.10	62 185.90	3 004.40	660.89	7
西和县	91 080.30	28 630.30	25 023.60	32 238.20	269.47	47
礼县	109 551.10	51 757.20	23 969.50	16 197.10	233.93	59
康县	59 723.90	25 315.90	22 742.60	3 533.40	305.18	36
武都县	91 494.80	36 072.90	22 347.60	16 811.90	188.18	65
文县	59 205.40	17 580.40	23 095.70	7 534.00	260.36	50
宕昌县	46 809.80	16 673.80	3 373.60	10 256.50	169.97	68
定西地区	740 381.20	356 465.10	23 555.50	135 273.80	276.62	8
定西县	138 526.00	68 195.80	1 424.00	17 639.20	321.70	32
通渭县	117 377.70	52 998.80	960.50	24 279.00	283.25	44
陇西县	105 629.60	54 058.70	4 840.60	17 748.30	236.31	58
渭源县	92 506.60	45 546.40	451.20	17 679.20	293.21	38
临洮县	153 245.80	88 517.40	15 736.20	31 927.40	312.62	34
漳县	64 028.60	29 651.00	136.00	6 036.60	376.20	26
岷县	69 066.90	17 497.00	7.00	19 964.10	169.03	69
武威地区	679 655.00	475 017.50	109 930.20	37 795.00	389.72	4
武威市	400 883.00	272 730.00	82 190.00	21 513.00	442.96	18
民勤县	132 622.50	96 982.60	25 430.20	3 367.70	748.76	13
古浪县	111 143.00	85 113.60	2 310.00	10 110.00	314.85	33
天祝县	35 006.50	20 191.30		2 812.00	163.58	71

19—17 续2

单位:吨

地 县	粮食	#小麦	#玉米	#薯类	人均粮食占有量(公斤)	
					绝对数	位次
张掖地区	844 680.00	473 642.00	243 055.00	16 330.00	719.73	1
张掖市	288 286.00	141 965.00	118 920.00	5 170.00	657.59	8
肃南县	6 184.00	3 480.00	45.00	282.00	175.68	67
民乐县	158 265.00	122 388.00		6 442.00	704.65	6
临泽县	123 036.00	48 772.00	64 748.00	955.00	890.92	3
高台县	148 971.00	77 114.00	58 952.00	1 037.00	995.13	1
山丹县	84 468.00	70 489.00	390.00	2 444.00	450.50	17
酒泉地区	601 725.70	367 715.30	199 196.30	4 953.00	703.47	2
酒泉市	243 437.10	127 349.30	100 494.60	4 778.70	792.18	5
金塔县	109 725.10	83 341.80	23 933.70	146.30	843.39	4
玉门市	96 436.00	59 326.00	25 987.00		476.93	14
安西县	70 798.10	48 615.10	19 184.20		917.07	2
敦煌市	77 534.80	45 856.40	29 446.80		645.59	9
肃北县	3 265.60	2 880.70			296.87	37
阿克塞县	529.00	346.00	150.00	28.00	69.61	79
临夏回族自治州	401 133.40	194 101.60	63 471.70	68 915.50	236.52	11
临夏市	21 596.60	6 949.90	11 814.70	1 174.30	121.81	76
临夏县	83 943.90	45 734.30	13 300.20	11 226.00	248.28	55
康乐县	64 714.90	34 738.90	3 017.60	6 301.60	307.43	35
永清县	51 715.20	21 918.10	10 884.30	13 716.40	275.08	46
广河县	45 311.50	18 159.20	13 365.80	8 927.20	264.21	48
和政县	39 585.30	19 167.80	831.30	5 485.20	226.46	61
东乡族自治县	49 770.00	20 864.00	7 557.00	14 774.00	219.62	63
积石山保安族东乡族撒拉族自治县	44 496.00	26 569.40	2 700.80	7311.20	213.33	64
甘南藏族自治州	90 151.00	29 894.00	4 843.00	8 072.00	148.43	12
临潭县	25 143.00	10 142.00		3 192.00	182.33	66
卓尼县	14 180.00	4 340.00		1 359.00	155.14	73
舟曲县	20 400.00	8 040.00	4 591.00	2 100.00	165.99	70
迭部县	13 000.00	4 566.00	252.00	946.00	247.15	57
玛曲县						85
碌曲县	1 410.00	21.00		62.00	50.90	81
夏河县	16 003.00	2 785.00		413.00	111.44	77

19—18 分县畜牧业和农民人均纯收入

地　县	大畜牲存栏（万头）	羊存栏（万只）	出栏肉牛（万头）	猪出栏（万头）	出栏肉用羊（万只）	绵羊毛产量（吨）	农民人均纯收入（元）
甘肃省	596.38	1 025.58	52.83	539.57	316.23	15 411.35	550.83
兰州市	15.02	53.40	0.24	32.30	16.20	867.14	722.92
榆中县	6.24	15.19	0.08	11.48	5.19	139.40	604.00
永登县	5.85	23.76	0.08	9.16	6.04	493.95	551.33
皋兰县	0.95	6.93		3.87	2.61	113.31	675.14
城关区	0.37	0.77	0.03	0.90	0.29	11.08	1 229.68
七里河	1.06	2.09	0.01	1.98	0.49	19.32	1 024.08
西固区	0.31	1.59		2.43	0.63	38.44	1 208.15
安宁区	0.03	0.50		0.45	0.27	11.87	1 291.15
红古区	0.21	2.57	0.04	2.03	0.68	39.77	986.97
嘉峪关市	0.62	2.40	0.01	1.67	0.93	35.07	1 015.86
金昌市	8.12	30.61	0.56	8.55	9.62	534.78	844.60
永川区	6.66	25.80	0.45	7.09	7.36	479.95	799.80
金川区	1.46	4.81	0.11	1.46	2.26	54.83	1 020.73
白银市	24.76	68.06	0.34	31.95	18.76	806.86	500.06
会宁县	14.04	19.60	0.32	12.41	5.85	281.90	405.32
靖远县	5.62	17.16	0.01	9.26	4.09	192.07	540.40
景泰县	2.78	18.78	0.01	5.17	5.32	184.40	551.49
白银区	0.67	5.02		3.32	1.32	80.49	801.01
平川区	1.65	7.50		1.79	2.18	68.00	500.50
天水市	43.75	23.48	2.22	51.62	4.75	273.43	538.43
清水县	8.41	3.96	0.50	5.32	0.87	42.41	488.23
秦安县	4.22	2.28		11.35	0.56	32.99	504.11
甘谷县	4.86	2.76	0.09	10.55	0.54	37.87	541.90
武山县	6.34	5.07	0.13	6.66	0.92	36.85	466.38
张川县	7.00	5.32	1.00	1.40	1.24	65.64	430.52
秦城区	7.41	1.96	0.18	6.29	0.22	26.58	610.02
北道区	5.51	2.13	0.32	10.05	0.40	31.09	666.94
市直							
酒泉地区	18.72	83.31	1.14	37.15	29.29	1 135.72	
酒泉市	7.12	12.26	0.45	15.94	5.52	306.28	1 255.47
金塔县	2.75	9.23	0.18	6.60	4.81	136.33	1 188.83
玉门市	2.96	7.64	0.13	5.19	3.05	122.13	1 182.00
安西县	1.90	8.72	0.16	3.74	3.22	72.54	1 226.88

19—18 续 1

地 县	大畜性存栏（万头）	羊存栏（万只）	出栏肉牛（万头）	猪出栏（万头）	出栏肉用羊（万只）	绵羊毛产量（吨）	农民人均纯收入（元）
敦煌市	1.98	11.41	0.02	5.59	4.50	59.17	1 255.26
肃北县	1.25	22.18	0.19	0.08	4.57	290.84	1 452.00
阿克塞县	0.76	11.87	0.01	0.01	3.62	148.43	1 948.00
张掖地区	43.99	116.27	3.76	50.58	36.99	3 087.55	851.90
张掖市	15.90	23.91	1.44	22.07	8.01	571.33	915.96
肃南县	4.90	43.37	0.80	0.30	11.00	1 691.91	1 055.00
民乐县	6.42	14.62	0.17	7.74	5.39	311.85	703.48
临泽县	5.40	5.57	0.39	7.66	1.90	91.78	862.41
高台县	4.32	8.77	0.36	9.33	4.30	148.70	981.46
山丹县	4.11	16.70	0.13	3.45	5.23	225.78	744.49
军马管理局	1.94	3.33	0.47	0.03	1.16	46.20	
武威地区	44.28	97.26	2.29	55.58	31.17	1 725.12	564.00
武威市	16.05	24.61	0.76	35.88	10.20	488.00	630.60
民勤县	7.84	19.31	0.13	8.82	6.27	226.00	630.00
古浪县	7.23	10.96	0.12	6.82	4.58	137.00	428.00
天祝县	13.16	42.38	1.28	4.06	10.12	874.12	457.26
定西地区	70.57	96.12	3.89	85.60	28.23	1 256.24	497.23
定西县	12.03	21.38	0.56	15.33	8.23	320.04	561.58
通渭县	12.09	8.98	0.23	13.31	3.23	241.53	486.86
陇西县	10.04	13.48	0.32	12.75	3.35	177.18	558.00
渭源县	7.57	11.42	0.49	10.48	1.80	159.21	469.31
临洮县	7.63	15.72	0.20	16.16	3.40	187.72	544.42
漳县	8.09	11.01	0.73	7.03	2.92	75.26	470.99
岷县	13.12	14.13	1.36	10.54	5.30	95.30	358.03
陇南地区	63.95	36.69	2.40	59.96	7.87	270.54	391.46
成县	4.09	0.76	0.35	6.01	0.27	15.00	517.57
两当县	1.89	0.05	0.09	1.73	0.03		496.66
徽县	5.35	0.30	0.61	8.63	0.10	1.77	610.91
西和县	6.07	2.91	0.06	8.13	0.51	77.66	393.18
礼县	15.37	6.43	0.57	7.79	0.58	63.95	336.61
康县	3.89	1.75	0.08	3.79	0.29	32.84	298.47
武都县	11.71	8.92	0.15	11.44	3.20	28.19	377.18
文县	6.47	6.86	0.04	5.88	1.38	3.02	414.91
宕昌县	9.11	8.71	0.45	6.56	1.51	48.11	285.86
平凉地区	56.10	26.34	6.59	43.16	8.10	355.60	553.68
平凉市	9.68	8.61	1.94	4.31	2.88	101.11	630.58

19—18 续 2

地 县	大畜牲存栏（万头）	羊存栏（万只）	出栏肉牛（万头）	猪出栏（万头）	出栏肉用羊（万只）	绵羊毛产量（吨）	农民人均纯收入（元）
泾川县	8.98	2.57	2.62	5.45	1.39	39.78	588.52
灵台县	9.69	5.83	1.30	3.38	1.54	54.87	580.78
崇信县	3.54	2.79	0.25	1.46	0.52	35.68	587.40
华亭县	5.56	2.77	0.44	3.17	0.76	27.33	582.40
庄浪县	8.04	0.13	0.02	10.24	0.02	0.68	496.44
静宁县	10.61	3.64	0.02	15.15	0.99	96.15	497.78
庆阳地区	63.32	133.95	8.05	50.33	50.03	2 426.16	602.05
西锋市	3.91	6.62	0.91	5.57	3.26	397.22	765.40
庆阳县	7.52	16.30	0.85	4.60	6.95	361.00	585.39
镇原县	15.45	21.27	1.87	11.53	8.79	590.00	580.58
宁县	9.19	10.91	1.91	11.04	3.82	295.62	597.93
正宁县	5.22	4.66	1.04	4.89	2.08	140.01	615.25
合水县	5.25	12.14	0.58	4.24	3.23	96.98	704.62
华池县	5.61	21.37	0.42	3.07	6.51	138.60	542.50
环县	11.06	40.14	0.47	5.33	15.31	406.73	491.29
林业处	0.11	0.54		0.06	0.08		
临夏回族自治州	35.90	89.03	5.20	19.00	28.84	1 593.69	383.44
临夏市	0.86	1.86	0.99	2.09	1.96	90.81	683.57
临夏县	6.90	14.30	0.91	6.07	4.86	378.86	430.00
康乐县	5.15	11.02	0.73	2.36	2.66	199.72	398.03
永靖县	4.21	15.52	0.04	3.83	2.99	118.05	335.80
广河县	3.94	10.23	1.30	0.04	4.50	271.92	435.83
和政县	4.49	10.01	0.26	1.92	1.65	173.73	368.00
东乡县	4.50	17.58	0.42	0.59	8.40	232.00	282.00
积石山	5.85	8.51	0.55	2.10	1.82	128.60	301.00
甘南藏族自治州	106.57	160.78	16.05	11.20	43.54	951.10	505.35
临潭县	4.95	11.44	0.63	2.55	3.11	71.00	370.15
卓尼县	12.99	13.12	1.73	2.87	4.26	81.41	493.35
舟曲县	5.90	9.27	0.20	2.82	1.53	32.60	380.03
迭部县	6.84	7.54	0.83	1.36	1.23	15.52	539.41
玛曲县	31.82	29.05	6.14		7.80	170.40	901.52
碌曲县	13.91	25.68	1.79	0.23	7.36	177.35	1 121.50
夏河县	27.61	63.86	4.29	1.37	17.83	398.34	589.71
州 级	2.55	0.82	0.44		0.42	4.48	
省农垦公司	0.68	7.43	0.09	0.56	1.81	84.35	
省劳改局	0.03	0.45		0.36	0.10	8.00	

19—19 分地区乡镇企业产值和收入

(1993年)　　单位:万元

地区	合计		农业		工业	
	产值	收入	产值	收入	产值	收入
兰州市	441 294.80	416 897.04			277 024.30	231 552.06
天水市	220 133.96	207 809.50	2 690.98	2 483.80	99 433.05	88014.50
白银市	104 729.09	89 211.50	1 259.00	1 090.80	46 358.60	38408.90
金昌市	39 664.79	31 301.00	1 647.50	1 405.80	16 947.30	11963.20
嘉峪关市	4 718.01	3 785.00	67.00	67.00	2 433.97	1 809.00
定西地区	114 301.81	95 369.00	649.68	406.00	46 550.48	32 704.00
庆阳地区	207 566.00	176 183.10	4 229.80	2 540.90	90 796.60	62938.50
平凉地区	146 200.90	124 833.70	2 211.50	2 132.90	74 898.90	49212.90
陇南地区	69 756.72	60 467.30	485.77	412.80	34 907.19	27 297.10
武威地区	77 269.60	71 470.40	1 999.00	1 753.20	28 831.50	27289.30
张掖地区	120 129.60	89 104.30	1 001.70	595.70	56 855.20	39 533.60
酒泉地区	122 537.28	84 612.70	1 862.52	1 184.50	67 121.42	37092.90
临夏回族自治州	86 979.80	87 981.80	82.60	82.60	38 028.10	33831.30
甘南藏族自治州	16 959.90	15 049.20	17.00	16.20	9 670.60	7266.00

19—19续1　　(1993年)　　单位:万元

地区	建筑业		交通运输业		商业饮食业	
	产值	收入	产值	收入	产值	收入
兰州市	49 393.90	40 211.24	58 668.20	57 916.80	56 208.40	84 303.24
天水市	44 400.04	38 373.30	27 544.85	27 560.40	46 065.04	49777.00
白银市	27 462.80	19 843.00	17 886.99	16 614.00	11 761.70	12477.30
金昌市	8 143.84	5 915.55	6 447.90	5 950.40	6 478.25	5921.75
嘉峪关市	1 029.74	671.00	962.20	962.00	225.10	225.00
定西地区	36 014.83	28 280.00	15 810.42	15 810.00	15 276.40	16547.00
庆阳地区	34 235.70	23 082.60	38 246.90	38 246.90	40 057.00	45792.00
平凉地区	32 525.42	19 905.70	18 073.21	16 948.30	18 491.87	35845.90
陇南地区	7 812.13	6 367.40	12 290.58	11 789.60	14 261.05	13194.90
武威地区	18 381.10	16 592.40	14 024.60	12 211.70	14 033.40	11367.20
张掖地区	32 797.80	10 123.50	15 246.00	15 267.00	14 229.80	21594.00
酒泉地区	28 875.92	19 136.00	16 903.12	16 865.30	7 774.30	9824.80
临夏回族自治州	25 127.60	23 044.00	12 587.10	12 531.50	11 154.40	17 519.90
甘南藏族自治州	1 038.00	800.30	3 324.10	3 324.10	2 910.20	3377.50

19—20 分地区粮食亩产及位次

(1993 年)　　　　单位:公斤/亩

地区	粮食		#小麦	#稻谷	#玉米	#薯类
	亩产	位次				
兰州市	134.20	11	129.70	141.00	340.10	129.90
天水市	150.60	8	146.40	296.00	252.60	135.20
白银市	117.30	14	120.40	359.80	373.10	84.00
金昌市	370.20	4	386.10		578.40	292.10
嘉峪关市	511.30	1	500.70		666.00	
定西地区	122.70	13	135.10		265.30	136.10
庆阳地区	142.00	10	171.60	395.20	247.20	152.90
平凉地区	143.00	9	143.90		247.10	138.80
陇南地区	152.90	7	151.20	343.20	222.60	148.90
武威地区	277.70	5	302.30		461.70	219.60
张掖地区	399.80	3	413.80	689.30	764.10	326.60
酒泉地区	507.30	2	460.20	460.00	671.60	454.40
临夏回族自治州	197.40	6	190.80		358.20	168.20
甘南藏族自治州	125.90	12	138.80		157.20	123.60

19—21 各地区经济作物产量

(1993 年)　　　　单位:吨

地区	棉花	油料	甜菜	药材
兰州市		15 270.71	18 321.10	510 499.96
天水市		32 417.42	6 162.90	254 687.24
白银市	23.44	19 231.54	18 631.50	195 133.70
金昌市		10 955.76	50 218.89	51 005.47
嘉峪关市		352.70	12 566.00	29 590.40
定西地区		47 868.03	15 175.27	75 231.61
庆阳地区		57 590.18	3 340.80	160 722.00
平凉地区		30 705.58	120.35	132 515.14
陇南地区	15.09	13 277.87	15 127.40	100 406.40
武威地区	221.80	29 878.10	334 601.50	232 937.27
张掖地区	517.70	74 448.16	245 929.28	361 422.40
酒泉地区	11 853.26	16 216.74	318 758.36	300 361.83
临夏回族自治州		18 257.31	2 421.22	80 236.20
甘南藏族自治州	2.15	7 990.24	154.40	6 287.75

19—22 分县工业总产值和增加值

单位：万元

地区	工业总产值	#国有工业	#集体工业	在工业总产值中		增加值
				轻工业	重工业	
兰州市	1 966 264	1 726 009	230 085	361 070	1 601 594	489 015
城关区	377 164	334 471	39 501	162 343	214 821	112 629
七里河区	278 246	241 565	36 077	75 380	202 866	15 927
西固区	898 372	826 749	71 518	94 078	804 294	238 967
安宁区	137 501	116 875	20 391	8 843	128 658	33 013
红古区	73 462	52 753	15 012	2 353	71 109	31 566
永登县	155 374	138 526	16 737	3 154	152 220	39 132
皋兰县	17 751	4 430	13 208	5 944	11 807	6 613
榆中县	28 394	10 640	17 641	8 975	19 419	11 168
嘉峪关市	216 298	194 378	20 931	13 716	202 582	86 815
嘉峪关区	216 298	194 378	20 931	13 716	202 582	86 815
金昌市	262 538	201 904	60 514	11 179	251 359	128 376
金川区	214 259	161 504	52 755	5 475	208 784	90 292
永昌县	48 279	40 400	7 759	5 704	42 575	35 367
白银市	530 379	450 313	80 066	27 755	502 624	183 101
白银区	419 458	359 688	59 770	17 120	402 338	111 284
平川区	72 199	67 272	4 927	193	72 006	56 882
靖远县	18 824	11 718	7 106	2 473	16 351	5 767
会宁县	5 866	1 812	4 054	3 499	2 367	2 325
景泰县	14 032	9 823	4 209	4 470	9 562	6 843
天水市	284 878	228 541	54 226	98 532	186 346	123 625
秦城区	149 087	118 299	28 832	31 216	117 871	56 553
北道区	83 567	72 299	11 236	41 772	41 795	41 697
清水县	3 736	2 409	1 275	2 115	1 621	1 441
秦安县	9 614	6 902	2 682	3 560	6 054	5 492
甘谷县	20 655	15 189	5 426	12 724	7 931	6 002
武山县	14 409	12 674	1 735	3 797	10 612	8 674
张家川县	3 809	769	3 040	3 347	462	3 766
酒泉地区	366 029	300 109	60 341	60 653	305 376	200 290
玉门市	254 865	241 004	13 861	3 142	251 723	111 494

单位:万元

地区	工业总产值	#国有工业	#集体工业	在工业总产值中		增加值
				轻工业	重工业	
酒泉市	58 809	39 406	13 824	37 153	21 656	57 226
敦煌县	18 811	5 464	13 347	9 095	9 716	18 550
金塔县	11 793	6 045	5 748	6 137	5 656	4 370
肃北自治县	3 995	2 262	1 733	105	3 890	1 989
阿克塞自治	7 741	1 145	6 596	191	7 550	3 419
安西县	10 015	4 783	5 232	4 830	5 185	3 242
张掖地区	103 217	66 089	37 128	49 337	53 880	50 400
张掖市	51 621	33 324	18 297	27 406	24 215	19 989
肃南自治县	3 494	1 376	2 118	450	3 044	1 651
民乐县	6 976	5 320	1 656	5 277	1 699	2 880
临泽县	9 479	7 002	2 477	7 467	2 012	3 716
高台县	9 863	2 967	6 896	4 175	5 688	6 664
山丹县	21 784	16 100	5 684	4 562	17 222	15 500
武威地区	84 507	56 337	28 144	47 422	37 085	29 139
武威市	60 495	42 755	17 714	39 024	21 471	21 613
民勤县	5 789	2 458	3 331	4 380	1 409	1 864
古浪县	5 586	2 723	2 863	1 643	3 943	1 985
天祝自治县	12 637	8 401	4 236	2 375	10 262	3 677
定西地区	133 852	92 653	28 905	47 943	85 909	67 315
定西县	39 499	28 792	10 687	15 558	23 941	33 436
通渭县	8 029	4 773	3 236	6 885	1 144	2 453
陇西县	70 334	51 450	6 670	15 689	54 645	20 199
渭源县	2 893	1 574	1 289	1 727	1 166	1 811
临洮县	8 182	3 334	4 838	5 280	2 902	5 701
漳县	2 672	1 774	898	1 944	728	2 432
岷县	2 243	956	1 287	860	1 383	1 283
陇南地区	63 213	43 260	19 953	20 020	43 193	51 966
武都县	4 909	3 314	1 595	2 468	2 441	3 683
宕昌县	1 673	1 395	278	352	1 321	1 495
成县	12 120	4 944	7 176	1 626	10 494	12 099

地区	工业总产值	#国有工业	#集体工业	在工业总产值中		增加值
				轻工业	重工业	
康县	4 514	2 823	1 691	2 203	2 311	3 355
文县	13 483	11 877	1 606	1 384	12 099	12 776
西和县	6 872	2 855	4 017	646	6 226	4 935
礼县	5 082	4 171	911	818	4 264	2 384
两当县	2 029	1 272	757	1 030	999	2 029
徽县	12 531	10 609	1 922	9 493	3 038	9 210
平凉地区	**96 426**	**61 814**	**33 348**	**35 698**	**60 728**	**47 574**
平凉市	45 365	33 594	11 731	16 265	29 100	27 174
泾川县	8 215	3 882	4 111	5 304	2 911	2 761
灵台县	4 438	1 999	2 439	2 639	1 799	1 177
崇信县	4 782	2 264	2 228	1 089	3 703	3 549
华亭县	21 614	15 948	5 616	2 817	18 787	9 408
庄浪县	4 061	1 009	3 052	2 502	1 559	998
静宁县	7 951	3 118	4 171	5 082	2 869	2 507
庆阳地区	**254 021**	**217 312**	**35 962**	**41 658**	**212 363**	**102 494**
西峰市	24 387	19 408	4 979	15 322	6 065	10 543
庆阳县	196 709	182 923	13 786	3 110	193 599	71 890
环县	7 323	4 324	2 999	4 074	3 249	7 247
华池县	1 983	1 486	497	1 317	666	1 088
合水县	4 309	2 114	2 195	3 430	879	1 994
正宁县	3 145	914	2 231	1 759	1 386	1 509
宁县	6 485	2 231	4 244	4 488	1 987	5 753
镇原县	9 680	3 912	5 031	8 158	1 532	2 470
临夏回族自治州	**88 241**	**79 977**	**8 115**	**14 626**	**73 615**	**57 749**
临夏市	14 784	10 208	4 576	10 065	4 719	5 314
临夏县	1 954	1 433	521	989	965	548
康乐县	1 001	735	266	646	355	88
永靖县	66 557	64 591	1 817	1 446	65 111	50 888
广河县	900	686	214	273	627	168
和政县	1 609	1 370	239	575	1 034	500
东乡自治县	983	719	263	378	604	219
积石山自治	453	235	219	254	200	24
甘南藏族自治州	**35 975**	**29 865**	**6 048**	**8 680**	**27 295**	**17 664**
临潭县	1 430	1 013	417	422	1 008	251
卓尼县	4 210	3 799	411	454	3 756	2 664
舟曲县	1 909	1 220	650	507	1 402	253
迭部县	17 302	15 575	1 727	1 725	15 577	11 870
玛曲县	776	454	322	313	463	48
碌曲县	774	531	243	202	572	120
夏河县	9 574	7 273	2 278	5 057	4 517	2 458

19—23 分地区全部独立核算工业企业主要财务指标

(1993 年) 单位:万元

地区	企业个数(个)	年末固定资产 原值	年末固定资产 净值	流动资产年平均余额
兰州市	1 204	2 074 927	1 270 453	1 233 981
天水市	61	207 524	135 002	126 855
白银市	191	225 403	172 204	160 260
金昌市	369	495 958	300 610	350 346
嘉峪关市	744	230 544	128 409	238 641
定西地区	624	236 493	116 776	134 312
庆阳地区	445	81 455	51 031	72 197
平凉地区	422	79 864	59 017	70 237
陇南地区	512	86 449	56 007	92 633
武威地区	369	27 551	20 664	19 574
张掖地区	640	104 718	69 223	76 499
酒泉地区	565	603 442	535 765	188 472
临夏回族自治州	149	56 783	36 844	39 880
甘南藏族自治州	95	39 905	25 080	22 320

19—23 续 1 (1993 年) 单位:万元

地区	提取折旧基金	增加值	销售收入	#销售税金	#销售成本
兰州市	766 974	489 015	2 279 992	189 341	1 816 601
天水市	70 285	86 815	261 368	24 852	163 114
白银市	65 855	128 376	232 631	23 214	164 162
金昌市	116 512	183 101	417 750	25 840	345 204
嘉峪关市	73 800	123 625	296 061	26 635	220 363
定西地区	136 222	200 290	243 757	12 811	182 062
庆阳地区	22 038	50 400	113 752	5 980	94 122
平凉地区	18 098	29 139	77 160	5 051	61 211
陇南地区	26 617	67 315	107 098	5 980	88 358
武威地区	5 731	51 966	26 323	2 569	18 445
张掖地区	28 993	47 574	84 145	4 743	65 277
酒泉地区	168 960	102 494	273 454	14 287	200 621
临夏回族自治州	15 745	57 749	48 740	2 580	38 508
甘南藏族自治州	13 221	17 664	26 887	2 035	16 296

19—23续2 (1993年) 单位:万元

地区	#销售费用	#销售利润	利税总额	亏损企业亏损总额
兰州市	31 048	241 225	255 587	32 404
天水市	5 850	67 332	53 963	1 839
白银市	5 755	39 155	40 921	1 782
金昌市	9 721	36 072	22 554	10 360
嘉峪关市	7 486	41 304	36 450	9 392
定西地区	2 994	15 972	16 413	48
庆阳地区	3 073	10 320	9 044	1 859
平凉地区	2 690	8 052	5 482	2 032
陇南地区	3 129	8 317	5 435	2 928
武威地区	1 037	4 254	17 112	653
张掖地区	2 394	10 486	6 875	4 629
酒泉地区	4 111	4 995	— 368	23 098
临夏回族自治州	1 019	6 611	3 366	1 344
甘南藏族自治州	536	8 034	6 826	564

19—24 分地区独立核算工业企业经济效益指标

(1993年) 单位:元

地区	每百元固定资产原值实现的增加值	每百元固定资产原值实现的利税	每百元资金实现的利税	每百元增加值实现的利税	每百元销售成本实现的利税
兰州市	23.57	12.32	10.21	52.27	14.07
嘉峪关市	41.83	26.00	20.61	62.16	33.08
金昌市	56.95	18.15	12.31	31.88	24.93
白银市	36.92	4.55	3.46	12.32	6.53
天水市	53.62	15.81	9.93	29.48	16.54
酒泉地区	84.69	6.94	6.54	8.19	9.02
张掖地区	61.87	11.10	7.34	17.94	9.61
武威地区	36.49	6.86	4.24	18.81	8.96
定西地区	77.87	6.29	3.66	8.07	6.15
陇南地区	188.62	62.11	42.53	32.93	92.77
平凉地区	45.43	6.57	4.72	14.45	10.53
庆阳地区	16.98	—0.06	—0.05	—0.36	—0.18
临夏回族自治州	101.70	5.93	4.39	5.83	8.74
甘南藏族自治州	44.27	17.11	14.40	38.64	41.89

19—25 分地区城镇合作、个体工业

(1993年)

地区	城镇合作经营工业		城镇个体工业	
	单位数(个)	产值(万元)	单位数(个)	产值(万元)
合计	269	8 010	7 489	22 469
兰州市	49	2 387	1 138	7 271
天水市	76	4 659	1 593	3 649
白银市			338	162
金昌市			274	284
嘉峪关市			190	1 590
定西地区	23	361	738	3 218
庆阳地区	53	480	712	2 583
平凉地区	27	25	281	698
陇南地区	39	63	264	216
武威地区			149	323
张掖地区			345	530
酒泉地区	2	35	775	633
临夏回族自治州			255	411
甘南藏族自治州			437	901

19—26 分地区村及村以下工业单位数和产值

(1993年)

地区	农村村办工业		农村合作经营工业		农村个体工业	
	单位数(个)	工业总产值(万元)	单位数(个)	工业总产值(万元)	单位数(个)	工业总产值(万元)
合计	4 026	183 453	4 761	90 453	73 003	262 255
兰州市	833	89 559	534	28 529	1 442	40 854
嘉峪关市	32	706			99	316
金昌市	145	4 081	34	894	273	2 377
白银市	201	11 224	85	2 013	888	6 431
天水市	528	15 380	1 135	17 681	11 328	43 907
酒泉地区	450	12 592	15	860	5 862	9 044
张掖地区	385	16 791	429	9 185	2 839	11 996
武威地区	179	3 883	176	2 164	3 746	7 578
定西地区	229	2 970	254	1 274	13 795	25 718
平凉地区	329	7 196	1 137	12 240	6 485	34 227
庆阳地区	430	11 871	1 257	11 899	7 369	45 161
陇南地区	180	3 522	407	2 591	12 997	14 738
甘南藏族自治州	33	349	45	256	2 886	3 468
临夏回族自治州	72	3 329	390	13 107	7 479	16 439

19—27 分地区城乡集市贸易情况

(1993 年)

地区	集市数(个)		集市贸易成交额(万元)		
	城市	乡村		城市	农村
合计	526	1 154	702 009	470 816	231 193
兰州市	203	54	307 466	303 834	3 632
天水市	48	77	73 223	21 570	51 653
白银市	30	68	21 139	13 985	7 154
金昌市	18		6 458	6 458	
嘉峪关市	9		10 059	10 059	
定西地区		234	41 727		41 727
庆阳地区	20	191	30 728	8 606	22 122
平凉地区	45	116	30 645	10 616	20 029
陇南地区		159	34 814		34 814
武威地区	48	25	39 662	33 829	5 833
张地地区	55	85	32 427	23 426	9 001
酒泉地区	35	18	3 363	27 232	6 131
临夏回族自治州	15	93	34 473	11 201	23 272
甘南藏族自治州		34	5 825		5 825

19—28 分地区社会消费品零售额(一)

(1993 年)

单位:万元

地区	社会消费品零售额	食品类	衣着类	日用品类	文化娱乐用品类	书报杂志类	药和医疗用品类	房屋及建筑材料类	燃料类
兰州市	656 823	70 059	32 773	85 077	9 293	7 019	23 498	2 509	34 061
天水市	137 213	20 806	8 669	20 619	699	1 465	3 844	4262	12 467
白银市	88 282	8 320	3 109	7 501	910	981	2 439	425	4 698
金昌市	49 951	13 319	2 185	4 765	660	281	505	720	127
嘉峪关市	28 308	3 579	1 147	4 288	453	180	498	927	349
定西地区	63 726	12 307	3 070	5 656	437	1 595	1 641	317	6 507
庆阳地区	65 517	7 391	2 864	3 732	496	1 263	1 535	345	2 804
平凉地区	66 424	11 745	2 019	4 957	646	960	1 822	361	2365
陇南地区	51 808	9 175	2 609	4 277	264	748	1 095	722	4436
武威地区	90 446	13 790	3 097	6 107	1 351	450	8 530	163	6 184
张地地区	76 884	12 163	5 145	6 406	673	1 026	3 080	752	4 656
酒泉地区	109 932	16 901	9 191	17 657	1 268	1 111	2 848	1123	5 513
临夏回族自治州	52 587	5 481	2 124	2 308	215	482	2 019	264	1 909
甘南藏族自治州	23 186	4 680	712	1 030	112	162	676	69	2 466

19—29 分地区社会消费品零售总额(二)

(1993年)　　　　单位:万元

地区	按经济类型分				按城乡分	
	国有经济	集体经济	个体	农民对非农业居民零售额	城镇	乡村
兰州市	253 646	143 555	179 853	52 642	635 073	21 750
天水市	49 653	33 461	35 019	14 204	118 874	18 339
白银市	33 266	23 279	14 775	13 698	73 681	14 601
金昌市	24 945	14 188	7 472	3 346	39 189	10 762
嘉峪关市	18 171	1 634	2 906	5 597	28 308	
定西地区	26 548	12 963	16 095	8 120	41 757	21 969
庆阳地区	18 545	16 538	21 651	8 668	33 613	31 904
平凉地区	23 037	15 532	18 468	9 366	51 400	15 024
陇南地区	26 109	11 181	9 789	4 729	35 496	16 312
武威地区	30 910	31 624	17 423	9 769	70 739	19 707
张地地区	32 110	13 733	23 828	7 213	57 454	19 430
酒泉地区	50 214	17 137	17 764	16 873	100 589	9 343
临夏回族自治州	13 405	6 944	24 046	7 718	41 803	10 784
甘南藏族自治州	1 178	2 652	7 585	1 161	18 608	4 578

19—30 分地区主要商品零售量

(1993年)

地区	粮食(万吨)	食用植物油(万吨)	猪肉(万头)	棉布(万米)	食糖(万吨)
兰州市	20.13	1.03	654.21	138.15	305.33
天水市	17.61	0.33	301.33	98.98	60.38
白银市	7.58	0.16	37.86	31.46	34.52
金昌市	8.85	0.68	15.23	55.47	26.27
嘉峪关市	0.54	0.03	11.22	10.75	36.57
定西地区	6.94	0.15	11.37	56.89	34.30
庆阳地区	3.44	0.20	246.47	61.80	67.34
平凉地区	7.60	0.16	11.60	59.11	50.19
陇南地区	7.01	0.13	0.46	39.26	57.97
武威地区	7.94	0.76	66.13	105.60	59.92
张地地区	6.06	5.75	38.36	85.67	74.22
酒泉地区	4.33	0.09	31.08	107.68	46.49
临夏回族自治州	4.39	0.02	1.25	43.44	34.35
甘南藏族自治州	3.56	0.16	2.36	27.47	9.80

19—31 分县社会消费品零售总额

（1993年）　　　　　　　　　　　　　　　　单位:万元

地　县	社会消费品零售总额	#农民对非农业居民零售	按销售地区分		
			市的零售额	县的零售额	县以下的零售额
兰州市	656 823	52 642	21 150	21 750	613 923
榆中县	9 991	263	5 646	4 345	
永登县	21 447	1 314	12 719	8 728	
皋兰县	4 571	23	2 785	1 786	
城关区	508 132	33 862		3 893	504 239
七里河区	51 962	11 914		306	51 656
西固区	26 920	2 682		465	26 455
安宁区	15 115	1 178		1 107	14 008
红古区	18 685	1 406		1 120	17 565
天水市	137 213	14 204	19 820	18 339	99 054
清水县	4 327	20	2 788	1 539	
秦安县	10 626	164	6 355	4 271	
甘谷县	8 455	556	3 506	4 949	
武山县	7 792	1 001	5 188	2 604	
张川县	2 684	31	1 983	701	
秦城区	56 424	5 623		2 201	54 223
北道区	46 905	6 309		2 074	44 831
白银市	88 282	13 698	16 163	14 601	57 518
会宁县	9 543	692	5 284	4 259	
靖远县	11 085	753	6 447	4 638	
景泰县	7 441	537	4 432	3 009	
白银区	52 532	8 752		2 695	49 837
平川区	7 681	2 964			7 681
金昌市	49 951	3 346	14 470	10 762	24 719
永昌县	25 232	520	14 470	10 762	
金川区	24 719	2 826			24 719
嘉峪关市	28 308	5 597			28 308
嘉峪关区	28 308	5 597			28 308
庆阳地区	65 517	8 668	22 639	31 904	10 974
西峰市	25 229	3 927		14 255	10 974
庆阳县	5 637	62	3 388	2 249	
镇原县	8 651	2 475	3 870	4 781	
宁县	7 963	316	4 571	3 392	

(1993年)　　单位:万元

地县	社会消费品零售总额	#农民对非农业居民零售	按销售地区分		
			市的零售额	县的零售额	县以下的零售额
正宁县	4 399	180	2 513	1 886	
合水县	4 369	687	2 969	1 400	
华池县	2 084	101	1 012	1 072	
环县	7 185	920	4 316	2 869	
平凉地区	**66 424**	**9 366**	**23 980**	**15 024**	**27 420**
平凉市	27 420	4 796			27 420
泾川县	8 666	435	5 555	3 111	
灵台县	8 762	1 124	6 996	1 766	
崇信县	2 222	277	1 451	771	
华亭县	6 337	538	3 470	2 867	
庄浪县	5 218	904	2 729	2 489	
静宁县	7 799	1 292	3 779	4 020	
陇南地区	**51 808**	**4 729**	**35 496**	**16 312**	
成县	7 163	619	4 793	2 370	
两当县	1 599	108	1 092	507	
徽县	4 896	525	2 981	1 915	
西和县	4 022	930	2 150	1 872	
礼县	4 928	473	2 406	2 522	
康县	4 167	570	1 986	1 281	
武都县	17 237	657	13 474	3 763	
文县	4 331	768	3 317	1 014	
宕昌县	3 465	79	3 297	168	
定西地区	**63 726**	**8 120**	**41 757**	**21 969**	
定西县	20 094	4 418	13 484	6 610	
通渭县	8 628	798	4 377	4 251	
陇西县	12 890	1 736	8 888	4 002	
渭源县	4 244	220	3 701	543	
临洮县	9 300	379	5 451	3 849	
漳县	3 472	98	2 363	1 109	
岷县	5 098	471	3 493	1 605	
武威地区	**90 446**	**9 769**	**21 349**	**19 707**	**49 390**
武威市	57 457	8 231		8 067	49 390
民勤县	13 597	84	9 085	4 512	
古浪县	8 008	440	4 557	3 451	
天祝县	11 384	1 014	7 707	3 677	

地　县	社会消费品零售总额	#农民对非农业居民零售	按销售地区分 市的零售额	县的零售额	县以下的零售额
张掖地区	76 884	7 213	22 814	19 430	34 640
张掖市	39 831	5 151		5 191	34 640
肃南县	5 869	159	1 984	3 885	
民乐县	7 408	327	5 156	2 252	
临泽县	6 982	444	4 407	2 575	
高台县	7 936	70	5 070	2 866	
山丹县	8 858	1 062	6 197	2 661	
酒泉地区	109 932	16 873	15 207	9 343	85 382
酒泉市	41 808	6 933		1 786	40 022
金塔县	8 176	2 030	6 549	1 627	
玉门市	24 586	4 329		1 609	22 977
安西县	8 777	932	6 427	2 350	
敦煌市	23 950	2 267		1 567	22 383
肃北县	1 722	366	1 398	324	
阿克塞县	913	16	833	80	
临夏回族自治州	52 587	7 418	17 899	10 784	23 904
临夏市	24 534	4 664		630	23 904
临夏县	3 822	216	2 164	1 658	
康乐县	3 495	233	2 238	1 257	
永靖县	9 307	643	6 238	3 069	
广河县	4 302	1 501	2 948	1 354	
和政县	1 759	142	1 208	551	
东乡族自治县	1 749	99	1 055	694	
积石山保安族东乡族撒拉族自治县	3 619	220	2 048	1 571	
甘南藏族自治州	23 186	1 161	18 608	4 578	
临潭县	1 870	136	1 560	310	
卓尼县	2 528	98	1 656	872	
舟曲县	2 694	108	2 544	150	
迭部县	1 969	33	707	1 262	
玛曲县	1 863	339	1 678	185	
碌曲县	1 472	239	1 314	158	
夏河县	10 790	203	9 149	1 641	

附录:私人企业概况

统计指标解释

·之二十·

【等级裁判员】指经考核正式批准授予等级裁判员称号的人数。裁判员等级分为国际裁判、国家级裁判、一级裁判、二级裁判、三级裁判。

【当年价格、可比价格、不变价格】当年价格是指报告期的实际价格,如工厂的出厂价格,农村产品的收购价格,商业的零售价格等。按当年价格计算,是指一些以货币表现的物量指标,如社会总产值、工农业总产值、国民收入、固定资产投资额等,按照当年的实际价格来计算总量。使用当年价格计算的数字,是为了使国民经济各项指标互相衔接,便于考察社会经济效益,便于对生产和流通、生产和分配、生产和消费进行综合平衡。

按当年价格计算的以货币表现的指标,在不同年份之间对比时,因为包含有多年之间价格变动的因素,不能确切地反映实物量的增减变动,必须消除价格变动因素后,才能真实地反映经济发展动态。因此,在计算增长速度时都使用按可比价格计算的数字。

可比价格是指在不同时期的价值指标对比时,扣除了价格变动因素,以确切表现物量的变化。按可比价格计算有两种方法:一种是直接按产品产量乘其不变价格计算;一种是用物价指数换算。

不变价格是用某一时期的同类产品的平均价格作为固定价格,来计算各时期的产品价值。新中国成立后,随着工农业产品价格水平的变化,国家统计局先后四次制定了全国统一的工业产品不变价格和农业产品不变价格。1949 年到 1957 年使用 1952 年工(农)业产品不变价格,从 1957 年到 1971 年使用 1957 年不变价格,从 1971 年到 1981 年使用 1970 年不变价格,从 1981 年到 1990 年使用 1980 年不变价格,从 1990 年开始使用 1990 年不变价格,本《年鉴》资料中所列按各时期不变价格计算,即指上述时期的不变价格。

【公证人员】指在国家公证机关依法办理公证事务的司法人员。包括公证员、助理公证员和在公证处工作的其他人员。

【离休金】指发给离休人员的离休费和按 1982 年国务院《关于发布老干部离职休养制度的几项规定的通知》发给符合规定的离休人员相当于 1—2 个月标准工资的生活补贴。

【退休金】指发给退休人员的退休费。

附1—1 私营企业单位数和注册资金

行 业	单位数(户)			注册资金(万元)		
	1990年	1992年	1993年	1990年	1992年	1993年
总 计	1 472	1 730	2 453	15 546	25 079	45 201
按行业分						
工业	901	953	1 245	9 633	12 357	20 015
建筑业	116	103	127	812	937	1 382
交通运输业	21	28	46	913	1 343	1 731
商业	282	441	718	3 148	7 942	17 237
饮食业	20	36	54	122	657	1 035
服务业	26	43	73	235	650	1 382
修理业	42	43	49	285	385	783
科技咨询业	6	61	95		533	983
其他	58	22	46	398	275	653

附1—2 私营企业投资者人数和雇工人数

单位:人

行 业	投资者人数			雇工人数		
	1990年	1992年	1993年	1990年	1992年	1993年
总 计	3 914	4 578	6 477	32 090	34 648	46 022
按行业分						
工业	2 318	2 424	3 103	21 771	22 169	27 394
建筑业	265	205	243	4 774	3 940	4 458
交通运输业	374	427	575	542	736	1 015
商业	651	1 042	1 823	2 833	5 097	8 872
饮食业	29	60	80	275	584	804
服务业	64	125	169	404	569	1 090
修理业	79	67	90	510	536	745
科技咨询业	18	166	274	165	630	1 057
其他	116	62	120	816	287	587

附 1—3 私营工业企业单位数和注册资金

行 业	单位数(户)			注册资金(万元)		
	1990 年	1992 年	1993 年	1990 年	1992 年	1993 年
合 计	901	953	1 245	9 633	12 357	20 015
一. 按城乡分						
城镇	208	332	459		5 282	9 192
农村	693	621	786		7 075	10 823
二. 按企业种类分						
独资企业	496	513	654	4 557	5 131	8 182
合作企业	400	410	505	4 995	5 191	6 768
有限责任公司	5	30	86	81	2 035	5 065

附 1—4 私营工业企业投资者人数和雇工人数

行 业	投资者人数(人)			雇工人数(人)		
	1990 年	1992 年	1993 年	1990 年	1992 年	1993 年
合 计	2 318	2 424	3 103	21 771	22 169	27 394
一. 按城乡分						
城镇	436	801	1 114		6 200	9 102
农村	1 882	1 623	1 989		15 969	18 292
二. 按企业种类分						
独资企业	496	513	654	9 423	10 191	12 736
合作企业	1 774	1 787	2 000	10 293	10 705	11 501
有限责任公司	48	124	449	40	1 273	3 157

附 1—5 私营企业总产值和营业额

行 业	总产值(万元)			营业额(万元)		
	1990 年	1992 年	1993 年	1990 年	1992 年	1993 年
总 计	13 969	15 609	41 256	7 419	12 872	22 936
按行业分						
工业	11 522	12 864	37 812			
建筑业	1 520	1 548	2 019			
交通运输业	927	1 197	1 425			
商业				6 139	10 707	18 599
饮食业				293	619	1 790
服务业				358	637	1 302
修理业				473	232	475
科技咨询业					495	428
其他				156	182	342

附1—6 各地区私营企业基本情况

(1992年)

地区	单位数(户)	投资者人数(人)	雇工人数(人)	注册资金(万元)	总产值(万元)	营业额(万元)
全省总计	1 730	4 578	34 648	25 079	15 609	12 872
兰州市	797	1 829	15 050	11 929	7 871	7 947
嘉峪关市	31	189	1 116	867	391	39
金昌市	65	133	1 271	948	518	488
白银市	81	155	1 986	1 851	585	130
天水市	182	455	3 341	1 763	1 921	1 774
酒泉地区	53	109	1 150	895	268	90
张掖地区	84	196	1 338	592	925	34
武威地区	70	215	1 710	709	438	504
定西地区	126	488	2 616	1 684	685	1 136
陇南地区	59	268	966	1 121	550	174
平凉地区	50	138	1 153	645	184	68
庆阳地区	48	122	906	710	369	240
临夏回族自治州	71	227	1 864	1 225	877	192
甘南藏族自治州	13	54	181	140	27	56

附1—7 各地区私营工业企业基本情况

(1992年)

地区	单位数(户)	投资者人数(人)	雇工人数(人)	注册资金(万元)	总产值(万元)
全省总计	953	2 424	22 169	12 357	12 864
兰州市	408	1 013	10 130	6 068	7 223
嘉峪关市	12	125	174	385	
金昌市	24	51	747	407	478
白银市	54	106	1 395	1 259	395
天水市	92	195	1 982	760	1 467
酒泉地区	28	73	699	502	199
张掖地区	76	169	1 205	409	925
武威地区	47	182	1 313	155	427
定西地区	64	144	1 500	694	251
陇南地区	26	44	360	313	183
平凉地区	32	80	771	209	144
庆阳地区	36	89	755	394	355
临夏回族自治州	49	144	1 075	789	802
甘南藏族自治州	5	9	63	13	15

附 1—8 各地区私营企业基本情况

(1993 年)

地区	单位数(户)	投资者人数(人)	雇工人数(人)	注册资金(万元)	总产值(万元)	营业额(万元)
全省总计	2 453	6 477	46 022	45 201	41 256	22 936
兰州市	1 073	2 345	18 698	19 636	9 661	14 160
嘉峪关市	36	223	1 247	1 302	1 661	359
金昌市	89	202	1 566	1 058	621	632
白银市	149	325	2 976	4 580	18 491	821
天水市	255	636	4 477	4 378	3 218	2 225
酒泉地区	81	210	1 746	1 797	368	359
张掖地区	103	370	1 702	1 600	977	114
武威地区	126	351	2 373	1 791	795	619
定西地区	154	549	3 551	2 877	1 495	1 378
陇南地区	109	577	1 564	1 977	1 316	1 165
平凉地区	89	194	1 793	1 221	863	509
庆阳地区	90	191	2 077	1 339	721	154
临夏回族自治州	84	251	2 056	1 461	1 017	385
甘南藏族自治州	15	53	196	184	52	56

附 1—9 各地区私营工业企业基本情况

(1993 年)

地区	单位数(户)	投资者人数(人)	雇工人数(人)	注册资金(万元)	总产值(万元)
全省总计	1 245	3 103	27 394	20 015	37 812
兰州市	495	1 027	10 592	7 527	8 958
嘉峪关市	50	165	458	767	1 186
金昌市	29	84	791	352	573
白银市	93	203	2 029	2 583	18 344
天水市	118	253	2 442	1 613	2 900
酒泉地区	33	97	1 004	804	285
张掖地区	83	294	1 480	1 112	948
武威地区	68	263	1 558	909	610
定西地区	78	190	2 117	1 373	1 038
陇南地区	49	114	782	610	726
平凉地区	49	104	1 152	492	617
庆阳地区	64	135	1 686	752	663
临夏回族自治州	60	160	1 215	1 058	927
甘南藏族自治州	6	14	88	63	37

1993年大事记

一月份

4日：省委、省政府在兰州宁卧庄礼堂召开全省农业工作广播电视大会，贯彻落实江泽民总书记和李鹏总理关于农业和农村工作的重要讲话精神及国务院保持农业稳定发展的10项重大措施，部署全省农村工作，确保农村经济持续稳定发展。

6日：在北京举行的中国首届美发美容明星大赛上，甘肃选手雷鸣丽夺得晚宴化妆季军。这是西北五省区参赛选手从大赛中获得的唯一一块奖牌。

7日：中共甘肃省委办公厅、甘肃省人民政府办公厅发布《关于重申严禁用公款吃喝、送礼挥霍浪费的通知》。

甘肃省政协七届一次会议在兰州开幕，省委书记顾金池作重要讲话，申效曾主持会议，朱宣人致开幕词。

8日：甘肃省八届人大第一次会议在兰州隆重开幕，许飞青主持大会，贾志杰省长代表甘肃省人民政府作《政府工作报告》，省计委主任郭琨作《关于甘肃省1992年国民经济和社会发展计划执行情况及1993年国民经济和社会发展计划(草案)的报告》、省财政厅厅长崔正华作《关于甘肃省1992年财政预算执行情况和1993年财政预算(草案)的报告》。

17日：在1993年中国数学奥林匹克暨第八届全国中学生数学冬令营竞赛中，第一次组队参赛的甘肃省代表队获团体第6名，甘肃省是西北地区唯一获得组队参赛资格的省份。中国奥林匹克竞赛主试委员特别授予甘肃省代表队进步奖，这在全国还是第一次。

二月份

4日：1992年盐锅峡化工厂工业总产值突破亿元大关，比上年增长7.2%，创历史最高纪录，销售收入7089万元，利税980万元。

8日：甘肃化工新技术有限公司面向市场，以高、新化工技术为企业服务。1992年，将DPT等3项填补国内空白的专利产品技术转让给全国6个省的生产厂家，所生产的产品已销往美国、日本、德国、西班牙，企业年创汇达160万美元。

10日：甘肃省目前最大的股份制企业——民百股份有限公司亚欧商厦奠基开工。

12日：中央纪委副书记候宗宾在我省调查研究时要求各级纪检、监察机关要适应新形势的要求，解放思想，振奋精神，转变作风，并就新形势下如何搞好纪检、监察工作与省委、省政府、省人大、省政协的领导同志交换了意见。

甘肃省经济体制改革工作会议在兰州召开，会议围绕建立社会主义市场经济体制的改革目标，提出了我省今年改革的总要求，明确了今年改革的主要任务。

14日：甘肃建筑工程总公司，获国家经贸部批准，取得了对外经营权。这是西北地区第一家获准这一权利的建筑企业。是我省建筑业走向世界的一件大事。

19日：郭琨同志在全省物价工作座谈会上代表省政府对我省的价格改革和物价工作讲了重要意见。会议决定了价格改革的重点和原则，一是要继续加快价格形成机制转换，该放的要尽量放开，该管的要认真管好；二是要重点解决铁路、石油、煤炭、电力和粮食的价格矛盾；三是要努力将物价总水平控制在6%左右；四是要进一步建立和完善必要的价格规章制度，以保障价格改革的顺利实施和市场价格机制的健康运行。

22日：省委书记顾金池在河西地区农村调查研究时指出：在全省放开农业种植计划的头一年，各地在发展社会主义市场经济中，更要加强农村工作，夯实农业在国民经济中的基础地位。并强调放开种植计划，有利于调整农业种植结构，有利于增加农民收入，有利于把农民引向市场。同时还要注意研究粮食价格放开以后，如何保护粮农经济利益的问题，制订相应的政策，防止谷贱伤农。

省长阎海旺带领省直有关部门的负责同志，先后来到定西、陇西、通渭、漳县等地检查了各地贯彻中央和省上有关农村工作会议精神的落实情况和春耕生产进展情况，详细考察了定西、文峰、首阳等经济开发区和部分乡镇、个体私营、股份合作制企业，走访了一些农民家庭，参加了定西、通渭县的三级干部会议，并同地区、县乡领导就进一步解放思想、深化改革、加快农村经济发展等问题交换了意见。并强调围绕春耕生产和乡镇企业两件大事下苦功夫。真抓实干，加快全省农村经济的发展。

24日：由兰州高德生命科学研究所研制成功的“丙型肝炎病毒抗体(抗——HCV)酶免疫诊断试剂盒”，正式通过了中国药品生物制品检定所的鉴定，各项指标均符合国家质控标准。该试剂的研制成功，填补了西北地区此项医学诊断试剂的空白。

甘肃省维护社会治安见义勇为奖励基金会在兰州成立，必将对维护我省治安秩序起到积极的推动作用。

26日：省委书记顾金池、省长阎海旺出席在兰州召开的省直和中央在兰单位房改实施动员大会并分别作了讲话。顾书记着重对加强房改中的思想工作和领导问题作了讲话。阎省长就如何搞好房改工作指出：一是要正确认识和处理好房改与建设社会主义市场经济体制的关系；二是要处理好长远利益和眼前利益的关系；三是正确认识和处理好提租补贴与其它房改政策的关系；四是要正确处理好房改起步和实现房改阶段目标的关系。

27日：省政府在兰州隆重召开全省乡镇企业家表彰大会，对来自全省各地的326名乡镇企业厂长(经理)，授予“甘肃省乡镇企业家”称号。其中，55名乡镇企业厂长(经理)被授予“甘肃省优秀乡镇企业家”称号。省委书记顾金池、省长阎海旺作了重要讲话。顾书记强调：各级领导、乡镇企业家和广大干部群众要统一思想，振奋精神，真抓实干，在提高经济效益的前提下，实现乡镇企业总产值在1992年的基础上，3年翻一番，5年翻两番的奋斗目标。阎省长指出，要千方百计创造人才脱颖而出的环境和条件，组织和动员成千上万的人才，到乡镇企业主战场施展才华，大显身手。

三月份

1日：省委在兰州宁卧庄礼堂举行第二期农村社教总结表彰大会。省长阎海旺主持会议，省委书记顾金池到会作了重要讲话。会上，表彰了96个先进单位和206名优秀工作队员，并向他们颁发了奖牌和荣誉证书。

3日：全省宣传部长会议在兰州召开，来自全省各地、州、市、省直宣教系统、企业、高等院校及部队的150多人出席了会议。会议由省人大常委会副主任、省委宣传部长姚文仓主持，省委书记顾金池作重要讲话，并强调指出：用建设有中国特色社会主义理论武装广大党员、干部和群众，是宣传思想战线的根本任务。

4日：靖远县中堡化工塑料厂与兰州塑料厂共同投资引进中美合资全新设备，生产出橡胶软管的替代产品PVC涂塑软管，填补了省内空白。据省有关部门检测，各项技术指标均达到或超过国家标准。

中科院兰州分院13名青年科技人员破格晋升，在中国科学院高级专业技术职务特批中，兰州分院有13名青年科技人员晋升为副研究员、研究员，占全部特批人员的1/10。其中两名年轻的助理研究员，被破格晋升为研究员。

省委、省政府、省军区在宁卧庄大礼堂隆重召开甘肃省学雷锋活动30周年纪念大会.陈绮玲副省长主持了大会，省委副书记孙英作了讲话，省军区副政委杜华在会上宣读了《中共甘肃省委、甘肃省人民政府、甘肃省军区关于表彰全省学雷锋活动先进集体和先进个人的决定》。

6日：中科院兰州沙漠所开辟中国沙漠第四纪地质研究新领域，使中国沙漠第四纪研究进入了一个定量的有年代标尺的新时期，从反映一般区域环境状况进入反映全球气候变化的新阶段，这表明我国该学科研究已经赶上和领先国际水平。

11日：由省政府批准发布施行的《甘肃省全民所有制工业企业转换经营机制实施办法》正式出台。在全省广播电视动员大会上，省委副书记孙英、副省长张吾乐分别在会上作了动员讲话。省委、省政府要求全省各有关方面立即行动起来，全面贯彻落实《条例》和我省制定的《实施办法》，进一步加快企业转换经营机制的步伐，推动建立社会主义市场经济体制的进程，促使我省经济发展既快又好地登上新台阶。

四月份

1日：甘肃省城乡放开粮食销价，取消城镇居民、经牧民、菜农的口粮和农村返销粮平价供应，价格随行就市，使实行了40年的粮食“统购统销”政策宣告结束。

兰州至乌鲁木齐开往哈萨克斯坦共和国首都阿拉木图的直通国际旅客列车驶出兰州站。至此，我省结束了没有对外开行国际列车的历史。

7日：在兰州召开的甘肃首次区调工作会议透露，省地矿局通过区调工作在我省新发现矿点63处，矿化点48处，各类异常619处。已形成矿床的有两座中型金矿以及大量有工作价值的煤、高铝原料、芒硝、白云岩、石墨及其他金属、非金属矿点。

10日：甘肃(香港)经贸洽谈会在香港展览中心大厦圆满结束，签约、成交总额达13.5亿美元，其中，签订项目合同67个，合同总金额8.1亿美元(外资额5.4亿美元)；签订项目协议37个，总金额3.4亿美元；进出口贸易成交总值1.6亿美元；签科技项目20个，总金额3211万元。

12日：在一年一度的全国29家重点涂料生产企业年度管理总结评比中，西北油漆厂17项经济、技术、管理指标总分名列第一，再次获得该项评比的第一名。这是该厂继“三连冠”之后又一次获得这项殊荣。

16日：当代地球化学研究中新兴的前沿学科——稀有气体同位素地球化学研究，经中科院兰州地质所的科研人员多年潜心研究，获得一系列重要成果，不仅填补了这一领域的一些空白，有些成果已处于国际同类研究的先进水平。

17日：由香港金海湾投资有限公司独资开发的兰州中港城，在兰州通过了规划设计评审，项目工程共分3期，将连片开发位于兰州市郑家庄一块21.45公顷(约322亩)的空地，这是迄今为止境外客商在我省最大的连片开发房地产项目。

18日：省委、省政府在白银召开全省双带整推现场会议。会议强调了在实施双带整推中突出要抓的几点：一是突出抓好“一厂两制”和城市集体经济的发展；二是大力促进乡镇企业的发展；三是大力促进第三产业和个体、私营经济的发展；四是要大力促进股份合作经济和“三资”企业的发展；五是加快小区建设的发展；六是大力发展高产、优质、高效农业。会议由省委副书记孙英主持，省委书记顾金池、省长阎海旺分别作了重要讲话。

20日：中科院兰州近物所“新核素合成和研究”重大项目科研组，在世界上首次全成了汞——208和铪——185两个新核素，与中科院上海原子核研究所合成的新核素铂——202一起，实现了我国在新核素合成领域零的突破，把五星红旗插在了核素图上。这项重大成果被评为全国十大科技成就之一，张立、袁双贵等科研人员受到各级组织的表彰奖励。

23日：国家科委在兰州隆重举行国家高新技术产业开发区授牌仪式，正式授予兰州高新技术产业开发区“国家高新技术产业开发区”铜牌。省上领导顾金池、阎海旺、卢克俭、孙英、李虎林、陈绮玲出席了授牌仪式。

26日：省长阎海旺、副省长陈绮玲在兰州宁卧庄宾馆亲切会见了前来我省参观考察的联合国人口基金会等援助甘肃项目考察团一行。考察联合国人口基金会援助我省的妇女参与发展项目、妇幼保健项目和计划生育基层工作人员培训项目。

五月份

1日：亚洲最大的镍闪速熔炼系统投产典礼在金川公司隆重举行。金川二期闪速熔炼系统的投产，标志着我国镍冶炼技术已进入八十年代国际先进水平。

2日：经甘肃省人民政府批准，对社会集团单位购买国家规定的专控商品恢复征收专控商品附加费，征收比例为5%——20%。

7日：一场罕见的特大沙尘风暴席卷了武威、古浪、民勤、金昌、景泰造成人员伤亡，农作物、树木、农电设施损失严重，工农业生产特别是农业生产损失惨重。

12日：甘肃太阳电照明基金会成立暨中美太阳电照明合作项目签字仪式在兰州龙首山庄举行。美国太阳电照明基金会将为此项目提供75%的经费。

19日：在北京召开的表彰全国质量效益型先进企业大会上，兰州钢铁集团公司榜上有名，领取了荣誉证书和奖牌。这次由国家技术监督局、中国质量管理协会联合表彰的单位共有110家，兰州钢铁集团公司是我省唯一一家获奖单位。

20日：兰州重离子加速器国家实验室学术委员会年会在兰州召开，兰州重离子加速器经过一万多小时正常运行，其主要束流指标达到国际先进水平，这标志着我国在中、低能重离子物理前沿领域的研究中有了一个国际水平的研究基地和先进设施。

23日：我国首家引进的万吨级高档钛白粉生产厂在甘肃酒泉的中国核工业总公司四O四厂建成投产，一次性生产成功，并已产出A——103型钛白粉，产品质量达到引进合同规定的指标。它的建成可大大扭转我国高档钛白粉长期依靠进口的局面。

27日：省委、省政府办公厅联合发出通知，要求各地切实纠正和制止用公款出国(境)旅游的问题。纪检、监察机关和财政、审计等部门要加强检查和监督。

六月份

2日：甘肃省邮电部门利用西班牙政府混合贷款引进程控交换设备10万门及长途自动交换、传输设备，在金昌、嘉峪关等地开始实施。

7日：由中国惠侨银行筹委会参资入股5亿美元，同兰州水电开发总公司联合建设黄河柴家峡水电站及连海铝业股份有限公司等项目的合同签字仪式在省城友谊饭店举行。美国文特尔国际投资集团、中国惠侨银行中方资金股东代表和李虎林、路明、柯茂盛等参加签字仪式。这也是我省迄今引进资金数额最大的联合开发项目。

16日：'93中国北京国际穆斯林经贸洽谈会开幕3天，我省代表团35个企业已同沙特、阿联酋、叙利亚、巴基斯坦、马来西亚、印度尼西亚、澳大利亚等国家的客商达成意向性协议11项，涉及机械、电子、纺织品、皮革、珠宝、地毯、工艺品、肉类、糖类、食品、房地产等方面。

17日：由我国现代清洗业的龙头企业中国蓝星化学清洗总公司建设的首期年产5000吨工业与民用清洗剂项目破土动工，计划完成后，将使兰州成为我国新型清洗剂生产基地。

18日：兰州证券交易厅正式开业，试运营两月成交突破4000万元。

19日：中共中央总书记、国家主席江泽民在西安主持西北五省(区)经济工作座谈会。研究进一步深化改革，扩大开放，促进西北经济发展问题，他强调指出：发展西北地区的经济，既要解放思想、抓住机遇、加快发展，又要实事求是、因地制宜、量力而行，争取有效益的发展速度。

20日：从中国五矿化工进出口商会硅铁分会成立大会上获悉：我省已成为国内最大的硅铁生产和出口基地。1992年共出口硅铁2.2万吨，创汇金额达到1000多万美元。

24日：省委书记顾金池、省长阎海旺和副省长张吾乐、崔正华召集省人行、工行、农行、省财政厅、省粮食局、计委、经贸委等部门负责人，专题研究、部署我省夏粮及农副产品收购资金工作，确保夏粮收购，努力实现不给农民打"白条"。

27日：在'93国际名酒(香港)博览会上，甘肃黄河啤酒厂的荣誉产品兰乐牌黄河啤酒一举夺得金奖，实现了甘肃啤酒业在国际性评比中"零"的突破。

28日：省科学院生物研究所与陇西酒精厂携手攻关，完成100立方米罐固定化酵母细胞淀粉质原料酒精发酵的工业大生产试验，实现了我国酒精工业中的一次"革命"。这一成果表明，在运用细胞固定化技术改造传统酒精发酵工艺方面，我省已处在先进水平。

七月份

1日：《兰州日报》正式创刊，为我省新闻战线又添一支新军。

4日：在兰州举行了同中国银行甘肃分行利用法国政府混合贷款8919万法国法郎转贷签字仪式，用于金昌化工总厂12万吨磷二铵扩建工程及技术、主要生产设备的引进。

8日：在北京召开的第六届国际冻土会议上，我国著名冻土学家、中国科学院兰州冰川冻土研究所所长、研究员程国栋当选为第七届国际冻土协会主席。

9日：中科院兰州近物所"新核素合成和研究"项目组，成功地合成和鉴别出重丰中子新核素钍——237。这是该所继去年合成并鉴别出汞——208和铪——185两个新核素以来，在世界上首次合成与鉴别的第三种新核素。这一成果把我国在原子核质量数大于170重质量丰中子区新核素的合成和研究又向前推进了一步，跨入难度更大的所谓"可裂变核区"，这一研究填补了核素图上的又一个空白。

12日：甘肃选手李彦新力拨男子1000米单人皮艇头筹，为我省捧回首枚金牌，从而也成为第一个在全国大型综合运动会水上项目中占有一席之地的西北人。

23日：甘肃有线电视台筹建顺利，试播成功。它标志着我省广播电视事业跨进一个新的发展阶段。

28日：我国第一台100吨全液压伸缩臂铁道救援起重机在兰州机车厂通过国家级技术鉴定。它的诞生，标志着我国在大型铁道救援设备的研制方面处于世界先进水平。

30日：酒泉钢铁公司丝绳厂暨酒港钢绳有限公司全面投产。随着第一根合格的6×19－15.5mm钢丝绳顺利诞生。我省不能生产钢丝绳的历史从此结束。

八月份

2日：我国第一条横跨黄河的索道——白塔山黄河索道奠基仪式在兰州滨河路隆重举行。该索道为单线脉动循环吊箱式，单向运输量每小时可达500人。

5日：以甘肃省委书记顾金池为首的中国共产党代表团访问了以色列，双方就双边关系和共同关心的国际问题交换了意见。

8日：电力部西北勘测设计研究院跻身全国勘测设计单位综合实力百强，名列第34位。这是由建设部、国家统计局、中国企业综合实力评估中心联合评估的。

11日：兰州平板玻璃厂跨省兼并青海乐都县平板玻璃厂取得成功。目前，兰州平板玻璃厂乐都分厂已恢复生产4个月，实现销售收入750万元，实现利税223万元，成为青海省乐都县的创利大户。

14日：省机械科学研究院继研制成功世界先进水平的蒙耐尔合金后，最近又研制成功ZA——27锌基合金，其铸造工艺性能优于美国1988年的标准要求，是国际上新型锌基合金中综合性能最好的一种，为使这一成果尽快得以推广应用，国家科委已将其列入国家的"火炬计划"。

18日：集经贸活动文艺演出旅游为一体的"93兰州丝绸之路经贸洽谈交易会"隆重开幕，以"8会1街"为主要内容的经贸活动已全部落实，30多场专业、业余文艺演出和省内7条专线及兰州市内景点的旅游观光活动也已全部就绪，已有5000多名宾客前来参加"兰交会"，东道主兰州市经过这次盛会的检验，也将会登上一个新台阶，树立起一个新的形象。

23日：以"友谊、开放、发展"为宗旨的"93兰州丝绸之路经贸洽谈交易会在取得丰硕成果后圆满结束。仅工业产品展销销售额达到29274.7万元，与外商正式签订合同10多个，总投资额达1024万美元。

26日：以国家民委副主任图道多吉为团长的国务院祝贺团，以顾金池为团长的甘肃省祝贺团和来自省内外兄弟州地市共40多个祝贺团参加了甘南藏族自治州成立40周年庆祝大会。

九月份

3日：中国蓝星化学清洗总公司加紧实施跨国经营战略，在对外合作方面取得了新的进展。蓝星总公司与澳大利亚梅姆泰克公司正式签订协议,合资成立中澳梅姆泰克水处理公司。这是蓝星总公司今年以来与外方合资成立的第 8 个合资企业。与乌克兰合资组建的蓝星顿涅茨克清洗装备有限公司,引进乌克兰的空气爆破清洗尖端技术,使蓝星总公司成为目前世界上掌握清洗技术最为全面的清洗企业集团。

8 日:兰州区域气象中心正式成立,这是全国继北京、上海、广州、武汉区域气象中心之后建成的第 5 个区域气象中心,它的成立,标志着我省气象现代化水平迈上了一个新的台阶,它将为推动我省和西北地区气象事业的进一步发展起到积极作用。

标志着金川有色金属公司跻身于世界大型现代化综合企业的'93 镍钴国际学术会议,在中国镍都金川召开。来自英国、日本、印度、芬兰、加拿大、俄罗斯、澳大利亚、香港等地的多 190 位专家、学者参加了会议。

9 日:我国核分析领域一项重大研究成果,可活化碳——13 示踪技术在兰州建立。这一成果将为新兴学科和技术,特别是生命科学研究提供了理论依据和实验手段,并将使人体研究跨入一个新的时期,核素示踪技术被认为是显微镜发明以来生物学、医学科学史上的重大成就之一。

12 日:我省夏粮获大丰收,创夏粮产量新纪录。总产达 47.5 亿公斤,比去年增产 9.48 亿公斤,增长 24.9%,创历史最高水平。

13 日:宋平同志来我省调查研究,与省、地、县领导共同商讨甘肃发展与建设大计,勉励干部、群众解放思想、实事求是,艰苦奋斗,加快经济发展和各项建设步伐。

14 日:由世界粮食计划署(WFP)无偿援助的甘肃省景泰川农业灌溉发展项目实施良好,该署聘请联合国粮农组织田间工程专家齐尔斯特拉先生等,实地考察后,给予很高评价。项目全部完成后,将从根本上改善景泰、古浪两县农业生产条件。

15 日:受国家对外贸易经济合作部委托,省治沙研究所为发展中国家在武威举办了一期“国际沙漠治理技术推广培训班”。来自叙利亚、沙特阿拉伯、埃及等 6 个国家的学员参加了这期培训班。

19 日:西北五省区党政主要领导联席会议第一次会议在乌鲁木齐市举行。陕西、甘肃、宁夏、青海、新疆五省区党政主要领导出席了会议。这次会议的中心议题是贯彻落实江泽民同志在西北五省区经济工作座谈会的讲话精神、共商西北地区加强区域联合协作,扩大对外开放,促进经济共同发展的问题。

20 日:甘肃证券公司同白银有色公贸股份有限公司在兰州签订企业内部股权证实行集中托管协议书。工业股份制企业内部股权证实行集中托管,这在我省尚属首家。

21 日:一项由国外投资并由外商负责招标的我国南海东部石油开发项目——惠州海上平台工程 HZ32——2/3 项目经过公开的国际招标,兰石所在共有 7 家投标者参加,其中美国、意大利、新加坡投标公司占 6 家的情况下,经过激烈的竞争,脱颖而出,一举中标。成为这一项目设计、制造、安装、调试的总承包单位。惠州海上平台项目是由美国和意大利 3 家公司组成的一个 ACT-OG 作业集团在国际上进行招标的工程项目之一。兰石所作为唯一的该项目国内投标单位,在这次国际投标中依靠自已多年从事陆地和海上油气水装备技术开发的业绩,通过了一道道难关,在国际竞争中获胜,成为总承包单位。

29 日:继人口普查和工业普查之后的又一次重大全国性社会调查工作——第三产业普查工作拉开序幕。全省第三产业普查动员会根据国务院的要求,对我省第三产业普查工作进行了安排和布署。这次普查工作的任务和目的是:摸清全省第三产业的底数、掌握现状,通过对普查统计数据资料的分析,找出第三产业在发展中存在的问题,提出相应的对策建议。为政府制定产业政策、就业政策、教育政策、分配政策以及其它各项政策提供依据。

十月份

4 日:省财政厅和省教委发出紧急通知,决定由省财政从专项补助费中划拨 1623 万元,由各地负责务必全部兑现拖欠教师的工资。这是我省落实中央有关精神,为教育办实事的一项措施。省财政厅、省教委在通知中要求各地专款专用、严禁截留,杜绝挪用,如有违犯,追究责任。

7 日:在中共甘肃省委书记顾金池带领下副省长郭琨,省委常委、兰州市委书记李虎林等一行 22 人,赴新疆进行了历时 13 天的学习考察。产生了西北地区经济发展史上的一个历史性文献《西北五省区党政主要领导联席会议第一次会议纪要》。会议向西北地区的广大干部群众发出了“共建国际大通道,联合起来走西口,加快经济发展”的号召,揭开了西北地区经济发展新的一页。

8 日:我国在酒泉卫星发射中心成功地发射了一颗科学探测与技术实验卫星。这次发射使用的是我国自行研制的“长征二号丙”运载火箭。

10 日:中科院学部委员、兰州冰川冻土所名誉所长施雅风教授获英国皇家地质学会名誉会员称号,这表明国际地质界对施雅风教授在人类地质研究方面的突出贡献的肯定,也标志着我国冰川冻土科学研究已跻身世界先进行列。

12日：我省又一个国际合作项目——中国粮农统计中心兰州分中心在兰州市城关区雁滩乡滩尖村隆重举行奠基仪式。中国粮农统计项目是意大利政府、联合国粮农组织、中国政府的一个多边合作项目，其中心的任务是，通过建立中国粮食及农业统计中心、各分中心，大规模培训农村统计人员，进行农业普查试点，将为开展农业普查作全面的组织和技术条件准备，最终将在中国建立常规性的农业普查制度，并参加联合国粮农组织统一规划的10年一次的世界农业普查。

20日：10年前就列入省城城市建设总体规划的兰州市东方红广场地下工程破土动工。该工程是一项合理利用地下空间的、平战结合的大型工程。其规划方案由清华大学建筑学院设计。工程总建筑面积约3万多平方米，大部分为地下一层、局部二层建筑，计划设商业网点，自动扶梯、瀑布水幕、彩电音乐喷泉和可停放100多车辆汽车，1000辆自行车的地下停车场。并安排有现代化的空气调节、报警消防和照明系统。承担工程建设任务的是兰州兴陇房地产开发有限公司。

21日：从在兰州召开的省直机关清理纠正乱收费工作汇报会上获悉，省公安厅等8个省直单位宣布取消85项不合理收费项目，兰州铁路局取消46项不合理收费项目。

28日：甘肃条山酒厂生产的52度条山玉液荣获布鲁塞尔1993年第31届世界名酒评比最高金奖。52度条山玉液还分获国际名酒联合会香港博览会金奖和香港国际食品博览会金奖。45度条山大曲也荣获香港国际食品博览会金奖。条山玉液在比利时荣获布鲁塞尔世界名酒评比最高金奖。这在我省酿酒行业还属首家。

30日：第七十四届广州交易会降下帷幕。甘肃交易团出口成交额达7000多万美元，同33个国家和地区签订了429份合同，成交商品包括32个大类、152个品种。

十一月份

3日：路明副省长与世界银行预评估团团长伏格洛先生，就马莲河流域水土保持项目甘肃分项目贷款等问题进行了会谈。马莲河流域水土保持项目是世界银行中国黄土高原水土保持项目的一部分，项目可行性研究报告通过了世行预评估。世行为马莲河项目拟贷款1.5亿美元，其中我省分项目4000万美元。

13日：省政府召开全省清理整顿乡镇煤矿工作会议，对开展此项工作进行了安排布署。郭琨副省长在会上作了动员讲话，方针是保护国有，扶持乡镇，限制村办，改造和取缔个体。

14日：省财政厅、省物价委员会发出《关于公布全省第一批取消的收费项目的通知》。报经省人民政府批准同意，现将第一批予以取消的80个收费项目发出通知，并向社会公布实行。

16日：兰州石油化工机器总厂在国际市场的竞争能力逐年增强，又在海上油田开发项目的国际招标中中标。

22日：中国唯一的通过冰雪研究环境的国家级开放实验室——“冰芯实验室”，已由中国科学院批准在兰州冰川冻土研究所兴建，著名科学家秦大河任实验室主任。

27日：省政府授权省财政厅、省物委公布第二批取消49项收费项目向社会公布.

28日：由省科委、省经贸委、省农委、省社科联联合主办的“抓联促转科技万里行”从兰州隆重出发。这次活动将历时10个月，行程万里，把先进适用的科技成果大规模向广大农村、企业转让、推广，以加快全省科技进步与经济建设的步伐。

十二月份

3日：一种通用型汉卡“万通38汉卡”由兰州春风电脑工程公司研制成功。这一国内独创的成果，将结束国内几十种汉卡相互隔绝不能通用的局面，使计算机用户避免了对价格昂贵的汉卡的重复购置，推动我国电脑的迅速普及。

4日：我国科学工作者在我省天水和陇南地区，首次发现了泥盆系与浊流有关的深海相遗迹化石20个属。为在这个地区预测金矿提供了有力的理论科学依据，丰富了世界痕迹学的内容。

7日：窑街矿物局海石湾矿井经国务院正式批准开工，是我省目前最大的大型矿井建设项目。

18日：经省人民政府批准，兰州陆运口岸正式开放。重点承担我省直接向香港、阿拉木图出口及开津、上海、黄浦、丹东、满洲里、阿拉山口等口岸转关出口的联检业务。

19日：中国共产党甘肃省第八次代表大会在省政府礼堂隆重开幕。张吾乐宣布大会开幕，阎海旺作题为《大力发展社会主义市场经济，为实现第二步战略目标努力奋斗》的报告。通过了关于七届省委报告的决议，省顾问委员会工作报告的决议，省纪律检查委员会工作报告的决议。选举产生了第八届省委和新一届省纪委。

28日：我省最大的年产1万吨农用塑料薄膜生产装置在兰州化学工业公司宏达公司建成投产，标志着我省农膜生产又上了一个新台阶，将对我省农业生产发挥进一步的推动作用。

29日：现任中科院兰州冰川冻土研究所所长、我省著名冻土学家程国栋研究员当选为中国科学院学部委员。

结束语

《甘肃年鉴》的编辑出版无疑是全省年鉴，地方志出版史上的一个里程碑，在全面反映甘肃省情，综合经济发展状况及行业、部门、企业微观经济和政府机关工作业绩等宏观政治导向方针方面也是富有开拓与创造的举动。在当前“让甘肃走向世界，让世界了解甘肃”的形势下具有很好的宣传效益和深远的社会历史效益。

省政府主持下首次出版的《甘肃年鉴》集往年的统计年鉴、行业年鉴、及地方志的特点为一书，首先是符合当前进一步改革、开放的形势，宣传党的政治经济指导方针，宣传行业领导的改革思想和主张，宣传甘肃省发展成就；其次是融政治、军事、法律、经济、社会为一体，宏观和微观为一体，具有往年无法比拟的广度、深度和综合性；再则是以统计系统的法定数字为基础，具有很强的真实性和可靠性，成为各级领导决策的依据，成为甘肃省的“窗口”。

每种新事物从产生到独树一帜都需要一个不断完善的过程，我们出版的这本书也是如此。所以，应始终遵循几个原则，一是遵循坚持以党的方针政策为指针，顺应改革形势的原则，准确反映浪头潮尖的重大改革政策，措施；二是遵循要办出地方特色和书本个体特色的原则，在内容上采用高、精、实的文章，在统计资料上扩充微观数据；三是遵循实事求是的原则，不仅要反映成绩，也要反映矛盾、困难；四是遵循不断开拓创新的原则，使《甘肃年鉴》一年比一年办得好。

《甘肃年鉴》应时应运而生，她将随着甘肃经济的不断发展而日臻完善，同时，她也将随着世界、全国、全省更多的人了解和帮助而独具风流，甘肃在走向世界，《甘肃年鉴》也将如此。

甘肃省政府副省长：郭琨

一九九四年七月

CONCLUDING REMARKS

The editing and publishing of GANSU YEARBOOK is undoubtedly amilestone in Gansu publishing history of yearbooks and local chronicles ,also is a opening and creative act in reflecting Gansu condition, synthetic economic development condition, trade , department andenterperise microcosmic economy, the government work achievement andmacroscopic political lead policy. Now it has a good propaganda benefitand profoud social historic benefit under the situation of LettingGansu move towards the world and letting the owrld understand Gansu.

GANSU YEARBOOK for the first publishing directed by Gansu Governmentis a book with the characteristics of the former statistical yearbooks, trade yearbooks and local chronicles together. First it accords withthe situation of further reform and open, propagates the party's political econonic lead policy, propagates the reform thought and standof trade leading, propagates Gansu development achievements, then mixespolitics, military affaixs, law, economy and society , together, mixesmicrocosmic and macroscopic together, and has the in comparable range, quality and synthetics than before, at last on the basis of thestatistical system's authoritative numbers, it has very strongtruthfulness and reliability, becomes the basis of leaders' decision atall levels, becomes the "window" of Gansu province.

Each new thing needs a continuously perfect course from energing toflying its owm colours, so is Gansu Yearbook. It follows sevealprinciples from beginning to end. The first principle is to followholding the Party's policy as pointer, going with the reform situation, exactly reflecting the important reform policy and measure in keymoment. The second principle is to follow the local characteristics andits individual characteristics, adopting high, essence, top, trutharticles fin the contents, enlarging miscrocosmic data in thestatsdtical materials. The third is following the practical andrealistic principle, it reflects not only achievements, but alsocontradictions and difficulties. The fourth is following the principleof continuously opening and blazing new trails and making GansuYearsbook betler and better.

GANSU YEARBOOK emerges at the temes require, it will be more ferfectday by day with the continuous development of Gansu economy, while itwill fly its own colours with the understanding and helping of morepeople in the world, China and Gansu province. Gansu province is goingtowards the world. So will be GANSU YEARBOOK.

Kuo Kuen

July, 1994.

中国统计出版社最新统计资料书简目

◆全国系列统计资料◆

《中国统计年鉴—1993》
《中国统计摘要—1994》
《中国农村统计年鉴—1994》
《中国工业经济统计年鉴—1993》
《中国市场统计年鉴—1993》
《中国生产资料市场统计年鉴—1993》
《中国经济科学年鉴—1993》
《中国社会统计资料—1993》
《国际经济和社会统计提要—1993》
《93′中国发展报告》
《全国主要社会经济指标排序年鉴—1993》
《环渤海:东北亚的黄金地带》

◆地方系列统计资料◆

《北京统计年鉴—1994》
《天津统计年鉴—1994》
《河北经济统计年鉴—1994》
《山西统计年鉴--1994》
《内蒙古统计年鉴—1994》
《辽宁年鉴—1994》
《辽宁统计年鉴—1994》
《吉林统计年鉴—1994》
《黑龙江经济统计年鉴—1994》
《上海统计年鉴—1994》
《江苏统计年鉴—1994》
《浙江统计年鉴—1994》
《安徽统计年鉴—1994》
《福建统计年鉴—1994》
《江西统计年鉴—1994》
《山东统计年鉴—1994》
《河南统计年鉴—1994》
《湖北统计年鉴—1994》
《湖南统计年鉴—1994》
《广东统计年鉴—1994》
《广西统计年鉴—1994》
《海南统计年鉴—1994》
《四川统计年鉴—1994》
《贵州统计年鉴—1994》
《云南统计年鉴—1994》
《西藏统计年鉴—1994》
《陕西统计年鉴—1994》
《西安统计年鉴—1994》
《甘肃年鉴—1994》
《青海统计年鉴—1994》
《宁夏统计年鉴—1994》
《新疆统计年鉴—1994》
《唐山统计年鉴—1994》
《张家口社会经济统计年鉴—1994》
《呼和浩特统计年鉴—1994》
《沈阳年鉴—1994》
《阜新统计年鉴—1994》
《长春经济统计年鉴—1994》
《延吉统计年鉴—1994》
《龙井社会经济统计年鉴—1994》
《哈尔滨统计年鉴—1994》
《齐齐哈尔经济统计年鉴—1994》
《双鸭山经济统计年鉴—1994》
《建三江农垦统计年鉴—1994》
《黑龙江垦区统计年鉴—1994》
《苏州统计年鉴—1994》
《无锡统计年鉴—1994》
《常州统计年鉴—1994》
《福州统计年鉴—1994》
《厦门经济特区年鉴—1994》
《九江统计年鉴—1994》
《济南统计年鉴—1994》
《青岛统计年鉴—1994》
《潍坊统计年鉴—1994》
《东营统计年鉴—1994》
《三门峡统计年鉴—1994》
《洛阳统计年鉴—1994》
《周口地区统计年鉴—1994》
《平顶山统计年鉴—1994》
《漯河统计年鉴—1994》
《衡阳社会经济统计年鉴—1994》
《广州统计年鉴—1994》
《深圳统计年鉴—1994》
《桂林社会经济统计年鉴—1994》
《柳州统计年鉴—1994》
《重庆统计年鉴—1994》
《西安统计年鉴—1994》
《天水统计年鉴—1994》
《吐鲁番统计年鉴—1994》
《奎屯统计年鉴—1994》
《新疆生产建设兵团统计年鉴—1994》
《巴音郭楞统计年鉴—1994》

酒泉鋼鐵公司

簡介

酒泉鋼鉄公司位于萬里長城西端的嘉峪關市，是西北地區規模最大的鋼鉄聯合企業，擁有職工 3.5 萬余人，現已形成年產鉄礦石 500 萬噸、生鉄 120 萬噸、鋼 60 萬噸、材 45 萬噸的生產規模。主要產品有生鉄、鋼錠(坯)、綫材、鋼絲繩及化工產品等 40 余種，均按國家標準和國際標準組織生產，產品輻射全國，并遠銷美國、日本、港澳和東南亞地區。還兼營工業、民用建築施工安裝和機電、內燃設備修理，以及商業和進出口貿易等。

目前，酒鋼公司正投資 20 多億元進行以中厚板軋鋼工程為主的改擴建工程，以進一步優化產品結構。到 1997 年可形成鋼、材雙 百萬噸的規模，將為西北經濟建設和國家鋼鉄工業作出更大的貢獻。

地址：甘肅省嘉峪關市雄關東路 12 號
郵編：735100
電話：09477—713294，222844
電掛：3932
電傳：72126 JQISC CN
傳真：09477—226872
經理：齊茂忠

JIUQUAN IRON AND STEEL COMPANY

The company, lying in Jiayuguan City to the west of the Great Wall, is the largest scaleiron and steel integrated complex in the Northwest area with over 35 thousand staff and workers. It has now formed the productive scale of the annual capacity of 5 million tons iron ore, 1.2million tons pig iron, 600 thousand tons steel, 450 thousand tons product. The main productshave over 40 kinds, such as pig iron, steel ingot, wirerod, steel cable and chemical products. which are produced by the national and international standard. The products are selling wellthroughout the country. and exported to the United States, Japan, Xianggang, Aomen, and theSoutheast areas. It also manages industrial and civil building construction installation, machine, internal–combustion equipments repaired, commerce, import and export trade, etc.

Now, the company is investing over 20 hundred million yuan to rebuild the project ofregarding the medium–thick board steel rolling as the main project in order to improve productconstruction. By 1997 it will form the scale of a million tons of iron and products. and willmake a greater contribution to the Northwest economic construction and the state iron and steelindustry.

①省優產品煉鋼生鉄、鑄造生鉄
②部優產品普通低碳鋼無扭控冷熱軋盤條，實物質量達到國際先進水平
③省優產品焦化苯、焦化甲苯、焦化二甲苯
④省優產品 150× 150mm 連鑄方坯
⑤省優產品冶金焦
⑥進口高速無扭控冷軋機，年產 40 萬噸

① The provincial excellent products ·· steelmaking pig iron, casting pig iron.
② The ministry excellent product ·· cold and heat rolling coil bar of ordinary low carbonsteel without button running. The material volume reaches the international advanced level.
③ The provical excellent products ·· coking benzol, coking toluene, coking Z toluene.
④ The provicial excellent product ·· 150× 150mm continuous casting square base.
⑤ The provincial excellent product ·· metallurgy coke
⑥ The import cold–rolling mill of high speed without button running, the annual productioncapacity is 400 thousand tons.

Add: No.12 Xiongguan East Road, Jiayuguan, Gansu.
Post Code: 735100
Tel: 09477–713294, 222844
Manager: Qi Mao Zhong

JIUQUAN IRON AND STEEL COMPANY

甘肅涼州皇臺酒廠

中國·甘肅涼州皇臺酒廠、甘肅涼州皇臺集團公司董事長：張景發1993年5月18日在北京"經濟聯合，產銷銜接"會上做報告。

簡介

甘肅涼州皇臺酒廠現有職工1800多人，占地面積53.4萬平方米，總建築面積22.65萬平方米，生產規模居全國酒類同行業第五位。

自1988年5月正式驗收投產至1993年10月底，全廠完成產量16122.2噸，完成產值7504.8萬元，上交稅金3434萬元，歸還貸款1835萬元，實現利潤168.1萬元，累計給國家貢獻6973.1萬元，等于賺回建廠初期的四個涼州皇臺酒廠，并先後榮獲國內外各種殊榮68項（其中國際性的5項，國家級的20項）。

經過8年的艱苦創業，1993年甘肅涼州皇臺酒廠進入中國企業最大市場占有份額，最佳經濟效益五百強之一，一百個優勝企業之一。1993年8月，又榮獲國家輕工總會、國家人事部命名的全國輕紡系統先進集體稱號。

1992年8月12日，江澤民總書記到武威視察，看了我廠拳頭產品涼州皇臺酒後說："涼州皇臺酒我知道，很不錯"；李鉄映、田紀雲、彭冲、李錫銘、王光英、王丙乾、趙補初等領導同志分別為酒廠題了"涼州雄風"、"皇臺美酒"、"中國名酒香飄九洲四海"、"南有茅臺、北有皇臺"、"香醇般若湯"、"中國名酒涼州皇臺"等題詞；省委書記顧金池視察酒廠時提出："以酒文化帶動武威經濟的發展"，題了"保銀牌，奪金牌，更上一層樓"等題詞，并說："奔馬已經站起來了，需要騰飛"。

地址：甘肅省武威市新建路55號
電話：0935·212830 213710
傳真：212830
郵編：733000
電掛：6974

GANSU LIANGZHOU HUANGTAI WINERY

The winery has over 1800 staff and workers, 53.4 thousand m2 area, 22. 65 thousand m2building area. Its productive scale is the 5th of China wine trade.

From May, 1988 of formal acceptance and production to the end of Oct, 1993, the winerycompleted 16122.2 tons of output, 75048 million yuan of output value, 34.34 million yuan of taxturned over to the state, 18.35 million yuan of returned loan, 1.681 million yuan of realizedprofit, 69.731 million yuan of contributed to the state, equaling 4 Liangzhou Huangtai Winerybuilt in the early days. The winery has won 68 special honour prize both of home and overseas.

After 8 years' hard work, the winery entered into one of 500 strong best economy benefit, one of 100 superior enetrprises in China enterprise markets in 1993. In Aug. 1993, the winerywon the advanced group title of the State Light Industry Society and the State Personal Ministry.

On Aug 12, 1992, General Secretary Jiang Ze Min visited Wuwei and saw Liangzhou HuangtaiWine, then "I know Liangzhou Huangtai Wine, it's good". The leaders of Li Tie Ying, Tian Ji Yun, Peng chong, Li Xi Ming, Wang guang Ying, Wang Bing Qian, Zhao Bu Chu seperately wrote a fewwords for the winery such as "Liangzhou magnificence" "Huangtai nice wine" "Maotai is in thesouth, Huangtai is in the north", etc. Gansu Provincial Committee Secretary Gu Jin Chi raised"Guarantee silver brand, contend for gold brand, go upstairs further," etc.

Add: Xinjian Road of Wuwei, Gansu.
Tel: 0935· 212830 213710
Fax: 212830
Post Code: 733000
Cable: 6974

中共中央政治局委員李鉄映來廠視察
Li Tie Ying visited the winery

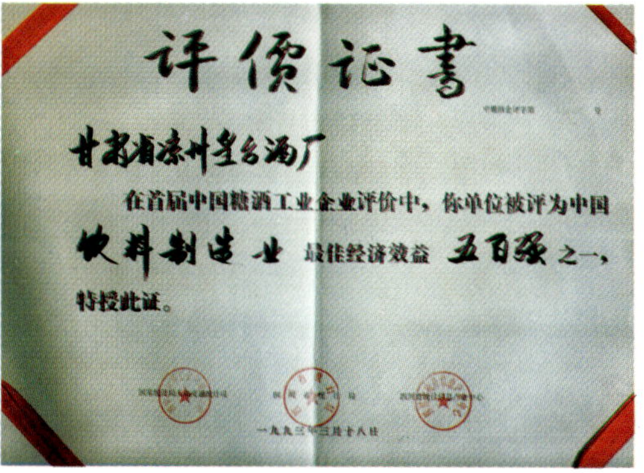

评價证書

甘肃省凉州皇台酒厂

在首届中国糖酒工业企业评价中，你单位被评为中国饮料制造业最佳经济效益五百强之一，特授此证。

GANSU LIANGZHOU HUANGTAI WINERY

原中共中央政治局常委宋平來廠視察
Song Ping visited the winery

全國人大副委員長李錫銘來廠視察
Li Xi Ming visited the winery

GANSU LIANGZHOU HUANGTAI WINERY

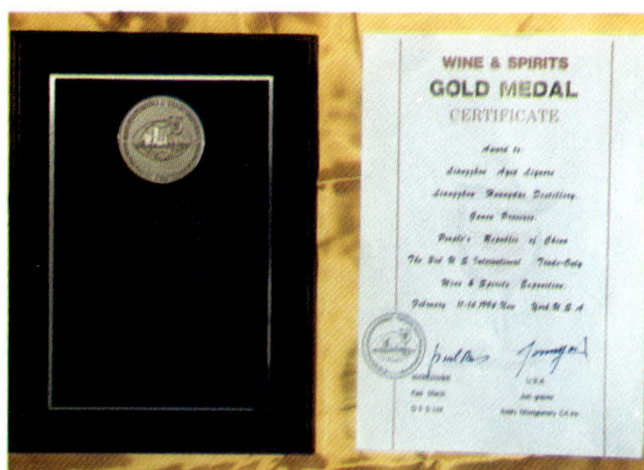
WINE & SPIRITS
GOLD MEDAL
CERTIFICATE

皇臺榮獲1994年美國第三屆酒飲國際博覽會金獎

Huangtai Wine won the gold prize of the third international wine fair in the United States.in 1994.

WINE & SPIRITS
GOLD MEDAL
CERTIFICATE

古酒榮獲1994年美國第三屆酒飲國際博覽會金獎

Gu Wine won the gold proze of the third international wine fair in the United States in 1994.

甘肅涼州皇臺酒廠

全國人大副委員長彭冲為我廠題詞
Peng Chong wrote a few words for the winery

涼州特曲

1993 年法國巴黎國際酒飲博覽會金獎
The wine won the gold Prize of Paris International Wine Fair in France in 1993.

1994 年皇臺、古酒評為國際名酒
Huangtai and Gu wine are elected as international famous wine in 1994.

GANSU LIANGZHOU HUANGTAI WINERY

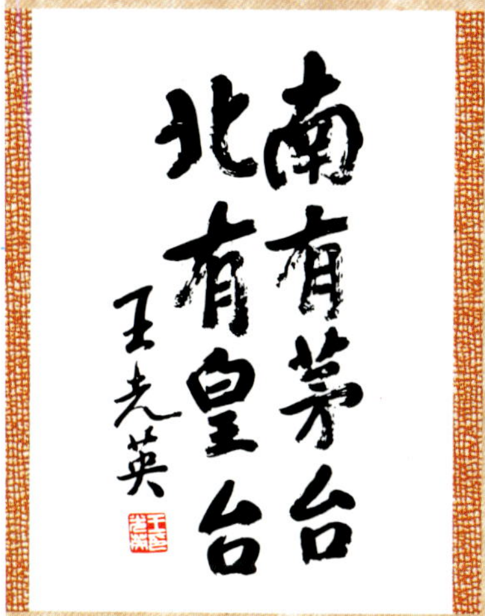

1993年元旦國家領導人王光英在北京人民大會堂為凉州皇臺、古酒榮獲日本第四屆國際博覽會金獎新聞發布會題詞。
In Jan. 1993, Wang Guang Ying, in Beijing Great Hall of the People wrote a few words at the news releasing meeting of that Huangtai, Gu Wine won the gold prize of the 4th international fair in Japan

蘭州鐵路局

地址：蘭州市和政路 156 號
電話：8821641（總值班室、市電）
22150（總值班室、路電）
郵編：730000

Add: No.156 Hezheng Road, Lanzhou
Tel: 8821641 22150
Post Code: 730000

路局領導班子研究全局發展規劃
The leader group is studying the bureau's development plan

簡介

蘭州鐵路局成立于 1956 年 3 月，到 1993 年底，全局營業里程 3485.6 公里，綫路總延展 5383.4 公里。管轄運營鐵路東起隴原重鎮天水，西至玉門關外的疏勒河，北達塞上煤城石嘴山，南迄昆侖山下的南山口，交匯聯結隴海、蘭新、包蘭、蘭青、干武、青藏 6 條鐵路干綫和嘉鏡、平汝等 10 條支綫，地跨甘肅、青海、寧夏三省區，形成以蘭州為中心的西北最大的鐵路交通樞紐。其中，更因其擁有我國第一條沙漠鐵路、第一條海拔最高的高原鐵路、第一條沿古絲綢之路修建的鐵路和第二座亞歐大陸橋而聞名全國。

蘭州鐵路局下設蘭州、武威、西寧、銀川 4 個分局和工程、工業 2 個總公司，全局共有職工近 12 萬人。建局 38 年來，全局鐵路職工在極其艱苦的自然條件下頑強拼搏，為開發建設大西北、促進國民經濟的發展做出了積極的貢獻，經濟吸引區已擴展到甘肅、青海、寧夏和新疆、內蒙、西藏等省區 140 多萬平方公里的地區。1993 年，全局廣大干部職工，面對運用車不足、施工緊張、自然災害嚴重等局面，克服重重困難，主要運輸指標創造了歷史最好成績。

“八五”期間，蘭州鐵路局進入了大發展、大改造的新時期，西北鐵路路網建設已全面鋪開。天蘭二期擴能工程已提前竣工，蘭武電化、武疏內燃改造已全綫投產，被列入國家重點建設項目的寶中鐵路已經接軌，蘭新復綫也將于 1994 年全綫鋪通，內燃化後的蘭青、青藏綫還在進一步擴能改造，包蘭電化改造已列入國家計劃。亞歐大陸橋的貫通和西北路網的逐步完善，必將為西北地區的經濟騰飛起到巨大的推動作用，蘭州鐵路局將以新的風姿迎接新世紀。

LANZHOU RAILWAY BUREAU

The bureau set up in March, 1956. By the end of 1993, its business mileage was 3485. 6km, its line total spread 5383.4km. The jurisdiction transport business railway·· The east, startsfrom Tianshui the west is to Shule River, the north starts from Shizui Mountains, the south isto Nanshankou. They unite and tie 6 railways of Longhai, Lanxin, Baolan, Lanqing, Ganwu, Qingzang and 10 branch railways of Jiajing, Pingru, etc. They extend acrorss Gansu, Qinghai, Ningxia and form the largest northwest railway communication hub taking Lanzhou as the centre. The bureau is famous for having the first desert railway, the first highest elevation plateaurailway, the first building railway along Ancient Silk Road and the second Asian and Europeancontinental bridge.

The bureau with 120000 staff and workers has 4 branch bureaus of Lanzhou, Wuwei, Xining, Yinchuan and 2 enginering, industrial companies under it. For 38 years, the staff and workershas tenaciously fought under the very hard natural conditions, and has made an activecontribution for building Northwest and promoting the development of National economy. Theeconomic appeal areal have spreaded to over 1.4 million km2 areas of Gansu, Qinghai, Ningxia, Xinjiang, Neimeng, Xizang, etc. In 1993, the vast cadres and workers overcame variousdifficulies of not enough transport trains, tense construction and serious natural calamities. The main transport indexes created the best historic results.

During the period of the 8th five–year–plan, Lanzhou Railway Bureau enters into a newperiod of large development and large reform. The northwest railway network built has allspreaded. The second period enlarging energy project of Tianlan has been completed ahead ofschedule Lanwu electric audiovisual aids and Wushu internal– combustion rebuilt has put intoproduction Baozhong railway·· the state key building item has connected tracks Lanxin multipletrack will be all spreaded in 1994. Lanqing and Qingzang lines after internal– combustion arestill further enlarged energy and rebuilt. Baolan electric audiovisual rebuilding has beenplaced on the state plan. Joining up of Asian and Europen Bridge and progressively perfectingof the northwest railway network will make a huge motive role for the economic soaring of thenorthwest areas. The bureau will greet a new century with new charm.

朱鎔基副總理視察蘭州鐵路局并題詞
Vice-primier Zhu Rong Ji visited Lanzhou Railway Bureau and wrote a few words.

蘭州鐵路局管轄示意圖 Its jurisdiction sketch map

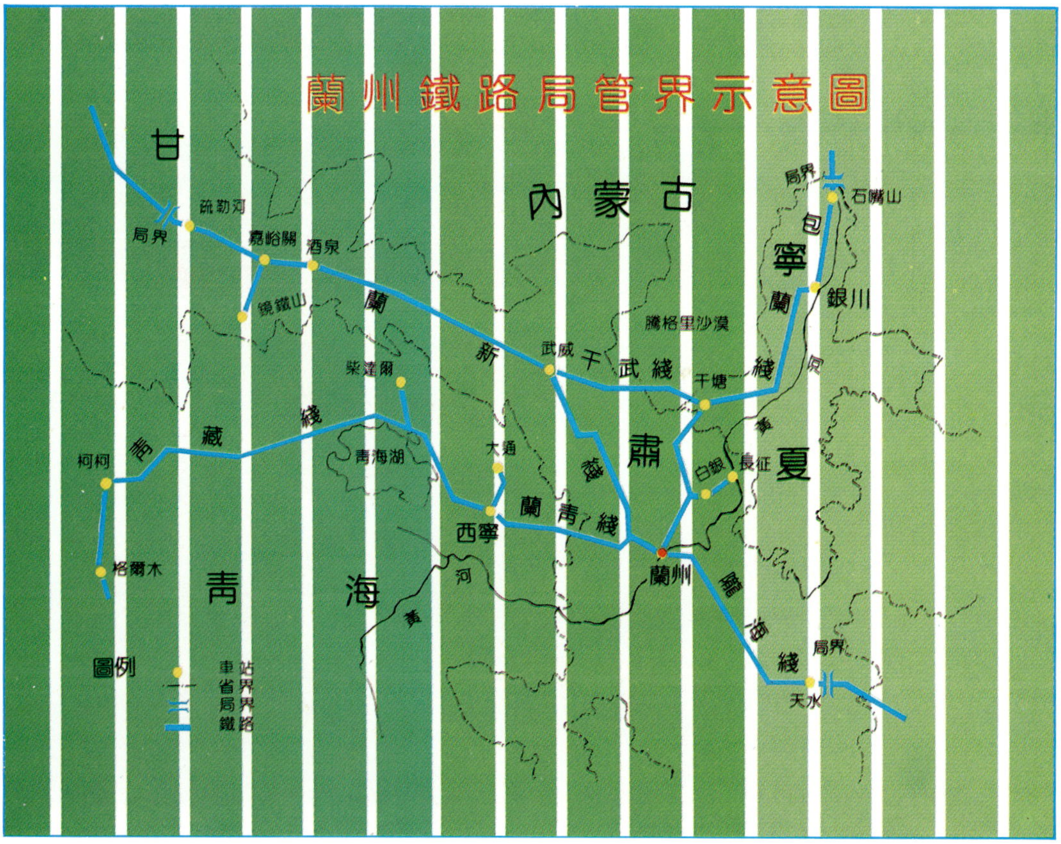

蘭州鐵路局管界示意圖

甘
內蒙古
寧
夏
肅
青
海
疏勒河
局界
嘉峪關
酒泉
鏡鐵山
蘭新線
武威
干武線
騰格里沙漠
干塘
包蘭線
石嘴山
銀川
局界
柴達爾
青藏線
柯柯
格爾木
青海湖
大通
西寧
蘭青線
白銀
長征
蘭州
隴海線
天水
局界
黃河

圖例
車站
省界
局界
鐵路

LANZHOU RAILWAY BUREAU

蘭州鐵路局

繁忙的蘭州西站編組場 The rich marshalling yard of Lanzhou west station

整裝待發 Ready and waiting

運輸綫上 On the transport line

蘭州西站貨場營業大廳
Business Hall of Lanzhou west goods yard

集裝箱運輸
Containerized traffic

沒有鉄軌的車站——臨夏鉄路代辦所
The railway station without rails——LinXia Railway Agency

武威南站晨景
Morning view of Wuwei South Station

蘭州鐵路局

在《世界建築史》上占有條目的客運站——蘭州車站
Lanzhou Railway Station— — The passenger transport station has an entry in the book of"The World Construction History".

"亞歐大陸橋"的咽喉—天水車站
The strategic passage of the Asian and European Bridge·· Tianshui Railway Station

英姿颯爽 Bright and brave

外國旅客 Foreign passengers

天(水)蘭(州)綫電氣化改造
Electric audiovisual rebuilding of Tianlan line.

中(衛)干(塘)復綫開通剪彩
Cut the ribbon at the opening of Zhonggang multiple track

邊施工邊運營的蘭新復綫
Lanxin multiple track of construction while transport

蘭州鐵路局

鉄道部長韓杼濱、甘肅省委書記閻海旺在蘭新復綫施工現場
Minister Han Shu Bin of the Railway Ministry and Gansu Provincial Committee Secretary YanHai Wang were in the construction site of Lanxin multiple track

蘭新復綫第一個區間開通儀式
Ceremony for opening of the first part of Lanxin multiple track

寶中綫鋪軌現場
The site of laying a railway track of Baozhong line

寶中綫鉄路鋪通慶典
Celebrations for opening of Baozhong railway

全路領先的尾部平面調車電氣化集中微機控制系統
Electric mass microcomputer control system of the final plane switch is always in the lead.

"五帶一體"固沙成果榮獲國家科技進步特等獎、1994 年全球五百佳環境獎。
Sand-fixation result of "Five belts and an organic whole" won a special- class prize ofthe State scientific and technical progress. and won the 500 best environment prize of thewhole world in 1994.

自動化净水處理設施
Automatic water treatment handling installations

聯合國慶祝世界環境日暨全球環保五百佳頒獎大會在英國倫敦伊麗沙白女王會議中心舉行，聯合國副秘書長、環境規劃署執行主任伊麗沙白·多德斯韋爾女士給蘭州鉄路局中衛固沙林場場長張克智同志授獎。
The world environment day celebrated by the United Nations and the issuing prizes meetingof the 500 best environmental protection in the world was held in Empress Yilishabai MeetingCentre in London, Britain. Miss Yilishabai · Dodeswer ·· Vice Secretarygeneral of the UnitedNations and Executive Director of Environmental Plan Office awarded a prize to Zhang Ke Zhi ofZhongwei sand-fixation forest farm of Lanzhou Railway Bureau.

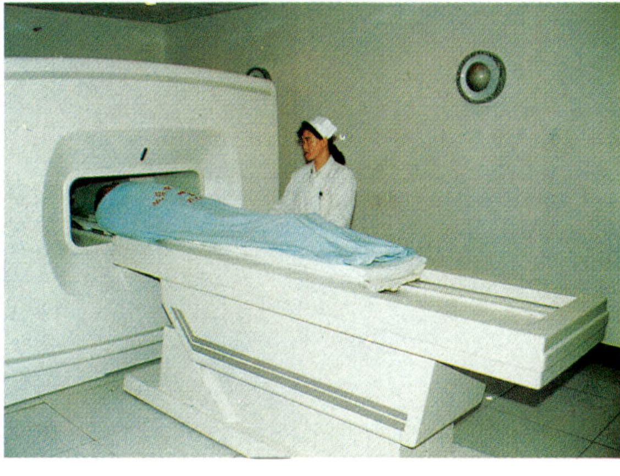

甘肅省首臺磁共振成像掃描儀
Gansu first magnetic resonant imagery scanner

蘭州鐵路局

與外國鉄路代表團洽談
Talking with the foreign railway delegation
外國鉄路專家參觀蘭州西站編組場
Fareign railway experts visited the marshalling yard of Lanzhou West Station
加拿大客人來路局共商合資建路
The Canadian guests came to talk cooperative-funds building railways with the buerau.

職工運動會
Worker's sports meet

閉路電視臺
Closed circuit television station

南京高原病康復院
Nanjing recovered hospital of highland diseases

電化教學
Teaching with electrical audiovisual aids.

蘭州煉油化工總廠

廠長李文成 Director: Li Wen Cheng

黨委書記戴年喜 Party Secretary: Dai Nian Xi

簡介

被譽為"中國煉油工業搖籃"的蘭州煉油化工總廠(簡稱蘭煉)占地500公頃，已發展成為集石油煉制加工、煉油催化劑與石油添加劑生產、煉油機械和儀表制造、石油煉制研究、自動化控制研究和建築安裝等綜合生產經營能力于一身；擁有員工2萬名，其中各類技術和管理人員約3千名；固定資產17億的全國特大型企業。躋身于全國500家最大工業企業前50名。

自"七·五"以來蘭煉對30多套裝置進行了更新、改造挖替，使其整體工藝達到世界先進水平。

蘭煉現擁有各類煉油化工裝置65套，其中有居國際和國內先進水平的同軸催化裂化、潤滑油深度精制、硫化烷基酚鈣、超穩分子篩等煉油化工生產裝置，能生產的石油產成品達360余種；還擁有FC系列儀表生產綫、大 功率烟氣輪機制造和計算機，MIS管理系統。產品廣泛應用于工農業生產和國防建設各個領域，為我國現代化作出了積極貢獻。

地址：蘭州市西固區玉門街10號
電話：7556160 7556011—32258
傳眞：0931·7558907
郵編：730060
電掛：3550

LANZHOU OIL REFINING CHEMICAL INDUSTRY PLANT

The plant named China Oil Refining Industrial Centre, with 500 ha area, has become extra-large scale enterprise in China with oil refining and processing, producing oil refiningcatalyst and oil additive, making oil refining machinery and equipments, studying oil refining, studying automatic contyol, building fixed together, also with 20000 staff and workers amongwhom there are 3000 various technical and management personnel, 17 hundred million fixed assets. It's the 50th of the 500 biggest industrial enterprises in China.

Since the Tth five-year plan, the plant has renewed, rebuilt and tapped the latent power ofover 30 sets of installations, And it has made its whole technology to reach the world'sadvanced level.

Now the plant has 65 sets of oil refining and chemical industrial installations among whomcoaxial catalytic cracking, lubricating oil depth precision, sulphur alkyl phenol calcium, superfirm molecular formula, etc. have reached the international and national advanced level. It can produce over 360 kinds of oil products, PC series of instrument produced line, big powervapour turbine made computers and over 350 kinds of its products, MIS management system. Theyare widely used in various fields of industrial and agricultural production, the building up ofnational defence. They has made an active contribution to our modernization.

Add: No.10 Yumen Street, Xigu, Lanzhou.
Tel: 7556160 7556011 · 32258
Fax: 0931 · 7558907
Post Code: 730060
Coble: 3550

1992年8月16日中共中央總書記江澤民來廠視察,幷為蘭煉題詞:"發揚高嚴細實廠風、創辦一流石化企業"
On Aug. 16, 1992, General secretary Jiang Ze Min was visiting the plant and wrote a fewwords to the plant · · "Carry forward plant style of high, strict, careful, done carefully,Build the first-class oil and chemical enterprise"

計算機中心站
Central station of Computers

中共中央政治局常委、國務院副總理朱鎔基帶領國務院有關部門領導來廠現場辦公。
Vice-premier Zhu Rong Ji came to work with the leaders of the departments concerned of theState Council in the plant

現代化的石油化工基地
Modern oil and chemical industry base

LANZHOU OIL REFINING CHEMICAL INDUSTRY PLANT

蘭州煉油化工總廠

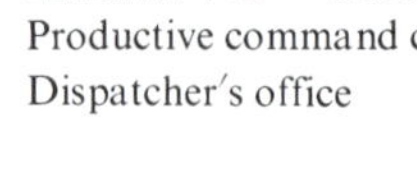
生產指揮中心一 調度室
Productive command centre··
Dispatcher's office

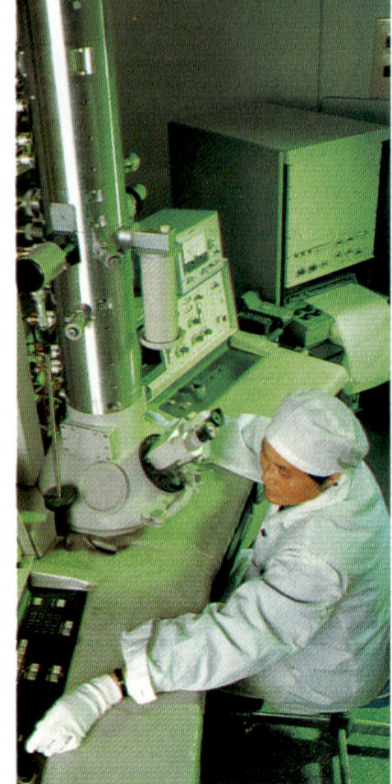
科研先行
Scientific research in advance

煉油生產裝置操作室
Operation room of oil refining productive installations

LANZHOU OIL REFINING CHEMICAL INDUSTRY PLANT

催化劑、添加劑產品商標“飛箭”
分子篩催化劑裝置
Feijian——catalyst, additive

分子篩催化剂装置
The zeolite catalyst manufacturing unit

Additive Manufacturing Plant of LPPCC

生產 3 個系列、12 個品種的蘭煉催化劑廠一角
A corner of the Catalyst Plant producing 3 series of 12 kinds.

蘭煉儀表廠的 FC 系列電動儀表裝配現場
Fixed site of FC series of eletric equip ments

生產 12 個系列、38 個品種，全國兩大石油添加劑基地之一的蘭煉添加劑廠一角
A corner of the Additive Plant producing 12 series of 38 kinds——One of the two biggestoil additive bases in China.

职工业余艺术团自编自演的节目也具感染力
A program written and performed by the Amateur Art Ensemble full of artistic appeal

組織豐富多彩的職工文化生活
Organize the worker's rich culour life

煉油生產裝置
Oil refining productive installations

蘭州平板玻璃廠

蘭州平板玻璃廠廠長兼黨委書記：張恩奎
Director as well as Party secretary: Zhang En Kui

地址：蘭州西固東路 49 號
電話：7556666· 7556688
電掛：5703
郵編：730060

攝影：白帆 Photographer: Bai Fan

簡介

蘭州平板玻璃廠是國家大型建材企業。主要生產藍天牌平板玻璃和加工玻璃產品。目前，又開工上馬一條 400 噸/日浮法玻璃生產綫。使技術和管理水平躍上一個新臺階，成為我國西北地區玻璃生產和深加工的基地。

LANZHOU PLATE GLASS FACTORY

The factory is a large-scale, building material, state enterprise. It mainly produces "Lantian" plate glass and processes glass products. Now, it has started a Fufa glass productionline of 400 tons per day which has made technology and management level to leap to a new stage. The factory has become the base of glass produced and processed in the northweat areas of China.

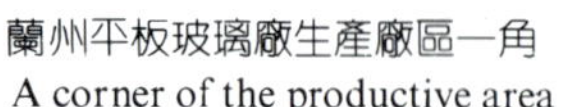

蘭州平板玻璃廠生產廠區一角
A corner of the productive area

蘭州平板玻璃廠1993年初兼并青海樂都玻璃廠
The factory annexed Ledu Glass Plant of Qinghai in 1993

九機窰全保溫技術改造，進一步提高了生產能力，節約了能源。
Insulating technical reform of Jiuji kiln has further raised the productive capacity, economized on energy resources.

Add: No.49 East Road, Xigu, Lanzhou.
Tel: 7556666 · 7556688
Cable: 5703
Post Code: 730060

該廠產品"雪鶴"牌超細玻璃棉榮獲部優產品。
Its product · · "Xuehe" superfine glass cotton won the Ministrial good product.

現代化管理窰爐儀表室
Kiln stove equipment room of modern management

嚴格管理，精心操作。
Rigorous management, meticulous operation

中日合資企業蘭州藍天玻璃制品有限公司生產磨邊倒邊玻璃生產綫。
The glass productive line of polishing siades of Lanzhou Lantian Glass Product LimitedCompany · · China and Japan cooperative funds enterprise.

LANZHOU PLATE GLASS FACTORY

蘭州水泥廠

廠長 陳貴庭 Director:Chen Gui Ting

簡介

蘭州水泥廠是工業廢渣(即電石渣、粉煤灰等)生產水泥的環境保護企業，80 年代被甘肅省計劃委員會和建設委員會列為"三廢"處理的重點工程，也是蘭州市首屈一指的環境治理企業。

本廠于 1985 年建成投產，現有固定資產近 2000 萬元，選用濕法長窰和機立窰二條生產綫，年生產能力 15 萬噸。主要設備有 Φ3.1m / 2.5m× 78m 迴轉窰一臺，Φ3.0× 10m 機立窰一臺，Φ1.83m× 7m 生料磨二臺，Φ2. 2m× 6.5m 水泥磨二臺。主要產品為"五泉山"牌硅酸鹽、普通硅酸鹽、粉煤灰硅酸鹽和 R 型早強水泥，標號為 625、525、425。產品質量高，性能穩定，被廣泛用于高層建築工程，暢銷省內外，深受廣大用戶的青睞。

LANZHOU CEMENT PLANT

The plant is an environmental protection enterprise producing cement with industry wasteresidue, the key project handling three waste listed by Gansu PLant Committee and ConstructionCommittee.

The plant, set up in 1985, uses two productive lines of Shifachang kiln and Jili kiln with 20 million Yuan, the annual production capacity of 150000 tons. The main equipments include oneΦ3.1m / 2.5m× 78m Junzhuan kiln, one Φ3.0× 10m Jili kiln, 2 Φ1.83m× 7m Shengliao mills, 2 Φ2.2m× 6.5m cement mills. The main products are Wuquan Mountain silicate, ordinary silicate, powder coal ash silicate, R type Zhaoqian cement with 625、525、 425 grades. The products, with high quality, are widely used in high layer construction project, selling well in both sides of Gansu province, are in users' good graces.

濕法工藝迴轉窰 Shifa technology Huizhuan Kiln

散裝水泥設施 Bulk cement equipments.

工廠全景 The whole view of Lanzhou Cement PLant

LANZHOU CEMENT PLANT

地址: 蘭州市西固區河口南新維路 9 號
聯系人: 陳貴庭 Connecter: Chen Gui Ting
電話: 7523630 (直撥) 7523483(總機)
郵編:730094
電掛:5809

Add: No.9 Xinwei Road, Hekounan, Xigu, Lanzhou
Tel: 7523630, 7523483
Post Code:730094
Cable:5809

用我廠高標號水泥建造的工貿商場
Lanzhou Industry and Trade Market built with high grade cement

用本廠625# 水泥建造的蘭州東崗立交橋
Lanzhou Donggang Upright Cross Bridge built with 625# cement

蘭州呢絨廠

LANZHOU WOOLLEN GOODS FACTORY

廠長兼黨委書記：雷萬靑
Director (Party Secretary): Lei Wan Qing

簡介

我廠系甘肅省輕紡工業廳直屬企業，是甘肅省定點生產各種粗紡呢絨和工業造紙毛毯的專業工廠。

我廠是八十年代新建的毛紡企業。設備齊全、工藝先進、擁有雄厚的設計、生產、科研力量和健全的質量保證體系以及先進的檢測手段。主要產品有全毛、混紡大衣呢、海軍呢、女式呢、法蘭絨、花呢、學生呢等 108 個品種，320 多個花色和 27 個規格的工業造紙毛毯。產品具有色澤艷麗、呢面豐滿、手感挺括、時興大方等特點。銷往全國 15 個省、市、自治區，以花色新穎繁多贏得市場，深受消費者的靑睞。

我廠還擁有甘肅省呢絨工貿公司、甘肅省輕工儀器儀表公司、綜合利用加工廠等獨立經營的下屬企業，主要經營針紡、五金交電、化工、儀器、儀表、建材、厚輔材料、農副等產品，全方位地為社會發展提供優質服務。

LANZHOU WOOLLEN GOODS FACTORY

It is an enterprise directly under the Light and Textile Industry Department of GansuProvince and a factory specialized to Gansu Province to produce all kinds of woollen goods andindustrial papermaking blanket.

It was set up in the 1980s. It has the complete equipments, the advanced technology, therich human of design, production and scientific reseach, the amplify system of quality guaranteeand the advanced test means, 108 varieties such as all-wool and blending cvercoating, navycloth, lady's cloth, student's cloth, flannel and facy suiting, and more than 320 designs andcolours as well as 27 standards of industrial papermaking blanket, which have the features ofbeautiful colour, rich face, well pressed handle, fashionable and tasteful, are sold to 15provinces, municipalities and autonomous regions and are in user good graces.

Besides it has some independent management enterprises such as the Woollen Goods TradeCompany of Gansu Province, the Light Industrial Instrument and Meter Company of Gansu Province, the Comprehensive Process and Utilization Plant and so on, which mainly engage in knit and textile goods, hardware and electrical appliance, chemical industrial products, instrument and meter, building materials, agricultural and by products.

地址：蘭州市七里河區西津西路 658 號
電話：2336700
郵編：730050
電報：9655

Add: No. 658 West Xijin Road, Qilihe, Lanzhou
Tel: 2336700
Post Code: 730050
Cable: 9655

地址：蘭州市一只船北街 3 號
電話：8821011—228
郵編：730000
Add: No.3 Yizhichuan North Street, Lanzhou
Tel: 8821011·228
Post Code: 730000

甘肅省農業生産資料總公司總經理、黨委書記張文杰同志
Manager and Party Secretary Zhang Wen Jie is working

甘肅省農業生産資料總公司

GANSU AGRICULTURAL MEANS OF PRODUCTION COMPANY

供銷社農資部門開辦的莊稼醫院已發展到 1078 所，集開方、配藥、咨詢、防治于一體，為農民提供了全方位的農資系列化服務，深受歡迎。

The Crop Hospitals run by the farm means department of the Supply and MarketingCooperation, have been developed into 1078 hospitals with writing out prescriptions, making upprescriptions, consulting, preventing and curing together. The hospitals have provided march- past service of the whole direction farm means to peasants and are warmly welcomed.

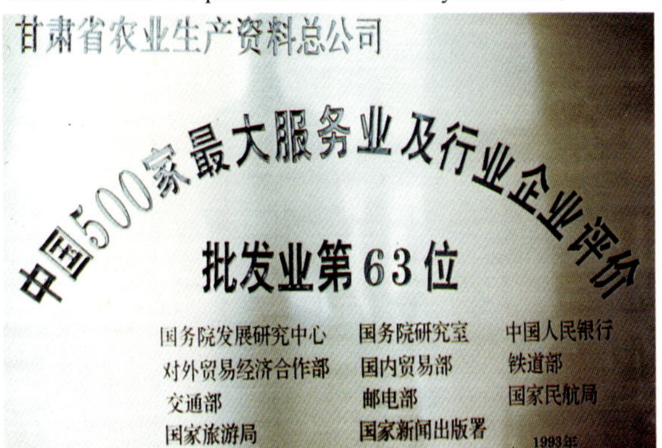

甘肃省农业生产资料总公司

中国500家最大服务业及行业企业评价

批发业第 63 位

国务院发展研究中心　国务院研究室　中国人民银行
对外贸易经济合作部　国内贸易部　铁道部
交通部　邮电部　国家民航局
国家旅游局　国家新闻出版署

1993年

簡介

甘肅省農業生產資料總公司是省供銷聯社直屬獨立核算、具有法人資格的大型批發企業，下屬化肥、農藥、農膜、農機具等九個經營、服務、儲運公司和一個農資系列化服務總站，職工 750 人。主營化肥、農膜、農藥三個大類，擴營商品二十個大類近 8000 個品種。固定資產達 3355 萬元，年銷售額近 5 億元。該公司在堅持服務三農，不斷提高社會效益的同時，企業經濟效益逐年遞增，1993 年被國務院發展研究中心等十一家部委評為中國最大服務業批發業第 63 位。

GANSU AGRICULTURAL MEANS OF PRODUCTION COMPANY

The company, with 750 staff and workers, is a large– scale independent accounting and wholesale enterprise with corporation qualifications under Gansu Supply and Marketing Cooperation. 9 management, service, storage and transportation companies of chemical fertilizer, farm chemial, farm film, farm mechanical instruments, etc. and a series sevice station of agricultural means. It mainly manages 3 types of chemical fertilizer, farm film, farm chemical,extending to manage 20 types of near 800 varieties products. The fixed assets reaches 33.55 million yuan. The annual selling volume is near 5 hundred million yuan. The company insistingon serving three farms and continuously raising social benefit, meanwhile enterprise economic benefit has been increasing progressively year after year. The company was elected as sixty–third of the largest service wholesale enterprise in China by the Research Centre of the State Council and other 11 Department Committees.

GANSU COTTON-LINEN COMPANY

總經理：薛廷璽 Manager:xue Ting Xi

電話：8821601
電掛：2236
傳眞：(0931) 8821690
郵編：730000
Tel:8821601
Cadle:2236
Fax:(0931) 8821690
Post Code:730000

甘肅省棉麻總公司

簡介

甘肅省棉麻總公司現有員工 420 人，擁有資產總額近 2 億元，下設 4 個分公司，7 個經營科室和 1 個綜合加工廠。主要經營棉花、棉紗、麻類、針紡織品、日雜百貨、農副土產、糧油副食、五金交電、化工建材。

GANSU COTTON-LINEN COMPANY

The company now has 420 staff and workers, near 2 hundred million yuan of total assets volume, 4 branches, 7 management offices, 1 synthetic processing factory under it. It mainly manages cotton, cotton yarn, linen, knit goods, articles of daily use, faroming products and by-products and local products, grain and oil and non-staple food,hard ware and traffic electric equipment, chemical industry and building materials.

廠長：蘭廣城
Dircetor: Lin Guan Cheng

LANZHOU COMMERCIAL UNIVERSAL MACHINE WORKS

蘭州商業通用機械廠

簡介

該廠始建于 1953 年，系國家重點中型企業，甘肅省一級企業，為第一批獲得國家工業鍋爐許可證的生產廠家，并取得一二類壓力容器制造許可證。主要生產 0.5～10 噸蒸氣熱水兩個系列 15 個規格的工業鍋爐。還生產石油庫、冷藏庫設備和配件，承擔全國大中型油冷庫設備和工藝安裝。具有生產大中型機械產品的能力。年加工能力為 2500 噸。

廠址：蘭州市龔家灣 187 號
電話：2336221－224
郵編：730050

雙鍋筒工業鍋爐 The industrial boiler with double tube

LANZHOU COMMERCIAL UNIVERSAL MACHINE WORKS

The works, set up in 1953, is a key, medium– scale, state enterprise, the first–classenterprise in Gansu province, one of the first production enterprises winning the stateindustrial boiler licence and the licence of making the first, second kinds of pressurecontainers. It mainly produces 0.5·10 rons vapour and hot water, two series of 15 standardsindustrial boilers. It also produces equipments and fittings of oil storage and cold storage, undertakes large–medium scale oil and cold storage equipments and technological installation inChina. It has the productive capacity of large–medium scale mechanical products with the annualprocessing capacity of 2500 tons.

Add: No.187 Gongjiawan, Lanzhou
Tel: 2336221· 224
Post Code: 730050

張掖石油公司油庫一側
A side of the oil storage of Zhangyue Oil Company

LANZHOU ALUMINIUM FACTORY

蘭州連海鋁業有限公司、中外合資海南中亞鋁業有限公司董事長、
蘭州鋁廠廠長、劉鉄軍 Liu Tie Jun : National model worker

地址：蘭州市西固區環行西路 6 號
郵編：730060
電掛：5732
電話：556511
傳真：555294
Add : No. 6 Huanxing West Road, Xigu. Lanzhou
Post Code : 730060
Cable : 5732
Tel : 7556511
Fax : 7555294

蘭州鋁廠

簡介

蘭州鋁廠是中國 500 家最大工業企業之一，國家一級企業。主導產品《蘭鋁牌》重熔用鋁錠、電工用鋁錠、稀土鋁合金錠、ZLD—102 鑄造鋁合金錠均獲甘肅省、中國有色金屬工業總公司優質產品獎，其中重熔用鋁錠又獲國家優質產品銀質獎。產品暢銷全國，并已進入國際市場。

LANZHOU ALUMINIUM FACTORY

The factory is one of the 500 largest, state-owned enterprises as well as the first- classenterprises in China. Its leading products ·· "LANLU" mark remeting aluminium ingot, electrial ingot, rare earth aluminium ingot, ZLD--102 casting aluminium alloy have gained thetitles of good quality products in Gansu Province and China National Nonferrous MetalIndustrial Corp. Among them remelting aluminium ingot has been awarded silver prize forexcellent quality by state. The products are selling well throughout China and broken in theinternational market.

蘭州卷烟廠

廠長範天才（市人大代表、省級勞模）
Director : Fan Tian Cai, Deputy to Lanzhou People's Congress, Gansu model worker

LANZHOU CIGARETTE FACTORY

簡介

蘭州卷烟廠始建于1937年，是中央在甘企業，隸屬于中國烟草總公司甘肅省烟草公司，為全國烟草行業57家大中型企業之一。現有職工1103人，占地面積70000平方米，總建築面積40000平方米，現已形成年產20萬箱卷烟能力。經國家烟草總公司確定，蘭州卷烟廠被列為總公司"七五"、"八五"技術改造重點企業之一。通過引進國外先進技術和設備，使工廠卷烟生產的蒸、打、切、卷、接、包六大主機成龍配套。其中引進西德HAUNI公司的梗絲膨脹生產綫；意大利SASIB公司的6000型横包機;英國MCLINS公司的MK8-MAXⅢ卷接機組和英國超九·五卷接機組標志着工廠的工藝裝備和技術裝備已達到八十年代先進水平。經過多年的生產實践，工廠定型生產混合型、烤烟型兩種烟型、3個系列、16個品種。包裝形式：84m/m硬盒翻蓋、84m/m全包裝、84m/m直包裝；老產品有："莫高"、"海洋"、"金城"、"蘭州"；新產品有"亞龍"、"魅力"、"大王"。其中84'S"莫高"牌系列高級旅游香烟以其裝璜精美、質量上乘、工藝考究享譽省內外，而且深受國外旅游者的喜愛。我廠產品現已打入廣東、福建、上海等27個省、市、縣、區。1993年工廠完成產量15萬箱，銷售收入3.05億元，上繳税金1.35億元；實現利潤580萬元。

LANZHOU CIGARETTE FACTORY

The factory, established in 1937, is a central enterprise in Gansu, under the commandof Gansu Tobacco Company of China Tobacco Company, one of the 57 large-medium scale enterprisesof China tobacco trade, with 1103 staff and workers, 70000 m2 area, 40000 m2 building area. Itsannual producing capacity is 200 thousand boxes now. The factory is rated as one of the keytechnical reform enterprises during the 7th-five- year and the 8th- five- year plan by theNational Tobacco Company. Through importing advanced technology and equipments from abroad the 6big key machines of steaming, beating, cutting, cigarating, contacting and packing have beenformed a complete irrigation system. The production line of pipe tobacco expanding is fromHauni Company of Germany, packing sideways machine of 6000 type from Sasib Company of Italy, cigaratting-contacting machine of MK8 XⅢ from Mclins Company of England. These marks that its technology and skill equipment has reached the advanced level of eighties. After many years' production practice, the factory has produce two tobacco types of mixed andflue-cured tobacco, three series of 16 varieties. Packing form : 84m/m hard box opened, 84m/mtotal packing, 84m/m straight packing. Its old products are Mogao, Haiyang, Jincheng, Lanzhou; Its new products are Yalong, Meili, Dawang, The high- quality tour cigarette of 84's Mogaoseries enjoys high prestige both at provicial inside and outside and are welcomed by foreigntourists. The products are selling well in Guangdong, Fujian, Shanghai, 27 provices, cities andcounties. In 1993, The factory completed 150000 boxes output, sales income is 305 million yuanthe tax turned overed to the state is 135 million yuan. the profit is 5800 thousand yuan.

地址：中國甘肅蘭州市酒泉路62號
郵編：730030
電話：8465311
電報：0356
傳真：8487748
Add : No.62 Jiuquan Road, Lanzhou, Gansu, China
Post Code : 730030
Tel : 8465311
Cable : 0356
Fax : 8487748

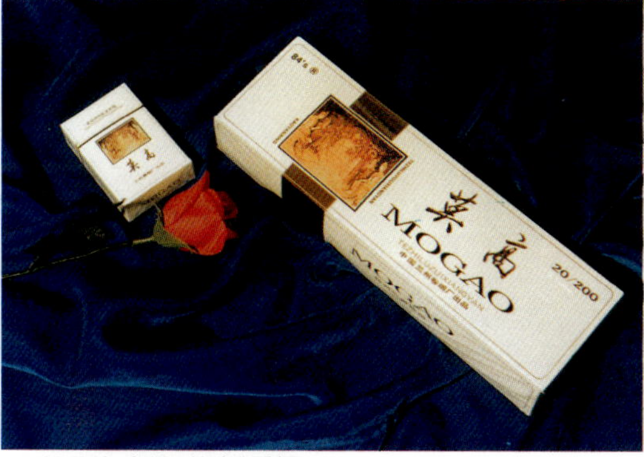

西部名牌,高級"莫高"香烟
West famous brand·· high quality Mogao cigarette

蘭州鍋爐廠

蘭州鍋爐廠法人代表、廠長孫世福
Legal Person as well as Director: Sun Shi Fu

LANZHOU BOILER FACTORY

簡介

蘭州鍋爐廠建于 1965 年，是機械電子工業部、勞動人事部定點鍋爐制造廠。主要生產 1～20 蒸噸各種系列、規格近 30 種蒸汽、熱水鍋爐和一、二類壓力容器。下屬經營公司生產各種鍋爐配套設備，并為用戶提供鍋爐裝置、修理、改造和技術咨詢等各種服務。

蘭州鍋爐廠以產品質量求生存、以技術進步求發展。近年來不斷加快改革步伐、加強內部管理；不斷開發新產品，加快產品的更新換代。

可靠的質量和周到的服務，使蘭州鍋爐廠的產品暢銷西北五省，·遍布全國各地。

地址：蘭州市西固區莊浪路 216 號
郵編：730060
電話：7555074

聯系人：張殿平（廠辦主任）
Contactor: Zhang Dian Ping
法人代表：孫世福（廠長）
Legal Person: Sun Shi Fu (Director)

LANZHOU BOILER FACTORY

The factory, set up in 1965, is a fixed factory making boilers of the Industrial Ministryof machinery and Electron, the Labour Personnel ministry. It mainly produces various series of 1· 20 tons, near 30 standards of steam and hot water boilers, one or two class pressurecontainers. The management companies under the factory produce various boiler necessaryaccessories and also provide various service of boiler installation, repairing, reform. technical consultation, etc. to customers.

The factory strives for living with product quality and strives for developing withtechnical progress. In recent years, the factory has continuously quickened reform steps, strengthened internal management; developed new products, quickened renewing and changinggeneration of its products.

Its reliable quality and thoughtful service make its products to sell well in fiveprovinces of Northwest and throughout China.

Add: No.216 Zhuanglang East Road, Xigu, Lanzhou.
Post Code: 730060
Tel: 7555074

蘭州鍋爐廠設計制造的 10T 蒸汽鍋爐進行省級鑒定的情況
10 T steam boiler is conducting Provincial-class appraisal.

蘭州鍋爐廠廠區 Factory area of Lanzhou Boiler Factory

甘肅省水利廳

簡介

甘肅省水利廳是甘肅省人民政府主管水行政的職能部門，統一管理全省水資源和河道、水庫、湖泊，主管全省防汛抗旱和水土保持工作，負責全省水利行業的管理。

GANSU IRRIGATION OFFICE

The office is a function department managing water administration of Gansu People's Government, It manages water resources, river courses, reservoirs, lakes, is in charge offlood control, drought resistance, water and soil conservation, also in charge of managingirrigation trades in Gansu.

省水利廳廳長：薛映承
Director: Xue Ying Cheng

上圖景泰川電力提灌工程一泵站
Jingtaichuan power irrigation by pumping project ·· pump station
中圖民樂縣翟寨子水庫
Zhaizhaizi Reservoir in Minle county
下圖張掖草灘莊水利樞紐
Zhangye grasslands is in the key water control project

地址：蘭州市臯蘭路 76 號
電話：8821630
郵編：730000
Add: No. 76 Gaolan Road, Lanzhou
Tel: 8821630
Post Code: 730000

GANSU IRRIGATION OFFICE

GAOAI CEMENT PLANT

高崖水泥廠廠長：于永平　Director: Yu Yong Ping

金城牌水泥

注册 商标

甘肅省高崖水泥廠

簡介

高崖水泥廠始建于1958年。年生產能力32萬噸，其中旋窰生產綫20萬噸，擁有固定資産7600多萬元，現有職工1700多人，是甘肅省大中型國有水泥骨干企業之一。30多年來企業立足技術進步，不斷挖潛，鋭意進取，所生産的“金城”牌水泥，暢銷全國20多個省市自治區，深受廣大用戶歡迎和好評。工廠整體實力雄厚，1990年被晉升為省二級企業，1992年進入全省工業企業經濟效益50強，名列第35位，被省委、省政府命名為省級“文明單位”，1993年工廠利税首次突破千萬元大關，被國家統計局列入中國最大的500家建材企業；在全國第五次水泥質量大對比中獲西北地區第一名；1990年以來，連續四年被定西地委、行署評為“文明單位”、“先進企業”；連續6年被榆中縣，蘭州市授于“重合同、守信用”企業、“納税先進單位”稱號，1993年被省政府命名為“重合同、守信用”企業。

地址：甘肅榆中縣高崖鎮
電話：(09440) 22834 22051
郵編：730113
電掛：3055
Add: Gaoai Town, Yuzhong County, Gansu.
Tel: (09440) 22834 22051
Post Coad: 730113
Cable: 3055

GAOAI CEMENT PLANT

The plant, set up in 1958, is one of the state, large—medium scale, key cement enterpriseswith the annual production capacity of 320000 tons including 200000 tons of rotary kilnproduction line, over 76 million yuan of fixed assets, over 1700 staff and workers. For over 30years, the enterprise has been based on technical progress, continuously tapping the latentpower, irresistibly keeping forging ahead. It's "Jincheng" cement are selling well inover 20 provinces, cities and autonomous regions of China, and well received by consumers. Itswhole strength is strong. It was promoted to Grade B enterprise in Gansu in 1990. In 1992 itbecame the thirty—fifth of the 50 best economic benefit enterprises in Gansu and won the titleof "Civilization Unit" of Gansu Provincial Committee and Government. In 1993 the plant firsttopped 10 million yuan of benefit tax. and was placed in the 500 largest building materialenterprises in China by China Statistical Bureau, and won the first title of the Northwestregion in the fifth cement quality competition. Since 1990, the plant has been continuously "Civilization Unit" and "Advanced Enterprise" of Dingxi Region Committee and Administrativeoffice. For six years, it has been continuously an enterprise of carrying out its promises andcomplying with contracts very well and an advanced unit of paying taxes of Yuzhong county andLanzhou city. In 1993, it was an enterprise of carrying out its promises and complying withcontracts very well of Gansu Provicial Government.

部分榮譽證書
Some honour certifications

GAOAI CEMENT PLANT

工廠大門
Gate of the plant.

12.4KM 長索道礦石運輸綫
12.4km cableway ore transportation line

金城牌水泥

甘肃省高崖水泥廠

該廠自己制造并安裝的大型設備增濕塔
Large-scale increasing wet tower made and fixed by the plant itself.

工廠外景 Outdoor view of the plant

GAOAI CEMENT PLANT

化驗室工作人員精心檢驗嚴把質量關
The workers in the lab meticulously examine and strictly guarantee the quality

空壓機站 Air compressor station

工廠全景 Full view of the plant

WUSHAN CEMENT PLANT

甘肅省武山水泥廠

廠長：石常海
Director: Shi Chang Hai

廠址：甘肅武山鴛鴦鎮
郵編：741316
電話：(09482)、21308

簡介

國家大型企業武山水泥廠，現有職工 1700 人，固定資產 2.5 億元，引進德國設備,建有兩條先進的回轉窰生產綫。年產優質高標號水泥 68 萬噸，主要產品有鴛鴦牌硅酸鹽、普通硅酸鹽兩大系列 8 個品種，其中：硅 525#R、525#R、425#R 獲省優，硅 525#R、普通硅 525#R 獲部優。產品行銷省內外及東南亞市場，在亞運場舘、國貿大廈、寶中鉄路等大型工程中獲得好評。

WUSHAN CEMENT PLANT

The plant is a large-scale enterprise in China! Now it has 1700 staff and workers, 2. 5hundred million yuan of fixed assets and imports some equipments from Germany. It has built twoadvanced productive lines of rotary kiln with the annual production capacity of 680000 tons ofhigh strength cement. The main products include Yuanyang mark silicate and ordinary silicate ·· two series of eight kinds among whom silicon 525#R, 525#R, 425#R won the provincial goodproducts, silicon 525# R and ordinary silicon 525#R won the ministry good products. Its productsare selling well throughout Gansu province and the Southeast Asia markets. Its products in thelarge-scale projects of the Asian sports Stadium, International Trade Building, Baozhong Railwayhave been well received.

Add: Yuanyang Town, Wushan County, Gansu.
Post Code: 741316
Tel: 09482· 21308

產品獲國家建材局優質產品獎

The product won the good quality product prize of the State Building Material Bureau.

榮獲甘肅省優質產品獎

The product won the good quality product prize of Gansu province.

工廠全貌

Full view of the plant

甘肅省武山水泥廠

石灰石礦山一角
A corner of limestone mine

索道運輸綫
Cableway transportation line

化驗室在做質量檢驗
The workers are testing quality in the lab.

我廠生產的525#R型水泥，遠銷國內各省，幷出口東南亞市場。
525# R cement is selling well throughout China and hss been exported to the Southeast Asianmarkets.

包裝站臺一角 A corner of packing station

LANZHOU HUAYI HOTEL

總經理：謝春生
General Manager: Xie Chun Sheng

蘭州華誼大酒店

地址：蘭州市西津西路 14 號
郵編：730050
電話：0931——2333051
電傳：72143 LFSHLCN
傳真：2330304

簡介

蘭州華誼大酒店是甘肅省首家中外合作經營(由香港華誠集團公司與友誼飯店合營)、外方管理的大型庭院式酒店。店內分前、後、西樓三幢客房樓，擁有豪華、高級、普通、經濟四種標準的客房 500 間，床位 1100 多個。各具規模的會議廳 20 余個。酒店自合資以來，積極引進外資對酒店進行全面裝修改造，同時不斷引入先進的管理經驗。改建完畢後，酒店將成為蘭州市規模最大、設施最全、功能最強的國際三星級標準酒店。酒店餐飲力量雄厚，擁有蘭州市第一流的集餐飲、娛樂于一體的大型粵菜宴會廳，設有可提供 500 人、300 人、100 人等同時進餐的各具規模和風味的餐廳十余個。由香港名廚主理的正宗粵菜、西餐、自助燒烤、廣東早茶、自助火鍋等更是在金城獨樹一幟。而設備一流設施齊全的健身康娛中心包括健身房、桑拿浴、美發美容、保健按摩室、醫療體檢、棋牌室、卡拉 OK 歌舞廳、鐳射電影院、華誼酒吧等則是賓客娛樂、消遣、休憩的理想場所。

此外，酒店還設有商務中心、多功能廳、購物中心、停車場、以及先進的中央控制系統、閉路電視系統和程控電話、計算機網絡系統等，為賓客提供郵政、電傳、電報、復印、打字、外幣兌換、客衣洗燙、出租車和代售機、車票等服務項目。

蘭州華誼大酒店奉行“賓客至上，服務第一”的辦店宗旨，為賓客提供一流的服務、一流的設施。不久的將來，她將以更快的步伐邁嚮國際先進酒店行列，為推動蘭州市旅游事業的發展作出積極的貢獻。

酒店總經理謝春生先生携全體員工隨時恭請各界朋友惠顧。

四季餐廳 Four Seasons Restaurant

酒店夜景圖 Night view of Huayi Hotel

豪華套房 Luxious suits

LANZHOU HUAYI HOTEL

The hotel is the first large-scale courtyard uineshop managed by China and foreign country (Xianggang Group Company and Friendship Hotel) and run by foreign country. It's divided intofront, back and west guest buildings with over 500 standard guest rooms of luxury, first-class, ordinary and economy, 1100 beds and 20 various scale meeting rooms. Since joint funds, the hotelcontinuously imported advanced management experience and also foreign funds to fit up andrebuild it. After rebuilt, the hotel will be the international three- star grade, standard hotel with the largest scale, the most complete equipments and the strongest function inLanzhou. The hotel, with stong power of dine and drink, has the first-class, largest scale Yuedishes banquet hall with dine, drink and recreation together in Lanzhou. It also has over 10various scale and flavour dining halls providing 500 persons, 300 persons, 100 persons to havedinner at the same time. Yue dishes, Western-style food, self-help roasting, Guangdong moming tea, self-help chafing dish made by the famous cooks of Hongkong flies its own colours in Jin City.

With the first-class equipment and complete installation, the health and recreation whichincludes gymnasium, Shana bath, beauty hair and parlour keep-fit massage room, medical check-up, chess and cards room, Kala OK song and dance hall, radium emanative cinema, Huayi bar etc. isan ideal place of recreation, diversion, and rest for guests.

Otherwise the hotel also has commercial service centre, many function hall, purchasing centre, car park, advanced central air regulation system, closed circuit television system, programme control telephones, computer newwork system, etc. It also provides postal service, telex, telegram, duplicating, typing, changing foreign money, washing and ironing clothes, taxi, commission engine, tickets, etc. to guests.

"Customer is God, service first" is the main policy pursued by the hotel. It provides thefirst class service and installation to guestes. In the near future, it will quicken its stepsto step up to the international advanced hotel and make an active contribution to developLanzhou tourist trade.

Welcome to Huayi Hotel

Add:No. 14 Xijin West Road, Lanzhou
Post Code:730050
Tel: 0931-----2333051
Telex: 72143 LFSHLCN
Fax: 2330304

LANZHOU HUAYI HOTEL

"燕樂廳"中餐廳 "Yan le ting" Chinese Restaurant

標準雙人房 Standard double room

中國民航甘肅省管理局

簡介

GANSU MANAGEMENT BUREAU OF CHINA CIVIL AVIATION

中國民航甘肅省管理局是 1985 年 11 月在原民航中川站的基礎上組建的，下設航行氣象、機務維修、通風導航、運輸服務、汽車運輸、場道維護、安檢消防等服務保障部門，管轄中川、敦煌、嘉峪關、慶陽四個機場，有職工 1000 余人,是國家計量二級企業。1992 年 9 月，民航甘肅省管理局全方位開放所轄四機場，歡迎全國各地航空公司前來甘肅開辟航班。

地址：蘭州市中川機場
郵編：730087
電話：8415926

GANSU MANAGEMENT BUREAU OF CHINA CIVIL AVIATION

The bureau set up in November, 1985 on the bases of Zhongchuan Station of the former civilaviation with navigte meteorology, maintenance service, communication nevigation, transportation service, car transportation, airport-way safeguarding, safaty examination, fireprotection, etc. under it. It manages the four airports of Zhongchuan, Dunhuang, Jiayuguan, Qingyang with over 1000 staff and workers. It's the second class, state measure enterprise. In September, 1992, the bureau opened the four airports in all directions. Welcomethe airline companies all over China to open flight numbers.

Add: Zhongchuan Airport, Lanzhou
Post Code: 730087
Tel: 8415926

蘭州中川機場 Zhongchuan Airport

敦煌機場 Dunhuang Airport

中川機場候機室服務人員接受旅客問詢
The service personnels accept passengers' inquiries in the waiting room of ZhongchuanAirport.

甘肅省交通廳公路局

THE HIGHWAY BUREAU OF GANSU TRAFFIC DEPARTMENT

簡介

甘肅省交通廳公路局是負責全省公路養護、管理的事業單位。管養着全省 34875 公里公路。其中：國道 11 條 5178 公里；省道 23 條 5320 公里；縣鄉公路 895 條 22496 公里；大中型橋梁 848 座；隧道 35 道(含明道)。近年來，全省公路職工發揚無私奉獻的精神，先後完成了河西千里"窗口路"、"蘭郎路"等的改造任務，建成了天水至北道、蘭州至中川機場高速公路和一大批橋梁隧道，大大改善了我省交通落後面貌。目前，公路職工正在為建設甘肅交通戰略目標—"兩縱兩橫"公路主骨架而繼續奮斗。

THE HIGHWAY BUREAU OF GANSU TRAFFIC DEPARTMENT

The bureau is a institution maintaining and managing the highway in Gansu. It maintains andmanaging 34875 km highway in the province among whom there are 11 state highway of 5178 km, 32provincial highway of 5320 km, 895 county and village highway of 22496 km, 848 large and mediumbridges, 35 tunnels. In recent years, the staff and workers have displayed their selflesstribution spirit, early or late completed remaking Hexi thousand "Window Road" and "LanlangRoad", built the expressways of Tiansui to Beidao, Lanzhou to Zhongchuan airport and largequantities of bridges, tunnels. These have improved the provincial traffic backwardness. Now, the staff and workers are continuously fighting for Gansu traffic strategic objective ·· building the key framework of "two length and two breadth"roads

地址：蘭州市濱河東路
443 號
電話：8481004 8480771
郵編：730030
傳真：8414973

Add: No. 443 Binhe East Road
Tel: 481004 480771
Post Code: 730030
Fax: 8414973

正在施工中的我省第 條高速公路—中川公路

The first expressway·· Zhongchuan Road in Gansu is under construction

為振興我省南部少數民族地區經濟，公路局利用GBM工程改建的蘭(州)郎(木寺)公路纏繞于群山中的部分路段。

In order to develop the minority nationality areas economy in the south of Gansu, part ofLanlang roads rebuilt by the bureau using GBM project twine round the mountains

甘肅省引大入秦工程指揮部

GANSU COMMAND POST OF YINDARUQIN IRRIGATION PROJECT

簡介

引大入秦工程是我省在建的一項跨流域引水的大型自流灌溉工程。工程從大通河天堂寺引水，灌溉蘭州市以北 60 多公里干旱缺水的秦王川地區。總干渠全長 87 公里，其中隧洞 33 座，75.14 公里，設計引水流量 32 秒立方米，3 條干渠總長 112 公里，支渠 45 條總長 687 公里。工程建成後，可灌地 86 萬畝，秦王川地區將成為蘭州市瓜果、蔬菜和肉禽蛋品的副食基地。有了大面積植樹造林的條件，將會在蘭州市西北部形成一條綠色屏障，帶來良好的生態效益和社會效益。

省委、省政府主持召開引大入秦工程專題會議

A special meeting on Yindaruqin Irrigation Project presided over by the ProvincialCommittee and Government.

世界銀行檢查團聽取引大入秦工程匯報。

The procua torial group of the world bank were listening to the report of YindaruqinIrrigation Project.

省引大入秦灌溉工程平面布置圖。

The plate assignment figure of Yindaruqin Irrigation Project.

GANSU COMMAND POST OF YINDARUQIN IRRIGATION PROJECT

Yindaruqin Irrigation Project, being under construction now, is a large-scale gravityirrigation project which draws water from Tiantangsi on Datong River to irrigate Qinwangchuanarea·· 60km in north of Lanzhou. The total canal is 87km long, including 33 tunnels of 75. 14kmlong. The designed flow capacity is 32m3 / s. In the project there are 3 main canals of 112 kmlong. and 45 branch canals of 687km long. After completion of the project, 860000 mu land can beirrigated and Qinwangchuan area will become a base of producing fruits, vegetables, meat andeggs for Lanzhou. With the condition of planting trees and afforesting, a green protectionscreen will be formed in North of Lanzhou which will bring about significant ecological andsocial efficiency.

地址：蘭州市永登縣民樂街 2 號
電話：09460——23827 轉
郵編：730300

Add: No. 2 Minle Street, Yongdeng County, Lanzhou
Tel: 09460——23827
Post Code:730300
聯系人：王國平 Contractor: Wang Guo Ping

簡 介

蘭山集團公司組建于 1988 年 4 月。下屬蘭山商場自 1986 年底開業以來，由一個兩千多平方米的零售商場，發展成為一個近萬平方米的大型商廈，設 18 個商品部，經營以家電、百貨、針紡織品、服裝鞋帽、金銀首飾、日化、五金交電、糖酒副食為主的 2 萬多種商品，成為西北供銷社系統最大的商業企業。公司連續五年、商場連續七年被評為重合同、守信用單位。商場還被團中央、國內貿易部評為優質服務先進單位。

總經理：紀蘊霞 Manager: Ji Yun Xia

黨委書記：孫玉芝 Party Secretary: Sun Yu Zhi

常務副總經理：趙小天 Vice Manager of the Standing Committee: Zhao Xiao Tian

副總經理：朱錫侖 Vice Manager: Zhu Xi Lun

副總經理兼蘭山商場總經理：李晉魯 Vice Manager and Concurrently Manager of Lanshan Market: Li Jin Lu

副總經理兼蘭山商場第一副總經理：李印奇 Vice Manager and Concurrently Vice Manager of Lanshan Market: Li Yin Qi

1994 年 2 月 8 日，省人大副主任穆永吉同志到公司視察。
Director Huping of Former Commercial Ministry on Nov. 17, 1993

甘肅省蘭山商業集團公司

LANSHAN COMMERCIAL GROUP COMPANY

LANSHAN COMMERCIAL GROUP COMPANY

The company set up in April, 1988. Lanshan Market under the command of the company hasdeveloped into a near 10000 m2, large-scale market with 18 commodity departments from an over2000 m2 retail market. It manages over 20000 commodities such as family electrical equipments, articles, knit goods, clothes and shoes and caps, gold and silver ornaments, chemical productsof daily use, hardware and traffic electrical equipments, sugar and wine, non- staple food. Ithas become the largest commerce enterprise of the Northwest Supply and Marketing CooperativeSystem. The company and the market have continuously been elected as units which carries outits promises and comply with contracts very well, seperately for five years and seven years. The market has also been elected as an advanced unit for excellent service by the CentralCommittee of the League and Domestic Trade Department.

地址：蘭州市天水路 2 號
電話：8885611 轉, 8823527 8827211 轉,
電掛：7369
Add:No. 2 Tianshui Road, Lanzhou
Tel: 8885611 8823527 8827211
Cable: 7369

1993 年 11 月 17 日原商業部部長胡平同志視察蘭山商場。
Vice-chairman Mu Yong Ji of Gansu Provincial People's longress was visiting the Company onFeb. 8, 1994

蘭山商場外貌 Appearance of Lanshan Market

蘭州飯店

一流服務

標準間 Standard room

LANZHOU HOTEL

簡介

蘭州飯店始建于 1956 年，占地面積 58400 平方米，建築面積 36400 平方米，座落于蘭州市繁華地段。

該店是中國旅游飯店協會的首批會員，國家審定的三星級涉外飯店。建店以來，一直是甘肅省內外政治、經貿、文化交流以及重大會議的主要場所，被中外嘉賓譽稱"隴上第一店"。

蘭州飯店服務配套、設施齊全。備有中、西式豪華套間、單人、雙人、三人套間，標準間，共 417 套(間)客房，以及大、中、小各類會議室，貴賓室、各式宴會廳、餐廳，餐位近 2000 個，且由高級、特級名廚主理，可供各種風味的名特佳肴。另有綜合商場，出租車隊，商務中心，電報、電傳、電話、傳眞直通世界各地。還設有國內外機票預訂，外幣兌換，通用中國長城卡、萬事達卡、牡丹卡。飯店設有各類娛樂健身服務系統。

根據總體規劃，店內將可再建兩幢高層四星或五星級飯店和一幢高層綜合寫字樓共十五萬平方米的投資項目，是海內外有志于在甘肅投資經營高檔次酒店及金融、商貿、娛樂、旅游等業務的最佳場所，熱忱歡迎合作洽談。

LANZHOU HOTEL

Lanzhou Hotel, set up in 1956, stands in Lanzhou busy section with 58400m^{2}area, 36400m^{2}building area.

The hotel is the first group of member of China Tourist Hotel Society, a tristart- gradeforeign nationals hotel examined and approved by the state. Since it was set up the hotel isalways the main place of politics, economy and trade, culture exchange and great meetings bothsides of Gansu. The hotel is named the First Hotel in Gansu by China and foreign honoured guests.

The hotel is with a complete set of service, complete installations, Chinese and Westernluxury apartments, single, double, triperson apartments, standard rooms, altogether 417 guestrooms, also with large, medium, small various meeting- rooms, honoured guest room, variousbanquet halls, restaurants, near 2000 dining places. The famous and special delicacies ofvarious special flavour can be provided by the senior and special grade, famous cooks. It alsohas synthetic markets, taxi group, commercial centre, telegram, telex telephone, facsimileputting through all over the world. It also set up scheduling internal and external plane tickets, exchanging foreign currency, current China Great Wall card, Wanshida card, Peony card, alsowith various recreation and gym service system.

According to synthetic plan, two four or five star-grade hotels and a synthetic writingbuilding will be built in the hotel, altogether 150000 m2 invest item. It is the best place forinvesting and managing high-grade wineshops, finance, commerce and trade, recreation, tourbusiness, etc. by persons with lofty ideals all over the world, Welcome to cooperate and talkwarmheartedly.

中式宴會廳 Chinese banquet hall

LANZHOU HOTEL

地址：中國蘭州市東崗西路 204 號
Add: No. 204 Donggang West Road, Lanzhou, China
電話：8416321　Tel: 8416321
電傳：72131 FANDN CN　Telex: 72131 FANDN, CN
傳眞：8418608　Fax: 8418608
郵編：730000　Post Code: 730000

蘭州飯店夜景 Night view of Lanzhou Hotel

隴上第一店